Blackstone's
EU Treaties
& Legislation

2021–2022

32nd edition

edited by

Professor Nigel Foster, FRSA

Visiting Professor of European Law at the Europa-Institut,
Universität des Saarlandes, Saarbrücken, Germany and, for the Law
Programme, North Borneo University College,
Professor of EU Law, South East European Law School Network (SEELS)
online EU Modules
LLM Degree Supervisor, Robert Kennedy College, Zürich, Switzerland

WITHDRAWN

OXFORD

UNIVE

OXFORD
UNIVERSITY PRESS

Great Clarendon Street, Oxford, OX2 6DP,
United Kingdom

Oxford University Press is a department of the University of Oxford.
It furthers the University's objective of excellence in research, scholarship,
and education by publishing worldwide. Oxford is a registered trade mark of
Oxford University Press in the UK and in certain other countries

First published by Blackstone Press 1990

Twenty-ninth edition 2018
Thirtieth edition 2019
Thirty-first edition 2020
Thirty-second edition 2021

Impression: 1

Published in the United States of America by Oxford University Press
198 Madison Avenue, New York, NY 10016, United States of America

British Library Cataloguing in Publication Data
Data available

ISBN 978–0–19–289840–1

Printed in Italy by
Rotolito SpA

Contents

Social policy: equal pay and treatment   397

Social policy: worker protection   448

Competition   497

Editor's preface to the 32nd edition

Dear lecturer, student buying this book, reviewer, or reader,

This 32nd edition is based on the foundations of the editions before and has been reviewed and updated subject, as ever, to space constraints, helpful advice from the editorial support team at OUP and the annual review amongst lecturers on the volume overall and its contents. It is the first edition following the UK exit from the EU. I have included the European Union (Withdrawal Agreement) Act 2020, selected extracts from The EU–UK Trade and Cooperation Agreement 2020, the Brexit Protocol on Ireland/Northern Ireland and extracts from the December 2020 Trade and Cooperation Agreement. Strictly, the last three as EU instruments should appear in Part I of this collection but because they are so obviously UK Brexit-associated they are included in Part III.

For further information on Brexit, please refer to the very helpful OUP site dedicated to it: **www.oxfordtextbooks.co.uk/brexit**

The contents of this edition of *Blackstone's EU Treaties & Legislation* were chosen based on material frequently used in university EU law courses and modules. Originally the updating was undertaken by consulting the printed version of the Official Journal to check for new material in the subject areas selected and amendments to the existing stock. Unsurprisingly, this is now undertaken entirely electronically, especially as the electronic version of the OJ is now the official version.

The Treaties are always updated and amended following the agreements of the member states to make such changes.

A thorough review of the contents is undertaken by myself and OUP on an annual basis and they are also reviewed in the light of any changes to university EU module contents. Having said that, the core material taught in EU law modules has remained extremely stable for decades now. However, Brexit may well change that in the future. I have introduced some new, Brexit-related materials.

In the competition law section, because I received advice that it has been repealed, I wish to repeat my advice from a number of previous years that Article 8(3) of the largely repealed Regulation 17 has not been repealed and remains in force because it continues the Commission's powers in respect of being able to review past Decisions. If you don't believe me, look it up in 'EU Legislation in force'. In that section I have removed Regulation 2014/104 as being more concerned with enforcement of competition law at the national level rather than the EU level.

As usual, I have made various corrections and amendments to the existing stock as required and as are noted throughout the volume.

I acknowledge with thanks the permission of the European Union to reproduce material taken historically from the OJ printed volumes. More recent provisions and additions have been taken from the online EUR-Lex website and, likewise, permission to reproduce these is gratefully acknowledged but with the clear proviso that from 1 July 2013 'only the Official Journal published in electronic form shall be authentic and shall produce legal effects' (Art 1 Regulation 216/2013). UK legislation is reproduced with the permission of HMSO (legislation.gov.uk) under the following terms: 'You may use and re-use the information featured on this website (not including logos) free of charge in any format or medium, under the terms of the Open Government Licence'. I am grateful to both for those permissions.

I am really thankful for the extensive support work and close attention to detail undertaken by the staff of OUP, in particular Sarah Stephenson, for another year of important and necessary behind-the-editor work and for enthusiastic support, and again for conducting a thorough review of the volume and its contents. Thanks also to Joy Ruskin-Tompkins for input in the production of this edition.

As ever, I would be most grateful to receive any comments, suggestions, hints, criticisms, or advice on the content, style, or indeed any other aspect of this publication or just to point out plain errors where they are noticed. Suggestions for additional material to be included are also most welcome. Whilst for each edition I am able to spot a few errors from the OJ and eradicate them, it is also perfectly possible that I introduce, inadvertently, some of my own. Thanks to those of you who have made such comments or provided much appreciated advice. I do reflect on each piece of advice provided.

The final note this year is to recognise that we are all in a time of unprecedented hardship and change around the world as a result of the Covid-19 pandemic which does not discriminate in who it infects and kills. It is my hope that the world will come out of this in a better and more humane shape. I would, though, like to lend my thanks to all the people in all countries who have gone beyond their calls of duty to help fellow citizens, in particular the front-line medical staff. Thank you so much.

Nigel Foster
Buckingham, UK
June 2021

Extracts from the editor's preface to the 1st edition

This collection of European Community legislation has been compiled with two main considerations in mind.

First, to compile an up-to-date selection of the Community primary and secondary legislation which is the subject of frequent reference and is therefore appropriate to include in an accessible reference work which will be useful to both students of Community law and the many others who now come into contact with it.

Secondly, to furnish a basic set of unannotated legislative provisions for those students of Community law who are permitted to take materials into examinations.

In attempting to fulfil these twin tasks, I have been acutely aware of the growing mass of Community law and the danger of trying to incorporate everything which may be considered relevant. Therefore, as demanded by a compilation attempting to achieve specific aims, I have been very selective in the material chosen, particularly with regard to the primary source material of the European Communities.

The first part of the compilation contains Community Treaty and other primary materials. The second part of the book includes secondary Community legislation taken from a number of areas of substantive law. Once again I have been necessarily selective and confined the scope to areas most commonly covered in Community law courses, although I am certain that I shall be unable to entirely satisfy all courses or perhaps even any course.

Finally I have included as a matter of necessity extracts from the European Communities Act 1972. For the latter item, I gratefully acknowledge HMSO.

The Community source material was taken predominantly from the Official Journal of the European Communities unless where otherwise stated and likewise I gratefully acknowledge the permission of the European Commission to reproduce those materials. Wherever they were noticed, errors in this material have been corrected; all other errors and omissions are my responsibility.

Nigel Foster
Cardiff
February 1990

New to this edition

The 32nd edition of *Blackstone's EU Treaties & Legislation* has been fully revised and updated with all relevant developments through to April 2021 including:

- The EU–UK Trade and Cooperation Agreement 2020 (selected extracts)
- Regulation 2019/515 European Parliament and Council on the mutual recognition of goods lawfully marketed in another Member State, replacing European Parliament and Council Regulation (EC) No 764/2008 (Application of technical rules)
- Removal of the old Table of Equivalences
- Updates to the Rules of Procedure of the Court of Justice of the European Union

Blackstone's Statutes
Unsurpassed in authority, reliability, and accuracy

The titles in the Blackstone's Statutes series are collections of carefully reviewed and selected unannotated legislative material and official documents.

We make every effort to ensure titles in the series meet the needs of their target market. They are reviewed by lecturers to match university courses closely and are expertly edited to be manageable in size, whilst retaining their comprehensive coverage.

The editors only include material that will be valuable to students and lecturers and it is therefore abridged where necessary.

Conventions used in *Blackstone's EU Treaties & Legislation*
The material in this book is reproduced in its most up-to-date form. Supplementary notes and details of amending provisions are generally not included.

 Visit **www.oup.com/uk/statutes** for accompanying online resources including video guides to reading and interpreting statutes, exam tips, and an interactive sample Act of Parliament.

Useful websites
Tables of equivalences for the Treaties on European Union and the Functioning of the European Union replacing the previous Treaty on European Union and the European Community Treaty as referred to in Article 5 of the Lisbon Treaty:

- Treaty on European Union and Treaty on the Functioning of the European Union: https://eur-lex.europa.eu/LexUriServ/LexUriServ.do?uri=OJ:C:2012:326:0363:0390:EN:PDF

Tables of equivalences for the Treaty on European Union and for the European Community Treaty as referred to in Article 12 of the Treaty of Amsterdam:

- Treaty on European Union (pre-Lisbon) and Treaty establishing the European Community: https://eur-lex.europa.eu/LexUriServ/LexUriServ.do?uri=CELEX:11997DNA:EN:HTML

Part I

EU Treaties

Consolidated Version of the Treaty on European Union*

Preamble

RESOLVED to mark a new stage in the process of European integration undertaken with the establishment of the European Communities,

DRAWING INSPIRATION from the cultural, religious and humanist inheritance of Europe, from which have developed the universal values of the inviolable and inalienable rights of the human person, freedom, democracy, equality and the rule of law,

RECALLING the historic importance of the ending of the division of the European continent and the need to create firm bases for the construction of the future Europe,

CONFIRMING their attachment to the principles of liberty, democracy and respect for human rights and fundamental freedoms and of the rule of law,

CONFIRMING their attachment to fundamental social rights as defined in the European Social Charter signed at Turin on 18 October 1961 and in the 1989 Community Charter of the Fundamental Social Rights of Workers,

DESIRING to deepen the solidarity between their peoples while respecting their history, their culture and their traditions,

DESIRING to enhance further the democratic and efficient functioning of the institutions so as to enable them better to carry out, within a single institutional framework, the tasks entrusted to them,

RESOLVED to achieve the strengthening and the convergence of their economies and to establish an economic and monetary union including, in accordance with the provisions of this Treaty and of the Treaty on the Functioning of the European Union, a single and stable currency,

DETERMINED to promote economic and social progress for their peoples, taking into account the principle of sustainable development and within the context of the accomplishment of the internal market and of reinforced cohesion and environmental protection, and to implement policies ensuring that advances in economic integration are accompanied by parallel progress in other fields,

RESOLVED to establish a citizenship common to nationals of their countries,

RESOLVED to implement a common foreign and security policy including the progressive framing of a common defence policy, which might lead to a common defence in accordance with the provisions of Article 42, thereby reinforcing the European identity and its independence in order to promote peace, security and progress in Europe and in the world,

RESOLVED to facilitate the free movement of persons, while ensuring the safety and security of their peoples, by establishing an area of freedom, security and justice, in accordance with the provisions of this Treaty and of the Treaty on the Functioning of the European Union,

---

* **Editor's Note:** Incorporating Lisbon Treaty changes. Signatures and contents omitted. This version incorporates the minor changes as reproduced in OJ 2016 C202/1 of 7 June 2016 and as amended by the Croatian Accession Treaty (OJ 2012 L112/1). See https://eur-lex.europa.eu/collection/eu-law/treaties/treaties-force.html#new-2-51. List of member states omitted.

RESOLVED to continue the process of creating an ever closer union among the peoples of Europe, in which decisions are taken as closely as possible to the citizen in accordance with the principle of subsidiarity,

IN VIEW of further steps to be taken in order to advance European integration,

HAVE DECIDED to establish a European Union and to this end have designated as their Plenipotentiaries:

(List of plenipotentiaries not reproduced.)

WHO, having exchanged their full powers, found in good and due form, have agreed as follows:

Title I Common provisions

Article 1   (ex Article 1 TEU)[1]

By this Treaty, the HIGH CONTRACTING PARTIES establish among themselves a EUROPEAN UNION, hereinafter called 'the Union' on which the Member States confer competences to attain objectives they have in common.

This Treaty marks a new stage in the process of creating an ever closer union among the peoples of Europe, in which decisions are taken as openly as possible and as closely as possible to the citizen.

The Union shall be founded on the present Treaty and on the Treaty on the Functioning of the European Union (hereinafter referred to as 'the Treaties'). Those two Treaties shall have the same legal value. The Union shall replace and succeed the European Community.

Article 2

The Union is founded on the values of respect for human dignity, freedom, democracy, equality, the rule of law and respect for human rights, including the rights of persons belonging to minorities. These values are common to the Member States in a society in which pluralism, non-discrimination, tolerance, justice, solidarity and equality between women and men prevail.

Article 3   (ex Article 2 TEU)

1. The Union's aim is to promote peace, its values and the well-being of its peoples.

2. The Union shall offer its citizens an area of freedom, security and justice without internal frontiers, in which the free movement of persons is ensured in conjunction with appropriate measures with respect to external border controls, asylum, immigration and the prevention and combating of crime.

3. The Union shall establish an internal market. It shall work for the sustainable development of Europe based on balanced economic growth and price stability, a highly competitive social market economy, aiming at full employment and social progress, and a high level of protection and improvement of the quality of the environment. It shall promote scientific and technological advance.

It shall combat social exclusion and discrimination, and shall promote social justice and protection, equality between women and men, solidarity between generations and protection of the rights of the child.

It shall promote economic, social and territorial cohesion, and solidarity among Member States.

It shall respect its rich cultural and linguistic diversity, and shall ensure that Europe's cultural heritage is safeguarded and enhanced.

4. The Union shall establish an economic and monetary union whose currency is the euro.

5. In its relations with the wider world, the Union shall uphold and promote its values and interests and contribute to the protection of its citizens. It shall contribute to peace, security, the sustainable development of the Earth, solidarity and mutual respect among peoples, free and fair trade, eradication of poverty and the protection of human rights, in particular the rights of the child, as

---

[1] These references are merely indicative. For more ample information, please refer to the tables of equivalences between the old and the new numbering of the Treaties.

well as to the strict observance and the development of international law, including respect for the principles of the United Nations Charter.

6. The Union shall pursue its objectives by appropriate means commensurate with the competences which are conferred upon it in the Treaties.

Article 4

1. In accordance with Article 5, competences not conferred upon the Union in the Treaties remain with the Member States.

2. The Union shall respect the equality of Member States before the Treaties as well as their national identities, inherent in their fundamental structures, political and constitutional, inclusive of regional and local self-government. It shall respect their essential State functions, including ensuring the territorial integrity of the State, maintaining law and order and safeguarding national security. In particular, national security remains the sole responsibility of each Member State.

3. Pursuant to the principle of sincere cooperation, the Union and the Member States shall, in full mutual respect, assist each other in carrying out tasks which flow from the Treaties.

The Member States shall take any appropriate measure, general or particular, to ensure fulfilment of the obligations arising out of the Treaties or resulting from the acts of the institutions of the Union.

The Member States shall facilitate the achievement of the Union's tasks and refrain from any measure which could jeopardise the attainment of the Union's objectives.

Article 5   (ex Article 5 TEC)

1. The limits of Union competences are governed by the principle of conferral. The use of Union competences is governed by the principles of subsidiarity and proportionality.

2. Under the principle of conferral, the Union shall act only within the limits of the competences conferred upon it by the Member States in the Treaties to attain the objectives set out therein. Competences not conferred upon the Union in the Treaties remain with the Member States.

3. Under the principle of subsidiarity, in areas which do not fall within its exclusive competence, the Union shall act only if and in so far as the objectives of the proposed action cannot be sufficiently achieved by the Member States, either at central level or at regional and local level, but can rather, by reason of the scale or effects of the proposed action, be better achieved at Union level.

The institutions of the Union shall apply the principle of subsidiarity as laid down in the Protocol on the application of the principles of subsidiarity and proportionality. National Parliaments ensure compliance with the principle of subsidiarity in accordance with the procedure set out in that Protocol.

4. Under the principle of proportionality, the content and form of Union action shall not exceed what is necessary to achieve the objectives of the Treaties.

The institutions of the Union shall apply the principle of proportionality as laid down in the Protocol on the application of the principles of subsidiarity and proportionality.

Article 6   (ex Article 6 TEU)

1. The Union recognises the rights, freedoms and principles set out in the Charter of Fundamental Rights of the European Union of 7 December 2000, as adapted at Strasbourg, on 12 December 2007, which shall have the same legal value as the Treaties.

The provisions of the Charter shall not extend in any way the competences of the Union as defined in the Treaties.

The rights, freedoms and principles in the Charter shall be interpreted in accordance with the general provisions in Title VII of the Charter governing its interpretation and application and with due regard to the explanations referred to in the Charter, that set out the sources of those provisions.

2. The Union shall accede to the European Convention for the Protection of Human Rights and Fundamental Freedoms. Such accession shall not affect the Union's competences as defined in the Treaties.

3. Fundamental rights, as guaranteed by the European Convention for the Protection of Human Rights and Fundamental Freedoms and as they result from the constitutional traditions common to the Member States, shall constitute general principles of the Union's law.

Article 7   (ex Article 7 TEU)

1. On a reasoned proposal by one-third of the Member States, by the European Parliament or by the European Commission, the Council, acting by a majority of four-fifths of its members after obtaining the consent of the European Parliament, may determine that there is a clear risk of a serious breach by a Member State of the values referred to in Article 2. Before making such a determination, the Council shall hear the Member State in question and may address recommendations to it, acting in accordance with the same procedure.

The Council shall regularly verify that the grounds on which such a determination was made continue to apply.

2. The European Council, acting by unanimity on a proposal by one-third of the Member States or by the Commission and after obtaining the consent of the European Parliament, may determine the existence of a serious and persistent breach by a Member State of the values referred to in Article 2, after inviting the Member State in question to submit its observations.

3. Where a determination under paragraph 2 has been made, the Council, acting by a qualified majority, may decide to suspend certain of the rights deriving from the application of the Treaties to the Member State in question, including the voting rights of the representative of the government of that Member State in the Council. In doing so, the Council shall take into account the possible consequences of such a suspension on the rights and obligations of natural and legal persons.

The obligations of the Member State in question under this Treaty shall in any case continue to be binding on that State.

4. The Council, acting by a qualified majority, may decide subsequently to vary or revoke measures taken under paragraph 3 in response to changes in the situation which led to their being imposed.

5. The voting arrangements applying to the European Parliament, the European Council and the Council for the purposes of this Article are laid down in Article 354 of the Treaty on the Functioning of the European Union.

Article 8

1. The Union shall develop a special relationship with neighbouring countries, aiming to establish an area of prosperity and good neighbourliness, founded on the values of the Union and characterised by close and peaceful relations based on cooperation.

2. For the purposes of paragraph 1, the Union may conclude specific agreements with the countries concerned. These agreements may contain reciprocal rights and obligations as well as the possibility of undertaking activities jointly. Their implementation shall be the subject of periodic consultation.

Title II Provisions on democratic principles

Article 9

In all its activities, the Union shall observe the principle of the equality of its citizens, who shall receive equal attention from its institutions, bodies, offices and agencies. Every national of a Member State shall be a citizen of the Union. Citizenship of the Union shall be additional to national citizenship and shall not replace it.

Article 10

1. The functioning of the Union shall be founded on representative democracy.

2. Citizens are directly represented at Union level in the European Parliament.

Member States are represented in the European Council by their Heads of State or Government and in the Council by their governments, themselves democratically accountable either to their national Parliaments, or to their citizens.

3. Every citizen shall have the right to participate in the democratic life of the Union. Decisions shall be taken as openly and as closely as possible to the citizen.

4. Political parties at European level contribute to forming European political awareness and to expressing the will of citizens of the Union.

Article 11

1. The institutions shall, by appropriate means, give citizens and representative associations the opportunity to make known and publicly exchange their views in all areas of Union action.

2. The institutions shall maintain an open, transparent and regular dialogue with representative associations and civil society.

3. The European Commission shall carry out broad consultations with parties concerned in order to ensure that the Union's actions are coherent and transparent.

4. Not less than one million citizens who are nationals of a significant number of Member States may take the initiative of inviting the European Commission, within the framework of its powers, to submit any appropriate proposal on matters where citizens consider that a legal act of the Union is required for the purpose of implementing the Treaties.

The procedures and conditions required for such a citizens' initiative shall be determined in accordance with the first paragraph of Article 24 of the Treaty on the Functioning of the European Union.

Article 12

National Parliaments contribute actively to the good functioning of the Union:

- (a) through being informed by the institutions of the Union and having draft legislative acts of the Union forwarded to them in accordance with the Protocol on the role of national Parliaments in the European Union;
- (b) by seeing to it that the principle of subsidiarity is respected in accordance with the procedures provided for in the Protocol on the application of the principles of subsidiarity and proportionality;
- (c) by taking part, within the framework of the area of freedom, security and justice, in the evaluation mechanisms for the implementation of the Union policies in that area, in accordance with Article 70 of the Treaty on the Functioning of the European Union, and through being involved in the political monitoring of Europol and the evaluation of Eurojust's activities in accordance with Articles 88 and 85 of that Treaty;
- (d) by taking part in the revision procedures of the Treaties, in accordance with Article 48 of this Treaty;
- (e) by being notified of applications for accession to the Union, in accordance with Article 49 of this Treaty;
- (f) by taking part in the inter-parliamentary cooperation between national Parliaments and with the European Parliament, in accordance with the Protocol on the role of national Parliaments in the European Union.

Title III Provisions on the institutions

Article 13

1. The Union shall have an institutional framework which shall aim to promote its values, advance its objectives, serve its interests, those of its citizens and those of the Member States, and ensure the consistency, effectiveness and continuity of its policies and actions.

The Union's institutions shall be:

- the European Parliament,
- the European Council,

- the Council,
- the European Commission (hereinafter referred to as 'the Commission'),
- the Court of Justice of the European Union,
- the European Central Bank,
- the Court of Auditors.

2. Each institution shall act within the limits of the powers conferred on it in the Treaties, and in conformity with the procedures, conditions and objectives set out in them. The institutions shall practice mutual sincere cooperation.

3. The provisions relating to the European Central Bank and the Court of Auditors and detailed provisions on the other institutions are set out in the Treaty on the Functioning of the European Union.

4. The European Parliament, the Council and the Commission shall be assisted by an Economic and Social Committee and a Committee of the Regions acting in an advisory capacity.

Article 14

1. The European Parliament shall, jointly with the Council, exercise legislative and budgetary functions. It shall exercise functions of political control and consultation as laid down in the Treaties. It shall elect the President of the Commission.

2. The European Parliament shall be composed of representatives of the Union's citizens. They shall not exceed seven hundred and fifty in number, plus the President. Representation of citizens shall be degressively proportional, with a minimum threshold of six members per Member State. No Member State shall be allocated more than ninety-six seats.

The European Council shall adopt by unanimity, on the initiative of the European Parliament and with its consent, a decision establishing the composition of the European Parliament, respecting the principles referred to in the first subparagraph.

3. The members of the European Parliament shall be elected for a term of five years by direct universal suffrage in a free and secret ballot.

4. The European Parliament shall elect its President and its officers from among its members.

Article 15

1. The European Council shall provide the Union with the necessary impetus for its development and shall define the general political directions and priorities thereof. It shall not exercise legislative functions.

2. The European Council shall consist of the Heads of State or Government of the Member States, together with its President and the President of the Commission. The High Representative of the Union for Foreign Affairs and Security Policy shall take part in its work.

3. The European Council shall meet twice every six months, convened by its President. When the agenda so requires, the members of the European Council may decide each to be assisted by a minister and, in the case of the President of the Commission, by a member of the Commission. When the situation so requires, the President shall convene a special meeting of the European Council.

4. Except where the Treaties provide otherwise, decisions of the European Council shall be taken by consensus.

5. The European Council shall elect its President, by a qualified majority, for a term of two and a half years, renewable once. In the event of an impediment or serious misconduct, the European Council can end the President's term of office in accordance with the same procedure.

6. The President of the European Council:
  (a) shall chair it and drive forward its work;
  (b) shall ensure the preparation and continuity of the work of the European Council in cooperation with the President of the Commission, and on the basis of the work of the General Affairs Council;
  (c) shall endeavour to facilitate cohesion and consensus within the European Council;
  (d) shall present a report to the European Parliament after each of the meetings of the European Council.

The President of the European Council shall, at his level and in that capacity, ensure the external representation of the Union on issues concerning its common foreign and security policy, without prejudice to the powers of the High Representative of the Union for Foreign Affairs and Security Policy.

The President of the European Council shall not hold a national office.

Article 16

1. The Council shall, jointly with the European Parliament, exercise legislative and budgetary functions. It shall carry out policy-making and coordinating functions as laid down in the Treaties.

2. The Council shall consist of a representative of each Member State at ministerial level, who may commit the government of the Member State in question and cast its vote.

3. The Council shall act by a qualified majority except where the Treaties provide otherwise.

4. As from 1 November 2014, a qualified majority shall be defined as at least 55 % of the members of the Council, comprising at least fifteen of them and representing Member States comprising at least 65 % of the population of the Union.

A blocking minority must include at least four Council members, failing which the qualified majority shall be deemed attained.

The other arrangements governing the qualified majority are laid down in Article 238(2) of the Treaty on the Functioning of the European Union.

5. The transitional provisions relating to the definition of the qualified majority which shall be applicable until 31 October 2014 and those which shall be applicable from 1 November 2014 to 31 March 2017 are laid down in the Protocol on transitional provisions.

6. The Council shall meet in different configurations, the list of which shall be adopted in accordance with Article 236 of the Treaty on the Functioning of the European Union.

The General Affairs Council shall ensure consistency in the work of the different Council configurations. It shall prepare and ensure the follow-up to meetings of the European Council, in liaison with the President of the European Council and the Commission.

The Foreign Affairs Council shall elaborate the Union's external action on the basis of strategic guidelines laid down by the European Council and ensure that the Union's action is consistent.

7. A Committee of Permanent Representatives of the Governments of the Member States shall be responsible for preparing the work of the Council.

8. The Council shall meet in public when it deliberates and votes on a draft legislative act. To this end, each Council meeting shall be divided into two parts, dealing respectively with deliberations on Union legislative acts and non-legislative activities.

9. The Presidency of Council configurations, other than that of Foreign Affairs, shall be held by Member State representatives in the Council on the basis of equal rotation, in accordance with the conditions established in accordance with Article 236 of the Treaty on the Functioning of the European Union.

Article 17

1. The Commission shall promote the general interest of the Union and take appropriate initiatives to that end. It shall ensure the application of the Treaties, and of measures adopted by the institutions pursuant to them. It shall oversee the application of Union law under the control of the Court of Justice of the European Union. It shall execute the budget and manage programmes. It shall exercise coordinating, executive and management functions, as laid down in the Treaties. With the exception of the common foreign and security policy, and other cases provided for in the Treaties, it shall ensure the Union's external representation. It shall initiate the Union's annual and multiannual programming with a view to achieving interinstitutional agreements.

2. Union legislative acts may only be adopted on the basis of a Commission proposal, except where the Treaties provide otherwise. Other acts shall be adopted on the basis of a Commission proposal where the Treaties so provide.

3. The Commission's term of office shall be five years.

The members of the Commission shall be chosen on the ground of their general competence and European commitment from persons whose independence is beyond doubt.

In carrying out its responsibilities, the Commission shall be completely independent. Without prejudice to Article 18(2), the members of the Commission shall neither seek nor take instructions from any Government or other institution, body, office or entity. They shall refrain from any action incompatible with their duties or the performance of their tasks.

4. The Commission appointed between the date of entry into force of the Treaty of Lisbon and 31 October 2014, shall consist of one national of each Member State, including its President and the High Representative of the Union for Foreign Affairs and Security Policy who shall be one of its Vice-Presidents.

5. As from 1 November 2014, the Commission shall consist of a number of members, including its President and the High Representative of the Union for Foreign Affairs and Security Policy, corresponding to two-thirds of the number of Member States, unless the European Council, acting unanimously, decides to alter this number.

The members of the Commission shall be chosen from among the nationals of the Member States on the basis of a system of strictly equal rotation between the Member States, reflecting the demographic and geographical range of all the Member States. This system shall be established unanimously by the European Council in accordance with Article 244 of the Treaty on the Functioning of the European Union.

6. The President of the Commission shall:
   (a) lay down guidelines within which the Commission is to work;
   (b) decide on the internal organisation of the Commission, ensuring that it acts consistently, efficiently and as a collegiate body;
   (c) appoint Vice-Presidents, other than the High Representative of the Union for Foreign Affairs and Security Policy, from among the members of the Commission.

A member of the Commission shall resign if the President so requests. The High Representative of the Union for Foreign Affairs and Security Policy shall resign, in accordance with the procedure set out in Article 18(1), if the President so requests.

7. Taking into account the elections to the European Parliament and after having held the appropriate consultations, the European Council, acting by a qualified majority, shall propose to the European Parliament a candidate for President of the Commission. This candidate shall be elected by the European Parliament by a majority of its component members. If he does not obtain the required majority, the European Council, acting by a qualified majority, shall within one month propose a new candidate who shall be elected by the European Parliament following the same procedure.

The Council, by common accord with the President-elect, shall adopt the list of the other persons whom it proposes for appointment as members of the Commission. They shall be selected, on the basis of the suggestions made by Member States, in accordance with the criteria set out in paragraph 3, second subparagraph, and paragraph 5, second subparagraph.

The President, the High Representative of the Union for Foreign Affairs and Security Policy and the other members of the Commission shall be subject as a body to a vote of consent by the European Parliament. On the basis of this consent the Commission shall be appointed by the European Council, acting by a qualified majority.

8. The Commission, as a body, shall be responsible to the European Parliament. In accordance with Article 234 of the Treaty on the Functioning of the European Union, the European Parliament may vote on a motion of censure of the Commission. If such a motion is carried, the members of the Commission shall resign as a body and the High Representative of the Union for Foreign Affairs and Security Policy shall resign from the duties that he carries out in the Commission.

Article 18

1. The European Council, acting by a qualified majority, with the agreement of the President of the Commission, shall appoint the High Representative of the Union for Foreign Affairs and Security Policy. The European Council may end his term of office by the same procedure.

2. The High Representative shall conduct the Union's common foreign and security policy. He shall contribute by his proposals to the development of that policy, which he shall carry out as mandated by the Council. The same shall apply to the common security and defence policy.

3. The High Representative shall preside over the Foreign Affairs Council.

4. The High Representative shall be one of the Vice-Presidents of the Commission. He shall ensure the consistency of the Union's external action. He shall be responsible within the Commission for responsibilities incumbent on it in external relations and for coordinating other aspects of the Union's external action. In exercising these responsibilities within the Commission, and only for these responsibilities, the High Representative shall be bound by Commission procedures to the extent that this is consistent with paragraphs 2 and 3.

Article 19

1. The Court of Justice of the European Union shall include the Court of Justice, the General Court and specialised courts. It shall ensure that in the interpretation and application of the Treaties the law is observed.

Member States shall provide remedies sufficient to ensure effective legal protection in the fields covered by Union law.

2. The Court of Justice shall consist of one judge from each Member State. It shall be assisted by Advocates-General.

The General Court shall include at least one judge per Member State.

The Judges and the Advocates-General of the Court of Justice and the Judges of the General Court shall be chosen from persons whose independence is beyond doubt and who satisfy the conditions set out in Articles 253 and 254 of the Treaty on the Functioning of the European Union. They shall be appointed by common accord of the governments of the Member States for six years. Retiring Judges and Advocates-General may be reappointed.

3. The Court of Justice of the European Union shall, in accordance with the Treaties:

    (a) rule on actions brought by a Member State, an institution or a natural or legal person;

    (b) give preliminary rulings, at the request of courts or tribunals of the Member States, on the interpretation of Union law or the validity of acts adopted by the institutions;

    (c) rule in other cases provided for in the Treaties.

Title IV Provisions on enhanced cooperation

Article 20   (ex Articles 27a to 27e, 40 to 40b and 43 to 45 TEU and ex Articles 11 and 11a TEC)

1. Member States which wish to establish enhanced cooperation between themselves within the framework of the Union's non-exclusive competences may make use of its institutions and exercise those competences by applying the relevant provisions of the Treaties, subject to the limits and in accordance with the detailed arrangements laid down in this Article and in Articles 326 to 334 of the Treaty on the Functioning of the European Union.

Enhanced cooperation shall aim to further the objectives of the Union, protect its interests and reinforce its integration process. Such cooperation shall be open at any time to all Member States, in accordance with Article 328 of the Treaty on the Functioning of the European Union.

2. The decision authorising enhanced cooperation shall be adopted by the Council as a last resort, when it has established that the objectives of such cooperation cannot be attained within a reasonable period by the Union as a whole, and provided that at least nine Member States participate in it. The Council shall act in accordance with the procedure laid down in Article 329 of the Treaty on the Functioning of the European Union.

3. All members of the Council may participate in its deliberations, but only members of the Council representing the Member States participating in enhanced cooperation shall take part in the vote. The voting rules are set out in Article 330 of the Treaty on the Functioning of the European Union.

4. Acts adopted in the framework of enhanced cooperation shall bind only participating Member States. They shall not be regarded as part of the *acquis* which has to be accepted by candidate States for accession to the Union.

Title V General provisions on the Union's external action and specific provisions on the common foreign and security policy

Chapter 1 General provisions on the Union's external action

Article 21

1. The Union's action on the international scene shall be guided by the principles which have inspired its own creation, development and enlargement, and which it seeks to advance in the wider world: democracy, the rule of law, the universality and indivisibility of human rights and fundamental freedoms, respect for human dignity, the principles of equality and solidarity, and respect for the principles of the United Nations Charter and international law.

The Union shall seek to develop relations and build partnerships with third countries, and international, regional or global organisations which share the principles referred to in the first subparagraph. It shall promote multilateral solutions to common problems, in particular in the framework of the United Nations.

2. The Union shall define and pursue common policies and actions, and shall work for a high degree of cooperation in all fields of international relations, in order to:

(a) safeguard its values, fundamental interests, security, independence and integrity;

(b) consolidate and support democracy, the rule of law, human rights and the principles of international law;

(c) preserve peace, prevent conflicts and strengthen international security, in accordance with the purposes and principles of the United Nations Charter, with the principles of the Helsinki Final Act and with the aims of the Charter of Paris, including those relating to external borders;

(d) foster the sustainable economic, social and environmental development of developing countries, with the primary aim of eradicating poverty;

(e) encourage the integration of all countries into the world economy, including through the progressive abolition of restrictions on international trade;

(f) help develop international measures to preserve and improve the quality of the environment and the sustainable management of global natural resources, in order to ensure sustainable development;

(g) assist populations, countries and regions confronting natural or man-made disasters; and

(h) promote an international system based on stronger multilateral cooperation and good global governance.

3. The Union shall respect the principles and pursue the objectives set out in paragraphs 1 and 2 in the development and implementation of the different areas of the Union's external action covered by this Title and by Part Five of the Treaty on the Functioning of the European Union, and of the external aspects of its other policies.

The Union shall ensure consistency between the different areas of its external action and between these and its other policies. The Council and the Commission, assisted by the High Representative of the Union for Foreign Affairs and Security Policy, shall ensure that consistency and shall cooperate to that effect.

Article 22

1. On the basis of the principles and objectives set out in Article 21, the European Council shall identify the strategic interests and objectives of the Union.

Decisions of the European Council on the strategic interests and objectives of the Union shall relate to the common foreign and security policy and to other areas of the external action of the Union. Such decisions may concern the relations of the Union with a specific country or region or may be thematic in approach. They shall define their duration, and the means to be made available by the Union and the Member States.

The European Council shall act unanimously on a recommendation from the Council, adopted by the latter under the arrangements laid down for each area. Decisions of the European Council shall be implemented in accordance with the procedures provided for in the Treaties.

2. The High Representative of the Union for Foreign Affairs and Security Policy, for the area of common foreign and security policy, and the Commission, for other areas of external action, may submit joint proposals to the Council.

Chapter 2 Specific provisions on the common foreign and security policy

Section 1 Common provisions

Article 23
The Union's action on the international scene, pursuant to this Chapter, shall be guided by the principles, shall pursue the objectives of, and be conducted in accordance with, the general provisions laid down in Chapter 1.

Article 24   (ex Article 11 TEU)
1. The Union's competence in matters of common foreign and security policy shall cover all areas of foreign policy and all questions relating to the Union's security, including the progressive framing of a common defence policy that might lead to a common defence.

The common foreign and security policy is subject to specific rules and procedures. It shall be defined and implemented by the European Council and the Council acting unanimously, except where the Treaties provide otherwise. The adoption of legislative acts shall be excluded. The common foreign and security policy shall be put into effect by the High Representative of the Union for Foreign Affairs and Security Policy and by Member States, in accordance with the Treaties. The specific role of the European Parliament and of the Commission in this area is defined by the Treaties. The Court of Justice of the European Union shall not have jurisdiction with respect to these provisions, with the exception of its jurisdiction to monitor compliance with Article 40 of this Treaty and to review the legality of certain decisions as provided for by the second paragraph of Article 275 of the Treaty on the Functioning of the European Union.

2. Within the framework of the principles and objectives of its external action, the Union shall conduct, define and implement a common foreign and security policy, based on the development of mutual political solidarity among Member States, the identification of questions of general interest and the achievement of an ever-increasing degree of convergence of Member States' actions.

3. The Member States shall support the Union's external and security policy actively and unreservedly in a spirit of loyalty and mutual solidarity and shall comply with the Union's action in this area.

The Member States shall work together to enhance and develop their mutual political solidarity. They shall refrain from any action which is contrary to the interests of the Union or likely to impair its effectiveness as a cohesive force in international relations.

The Council and the High Representative shall ensure compliance with these principles.

Article 25   (ex Article 12 TEU)
The Union shall conduct the common foreign and security policy by:
    (a) defining the general guidelines;
    (b) adopting decisions defining:
        (i)   actions to be undertaken by the Union;
        (ii) positions to be taken by the Union;
        (iii) arrangements for the implementation of the decisions referred to in points (i) and (ii); and by
    (c) strengthening systematic cooperation between Member States in the conduct of policy.

Article 26   (ex Article 13 TEU)

1. The European Council shall identify the Union's strategic interests, determine the objectives of and define general guidelines for the common foreign and security policy, including for matters with defence implications. It shall adopt the necessary decisions.

If international developments so require, the President of the European Council shall convene an extraordinary meeting of the European Council in order to define the strategic lines of the Union's policy in the face of such developments.

2. The Council shall frame the common foreign and security policy and take the decisions necessary for defining and implementing it on the basis of the general guidelines and strategic lines defined by the European Council.

The Council and the High Representative of the Union for Foreign Affairs and Security Policy shall ensure the unity, consistency and effectiveness of action by the Union.

3. The common foreign and security policy shall be put into effect by the High Representative and by the Member States, using national and Union resources.

Article 27

1. The High Representative of the Union for Foreign Affairs and Security Policy, who shall chair the Foreign Affairs Council, shall contribute through his proposals towards the preparation of the common foreign and security policy and shall ensure implementation of the decisions adopted by the European Council and the Council.

2. The High Representative shall represent the Union for matters relating to the common foreign and security policy. He shall conduct political dialogue with third parties on the Union's behalf and shall express the Union's position in international organisations and at international conferences.

3. In fulfilling his mandate, the High Representative shall be assisted by a European External Action Service. This service shall work in cooperation with the diplomatic services of the Member States and shall comprise officials from relevant departments of the General Secretariat of the Council and of the Commission as well as staff seconded from national diplomatic services of the Member States. The organisation and functioning of the European External Action Service shall be established by a decision of the Council. The Council shall act on a proposal from the High Representative after consulting the European Parliament and after obtaining the consent of the Commission.

Article 28   (ex Article 14 TEU)

1. Where the international situation requires operational action by the Union, the Council shall adopt the necessary decisions. They shall lay down their objectives, scope, the means to be made available to the Union, if necessary their duration, and the conditions for their implementation.

If there is a change in circumstances having a substantial effect on a question subject to such a decision, the Council shall review the principles and objectives of that decision and take the necessary decisions.

2. Decisions referred to in paragraph 1 shall commit the Member States in the positions they adopt and in the conduct of their activity.

3. Whenever there is any plan to adopt a national position or take national action pursuant to a decision as referred to in paragraph 1, information shall be provided by the Member State concerned in time to allow, if necessary, for prior consultations within the Council. The obligation to provide prior information shall not apply to measures which are merely a national transposition of Council decisions.

4. In cases of imperative need arising from changes in the situation and failing a review of the Council decision as referred to in paragraph 1, Member States may take the necessary measures as a matter of urgency having regard to the general objectives of that decision. The Member State concerned shall inform the Council immediately of any such measures.

5. Should there be any major difficulties in implementing a decision as referred to in this Article, a Member State shall refer them to the Council which shall discuss them and seek appropriate solutions. Such solutions shall not run counter to the objectives of the decision referred to in paragraph 1 or impair its effectiveness.

Article 29   (ex Article 15 TEU)

The Council shall adopt decisions which shall define the approach of the Union to a particular matter of a geographical or thematic nature. Member States shall ensure that their national policies conform to the Union positions.

Article 30   (ex Article 22 TEU)

1. Any Member State, the High Representative of the Union for Foreign Affairs and Security Policy, or the High Representative with the Commission's support, may refer any question relating to the common foreign and security policy to the Council and may submit to it initiatives or proposals as appropriate.

2. In cases requiring a rapid decision, the High Representative, of his own motion, or at the request of a Member State, shall convene an extraordinary Council meeting within 48 hours or, in an emergency, within a shorter period.

Article 31   (ex Article 23 TEU)

1. Decisions under this Chapter shall be taken by the European Council and the Council acting unanimously, except where this Chapter provides otherwise. The adoption of legislative acts shall be excluded.

When abstaining in a vote, any member of the Council may qualify its abstention by making a formal declaration under the present subparagraph. In that case, it shall not be obliged to apply the decision, but shall accept that the decision commits the Union. In a spirit of mutual solidarity, the Member State concerned shall refrain from any action likely to conflict with or impede Union action based on that decision and the other Member States shall respect its position. If the members of the Council qualifying their abstention in this way represent at least one third of the Member States comprising at least one-third of the population of the Union, the decision shall not be adopted.

2. By derogation from the provisions of paragraph 1, the Council shall act by qualified majority:
   - when adopting a decision defining a Union action or position on the basis of a decision of the European Council relating to the Union's strategic interests and objectives, as referred to in Article 22(1),
   - when adopting a decision defining a Union action or position, on a proposal which the High Representative of the Union for Foreign Affairs and Security Policy has presented following a specific request from the European Council, made on its own initiative or that of the High Representative,
   - when adopting any decision implementing a decision defining a Union action or position,
   - when appointing a special representative in accordance with Article 33.

If a member of the Council declares that, for vital and stated reasons of national policy, it intends to oppose the adoption of a decision to be taken by qualified majority, a vote shall not be taken. The High Representative will, in close consultation with the Member State involved, search for a solution acceptable to it. If he does not succeed, the Council may, acting by a qualified majority, request that the matter be referred to the European Council for a decision by unanimity.

3. The European Council may unanimously adopt a decision stipulating that the Council shall act by a qualified majority in cases other than those referred to in paragraph 2.

4. Paragraphs 2 and 3 shall not apply to decisions having military or defence implications.

5. For procedural questions, the Council shall act by a majority of its members.

Article 32   (ex Article 16 TEU)

Member States shall consult one another within the European Council and the Council on any matter of foreign and security policy of general interest in order to determine a common approach. Before undertaking any action on the international scene or entering into any commitment which could affect the Union's interests, each Member State shall consult the others within the European Council or the Council. Member States shall ensure, through the convergence of their actions, that the Union is able to assert its interests and values on the international scene. Member States shall show mutual solidarity.

When the European Council or the Council has defined a common approach of the Union within the meaning of the first paragraph, the High Representative of the Union for Foreign Affairs and Security Policy and the Ministers for Foreign Affairs of the Member States shall coordinate their activities within the Council.

The diplomatic missions of the Member States and the Union delegations in third countries and at international organisations shall cooperate and shall contribute to formulating and implementing the common approach.

Article 33   (ex Article 18 TEU)

The Council may, on a proposal from the High Representative of the Union for Foreign Affairs and Security Policy, appoint a special representative with a mandate in relation to particular policy issues. The special representative shall carry out his mandate under the authority of the High Representative.

Article 34   (ex Article 19 TEU)

1. Member States shall coordinate their action in international organisations and at international conferences. They shall uphold the Union's positions in such forums. The High Representative of the Union for Foreign Affairs and Security Policy shall organise this coordination.

In international organisations and at international conferences where not all the Member States participate, those which do take part shall uphold the Union's positions.

2. In accordance with Article 24(3), Member States represented in international organisations or international conferences where not all the Member States participate shall keep the other Member States and the High Representative informed of any matter of common interest.

Member States which are also members of the United Nations Security Council will concert and keep the other Member States and the High Representative fully informed. Member States which are members of the Security Council will, in the execution of their functions, defend the positions and the interests of the Union, without prejudice to their responsibilities under the provisions of the United Nations Charter.

When the Union has defined a position on a subject which is on the United Nations Security Council agenda, those Member States which sit on the Security Council shall request that the High Representative be invited to present the Union's position.

Article 35   (ex Article 20 TEU)

The diplomatic and consular missions of the Member States and the Union delegations in third countries and international conferences, and their representations to international organisations, shall cooperate in ensuring that decisions defining Union positions and actions adopted pursuant to this Chapter are complied with and implemented.

They shall step up cooperation by exchanging information and carrying out joint assessments.

They shall contribute to the implementation of the right of citizens of the Union to protection in the territory of third countries as referred to in Article 20(2)(c) of the Treaty on the Functioning of the European Union and of the measures adopted pursuant to Article 23 of that Treaty.

Article 36   (ex Article 21 TEU)

The High Representative of the Union for Foreign Affairs and Security Policy shall regularly consult the European Parliament on the main aspects and the basic choices of the common foreign and security policy and the common security and defence policy and inform it of how those policies evolve. He shall ensure that the views of the European Parliament are duly taken into consideration. Special representatives may be involved in briefing the European Parliament.

The European Parliament may ask questions of the Council or make recommendations to it and to the High Representative. Twice a year it shall hold a debate on progress in implementing the common foreign and security policy, including the common security and defence policy.

Article 37   (ex Article 24 TEU)

The Union may conclude agreements with one or more States or international organisations in areas covered by this Chapter.

Article 38   (ex Article 25 TEU)

Without prejudice to Article 240 of the Treaty on the Functioning of the European Union, a Political and Security Committee shall monitor the international situation in the areas covered by the common foreign and security policy and contribute to the definition of policies by delivering opinions to the Council at the request of the Council or of the High Representative of the Union for Foreign Affairs and Security Policy or on its own initiative. It shall also monitor the implementation of agreed policies, without prejudice to the powers of the High Representative.

Within the scope of this Chapter, the Political and Security Committee shall exercise, under the responsibility of the Council and of the High Representative, the political control and strategic direction of the crisis management operations referred to in Article 43.

The Council may authorise the Committee, for the purpose and for the duration of a crisis management operation, as determined by the Council, to take the relevant decisions concerning the political control and strategic direction of the operation.

Article 39

In accordance with Article 16 of the Treaty on the Functioning of the European Union and by way of derogation from paragraph 2 thereof, the Council shall adopt a decision laying down the rules relating to the protection of individuals with regard to the processing of personal data by the Member States when carrying out activities which fall within the scope of this Chapter, and the rules relating to the free movement of such data. Compliance with these rules shall be subject to the control of independent authorities.

Article 40   (ex Article 47 TEU)

The implementation of the common foreign and security policy shall not affect the application of the procedures and the extent of the powers of the institutions laid down by the Treaties for the exercise of the Union competences referred to in Articles 3 to 6 of the Treaty on the Functioning of the European Union.

Similarly, the implementation of the policies listed in those Articles shall not affect the application of the procedures and the extent of the powers of the institutions laid down by the Treaties for the exercise of the Union competences under this Chapter.

Article 41   (ex Article 28 TEU)

1. Administrative expenditure to which the implementation of this Chapter gives rise for the institutions shall be charged to the Union budget.

2. Operating expenditure to which the implementation of this Chapter gives rise shall also be charged to the Union budget, except for such expenditure arising from operations having military or defence implications and cases where the Council acting unanimously decides otherwise.

In cases where expenditure is not charged to the Union budget, it shall be charged to the Member States in accordance with the gross national product scale, unless the Council acting unanimously decides otherwise. As for expenditure arising from operations having military or defence implications, Member States whose representatives in the Council have made a formal declaration under Article 31(1), second subparagraph, shall not be obliged to contribute to the financing thereof.

3. The Council shall adopt a decision establishing the specific procedures for guaranteeing rapid access to appropriations in the Union budget for urgent financing of initiatives in the framework of the common foreign and security policy, and in particular for preparatory activities for the tasks referred to in Article 42(1) and Article 43. It shall act after consulting the European Parliament.

Preparatory activities for the tasks referred to in Article 42(1) and Article 43 which are not charged to the Union budget shall be financed by a start-up fund made up of Member States' contributions.

The Council shall adopt by a qualified majority, on a proposal from the High Representative of the Union for Foreign Affairs and Security Policy, decisions establishing:

(a) the procedures for setting up and financing the start-up fund, in particular the amounts allocated to the fund;

(b) the procedures for administering the start-up fund;

(c) the financial control procedures.

When the task planned in accordance with Article 42(1) and Article 43 cannot be charged to the Union budget, the Council shall authorise the High Representative to use the fund. The High Representative shall report to the Council on the implementation of this remit.

Section 2   Provisions on the common security and defence policy

Article 42   (ex Article 17 TEU)

1. The common security and defence policy shall be an integral part of the common foreign and security policy. It shall provide the Union with an operational capacity drawing on civilian and military assets. The Union may use them on missions outside the Union for peace-keeping, conflict prevention and strengthening international security in accordance with the principles of the United Nations Charter. The performance of these tasks shall be undertaken using capabilities provided by the Member States.

2. The common security and defence policy shall include the progressive framing of a common Union defence policy. This will lead to a common defence, when the European Council, acting unanimously, so decides. It shall in that case recommend to the Member States the adoption of such a decision in accordance with their respective constitutional requirements.

The policy of the Union in accordance with this Section shall not prejudice the specific character of the security and defence policy of certain Member States and shall respect the obligations of certain Member States, which see their common defence realised in the North Atlantic Treaty Organisation (NATO), under the North Atlantic Treaty and be compatible with the common security and defence policy established within that framework.

3. Member States shall make civilian and military capabilities available to the Union for the implementation of the common security and defence policy, to contribute to the objectives defined by the Council. Those Member States which together establish multinational forces may also make them available to the common security and defence policy.

Member States shall undertake progressively to improve their military capabilities. The Agency in the field of defence capabilities development, research, acquisition and armaments (hereinafter referred to as 'the European Defence Agency') shall identify operational requirements, shall promote measures to satisfy those requirements, shall contribute to identifying and, where appropriate, implementing any measure needed to strengthen the industrial and technological base of the defence sector, shall participate in defining a European capabilities and armaments policy, and shall assist the Council in evaluating the improvement of military capabilities.

4. Decisions relating to the common security and defence policy, including those initiating a mission as referred to in this Article, shall be adopted by the Council acting unanimously on a proposal from the High Representative of the Union for Foreign Affairs and Security Policy or an initiative from a Member State. The High Representative may propose the use of both national resources and Union instruments, together with the Commission where appropriate.

5. The Council may entrust the execution of a task, within the Union framework, to a group of Member States in order to protect the Union's values and serve its interests. The execution of such a task shall be governed by Article 44.

6. Those Member States whose military capabilities fulfil higher criteria and which have made more binding commitments to one another in this area with a view to the most demanding missions shall establish permanent structured cooperation within the Union framework. Such cooperation shall be governed by Article 46. It shall not affect the provisions of Article 43.

7. If a Member State is the victim of armed aggression on its territory, the other Member States shall have towards it an obligation of aid and assistance by all the means in their power, in

accordance with Article 51 of the United Nations Charter. This shall not prejudice the specific character of the security and defence policy of certain Member States.

Commitments and cooperation in this area shall be consistent with commitments under the North Atlantic Treaty Organisation, which, for those States which are members of it, remains the foundation of their collective defence and the forum for its implementation.

Article 43

1. The tasks referred to in Article 42(1), in the course of which the Union may use civilian and military means, shall include joint disarmament operations, humanitarian and rescue tasks, military advice and assistance tasks, conflict prevention and peace-keeping tasks, tasks of combat forces in crisis management, including peace-making and post-conflict stabilisation. All these tasks may contribute to the fight against terrorism, including by supporting third countries in combating terrorism in their territories.

2. The Council shall adopt decisions relating to the tasks referred to in paragraph 1, defining their objectives and scope and the general conditions for their implementation. The High Representative of the Union for Foreign Affairs and Security Policy, acting under the authority of the Council and in close and constant contact with the Political and Security Committee, shall ensure coordination of the civilian and military aspects of such tasks.

Article 44

1. Within the framework of the decisions adopted in accordance with Article 43, the Council may entrust the implementation of a task to a group of Member States which are willing and have the necessary capability for such a task. Those Member States, in association with the High Representative of the Union for Foreign Affairs and Security Policy, shall agree among themselves on the management of the task.

2. Member States participating in the task shall keep the Council regularly informed of its progress on their own initiative or at the request of another Member State. Those States shall inform the Council immediately should the completion of the task entail major consequences or require amendment of the objective, scope and conditions determined for the task in the decisions referred to in paragraph 1. In such cases, the Council shall adopt the necessary decisions.

Article 45

1. The European Defence Agency referred to in Article 42(3), subject to the authority of the Council, shall have as its task to:
    (a) contribute to identifying the Member States' military capability objectives and evaluating observance of the capability commitments given by the Member States;
    (b) promote harmonisation of operational needs and adoption of effective, compatible procurement methods;
    (c) propose multilateral projects to fulfil the objectives in terms of military capabilities, ensure coordination of the programmes implemented by the Member States and management of specific cooperation programmes;
    (d) support defence technology research, and coordinate and plan joint research activities and the study of technical solutions meeting future operational needs;
    (e) contribute to identifying and, if necessary, implementing any useful measure for strengthening the industrial and technological base of the defence sector and for improving the effectiveness of military expenditure.

2. The European Defence Agency shall be open to all Member States wishing to be part of it. The Council, acting by a qualified majority, shall adopt a decision defining the Agency's statute, seat and operational rules. That decision should take account of the level of effective participation in the Agency's activities. Specific groups shall be set up within the Agency bringing together Member States engaged in joint projects. The Agency shall carry out its tasks in liaison with the Commission where necessary.

Article 46

1. Those Member States which wish to participate in the permanent structured cooperation referred to in Article 42(6), which fulfil the criteria and have made the commitments on military

capabilities set out in the Protocol on permanent structured cooperation, shall notify their intention to the Council and to the High Representative of the Union for Foreign Affairs and Security Policy.

2. Within three months following the notification referred to in paragraph 1 the Council shall adopt a decision establishing permanent structured cooperation and determining the list of participating Member States. The Council shall act by a qualified majority after consulting the High Representative.

3. Any Member State which, at a later stage, wishes to participate in the permanent structured cooperation shall notify its intention to the Council and to the High Representative.

The Council shall adopt a decision confirming the participation of the Member State concerned which fulfils the criteria and makes the commitments referred to in Articles 1 and 2 of the Protocol on permanent structured cooperation. The Council shall act by a qualified majority after consulting the High Representative. Only members of the Council representing the participating Member States shall take part in the vote.

A qualified majority shall be defined in accordance with Article 238(3)(a) of the Treaty on the Functioning of the European Union.

4. If a participating Member State no longer fulfils the criteria or is no longer able to meet the commitments referred to in Articles 1 and 2 of the Protocol on permanent structured cooperation, the Council may adopt a decision suspending the participation of the Member State concerned.

The Council shall act by a qualified majority. Only members of the Council representing the participating Member States, with the exception of the Member State in question, shall take part in the vote.

A qualified majority shall be defined in accordance with Article 238(3)(a) of the Treaty on the Functioning of the European Union.

5. Any participating Member State which wishes to withdraw from permanent structured cooperation shall notify its intention to the Council, which shall take note that the Member State in question has ceased to participate.

6. The decisions and recommendations of the Council within the framework of permanent structured cooperation, other than those provided for in paragraphs 2 to 5, shall be adopted by unanimity. For the purposes of this paragraph, unanimity shall be constituted by the votes of the representatives of the participating Member States only.

Title VI Final provisions

Article 47
The Union shall have legal personality.

Article 48   (ex Article 48 TEU)
1. The Treaties may be amended in accordance with an ordinary revision procedure. They may also be amended in accordance with simplified revision procedures.

Ordinary revision procedure
2. The Government of any Member State, the European Parliament or the Commission may submit to the Council proposals for the amendment of the Treaties. These proposals may, *inter alia*, serve either to increase or to reduce the competences conferred on the Union in the Treaties. These proposals shall be submitted to the European Council by the Council and the national Parliaments shall be notified.

3. If the European Council, after consulting the European Parliament and the Commission, adopts by a simple majority a decision in favour of examining the proposed amendments, the President of the European Council shall convene a Convention composed of representatives of the national Parliaments, of the Heads of State or Government of the Member States, of the European Parliament and of the Commission. The European Central Bank shall also be consulted in the case of institutional changes in the monetary area. The Convention shall examine the proposals for

amendments and shall adopt by consensus a recommendation to a conference of representatives of the governments of the Member States as provided for in paragraph 4.

The European Council may decide by a simple majority, after obtaining the consent of the European Parliament, not to convene a Convention should this not be justified by the extent of the proposed amendments. In the latter case, the European Council shall define the terms of reference for a conference of representatives of the governments of the Member States.

4. A conference of representatives of the governments of the Member States shall be convened by the President of the Council for the purpose of determining by common accord the amendments to be made to the Treaties.

The amendments shall enter into force after being ratified by all the Member States in accordance with their respective constitutional requirements.

5. If, two years after the signature of a treaty amending the Treaties, four fifths of the Member States have ratified it and one or more Member States have encountered difficulties in proceeding with ratification, the matter shall be referred to the European Council.

Simplified revision procedures

6. The Government of any Member State, the European Parliament or the Commission may submit to the European Council proposals for revising all or part of the provisions of Part Three of the Treaty on the Functioning of the European Union relating to the internal policies and action of the Union.

The European Council may adopt a decision amending all or part of the provisions of Part Three of the Treaty on the Functioning of the European Union. The European Council shall act by unanimity after consulting the European Parliament and the Commission, and the European Central Bank in the case of institutional changes in the monetary area. That decision shall not enter into force until it is approved by the Member States in accordance with their respective constitutional requirements.

The decision referred to in the second subparagraph shall not increase the competences conferred on the Union in the Treaties.

7. Where the Treaty on the Functioning of the European Union or Title V of this Treaty provides for the Council to act by unanimity in a given area or case, the European Council may adopt a decision authorising the Council to act by a qualified majority in that area or in that case. This subparagraph shall not apply to decisions with military implications or those in the area of defence.

Where the Treaty on the Functioning of the European Union provides for legislative acts to be adopted by the Council in accordance with a special legislative procedure, the European Council may adopt a decision allowing for the adoption of such acts in accordance with the ordinary legislative procedure.

Any initiative taken by the European Council on the basis of the first or the second subparagraph shall be notified to the national Parliaments. If a national Parliament makes known its opposition within six months of the date of such notification, the decision referred to in the first or the second subparagraph shall not be adopted. In the absence of opposition, the European Council may adopt the decision.

For the adoption of the decisions referred to in the first and second subparagraphs, the European Council shall act by unanimity after obtaining the consent of the European Parliament, which shall be given by a majority of its component members.

Article 49   (ex Article 49 TEU)

Any European State which respects the values referred to in Article 2 and is committed to promoting them may apply to become a member of the Union. The European Parliament and national Parliaments shall be notified of this application. The applicant State shall address its application to the Council, which shall act unanimously after consulting the Commission and after receiving the consent of the European Parliament, which shall act by a majority of its component members. The conditions of eligibility agreed upon by the European Council shall be taken into account.

The conditions of admission and the adjustments to the Treaties on which the Union is founded, which such admission entails, shall be the subject of an agreement between the Member States and the applicant State. This agreement shall be submitted for ratification by all the contracting States in accordance with their respective constitutional requirements.

Article 50

1. Any Member State may decide to withdraw from the Union in accordance with its own constitutional requirements.

2. A Member State which decides to withdraw shall notify the European Council of its intention. In the light of the guidelines provided by the European Council, the Union shall negotiate and conclude an agreement with that State, setting out the arrangements for its withdrawal, taking account of the framework for its future relationship with the Union. That agreement shall be negotiated in accordance with Article 218(3) of the Treaty on the Functioning of the European Union. It shall be concluded on behalf of the Union by the Council, acting by a qualified majority, after obtaining the consent of the European Parliament.

3. The Treaties shall cease to apply to the State in question from the date of entry into force of the withdrawal agreement or, failing that, two years after the notification referred to in paragraph 2, unless the European Council, in agreement with the Member State concerned, unanimously decides to extend this period.

4. For the purposes of paragraphs 2 and 3, the member of the European Council or of the Council representing the withdrawing Member State shall not participate in the discussions of the European Council or Council or in decisions concerning it.

A qualified majority shall be defined in accordance with Article 238(3)(b) of the Treaty on the Functioning of the European Union.

5. If a State which has withdrawn from the Union asks to rejoin, its request shall be subject to the procedure referred to in Article 49.

Article 51

The Protocols and Annexes to the Treaties shall form an integral part thereof.

Article 52

1. The Treaties shall apply to the Kingdom of Belgium, the Republic of Bulgaria, the Czech Republic, the Kingdom of Denmark, the Federal Republic of Germany, the Republic of Estonia, Ireland, the Hellenic Republic, the Kingdom of Spain, the French Republic, the Republic of Croatia, the Italian Republic, the Republic of Cyprus, the Republic of Latvia, the Republic of Lithuania, the Grand Duchy of Luxembourg, the Republic of Hungary, the Republic of Malta, the Kingdom of the Netherlands, the Republic of Austria, the Republic of Poland, the Portuguese Republic, Romania, the Republic of Slovenia, the Slovak Republic, the Republic of Finland, the Kingdom of Sweden and the United Kingdom of Great Britain and Northern Ireland.

2. The territorial scope of the Treaties is specified in Article 355 of the Treaty on the Functioning of the European Union.

Article 53   (ex Article 51 TEU)

This Treaty is concluded for an unlimited period.

Article 54   (ex Article 52 TEU)

1. This Treaty shall be ratified by the High Contracting Parties in accordance with their respective constitutional requirements. The instruments of ratification shall be deposited with the Government of the Italian Republic.

2. This Treaty shall enter into force on 1 January 1993, provided that all the Instruments of ratification have been deposited, or, failing that, on the first day of the month following the deposit of the Instrument of ratification by the last signatory State to take this step.

Article 55   (ex Article 53 TEU)

1. This Treaty, drawn up in a single original in the Bulgarian, Croatian, Czech, Danish, Dutch, English, Estonian, Finnish, French, German, Greek, Hungarian, Irish, Italian, Latvian, Lithuanian, Maltese, Polish, Portuguese, Romanian, Slovak, Slovenian, Spanish and Swedish languages, the texts in each of these languages being equally authentic, shall be deposited in the archives of the Government of the Italian Republic, which will transmit a certified copy to each of the governments of the other signatory States.

2. This Treaty may also be translated into any other languages as determined by Member States among those which, in accordance with their constitutional order, enjoy official status in all or part of their territory. A certified copy of such translations shall be provided by the Member States concerned to be deposited in the archives of the Council.

IN WITNESS WHEREOF the undersigned Plenipotentiaries have signed this Treaty.

Done at Maastricht on the seventh day of February in the year one thousand nine hundred and ninety-two.

(List of signatories not reproduced.)

Consolidated Version of the Treaty on the Functioning of the European Union*

Preamble

DETERMINED to lay the foundations of an ever closer union among the peoples of Europe,

RESOLVED to ensure the economic and social progress of their States by common action to eliminate the barriers which divide Europe,

AFFIRMING as the essential objective of their efforts the constant improvements of the living and working conditions of their peoples,

RECOGNISING that the removal of existing obstacles calls for concerted action in order to guarantee steady expansion, balanced trade and fair competition,

ANXIOUS to strengthen the unity of their economies and to ensure their harmonious development by reducing the differences existing between the various regions and the backwardness of the less favoured regions,

DESIRING to contribute, by means of a common commercial policy, to the progressive abolition of restrictions on international trade,

INTENDING to confirm the solidarity which binds Europe and the overseas countries and desiring to ensure the development of their prosperity, in accordance with the principles of the Charter of the United Nations,

RESOLVED by thus pooling their resources to preserve and strengthen peace and liberty, and calling upon the other peoples of Europe who share their ideal to join in their efforts,

DETERMINED to promote the development of the highest possible level of knowledge for their peoples through a wide access to education and through its continuous updating,

and to this end have designated as their Plenipotentiaries:

(List of plenipotentiaries not reproduced.)

WHO, having exchanged their full powers, found in good and due form, have agreed as follows.

---

* **Editor's Note:** Incorporating Lisbon Treaty changes. Signatures, list of States and contents omitted. This version incorporates the changes as reproduced in OJ 2016 C202/1 of 7 June 2016 and as amended by the Croatian Accession Treaty (OJ 2012 L112/1). See https://eur-lex.europa.eu/legal-content/EN/TXT/?uri=OJ:C:2016:202:TOC.

PART ONE PRINCIPLES

Article 1

1. This Treaty organises the functioning of the Union and determines the areas of, delimitation of, and arrangements for exercising its competences.

2. This Treaty and the Treaty on European Union constitute the Treaties on which the Union is founded. These two Treaties, which have the same legal value, shall be referred to as 'the Treaties'.

Title I Categories and areas of Union competence

Article 2

1. When the Treaties confer on the Union exclusive competence in a specific area, only the Union may legislate and adopt legally binding acts, the Member States being able to do so themselves only if so empowered by the Union or for the implementation of Union acts.

2. When the Treaties confer on the Union a competence shared with the Member States in a specific area, the Union and the Member States may legislate and adopt legally binding acts in that area. The Member States shall exercise their competence to the extent that the Union has not exercised its competence. The Member States shall again exercise their competence to the extent that the Union has decided to cease exercising its competence.

3. The Member States shall coordinate their economic and employment policies within arrangements as determined by this Treaty, which the Union shall have competence to provide.

4. The Union shall have competence, in accordance with the provisions of the Treaty on European Union, to define and implement a common foreign and security policy, including the progressive framing of a common defence policy.

5. In certain areas and under the conditions laid down in the Treaties, the Union shall have competence to carry out actions to support, coordinate or supplement the actions of the Member States, without thereby superseding their competence in these areas.

Legally binding acts of the Union adopted on the basis of the provisions of the Treaties relating to these areas shall not entail harmonisation of Member States' laws or regulations.

6. The scope of and arrangements for exercising the Union's competences shall be determined by the provisions of the Treaties relating to each area.

Article 3

1. The Union shall have exclusive competence in the following areas:
    (a) customs union;
    (b) the establishing of the competition rules necessary for the functioning of the internal market;
    (c) monetary policy for the Member States whose currency is the euro;
    (d) the conservation of marine biological resources under the common fisheries policy;
    (e) common commercial policy.

2. The Union shall also have exclusive competence for the conclusion of an international agreement when its conclusion is provided for in a legislative act of the Union or is necessary to enable the Union to exercise its internal competence, or in so far as its conclusion may affect common rules or alter their scope.

Article 4

1. The Union shall share competence with the Member States where the Treaties confer on it a competence which does not relate to the areas referred to in Articles 3 and 6.

2. Shared competence between the Union and the Member States applies in the following principal areas:
    (a) internal market;
    (b) social policy, for the aspects defined in this Treaty;

    (c) economic, social and territorial cohesion;

    (d) agriculture and fisheries, excluding the conservation of marine biological resources;

    (e) environment;

    (f) consumer protection;

    (g) transport;

    (h) trans-European networks;

    (i) energy;

    (j) area of freedom, security and justice;

    (k) common safety concerns in public health matters, for the aspects defined in this Treaty.

3. In the areas of research, technological development and space, the Union shall have competence to carry out activities, in particular to define and implement programmes; however, the exercise of that competence shall not result in Member States being prevented from exercising theirs.

4. In the areas of development cooperation and humanitarian aid, the Union shall have competence to carry out activities and conduct a common policy; however, the exercise of that competence shall not result in Member States being prevented from exercising theirs.

Article 5

1. The Member States shall coordinate their economic policies within the Union. To this end, the Council shall adopt measures, in particular broad guidelines for these policies.

Specific provisions shall apply to those Member States whose currency is the euro.

2. The Union shall take measures to ensure coordination of the employment policies of the Member States, in particular by defining guidelines for these policies.

3. The Union may take initiatives to ensure coordination of Member States' social policies.

Article 6

The Union shall have competence to carry out actions to support, coordinate or supplement the actions of the Member States. The areas of such action shall, at European level, be:

    (a) protection and improvement of human health;

    (b) industry;

    (c) culture;

    (d) tourism;

    (e) education, vocational training, youth and sport;

    (f) civil protection;

    (g) administrative cooperation.

Title II Provisions having general application

Article 7

The Union shall ensure consistency between its policies and activities, taking all of its objectives into account and in accordance with the principle of conferral of powers.

Article 8   (ex Article 3(2) TEC)[1]

In all its activities, the Union shall aim to eliminate inequalities, and to promote equality, between men and women.

Article 9

In defining and implementing its policies and activities, the Union shall take into account requirements linked to the promotion of a high level of employment, the guarantee of adequate social protection, the fight against social exclusion, and a high level of education, training and protection of human health.

---

[1] These references are merely indicative. For more ample information, please refer to the tables of equivalences between the old and the new numbering of the Treaties.

Article 10

In defining and implementing its policies and activities, the Union shall aim to combat discrimination based on sex, racial or ethnic origin, religion or belief, disability, age or sexual orientation.

Article 11   (ex Article 6 TEC)

Environmental protection requirements must be integrated into the definition and implementation of the Union policies and activities, in particular with a view to promoting sustainable development.

Article 12   (ex Article 153(2) TEC)

Consumer protection requirements shall be taken into account in defining and implementing other Union policies and activities.

Article 13

In formulating and implementing the Union's agriculture, fisheries, transport, internal market, research and technological development and space policies, the Union and the Member States shall, since animals are sentient beings, pay full regard to the welfare requirements of animals, while respecting the legislative or administrative provisions and customs of the Member States relating in particular to religious rites, cultural traditions and regional heritage.

Article 14   (ex Article 16 TEC)

Without prejudice to Article 4 of the Treaty on European Union or to Articles 93, 106 and 107 of this Treaty, and given the place occupied by services of general economic interest in the shared values of the Union as well as their role in promoting social and territorial cohesion, the Union and the Member States, each within their respective powers and within the scope of application of the Treaties, shall take care that such services operate on the basis of principles and conditions, particularly economic and financial conditions, which enable them to fulfil their missions. The European Parliament and the Council, acting by means of regulations in accordance with the ordinary legislative procedure, shall establish these principles and set these conditions without prejudice to the competence of Member States, in compliance with the Treaties, to provide, to commission and to fund such services.

Article 15   (ex Article 255 TEC)

1. In order to promote good governance and ensure the participation of civil society, the Union institutions, bodies, offices and agencies shall conduct their work as openly as possible.

2. The European Parliament shall meet in public, as shall the Council when considering and voting on a draft legislative act.

3. Any citizen of the Union, and any natural or legal person residing or having its registered office in a Member State, shall have a right of access to documents of the Union institutions, bodies, offices and agencies, whatever their medium, subject to the principles and the conditions to be defined in accordance with this paragraph.

General principles and limits on grounds of public or private interest governing this right of access to documents shall be determined by the European Parliament and the Council, by means of regulations, acting in accordance with the ordinary legislative procedure.

Each institution, body, office or agency shall ensure that its proceedings are transparent and shall elaborate in its own Rules of Procedure specific provisions regarding access to its documents, in accordance with the regulations referred to in the second subparagraph.

The Court of Justice of the European Union, the European Central Bank and the European Investment Bank shall be subject to this paragraph only when exercising their administrative tasks.

The European Parliament and the Council shall ensure publication of the documents relating to the legislative procedures under the terms laid down by the regulations referred to in the second subparagraph.

Article 16   (ex Article 286 TEC)

1. Everyone has the right to the protection of personal data concerning them.

2. The European Parliament and the Council, acting in accordance with the ordinary legislative procedure, shall lay down the rules relating to the protection of individuals with regard to the

processing of personal data by Union institutions, bodies, offices and agencies, and by the Member States when carrying out activities which fall within the scope of Union law, and the rules relating to the free movement of such data.

Compliance with these rules shall be subject to the control of independent authorities.

The rules adopted on the basis of this Article shall be without prejudice to the specific rules laid down in Article 39 of the Treaty on European Union.

Article 17

1. The Union respects and does not prejudice the status under national law of churches and religious associations or communities in the Member States.

2. The Union equally respects the status under national law of philosophical and non-confessional organisations.

3. Recognising their identity and their specific contribution, the Union shall maintain an open, transparent and regular dialogue with these churches and organisations.

PART TWO NON-DISCRIMINATION AND CITIZENSHIP OF THE UNION

Article 18   (ex Article 12 TEC)

Within the scope of application of the Treaties, and without prejudice to any special provisions contained therein, any discrimination on grounds of nationality shall be prohibited.

The European Parliament and the Council, acting in accordance with the ordinary legislative procedure, may adopt rules designed to prohibit such discrimination.

Article 19   (ex Article 13 TEC)

1. Without prejudice to the other provisions of the Treaties and within the limits of the powers conferred by them upon the Union, the Council, acting unanimously in accordance with a special legislative procedure and after obtaining the consent of the European Parliament, may take appropriate action to combat discrimination based on sex, racial or ethnic origin, religion or belief, disability, age or sexual orientation.

2. By way of derogation from paragraph 1, the European Parliament and the Council, acting in accordance with the ordinary legislative procedure, may adopt the basic principles of Union incentive measures, excluding any harmonisation of the laws and regulations of the Member States, to support action taken by the Member States in order to contribute to the achievement of the objectives referred to in paragraph 1.

Article 20   (ex Article 17 TEC)

1. Citizenship of the Union is hereby established. Every person holding the nationality of a Member State shall be a citizen of the Union. Citizenship of the Union shall be additional to and not replace national citizenship.

2. Citizens of the Union shall enjoy the rights and be subject to the duties provided for in the Treaties. They shall have, *inter alia*:

    (a) the right to move and reside freely within the territory of the Member States;

    (b) the right to vote and to stand as candidates in elections to the European Parliament and in municipal elections in their Member State of residence, under the same conditions as nationals of that State;

    (c) the right to enjoy, in the territory of a third country in which the Member State of which they are nationals is not represented, the protection of the diplomatic and consular authorities of any Member State on the same conditions as the nationals of that State;

    (d) the right to petition the European Parliament, to apply to the European Ombudsman, and to address the institutions and advisory bodies of the Union in any of the Treaty languages and to obtain a reply in the same language.

These rights shall be exercised in accordance with the conditions and limits defined by the Treaties and by the measures adopted thereunder.

Article 21   (ex Article 18 TEC)

1. Every citizen of the Union shall have the right to move and reside freely within the territory of the Member States, subject to the limitations and conditions laid down in the Treaties and by the measures adopted to give them effect.

2. If action by the Union should prove necessary to attain this objective and the Treaties have not provided the necessary powers, the European Parliament and the Council, acting in accordance with the ordinary legislative procedure, may adopt provisions with a view to facilitating the exercise of the rights referred to in paragraph 1.

3. For the same purposes as those referred to in paragraph 1 and if the Treaties have not provided the necessary powers, the Council, acting in accordance with a special legislative procedure, may adopt measures concerning social security or social protection. The Council shall act unanimously after consulting the European Parliament.

Article 22   (ex Article 19 TEC)

1. Every citizen of the Union residing in a Member State of which he is not a national shall have the right to vote and to stand as a candidate at municipal elections in the Member State in which he resides, under the same conditions as nationals of that State. This right shall be exercised subject to detailed arrangements adopted by the Council, acting unanimously in accordance with a special legislative procedure and after consulting the European Parliament; these arrangements may provide for derogations where warranted by problems specific to a Member State.

2. Without prejudice to Article 223(1) and to the provisions adopted for its implementation, every citizen of the Union residing in a Member State of which he is not a national shall have the right to vote and to stand as a candidate in elections to the European Parliament in the Member State in which he resides, under the same conditions as nationals of that State. This right shall be exercised subject to detailed arrangements adopted by the Council, acting unanimously in accordance with a special legislative procedure and after consulting the European Parliament; these arrangements may provide for derogations where warranted by problems specific to a Member State.

Article 23   (ex Article 20 TEC)

Every citizen of the Union shall, in the territory of a third country in which the Member State of which he is a national is not represented, be entitled to protection by the diplomatic or consular authorities of any Member State, on the same conditions as the nationals of that State. Member States shall adopt the necessary provisions and start the international negotiations required to secure this protection.

The Council, acting in accordance with a special legislative procedure and after consulting the European Parliament, may adopt directives establishing the coordination and cooperation measures necessary to facilitate such protection.

Article 24   (ex Article 21 TEC)

The European Parliament and the Council, acting by means of regulations in accordance with the ordinary legislative procedure, shall adopt the provisions for the procedures and conditions required for a citizens' initiative within the meaning of Article 11 of the Treaty on European Union, including the minimum number of Member States from which such citizens must come.

Every citizen of the Union shall have the right to petition the European Parliament in accordance with Article 227.

Every citizen of the Union may apply to the Ombudsman established in accordance with Article 228.

Every citizen of the Union may write to any of the institutions, bodies, offices or agencies referred to in this Article or in Article 13 of the Treaty on European Union in one of the languages mentioned in Article 55(1) of the Treaty on European Union and have an answer in the same language.

Article 25   (ex Article 22 TEC)

The Commission shall report to the European Parliament, to the Council and to the Economic and Social Committee every three years on the application of the provisions of this Part. This report shall take account of the development of the Union.

On this basis, and without prejudice to the other provisions of the Treaties, the Council, acting unanimously in accordance with a special legislative procedure and after obtaining the consent of the European Parliament, may adopt provisions to strengthen or to add to the rights listed in Article 20(2). These provisions shall enter into force after their approval by the Member States in accordance with their respective constitutional requirements.

PART THREE UNION POLICIES AND INTERNAL ACTIONS

Title I The internal market

Article 26   (ex Article 14 TEC)

1. The Union shall adopt measures with the aim of establishing or ensuring the functioning of the internal market, in accordance with the relevant provisions of the Treaties.

2. The internal market shall comprise an area without internal frontiers in which the free movement of goods, persons, services and capital is ensured in accordance with the provisions of the Treaties.

3. The Council, on a proposal from the Commission, shall determine the guidelines and conditions necessary to ensure balanced progress in all the sectors concerned.

Article 27   (ex Article 15 TEC)

When drawing up its proposals with a view to achieving the objectives set out in Article 26, the Commission shall take into account the extent of the effort that certain economies showing differences in development will have to sustain for the establishment of the internal market and it may propose appropriate provisions.

If these provisions take the form of derogations, they must be of a temporary nature and must cause the least possible disturbance to the functioning of the internal market.

Title II Free movement of goods

Article 28   (ex Article 23 TEC)

1. The Union shall comprise a customs union which shall cover all trade in goods and which shall involve the prohibition between Member States of customs duties on imports and exports and of all charges having equivalent effect, and the adoption of a common customs tariff in their relations with third countries.

2. The provisions of Article 30 and of Chapter 3 of this Title shall apply to products originating in Member States and to products coming from third countries which are in free circulation in Member States.*

Article 29   (ex Article 24 TEC)

Products coming from a third country shall be considered to be in free circulation in a Member State if the import formalities have been complied with and any customs duties or charges having equivalent effect which are payable have been levied in that Member State, and if they have not benefited from a total or partial drawback of such duties or charges.

---

* **Editor's Note**: Second paragraph as corrected in the Consolidated Treaties' version published in OJ 2012 C326/60.

Chapter 1 The customs union

Article 30 (ex Article 25 TEC)

Customs duties on imports and exports and charges having equivalent effect shall be prohibited between Member States. This prohibition shall also apply to customs duties of a fiscal nature.

Article 31 (ex Article 26 TEC)

Common Customs Tariff duties shall be fixed by the Council on a proposal from the Commission.

Article 32 (ex Article 27 TEC)

In carrying out the tasks entrusted to it under this Chapter the Commission shall be guided by:
- (a) the need to promote trade between Member States and third countries;
- (b) developments in conditions of competition within the Union in so far as they lead to an improvement in the competitive capacity of undertakings;
- (c) the requirements of the Union as regards the supply of raw materials and semi-finished goods; in this connection the Commission shall take care to avoid distorting conditions of competition between Member States in respect of finished goods;
- (d) the need to avoid serious disturbances in the economies of Member States and to ensure rational development of production and an expansion of consumption within the Union.

Chapter 2 Customs cooperation

Article 33 (ex Article 135 TEC)

Within the scope of application of the Treaties, the European Parliament and the Council, acting in accordance with the ordinary legislative procedure, shall take measures in order to strengthen customs cooperation between Member States and between the latter and the Commission.

Chapter 3 Prohibition of quantitative restrictions between Member States

Article 34 (ex Article 28 TEC)

Quantitative restrictions on imports and all measures having equivalent effect shall be prohibited between Member States.

Article 35 (ex Article 29 TEC)

Quantitative restrictions on exports, and all measures having equivalent effect, shall be prohibited between Member States.

Article 36 (ex Article 30 TEC)

The provisions of Articles 34 and 35 shall not preclude prohibitions or restrictions on imports, exports or goods in transit justified on grounds of public morality, public policy or public security; the protection of health and life of humans, animals or plants; the protection of national treasures possessing artistic, historic or archaeological value; or the protection of industrial and commercial property. Such prohibitions or restrictions shall not, however, constitute a means of arbitrary discrimination or a disguised restriction on trade between Member States.

Article 37 (ex Article 31 TEC)

1. Member States shall adjust any State monopolies of a commercial character so as to ensure that no discrimination regarding the conditions under which goods are procured and marketed exists between nationals of Member States.

The provisions of this Article shall apply to any body through which a Member State, in law or in fact, either directly or indirectly supervises, determines or appreciably influences imports or exports between Member States. These provisions shall likewise apply to monopolies delegated by the State to others.

2. Member States shall refrain from introducing any new measure which is contrary to the principles laid down in paragraph 1 or which restricts the scope of the articles dealing with the prohibition of customs duties and quantitative restrictions between Member States.

3. If a State monopoly of a commercial character has rules which are designed to make it easier to dispose of agricultural products or obtain for them the best return, steps should be taken in applying the rules contained in this Article to ensure equivalent safeguards for the employment and standard of living of the producers concerned.

Title III Agriculture and fisheries

Article 38   (ex Article 32 TEC)

1. The Union shall define and implement a common agriculture and fisheries policy.

'The internal market' shall extend to agriculture, fisheries and trade in agricultural products. 'Agricultural products' means the products of the soil, of stockfarming and of fisheries and products of first-stage processing directly related to these products. References to the common agricultural policy or to agriculture, and the use of the term 'agricultural', shall be understood as also referring to fisheries, having regard to the specific characteristics of this sector.

2. Save as otherwise provided in Articles 39 to 44, the rules laid down for the establishment and functioning of the internal market shall apply to agricultural products.

3. The products subject to the provisions of Articles 39 to 44 are listed in Annex I.

4. The operation and development of the internal market for agricultural products must be accompanied by the establishment of a common agricultural policy.

Article 39   (ex Article 33 TEC)

1. The objectives of the common agricultural policy shall be:
   - (a) to increase agricultural productivity by promoting technical progress and by ensuring the rational development of agricultural production and the optimum utilisation of the factors of production, in particular labour;
   - (b) thus to ensure a fair standard of living for the agricultural community, in particular by increasing the individual earnings of persons engaged in agriculture;
   - (c) to stabilise markets;
   - (d) to assure the availability of supplies;
   - (e) to ensure that supplies reach consumers at reasonable prices.

2. In working out the common agricultural policy and the special methods for its application, account shall be taken of:
   - (a) the particular nature of agricultural activity, which results from the social structure of agriculture and from structural and natural disparities between the various agricultural regions;
   - (b) the need to effect the appropriate adjustments by degrees;
   - (c) the fact that in the Member States agriculture constitutes a sector closely linked with the economy as a whole.

Article 40   (ex Article 34 TEC)

1. In order to attain the objectives set out in Article 39, a common organisation of agricultural markets shall be established.

This organisation shall take one of the following forms, depending on the product concerned:
   - (a) common rules on competition;
   - (b) compulsory coordination of the various national market organisations;
   - (c) a European market organisation.

2. The common organisation established in accordance with paragraph 1 may include all measures required to attain the objectives set out in Article 39, in particular regulation of prices, aids for the production and marketing of the various products, storage and carryover arrangements and common machinery for stabilising imports or exports.

The common organisation shall be limited to pursuit of the objectives set out in Article 39 and shall exclude any discrimination between producers or consumers within the Union.

Any common price policy shall be based on common criteria and uniform methods of calculation.

3. In order to enable the common organisation referred to in paragraph 1 to attain its objectives, one or more agricultural guidance and guarantee funds may be set up.

Article 41   (ex Article 35 TEC)

To enable the objectives set out in Article 39 to be attained, provision may be made within the framework of the common agricultural policy for measures such as:

(a) an effective coordination of efforts in the spheres of vocational training, of research and of the dissemination of agricultural knowledge; this may include joint financing of projects or institutions;

(b) joint measures to promote consumption of certain products.

Article 42   (ex Article 36 TEC)

The provisions of the Chapter relating to rules on competition shall apply to production of and trade in agricultural products only to the extent determined by the European Parliament and the Council within the framework of Article 43(2) and in accordance with the procedure laid down therein, account being taken of the objectives set out in Article 39.

The Council, on a proposal from the Commission, may authorise the granting of aid:

(a) for the protection of enterprises handicapped by structural or natural conditions;

(b) within the framework of economic development programmes.

Article 43   (ex Article 37 TEC)

1. The Commission shall submit proposals for working out and implementing the common agricultural policy, including the replacement of the national organisations by one of the forms of common organisation provided for in Article 40(1), and for implementing the measures specified in this Title.

These proposals shall take account of the interdependence of the agricultural matters mentioned in this Title.

2. The European Parliament and the Council, acting in accordance with the ordinary legislative procedure and after consulting the Economic and Social Committee, shall establish the common organisation of agricultural markets provided for in Article 40(1) and the other provisions necessary for the pursuit of the objectives of the common agricultural policy and the common fisheries policy.

3. The Council, on a proposal from the Commission, shall adopt measures on fixing prices, levies, aid and quantitative limitations and on the fixing and allocation of fishing opportunities.

4. In accordance with paragraph 1, the national market organisations may be replaced by the common organisation provided for in Article 40(1) if:

(a) the common organisation offers Member States which are opposed to this measure and which have an organisation of their own for the production in question equivalent safeguards for the employment and standard of living of the producers concerned, account being taken of the adjustments that will be possible and the specialisation that will be needed with the passage of time;

(b) such an organisation ensures conditions for trade within the Union similar to those existing in a national market.

5. If a common organisation for certain raw materials is established before a common organisation exists for the corresponding processed products, such raw materials as are used for processed products intended for export to third countries may be imported from outside the Union.

Article 44   (ex Article 38 TEC)

Where in a Member State a product is subject to a national market organisation or to internal rules having equivalent effect which affect the competitive position of similar production in another Member State, a countervailing charge shall be applied by Member States to imports of this product coming from the Member State where such organisation or rules exist, unless that State applies a countervailing charge on export.

The Commission shall fix the amount of these charges at the level required to redress the balance; it may also authorise other measures, the conditions and details of which it shall determine.

Title IV Free movement of persons, services and capital

Chapter 1 Workers

Article 45   (ex Article 39 TEC)

1. Freedom of movement for workers shall be secured within the Union.

2. Such freedom of movement shall entail the abolition of any discrimination based on nationality between workers of the Member States as regards employment, remuneration and other conditions of work and employment.

3. It shall entail the right, subject to limitations justified on grounds of public policy, public security or public health:

   (a) to accept offers of employment actually made;
   (b) to move freely within the territory of Member States for this purpose;
   (c) to stay in a Member State for the purpose of employment in accordance with the provisions governing the employment of nationals of that State laid down by law, regulation or administrative action;
   (d) to remain in the territory of a Member State after having been employed in that State, subject to conditions which shall be embodied in regulations to be drawn up by the Commission.

4. The provisions of this Article shall not apply to employment in the public service.

Article 46   (ex Article 40 TEC)

The European Parliament and the Council shall, acting in accordance with the ordinary legislative procedure and after consulting the Economic and Social Committee, issue directives or make regulations setting out the measures required to bring about freedom of movement for workers, as defined in Article 45, in particular:

   (a) by ensuring close cooperation between national employment services;
   (b) by abolishing those administrative procedures and practices and those qualifying periods in respect of eligibility for available employment, whether resulting from national legislation or from agreements previously concluded between Member States, the maintenance of which would form an obstacle to liberalisation of the movement of workers;
   (c) by abolishing all such qualifying periods and other restrictions provided for either under national legislation or under agreements previously concluded between Member States as imposed on workers of other Member States conditions regarding the free choice of employment other than those imposed on workers of the State concerned;
   (d) by setting up appropriate machinery to bring offers of employment into touch with applications for employment and to facilitate the achievement of a balance between supply and demand in the employment market in such a way as to avoid serious threats to the standard of living and level of employment in the various regions and industries.

Article 47   (ex Article 41 TEC)

Member States shall, within the framework of a joint programme, encourage the exchange of young workers.

Article 48   (ex Article 42 TEC)

The European Parliament and the Council shall, acting in accordance with the ordinary legislative procedure, adopt such measures in the field of social security as are necessary to provide freedom of movement for workers; to this end, they shall make arrangements to secure for employed and self-employed migrant workers and their dependants:

   (a) aggregation, for the purpose of acquiring and retaining the right to benefit and of calculating the amount of benefit, of all periods taken into account under the laws of the several countries;

(b) payment of benefits to persons resident in the territories of Member States.

Where a member of the Council declares that a draft legislative act referred to in the first sub-paragraph would affect important aspects of its social security system, including its scope, cost or financial structure, or would affect the financial balance of that system, it may request that the matter be referred to the European Council. In that case, the ordinary legislative procedure shall be suspended. After discussion, the European Council shall, within four months of this suspension, either:

(a) refer the draft back to the Council, which shall terminate the suspension of the ordinary legislative procedure; or

(b) take no action or request the Commission to submit a new proposal; in that case, the act originally proposed shall be deemed not to have been adopted.

Chapter 2 Right of establishment

Article 49   (ex Article 43 TEC)

Within the framework of the provisions set out below, restrictions on the freedom of establishment of nationals of a Member State in the territory of another Member State shall be prohibited. Such prohibition shall also apply to restrictions on the setting-up of agencies, branches or subsidiaries by nationals of any Member State established in the territory of any Member State.

Freedom of establishment shall include the right to take up and pursue activities as self-employed persons and to set up and manage undertakings, in particular companies or firms within the meaning of the second paragraph of Article 54, under the conditions laid down for its own nationals by the law of the country where such establishment is effected, subject to the provisions of the Chapter relating to capital.

Article 50   (ex Article 44 TEC)

1. In order to attain freedom of establishment as regards a particular activity, the European Parliament and the Council, acting in accordance with the ordinary legislative procedure and after consulting the Economic and Social Committee, shall act by means of directives.

2. The European Parliament, the Council and the Commission shall carry out the duties devolving upon them under the preceding provisions, in particular:

(a) by according, as a general rule, priority treatment to activities where freedom of establishment makes a particularly valuable contribution to the development of production and trade;

(b) by ensuring close cooperation between the competent authorities in the Member States in order to ascertain the particular situation within the Union of the various activities concerned;

(c) by abolishing those administrative procedures and practices, whether resulting from national legislation or from agreements previously concluded between Member States, the maintenance of which would form an obstacle to freedom of establishment;

(d) by ensuring that workers of one Member State employed in the territory of another Member State may remain in that territory for the purpose of taking up activities therein as self-employed persons, where they satisfy the conditions which they would be required to satisfy if they were entering that State at the time when they intended to take up such activities;

(e) by enabling a national of one Member State to acquire and use land and buildings situated in the territory of another Member State, in so far as this does not conflict with the principles laid down in Article 39(2);

(f) by effecting the progressive abolition of restrictions on freedom of establishment in every branch of activity under consideration, both as regards the conditions for setting up agencies, branches or subsidiaries in the territory of a Member State and as regards the subsidiaries in the territory of a Member State and as regards the conditions governing the entry of personnel belonging to the main establishment into managerial or supervisory posts in such agencies, branches or subsidiaries;

(g) by coordinating to the necessary extent the safeguards which, for the protection of the interests of members and others, are required by Member States of companies or firms within the meaning of the second paragraph of Article 54 with a view to making such safeguards equivalent throughout the Union;

(h) by satisfying themselves that the conditions of establishment are not distorted by aids granted by Member States.

Article 51   (ex Article 45 TEC)

The provisions of this Chapter shall not apply, so far as any given Member State is concerned, to activities which in that State are connected, even occasionally, with the exercise of official authority.

The European Parliament and the Council, acting in accordance with the ordinary legislative procedure, may rule that the provisions of this Chapter shall not apply to certain activities.

Article 52   (ex Article 46 TEC)

1. The provisions of this Chapter and measures taken in pursuance thereof shall not prejudice the applicability of provisions laid down by law, regulation or administrative action providing for special treatment for foreign nationals on grounds of public policy, public security or public health.

2. The European Parliament and the Council shall, acting in accordance with the ordinary legislative procedure, issue directives for the coordination of the abovementioned provisions.

Article 53   (ex Article 47 TEC)

1. In order to make it easier for persons to take up and pursue activities as self-employed persons, the European Parliament and the Council shall, acting in accordance with the ordinary legislative procedure, issue directives for the mutual recognition of diplomas, certificates and other evidence of formal qualifications and for the coordination of the provisions laid down by law, regulation or administrative action in Member States concerning the taking-up and pursuit of activities as self-employed persons.

2. In the case of the medical and allied and pharmaceutical professions, the progressive abolition of restrictions shall be dependent upon coordination of the conditions for their exercise in the various Member States.

Article 54   (ex Article 48 TEC)

Companies or firms formed in accordance with the law of a Member State and having their registered office, central administration or principal place of business within the Union shall, for the purposes of this Chapter, be treated in the same way as natural persons who are nationals of Member States.,

'Companies or firms' means companies or firms constituted under civil or commercial law, including cooperative societies, and other legal persons governed by public or private law, save for those which are non-profit-making.

Article 55   (ex Article 294 TEC)

Member States shall accord nationals of the other Member States the same treatment as their own nationals as regards participation in the capital of companies or firms within the meaning of Article 54, without prejudice to the application of the other provisions of the Treaties.

Chapter 3   Services

Article 56   (ex Article 49 TEC)

Within the framework of the provisions set out below, restrictions on freedom to provide services within the Union shall be prohibited in respect of nationals of Member States who are established in a Member State other than that of the person for whom the services are intended.

The European Parliament and the Council, acting in accordance with the ordinary legislative procedure, may extend the provisions of the Chapter to nationals of a third country who provide services and who are established within the Union.

Article 57   (ex Article 50 TEC)

Services shall be considered to be 'services' within the meaning of the Treaties where they are normally provided for remuneration, in so far as they are not governed by the provisions relating to freedom of movement for goods, capital and persons.

'Services' shall in particular include:

(a) activities of an industrial character;

(b) activities of a commercial character;

(c) activities of craftsmen;

(d) activities of the professions.

Without prejudice to the provisions of the Chapter relating to the right of establishment, the person providing a service may, in order to do so, temporarily pursue his activity in the Member State where the service is provided, under the same conditions as are imposed by that State on its own nationals.

Article 58   (ex Article 51 TEC)

1. Freedom to provide services in the field of transport shall be governed by the provisions of the Title relating to transport.

2. The liberalisation of banking and insurance services connected with movements of capital shall be effected in step with the liberalisation of movement of capital.

Article 59   (ex Article 52 TEC)

1. In order to achieve the liberalisation of a specific service, the European Parliament and the Council, acting in accordance with the ordinary legislative procedure and after consulting the Economic and Social Committee, shall issue directives.

2. As regards the directives referred to in paragraph 1, priority shall as a general rule be given to those services which directly affect production costs or the liberalisation of which helps to promote trade in goods.

Article 60   (ex Article 53 TEC)

The Member States shall endeavour to undertake the liberalisation of services beyond the extent required by the directives issued pursuant to Article 59(1), if their general economic situation and the situation of the economic sector concerned so permit.

To this end, the Commission shall make recommendations to the Member States concerned.

Article 61   (ex Article 54 TEC)

As long as restrictions on freedom to provide services have not been abolished, each Member State shall apply such restrictions without distinction on grounds of nationality or residence to all persons providing services within the meaning of the first paragraph of Article 56.

Article 62   (ex Article 55 TEC)

The provisions of Articles 51 to 54 shall apply to the matters covered by this Chapter.

Chapter 4 Capital and payments

Article 63   (ex Article 56 TEC)

1. Within the framework of the provisions set out in this Chapter, all restrictions on the movement of capital between Member States and between Member States and third countries shall be prohibited.

2. Within the framework of the provisions set out in this Chapter, all restrictions on payments between Member States and between Member States and third countries shall be prohibited.

Article 64   (ex Article 57 TEC)

1. The provisions of Article 63 shall be without prejudice to the application to third countries of any restrictions which exist on 31 December 1993 under national or Union law adopted in respect of the movement of capital to or from third countries involving direct investment—including in

real estate—establishment, the provision of financial services or the admission of securities to capital markets. In respect of restrictions existing under national law in Bulgaria, Estonia and Hungary, the relevant date shall be 31 December 1999. In respect of restrictions existing under national law in Croatia, the relevant date shall be 31 December 2002.

2. Whilst endeavouring to achieve the objective of free movement of capital between Member States and third countries to the greatest extent possible and without prejudice to the other Chapters of the Treaties, the European Parliament and the Council, acting in accordance with the ordinary legislative procedure, shall adopt the measures on the movement of capital to or from third countries involving direct investment—including investment in real estate—establishment, the provision of financial services or the admission of securities to capital markets.

3. Notwithstanding paragraph 2, only the Council, acting in accordance with a special legislative procedure, may unanimously, and after consulting the European Parliament, adopt measures which constitute a step backwards in Union law as regards the liberalisation of the movement of capital to or from third countries.

Article 65   (ex Article 58 TEC)

1. The provisions of Article 63 shall be without prejudice to the right of Member States:
    (a) to apply the relevant provisions of their tax law which distinguish between taxpayers who are not in the same situation with regard to their place of residence or with regard to the place where their capital is invested;
    (b) to take all requisite measures to prevent infringements of national law and regulations, in particular in the field of taxation and the prudential supervision of financial institutions, or to lay down procedures for the declaration of capital movements for purposes of administrative or statistical information, or to take measures which are justified on grounds of public policy or public security.

2. The provisions of this Chapter shall be without prejudice to the applicability of restrictions on the right of establishment which are compatible with the Treaties.

3. The measures and procedures referred to in paragraphs 1 and 2 shall not constitute a means of arbitrary discrimination or a disguised restriction on the free movement of capital and payments as defined in Article 63.

4. In the absence of measures pursuant to Article 64(3), the Commission or, in the absence of a Commission decision within three months from the request of the Member State concerned, the Council, may adopt a decision stating that restrictive tax measures adopted by a Member State concerning one or more third countries are to be considered compatible with the Treaties in so far as they are justified by one of the objectives of the Union and compatible with the proper functioning of the internal market. The Council shall act unanimously on application by a Member State.

Article 66   (ex Article 59 TEC)

Where, in exceptional circumstances, movements of capital to or from third countries cause, or threaten to cause, serious difficulties for the operation of economic and monetary union, the Council, on a proposal from the Commission and after consulting the European Central Bank, may take safeguard measures with regard to third countries for a period not exceeding six months if such measures are strictly necessary.

Title V Area of freedom, security and justice

Chapter 1 General provisions

Article 67   (ex Article 61 TEC and ex Article 29 TEU)

1. The Union shall constitute an area of freedom, security and justice with respect for fundamental rights and the different legal systems and traditions of the Member States.

2. It shall ensure the absence of internal border controls for persons and shall frame a common policy on asylum, immigration and external border control, based on solidarity between Member

States, which is fair towards third-country nationals. For the purpose of this Title, stateless persons shall be treated as third-country nationals.

3. The Union shall endeavour to ensure a high level of security through measures to prevent and combat crime, racism and xenophobia, and through measures for coordination and cooperation between police and judicial authorities and other competent authorities, as well as through the mutual recognition of judgments in criminal matters and, if necessary, through the approximation of criminal laws.

4. The Union shall facilitate access to justice, in particular through the principle of mutual recognition of judicial and extrajudicial decisions in civil matters.

Article 68
The European Council shall define the strategic guidelines for legislative and operational planning within the area of freedom, security and justice.

Article 69
National Parliaments ensure that the proposals and legislative initiatives submitted under Chapters 4 and 5 comply with the principle of subsidiarity, in accordance with the arrangements laid down by the Protocol on the application of the principles of subsidiarity and proportionality.

Article 70
Without prejudice to Articles 258, 259 and 260, the Council may, on a proposal from the Commission, adopt measures laying down the arrangements whereby Member States, in collaboration with the Commission, conduct objective and impartial evaluation of the implementation of the Union policies referred to in this Title by Member States' authorities, in particular in order to facilitate full application of the principle of mutual recognition. The European Parliament and national Parliaments shall be informed of the content and results of the evaluation.

Article 71   (ex Article 36 TEU)
A standing committee shall be set up within the Council in order to ensure that operational cooperation on internal security is promoted and strengthened within the Union. Without prejudice to Article 240, it shall facilitate coordination of the action of Member States' competent authorities. Representatives of the Union bodies, offices and agencies concerned may be involved in the proceedings of this committee. The European Parliament and national Parliaments shall be kept informed of the proceedings.

Article 72   (ex Article 64(1) TEC and ex Article 33 TEU)
This Title shall not affect the exercise of the responsibilities incumbent upon Member States with regard to the maintenance of law and order and the safeguarding of internal security.

Article 73
It shall be open to Member States to organise between themselves and under their responsibility such forms of cooperation and coordination as they deem appropriate between the competent departments of their administrations responsible for safeguarding national security.

Article 74   (ex Article 66 TEC)
The Council shall adopt measures to ensure administrative cooperation between the relevant departments of the Member States in the areas covered by this Title, as well as between those departments and the Commission. It shall act on a Commission proposal, subject to Article 76, and after consulting the European Parliament.

Article 75   (ex Article 60 TEC)
Where necessary to achieve the objectives set out in Article 67, as regards preventing and combating terrorism and related activities, the European Parliament and the Council, acting by means of regulations in accordance with the ordinary legislative procedure, shall define a framework for administrative measures with regard to capital movements and payments, such as the freezing of funds,

financial assets or economic gains belonging to, or owned or held by, natural or legal persons, groups or non-State entities.

The Council, on a proposal from the Commission, shall adopt measures to implement the framework referred to in the first paragraph.

The acts referred to in this Article shall include necessary provisions on legal safeguards.

Article 76
The acts referred to in Chapters 4 and 5, together with the measures referred to in Article 74 which ensure administrative cooperation in the areas covered by these Chapters, shall be adopted:
   (a) on a proposal from the Commission, or
   (b) on the initiative of a quarter of the Member States.

Chapter 2 Policies on border checks, asylum and immigration

Article 77   (ex Article 62 TEC)
   1. The Union shall develop a policy with a view to:
   (a) ensuring the absence of any controls on persons, whatever their nationality, when crossing internal borders;
   (b) carrying out checks on persons and efficient monitoring of the crossing of external borders;
   (c) the gradual introduction of an integrated management system for external borders.
   2. For the purposes of paragraph 1, the European Parliament and the Council, acting in accordance with the ordinary legislative procedure, shall adopt measures concerning:
   (a) the common policy on visas and other short-stay residence permits;
   (b) the checks to which persons crossing external borders are subject;
   (c) the conditions under which nationals of third countries shall have the freedom to travel within the Union for a short period;
   (d) any measure necessary for the gradual establishment of an integrated management system for external borders;
   (e) the absence of any controls on persons, whatever their nationality, when crossing internal borders.
   3. If action by the Union should prove necessary to facilitate the exercise of the right referred to in Article 20(2)(a), and if the Treaties have not provided the necessary powers, the Council, acting in accordance with a special legislative procedure, may adopt provisions concerning passports, identity cards, residence permits or any other such document. The Council shall act unanimously after consulting the European Parliament.
   4. This Article shall not affect the competence of the Member States concerning the geographical demarcation of their borders, in accordance with international law.

Article 78   (ex Articles 63, points 1 and 2, and 64(2) TEC)
   1. The Union shall develop a common policy on asylum, subsidiary protection and temporary protection with a view to offering appropriate status to any third-country national requiring international protection and ensuring compliance with the principle of *non-refoulement*. This policy must be in accordance with the Geneva Convention of 28 July 1951 and the Protocol of 31 January 1967 relating to the status of refugees, and other relevant treaties.
   2. For the purposes of paragraph 1, the European Parliament and the Council, acting in accordance with the ordinary legislative procedure, shall adopt measures for a common European asylum system comprising:
   (a) a uniform status of asylum for nationals of third countries, valid throughout the Union;
   (b) a uniform status of subsidiary protection for nationals of third countries who, without obtaining European asylum, are in need of international protection;
   (c) a common system of temporary protection for displaced persons in the event of a massive inflow;

(d) common procedures for the granting and withdrawing of uniform asylum or subsidiary protection status;

(e) criteria and mechanisms for determining which Member State is responsible for considering an application for asylum or subsidiary protection;

(f) standards concerning the conditions for the reception of applicants for asylum or subsidiary protection;

(g) partnership and cooperation with third countries for the purpose of managing inflows of people applying for asylum or subsidiary or temporary protection.

3. In the event of one or more Member States being confronted by an emergency situation characterised by a sudden inflow of nationals of third countries, the Council, on a proposal from the Commission, may adopt provisional measures for the benefit of the Member State(s) concerned. It shall act after consulting the European Parliament.

Article 79   (ex Article 63, points 3 and 4, TEC)

1. The Union shall develop a common immigration policy aimed at ensuring, at all stages, the efficient management of migration flows, fair treatment of third-country nationals residing legally in Member States, and the prevention of, and enhanced measures to combat, illegal immigration and trafficking in human beings.

2. For the purposes of paragraph 1, the European Parliament and the Council, acting in accordance with the ordinary legislative procedure, shall adopt measures in the following areas:

(a) the conditions of entry and residence, and standards on the issue by Member States of long-term visas and residence permits, including those for the purpose of family reunification;

(b) the definition of the rights of third-country nationals residing legally in a Member State, including the conditions governing freedom of movement and of residence in other Member States;

(c) illegal immigration and unauthorised residence, including removal and repatriation of persons residing without authorisation;

(d) combating trafficking in persons, in particular women and children.

3. The Union may conclude agreements with third countries for the readmission to their countries of origin or provenance of third-country nationals who do not or who no longer fulfil the conditions for entry, presence or residence in the territory of one of the Member States.

4. The European Parliament and the Council, acting in accordance with the ordinary legislative procedure, may establish measures to provide incentives and support for the action of Member States with a view to promoting the integration of third-country nationals residing legally in their territories, excluding any harmonisation of the laws and regulations of the Member States.

5. This Article shall not affect the right of Member States to determine volumes of admission of third-country nationals coming from third countries to their territory in order to seek work, whether employed or self-employed.

Article 80

The policies of the Union set out in this Chapter and their implementation shall be governed by the principle of solidarity and fair sharing of responsibility, including its financial implications, between the Member States. Whenever necessary, the Union acts adopted pursuant to this Chapter shall contain appropriate measures to give effect to this principle.

Chapter 3   Judicial cooperation in civil matters

Article 81   (ex Article 65 TEC)

1. The Union shall develop judicial cooperation in civil matters having cross-border implications, based on the principle of mutual recognition of judgments and of decisions in extrajudicial cases. Such cooperation may include the adoption of measures for the approximation of the laws and regulations of the Member States.

2. For the purposes of paragraph 1, the European Parliament and the Council, acting in accordance with the ordinary legislative procedure, shall adopt measures, particularly when necessary for the proper functioning of the internal market, aimed at ensuring:

(a) the mutual recognition and enforcement between Member States of judgments and of decisions in extrajudicial cases;

(b) the cross-border service of judicial and extrajudicial documents;

(c) the compatibility of the rules applicable in the Member States concerning conflict of laws and of jurisdiction;

(d) cooperation in the taking of evidence;

(e) effective access to justice;

(f) the elimination of obstacles to the proper functioning of civil proceedings, if necessary by promoting the compatibility of the rules on civil procedure applicable in the Member States;

(g) the development of alternative methods of dispute settlement;

(h) support for the training of the judiciary and judicial staff.

3. Notwithstanding paragraph 2, measures concerning family law with cross-border implications shall be established by the Council, acting in accordance with a special legislative procedure. The Council shall act unanimously after consulting the European Parliament.

The Council, on a proposal from the Commission, may adopt a decision determining those aspects of family law with cross-border implications which may be the subject of acts adopted by the ordinary legislative procedure. The Council shall act unanimously after consulting the European Parliament.

The proposal referred to in the second subparagraph shall be notified to the national Parliaments. If a national Parliament makes known its opposition within six months of the date of such notification, the decision shall not be adopted. In the absence of opposition, the Council may adopt the decision.

Chapter 4 Judicial cooperation in criminal matters

Article 82 (ex Article 31 TEU)

1. Judicial cooperation in criminal matters in the Union shall be based on the principle of mutual recognition of judgments and judicial decisions and shall include the approximation of the laws and regulations of the Member States in the areas referred to in paragraph 2 and in Article 83.

The European Parliament and the Council, acting in accordance with the ordinary legislative procedure, shall adopt measures to:

(a) lay down rules and procedures for ensuring recognition throughout the Union of all forms of judgments and judicial decisions;

(b) prevent and settle conflicts of jurisdiction between Member States;

(c) support the training of the judiciary and judicial staff;

(d) facilitate cooperation between judicial or equivalent authorities of the Member States in relation to proceedings in criminal matters and the enforcement of decisions.

2. To the extent necessary to facilitate mutual recognition of judgments and judicial decisions and police and judicial cooperation in criminal matters having a cross-border dimension, the European Parliament and the Council may, by means of directives adopted in accordance with the ordinary legislative procedure, establish minimum rules. Such rules shall take into account the differences between the legal traditions and systems of the Member States.

They shall concern:

(a) mutual admissibility of evidence between Member States;

(b) the rights of individuals in criminal procedure;

(c) the rights of victims of crime;

(d) any other specific aspects of criminal procedure which the Council has identified in advance by a decision; for the adoption of such a decision, the Council shall act unanimously after obtaining the consent of the European Parliament.

Adoption of the minimum rules referred to in this paragraph shall not prevent Member States from maintaining or introducing a higher level of protection for individuals.

3. Where a member of the Council considers that a draft directive as referred to in paragraph 2 would affect fundamental aspects of its criminal justice system, it may request that the draft directive be referred to the European Council. In that case, the ordinary legislative procedure shall be suspended. After discussion, and in case of a consensus, the European Council shall, within four months of this suspension, refer the draft back to the Council, which shall terminate the suspension of the ordinary legislative procedure.

Within the same timeframe, in case of disagreement, and if at least nine Member States wish to establish enhanced cooperation on the basis of the draft directive concerned, they shall notify the European Parliament, the Council and the Commission accordingly. In such a case, the authorisation to proceed with enhanced cooperation referred to in Article 20(2) of the Treaty on European Union and Article 329(1) of this Treaty shall be deemed to be granted and the provisions on enhanced cooperation shall apply.

Article 83   (ex Article 31 TEU)

1. The European Parliament and the Council may, by means of directives adopted in accordance with the ordinary legislative procedure, establish minimum rules concerning the definition of criminal offences and sanctions in the areas of particularly serious crime with a cross-border dimension resulting from the nature or impact of such offences or from a special need to combat them on a common basis.

These areas of crime are the following: terrorism, trafficking in human beings and sexual exploitation of women and children, illicit drug trafficking, illicit arms trafficking, money laundering, corruption, counterfeiting of means of payment, computer crime and organised crime.

On the basis of developments in crime, the Council may adopt a decision identifying other areas of crime that meet the criteria specified in this paragraph. It shall act unanimously after obtaining the consent of the European Parliament.

2. If the approximation of criminal laws and regulations of the Member States proves essential to ensure the effective implementation of a Union policy in an area which has been subject to harmonisation measures, directives may establish minimum rules with regard to the definition of criminal offences and sanctions in the area concerned.

Such directives shall be adopted by the same ordinary or special legislative procedure as was followed for the adoption of the harmonisation measures in question, without prejudice to Article 76.

3. Where a member of the Council considers that a draft directive as referred to in paragraph 1 or 2 would affect fundamental aspects of its criminal justice system, it may request that the draft directive be referred to the European Council. In that case, the ordinary legislative procedure shall be suspended. After discussion, and in case of a consensus, the European Council shall, within four months of this suspension, refer the draft back to the Council, which shall terminate the suspension of the ordinary legislative procedure.

Within the same timeframe, in case of disagreement, and if at least nine Member States wish to establish enhanced cooperation on the basis of the draft directive concerned, they shall notify the European Parliament, the Council and the Commission accordingly. In such a case, the authorisation to proceed with enhanced cooperation referred to in Article 20(2) of the Treaty on European Union and Article 329(1) of this Treaty shall be deemed to be granted and the provisions on enhanced cooperation shall apply.

Article 84

The European Parliament and the Council, acting in accordance with the ordinary legislative procedure, may establish measures to promote and support the action of Member States in the field of crime prevention, excluding any harmonisation of the laws and regulations of the Member States.

Article 85   (ex Article 31 TEU)

1. Eurojust's mission shall be to support and strengthen coordination and cooperation between national investigating and prosecuting authorities in relation to serious crime affecting two or more Member States or requiring a prosecution on common bases, on the basis of operations conducted and information supplied by the Member States' authorities and by Europol.

In this context, the European Parliament and the Council, by means of regulations adopted in accordance with the ordinary legislative procedure, shall determine Eurojust's structure, operation, field of action and tasks. These tasks may include:

(a) the initiation of criminal investigations, as well as proposing the initiation of prosecutions conducted by competent national authorities, particularly those relating to offences against the financial interests of the Union;

(b) the coordination of investigations and prosecutions referred to in point (a);

(c) the strengthening of judicial cooperation, including by resolution of conflicts of jurisdiction and by close cooperation with the European Judicial Network.

These regulations shall also determine arrangements for involving the European Parliament and national Parliaments in the evaluation of Eurojust's activities.

2. In the prosecutions referred to in paragraph 1, and without prejudice to Article 86, formal acts of judicial procedure shall be carried out by the competent national officials.

Article 86

1. In order to combat crimes affecting the financial interests of the Union, the Council, by means of regulations adopted in accordance with a special legislative procedure, may establish a European Public Prosecutor's Office from Eurojust. The Council shall act unanimously after obtaining the consent of the European Parliament.

In the absence of unanimity in the Council, a group of at least nine Member States may request that the draft regulation be referred to the European Council. In that case, the procedure in the Council shall be suspended. After discussion, and in case of a consensus, the European Council shall, within four months of this suspension, refer the draft back to the Council for adoption.

Within the same timeframe, in case of disagreement, and if at least nine Member States wish to establish enhanced cooperation on the basis of the draft regulation concerned, they shall notify the European Parliament, the Council and the Commission accordingly. In such a case, the authorisation to proceed with enhanced cooperation referred to in Article 20(2) of the Treaty on European Union and Article 329(1) of this Treaty shall be deemed to be granted and the provisions on enhanced cooperation shall apply.

2. The European Public Prosecutor's Office shall be responsible for investigating, prosecuting and bringing to judgment, where appropriate in liaison with Europol, the perpetrators of, and accomplices in, offences against the Union's financial interests, as determined by the regulation provided for in paragraph 1. It shall exercise the functions of prosecutor in the competent courts of the Member States in relation to such offences.

3. The regulations referred to in paragraph 1 shall determine the general rules applicable to the European Public Prosecutor's Office, the conditions governing the performance of its functions, the rules of procedure applicable to its activities, as well as those governing the admissibility of evidence, and the rules applicable to the judicial review of procedural measures taken by it in the performance of its functions.

4. The European Council may, at the same time or subsequently, adopt a decision amending paragraph 1 in order to extend the powers of the European Public Prosecutor's Office to include serious crime having a cross-border dimension and amending accordingly paragraph 2 as regards the perpetrators of, and accomplices in, serious crimes affecting more than one Member State. The European Council shall act unanimously after obtaining the consent of the European Parliament and after consulting the Commission.

Chapter 5 Police cooperation

Article 87 (ex Article 30 TEU)

1. The Union shall establish police cooperation involving all the Member States' competent authorities, including police, customs and other specialised law enforcement services in relation to the prevention, detection and investigation of criminal offences.

2. For the purposes of paragraph 1, the European Parliament and the Council, acting in accordance with the ordinary legislative procedure, may establish measures concerning:

(a) the collection, storage, processing, analysis and exchange of relevant information;

(b) support for the training of staff, and cooperation on the exchange of staff, on equipment and on research into crime-detection;

(c) common investigative techniques in relation to the detection of serious forms of organised crime.

3. The Council, acting in accordance with a special legislative procedure, may establish measures concerning operational cooperation between the authorities referred to in this Article. The Council shall act unanimously after consulting the European Parliament.

In case of the absence of unanimity in the Council, a group of at least nine Member States may request that the draft measures be referred to the European Council. In that case, the procedure in the Council shall be suspended. After discussion, and in case of a consensus, the European Council shall, within four months of this suspension, refer the draft back to the Council for adoption.

Within the same timeframe, in case of disagreement, and if at least nine Member States wish to establish enhanced cooperation on the basis of the draft measures concerned, they shall notify the European Parliament, the Council and the Commission accordingly. In such a case, the authorisation to proceed with enhanced cooperation referred to in Article 20(2) of the Treaty on European Union and Article 329(1) of this Treaty shall be deemed to be granted and the provisions on enhanced cooperation shall apply.

The specific procedure provided for in the second and third subparagraphs shall not apply to acts which constitute a development of the Schengen *acquis*.

Article 88   (ex Article 30 TEU)

1. Europol's mission shall be to support and strengthen action by the Member States' police authorities and other law enforcement services and their mutual cooperation in preventing and combating serious crime affecting two or more Member States, terrorism and forms of crime which affect a common interest covered by a Union policy.

2. The European Parliament and the Council, by means of regulations adopted in accordance with the ordinary legislative procedure, shall determine Europol's structure, operation, field of action and tasks. These tasks may include:

(a) the collection, storage, processing, analysis and exchange of information, in particular that forwarded by the authorities of the Member States or third countries or bodies;

(b) the coordination, organisation and implementation of investigative and operational action carried out jointly with the Member States' competent authorities or in the context of joint investigative teams, where appropriate in liaison with Eurojust.

These regulations shall also lay down the procedures for scrutiny of Europol's activities by the European Parliament, together with national Parliaments.

3. Any operational action by Europol must be carried out in liaison and in agreement with the authorities of the Member State or States whose territory is concerned. The application of coercive measures shall be the exclusive responsibility of the competent national authorities.

Article 89   (ex Article 32 TEU)

The Council, acting in accordance with a special legislative procedure, shall lay down the conditions and limitations under which the competent authorities of the Member States referred to in Articles 82 and 87 may operate in the territory of another Member State in liaison and in agreement with the authorities of that State. The Council shall act unanimously after consulting the European Parliament.

Title VI Transport

Article 90   (ex Article 70 TEC)

The objectives of the Treaties shall, in matters governed by this Title, be pursued within the framework of a common transport policy.

Article 91 (ex Article 71 TEC)

1. For the purpose of implementing Article 90, and taking into account the distinctive features of transport, the European Parliament and the Council shall, acting in accordance with the ordinary legislative procedure and after consulting the Economic and Social Committee and the Committee of the Regions, lay down:

(a) common rules applicable to international transport to or from the territory of a Member State or passing across the territory of one or more Member States;

(b) the conditions under which non-resident carriers may operate transport services within a Member State;

(c) measures to improve transport safety;

(d) any other appropriate provisions.

2. When the measures referred to in paragraph 1 are adopted, account shall be taken of cases where their application might seriously affect the standard of living and level of employment in certain regions, and the operation of transport facilities.

Article 92 (ex Article 72 TEC)

Until the provisions referred to in Article 91(1) have been laid down, no Member State may, unless the Council has unanimously adopted a measure granting a derogation, make the various provisions governing the subject on 1 January 1958 or, for acceding States, the date of their accession less favourable in their direct or indirect effect on carriers of other Member States as compared with carriers who are nationals of that State.

Article 93 (ex Article 73 TEC)

Aids shall be compatible with the Treaties if they meet the needs of coordination of transport or if they represent reimbursement for the discharge of certain obligations inherent in the concept of a public service.

Article 94 (ex Article 74 TEC)

Any measures taken within the framework of the Treaties in respect of transport rates and conditions shall take account of the economic circumstances of carriers.

Article 95 (ex Article 75 TEC)

1. In the case of transport within the Union, discrimination which takes the form of carriers charging different rates and imposing different conditions for the carriage of the same goods over the same transport links on grounds of the country of origin or of destination of the goods in question shall be prohibited.

2. Paragraph 1 shall not prevent the European Parliament and the Council from adopting other measures pursuant to Article 91(1).

3. The Council shall, on a proposal from the Commission and after consulting the European Parliament and the Economic and Social Committee, lay down rules for implementing the provisions of paragraph 1.

The Council may in particular lay down the provisions needed to enable the institutions of the Union to secure compliance with the rule laid down in paragraph 1 and to ensure that users benefit from it to the full.

4. The Commission shall, acting on its own initiative or on application by a Member State, investigate any cases of discrimination falling within paragraph 1 and, after consulting any Member State concerned, shall take the necessary decisions within the framework of the rules laid down in accordance with the provisions of paragraph 3.

Article 96 (ex Article 76 TEC)

1. The imposition by a Member State, in respect of transport operations carried out within the Union, of rates and conditions involving any element of support or protection in the interest of one or more particular undertakings or industries shall be prohibited, unless authorised by the Commission.

2. The Commission shall, acting on its own initiative or on application by a Member State, examine the rates and conditions referred to in paragraph 1, taking account in particular of the requirements of an appropriate regional economic policy, the needs of underdeveloped areas and the problems of areas seriously affected by political circumstances on the one hand, and of the effects of such rates and conditions on competition between the different modes of transport on the other.

After consulting each Member State concerned, the Commission shall take the necessary decisions.

3. The prohibition provided for in paragraph 1 shall not apply to tariffs fixed to meet competition.

Article 97   (ex Article 77 TEC)

Charges or dues in respect of the crossing of frontiers which are charged by a carrier in addition to the transport rates shall not exceed a reasonable level after taking the costs actually incurred thereby into account.

Member States shall endeavour to reduce these costs progressively.

The Commission may make recommendations to Member States for the application of this Article.

Article 98   (ex Article 78 TEC)

The provisions of this Title shall not form an obstacle to the application of measures taken in the Federal Republic of Germany to the extent that such measures are required in order to compensate for the economic disadvantages caused by the division of Germany to the economy of certain areas of the Federal Republic affected by that division. Five years after the entry into force of the Treaty of Lisbon, the Council, acting on a proposal from the Commission, may adopt a decision repealing this Article.

Article 99   (ex Article 79 TEC)

An Advisory Committee consisting of experts designated by the governments of Member States shall be attached to the Commission. The Commission, whenever it considers it desirable, shall consult the Committee on transport matters.

Article 100   (ex Article 80 TEC)

1. The provisions of this Title shall apply to transport by rail, road and inland waterway.

2. The European Parliament and the Council, acting in accordance with the ordinary legislative procedure, may lay down appropriate provisions for sea and air transport. They shall act after consulting the Economic and Social Committee and the Committee of the Regions.

Title VII Common rules on competition, taxation and approximation of laws

Chapter 1 Rules on competition

Section 1 Rules applying to undertakings

Article 101   (ex Article 81 TEC)

1. The following shall be prohibited as incompatible with the internal market: all agreements between undertakings, decisions by associations of undertakings and concerted practices which may affect trade between Member States and which have as their object or effect the prevention, restriction or distortion of competition within the internal market, and in particular those which:

    (a) directly or indirectly fix purchase or selling prices or any other trading conditions;

    (b) limit or control production, markets, technical development, or investment;

    (c) share markets or sources of supply;

    (d) apply dissimilar conditions to equivalent transactions with other trading parties, thereby placing them at a competitive disadvantage;

    (e) make the conclusion of contracts subject to acceptance by the other parties of supplementary obligations which, by their nature or according to commercial usage, have no connection with the subject of such contracts.

2. Any agreements or decisions prohibited pursuant to this Article shall be automatically void.
3. The provisions of paragraph 1 may, however, be declared inapplicable in the case of:
   - any agreement or category of agreements between undertakings,
   - any decision or category of decisions by associations of undertakings,
   - any concerted practice or category of concerted practices,

which contributes to improving the production or distribution of goods or to promoting technical or economic progress, while allowing consumers a fair share of the resulting benefit, and which does not:

 (a) impose on the undertakings concerned restrictions which are not indispensable to the attainment of these objectives;

 (b) afford such undertakings the possibility of eliminating competition in respect of a substantial part of the products in question.

Article 102   (ex Article 82 TEC)

Any abuse by one or more undertakings of a dominant position within the internal market or in a substantial part of it shall be prohibited as incompatible with the internal market in so far as it may affect trade between Member States.

Such abuse may, in particular, consist in:

 (a) directly or indirectly imposing unfair purchase or selling prices or other unfair trading conditions;

 (b) limiting production, markets or technical development to the prejudice of consumers;

 (c) applying dissimilar conditions to equivalent transactions with other trading parties, thereby placing them at a competitive disadvantage;

 (d) making the conclusion of contracts subject to acceptance by the other parties of supplementary obligations which, by their nature or according to commercial usage, have no connection with the subject of such contracts.

Article 103   (ex Article 83 TEC)

1. The appropriate regulations or directives to give effect to the principles set out in Articles 101 and 102 shall be laid down by the Council, on a proposal from the Commission and after consulting the European Parliament.
2. The regulations or directives referred to in paragraph 1 shall be designed in particular:

 (a) to ensure compliance with the prohibitions laid down in Article 101(1) and in Article 102 by making provision for fines and periodic penalty payments;

 (b) to lay down detailed rules for the application of Article 101(3), taking into account the need to ensure effective supervision on the one hand, and to simplify administration to the greatest possible extent on the other;

 (c) to define, if need be, in the various branches of the economy, the scope of the provisions of Articles 101 and 102;

 (d) to define the respective functions of the Commission and of the Court of Justice of the European Union in applying the provisions laid down in this paragraph;

 (e) to determine the relationship between national laws and the provisions contained in this Section or adopted pursuant to this Article.

Article 104   (ex Article 84 TEC)

Until the entry into force of the provisions adopted in pursuance of Article 103, the authorities in Member States shall rule on the admissibility of agreements, decisions and concerted practices and on abuse of a dominant position in the internal market in accordance with the law of their country and with the provisions of Article 101, in particular paragraph 3, and of Article 102.

Article 105   (ex Article 85 TEC)

1. Without prejudice to Article 104, the Commission shall ensure the application of the principles laid down in Articles 101 and 102. On application by a Member State or on its own initiative, and in cooperation with the competent authorities in the Member States, which shall give it their

assistance, the Commission shall investigate cases of suspected infringement of these principles. If it finds that there has been an infringement, it shall propose appropriate measures to bring it to an end.

2. If the infringement is not brought to an end, the Commission shall record such infringement of the principles in a reasoned decision. The Commission may publish its decision and authorise Member States to take the measures, the conditions and details of which it shall determine, needed to remedy the situation.

3. The Commission may adopt regulations relating to the categories of agreement in respect of which the Council has adopted a regulation or a directive pursuant to Article 103(2)(b).

Article 106   (ex Article 86 TEC)

1. In the case of public undertakings and undertakings to which Member States grant special or exclusive rights, Member States shall neither enact nor maintain in force any measure contrary to the rules contained in the Treaties, in particular to those rules provided for in Article 18 and Articles 101 to 109.

2. Undertakings entrusted with the operation of services of general economic interest or having the character of a revenue-producing monopoly shall be subject to the rules contained in the Treaties, in particular to the rules on competition, in so far as the application of such rules does not obstruct the performance, in law or in fact, of the particular tasks assigned to them. The development of trade must not be affected to such an extent as would be contrary to the interests of the Union.

3. The Commission shall ensure the application of the provisions of this Article and shall, where necessary, address appropriate directives or decisions to Member States.

Section 2 Aids granted by States

Article 107   (ex Article 87 TEC)

1. Save as otherwise provided in the Treaties, any aid granted by a Member State or through State resources in any form whatsoever which distorts or threatens to distort competition by favouring certain undertakings or the production of certain goods shall, in so far as it affects trade between Member States, be incompatible with the internal market.

2. The following shall be compatible with the internal market:
   - (a) aid having a social character, granted to individual consumers, provided that such aid is granted without discrimination related to the origin of the products concerned;
   - (b) aid to make good the damage caused by natural disasters or exceptional occurrences;
   - (c) aid granted to the economy of certain areas of the Federal Republic of Germany affected by the division of Germany, in so far as such aid is required in order to compensate for the economic disadvantages caused by that division. Five years after the entry into force of the Treaty of Lisbon, the Council, acting on a proposal from the Commission, may adopt a decision repealing this point.

3. The following may be considered to be compatible with the internal market:
   - (a) aid to promote the economic development of areas where the standard of living is abnormally low or where there is serious underemployment, and of the regions referred to in Article 349, in view of their structural, economic and social situation;
   - (b) aid to promote the execution of an important project of common European interest or to remedy a serious disturbance in the economy of a Member State;
   - (c) aid to facilitate the development of certain economic activities or of certain economic areas, where such aid does not adversely affect trading conditions to an extent contrary to the common interest;
   - (d) aid to promote culture and heritage conservation where such aid does not affect trading conditions and competition in the Union to an extent that is contrary to the common interest;
   - (e) such other categories of aid as may be specified by decision of the Council on a proposal from the Commission.

Article 108   (ex Article 88 TEC)

1. The Commission shall, in cooperation with Member States, keep under constant review all systems of aid existing in those States. It shall propose to the latter any appropriate measures required by the progressive development or by the functioning of the internal market.

2. If, after giving notice to the parties concerned to submit their comments, the Commission finds that aid granted by a State or through State resources is not compatible with the internal market having regard to Article 107, or that such aid is being misused, it shall decide that the State concerned shall abolish or alter such aid within a period of time to be determined by the Commission.

If the State concerned does not comply with this decision within the prescribed time, the Commission or any other interested State may, in derogation from the provisions of Articles 258 and 259, refer the matter to the Court of Justice of the European Union direct.

On application by a Member State, the Council may, acting unanimously, decide that aid which that State is granting or intends to grant shall be considered to be compatible with the internal market, in derogation from the provisions of Article 107 or from the regulations provided for in Article 109, if such a decision is justified by exceptional circumstances. If, as regards the aid in question, the Commission has already initiated the procedure provided for in the first subparagraph of this paragraph, the fact that the State concerned has made its application to the Council shall have the effect of suspending that procedure until the Council has made its attitude known.

If, however, the Council has not made its attitude known within three months of the said application being made, the Commission shall give its decision on the case.

3. The Commission shall be informed, in sufficient time to enable it to submit its comments, of any plans to grant or alter aid. If it considers that any such plan is not compatible with the internal market having regard to Article 107, it shall without delay initiate the procedure provided for in paragraph 2. The Member State concerned shall not put its proposed measures into effect until this procedure has resulted in a final decision.

4. The Commission may adopt regulations relating to the categories of State aid that the Council has, pursuant to Article 109, determined may be exempted from the procedure provided for by paragraph 3 of this Article.

Article 109   (ex Article 89 TEC)

The Council, on a proposal from the Commission and after consulting the European Parliament, may make any appropriate regulations for the application of Articles 107 and 108 and may in particular determine the conditions in which Article 108(3) shall apply and the categories of aid exempted from this procedure.

Chapter 2 Tax provisions

Article 110   (ex Article 90 TEC)

No Member State shall impose, directly or indirectly, on the products of other Member States any internal taxation of any kind in excess of that imposed directly or indirectly on similar domestic products.

Furthermore, no Member State shall impose on the products of other Member States any internal taxation of such a nature as to afford indirect protection to other products.

Article 111   (ex Article 91 TEC)

Where products are exported to the territory of any Member State, any repayment of internal taxation shall not exceed the internal taxation imposed on them whether directly or indirectly.

Article 112   (ex Article 92 TEC)

In the case of charges other than turnover taxes, excise duties and other forms of indirect taxation, remissions and repayments in respect of exports to other Member States may not be granted and countervailing charges in respect of imports from Member States may not be imposed unless the measures contemplated have been previously approved for a limited period by the Council on a proposal from the Commission.

Article 113   (ex Article 93 TEC)

The Council shall, acting unanimously in accordance with a special legislative procedure and after consulting the European Parliament and the Economic and Social Committee, adopt provisions for the harmonisation of legislation concerning turnover taxes, excise duties and other forms of indirect taxation to the extent that such harmonisation is necessary to ensure the establishment and the functioning of the internal market and to avoid distortion of competition.

Chapter 3   Approximation of laws

Article 114   (ex Article 95 TEC)

1. Save where otherwise provided in the Treaties, the following provisions shall apply for the achievement of the objectives set out in Article 26. The European Parliament and the Council shall, acting in accordance with the ordinary legislative procedure and after consulting the Economic and Social Committee, adopt the measures for the approximation of the provisions laid down by law, regulation or administrative action in Member States which have as their object the establishment and functioning of the internal market.

2. Paragraph 1 shall not apply to fiscal provisions, to those relating to the free movement of persons nor to those relating to the rights and interests of employed persons.

3. The Commission, in its proposals envisaged in paragraph 1 concerning health, safety, environmental protection and consumer protection, will take as a base a high level of protection, taking account in particular of any new development based on scientific facts. Within their respective powers, the European Parliament and the Council will also seek to achieve this objective.

4. If, after the adoption of a harmonisation measure by the European Parliament and the Council, by the Council or by the Commission, a Member State deems it necessary to maintain national provisions on grounds of major needs referred to in Article 36, or relating to the protection of the environment or the working environment, it shall notify the Commission of these provisions as well as the grounds for maintaining them.

5. Moreover, without prejudice to paragraph 4, if, after the adoption of a harmonisation measure by the European Parliament and the Council, by the Council or by the Commission, a Member State deems it necessary to introduce national provisions based on new scientific evidence relating to the protection of the environment or the working environment on grounds of a problem specific to that Member State arising after the adoption of the harmonisation measure, it shall notify the Commission of the envisaged provisions as well as the grounds for introducing them.

6. The Commission shall, within six months of the notifications as referred to in paragraphs 4 and 5, approve or reject the national provisions involved after having verified whether or not they are a means of arbitrary discrimination or a disguised restriction on trade between Member States and whether or not they shall constitute an obstacle to the functioning of the internal market.

In the absence of a decision by the Commission within this period the national provisions referred to in paragraphs 4 and 5 shall be deemed to have been approved.

When justified by the complexity of the matter and in the absence of danger for human health, the Commission may notify the Member State concerned that the period referred to in this paragraph may be extended for a further period of up to six months.

7. When, pursuant to paragraph 6, a Member State is authorised to maintain or introduce national provisions derogating from a harmonisation measure, the Commission shall immediately examine whether to propose an adaptation to that measure.

8. When a Member State raises a specific problem on public health in a field which has been the subject of prior harmonisation measures, it shall bring it to the attention of the Commission which shall immediately examine whether to propose appropriate measures to the Council.

9. By way of derogation from the procedure laid down in Articles 258 and 259, the Commission and any Member State may bring the matter directly before the Court of Justice of the European Union if it considers that another Member State is making improper use of the powers provided for in this Article.

10. The harmonisation measures referred to above shall, in appropriate cases, include a safeguard clause authorising the Member States to take, for one or more of the non-economic reasons referred to in Article 36, provisional measures subject to a Union control procedure.

Article 115   (ex Article 94 TEC)

Without prejudice to Article 114, the Council shall, acting unanimously in accordance with a special legislative procedure and after consulting the European Parliament and the Economic and Social Committee, issue directives for the approximation of such laws, regulations or administrative provisions of the Member States as directly affect the establishment or functioning of the internal market.

Article 116   (ex Article 96 TEC)

Where the Commission finds that a difference between the provisions laid down by law, regulation or administrative action in Member States is distorting the conditions of competition in the internal market and that the resultant distortion needs to be eliminated, it shall consult the Member States concerned.

If such consultation does not result in an agreement eliminating the distortion in question, the European, Parliament and the Council, acting in accordance with the ordinary legislative procedure, shall issue the necessary directives. Any other appropriate measures provided for in the Treaties may be adopted.

Article 117   (ex Article 97 TEC)

1. Where there is a reason to fear that the adoption or amendment of a provision laid down by law, regulation or administrative action may cause distortion within the meaning of Article 116, a Member State desiring to proceed therewith shall consult the Commission. After consulting the Member States, the Commission shall recommend to the States concerned such measures as may be appropriate to avoid the distortion in question.

2. If a State desiring to introduce or amend its own provisions does not comply with the recommendation addressed to it by the Commission, other Member States shall not be required, pursuant to Article 116, to amend their own provisions in order to eliminate such distortion. If the Member State which has ignored the recommendation of the Commission causes distortion detrimental only to itself, the provisions of Article 116 shall not apply.

Article 118

In the context of the establishment and functioning of the internal market, the European Parliament and the Council, acting in accordance with the ordinary legislative procedure, shall establish measures for the creation of European intellectual property rights to provide uniform protection of intellectual property rights throughout the Union and for the setting up of centralised Union-wide authorisation, coordination and supervision arrangements.

The Council, acting in accordance with a special legislative procedure, shall by means of regulations establish language arrangements for the European intellectual property rights. The Council shall act unanimously after consulting the European Parliament.

Title VIII Economic and monetary policy

Article 119   (ex Article 4 TEC)

1. For the purposes set out in Article 3 of the Treaty on European Union, the activities of the Member States and the Union shall include, as provided in the Treaties, the adoption of an economic policy which is based on the close coordination of Member States' economic policies, on the internal market and on the definition of common objectives, and conducted in accordance with the principle of an open market economy with free competition.

2. Concurrently with the foregoing, and as provided in the Treaties and in accordance with the procedures set out therein, these activities shall include a single currency, the euro, and the definition and conduct of a single monetary policy and exchange-rate policy the primary objective of both of which shall be to maintain price stability and, without prejudice to this objective, to support the

general economic policies in the Union, in accordance with the principle of an open market economy with free competition.

3. These activities of the Member States and the Union shall entail compliance with the following guiding principles: stable prices, sound public finances and monetary conditions and a sustainable balance of payments.

Chapter 1 Economic policy

Article 120   (ex Article 98 TEC)

Member States shall conduct their economic policies with a view to contributing to the achievement of the objectives of the Union, as defined in Article 3 of the Treaty on European Union, and in the context of the broad guidelines referred to in Article 121(2). The Member States and the Union shall act in accordance with the principle of an open market economy with free competition, favouring an efficient allocation of resources, and in compliance with the principles set out in Article 119.

Article 121   (ex Article 99 TEC)

1. Member States shall regard their economic policies as a matter of common concern and shall coordinate them within the Council, in accordance with the provisions of Article 120.

2. The Council shall, on a recommendation from the Commission, formulate a draft for the broad guidelines of the economic policies of the Member States and of the Union, and shall report its findings to the European Council.

The European Council shall, acting on the basis of the report from the Council, discuss a conclusion on the broad guidelines of the economic policies of the Member States and of the Union.

On the basis of this conclusion, the Council shall adopt a recommendation setting out these broad guidelines. The Council shall inform the European Parliament of its recommendation.

3. In order to ensure closer coordination of economic policies and sustained convergence of the economic performances of the Member States, the Council shall, on the basis of reports submitted by the Commission, monitor economic developments in each of the Member States and in the Union as well as the consistency of economic policies with the broad guidelines referred to in paragraph 2, and regularly carry out an overall assessment.

For the purpose of this multilateral surveillance, Member States shall forward information to the Commission about important measures taken by them in the field of their economic policy and such other information as they deem necessary.

4. Where it is established, under the procedure referred to in paragraph 3, that the economic policies of a Member State are not consistent with the broad guidelines referred to in paragraph 2 or that they risk jeopardising the proper functioning of economic and monetary union, the Commission may address a warning to the Member State concerned. The Council, on a recommendation from the Commission, may address the necessary recommendations to the Member State concerned. The Council may, on a proposal from the Commission, decide to make its recommendations public.

Within the scope of this paragraph, the Council shall act without taking into account the vote of the member of the Council representing the Member State concerned.

A qualified majority of the other members of the Council shall be defined in accordance with Article 238(3)(a).

5. The President of the Council and the Commission shall report to the European Parliament on the results of multilateral surveillance. The President of the Council may be invited to appear before the competent committee of the European Parliament if the Council has made its recommendations public.

6. The European Parliament and the Council, acting by means of regulations in accordance with the ordinary legislative procedure, may adopt detailed rules for the multilateral surveillance procedure referred to in paragraphs 3 and 4.

Article 122   (ex Article 100 TEC)

1. Without prejudice to any other procedures provided for in the Treaties, the Council, on a proposal from the Commission, may decide, in a spirit of solidarity between Member States, upon the

measures appropriate to the economic situation, in particular if severe difficulties arise in the supply of certain products, notably in the area of energy.

2. Where a Member State is in difficulties or is seriously threatened with severe difficulties caused by natural disasters or exceptional occurrences beyond its control, the Council, on a proposal from the Commission, may grant, under certain conditions, Union financial assistance to the Member State concerned. The President of the Council shall inform the European Parliament of the decision taken.

Article 123   (ex Article 101 TEC)

1. Overdraft facilities or any other type of credit facility with the European Central Bank or with the central banks of the Member States (hereinafter referred to as 'national central banks') in favour of Union institutions, bodies, offices or agencies, central governments, regional, local or other public authorities, other bodies governed by public law, or public undertakings of Member States shall be prohibited, as shall the purchase directly from them by the European Central Bank or national central banks of debt instruments.

2. Paragraph 1 shall not apply to publicly owned credit institutions which, in the context of the supply of reserves by central banks, shall be given the same treatment by national central banks and the European Central Bank as private credit institutions.

Article 124   (ex Article 102 TEC)

Any measure, not based on prudential considerations, establishing privileged access by Union institutions, bodies, offices or agencies, central governments, regional, local or other public authorities, other bodies governed by public law, or public undertakings of Member States to financial institutions, shall be prohibited.

Article 125   (ex Article 103 TEC)

1. The Union shall not be liable for or assume the commitments of central governments, regional, local or other public authorities, other bodies governed by public law, or public undertakings of any Member State, without prejudice to mutual financial guarantees for the joint execution of a specific project. A Member State shall not be liable for or assume the commitments of central governments, regional, local or other public authorities, other bodies governed by public law, or public undertakings of another Member State, without prejudice to mutual financial guarantees for the joint execution of a specific project.

2. The Council, on a proposal from the Commission and after consulting the European Parliament, may, as required, specify definitions for the application of the prohibitions referred to in Articles 123 and 124 and in this Article.

Article 126   (ex Article 104 TEC)

1. Member States shall avoid excessive government deficits.

2. The Commission shall monitor the development of the budgetary situation and of the stock of government debt in the Member States with a view to identifying gross errors. In particular it shall examine compliance with budgetary discipline on the basis of the following two criteria:

(a) whether the ratio of the planned or actual government deficit to gross domestic product exceeds a reference value, unless:
- either the ratio has declined substantially and continuously and reached a level that comes close to the reference value,
- or, alternatively, the excess over the reference value is only exceptional and temporary and the ratio remains close to the reference value;

(b) whether the ratio of government debt to gross domestic product exceeds a reference value, unless the ratio is sufficiently diminishing and approaching the reference value at a satisfactory pace.

The reference values are specified in the Protocol on the excessive deficit procedure annexed to the Treaties.

3. If a Member State does not fulfil the requirements under one or both of these criteria, the Commission shall prepare a report. The report of the Commission shall also take into account

whether the government deficit exceeds government investment expenditure and take into account all other relevant factors, including the medium-term economic and budgetary position of the Member State.

The Commission may also prepare a report if, notwithstanding the fulfilment of the requirements under the criteria, it is of the opinion that there is a risk of an excessive deficit in a Member State.

4. The Economic and Financial Committee shall formulate an opinion on the report of the Commission.

5. If the Commission considers that an excessive deficit in a Member State exists or may occur, it shall address an opinion to the Member State concerned and shall inform the Council accordingly.

6. The Council shall, on a proposal from the Commission, and having considered any observations which the Member State concerned may wish to make, decide after an overall assessment whether an excessive deficit exists.

7. Where the Council decides, in accordance with paragraph 6, that an excessive deficit exists, it shall adopt, without undue delay, on a recommendation from the Commission, recommendations addressed to the Member State concerned with a view to bringing that situation to an end within a given period. Subject to the provisions of paragraph 8, these recommendations shall not be made public.

8. Where it establishes that there has been no effective action in response to its recommendations within the period laid down, the Council may make its recommendations public.

9. If a Member State persists in failing to put into practice the recommendations of the Council, the Council may decide to give notice to the Member State to take, within a specified time limit, measures for the deficit reduction which is judged necessary by the Council in order to remedy the situation.

In such a case, the Council may request the Member State concerned to submit reports in accordance with a specific timetable in order to examine the adjustment efforts of that Member State.

10. The rights to bring actions provided for in Articles 258 and 259 may not be exercised within the framework of paragraphs 1 to 9 of this Article.

11. As long as a Member State fails to comply with a decision taken in accordance with paragraph 9, the Council may decide to apply or, as the case may be, intensify one or more of the following measures:

– to require the Member State concerned to publish additional information, to be specified by the Council, before issuing bonds and securities,

– to invite the European Investment Bank to reconsider its lending policy towards the Member State concerned,

– to require the Member State concerned to make a non-interest-bearing deposit of an appropriate size with the Union until the excessive deficit has, in the view of the Council, been corrected,

– to impose fines of an appropriate size.

The President of the Council shall inform the European Parliament of the decisions taken.

12. The Council shall abrogate some or all of its decisions or recommendations referred to in paragraphs 6 to 9 and 11 to the extent that the excessive deficit in the Member State concerned has, in the view of the Council, been corrected. If the Council has previously made public recommendations, it shall, as soon as the decision under paragraph 8 has been abrogated, make a public statement that an excessive deficit in the Member State concerned no longer exists.

13. When taking the decisions or recommendations referred to in paragraphs 8, 9, 11 and 12, the Council shall act on a recommendation from the Commission.

When the Council adopts the measures referred to in paragraphs 6 to 9, 11 and 12, it shall act without taking into account the vote of the member of the Council representing the Member State concerned.

A qualified majority of the other members of the Council shall be defined in accordance with Article 238(3)(a).

14. Further provisions relating to the implementation of the procedure described in this Article are set out in the Protocol on the excessive deficit procedure annexed to the Treaties.

The Council shall, acting unanimously in accordance with a special legislative procedure and after consulting the European Parliament and the European Central Bank, adopt the appropriate provisions which shall then replace the said Protocol.

Subject to the other provisions of this paragraph, the Council shall, on a proposal from the Commission and after consulting the European Parliament, lay down detailed rules and definitions for the application of the provisions of the said Protocol.

Chapter 2 Monetary policy

Article 127   (ex Article 105 TEC)

1. The primary objective of the European System of Central Banks (hereinafter referred to as 'the ESCB') shall be to maintain price stability. Without prejudice to the objective of price stability, the ESCB shall support the general economic policies in the Union with a view to contributing to the achievement of the objectives of the Union as laid down in Article 3 of the Treaty on European Union. The ESCB shall act in accordance with the principle of an open market economy with free competition, favouring an efficient allocation of resources, and in compliance with the principles set out in Article 119.

2. The basic tasks to be carried out through the ESCB shall be:
   – to define and implement the monetary policy of the Union,
   – to conduct foreign-exchange operations consistent with the provisions of Article 219,
   – to hold and manage the official foreign reserves of the Member States,
   – to promote the smooth operation of payment systems.

3. The third indent of paragraph 2 shall be without prejudice to the holding and management by the governments of Member States of foreign-exchange working balances.

4. The European Central Bank shall be consulted:
   – on any proposed Union act in its fields of competence,
   – by national authorities regarding any draft legislative provision in its fields of competence, but within the limits and under the conditions set out by the Council in accordance with the procedure laid down in Article 129(4).

The European Central Bank may submit opinions to the appropriate Union institutions, bodies, offices or agencies or to national authorities on matters in its fields of competence.

5. The ESCB shall contribute to the smooth conduct of policies pursued by the competent authorities relating to the prudential supervision of credit institutions and the stability of the financial system.

6. The Council, acting by means of regulations in accordance with a special legislative procedure, may unanimously, and after consulting the European Parliament and the European Central Bank, confer specific tasks upon the European Central Bank concerning policies relating to the prudential supervision of credit institutions and other financial institutions with the exception of insurance undertakings.

Article 128   (ex Article 106 TEC)

1. The European Central Bank shall have the exclusive right to authorise the issue of euro banknotes within the Union. The European Central Bank and the national central banks may issue such notes. The banknotes issued by the European Central Bank and the national central banks shall be the only such notes to have the status of legal tender within the Union.

2. Member States may issue euro coins subject to approval by the European Central Bank of the volume of the issue. The Council, on a proposal from the Commission and after consulting the European Parliament and the European Central Bank, may adopt measures to harmonise the denominations and technical specifications of all coins intended for circulation to the extent necessary to permit their smooth circulation within the Union.

Article 129   (ex Article 107 TEC)

1. The ESCB shall be governed by the decision-making bodies of the European Central Bank which shall be the Governing Council and the Executive Board.

2. The Statute of the European System of Central Banks and of the European Central Bank (hereinafter referred to as 'the Statute of the ESCB and of the ECB') is laid down in a Protocol annexed to the Treaties.

3. Articles 5.1, 5.2, 5.3, 17, 18, 19.1, 22, 23, 24, 26, 32.2, 32.3, 32.4, 32.6, 33.1(a) and 36 of the Statute of the ESCB and of the ECB may be amended by the European Parliament and the Council, acting in accordance with the ordinary legislative procedure. They shall act either on a recommendation from the European Central Bank and after consulting the Commission or on a proposal from the Commission and after consulting the European Central Bank.

4. The Council, either on a proposal from the Commission and after consulting the European Parliament and the European Central Bank or on a recommendation from the European Central Bank and after consulting the European Parliament and the Commission, shall adopt the provisions referred to in Articles 4, 5.4, 19.2, 20, 28.1, 29.2, 30.4 and 34.3 of the Statute of the ESCB and of the ECB.

Article 130   (ex Article 108 TEC)

When exercising the powers and carrying out the tasks and duties conferred upon them by the Treaties and the Statute of the ESCB and of the ECB, neither the European Central Bank, nor a national central bank, nor any member of their decision-making bodies shall seek or take instructions from Union institutions, bodies, offices or agencies, from any government of a Member State or from any other body. The Union institutions, bodies, offices or agencies and the governments of the Member States undertake to respect this principle and not to seek to influence the members of the decision-making bodies of the European Central Bank or of the national central banks in the performance of their tasks.

Article 131   (ex Article 109 TEC)

Each Member State shall ensure that its national legislation including the statutes of its national central bank is compatible with the Treaties and the Statute of the ESCB and of the ECB.

Article 132   (ex Article 110 TEC)

1. In order to carry out the tasks entrusted to the ESCB, the European Central Bank shall, in accordance with the provisions of the Treaties and under the conditions laid down in the Statute of the ESCB and of the ECB:

- make regulations to the extent necessary to implement the tasks defined in Article 3.1, first indent, Articles 19.1, 22 and 25.2 of the Statute of the ESCB and of the ECB in cases which shall be laid down in the acts of the Council referred to in Article 129(4),
- take decisions necessary for carrying out the tasks entrusted to the ESCB under the Treaties and the Statute of the ESCB and of the ECB,
- make recommendations and deliver opinions.

2. The European Central Bank may decide to publish its decisions, recommendations and opinions.

3. Within the limits and under the conditions adopted by the Council under the procedure laid down in Article 129(4), the European Central Bank shall be entitled to impose fines or periodic penalty payments on undertakings for failure to comply with obligations under its regulations and decisions.

Article 133

Without prejudice to the powers of the European Central Bank, the European Parliament and the Council, acting in accordance with the ordinary legislative procedure, shall lay down the measures necessary for the use of the euro as the single currency. Such measures shall be adopted after consultation of the European Central Bank.

Chapter 3 Institutional provisions

Article 134   (ex Article 114 TEC)

1. In order to promote coordination of the policies of Member States to the full extent needed for the functioning of the internal market, an Economic and Financial Committee is hereby set up.

2. The Economic and Financial Committee shall have the following tasks:

- to deliver opinions at the request of the Council or of the Commission, or on its own initiative for submission to those institutions,

- to keep under review the economic and financial situation of the Member States and of the Union and to report regularly thereon to the Council and to the Commission, in particular on financial relations with third countries and international institutions,
- without prejudice to Article 240, to contribute to the preparation of the work of the Council referred to in Articles 66, 75, 121(2), (3), (4) and (6), 122, 124, 125, 126, 127(6), 128(2), 129(3) and (4), 138, 140(2) and (3), 143, 144(2) and (3), and in Article 219, and to carry out other advisory and preparatory tasks assigned to it by the Council,
- to examine, at least once a year, the situation regarding the movement of capital and the freedom of payments, as they result from the application of the Treaties and of measures adopted by the Council; the examination shall cover all measures relating to capital movements and payments; the Committee shall report to the Commission and to the Council on the outcome of this examination.

The Member States, the Commission and the European Central Bank shall each appoint no more than two members of the Committee.

3. The Council shall, on a proposal from the Commission and after consulting the European Central Bank and the Committee referred to in this Article, lay down detailed provisions concerning the composition of the Economic and Financial Committee. The President of the Council shall inform the European Parliament of such a decision.

4. In addition to the tasks set out in paragraph 2, if and as long as there are Member States with a derogation as referred to in Article 139, the Committee shall keep under review the monetary and financial situation and the general payments system of those Member States and report regularly thereon to the Council and to the Commission.

Article 135 (ex Article 115 TEC)

For matters within the scope of Articles 121(4), 126 with the exception of paragraph 14, 138, 140(1), 140(2), first subparagraph, 140(3) and 219, the Council or a Member State may request the Commission to make a recommendation or a proposal, as appropriate. The Commission shall examine this request and submit its conclusions to the Council without delay.

Chapter 4 Provisions specific to Member States whose currency is the euro

Article 136*

1. In order to ensure the proper functioning of economic and monetary union, and in accordance with the relevant provisions of the Treaties, the Council shall, in accordance with the relevant procedure from among those referred to in Articles 121 and 126, with the exception of the procedure set out in Article 126(14), adopt measures specific to those Member States whose currency is the euro:

(a) to strengthen the coordination and surveillance of their budgetary discipline;
(b) to set out economic policy guidelines for them, while ensuring that they are compatible with those adopted for the whole of the Union and are kept under surveillance.

2. For those measures set out in paragraph 1, only members of the Council representing Member States whose currency is the euro shall take part in the vote.

A qualified majority of the said members shall be defined in accordance with Article 238(3)(a).

3. The Member States whose currency is the euro may establish a stability mechanism to be activated if indispensable to safeguard the stability of the euro area as a whole. The granting of any required financial assistance under the mechanism will be made subject to strict conditionality.

Article 137

Arrangements for meetings between ministers of those Member States whose currency is the euro are laid down by the Protocol on the Euro Group.

---

* **Editor's Note**: As amended by Decision 2011/199 (OJ 2011 L91/1).

Article 138   (ex Article 111(4), TEC)

1. In order to secure the euro's place in the international monetary system, the Council, on a proposal from the Commission, shall adopt a decision establishing common positions on matters of particular interest for economic and monetary union within the competent international financial institutions and conferences. The Council shall act after consulting the European Central Bank.

2. The Council, on a proposal from the Commission, may adopt appropriate measures to ensure unified representation within the international financial institutions and conferences. The Council shall act after consulting the European Central Bank.

3. For the measures referred to in paragraphs 1 and 2, only members of the Council representing Member States whose currency is the euro shall take part in the vote.

A qualified majority of the said members shall be defined in accordance with Article 238(3)(a).

Chapter 5 Transitional provisions

Article 139

1. Member States in respect of which the Council has not decided that they fulfil the necessary conditions for the adoption of the euro shall hereinafter be referred to as 'Member States with a derogation'.

2. The following provisions of the Treaties shall not apply to Member States with a derogation:

(a) adoption of the parts of the broad economic policy guidelines which concern the euro area generally (Article 121(2));

(b) coercive means of remedying excessive deficits (Article 126(9) and (11));

(c) the objectives and tasks of the ESCB (Article 127(1) to (3) and (5));

(d) issue of the euro (Article 128);

(e) acts of the European Central Bank (Article 132);

(f) measures governing the use of the euro (Article 133);

(g) monetary agreements and other measures relating to exchange-rate policy (Article 219);

(h) appointment of members of the Executive Board of the European Central Bank (Article 283(2));

(i) decisions establishing common positions on issues of particular relevance for economic and monetary union within the competent international financial institutions and conferences (Article 138(1));

(j) measures to ensure unified representation within the international financial institutions and conferences (Article 138(2)).

In the Articles referred to in points (a) to (j), 'Member States' shall therefore mean Member States whose currency is the euro.

3. Under Chapter IX of the Statute of the ESCB and of the ECB, Member States with a derogation and their national central banks are excluded from rights and obligations within the ESCB.

4. The voting rights of members of the Council representing Member States with a derogation shall be suspended for the adoption by the Council of the measures referred to in the Articles listed in paragraph 2, and in the following instances:

(a) recommendations made to those Member States whose currency is the euro in the framework of multilateral surveillance, including on stability programmes and warnings (Article 121(4));

(b) measures relating to excessive deficits concerning those Member States whose currency is the euro (Article 126(6), (7), (8), (12) and (13)).

A qualified majority of the other members of the Council shall be defined in accordance with Article 238(3)(a).

Article 140   (ex Articles 121(1), 122(2), second sentence, and 123(5) TEC)

1. At least once every two years, or at the request of a Member State with a derogation, the Commission and the European Central Bank shall report to the Council on the progress made by the Member States with a derogation in fulfilling their obligations regarding the achievement of economic

and monetary union. These reports shall include an examination of the compatibility between the national legislation of each of these Member States, including the statutes of its national central bank, and Articles 130 and 131 and the Statute of the ESCB and of the ECB. The reports shall also examine the achievement of a high degree of sustainable convergence by reference to the fulfilment by each Member State of the following criteria:

- the achievement of a high degree of price stability; this will be apparent from a rate of inflation which is close to that of, at most, the three best performing Member States in terms of price stability,
- the sustainability of the government financial position; this will be apparent from having achieved a government budgetary position without a deficit that is excessive as determined in accordance with Article 126(6),
- the observance of the normal fluctuation margins provided for by the exchange-rate mechanism of the European Monetary System, for at least two years, without devaluing against the euro,
- the durability of convergence achieved by the Member State with a derogation and of its participation in the exchange-rate mechanism being reflected in the long-term interest-rate levels.

The four criteria mentioned in this paragraph and the relevant periods over which they are to be respected are developed further in a Protocol annexed to the Treaties. The reports of the Commission and the European Central Bank shall also take account of the results of the integration of markets, the situation and development of the balances of payments on current account and an examination of the development of unit labour costs and other price indices.

2. After consulting the European Parliament and after discussion in the European Council, the Council shall, on a proposal from the Commission, decide which Member States with a derogation fulfil the necessary conditions on the basis of the criteria set out in paragraph 1, and abrogate the derogations of the Member States concerned.

The Council shall act having received a recommendation of a qualified majority of those among its members representing Member States whose currency is the euro. These members shall act within six months of the Council receiving the Commission's proposal.

The qualified majority of the said members, as referred to in the second subparagraph, shall be defined in accordance with Article 238(3)(a).

3. If it is decided, in accordance with the procedure set out in paragraph 2, to abrogate a derogation, the Council shall, acting with the unanimity of the Member States whose currency is the euro and the Member State concerned, on a proposal from the Commission and after consulting the European Central Bank, irrevocably fix the rate at which the euro shall be substituted for the currency of the Member State concerned, and take the other measures necessary for the introduction of the euro as the single currency in the Member State concerned.

Article 141   (ex Articles 123(3) and 117(2) first five indents, TEC)

1. If and as long as there are Member States with a derogation, and without prejudice to Article 129(1), the General Council of the European Central Bank referred to in Article 44 of the Statute of the ESCB and of the ECB shall be constituted as a third decision-making body of the European Central Bank.

2. If and as long as there are Member States with a derogation, the European Central Bank shall, as regards those Member States:

- strengthen cooperation between the national central banks,
- strengthen the coordination of the monetary policies of the Member States, with the aim of ensuring price stability,
- monitor the functioning of the exchange-rate mechanism,
- hold consultations concerning issues falling within the competence of the national central banks and affecting the stability of financial institutions and markets,
- carry out the former tasks of the European Monetary Cooperation Fund which had subsequently been taken over by the European Monetary Institute.

Article 142   (ex Article 124(1) TEC)

Each Member State with a derogation shall treat its exchange-rate policy as a matter of common interest. In so doing, Member States shall take account of the experience acquired in cooperation within the framework of the exchange-rate mechanism.

Article 143   (ex Article 119 TEC)

1. Where a Member State with a derogation is in difficulties or is seriously threatened with difficulties as regards its balance of payments either as a result of an overall disequilibrium in its balance of payments, or as a result of the type of currency at its disposal, and where such difficulties are liable in particular to jeopardise the functioning of the internal market or the implementation of the common commercial policy, the Commission shall immediately investigate the position of the State in question and the action which, making use of all the means at its disposal, that State has taken or may take in accordance with the provisions of the Treaties. The Commission shall state what measures it recommends the State concerned to take.

If the action taken by a Member State with a derogation and the measures suggested by the Commission do not prove sufficient to overcome the difficulties which have arisen or which threaten, the Commission shall, after consulting the Economic and Financial Committee, recommend to the Council the granting of mutual assistance and appropriate methods therefore.

The Commission shall keep the Council regularly informed of the situation and of how it is developing.

2. The Council shall grant such mutual assistance; it shall adopt directives or decisions laying down the conditions and details of such assistance, which may take such forms as:

(a) a concerted approach to or within any other international organisations to which Member States with a derogation may have recourse;

(b) measures needed to avoid deflection of trade where the Member State with a derogation which is in difficulties maintains or reintroduces quantitative restrictions against third countries;

(c) the granting of limited credits by other Member States, subject to their agreement.

3. If the mutual assistance recommended by the Commission is not granted by the Council or if the mutual assistance granted and the measures taken are insufficient, the Commission shall authorise the Member State with a derogation which is in difficulties to take protective measures, the conditions and details of which the Commission shall determine.

Such authorisation may be revoked and such conditions and details may be changed by the Council.

Article 144   (ex Article 120 TEC)

1. Where a sudden crisis in the balance of payments occurs and a decision within the meaning of Article 143(2) is not immediately taken, a Member State with a derogation may, as a precaution, take the necessary protective measures. Such measures must cause the least possible disturbance in the functioning of the internal market and must not be wider in scope than is strictly necessary to remedy the sudden difficulties which have arisen.

2. The Commission and the other Member States shall be informed of such protective measures not later than when they enter into force. The Commission may recommend to the Council the granting of mutual assistance under Article 143.

3. After the Commission has delivered a recommendation and the Economic and Financial Committee has been consulted, the Council may decide that the Member State concerned shall amend, suspend or abolish the protective measures referred to above.

Title IX Employment

Article 145   (ex Article 125 TEC)

Member States and the Union shall, in accordance with this Title, work towards developing a coordinated strategy for employment and particularly for promoting a skilled, trained and adaptable workforce and labour markets responsive to economic change with a view to achieving the objectives defined in Article 3 of the Treaty on European Union.

Article 146   (ex Article 126 TEC)

1. Member States, through their employment policies, shall contribute to the achievement of the objectives referred to in Article 145 in a way consistent with the broad guidelines of the economic policies of the Member States and of the Union adopted pursuant to Article 121(2).

2. Member States, having regard to national practices related to the responsibilities of management and labour, shall regard promoting employment as a matter of common concern and shall coordinate their action in this respect within the Council, in accordance with the provisions of Article 148.

Article 147   (ex Article 127 TEC)

1. The Union shall contribute to a high level of employment by encouraging cooperation between Member States and by supporting and, if necessary, complementing their action. In doing so, the competences of the Member States shall be respected.

2. The objective of a high level of employment shall be taken into consideration in the formulation and implementation of Union policies and activities.

Article 148   (ex Article 128 TEC)

1. The European Council shall each year consider the employment situation in the Union and adopt conclusions thereon, on the basis of a joint annual report by the Council and the Commission.

2. On the basis of the conclusions of the European Council, the Council, on a proposal from the Commission and after consulting the European Parliament, the Economic and Social Committee, the Committee of the Regions and the Employment Committee referred to in Article 150, shall each year draw up guidelines which the Member States shall take into account in their employment policies. These guidelines shall be consistent with the broad guidelines adopted pursuant to Article 121(2).

3. Each Member State shall provide the Council and the Commission with an annual report on the principal measures taken to implement its employment policy in the light of the guidelines for employment as referred to in paragraph 2.

4. The Council, on the basis of the reports referred to in paragraph 3 and having received the views of the Employment Committee, shall each year carry out an examination of the implementation of the employment policies of the Member States in the light of the guidelines for employment. The Council, on a recommendation from the Commission, may, if it considers it appropriate in the light of that examination, make recommendations to Member States.

5. On the basis of the results of that examination, the Council and the Commission shall make a joint annual report to the European Council on the employment situation in the Union and on the implementation of the guidelines for employment.

Article 149   (ex Article 129 TEC)

The European Parliament and the Council, acting in accordance with the ordinary legislative procedure and after consulting the Economic and Social Committee and the Committee of the Regions, may adopt incentive measures designed to encourage cooperation between Member States and to support their action in the field of employment through initiatives aimed at developing exchanges of information and best practices, providing comparative analysis and advice as well as promoting innovative approaches and evaluating experiences, in particular by recourse to pilot projects.

Those measures shall not include harmonisation of the laws and regulations of the Member States.

Article 150   (ex Article 130 TEC)

The Council, acting by a simple majority after consulting the European Parliament, shall establish an Employment Committee with advisory status to promote coordination between Member States on employment and labour market policies. The tasks of the Committee shall be:

- to monitor the employment situation and employment policies in the Member States and the Union,

> – without prejudice to Article 240, to formulate opinions at the request of either the Council or the Commission or on its own initiative, and to contribute to the preparation of the Council proceedings referred to in Article 148.

In fulfilling its mandate, the Committee shall consult management and labour.

Each Member State and the Commission shall appoint two members of the Committee.

Title X Social policy

Article 151   (ex Article 136 TEC)

The Union and the Member States, having in mind fundamental social rights such as those set out in the European Social Charter signed at Turin on 18 October 1961 and in the 1989 Community Charter of the Fundamental Social Rights of Workers, shall have as their objectives the promotion of employment, improved living and working conditions, so as to make possible their harmonisation while the improvement is being maintained, proper social protection, dialogue between management and labour, the development of human resources with a view to lasting high employment and the combating of exclusion.

To this end the Union and the Member States shall implement measures which take account of the diverse forms of national practices, in particular in the field of contractual relations, and the need to maintain the competitiveness of the Union economy.

They believe that such a development will ensue not only from the functioning of the internal market, which will favour the harmonisation of social systems, but also from the procedures provided for in the Treaties and from the approximation of provisions laid down by law, regulation or administrative action.

Article 152

The Union recognises and promotes the role of the social partners at its level, taking into account the diversity of national systems. It shall facilitate dialogue between the social partners, respecting their autonomy.

The Tripartite Social Summit for Growth and Employment shall contribute to social dialogue.

Article 153   (ex Article 137 TEC)

1. With a view to achieving the objectives of Article 151, the Union shall support and complement the activities of the Member States in the following fields:

   (a) improvement in particular of the working environment to protect workers' health and safety;
   (b) working conditions;
   (c) social security and social protection of workers;
   (d) protection of workers where their employment contract is terminated;
   (e) the information and consultation of workers;
   (f) representation and collective defence of the interests of workers and employers, including co-determination, subject to paragraph 5;
   (g) conditions of employment for third-country nationals legally residing in Union territory;
   (h) the integration of persons excluded from the labour market, without prejudice to Article 166;
   (i) equality between men and women with regard to labour market opportunities and treatment at work;
   (j) the combating of social exclusion;
   (k) the modernisation of social protection systems without prejudice to point (c).

2. To this end, the European Parliament and the Council:

   (a) may adopt measures designed to encourage cooperation between Member States through initiatives aimed at improving knowledge, developing exchanges of information and best practices, promoting innovative approaches and evaluating experiences, excluding any harmonisation of the laws and regulations of the Member States;

(b) may adopt, in the fields referred to in paragraph 1(a) to (i), by means of directives, minimum requirements for gradual implementation, having regard to the conditions and technical rules obtaining in each of the Member States. Such directives shall avoid imposing administrative, financial and legal constraints in a way which would hold back the creation and development of small and medium-sized undertakings.

The European Parliament and the Council shall act in accordance with the ordinary legislative procedure after consulting the Economic and Social Committee and the Committee of the Regions.

In the fields referred to in paragraph 1(c), (d), (f) and (g), the Council shall act unanimously, in accordance with a special legislative procedure, after consulting the European Parliament and the said Committees.

The Council, acting unanimously on a proposal from the Commission, after consulting the European Parliament, may decide to render the ordinary legislative procedure applicable to paragraph 1(d), (f) and (g).

3. A Member State may entrust management and labour, at their joint request, with the implementation of directives adopted pursuant to paragraph 2, or, where appropriate, with the implementation of a Council decision adopted in accordance with Article 155.

In this case, it shall ensure that, no later than the date on which a directive or a decision must be transposed or implemented, management and labour have introduced the necessary measures by agreement, the Member State concerned being required to take any necessary measure enabling it at any time to be in a position to guarantee the results imposed by that directive or that decision.

4. The provisions adopted pursuant to this Article:
   – shall not affect the right of Member States to define the fundamental principles of their social security systems and must not significantly affect the financial equilibrium thereof,
   – shall not prevent any Member State from maintaining or introducing more stringent protective measures compatible with the Treaties.

5. The provisions of this Article shall not apply to pay, the right of association, the right to strike or the right to impose lock-outs.

Article 154 (ex Article 138 TEC)

1. The Commission shall have the task of promoting the consultation of management and labour at Union level and shall take any relevant measure to facilitate their dialogue by ensuring balanced support for the parties.

2. To this end, before submitting proposals in the social policy field, the Commission shall consult management and labour on the possible direction of Union action.

3. If, after such consultation, the Commission considers Union action advisable, it shall consult management and labour on the content of the envisaged proposal.

Management and labour shall forward to the Commission an opinion or, where appropriate, a recommendation.

4. On the occasion of the consultation referred to in paragraphs 2 and 3, management and labour may inform the Commission of their wish to initiate the process provided for in Article 155. The duration of this process shall not exceed nine months, unless the management and labour concerned and the Commission decide jointly to extend it.

Article 155 (ex Article 139 TEC)

1. Should management and labour so desire, the dialogue between them at Union level may lead to contractual relations, including agreements.

2. Agreements concluded at Union level shall be implemented either in accordance with the procedures and practices specific to management and labour and the Member States or, in matters covered by Article 153, at the joint request of the signatory parties, by a Council decision on a proposal from the Commission. The European Parliament shall be informed.

The Council shall act unanimously where the agreement in question contains one or more provisions relating to one of the areas for which unanimity is required pursuant to Article 153(2).

Article 156 (ex Article 140 TEC)

With a view to achieving the objectives of Article 151 and without prejudice to the other provisions of the Treaties, the Commission shall encourage cooperation between the Member States and facilitate the coordination of their action in all social policy fields under this Chapter, particularly in matters relating to:
- employment,
- labour law and working conditions,
- basic and advanced vocational training,
- social security,
- prevention of occupational accidents and diseases,
- occupational hygiene,
- the right of association and collective bargaining between employers and workers.

To this end, the Commission shall act in close contact with Member States by making studies, delivering opinions and arranging consultations both on problems arising at national level and on those of concern to international organisations, in particular initiatives aiming at the establishment of guidelines and indicators, the organisation of exchange of best practice, and the preparation of the necessary elements for periodic monitoring and evaluation. The European Parliament shall be kept fully informed.

Before delivering the opinions provided for in this Article, the Commission shall consult the Economic and Social Committee.

Article 157 (ex Article 141 TEC)

1. Each Member State shall ensure that the principle of equal pay for male and female workers for equal work or work of equal value is applied.

2. For the purpose of this Article, 'pay' means the ordinary basic or minimum wage or salary and any other consideration, whether in cash or in kind, which the worker receives directly or indirectly, in respect of his employment, from his employer.

Equal pay without discrimination based on sex means:
   (a) that pay for the same work at piece rates shall be calculated on the basis of the same unit of measurement;
   (b) that pay for work at time rates shall be the same for the same job.

3. The European Parliament and the Council, acting in accordance with the ordinary legislative procedure, and after consulting the Economic and Social Committee, shall adopt measures to ensure the application of the principle of equal opportunities and equal treatment of men and women in matters of employment and occupation, including the principle of equal pay for equal work or work of equal value.

4. With a view to ensuring full equality in practice between men and women in working life, the principle of equal treatment shall not prevent any Member State from maintaining or adopting measures providing for specific advantages in order to make it easier for the underrepresented sex to pursue a vocational activity or to prevent or compensate for disadvantages in professional careers.

Article 158 (ex Article 142 TEC)

Member States shall endeavour to maintain the existing equivalence between paid holiday schemes.

Article 159 (ex Article 143 TEC)

The Commission shall draw up a report each year on progress in achieving the objectives of Article 151, including the demographic situation in the Union. It shall forward the report to the European Parliament, the Council and the Economic and Social Committee.

Article 160 (ex Article 144 TEC)

The Council, acting by a simple majority after consulting the European Parliament, shall establish a Social Protection Committee with advisory status to promote cooperation on social protection policies between Member States and with the Commission. The tasks of the Committee shall be:
- to monitor the social situation and the development of social protection policies in the Member States and the Union,

- to promote exchanges of information, experience and good practice between Member States and with the Commission,
- without prejudice to Article 240, to prepare reports, formulate opinions or undertake other work within its fields of competence, at the request of either the Council or the Commission or on its own initiative.

In fulfilling its mandate, the Committee shall establish appropriate contacts with management and labour.

Each Member State and the Commission shall appoint two members of the Committee.

Article 161 (ex Article 145 TEC)

The Commission shall include a separate chapter on social developments within the Union in its annual report to the European Parliament.

The European Parliament may invite the Commission to draw up reports on any particular problems concerning social conditions.

Title XI The European Social Fund

Article 162 (ex Article 146 TEC)

In order to improve employment opportunities for workers in the internal market and to contribute thereby to raising the standard of living, a European Social Fund is hereby established in accordance with the provisions set out below; it shall aim to render the employment of workers easier and to increase their geographical and occupational mobility within the Union, and to facilitate their adaptation to industrial changes and to changes in production systems, in particular through vocational training and retraining.

Article 163 (ex Article 147 TEC)

The Fund shall be administered by the Commission.

The Commission shall be assisted in this task by a Committee presided over by a Member of the Commission and composed of representatives of governments, trade unions and employers' organisations.

Article 164 (ex Article 148 TEC)

The European Parliament and the Council, acting in accordance with the ordinary legislative procedure and after consulting the Economic and Social Committee and the Committee of the Regions, shall adopt implementing regulations relating to the European Social Fund.

Title XII Education, vocational training, youth and sport

Article 165 (ex Article 149 TEC)

1. The Union shall contribute to the development of quality education by encouraging cooperation between Member States and, if necessary, by supporting and supplementing their action, while fully respecting the responsibility of the Member States for the content of teaching and the organisation of education systems and their cultural and linguistic diversity.

The Union shall contribute to the promotion of European sporting issues, while taking account of the specific nature of sport, its structures based on voluntary activity and its social and educational function.

2. Union action shall be aimed at:
    - developing the European dimension in education, particularly through the teaching and dissemination of the languages of the Member States,
    - encouraging mobility of students and teachers, by encouraging *inter alia*, the academic recognition of diplomas and periods of study,
    - promoting cooperation between educational establishments,

- developing exchanges of information and experience on issues common to the education systems of the Member States,
- encouraging the development of youth exchanges and of exchanges of socio-educational instructors, and encouraging the participation of young people in democratic life in Europe,
- encouraging the development of distance education,
- developing the European dimension in sport, by promoting fairness and openness in sporting competitions and cooperation between bodies responsible for sports, and by protecting the physical and moral integrity of sportsmen and sportswomen, especially the youngest sportsmen and sportswomen.

3. The Union and the Member States shall foster cooperation with third countries and the competent international organisations in the field of education and sport, in particular the Council of Europe.

4. In order to contribute to the achievement of the objectives referred to in this Article:
- the European Parliament and the Council, acting in accordance with the ordinary legislative procedure, after consulting the Economic and Social Committee and the Committee of the Regions, shall adopt incentive measures, excluding any harmonisation of the laws and regulations of the Member States,
- the Council, on a proposal from the Commission, shall adopt recommendations.

Article 166   (ex Article 150 TEC)

1. The Union shall implement a vocational training policy which shall support and supplement the action of the Member States, while fully respecting the responsibility of the Member States for the content and organisation of vocational training.

2. Union action shall aim to:
- facilitate adaptation to industrial changes, in particular through vocational training and retraining,
- improve initial and continuing vocational training in order to facilitate vocational integration and reintegration into the labour market,
- facilitate access to vocational training and encourage mobility of instructors and trainees and particularly young people,
- stimulate cooperation on training between educational or training establishments and firms,
- develop exchanges of information and experience on issues common to the training systems of the Member States.

3. The Union and the Member States shall foster cooperation with third countries and the competent international organisations in the sphere of vocational training.

4. The European Parliament and the Council, acting in accordance with the ordinary legislative procedure and after consulting the Economic and Social Committee and the Committee of the Regions, shall adopt measures to contribute to the achievement of the objectives referred to in this Article, excluding any harmonisation of the laws and regulations of the Member States, and the Council, on a proposal from the Commission, shall adopt recommendations.

Title XIII Culture

Article 167   (ex Article 151 TEC)

1. The Union shall contribute to the flowering of the cultures of the Member States, while respecting their national and regional diversity and at the same time bringing the common cultural heritage to the fore.

2. Action by the Union shall be aimed at encouraging cooperation between Member States and, if necessary, supporting and supplementing their action in the following areas:
- improvement of the knowledge and dissemination of the culture and history of the European peoples,

- conservation and safeguarding of cultural heritage of European significance,
- non-commercial cultural exchanges,
- artistic and literary creation, including in the audiovisual sector.

3. The Union and the Member States shall foster cooperation with third countries and the competent international organisations in the sphere of culture, in particular the Council of Europe.

4. The Union shall take cultural aspects into account in its action under other provisions of the Treaties, in particular in order to respect and to promote the diversity of its cultures.

5. In order to contribute to the achievement of the objectives referred to in this Article:
- the European Parliament and the Council acting in accordance with the ordinary legislative procedure and after consulting the Committee of the Regions, shall adopt incentive measures, excluding any harmonisation of the laws and regulations of the Member States.
- the Council, on a proposal from the Commission, shall adopt recommendations.

Title XIV Public health

Article 168 (ex Article 152 TEC)

1. A high level of human health protection shall be ensured in the definition and implementation of all Union policies and activities.

Union action, which shall complement national policies, shall be directed towards improving public health, preventing physical and mental illness and diseases, and obviating sources of danger to physical and mental health. Such action shall cover the fight against the major health scourges, by promoting research into their causes, their transmission and their prevention, as well as health information and education, and monitoring, early warning of and combating serious cross-border threats to health.

The Union shall complement the Member States' action in reducing drugs-related health damage, including information and prevention.

2. The Union shall encourage cooperation between the Member States in the areas referred to in this Article and, if necessary, lend support to their action. It shall in particular encourage cooperation between the Member States to improve the complementarity of their health services in cross-border areas.

Member States shall, in liaison with the Commission, coordinate among themselves their policies and programmes in the areas referred to in paragraph 1. The Commission may, in close contact with the Member States, take any useful initiative to promote such coordination, in particular initiatives aiming at the establishment of guidelines and indicators, the organisation of exchange of best practice, and the preparation of the necessary elements for periodic monitoring and evaluation. The European Parliament shall be kept fully informed.

3. The Union and the Member States shall foster cooperation with third countries and the competent international organisations in the sphere of public health.

4. By way of derogation from Article 2(5) and Article 6(a) and in accordance with Article 4(2)(k) the European Parliament and the Council, acting in accordance with the ordinary legislative procedure and after consulting the Economic and Social Committee and the Committee of the Regions, shall contribute to the achievement of the objectives referred to in this Article through adopting in order to meet common safety concerns:
- (a) measures setting high standards of quality and safety of organs and substances of human origin, blood and blood derivatives; these measures shall not prevent any Member State from maintaining or introducing more stringent protective measures;
- (b) measures in the veterinary and phytosanitary fields which have as their direct objective the protection of public health;
- (c) measures setting high standards of quality and safety for medicinal products and devices for medical use.

5. The European Parliament and the Council, acting in accordance with the ordinary legislative procedure and after consulting the Economic and Social Committee and the Committee of the Regions, may also adopt incentive measures designed to protect and improve human health and in

particular to combat the major cross-border health scourges, measures concerning monitoring, early warning of and combating serious cross-border threats to health, and measures which have as their direct objective the protection of public health regarding tobacco and the abuse of alcohol, excluding any harmonisation of the laws and regulations of the Member States.

6. The Council, on a proposal from the Commission, may also adopt recommendations for the purposes set out in this Article.

7. Union action shall respect the responsibilities of the Member States for the definition of their health policy and for the organisation and delivery of health services and medical care. The responsibilities of the Member States shall include the management of health services and medical care and the allocation of the resources assigned to them. The measures referred to in paragraph 4(a) shall not affect national provisions on the donation or medical use of organs and blood.

Title XV Consumer protection

Article 169   (ex Article 153 TEC)

1. In order to promote the interests of consumers and to ensure a high level of consumer protection, the Union shall contribute to protecting the health, safety and economic interests of consumers, as well as to promoting their right to information, education and to organise themselves in order to safeguard their interests.

2. The Union shall contribute to the attainment of the objectives referred to in paragraph 1 through:
    (a) measures adopted pursuant to Article 114 in the context of the completion of the internal market;
    (b) measures which support, supplement and monitor the policy pursued by the Member States.

3. The European Parliament and the Council, acting in accordance with the ordinary legislative procedure and after consulting the Economic and Social Committee, shall adopt the measures referred to in paragraph 2(b).

4. Measures adopted pursuant to paragraph 3 shall not prevent any Member State from maintaining or introducing more stringent protective measures. Such measures must be compatible with the Treaties. The Commission shall be notified of them.

Title XVI Trans-European networks

Article 170   (ex Article 154 TEC)

1. To help achieve the objectives referred to in Articles 26 and 174 and to enable citizens of the Union, economic operators and regional and local communities to derive full benefit from the setting-up of an area without internal frontiers, the Union shall contribute to the establishment and development of trans-European networks in the areas of transport, telecommunications and energy infrastructures.

2. Within the framework of a system of open and competitive markets, action by the Union shall aim at promoting the interconnection and interoperability of national networks as well as access to such networks. It shall take account in particular of the need to link island, landlocked and peripheral regions with the central regions of the Union.

Article 171   (ex Article 155 TEC)

1. In order to achieve the objectives referred to in Article 170, the Union:
    – shall establish a series of guidelines covering the objectives, priorities and broad lines of measures envisaged in the sphere of trans-European networks; these guidelines shall identify projects of common interest,

 – shall implement any measures that may prove necessary to ensure the interoperability of the networks, in particular in the field of technical standardisation,
 – may support projects of common interest supported by Member States, which are identified in the framework of the guidelines referred to in the first indent, particularly through feasibility studies, loan guarantees or interest-rate subsidies; the Union may also contribute, through the Cohesion Fund set up pursuant to Article 177, to the financing of specific projects in Member States in the area of transport infrastructure.

The Union's activities shall take into account the potential economic viability of the projects.

2. Member States shall, in liaison with the Commission, coordinate among themselves the policies pursued at national level which may have a significant impact on the achievement of the objectives referred to in Article 170. The Commission may, in close cooperation with the Member State, take any useful initiative to promote such coordination.

3. The Union may decide to cooperate with third countries to promote projects of mutual interest and to ensure the interoperability of networks.

Article 172   (ex Article 156 TEC)

The guidelines and other measures referred to in Article 171(1) shall be adopted by the European Parliament and the Council, acting in accordance with the ordinary legislative procedure and after consulting the Economic and Social Committee and the Committee of the Regions.

Guidelines and projects of common interest which relate to the territory of a Member State shall require the approval of the Member State concerned.

Title XVII Industry

Article 173   (ex Article 157 TEC)

1. The Union and the Member States shall ensure that the conditions necessary for the competitiveness of the Union's industry exist.

For that purpose, in accordance with a system of open and competitive markets, their action shall be aimed at:
 – speeding up the adjustment of industry to structural changes,
 – encouraging an environment favourable to initiative and to the development of undertakings throughout the Union, particularly small and medium-sized undertakings,
 – encouraging an environment favourable to cooperation between undertakings,
 – fostering better exploitation of the industrial potential of policies of innovation, research and technological development.

2. The Member States shall consult each other in liaison with the Commission and, where necessary, shall coordinate their action. The Commission may take any useful initiative to promote such coordination, in particular initiatives aiming at the establishment of guidelines and indicators, the organisation of exchange of best practice, and the preparation of the necessary elements for periodic monitoring and evaluation. The European Parliament shall be kept fully informed.

3. The Union shall contribute to the achievement of the objectives set out in paragraph 1 through the policies and activities it pursues under other provisions of the Treaties. The European Parliament and the Council, acting in accordance with the ordinary legislative procedure and after consulting the Economic and Social Committee, may decide on specific measures in support of action taken in the Member States to achieve the objectives set out in paragraph 1, excluding any harmonisation of the laws and regulations of the Member States.

This Title shall not provide a basis for the introduction by the Union of any measure which could lead to a distortion of competition or contains tax provisions or provisions relating to the rights and interests of employed persons.

Title XVIII Economic, social and territorial cohesion

Article 174   (ex Article 158 TEC)

In order to promote its overall harmonious development, the Union shall develop and pursue its actions leading to the strengthening of its economic, social and territorial cohesion.

In particular, the Union shall aim at reducing disparities between the levels of development of the various regions and the backwardness of the least favoured regions.

Among the regions concerned, particular attention shall be paid to rural areas, areas affected by industrial transition, and regions which suffer from severe and permanent natural or demographic handicaps such as the northernmost regions with very low population density and island, cross-border and mountain regions.

Article 175   (ex Article 159 TEC)

Member States shall conduct their economic policies and shall coordinate them in such a way as, in addition, to attain the objectives set out in Article 174. The formulation and implementation of the Union's policies and actions and the implementation of the internal market shall take into account the objectives set out in Article 174 and shall contribute to their achievement. The Union shall also support the achievement of these objectives by the action it takes through the Structural Funds (European Agricultural Guidance and Guarantee Fund, Guidance Section; European Social Fund; European Regional Development Fund), the European Investment Bank and the other existing Financial Instruments.

The Commission shall submit a report to the European Parliament, the Council, the Economic and Social Committee and the Committee of the Regions every three years on the progress made towards achieving economic, social and territorial cohesion and on the manner in which the various means provided for in this Article have contributed to it. This report shall, if necessary, be accompanied by appropriate proposals.

If specific actions prove necessary outside the Funds and without prejudice to the measures decided upon within the framework of the other Union policies, such actions may be adopted by the Council acting in accordance with the ordinary legislative procedure and after consulting the Economic and Social Committee and the Committee of the Regions.

Article 176   (ex Article 160 TEC)

The European Regional Development Fund is intended to help to redress the main regional imbalances in the Union through participation in the development and structural adjustment of regions whose development is lagging behind and in the conversion of declining industrial regions.

Article 177   (ex Article 161 TEC)

Without prejudice to Article 178, the European Parliament and the Council, acting by means of regulations in accordance with the ordinary legislative procedure and consulting the Economic and Social Committee and the Committee of the Regions, shall define the tasks, priority objectives and the organisation of the Structural Funds, which may involve grouping the Funds. The general rules applicable to them and the provisions necessary to ensure their effectiveness and the coordination of the Funds with one another and with the other existing Financial Instruments shall also be defined by the same procedure.

A Cohesion Fund set up in accordance with the same procedure shall provide a financial contribution to projects in the fields of environment and trans-European networks in the area of transport infrastructure.

Article 178   (ex Article 162 TEC)

Implementing regulations relating to the European Regional Development Fund shall be taken by the European Parliament and the Council, acting in accordance with the ordinary legislative procedure and after consulting the Economic and Social Committee and the Committee of the Regions.

With regard to the European Agricultural Guidance and Guarantee Fund, Guidance Section, and the European Social Fund, Articles 43 and 164 respectively shall continue to apply.

Title XIX Research and technological development and space

Article 179   (ex Article 163 TEC)

1. The Union shall have the objective of strengthening its scientific and technological bases by achieving a European research area in which researchers, scientific knowledge and technology circulate freely, and encouraging it to become more competitive, including in its industry, while promoting all the research activities deemed necessary by virtue of other Chapters of the Treaties.

2. For this purpose the Union shall, throughout the Union, encourage undertakings, including small and medium-sized undertakings, research centres and universities in their research and technological development activities of high quality; it shall support their efforts to cooperate with one another, aiming, notably, at permitting researchers to cooperate freely across borders and at enabling undertakings to exploit the internal market potential to the full, in particular through the opening-up of national public contracts, the definition of common standards and the removal of legal and fiscal obstacles to that cooperation.

3. All Union activities under the Treaties in the area of research and technological development, including demonstration projects, shall be decided on and implemented in accordance with the provisions of this Title.

Article 180   (ex Article 164 TEC)

In pursuing these objectives, the Union shall carry out the following activities, complementing the activities carried out in the Member States:

- (a) implementation of research, technological development and demonstration programmes, by promoting cooperation with and between undertakings, research centres and universities;
- (b) promotion of cooperation in the field of Union research, technological development and demonstration with third countries and international organisations;
- (c) dissemination and optimisation of the results of activities in Union research, technological development and demonstration;
- (d) stimulation of the training and mobility of researchers in the Union.

Article 181   (ex Article 165 TEC)

1. The Union and the Member States shall coordinate their research and technological development activities so as to ensure that national policies and Union policy are mutually consistent.

2. In close cooperation with the Member State, the Commission may take any useful initiative to promote the coordination referred to in paragraph 1, in particular initiatives aiming at the establishment of guidelines and indicators, the organisation of exchange of best practice, and the preparation of the necessary elements for periodic monitoring and evaluation. The European Parliament shall be kept fully informed.

Article 182   (ex Article 166 TEC)

1. A multiannual framework programme, setting out all the activities of the Union, shall be adopted by the European Parliament and the Council, acting in accordance with the ordinary legislative procedure after consulting the Economic and Social Committee.

The framework programme shall:

- – establish the scientific and technological objectives to be achieved by the activities provided for in Article 180 and fix the relevant priorities,
- – indicate the broad lines of such activities,
- – fix the maximum overall amount and the detailed rules for Union financial participation in the framework programme and the respective shares in each of the activities provided for.

2. The framework programme shall be adapted or supplemented as the situation changes.

3. The framework programme shall be implemented through specific programmes developed within each activity. Each specific programme shall define the detailed rules for implementing it, fix its duration and provide for the means deemed necessary. The sum of the amounts deemed necessary, fixed in the specific programmes, may not exceed the overall maximum amount fixed for the framework programme and each activity.

4. The Council, acting in accordance with a special legislative procedure and after consulting the European Parliament and the Economic and Social Committee, shall adopt the specific programmes.

5. As a complement to the activities planned in the multiannual framework programme, the European Parliament and the Council, acting in accordance with the ordinary legislative procedure and after consulting the Economic and Social Committee, shall establish the measures necessary for the implementation of the European research area.

Article 183   (ex Article 167 TEC)

For the implementation of the multiannual framework programme the Union shall:
- determine the rules for the participation of undertakings, research centres and universities,
- lay down the rules governing the dissemination of research results.

Article 184   (ex Article 168 TEC)

In implementing the multiannual framework programme, supplementary programmes may be decided on involving the participation of certain Member States only, which shall finance them subject to possible Union participation.

The Union shall adopt the rules applicable to supplementary programmes, particularly as regards the dissemination of knowledge and access by other Member States.

Article 185   (ex Article 169 TEC)

In implementing the multiannual framework programme, the Union may make provision, in agreement with the Member States concerned, for participation in research and development programmes undertaken by several Member States, including participation in the structures created for the execution of those programmes.

Article 186   (ex Article 170 TEC)

In implementing the multiannual framework programme the Union may make provision for cooperation in Union research, technological development and demonstration with third countries or international organisations.

The detailed arrangements for such cooperation may be the subject of agreements between the Union and the third parties concerned.

Article 187   (ex Article 171 TEC)

The Union may set up joint undertakings or any other structure necessary for the efficient execution of Union research, technological development and demonstration programmes.

Article 188   (ex Article 172 TEC)

The Council, on a proposal from the Commission and after consulting the European Parliament and the Economic and Social Committee, shall adopt the provisions referred to in Article 187.

The European Parliament and the Council, acting in accordance with the ordinary legislative procedure and after consulting the Economic and Social Committee, shall adopt the provisions referred to in Articles 183, 184 and 185. Adoption of the supplementary programmes shall require the agreement of the Member States concerned.

Article 189

1. To promote scientific and technical progress, industrial competitiveness and the implementation of its policies, the Union shall draw up a European space policy. To this end, it may promote joint

initiatives, support research and technological development and coordinate the efforts needed for the exploration and exploitation of space.

2. To contribute to attaining the objectives referred to in paragraph 1, the European Parliament and the Council, acting in accordance with the ordinary legislative procedure, shall establish the necessary measures, which may take the form of a European space programme, excluding any harmonisation of the laws and regulations of the Member States.

3. The Union shall establish any appropriate relations with the European Space Agency.

4. This Article shall be without prejudice to the other provisions of this Title.

Article 190   (ex Article 173 TEC)

At the beginning of each year the Commission shall send a report to the European Parliament and to the Council. The report shall include information on research and technological development activities and the dissemination of results during the previous year, and the work programme for the current year.

Title XX Environment

Article 191   (ex Article 174 TEC)

1. Union policy on the environment shall contribute to pursuit of the following objectives:
    – preserving, protecting and improving the quality of the environment,
    – protecting human health,
    – prudent and rational utilisation of natural resources,
    – promoting measures at international level to deal with regional or worldwide environmental problems, and in particular combating climate change.

2. Union policy on the environment shall aim at a high level of protection taking into account the diversity of situations in the various regions of the Union. It shall be based on the precautionary principle and on the principles that preventive action should be taken, that environmental damage should as a priority be rectified at source and that the polluter should pay.

In this context, harmonisation measures answering environmental protection requirements shall include, where appropriate, a safeguard clause allowing Member States to take provisional measures, for non-economic environmental reasons, subject to a procedure of inspection by the Union.

3. In preparing its policy on the environment, the Union shall take account of:
    – available scientific and technical data,
    – environmental conditions in the various regions of the Union,
    – the potential benefits and costs of action or lack of action,
    – the economic and social development of the Union as a whole and the balanced development of its regions.

4. Within their respective spheres of competence, the Union and the Member States shall cooperate with third countries and with the competent international organisations. The arrangements for Union cooperation may be the subject of agreements between the Union and the third parties concerned.

The previous subparagraph shall be without prejudice to Member States' competence to negotiate in international bodies and to conclude international agreements.

Article 192   (ex Article 175 TEC)

1. The European Parliament and the Council, acting in accordance with the ordinary legislative procedure and after consulting the Economic and Social Committee and the Committee of the Regions, shall decide what action is to be taken by the Union in order to achieve the objectives referred to in Article 191.

2. By way of derogation from the decision-making procedure provided for in paragraph 1 and without prejudice to Article 114, the Council acting unanimously in accordance with a special legislative

procedure and after consulting the European Parliament, the Economic and Social Committee and the Committee of the Regions, shall adopt:

    (a) provisions primarily of a fiscal nature;

    (b) measures affecting:

      – town and country planning,

      – quantitative management of water resources or affecting, directly or indirectly, the availability of those resources,

      – land use, with the exception of waste management;

    (c) measures significantly affecting a Member State's choice between different energy sources and the general structure of its energy supply.

The Council, acting unanimously on a proposal from the Commission and after consulting the European Parliament, the Economic and Social Committee and the Committee of the Regions, may make the ordinary legislative procedure applicable to the matters referred to in the first subparagraph.

3. General action programmes setting out priority objectives to be attained shall be adopted by the European Parliament and the Council, acting in accordance with the ordinary legislative procedure and after consulting the Economic and Social Committee and the Committee of the Regions.

The measures necessary for the implementation of these programmes shall be adopted under the terms of paragraph 1 or 2, as the case may be.

4. Without prejudice to certain measures adopted by the Union, the Member States shall finance and implement the environment policy.

5. Without prejudice to the principle that the polluter should pay, if a measure based on the provisions of paragraph 1 involves costs deemed disproportionate for the public authorities of a Member State, such measure shall lay down appropriate provisions in the form of:

    – temporary derogations, and/or

    – financial support from the Cohesion Fund set up pursuant to Article 177.

Article 193   (ex Article 176 TEC)

The protective measures adopted pursuant to Article 192 shall not prevent any Member State from maintaining or introducing more stringent protective measures. Such measures must be compatible with the Treaties. They shall be notified to the Commission.

Title XXI Energy

Article 194

1. In the context of the establishment and functioning of the internal market and with regard for the need to preserve and improve the environment, Union policy on energy shall aim, in a spirit of solidarity between Member States, to:

    (a) ensure the functioning of the energy market;

    (b) ensure security of energy supply in the Union;

    (c) promote energy efficiency and energy saving and the development of new and renewable forms of energy; and

    (d) promote the interconnection of energy networks.

2. Without prejudice to the application of other provisions of the Treaties, the European Parliament and the Council, acting in accordance with the ordinary legislative procedure, shall establish the measures necessary to achieve the objectives in paragraph 1. Such measures shall be adopted after consultation of the Economic and Social Committee and the Committee of the Regions.

Such measures shall not affect a Member State's right to determine the conditions for exploiting its energy resources, its choice between different energy sources and the general structure of its energy supply, without prejudice to Article 192(2)(c).

3. By way of derogation from paragraph 2, the Council, acting in accordance with a special legislative procedure, shall unanimously and after consulting the European Parliament, establish the measures referred to therein when they are primarily of a fiscal nature.

Title XXII Tourism

Article 195

1. The Union shall complement the action of the Member States in the tourism sector, in particular by promoting the competitiveness of Union undertakings in that sector.

To that end, Union action shall be aimed at:

(a) encouraging the creation of a favourable environment for the development of undertakings in this sector;

(b) promoting cooperation between the Member States, particularly by the exchange of good practice.

2. The European Parliament and the Council, acting in accordance with the ordinary legislative procedure, shall establish specific measures to complement actions within the Member States to achieve the objectives referred to in this Article, excluding any harmonisation of the laws and regulations of the Member States.

Title XXIII Civil protection

Article 196

1. The Union shall encourage cooperation between Member States in order to improve the effectiveness of systems for preventing and protecting against natural or man-made disasters.

Union action shall aim to:

(a) support and complement Member States' action at national, regional and local level in risk prevention, in preparing their civil-protection personnel and in responding to natural or man-made disasters within the Union;

(b) promote swift, effective operational cooperation within the Union between national civil-protection services;

(c) promote consistency in international civil-protection work.

2. The European Parliament and the Council, acting in accordance with the ordinary legislative procedure shall establish the measures necessary to help achieve the objectives referred to in paragraph 1, excluding any harmonisation of the laws and regulations of the Member States.

Title XXIV Administrative cooperation

Article 197

1. Effective implementation of Union law by the Member States, which is essential for the proper functioning of the Union, shall be regarded as a matter of common interest.

2. The Union may support the efforts of Member States to improve their administrative capacity to implement Union law. Such action may include facilitating the exchange of information and of civil servants as well as supporting training schemes. No Member State shall be obliged to avail itself of such support. The European Parliament and the Council, acting by means of regulations in accordance with the ordinary legislative procedure, shall establish the necessary measures to this end, excluding any harmonisation of the laws and regulations of the Member States.

3. This Article shall be without prejudice to the obligations of the Member States to implement Union law or to the prerogatives and duties of the Commission. It shall also be without prejudice to other provisions of the Treaties providing for administrative cooperation among the Member States and between them and the Union.

PART FOUR ASSOCIATION OF THE OVERSEAS COUNTRIES AND TERRITORIES

Article 198   (ex Article 182 TEC)

The Member States agree to associate with the Union the non-European countries and territories which have special relations with Denmark, France, the Netherlands and the United Kingdom. These countries and territories (hereinafter called the 'countries and territories') are listed in Annex II.

The purpose of association shall be to promote the economic and social development of the countries and territories and to establish close economic relations between them and the Union as a whole.

In accordance with the principles set out in the preamble to this Treaty, association shall serve primarily to further the interests and prosperity of the inhabitants of these countries and territories in order to lead them to the economic, social and cultural development to which they aspire.

Article 199   (ex Article 183 TEC)

Association shall have the following objectives.

1. Member States shall apply to their trade with the countries and territories the same treatment as they accord each other pursuant to the Treaties.

2. Each country or territory shall apply to its trade with Member States and with the other countries and territories the same treatment as that which it applies to the European State with which it has special relations.

3. The Member States shall contribute to the investments required for the progressive development of these countries and territories.

4. For investments financed by the Union, participation in tenders and supplies shall be open on equal terms to all natural and legal persons who are nationals of a Member State or of one of the countries and territories.

5. In relations between Member States and the countries and territories the right of establishment of nationals and companies or firms shall be regulated in accordance with the provisions and procedures laid down in the Chapter relating to the right of establishment and on a non-discriminatory basis, subject to any special provisions laid down pursuant to Article 203.

Article 200   (ex Article 184 TEC)

1. Customs duties on imports into the Member States of goods originating in the countries and territories shall be prohibited in conformity with the prohibition of customs duties between Member States in accordance with the provisions of the Treaties.

2. Customs duties on imports into each country or territory from Member States or from the other countries or territories shall be prohibited in accordance with the provisions of Article 30.

3. The countries and territories may, however, levy customs duties which meet the needs of their development and industrialisation or produce revenue for their budgets.

The duties referred to in the preceding subparagraph may not exceed the level of those imposed on imports of products from the Member State with which each country or territory has special relations.

4. Paragraph 2 shall not apply to countries and territories which, by reason of the particular international obligations by which they are bound, already apply a non-discriminatory customs tariff.

5. The introduction of or any change in customs duties imposed on goods imported into the countries and territories shall not, either in law or in fact, give rise to any direct or indirect discrimination between imports from the various Member States.

Article 201   (ex Article 185 TEC)

If the level of the duties applicable to goods from a third country on entry into a country or territory is liable, when the provisions of Article 200(1) have been applied, to cause deflections of trade to the detriment of any Member State, the latter may request the Commission to propose to the other Member States the measures needed to remedy the situation.

Article 202   (ex Article 186 TEC)

Subject to the provisions relating to public health, public security or public policy, freedom of movement within Member States for workers from the countries and territories, and within the countries and territories for workers from Member States, shall be regulated by acts adopted in accordance with Article 203.

Article 203   (ex Article 187 TEC)

The Council, acting unanimously on a proposal from the Commission, shall, on the basis of the experience acquired under the association of the countries and territories with the Union and of the principles set out in the Treaties, lay down provisions as regards the detailed rules and the procedure for the association of the countries and territories with the Union. Where the provisions in question are adopted by the Council in accordance with a special legislative procedure, it shall act unanimously on a proposal from the Commission and after consulting the European Parliament.

Article 204   (ex Article 188 TEC)

The provisions of Articles 198 to 203 shall apply to Greenland, subject to the specific provisions for Greenland set out in the Protocol on special arrangements for Greenland, annexed to the Treaties.

PART FIVE EXTERNAL ACTION BY THE UNION

Title I General provisions on the Union's external action

Article 205

The Union's action on the international scene, pursuant to this Part, shall be guided by the principles, pursue the objectives and be conducted in accordance with the general provisions laid down in Chapter 1 of Title V of the Treaty on European Union.

Title II Common commercial policy

Article 206   (ex Article 131 TEC)

By establishing a customs union in accordance with Articles 28 to 32, the Union shall contribute, in the common interest, to the harmonious development of world trade, the progressive abolition of restrictions on international trade and on foreign direct investment, and the lowering of customs and other barriers.

Article 207   (ex Article 133 TEC)

1. The common commercial policy shall be based on uniform principles, particularly with regard to changes in tariff rates, the conclusion of tariff and trade agreements relating to trade in goods and services, and the commercial aspects of intellectual property, foreign direct investment, the achievement of uniformity in measures of liberalisation, export policy and measures to protect trade such as those to be taken in the event of dumping or subsidies. The common commercial policy shall be conducted in the context of the principles and objectives of the Union's external action.

2. The European Parliament and the Council, acting by means of regulations in accordance with the ordinary legislative procedure, shall adopt the measures defining the framework for implementing the common commercial policy.

3. Where agreements with one or more third countries or international organisations need to be negotiated and concluded, Article 218 shall apply, subject to the special provisions of this Article.

   The Commission shall make recommendations to the Council, which shall authorise it to open the necessary negotiations. The Council and the Commission shall be responsible for ensuring that the agreements negotiated are compatible with internal Union policies and rules.

The Commission shall conduct these negotiations in consultation with a special committee appointed by the Council to assist the Commission in this task and within the framework of such directives as the Council may issue to it. The Commission shall report regularly to the special committee and to the European Parliament on the progress of negotiations.

4. For the negotiation and conclusion of the agreements referred to in paragraph 3, the Council shall act by a qualified majority.

For the negotiation and conclusion of agreements in the fields of trade in services and the commercial aspects of intellectual property, as well as foreign direct investment, the Council shall act unanimously where such agreements include provisions for which unanimity is required for the adoption of internal rules.

The Council shall also act unanimously for the negotiation and conclusion of agreements:

(a) in the field of trade in cultural and audiovisual services, where these agreements risk prejudicing the Union's cultural and linguistic diversity;

(b) in the field of trade in social, education and health services, where these agreements risk seriously disturbing the national organisation of such services and prejudicing the responsibility of Member States to deliver them.

5. The negotiation and conclusion of international agreements in the field of transport shall be subject to Title VI of Part Three and to Article 218.

6. The exercise of the competences conferred by this Article in the field of the common commercial policy shall not affect the delimitation of competences between the Union and the Member States, and shall not lead to harmonisation of legislative or regulatory provisions of the Member States in so far as the Treaties exclude such harmonisation.

Title III Cooperation with third countries and humanitarian aid

Chapter 1 Development cooperation

Article 208   (ex Article 177 TEC)

1. Union policy in the field of development cooperation shall be conducted within the framework of the principles and objectives of the Union's external action. The Union's development cooperation policy and that of the Member States complement and reinforce each other.

Union development cooperation policy shall have as its primary objective the reduction and, in the long term, the eradication of poverty. The Union shall take account of the objectives of development cooperation in the policies that it implements which are likely to affect developing countries.

2. The Union and the Member States shall comply with the commitments and take account of the objectives they have approved in the context of the United Nations and other competent international organisations.

Article 209 (ex Article 179 TEC)

1. The European Parliament and the Council, acting in accordance with the ordinary legislative procedure, shall adopt the measures necessary for the implementation of development cooperation policy, which may relate to multiannual cooperation programmes with developing countries or programmes with a thematic approach.

2. The Union may conclude with third countries and competent international organisations any agreement helping to achieve the objectives referred to in Article 21 of the Treaty on European Union and in Article 208 of this Treaty.

The first subparagraph shall be without prejudice to Member States' competence to negotiate in international bodies and to conclude agreements.

3. The European Investment Bank shall contribute, under the terms laid down in its Statute, to the implementation of the measures referred to in paragraph 1.

Article 210　(ex Article 180 TEC)

1. In order to promote the complementarity and efficiency of their action, the Union and the Member States shall coordinate their policies on development cooperation and shall consult each other on their aid programmes, including in international organisations and during international conferences. They may undertake joint action. Member States shall contribute if necessary to the implementation of Union aid programmes.

2. The Commission may take any useful initiative to promote the coordination referred to in paragraph 1.

Article 211　(ex Article 181 TEC)

Within their respective spheres of competence, the Union and the Member States shall cooperate with third countries and with the competent international organisations.

Chapter 2　Economic, financial and technical cooperation with third countries

Article 212　(ex Article 181a TEC)

1. Without prejudice to the other provisions of the Treaties, and in particular Articles 208 to 211, the Union shall carry out economic, financial and technical cooperation measures, including assistance, in particular financial assistance, with third countries other than developing countries. Such measures shall be consistent with the development policy of the Union and shall be carried out within the framework of the principles and objectives of its external action. The Union's operations and those of the Member States shall complement and reinforce each other.

2. The European Parliament and the Council, acting in accordance with the ordinary legislative procedure, shall adopt the measures necessary for the implementation of paragraph 1.

3. Within their respective spheres of competence, the Union and the Member States shall cooperate with third countries and the competent international organisations. The arrangements for Union cooperation may be the subject of agreements between the Union and the third parties concerned.

The first subparagraph shall be without prejudice to the Member States' competence to negotiate in international bodies and to conclude international agreements.

Article 213

When the situation in a third country requires urgent financial assistance from the Union, the Council shall adopt the necessary decisions on a proposal from the Commission.

Chapter 3　Humanitarian aid

Article 214

1. The Union's operations in the field of humanitarian aid shall be conducted within the framework of the principles and objectives of the external action of the Union. Such operations shall be intended to provide *ad hoc* assistance and relief and protection for people in third countries who are victims of natural or man-made disasters, in order to meet the humanitarian needs resulting from these different situations. The Union's measures and those of the Member States shall complement and reinforce each other.

2. Humanitarian aid operations shall be conducted in compliance with the principles of international law and with the principles of impartiality, neutrality and non-discrimination.

3. The European Parliament and the Council, acting in accordance with the ordinary legislative procedure, shall establish the measures defining the framework within which the Union's humanitarian aid operations shall be implemented.

4. The Union may conclude with third countries and competent international organisations any agreement helping to achieve the objectives referred to in paragraph 1 and in Article 21 of the Treaty on European Union.

The first subparagraph shall be without prejudice to Member States' competence to negotiate in international bodies and to conclude agreements.

5. In order to establish a framework for joint contributions from young Europeans to the humanitarian aid operations of the Union, a European Voluntary Humanitarian Aid Corps shall be set up. The European Parliament and the Council, acting by means of regulations in accordance with the ordinary legislative procedure, shall determine the rules and procedures for the operation of the Corps.

6. The Commission may take any useful initiative to promote coordination between actions of the Union and those of the Member States, in order to enhance the efficiency and complementarity of Union and national humanitarian aid measures.

7. The Union shall ensure that its humanitarian aid operations are coordinated and consistent with those of international organisations and bodies, in particular those forming part of the United Nations system.

Title IV Restrictive measures

Article 215   (ex Article 301 TEC)

1. Where a decision, adopted in accordance with Chapter 2 of Title V of the Treaty on European Union, provides for the interruption or reduction, in part or completely, of economic and financial relations with one or more third countries, the Council, acting by a qualified majority on a joint proposal from the High Representative of the Union for Foreign Affairs and Security Policy and the Commission, shall adopt the necessary measures. It shall inform the European Parliament thereof.

2. Where a decision adopted in accordance with Chapter 2 of Title V of the Treaty on European Union so provides, the Council may adopt restrictive measures under the procedure referred to in paragraph 1 against natural or legal persons and groups or non-State entities.

3. The acts referred to in this Article shall include necessary provisions on legal safeguards.

Title V International agreements

Article 216

1. The Union may conclude an agreement with one or more third countries or international organisations where the Treaties so provide or where the conclusion of an agreement is necessary in order to achieve, within the framework of the Union's policies, one of the objectives referred to in the Treaties, or is provided for in a legally binding Union act or is likely to affect common rules or alter their scope.

2. Agreements concluded by the Union are binding upon the institutions of the Union and on its Member States.

Article 217   (ex Article 310 TEC)

The Union may conclude with one or more third countries or international organisations agreements establishing an association involving reciprocal rights and obligations, common action and special procedure.

Article 218   (ex Article 300 TEC)

1. Without prejudice to the specific provisions laid down in Article 207, agreements between the Union and third countries or international organisations shall be negotiated and concluded in accordance with the following procedure.

2. The Council shall authorise the opening of negotiations, adopt negotiating directives, authorise the signing of agreements and conclude them.

3. The Commission, or the High Representative of the Union for Foreign Affairs and Security Policy where the agreement envisaged relates exclusively or principally to the common foreign and security policy, shall submit recommendations to the Council, which shall adopt a decision authorising

the opening of negotiations and, depending on the subject of the agreement envisaged, nominating the Union negotiator or the head of the Union's negotiating team.

4. The Council may address directives to the negotiator and designate a special committee in consultation with which the negotiations must be conducted.

5. The Council, on a proposal by the negotiator, shall adopt a decision authorising the signing of the agreement and, if necessary, its provisional application before entry into force.

6. The Council, on a proposal by the negotiator, shall adopt a decision concluding the agreement.

Except where agreements relate exclusively to the common foreign and security policy, the Council shall adopt the decision concluding the agreement:

    (a) after obtaining the consent of the European Parliament in the following cases:

        (i) association agreements;

        (ii) agreement on Union accession to the European Convention for the Protection of Human Rights and Fundamental Freedoms;

        (iii) agreements establishing a specific institutional framework by organising cooperation procedures;

        (iv) agreements with important budgetary implications for the Union;

        (v) agreements covering fields to which either the ordinary legislative procedure applies, or the special legislative procedure where consent by the European Parliament is required.

        The European Parliament and the Council may, in an urgent situation, agree upon a time-limit for consent.

    (b) after consulting the European Parliament in other cases. The European Parliament shall deliver its opinion within a time-limit which the Council may set depending on the urgency of the matter. In the absence of an opinion within that time-limit, the Council may act.

7. When concluding an agreement, the Council may, by way of derogation from paragraphs 5, 6 and 9, authorise the negotiator to approve on the Union's behalf modifications to the agreement where it provides for them to be adopted by a simplified procedure or by a body set up by the agreement. The Council may attach specific conditions to such authorisation.

8. The Council shall act by a qualified majority throughout the procedure.

However, it shall act unanimously when the agreement covers a field for which unanimity is required for the adoption of a Union act as well as for association agreements and the agreements referred to in Article 212 with the States which are candidates for accession. The Council shall also act unanimously for the agreement on accession of the Union to the European Convention for the Protection of Human Rights and Fundamental Freedoms; the decision concluding this agreement shall enter into force after it has been approved by the Member States in accordance with their respective constitutional requirements.

9. The Council, on a proposal from the Commission or the High Representative of the Union for Foreign Affairs and Security Policy, shall adopt a decision suspending application of an agreement and establishing the positions to be adopted on the Union's behalf in a body set up by an agreement, when that body is called upon to adopt acts having legal effects, with the exception of acts supplementing or amending the institutional framework of the agreement.

10. The European Parliament shall be immediately and fully informed at all stages of the procedure.

11. A Member State, the European Parliament, the Council or the Commission may obtain the opinion of the Court of Justice as to whether an agreement envisaged is compatible with the Treaties. Where the opinion of the Court is adverse, the agreement envisaged may not enter into force unless it is amended or the Treaties are revised.

Article 219   (ex Article 111(1) to (3) and (5) TEC)

1. By way of derogation from Article 218, the Council, either on a recommendation from the European Central Bank or on a recommendation from the Commission and after consulting the European Central Bank, in an endeavour to reach a consensus consistent with the objective of price

stability, may conclude formal agreements on an exchange-rate system for the euro in relation to the currencies of third States. The Council shall act unanimously after consulting the European Parliament and in accordance with the procedure provided for in paragraph 3.

The Council may, either on a recommendation from the European Central Bank or on a recommendation from the Commission, and after consulting the European Central Bank, in an endeavour to reach a consensus consistent with the objective of price stability, adopt, adjust or abandon the central rates of the euro within the exchange-rate system. The President of the Council shall inform the European Parliament of the adoption, adjustment or abandonment of the euro central rates.

2. In the absence of an exchange-rate system in relation to one or more currencies of third States as referred to in paragraph 1, the Council, either on a recommendation from the Commission and after consulting the European Central Bank or on a recommendation from the European Central Bank, may formulate general orientations for exchange-rate policy in relation to these currencies. These general orientations shall be without prejudice to the primary objective of the ESCB to maintain price stability.

3. By way of derogation from Article 218, where agreements concerning monetary or foreign exchange regime matters need to be negotiated by the Union with one or more third States or international organisations, the Council, on a recommendation from the Commission and after consulting the European Central Bank, shall decide the arrangements for the negotiation and for the conclusion of such agreements. These arrangements shall ensure that the Union expresses a single position. The Commission shall be fully associated with the negotiations.

4. Without prejudice to Union competence and Union agreements as regards economic and monetary union, Member States may negotiate in international bodies and conclude international agreements.

Title VI The Union's relations with international organisations and third countries and Union delegations

Article 220   (ex Articles 302 to 304 TEC)

1. The Union shall establish all appropriate forms of cooperation with the organs of the United Nations and its specialised agencies, the Council of Europe, the Organisation for Security and Cooperation in Europe and the Organisation for Economic Cooperation and Development.

The Union shall also maintain such relations as are appropriate with other international organisations.

2. The High Representative of the Union for Foreign Affairs and Security Policy and the Commission shall be instructed to implement this Article.

Article 221

1. Union delegations in third countries and at international organisations shall represent the Union.

2. Union delegations shall be placed under the authority of the High Representative of the Union for Foreign Affairs and Security Policy. They shall act in close cooperation with Member States' diplomatic and consular missions.

Title VII Solidarity clause

Article 222

1. The Union and its Member States shall act jointly in a spirit of solidarity if a Member State is the object of a terrorist attack or the victim of a natural or man-made disaster. The Union shall mobilise all the instruments at its disposal, including the military resources made available by the Member States, to:

    (a) – prevent the terrorist threat in the territory of the Member States;

        – protect democratic institutions and the civilian population from any terrorist attack;

– assist a Member State in its territory, at the request of its political authorities, in the event of a terrorist attack;

(b) assist a Member State in its territory, at the request of its political authorities, in the event of a natural or man-made disaster.

2. Should a Member State be the object of a terrorist attack or the victim of a natural or man-made disaster, the other Member States shall assist it at the request of its political authorities. To that end, the Member States shall coordinate between themselves in the Council.

3. The arrangements for the implementation by the Union of the solidarity clause shall be defined by a decision adopted by the Council acting on a joint proposal by the Commission and the High Representative of the Union for Foreign Affairs and Security Policy. The Council shall act in accordance with Article 31(1) of the Treaty on European Union where this decision has defence implications. The European Parliament shall be informed.

For the purposes of this paragraph and without prejudice to Article 240, the Council shall be assisted by the Political and Security Committee with the support of the structures developed in the context of the common security and defence policy and by the Committee referred to in Article 71; the two committees shall, if necessary, submit joint opinions.

4. The European Council shall regularly assess the threats facing the Union in order to enable the Union and its Member States to take effective action.

PART SIX INSTITUTIONAL AND FINANCIAL PROVISIONS

Title I Institutional provisions

Chapter 1 The institutions

Section 1 The European Parliament

Article 223   (ex Article 190(4) and (5) TEC)

1. The European Parliament shall draw up a proposal to lay down the provisions necessary for the election of its Members by direct universal suffrage in accordance with a uniform procedure in all Member States or in accordance with principles common to all Member States.

The Council, acting unanimously in accordance with a special legislative procedure and after obtaining the consent of the European Parliament, which shall act by a majority of its component Members, shall lay down the necessary provisions. These provisions shall enter into force following their approval by the Member States in accordance with their respective constitutional requirements.

2. The European Parliament, acting by means of regulations on its own initiative in accordance with a special legislative procedure after seeking an opinion from the Commission and with the approval of the Council, shall lay down the regulations and general conditions governing the performance of the duties of its Members. All rules or conditions relating to the taxation of Members or former Members shall require unanimity within the Council.

Article 224   (ex Article 191, second subparagraph, TEC)

The European Parliament and the Council, acting in accordance with the ordinary legislative procedure, by means of regulations, shall lay down the regulations governing political parties at European level referred to in Article 10(4) of the Treaty on European Union and in particular the rules regarding their funding.

Article 225   (ex Article 192, second subparagraph, TEC)

The European Parliament may, acting by a majority of its component Members, request the Commission to submit any appropriate proposal on matters on which it considers that a Union act is required for the purpose of implementing the Treaties. If the Commission does not submit a proposal, it shall inform the European Parliament of the reasons.

Article 226   (ex Article 193 TEC)

In the course of its duties, the European Parliament may, at the request of a quarter of its component Members, set up a temporary Committee of Inquiry to investigate, without prejudice to the powers conferred by the Treaties on other institutions or bodies, alleged contraventions or maladministration in the implementation of Union law, except where the alleged facts are being examined before a court and while the case is still subject to legal proceedings.

The temporary Committee of Inquiry shall cease to exist on the submission of its report.

The detailed provisions governing the exercise of the right of inquiry shall be determined by the European Parliament, acting by means of regulations on its own initiative in accordance with a special legislative procedure, after obtaining the consent of the Council and the Commission.

Article 227   (ex Article 194 TEC)

Any citizen of the Union, and any natural or legal person residing or having its registered office in a Member State, shall have the right to address, individually or in association with other citizens or persons, a petition to the European Parliament on a matter which comes within the Union's fields of activity and which affects him, her or it directly.

Article 228   (ex Article 195 TEC)

1. A European Ombudsman, elected by the European Parliament, shall be empowered to receive complaints from any citizen of the Union or any natural or legal person residing or having its registered office in a Member State concerning instances of maladministration in the activities of the Union institutions, bodies, offices or agencies, with the exception of the Court of Justice of the European Union acting in its judicial role. He or she shall examine such complaints and report on them.

In accordance with his duties, the Ombudsman shall conduct inquiries for which he finds grounds, either on his own initiative or on the basis of complaints submitted to him direct or through a Member of the European Parliament, except where the alleged facts are or have been the subject of legal proceedings. Where the Ombudsman establishes an instance of maladministration, he shall refer the matter to the institution, body, office or agency concerned, which shall have a period of three months in which to inform him of its views. The Ombudsman shall then forward a report to the European Parliament and the institution, body, office or agency concerned. The person lodging the complaint shall be informed of the outcome of such inquiries.

The Ombudsman shall submit an annual report to the European Parliament on the outcome of his inquiries.

2. The Ombudsman shall be elected after each election of the European Parliament for the duration of its term of office. The Ombudsman shall be eligible for reappointment.

The Ombudsman may be dismissed by the Court of Justice at the request of the European Parliament if he no longer fulfils the conditions required for the performance of his duties or if he is guilty of serious misconduct.

3. The Ombudsman shall be completely independent in the performance of his duties. In the performance of those duties he shall neither seek nor take instructions from any Government, institution, body, office or entity. The Ombudsman may not, during his term of office, engage in any other occupation, whether gainful or not.

4. The European Parliament acting by means of regulations on its own initiative in accordance with a special legislative procedure shall, after seeking an opinion from the Commission and with the approval of the Council, lay down the regulations and general conditions governing the performance of the Ombudsman's duties.

Article 229   (ex Article 196 TEC)

The European Parliament shall hold an annual session. It shall meet, without requiring to be convened, on the second Tuesday in March.

The European Parliament may meet in extraordinary part-session at the request of a majority of its component Members or at the request of the Council or of the Commission.

Article 230   (ex Article 197, second, third and fourth paragraph, TEC)

The Commission may attend all the meetings and shall, at its request, be heard.

The Commission shall reply orally or in writing to questions put to it by the European Parliament or by its Members.

The European Council and the Council shall be heard by the European Parliament in accordance with the conditions laid down in the Rules of Procedure of the European Council and those of the Council.

Article 231   (ex Article 198 TEC)

Save as otherwise provided in the Treaties, the European Parliament shall act by a majority of the votes cast.

The Rules of Procedure shall determine the quorum.

Article 232   (ex Article 199 TEC)

The European Parliament shall adopt its Rules of Procedure, acting by a majority of its Members.

The proceedings of the European Parliament shall be published in the manner laid down in the Treaties and in its Rules of Procedure.

Article 233   (ex Article 200 TEC)

The European Parliament shall discuss in open session the annual general report submitted to it by the Commission.

Article 234   (ex Article 201 TEC)

If a motion of censure on the activities of the Commission is tabled before it, the European Parliament shall not vote thereon until at least three days after the motion has been tabled and only by open vote.

If the motion of censure is carried by a two-thirds majority of the votes cast, representing a majority of the component Members of the European Parliament, the members of the Commission shall resign as a body and the High Representative of the Union for Foreign Affairs and Security Policy shall resign from duties that he or she carries out in the Commission. They shall remain in office and continue to deal with current business until they are replaced in accordance with Article 17 of the Treaty on European Union. In this case, the term of office of the members of the Commission appointed to replace them shall expire on the date on which the term of office of the members of the Commission obliged to resign as a body would have expired.

Section 2 The European Council

Article 235

1. Where a vote is taken, any member of the European Council may also act on behalf of not more than one other member.

Article 16(4) of the Treaty on European Union and Article 238(2) of this Treaty shall apply to the European Council when it is acting by a qualified majority. Where the European Council decides by vote, its President and the President of the Commission shall not take part in the vote.

Abstentions by members present in person or represented shall not prevent the adoption by the European Council of acts which require unanimity.

2. The President of the European Parliament may be invited to be heard by the European Council.

3. The European Council shall act by a simple majority for procedural questions and for the adoption of its Rules of Procedure.

4. The European Council shall be assisted by the General Secretariat of the Council.

Article 236

The European Council shall adopt by a qualified majority:

    (a) a decision establishing the list of Council configurations, other than those of the General Affairs Council and of the Foreign Affairs Council, in accordance with Article 16(6) of the Treaty on European Union;

    (b) a decision on the Presidency of Council configurations, other than that of Foreign Affairs, in accordance with Article 16(9) of the Treaty on European Union.

Section 3 The Council

Article 237   (ex Article 204 TEC)

The Council shall meet when convened by its President on his own initiative or at the request of one of its Members or of the Commission.

Article 238   (ex Article 205(1) and (2), TEC)

1. Where it is required to act by a simple majority, the Council shall act by a majority of its component members.

2. By way of derogation from Article 16(4) of the Treaty on European Union, as from 1 November 2014 and subject to the provisions laid down in the Protocol on transitional provisions, where the Council does not act on a proposal from the Commission or from the High Representative of the Union for Foreign Affairs and Security Policy, the qualified majority shall be defined as at least 72 % of the members of the Council, representing Member States comprising at least 65 % of the population of the Union.

3. As from 1 November 2014 and subject to the provisions laid down in the Protocol on transitional provisions, in cases where, under the Treaties, not all the members of the Council participate in voting, a qualified majority shall be defined as follows:

    (a) A qualified majority shall be defined as at least 55 % of the members of the Council representing the participating Member States, comprising at least 65 % of the population of these States.

        A blocking minority must include at least the minimum number of Council members representing more than 35 % of the population of the participating Member States, plus one member, failing which the qualified majority shall be deemed attained;

    (b) By way of derogation from point (a), where the Council does not act on a proposal from the Commission or from the High Representative of the Union for Foreign Affairs and Security Policy, the qualified majority shall be defined as at least 72 % of the members of the Council representing the participating Member States, comprising at least 65 % of the population of these States.

4. Abstentions by Members present in person or represented shall not prevent the adoption by the Council of acts which require unanimity.

Article 239   (ex Article 206 TEC)

Where a vote is taken, any Member of the Council may also act on behalf of not more than one other member.

Article 240   (ex Article 207 TEC)

1. A committee consisting of the Permanent Representatives of the Governments of the Member States shall be responsible for preparing the work of the Council and for carrying out the tasks assigned to it by the latter. The Committee may adopt procedural decisions in cases provided for in the Council's Rules of Procedure.

2. The Council shall be assisted by a General Secretariat, under the responsibility of a Secretary-General appointed by the Council.

    The Council shall decide on the organisation of the General Secretariat by a simple majority.

3. The Council shall act by a simple majority regarding procedural matters and for the adoption of its Rules of Procedure.

Article 241   (ex Article 208 TEC)

The Council acting by a simple majority may request the Commission to undertake any studies the Council considers desirable for the attainment of the common objectives, and to submit to it any appropriate proposals. If the Commission does not submit a proposal, it shall inform the Council of the reasons.

Article 242   (ex Article 209 TEC)

The Council, acting by a simple majority shall, after consulting the Commission, determine the rules governing the committees provided for in the Treaties.

Article 243   (ex Article 210 TEC)

The Council shall determine the salaries, allowances and pensions of the President of the European Council, the President of the Commission, the High Representative of the Union for Foreign Affairs and Security Policy, the Members of the Commission, the Presidents, Members and Registrars of the Court of Justice of the European Union, and the Secretary-General of the Council. It shall also determine any payment to be made instead of remuneration.

Section 4 The Commission

Article 244

In accordance with Article 17(5) of the Treaty on European Union, the Members of the Commission shall be chosen on the basis of a system of rotation established unanimously by the European Council and on the basis of the following principles:

> (a) Member States shall be treated on a strictly equal footing as regards determination of the sequence of, and the time spent by, their nationals as members of the Commission; consequently, the difference between the total number of terms of office held by nationals of any given pair of Member States may never be more than one;
>
> (b) subject to point (a), each successive Commission shall be so composed as to reflect satisfactorily the demographic and geographical range of all the Member States.

Article 245   (ex Article 213 TEC)

The Members of the Commission shall refrain from any action incompatible with their duties. Member States shall respect their independence and shall not seek to influence them in the performance of their tasks.

The Members of the Commission may not, during their term of office, engage in any other occupation, whether gainful or not. When entering upon their duties they shall give a solemn undertaking that, both during and after their term of office, they will respect the obligations arising therefrom and in particular their duty to behave with integrity and discretion as regards the acceptance, after they have ceased to hold office, of certain appointments or benefits. In the event of any breach of these obligations, the Court of Justice may, on application by the Council acting by a simple majority or the Commission, rule that the Member concerned be, according to the circumstances, either compulsorily retired in accordance with Article 247 or deprived of his right to a pension or other benefits in its stead.

Article 246   (ex Article 215 TEC)

Apart from normal replacement, or death, the duties of a Member of the Commission shall end when he resigns or is compulsorily retired.

A vacancy caused by resignation, compulsory retirement or death shall be filled for the remainder of the Member's term of office by a new Member of the same nationality appointed by the Council, by common accord with the President of the Commission, after consulting the European Parliament and in accordance with the criteria set out in the second subparagraph of Article 17(3) of the Treaty on European Union.

The Council may, acting unanimously on a proposal from the President of the Commission, decide that such a vacancy need not be filled, in particular when the remainder of the Member's term of office is short.

In the event of resignation, compulsory retirement or death, the President shall be replaced for the remainder of his term of office. The procedure laid down in the first subparagraph of Article 17(7) of the Treaty on European Union shall be applicable for the replacement of the President.

In the event of resignation, compulsory retirement or death, the High Representative of the Union for Foreign Affairs and Security Policy shall be replaced, for the remainder of his or her term of office, in accordance with Article 18(1) of the Treaty on European Union.

In the case of the resignation of all the Members of the Commission, they shall remain in office and continue to deal with current business until they have been replaced, for the remainder of their term of office, in accordance with Article 17 of the Treaty on European Union.

Article 247   (ex Article 216 TEC)

If any Member of the Commission no longer fulfils the conditions required for the performance of his duties or if he has been guilty of serious misconduct, the Court of Justice may, on application by the Council acting by a simple majority or the Commission, compulsorily retire him.

Article 248   (ex Article 217(2), TEC)

Without prejudice to Article 18(4) of the Treaty on European Union, the responsibilities incumbent upon the Commission shall be structured and allocated among its members by its President, in accordance with Article 17(6) of that Treaty. The President may reshuffle the allocation of those responsibilities during the Commission's term of office. The Members of the Commission shall carry out the duties devolved upon them by the President under his authority.

Article 249   (ex Articles 218(2) and 212 TEC)

1. The Commission shall adopt its Rules of Procedure so as to ensure that both it and its departments operate. It shall ensure that these Rules are published.

2. The Commission shall publish annually, not later than one month before the opening of the session of the European Parliament, a general report on the activities of the Union.

Article 250   (ex Article 219 TEC)

The Commission shall act by a majority of its Members.

Its Rules of Procedure shall determine the quorum.

Section 5 The Court of Justice of the European Union

Article 251   (ex Article 221 TEC)

The Court of Justice shall sit in chambers or in a Grand Chamber, in accordance with the rules laid down for that purpose in the Statute of the Court of Justice of the European Union.

When provided for in the Statute, the Court of Justice may also sit as a full Court.

Article 252   (ex Article 222 TEC)

The Court of Justice shall be assisted by eight Advocates-General. Should the Court of Justice so request, the Council, acting unanimously, may increase the number of Advocates-General.*

It shall be the duty of the Advocate-General, acting with complete impartiality and independence, to make, in open court, reasoned submissions on cases which, in accordance with the Statute of the Court of Justice of the European Union, require his involvement.

Article 253   (ex Article 223 TEC)

The Judges and Advocates-General of the Court of Justice shall be chosen from persons whose independence is beyond doubt and who possess the qualifications required for appointment to the highest judicial offices in their respective countries or who are jurisconsults of recognised competence; they shall be appointed by common accord of the governments of the Member States for a term of six years, after consultation of the panel provided for in Article 255.

Every three years there shall be a partial replacement of the Judges and Advocates-General, in accordance with the conditions laid down in the Statute of the Court of Justice of the European Union.

---

* **Editor's Note**: Declaration 38 attached to the Treaties allows for the Court to request an increase in the number of Advocates-General, which has now taken place and has been unanimously approved by the Council in Decision 2013/336 (OJ 2013 L179/92), so the number of Advocates-General now stands at nine. Note though that the Decision also agreed an increase in the number of Advocates-General to 11 with effect from 7 October 2015.

The Judges shall elect the President of the Court of Justice from among their number for a term of three years. He may be re-elected.

Retiring Judges and Advocates-General may be reappointed.

The Court of Justice shall appoint its Registrar and lay down the rules governing his service.

The Court of Justice shall establish its Rules of Procedure. Those Rules shall require the approval of the Council.

Article 254   (ex Article 224 TEC)

The number of Judges of the General Court shall be determined by the Statute of the Court of Justice of the European Union. The Statute may provide for the General Court to be assisted by Advocates-General.

The members of the General Court shall be chosen from persons whose independence is beyond doubt and who possess the ability required for appointment to high judicial office. They shall be appointed by common accord of the governments of the Member States for a term of six years, after consultation of the panel provided for in Article 255. The membership shall be partially renewed every three years. Retiring members shall be eligible for reappointment.

The Judges shall elect the President of the General Court from among their number for a term of three years. He may be re-elected.

The General Court shall appoint its Registrar and lay down the rules governing his service.

The General Court shall establish its Rules of Procedure in agreement with the Court of Justice. Those Rules shall require the approval of the Council.

Unless the Statute of the Court of Justice of the European Union provides otherwise, the provisions of the Treaties relating to the Court of Justice shall apply to the General Court.

Article 255

A panel shall be set up in order to give an opinion on candidates' suitability to perform the duties of Judge and Advocate-General of the Court of Justice and the General Court before the governments of the Member States make the appointments referred to in Articles 253 and 254.

The panel shall comprise seven persons chosen from among former members of the Court of Justice and the General Court, members of national supreme courts and lawyers of recognised competence, one of whom shall be proposed by the European Parliament. The Council shall adopt a decision establishing the panel's operating rules and a decision appointing its members. It shall act on the initiative of the President of the Court of Justice.

Article 256   (ex Article 225 TEC)

1. The General Court shall have jurisdiction to hear and determine at first instance actions or proceedings referred to in Articles 263, 265, 268, 270 and 272, with the exception of those assigned to a specialised court set up under Article 257 and those reserved in the Statute for the Court of Justice. The Statute may provide for the General Court to have jurisdiction for other classes of action or proceeding.

Decisions given by the General Court under this paragraph may be subject to a right of appeal to the Court of Justice on points of law only, under the conditions and within the limits laid down by the Statute.

2. The General Court shall have jurisdiction to hear and determine actions or proceedings brought against decisions of the specialised courts.

Decisions given by the General Court under this paragraph may exceptionally be subject to review by the Court of Justice, under the conditions and within the limits laid down by the Statute, where there is a serious risk of the unity or consistency of Union law being affected.

3. The General Court shall have jurisdiction to hear and determine questions referred for a preliminary ruling under Article 267, in specific areas laid down by the Statute.

Where the General Court considers that the case requires a decision of principle likely to affect the unity or consistency of Union law, it may refer the case to the Court of Justice for a ruling.

Decisions given by the General Court on questions referred for a preliminary ruling may exceptionally be subject to review by the Court of Justice, under the conditions and within the limits laid down by the Statute, where there is a serious risk of the unity or consistency of Union law being affected.

Article 257   (ex Article 225a TEC)

The European Parliament and the Council, acting in accordance with the ordinary legislative procedure, may establish specialised courts attached to the General Court to hear and determine at first instance certain classes of action or proceeding brought in specific areas. The European Parliament and the Council shall act by means of regulations either on a proposal from the Commission after consultation of the Court of Justice or at the request of the Court of Justice after consultation of the Commission.

The regulation establishing a specialised court shall lay down the rules on the organisation of the court and the extent of the jurisdiction conferred upon it.

Decisions given by specialised courts may be subject to a right of appeal on points of law only or, when provided for in the regulation establishing the specialised court, a right of appeal also on matters of fact, before the General Court.

The members of the specialised courts shall be chosen from persons whose independence is beyond doubt and who possess the ability required for appointment to judicial office. They shall be appointed by the Council, acting unanimously.

The specialised courts shall establish their Rules of Procedure in agreement with the Court of Justice. Those Rules shall require the approval of the Council.

Unless the regulation establishing the specialised court provides otherwise, the provisions of the Treaties relating to the Court of Justice of the European Union and the provisions of the Statute of the Court of Justice of the European Union shall apply to the specialised courts. Title I of the Statute and Article 64 thereof shall in any case apply to the specialised courts.

Article 258   (ex Article 226 TEC)

If the Commission considers that a Member State has failed to fulfil an obligation under the Treaties, it shall deliver a reasoned opinion on the matter after giving the State concerned the opportunity to submit its observations.

If the State concerned does not comply with the opinion within the period laid down by the Commission, the latter may bring the matter before the Court of Justice of the European Union.

Article 259   (ex Article 227 TEC)

A Member State which considers that another Member State has failed to fulfil an obligation under the Treaties may bring the matter before the Court of Justice of the European Union.

Before a Member State brings an action against another Member State for an alleged infringement of an obligation under the Treaties, it shall bring the matter before the Commission.

The Commission shall deliver a reasoned opinion after each of the States concerned has been given the opportunity to submit its own case and its observations on the other party's case both orally and in writing.

If the Commission has not delivered an opinion within three months of the date on which the matter was brought before it, the absence of such opinion shall not prevent the matter from being brought before the Court.

Article 260   (ex Article 228 TEC)

1. If the Court of Justice of the European Union finds that a Member State has failed to fulfil an obligation under the Treaties, the State shall be required to take the necessary measures to comply with the judgment of the Court.

2. If the Commission considers that the Member State concerned has not taken the necessary measures to comply with the judgment of the Court, it may bring the case before the Court after giving that State the opportunity to submit its observations. It shall specify the amount of the lump sum or penalty payment to be paid by the Member State concerned which it considers appropriate in the circumstances.

If the Court finds that the Member State concerned has not complied with its judgment it may impose a lump sum or penalty payment on it.

This procedure shall be without prejudice to Article 259.

3. When the Commission brings a case before the Court pursuant to Article 258 on the grounds that the Member State concerned has failed to fulfil its obligation to notify measures transposing

a directive adopted under a legislative procedure, it may, when it deems appropriate, specify the amount of the lump sum or penalty payment to be paid by the Member State concerned which it considers appropriate in the circumstances.

If the Court finds that there is an infringement it may impose a lump sum or penalty payment on the Member State concerned not exceeding the amount specified by the Commission. The payment obligation shall take effect on the date set by the Court in its judgment.

Article 261   (ex Article 229 TEC)

Regulations adopted jointly by the European Parliament and the Council, and by the Council, pursuant to the provisions of the Treaties, may give the Court of Justice of the European Union unlimited jurisdiction with regard to the penalties provided for in such regulations.

Article 262   (ex Article 229a TEC)

Without prejudice to the other provisions of the Treaties, the Council, acting unanimously in accordance with a special legislative procedure and after consulting the European Parliament, may adopt provisions to confer jurisdiction, to the extent that it shall determine, on the Court of Justice of the European Union in disputes relating to the application of acts adopted on the basis of the Treaties which create European intellectual property rights. These provisions shall enter into force after their approval by the Member States in accordance with their respective constitutional requirements.

Article 263   (ex Article 230 TEC)

The Court of Justice of the European Union shall review the legality of legislative acts, of acts of the Council, of the Commission and of the European Central Bank, other than recommendations and opinions, and of acts of the European Parliament and of the European Council intended to produce legal effects *vis-à-vis* third parties. It shall also review the legality of acts of bodies, offices or agencies of the Union intended to produce legal effects *vis-à-vis* third parties.

It shall for this purpose have jurisdiction in actions brought by a Member State, the European Parliament, the Council or the Commission on grounds of lack of competence, infringement of an essential procedural requirement, infringement of the Treaties or of any rule of law relating to their application, or misuse of powers.

The Court shall have jurisdiction under the same conditions in actions brought by the Court of Auditors, by the European Central Bank and by the Committee of the Regions for the purpose of protecting their prerogatives.

Any natural or legal person may, under the conditions laid down in the first and second paragraphs, institute proceedings against an act addressed to that person or which is of direct and individual concern to them, and against a regulatory act which is of direct concern to them and does not entail implementing measures.

Acts setting up bodies, offices and agencies of the Union may lay down specific conditions and arrangements concerning actions brought by natural or legal persons against acts of these bodies, offices or agencies intended to produce legal effects in relation to them.

The proceedings provided for in this Article shall be instituted within two months of the publication of the measure, or of its notification to the plaintiff, or, in the absence thereof, of the day on which it came to the knowledge of the latter, as the case may be.

Article 264   (ex Article 231 TEC)

If the action is well founded, the Court of Justice of the European Union shall declare the act concerned to be void.

However, the Court shall, if it considers this necessary, state which of the effects of the act which it has declared void shall be considered as definitive.

Article 265   (ex Article 232 TEC)

Should the European Parliament, the European Council, the Council, the Commission or the European Central Bank, in infringement of the Treaties, fail to act, the Member States and the other institutions of the Union may bring an action before the Court of Justice of the European Union to have the infringement established. This Article shall apply, under the same conditions, to bodies, offices and agencies of the Union which fail to act.

The action shall be admissible only if the institution, body, office or agency concerned has first been called upon to act. If, within two months of being so called upon, the institution, body, office or agency concerned has not defined its position, the action may be brought within a further period of two months.

Any natural or legal person may, under the conditions laid down in the preceding paragraphs, complain to the Court that an institution, body, office or agency of the Union has failed to address to that person any act other than a recommendation or an opinion.

Article 266   (ex Article 233 TEC)

The institution whose act has been declared void or whose failure to act has been declared contrary to the Treaties shall be required to take the necessary measures to comply with the judgment of the Court of Justice of the European Union.

This obligation shall not affect any obligation which may result from the application of the second paragraph of Article 340.

Article 267   (ex Article 234 TEC)

The Court of Justice of the European Union shall have jurisdiction to give preliminary rulings concerning:

  (a) the interpretation of the Treaties;
  (b) the validity and interpretation of acts of the institutions, bodies, offices or agencies of the Union;

Where such a question is raised before any court or tribunal of a Member State, that court or tribunal may, if it considers that a decision on the question is necessary to enable it to give judgment, request the Court to give a ruling thereon.

Where any such question is raised in a case pending before a court or tribunal of a Member State against whose decisions there is no judicial remedy under national law, that court or tribunal shall bring the matter before the Court.

If such a question is raised in a case pending before a court or tribunal of a Member State with regard to a person in custody, the Court of Justice of the European Union shall act with the minimum of delay.

Article 268   (ex Article 235 TEC)

The Court of Justice of the European Union shall have jurisdiction in disputes relating to compensation for damage provided for in the second and third paragraphs of Article 340.

Article 269

The Court of Justice shall have jurisdiction to decide on the legality of an act adopted by the European Council or by the Council pursuant to Article 7 of the Treaty on European Union solely at the request of the Member State concerned by a determination of the European Council or of the Council and in respect solely of the procedural stipulations contained in that Article.

Such a request must be made within one month from the date of such determination.

The Court shall rule within one month from the date of the request.

Article 270   (ex Article 236 TEC)

The Court of Justice of the European Union shall have jurisdiction in any dispute between the Union and its servants within the limits and under the conditions laid down in the Staff Regulations of Officials and the Conditions of Employment of other servants of the Union.

Article 271   (ex Article 237 TEC)

The Court of Justice of the European Union shall, within the limits hereinafter laid down, have jurisdiction in disputes concerning:

(a) the fulfilment by Member States of obligations under the Statute of the European Investment Bank. In this connection, the Board of Directors of the Bank shall enjoy the powers conferred upon the Commission by Article 258;

(b) measures adopted by the Board of Governors of the European Investment Bank. In this connection, any Member State, the Commission or the Board of Directors of the Bank may institute proceedings under the conditions laid down in Article 263;

(c) measures adopted by the Board of Directors of the European Investment Bank. Proceedings against such measures may be instituted only by Member States or by the Commission, under the conditions laid down in Article 263, and solely on the grounds of non-compliance with the procedure provided for in Article 19(2), (5), (6) and (7) of the Statute of the Bank;

(d) the fulfilment by national central banks of obligations under the Treaties and the Statute of the ESCB and of the ECB. In this connection the powers of the Governing Council of the European Central Bank in respect of national central banks shall be the same as those conferred upon the Commission in respect of Member States by Article 258. If the Court finds that a national central bank has failed to fulfil an obligation under the Treaties, that bank shall be required to take the necessary measures to comply with the judgment of the Court.

Article 272   (ex Article 238 TEC)

The Court of Justice of the European Union shall have jurisdiction to give judgment pursuant to any arbitration clause contained in a contract concluded by or on behalf of the Union, whether that contract be governed by public or private law.

Article 273   (ex Article 239 TEC)

The Court of Justice shall have jurisdiction in any dispute between Member States which relates to the subject matter of the Treaties if the dispute is submitted to it under a special agreement between the parties.

Article 274   (ex Article 240 TEC)

Save where jurisdiction is conferred on the Court of Justice of the European Union by the Treaties, disputes to which the Union is a party shall not on that ground be excluded from the jurisdiction of the courts or tribunals of the Member States.

Article 275

The Court of Justice of the European Union shall not have jurisdiction with respect to the provisions relating to the common foreign and security policy nor with respect to acts adopted on the basis of those provisions.

However, the Court shall have jurisdiction to monitor compliance with Article 40 of the Treaty on European Union and to rule on proceedings, brought in accordance with the conditions laid down in the fourth paragraph of Article 263 of this Treaty, reviewing the legality of decisions providing for restrictive measures against natural or legal persons adopted by the Council on the basis of Chapter 2 of Title V of the Treaty on European Union.

Article 276

In exercising its powers regarding the provisions of Chapters 4 and 5 of Title V of Part Three relating to the area of freedom, security and justice, the Court of Justice of the European Union shall have no jurisdiction to review the validity or proportionality of operations carried out by the police or other law-enforcement services of a Member State or the exercise of the responsibilities incumbent upon Member States with regard to the maintenance of law and order and the safeguarding of internal security.

Article 277   (ex Article 241 TEC)

Notwithstanding the expiry of the period laid down in Article 263, sixth paragraph, any party may, in proceedings in which an act of general application adopted by an institution, body, office or agency of the Union is at issue, plead the grounds specified in Article 263, second paragraph, in order to invoke before the Court of Justice of the European Union the inapplicability of that act.

Article 278   (ex Article 242 TEC)

Actions brought before the Court of Justice of the European Union shall not have suspensory effect. The Court may, however, if it considers that circumstances so require, order that application of the contested act be suspended.

Article 279   (ex Article 243 TEC)

The Court of Justice of the European Union may in any cases before it prescribe any necessary interim measures.

Article 280   (ex Article 244 TEC)

The judgments of the Court of Justice of the European Union shall be enforceable under the conditions laid down in Article 299.

Article 281   (ex Article 245 TEC)

The Statute of the Court of Justice of the European Union shall be laid down in a separate Protocol.

The European Parliament and the Council, acting in accordance with the ordinary legislative procedure, may amend the provisions of the Statute, with the exception of Title I and Article 64. The European Parliament and the Council shall act either at the request of the Court of Justice and after consultation of the Commission, or on a proposal from the Commission and after consultation of the Court of Justice.

Section 6 The European Central Bank

Article 282

1. The European Central Bank, together with the national central banks, shall constitute the European System of Central Banks (ESCB). The European Central Bank, together with the national central banks of the Member States whose currency is the euro, which constitute the Eurosystem, shall conduct the monetary policy of the Union.

2. The ESCB shall be governed by the decision-making bodies of the European Central Bank. The primary objective of the ESCB shall be to maintain price stability. Without prejudice to that objective, it shall support the general economic policies in the Union in order to contribute to the achievement of the latter's objectives.

3. The European Central Bank shall have legal personality. It alone may authorise the issue of the euro. It shall be independent in the exercise of its powers and in the management of its finances. Union institutions, bodies, offices and agencies and the governments of the Member States shall respect that independence.

4. The European Central Bank shall adopt such measures as are necessary to carry out its tasks in accordance with Articles 127 to 133, with Article 138, and with the conditions laid down in the Statute of the ESCB and of the ECB. In accordance with these same Articles, those Member States whose currency is not the euro, and their central banks, shall retain their powers in monetary matters.

5. Within the areas falling within its responsibilities, the European Central Bank shall be consulted on all proposed Union acts, and all proposals for regulation at national level, and may give an opinion.

Article 283   (ex Article 112 TEC)

1. The Governing Council of the European Central Bank shall comprise the members of the Executive Board of the European Central Bank and the Governors of the national central banks of the Member States whose currency is the euro.

2. The Executive Board shall comprise the President, the Vice-President and four other members.

The President, the Vice-President and the other members of the Executive Board shall be appointed by the European Council, acting by a qualified majority, from among persons of recognised standing and professional experience in monetary or banking matters, on a recommendation from the Council, after it has consulted the European Parliament and the Governing Council of the European Central Bank.

Their term of office shall be eight years and shall not be renewable.

Only nationals of Member States may be members of the Executive Board.

Article 284   (ex Article 113 TEC)

1. The President of the Council and a Member of the Commission may participate, without having the right to vote, in meetings of the Governing Council of the European Central Bank.

The President of the Council may submit a motion for deliberation to the Governing Council of the European Central Bank.

2. The President of the European Central Bank shall be invited to participate in Council meetings when the Council is discussing matters relating to the objectives and tasks of the ESCB.

3. The European Central Bank shall address an annual report on the activities of the ESCB and on the monetary policy of both the previous and current year to the European Parliament, the Council and the Commission, and also to the European Council. The President of the European Central Bank shall present this report to the Council and to the European Parliament, which may hold a general debate on that basis.

The President of the European Central Bank and the other members of the Executive Board may, at the request of the European Parliament or on their own initiative, be heard by the competent committees of the European Parliament.

Section 7 The Court of Auditors

Article 285   (ex Article 246 TEC)

The Court of Auditors shall carry out the Union's audit.

It shall consist of one national of each Member State. Its Members shall be completely independent in the performance of their duties, in the Union's general interest.

Article 286   (ex Article 247 TEC)

1. The Members of the Court of Auditors shall be chosen from among persons who belong or have belonged in their respective States to external audit bodies or who are especially qualified for this office. Their independence must be beyond doubt.

2. The Members of the Court of Auditors shall be appointed for a term of six years. The Council, after consulting the European Parliament, shall adopt the list of Members drawn up in accordance with the proposals made by each Member State. The term of office of the Members of the Court of Auditors shall be renewable.

They shall elect the President of the Court of Auditors from among their number for a term of three years. The President may be re-elected.

3. In the performance of these duties, the Members of the Court of Auditors shall neither seek nor take instructions from any government or from any other body. The Members of the Court of Auditors shall refrain from any action incompatible with their duties.

4. The Members of the Court of Auditors may not, during their term of office, engage in any other occupation, whether gainful or not. When entering upon their duties they shall give a solemn undertaking that, both during and after their term of office, they will respect the obligations arising therefrom and in particular their duty to behave with integrity and discretion as regards the acceptance, after they have ceased to hold office, of certain appointments or benefits.

5. Apart from normal replacement, or death, the duties of a Member of the Court of Auditors shall end when he resigns, or is compulsorily retired by a ruling of the Court of Justice pursuant to paragraph 6.

The vacancy thus caused shall be filled for the remainder of the Member's term of office.

Save in the case of compulsory retirement, Members of the Court of Auditors shall remain in office until they have been replaced.

6. A Member of the Court of Auditors may be deprived of his office or of his right to a pension or other benefits in its stead only if the Court of Justice, at the request of the Court of Auditors, finds that he no longer fulfils the requisite conditions or meets the obligations arising from his office.

7. The Council shall determine the conditions of employment of the President and the Members of the Court of Auditors and in particular their salaries, allowances and pensions. It shall also determine any payment to be made instead of remuneration.

8. The provisions of the Protocol on the privileges and immunities of the European Union applicable to the Judges of the Court of Justice of the European Union shall also apply to the Members of the Court of Auditors.

Article 287   (ex Article 248 TEC)

1. The Court of Auditors shall examine the accounts of all revenue and expenditure of the Union. It shall also examine the accounts of all revenue and expenditure of all bodies, offices or agencies set up by the Union in so far as the relevant constituent instrument does not preclude such examination.

The Court of Auditors shall provide the European Parliament and the Council with a statement of assurance as to the reliability of the accounts and the legality and regularity of the underlying transactions which shall be published in the *Official Journal of the European Union*. This statement may be supplemented by specific assessments for each major area of Union activity.

2. The Court of Auditors shall examine whether all revenue has been received and all expenditure incurred in a lawful and regular manner and whether the financial management has been sound. In doing so, it shall report in particular on any cases of irregularity.

The audit of revenue shall be carried out on the basis both of the amounts established as due and the amounts actually paid to the Union.

The audit of expenditure shall be carried out on the basis both of commitments undertaken and payments made.

These audits may be carried out before the closure of accounts for the financial year in question.

3. The audit shall be based on records and, if necessary, performed on the spot in the other institutions of the Union, on the premises of any body, office or agency which manages revenue or expenditure on behalf of the Union and in the Member States, including on the premises of any natural or legal person in receipt of payments from the budget. In the Member States the audit shall be carried out in liaison with national audit bodies or, if these do not have the necessary powers, with the competent national departments. The Court of Auditors and the national audit bodies of the Member States shall cooperate in a spirit of trust while maintaining their independence. These bodies or departments shall inform the Court of Auditors whether they intend to take part in the audit.

The other institutions of the Union, any bodies, offices or agencies managing revenue or expenditure on behalf of the Union, any natural or legal person in receipt of payments from the budget, and the national audit bodies or, if these do not have the necessary powers, the competent national departments, shall forward to the Court of Auditors, at its request, any document or information necessary to carry out its task.

In respect of the European Investment Bank's activity in managing Union expenditure and revenue, the Court's rights of access to information held by the Bank shall be governed by an agreement between the Court, the Bank and the Commission. In the absence of an agreement, the Court shall nevertheless have access to information necessary for the audit of Union expenditure and revenue managed by the Bank.

4. The Court of Auditors shall draw up an annual report after the close of each financial year. It shall be forwarded to the other institutions of the Union and shall be published, together with the replies of these institutions to the observations of the Court of Auditors, in the *Official Journal of the European Union*.

The Court of Auditors may also, at any time, submit observations, particularly in the form of special reports, on specific questions and deliver opinions at the request of one of the other institutions of the Union.

It shall adopt its annual reports, special reports or opinions by a majority of its Members. However, it may establish internal chambers in order to adopt certain categories of reports or opinions under the conditions laid down by its Rules of Procedure.

It shall assist the European Parliament and the Council in exercising their powers of control over the implementation of the budget.

The Court of Auditors shall draw up its Rules of Procedure. Those rules shall require the approval of the Council.

Chapter 2 Legal acts of the Union, adoption procedures and other provisions

Section 1 The legal acts of the Union

Article 288   (ex Article 249 TEC)

To exercise the Union's competences, the institutions shall adopt regulations, directives, decisions, recommendations and opinions.

A regulation shall have general application. It shall be binding in its entirety and directly applicable in all Member States.

A directive shall be binding, as to the result to be achieved, upon each Member State to which it is addressed, but shall leave to the national authorities the choice of form and methods.

A decision shall be binding in its entirety. A decision which specifies those to whom it is addressed shall be binding only on them.

Recommendations and opinions shall have no binding force.

Article 289

1. The ordinary legislative procedure shall consist in the joint adoption by the European Parliament and the Council of a regulation, directive or decision on a proposal from the Commission. This procedure is defined in Article 294.

2. In the specific cases provided for by the Treaties, the adoption of a regulation, directive or decision by the European Parliament with the participation of the Council, or by the latter with the participation of the European Parliament, shall constitute a special legislative procedure.

3. Legal acts adopted by legislative procedure shall constitute legislative acts.

4. In the specific cases provided for by the Treaties, legislative acts may be adopted on the initiative of a group of Member States or of the European Parliament, on a recommendation from the European Central Bank or at the request of the Court of Justice or the European Investment Bank.

Article 290

1. A legislative act may delegate to the Commission the power to adopt non-legislative acts of general application to supplement or amend certain non-essential elements of the legislative act.

The objectives, content, scope and duration of the delegation of power shall be explicitly defined in the legislative acts. The essential elements of an area shall be reserved for the legislative act and accordingly shall not be the subject of a delegation of power.

2. Legislative acts shall explicitly lay down the conditions to which the delegation is subject; these conditions may be as follows:

(a) the European Parliament or the Council may decide to revoke the delegation;

(b) the delegated act may enter into force only if no objection has been expressed by the European Parliament or the Council within a period set by the legislative act.

For the purposes of (a) and (b), the European Parliament shall act by a majority of its component members, and the Council by a qualified majority.

3. The adjective 'delegated' shall be inserted in the title of delegated acts.

Article 291

1. Member States shall adopt all measures of national law necessary to implement legally binding Union acts.

2. Where uniform conditions for implementing legally binding Union acts are needed, those acts shall confer implementing powers on the Commission, or, in duly justified specific cases and in the cases provided for in Articles 24 and 26 of the Treaty on European Union, on the Council.

3. For the purposes of paragraph 2, the European Parliament and the Council, acting by means of regulations in accordance with the ordinary legislative procedure, shall lay down in advance the rules and general principles concerning mechanisms for control by Member States of the Commission's exercise of implementing powers.

4. The word 'implementing' shall be inserted in the title of implementing acts.

Article 292

The Council shall adopt recommendations. It shall act on a proposal from the Commission in all cases where the Treaties provide that it shall adopt acts on a proposal from the Commission. It shall act unanimously in those areas in which unanimity is required for the adoption of a Union act. The Commission, and the European Central Bank in the specific cases provided for in the Treaties, shall adopt recommendations.

Section 2 Procedures for the adoption of acts and other provisions

Article 293   (ex Article 250 TEC)

1. Where, pursuant to the Treaties, the Council acts on a proposal from the Commission, it may amend that proposal only by acting unanimously, except in the cases referred to in paragraphs 10 and 13 of Article 294, in Articles 310, 312 and 314 and in the second paragraph of Article 315.

2. As long as the Council has not acted, the Commission may alter its proposal at any time during the procedures leading to the adoption of a Union act.

Article 294   (ex Article 251 TEC)

1. Where reference is made in the Treaties to the ordinary legislative procedure for the adoption of an act, the following procedure shall apply.

2. The Commission shall submit a proposal to the European Parliament and the Council.

First reading

3. The European Parliament shall adopt its position at first reading and communicate it to the Council.

4. If the Council approves the European Parliament's position, the act concerned shall be adopted in the wording which corresponds to the position of the European Parliament.

5. If the Council does not approve the European Parliament's position, it shall adopt its position at first reading and communicate it to the European Parliament.

6. The Council shall inform the European Parliament fully of the reasons which led it to adopt its position at first reading. The Commission shall inform the European Parliament fully of its position.

Second reading

7. If, within three months of such communication, the European Parliament:
   (a) approves the Council's position at first reading or has not taken a decision, the act concerned shall be deemed to have been adopted in the wording which corresponds to the position of the Council;
   (b) rejects, by a majority of its component members, the Council's position at first reading, the proposed act shall be deemed not to have been adopted;
   (c) proposes, by a majority of its component members, amendments to the Council's position at first reading, the text thus amended shall be forwarded to the Council and to the Commission, which shall deliver an opinion on those amendments.

8. If, within three months of receiving the European Parliament's amendments, the Council, acting by a qualified majority:

    (a) approves all those amendments, the act in question shall be deemed to have been adopted;

    (b) does not approve all the amendments, the President of the Council, in agreement with the President of the European Parliament, shall within six weeks convene a meeting of the Conciliation Committee.

9. The Council shall act unanimously on the amendments on which the Commission has delivered a negative opinion.

Conciliation

10. The Conciliation Committee, which shall be composed of the members of the Council or their representatives and an equal number of members representing the European Parliament, shall have the task of reaching agreement on a joint text, by a qualified majority of the members of the Council or their representatives and by a majority of the members representing the European Parliament within six weeks of its being convened, on the basis of the positions of the European Parliament and the Council at second reading.

11. The Commission shall take part in the Conciliation Committee's proceedings and shall take all necessary initiatives with a view to reconciling the positions of the European Parliament and the Council.

12. If, within six weeks of its being convened, the Conciliation Committee does not approve the joint text, the proposed act shall be deemed not to have been adopted.

Third reading

13. If, within that period, the Conciliation Committee approves a joint text, the European Parliament, acting by a majority of the votes cast, and the Council, acting by a qualified majority, shall each have a period of six weeks from that approval in which to adopt the act in question in accordance with the joint text. If they fail to do so, the proposed act shall be deemed not to have been adopted.

14. The periods of three months and six weeks referred to in this Article shall be extended by a maximum of one month and two weeks respectively at the initiative of the European Parliament or the Council.

Special provisions

15. Where, in the cases provided for in the Treaties, a legislative act is submitted to the ordinary legislative procedure on the initiative of a group of Member States, on a recommendation by the European Central Bank, or at the request of the Court of Justice, paragraph 2, the second sentence of paragraph 6, and paragraph 9 shall not apply.

In such cases, the European Parliament and the Council shall communicate the proposed act to the Commission with their positions at first and second readings. The European Parliament or the Council may request the opinion of the Commission throughout the procedure, which the Commission may also deliver on its own initiative. It may also, if it deems it necessary, take part in the Conciliation Committee in accordance with paragraph 11.

Article 295

The European Parliament, the Council and the Commission shall consult each other and by common agreement make arrangements for their cooperation. To that end, they may, in compliance with the Treaties, conclude interinstitutional agreements which may be of a binding nature.

Article 296   (ex Article 253 TEC)

Where the Treaties do not specify the type of act to be adopted, the institutions shall select it on a case-by-case basis, in compliance with the applicable procedures and with the principle of proportionality.

Legal acts shall state the reasons on which they are based and shall refer to any proposals, initiatives, recommendations, requests or opinions required by the Treaties.

When considering draft legislative acts, the European Parliament and the Council shall refrain from adopting acts not provided for by the relevant legislative procedure in the area in question.

Article 297   (ex Article 254 TEC)

1. Legislative acts adopted under the ordinary legislative procedure shall be signed by the President of the European Parliament and by the President of the Council.

Legislative acts adopted under a special legislative procedure shall be signed by the President of the institution which adopted them.

Legislative acts shall be published in the *Official Journal of the European Union*. They shall enter into force on the date specified in them or, in the absence thereof, on the twentieth day following that of their publication.

2. Non-legislative acts adopted in the form of regulations, directives or decisions, when the latter do not specify to whom they are addressed, shall be signed by the President of the institution which adopted them.

Regulations and directives which are addressed to all Member States, as well as decisions which do not specify to whom they are addressed, shall be published in the *Official Journal of the European Union*. They shall enter into force on the date specified in them or, in the absence thereof, on the twentieth day following that of their publication.

Other directives, and decisions which specify to whom they are addressed, shall be notified to those to whom they are addressed and shall take effect upon such notification.

Article 298

1. In carrying out their missions, the institutions, bodies, offices and agencies of the Union shall have the support of an open, efficient and independent European administration.

2. In compliance with the Staff Regulations and the Conditions of Employment adopted on the basis of Article 336, the European Parliament and the Council, acting by means of regulations in accordance with the ordinary legislative procedure, shall establish provisions to that end.

Article 299   (ex Article 256 TEC)

Acts of the Council, the Commission or the European Central Bank which impose a pecuniary obligation on persons other than States, shall be enforceable.

Enforcement shall be governed by the rules of civil procedure in force in the State in the territory of which it is carried out. The order for its enforcement shall be appended to the decision, without other formality than verification of the authenticity of the decision, by the national authority which the government of each Member State shall designate for this purpose and shall make known to the Commission and to the Court of Justice of the European Union.

When these formalities have been completed on application by the party concerned, the latter may proceed to enforcement in accordance with the national law, by bringing the matter directly before the competent authority.

Enforcement may be suspended only by a decision of the Court. However, the courts of the country concerned shall have jurisdiction over complaints that enforcement is being carried out in an irregular manner.

Chapter 3   The Union's advisory bodies

Article 300

1. The European Parliament, the Council and the Commission shall be assisted by an Economic and Social Committee and a Committee of the Regions, exercising advisory functions.

2. The Economic and Social Committee shall consist of representatives of organisations of employers, of the employed, and of other parties representative of civil society, notably in socio-economic, civic, professional and cultural areas.

3. The Committee of the Regions shall consist of representatives of regional and local bodies who either hold a regional or local authority electoral mandate or are politically accountable to an elected assembly.

4. The members of the Economic and Social Committee and of the Committee of the Regions shall not be bound by any mandatory instructions. They shall be completely independent in the performance of their duties, in the Union's general interest.

5. The rules referred to in paragraphs 2 and 3 governing the nature of the composition of the Committees shall be reviewed at regular intervals by the Council to take account of economic, social and demographic developments within the Union. The Council, on a proposal from the Commission, shall adopt decisions to that end.

Section 1 The Economic and Social Committee

Article 301   (ex Article 258 TEC)

The number of members of the Economic and Social Committee shall not exceed 350.

The Council, acting unanimously on a proposal from the Commission, shall adopt a decision determining the Committee's composition.

The Council shall determine the allowances of members of the Committee.

Article 302   (ex Article 259 TEC)

1. The members of the Committee shall be appointed for five years The Council shall adopt the list of members drawn up in accordance with the proposals made by each Member State. The term of office of the members of the Committee shall be renewable.

2. The Council shall act after consulting the Commission. It may obtain the opinion of European bodies which are representative of the various economic and social sectors and of civil society to which the Union's activities are of concern.

Article 303   (ex Article 260 TEC)

The Committee shall elect its chairman and officers from among its members for a term of two and a half years.

It shall adopt its Rules of Procedure.

The Committee shall be convened by its chairman at the request of the European Parliament, the Council or of the Commission. It may also meet on its own initiative.

Article 304   (ex Article 262 TEC)

The Committee shall be consulted by the European Parliament, by the Council or by the Commission where the Treaties so provide. The Committee may be consulted by these institutions in all cases in which they consider it appropriate. It may issue an opinion on its own initiative in cases in which it considers such action appropriate.

The European Parliament, the Council or the Commission shall, if it considers it necessary, set the Committee, for the submission of its opinion, a time limit which may not be less than one month from the date on which the chairman receives notification to this effect. Upon expiry of the time limit, the absence of an opinion shall not prevent further action.

The opinion of the Committee, together with a record of the proceedings, shall be forwarded to the European Parliament, to the Council and to the Commission.

Section 2 The Committee of the Regions

Article 305   (ex Article 263, second, third and fourth paragraphs, TEC)

The number of members of the Committee of the Regions shall not exceed 350.

The Council, acting unanimously on a proposal from the Commission, shall adopt a decision determining the Committee's composition.

The members of the Committee and an equal number of alternate members shall be appointed for five years. Their term of office shall be renewable. The Council shall adopt the list of members and alternate members drawn up in accordance with the proposals made by each Member State. When the mandate referred to in Article 300(3) on the basis of which they were proposed comes to an end, the term of office of members of the Committee shall terminate automatically and they shall then be replaced for the remainder of the said term of office in accordance with the same procedure. No member of the Committee shall at the same time be a Member of the European Parliament.

Article 306   (ex Article 264 TEC)

The Committee of the Regions shall elect its chairman and officers from among its members for a term of two and a half years.

It shall adopt its Rules of Procedure.

The Committee shall be convened by its chairman at the request of the European Parliament, the Council or of the Commission. It may also meet on its own initiative.

Article 307   (ex Article 265 TEC)

The Committee of the Regions shall be consulted by the European Parliament, by the Council or by the Commission where the Treaties so provide and in all other cases, in particular those which concern cross-border cooperation, in which one of these institutions considers it appropriate.

The European Parliament, the Council or the Commission shall, if it considers it necessary, set the Committee, for the submission of its opinion, a time limit which may not be less than one month from the date on which the chairman receives notification to this effect. Upon expiry of the time limit, the absence of an opinion shall not prevent further action.

Where the Economic and Social Committee is consulted pursuant to Article 304, the Committee of the Regions shall be informed by the European Parliament, the Council or the Commission of the request for an opinion. Where it considers that specific regional interests are involved, the Committee of the Regions may issue an opinion on the matter.

It may issue an opinion on its own initiative in cases in which it considers such action appropriate.

The opinion of the Committee, together with a record of the proceedings, shall be forwarded to the European Parliament, to the Council and to the Commission.

Chapter 4 The European Investment Bank

Article 308   (ex Article 266 TEC)

The European Investment Bank shall have legal personality.

The members of the European Investment Bank shall be the Member States.

The Statute of the European Investment Bank is laid down in a Protocol annexed to the Treaties. The Council acting unanimously in accordance with a special legislative procedure, at the request of the European Investment Bank and after consulting the European Parliament and the Commission, or on a proposal from the Commission and after consulting the European Parliament and the European Investment Bank, may amend the Statute of the Bank.

Article 309   (ex Article 267 TEC)

The task of the European Investment Bank shall be to contribute, by having recourse to the capital market and utilising its own resources, to the balanced and steady development of the internal market in the interest of the Union. For this purpose the Bank shall, operating on a non-profit-making basis, grant loans and give guarantees which facilitate the financing of the following projects in all sectors of the economy:

    (a) projects for developing less-developed regions;

    (b) projects for modernising or converting undertakings or for developing fresh activities called for by the establishment or functioning of the internal market, where these projects are of such a size or nature that they cannot be entirely financed by the various means available in the individual Member States;

    (c) projects of common interest to several Member States which are of such a size or nature that they cannot be entirely financed by the various means available in the individual Member States.

In carrying out its task, the Bank shall facilitate the financing of investment programmes in conjunction with assistance from the Structural Funds and other Union Financial Instruments.

Title II Financial provisions

Article 310   (ex Article 268 TEC)

1. All items of revenue and expenditure of the Union shall be included in estimates to be drawn up for each financial year and shall be shown in the budget.

The Union's annual budget shall be established by the European Parliament and the Council in accordance with Article 314.

The revenue and expenditure shown in the budget shall be in balance.

2. The expenditure shown in the budget shall be authorised for the annual budgetary period in accordance with the regulation referred to in Article 322.

3. The implementation of expenditure shown in the budget shall require the prior adoption of a legally binding Union act providing a legal basis for its action and for the implementation of the corresponding expenditure in accordance with the regulation referred to in Article 322, except in cases for which that law provides.

4. With a view to maintaining budgetary discipline, the Union shall not adopt any act which is likely to have appreciable implications for the budget without providing an assurance that the expenditure arising from such an act is capable of being financed within the limit of the Union's own resources and in compliance with the multiannual financial framework referred to in Article 312.

5. The budget shall be implemented in accordance with the principle of sound financial management. Member States shall cooperate with the Union to ensure that the appropriations entered in the budget are used in accordance with this principle.

6. The Union and the Member States, in accordance with Article 325, shall counter fraud and any other illegal activities affecting the financial interests of the Union.

Chapter 1 The Union's own resources

Article 311   (ex Article 269 TEC)

The Union shall provide itself with the means necessary to attain its objectives and carry through its policies.

Without prejudice to other revenue, the budget shall be financed wholly from own resources.

The Council, acting in accordance with a special legislative procedure, shall unanimously and after consulting the European Parliament adopt a decision laying down the provisions relating to the system of own resources of the Union. In this context it may establish new categories of own resources or abolish an existing category. That decision shall not enter into force until it is approved by the Member States in accordance with their respective constitutional requirements.

The Council, acting by means of regulations in accordance with a special legislative procedure, shall lay down implementing measures for the Union's own resources system in so far as this is provided for in the decision adopted on the basis of the third paragraph. The Council shall act after obtaining the consent of the European Parliament.

Chapter 2 The multiannual financial framework

Article 312

1. The multiannual financial framework shall ensure that Union expenditure develops in an orderly manner and within the limits of its own resources.

It shall be established for a period of at least five years.

The annual budget of the Union shall comply with the multiannual financial framework.

2. The Council, acting in accordance with a special legislative procedure, shall adopt a regulation laying down the multiannual financial framework. The Council shall act unanimously after obtaining the consent of the European Parliament, which shall be given by a majority of its component members.

The European Council may, unanimously, adopt a decision authorising the Council to act by a qualified majority when adopting the regulation referred to in the first subparagraph.

3. The financial framework shall determine the amounts of the annual ceilings on commitment appropriations by category of expenditure and of the annual ceiling on payment appropriations. The categories of expenditure, limited in number, shall correspond to the Union's major sectors of activity.

The financial framework shall lay down any other provisions required for the annual budgetary procedure to run smoothly.

4. Where no Council regulation determining a new financial framework has been adopted by the end of the previous financial framework, the ceilings and other provisions corresponding to the last year of that framework shall be extended until such time as that act is adopted.

5. Throughout the procedure leading to the adoption of the financial framework, the European Parliament, the Council and the Commission shall take any measure necessary to facilitate its adoption.

Chapter 3 The Union's annual budget

Article 313   (ex Article 272(1), TEC)

The financial year shall run from 1 January to 31 December.

Article 314   (ex Article 272(2) to (10), TEC)

The European Parliament and the Council, acting in accordance with a special legislative procedure, shall establish the Union's annual budget in accordance with the following provisions.

1. With the exception of the European Central Bank, each institution shall, before 1 July, draw up estimates of its expenditure for the following financial year. The Commission shall consolidate these estimates in a draft budget which may contain different estimates.

The draft budget shall contain an estimate of revenue and an estimate of expenditure.

2. The Commission shall submit a proposal containing the draft budget to the European Parliament and to the Council not later than 1 September of the year preceding that in which the budget is to be implemented.

The Commission may amend the draft budget during the procedure until such time as the Conciliation Committee, referred to in paragraph 5, is convened.

3. The Council shall adopt its position on the draft budget and forward it to the European Parliament not later than 1 October of the year preceding that in which the budget is to be implemented. The Council shall inform the European Parliament in full of the reasons which led it to adopt its position.

4. If, within forty-two days of such communication, the European Parliament:
   (a) approves the position of the Council, the budget shall be adopted;
   (b) has not taken a decision, the budget shall be deemed to have been adopted;
   (c) adopts amendments by a majority of its component members, the amended draft shall be forwarded to the Council and to the Commission. The President of the European Parliament, in agreement with the President of the Council, shall immediately convene a meeting of the Conciliation Committee. However, if within ten days of the draft being forwarded the Council informs the European Parliament that it has approved all its amendments, the Conciliation Committee shall not meet.

5. The Conciliation Committee, which shall be composed of the members of the Council or their representatives and an equal number of members representing the European Parliament, shall have the task of reaching agreement on a joint text, by a qualified majority of the members of the Council or their representatives and by a majority of the representatives of the European Parliament within twenty-one days of its being convened, on the basis of the positions of the European Parliament and the Council.

The Commission shall take part in the Conciliation Committee's proceedings and shall take all the necessary initiatives with a view to reconciling the positions of the European Parliament and the Council.

6. If, within the twenty-one days referred to in paragraph 5, the Conciliation Committee agrees on a joint text, the European Parliament and the Council shall each have a period of fourteen days from the date of that agreement in which to approve the joint text.

7. If, within the period of fourteen days referred to in paragraph 6:

(a) the European Parliament and the Council both approve the joint text or fail to take a decision, or if one of these institutions approves the joint text while the other one fails to take a decision, the budget shall be deemed to be definitively adopted in accordance with the joint text; or

(b) the European Parliament, acting by a majority of its component members, and the Council both reject the joint text, or if one of these institutions rejects the joint text while the other one fails to take a decision, a new draft budget shall be submitted by the Commission; or

(c) the European Parliament, acting by a majority of its component members, rejects the joint text while the Council approves it, a new draft budget shall be submitted by the Commission; or

(d) the European Parliament approves the joint text whilst the Council rejects it, the European Parliament may, within fourteen days from the date of the rejection by the Council and acting by a majority of its component members and three-fifths of the votes cast, decide to confirm all or some of the amendments referred to in paragraph 4(c). Where a European Parliament amendment is not confirmed, the position agreed in the Conciliation Committee on the budget heading which is the subject of the amendment shall be retained. The budget shall be deemed to be definitively adopted on this basis.

8. If, within the twenty-one days referred to in paragraph 5, the Conciliation Committee does not agree on a joint text, a new draft budget shall be submitted by the Commission.

9. When the procedure provided for in this Article has been completed, the President of the European Parliament shall declare that the budget has been definitively adopted.

10. Each institution shall exercise the powers conferred upon it under this Article in compliance with the Treaties and the acts adopted thereunder, with particular regard to the Union's own resources and the balance between revenue and expenditure.

Article 315   (ex Article 273 TEC)

If, at the beginning of a financial year, the budget has not yet been definitively adopted, a sum equivalent to not more than one-twelfth of the budget appropriations for the preceding financial year may be spent each month in respect of any chapter of the budget in accordance with the provisions of the Regulations made pursuant to Article 322; that sum shall not, however, exceed one-twelfth of the appropriations provided for in the same chapter of the draft budget.

The Council on a proposal by the Commission, may, provided that the other conditions laid down in the first paragraph are observed, authorise expenditure in excess of one-twelfth in accordance with the regulations made pursuant to Article 322. The Council shall forward the decision immediately to the European Parliament.

The decision referred to in the second paragraph shall lay down the necessary measures relating to resources to ensure application of this Article, in accordance with the acts referred to in Article 311.

It shall enter into force thirty days following its adoption if the European Parliament, acting by a majority of its component Members, has not decided to reduce this expenditure within that time limit.

Article 316   (ex Article 271 TEC)

In accordance with conditions to be laid down pursuant to Article 322, any appropriations, other than those relating to staff expenditure, that are unexpended at the end of the financial year may be carried forward to the next financial year only.

Appropriations shall be classified under different chapters grouping items of expenditure according to their nature or purpose and subdivided in accordance with the regulations made pursuant to Article 322.

The expenditure of the European Parliament, the European Council and the Council, the Commission and the Court of Justice of the European Union shall be set out in separate parts of the budget, without prejudice to special arrangements for certain common items of expenditure.

Chapter 4 Implementation of the budget and discharge

Article 317   (ex Article 274 TEC)

The Commission shall implement the budget in cooperation with the Member States, in accordance with the provisions of the regulations made pursuant to Article 322, on its own responsibility and within the limits of the appropriations, having regard to the principles of sound financial management. Member States shall cooperate with the Commission to ensure that the appropriations are used in accordance with the principles of sound financial management.

The regulations shall lay down the control and audit obligations of the Member States in the implementation of the budget and the resulting responsibilities. They shall also lay down the responsibilities and detailed rules for each institution concerning its part in effecting its own expenditure.

Within the budget, the Commission may, subject to the limits and conditions laid down in the regulations made pursuant to Article 322, transfer appropriations from one chapter to another or from one subdivision to another.

Article 318   (ex Article 275 TEC)

The Commission shall submit annually to the European Parliament and to the Council the accounts of the preceding financial year relating to the implementation of the budget. The Commission shall also forward to them a financial statement of the assets and liabilities of the Union.

The Commission shall also submit to the European Parliament and to the Council an evaluation report on the Union's finances based on the results achieved, in particular in relation to the indications given by the European Parliament and the Council pursuant to Article 319.

Article 319   (ex Article 276 TEC)

1. The European Parliament, acting on a recommendation from the Council, shall give a discharge to the Commission in respect of the implementation of the budget. To this end, the Council and the European Parliament in turn shall examine the accounts, the financial statement and the evaluation report referred to in Article 318, the annual report by the Court of Auditors together with the replies of the institutions under audit to the observations of the Court of Auditors, the statement of assurance referred to in Article 287(1), second subparagraph and any relevant special reports by the Court of Auditors.

2. Before giving a discharge to the Commission, or for any other purpose in connection with the exercise of its powers over the implementation of the budget, the European Parliament may ask to hear the Commission give evidence with regard to the execution of expenditure or the operation of financial control systems. The Commission shall submit any necessary information to the European Parliament at the latter's request.

3. The Commission shall take all appropriate steps to act on the observations in the decisions giving discharge and on other observations by the European Parliament relating to the execution of expenditure, as well as on comments accompanying the recommendations on discharge adopted by the Council.

At the request of the European Parliament or the Council, the Commission shall report on the measures taken in the light of these observations and comments and in particular on the instructions given to the departments which are responsible for the implementation of the budget. These reports shall also be forwarded to the Court of Auditors.

Chapter 5 Common provisions

Article 320   (ex Article 277 TEC)

The multiannual financial framework and the annual budget shall be drawn up in euro.

Article 321   (ex Article 278 TEC)

The Commission may, provided it notifies the competent authorities of the Member States concerned, transfer into the currency of one of the Member States its holdings in the currency of another Member State, to the extent necessary to enable them to be used for purposes which come within the scope of the Treaties. The Commission shall as far as possible avoid making such transfers if it possesses cash or liquid assets in the currencies which it needs.

The Commission shall deal with each Member State through the authority designated by the State concerned. In carrying out financial operations the Commission shall employ the services of the bank of issue of the Member State concerned or of any other financial institution approved by that State.

Article 322   (ex Article 279 TEC)

1. The European Parliament and the Council, acting in accordance with the ordinary legislative procedure, and after consulting the Court of Auditors, shall adopt by means of regulations:
    (a) the financial rules which determine in particular the procedure to be adopted for establishing and implementing the budget and for presenting and auditing accounts;
    (b) rules providing for checks on the responsibility of financial actors, in particular authorising officers and accounting officers.

2. The Council, acting on a proposal from the Commission and after consulting the European Parliament and the Court of Auditors, shall determine the methods and procedure whereby the budget revenue provided under the arrangements relating to the Union's own resources shall be made available to the Commission, and determine the measures to be applied, if need be, to meet cash requirements.

Article 323

The European Parliament, the Council and the Commission shall ensure that the financial means are made available to allow the Union to fulfil its legal obligations in respect of third parties.

Article 324

Regular meetings between the Presidents of the European Parliament, the Council and the Commission shall be convened, on the initiative of the Commission, under the budgetary procedures referred to in this Title. The Presidents shall take all the necessary steps to promote consultation and the reconciliation of the positions of the institutions over which they preside in order to facilitate the implementation of this Title.

Chapter 6 Combating fraud

Article 325   (ex Article 280 TEC)

1. The Union and the Member States shall counter fraud and any other illegal activities affecting the financial interests of the Union through measures to be taken in accordance with this Article, which shall act as a deterrent and be such as to afford effective protection in the Member States, and in all the Union's institutions, bodies, offices and agencies.

2. Member States shall take the same measures to counter fraud affecting the financial interests of the Union as they take to counter fraud affecting their own financial interests.

3. Without prejudice to other provisions of the Treaties, the Member States shall coordinate their action aimed at protecting the financial interests of the Union against fraud. To this end they shall organise, together with the Commission, close and regular cooperation between the competent authorities.

4. The European Parliament and the Council, acting in accordance with the ordinary legislative procedure, after consulting the Court of Auditors, shall adopt the necessary measures in the fields of

the prevention of and fight against fraud affecting the financial interests of the Union with a view to affording effective and equivalent protection in the Member States and in all the Union's institutions, bodies, offices and agencies.

5. The Commission, in cooperation with Member States, shall each year submit to the European Parliament and to the Council a report on the measures taken for the implementation of this Article.

Title III Enhanced cooperation

Article 326   (ex Articles 27a to 27e, 40 to 40b and 43 to 45 TEU and ex Articles 11 and 11a TEC)

Any enhanced cooperation shall comply with the Treaties and Union law.

Such cooperation shall not undermine the internal market or economic, social and territorial cohesion. It shall not constitute a barrier to or discrimination in trade between Member States, nor shall it distort competition between them.

Article 327   (ex Articles 27a to 27e, 40 to 40b and 43 to 45 TEU and ex Articles 11 and 11a TEC)

Any enhanced cooperation shall respect the competences, rights and obligations of those Member States which do not participate in it. Those Member States shall not impede its implementation by the participating Member States.

Article 328   (ex Articles 27a to 27e, 40 to 40b and 43 to 45 TEU and ex Articles 11 and 11a TEC)

1. When enhanced cooperation is being established, it shall be open to all Member States, subject to compliance with any conditions of participation laid down by the authorising decision. It shall also be open to them at any other time, subject to compliance with the acts already adopted within that framework, in addition to those conditions.

The Commission and the Member States participating in enhanced cooperation shall ensure that they promote participation by as many Member States as possible.

2. The Commission and, where appropriate, the High Representative of the Union for Foreign Affairs and Security Policy shall keep the European Parliament and the Council regularly informed regarding developments in enhanced cooperation.

Article 329   (ex Articles 27a to 27e, 40 to 40b and 43 to 45 TEU and ex Articles 11 and 11a TEC)

1. Member States which wish to establish enhanced cooperation between themselves in one of the areas covered by the Treaties, with the exception of fields of exclusive competence and the common foreign and security policy, shall address a request to the Commission, specifying the scope and objectives of the enhanced cooperation proposed. The Commission may submit a proposal to the Council to that effect. In the event of the Commission not submitting a proposal, it shall inform the Member States concerned of the reasons for not doing so.

Authorisation to proceed with the enhanced cooperation referred to in the first subparagraph shall be granted by the Council, on a proposal from the Commission and after obtaining the consent of the European Parliament.

2. The request of the Member States which wish to establish enhanced cooperation between themselves within the framework of the common foreign and security policy shall be addressed to the Council. It shall be forwarded to the High Representative of the Union for Foreign Affairs and Security Policy, who shall give an opinion on whether the enhanced cooperation proposed is consistent with the Union's common foreign and security policy, and to the Commission, which shall give its opinion in particular on whether the enhanced cooperation proposed is consistent with other Union policies. It shall also be forwarded to the European Parliament for information.

Authorisation to proceed with enhanced cooperation shall be granted by a decision of the Council acting unanimously.

Article 330 (ex Articles 27a to 27e, 40 to 40b and 43 to 45 TEU and ex Articles 11 and 11a TEC)

All members of the Council may participate in its deliberations, but only members of the Council representing the Member States participating in enhanced cooperation shall take part in the vote.

Unanimity shall be constituted by the votes of the representatives of the participating Member States only.

A qualified majority shall be defined in accordance with Article 238(3).

Article 331 (ex Articles 27a to 27e, 40 to 40b and 43 to 45 TEU and ex Articles 11 and 11a TEC)

1. Any Member State which wishes to participate in enhanced cooperation in progress in one of the areas referred to in Article 329(1) shall notify its intention to the Council and the Commission.

The Commission shall, within four months of the date of receipt of the notification, confirm the participation of the Member State concerned. It shall note where necessary that the conditions of participation have been fulfilled and shall adopt any transitional measures necessary with regard to the application of the acts already adopted within the framework of enhanced cooperation.

However, if the Commission considers that the conditions of participation have not been fulfilled, it shall indicate the arrangements to be adopted to fulfil those conditions and shall set a deadline for re-examining the request. On the expiry of that deadline, it shall re-examine the request, in accordance with the procedure set out in the second subparagraph. If the Commission considers that the conditions of participation have still not been met, the Member State concerned may refer the matter to the Council, which shall decide on the request. The Council shall act in accordance with Article 330. It may also adopt the transitional measures referred to in the second subparagraph on a proposal from the Commission.

2. Any Member State which wishes to participate in enhanced cooperation in progress in the framework of the common foreign and security policy shall notify its intention to the Council, the High Representative of the Union for Foreign Affairs and Security Policy and the Commission.

The Council shall confirm the participation of the Member State concerned, after consulting the High Representative of the Union for Foreign Affairs and Security Policy and after noting, where necessary, that the conditions of participation have been fulfilled. The Council, on a proposal from the High Representative, may also adopt any transitional measures necessary with regard to the application of the acts already adopted within the framework of enhanced cooperation. However, if the Council considers that the conditions of participation have not been fulfilled, it shall indicate the arrangements to be adopted to fulfil those conditions and shall set a deadline for re-examining the request for participation.

For the purposes of this paragraph, the Council shall act unanimously and in accordance with Article 330.

Article 332 (ex Articles 27a to 27e, 40 to 40b and 43 to 45 TEU and ex Articles 11 and 11a TEC)

Expenditure resulting from implementation of enhanced cooperation, other than administrative costs entailed for the institutions, shall be borne by the participating Member States, unless all members of the Council, acting unanimously after consulting the European Parliament, decide otherwise.

Article 333 (ex Articles 27a to 27e, 40 to 40b and 43 to 45 TEU and ex Articles 11 and 11a TEC)

1. Where a provision of the Treaties which may be applied in the context of enhanced cooperation stipulates that the Council shall act unanimously, the Council, acting unanimously in accordance with the arrangements laid down in Article 330, may adopt a decision stipulating that it will act by a qualified majority.

2. Where a provision of the Treaties which may be applied in the context of enhanced cooperation stipulates that the Council shall adopt acts under a special legislative procedure, the Council, acting unanimously in accordance with the arrangements laid down in Article 330, may adopt a decision stipulating that it will act under the ordinary legislative procedure. The Council shall act after consulting the European Parliament.

3. Paragraphs 1 and 2 shall not apply to decisions having military or defence implications.

Article 334   (ex Articles 27a to 27e, 40 to 40b and 43 to 45 TEU and ex Articles 11 and 11a TEC)

The Council and the Commission shall ensure the consistency of activities undertaken in the context of enhanced cooperation and the consistency of such activities with the policies of the Union, and shall cooperate to that end.

PART SEVEN GENERAL AND FINAL PROVISIONS

Article 335   (ex Article 282 TEC)

In each of the Member States, the Union shall enjoy the most extensive legal capacity accorded to legal persons under their laws; it may, in particular, acquire or dispose of movable and immovable property and may be a party to legal proceedings. To this end, the Union shall be represented by the Commission. However, the Union shall be represented by each of the institutions, by virtue of their administrative autonomy, in matters relating to their respective operation.

Article 336   (ex Article 283 TEC)

The European Parliament and the Council shall, acting by means of regulations in accordance with the ordinary legislative procedure on a proposal from the Commission and after consulting the other institutions concerned, lay down the Staff Regulations of Officials of the European Union and the Conditions of Employment of other servants of the Union.

Article 337   (ex Article 284 TEC)

The Commission may, within the limits and under conditions laid down by the Council acting by a simple majority in accordance with the provisions of the Treaties, collect any information and carry out any checks required for the performance of the tasks entrusted to it.

Article 338   (ex Article 285 TEC)

1. Without prejudice to Article 5 of the Protocol on the Statute of the European System of Central Banks and of the European Central Bank, the European Parliament and the Council, acting in accordance with the ordinary legislative procedure, shall adopt measures for the production of statistics where necessary for the performance of the activities of the Union.

2. The production of Union statistics shall conform to impartiality, reliability, objectivity, scientific independence, cost-effectiveness and statistical confidentiality; it shall not entail excessive burdens on economic operators.

Article 339   (ex Article 287 TEC)

The members of the institutions of the Union, the members of committees, and the officials and other servants of the Union shall be required, even after their duties have ceased, not to disclose information of the kind covered by the obligation of professional secrecy, in particular information about undertakings, their business relations or their cost components.

Article 340   (ex Article 288 TEC)

The contractual liability of the Union shall be governed by the law applicable to the contract in question.

In the case of non-contractual liability, the Union shall, in accordance with the general principles common to the laws of the Member States, make good any damage caused by its institutions or by its servants in the performance of their duties.

Notwithstanding the second paragraph, the European Central Bank shall, in accordance with the general principles common to the laws of the Member States, make good any damage caused by it or by its servants in the performance of their duties.

The personal liability of its servants towards the Union shall be governed by the provisions laid down in their Staff Regulations or in the Conditions of Employment applicable to them.

Article 341   (ex Article 289 TEC)

The seat of the institutions of the Union shall be determined by common accord of the governments of the Member States.

Article 342   (ex Article 290 TEC)

The rules governing the languages of the institutions of the Union shall, without prejudice to the provisions contained in the Statute of the Court of Justice of the European Union, be determined by the Council, acting unanimously by means of regulations.

Article 343   (ex Article 291 TEC)

The Union shall enjoy in the territories of the Member States such privileges and immunities as are necessary for the performance of its tasks, under the conditions laid down in the Protocol of 8 April 1965 on the privileges and immunities of the European Union. The same shall apply to the European Central Bank and the European Investment Bank.

Article 344   (ex Article 292 TEC)

Member States undertake not to submit a dispute concerning the interpretation or application of the Treaties to any method of settlement other than those provided for therein.

Article 345   (ex Article 295 TEC)

The Treaties shall in no way prejudice the rules in Member States governing the system of property ownership.

Article 346   (ex Article 296 TEC)

1. The provisions of the Treaties shall not preclude the application of the following rules:
   (a) no Member State shall be obliged to supply information the disclosure of which it considers contrary to the essential interests of its security;
   (b) any Member State may take such measures as it considers necessary for the protection of the essential interests of its security which are connected with the production of or trade in arms, munitions and war material; such measures shall not adversely affect the conditions of competition in the internal market regarding products which are not intended for specifically military purposes.

2. The Council may, acting unanimously on a proposal from the Commission, make changes to the list, which it drew up on 15 April 1958, of the products to which the provisions of paragraph 1(b) apply.

Article 347   (ex Article 297 TEC)

Member States shall consult each other with a view to taking together the steps needed to prevent the functioning of the internal market being affected by measures which a Member State may be called upon to take in the event of serious internal disturbances affecting the maintenance of law and order, in the event of war, serious international tension constituting a threat of war, or in order to carry out obligations it has accepted for the purpose of maintaining peace and international security.

Article 348   (ex Article 298 TEC)

If measures taken in the circumstances referred to in Articles 346 and 347 have the effect of distorting the conditions of competition in the internal market, the Commission shall, together with the State concerned, examine how these measures can be adjusted to the rules laid down in the Treaties.

By way of derogation from the procedure laid down in Articles 258 and 259, the Commission or any Member State may bring the matter directly before the Court of Justice if it considers that another Member State is making improper use of the powers provided for in Articles 346 and 347. The Court of Justice shall give its ruling in camera.

Article 349   (ex Article 299(2), second, third and fourth subparagraphs, TEC)

Taking account of the structural social and economic situation of Guadeloupe, French Guiana, Martinique, Réunion, Saint-Barthélemy, Saint-Martin, the Azores, Madeira and the Canary Islands, which is compounded by their remoteness, insularity, small size, difficult topography and climate, economic dependence on a few products, the permanence and combination of which severely restrain their development, the Council, on a proposal from the Commission and after consulting the European Parliament, shall adopt specific measures aimed, in particular, at laying down the conditions of application of the Treaties to those regions, including common policies. Where the specific measures in question are adopted by the Council in accordance with a special legislative procedure, it shall also act on a proposal from the Commission and after consulting the European Parliament.

The measures referred to in the first paragraph concern in particular areas such as customs and trade policies, fiscal policy, free zones, agriculture and fisheries policies, conditions for supply of raw materials and essential consumer goods, State aids and conditions of access to structural funds and to horizontal Union programmes.

The Council shall adopt the measures referred to in the first paragraph taking into account the special characteristics and constraints of the outermost regions without undermining the integrity and the coherence of the Union legal order, including the internal market and common policies.

Article 350   (ex Article 306 TEC)

The provisions of the Treaties shall not preclude the existence or completion of regional unions between Belgium and Luxembourg, or between Belgium, Luxembourg and the Netherlands, to the extent that the objectives of these regional unions are not attained by application of the Treaties.

Article 351   (ex Article 307 TEC)

The rights and obligations arising from agreements concluded before 1 January 1958 or, for acceding States, before the date of their accession, between one or more Member States on the one hand, and one or more third countries on the other, shall not be affected by the provisions of the Treaties.

To the extent that such agreements are not compatible with the Treaties, the Member State or States concerned shall take all appropriate steps to eliminate the incompatibilities established. Member States shall, where necessary, assist each other to this end and shall, where appropriate, adopt a common attitude.

In applying the agreements referred to in the first paragraph, Member States shall take into account the fact that the advantages accorded under the Treaties by each Member State form an integral part of the establishment of the Union and are thereby inseparably linked with the creation of common institutions, the conferring of powers upon them and the granting of the same advantages by all the other Member States.

Article 352   (ex Article 308 TEC)

1. If action by the Union should prove necessary, within the framework of the policies defined in the Treaties, to attain one of the objectives set out in the Treaties, and the Treaties have not provided the necessary powers, the Council, acting unanimously on a proposal from the Commission and after obtaining the consent of the European Parliament, shall adopt the appropriate measures. Where the measures in question are adopted by the Council in accordance with a special legislative procedure, it shall also act unanimously on a proposal from the Commission and after obtaining the consent of the European Parliament.

2. Using the procedure for monitoring the subsidiarity principle referred to in Article 5(3) of the Treaty on European Union, the Commission shall draw national Parliaments' attention to proposals based on this Article.

3. Measures based on this Article shall not entail harmonisation of Member States' laws or regulations in cases where the Treaties exclude such harmonisation.

4. This Article cannot serve as a basis for attaining objectives pertaining to the common foreign and security policy and any acts adopted pursuant to this Article shall respect the limits set out in Article 40, second paragraph, of the Treaty on European Union.

Article 353

Article 48(7) of the Treaty on European Union shall not apply to the following Articles:
   - Article 311, third and fourth paragraphs,
   - Article 312(2), first subparagraph,
   - Article 352, and
   - Article 354.

Article 354 (ex Article 309 TEC)

For the purposes of Article 7 of the Treaty on European Union on the suspension of certain rights resulting from Union membership, the member of the European Council or of the Council representing the Member State in question shall not take part in the vote and the Member State in question shall not be counted in the calculation of the one-third or four-fifths of Member States referred to in paragraphs 1 and 2 of that Article. Abstentions by members present in person or represented shall not prevent the adoption of decisions referred to in paragraph 2 of that Article.

For the adoption of the decisions referred to in paragraphs 3 and 4 of Article 7 of the Treaty on European Union, a qualified majority shall be defined in accordance with Article 238(3)(b) of this Treaty.

Where, following a decision to suspend voting rights adopted pursuant to paragraph 3 of Article 7 of the Treaty on European Union, the Council acts by a qualified majority on the basis of a provision of the Treaties, that qualified majority shall be defined in accordance with Article 238(3)(b) of this Treaty, or, where the Council acts on a proposal from the Commission or from the High Representative of the Union for Foreign Affairs and Security Policy, in accordance with Article 238(3)(a).

For the purposes of Article 7 of the Treaty on European Union, the European Parliament shall act by a two-thirds majority of the votes cast, representing the majority of its component Members.

Article 355 (ex Article 299(2), first subparagraph, and Article 299(3) to (6) TEC)

In addition to the provisions of Article 52 of the Treaty on European Union relating to the territorial scope of the Treaties, the following provisions shall apply:

1. The provisions of the Treaties shall apply to Guadeloupe, French Guiana, Martinique, Réunion, Saint-Barthélemy, Saint-Martin, the Azores, Madeira and the Canary Islands in accordance with Article 349.

2. The special arrangements for association set out in Part Four shall apply to the overseas countries and territories listed in Annex II.

The Treaties shall not apply to those overseas countries and territories having special relations with the United Kingdom of Great Britain and Northern Ireland which are not included in the aforementioned list.

3. The provisions of the Treaties shall apply to the European territories for whose external relations a Member State is responsible.

4. The provisions of the Treaties shall apply to the Åland Islands in accordance with the provisions set out in Protocol 2 to the Act concerning the conditions of accession of the Republic of Austria, the Republic of Finland and the Kingdom of Sweden.

5. Notwithstanding Article 52 of the Treaty on European Union and paragraphs 1 to 4 of this Article:

(a) the Treaties shall not apply to the Faeroe Islands;

(b) the Treaties shall not apply to the United Kingdom Sovereign Base Areas of Akrotiri and Dhekelia in Cyprus except to the extent necessary to ensure the implementation of the arrangements set out in the Protocol on the Sovereign Base Areas of the United Kingdom of Great Britain and Northern Ireland in Cyprus annexed to the Act concerning the conditions of accession of the Czech Republic, the Republic of Estonia, the Republic of Cyprus, the Republic of Latvia, the Republic of Lithuania, the Republic of Hungary, the Republic of Malta, the Republic of Poland, the Republic of Slovenia and the Slovak Republic to the European Union and in accordance with the terms of that Protocol;

(c) the Treaties shall apply to the Channel Islands and the Isle of Man only to the extent necessary to ensure the implementation of the arrangements for those islands set out in the Treaty concerning the accession of new Member States to the European Economic Community and to the European Atomic Energy Community signed on 22 January 1972.

6. The European Council may, on the initiative of the Member State concerned, adopt a decision amending the status, with regard to the Union, of a Danish, French or Netherlands country or territory referred to in paragraphs 1 and 2. The European Council shall act unanimously after consulting the Commission.

Article 356   (ex Article 312 TEC)

This Treaty is concluded for an unlimited period.

Article 357   (ex Article 313 TEC)

This Treaty shall be ratified by the High Contracting Parties in accordance with their respective constitutional requirements. The Instruments of ratification shall be deposited with the Government of the Italian Republic.

This Treaty shall enter into force on the first day of the month following the deposit of the Instrument of ratification by the last signatory State to take this step. If, however, such deposit is made less than 15 days before the beginning of the following month, this Treaty shall not enter into force until the first day of the second month after the date of such deposit.

Article 358

The provisions of Article 55 of the Treaty on European Union shall apply to this Treaty.

IN WITNESS WHEREOF, the undersigned Plenipotentiaries have signed this Treaty.

Done at Rome this twenty-fifth day of March in the year one thousand nine hundred and fifty-seven. *(List of signatories not reproduced.)*

Charter of Fundamental Rights of the European Union

[OJ 2016 C202/389]*

Preamble

The peoples of Europe, in creating an ever closer union among them, are resolved to share a peaceful future based on common values.

Conscious of its spiritual and moral heritage, the Union is founded on the indivisible, universal values of human dignity, freedom, equality and solidarity; it is based on the principles of democracy and the rule of law. It places the individual at the heart of its activities, by establishing the citizenship of the Union and by creating an area of freedom, security and justice.

The Union contributes to the preservation and to the development of these common values while respecting the diversity of the cultures and traditions of the peoples of Europe as well as the national identities of the Member States and the organisation of their public authorities at national, regional and local levels; it seeks to promote balanced and sustainable development and ensures free movement of persons, goods, services and capital, and the freedom of establishment.

To this end, it is necessary to strengthen the protection of fundamental rights in the light of changes in society, social progress and scientific and technological developments by making those rights more visible in a Charter.

This Charter reaffirms, with due regard for the powers and tasks of the Community and the Union and the principle of subsidiarity, the rights as they result, in particular, from the constitutional traditions and international obligations common to the Member States, the Treaty on European Union, the Community Treaties, the European Convention for the Protection of Human Rights and Fundamental Freedoms, the Social Charters adopted by the Community and by the Council of Europe and the case-law of the Court of Justice of the European Communities and of the European Court of Human Rights. In this context the Charter will be interpreted by the courts of the Union and the Member States with due regard to the explanations prepared under the authority of the Praesidium of the Convention which drafted the Charter and updated under the responsibility of the Praesidium of the European Convention.

Enjoyment of these rights entails responsibilities and duties with regard to other persons, to the human community and to future generations.

The Union therefore recognises the rights, freedoms and principles set out hereafter.

---

* **Editor's Note:** Proclaimations and signatures omitted. This is the version re-proclaimed in 2007 and subsequently reproduced in the OJ in 2010. It remains, however, largely the text of 2000.

Chapter I Dignity

Article 1   Human dignity

Human dignity is inviolable. It must be respected and protected.

Article 2   Right to life

1. Everyone has the right to life.
2. No one shall be condemned to the death penalty, or executed.

Article 3   Right to the integrity of the person

1. Everyone has the right to respect for his or her physical and mental integrity.
2. In the fields of medicine and biology, the following must be respected in particular:
   - the free and informed consent of the person concerned, according to the procedures laid down by law,
   - the prohibition of eugenic practices, in particular those aiming at the selection of persons,
   - the prohibition on making the human body and its parts as such a source of financial gain,
   - the prohibition of the reproductive cloning of human beings.

Article 4   Prohibition of torture and inhuman or degrading treatment or punishment

No one shall be subjected to torture or to inhuman or degrading treatment or punishment.

Article 5   Prohibition of slavery and forced labour

1. No one shall be held in slavery or servitude.
2. No one shall be required to perform forced or compulsory labour.
3. Trafficking in human beings is prohibited.

Chapter II Freedoms

Article 6   Right to liberty and security

Everyone has the right to liberty and security of person.

Article 7   Respect for private and family life

Everyone has the right to respect for his or her private and family life, home and communications.

Article 8   Protection of personal data

1. Everyone has the right to the protection of personal data concerning him or her.
2. Such data must be processed fairly for specified purposes and on the basis of the consent of the person concerned or some other legitimate basis laid down by law. Everyone has the right of access to data which has been collected concerning him or her, and the right to have it rectified.
3. Compliance with these rules shall be subject to control by an independent authority.

Article 9   Right to marry and right to found a family

The right to marry and the right to found a family shall be guaranteed in accordance with the national laws governing the exercise of these rights.

Article 10   Freedom of thought, conscience and religion

1. Everyone has the right to freedom of thought, conscience and religion. This right includes freedom to change religion or belief and freedom, either alone or in community with others and in public or in private, to manifest religion or belief, in worship, teaching, practice and observance.
2. The right to conscientious objection is recognised, in accordance with the national laws governing the exercise of this right.

Article 11   Freedom of expression and information

1. Everyone has the right to freedom of expression. This right shall include freedom to hold opinions and to receive and impart information and ideas without interference by public authority and regardless of frontiers.
2. The freedom and pluralism of the media shall be respected.

Article 12   Freedom of assembly and of association

1. Everyone has the right to freedom of peaceful assembly and to freedom of association at all levels, in particular in political, trade union and civic matters, which implies the right of everyone to form and to join trade unions for the protection of his or her interests.

2. Political parties at Union level contribute to expressing the political will of the citizens of the Union.

Article 13   Freedom of the arts and sciences

The arts and scientific research shall be free of constraint. Academic freedom shall be respected.

Article 14   Right to education

1. Everyone has the right to education and to have access to vocational and continuing training.

2. This right includes the possibility to receive free compulsory education.

3. The freedom to found educational establishments with due respect for democratic principles and the right of parents to ensure the education and teaching of their children in conformity with their religious, philosophical and pedagogical convictions shall be respected, in accordance with the national laws governing the exercise of such freedom and right.

Article 15   Freedom to choose an occupation and right to engage in work

1. Everyone has the right to engage in work and to pursue a freely chosen or accepted occupation.

2. Every citizen of the Union has the freedom to seek employment, to work, to exercise the right of establishment and to provide services in any Member State.

3. Nationals of third countries who are authorised to work in the territories of the Member States are entitled to working conditions equivalent to those of citizens of the Union.

Article 16   Freedom to conduct a business

The freedom to conduct a business in accordance with Union law and national laws and practices is recognised.

Article 17   Right to property

1. Everyone has the right to own, use, dispose of and bequeath his or her lawfully acquired possessions. No one may be deprived of his or her possessions, except in the public interest and in the cases and under the conditions provided for by law, subject to fair compensation being paid in good time for their loss. The use of property may be regulated by law in so far as is necessary for the general interest.

2. Intellectual property shall be protected.

Article 18   Right to asylum

The right to asylum shall be guaranteed with due respect for the rules of the Geneva Convention of 28 July 1951 and the Protocol of 31 January 1967 relating to the status of refugees and in accordance with the Treaty on European Union and the Treaty on the Functioning of the European Union (hereinafter referred to as 'the Treaties').

Article 19   Protection in the event of removal, expulsion or extradition

1. Collective expulsions are prohibited.

2. No one may be removed, expelled or extradited to a State where there is a serious risk that he or she would be subjected to the death penalty, torture or other inhuman or degrading treatment or punishment.

Chapter III Equality

Article 20   Equality before the law

Everyone is equal before the law.

Article 21   Non-discrimination

1. Any discrimination based on any ground such as sex, race, colour, ethnic or social origin, genetic features, language, religion or belief, political or any other opinion, membership of a national minority, property, birth, disability, age or sexual orientation shall be prohibited.

2. Within the scope of application of the Treaties and without prejudice to the special provisions of those Treaties, any discrimination on grounds of nationality shall be prohibited.

Article 22   Cultural, religious and linguistic diversity

The Union shall respect cultural, religious and linguistic diversity.

Article 23   Equality between men and women

Equality between men and women must be ensured in all areas, including employment, work and pay.

The principle of equality shall not prevent the maintenance or adoption of measures providing for specific advantages in favour of the under-represented sex.

Article 24   The rights of the child

1. Children shall have the right to such protection and care as is necessary for their well-being. They may express their views freely. Such views shall be taken into consideration on matters which concern them in accordance with their age and maturity.

2. In all actions relating to children, whether taken by public authorities or private institutions, the child's best interests must be a primary consideration.

3. Every child shall have the right to maintain on a regular basis a personal relationship and direct contact with both his or her parents, unless that is contrary to his or her interests.

Article 25   The rights of the elderly

The Union recognises and respects the rights of the elderly to lead a life of dignity and independence and to participate in social and cultural life.

Article 26   Integration of persons with disabilities

The Union recognises and respects the right of persons with disabilities to benefit from measures designed to ensure their independence, social and occupational integration and participation in the life of the community.

Chapter IV Solidarity

Article 27   Workers' right to information and consultation within the undertaking

Workers or their representatives must, at the appropriate levels, be guaranteed information and consultation in good time in the cases and under the conditions provided for by Community law and national laws and practices.

Article 28   Right of collective bargaining and action

Workers and employers, or their respective organisations, have, in accordance with Community law and national laws and practices, the right to negotiate and conclude collective agreements at the appropriate levels and, in cases of conflicts of interest, to take collective action to defend their interests, including strike action.

Article 29   Right of access to placement services

Everyone has the right of access to a free placement service.

Article 30   Protection in the event of unjustified dismissal

Every worker has the right to protection against unjustified dismissal, in accordance with Union law and national laws and practices.

Article 31   Fair and just working conditions

1. Every worker has the right to working conditions which respect his or her health, safety and dignity.

2. Every worker has the right to limitation of maximum working hours, to daily and weekly rest periods and to an annual period of paid leave.

Article 32   Prohibition of child labour and protection of young people at work

The employment of children is prohibited. The minimum age of admission to employment may not be lower than the minimum school-leaving age, without prejudice to such rules as may be more favourable to young people and except for limited derogations.

Young people admitted to work must have working conditions appropriate to their age and be protected against economic exploitation and any work likely to harm their safety, health or physical, mental, moral or social development or to interfere with their education.

Article 33   Family and professional life

1. The family shall enjoy legal, economic and social protection.

2. To reconcile family and professional life, everyone shall have the right to protection from dismissal for a reason connected with maternity and the right to paid maternity leave and to parental leave following the birth or adoption of a child.

Article 34   Social security and social assistance

1. The Union recognises and respects the entitlement to social security benefits and social services providing protection in cases such as maternity, illness, industrial accidents, dependency or old age, and in the case of loss of employment, in accordance with the rules laid down by Union law and national laws and practices.

2. Everyone residing and moving legally within the European Union is entitled to social security benefits and social advantages in accordance with Union law and national laws and practices.

3. In order to combat social exclusion and poverty, the Union recognises and respects the right to social and housing assistance so as to ensure a decent existence for all those who lack sufficient resources, in accordance with the rules laid down by Union law and national laws and practices.

Article 35   Health care

Everyone has the right of access to preventive health care and the right to benefit from medical treatment under the conditions established by national laws and practices. A high level of human health protection shall be ensured in the definition and implementation of all Union policies and activities.

Article 36   Access to services of general economic interest

The Union recognises and respects access to services of general economic interest as provided for in national laws and practices, in accordance with the Treaties, in order to promote the social and territorial cohesion of the Union.

Article 37   Environmental protection

A high level of environmental protection and the improvement of the quality of the environment must be integrated into the policies of the Union and ensured in accordance with the principle of sustainable development.

Article 38   Consumer protection

Union policies shall ensure a high level of consumer protection.

Chapter V Citizens' rights

Article 39   Right to vote and to stand as a candidate at elections to the European Parliament

1. Every citizen of the Union has the right to vote and to stand as a candidate at elections to the European Parliament in the Member State in which he or she resides, under the same conditions as nationals of that State.

2. Members of the European Parliament shall be elected by direct universal suffrage in a free and secret ballot.

Article 40   Right to vote and to stand as a candidate at municipal elections

Every citizen of the Union has the right to vote and to stand as a candidate at municipal elections in the Member State in which he or she resides under the same conditions as nationals of that State.

Article 41   Right to good administration

1. Every person has the right to have his or her affairs handled impartially, fairly and within a reasonable time by the institutions, bodies, offices and agencies of the Union.

2. This right includes:
  - the right of every person to be heard, before any individual measure which would affect him or her adversely is taken;
  - the right of every person to have access to his or her file, while respecting the legitimate interests of confidentiality and of professional and business secrecy;
  - the obligation of the administration to give reasons for its decisions.

3. Every person has the right to have the Community make good any damage caused by its institutions or by its servants in the performance of their duties, in accordance with the general principles common to the laws of the Member States.

4. Every person may write to the institutions of the Union in one of the languages of the Treaties and must have an answer in the same language.

Article 42   Right of access to documents

Any citizen of the Union, and any natural or legal person residing or having its registered office in a Member State, has a right of access to documents of the institutions, bodies, offices and agencies of the Union, whatever their medium.

Article 43   Ombudsman

Any citizen of the Union and any natural or legal person residing or having its registered office in a Member State has the right to refer to the European Ombudsman cases of maladministration in the activities of the institutions, bodies, offices or agencies of the Union, with the exception of the Court of Justice of the European Union acting in its judicial role.

Article 44   Right to petition

Any citizen of the Union and any natural or legal person residing or having its registered office in a Member State has the right to petition the European Parliament.

Article 45   Freedom of movement and of residence

1. Every citizen of the Union has the right to move and reside freely within the territory of the Member States.

2. Freedom of movement and residence may be granted, in accordance with the Treaties, to nationals of third countries legally resident in the territory of a Member State.

Article 46   Diplomatic and consular protection

Every citizen of the Union shall, in the territory of a third country in which the Member State of which he or she is a national is not represented, be entitled to protection by the diplomatic or consular authorities of any Member State, on the same conditions as the nationals of that Member State.

Chapter VI Justice

Article 47   Right to an effective remedy and to a fair trial

Everyone whose rights and freedoms guaranteed by the law of the Union are violated has the right to an effective remedy before a tribunal in compliance with the conditions laid down in this Article.

Everyone is entitled to a fair and public hearing within a reasonable time by an independent and impartial tribunal previously established by law. Everyone shall have the possibility of being advised, defended and represented.

Legal aid shall be made available to those who lack sufficient resources in so far as such aid is necessary to ensure effective access to justice.

Article 48   Presumption of innocence and right of defence

1. Everyone who has been charged shall be presumed innocent until proved guilty according to law.

2. Respect for the rights of the defence of anyone who has been charged shall be guaranteed.

Article 49   Principles of legality and proportionality of criminal offences and penalties

1. No one shall be held guilty of any criminal offence on account of any act or omission which did not constitute a criminal offence under national law or international law at the time when it was committed. Nor shall a heavier penalty be imposed than that which was applicable at the time the criminal offence was committed. If, subsequent to the commission of a criminal offence, the law provides for a lighter penalty, that penalty shall be applicable.

2. This Article shall not prejudice the trial and punishment of any person for any act or omission which, at the time when it was committed, was criminal according to the general principles recognised by the community of nations.

3. The severity of penalties must not be disproportionate to the criminal offence.

Article 50 Right not to be tried or punished twice in criminal proceedings for the same criminal offence

No one shall be liable to be tried or punished again in criminal proceedings for an offence for which he or she has already been finally acquitted or convicted within the Union in accordance with the law.

Chapter VII General provisions

Article 51 Scope

1. The provisions of this Charter are addressed to the institutions, bodies, offices and agencies of the Union with due regard for the principle of subsidiarity and to the Member States only when they are implementing Union law. They shall therefore respect the rights, observe the principles and promote the application thereof in accordance with their respective powers and respecting the limits of the powers of the Union as conferred on it in the Treaties.

2. The Charter does not extend the field of application of Union law beyond the powers of the Union or establish any new power or task for the Union, or modify powers and tasks as defined in the Treaties.

Article 52 Scope of guaranteed rights

1. Any limitation on the exercise of the rights and freedoms recognised by this Charter must be provided for by law and respect the essence of those rights and freedoms. Subject to the principle of proportionality, limitations may be made only if they are necessary and genuinely meet objectives of general interest recognised by the Union or the need to protect the rights and freedoms of others.

2. Rights recognised by this Charter for which provision is made in the Treaties shall be exercised under the conditions and within the limits defined by those Treaties.

3. In so far as this Charter contains rights which correspond to rights guaranteed by the Convention for the Protection of Human Rights and Fundamental Freedoms, the meaning and scope of those rights shall be the same as those laid down by the said Convention. This provision shall not prevent Union law providing more extensive protection.

4. In so far as this Charter recognises fundamental rights as they result from the constitutional traditions common to the Member States, those rights shall be interpreted in harmony with those traditions.

5. The provisions of this Charter which contain principles may be implemented by legislative and executive acts taken by institutions, bodies, offices and agencies of the Union, and by acts of Member States when they are implementing Union law, in the exercise of their respective powers. They shall be judicially cognisable only in the interpretation of such acts and in the ruling on their legality.

6. Full account shall be taken of national laws and practices as specified in this Charter.

7. The explanations drawn up as a way of providing guidance in the interpretation of this Charter shall be given due regard by the courts of the Union and of the Member States.

Article 53 Level of protection

Nothing in this Charter shall be interpreted as restricting or adversely affecting human rights and fundamental freedoms as recognised, in their respective fields of application, by Union law and international law and by international agreements to which the Union, the Community or all the Member States are party, including the European Convention for the Protection of Human Rights and Fundamental Freedoms, and by the Member States' constitutions.

Article 54 Prohibition of abuse of rights

Nothing in this Charter shall be interpreted as implying any right to engage in any activity or to perform any act aimed at the destruction of any of the rights and freedoms recognised in this Charter or at their limitation to a greater extent than is provided for herein.

The above text adapts the wording of the Charter proclaimed on 7 December 2000, and will replace it as from the date of entry into force of the Treaty of Lisbon.

Selected Protocols attached to the Treaties by the Lisbon Treaty

Protocol (No 1) on the Role of National Parliaments in the European Union

THE HIGH CONTRACTING PARTIES

RECALLING that the way in which national Parliaments scrutinise their governments in relation to the activities of the Union is a matter for the particular constitutional organisation and practice of each Member State,

DESIRING to encourage greater involvement of national Parliaments in the activities of the European Union and to enhance their ability to express their views on draft legislative acts of the Union as well as on other matters which may be of particular interest to them,

HAVE AGREED UPON the following provisions, which shall be annexed to the Treaty on European Union, to the Treaty on the Functioning of the European Union and to the Treaty establishing the European Atomic Energy Community:

Title I Information for national Parliaments

Article 1

Commission consultation documents (green and white papers and communications) shall be forwarded directly by the Commission to national Parliaments upon publication. The Commission shall also forward the annual legislative programme as well as any other instrument of legislative planning or policy to national Parliaments, at the same time as to the European Parliament and the Council.

Article 2

Draft legislative acts sent to the European Parliament and to the Council shall be forwarded to national Parliaments.

For the purposes of this Protocol, 'draft legislative acts' shall mean proposals from the Commission, initiatives from a group of Member States, initiatives from the European Parliament, requests from the Court of Justice, recommendations from the European Central Bank and requests from the European Investment Bank for the adoption of a legislative act.

Draft legislative acts originating from the Commission shall be forwarded to national Parliaments directly by the Commission, at the same time as to the European Parliament and the Council.

Draft legislative acts originating from the European Parliament shall be forwarded to national Parliaments directly by the European Parliament.

Draft legislative acts originating from a group of Member States, the Court of Justice, the European Central Bank or the European Investment Bank shall be forwarded to national Parliaments by the Council.

Article 3

National Parliaments may send to the Presidents of the European Parliament, the Council and the Commission a reasoned opinion on whether a draft legislative act complies with the principle of subsidiarity, in accordance with the procedure laid down in the Protocol on the application of the principles of subsidiarity and proportionality.

If the draft legislative act originates from a group of Member States, the President of the Council shall forward the reasoned opinion or opinions to the governments of those Member States.

If the draft legislative act originates from the Court of Justice, the European Central Bank or the European Investment Bank, the President of the Council shall forward the reasoned opinion or opinions to the institution or body concerned.

Article 4

An eight-week period shall elapse between a draft legislative act being made available to national Parliaments in the official languages of the Union and the date when it is placed on a provisional agenda for the Council for its adoption or for adoption of a position under a legislative procedure. Exceptions shall be possible in cases of urgency, the reasons for which shall be stated in the act or position of the Council. Save in urgent cases for which due reasons have been given, no agreement may be reached on a draft legislative act during those eight weeks. Save in urgent cases for which due reasons have been given, a ten-day period shall elapse between the placing of a draft legislative act on the provisional agenda for the Council and the adoption of a position.

Article 5

The agendas for and the outcome of meetings of the Council, including the minutes of meetings where the Council is deliberating on draft legislative acts, shall be forwarded directly to national Parliaments, at the same time as to Member States' governments.

Article 6

When the European Council intends to make use of the first or second subparagraphs of Article 48(7) of the Treaty on European Union, national Parliaments shall be informed of the initiative of the European Council at least six months before any decision is adopted.

Article 7

The Court of Auditors shall forward its annual report to national Parliaments, for information, at the same time as to the European Parliament and to the Council.

Article 8

Where the national Parliamentary system is not unicameral, Articles 1 to 7 shall apply to the component chambers.

Title II Interparliamentary cooperation

Article 9

The European Parliament and national Parliaments shall together determine the organisation and promotion of effective and regular interparliamentary cooperation within the Union.

Article 10

A conference of Parliamentary Committees for Union Affairs may submit any contribution it deems appropriate for the attention of the European Parliament, the Council and the Commission. That conference shall in addition promote the exchange of information and best practice between national Parliaments and the European Parliament, including their special committees. It may also organise interparliamentary conferences on specific topics, in particular to debate matters of common foreign and security policy, including common security and defence policy. Contributions from the conference shall not bind national Parliaments and shall not prejudge their positions.

Protocol (No 2) on the Application of the Principles of Subsidiarity and Proportionality

THE HIGH CONTRACTING PARTIES,

WISHING to ensure that decisions are taken as closely as possible to the citizens of the Union,

RESOLVED to establish the conditions for the application of the principles of subsidiarity and proportionality, as laid down in Article 5 of the Treaty on European Union, and to establish a system for monitoring the application of those principles,

HAVE AGREED UPON the following provisions, which shall be annexed to the Treaty on European Union and to the Treaty on the Functioning of the European Union:

Article 1

Each institution shall ensure constant respect for the principles of subsidiarity and proportionality, as laid down in Article 5 of the Treaty on European Union.

Article 2

Before proposing legislative acts, the Commission shall consult widely. Such consultations shall, where appropriate, take into account the regional and local dimension of the action envisaged. In cases of exceptional urgency, the Commission shall not conduct such consultations. It shall give reasons for its decision in its proposal.

Article 3

For the purposes of this Protocol, 'draft legislative acts' shall mean proposals from the Commission, initiatives from a group of Member States, initiatives from the European Parliament, requests from the Court of Justice, recommendations from the European Central Bank and requests from the European Investment Bank for the adoption of a legislative act.

Article 4

The Commission shall forward its draft legislative acts and its amended drafts to national Parliaments at the same time as to the Union legislator.

The European Parliament shall forward its draft legislative acts and its amended drafts to national Parliaments.

The Council shall forward draft legislative acts originating from a group of Member States, the Court of Justice, the European Central Bank or the European Investment Bank and amended drafts to national Parliaments.

Upon adoption, legislative resolutions of the European Parliament and positions of the Council shall be forwarded by them to national Parliaments.

Article 5

Draft legislative acts shall be justified with regard to the principles of subsidiarity and proportionality. Any draft legislative act should contain a detailed statement making it possible to appraise compliance with the principles of subsidiarity and proportionality. This statement should contain some assessment of the proposal's financial impact and, in the case of a directive, of its implications for the rules to be put in place by Member States, including, where necessary, the regional legislation. The reasons for concluding that a Union objective can be better achieved at Union level shall be substantiated by qualitative and, wherever possible, quantitative indicators. Draft legislative acts shall take account of the need for any burden, whether financial or administrative, falling upon the Union, national governments, regional or local authorities, economic operators and citizens, to be minimised and commensurate with the objective to be achieved.

Article 6

Any national Parliament or any chamber of a national Parliament may, within eight weeks from the date of transmission of a draft legislative act, in the official languages of the Union, send to the Presidents of the European Parliament, the Council and the Commission a reasoned opinion stating why it considers that the draft in question does not comply with the principle of subsidiarity. It will be for each national Parliament or each chamber of a national Parliament to consult, where appropriate, regional parliaments with legislative powers.

If the draft legislative act originates from a group of Member States, the President of the Council shall forward the opinion to the governments of those Member States.

If the draft legislative act originates from the Court of Justice, the European Central Bank or the European Investment Bank, the President of the Council shall forward the opinion to the institution or body concerned.

Article 7

1. The European Parliament, the Council and the Commission, and, where appropriate, the group of Member States, the Court of Justice, the European Central Bank or the European Investment Bank, if the draft legislative act originates from them, shall take account of the reasoned opinions issued by national Parliaments or by a chamber of a national Parliament.

Each national Parliament shall have two votes, shared out on the basis of the national Parliamentary system. In the case of a bicameral Parliamentary system, each of the two chambers shall have one vote.

2. Where reasoned opinions on a draft legislative act's non-compliance with the principle of subsidiarity represent at least one third of all the votes allocated to the national Parliaments in accordance with the second subparagraph of paragraph 1, the draft must be reviewed. This threshold shall be a quarter in the case of a draft legislative act submitted on the basis of Article 76 of the Treaty on the Functioning of the European Union on the area of freedom, security and justice.

After such review, the Commission or, where appropriate, the group of Member States, the European Parliament, the Court of Justice, the European Central Bank or the European Investment Bank, if the draft legislative act originates from them, may decide to maintain, amend or withdraw the draft. Reasons must be given for this decision.

3. Furthermore, under the ordinary legislative procedure, where reasoned opinions on the non-compliance of a proposal for a legislative act with the principle of subsidiarity represent at least a simple majority of the votes allocated to the national Parliaments in accordance with the second subparagraph of paragraph 1, the proposal must be reviewed. After such review, the Commission may decide to maintain, amend or withdraw the proposal.

If it chooses to maintain the proposal, the Commission will have, in a reasoned opinion, to justify why it considers that the proposal complies with the principle of subsidiarity. This reasoned opinion, as well as the reasoned opinions of the national Parliaments, will have to be submitted to the Union legislator, for consideration in the procedure:

(a) before concluding the first reading, the legislator (the European Parliament and the Council) shall consider whether the legislative proposal is compatible with the principle of subsidiarity, taking particular account of the reasons expressed and shared by the majority of national Parliaments as well as the reasoned opinion of the Commission;

(b) if, by a majority of 55 % of the members of the Council or a majority of the votes cast in the European Parliament, the legislator is of the opinion that the proposal is not compatible with the principle of subsidiarity, the legislative proposal shall not be given further consideration.

Article 8

The Court of Justice of the European Union shall have jurisdiction in actions on grounds of infringement of the principle of subsidiarity by a legislative act, brought in accordance with the rules laid down in Article 263 of the Treaty on the Functioning of the European Union by Member States, or notified by them in accordance with their legal order on behalf of their national Parliament or a chamber thereof.

In accordance with the rules laid down in the said Article, the Committee of the Regions may also bring such actions against legislative acts for the adoption of which the Treaty on the Functioning of the European Union provides that it be consulted.

Article 9

The Commission shall submit each year to the European Council, the European Parliament, the Council and national Parliaments a report on the application of Article 5 of the Treaty on European Union. This annual report shall also be forwarded to the Economic and Social Committee and the Committee of the Regions.

Protocol (No 3) on the Statute of the Court of Justice of the European Union*

THE HIGH CONTRACTING PARTIES,

DESIRING to lay down the Statute of the Court of Justice of the European Union provided for in Article 281 of the Treaty on the Functioning of the European Union,

HAVE AGREED UPON the following provisions, which shall be annexed to the Treaty on European Union, the Treaty on the Functioning of the European Union and the Treaty establishing the European Atomic Energy Community:

Article 1

The Court of Justice of the European Union shall be constituted and shall function in accordance with the provisions of the Treaties, of the Treaty establishing the European Atomic Energy Community (EAEC Treaty) and of this Statute.

Title I Judges and Advocates-General

Article 2

Before taking up his duties each Judge shall, before the Court of Justice sitting in open court, take an oath to perform his duties impartially and conscientiously and to preserve the secrecy of the deliberations of the Court.

Article 3

The Judges shall be immune from legal proceedings. After they have ceased to hold office, they shall continue to enjoy immunity in respect of acts performed by them in their official capacity, including words spoken or written.

The Court of Justice, sitting as a full Court, may waive the immunity. If the decision concerns a member of the General Court or of a specialised court, the Court shall decide after consulting the court concerned.

Where immunity has been waived and criminal proceedings are instituted against a Judge, he shall be tried, in any of the Member States, only by the court competent to judge the members of the highest national judiciary.

Articles 11 to 14 and Article 17 of the Protocol on the privileges and immunities of the European Union shall apply to the Judges, Advocates-General, Registrar and Assistant Rapporteurs of the Court of Justice of the European Union, without prejudice to the provisions relating to immunity from legal proceedings of Judges which are set out in the preceding paragraphs.

Article 4

The Judges may not hold any political or administrative office.

They may not engage in any occupation, whether gainful or not, unless exemption is exceptionally granted by the Council, acting by a simple majority.

When taking up their duties, they shall give a solemn undertaking that, both during and after their term of office, they will respect the obligations arising therefrom, in particular the duty to behave with integrity and discretion as regards the acceptance, after they have ceased to hold office, of certain appointments or benefits.

Any doubt on this point shall be settled by decision of the Court of Justice. If the decision concerns a member of the General Court or of a specialised court, the Court shall decide after consulting the court concerned.

---

* **Editor's Note:** As amended up to 17 April 2019 (OJ 2019 L111/1).

Article 5

Apart from normal replacement, or death, the duties of a Judge shall end when he resigns.

Where a Judge resigns, his letter of resignation shall be addressed to the President of the Court of Justice for transmission to the President of the Council. Upon this notification a vacancy shall arise on the bench.

Save where Article 6 applies, a Judge shall continue to hold office until his successor takes up his duties.

Article 6

A Judge may be deprived of his office or of his right to a pension or other benefits in its stead only if, in the unanimous opinion of the Judges and Advocates-General of the Court of Justice, he no longer fulfils the requisite conditions or meets the obligations arising from his office. The Judge concerned shall not take part in any such deliberations. If the person concerned is a member of the General Court or of a specialised court, the Court shall decide after consulting the court concerned.

The Registrar of the Court shall communicate the decision of the Court to the President of the European Parliament and to the President of the Commission and shall notify it to the President of the Council.

In the case of a decision depriving a Judge of his office, a vacancy shall arise on the bench upon this latter notification.

Article 7

A Judge who is to replace a member of the Court whose term of office has not expired shall be appointed for the remainder of his predecessor's term.

Article 8

The provisions of Articles 2 to 7 shall apply to the Advocates-General.

Title II Organisation of the Court of Justice

Article 9

When, every three years, the Judges are partially replaced, one half of the number of Judges shall be replaced. If the number of Judges is an uneven number, the number of Judges who shall be replaced shall alternately be the number which is the next above one half of the number of Judges and the number which is next below one half. The first paragraph shall also apply when the Advocates-General are partially replaced, every three years.

Article 9a

The Judges shall elect the President and the Vice-President of the Court of Justice from among their number for a term of three years. They may be re-elected.

The Vice-President shall assist the President in accordance with the conditions laid down in the Rules of Procedure. He shall take the President's place when the latter is prevented from attending or when the office of President is vacant.

Article 10

The Registrar shall take an oath before the Court of Justice to perform his duties impartially and conscientiously and to preserve the secrecy of the deliberations of the Court of Justice.

Article 11

The Court of Justice shall arrange for replacement of the Registrar on occasions when he is prevented from attending the Court of Justice.

Article 12

Officials and other servants shall be attached to the Court of Justice to enable it to function. They shall be responsible to the Registrar under the authority of the President.

Article 13

At the request of the Court of Justice, the European Parliament and the Council may, acting in accordance with the ordinary legislative procedure, provide for the appointment of Assistant Rapporteurs and lay down the rules governing their service. The Assistant Rapporteurs may be required, under conditions laid down in the Rules of Procedure, to participate in preparatory inquiries in cases pending before the Court and to cooperate with the Judge who acts as Rapporteur.

The Assistant Rapporteurs shall be chosen from persons whose independence is beyond doubt and who possess the necessary legal qualifications; they shall be appointed by the Council, acting by a simple majority. They shall take an oath before the Court to perform their duties impartially and conscientiously and to preserve the secrecy of the deliberations of the Court.

Article 14

The Judges, the Advocates-General and the Registrar shall be required to reside at the place where the Court of Justice has its seat.

Article 15

The Court of Justice shall remain permanently in session. The duration of the judicial vacations shall be determined by the Court with due regard to the needs of its business.

Article 16

The Court of Justice shall form chambers consisting of three and five Judges. The Judges shall elect the Presidents of the chambers from among their number. The Presidents of the chambers of five Judges shall be elected for three years. They may be re-elected once.

The Grand Chamber shall consist of 15 Judges. It shall be presided over by the President of the Court. The Vice-President of the Court and, in accordance with the conditions laid down in the Rules of Procedure, three of the Presidents of the chambers of five Judges and other Judges shall also form part of the Grand Chamber.

The Court shall sit in a Grand Chamber when a Member State or an institution of the Union that is party to the proceedings so requests.

The Court shall sit as a full Court where cases are brought before it pursuant to Article 228(2), Article 245(2), Article 247 or Article 286(7) of the Treaty on the Functioning of the European Union.

Moreover, where it considers that a case before it is of exceptional importance, the Court may decide, after hearing the Advocate-General, to refer the case to the full Court.

Article 17

Decisions of the Court of Justice shall be valid only when an uneven number of its members is sitting in the deliberations.

Decisions of the chambers consisting of either three or five Judges shall be valid only if they are taken by three Judges.

Decisions of the Grand Chamber shall be valid only if 11 Judges are sitting.

Decisions of the full Court shall be valid only if 17 Judges are sitting.

In the event of one of the Judges of a chamber being prevented from attending, a Judge of another chamber may be called upon to sit in accordance with conditions laid down in the Rules of Procedure.

Article 18

No Judge or Advocate-General may take part in the disposal of any case in which he has previously taken part as agent or adviser or has acted for one of the parties, or in which he has been called upon to pronounce as a member of a court or tribunal, of a commission of inquiry or in any other capacity.

If, for some special reason, any Judge or Advocate-General considers that he should not take part in the judgment or examination of a particular case, he shall so inform the President. If, for some special reason, the President considers that any Judge or Advocate-General should not sit or make submissions in a particular case, he shall notify him accordingly.

Any difficulty arising as to the application of this Article shall be settled by decision of the Court of Justice.

A party may not apply for a change in the composition of the Court or of one of its chambers on the grounds of either the nationality of a Judge or the absence from the Court or from the chamber of a Judge of the nationality of that party.

Title III Procedure before the Court of Justice

Article 19

The Member States and the institutions of the Union shall be represented before the Court of Justice by an agent appointed for each case; the agent may be assisted by an adviser or by a lawyer.

The States, other than the Member States, which are parties to the Agreement on the European Economic Area and also the EFTA Surveillance Authority referred to in that Agreement shall be represented in same manner.

Other parties must be represented by a lawyer.

Only a lawyer authorised to practise before a court of a Member State or of another State which is a party to the Agreement on the European Economic Area may represent or assist a party before the Court.

Such agents, advisers and lawyers shall, when they appear before the Court, enjoy the rights and immunities necessary to the independent exercise of their duties, under conditions laid down in the Rules of Procedure.

As regards such advisers and lawyers who appear before it, the Court shall have the powers normally accorded to courts of law, under conditions laid down in the Rules of Procedure.

University teachers being nationals of a Member State whose law accords them a right of audience shall have the same rights before the Court as are accorded by this Article to lawyers.

Article 20

The procedure before the Court of Justice shall consist of two parts: written and oral.

The written procedure shall consist of the communication to the parties and to the institutions of the Union whose decisions are in dispute, of applications, statements of case, defences and observations, and of replies, if any, as well as of all papers and documents in support or of certified copies of them.

Communications shall be made by the Registrar in the order and within the time laid down in the Rules of Procedure.

The oral procedure shall consist of the hearing by the Court of agents, advisers and lawyers and of the submissions of the Advocate-General, as well as the hearing, if any, of witnesses and experts.

Where it considers that the case raises no new point of law, the Court may decide, after hearing the Advocate-General, that the case shall be determined without a submission from the Advocate-General.

Article 21

A case shall be brought before the Court of Justice by a written application addressed to the Registrar. The application shall contain the applicant's name and permanent address and the description of the signatory, the name of the party or names of the parties against whom the application is made, the subject-matter of the dispute, the form of order sought and a brief statement of the pleas in law on which the application is based.

The application shall be accompanied, where appropriate, by the measure the annulment of which is sought or, in the circumstances referred to in Article 265 of the Treaty on the Functioning of the European Union, by documentary evidence of the date on which an institution was, in accordance with those Articles, requested to act. If the documents are not submitted with the application, the Registrar shall ask the party concerned to produce them within a reasonable period, but in that event the rights of the party shall not lapse even if such documents are produced after the time limit for bringing proceedings.

Article 22

A case governed by Article 18 of the EAEC Treaty shall be brought before the Court of Justice by an appeal addressed to the Registrar. The appeal shall contain the name and permanent address of the applicant and the description of the signatory, a reference to the decision against which the appeal is brought, the names of the respondents, the subject-matter of the dispute, the submissions and a brief statement of the grounds on which the appeal is based.

The appeal shall be accompanied by a certified copy of the decision of the Arbitration Committee which is contested.

If the Court rejects the appeal, the decision of the Arbitration Committee shall become final.

If the Court annuls the decision of the Arbitration Committee, the matter may be re-opened, where appropriate, on the initiative of one of the parties in the case, before the Arbitration Committee. The latter shall conform to any decisions on points of law given by the Court.

Article 23

In the cases governed by Article 267 of the Treaty on the Functioning of the European Union, the decision of the court or tribunal of a Member State which suspends its proceedings and refers a case to the Court of Justice shall be notified to the Court by the court or tribunal concerned. The decision shall then be notified by the Registrar of the Court to the parties, to the Member States and to the Commission, and to the institution, body, office or agency of the Union which adopted the act the validity or interpretation of which is in dispute.

Within two months of this notification, the parties, the Member States, the Commission and, where appropriate, the institution, body, office or agency which adopted the act the validity or interpretation of which is in dispute, shall be entitled to submit statements of case or written observations to the Court.

In the cases governed by Article 267 of the Treaty on the Functioning of the European Union, the decision of the national court or tribunal shall, moreover, be notified by the Registrar of the Court to the States, other than the Member States, which are parties to the Agreement on the European Economic Area and also to the EFTA Surveillance Authority referred to in that Agreement which may, within two months of notification, where one of the fields of application of that Agreement is concerned, submit statements of case or written observations to the Court.

Where an agreement relating to a specific subject matter, concluded by the Council and one or more non-member States, provides that those States are to be entitled to submit statements of case or written observations where a court or tribunal of a Member State refers to the Court of Justice for a preliminary ruling a question falling within the scope of the agreement, the decision of the national court or tribunal containing that question shall also be notified to the non-member States concerned. Within two months from such notification, those States may lodge at the Court statements of case or written observations.

Article 23a[1]

The Rules of Procedure may provide for an expedited or accelerated procedure and, for references for a preliminary ruling relating to the area of freedom, security and justice, an urgent procedure.

Those procedures may provide, in respect of the submission of statements of case or written observations, for a shorter period than that provided for by Article 23, and, in derogation from the fourth paragraph of Article 20, for the case to be determined without a submission from the Advocate General.

In addition, the urgent procedure may provide for restriction of the parties and other interested persons mentioned in Article 23, authorised to submit statements of case or written observations and, in cases of extreme urgency, for the written stage of the procedure to be omitted.

Article 24

The Court of Justice may require the parties to produce all documents and to supply all information which the Court considers desirable. Formal note shall be taken of any refusal.

The Court may also require the Member States and institutions, bodies, offices and agencies not being parties to the case to supply all information which the Court considers necessary for the proceedings.

---

[1] Article inserted by Decision 2008/79/EC, Euratom (OJ L 24, 29.1.2008, p. 42).

Article 25

The Court of Justice may at any time entrust any individual, body, authority, committee or other organisation it chooses with the task of giving an expert opinion.

Article 26

Witnesses may be heard under conditions laid down in the Rules of Procedure.

Article 27

With respect to defaulting witnesses the Court of Justice shall have the powers generally granted to courts and tribunals and may impose pecuniary penalties under conditions laid down in the Rules of Procedure.

Article 28

Witnesses and experts may be heard on oath taken in the form laid down in the Rules of Procedure or in the manner laid down by the law of the country of the witness or expert.

Article 29

The Court of Justice may order that a witness or expert be heard by the judicial authority of his place of permanent residence.

The order shall be sent for implementation to the competent judicial authority under conditions laid down in the Rules of Procedure. The documents drawn up in compliance with the letters roga-tory shall be returned to the Court under the same conditions.

The Court shall defray the expenses, without prejudice to the right to charge them, where appro-priate, to the parties.

Article 30

A Member State shall treat any violation of an oath by a witness or expert in the same manner as if the offence had been committed before one of its courts with jurisdiction in civil proceedings. At the instance of the Court of Justice, the Member State concerned shall prosecute the offender before its competent court.

Article 31

The hearing in court shall be public, unless the Court of Justice, of its own motion or on application by the parties, decides otherwise for serious reasons.

Article 32

During the hearings the Court of Justice may examine the experts, the witnesses and the par-ties themselves. The latter, however, may address the Court of Justice only through their representatives.

Article 33

Minutes shall be made of each hearing and signed by the President and the Registrar.

Article 34

The case list shall be established by the President.

Article 35

The deliberations of the Court of Justice shall be and shall remain secret.

Article 36

Judgments shall state the reasons on which they are based. They shall contain the names of the Judges who took part in the deliberations.

Article 37

Judgments shall be signed by the President and the Registrar. They shall be read in open court.

Article 38

The Court of Justice shall adjudicate upon costs.

Article 39

The President of the Court of Justice may, by way of summary procedure, which may, in so far as necessary, differ from some of the rules contained in this Statute and which shall be laid down in the Rules of Procedure, adjudicate upon applications to suspend execution, as provided for in Article 278 of the Treaty on the Functioning of the European Union and Article 157 of the EAEC Treaty, or to prescribe interim measures pursuant to Article 279 of the Treaty on the Functioning of the European Union, or to suspend enforcement in accordance with the fourth paragraph of Article 299 of the Treaty on the Functioning of the European Union or the third paragraph of Article 164 of the EAEC Treaty.

The powers referred to in the first paragraph may, under the conditions laid down in the Rules of Procedure, be exercised by the Vice-President of the Court of Justice.

Should the President and the Vice-President be prevented from attending, another Judge shall take their place under the conditions laid down in the Rules of Procedure.

The ruling of the President or of the Judge replacing him shall be provisional and shall in no way prejudice the decision of the Court on the substance of the case.

Article 40

Member States and institutions of the Union may intervene in cases before the Court of Justice.

The same right shall be open to the bodies, offices and agencies of the Union and to any other person which can establish an interest in the result of a case submitted to the Court. Natural or legal persons shall not intervene in cases between Member States, between institutions of the Union or between Member States and institutions of the Union.

Without prejudice to the second paragraph, the States, other than the Member States, which are parties to the Agreement on the European Economic Area, and also the EFTA Surveillance Authority referred to in that Agreement, may intervene in cases before the Court where one of the fields of application of that Agreement is concerned.

An application to intervene shall be limited to supporting the form of order sought by one of the parties.

Article 41

Where the defending party, after having been duly summoned, fails to file written submissions in defence, judgment shall be given against that party by default. An objection may be lodged against the judgment within one month of it being notified. The objection shall not have the effect of staying enforcement of the judgment by default unless the Court of Justice decides otherwise.

Article 42

Member States, institutions, bodies, offices and agencies of the Union and any other natural or legal persons may, in cases and under conditions to be determined by the Rules of Procedure, institute third-party proceedings to contest a judgment rendered without their being heard, where the judgment is prejudicial to their rights.

Article 43

If the meaning or scope of a judgment is in doubt, the Court of Justice shall construe it on application by any party or any institution of the Union establishing an interest therein.

Article 44

An application for revision of a judgment may be made to the Court of Justice only on discovery of a fact which is of such a nature as to be a decisive factor, and which, when the judgment was given, was unknown to the Court and to the party claiming the revision.

The revision shall be opened by a judgment of the Court expressly recording the existence of a new fact, recognising that it is of such a character as to lay the case open to revision and declaring the application admissible on this ground.

No application for revision may be made after the lapse of 10 years from the date of the judgment.

Article 45

Periods of grace based on considerations of distance shall be determined by the Rules of Procedure.

No right shall be prejudiced in consequence of the expiry of a time limit if the party concerned proves the existence of unforeseeable circumstances or of *force majeure*.

Article 46

Proceedings against the Union in matters arising from non-contractual liability shall be barred after a period of five years from the occurrence of the event giving rise thereto. The period of limitation shall be interrupted if proceedings are instituted before the Court of Justice or if prior to such proceedings an application is made by the aggrieved party to the relevant institution of the Union. In the latter event the proceedings must be instituted within the period of two months provided for in Article 263 of the Treaty on the Functioning of the European Union; the provisions of the second paragraph of Article 265 of the Treaty on the Functioning of the European Union shall apply where appropriate.

This Article shall also apply to proceedings against the European Central Bank regarding non-contractual liability.

Title IV General Court

Article 47

The first paragraph of Article 9, Article 9a, Articles 14 and 15, the first, second, fourth and fifth paragraphs of Article 17 and Article 18 shall apply to the General Court and its members.

The fourth paragraph of Article 3 and Articles 10, 11 and 14 shall apply to the Registrar of the General Court *mutatis mutandis*.

Article 48*

The General Court shall consist of:
    (a) 40 Judges as from 25 December 2015;
    (b) 47 Judges as from 1 September 2016;
    (c) two Judges per Member State as from 1 September 2019.

Article 49

The Members of the General Court may be called upon to perform the task of an Advocate-General.

It shall be the duty of the Advocate-General, acting with complete impartiality and independence, to make, in open court, reasoned submissions on certain cases brought before the General Court in order to assist the General Court in the performance of its task.

The criteria for selecting such cases, as well as the procedures for designating the Advocates-General, shall be laid down in the Rules of Procedure of the General Court.

A Member called upon to perform the task of Advocate-General in a case may not take part in the judgment of the case.

Article 50

The General Court shall sit in chambers of three or five Judges. The Judges shall elect the Presidents of the chambers from among their number. The Presidents of the chambers of five Judges shall be elected for three years. They may be re-elected once.

The composition of the chambers and the assignment of cases to them shall be governed by the Rules of Procedure. In certain cases governed by the Rules of Procedure, the General Court may sit as a full court or be constituted by a single Judge.

The Rules of Procedure may also provide that the General Court may sit in a Grand Chamber in cases and under the conditions specified therein.

Article 50a

    1. The General Court shall exercise at first instance jurisdiction in disputes between the Union and its servants as referred to in Article 270 of the Treaty on the Functioning of the European Union, including disputes between all institutions, bodies, offices or agencies, on the one hand, and their

---

* **Editor's Note:** The details of the appointment process and terms of office are contained within Articles 2 and 3 of the amending Regulation.

servants, on the other, in respect of which jurisdiction is conferred on the Court of Justice of the European Union.

2. At all stages of the procedure, including the time when the application is filed, the General Court may examine the possibilities of an amicable settlement of the dispute and may try to facilitate such settlement.

Article 51

By way of derogation from the rule laid down in Article 256(1) of the Treaty on the Functioning of the European Union, jurisdiction shall be reserved to the Court of Justice:

> (a) in actions referred to in Articles 263 and 265 of the Treaty on the Functioning of the European Union which are brought by a Member State against:
>> (i) a legislative act, an act of the European Parliament, of the European Council or of the Council, or against a failure to act by one or more of those institutions, except for:
>>> – decisions taken by the Council under the third subparagraph of Article 108(2) of the Treaty on the Functioning of the European Union,
>>> – acts of the Council adopted pursuant to a Council regulation concerning measures to protect trade within the meaning of Article 207 of the Treaty on the Functioning of the European Union,
>>> – acts of the Council by which the Council exercises implementing powers in accordance with Article 291(2) of the Treaty on the Functioning of the European Union;
>> (ii) an act of, or a failure to act by, the Commission under Article 331(1) of the Treaty on the Functioning of the European Union;
> (b) in actions referred to in Articles 263 and 265 of the Treaty on the Functioning of the European Union which are brought by an institution of the Union against a legislative act, an act of the European Parliament, of the European Council, of the Council, of the Commission or of the European Central Bank, or against a failure to act by one or more of those institutions;
> (c) in actions referred to in Article 263 of the Treaty on the Functioning of the European Union which are brought by a Member State against an act of the Commission relating to a failure to comply with a judgment delivered by the Court under the second subparagraph of Article 260(2), or the second subparagraph of Article 260(3), of the Treaty on the Functioning of the European Union.

Article 52

The President of the Court of Justice and the President of the General Court shall determine, by common accord, the conditions under which officials and other servants attached to the Court of Justice shall render their services to the General Court to enable it to function. Certain officials or other servants shall be responsible to the Registrar of the General Court under the authority of the President of the General Court.

Article 53

The procedure before the General Court shall be governed by Title III.

Such further and more detailed provisions as may be necessary shall be laid down in its Rules of Procedure. The Rules of Procedure may derogate from the fourth paragraph of Article 40 and from Article 41 in order to take account of the specific features of litigation in the field of intellectual property.

Notwithstanding the fourth paragraph of Article 20, the Advocate-General may make his reasoned submissions in writing.

Article 54

Where an application or other procedural document addressed to the General Court is lodged by mistake with the Registrar of the Court of Justice, it shall be transmitted immediately by that Registrar to the Registrar of the General Court; likewise, where an application or other procedural document addressed to the Court of Justice is lodged by mistake with the Registrar of the General Court, it shall be transmitted immediately by that Registrar to the Registrar of the Court of Justice.

Where the General Court finds that it does not have jurisdiction to hear and determine an action in respect of which the Court of Justice has jurisdiction, it shall refer that action to the Court of Justice; likewise, where the Court of Justice finds that an action falls within the jurisdiction of the General Court, it shall refer that action to the General Court, whereupon that Court may not decline jurisdiction.

Where the Court of Justice and the General Court are seised of cases in which the same relief is sought, the same issue of interpretation is raised or the validity of the same act is called in question, the General Court may, after hearing the parties, stay the proceedings before it until such time as the Court of Justice has delivered judgment or, where the action is one brought pursuant to Article 263 of the Treaty on the Functioning of the European Union, may decline jurisdiction so as to allow the Court of Justice to rule on such actions. In the same circumstances, the Court of Justice may also decide to stay the proceedings before it; in that event, the proceedings before the General Court shall continue.

Where a Member State and an institution of the Union are challenging the same act, the General Court shall decline jurisdiction so that the Court of Justice may rule on those applications.

Article 55

Final decisions of the General Court, decisions disposing of the substantive issues in part only or disposing of a procedural issue concerning a plea of lack of competence or inadmissibility, shall be notified by the Registrar of the General Court to all parties as well as all Member States and the institutions of the Union even if they did not intervene in the case before the General Court.

Article 56

An appeal may be brought before the Court of Justice, within two months of the notification of the decision appealed against, against final decisions of the General Court and decisions of that Court disposing of the substantive issues in part only or disposing of a procedural issue concerning a plea of lack of competence or inadmissibility.

Such an appeal may be brought by any party which has been unsuccessful, in whole or in part, in its submissions. However, interveners other than the Member States and the institutions of the Union may bring such an appeal only where the decision of the General Court directly affects them.

With the exception of cases relating to disputes between the Union and its servants, an appeal may also be brought by Member States and institutions of the Union which did not intervene in the proceedings before the General Court. Such Member States and institutions shall be in the same position as Member States or institutions which intervened at first instance.

Article 57

Any person whose application to intervene has been dismissed by the General Court may appeal to the Court of Justice within two weeks from the notification of the decision dismissing the application.

The parties to the proceedings may appeal to the Court of Justice against any decision of the General Court made pursuant to Article 278 or Article 279 or the fourth paragraph of Article 299 of the Treaty on the Functioning of the European Union or Article 157 or the third paragraph of Article 164 of the EAEC Treaty within two months from their notification.

The appeal referred to in the first two paragraphs of this Article shall be heard and determined under the procedure referred to in Article 39.

Article 58

An appeal to the Court of Justice shall be limited to points of law. It shall lie on the grounds of lack of competence of the General Court, a breach of procedure before it which adversely affects the interests of the appellant as well as the infringement of Union law by the General Court.

No appeal shall lie regarding only the amount of the costs or the party ordered to pay them.

Article 58a

An appeal brought against a decision of the General Court concerning a decision of an independent board of appeal of one of the following offices and agencies of the Union shall not proceed unless the Court of Justice first decides that it should be allowed to do so:

    (a) the European Union Intellectual Property Office;

    (b) the Community Plant Variety Office;

    (c) the European Chemicals Agency;

    (d) the European Union Aviation Safety Agency.

The procedure referred to in the first paragraph shall also apply to appeals brought against decisions of the General Court concerning a decision of an independent board of appeal, set up after 1 May 2019 within any other office or agency of the Union, which has to be seised before an action can be brought before the General Court.

An appeal shall be allowed to proceed, wholly or in part, in accordance with the detailed rules set out in the Rules of Procedure, where it raises an issue that is significant with respect to the unity, consistency or development of Union law.

The decision as to whether the appeal should be allowed to proceed or not shall be reasoned, and it shall be published.

Article 59

Where an appeal is brought against a decision of the General Court, the procedure before the Court of Justice shall consist of a written part and an oral part. In accordance with conditions laid down in the Rules of Procedure, the Court of Justice, having heard the Advocate-General and the parties, may dispense with the oral procedure.

Article 60

Without prejudice to Articles 278 and 279 of the Treaty on the Functioning of the European Union or Article 157 of the EAEC Treaty, an appeal shall not have suspensory effect.

By way of derogation from Article 280 of the Treaty on the Functioning of the European Union, decisions of the General Court declaring a regulation to be void shall take effect only as from the date of expiry of the period referred to in the first paragraph of Article 56 of this Statute or, if an appeal shall have been brought within that period, as from the date of dismissal of the appeal, without prejudice, however, to the right of a party to apply to the Court of Justice, pursuant to Articles 278 and 279 of the Treaty on the Functioning of the European Union or Article 157 of the EAEC Treaty, for the suspension of the effects of the regulation which has been declared void or for the prescription of any other interim measure.

Article 61

If the appeal is well founded, the Court of Justice shall quash the decision of the General Court. It may itself give final judgment in the matter, where the state of the proceedings so permits, or refer the case back to the General Court for judgment.

Where a case is referred back to the General Court, that Court shall be bound by the decision of the Court of Justice on points of law.

When an appeal brought by a Member State or an institution of the Union, which did not intervene in the proceedings before the General Court, is well founded, the Court of Justice may, if it considers this necessary, state which of the effects of the decision of the General Court which has been quashed shall be considered as definitive in respect of the parties to the litigation.

Article 62

In the cases provided for in Article 256(2) and (3) of the Treaty on the Functioning of the European Union, where the First Advocate-General considers that there is a serious risk of the unity or consistency of Union law being affected, he may propose that the Court of Justice review the decision of the General Court.

The proposal must be made within one month of delivery of the decision by the General Court. Within one month of receiving the proposal made by the First Advocate-General, the Court of Justice shall decide whether or not the decision should be reviewed.

Article 62a

The Court of Justice shall give a ruling on the questions which are subject to review by means of an urgent procedure on the basis of the file forwarded to it by the General Court.

Those referred to in Article 23 of this Statute and, in the cases provided for in Article 256(2) of the EC Treaty, the parties to the proceedings before the General Court shall be entitled to lodge statements or written observations with the Court of Justice relating to questions which are subject to review within a period prescribed for that purpose.

The Court of Justice may decide to open the oral procedure before giving a ruling.

Article 62b

In the cases provided for in Article 256(2) of the Treaty on the Functioning of the European Union, without prejudice to Articles 278 and 279 of the Treaty on the Functioning of the European Union, proposals for review and decisions to open the review procedure shall not have suspensory effect. If the Court of Justice finds that the decision of the General Court affects the unity or consistency of Union law, it shall refer the case back to the General Court which shall be bound by the points of law decided by the Court of Justice; the Court of Justice may state which of the effects of the decision of the General Court are to be considered as definitive in respect of the parties to the litigation. If, however, having regard to the result of the review, the outcome of the proceedings flows from the findings of fact on which the decision of the General Court was based, the Court of Justice shall give final judgment.

In the cases provided for in Article 256(3) of the Treaty on the Functioning of the European Union, in the absence of proposals for review or decisions to open the review procedure, the answer(s) given by the General Court to the questions submitted to it shall take effect upon expiry of the periods prescribed for that purpose in the second paragraph of Article 62. Should a review procedure be opened, the answer(s) subject to review shall take effect following that procedure, unless the Court of Justice decides otherwise. If the Court of Justice finds that the decision of the General Court affects the unity or consistency of Union law, the answer given by the Court of Justice to the questions subject to review shall be substituted for that given by the General Court.

Title IVa Specialised courts

Article 62c

The provisions relating to the jurisdiction, composition, organisation and procedure of any specialised court established under Article 257 of the Treaty on the Functioning of the European Union shall be contained in an Annex to this Statute.

Title V Final provisions

Article 63

The Rules of Procedure of the Court of Justice and of the General Court shall contain any provisions necessary for applying and, where required, supplementing this Statute.

Article 64

The rules governing the language arrangements applicable at the Court of Justice of the European Union shall be laid down by a regulation of the Council acting unanimously. This regulation shall be adopted either at the request of the Court of Justice and after consultation of the Commission and the European Parliament, or on a proposal from the Commission and after consultation of the Court of Justice and of the European Parliament.

Until those rules have been adopted, the provisions of the Rules of Procedure of the Court of Justice and of the Rules of Procedure of the General Court governing language arrangements shall continue to apply. By way of derogation from Articles 253 and 254 of the Treaty on the Functioning of the European Union, those provisions may only be amended or repealed with the unanimous consent of the Council.

Protocol (No 6) on the Location of the Seats of the Institutions and of Certain Bodies, Offices, Agencies and Departments of the European Union

THE REPRESENTATIVES OF THE GOVERNMENTS OF THE MEMBER STATES,

HAVING REGARD to Article 341 of the Treaty on the Functioning of the European Union and Article 189 of the Treaty establishing the European Atomic Energy Community,

RECALLING AND CONFIRMING the Decision of 8 April 1965, and without prejudice to the decisions concerning the seat of future institutions, bodies, offices, agencies and departments,

HAVE AGREED UPON the following provisions, which shall be annexed to the Treaty on European Union and to the Treaty on the Functioning of the European Union, and to the Treaty establishing the European Atomic Energy Community:

Sole Article

(a) The European Parliament shall have its seat in Strasbourg where the 12 periods of monthly plenary sessions, including the budget session, shall be held. The periods of additional plenary sessions shall be held in Brussels. The committees of the European Parliament shall meet in Brussels. The General Secretariat of the European Parliament and its departments shall remain in Luxembourg.

(b) The Council shall have its seat in Brussels. During the months of April, June and October, the Council shall hold its meetings in Luxembourg.

(c) The Commission shall have its seat in Brussels. The departments listed in Articles 7, 8 and 9 of the Decision of 8 April 1965 shall be established in Luxembourg.

(d) The Court of Justice of the European Union shall have its seat in Luxembourg.

(e) The Court of Auditors shall have its seat in Luxembourg.

(f) The Economic and Social Committee shall have its seat in Brussels.

(g) The Committee of the Regions shall have its seat in Brussels.

(h) The European Investment Bank shall have its seat in Luxembourg.

(i) The European Central Bank shall have its seat in Frankfurt.

(j) The European Police Office (Europol) shall have its seat in The Hague.

Protocol (No 8) Relating to Article 6(2) of the Treaty on European Union on the Accession of the Union to the European Convention on the Protection of Human Rights and Fundamental Freedoms

THE HIGH CONTRACTING PARTIES,

HAVE AGREED UPON the following provisions, which shall be annexed to the Treaty on European Union and to the Treaty on the Functioning of the European Union:

Article 1

The agreement relating to the accession of the Union to the European Convention on the Protection of Human Rights and Fundamental Freedoms (hereinafter referred to as the 'European Convention') provided for in Article 6(2) of the Treaty on European Union shall make provision for preserving the specific characteristics of the Union and Union law, in particular with regard to:

(a) the specific arrangements for the Union's possible participation in the control bodies of the European Convention;

(b) the mechanisms necessary to ensure that proceedings by non-Member States and individual applications are correctly addressed to Member States and/or the Union as appropriate.

Article 2

The agreement referred to in Article 1 shall ensure that accession of the Union shall not affect the competences of the Union or the powers of its institutions. It shall ensure that nothing therein affects the situation of Member States in relation to the European Convention, in particular in relation to the Protocols thereto, measures taken by Member States derogating from the European Convention in accordance with Article 15 thereof and reservations to the European Convention made by Member States in accordance with Article 57 thereof.

Article 3

Nothing in the agreement referred to in Article 1 shall affect Article 344 of the Treaty on the Functioning of the European Union.

Protocol (No 25) on the Exercise of Shared Competence

THE HIGH CONTRACTING PARTIES,

HAVE AGREED UPON the following provisions, which shall be annexed to the Treaty on European Union and to the Treaty on the Functioning of the European Union:

Sole Article

With reference to Article 2 (2) of the Treaty on the Functioning of the European Union on shared competence, when the Union has taken action in a certain area, the scope of this exercise of competence only covers those elements governed by the Union act in question and therefore does not cover the whole area.

Protocol (No 30) on the Application of the Charter of Fundamental Rights of the European Union to Poland and to the United Kingdom

THE HIGH CONTRACTING PARTIES,

WHEREAS in Article 6 of the Treaty on European Union, the Union recognises the rights, freedoms and principles set out in the Charter of Fundamental Rights of the European Union,

WHEREAS the Charter is to be applied in strict accordance with the provisions of the aforementioned Article 6 and Title VII of the Charter itself,

WHEREAS the aforementioned Article 6 requires the Charter to be applied and interpreted by the courts of Poland and of the United Kingdom strictly in accordance with the explanations referred to in that Article,

WHEREAS the Charter contains both rights and principles,

WHEREAS the Charter contains both provisions which are civil and political in character and those which are economic and social in character,

WHEREAS the Charter reaffirms the rights, freedoms and principles recognised in the Union and makes those rights more visible, but does not create new rights or principles,

RECALLING the obligations devolving upon Poland and the United Kingdom under the Treaty on European Union, the Treaty on the Functioning of the European Union, and Union law generally,

NOTING the wish of Poland and the United Kingdom to clarify certain aspects of the application of the Charter,

DESIROUS therefore of clarifying the application of the Charter in relation to the laws and administrative action of Poland and of the United Kingdom and of its justiciability within Poland and within the United Kingdom,

REAFFIRMING that references in this Protocol to the operation of specific provisions of the Charter are strictly without prejudice to the operation of other provisions of the Charter,

REAFFIRMING that this Protocol is without prejudice to the application of the Charter to other Member States,

REAFFIRMING that this Protocol is without prejudice to other obligations devolving upon Poland and the United Kingdom under the Treaty on European Union, the Treaty on the Functioning of the European Union, and Union law generally,

HAVE AGREED UPON the following provisions, which shall be annexed to the Treaty on European Union and to the Treaty on the Functioning of the European Union:

Article 1

1. The Charter does not extend the ability of the Court of Justice of the European Union, or any court or tribunal of Poland or of the United Kingdom, to find that the laws, regulations or administrative provisions, practices or action of Poland or of the United Kingdom are inconsistent with the fundamental rights, freedoms and principles that it reaffirms.

2. In particular, and for the avoidance of doubt, nothing in Title IV of the Charter creates justiciable rights applicable to Poland or the United Kingdom except in so far as Poland or the United Kingdom has provided for such rights in its national law.

Article 2

To the extent that a provision of the Charter refers to national laws and practices, it shall only apply to Poland or the United Kingdom to the extent that the rights or principles that it contains are recognised in the law or practices of Poland or of the United Kingdom.

Protocol (No 33) Concerning Article 157 of the Treaty on the Functioning of the European Union

THE HIGH CONTRACTING PARTIES,

HAVE AGREED UPON the following provision, which shall be annexed to the Treaty on European Union and to the Treaty on the Functioning of the European Union:

For the purposes of Article 157 of the Treaty on the Functioning of the European Union, benefits under occupational social security schemes shall not be considered as remuneration if and in so far as they are attributable to periods of employment prior to 17 May 1990, except in the case of workers or those claiming under them who have before that date initiated legal proceedings or introduced an equivalent claim under the applicable national law.

Protocol on the concerns of the Irish people on the Treaty of Lisbon*

THE HIGH CONTRACTING PARTIES,

RECALLING the Decision of the Heads of State or Government of the 27 Member States of the European Union, meeting within the European Council, on 18–19 June 2009, on the concerns of the Irish people on the Treaty of Lisbon;

RECALLING the declaration of the Heads of State or Government, meeting within the European Council, on 18–19 June 2009, that they would, at the time of the conclusion of the next Accession Treaty, set out the provisions of that Decision in a Protocol to be attached, in accordance with their respective constitutional requirements, to the Treaty on European Union and the Treaty on the Functioning of the European Union;

NOTING the signature by the High Contracting Parties of the Treaty between the High Contracting Parties and the Republic of Croatia concerning the accession of the Republic of Croatia to the European Union;

* (OJ 2013 L60/131) **Editor's Note:** See Decision 2013/272 confirming the agreement for one Commissioner for each state (OJ 2013 L165/98).

HAVE AGREED UPON the following provisions, which shall be annexed to the Treaty on European Union and to the Treaty on the Functioning of the European Union:

Title I Right to life, family and education

Article 1

Nothing in the Treaty of Lisbon attributing legal status to the Charter of Fundamental Rights of the European Union, or in the provisions of that Treaty in the area of Freedom, Security and Justice affects in any way the scope and applicability of the protection of the right to life in Article 40.3.1, 40.3.2 and 40.3.3, the protection of the family in Article 41 and the protection of the rights in respect of education in Articles 42 and 44.2.4 and 44.2.5 provided by the Constitution of Ireland.

Title II Taxation

Article 2

Nothing in the Treaty of Lisbon makes any change of any kind, for any Member State, to the extent or operation of the competence of the European Union in relation to taxation.

Title III Security and defence

Article 3

The Union's action on the international scene is guided by the principles of democracy, the rule of law, the universality and indivisibility of human rights and fundamental freedoms, respect for human dignity, the principles of equality and solidarity, and respect for the principles of the United Nations Charter and international law.

The Union's common security and defence policy is an integral part of the common foreign and security policy and provides the Union with an operational capacity to undertake missions outside the Union for peace-keeping, conflict prevention and strengthening international security in accordance with the principles of the United Nations Charter.

It does not prejudice the security and defence policy of each Member State, including Ireland, or the obligations of any Member State.

The Treaty of Lisbon does not affect or prejudice Ireland's traditional policy of military neutrality.

It will be for Member States—including Ireland, acting in a spirit of solidarity and without prejudice to its traditional policy of military neutrality—to determine the nature of aid or assistance to be provided to a Member State which is the object of a terrorist attack or the victim of armed aggression on its territory.

Any decision to move to a common defence will require a unanimous decision of the European Council. It would be a matter for the Member States, including Ireland, to decide, in accordance with the provisions of the Treaty of Lisbon and with their respective constitutional requirements, whether or not to adopt a common defence.

Nothing in this Title affects or prejudices the position or policy of any other Member State on security and defence.

It is also a matter for each Member State to decide, in accordance with the provisions of the Treaty of Lisbon and any domestic legal requirements, whether to participate in permanent structured cooperation or the European Defence Agency.

The Treaty of Lisbon does not provide for the creation of a European army or for conscription to any military formation.

It does not affect the right of Ireland or any other Member State to determine the nature and volume of its defence and security expenditure and the nature of its defence capabilities.

It will be a matter for Ireland or any other Member State, to decide, in accordance with any domestic legal requirements, whether or not to participate in any military operation.

Title IV Final provisions

Article 4

This Protocol shall remain open for signature by the High Contracting Parties until 30 June 2012.

This Protocol shall be ratified by the High Contracting Parties, and by the Republic of Croatia in the event that this Protocol has not entered into force by the date of accession of the Republic of Croatia to the European Union, in accordance with their respective constitutional requirements. The instruments of ratification shall be deposited with the Government of the Italian Republic.

This Protocol shall enter into force if possible on 30 June 2013, provided that all the instruments of ratification have been deposited, or, failing that, on the first day of the month following the deposit of the instrument of ratification by the last Member State to take this step.

Article 5

This Protocol, drawn up in a single original in the Bulgarian, Czech, Danish, Dutch, English, Estonian, Finnish, French, German, Greek, Hungarian, Irish, Italian, Latvian, Lithuanian, Maltese, Polish, Portuguese, Romanian, Slovak, Slovenian, Spanish and Swedish languages, each text being equally authentic, shall be deposited in the archives of the Government of the Italian Republic, which shall transmit a certified copy to each of the governments of the other Member States.

Once the Republic of Croatia has become bound by this Protocol pursuant to Article 2 of the Act concerning the conditions of accession of the Republic of Croatia, the Croatian text of this Protocol, which shall be equally authentic to the texts referred to in the first paragraph, shall also be deposited in the archives of the Government of the Italian Republic, which shall transmit a certified copy to each of the governments of the other Member States.

IN WITNESS WHEREOF, the undersigned Plenipotentiaries have signed this Protocol.
(Signatures omitted.)

Selected Declarations concerning provisions of the Treaties

1. Declaration concerning the Charter of Fundamental Rights of the European Union

The Charter of Fundamental Rights of the European Union, which has legally binding force, confirms the fundamental rights guaranteed by the European Convention for the Protection of Human Rights and Fundamental Freedoms and as they result from the constitutional traditions common to the Member States.

The Charter does not extend the field of application of Union law beyond the powers of the Union or establish any new power or task for the Union, or modify powers and tasks as defined by the Treaties.

2. Declaration on Article 6(2) of the Treaty on European Union

The Conference agrees that the Union's accession to the European Convention for the Protection of Human Rights and Fundamental Freedoms should be arranged in such a way as to preserve the specific features of Union law. In this connection, the Conference notes the existence of a regular dialogue between the Court of Justice of the European Union and the European Court of Human Rights; such dialogue could be reinforced when the Union accedes to that Convention.

7. Declaration on Article 16(4) of the Treaty on European Union and Article 238(2) of the Treaty on the Functioning of the European Union (Extracts)*

The Conference declares that the decision relating to the implementation of Article 16(4) of the Treaty on European Union and Article 238(2) of the Treaty on the Functioning of the European Union will be adopted by the Council on the date of the signature of the Treaty of Lisbon and will enter into force on the day that Treaty enters into force. The draft decision is set out below:

Draft decision of the Council relating to the implementation of Article 16(4) of the Treaty on European Union and Article 238(2) of the Treaty on the Functioning of the European Union between 1 November 2014 and 31 March 2017 on the one hand, and as from 1 April 2017 on the other

THE COUNCIL OF THE EUROPEAN UNION,

Whereas:

(1) Provisions should be adopted allowing for a smooth transition from the system for decision-making in the Council by a qualified majority as defined in Article 3(3) of the Protocol on the transitional provisions, which will continue to apply until 31 October 2014, to the voting system provided for in Article 16(4) of the Treaty on European Union and Article 238(2) of the Treaty on the Functioning of the European Union, which will apply with effect from 1 November 2014, including, during a transitional period until 31 March 2017, specific provisions laid down in Article 3(2) of that Protocol.

(2) It is recalled that it is the practice of the Council to devote every effort to strengthening the democratic legitimacy of decisions taken by a qualified majority,

HAS DECIDED AS FOLLOWS:

Section 1 (Omitted)

Section 2 Provisions to be applied as from 1 April 2017

Article 4
As from 1 April 2017, if members of the Council, representing:
1. at least 55 % of the population, or
2. at least 55 % of the number of Member States

necessary to constitute a blocking minority resulting from the application of Article 16(4), first subparagraph, of the Treaty on European Union or Article 238(2) of the Treaty on the Functioning of the European Union, indicate their opposition to the Council adopting an act by a qualified majority, the Council shall discuss the issue.

Article 5
The Council shall, in the course of these discussions, do all in its power to reach, within a reasonable time and without prejudicing obligatory time limits laid down by Union law, a satisfactory solution to address concerns raised by the members of the Council referred to in Article 4.

Article 6
To this end, the President of the Council, with the assistance of the Commission and in compliance with the Rules of Procedure of the Council, shall undertake any initiative necessary to facilitate a wider basis of agreement in the Council. The members of the Council shall lend him or her their assistance.

Section 3 Entry into force

Article 7
This Decision shall enter into force on the date of the entry into force of the Treaty of Lisbon.

---

* **Editor's Note:** Only the Section and Articles still relevant are included here.

17. Declaration concerning primacy

The Conference recalls that, in accordance with well settled case law of the Court of Justice of the European Union, the Treaties and the law adopted by the Union on the basis of the Treaties have primacy over the law of Member States, under the conditions laid down by the said case law.

The Conference has also decided to attach as an Annex to this Final Act the Opinion of the Council Legal Service on the primacy of EC law as set out in 11197/07 (JUR 260):

'Opinion of the Council Legal Service of 22 June 2007

It results from the case-law of the Court of Justice that primacy of EC law is a cornerstone principle of Community law. According to the Court, this principle is inherent to the specific nature of the European Community. At the time of the first judgment of this established case law (Costa/ENEL, 15 July 1964, Case 6/641[1]) there was no mention of primacy in the treaty. It is still the case today. The fact that the principle of primacy will not be included in the future treaty shall not in any way change the existence of the principle and the existing case-law of the Court of Justice.'

18. Declaration in relation to the delimitation of competences

The Conference underlines that, in accordance with the system of division of competences between the Union and the Member States as provided for in the Treaty on European Union and the Treaty on the Functioning of the European Union, competences not conferred upon the Union in the Treaties remain with the Member States.

When the Treaties confer on the Union a competence shared with the Member States in a specific area, the Member States shall exercise their competence to the extent that the Union has not exercised, or has decided to cease exercising, its competence. The latter situation arises when the relevant EU institutions decide to repeal a legislative act, in particular better to ensure constant respect for the principles of subsidiarity and proportionality. The Council may, at the initiative of one or several of its members (representatives of Member States) and in accordance with Article 241 of the Treaty on the Functioning of the European Union, request the Commission to submit proposals for repealing a legislative act. The Conference welcomes the Commission's declaration that it will devote particular attention to these requests.

Equally, the representatives of the governments of the Member States, meeting in an Intergovernmental Conference, in accordance with the ordinary revision procedure provided for in Article 48(2) to (5) of the Treaty on European Union, may decide to amend the Treaties upon which the Union is founded, including either to increase or to reduce the competences conferred on the Union in the said Treaties.

24. Declaration concerning the legal personality of the European Union

The Conference confirms that the fact that the European Union has a legal personality will not in any way authorise the Union to legislate or to act beyond the competences conferred upon it by the Member States in the Treaties.

---

[1] *'It follows (. . .) that the law stemming from the treaty, an independent source of law, could not, because of its special and original nature, be overridden by domestic legal provisions, however framed, without being deprived of its character as Community law and without the legal basis of the Community itself being called into question.'*

41. Declaration on Article 352 of the Treaty on the Functioning of the European Union

The Conference declares that the reference in Article 352(1) of the Treaty on the Functioning of the European Union to objectives of the Union refers to the objectives as set out in Article 3(2) and (3) of the Treaty on European Union and to the objectives of Article 3(5) of the said Treaty with respect to external action under Part Five of the Treaty on the Functioning of the European Union. It is therefore excluded that an action based on Article 352 of the Treaty on the Functioning of the European Union would only pursue objectives set out in Article 3(1) of the Treaty on European Union. In this connection, the Conference notes that in accordance with Article 31(1) of the Treaty on European Union, legislative acts may not be adopted in the area of the Common Foreign and Security Policy.

42. Declaration on Article 352 of the Treaty on the Functioning of the European Union

The Conference underlines that, in accordance with the settled case law of the Court of Justice of the European Union, Article 352 of the Treaty on the Functioning of the European Union, being an integral part of an institutional system based on the principle of conferred powers, cannot serve as a basis for widening the scope of Union powers beyond the general framework created by the provisions of the Treaties as a whole and, in particular, by those that define the tasks and the activities of the Union. In any event, this Article cannot be used as a basis for the adoption of provisions whose effect would, in substance, be to amend the Treaties without following the procedure which they provide for that purpose.

Additional legislation and agreements affecting the institutions

Majority voting procedure extract from the Luxembourg Accords

[EEC Bulletin 1966 No 3, p. 9]*

   I. Where, in the case of decisions which may be taken by majority vote on a proposal of the Commission, very important interests of one or more partners are at stake, the Members of the Council will endeavour, within a reasonable time, to reach solutions which can be adopted by all the Members of the Council while respecting their mutual interests and those of the Community, in accordance with Article 2 of the Treaty.

   II. With regard to the preceding paragraph, the French delegation considers that where very important interests are at stake the discussion must be continued until unanimous agreement is reached.

   III. The six delegations note that there is a divergence of views on what should be done in the event of a failure to reach complete agreement.

   IV. The six delegations nevertheless consider that this divergence does not prevent the Community's work being resumed in accordance with the normal procedure.

---

* **Editor's Note:** Permission to reproduce gratefully acknowledged but please note that 'Only European Community legislation printed in the paper edition of the *Official Journal of the European Union* is deemed authentic'.

Regulation (EC) No 1049/2001 of the European Parliament and of the Council of 30 May 2001 regarding public access to European Parliament, Council and Commission documents

[OJ 2001 L145/43]

THE EUROPEAN PARLIAMENT AND THE COUNCIL OF THE EUROPEAN UNION,

Having regard to the Treaty establishing the European Community, and in particular Article 255(2) thereof,

Having regard to the proposal from the Commission[1],

Acting in accordance with the procedure referred to in Article 251 of the Treaty[2],

Whereas:

(1) The second subparagraph of Article 1 of the Treaty on European Union enshrines the concept of openness, stating that the Treaty marks a new stage in the process of creating an ever closer union among the peoples of Europe, in which decisions are taken as openly as possible and as closely as possible to the citizen.

(2) Openness enables citizens to participate more closely in the decision-making process and guarantees that the administration enjoys greater legitimacy and is more effective and more accountable to the citizen in a democratic system. Openness contributes to strengthening the principles of democracy and respect for fundamental rights as laid down in Article 6 of the EU Treaty and in the Charter of Fundamental Rights of the European Union.

(3) The conclusions of the European Council meetings held at Birmingham, Edinburgh and Copenhagen stressed the need to introduce greater transparency into the work of the Union institutions. This Regulation consolidates the initiatives that the institutions have already taken with a view to improving the transparency of the decision-making process.

(4) The purpose of this Regulation is to give the fullest possible effect to the right of public access to documents and to lay down the general principles and limits on such access in accordance with Article 255(2) of the EC Treaty.

(5) Since the question of access of documents is not covered by provisions of the Treaty establishing the European Coal and Steel Community and the Treaty establishing the European Atomic Energy Community, the European Parliament, the Council and the Commission should, in accordance with Declaration No 41 attached to the Final Act of the Treaty of Amsterdam, draw guidance from this Regulation as regards documents concerning the activities covered by those two Treaties.

(6) Wider access should be granted to documents in cases where the institutions are acting in their legislative capacity, including under delegated powers, while at the same time preserving the effectiveness of the institutions' decision-making process. Such documents should be made directly accessible to the greatest possible extent.

(7) In accordance with Articles 28(1) and 41(1) of the EU Treaty, the right of access also applies to documents relating to the common foreign and security policy and to police and judicial cooperation in criminal matters. Each institution should respect its security rules.

(8) In order to ensure the full application of this Regulation to all activities of the Union, all agencies established by the institutions should apply the principles laid down in this Regulation.

(9) On account of their highly sensitive content, certain documents should be given special treatment. Arrangements for informing the European Parliament of the content of such documents should be made through interinstitutional agreement.

(10) In order to bring about greater openness in the work of the institutions, access to documents should be granted by the European Parliament, the Council and the Commission not only to documents drawn up by the institutions, but also to documents received by them. In this context, it

[1] OJ C 177 E, 27.6.2000, p. 70.

[2] Opinion of the European Parliament of 3 May 2001 (not yet published in the Official Journal) and Council Decision of 28 May 2001.

is recalled that Declaration No 35 attached to the Final Act of the Treaty of Amsterdam provides that a Member State may request the Commission or the Council not to communicate to third parties a document originating from that State without its prior agreement.

(11) In principle, all documents of the institutions should be accessible to the public. However, certain public and private interests should be protected by way of exceptions. The institutions should be entitled to protect their internal consultations and deliberations where necessary to safeguard their ability to carry out their tasks. In assessing the exceptions, the institutions should take account of the principles in Community legislation concerning the protection of personal data, in all areas of Union activities.

(12) All rules concerning access to documents of the institutions should be in conformity with this Regulation.

(13) In order to ensure that the right of access is fully respected, a two-stage administrative procedure should apply, with the additional possibility of court proceedings or complaints to the Ombudsman.

(14) Each institution should take the measures necessary to inform the public of the new provisions in force and to train its staff to assist citizens exercising their rights under this Regulation. In order to make it easier for citizens to exercise their rights, each institution should provide access to a register of documents.

(15) Even though it is neither the object nor the effect of this Regulation to amend national legislation on access to documents, it is nevertheless clear that, by virtue of the principle of loyal cooperation which governs relations between the institutions and the Member States, Member States should take care not to hamper the proper application of this Regulation and should respect the security rules of the institutions.

(16) This Regulation is without prejudice to existing rights of access to documents for Member States, judicial authorities or investigative bodies.

(17) In accordance with Article 255(3) of the EC Treaty, each institution lays down specific provisions regarding access to its documents in its rules of procedure. Council Decision 93/731/EC of 20 December 1993 on public access to Council documents[3], Commission Decision 94/90/ECSC, EC, Euratom of 8 February 1994 on public access to Commission documents[4], European Parliament Decision 97/632/EC, ECSC, Euratom of 10 July 1997 on public access to European Parliament documents[5], and the rules on confidentiality of Schengen documents should therefore, if necessary, be modified or be repealed,

HAVE ADOPTED THIS REGULATION:

Article 1 Purpose
The purpose of this Regulation is:
- (a) to define the principles, conditions and limits on grounds of public or private interest governing the right of access to European Parliament, Council and Commission (hereinafter referred to as 'the institutions') documents provided for in Article 255 of the EC Treaty in such a way as to ensure the widest possible access to documents,
- (b) to establish rules ensuring the easiest possible exercise of this right, and
- (c) to promote good administrative practice on access to documents.

Article 2 Beneficiaries and scope
1. Any citizen of the Union, and any natural or legal person residing or having its registered office in a Member State, has a right of access to documents of the institutions, subject to the principles, conditions and limits defined in this Regulation.

[3] OJ L 340, 31.12.1993, p. 43. Decision as last amended by Decision 2000/527/EC (OJ L 212, 23.8.2000, p. 9).
[4] OJ L 46, 18.2.1994, p. 58. Decision as amended by Decision 96/567/EC, ECSC, Euratom (OJ L 247, 28.9.1996, p. 45).
[5] OJ L 263, 25.9.1997, p. 27.

2. The institutions may, subject to the same principles, conditions and limits, grant access to documents to any natural or legal person not residing or not having its registered office in a Member State.

3. This Regulation shall apply to all documents held by an institution, that is to say, documents drawn up or received by it and in its possession, in all areas of activity of the European Union.

4. Without prejudice to Articles 4 and 9, documents shall be made accessible to the public either following a written application or directly in electronic form or through a register. In particular, documents drawn up or received in the course of a legislative procedure shall be made directly accessible in accordance with Article 12.

5. Sensitive documents as defined in Article 9(1) shall be subject to special treatment in accordance with that Article.

6. This Regulation shall be without prejudice to rights of public access to documents held by the institutions which might follow from instruments of international law or acts of the institutions implementing them.

Article 3   Definitions

For the purpose of this Regulation:
> (a) 'document' shall mean any content whatever its medium (written on paper or stored in electronic form or as a sound, visual or audiovisual recording) concerning a matter relating to the policies, activities and decisions falling within the institution's sphere of responsibility;
> (b) 'third party' shall mean any natural or legal person, or any entity outside the institution concerned, including the Member States, other Community or non-Community institutions and bodies and third countries.

Article 4   Exceptions

1. The institutions shall refuse access to a document where disclosure would undermine the protection of:
> (a) the public interest as regards:
>> – public security,
>> – defence and military matters,
>> – international relations,
>> – the financial, monetary or economic policy of the Community or a Member State;
> (b) privacy and the integrity of the individual, in particular in accordance with Community legislation regarding the protection of personal data.

2. The institutions shall refuse access to a document where disclosure would undermine the protection of:
> – commercial interests of a natural or legal person, including intellectual property,
> – court proceedings and legal advice,
> – the purpose of inspections, investigations and audits,

unless there is an overriding public interest in disclosure.

3. Access to a document, drawn up by an institution for internal use or received by an institution, which relates to a matter where the decision has not been taken by the institution, shall be refused if disclosure of the document would seriously undermine the institution's decision-making process, unless there is an overriding public interest in disclosure. Access to a document containing opinions for internal use as part of deliberations and preliminary consultations within the institution concerned shall be refused even after the decision has been taken if disclosure of the document would seriously undermine the institution's decision-making process, unless there is an overriding public interest in disclosure.

4. As regards third-party documents, the institution shall consult the third party with a view to assessing whether an exception in paragraph 1 or 2 is applicable, unless it is clear that the document shall or shall not be disclosed.

5. A Member State may request the institution not to disclose a document originating from that Member State without its prior agreement.

6. If only parts of the requested document are covered by any of the exceptions, the remaining parts of the document shall be released.

7. The exceptions as laid down in paragraphs 1 to 3 shall only apply for the period during which protection is justified on the basis of the content of the document. The exceptions may apply for a maximum period of 30 years. In the case of documents covered by the exceptions relating to privacy or commercial interests and in the case of sensitive documents, the exceptions may, if necessary, continue to apply after this period.

Article 5   Documents in the Member States

Where a Member State receives a request for a document in its possession, originating from an institution, unless it is clear that the document shall or shall not be disclosed, the Member State shall consult with the institution concerned in order to take a decision that does not jeopardise the attainment of the objectives of this Regulation. The Member State may instead refer the request to the institution.

Article 6   Applications

1. Applications for access to a document shall be made in any written form, including electronic form, in one of the languages referred to in Article 314 of the EC Treaty and in a sufficiently precise manner to enable the institution to identify the document. The applicant is not obliged to state reasons for the application.

2. If an application is not sufficiently precise, the institution shall ask the applicant to clarify the application and shall assist the applicant in doing so, for example, by providing information on the use of the public registers of documents.

3. In the event of an application relating to a very long document or to a very large number of documents, the institution concerned may confer with the applicant informally, with a view to finding a fair solution.

4. The institutions shall provide information and assistance to citizens on how and where applications for access to documents can be made.

Article 7   Processing of initial applications

1. An application for access to a document shall be handled promptly. An acknowledgement of receipt shall be sent to the applicant. Within 15 working days from registration of the application, the institution shall either grant access to the document requested and provide access in accordance with Article 10 within that period or, in a written reply, state the reasons for the total or partial refusal and inform the applicant of his or her right to make a confirmatory application in accordance with paragraph 2 of this Article.

2. In the event of a total or partial refusal, the applicant may, within 15 working days of receiving the institution's reply, make a confirmatory application asking the institution to reconsider its position.

3. In exceptional cases, for example, in the event of an application relating to a very long document or to a very large number of documents, the time-limit provided for in paragraph 1 may be extended by 15 working days, provided that the applicant is notified in advance and that detailed reasons are given.

4. Failure by the institution to reply within the prescribed time-limit shall entitle the applicant to make a confirmatory application.

Article 8   Processing of confirmatory applications

1. A confirmatory application shall be handled promptly. Within 15 working days from registration of such an application, the institution shall either grant access to the document requested and provide access in accordance with Article 10 within that period or, in a written reply, state the reasons for the total or partial refusal. In the event of a total or partial refusal, the institution

shall inform the applicant of the remedies open to him or her, namely instituting court proceedings against the institution and/or making a complaint to the Ombudsman, under the conditions laid down in Articles 230 and 195 of the EC Treaty, respectively.

2. In exceptional cases, for example, in the event of an application relating to a very long document or to a very large number of documents, the time limit provided for in paragraph 1 may be extended by 15 working days, provided that the applicant is notified in advance and that detailed reasons are given.

3. Failure by the institution to reply within the prescribed time limit shall be considered as a negative reply and entitle the applicant to institute court proceedings against the institution and/or make a complaint to the Ombudsman, under the relevant provisions of the EC Treaty.

Article 9   Treatment of sensitive documents

1. Sensitive documents are documents originating from the institutions or the agencies established by them, from Member States, third countries or International Organisations, classified as 'TRÈS SECRET/TOP SECRET', 'SECRET' or 'CONFIDENTIEL' in accordance with the rules of the institution concerned, which protect essential interests of the European Union or of one or more of its Member States in the areas covered by Article 4(1)(a), notably public security, defence and military matters.

2. Applications for access to sensitive documents under the procedures laid down in Articles 7 and 8 shall be handled only by those persons who have a right to acquaint themselves with those documents. These persons shall also, without prejudice to Article 11(2), assess which references to sensitive documents could be made in the public register.

3. Sensitive documents shall be recorded in the register or released only with the consent of the originator.

4. An institution which decides to refuse access to a sensitive document shall give the reasons for its decision in a manner which does not harm the interests protected in Article 4.

5. Member States shall take appropriate measures to ensure that when handling applications for sensitive documents the principles in this Article and Article 4 are respected.

6. The rules of the institutions concerning sensitive documents shall be made public.

7. The Commission and the Council shall inform the European Parliament regarding sensitive documents in accordance with arrangements agreed between the institutions.

Article 10   Access following an application

1. The applicant shall have access to documents either by consulting them on the spot or by receiving a copy, including, where available, an electronic copy, according to the applicant's preference. The cost of producing and sending copies may be charged to the applicant. This charge shall not exceed the real cost of producing and sending the copies. Consultation on the spot, copies of less than 20 A4 pages and direct access in electronic form or through the register shall be free of charge.

2. If a document has already been released by the institution concerned and is easily accessible to the applicant, the institution may fulfil its obligation of granting access to documents by informing the applicant how to obtain the requested document.

3. Documents shall be supplied in an existing version and format (including electronically or in an alternative format such as Braille, large print or tape) with full regard to the applicant's preference.

Article 11   Registers

1. To make citizens' rights under this Regulation effective, each institution shall provide public access to a register of documents. Access to the register should be provided in electronic form. References to documents shall be recorded in the register without delay.

2. For each document the register shall contain a reference number (including, where applicable, the interinstitutional reference), the subject matter and/or a short description of the content of the document and the date on which it was received or drawn up and recorded in the register.

References shall be made in a manner which does not undermine protection of the interests in Article 4.

3. The institutions shall immediately take the measures necessary to establish a register which shall be operational by 3 June 2002.

Article 12   Direct access in electronic form or through a register

1. The institutions shall as far as possible make documents directly accessible to the public in electronic form or through a register in accordance with the rules of the institution concerned.

2. In particular, legislative documents, that is to say, documents drawn up or received in the course of procedures for the adoption of acts which are legally binding in or for the Member States, should, subject to Articles 4 and 9, be made directly accessible.

3. Where possible, other documents, notably documents relating to the development of policy or strategy, should be made directly accessible.

4. Where direct access is not given through the register, the register shall as far as possible indicate where the document is located.

Article 13   Publication in the Official Journal

1. In addition to the acts referred to in Article 254(1) and (2) of the EC Treaty and the first paragraph of Article 163 of the Euratom Treaty, the following documents shall, subject to Articles 4 and 9 of this Regulation, be published in the Official Journal:

(a) Commission proposals;

(b) common positions adopted by the Council in accordance with the procedures referred to in Articles 251 and 252 of the EC Treaty and the reasons underlying those common positions, as well as the European Parliament's positions in these procedures;

(c) framework decisions and decisions referred to in Article 34(2) of the EU Treaty;

(d) conventions established by the Council in accordance with Article 34(2) of the EU Treaty;

(e) conventions signed between Member States on the basis of Article 293 of the EC Treaty;

(f) international agreements concluded by the Community or in accordance with Article 24 of the EU Treaty.

2. As far as possible, the following documents shall be published in the Official Journal:

(a) initiatives presented to the Council by a Member State pursuant to Article 67(1) of the EC Treaty or pursuant to Article 34(2) of the EU Treaty;

(b) common positions referred to in Article 34(2) of the EU Treaty;

(c) directives other than those referred to in Article 254(1) and (2) of the EC Treaty, decisions other than those referred to in Article 254(1) of the EC Treaty, recommendations and opinions.

3. Each institution may in its rules of procedure establish which further documents shall be published in the Official Journal.

Article 14   Information

1. Each institution shall take the requisite measures to inform the public of the rights they enjoy under this Regulation.

2. The Member States shall cooperate with the institutions in providing information to the citizens.

Article 15   Administrative practice in the institutions

1. The institutions shall develop good administrative practices in order to facilitate the exercise of the right of access guaranteed by this Regulation.

2. The institutions shall establish an interinstitutional committee to examine best practice, address possible conflicts and discuss future developments on public access to documents.

Article 16   Reproduction of documents

This Regulation shall be without prejudice to any existing rules on copyright which may limit a third party's right to reproduce or exploit released documents.

Article 17   Reports

1. Each institution shall publish annually a report for the preceding year including the number of cases in which the institution refused to grant access to documents, the reasons for such refusals and the number of sensitive documents not recorded in the register.

2. At the latest by 31 January 2004, the Commission shall publish a report on the implementation of the principles of this Regulation and shall make recommendations, including, if appropriate, proposals for the revision of this Regulation and an action programme of measures to be taken by the institutions.

Article 18   Application measures

1. Each institution shall adapt its rules of procedure to the provisions of this Regulation. The adaptations shall take effect from 3 December 2001.

2. Within six months of the entry into force of this Regulation, the Commission shall examine the conformity of Council Regulation (EEC, Euratom) No 354/83 of 1 February 1983 concerning the opening to the public of the historical archives of the European Economic Community and the European Atomic Energy Community[6] with this Regulation in order to ensure the preservation and archiving of documents to the fullest extent possible.

3. Within six months of the entry into force of this Regulation, the Commission shall examine the conformity of the existing rules on access to documents with this Regulation.

Article 19   Entry into force

This Regulation shall enter into force on the third day following that of its publication in the Official Journal of the European Communities. It shall be applicable from 3 December 2001.

This Regulation shall be binding in its entirety and directly applicable in all Member States.

Done at Brussels, 30 May 2001.

Joint declaration relating to Regulation 1049/2001 of the European Parliament and of the Council regarding public access to European Parliament, Council and Commission documents

[OJ 2001 L173/5]

1. The European Parliament, the Council and the Commission agree that the agencies and similar bodies created by the legislator should have rules on access to their documents which conform to those of this Regulation. To this effect, the European Parliament and the Council welcome the Commission's intention to propose, as soon as possible, amendments to the acts establishing the existing agencies and bodies and to include provisions in future proposals concerning the establishment of such agencies and bodies. They undertake to adopt the necessary acts rapidly.

2. The European Parliament, the Council and the Commission call on the institutions and bodies not covered by paragraph 1 to adopt internal rules on public access to documents which take account of the principles and limits in this Regulation.

---

[6] OJ L 43, 15.2.1983, p. 1.

Joint declaration on practical arrangements for the codecision procedure (Article 251 of the EC Treaty)

[OJ 2007 C145/02]

General principles

1. The European Parliament, the Council and the Commission, hereinafter referred to collectively as 'the institutions', note that current practice involving talks between the Council Presidency, the Commission and the chairs of the relevant committees and/or rapporteurs of the European Parliament and between the co-chairs of the Conciliation Committee has proved its worth.

2. The institutions confirm that this practice, which has developed at all stages of the codecision procedure, must continue to be encouraged. The institutions undertake to examine their working methods with a view to making even more effective use of the full scope of the codecision procedure as established by the EC Treaty.

3. This Joint Declaration clarifies these working methods, and the practical arrangements for pursuing them. It complements the Interinstitutional Agreement on Better Lawmaking[1] and notably its provisions relating to the co-decision procedure. The institutions undertake fully to respect such commitments in line with the principles of transparency, accountability and efficiency. In this respect, the institutions should pay particular attention to making progress on simplification proposals while respecting the acquis communautaire.

4. The institutions shall cooperate in good faith throughout the procedure with a view to reconciling their positions as far as possible and thereby clearing the way, where appropriate, for the adoption of the act concerned at an early stage of the procedure.

5. With that aim in view, they shall cooperate through appropriate interinstitutional contacts to monitor the progress of the work and analyse the degree of convergence at all stages of the codecision procedure.

6. The institutions, in accordance with their internal rules of procedure, undertake to exchange information regularly on the progress of codecision files. They shall ensure that their respective calendars of work are coordinated as far as possible in order to enable proceedings to be conducted in a coherent and convergent fashion. They will therefore seek to establish an indicative timetable for the various stages leading to the final adoption of different legislative proposals, while fully respecting the political nature of the decision-making process.

7. Cooperation between the institutions in the context of codecision often takes the form of tripartite meetings ('trilogues'). This trilogue system has demonstrated its vitality and flexibility in increasing significantly the possibilities for agreement at first and second reading stages, as well as contributing to the preparation of the work of the Conciliation Committee.

8. Such trilogues are usually conducted in an informal framework. They may be held at all stages of the procedure and at different levels of representation, depending on the nature of the expected discussion. Each institution, in accordance with its own rules of procedure, will designate its participants for each meeting, define its mandate for the negotiations and inform the other institutions of arrangements for the meetings in good time.

9. As far as possible, any draft compromise texts submitted for discussion at a forthcoming meeting shall be circulated in advance to all participants. In order to enhance transparency, trilogues taking place within the European Parliament and Council shall be announced, where practicable.

10. The Council Presidency will endeavour to attend the meetings of the parliamentary committees. It will carefully consider any request it receives to provide information related to the Council position, as appropriate.

---

[1] OJ C 321, 31.12.2003, p. 1.

FIRST READING

11. The institutions shall cooperate in good faith with a view to reconciling their positions as far as possible so that, wherever possible, acts can be adopted at first reading.

Agreement at the stage of first reading in the European Parliament

12. Appropriate contacts shall be established to facilitate the conduct of proceedings at first reading.

13. The Commission shall facilitate such contacts and shall exercise its right of initiative in a constructive manner with a view to reconciling the positions of the European Parliament and the Council, with due regard for the balance between the institutions and the role conferred on it by the Treaty.

14. Where an agreement is reached through informal negotiations in trilogues, the chair of Coreper shall forward, in a letter to the chair of the relevant parliamentary committee, details of the substance of the agreement, in the form of amendments to the Commission proposal. That letter shall indicate the Council's willingness to accept that outcome, subject to legal-linguistic verification, should it be confirmed by the vote in plenary. A copy of that letter shall be forwarded to the Commission.

15. In this context, where conclusion of a dossier at first reading is imminent, information on the intention to conclude an agreement should be made readily available as early as possible.

Agreement at the stage of Council common position

16. Where no agreement is reached at the European Parliament's first reading, contacts may be continued with a view to concluding an agreement at the common position stage.

17. The Commission shall facilitate such contacts and shall exercise its right of initiative in a constructive manner with a view to reconciling the positions of the European Parliament and the Council, with due regard for the balance between the institutions and the role conferred on it by the Treaty.

18. Where an agreement is reached at this stage, the chair of the relevant parliamentary committee shall indicate, in a letter to the chair of Coreper, his recommendation to the plenary to accept the Council common position without amendment, subject to confirmation of the common position by the Council and to legal-linguistic verification. A copy of the letter shall be forwarded to the Commission.

SECOND READING

19. In its statement of reasons, the Council shall explain as clearly as possible the reasons that led it to adopt its common position. During its second reading, the European Parliament shall take the greatest possible account of those reasons and of the Commission's position.

20. Before transmitting the common position, the Council shall endeavour to consider in consultation with the European Parliament and the Commission the date for its transmission in order to ensure the maximum efficiency of the legislative procedure at second reading.

Agreement at the stage of second reading in the European Parliament

21. Appropriate contacts will continue as soon as the Council common position is forwarded to the European Parliament, with a view to achieving a better understanding of the respective positions and thus to bringing the legislative procedure to a conclusion as quickly as possible.

22. The Commission shall facilitate such contacts and give its opinion with a view to reconciling the positions of the European Parliament and the Council, with due regard for the balance between the institutions and the role conferred on it by the Treaty.

23. Where an agreement is reached through informal negotiations in trilogues, the chair of Coreper shall forward, in a letter to the chair of the relevant parliamentary committee, details of the substance of the agreement, in the form of amendments to the Council common position. That

letter shall indicate the Council's willingness to accept that outcome, subject to legal-linguistic verification, should it be confirmed by the vote in plenary. A copy of that letter shall be forwarded to the Commission.

CONCILIATION

24. If it becomes clear that the Council will not be in a position to accept all the amendments of the European Parliament at second reading and when the Council is ready to present its position, a first trilogue will be organised. Each institution, in accordance with its own rules of procedure, will designate its participants for each meeting and define its mandate for the negotiations. The Commission will indicate to both delegations at the earliest possible stage its intentions with regard to its opinion on the European Parliament's second reading amendments.

25. Trilogues shall take place throughout the conciliation procedure with the aim of resolving outstanding issues and preparing the ground for an agreement to be reached in the Conciliation Committee. The results of the trilogues shall be discussed and possibly approved at the meetings of the respective institutions.

26. The Conciliation Committee shall be convened by the President of the Council, with the agreement of the President of the European Parliament and with due regard to the provisions of the Treaty.

27. The Commission shall take part in the conciliation proceedings and shall take all the necessary initiatives with a view to reconciling the positions of the European Parliament and the Council. Such initiatives may include, draft compromise texts having regard to the positions of the European Parliament and of the Council and with due regard for the role conferred upon the Commission by the Treaty.

28. The Conciliation Committee shall be chaired jointly by the President of the European Parliament and the President of the Council. Committee meetings shall be chaired alternately by each co-chair.

29. The dates and the agendas for the Conciliation Committee's meetings shall be set jointly by the co-chairs with a view to the effective functioning of the Conciliation Committee throughout the conciliation procedure. The Commission shall be consulted on the dates envisaged. The European Parliament and the Council shall set aside, for guidance, appropriate dates for conciliation proceedings and shall notify the Commission thereof.

30. The co-chairs may put several dossiers on the agenda of any one meeting of the Conciliation Committee. As well as the principal topic ('B-item'), where agreement has not yet been reached, conciliation procedures on other topics may be opened and/or closed without discussion on these items ('A-item').

31. While respecting the Treaty provisions regarding time-limits, the European Parliament and the Council shall, as far as possible, take account of scheduling requirements, in particular those resulting from breaks in the institutions' activities and from the European Parliament's elections. At all events, the break in activities shall be as short as possible.

32. The Conciliation Committee shall meet alternately at the premises of the European Parliament and the Council, with a view to an equal sharing of facilities, including interpretation facilities.

33. The Conciliation Committee shall have available to it the Commission proposal, the Council common position and the Commission's opinion thereon, the amendments proposed by the European Parliament and the Commission's opinion thereon, and a joint working document by the European Parliament and Council delegations. This working document should enable users to identify the issues at stake easily and to refer to them efficiently. The Commission shall, as a general rule, submit its opinion within three weeks of official receipt of the outcome of the European Parliament's vote and at the latest by the commencement of conciliation proceedings.

34. The co-chairs may submit texts for the Conciliation Committee's approval.

35. Agreement on a joint text shall be established at a meeting of the Conciliation Committee or, subsequently, by an exchange of letters between the co-chairs. Copies of such letters shall be forwarded to the Commission.

36. If the Conciliation Committee reaches agreement on a joint text, the text shall, after legal-linguistic finalisation, be submitted to the co-chairs for formal approval. However, in exceptional cases in order to respect the deadlines, a draft joint text may be submitted to the co-chairs for approval.

37. The co-chairs shall forward the approved joint text to the Presidents of the European Parliament and of the Council by means of a jointly signed letter. Where the Conciliation Committee is unable to agree on a joint text, the co-chairs shall notify the Presidents of the European Parliament and of the Council thereof in a jointly signed letter. Such letters shall serve as an official record. Copies of such letters shall be forwarded to the Commission for information. The working documents used during the conciliation procedure will be accessible in the Register of each institution once the procedure has been concluded.

38. The Secretariat of the European Parliament and the General-Secretariat of the Council shall act jointly as the Conciliation Committee's secretariat, in association with the Secretariat-General of the Commission.

GENERAL PROVISIONS

39. Should the European Parliament or the Council deem it essential to extend the time-limits referred to in Article 251 of the Treaty, they shall notify the President of the other institution and the Commission accordingly.

40. Where an agreement is reached at first or second reading, or during conciliation, the agreed text shall be finalised by the legal-linguistic services of the European Parliament and of the Council acting in close cooperation and by mutual agreement.

41. No changes shall be made to any agreed texts without the explicit agreement, at the appropriate level, of both the European Parliament and the Council.

42. Finalisation shall be carried out with due regard to the different procedures of the European Parliament and the Council, in particular with respect to deadlines for conclusion of internal procedures. The institutions undertake not to use the time-limits laid down for the legal-linguistic finalisation of acts to reopen discussions on substantive issues.

43. The European Parliament and the Council shall agree on a common presentation of the texts prepared jointly by those institutions.

44. As far as possible, the institutions undertake to use mutually acceptable standard clauses to be incorporated in the acts adopted under codecision in particular as regards provisions concerning the exercise of implementing powers (in accordance with the 'comitology' decision[2]), entry into force, transposition and the application of acts and respect for the Commission's right of initiative.

45. The institutions will endeavour to hold a joint press conference to announce the successful outcome of the legislative process at first or second reading or during conciliation. They will also endeavour to issue joint press releases.

46. Following adoption of a legislative act under the codecision procedure by the European Parliament and the Council, the text shall be submitted, for signature, to the President of the European Parliament and the President of the Council and to the Secretaries-General of those institutions.

47. The Presidents of the European Parliament and the Council shall receive the text for signature in their respective languages and shall, as far as possible, sign the text together at a joint ceremony to be organised on a monthly basis with a view to signing important acts in the presence of the media.

---

[2] Council Decision 1999/468/EC of 28 June 1999 laying down the procedures for the exercise of implementing powers conferred on the Commission (OJ L 184, 17.7.1999, p. 23). Decision as amended by Decision 2006/512/EC (OJ L 200, 27.7.2006, p. 11).

48. The jointly signed text shall be forwarded for publication in the *Official Journal of the European Union*. Publication shall normally follow within two months of the adoption of the legislative act by the European Parliament and the Council.

49. If one of the institutions identifies a clerical or obvious error in a text (or in one of the language versions thereof), it shall immediately notify the other institutions. If the error concerns an act that has not yet been adopted by either the European Parliament or the Council, the legal-linguistic services of the European Parliament and the Council shall prepare the necessary corrigendum in close cooperation.

Where this error concerns an act that has already been adopted by one or both of those institutions, whether published or not, the European Parliament and the Council shall adopt, by common agreement, a corrigendum drawn up under their respective procedures.

Done at Brussels, on the thirteenth day of June in the year two thousand and seven.
(Signatures omitted.)

Regulation (EU) No 182/2011 of the European Parliament and of the Council of 16 February 2011 laying down the rules and general principles concerning mechanisms for control by Member States of the Commission's exercise of implementing powers

[OJ 2011 L55/13]

THE EUROPEAN PARLIAMENT AND THE COUNCIL OF THE EUROPEAN UNION,

Having regard to the Treaty on the Functioning of the European Union, and in particular Article 291(3) thereof,

Having regard to the proposal from the Commission,

After transmission of the draft legislative act to the national parliaments,

Acting in accordance with the ordinary legislative procedure[1],

Whereas:

(1) Where uniform conditions for the implementation of legally binding Union acts are needed, those acts (hereinafter 'basic acts') are to confer implementing powers on the Commission, or, in duly justified specific cases and in the cases provided for in Articles 24 and 26 of the Treaty on European Union, on the Council.

(2) It is for the legislator, fully respecting the criteria laid down in the Treaty on the Functioning of the European Union ('TFEU'), to decide in respect of each basic act whether to confer implementing powers on the Commission in accordance with Article 291(2) of that Treaty.

(3) Hitherto, the exercise of implementing powers by the Commission has been governed by Council Decision 1999/468/EC[2].

(4) The TFEU now requires the European Parliament and the Council to lay down the rules and general principles concerning mechanisms for control by Member States of the Commission's exercise of implementing powers.

(5) It is necessary to ensure that the procedures for such control are clear, effective and proportionate to the nature of the implementing acts and that they reflect the institutional requirements of the TFEU as well as the experience gained and the common practice followed in the implementation of Decision 1999/468/EC.

---

[1] Position of the European Parliament of 16 December 2010 (not yet published in the Official Journal) and decision of the Council of 14 February 2011.

[2] OJ L 184, 17.7.1999, p. 23.

(6) In those basic acts which require the control of the Member States for the adoption by the Commission of implementing acts, it is appropriate, for the purposes of such control, that committees composed of the representatives of the Member States and chaired by the Commission be set up.

(7) Where appropriate, the control mechanism should include referral to an appeal committee which should meet at the appropriate level.

(8) In the interests of simplification, the Commission should exercise implementing powers in accordance with one of only two procedures, namely the advisory procedure or the examination procedure.

(9) In order to simplify further, common procedural rules should apply to the committees, including the key provisions relating to their functioning and the possibility of delivering an opinion by written procedure.

(10) Criteria should be laid down to determine the procedure to be used for the adoption of implementing acts by the Commission. In order to achieve greater consistency, the procedural requirements should be proportionate to the nature and impact of the implementing acts to be adopted.

(11) The examination procedure should in particular apply for the adoption of acts of general scope designed to implement basic acts and specific implementing acts with a potentially important impact. That procedure should ensure that implementing acts cannot be adopted by the Commission if they are not in accordance with the opinion of the committee, except in very exceptional circumstances, where they may apply for a limited period of time. The procedure should also ensure that the Commission is able to review the draft implementing acts where no opinion is delivered by the committee, taking into account the views expressed within the committee.

(12) Provided that the basic act confers implementing powers on the Commission relating to programmes with substantial budgetary implications or directed to third countries, the examination procedure should apply.

(13) The chair of a committee should endeavour to find solutions which command the widest possible support within the committee or the appeal committee and should explain the manner in which the discussions and suggestions for amendments have been taken into account. For that purpose, the Commission should pay particular attention to the views expressed within the committee or the appeal committee as regards draft definitive anti-dumping or countervailing measures.

(14) When considering the adoption of other draft implementing acts concerning particularly sensitive sectors, notably taxation, consumer health, food safety and protection of the environment, the Commission, in order to find a balanced solution, will, as far as possible, act in such a way as to avoid going against any predominant position which might emerge within the appeal committee against the appropriateness of an implementing act.

(15) The advisory procedure should, as a general rule, apply in all other cases or where it is considered more appropriate.

(16) It should be possible, where this is provided for in a basic act, to adopt implementing acts which are to apply immediately on imperative grounds of urgency.

(17) The European Parliament and the Council should be promptly informed of committee proceedings on a regular basis.

(18) Either the European Parliament or the Council should be able at any time to indicate to the Commission that, in its view, a draft implementing act exceeds the implementing powers provided for in the basic act, taking into account their rights relating to the review of the legality of Union acts.

(19) Public access to information on committee proceedings should be ensured in accordance with Regulation (EC) No 1049/2001 of the European Parliament and of the Council of 30 May 2001 regarding public access to European Parliament, Council and Commission documents[3].

(20) A register containing information on committee proceedings should be kept by the Commission. Consequently, rules relating to the protection of classified documents applicable to the Commission should also apply to the use of the register.

---

[3] OJ L 145, 31.5.2001, p. 43.

(21) Decision 1999/468/EC should be repealed. In order to ensure the transition between the regime provided for in Decision 1999/468/EC and this Regulation, any reference in existing legislation to the procedures provided for in that Decision should, with the exception of the regulatory procedure with scrutiny provided for in Article 5a thereof, be understood as a reference to the corresponding procedures provided for in this Regulation. The effects of Article 5a of Decision 1999/468/EC should be provisionally maintained for the purposes of existing basic acts which refer to that Article.

(22) The Commission's powers, as laid down by the TFEU, concerning the implementation of the competition rules are not affected by this Regulation,

HAVE ADOPTED THIS REGULATION:

Article 1   Subject-matter

This Regulation lays down the rules and general principles governing the mechanisms which apply where a legally binding Union act (hereinafter a 'basic act') identifies the need for uniform conditions of implementation and requires that the adoption of implementing acts by the Commission be subject to the control of Member States.

Article 2   Selection of procedures

1. A basic act may provide for the application of the advisory procedure or the examination procedure, taking into account the nature or the impact of the implementing act required.

2. The examination procedure applies, in particular, for the adoption of:
(a) implementing acts of general scope;
(b) other implementing acts relating to:
(i)   programmes with substantial implications;
(ii)   the common agricultural and common fisheries policies;
(iii) the environment, security and safety, or protection of the health or safety, of humans, animals or plants;
(iv)   the common commercial policy;
(v)   taxation.

3. The advisory procedure applies, as a general rule, for the adoption of implementing acts not falling within the ambit of paragraph 2. However, the advisory procedure may apply for the adoption of the implementing acts referred to in paragraph 2 in duly justified cases.

Article 3   Common provisions

1. The common provisions set out in this Article shall apply to all the procedures referred to in Articles 4 to 8.

2. The Commission shall be assisted by a committee composed of representatives of the Member States. The committee shall be chaired by a representative of the Commission. The chair shall not take part in the committee vote.

3. The chair shall submit to the committee the draft implementing act to be adopted by the Commission.

Except in duly justified cases, the chair shall convene a meeting not less than 14 days from submission of the draft implementing act and of the draft agenda to the committee. The committee shall deliver its opinion on the draft implementing act within a time limit which the chair may lay down according to the urgency of the matter. Time limits shall be proportionate and shall afford committee members early and effective opportunities to examine the draft implementing act and express their views.

4. Until the committee delivers an opinion, any committee member may suggest amendments and the chair may present amended versions of the draft implementing act.

The chair shall endeavour to find solutions which command the widest possible support within the committee. The chair shall inform the committee of the manner in which the discussions and suggestions for amendments have been taken into account, in particular as regards those suggestions which have been largely supported within the committee.

5. In duly justified cases, the chair may obtain the committee's opinion by written procedure. The chair shall send the committee members the draft implementing act and shall lay down a time limit for delivery of an opinion according to the urgency of the matter. Any committee member who does not oppose the draft implementing act or who does not explicitly abstain from voting thereon before the expiry of that time limit shall be regarded as having tacitly agreed to the draft implementing act.

Unless otherwise provided in the basic act, the written procedure shall be terminated without result where, within the time limit referred to in the first subparagraph, the chair so decides or a committee member so requests. In such a case, the chair shall convene a committee meeting within a reasonable time.

6. The committee's opinion shall be recorded in the minutes. Committee members shall have the right to ask for their position to be recorded in the minutes. The chair shall send the minutes to the committee members without delay.

7. Where applicable, the control mechanism shall include referral to an appeal committee.

The appeal committee shall adopt its own rules of procedure by a simple majority of its component members, on a proposal from the Commission.

Where the appeal committee is seised, it shall meet at the earliest 14 days, except in duly justified cases, and at the latest 6 weeks, after the date of referral. Without prejudice to paragraph 3, the appeal committee shall deliver its opinion within 2 months of the date of referral.

A representative of the Commission shall chair the appeal committee.

The chair shall set the date of the appeal committee meeting in close cooperation with the members of the committee, in order to enable Member States and the Commission to ensure an appropriate level of representation. By 1 April 2011, the Commission shall convene the first meeting of the appeal committee in order to adopt its rules of procedure.

Article 4   Advisory procedure

1. Where the advisory procedure applies, the committee shall deliver its opinion, if necessary by taking a vote. If the committee takes a vote, the opinion shall be delivered by a simple majority of its component members.

2. The Commission shall decide on the draft implementing act to be adopted, taking the utmost account of the conclusions drawn from the discussions within the committee and of the opinion delivered.

Article 5   Examination procedure

1. Where the examination procedure applies, the committee shall deliver its opinion by the majority laid down in Article 16(4) and (5) of the Treaty on European Union and, where applicable, Article 238(3) TFEU, for acts to be adopted on a proposal from the Commission. The votes of the representatives of the Member States within the committee shall be weighted in the manner set out in those Articles.

2. Where the committee delivers a positive opinion, the Commission shall adopt the draft implementing act.

3. Without prejudice to Article 7, if the committee delivers a negative opinion, the Commission shall not adopt the draft implementing act. Where an implementing act is deemed to be necessary, the chair may either submit an amended version of the draft implementing act to the same committee within 2 months of delivery of the negative opinion, or submit the draft implementing act within 1 month of such delivery to the appeal committee for further deliberation.

4. Where no opinion is delivered, the Commission may adopt the draft implementing act, except in the cases provided for in the second subparagraph. Where the Commission does not adopt the draft implementing act, the chair may submit to the committee an amended version thereof.

Without prejudice to Article 7, the Commission shall not adopt the draft implementing act where:

(a) that act concerns taxation, financial services, the protection of the health or safety of humans, animals or plants, or definitive multilateral safeguard measures;

(b) the basic act provides that the draft implementing act may not be adopted where no opinion is delivered; or

(c) a simple majority of the component members of the committee opposes it.

In any of the cases referred to in the second subparagraph, where an implementing act is deemed to be necessary, the chair may either submit an amended version of that act to the same committee within 2 months of the vote, or submit the draft implementing act within 1 month of the vote to the appeal committee for further deliberation.

5. By way of derogation from paragraph 4, the following procedure shall apply for the adoption of draft definitive anti-dumping or countervailing measures, where no opinion is delivered by the committee and a simple majority of its component members opposes the draft implementing act.

The Commission shall conduct consultations with the Member States. 14 days at the earliest and 1 month at the latest after the committee meeting, the Commission shall inform the committee members of the results of those consultations and submit a draft implementing act to the appeal committee. By way of derogation from Article 3(7), the appeal committee shall meet 14 days at the earliest and 1 month at the latest after the submission of the draft implementing act. The appeal committee shall deliver its opinion in accordance with Article 6. The time limits laid down in this paragraph shall be without prejudice to the need to respect the deadlines laid down in the relevant basic acts.

Article 6   Referral to the appeal committee

1. The appeal committee shall deliver its opinion by the majority provided for in Article 5(1).

2. Until an opinion is delivered, any member of the appeal committee may suggest amendments to the draft implementing act and the chair may decide whether or not to modify it.

The chair shall endeavour to find solutions which command the widest possible support within the appeal committee.

The chair shall inform the appeal committee of the manner in which the discussions and suggestions for amendments have been taken into account, in particular as regards suggestions for amendments which have been largely supported within the appeal committee.

3. Where the appeal committee delivers a positive opinion, the Commission shall adopt the draft implementing act.

Where no opinion is delivered, the Commission may adopt the draft implementing act.

Where the appeal committee delivers a negative opinion, the Commission shall not adopt the draft implementing act.

4. By way of derogation from paragraph 3, for the adoption of definitive multilateral safeguard measures, in the absence of a positive opinion voted by the majority provided for in Article 5(1), the Commission shall not adopt the draft measures.

5. By way of derogation from paragraph 1, until 1 September 2012, the appeal committee shall deliver its opinion on draft definitive anti-dumping or countervailing measures by a simple majority of its component members.

Article 7   Adoption of implementing acts in exceptional cases

By way of derogation from Article 5(3) and the second subparagraph of Article 5(4), the Commission may adopt a draft implementing act where it needs to be adopted without delay in order to avoid creating a significant disruption of the markets in the area of agriculture or a risk for the financial interests of the Union within the meaning of Article 325 TFEU.

In such a case, the Commission shall immediately submit the adopted implementing act to the appeal committee. Where the appeal committee delivers a negative opinion on the adopted implementing act, the Commission shall repeal that act immediately. Where the appeal committee delivers a positive opinion or no opinion is delivered, the implementing act shall remain in force.

Article 8   Immediately applicable implementing acts

1. By way of derogation from Articles 4 and 5, a basic act may provide that, on duly justified imperative grounds of urgency, this Article is to apply.

2. The Commission shall adopt an implementing act which shall apply immediately, without its prior submission to a committee, and shall remain in force for a period not exceeding 6 months unless the basic act provides otherwise.

3. At the latest 14 days after its adoption, the chair shall submit the act referred to in paragraph 2 to the relevant committee in order to obtain its opinion.

4. Where the examination procedure applies, in the event of the committee delivering a negative opinion, the Commission shall immediately repeal the implementing act adopted in accordance with paragraph 2.

5. Where the Commission adopts provisional anti-dumping or countervailing measures, the procedure provided for in this Article shall apply. The Commission shall adopt such measures after consulting or, in cases of extreme urgency, after informing the Member States. In the latter case, consultations shall take place 10 days at the latest after notification to the Member States of the measures adopted by the Commission.

Article 9   Rules of procedure

1. Each committee shall adopt by a simple majority of its component members its own rules of procedure on the proposal of its chair, on the basis of standard rules to be drawn up by the Commission following consultation with Member States. Such standard rules shall be published by the Commission in the *Official Journal of the European Union*.

In so far as may be necessary, existing committees shall adapt their rules of procedure to the standard rules.

2. The principles and conditions on public access to documents and the rules on data protection applicable to the Commission shall apply to the committees.

Article 10   Information on committee proceedings

1. The Commission shall keep a register of committee proceedings which shall contain:
   (a) a list of committees;
   (b) the agendas of committee meetings;
   (c) the summary records, together with the lists of the authorities and organisations to which the persons designated by the Member States to represent them belong;
   (d) the draft implementing acts on which the committees are asked to deliver an opinion;
   (e) the voting results;
   (f) the final draft implementing acts following delivery of the opinion of the committees;
   (g) information concerning the adoption of the final draft implementing acts by the Commission; and
   (h) statistical data on the work of the committees.

2. The Commission shall also publish an annual report on the work of the committees.

3. The European Parliament and the Council shall have access to the information referred to in paragraph 1 in accordance with the applicable rules.

4. At the same time as they are sent to the committee members, the Commission shall make available to the European Parliament and the Council the documents referred to in points (b), (d) and (f) of paragraph 1 whilst also informing them of the availability of such documents.

5. The references of all documents referred to in points (a) to (g) of paragraph 1 as well as the information referred to in paragraph 1(h) shall be made public in the register.

Article 11   Right of scrutiny for the European Parliament and the Council

Where a basic act is adopted under the ordinary legislative procedure, either the European Parliament or the Council may at any time indicate to the Commission that, in its view, a draft implementing act exceeds the implementing powers provided for in the basic act. In such a case, the Commission shall review the draft implementing act, taking account of the positions expressed, and shall inform the European Parliament and the Council whether it intends to maintain, amend or withdraw the draft implementing act.

Article 12   Repeal of Decision 1999/468/EC

Decision 1999/468/EC is hereby repealed.

The effects of Article 5a of Decision 1999/468/EC shall be maintained for the purposes of existing basic acts making reference thereto.

Article 13   Transitional provisions: adaptation of existing basic acts

1. Where basic acts adopted before the entry into force of this Regulation provide for the exercise of implementing powers by the Commission in accordance with Decision 1999/468/EC, the following rules shall apply:

    (a) where the basic act makes reference to Article 3 of Decision 1999/468/EC, the advisory procedure referred to in Article 4 of this Regulation shall apply;

    (b) where the basic act makes reference to Article 4 of Decision 1999/468/EC, the examination procedure referred to in Article 5 of this Regulation shall apply, with the exception of the second and third subparagraphs of Article 5(4);

    (c) where the basic act makes reference to Article 5 of Decision 1999/468/EC, the examination procedure referred to in Article 5 of this Regulation shall apply and the basic act shall be deemed to provide that, in the absence of an opinion, the Commission may not adopt the draft implementing act, as envisaged in point (b) of the second subparagraph of Article 5(4);

    (d) where the basic act makes reference to Article 6 of Decision 1999/468/EC, Article 8 of this Regulation shall apply;

    (e) where the basic act makes reference to Articles 7 and 8 of Decision 1999/468/EC, Articles 10 and 11 of this Regulation shall apply.

2. Articles 3 and 9 of this Regulation shall apply to all existing committees for the purposes of paragraph 1.

3. Article 7 of this Regulation shall apply only to existing procedures which make reference to Article 4 of Decision 1999/468/EC.

4. The transitional provisions laid down in this Article shall not prejudge the nature of the acts concerned.

Article 14   Transitional arrangement

This Regulation shall not affect pending procedures in which a committee has already delivered its opinion in accordance with Decision 1999/468/EC.

Article 15   Review

By 1 March 2016, the Commission shall present a report to the European Parliament and the Council on the implementation of this Regulation, accompanied, if necessary, by appropriate legislative proposals.

Article 16   Entry into force

This Regulation shall enter into force on 1 March 2011.

This Regulation is binding in its entirety and directly applicable in all Member States.

Done at Strasbourg, 16 February 2011.
For the European Parliament
The President
J. BUZEK
For the Council
The President
MARTONYI J.

RECOMMENDATIONS to national courts and tribunals, in relation to the initiation of preliminary ruling proceedings

(2019/C380/01)*

Introduction

1. The reference for a preliminary ruling, provided for in Article 19(3)(b) of the Treaty on European Union ('TEU') and Article 267 of the Treaty on the Functioning of the European Union ('TFEU'), is a fundamental mechanism of EU law. It is designed to ensure the uniform interpretation and application of EU law within the European Union, by offering the courts and tribunals of the Member States a means of bringing before the Court of Justice of the European Union ('the Court') for a preliminary ruling questions concerning the interpretation of EU law or the validity of acts adopted by the institutions, bodies, offices or agencies of the Union.

2. The preliminary ruling procedure is based on close cooperation between the Court and the courts and tribunals of the Member States. In order to ensure that that procedure is fully effective, it is necessary to recall its essential characteristics and to provide further information to clarify the provisions of the rules of procedure relating, in particular, to the originator, subject matter and scope of a request for a preliminary ruling, as well as to the form and content of such a request. That information—which applies to all requests for a preliminary ruling (I)—is supplemented by provisions concerning requests for a preliminary ruling requiring particularly expeditious handling (II) and by an annex which summarises, by way of a reminder, all the elements that must be included in a request for a preliminary ruling.

I. Provisions which apply to all requests for a preliminary ruling

The originator of the request for a preliminary ruling

3. The jurisdiction of the Court to give a preliminary ruling on the interpretation or validity of EU law is exercised exclusively on the initiative of the national courts and tribunals, whether or not the parties to the main proceedings have expressed the wish that a question be referred to the Court. In so far as it is called upon to assume responsibility for the subsequent judicial decision, it is for the national court or tribunal before which a dispute has been brought—and for that court or tribunal alone—to determine, in the light of the particular circumstances of each case, both the need for a request for a preliminary ruling in order to enable it to deliver its decision and the relevance of the questions which it submits to the Court.

4. Status as a court or tribunal is interpreted by the Court as an autonomous concept of EU law. The Court takes account of a number of factors such as whether the body making the reference is established by law, whether it is permanent, whether its jurisdiction is compulsory, whether its procedure is *inter partes*, whether it applies rules of law and whether it is independent.

5. The courts and tribunals of the Member States may refer a question to the Court on the interpretation or validity of EU law where they consider that a decision of the Court on the question is necessary to enable them to give judgment (see second paragraph of Article 267 TFEU). A reference for a preliminary ruling may, inter alia, prove particularly useful when a question of interpretation is raised before the national court or tribunal that is new and of general interest for the uniform application of EU law, or where the existing case-law does not appear to provide the necessary guidance in a new legal context or set of facts.

---

* **Editor's Note:** This version of the Recommendations is the version from 2019, OJ 2019/C380/01.

6. Where a question is raised in the context of a case that is pending before a court or tribunal against whose decisions there is no judicial remedy under national law, that court or tribunal is nonetheless required to bring a request for a preliminary ruling before the Court (see third paragraph of Article 267 TFEU), unless there is already well-established case-law on the point or unless the correct interpretation of the rule of law in question admits of no reasonable doubt.

7. It follows, moreover, from settled case-law that although national courts and tribunals may reject pleas raised before them challenging the validity of acts of an institution, body, office or agency of the Union, the Court has exclusive jurisdiction to declare such acts invalid. When it has doubts about the validity of such an act, a court or tribunal of a Member State must therefore refer the matter to the Court, stating the reasons why it has such doubts.

The subject matter and scope of the request for a preliminary ruling

8. A request for a preliminary ruling must concern the interpretation or validity of EU law, not the interpretation of rules of national law or issues of fact raised in the main proceedings.

9. *The Court can give a preliminary ruling only if EU law applies to the case in the main proceedings.* It is essential, in that respect, that the referring court or tribunal set out all the relevant matters of fact and of law that have prompted it to consider that any provisions of EU law may be applicable in the case.

10. With regard to references for a preliminary ruling concerning the interpretation of the Charter of Fundamental Rights of the European Union, it must be noted that, under Article 51(1) of the Charter, the provisions of the Charter are addressed to the Member States only when they are implementing EU law. While the circumstances of such implementation can vary, it must nevertheless be clearly and unequivocally apparent from the request for a preliminary ruling that a rule of EU law other than the Charter is applicable to the case in the main proceedings. Since the Court has no jurisdiction to give a preliminary ruling where a legal situation does not come within the scope of EU law, any *provisions of the Charter* that may be relied upon by the referring court or tribunal *cannot, of themselves, form the basis for such jurisdiction.*

11. Lastly, although, in order to deliver its decision, the Court necessarily takes into account the legal and factual context of the dispute in the main proceedings, as defined by the referring court or tribunal in its request for a preliminary ruling, it does not itself apply EU law to that dispute. When ruling on the interpretation or validity of EU law, the Court makes every effort to give a reply which will be of assistance in resolving the dispute in the main proceedings, but it is for the referring court or tribunal to draw case-specific conclusions, if necessary by disapplying the rule of national law that has been held to be incompatible with EU law.

The appropriate stage at which to make a reference for a preliminary ruling

12. A national court or tribunal may submit a request for a preliminary ruling to the Court as soon as it finds that a ruling on the interpretation or validity of EU law is necessary to enable it to give judgment. It is that court or tribunal which is in fact in the best position to decide at what stage of the national proceedings such a request should be made.

13. Since, however, that request will serve as the basis of the proceedings before the Court and the Court must therefore have available to it all the information that will enable it both to assess whether it has jurisdiction to give a reply to the questions raised and, if so, to give a useful reply to those questions, it is necessary that a decision to make a reference for a preliminary ruling be taken when the national proceedings have reached a stage at which the referring court or tribunal is able to *define, in sufficient detail, the legal and factual context of the case in the main proceedings, and the legal issues which it raises.* In the interests of the proper administration of justice, it may also be appropriate for the reference to be made only after both sides have been heard.

The form and content of the request for a preliminary ruling

14. The request for a preliminary ruling may be in any form allowed by national law, but it should be borne in mind that that request serves as the basis of the proceedings before the Court and

is served on all the interested persons referred to in Article 23 of the Protocol on the Statute of the Court of Justice of the European Union ('the Statute') and, in particular, on all the Member States, with a view to obtaining any observations they may wish to make. Owing to the consequential need to translate it into all the official languages of the European Union, the request for a preliminary ruling should therefore be drafted simply, clearly and precisely by the referring court or tribunal, avoiding superfluous detail. As experience has shown, about 10 pages are often sufficient to set out adequately the legal and factual context of a request for a preliminary ruling and the grounds for making the reference to the Court.

15. The content of any request for a preliminary ruling is prescribed by Article 94 of the Rules of Procedure of the Court and is summarised, by way of a reminder, in the annex hereto. In addition to the text of the questions referred to the Court for a preliminary ruling, *the request for a preliminary ruling must contain*:

- a summary of the subject matter of the dispute in the main proceedings and the relevant findings of fact as determined by the referring court or tribunal, or, at the very least, an account of the facts on which the questions referred are based,
- the tenor of any national provisions applicable in the case and, where appropriate, the relevant national case-law, and
- a statement of the reasons which prompted the referring court or tribunal to inquire about the interpretation or validity of certain provisions of EU law, and the relationship between those provisions and the national legislation applicable to the main proceedings.

In the absence of one or more of the above, the Court may find it necessary, notably on the basis of Article 53(2) of the Rules of Procedure, to decline jurisdiction to give a preliminary ruling on the questions referred or dismiss the request for a preliminary ruling as inadmissible.

16. In its request for a preliminary ruling, the referring court or tribunal must provide the *precise references for the national provisions applicable to the facts of the dispute in the main proceedings and for the provisions of EU law* whose interpretation is sought or whose validity is challenged. Those references must, as far as possible, include both the exact title and date of adoption of the acts containing the provisions concerned and the publication references for those acts. When referring to case-law, the referring court or tribunal is also requested to mention the European Case Law Identifier (ECLI) of the decision concerned.

17. If it considers it necessary for the purpose of understanding the case, the referring court or tribunal may briefly set out the *main arguments of the parties to the main proceedings*. It should be borne in mind in that context that only the request for a preliminary ruling will be translated, not any annexes to that request.

18. The referring court or tribunal may also briefly state *its view on the answer to be given to the questions referred for a preliminary ruling*. That information may be useful to the Court, particularly where it is called upon to give a preliminary ruling in an expedited or urgent procedure.

19. Lastly, *the questions referred* to the Court for a preliminary ruling must appear *in a separate and clearly identified section of the order for reference*, preferably at the beginning or the end. It must be possible to understand them on their own terms, without it being necessary to refer to the statement of the grounds for the request.

20. In order to make the request for a preliminary ruling easier to read, it is essential that the Court receive it in typewritten form and that the pages and paragraphs of the order for reference be numbered. Handwritten requests for a preliminary ruling will not be processed by the Court.

Protection of personal data and anonymisation of the request for a preliminary ruling

21. In order to ensure optimal protection of personal data in the Court's handling of the case, service of the request for a preliminary ruling on the interested persons referred to in Article 23 of the Statute and the subsequent dissemination, in all official languages of the European Union, of the decision closing the proceedings, *the referring court or tribunal*—which alone has full knowledge of the file submitted to the Court—*is invited to anonymise the case by replacing, for example using initials or a combination of letters, the names of individuals* referred to in the request *and by redacting*

information that might enable them to be identified. Given the increasing use of new information technologies and, in particular, the use of search engines, any anonymisation effected after the request for a preliminary ruling has been served on the interested persons referred to in Article 23 of the Statute and publication of the notice relating to the case in the *Official Journal of the European Union* is likely to be less effective.

22. If the referring court or tribunal has a nominative version of the request for a preliminary ruling, containing the full names and contact details of the parties to the main proceedings, and an anonymised version of that request, it is requested to send both versions to the Court to facilitate the Court's handling of the case.

Transmission to the Court of the request for a preliminary ruling and of the case file in the national proceedings

23. The request for a preliminary ruling must be dated and signed, then sent to the Court Registry electronically or by post (Registry of the Court of Justice, Rue du Fort Niedergrünewald, L-2925 Luxembourg). For reasons connected, in particular, with the need to ensure expeditious handling of the case and optimal communication with the referring court or tribunal, the Court recommends that national courts and tribunals use the e-Curia application. The rules on access to that application, which enables procedural documents to be lodged and served electronically, and the conditions of use of e-Curia may be viewed on the institution's website (https://curia.europa.eu/jcms/jcms/P_78957/en/). In order to facilitate the Court's processing of requests for a preliminary ruling and, in particular, their translation into all the official languages of the European Union, national courts and tribunals are requested, in addition to sending the original version of the request for a preliminary ruling via e-Curia, to send an editable version (word processing software such as 'Word', 'OpenOffice' or 'LibreOffice') of that request to the following address: DDP-GreffeCour@curia.europa.eu.

24. The request for a preliminary ruling must reach the Registry together with all the relevant documents and documents useful for the Court's handling of the case and, in particular, the precise contact details for the parties to the main proceedings and their representatives, if any, as well as the file of the case in the main proceedings or a copy of it. The file (or copy file)—which may be sent electronically or by post—will be retained at the Registry throughout the proceedings before the Court where, unless otherwise indicated by the referring court or tribunal, it may be consulted by the interested persons referred to in Article 23 of the Statute.

Interaction between the reference for a preliminary ruling and the national proceedings

25. Although the referring court or tribunal may still order protective measures, particularly in connection with a reference on determination of validity, the lodging of a request for a preliminary ruling nevertheless calls for the national proceedings to be stayed until the Court has given its ruling.

26. While the Court, in principle, remains seised of a request for a preliminary ruling for so long as that request is not withdrawn by the referring court or tribunal, it must nevertheless be borne in mind that the Court's role in the preliminary ruling procedure is to contribute to the effective administration of justice in the Member States, and not to give opinions on general or hypothetical questions. Since the preliminary ruling procedure is predicated on there being proceedings actually pending before the referring court or tribunal, it is incumbent on that court or tribunal to inform the Court of any procedural step that may affect the referral and, in particular, of any discontinuance or withdrawal or of any amicable settlement of the dispute in the main proceedings, and of any other event leading to the termination of the proceedings. The referring court or tribunal must also inform the Court of any decision delivered in the context of an appeal against the order for reference and of the consequences of that decision for the request for a preliminary ruling. In the interests of the proper conduct of the preliminary ruling proceedings before the Court and, in particular, to ensure that the Court does not devote time and resources to a case that is likely to be withdrawn or become devoid of purpose, it is important that such information is communicated to the Court with the minimum of delay.

27. National courts and tribunals should also note that the withdrawal of a request for a preliminary ruling may have an impact on the management of similar cases by the referring court or

tribunal. Where the outcome of a number of cases pending before the referring court or tribunal depends on the reply to be given by the Court to the questions submitted by that court or tribunal, it is appropriate for that court or tribunal to join those cases before submitting to the Court its request for a preliminary ruling in order to enable the Court to reply to the questions referred notwithstanding any withdrawal of one or more cases.

Costs and legal aid

28. Preliminary ruling proceedings before the Court are free of charge and the Court does not rule on the costs of the parties to the proceedings pending before the referring court or tribunal. It is for the referring court or tribunal to rule on those costs.

29. If a party to the main proceedings has insufficient means, the Court may grant that party legal aid to cover the costs, particularly those in respect of its representation, which it incurs before the Court. That aid can, however, be granted only if the party in question is not already in receipt of aid under national rules or to the extent to which that aid does not cover, or covers only partly, costs incurred before the Court. That party is requested in any event to send to the Court all information and supporting documents that will enable his or her true financial situation to be assessed.

Conduct of the proceedings before the Court and the action taken by the referring court or tribunal upon the Court's decision

30. The Court Registry will remain in contact with the referring court or tribunal throughout the proceedings, and will send it copies of all procedural documents and any requests for information or clarification deemed necessary in order for a useful reply to be given to the questions referred by that court or tribunal.

31. At the end of the proceedings which, as a rule, comprise a written part and an oral part, the Court gives its ruling in the form of a judgment on the questions put by the referring court or tribunal. In some cases, however, the Court may find it necessary to rule on those questions without an oral part of the procedure, or even without seeking the written observations of the interested persons referred to in Article 23 of the Statute. That is the case, in particular, when the question referred for a preliminary ruling is identical to a question on which the Court has already ruled, or where the answer to such a question may be clearly deduced from existing case-law or admits of no reasonable doubt. In such cases, the Court will, on the basis of Article 99 of its Rules of Procedure, rule expeditiously on the question put, by a reasoned order which has the same scope and the same binding force as a judgment.

32. After the judgment has been delivered or the order closing the proceedings has been signed, the Registry will send the Court's decision to the referring court or tribunal, which is requested to inform the Court of the action taken upon that decision in the case in the main proceedings. The final decision of the referring court or tribunal must be sent, with an express reference to the case number of the case before the Court, to the following address: Follow-up-DDP@curia.europa.eu.

II. Provisions applicable to requests for a preliminary ruling requiring particularly expeditious handling

33. As provided in Article 23a of the Statute and Articles 105 to 114 of the Rules of Procedure, a reference for a preliminary ruling may, in certain circumstances, be determined pursuant to an expedited procedure or an urgent procedure. The Court will decide whether these procedures are to be applied, either on submission by the referring court or tribunal of a separate, duly reasoned, request setting out the matters of fact or of law which justify the application of such procedure(s), or, exceptionally, of its own motion, where that appears to be required by the nature or the particular circumstances of the case.

Conditions for the application of the expedited procedure and the urgent procedure

34. Article 105 of the Rules of Procedure provides that a reference for a preliminary ruling may thus be determined pursuant to *an expedited procedure*, derogating from the provisions of those rules, where the nature of the case requires that it be dealt with within a short time. Since that procedure

imposes significant constraints on all those involved in it, and, in particular, on all the Member States called upon to lodge observations, whether written or oral, within much shorter time limits than would ordinarily apply, its application must be sought only when particular circumstances create an emergency that warrants the Court ruling quickly on the questions referred. That may be the case, inter alia, if there is a serious and immediate danger to public health or to the environment which a prompt decision by the Court might help to avert, or if particular circumstances require uncertainties concerning fundamental issues of national constitutional law and of EU law to be resolved within a very short time. According to settled case-law, the large number of persons or legal situations potentially affected by the decision that the referring court or tribunal has to deliver after bringing the matter before the Court for a preliminary ruling, the fact that there may be important economic issues at stake or that the referring court or tribunal is obliged to rule expeditiously do not, however, in themselves constitute exceptional circumstances that would justify the use of the expedited procedure.

35. The same applies *a fortiori* to *the urgent preliminary ruling procedure*, provided for in Article 107 of the Rules of Procedure. That procedure, which applies only in the areas covered by Title V of Part Three of the TFEU, relating to the area of freedom, security and justice, imposes even greater constraints on those concerned, since it limits the number of parties authorised to lodge written observations and, in cases of extreme urgency, allows the written part of the procedure before the Court to be omitted altogether. The application of the urgent procedure must therefore be requested only where it is absolutely necessary for the Court to give its ruling very quickly on the questions submitted by the referring court or tribunal.

36. Although it is not possible to provide an exhaustive list of such circumstances, particularly because of the varied and evolving nature of the rules of EU law governing the area of freedom, security and justice, a national court or tribunal may, for example, consider submitting a request for the urgent preliminary ruling procedure to be applied in the case, referred to in the fourth paragraph of Article 267 TFEU, of a person in custody or deprived of his or her liberty, where the answer to the question raised is decisive as to the assessment of that person's legal situation, or in proceedings concerning parental authority or custody of young children, in so far, in particular, as the outcome of the dispute in the main proceedings depends on the answer to the question referred for a preliminary ruling and the use of the ordinary procedure could cause serious, and perhaps irreparable, harm to the relationship between a child and (one of) that child's parents or to the child's development and integration into his or her family and social environment. By contrast, mere economic interests, however substantial and legitimate they may be, the legal uncertainty affecting the parties to the main proceedings or other parties to similar disputes, the large number of persons or legal situations potentially affected by the decision that a referring court has to deliver after bringing a matter before the Court for a preliminary ruling, or the large number of cases that may be affected by the decision of the Court do not constitute, as such, circumstances that would justify the application of the urgent preliminary ruling procedure.

The request for application of the expedited procedure or the urgent procedure

37. To enable the Court to decide quickly whether the expedited procedure or the urgent preliminary ruling procedure should be applied, the request must *set out precisely the matters of fact and law which establish the urgency* and, in particular, the risks involved in following the ordinary procedure. In so far as it is possible to do so, the referring court or tribunal must also briefly state its view on the answer to be given to the questions referred. Such a statement makes it easier for the parties to the main proceedings and the other interested persons participating in the procedure to define their positions, and therefore contributes to the rapidity of the procedure.

38. The request for the application of the expedited procedure or the urgent procedure must in any event be submitted in an unambiguous form that enables the Registry to establish immediately that the file has to be dealt with in a particular way. Accordingly, the referring court or tribunal is requested to specify which of the two procedures is required in the particular case, and to mention in its request the relevant article of the Rules of Procedure (Article 105 for the expedited procedure or Article 107 for the urgent procedure). That mention must be included in a clearly identifiable place in its order for reference or in a separate letter from the referring court or tribunal.

39. As regards the order for reference itself, it is particularly important that it should be concise where the matter is urgent, as this will help to ensure the rapidity of the procedure.

Communication between the Court, the referring court or tribunal and the parties to the main proceedings

40. A court or tribunal submitting a request for the expedited procedure or the urgent procedure to be applied is requested to send that request and the order for reference itself—together with the text of the latter in an editable format (word processing software such as 'Word', 'Open Office' or 'LibreOffice')—by means of the e-Curia application or by email (DDP-GreffeCour@curia.europa.eu).

41. In order to facilitate subsequent communication by the Court with the referring court or tribunal and with the parties to the main proceedings, the referring court or tribunal is also requested to state its email address and any fax number which may be used by the Court, together with the email addresses and any fax numbers of the representatives of the parties to the main proceedings.

ANNEX
The essential elements of a request for a preliminary ruling

This annex summarises, by way of a reminder, the main elements that must be included in a request for a preliminary ruling. These are followed by an indication of the paragraphs in the present recommendations in which those elements are discussed in more detail.

Whether transmitted electronically or by post, all requests for a preliminary ruling must mention:

1. the identity of the court or tribunal making the reference and, where appropriate, the chamber or formation of the court or tribunal having jurisdiction (see, in that respect, paragraphs 3 to 7);

2. the precise identity of the parties to the main proceedings and of anyone representing them before the referring court or tribunal (with regard to the parties to the main proceedings, see, however, paragraphs 21 and 22 of the present recommendations, in relation to the protection of personal data);

3. the subject matter of the dispute in the main proceedings and the relevant facts (see paragraph 15);

4. the relevant provisions of national law and of EU law (see paragraphs 15 and 16);

5. the reasons that prompted the referring court or tribunal to inquire about the interpretation or validity of EU law (see paragraphs 8 to 11 and 15 to 18);

6. the questions referred for a preliminary ruling (see paragraph 19) and, if applicable,

7. the possible need for specific treatment of the request, related, for example, to the need to preserve the anonymity of individuals concerned by the dispute or to the particularly expeditious way in which the request should be dealt with by the Court (see paragraph 33 et seq.).

As regards form, requests for a preliminary ruling must be typewritten, dated and signed and must be received at the Court Registry, preferably electronically, together with all the documents that are relevant and useful for the handling of the case (see, in that respect, paragraphs 20 to 24 of the present recommendations and, with regard to requests requiring particularly expeditious treatment, paragraphs 40 and 41).

Transmission channels recommended by the Court

In order to ensure the best possible communication with courts and tribunals that have referred questions to the Court for a preliminary ruling, the Court recommends the use of the following transmission channels:

(1) Lodging of the request for a preliminary ruling (or of other relevant documents linked to that request):

- Signed original of the request for a preliminary ruling (or of the other documents linked to that request): to be sent via the e-Curia application. The rules on access to that application, which is free of charge and secure, and the conditions of use of e-Curia, are available here: https://curia.europa.eu/jcms/jcms/P_78957/en/

    – Editable version of the request for a preliminary ruling (or of the other documents linked to it): DDP-GreffeCour@curia.europa.eu

    (2) Transmission of the final decision of the referring court or tribunal (anonymised, if necessary, including for the purposes of being placed online), following the Court's decision on the request for a preliminary ruling: Follow-up-DDP@curia.europa.eu

Rules of Procedure of the Court of Justice

THE COURT OF JUSTICE*

    Having regard to the Treaty on European Union, and in particular Article 19 thereof,

    Having regard to the Treaty on the Functioning of the European Union, and in particular the sixth paragraph of Article 253 thereof,

    Having regard to the Treaty establishing the European Atomic Energy Community, and in particular Article 106a(1) thereof,

    Having regard to the Protocol on the Statute of the Court of Justice of the European Union, and in particular Article 63 and the second paragraph of Article 64 thereof,

    Whereas:

    (1) Despite having been amended on several occasions over the years, the Rules of Procedure of the Court of Justice have remained fundamentally unchanged in structure since their original adoption on 4 March 1953. The Rules of Procedure of 19 June 1991, which are currently in force, still reflect the initial preponderance of direct actions, whereas in fact the majority of such actions now fall within the jurisdiction of the General Court, and references for a preliminary ruling from the courts and tribunals of the Member States represent, quantitatively, the primary category of cases brought before the Court. That fact should be taken into account and the structure and content of the Rules of Procedure of the Court adapted, in consequence, to changes in its caseload.

    (2) While references for a preliminary ruling should be given their proper place in the Rules of Procedure, it is also appropriate to draw a clearer distinction between the rules that apply to all types of action and those that are specific to each type, to be contained in separate titles. In the interests of clarification, procedural provisions common to all cases brought before the Court should, therefore, all be contained in an initial title.

    (3) In the light of experience gained in the course of implementing the various procedures, it is also necessary to supplement or to clarify, for the benefit of litigants as well as of national courts and tribunals, the rules that apply to each procedure. The rules in question concern, in particular, the concepts of party to the main proceedings, intervener and party to the proceedings before the General Court, or, in preliminary rulings, the rules governing the bringing of matters before the Court and the content of the order for reference. With regard to appeals against decisions of the General Court, a clearer distinction must also be drawn between appeals and cross-appeals in consequence of the service of an appeal on the cross-appellant.

    (4) Conversely, the excessive complexity of certain procedures, such as the review procedure, has come to light on their implementation. Accordingly, they should be simplified by providing, inter alia, for a Chamber of five Judges to be designated for a period of one year to be responsible for ruling both on the First Advocate General's proposal to review and on the questions to be reviewed.

    (5) Similarly, the procedural arrangements for dealing with requests for Opinions should be eased by aligning them with those that apply to other cases and by providing, in consequence, for a single Advocate General to be involved in dealing with the request for an Opinion. In the interests of making the Rules easier to understand, all the particular procedures currently to be found in a number of separate titles and chapters of the Rules of Procedure should also be brought together in a single title.

    (6) In order to maintain the Court's capacity, in the face of an ever-increasing caseload, to dispose within a reasonable period of time of the cases brought before it, it is also necessary to continue

---

* **Editor's Note:** Of 25 September 2012 (OJ 2012 L265/1) as amended to 18 June 2013 (OJ 2013 L173/65), 19 July 2016 (OJ 2016 L217/69), which replaced entirely the previously much amended rules of procedure from 1991, 9 April 2019 (OJ 2019 L111/73) and 8 November 2019 (OJ 2019 L316/103).

the efforts made to reduce the duration of proceedings before the Court, in particular by extending the opportunities for the Court to rule by reasoned order, simplifying the rules relating to the intervention of the States and institutions referred to in the first and third paragraphs of Article 40 of the Statute and providing for the Court to be able to rule without a hearing if it considers that it has sufficient information on the basis of all the written observations lodged in a case.

(7) In the interests of making the Rules applied by the Court easier to understand, lastly, certain rules which are outdated or not applied should be deleted, every paragraph of the present Rules numbered, each article given a specific heading summarising its content and the terminology harmonised.

With the Council's approval given on 24 September 2012.

HAS ADOPTED THESE RULES OF PROCEDURE:

Introductory provisions

Article 1   Definitions

1. In these Rules:
   (a) provisions of the Treaty on European Union are referred to by the number of the article concerned followed by 'TEU',
   (b) provisions of the Treaty on the Functioning of the European Union are referred to by the number of the article concerned followed by 'TFEU',
   (c) provisions of the Treaty establishing the European Atomic Energy Community are referred to by the number of the article concerned followed by 'TEAEC',
   (d) 'Statute' means the Protocol on the Statute of the Court of Justice of the European Union,
   (e) 'EEA Agreement' means the Agreement on the European Economic Area,[1]
   (f) 'Council Regulation No 1' means Council Regulation No 1 of 15 April 1958 determining the languages to be used by the European Economic Community.[2]

2. For the purposes of these Rules:
   (a) 'institutions' means the institutions of the European Union referred to in Article 13(1) TEU and bodies, offices and agencies established by the Treaties, or by an act adopted in implementation thereof, which may be parties before the Court,
   (b) 'EFTA Surveillance Authority' means the surveillance authority referred to in the EEA Agreement,
   (c) 'interested persons referred to in Article 23 of the Statute' means all the parties, States, institutions, bodies, offices and agencies authorised, pursuant to that Article, to submit statements of case or observations in the context of a reference for a preliminary ruling.

Article 2   Purport of these Rules

These Rules implement and supplement, so far as necessary, the relevant provisions of the EU, FEU and EAEC Treaties, and the Statute.

Title I Organisation of the Court

Chapter 1 Judges and Advocates General

Article 3   Commencement of the term of office of Judges and Advocates General

The term of office of a Judge or Advocate General shall begin on the date fixed for that purpose in the instrument of appointment. In the absence of any provisions in that instrument regarding the date of commencement of the term of office, that term shall begin on the date of publication of the instrument in the *Official Journal of the European Union*.

---

[1] OJ L 1, 3.1.1994, p. 27.
[2] OJ, English Special Edition 1952–1958 (I), p. 59.

Article 4   Taking of the oath

Before taking up his duties, a Judge or Advocate General shall, at the first public sitting of the Court which he attends after his appointment, take the following oath provided for in Article 2 of the Statute:

'I swear that I will perform my duties impartially and conscientiously; I swear that I will preserve the secrecy of the deliberations of the Court.'

Article 5   Solemn undertaking

Immediately after taking the oath, a Judge or Advocate General shall sign a declaration by which he gives the solemn undertaking provided for in the third paragraph of Article 4 of the Statute.

Article 6   Depriving a Judge or Advocate General of his office

1. Where the Court is called upon, pursuant to Article 6 of the Statute, to decide whether a Judge or Advocate General no longer fulfils the requisite conditions or no longer meets the obligations arising from his office, the President shall invite the Judge or Advocate General concerned to make representations.

2. The Court shall give a decision in the absence of the Registrar.

Article 7   Order of seniority

1. The seniority of Judges and Advocates General shall be calculated without distinction according to the date on which they took up their duties.

2. Where there is equal seniority on that basis, the order of seniority shall be determined by age.

3. Judges and Advocates General whose terms of office are renewed shall retain their former seniority.

Chapter 2   Presidency of the Court, constitution of the Chambers and election of the first Advocate General

Article 8   Election of the President and of the Vice-President of the Court

1. The Judges shall, immediately after the partial replacement provided for in the second paragraph of Article 253 TFEU, elect one of their number as President of the Court for a term of three years.

2. If the office of the President falls vacant before the normal date of expiry of the term thereof, the Court shall elect a successor for the remainder of the term.

3. The elections provided for in this Article shall be by secret ballot. The Judge obtaining the votes of more than half the Judges of the Court shall be elected. If no Judge obtains that majority, further ballots shall be held until that majority is attained.

4. The Judges shall then elect one of their number as Vice-President of the Court for a term of three years, in accordance with the procedures laid down in the preceding paragraph. Paragraph 2 shall apply if the office of the Vice-President of the Court falls vacant before the normal date of expiry of the term thereof.

5. The names of the President and Vice-President elected in accordance with this Article shall be published in the *Official Journal of the European Union*.

Article 9   Responsibilities of the President of the Court

1. The President shall represent the Court.

2. The President shall direct the judicial business of the Court. He shall preside at general meetings of the Members of the Court and at hearings before and deliberations of the full Court and the Grand Chamber.

3. The President shall ensure the proper functioning of the services of the Court.

Article 10   Responsibilities of the Vice-President of the Court

1. The Vice-President shall assist the President of the Court in the performance of his duties and shall take the President's place when the latter is prevented from acting.

2. He shall take the President's place, at his request, in performing the duties referred to in Article 9(1) and (3) of these Rules.

3. The Court shall, by decision, specify the conditions under which the Vice-President shall take the place of the President of the Court in the performance of his judicial duties. That decision shall be published in the *Official Journal of the European Union*.

Article 11   Constitution of Chambers

1. The Court shall set up Chambers of five and three Judges in accordance with Article 16 of the Statute and shall decide which Judges shall be attached to them.

2. The Court shall designate the Chambers of five Judges which, for a period of one year, shall be responsible for cases of the kind referred to in Article 107 and Articles 193 and 194.

3. In respect of cases assigned to a formation of the Court in accordance with Article 60, the word 'Court' in these Rules shall mean that formation.

4. In respect of cases assigned to a Chamber of five or three Judges, the powers of the President of the Court shall be exercised by the President of the Chamber.

5. The composition of the Chambers and the designation of the Chambers responsible for cases of the kind referred to in Article 107 and Articles 193 and 194 shall be published in the *Official Journal of the European Union*.

Article 12   Election of Presidents of Chambers

1. The Judges shall, immediately after the election of the President and Vice-President of the Court, elect the Presidents of the Chambers of five Judges for a term of three years.

2. The Judges shall then elect the Presidents of the Chambers of three Judges for a term of one year.

3. The provisions of Article 8(2) and (3) shall apply.

4. The names of the Presidents of Chambers elected in accordance with this Article shall be published in the *Official Journal of the European Union*.

Article 13   Where the President and Vice-President of the Court are prevented from acting

When the President and the Vice-President of the Court are prevented from acting, the functions of President shall be exercised by one of the Presidents of the Chambers of five Judges or, failing that, by one of the Presidents of the Chambers of three Judges or, failing that, by one of the other Judges, according to the order of seniority laid down in Article 7.

Article 14   Election of the First Advocate General

1. The Advocates General shall, immediately after the partial replacement provided for in the second paragraph of Article 253 TFEU, elect one of their number as First Advocate General for a term of three years.

2. If the office of the First Advocate General falls vacant before the normal date of expiry of the term thereof, he shall be replaced for the remainder of the term.

3. The elections provided for in this Article shall be by secret ballot. The Advocate General obtaining the votes of more than half of the Advocates General of the Court shall be elected. If no Advocate General obtains that majority, further ballots shall be held until that majority is obtained.

4. The name of the First Advocate General elected in accordance with this Article shall be published in the *Official Journal of the European Union*.

Chapter 3 Assignment of cases to Judge-Rapporteurs and Advocates General

Article 15   Designation of the Judge-Rapporteur

1. As soon as possible after the document initiating proceedings has been lodged, the President of the Court s hall designate a Judge to act as Rapporteur in the case.

2. For cases of the kind referred to in Article 107 and Articles 193 and 194, the Judge-Rapporteur shall be selected from among the Judges of the Chamber designated in accordance with Article 11(2), on a proposal from the President of that Chamber. If, pursuant to Article 109, the Chamber decides that the reference is not to be dealt with under the urgent procedure, the President of the Court may reassign the case to a Judge-Rapporteur attached to another Chamber.

3. The President of the Court shall take the necessary steps if a Judge-Rapporteur is prevented from acting.

Article 16 Designation of the Advocate General

1. The First Advocate General shall assign each case to an Advocate General.

2. The First Advocate General shall take the necessary steps if an Advocate General is prevented from acting.

Chapter 4 Assistant Rapporteurs

Article 17 Assistant Rapporteurs

1. Where the Court is of the opinion that the consideration of and preparatory inquiries in cases before it so require, it shall, pursuant to Article 13 of the Statute, propose the appointment of Assistant Rapporteurs.

2. Assistant Rapporteurs shall in particular:

(a) assist the President of the Court in interim proceedings and

(b) assist the Judge-Rapporteurs in their work.

3. In the performance of their duties the Assistant Rapporteurs shall be responsible to the President of the Court, the President of a Chamber or a Judge-Rapporteur, as the case may be.

4. Before taking up his duties, an Assistant Rapporteur shall take before the Court the oath set out in Article 4 of these Rules.

Chapter 5 Registry

Article 18 Appointment of the Registrar

1. The Court shall appoint the Registrar.

2. When the post of Registrar is vacant, an advertisement shall be published in the *Official Journal of the European Union*. Interested persons shall be invited to submit their applications within a time-limit of not less than three weeks, accompanied by full details of their nationality, university degrees, knowledge of languages, present and past occupations, and experience, if any, in judicial and international fields.

3. The vote, in which the Judges and the Advocates General shall take part, shall take place in accordance with the procedure laid down in Article 8(3) of these Rules.

4. The Registrar shall be appointed for a term of six years. He may be reappointed. The Court may decide to renew the term of office of the incumbent Registrar without availing itself of the procedure laid down in paragraph 2 of this Article.

5. The Registrar shall take the oath set out in Article 4 and sign the declaration provided for in Article 5.

6. The Registrar may be deprived of his office only if he no longer fulfils the requisite conditions or no longer meets the obligations arising from his office. The Court shall take its decision after giving the Registrar an opportunity to make representations.

7. If the office of Registrar falls vacant before the normal date of expiry of the term thereof, the Court shall appoint a new Registrar for a term of six years.

8. The name of the Registrar elected in accordance with this Article shall be published in the *Official Journal of the European Union*.

Article 19 Deputy Registrar

The Court may, in accordance with the procedure laid down in respect of the Registrar, appoint a Deputy Registrar to assist the Registrar and to take his place if he is prevented from acting.

Article 20 Responsibilities of the Registrar

1. The Registrar shall be responsible, under the authority of the President of the Court, for the acceptance, transmission and custody of all documents and for effecting service as provided for by these Rules.

2. The Registrar shall assist the Members of the Court in all their official functions.

3. The Registrar shall have custody of the seals and shall be responsible for the records. He shall be in charge of the publications of the Court and, in particular, the European Court Reports.

4. The Registrar shall direct the services of the Court under the authority of the President of the Court. He shall be responsible for the management of the staff and the administration, and for the preparation and implementation of the budget.

Article 21   Keeping of the register

1. There shall be kept in the Registry, under the responsibility of the Registrar, a register in which all procedural documents and supporting items and documents lodged shall be entered in the order in which they are submitted.

2. When a document has been registered, the Registrar shall make a note to that effect on the original and, if a party so requests, on any copy submitted for the purpose.

3. Entries in the register and the notes provided for in the preceding paragraph shall be authentic.

4. A notice shall be published in the *Official Journal of the European Union* indicating the date of registration of an application initiating proceedings, the names of the parties or, as the case may be, initials replacing a name, the form of order sought by the applicant and a summary of the pleas in law and of the main supporting arguments.

5. In the cases referred to in Title III of these Rules, the notice published in the *Official Journal of the European Union* shall indicate the date of lodging of a request for a preliminary ruling, the referring court or tribunal, the names of the parties to the main proceedings or, as the case may be, initials replacing a name, as well as the questions referred to the Court.

Article 22   Consultation of the register and of judgments and orders

1. Anyone may consult the register at the Registry and may obtain copies or extracts on payment of a charge on a scale fixed by the Court on a proposal from the Registrar.

2. The parties to a case may, on payment of the appropriate charge, obtain certified copies of procedural documents.

3. Anyone may, on payment of the appropriate charge, also obtain certified copies of judgments and orders.

Chapter 6 The working of the Court

Article 23   Location of the sittings of the Court

The Court may choose to hold one or more specific sittings in a place other than that in which it has its seat.

Article 24   Calendar of the Court's judicial business

1. The judicial year shall begin on 7 October of each calendar year and end on 6 October of the following year.

2. The judicial vacations shall be determined by the Court.

3. In a case of urgency, the President may convene the Judges and the Advocates General during the judicial vacations.

4. The Court shall observe the official holidays of the place in which it has its seat.

5. The Court may, in proper circumstances, grant leave of absence to any Judge or Advocate General.

6. The dates of the judicial vacations and the list of official holidays shall be published annually in the *Official Journal of the European Union*.

Article 25   General meeting

Decisions concerning administrative issues or the action to be taken upon the proposals contained in the preliminary report referred to in Article 59 of these Rules shall be taken by the Court at the general meeting in which all the Judges and Advocates General shall take part and have a vote. The Registrar shall be present, unless the Court decides to the contrary.

Article 26 Drawing-up of minutes

Where the Court sits without the Registrar being present it shall, if necessary, instruct the most junior Judge for the purposes of Article 7 of these Rules to draw up minutes, which shall be signed by that Judge and by the President.

Chapter 7 Formations of the Court

Section 1 Composition of the formations of the Court

Article 27 Composition of the Grand Chamber

1. The Grand Chamber shall, for each case, be composed of the President and the Vice-President of the Court, three Presidents of Chambers of five Judges, the Judge-Rapporteur and the number of Judges necessary to reach 15. The last-mentioned Judges and the three Presidents of Chambers of five Judges shall be designated from the lists referred to in paragraphs 3 and 4 of this Article, following the order laid down therein. The starting-point on each of those lists, in every case assigned to the Grand Chamber, shall be the name of the Judge immediately following the last Judge designated from the list concerned for the preceding case assigned to that formation of the Court.

2. After the election of the President and the Vice-President of the Court, and then of the Presidents of the Chambers of five Judges, a list of the Presidents of Chambers of five Judges and a list of the other Judges shall be drawn up for the purposes of determining the composition of the Grand Chamber.

3. The list of the Presidents of Chambers of five Judges shall be drawn up according to the order laid down in Article 7 of these Rules.

4. The list of the other Judges shall be drawn up according to the order laid down in Article 7 of these Rules, alternating with the reverse order: the first Judge on that list shall be the first according to the order laid down in that Article, the second Judge shall be the last according to that order, the third Judge shall be the second according to that order, the fourth Judge the penultimate according to that order, and so on.

5. The lists referred to in paragraphs 3 and 4 shall be published in the *Official Journal of the European Union*.

6. In cases which are assigned to the Grand Chamber between the beginning of a calendar year in which there is a partial replacement of Judges and the moment when that replacement has taken place, two substitute Judges may be designated to complete the formation of the Court for so long as the attainment of the quorum referred to in the third paragraph of Article 17 of the Statute is in doubt. Those substitute Judges shall be the two Judges appearing on the list referred to in paragraph 4 immediately after the last Judge designated for the composition of the Grand Chamber in the case.

7. The substitute Judges shall replace, in the order of the list referred to in paragraph 4, such Judges as are unable to take part in the determination of the case.

Article 28 Composition of the Chambers of five and of three Judges

1. The Chambers of five Judges and of three Judges shall, for each case, be composed of the President of the Chamber, the Judge-Rapporteur and the number of Judges required to attain the number of five and three Judges respectively. Those last-mentioned Judges shall be designated from the lists referred to in paragraphs 2 and 3, following the order laid down therein. The starting-point on those lists, in every case assigned to a Chamber, shall be the name of the Judge immediately following the last Judge designated from the list for the preceding case assigned to the Chamber concerned.

2. For the composition of the Chambers of five Judges, after the election of the Presidents of those Chambers lists shall be drawn up including all the Judges attached to the Chamber concerned, with the exception of its President. The lists shall be drawn up in the same way as the list referred to in Article 27(4).

3. For the composition of the Chambers of three Judges, after the election of the Presidents of those Chambers lists shall be drawn up including all the Judges attached to the Chamber concerned,

with the exception of its President. The lists shall be drawn up according to the order laid down in Article 7.

4. The lists referred to in paragraphs 2 and 3 shall be published in the *Official Journal of the European Union*.

Article 29   Composition of Chambers where cases are related or referred back

1. Where the Court considers that a number of cases must be heard and determined together by one and the same formation of the Court, the composition of that formation shall be that fixed for the case in respect of which the preliminary report was examined first.

2. Where a Chamber to which a case has been assigned requests the Court, pursuant to Article 60(3) of these Rules, to assign the case to a formation composed of a greater number of Judges, that formation shall include the members of the Chamber which has referred the case back.

Article 30   Where a President of a Chamber is prevented from acting

1. When the President of a Chamber of five Judges is prevented from acting, the functions of President of the Chamber shall be exercised by a President of a Chamber of three Judges, where necessary according to the order laid down in Article 7 of these Rules, or, if that formation of the Court does not include a President of a Chamber of three Judges, by one of the other Judges according to the order laid down in Article 7.

2. When the President of a Chamber of three Judges is prevented from acting, the functions of President of the Chamber shall be exercised by a Judge of that formation of the Court according to the order laid down in Article 7.

Article 31   Where a member of the formation of the Court is prevented from acting

1. When a member of the Grand Chamber is prevented from acting, he shall be replaced by another Judge according to the order of the list referred to in Article 27(4).

2. When a member of a Chamber of five Judges is prevented from acting, he shall be replaced by another Judge of that Chamber, according to the order of the list referred to in Article 28(2). If it is not possible to replace the Judge prevented from acting by a Judge of the same Chamber, the President of that Chamber shall so inform the President of the Court who may designate another Judge to complete the Chamber.

3. When a member of a Chamber of three Judges is prevented from acting, he shall be replaced by another Judge of that Chamber, according to the order of the list referred to in Article 28(3). If it is not possible to replace the Judge prevented from acting by a Judge of the same Chamber, the President of that Chamber shall so inform the President of the Court who may designate another Judge to complete the Chamber.

Section 2   Deliberations

Article 32   Procedures concerning deliberations

1. The deliberations of the Court shall be and shall remain secret.

2. When a hearing has taken place, only those Judges who participated in that hearing and, where relevant, the Assistant Rapporteur responsible for the consideration of the case shall take part in the deliberations.

3. Every Judge taking part in the deliberations shall state his opinion and the reasons for it.

4. The conclusions reached by the majority of the Judges after final discussion shall determine the decision of the Court.

Article 33   Number of Judges taking part in the deliberations

Where, by reason of a Judge being prevented from acting, there is an even number of Judges, the most junior Judge for the purposes of Article 7 of these Rules shall abstain from taking part in the deliberations unless he is the Judge-Rapporteur. In that case the Judge immediately senior to him shall abstain from taking part in the deliberations.

Article 34   Quorum of the Grand Chamber

1. If, for a case assigned to the Grand Chamber, it is not possible to attain the quorum referred to in the third paragraph of Article 17 of the Statute, the President of the Court shall designate one or more other Judges according to the order of the list referred to in Article 27(4) of these Rules.

2. If a hearing has taken place before that designation, the Court shall rehear oral argument from the parties and the Opinion of the Advocate General.

Article 35   Quorum of the Chambers of five and of three Judges

1. If, for a case assigned to a Chamber of five or of three Judges, it is not possible to attain the quorum referred to in the second paragraph of Article 17 of the Statute, the President of the Court shall designate one or more other Judges according to the order of the list referred to in Article 28(2) or (3), respectively, of these Rules. If it is not possible to replace the Judge prevented from acting by a Judge of the same Chamber, the President of that Chamber shall so inform the President of the Court forthwith who shall designate another Judge to complete the Chamber.

2. Article 34(2) shall apply, *mutatis mutandis*, to the Chambers of five and of three Judges.

Chapter 8 Languages

Article 36   Language of a case

The language of a case shall be Bulgarian, Croatian, Czech, Danish, Dutch, English, Estonian, Finnish, French, German, Greek, Hungarian, Irish, Italian, Latvian, Lithuanian, Maltese, Polish, Portuguese, Romanian, Slovak, Slovene, Spanish or Swedish.

Article 37   Determination of the language of a case

1. In direct actions, the language of a case shall be chosen by the applicant, except that:

   (a) where the defendant is a Member State, the language of the case shall be the official language of that State; where that State has more than one official language, the applicant may choose between them;

   (b) at the joint request of the parties, the use of another of the languages mentioned in Article 36 for all or part of the proceedings may be authorised;

   (c) at the request of one of the parties, and after the opposite party and the Advocate General have been heard, the use of another of the languages mentioned in Article 36 may be authorised as the language of the case for all or part of the proceedings by way of derogation from subparagraphs (a) and (b); such a request may not be submitted by one of the institutions of the European Union.

2. Without prejudice to the provisions of paragraph 1(b) and (c), and of Article 38(4) and (5) of these Rules,

   (a) in appeals against decisions of the General Court as referred to in Articles 56 and 57 of the Statute, the language of the case shall be the language of the decision of the General Court against which the appeal is brought;

   (b) where, in accordance with the second paragraph of Article 62 of the Statute, the Court decides to review a decision of the General Court, the language of the case shall be the language of the decision of the General Court which is the subject of review;

   (c) in the case of challenges concerning the costs to be recovered, applications to set aside judgments by default, third-party proceedings and applications for interpretation or revision of a judgment or for the Court to remedy a failure to adjudicate, the language of the case shall be the language of the decision to which those applications or challenges relate.

3. In preliminary ruling proceedings, the language of the case shall be the language of the referring court or tribunal. At the duly substantiated request of one of the parties to the main proceedings, and after the other party to the main proceedings and the Advocate General have been heard, the use of another of the languages mentioned in Article 36 may be authorised for the oral

part of the procedure. Where granted, the authorisation to use that other language shall apply in respect of all the interested persons referred to in Article 23 of the Statute.

4. Requests as above may be decided on by the President; the latter may, and where he wishes to accede to a request without the agreement of all the parties must, refer the request to the Court.

Article 38   Use of the language of the case

1. The language of the case shall in particular be used in the written and oral pleadings of the parties, including the items and documents produced or annexed to them, and also in the minutes and decisions of the Court.

2. Any item or document produced or annexed that is expressed in another language must be accompanied by a translation into the language of the case.

3. However, in the case of substantial items or lengthy documents, translations may be confined to extracts. At any time the Court may, of its own motion or at the request of one of the parties, call for a complete or fuller translation.

4. Notwithstanding the foregoing provisions, a Member State shall be entitled to use its official language when taking part in preliminary ruling proceedings, when intervening in a case before the Court or when bringing a matter before the Court pursuant to Article 259 TFEU. This provision shall apply both to written documents and to oral statements. The Registrar shall arrange in each instance for translation into the language of the case.

5. The States, other than the Member States, which are parties to the EEA Agreement, and also the EFTA Surveillance Authority, shall be entitled to use one of the languages mentioned in Article 36, other than the language of the case, when they take part in preliminary ruling proceedings or intervene in a case before the Court. This provision shall apply both to written documents and to oral statements. The Registrar shall arrange in each instance for translation into the language of the case.

6. Non-Member States taking part in preliminary ruling proceedings pursuant to the fourth paragraph of Article 23 of the Statute shall be entitled to use one of the languages mentioned in Article 36 other than the language of the case. This provision shall apply both to written documents and to oral statements. The Registrar shall arrange in each instance for translation into the language of the case.

7. Where a witness or expert states that he is unable adequately to express himself in one of the languages referred to in Article 36, the Court may authorise him to give his evidence in another language. The Registrar shall arrange for translation into the language of the case.

8. The President and the Vice-President of the Court and also the Presidents of Chambers in conducting oral proceedings, Judges and Advocates General in putting questions and Advocates General in delivering their Opinions may use one of the languages referred to in Article 36 other than the language of the case. The Registrar shall arrange for translation into the language of the case.

Article 39   Responsibility of the Registrar concerning language arrangements

1. The Registrar shall arrange for procedural documents lodged during the written part of the procedure to be translated into the language of the case and, as the case may be, into another language mentioned in Article 36.

2. The Registrar shall also ensure that what is said at the hearing is interpreted into the language of the case and into the other languages that are mentioned in Article 36 and are used by the parties present at the hearing or considered necessary for the efficient conduct of that hearing.

Article 40   Languages of the publications of the Court

Publications of the Court shall be issued in the languages referred to in Article 1 of Council Regulation No 1.

Article 41   Authentic texts

The texts of documents drawn up in the language of the case or, where applicable, in another language authorised pursuant to Articles 37 or 38 of these Rules shall be authentic.

Article 42   Language service of the Court

The Court shall set up a language service staffed by experts with adequate legal training and a thorough knowledge of several official languages of the European Union.

Title II Common procedural provisions

Chapter 1 Rights and obligations of agents, advisers and lawyers

Article 43   Privileges, immunities and facilities

1. Agents, advisers and lawyers who appear before the Court or before any judicial authority to which the Court has addressed letters rogatory shall enjoy immunity in respect of words spoken or written by them concerning the case or the parties.

2. Agents, advisers and lawyers shall also enjoy the following privileges and facilities:

  (a) any papers and documents relating to the proceedings shall be exempt from both search and seizure. In the event of a dispute, the customs officials or police may seal those papers and documents; they shall then be immediately forwarded to the Court for inspection in the presence of the Registrar and of the person concerned;

  (b) agents, advisers and lawyers shall be entitled to travel in the course of duty without hindrance.

Article 44   Status of the parties' representatives

1. In order to qualify for the privileges, immunities and facilities specified in Article 43, persons entitled to them shall furnish proof of their status as follows:

  (a) agents shall produce an official document issued by the party for whom they act, who shall immediately serve a copy thereof on the Registrar;

  (b) lawyers shall produce a certificate that they are authorised to practise before a court of a Member State or of another State which is a party to the EEA Agreement, and, where the party which they represent is a legal person governed by private law, an authority to act issued by that person;

  (c) advisers shall produce an authority to act issued by the party whom they are assisting.

2. The Registrar of the Court shall issue them with a certificate, as required. The validity of this certificate shall be limited to a specified period, which may be extended or curtailed according to the duration of the proceedings.

Article 45   Waiver of immunity

1. The privileges, immunities and facilities specified in Article 43 of these Rules are granted exclusively in the interests of the proper conduct of proceedings.

2. The Court may waive immunity where it considers that the proper conduct of proceedings will not be hindered thereby.

Article 46   Exclusion from the proceedings

1. If the Court considers that the conduct of an agent, adviser or lawyer before the Court is incompatible with the dignity of the Court or with the requirements of the proper administration of justice, or that such agent, adviser or lawyer is using his rights for purposes other than those for which they were granted, it shall inform the person concerned. If the Court informs the competent authorities to whom the person concerned is answerable, a copy of the letter sent to those authorities shall be forwarded to the person concerned.

2. On the same grounds, the Court may at any time, having heard the person concerned and the Advocate General, decide to exclude an agent, adviser or lawyer from the proceedings by reasoned order. That order shall have immediate effect.

3. Where an agent, adviser or lawyer is excluded from the proceedings, the proceedings shall be suspended for a period fixed by the President in order to allow the party concerned to appoint another agent, adviser or lawyer.

4. Decisions taken under this Article may be rescinded.

Article 47 University teachers and parties to the main proceedings

1. The provisions of this Chapter shall apply to university teachers who have a right of audience before the Court in accordance with Article 19 of the Statute.

2. They shall also apply, in the context of references for a preliminary ruling, to the parties to the main proceedings where, in accordance with the national rules of procedure applicable, those parties are permitted to bring or defend court proceedings without being represented by a lawyer, and to persons authorised under those rules to represent them.

Chapter 2 Service

Article 48 Methods of service

1. Where these Rules require that a document be served on a person, the Registrar shall ensure that service is effected at that person's address for service either by the dispatch of a copy of the document by registered post with a form for acknowledgement of receipt or by personal delivery of the copy against a receipt. The Registrar shall prepare and certify the copies of documents to be served, save where the parties themselves supply the copies in accordance with Article 57(2) of these Rules.

2. Where the addressee has agreed that service is to be effected on him by telefax or any other technical means of communication, any procedural document, including a judgment or order of the Court, may be served by the transmission of a copy of the document by such means.

3. Where, for technical reasons or on account of the nature or length of the document, such transmission is impossible or impracticable, the document shall be served, if the addressee has not specified an address for service, at his address in accordance with the procedures laid down in paragraph 1 of this Article. The addressee shall be so informed by telefax or any other technical means of communication. Service shall then be deemed to have been effected on the addressee by registered post on the 10th day following the lodging of the registered letter at the post office of the place in which the Court has its seat, unless it is shown by the acknowledgement of receipt that the letter was received on a different date or the addressee informs the Registrar, within three weeks of being informed by telefax or any other technical means of communication, that the document to be served has not reached him.

4. The Court may, by decision, determine the criteria for a procedural document to be served by electronic means. That decision shall be published in the *Official Journal of the European Union*.

Chapter 3 Time-limits

Article 49 Calculation of time-limits

1. Any procedural time-limit prescribed by the Treaties, the Statute or these Rules shall be calculated as follows:

  (a) where a time-limit expressed in days, weeks, months or years is to be calculated from the moment at which an event occurs or an action takes place, the day during which that event occurs or that action takes place shall not be counted as falling within the time-limit in question;

  (b) a time-limit expressed in weeks, months or years shall end with the expiry of whichever day in the last week, month or year is the same day of the week, or falls on the same date, as the day during which the event or action from which the time-limit is to be calculated occurred or took place. If, in a time-limit expressed in months or years, the day on which it should expire does not occur in the last month, the time-limit shall end with the expiry of the last day of that month;

  (c) where a time-limit is expressed in months and days, it shall first be calculated in whole months, then in days;

  (d) time-limits shall include Saturdays, Sundays and the official holidays referred to in Article 24(6) of these Rules;

  (e) time-limits shall not be suspended during the judicial vacations.

2. If the time-limit would otherwise end on a Saturday, Sunday or an official holiday, it shall be extended until the end of the first subsequent working day.

Article 50   Proceedings against a measure adopted by an institution

Where the time-limit allowed for initiating proceedings against a measure adopted by an institution runs from the publication of that measure, that time-limit shall be calculated, for the purposes of Article 49(1)(a), from the end of the 14th day after publication of the measure in the *Official Journal of the European Union*.

Article 51   Extension on account of distance

The procedural time-limits shall be extended on account of distance by a single period of 10 days.

Article 52   Setting and extension of time-limits

1. Any time-limit prescribed by the Court pursuant to these Rules may be extended.

2. The President and the Presidents of Chambers may delegate to the Registrar power of signature for the purposes of setting certain time-limits which, pursuant to these Rules, it falls to them to prescribe, or of extending such time-limits.

Chapter 4   Different procedures for dealing with cases

Article 53   Procedures for dealing with cases

1. Without prejudice to the special provisions laid down in the Statute or in these Rules, the procedure before the Court shall consist of a written part and an oral part.

2. Where it is clear that the Court has no jurisdiction to hear and determine a case or where a request or an application is manifestly inadmissible, the Court may, after hearing the Advocate General, at any time decide to give a decision by reasoned order without taking further steps in the proceedings.

3. The President may in special circumstances decide that a case be given priority over others.

4. A case may be dealt with under an expedited procedure in accordance with the conditions provided by these Rules.

5. A reference for a preliminary ruling may be dealt with under an urgent procedure in accordance with the conditions provided by these Rules.

Article 54   Joinder

1. Two or more cases of the same type concerning the same subject-matter may at any time be joined, on account of the connection between them, for the purposes of the written or oral part of the procedure or of the judgment which closes the proceedings.

2. A decision on whether cases should be joined shall be taken by the President after hearing the Judge-Rapporteur and the Advocate General, if the cases concerned have already been assigned, and, save in the case of references for a preliminary ruling, after also hearing the parties. The President may refer the decision on this matter to the Court.

3. Joined cases may be disjoined, in accordance with the provisions of paragraph 2.

Article 55   Stay of proceedings

1. The proceedings may be stayed:

    (a) in the circumstances specified in the third paragraph of Article 54 of the Statute, by order of the Court, made after hearing the Advocate General;

    (b) in all other cases, by decision of the President adopted after hearing the Judge-Rapporteur and the Advocate General and, save in the case of references for a preliminary ruling, the parties.

2. The proceedings may be resumed by order or decision, following the same procedure.

3. The orders or decisions referred to in paragraphs 1 and 2 shall be served on the parties or interested persons referred to in Article 23 of the Statute.

4. The stay of proceedings shall take effect on the date indicated in the order or decision of stay or, in the absence of such indication, on the date of that order or decision.

5. While proceedings are stayed time shall cease to run for the parties or interested persons referred to in Article 23 of the Statute for the purposes of procedural time-limits.

6. Where the order or decision of stay does not fix the length of stay, it shall end on the date indicated in the order or decision of resumption or, in the absence of such indication, on the date of the order or decision of resumption.

7. From the date of resumption of proceedings following a stay, the suspended procedural time-limits shall be replaced by new time-limits and time shall begin to run from the date of that resumption.

Article 56   Deferment of the determination of a case

After hearing the Judge-Rapporteur, the Advocate General and the parties, the President may in special circumstances, either of his own motion or at the request of one of the parties, defer a case to be dealt with at a later date.

Chapter 5 Written part of the procedure

Article 57   Lodging of procedural documents

1. The original of every procedural document must bear the handwritten signature of the party's agent or lawyer or, in the case of observations submitted in the context of preliminary ruling proceedings, that of the party to the main proceedings or his representative, if the national rules of procedure applicable to those main proceedings so permit.

2. The original, accompanied by all annexes referred to therein, shall be submitted together with five copies for the Court and, in the case of proceedings other than preliminary ruling proceedings, a copy for every other party to the proceedings. Copies shall be certified by the party lodging them.

3. The institutions shall in addition produce, within time-limits laid down by the Court, translations of any procedural document into the other languages provided for by Article 1 of Council Regulation No 1. The preceding paragraph of this Article shall apply.

4. To every procedural document there shall be annexed a file containing the items and documents relied on in support of it, together with a schedule listing them.

5. Where in view of the length of an item or document only extracts from it are annexed to the procedural document, the whole item or document or a full copy of it shall be lodged at the Registry.

6. All procedural documents shall bear a date. In the calculation of procedural time-limits, only the date and time of lodgment of the original at the Registry shall be taken into account.

7. Without prejudice to the provisions of paragraphs 1 to 6, the date on and time at which a copy of the signed original of a procedural document, including the schedule of items and documents referred to in paragraph 4, is received at the Registry by telefax or any other technical means of communication available to the Court shall be deemed to be the date and time of lodgment for the purposes of compliance with the procedural time-limits, provided that the signed original of the procedural document, accompanied by the annexes and copies referred to in paragraph 2, is lodged at the Registry no later than 10 days thereafter. Article 51 of these Rules shall not apply to the latter time limit.

8. Without prejudice to paragraphs 3 to 6, the Court may, by decision, determine the criteria for a procedural document sent to the Registry by electronic means to be deemed to be the original of that document. That decision shall be published in the *Official Journal of the European Union*.

Article 58   Length of procedural documents

Without prejudice to any special provisions laid down in these Rules, the Court may, by decision, set the maximum length of written pleadings or observations lodged before it. That decision shall be published in the *Official Journal of the European Union*.

Chapter 6 The preliminary report and assignment of cases to formations of the Court

Article 59 Preliminary report

1. When the written part of the procedure is closed, the President shall fix a date on which the Judge-Rapporteur is to present a preliminary report to the general meeting of the Court.

2. The preliminary report shall contain proposals as to whether particular measures of organisation of procedure, measures of inquiry or, if appropriate, requests to the referring court or tribunal for clarification should be undertaken, and as to the formation to which the case should be assigned. It shall also contain the Judge-Rapporteur's proposals, if any, as to whether to dispense with a hearing and as to whether to dispense with an Opinion of the Advocate General pursuant to the fifth paragraph of Article 20 of the Statute.

3. The Court shall decide, after hearing the Advocate General, what action to take on the proposals of the Judge-Rapporteur.

Article 60 Assignment of cases to formations of the Court

1. The Court shall assign to the Chambers of five and of three Judges any case brought before it in so far as the difficulty or importance of the case or particular circumstances are not such as to require that it should be assigned to the Grand Chamber, unless a Member State or an institution of the European Union participating in the proceedings has requested that the case be assigned to the Grand Chamber, pursuant to the third paragraph of Article 16 of the Statute.

2. The Court shall sit as a full Court where cases are brought before it pursuant to the provisions referred to in the fourth paragraph of Article 16 of the Statute. It may assign a case to the full Court where, in accordance with the fifth paragraph of Article 16 of the Statute, it considers that the case is of exceptional importance.

3. The formation to which a case has been assigned may, at any stage of the proceedings, request the Court to assign the case to a formation composed of a greater number of Judges.

4. Where the oral part of the procedure is opened without an inquiry, the President of the formation determining the case shall fix the opening date.

Chapter 7 Measures of organisation of procedure and measures of inquiry

Section 1 Measures of organisation of procedure

Article 61 Measures of organisation prescribed by the Court

1. In addition to the measures which may be prescribed in accordance with Article 24 of the Statute, the Court may invite the parties or the interested persons referred to in Article 23 of the Statute to answer certain questions in writing, within the time-limit laid down by the Court, or at the hearing. The written replies shall be communicated to the other parties or the interested persons referred to in Article 23 of the Statute.

2. Where a hearing is organised, the Court shall, in so far as possible, invite the participants in that hearing to concentrate in their oral pleadings on one or more specified issues.

Article 62 Measures of organisation prescribed by the Judge-Rapporteur or the Advocate General

1. The Judge-Rapporteur or the Advocate General may request the parties or the interested persons referred to in Article 23 of the Statute to submit within a specified time-limit all such information relating to the facts, and all such documents or other particulars, as they may consider relevant. The replies and documents provided shall be communicated to the other parties or the interested persons referred to in Article 23 of the Statute.

2. The Judge-Rapporteur or the Advocate General may also send to the parties or the interested persons referred to in Article 23 of the Statute questions to be answered at the hearing.

Section 2 Measures of inquiry

Article 63 Decision on measures of inquiry

1. The Court shall decide in its general meeting whether a measure of inquiry is necessary.

2. Where the case has already been assigned to a formation of the Court, the decision shall be taken by that formation.

Article 64 Determination of measures of inquiry

1. The Court, after hearing the Advocate General, shall prescribe the measures of inquiry that it considers appropriate by means of an order setting out the facts to be proved.

2. Without prejudice to Articles 24 and 25 of the Statute, the following measures of inquiry may be adopted:

    (a) the personal appearance of the parties;

    (b) a request for information and production of documents;

    (c) oral testimony;

    (d) the commissioning of an expert's report;

    (e) an inspection of the place or thing in question.

3. Evidence may be submitted in rebuttal and previous evidence may be amplified.

Article 65 Participation in measures of inquiry

1. Where the formation of the Court does not undertake the inquiry itself, it shall entrust the task of so doing to the Judge-Rapporteur.

2. The Advocate General shall take part in the measures of inquiry.

3. The parties shall be entitled to attend the measures of inquiry.

Article 66 Oral testimony

1. The Court may, either of its own motion or at the request of one of the parties, and after hearing the Advocate General, order that certain facts be proved by witnesses.

2. A request by a party for the examination of a witness shall state precisely about what facts and for what reasons the witness should be examined.

3. The Court shall rule by reasoned order on the request referred to in the preceding paragraph. If the request is granted, the order shall set out the facts to be established and state which witnesses are to be heard in respect of each of those facts.

4. Witnesses shall be summoned by the Court, where appropriate after lodgment of the security provided for in Article 73(1) of these Rules.

Article 67 Examination of witnesses

1. After the identity of the witness has been established, the President shall inform him that he will be required to vouch the truth of his evidence in the manner laid down in these Rules.

2. The witness shall give his evidence to the Court, the parties having been given notice to attend. After the witness has given his evidence the President may, at the request of one of the parties or of his own motion, put questions to him.

3. The other Judges and the Advocate General may do likewise.

4. Subject to the control of the President, questions may be put to witnesses by the representatives of the parties.

Article 68 Witnesses' oath

1. After giving his evidence, the witness shall take the following oath:

'I swear that I have spoken the truth, the whole truth and nothing but the truth.'

2. The Court may, after hearing the parties, exempt a witness from taking the oath.

Article 69 Pecuniary penalties

1. Witnesses who have been duly summoned shall obey the summons and attend for examination.

2. If, without good reason, a witness who has been duly summoned fails to appear before the Court, the Court may impose upon him a pecuniary penalty not exceeding EUR 5000 and may order that a further summons be served on the witness at his own expense.

3. The same penalty may be imposed upon a witness who, without good reason, refuses to give evidence or to take the oath.

Article 70   Expert's report

1. The Court may order that an expert's report be obtained. The order appointing the expert shall define his task and set a time-limit within which he is to submit his report.

2. After the expert has submitted his report and that report has been served on the parties, the Court may order that the expert be examined, the parties having been given notice to attend. At the request of one of the parties or of his own motion, the President may put questions to the expert.

3. The other Judges and the Advocate General may do likewise.

4. Subject to the control of the President, questions may be put to the expert by the representatives of the parties.

Article 71   Expert's oath

1. After making his report, the expert shall take the following oath:
'I swear that I have conscientiously and impartially carried out my task.'

2. The Court may, after hearing the parties, exempt the expert from taking the oath.

Article 72   Objection to a witness or expert

1. If one of the parties objects to a witness or an expert on the ground that he is not a competent or proper person to act as a witness or expert or for any other reason, or if a witness or expert refuses to give evidence or to take the oath, the matter shall be resolved by the Court.

2. An objection to a witness or an expert shall be raised within two weeks after service of the order summoning the witness or appointing the expert; the statement of objection must set out the grounds of objection and indicate the nature of any evidence offered.

Article 73   Witnesses' and experts' costs

1. Where the Court orders the examination of witnesses or an expert's report, it may request the parties or one of them to lodge security for the witnesses' costs or the costs of the expert's report.

2. Witnesses and experts shall be entitled to reimbursement of their travel and subsistence expenses. The cashier of the Court may make an advance payment towards these expenses.

3. Witnesses shall be entitled to compensation for loss of earnings, and experts to fees for their services. The cashier of the Court shall pay witnesses and experts these sums after they have carried out their respective duties or tasks.

Article 74   Minutes of inquiry hearings

1. The Registrar shall draw up minutes of every inquiry hearing. The minutes shall be signed by the President and by the Registrar. They shall constitute an official record.

2. In the case of the examination of witnesses or experts, the minutes shall be signed by the President or by the Judge-Rapporteur responsible for conducting the examination of the witness or expert, and by the Registrar. Before the minutes are thus signed, the witness or expert must be given an opportunity to check the content of the minutes and to sign them.

3. The minutes shall be served on the parties.

Article 75   Opening of the oral part of the procedure after the inquiry

1. Unless the Court decides to prescribe a time-limit within which the parties may submit written observations, the President shall fix the date for the opening of the oral part of the procedure after the measures of inquiry have been completed.

2. Where a time-limit has been prescribed for the submission of written observations, the President shall fix the date for the opening of the oral part of the procedure after that time-limit has expired.

Chapter 8 Oral part of the procedure

Article 76   Hearing

1. Any reasoned requests for a hearing shall be submitted within three weeks after service on the parties or the interested persons referred to in Article 23 of the Statute of notification of the close of the written part of the procedure. That time-limit may be extended by the President.

2. On a proposal from the Judge-Rapporteur and after hearing the Advocate General, the Court may decide not to hold a hearing if it considers, on reading the written pleadings or observations lodged during the written part of the procedure, that it has sufficient information to give a ruling.

3. The preceding paragraph shall not apply where a request for a hearing, stating reasons, has been submitted by an interested person referred to in Article 23 of the Statute who did not participate in the written part of the procedure.

Article 77   Joint hearing

If the similarities between two or more cases of the same type so permit, the Court may decide to organise a joint hearing of those cases.

Article 78   Conduct of oral proceedings

Oral proceedings shall be opened and directed by the President, who shall be responsible for the proper conduct of the hearing.

Article 79   Cases heard in camera

1. For serious reasons related, in particular, to the security of the Member States or to the protection of minors, the Court may decide to hear a case *in camera*.

2. The oral proceedings in cases heard *in camera* shall not be published.

Article 80   Questions

The members of the formation of the Court and the Advocate General may in the course of the hearing put questions to the agents, advisers or lawyers of the parties and, in the circumstances referred to in Article 47(2) of these Rules, to the parties to the main proceedings or to their representatives.

Article 81   Close of the hearing

After the parties or the interested persons referred to in Article 23 of the Statute have presented oral argument, the President shall declare the hearing closed.

Article 82   Delivery of the Opinion of the Advocate General

1. Where a hearing takes place, the Opinion of the Advocate General shall be delivered after the close of that hearing.

2. The President shall declare the oral part of the procedure closed after the Advocate General has delivered his Opinion.

Article 83   Opening or reopening of the oral part of the procedure

The Court may at any time, after hearing the Advocate General, order the opening or reopening of the oral part of the procedure, in particular if it considers that it lacks sufficient information or where a party has, after the close of that part of the procedure, submitted a new fact which is of such a nature as to be a decisive factor for the decision of the Court, or where the case must be decided on the basis of an argument which has not been debated between the parties or the interested persons referred to in Article 23 of the Statute.

Article 84   Minutes of hearings

1. The Registrar shall draw up minutes of every hearing. The minutes shall be signed by the President and by the Registrar. They shall constitute an official record.

2. The parties and interested persons referred to in Article 23 of the Statute may inspect the minutes at the Registry and obtain copies.

Article 85   Recording of the hearing

The President may, on a duly substantiated request, authorise a party or an interested person referred to in Article 23 of the Statute who has participated in the written or oral part of the proceedings to listen, on the Court's premises, to the soundtrack of the hearing in the language used by the speaker during that hearing.

Chapter 9   Judgments and orders

Article 86   Date of delivery of a judgment

The parties or interested persons referred to in Article 23 of the Statute shall be informed of the date of delivery of a judgment.

Article 87   Content of a judgment

A judgment shall contain:

- (a) a statement that it is the judgment of the Court,
- (b) an indication as to the formation of the Court,
- (c) the date of delivery,
- (d) the names of the President and of the Judges who took part in the deliberations, with an indication as to the name of the Judge-Rapporteur,
- (e) the name of the Advocate General,
- (f) the name of the Registrar,
- (g) a description of the parties or of the interested persons referred to in Article 23 of the Statute who participated in the proceedings,
- (h) the names of their representatives,
- (i) in the case of direct actions and appeals, a statement of the forms of order sought by the parties,
- (j) where applicable, the date of the hearing,
- (k) a statement that the Advocate General has been heard and, where applicable, the date of his Opinion,
- (l) a summary of the facts,
- (m) the grounds for the decision,
- (n) the operative part of the judgment, including, where appropriate, the decision as to costs.

Article 88   Delivery and service of the judgment

1. The judgment shall be delivered in open court.

2. The original of the judgment, signed by the President, by the Judges who took part in the deliberations and by the Registrar, shall be sealed and deposited at the Registry; certified copies of the judgment shall be served on the parties and, where applicable, the referring court or tribunal, the interested persons referred to in Article 23 of the Statute and the General Court.

Article 89   Content of an order

1. An order shall contain:

- (a) a statement that it is the order of the Court,
- (b) an indication as to the formation of the Court,
- (c) the date of its adoption,
- (d) an indication as to the legal basis of the order,
- (e) the names of the President and, where applicable, the Judges who took part in the deliberations, with an indication as to the name of the Judge-Rapporteur,
- (f) the name of the Advocate General,
- (g) the name of the Registrar,
- (h) a description of the parties or of the interested persons referred to in Article 23 of the Statute who participated in the proceedings,

(i) the names of their representatives,

(j) a statement that the Advocate General has been heard,

(k) the operative part of the order, including, where appropriate, the decision as to costs.

2. Where, in accordance with these Rules, an order must be reasoned, it shall in addition contain:

(a) in the case of direct actions and appeals, a statement of the forms of order sought by the parties,

(b) a summary of the facts,

(c) the grounds for the decision.

Article 90   Signature and service of the order

The original of the order, signed by the President and by the Registrar, shall be sealed and deposited at the Registry; certified copies of the order shall be served on the parties and, where applicable, the referring court or tribunal, the interested persons referred to in Article 23 of the Statute and the General Court.

Article 91   Binding nature of judgments and orders

1. A judgment shall be binding from the date of its delivery.

2. An order shall be binding from the date of its service.

Article 92   Publication in the Official Journal of the European Union

A notice containing the date and the operative part of the judgment or order of the Court which closes the proceedings shall be published in the *Official Journal of the European Union*.

Title III References for a preliminary ruling

Chapter 1 General provisions

Article 93   Scope

The procedure shall be governed by the provisions of this Title:

(a) in the cases covered by Article 23 of the Statute,

(b) as regards references for interpretation which may be provided for by agreements to which the European Union or the Member States are parties.

Article 94   Content of the request for a preliminary ruling

In addition to the text of the questions referred to the Court for a preliminary ruling, the request for a preliminary ruling shall contain:

(a) a summary of the subject-matter of the dispute and the relevant findings of fact as determined by the referring court or tribunal, or, at least, an account of the facts on which the questions are based;

(b) the tenor of any national provisions applicable in the case and, where appropriate, the relevant national case-law;

(c) a statement of the reasons which prompted the referring court or tribunal to inquire about the interpretation or validity of certain provisions of European Union law, and the relationship between those provisions and the national legislation applicable to the main proceedings.

Article 95   Anonymity

1. Where anonymity has been granted by the referring court or tribunal, the Court shall respect that anonymity in the proceedings pending before it.

2. At the request of the referring court or tribunal, of a party to the main proceedings or of its own motion, the Court may also render anonymous one or more persons or entities concerned by the case.

Article 96   Participation in preliminary ruling proceedings

1. Pursuant to Article 23 of the Statute, the following shall be authorised to submit observations to the Court:

    (a) the parties to the main proceedings,

    (b) the Member States,

    (c) the European Commission,

    (d) the institution which adopted the act the validity or interpretation of which is in dispute,

    (e) the States, other than the Member States, which are parties to the EEA Agreement, and also the EFTA Surveillance Authority, where a question concerning one of the fields of application of that Agreement is referred to the Court for a preliminary ruling,

    (f) non-Member States which are parties to an agreement relating to a specific subject-matter, concluded with the Council, where the agreement so provides and where a court or tribunal of a Member State refers to the Court of Justice for a preliminary ruling a question falling within the scope of that agreement.

2. Non-participation in the written part of the procedure does not preclude participation in the oral part of the procedure.

Article 97   Parties to the main proceedings

1. The parties to the main proceedings are those who are determined as such by the referring court or tribunal in accordance with national rules of procedure.

2. Where the referring court or tribunal informs the Court that a new party has been admitted to the main proceedings, when the proceedings before the Court are already pending, that party must accept the case as he finds it at the time when the Court was so informed. That party shall receive a copy of every procedural document already served on the interested persons referred to in Article 23 of the Statute.

3. As regards the representation and attendance of the parties to the main proceedings, the Court shall take account of the rules of procedure in force before the court or tribunal which made the reference. In the event of any doubt as to whether a person may under national law represent a party to the main proceedings, the Court may obtain information from the referring court or tribunal on the rules of procedure applicable.

Article 98   Translation and service of the request for a preliminary ruling

1. The requests for a preliminary ruling referred to in this Title shall be served on the Member States in the original version, accompanied by a translation into the official language of the State to which they are being addressed. Where appropriate, on account of the length of the request, such translation shall be replaced by the translation into the official language of the State to which it is addressed of a summary of that request, which will serve as a basis for the position to be adopted by that State. The summary shall include the full text of the question or questions referred for a preliminary ruling. That summary shall contain, in particular, in so far as that information appears in the request for a preliminary ruling, the subject-matter of the main proceedings, the essential arguments of the parties to those proceedings, a succinct presentation of the reasons for the reference for a preliminary ruling and the case-law and the provisions of national law and European Union law relied on.

2. In the cases covered by the third paragraph of Article 23 of the Statute, the requests for a preliminary ruling shall be served on the States, other than the Member States, which are parties to the EEA Agreement and also on the EFTA Surveillance Authority in the original version, accompanied by a translation of the request, or where appropriate of a summary, into one of the languages referred to in Article 36, to be chosen by the addressee.

3. Where a non-Member State has the right to take part in preliminary ruling proceedings pursuant to the fourth paragraph of Article 23 of the Statute, the original version of the request for a preliminary ruling shall be served on it accompanied by a translation of the request, or where appropriate of a summary, into one of the languages referred to in Article 36, to be chosen by the non-Member State concerned.

Article 99   Reply by reasoned order

Where a question referred to the Court for a preliminary ruling is identical to a question on which the Court has already ruled, where the reply to such a question may be clearly deduced from existing case-law or where the answer to the question referred for a preliminary ruling admits of no reasonable doubt, the Court may at any time, on a proposal from the Judge-Rapporteur and after hearing the Advocate General, decide to rule by reasoned order.

Article 100   Circumstances in which the Court remains seised

1. The Court shall remain seised of a request for a preliminary ruling for as long as it is not withdrawn by the court or tribunal which made that request to the Court. The withdrawal of a request may be taken into account until notice of the date of delivery of the judgment has been served on the interested persons referred to in Article 23 of the Statute.

2. However, the Court may at any time declare that the conditions of its jurisdiction are no longer fulfilled.

Article 101   Request for clarification

1. Without prejudice to the measures of organisation of procedure and measures of inquiry provided for in these Rules, the Court may, after hearing the Advocate General, request clarification from the referring court or tribunal within a time-limit prescribed by the Court.

2. The reply of the referring court or tribunal to that request shall be served on the interested persons referred to in Article 23 of the Statute.

Article 102   Costs of the preliminary ruling proceedings

It shall be for the referring court or tribunal to decide as to the costs of the preliminary ruling proceedings.

Article 103   Rectification of judgments and orders

1. Clerical mistakes, errors in calculation and obvious inaccuracies affecting judgments or orders may be rectified by the Court, of its own motion or at the request of an interested person referred to in Article 23 of the Statute made within two weeks after delivery of the judgment or service of the order.

2. The Court shall take its decision after hearing the Advocate General.

3. The original of the rectification order shall be annexed to the original of the rectified decision. A note of this order shall be made in the margin of the original of the rectified decision.

Article 104   Interpretation of preliminary rulings

1. Article 158 of these Rules relating to the interpretation of judgments and orders shall not apply to decisions given in reply to a request for a preliminary ruling.

2. It shall be for the national courts or tribunals to assess whether they consider that sufficient guidance is given by a preliminary ruling, or whether it appears to them that a further reference to the Court is required.

Chapter 2 Expedited preliminary ruling procedure

Article 105   Expedited procedure

1. At the request of the referring court or tribunal or, exceptionally, of his own motion, the President of the Court may, where the nature of the case requires that it be dealt with within a short time, after hearing the Judge-Rapporteur and the Advocate General, decide that a reference for a preliminary ruling is to be determined pursuant to an expedited procedure derogating from the provisions of these Rules.

2. In that event, the President shall immediately fix the date for the hearing, which shall be communicated to the interested persons referred to in Article 23 of the Statute when the request for a preliminary ruling is served.

3. The interested persons referred to in the preceding paragraph may lodge statements of case or written observations within a time-limit prescribed by the President, which shall not be less than

15 days. The President may request those interested persons to restrict the matters addressed in their statement of case or written observations to the essential points of law raised by the request for a preliminary ruling.

4. The statements of case or written observations, if any, shall be communicated to all the interested persons referred to in Article 23 of the Statute prior to the hearing.

5. The Court shall rule after hearing the Advocate General.

Article 106   Transmission of procedural documents

1. The procedural documents referred to in the preceding Article shall be deemed to have been lodged on the transmission to the Registry, by telefax or any other technical means of communication available to the Court, of a copy of the signed original and the items and documents relied on in support of it, together with the schedule referred to in Article 57(4). The original of the document and the annexes referred to above shall be sent to the Registry immediately.

2. Where the preceding Article requires that a document be served on or communicated to a person, such service or communication may be effected by transmission of a copy of the document by telefax or any other technical means of communication available to the Court and the addressee.

Chapter 3 Urgent preliminary ruling procedure

Article 107   Scope of the urgent preliminary ruling procedure

1. A reference for a preliminary ruling which raises one or more questions in the areas covered by Title V of Part Three of the Treaty on the Functioning of the European Union may, at the request of the referring court or tribunal or, exceptionally, of the Court's own motion, be dealt with under an urgent procedure derogating from the provisions of these Rules.

2. The referring court or tribunal shall set out the matters of fact and law which establish the urgency and justify the application of that exceptional procedure and shall, in so far as possible, indicate the answer that it proposes to the questions referred.

3. If the referring court or tribunal has not submitted a request for the urgent procedure to be applied, the President of the Court may, if the application of that procedure appears, prima facie, to be required, ask the Chamber referred to in Article 108 to consider whether it is necessary to deal with the reference under that procedure.

Article 108   Decision as to urgency

1. The decision to deal with a reference for a preliminary ruling under the urgent procedure shall be taken by the designated Chamber, acting on a proposal from the Judge-Rapporteur and after hearing the Advocate General. The composition of that Chamber shall be determined in accordance with Article 28(2) on the day on which the case is assigned to the Judge-Rapporteur if the application of the urgent procedure is requested by the referring court or tribunal, or, if the application of that procedure is considered at the request of the President of the Court, on the day on which that request is made.

2. If the case is connected with a pending case assigned to a Judge-Rapporteur who is not a member of the designated Chamber, that Chamber may propose to the President of the Court that the case be assigned to that Judge-Rapporteur. Where the case is reassigned to that Judge-Rapporteur, the Chamber of five Judges which includes him shall carry out the duties of the designated Chamber in respect of that case. Article 29(1) shall apply.

Article 109   Written part of the urgent procedure

1. A request for a preliminary ruling shall, where the referring court or tribunal has requested the application of the urgent procedure or where the President has requested the designated Chamber to consider whether it is necessary to deal with the reference under that procedure, be served forthwith by the Registrar on the parties to the main proceedings, on the Member State from which the reference is made, on the European Commission and on the institution which adopted the act the validity or interpretation of which is in dispute.

2. The decision as to whether or not to deal with the reference for a preliminary ruling under the urgent procedure shall be served immediately on the referring court or tribunal and on the parties, Member State and institutions referred to in the preceding paragraph. The decision to deal with the reference under the urgent procedure shall prescribe the time-limit within which those parties or entities may lodge statements of case or written observations. The decision may specify the matters of law to which such statements of case or written observations must relate and may specify the maximum length of those documents.

3. Where a request for a preliminary ruling refers to an administrative procedure or judicial proceedings conducted in a Member State other than that from which the reference is made, the Court may invite that first Member State to provide all relevant information in writing or at the hearing.

4. As soon as the service referred to in paragraph 1 above has been effected, the request for a preliminary ruling shall also be communicated to the interested persons referred to in Article 23 of the Statute, other than the persons served, and the decision whether or not to deal with the reference for a preliminary ruling under the urgent procedure shall be communicated to those interested persons as soon as the service referred to in paragraph 2 has been effected.

5. The interested persons referred to in Article 23 of the Statute shall be informed as soon as possible of the likely date of the hearing.

6. Where the reference is not to be dealt with under the urgent procedure, the proceedings shall continue in accordance with the provisions of Article 23 of the Statute and the applicable provisions of these Rules.

Article 110   Service and information following the close of the written part of the procedure

1. Where a reference for a preliminary ruling is to be dealt with under the urgent procedure, the request for a preliminary ruling and the statements of case or written observations which have been lodged shall be served on the interested persons referred to in Article 23 of the Statute other than the parties and entities referred to in Article 109(1). The request for a preliminary ruling shall be accompanied by a translation, where appropriate of a summary, in accordance with Article 98.

2. The statements of case or written observations which have been lodged shall also be served on the parties and other interested persons referred to in Article 109(1).

3. The date of the hearing shall be communicated to the interested persons referred to in Article 23 of the Statute at the same time as the documents referred to in the preceding paragraphs are served.

Article 111   Omission of the written part of the procedure

The designated Chamber may, in cases of extreme urgency, decide to omit the written part of the procedure referred to in Article 109(2).

Article 112   Decision on the substance

The designated Chamber shall rule after hearing the Advocate General.

Article 113   Formation of the Court

1. The designated Chamber may decide to sit in a formation of three Judges. In that event, it shall be composed of the President of the designated Chamber, the Judge-Rapporteur and the first Judge or, as the case may be, the first two Judges designated from the list referred to in Article 28(2) on the date on which the composition of the designated Chamber is determined in accordance with Article 108(1).

2. The designated Chamber may also request the Court to assign the case to a formation composed of a greater number of Judges. The urgent procedure shall continue before the new formation of the Court, where necessary after the reopening of the oral part of the procedure.

Article 114   Transmission of procedural documents

Procedural documents shall be transmitted in accordance with Article 106.

Chapter 4 Legal aid

Article 115   Application for legal aid

1. A party to the main proceedings who is wholly or in part unable to meet the costs of the proceedings before the Court may at any time apply for legal aid.

2. The application shall be accompanied by all information and supporting documents making it possible to assess the applicant's financial situation, such as a certificate issued by a competent national authority attesting to his financial situation.

3. If the applicant has already obtained legal aid before the referring court or tribunal, he shall produce the decision of that court or tribunal and specify what is covered by the sums already granted.

Article 116   Decision on the application for legal aid

1. As soon as the application for legal aid has been lodged it shall be assigned by the President to the Judge-Rapporteur responsible for the case in the context of which the application has been made.

2. The decision to grant legal aid, in full or in part, or to refuse it shall be taken, on a proposal from the Judge-Rapporteur and after hearing the Advocate General, by the Chamber of three Judges to which the Judge-Rapporteur is assigned. The formation of the Court shall, in that event, be composed of the President of that Chamber, the Judge-Rapporteur and the first Judge or, as the case may be, the first two Judges designated from the list referred to in Article 28(3) on the date on which the application for legal aid is brought before that Chamber by the Judge-Rapporteur.

3. If the Judge-Rapporteur is not a member of a Chamber of three Judges, the decision shall be taken, under the same conditions, by the Chamber of five Judges to which he is assigned. In addition to the Judge-Rapporteur, the formation of the Court shall be composed of four Judges designated from the list referred to in Article 28(2) on the date on which the application for legal aid is brought before that Chamber by the Judge-Rapporteur.

4. The formation of the Court shall give its decision by way of order. Where the application for legal aid is refused in whole or in part, the order shall state the reasons for that refusal.

Article 117   Sums to be advanced as legal aid

Where legal aid is granted, the cashier of the Court shall be responsible, where applicable within the limits set by the formation of the Court, for costs involved in the assistance and representation of the applicant before the Court. At the request of the applicant or his representative, an advance on those costs may be paid.

Article 118   Withdrawal of legal aid

The formation of the Court which gave a decision on the application for legal aid may at any time, either of its own motion or on request, withdraw that legal aid if the circumstances which led to its being granted alter during the proceedings.

Title IV Direct actions

Chapter 1 Representation of the parties

Article 119   Obligation to be represented

1. A party may be represented only by his agent or lawyer.

2. Agents and lawyers must lodge at the Registry an official document or an authority to act issued by the party whom they represent.

3. The lawyer acting for a party must also lodge at the Registry a certificate that he is authorised to practise before a court of a Member State or of another State which is a party to the EEA Agreement.

4. If those documents are not lodged, the Registrar shall prescribe a reasonable time limit within which the party concerned is to produce them. If the party concerned fails to produce the

required documents within the time limit prescribed, the President shall, after hearing the Judge-Rapporteur and the Advocate General, decide whether the non-compliance with that procedural requirement renders the application or written pleading formally inadmissible. If he considers it necessary, the President may refer that question to the Court of Justice.

Chapter 2   Written part of the procedure

Article 120   Content of the application

An application of the kind referred to in Article 21 of the Statute shall state:

- (a) the name and address of the applicant;
- (b) the name of the party against whom the application is made;
- (c) the subject-matter of the proceedings, the pleas in law and arguments relied on and a summary of those pleas in law;
- (d) the form of order sought by the applicant;
- (e) where appropriate, any evidence produced or offered.

Article 121   Information relating to service

1. For the purpose of the proceedings, the application shall state an address for service. It shall indicate the name of the person who is authorised and has expressed willingness to accept service.

2. In addition to, or instead of, specifying an address for service as referred to in paragraph 1, the application may state that the lawyer or agent agrees that service is to be effected on him by telefax or any other technical means of communication.

3. If the application does not comply with the requirements referred to in paragraphs 1 or 2, all service on the party concerned for the purpose of the proceedings shall be effected, for so long as the defect has not been cured, by registered letter addressed to the agent or lawyer of that party. By way of derogation from Article 48, service shall then be deemed to be duly effected by the lodging of the registered letter at the post office of the place in which the Court has its seat.

Article 122   Annexes to the application

1. The application shall be accompanied, where appropriate, by the documents specified in the second paragraph of Article 21 of the Statute.

2. An application submitted under Article 273 TFEU shall be accompanied by a copy of the special agreement concluded between the Member States concerned.

3. If an application does not comply with the requirements set out in paragraphs 1 or 2 of this Article, the Registrar shall prescribe a reasonable time limit within which the applicant is to produce the abovementioned documents. If the applicant fails to put the application in order, the President shall, after hearing the Judge-Rapporteur and the Advocate General, decide whether the non-compliance with these conditions renders the application formally inadmissible. If he considers it necessary, the President may refer that question to the Court of Justice.

Article 123   Service of the application

The application shall be served on the defendant. In cases where Article 119(4) or Article 122(3) applies, service shall be effected as soon as the application has been put in order or the President or the Court has declared it admissible notwithstanding the failure to observe the requirements set out in those two Articles.

Article 124   Content of the defence

1. Within two months after service on him of the application, the defendant shall lodge a defence, stating:

- (a) the name and address of the defendant;
- (b) the pleas in law and arguments relied on;
- (c) the form of order sought by the defendant;
- (d) where appropriate, any evidence produced or offered.

2. Article 121 shall apply to the defence.

3. The time-limit laid down in paragraph 1 may exceptionally be extended by the President at the duly reasoned request of the defendant.

Article 125   Transmission of documents

Where the European Parliament, the Council or the European Commission is not a party to a case, the Court shall send to them copies of the application and of the defence, without the annexes thereto, to enable them to assess whether the inapplicability of one of their acts is being invoked under Article 277 TFEU.

Article 126   Reply and rejoinder

1. The application initiating proceedings and the defence may be supplemented by a reply from the applicant and by a rejoinder from the defendant.

2. The President shall prescribe the time-limits within which those procedural documents are to be produced. He may specify the matters to which the reply or the rejoinder should relate.

Chapter 3 Pleas in law and evidence

Article 127   New pleas in law

1. No new plea in law may be introduced in the course of proceedings unless it is based on matters of law or of fact which come to light in the course of the procedure.

2. Without prejudice to the decision to be taken on the admissibility of the plea in law, the President may, on a proposal from the Judge-Rapporteur and after hearing the Advocate General, prescribe a time-limit within which the other party may respond to that plea.

Article 128   Evidence produced or offered

1. In reply or rejoinder a party may produce or offer further evidence in support of his arguments. The party must give reasons for the delay in submitting such evidence.

2. The parties may, exceptionally, produce or offer further evidence after the close of the written part of the procedure. They must give reasons for the delay in submitting such evidence. The President may, on a proposal from the Judge-Rapporteur and after hearing the Advocate General, prescribe a time-limit within which the other party may comment on such evidence.

Chapter 4 Intervention

Article 129   Object and effects of the intervention

1. The intervention shall be limited to supporting, in whole or in part, the form of order sought by one of the parties. It shall not confer the same procedural rights as those conferred on the parties and, in particular, shall not give rise to any right to request that a hearing be held.

2. The intervention shall be ancillary to the main proceedings. It shall become devoid of purpose if the case is removed from the register of the Court as a result of a party's discontinuance or withdrawal from the proceedings or of an agreement between the parties, or where the application is declared inadmissible.

3. The intervener must accept the case as he finds it at the time of his intervention.

4. Consideration may be given to an application to intervene which is made after the expiry of the time-limit prescribed in Article 130 but before the decision to open the oral part of the procedure provided for in Article 60(4). In that event, if the President allows the intervention, the intervener may submit his observations during the hearing, if it takes place.

Article 130   Application to intervene

1. An application to intervene must be submitted within six weeks of the publication of the notice referred to in Article 21(4).

2. The application to intervene shall contain:
    (a) a description of the case;
    (b) a description of the main parties;
    (c) the name and address of the intervener;

(d) the form of order sought, in support of which the intervener is applying for leave to intervene;

(e) a statement of the circumstances establishing the right to intervene, where the application is submitted pursuant to the second or third paragraph of Article 40 of the Statute.

3. The intervener shall be represented in accordance with Article 19 of the Statute.

4. Articles 119, 121 and 122 of these Rules shall apply.

Article 131   Decision on applications to intervene

1. The application to intervene shall be served on the parties in order to obtain any written or oral observations they may wish to make on that application.

2. Where the application is submitted pursuant to the first paragraph of Article 40 of the Statute, the intervention shall be allowed by decision of the President and the intervener shall receive a copy of every procedural document served on the parties, unless the parties have, within 10 days after the service referred to in paragraph 1 has been effected, identified secret or confidential items or documents which, if communicated to the intervener, the parties claim would be prejudicial to them. In that case, the President shall decide on the application to intervene by order, after hearing the Judge-Rapporteur and the Advocate General, and the intervener shall receive a copy of every procedural document served on the parties, save, where applicable, for the secret or confidential items or documents excluded from such communication.

3. Where the application is submitted pursuant to the second paragraph of Article 40 of the Statute, the President shall decide on the application to intervene by order, after hearing the Judge-Rapporteur and the Advocate General, or shall refer the application to the Court. If the application to intervene is granted, the intervener shall receive a copy of every procedural document served on the parties, save, where applicable, for the secret or confidential items or documents excluded from such communication.

4. Where the application is submitted pursuant to the third paragraph of Article 40 of the Statute, the intervention shall be allowed by decision of the President and the intervener shall receive a copy of every procedural document served on the parties unless those parties have, within 10 days after the service referred to in paragraph 1 has been effected, put forward observations on the application to intervene or identified secret or confidential items or documents which, if communicated to the intervener, the parties claim would be prejudicial to them. In such cases, the President shall decide on the application to intervene by order, after hearing the Judge-Rapporteur and the Advocate General, and the intervener shall receive a copy of every procedural document served on the parties, save, where applicable, for the secret or confidential items or documents excluded from such communication.

Article 132   Submission of statements

1. The intervener may submit a statement in intervention within one month after communication of the procedural documents referred to in the preceding Article. That time-limit may be extended by the President at the duly reasoned request of the intervener.

2. The statement in intervention shall contain:

(a) the form of order sought by the intervener in support, in whole or in part, of the form of order sought by one of the parties;

(b) the pleas in law and arguments relied on by the intervener;

(c) where appropriate, any evidence produced or offered.

3. After the statement in intervention has been lodged, the President shall, where necessary, prescribe a time-limit within which the parties may reply to that statement.

Chapter 5   Expedited procedure

Article 133   Decision relating to the expedited procedure

1. At the request of the applicant or the defendant, the President of the Court may, where the nature of the case requires that it be dealt with within a short time, after hearing the other party, the Judge-Rapporteur and the Advocate General, decide that a case is to be determined pursuant to an expedited procedure derogating from the provisions of these Rules.

2. The request for a case to be determined pursuant to an expedited procedure must be made by a separate document submitted at the same time as the application initiating proceedings or the defence, as the case may be, is lodged.

3. Exceptionally the President may also take such a decision of his own motion, after hearing the parties, the Judge-Rapporteur and the Advocate General.

Article 134   Written part of the procedure

1. Under the expedited procedure, the application initiating proceedings and the defence may be supplemented by a reply and a rejoinder only if the President, after hearing the Judge-Rapporteur and the Advocate General, considers this to be necessary.

2. An intervener may submit a statement in intervention only if the President, after hearing the Judge-Rapporteur and the Advocate General, considers this to be necessary.

Article 135   Oral part of the procedure

1. Once the defence has been submitted or, if the decision to determine the case pursuant to an expedited procedure is not made until after that pleading has been lodged, once that decision has been taken, the President shall fix a date for the hearing, which shall be communicated forthwith to the parties. He may postpone the date of the hearing where it is necessary to undertake measures of inquiry or where measures of organisation of procedure so require.

2. Without prejudice to Articles 127 and 128, a party may supplement his arguments and produce or offer evidence during the oral part of the procedure. The party must, however, give reasons for the delay in producing such further arguments or evidence.

Article 136   Decision on the substance

The Court shall give its ruling after hearing the Advocate General.

Chapter 6 Costs

Article 137   Decision as to costs

A decision as to costs shall be given in the judgment or order which closes the proceedings.

Article 138   General rules as to allocation of costs

1. The unsuccessful party shall be ordered to pay the costs if they have been applied for in the successful party's pleadings.

2. Where there is more than one unsuccessful party the Court shall decide how the costs are to be shared.

3. Where each party succeeds on some and fails on other heads, the parties shall bear their own costs. However, if it appears justified in the circumstances of the case, the Court may order that one party, in addition to bearing its own costs, pay a proportion of the costs of the other party.

Article 139   Unreasonable or vexatious costs

The Court may order a party, even if successful, to pay costs which the Court considers that party to have unreasonably or vexatiously caused the opposite party to incur.

Article 140   Costs of interveners

1. The Member States and institutions which have intervened in the proceedings shall bear their own costs.

2. The States, other than the Member States, which are parties to the EEA Agreement, and also the EFTA Surveillance Authority, shall similarly bear their own costs if they have intervened in the proceedings.

3. The Court may order an intervener other than those referred to in the preceding paragraphs to bear his own costs.

Article 141   Costs in the event of discontinuance or withdrawal

1. A party who discontinues or withdraws from proceedings shall be ordered to pay the costs if they have been applied for in the other party's observations on the discontinuance.

2. However, at the request of the party who discontinues or withdraws from proceedings, the costs shall be borne by the other party if this appears justified by the conduct of that party.

3. Where the parties have come to an agreement on costs, the decision as to costs shall be in accordance with that agreement.

4. If costs are not claimed, the parties shall bear their own costs.

Article 142   Costs where a case does not proceed to judgment
Where a case does not proceed to judgment the costs shall be in the discretion of the Court.

Article 143   Costs of proceedings
Proceedings before the Court shall be free of charge, except that:
> (a) where a party has caused the Court to incur avoidable costs the Court may, after hearing the Advocate General, order that party to refund them;
> (b) where copying or translation work is carried out at the request of a party, the cost shall, in so far as the Registrar considers it excessive, be paid for by that party on the Registry's scale of charges referred to in Article 22.

Article 144   Recoverable costs
Without prejudice to the preceding Article, the following shall be regarded as recoverable costs:
> (a) sums payable to witnesses and experts under Article 73 of these Rules;
> (b) expenses necessarily incurred by the parties for the purpose of the proceedings, in particular the travel and subsistence expenses and the remuneration of agents, advisers or lawyers.

Article 145   Dispute concerning the costs to be recovered
1. If there is a dispute concerning the costs to be recovered, the Chamber of three Judges to which the Judge-Rapporteur who dealt with the case is assigned shall, on application by the party concerned and after hearing the opposite party and the Advocate General, make an order. In that event, the formation of the Court shall be composed of the President of that Chamber, the Judge-Rapporteur and the first Judge or, as the case may be, the first two Judges designated from the list referred to in Article 28(3) on the date on which the dispute is brought before that Chamber by the Judge-Rapporteur.

2. If the Judge-Rapporteur is not a member of a Chamber of three Judges, the decision shall be taken, under the same conditions, by the Chamber of five Judges to which he is assigned. In addition to the Judge-Rapporteur, the formation of the Court shall be composed of four Judges designated from the list referred to in Article 28(2) on the date on which the dispute is brought before that Chamber by the Judge-Rapporteur.

3. The parties may, for the purposes of enforcement, apply for an authenticated copy of the order.

Article 146   Procedure for payment
1. Sums due from the cashier of the Court and from its debtors shall be paid in euro.

2. Where costs to be recovered have been incurred in a currency other than the euro or where the steps in respect of which payment is due were taken in a country of which the euro is not the currency, the conversion shall be effected at the European Central Bank's official rates of exchange on the day of payment.

Chapter 7   Amicable settlement, discontinuance, cases that do not proceed to judgment and preliminary issues

Article 147   Amicable settlement
1. If, before the Court has given its decision, the parties reach a settlement of their dispute and inform the Court of the abandonment of their claims, the President shall order the case to be removed from the register and shall give a decision as to costs in accordance with Article 141, having regard to any proposals made by the parties on the matter.

2. This provision shall not apply to proceedings under Articles 263 TFEU and 265 TFEU.

Article 148 Discontinuance

If the applicant informs the Court in writing or at the hearing that he wishes to discontinue the proceedings, the President shall order the case to be removed from the register and shall give a decision as to costs in accordance with Article 141.

Article 149 Cases that do not proceed to judgment

If the Court declares that the action has become devoid of purpose and that there is no longer any need to adjudicate on it, the Court may at any time of its own motion, on a proposal from the Judge-Rapporteur and after hearing the parties and the Advocate General, decide to rule by reasoned order. It shall give a decision as to costs.

Article 150 Absolute bar to proceeding with a case

On a proposal from the Judge-Rapporteur, the Court may at any time of its own motion, after hearing the parties and the Advocate General, decide to rule by reasoned order on whether there exists any absolute bar to proceeding with a case.

Article 151 Preliminary objections and issues

1. A party applying to the Court for a decision on a preliminary objection or issue not going to the substance of the case shall submit the application by a separate document.

2. The application must state the pleas of law and arguments relied on and the form of order sought by the applicant; any supporting items and documents must be annexed to it.

3. As soon as the application has been submitted, the President shall prescribe a time-limit within which the opposite party may submit in writing his pleas in law and the form of order which he seeks.

4. Unless the Court decides otherwise, the remainder of the proceedings on the application shall be oral.

5. The Court shall, after hearing the Advocate General, decide on the application as soon as possible or, where special circumstances so justify, reserve its decision until it rules on the substance of the case.

6. If the Court refuses the application or reserves its decision, the President shall prescribe new time-limits for the further steps in the proceedings.

Chapter 8 Judgments by default

Article 152 Judgments by default

1. If a defendant on whom an application initiating proceedings has been duly served fails to respond to the application in the proper form and within the time-limit prescribed, the applicant may apply to the Court for judgment by default.

2. The application for judgment by default shall be served on the defendant. The Court may decide to open the oral part of the procedure on the application.

3. Before giving judgment by default the Court shall, after hearing the Advocate General, consider whether the application initiating proceedings is admissible, whether the appropriate formalities have been complied with, and whether the applicant's claims appear well founded. The Court may adopt measures of organisation of procedure or order measures of inquiry.

4. A judgment by default shall be enforceable. The Court may, however, grant a stay of execution until the Court has given its decision on any application under Article 156 to set aside the judgment, or it may make execution subject to the provision of security of an amount and nature to be fixed in the light of the circumstances; this security shall be released if no such application is made or if the application fails.

Chapter 9 Requests and applications relating to judgments and orders

Article 153 Competent formation of the Court

1. With the exception of applications referred to in Article 159, the requests and applications referred to in this Chapter shall be assigned to the Judge-Rapporteur who was responsible for the

case to which the request or application relates, and shall be assigned to the formation of the Court which gave a decision in that case.

2. If the Judge-Rapporteur is prevented from acting, the President of the Court shall assign the request or application referred to in this Chapter to a Judge who was a member of the formation of the Court which gave a decision in the case to which that request or application relates.

3. If the quorum referred to in Article 17 of the Statute can no longer be attained, the Court shall, on a proposal from the Judge-Rapporteur and after hearing the Advocate General, assign the request or application to a new formation of the Court.

Article 154   Rectification

1. Without prejudice to the provisions relating to the interpretation of judgments and orders, clerical mistakes, errors in calculation and obvious inaccuracies may be rectified by the Court, of its own motion or at the request of a party made within two weeks after delivery of the judgment or service of the order.

2. Where the request for rectification concerns the operative part or one of the grounds constituting the necessary support for the operative part, the parties, whom the Registrar shall duly inform, may submit written observations within a time-limit prescribed by the President.

3. The Court shall take its decision after hearing the Advocate General.

4. The original of the rectification order shall be annexed to the original of the rectified decision. A note of this order shall be made in the margin of the original of the rectified decision.

Article 155   Failure to adjudicate

1. If the Court has failed to adjudicate on a specific head of claim or on costs, any party wishing to rely on that may, within a month after service of the decision, apply to the Court to supplement its decision.

2. The application shall be served on the opposite party and the President shall prescribe a time-limit within which that party may submit written observations.

3. After these observations have been submitted, the Court shall, after hearing the Advocate General, decide both on the admissibility and on the substance of the application.

Article 156   Application to set aside

1. Application may be made pursuant to Article 41 of the Statute to set aside a judgment delivered by default.

2. The application to set aside the judgment must be made within one month from the date of service of the judgment and must be submitted in the form prescribed by Articles 120 to 122 of these Rules.

3. After the application has been served, the President shall prescribe a time-limit within which the other party may submit his written observations.

4. The proceedings shall be conducted in accordance with Articles 59 to 92 of these Rules.

5. The Court shall decide by way of a judgment which may not be set aside.

6. The original of this judgment shall be annexed to the original of the judgment by default. A note of the judgment on the application to set aside shall be made in the margin of the original of the judgment by default.

Article 157   Third-party proceedings

1. Articles 120 to 122 of these Rules shall apply to an application initiating third-party proceedings made pursuant to Article 42 of the Statute. In addition such an application shall:

    (a) specify the judgment or order contested;

    (b) state how the contested decision is prejudicial to the rights of the third party;

    (c) indicate the reasons for which the third party was unable to take part in the original case.

2. The application must be made against all the parties to the original case.

3. The application must be submitted within two months of publication of the decision in the *Official Journal of the European Union*.

4. The Court may, on application by the third party, order a stay of execution of the contested decision. The provisions of Chapter 10 of this Title shall apply.

5. The contested decision shall be varied on the points on which the submissions of the third party are upheld.

6. The original of the judgment in the third-party proceedings shall be annexed to the original of the contested decision. A note of the judgment in the third-party proceedings shall be made in the margin of the original of the contested decision.

Article 158   Interpretation

1. In accordance with Article 43 of the Statute, if the meaning or scope of a judgment or order is in doubt, the Court shall construe it on application by any party or any institution of the European Union establishing an interest therein.

2. An application for interpretation must be made within two years after the date of delivery of the judgment or service of the order.

3. An application for interpretation shall be made in accordance with Articles 120 to 122 of these Rules. In addition it shall specify:
  (a) the decision in question;
  (b) the passages of which interpretation is sought.

4. The application must be made against all the parties to the case in which the decision of which interpretation is sought was given.

5. The Court shall give its decision after having given the parties an opportunity to submit their observations and after hearing the Advocate General.

6. The original of the interpreting decision shall be annexed to the original of the decision interpreted. A note of the interpreting decision shall be made in the margin of the original of the decision interpreted.

Article 159   Revision

1. In accordance with Article 44 of the Statute, an application for revision of a decision of the Court may be made only on discovery of a fact which is of such a nature as to be a decisive factor and which, when the judgment was delivered or the order served, was unknown to the Court and to the party claiming the revision.

2. Without prejudice to the time-limit of 10 years prescribed in the third paragraph of Article 44 of the Statute, an application for revision shall be made within three months of the date on which the facts on which the application is founded came to the applicant's knowledge.

3. Articles 120 to 122 of these Rules shall apply to an application for revision. In addition such an application shall:
  (a) specify the judgment or order contested;
  (b) indicate the points on which the decision is contested;
  (c) set out the facts on which the application is founded;
  (d) indicate the nature of the evidence to show that there are facts justifying revision, and that the time-limits laid down in paragraph 2 have been observed.

4. The application for revision must be made against all parties to the case in which the contested decision was given.

5. Without prejudice to its decision on the substance, the Court shall, after hearing the Advocate General, give in the form of an order its decision on the admissibility of the application, having regard to the written observations of the parties.

6. If the Court declares the application admissible, it shall proceed to consider the substance of the application and shall give its decision in the form of a judgment in accordance with these Rules.

7. The original of the revising judgment shall be annexed to the original of the decision revised. A note of the revising judgment shall be made in the margin of the original of the decision revised.

Article 159a   Manifestly inadmissible or manifestly unfounded requests and applications

Where a request or an application referred to in this Chapter is, in whole or in part, manifestly inadmissible or manifestly unfounded, the Court may, having heard the Judge-Rapporteur and the Advocate General, at any time decide to dismiss it, in whole or in part, by reasoned order.

Chapter 10 Suspension of operation or enforcement and other interim measures

Article 160   Application for suspension or for interim measures

1. An application to suspend the operation of any measure adopted by an institution, made pursuant to Article 278 TFEU or Article 157 TEAEC, shall be admissible only if the applicant has challenged that measure in an action before the Court.

2. An application for the adoption of one of the other interim measures referred to in Article 279 TFEU shall be admissible only if it is made by a party to a case before the Court and relates to that case.

3. An application of a kind referred to in the preceding paragraphs shall state the subject-matter of the proceedings, the circumstances giving rise to urgency and the pleas of fact and law establishing a prima facie case for the interim measure applied for.

4. The application shall be made by a separate document and in accordance with the provisions of Articles 120 to 122 of these Rules.

5. The application shall be served on the opposite party, and the President shall prescribe a short time-limit within which that party may submit written or oral observations.

6. The President may order a preparatory inquiry.

7. The President may grant the application even before the observations of the opposite party have been submitted. This decision may be varied or cancelled even without any application being made by any party.

Article 161   Decision on the application

1. The President shall either decide on the application himself or refer it immediately to the Court.

2. If the President is prevented from acting, Articles 10 and 13 of these Rules shall apply.

3. Where the application is referred to it, the Court shall give a decision immediately, after hearing the Advocate General.

Article 162   Order for suspension of operation or for interim measures

1. The decision on the application shall take the form of a reasoned order, from which no appeal shall lie. The order shall be served on the parties forthwith.

2. The execution of the order may be made conditional on the lodging by the applicant of security, of an amount and nature to be fixed in the light of the circumstances.

3. Unless the order fixes the date on which the interim measure is to lapse, the measure shall lapse when the judgment which closes the proceedings is delivered.

4. The order shall have only an interim effect, and shall be without prejudice to the decision of the Court on the substance of the case.

Article 163   Change in circumstances

On application by a party, the order may at any time be varied or cancelled on account of a change in circumstances.

Article 164   New application

Rejection of an application for an interim measure shall not bar the party who made it from making a further application on the basis of new facts.

Article 165   Applications pursuant to Articles 280 TFEU and 299 TFEU and Article 164 TEAEC

1. The provisions of this Chapter shall apply to applications to suspend the enforcement of a decision of the Court or of any measure adopted by the Council, the European Commission or the European Central Bank, submitted pursuant to Articles 280 TFEU and 299 TFEU or Article 164 TEAEC.

2. The order granting the application shall fix, where appropriate, a date on which the interim measure is to lapse.

Article 166   Application pursuant to Article 81 TEAEC

1. An application of a kind referred to in the third and fourth paragraphs of Article 81 TEAEC shall contain:
   (a) the names and addresses of the persons or undertakings to be inspected;
   (b) an indication of what is to be inspected and of the purpose of the inspection.

2. The President shall give his decision in the form of an order. Article 162 of these Rules shall apply.

3. If the President is prevented from acting, Articles 10 and 13 of these Rules shall apply.

Title V   Appeals against decisions of the General Court

Chapter 1   Form and content of the appeal, and form of order sought

Article 167   Lodging of the appeal

1. An appeal shall be brought by lodging an application at the Registry of the Court of Justice or of the General Court. When that application is lodged at the Registry of the General Court, it shall be transmitted forthwith to the Registry of the Court of Justice.

2. As soon as it is informed of the existence of an appeal, the Registry of the General Court shall forthwith transmit to the Registry of the Court of Justice the file in the case at first instance and any procedural file of the Board of Appeal transmitted to the General Court pursuant to the provisions of the Rules of Procedure of the General Court concerning proceedings relating to intellectual property rights.

Article 168   Content of the appeal

1. An appeal shall contain:
   (a) the name and address of the appellant;
   (b) a reference to the decision of the General Court appealed against;
   (c) the names of the other parties to the relevant case before the General Court;
   (d) the pleas in law and legal arguments relied on, and a summary of those pleas in law;
   (e) the form of order sought by the appellant.

2. Articles 119, 121 and 122(1) of these Rules shall apply to appeals.

3. The appeal shall state the date on which the decision appealed against was served on the appellant.

4. If an appeal does not comply with paragraphs 1 to 3 of this Article, the Registrar shall prescribe a reasonable time limit within which the appellant is to put the appeal in order. If the appellant fails to put the appeal in order within the time limit prescribed, the President shall, after hearing the Judge-Rapporteur and the Advocate General, decide whether the non-compliance with that formal requirement renders the appeal formally inadmissible. If he considers it necessary, the President may refer that question to the Court of Justice.

Article 169 Form of order sought, pleas in law and arguments of the appeal

1. An appeal shall seek to have set aside, in whole or in part, the decision of the General Court as set out in the operative part of that decision.

2. The pleas in law and legal arguments relied on shall identify precisely those points in the grounds of the decision of the General Court which are contested.

Article 170 Form of order sought in the event that the appeal is allowed

1. An appeal shall seek, in the event that it is declared well founded, the same form of order, in whole or in part, as that sought at first instance and shall not seek a different form of order. The subject-matter of the proceedings before the General Court may not be changed in the appeal.

2. Where the appellant requests that the case be referred back to the General Court if the decision appealed against is set aside, he shall set out the reasons why the state of the proceedings does not permit a decision by the Court of Justice.

Chapter 1a Prior determination as to whether appeals under Article 58a of the Statute should be allowed to proceed

Article 170a Request that the appeal be allowed to proceed

1. In the situations referred to in the first and second paragraphs of Article 58a of the Statute, the appellant shall annex to the appeal a request that the appeal be allowed to proceed, setting out the issue raised by the appeal that is significant with respect to the unity, consistency or development of European Union law and containing all the information necessary to enable the Court of Justice to rule on that request. If there is no such request, the Vice-President of the Court shall declare the appeal inadmissible.

2. The request that the appeal be allowed to proceed shall not exceed seven pages and shall be drawn up taking into account all the formal requirements contained in the Practice Directions to parties concerning cases brought before the Court, adopted on the basis of these Rules.

3. If the request that the appeal be allowed to proceed does not comply with the requirements set out in the preceding paragraph, the Registrar shall prescribe a reasonable time-limit within which the appellant is to put the request in order. If the appellant fails to put the request in order within the time-limit prescribed, the Vice-President of the Court shall decide, on a proposal from the Judge-Rapporteur and after hearing the Advocate General, whether the non-compliance with that formal requirement renders the appeal formally inadmissible.

Article 170b Decision on the request that the appeal be allowed to proceed

1. The Court of Justice shall rule as soon as possible on the request that the appeal be allowed to proceed.

2. The decision on that request shall be taken, on a proposal from the Judge-Rapporteur and after hearing the Advocate General, by a Chamber specially established for that purpose, presided over by the Vice-President of the Court and including also the Judge-Rapporteur and the President of the Chamber of three Judges to which the Judge-Rapporteur is attached on the date on which the request is made.

3. The decision on the request that the appeal be allowed to proceed shall take the form of a reasoned order.

4. Where the Court of Justice decides that the appeal should be allowed to proceed, wholly or in part, having regard to the criteria set out in the third paragraph of Article 58a of the Statute, the proceedings shall continue in accordance with Articles 171 to 190a of these Rules. The order referred to in the preceding paragraph shall be served, together with the appeal, on the parties to the relevant case before the General Court and shall specify, where the appeal is to be allowed to proceed in part, the pleas in law or parts of the appeal to which the response must relate.

5. The General Court and, if they were not parties to the proceedings before it, the Member States, the European Parliament, the Council and the European Commission shall forthwith be informed by the Registrar of the decision that the appeal should be allowed to proceed.

Chapter 2 Responses, replies and rejoinders

Article 171 Service of the appeal

1. The appeal shall be served on the other parties to the relevant case before the General Court.

2. In a case where Article 168(4) of these Rules applies, service shall be effected as soon as the appeal has been put in order or the President or the Court of Justice has declared it admissible notwithstanding the failure to observe the formal requirements laid down by that Article.

Article 172 Parties authorised to lodge a response

Any party to the relevant case before the General Court having an interest in the appeal being allowed or dismissed may submit a response within two months after service on him of the appeal. The time-limit for submitting a response shall not be extended.

Article 173 Content of the response

1. A response shall contain:
    (a) the name and address of the party submitting it;
    (b) the date on which the appeal was served on him;
    (c) the pleas in law and legal arguments relied on;
    (d) the form of order sought.

2. Articles 119 and 121 of these Rules shall apply to responses.

Article 174 Form of order sought in the response

A response shall seek to have the appeal allowed or dismissed, in whole or in part.

Article 175 Reply and rejoinder

1. The appeal and the response may be supplemented by a reply and a rejoinder only where the President, on a duly reasoned application submitted by the appellant within seven days of service of the response, considers it necessary, after hearing the Judge-Rapporteur and the Advocate General, in particular to enable the appellant to present his views on a plea of inadmissibility or on new matters relied on in the response.

2. The President shall fix the date by which the reply is to be produced and, upon service of that pleading, the date by which the rejoinder is to be produced. He may limit the number of pages and the subject-matter of those pleadings.

Chapter 3 Form and content of the cross-appeal, and form of order sought

Article 176 Cross-appeal

1. The parties referred to in Article 172 of these Rules may submit a cross-appeal within the same time-limit as that prescribed for the submission of a response.

2. A cross-appeal must be introduced by a document separate from the response.

Article 177 Content of the cross-appeal

1. A cross-appeal shall contain:
    (a) the name and address of the party bringing the cross-appeal;
    (b) the date on which the appeal was served on him;
    (c) the pleas in law and legal arguments relied on;
    (d) the form of order sought.

2. Articles 119, 121 and 122(1) and (3) of these Rules shall apply to cross-appeals.

Article 178 Form of order sought, pleas in law and arguments of the cross-appeal

1. A cross-appeal shall seek to have set aside, in whole or in part, the decision of the General Court.

2. It may also seek to have set aside an express or implied decision relating to the admissibility of the action before the General Court.

3. The pleas in law and legal arguments relied on shall identify precisely those points in the grounds of the decision of the General Court which are contested. The pleas in law and arguments must be separate from those relied on in the response.

Chapter 4   Pleadings consequent on the cross-appeal

Article 179   Response to the cross-appeal
Where a cross-appeal is brought, the applicant at first instance or any other party to the relevant case before the General Court having an interest in the cross-appeal being allowed or dismissed may submit a response, which must be limited to the pleas in law relied on in that cross-appeal, within two months after its being served on him. That time-limit shall not be extended.

Article 180   Reply and rejoinder on a cross-appeal
1. The cross-appeal and the response thereto may be supplemented by a reply and a rejoinder only where the President, on a duly reasoned application submitted by the party who brought the cross-appeal within seven days of service of the response to the cross-appeal, considers it necessary, after hearing the Judge-Rapporteur and the Advocate General, in particular to enable that party to present his views on a plea of inadmissibility or on new matters relied on in the response to the cross-appeal.

2. The President shall fix the date by which that reply is to be produced and, upon service of that pleading, the date by which the rejoinder is to be produced. He may limit the number of pages and the subject-matter of those pleadings.

Chapter 5   Appeals determined by order

Article 181   Manifestly inadmissible or manifestly unfounded appeal or cross-appeal
Where the appeal or cross-appeal is, in whole or in part, manifestly inadmissible or manifestly unfounded, the Court may at any time, acting on a proposal from the Judge-Rapporteur and after hearing the Advocate General, decide by reasoned order to dismiss that appeal or cross-appeal in whole or in part.

Article 182   Manifestly well-founded appeal or cross-appeal
Where the Court has already ruled on one or more questions of law identical to those raised by the pleas in law of the appeal or cross-appeal and considers the appeal or cross-appeal to be manifestly well founded, it may, acting on a proposal from the Judge-Rapporteur and after hearing the parties and the Advocate General, decide by reasoned order in which reference is made to the relevant case-law to declare the appeal or cross-appeal manifestly well founded.

Chapter 6   Effect on a cross-appeal of the removal of the appeal from the register

Article 183   Effect on a cross-appeal of the discontinuance or manifest inadmissibility of the appeal
A cross-appeal shall be deemed to be devoid of purpose:
- (a) if the appellant discontinues his appeal;
- (b) if the appeal is declared manifestly inadmissible for non-compliance with the time-limit for lodging an appeal;
- (c) if the appeal is declared manifestly inadmissible on the sole ground that it is not directed against a final decision of the General Court or against a decision disposing of the substantive issues in part only or disposing of a procedural issue concerning a plea of lack of competence or inadmissibility within the meaning of the first paragraph of Article 56 of the Statute.

Chapter 7   Costs and legal aid in appeals

Article 184   Costs in appeals

1. Subject to the following provisions, Articles 137 to 146 of these Rules shall apply, *mutatis mutandis*, to the procedure before the Court of Justice on an appeal against a decision of the General Court.

2. Where the appeal is unfounded or where the appeal is well founded and the Court itself gives final judgment in the case, the Court shall make a decision as to the costs.

3. When an appeal brought by a Member State or an institution of the European Union which did not intervene in the proceedings before the General Court is well founded, the Court of Justice may order that the parties share the costs or that the successful appellant pay the costs which the appeal has caused an unsuccessful party to incur.

4. Where the appeal has not been brought by an intervener at first instance, he may not be ordered to pay costs in the appeal proceedings unless he participated in the written or oral part of the proceedings before the Court of Justice. Where an intervener at first instance takes part in the proceedings, the Court may decide that he shall bear his own costs.

Article 185   Legal aid

1. A party who is wholly or in part unable to meet the costs of the proceedings may at any time apply for legal aid.

2. The application shall be accompanied by all information and supporting documents making it possible to assess the applicant's financial situation, such as a certificate issued by a competent national authority attesting to his financial situation.

Article 186   Prior application for legal aid

1. If the application is made prior to the appeal which the applicant for legal aid intends to commence, it shall briefly state the subject of the appeal.

2. The application for legal aid need not be made through a lawyer.

3. The introduction of an application for legal aid shall, with regard to the person who made that application, suspend the time-limit prescribed for the bringing of the appeal until the date of service of the order making a decision on that application.

4. The President shall assign the application for legal aid, as soon as it is lodged, to a Judge-Rapporteur who shall put forward, promptly, a proposal as to the action to be taken on it.

Article 187   Decision on the application for legal aid

1. The decision to grant legal aid, in whole or in part, or to refuse it shall be taken, on a proposal from the Judge-Rapporteur and after hearing the Advocate General, by the Chamber of three Judges to which the Judge-Rapporteur is assigned. In that event, the formation of the Court shall be composed of the President of that Chamber, the Judge-Rapporteur and the first Judge or, as the case may be, the first two Judges designated from the list referred to in Article 28(3) on the date on which the application for legal aid is brought before that Chamber by the Judge-Rapporteur. It shall consider, if appropriate, whether the appeal is manifestly unfounded.

2. If the Judge-Rapporteur is not a member of a Chamber of three Judges, the decision shall be taken, under the same conditions, by the Chamber of five Judges to which he is assigned. In addition to the Judge-Rapporteur, the formation of the Court shall be composed of four Judges designated from the list referred to in Article 28(2) on the date on which the application for legal aid is brought before that Chamber by the Judge-Rapporteur.

3. The formation of the Court shall give its decision by way of order. Where the application for legal aid is refused in whole or in part, the order shall state the reasons for that refusal.

Article 188   Sums to be advanced as legal aid

1. Where legal aid is granted, the cashier of the Court shall be responsible, where applicable within the limits set by the formation of the Court, for costs involved in the assistance and

representation of the applicant before the Court. At the request of the applicant or his representative, an advance on those costs may be paid.

2. In its decision as to costs the Court may order the payment to the cashier of the Court of sums advanced as legal aid.

3. The Registrar shall take steps to obtain the recovery of these sums from the party ordered to pay them.

Article 189   Withdrawal of legal aid

The formation of the Court which gave a decision on the application for legal aid may at any time, either of its own motion or on request, withdraw that legal aid if the circumstances which led to its being granted alter during the proceedings.

Chapter 8 Other provisions applicable to appeals

Article 190   Other provisions applicable to appeals

1. Articles 127, 129 to 136, 147 to 150, 153 to 155 and 157 to 166 of these Rules shall apply to the procedure before the Court of Justice on an appeal against decisions of the General Court.

2. By way of derogation from Article 130(1), an application to intervene shall, however, be made within one month of the publication of the notice referred to in Article 21(4).

3. Article 95 shall apply, *mutatis mutandis*, to the procedure before the Court of Justice on an appeal against decisions of the General Court.

Article 190a   Treatment of information or material produced before the General Court in accordance with Article 105 of its Rules of Procedure

1. Where an appeal is brought against a decision of the General Court adopted in proceedings in which information or material has been produced by a main party in accordance with Article 105 of the Rules of Procedure of the General Court and has not been communicated to the other main party, the Registry of the General Court shall make that information or material available to the Court of Justice, on the conditions laid down in the decision referred to in paragraph 11 of that Article.

2. The information or material referred to in paragraph 1 shall not be communicated to the parties to the proceedings before the Court of Justice.

3. The Court of Justice shall ensure that the confidential matters contained in the information or material referred to in paragraph 1 are not disclosed in the decision which closes the proceedings or in any Opinion of the Advocate General.

4. The information or material referred to in paragraph 1 shall be returned to the party that produced it before the General Court as soon as the decision closing the proceedings before the Court of Justice has been served, save where the case is referred back to the General Court. In the latter case, the information or material concerned shall again be made available to the General Court, on the conditions laid down in the decision referred to in paragraph 5.

5. The Court of Justice shall adopt, by decision, the security rules for protecting the information or material referred to in paragraph 1. That decision shall be published in the *Official Journal of the European Union*.

Title VI Review of decisions of the General Court

Article 191   Reviewing Chamber

A Chamber of five Judges shall be designated for a period of one year for the purpose of deciding, in accordance with Articles 193 and 194 of these Rules, whether a decision of the General Court is to be reviewed in accordance with Article 62 of the Statute.

Article 192   Information and communication of decisions which may be reviewed

1. As soon as the date for the delivery or signature of a decision to be given under Article 256(2) or (3) TFEU is fixed, the Registry of the General Court shall inform the Registry of the Court of Justice.

2. The decision shall be communicated to the Registry of the Court of Justice immediately upon its delivery or signature, as shall the file in the case, which shall be made available forthwith to the First Advocate General.

Article 193   Review of decisions given on appeal

1. The proposal of the First Advocate General to review a decision of the General Court given under Article 256(2) TFEU shall be forwarded to the President of the Court of Justice and to the President of the reviewing Chamber. Notice of that transmission shall be given to the Registrar at the same time.

2. As soon as he is informed of the existence of a proposal, the Registrar shall communicate the file in the case before the General Court to the members of the reviewing Chamber.

3. As soon as the proposal to review has been received, the President of the Court shall designate the Judge-Rapporteur from among the Judges of the reviewing Chamber on a proposal from the President of that Chamber. The composition of the formation of the Court shall be determined in accordance with Article 28(2) of these Rules on the day on which the case is assigned to the Judge-Rapporteur.

4. That Chamber, acting on a proposal from the Judge-Rapporteur, shall decide whether the decision of the General Court is to be reviewed. The decision to review the decision of the General Court shall indicate only the questions which are to be reviewed.

5. The General Court, the parties to the proceedings before it and the other interested persons referred to in the second paragraph of Article 62a of the Statute shall forthwith be informed by the Registrar of the decision of the Court of Justice to review the decision of the General Court.

6. Notice of the date of the decision to review the decision of the General Court and of the questions which are to be reviewed shall be published in the *Official Journal of the European Union*.

Article 194   Review of preliminary rulings

1. The proposal of the First Advocate General to review a decision of the General Court given under Article 256(3) TFEU shall be forwarded to the President of the Court of Justice and to the President of the reviewing Chamber. Notice of that transmission shall be given to the Registrar at the same time.

2. As soon as he is informed of the existence of a proposal, the Registrar shall communicate the file in the case before the General Court to the members of the reviewing Chamber.

3. The Registrar shall also inform the General Court, the referring court or tribunal, the parties to the main proceedings and the other interested persons referred to in the second paragraph of Article 62a of the Statute of the existence of a proposal to review.

4. As soon as the proposal to review has been received, the President of the Court shall designate the Judge-Rapporteur from among the Judges of the reviewing Chamber on a proposal from the President of that Chamber. The composition of the formation of the Court shall be determined in accordance with Article 28(2) of these Rules on the day on which the case is assigned to the Judge-Rapporteur.

5. That Chamber, acting on a proposal from the Judge-Rapporteur, shall decide whether the decision of the General Court is to be reviewed. The decision to review the decision of the General Court shall indicate only the questions which are to be reviewed.

6. The General Court, the referring court or tribunal, the parties to the main proceedings and the other interested persons referred to in the second paragraph of Article 62a of the Statute shall

forthwith be informed by the Registrar of the decision of the Court of Justice as to whether or not the decision of the General Court is to be reviewed.

7. Notice of the date of the decision to review the decision of the General Court and of the questions which are to be reviewed shall be published in the *Official Journal of the European Union*.

Article 195   Judgment on the substance of the case after a decision to review

1. The decision to review a decision of the General Court shall be served on the parties and other interested persons referred to in the second paragraph of Article 62a of the Statute. The decision served on the Member States, and the States, other than the Member States, which are parties to the EEA Agreement, as well as the EFTA Surveillance Authority, shall be accompanied by a translation of the decision of the Court of Justice in accordance with the provisions of Article 98 of these Rules. The decision of the Court of Justice shall also be communicated to the General Court and, if applicable, to the referring court or tribunal.

2. Within one month of the date of service referred to in paragraph 1, the parties and other interested persons on whom the decision of the Court of Justice has been served may lodge statements or written observations on the questions which are subject to review.

3. As soon as a decision to review a decision of the General Court has been taken, the First Advocate General shall assign the review to an Advocate General.

4. The reviewing Chamber shall rule on the substance of the case, after hearing the Advocate General.

5. It may, however, request the Court of Justice to assign the case to a formation of the Court composed of a greater number of Judges.

6. Where the decision of the General Court which is subject to review was given under Article 256(2) TFEU, the Court of Justice shall make a decision as to costs.

Title VII Requests for Opinions

Article 196   Written part of the procedure

1. In accordance with Article 218(11) TFEU, a request for an Opinion may be made by a Member State, by the European Parliament, by the Council or by the European Commission.

2. A request for an Opinion may relate both to whether the envisaged agreement is compatible with the provisions of the Treaties and to whether the European Union or any institution of the European Union has the power to enter into that agreement.

3. It shall be served on the Member States and on the institutions referred to in paragraph 1, and the President shall prescribe a time-limit within which they may submit written observations.

Article 197   Designation of the Judge-Rapporteur and of the Advocate General

As soon as the request for an Opinion has been submitted, the President shall designate a Judge-Rapporteur and the First Advocate General shall assign the case to an Advocate General.

Article 198   Hearing

The Court may decide that the procedure before it shall also include a hearing.

Article 199   Time-limit for delivering the Opinion

The Court shall deliver its Opinion as soon as possible, after hearing the Advocate General.

Article 200   Delivery of the Opinion

1. The Opinion, signed by the President, the Judges who took part in the deliberations and the Registrar, shall be delivered in open court.

2. It shall be served on all the Member States and on the institutions referred to in Article 196(1).

Title VIII   Particular forms of procedure

Article 201   Appeals against decisions of the arbitration committee

1. An application initiating an appeal under the second paragraph of Article 18 TEAEC shall state:

   (a) the name and permanent address of the applicant;
   (b) the description of the signatory;
   (c) a reference to the arbitration committee's decision against which the appeal is made;
   (d) the names of the respondents;
   (e) a summary of the facts;
   (f) the grounds on which the appeal is based and arguments relied on, and a brief statement of those grounds;
   (g) the form of order sought by the applicant.

2. Articles 119 and 121 of these Rules shall apply to the application.

3. A certified copy of the contested decision shall be annexed to the application.

4. As soon as the application has been lodged, the Registrar of the Court shall request the arbitration committee registry to transmit to the Court the file in the case.

5. Articles 123 and 124 of these Rules shall apply to this procedure. The Court may decide that the procedure before it shall also include a hearing.

6. The Court shall give its decision in the form of a judgment. Where the Court sets aside the decision of the arbitration committee it may refer the case back to the committee.

Article 202   Procedure under Article 103 TEAEC

1. Four certified copies shall be lodged of an application under the third paragraph of Article 103 TEAEC. The application shall be accompanied by the draft of the agreement or contract concerned, by the observations of the European Commission addressed to the State concerned and by all other supporting documents.

2. The application and annexes thereto shall be served on the European Commission, which shall have a time-limit of 10 days from such service to submit its written observations. This time-limit may be extended by the President after the State concerned has been heard.

3. Following the lodging of such observations, which shall be served on the State concerned, the Court shall give its decision promptly, after hearing the Advocate General and, if they so request, the State concerned and the European Commission.

Article 203   Procedures under Articles 104 TEAEC and 105 TEAEC

Applications under the third paragraph of Article 104 TEAEC and the second paragraph of Article 105 TEAEC shall be governed by the provisions of Titles II and IV of these Rules. Such applications shall also be served on the State to which the respondent person or undertaking belongs.

Article 204   Procedure provided for by Article 111(3) of the EEA Agreement

1. In the case governed by Article 111(3) of the EEA Agreement, the matter shall be brought before the Court by a request submitted by the Contracting Parties which are parties to the dispute. The request shall be served on the other Contracting Parties, on the European Commission, on the EFTA Surveillance Authority and, where appropriate, on the other interested persons on whom a request for a preliminary ruling raising the same question of interpretation of European Union legislation would be served.

2. The President shall prescribe a time-limit within which the Contracting Parties and the other interested persons on whom the request has been served may submit written observations.

3. The request shall be made in one of the languages referred to in Article 36 of these Rules. Article 38 shall apply. The provisions of Article 98 shall apply mutatis mutandis.

4. As soon as the request referred to in paragraph 1 of this Article has been submitted, the President shall designate a Judge-Rapporteur. The First Advocate General shall, immediately afterwards, assign the request to an Advocate General.

5. The Court shall, after hearing the Advocate General, give a reasoned decision on the request.

6. The decision of the Court, signed by the President, the Judges who took part in the deliberations and the Registrar, shall be served on the Contracting Parties and on the other interested persons referred to in paragraphs 1 and 2.

Article 205   (Repealed)

Article 206   Requests under Article 269 TFEU

1. Four certified copies shall be submitted of a request under Article 269 TFEU. The request shall be accompanied by any relevant document and, in particular, any observations and recommendations made pursuant to Article 7 TEU.

2. The request and annexes thereto shall be served on the European Council or on the Council, as appropriate, each of which shall have a non-extendible time limit of 10 days from such service to submit its written observations. Article 51 shall not apply to that time limit.

3. The request and annexes thereto shall also be communicated to the Member States other than the State in question, to the European Parliament and to the European Commission.

4. Following the lodging of the observations referred to in paragraph 2, which shall be served on the Member State concerned and on the States and institutions referred to in paragraph 3, the Court shall give its decision within a time-limit of one month from the lodging of the request and after hearing the Advocate General. At the request of the Member State concerned, the European Council or the Council, or of its own motion, the Court may decide that the procedure before it shall also include a hearing, which all the States and institutions referred to in this Article shall be given notice to attend.

Final provisions

Article 207   Supplementary rules

Subject to the provisions of Article 253 TFEU and after consultation with the Governments concerned, the Court shall adopt supplementary rules concerning its practice in relation to:

    (a) letters rogatory;

    (b) applications for legal aid;

    (c) reports by the Court of perjury by witnesses or experts, delivered pursuant to Article 30 of the Statute.

Article 208   Implementing rules

The Court may, by a separate act, adopt practice rules for the implementation of these Rules.

Article 209   Repeal

These Rules replace the Rules of Procedure of the Court of Justice of the European Communities adopted on 19 June 1991, as last amended on 24 May 2011 (*Official Journal of the European Union*, L 162 of 22 June 2011, p. 17).

Article 210   Publication and entry into force of these Rules

These Rules, which are authentic in the languages referred to in Article 36 of these Rules, shall be published in the *Official Journal of the European Union* and shall enter into force on the first day of the second month following their publication.

Done at Luxembourg, 25 September 2012.

Part II

Secondary Legislation

Free movement of goods

Commission Directive of 22 December 1969 based on the provisions of Article 33(7), on the abolition of measures which have an effect equivalent to quantitative restrictions on imports and are not covered by other provisions adopted in pursuance of the EEC Treaty (70/50/EEC)*

[OJ Sp. Ed. 1970, I No L13/29, p. 17]

(Preamble omitted.)

Article 1
The purpose of this Directive is to abolish the measures referred to in Articles 2 and 3, which were operative at the date of entry into force of the EEC Treaty.

Article 2
1. This Directive covers measures, other than those applicable equally to domestic or imported products, which hinder imports which could otherwise take place, including measures which make importation more difficult or costly than the disposal of domestic production.

2. In particular, it covers measures which make imports or the disposal, at any marketing stage, of imported products subject to a condition—other than a formality—which is required in respect of imported products only, or a condition differing from that required for domestic products and more difficult to satisfy. Equally, it covers, in particular, measures which favour domestic products or grant them a preference, other than an aid, to which conditions may or may not be attached.

3. The measures referred to must be taken to include those measures which:
   (a) lay down, for imported products only, minimum or maximum prices below or above which imports are prohibited, reduced or made subject to conditions liable to hinder importation;
   (b) lay down less favourable prices for imported products than for domestic products;
   (c) fix profit margins or any other price components for imported products only or fix these differently for domestic products and for imported products, to the detriment of the latter;

---

* **Editor's Note:** As clarified in the Preface, this is still in force. See http://data.europa.eu/eli/dir/1970/50/oj.

(d) preclude any increase in the price of the imported product corresponding to the supplementary costs and charges inherent in importation;

(e) fix the prices of products solely on the basis of the cost price or the quality of domestic products at such a level as to create a hindrance to importation;

(f) lower the value of an imported product, in particular by causing a reduction in its intrinsic value, or increase its costs;

(g) make access of imported products to the domestic market conditional upon having an agent or representative in the territory of the importing Member State;

(h) lay down conditions of payment in respect of imported products only, or subject imported products to conditions which are different from those laid down for domestic products and more difficult to satisfy;

(i) require, for imports only, the giving of guarantees or making of payments on account;

(j) subject imported products only to conditions, in respect, in particular of shape, size, weight, composition, presentation, identification or putting up, or subject imported products to conditions which are different from those for domestic products and more difficult to satisfy;

(k) hinder the purchase by private individuals of imported products only, or encourage, require or give preference to the purchase of domestic products only;

(l) totally or partially preclude the use of national facilities or equipment in respect of imported products only, or totally or partially confine the use of such facilities or equipment to domestic products only;

(m) prohibit or limit publicity in respect of imported products only, or totally or partially confine publicity to domestic products only;

(n) prohibit, limit or require stocking in respect of imported products only; totally or partially confine the use of stocking facilities to domestic products only, or make the stocking of imported products subject to conditions which are different from those required for domestic products and more difficult to satisfy;

(o) make importation subject to the granting of reciprocity by one or more Member States;

(p) prescribe that imported products are to conform, totally or partially, to rules other than those of the importing country;

(q) specify time limits for imported products which are insufficient or excessive in relation to the normal course of the various transactions to which these time limits apply;

(r) subject imported products to controls or, other than those inherent in the customs clearance procedure, to which domestic products are not subject or which are stricter in respect of imported products than they are in respect of domestic products, without this being necessary in order to ensure equivalent protection;

(s) confine names which are not indicative of origin or source to domestic products only.

Article 3

This Directive also covers measures governing the marketing of products which deal, in particular, with shape, size, weight, composition, presentation, identification or putting up and which are equally applicable to domestic and imported products, where the restrictive effect of such measures on the free movement of goods exceeds the effects intrinsic to trade rules.

This is the case, in particular, where:

– the restrictive effects on the free movement of goods are out of proportion to their purpose;
– the same objective can be attained by other means which are less of a hindrance to trade.

(All remaining provisions omitted.)

Commission Practice Note on Import Prohibitions

Communication from the Commission concerning the consequences of the judgment given by the Court of Justice on 20 February 1979 in Case 120/78 ('Cassis de Dijon')

[OJ 1980 C256/2]

The following is the text of a letter which has been sent to the Member States; the European Parliament and the Council have also been notified of it.

In the Commission's Communication of 6 November 1978 on 'Safeguarding free trade within the Community', it was emphasised that the free movement of goods is being affected by a growing number of restrictive measures.

The judgment delivered by the Court of Justice on 20 February 1979 in Case 120/78 (the 'Cassis de Dijon' case), and recently reaffirmed in the judgment of 26 June 1980 in Case 788/79, has given the Commission some interpretative guidance enabling it to monitor more strictly the application of the Treaty rules on the free movement of goods, particularly Articles 30 to 36 of the EEC Treaty.

The Court gives a very general definition of the barriers to free trade which are prohibited by the provisions of Article 30 et seq. of the EEC Treaty. These are taken to include 'any national measure capable of hindering, directly or indirectly, actually or potentially, intra-Community trade'.

In its judgment of 20 February 1979 the Court indicates the scope of this definition as it applies to technical and commercial rules.

Any product lawfully produced and marketed in one Member State must, in principle, be admitted to the market of any other Member State.

Technical and commercial rules, even those equally applicable to national and imported products, may create barriers to trade only where those rules are necessary to satisfy mandatory requirements and to serve a purpose which is in the general interest and for which they are an essential guarantee. This purpose must be such as to take precedence over the requirements of the free movement of goods, which constitutes one of the fundamental rules of the Community.

The conclusions in terms of policy which the Commission draws from this new guidance are set out below.

  – Whereas Member States may, with respect to domestic products and in the absence of relevant Community provisions, regulate the terms on which such products are marketed, the case is different for products imported from other Member States.

Any product imported from another Member State must in principle be admitted to the territory of the importing Member State if it has been lawfully produced, that is, conforms to the rules and processes of manufacture that are customarily and traditionally accepted in the exporting country, and is marketed in the territory of the latter.

This principle implies that Member States, when drawing up commercial or technical rules liable to affect the free movement of goods, may not take an exclusively national viewpoint and take account only of requirements confined to domestic products. The proper functioning of the common market demands that each Member State also give consideration to the legitimate requirements of the other Member States.

  – Only under very strict conditions does the Court accept exceptions to this principle; barriers to trade resulting from differences between commercial and technical rules are only admissible:

- if the rules are necessary, that is appropriate and not excessive, in order to satisfy manda- tory requirements (public health, protection of consumers or the environment, the fair- ness of commercial transactions, etc.);
- if the rules serve a purpose in the general interest which is compelling enough to justify an exception to a fundamental rule of the Treaty such as the free movement of goods;
- if the rules are essential for such a purpose to be attained, i.e. are the means which are the most appropriate and at the same time least hinder trade.

The Court's interpretation has induced the Commission to set out a number of guidelines.

- The principles deduced by the Court imply that a Member State may not in principle pro- hibit the sale in its territory of a product lawfully produced and marketed in another Member State even if the product is produced according to technical or quality require- ments which differ from those imposed on its domestic products. Where a product 'suitably and satisfactorily' fulfils the legitimate objective of a Member State's own rules (public safety, protection of the consumer or the environment, etc.), the importing country can- not justify prohibiting its sale in its territory by claiming that the way it fulfils the objective is different from that imposed on domestic products.

In such a case, an absolute prohibition of sale could not be considered 'necessary' to satisfy a 'mandatory requirement' because it would not be an 'essential guarantee' in the sense defined in the Court's judgment.

The Commission will therefore have to tackle a whole body of commercial rules which lay down that products manufactured and marketed in one Member State must fulfil technical or qualitative conditions in order to be admitted to the market of another and specifically in all cases where the trade barriers occasioned by such rules are inadmissible according to the very strict criteria set out by the Court.

The Commission is referring in particular to rules covering the composition, designation, pres- entation and packaging of products as well as rules requiring compliance with certain technical standards.

The Commission's work of harmonisation will henceforth have to be directed mainly at national laws having an impact on the functioning of the common market where barriers to trade to be removed arise from national provisions which are admissible under the criteria set by the Court.

The Commission will be concentrating on sectors deserving priority because of their economic relevance to the creation of a single internal market.

To forestall later difficulties, the Commission will be informing Member States of potential objec- tions, under the terms of Community law, to provisions they may be considering introducing which come to the attention of the Commission.

It will be producing suggestions soon on the procedures to be followed in such cases.

The Commission is confident that this approach will secure greater freedom of trade for the Community's manufacturers, so strengthening the industrial base of the Community, while meet- ing the expectations of consumers.

Council Regulation 2679/98 of 7 December 1998 on the functioning of the internal market in relation to the free movement of goods among the Member States

[OJ 1998 L337/8]

THE COUNCIL OF THE EUROPEAN UNION,

Having regard to the Treaty establishing the European Community, and in particular Article 235 thereof,

Having regard to the proposal from the Commission,[1]

Having regard to the opinion of the European Parliament,[2]

Having regard to the opinion of the Economic and Social Committee,[3]

(1) Whereas, as provided for in Article 7a of the Treaty, the internal market comprises an area without internal frontiers in which, in particular, the free movement of goods is ensured in accordance with Articles 30 to 36 of the Treaty;

(2) Whereas breaches of this principle, such as occur when in a given Member State the free movement of goods is obstructed by actions of private individuals, may cause grave disruption to the proper functioning of the internal market and inflict serious losses on the individuals affected;

(3) Whereas, in order to ensure fulfilment of the obligations arising from the Treaty, and, in particular, to ensure the proper functioning of the internal market, Member States should, on the one hand, abstain from adopting measures or engaging in conduct liable to constitute an obstacle to trade and, on the other hand, take all necessary and proportionate measures with a view to facilitating the free movement of goods in their territory;

(4) Whereas such measures must not affect the exercise of fundamental rights, including the right or freedom to strike;

(5) Whereas this Regulation does not prevent any actions which may be necessary in certain cases at Community level to respond to problems in the functioning of the internal market, taking into account, where appropriate, the application of this Regulation;

(6) Whereas Member States have exclusive competence as regards the maintenance of public order and the safeguarding of internal security as well as in determining whether, when and which measures are necessary and proportionate in order to facilitate the free movement of goods in their territory in a given situation;

(7) Whereas there should be adequate and rapid exchange of information between the Member States and the Commission on obstacles to the free movement of goods;

(8) Whereas a Member State on the territory of which obstacles to the free movement of goods occur should take all necessary and proportionate measures to restore as soon as possible the free movement of goods in their territory in order to avoid the risk that the disruption or loss in question will continue, increase or intensify and that there may be a breakdown in trade and in the contractual relations which underlie it; whereas such Member State should inform the Commission and, if requested, other Member States of the measures it has taken or intends to take in order to fulfil this objective;

(9) Whereas the Commission, in fulfilment of its duty under the Treaty, should notify the Member State concerned of its view that a breach has occurred and the Member State should respond to that notification;

(10) Whereas the Treaty provides for no powers, other than those in Article 235 thereof, for the adoption of this Regulation,

HAS ADOPTED THIS REGULATION:

Article 1

For the purpose of this Regulation:

1. the term 'obstacle' shall mean an obstacle to the free movement of goods among Member States which is attributable to a Member State, whether it involves action or inaction on its part, which may constitute a breach of Articles 30 to 36 of the Treaty and which:

    (a) leads to serious disruption of the free movement of goods by physically or otherwise preventing, delaying or diverting their import into, export from or transport across a Member State,

    (b) causes serious loss to the individuals affected, and

---

[1] OJ C 10, 15.1.1998, p. 14.

[2] OJ C 359, 23.11.1998.

[3] OJ C 214, 10.7.1998, p. 90.

(c) requires immediate action in order to prevent any continuation, increase or intensification of the disruption or loss in question;

2. the term 'inaction' shall cover the case when the competent authorities of a Member State, in the presence of an obstacle caused by actions taken by private individuals, fail to take all necessary and proportionate measures within their powers with a view to removing the obstacle and ensuring the free movement of goods in their territory.

Article 2

This Regulation may not be interpreted as affecting in any way the exercise of fundamental rights as recognised in Member States, including the right or freedom to strike. These rights may also include the right or freedom to take other actions covered by the specific industrial relations systems in Member States.

Article 3

1. When an obstacle occurs or when there is a threat thereof

(a) any Member State (whether or not it is the Member State concerned) which has relevant information shall immediately transmit it to the Commission, and

(b) the Commission shall immediately transmit to the Member States that information and any information from any other source which it may consider relevant.

2. The Member State concerned shall respond as soon as possible to requests for information from the Commission and from other Member States concerning the nature of the obstacle or threat and the action which it has taken or proposes to take. Information exchange between Member States shall also be transmitted to the Commission.

Article 4

1. When an obstacle occurs, and subject to Article 2, the Member State concerned shall

(a) take all necessary and proportionate measures so that the free movement of goods is assured in the territory of the Member State in accordance with the Treaty, and

(b) inform the Commission of the actions which its authorities have taken or intend to take.

2. The Commission shall immediately transmit the information received under paragraph 1(b) to the other Member States.

Article 5

1. Where the Commission considers that an obstacle is occurring in a Member State, it shall notify the Member State concerned of the reasons that have led the Commission to such a conclusion and shall request the Member State to take all necessary and proportionate measures to remove the said obstacle within a period which it shall determine with reference to the urgency of the case.

2. In reaching its conclusion, the Commission shall have regard to Article 2.

3. The Commission may publish in the Official Journal of the European Communities the text of the notification which it has sent to the Member State concerned and shall immediately transmit the text to any party which requests it.

4. The Member State shall, within five working days of receipt of the text, either:

– inform the Commission of the steps which it has taken or intends to take to implement paragraph 1, or

– communicate a reasoned submission as to why there is no obstacle constituting a breach of Articles 30 to 36 of the Treaty.

5. In exceptional cases, the Commission may allow an extension of the deadline mentioned in paragraph 4 if the Member State submits a duly substantiated request and the grounds cited are deemed acceptable.

This Regulation shall be binding in its entirety and directly applicable in all Member States.

Done at Brussels, 7 December 1998.

Directive (EU) 2015/1535 of the European Parliament and of the Council of 9 September 2015 laying down a procedure for the provision of information in the field of technical regulations and of rules on Information Society services (codification)

[OJ 2015 L241/1]*

THE EUROPEAN PARLIAMENT AND THE COUNCIL OF THE EUROPEAN UNION,

Having regard to the Treaty on the Functioning of the European Union, and in particular Articles 114, 337 and 43 thereof,

Having regard to the proposal from the European Commission,

After transmission of the draft legislative act to the national parliaments,

Having regard to the opinions of the European Economic and Social Committee[1],

Acting in accordance with the ordinary legislative procedure[2],

Whereas:

(1) Directive 98/34/EC of the European Parliament and of the Council[3] has been substantially amended several times[4]. In the interests of clarity and rationality, that Directive should be codified.

(2) The internal market comprises an area without internal frontiers in which the free movement of goods, persons, services and capital is ensured. Therefore, the prohibition of quantitative restrictions on the movement of goods and of measures having an equivalent effect is one of the basic principles of the Union.

(3) In order to promote the smooth functioning of the internal market, as much transparency as possible should be ensured as regards national initiatives for the establishment of technical regulations.

(4) Barriers to trade resulting from technical regulations relating to products may be allowed only where they are necessary in order to meet essential requirements and have an objective in the public interest of which they constitute the main guarantee.

(5) It is essential for the Commission to have the necessary information at its disposal before the adoption of technical provisions. Consequently, the Member States, which are required to facilitate the achievement of its task pursuant to Article 4(3) of the Treaty on European Union (TEU), must notify it of their projects in the field of technical regulations.

(6) All the Member States must also be informed of the technical regulations envisaged by any one Member State.

(7) The aim of the internal market is to create an environment that is conducive to the competitiveness of undertakings. Increased provision of information is one way of helping undertakings to make more of the advantages inherent in this market. It is therefore necessary to enable economic operators to give their assessment of the impact of the national technical regulations proposed by

---

* **Editor's Note:** Annex III omitted.
[1] Opinion of 14 July 2010 (OJ C 44, 11.2.2011, p. 142) and opinion of 26 February 2014 (OJ C 214, 8.7.2014, p. 55).
[2] Position of the European Parliament of 15 April 2014 (not yet published in the Official Journal) and decision of the Council of 13 July 2015.
[3] Directive 98/34/EC of the European Parliament and of the Council of 22 June 1998 laying down a procedure for the provision of information in the field of technical standards and regulations and of rules on Information Society services (OJ L 204, 21.7.1998, p. 37). The original title was 'Directive 98/34/EC of the European Parliament and of the Council of 22 June 1998 laying down a procedure for the provision of information in the field of technical standards and regulations'. It was amended by Directive 98/48/EC of the European Parliament and of the Council of 20 July 1998 amending Directive 98/34/EC laying down a procedure for the provision of information in the field of technical standards and regulations (OJ L 217, 5.8.1998, p. 18).
[4] See Annex III, Part A.

other Member States, by providing for the regular publication of the titles of notified drafts and by means of the provisions relating to the confidentiality of such drafts.

(8) It is appropriate, in the interests of legal certainty, that Member States publicly announce that a national technical regulation has been adopted in accordance with the formalities laid down in this Directive.

(9) As far as technical regulations for products are concerned, the measures designed to ensure the proper functioning or the continued development of the market include greater transparency of national intentions and a broadening of the criteria and conditions for assessing the potential effect of the proposed regulations on the market.

(10) It is therefore necessary to assess all the requirements laid down in respect of a product and to take account of developments in national practices for the regulation of products.

(11) Requirements, other than technical specifications, referring to the life cycle of a product after it has been placed on the market are liable to affect the free movement of that product or to create obstacles to the proper functioning of the internal market.

(12) It is necessary to clarify the concept of a de facto technical regulation. In particular, the provisions by which the public authority refers to technical specifications or other requirements, or encourages the observance thereof, and the provisions referring to products with which the public authority is associated, in the public interest, have the effect of conferring on such requirements or specifications a more binding value than they would otherwise have by virtue of their private origin.

(13) The Commission and the Member States must also be allowed sufficient time in which to propose amendments to an envisaged measure, in order to remove or reduce any barriers which it might create to the free movement of goods.

(14) The Member State concerned must take account of those amendments when formulating the definitive text of the measure envisaged.

(15) It is inherent in the internal market that, in particular where the principle of mutual recognition cannot be implemented by the Member States, the Commission adopts or proposes the adoption of binding acts. A specific temporary standstill period has been established in order to prevent the introduction of national measures from compromising the adoption of binding acts by the European Parliament and the Council or by the Commission in the same field.

(16) The Member State concerned is to, pursuant to the general obligations laid down in Article 4(3) TEU, defer implementation of the envisaged measure for a period sufficient to allow either a joint examination of the proposed amendments or the preparation of a proposal for a legislative act or the adoption of a binding act of the Commission.

(17) With a view to facilitating the adoption of measures by the European Parliament and the Council, Member States should refrain from adopting technical regulations once the Council has adopted a position at first reading on a Commission proposal concerning that sector.

(18) It is necessary to provide for a Standing Committee, the members of which are appointed by the Member States, with the task of cooperating in the efforts of the Commission to lessen any adverse effects on the free movement of goods.

(19) This Directive should be without prejudice to the obligations of the Member States relating to the time limits for the transposition into national law of the Directives set out in Part B of Annex III,

HAVE ADOPTED THIS DIRECTIVE:

Article 1

1. For the purposes of this Directive, the following definitions apply:

    (a) 'product' means any industrially manufactured product and any agricultural product, including fish products;

    (b) 'service' means any Information Society service, that is to say, any service normally provided for remuneration, at a distance, by electronic means and at the individual request of a recipient of services.

        For the purposes of this definition:

        (i) 'at a distance' means that the service is provided without the parties being simultaneously present;

(ii) 'by electronic means' means that the service is sent initially and received at its destination by means of electronic equipment for the processing (including digital compression) and storage of data, and entirely transmitted, conveyed and received by wire, by radio, by optical means or by other electromagnetic means;

(iii) 'at the individual request of a recipient of services' means that the service is provided through the transmission of data on individual request.

An indicative list of services not covered by this definition is set out in Annex I;

(c) 'technical specification' means a specification contained in a document which lays down the characteristics required of a product such as levels of quality, performance, safety or dimensions, including the requirements applicable to the product as regards the name under which the product is sold, terminology, symbols, testing and test methods, packaging, marking or labelling and conformity assessment procedures.

The term 'technical specification' also covers production methods and processes used in respect of agricultural products, as referred to in the second subparagraph of Article 38(1) of the Treaty on the Functioning of the European Union (TFEU), products intended for human and animal consumption, and medicinal products as defined in Article 1 of Directive 2001/83/EC of the European Parliament and of the Council[5], as well as production methods and processes relating to other products, where these have an effect on their characteristics;

(d) 'other requirements' means a requirement, other than a technical specification, imposed on a product for the purpose of protecting, in particular, consumers or the environment, and which affects its life cycle after it has been placed on the market, such as conditions of use, recycling, reuse or disposal, where such conditions can significantly influence the composition or nature of the product or its marketing;

(e) 'rule on services' means a requirement of a general nature relating to the taking-up and pursuit of service activities within the meaning of point (b), in particular provisions concerning the service provider, the services and the recipient of services, excluding any rules which are not specifically aimed at the services defined in that point.

For the purposes of this definition:

(i) a rule shall be considered to be specifically aimed at Information Society services where, having regard to its statement of reasons and its operative part, the specific aim and object of all or some of its individual provisions is to regulate such services in an explicit and targeted manner;

(ii) a rule shall not be considered to be specifically aimed at Information Society services if it affects such services only in an implicit or incidental manner;

(f) 'technical regulation' means technical specifications and other requirements or rules on services, including the relevant administrative provisions, the observance of which is compulsory, de jure or de facto, in the case of marketing, provision of a service, establishment of a service operator or use in a Member State or a major part thereof, as well as laws, regulations or administrative provisions of Member States, except those provided for in Article 7, prohibiting the manufacture, importation, marketing or use of a product or prohibiting the provision or use of a service, or establishment as a service provider.

De facto technical regulations shall include:

(i) laws, regulations or administrative provisions of a Member State which refer either to technical specifications or to other requirements or to rules on services, or to professional codes or codes of practice which in turn refer to technical specifications or to other requirements or to rules on services, compliance with which confers a presumption of conformity with the obligations imposed by the aforementioned laws, regulations or administrative provisions;

---

[5] Directive 2001/83/EC of the European Parliament and of the Council of 6 November 2001 on the Community code relating to medicinal products for human use (OJ L 311, 28.11.2001, p. 67).

(ii) voluntary agreements to which a public authority is a contracting party and which provide, in the general interest, for compliance with technical specifications or other requirements or rules on services, excluding public procurement tender specifications;

(iii) technical specifications or other requirements or rules on services which are linked to fiscal or financial measures affecting the consumption of products or services by encouraging compliance with such technical specifications or other requirements or rules on services; technical specifications or other requirements or rules on services linked to national social security systems are not included.

This comprises technical regulations imposed by the authorities designated by the Member States and appearing on a list drawn up and updated, where appropriate, by the Commission, in the framework of the Committee referred to in Article 2.

The same procedure shall be used for amending this list;

(g) 'draft technical regulation' means the text of a technical specification or other requirement or of a rule on services, including administrative provisions, formulated with the aim of enacting it or of ultimately having it enacted as a technical regulation, the text being at a stage of preparation at which substantial amendments can still be made.

2. This Directive shall not apply to:

(a) radio broadcasting services;

(b) television broadcasting services covered by point (e) of Article 1(1) of Directive 2010/13/EU of the European Parliament and of the Council[6].

3. This Directive shall not apply to rules relating to matters which are covered by Union legislation in the field of telecommunications services, as covered by Directive 2002/21/EC of the European Parliament and of the Council[7].

4. This Directive shall not apply to rules relating to matters which are covered by Union legislation in the field of financial services, as listed non-exhaustively in Annex II to this Directive.

5. With the exception of Article 5(3), this Directive shall not apply to rules enacted by or for regulated markets within the meaning of Directive 2004/39/EC of the European Parliament and of the Council[8] or by or for other markets or bodies carrying out clearing or settlement functions for those markets.

6. This Directive shall not apply to those measures Member States consider necessary under the Treaties for the protection of persons, in particular workers, when products are used, provided that such measures do not affect the products.

Article 2

A Standing Committee shall be set up consisting of representatives appointed by the Member States who may call on the assistance of experts or advisers; its chairman shall be a representative of the Commission.

The Committee shall draw up its own rules of procedure.

Article 3

1. The Committee shall meet at least twice a year.

The Committee shall meet in a specific composition to examine questions concerning Information Society services.

2. The Commission shall submit to the Committee a report on the implementation and application of the procedures set out in this Directive, and shall present proposals aimed at eliminating existing or foreseeable barriers to trade.

---

[6] Directive 2010/13/EU of the European Parliament and of the Council of 10 March 2010 on the coordination of certain provisions laid down by law, regulation or administrative action in Member States concerning the provision of audiovisual media services (Audiovisual Media Services Directive) (OJ L 95, 15.4.2010, p. 1).

[7] Directive 2002/21/EC of the European Parliament and of the Council of 7 March 2002 on a common regulatory framework for electronic communications networks and services (Framework Directive) (OJ L 108, 24.4.2002, p. 33).

[8] Directive 2004/39/EC of the European Parliament and of the Council of 21 April 2004 on markets in financial instruments amending Council Directives 85/611/EEC and 93/6/EEC and Directive 2000/12/EC of the European Parliament and of the Council and repealing Council Directive 93/22/EEC (OJ L 145, 30.4.2004, p. 1).

3. The Committee shall express its opinion on the communications and proposals referred to in paragraph 2 and may, in that regard, propose, in particular, that the Commission:

(a) ensure where necessary, in order to avoid the risk of barriers to trade, that initially the Member States concerned decide amongst themselves on appropriate measures;

(b) take all appropriate measures;

(c) identify the areas where harmonisation appears necessary, and, should the case arise, undertake appropriate harmonisation in a given sector.

4. The Committee must be consulted by the Commission:

(a) when deciding on the actual system through which the exchange of information provided for in this Directive is to be effected and on any change to it;

(b) when reviewing the operation of the system provided for in this Directive.

5. The Committee may be consulted by the Commission on any preliminary draft technical regulation received by the latter.

6. Any question regarding the implementation of this Directive may be submitted to the Committee at the request of its chairman or of a Member State.

7. The proceedings of the Committee and the information to be submitted to it shall be confidential.

However, the Committee and the national authorities may, provided that the necessary precautions are taken, consult, for an expert opinion, natural or legal persons, including persons in the private sector.

8. With respect to rules on services, the Commission and the Committee may consult natural or legal persons from industry or academia, and where possible representative bodies, capable of delivering an expert opinion on the social and societal aims and consequences of any draft rule on services, and take note of their advice whenever requested to do so.

Article 4

Member States shall communicate to the Commission, in accordance with Article 5(1), all requests made to standards institutions to draw up technical specifications or a standard for specific products for the purpose of enacting a technical regulation for such products in the form of draft technical regulations, and shall state the grounds for their enactment.

Article 5

1. Subject to Article 7, Member States shall immediately communicate to the Commission any draft technical regulation, except where it merely transposes the full text of an international or European standard, in which case information regarding the relevant standard shall suffice; they shall also let the Commission have a statement of the grounds which make the enactment of such a technical regulation necessary, where those grounds have not already been made clear in the draft.

Where appropriate, and unless it has already been sent with a prior communication, Member States shall simultaneously communicate the text of the basic legislative or regulatory provisions principally and directly concerned to the Commission, should knowledge of such text be necessary to assess the implications of the draft technical regulation.

Member States shall communicate the draft technical regulation again to the Commission under the conditions set out in the first and second subparagraphs of this paragraph if they make changes to the draft that have the effect of significantly altering its scope, shortening the timetable originally envisaged for implementation, adding specifications or requirements, or making the latter more restrictive.

Where, in particular, the draft technical regulation seeks to limit the marketing or use of a chemical substance, preparation or product on grounds of public health or of the protection of consumers or the environment, Member States shall also forward either a summary or the references of all relevant data relating to the substance, preparation or product concerned and to known and available substitutes, where such information may be available, and communicate the anticipated effects of the measure on public health and the protection of the consumer and the environment, together with an analysis of the risk carried out as appropriate in accordance with the principles provided for in the relevant part of Section II.3 of Annex XV to Regulation (EC) No 1907/2006 of the European Parliament and of the Council[9].

The Commission shall immediately notify the other Member States of the draft technical regulation and all documents which have been forwarded to it; it may also refer this draft, for an opinion, to the Committee referred to in Article 2 of this Directive and, where appropriate, to the committee responsible for the field in question.

With respect to the technical specifications or other requirements or rules on services referred to in point (iii) of the second subparagraph of point (f) of Article 1(1) of this Directive, the comments or detailed opinions of the Commission or Member States may concern only aspects which may hinder trade or, in respect of rules on services, the free movement of services or the freedom of establishment of service operators and not the fiscal or financial aspects of the measure.

2. The Commission and the Member States may make comments to the Member State which has forwarded a draft technical regulation; that Member State shall take such comments into account as far as possible in the subsequent preparation of the technical regulation.

3. Member States shall communicate the definitive text of a technical regulation to the Commission without delay.

4. Information supplied under this Article shall not be confidential except at the express request of the notifying Member State. Any such request shall be supported by reasons.

In cases of that kind, if the necessary precautions are taken, the Committee referred to in Article 2 and the national authorities may seek expert advice from physical or legal persons in the private sector.

5. When draft technical regulations form part of measures which are required to be communicated to the Commission at the draft stage under another Union act, Member States may make a communication within the meaning of paragraph 1 under that other act, provided that they formally indicate that the said communication also constitutes a communication for the purposes of this Directive.

The absence of a reaction from the Commission under this Directive to a draft technical regulation shall not prejudice any decision which might be taken under other Union acts.

Article 6

1. Member States shall postpone the adoption of a draft technical regulation for three months from the date of receipt by the Commission of the communication referred to in Article 5(1).

2. Member States shall postpone:
- for four months the adoption of a draft technical regulation in the form of a voluntary agreement within the meaning of point (ii) of the second subparagraph of point (f) of Article 1(1),
- without prejudice to paragraphs 3, 4 and 5 of this article, for six months the adoption of any other draft technical regulation except for draft rules on services,

from the date of receipt by the Commission of the communication referred to in Article 5(1), if the Commission or another Member State delivers a detailed opinion, within three months of that date, to the effect that the measure envisaged may create obstacles to the free movement of goods within the internal market,
- without prejudice to paragraphs 4 and 5, for four months the adoption of any draft rule on services, from the date of receipt by the Commission of the communication referred to in Article 5(1), if the Commission or another Member State delivers a detailed opinion, within three months of that date, to the effect that the measure envisaged may create obstacles to the free movement of services or to the freedom of establishment of service operators within the internal market.

With regard to draft rules on services, detailed opinions from the Commission or Member States may not affect any cultural policy measures, in particular in the audiovisual sphere, which Member

---

[9] Regulation (EC) No 1907/2006 of the European Parliament and of the Council of 18 December 2006 concerning the Registration, Evaluation, Authorisation and Restriction of Chemicals (REACH), establishing a European Chemicals Agency, amending Directive 1999/45/EC and repealing Council Regulation (EEC) No 793/93 and Commission Regulation (EC) No 1488/94 as well as Council Directive 76/769/EEC and Commission Directives 91/155/EEC, 93/67/EEC, 93/105/EC and 2000/21/EC (OJ L 396, 30.12.2006, p. 1).

States might adopt in accordance with the law of the Union, taking account of their linguistic diversity, their specific national and regional characteristics and their cultural heritage.

The Member State concerned shall report to the Commission on the action it proposes to take on such detailed opinions. The Commission shall comment on this reaction.

With respect to rules on services, the Member State concerned shall indicate, where appropriate, the reasons why the detailed opinions cannot be taken into account.

3. With the exclusion of draft rules relating to services, Member States shall postpone the adoption of a draft technical regulation for 12 months from the date of receipt by the Commission of the communication referred to in Article 5(1) of this Directive, if, within three months of that date, the Commission announces its intention to propose or adopt a directive, regulation or decision on the matter in accordance with Article 288 TFEU.

4. Member States shall postpone the adoption of a draft technical regulation for 12 months from the date of receipt by the Commission of the communication referred to in Article 5(1) of this Directive, if, within the three months following that date, the Commission announces its finding that the draft technical regulation concerns a matter which is covered by a proposal for a directive, regulation or decision presented to the European Parliament and the Council in accordance with Article 288 TFEU.

5. If the Council adopts a position at first reading during the standstill period referred to in paragraphs 3 and 4, that period shall, subject to paragraph 6, be extended to 18 months.

6. The obligations referred to in paragraphs 3, 4 and 5 shall lapse:
   (a) when the Commission informs the Member States that it no longer intends to propose or adopt a binding act;
   (b) when the Commission informs the Member States of the withdrawal of its draft or proposal;
   (c) when a binding act has been adopted by the European Parliament and the Council or by the Commission.

7. Paragraphs 1 to 5 shall not apply in cases where:
   (a) for urgent reasons, occasioned by serious and unforeseeable circumstances relating to the protection of public health or safety, the protection of animals or the preservation of plants, and for rules on services, also for public policy, in particular the protection of minors, a Member State is obliged to prepare technical regulations in a very short space of time in order to enact and introduce them immediately without any consultations being possible; or
   (b) for urgent reasons occasioned by serious circumstances relating to the protection of the security and the integrity of the financial system, in particular the protection of depositors, investors and insured persons, a Member State is obliged to enact and implement rules on financial services immediately.

In the communication referred to in Article 5, the Member State shall give reasons for the urgency of the measures taken. The Commission shall give its views on the communication as soon as possible. It shall take appropriate action in cases where improper use is made of this procedure. The European Parliament shall be kept informed by the Commission.

Article 7

1. Articles 5 and 6 shall not apply to those laws, regulations and administrative provisions of the Member States or voluntary agreements by means of which Member States:
   (a) comply with binding Union acts which result in the adoption of technical specifications or rules on services;
   (b) fulfil the obligations arising out of international agreements which result in the adoption of common technical specifications or rules on services in the Union;
   (c) make use of safeguard clauses provided for in binding Union acts;
   (d) apply Article 12(1) of Directive 2001/95/EC of the European Parliament and of the Council[10];

---

[10] Directive 2001/95/EC of the European Parliament and of the Council of 3 December 2001 on general product safety (OJ L 11, 15.1.2002, p. 4).

(e) restrict themselves to implementing a judgment of the Court of Justice of the European Union;

(f) restrict themselves to amending a technical regulation within the meaning of point (f) of Article 1(1), in accordance with a Commission request, with a view to removing a barrier to trade or, in the case of rules on services, to the free movement of services or the freedom of establishment of service operators.

2. Article 6 shall not apply to the laws, regulations and administrative provisions of the Member States prohibiting manufacture in so far as they do not impede the free movement of products.

3. Paragraphs 3 to 6 of Article 6 shall not apply to the voluntary agreements referred to in point (ii) of the second subparagraph of point (f) of Article 1(1).

4. Article 6 shall not apply to the technical specifications or other requirements or the rules on services referred to in point (iii) of the second subparagraph of point (f) of Article 1(1).

Article 8

The Commission shall report every two years to the European Parliament, the Council and the European Economic and Social Committee on the results of the application of this Directive.

The Commission shall publish annual statistics on the notifications received in the *Official Journal of the European Union*.

Article 9

When Member States adopt a technical regulation, it shall contain a reference to this Directive or shall be accompanied by such reference on the occasion of its official publication. The methods of making such reference shall be laid down by Member States.

Article 10

Directive 98/34/EC, as amended by the acts listed in Part A of Annex III to this Directive, is repealed, without prejudice to the obligations of the Member States relating to the time limits for the transposition into national law of the Directives set out in Part B of Annex III to the repealed Directive and in Part B of Annex III to this Directive.

References to the repealed Directive shall be construed as references to this Directive and shall be read in accordance with the correlation table in Annex IV.

Article 11

This Directive shall enter into force on the twentieth day following that of its publication in the *Official Journal of the European Union*.

Article 12

This Directive is addressed to the Member States.

Done at Strasbourg, 9 September 2015.
For the European Parliament
The President
M. SCHULZ
For the Council
The President
N. SCHMIT

ANNEX I

Indicative list of services not covered by the second subparagraph of point (b) of Article 1(1)

1. Services not provided 'at a distance'

Services provided in the physical presence of the provider and the recipient, even if they involve the use of electronic devices:

(a) medical examinations or treatment at a doctor's surgery using electronic equipment where the patient is physically present;

(b) consultation of an electronic catalogue in a shop with the customer on site;

(c) plane ticket reservation at a travel agency in the physical presence of the customer by means of a network of computers;

(d) electronic games made available in a video arcade where the customer is physically present.

2. Services not provided 'by electronic means'

- services having material content even though provided via electronic devices:
    (a) automatic cash or ticket dispensing machines (banknotes, rail tickets);
    (b) access to road networks, car parks, etc., charging for use, even if there are electronic devices at the entrance/exit controlling access and/or ensuring correct payment is made,
- offline services: distribution of CD-ROMs or software on diskettes,
- services which are not provided via electronic processing/inventory systems:
    (a) voice telephony services;
    (b) telefax/telex services;
    (c) services provided via voice telephony or fax;
    (d) telephone/telefax consultation of a doctor;
    (e) telephone/telefax consultation of a lawyer;
    (f) telephone/telefax direct marketing.

3. Services not supplied 'at the individual request of a recipient of services'

Services provided by transmitting data without individual demand for simultaneous reception by an unlimited number of individual receivers (point to multipoint transmission):

(a) television broadcasting services (including near-video on-demand services), covered by point (e) of Article 1(1) of Directive 2010/13/EU;

(b) radio broadcasting services;

(c) (televised) teletext.

ANNEX II

Indicative list of the financial services covered by Article 1(4)

- Investment services,
- insurance and reinsurance operations,
- banking services,
- operations relating to pension funds,
- services relating to dealings in futures or options.

Such services include in particular:

(a) investment services referred to in the Annex to Directive 2004/39/EC; services of collective investment undertakings;

(b) services covered by the activities subject to mutual recognition referred to in Annex I to Directive 2013/36/EU of the European Parliament and of the Council[11];

(c) operations covered by the insurance and reinsurance activities referred to in Directive 2009/138/EC of the European Parliament and of the Council[12].

---

[11] Directive 2013/36/EU of the European Parliament and of the Council of 26 June 2013 on access to the activity of credit institutions and the prudential supervision of credit institutions and investment firms, amending Directive 2002/87/EC and repealing Directives 2006/48/EC and 2006/49/EC (OJ L 176, 27.6.2013, p. 338).

[12] Directive 2009/138/EC of the European Parliament and of the Council of 25 November 2009 on the taking-up and pursuit of the business of Insurance and Reinsurance (Solvency II) (OJ L 335, 17.12.2009, p. 1).

Regulation (EU) 2019/515 of the European Parliament and of the Council of 19 March 2019 on the mutual recognition of goods lawfully marketed in another Member State

[OJ 2019 L91/1]*

THE EUROPEAN PARLIAMENT AND THE COUNCIL OF THE EUROPEAN UNION,

Having regard to the Treaty on the Functioning of the European Union, and in particular Article 114 thereof,

Having regard to the proposal from the European Commission,

After transmission of the draft legislative act to the national parliaments,

Having regard to the opinion of the European Economic and Social Committee[1],

Acting in accordance with the ordinary legislative procedure[2],

Whereas:

(1) The internal market comprises an area without internal frontiers in which the free movement of goods is ensured in accordance with the Treaties. Quantitative restrictions on imports and all measures having equivalent effect are prohibited between Member States. That prohibition covers any national measure which is capable of hindering, directly or indirectly, actually or potentially, intra-Union trade in goods. The free movement of goods is ensured in the internal market by the harmonisation of rules at Union level that set common requirements for the marketing of certain goods or, for goods or aspects of goods not exhaustively covered by Union harmonisation rules, by the application of the principle of mutual recognition as defined by the Court of Justice of the European Union.

(2) A well-functioning principle of mutual recognition is an essential complement to harmonisation of rules at Union level, especially considering that many goods have both harmonised and non-harmonised aspects.

(3) Obstacles to the free movement of goods between Member States may be unlawfully created if, in the absence of Union harmonisation rules covering goods or certain aspects of goods, a Member State's competent authority applies national rules to goods that are lawfully marketed in another Member State, requiring the goods to meet certain technical requirements, for example, requirements relating to designation, form, size, weight, composition, presentation, labelling or packaging. The application of such rules to goods that are lawfully marketed in another Member State could be contrary to Articles 34 and 36 of the Treaty on the Functioning of the European Union (TFEU), even if the rules apply to all goods without distinction.

(4) The principle of mutual recognition derives from the case-law of the Court of Justice of the European Union. According to this principle, Member States may not prohibit the sale on their territory of goods which are lawfully marketed in another Member State, even where those goods have been produced in accordance with different technical rules, including goods that are not the result of a manufacturing process. But the principle of mutual recognition is not absolute. Member States can restrict the marketing of goods that have been lawfully marketed in another Member State, where such restrictions are justified on the grounds set out in Article 36 TFEU or on the basis of other overriding reasons of public interest, recognised by the case-law of the Court of Justice of the European Union in relation to the free movement of goods, and where those restrictions are proportionate to the aim pursued. This Regulation imposes the obligation to clearly justify why market access has been restricted or denied.

(5) The concept of overriding reasons of public interest is an evolving concept developed by the Court of Justice of the European Union in its case-law in relation to Articles 34 and 36 TFEU. Where

---

* **Editor's Note:** Repealing Regulation 764/2008.
[1] OJ C 283, 10.8.2018, p. 19.
[2] Position of the European Parliament of 14 February 2019 (not yet published in the Official Journal) and decision of the Council of 5 March 2019.

legitimate differences exist from one Member State to another, such overriding reasons might justify the application of national technical rules by the competent authorities. However, administrative decisions always need to be duly justified, to be legitimate, to be appropriate and to respect the principle of proportionality, and the competent authority has to make the least restrictive decision possible. In order to improve the functioning of the internal market for goods, the national technical rules should be fit for purpose and should not create disproportionate non-tariff barriers. Furthermore, administrative decisions restricting or denying market access in respect of goods that are lawfully marketed in another Member State must not be based on the mere fact that the goods under assessment fulfil the legitimate public objective pursued by the Member State in a different way from the way in which goods in that Member State fulfil that objective. In order to assist Member States, the Commission should provide non-binding guidance in relation to the case-law of the Court of Justice of the European Union on the concept of overriding reasons of public interest and how to apply the principle of mutual recognition. Competent authorities should have the opportunity to provide contributions and deliver feedback on the guidance.

(6) In its Conclusions on the Single Market Policy of December 2013, the Competitiveness Council noted that to improve framework conditions for businesses and consumers in the Single Market, all relevant instruments should be appropriately employed, including mutual recognition. The Council invited the Commission to report on cases where the functioning of the principle of mutual recognition is still inadequate or problematic. In its Conclusions on the Single Market Policy of February 2015, the Competitiveness Council urged the Commission to take steps to ensure that the principle of mutual recognition functioned effectively and to bring forward proposals to that effect.

(7) Regulation (EC) No 764/2008 of the European Parliament and of the Council[3] was adopted in order to facilitate the application of the principle of mutual recognition by establishing procedures to minimise the possibility of creating unlawful obstacles to the free movement of goods which have already been lawfully marketed in another Member State. Despite the adoption of that Regulation, many problems still exist as regards the application of the principle of mutual recognition. The evaluation carried out between 2014 and 2016 showed that the principle of mutual recognition does not function as it should, and that Regulation (EC) No 764/2008 has had limited effect in facilitating the application of that principle. The tools and procedural guarantees put in place by that Regulation failed in their aim of improving the application of the principle of mutual recognition. For example, the Product Contact Points network which was put in place in order to provide information to economic operators on applicable national rules and the application of the principle of mutual recognition is barely known or used by economic operators. Within that network, national authorities do not cooperate sufficiently. The requirement to notify administrative decisions restricting or denying market access is rarely complied with. As a result, obstacles to the free movement of goods in the internal market remain.

(8) Regulation (EC) No 764/2008 has several shortcomings, and should therefore be revised and strengthened. For the sake of clarity, Regulation (EC) No 764/2008 should be replaced by this Regulation. This Regulation should establish clear procedures to ensure the free movement of goods lawfully marketed in another Member State and to ensure that free movement can be restricted only where Member States have legitimate public interest grounds for doing so and that the restriction is justified and proportionate. This Regulation should also ensure that existing rights and obligations deriving from the principle of mutual recognition are observed, by both economic operators and national authorities.

(9) This Regulation should not prejudice the further harmonisation of conditions for the marketing of goods with a view to improving the functioning of the internal market, where appropriate.

(10) It is also possible for trade barriers to result from other types of measures falling under the scope of Articles 34 and 36 TFEU. Those measures can include, for example, technical specifications

---

[3] Regulation (EC) No 764/2008 of the European Parliament and of the Council of 9 July 2008 laying down procedures relating to the application of certain national technical rules to products lawfully marketed in another Member State and repealing Decision No 3052/95/EC (OJ L 218, 13.8.2008, p. 21).

drawn up for public procurement procedures or requirements to use official languages in the Member States. However, such measures should not constitute national technical rules within the meaning of this Regulation and should not fall within its scope.

(11) National technical rules are sometimes given effect in a Member State by means of a prior authorisation procedure, under which formal approval has to be obtained from a competent authority before the goods can be placed on the market there. The existence of a prior authorisation procedure in itself restricts the free movement of goods. Therefore, in order to be justified with regard to the fundamental principle of the free movement of goods within the internal market, such a procedure has to pursue a public interest objective recognised by Union law, and it has to be proportionate and non-discriminatory. The compliance of such a procedure with Union law is to be assessed in the light of the considerations set out in the case-law of the Court of Justice of the European Union. Therefore, administrative decisions restricting or denying market access exclusively on the grounds that the goods do not have a valid prior authorisation should be excluded from the scope of this Regulation. When, however, an application for mandatory prior authorisation of goods is made, any administrative decision to reject the application on the basis of a national technical rule applicable in that Member State should only be taken in accordance with this Regulation, so that the applicant can benefit from the procedural protection which this Regulation provides. The same applies to voluntary prior authorisation of goods, where it exists.

(12) It is important to clarify that the types of goods covered by this Regulation include agricultural products. The term 'agricultural products' includes products of fisheries, as provided for in Article 38(1) TFEU. In order to help to identify which types of goods are subject to this Regulation, the Commission should assess the feasibility and benefits of further developing an indicative product list for mutual recognition.

(13) It is also important to clarify that the term 'producer' includes not only manufacturers of goods, but also persons who produce goods which were not the result of a manufacturing process, including agricultural products, as well as persons who present themselves as the producers of goods.

(14) Decisions of national courts or tribunals assessing the legality of cases in which, on account of the application of a national technical rule, goods lawfully marketed in one Member State are not granted access to the market in another Member State, and decisions of national courts or tribunals applying penalties, should be excluded from the scope of this Regulation.

(15) To benefit from the principle of mutual recognition, goods must be lawfully marketed in another Member State. It should be clarified that, for goods to be considered to be lawfully marketed in another Member State, the goods need to comply with the relevant rules applicable in that Member State, and need to be made available to end users in that Member State.

(16) To raise awareness on the part of national authorities and economic operators of the principle of mutual recognition, Member States should consider providing for clear and unambiguous 'single market clauses' in their national technical rules with a view to facilitating the application of that principle.

(17) The evidence required to demonstrate that goods are lawfully marketed in another Member State varies significantly from Member State to Member State. This causes unnecessary burdens, delays and additional costs for economic operators, and prevents national authorities from obtaining the information necessary for assessing the goods in a timely manner. This may inhibit the application of the principle of mutual recognition. It is therefore essential to make it easier for economic operators to demonstrate that their goods are lawfully marketed in another Member State. Economic operators should benefit from a self-declaration that provides competent authorities with all necessary information on the goods and on their compliance with the rules applicable in that other Member State. The use of voluntary declarations should not prevent national authorities from taking administrative decisions restricting or denying market access, provided that such decisions are proportionate, justified and respect the principle of mutual recognition and are in accordance with this Regulation.

(18) It should be possible for the producer, importer or distributor to draw up a declaration of lawful marketing of goods for the purposes of mutual recognition ('mutual recognition declaration'). The producer is best placed to provide the information in the mutual recognition declaration as the producer knows the goods best and is in possession of the evidence necessary to verify the information in the mutual recognition declaration. The producer should be able to mandate an authorised representative to draw up such declarations on the producer's behalf and under the responsibility of the producer. However, where an economic operator is only able to provide the information on the lawfulness of the marketing of the goods in the declaration, it should be possible for another economic operator to provide the information that the goods are being made available to end users in the Member State concerned, provided that that economic operator takes responsibility for the information that it provided in the mutual recognition declaration and is able to provide the necessary evidence to verify this information.

(19) The mutual recognition declaration should always contain accurate and complete information on the goods. The declaration should therefore be kept up to date in order to reflect changes, for example changes in the relevant national technical rules.

(20) In order to ensure that the information provided in a mutual recognition declaration is comprehensive, a harmonised structure for such declarations should be laid down for use by economic operators wishing to make such declarations.

(21) It is important to ensure that the mutual recognition declaration is filled in truthfully and accurately. It is therefore necessary to require economic operators to be responsible for the information provided by them in the mutual recognition declaration.

(22) In order to enhance the efficiency and competitiveness of businesses operating in the field of goods that are not covered by Union harmonisation legislation, it should be possible to benefit from new information technologies for the purpose of facilitating the provision of the mutual recognition declaration. Therefore, economic operators should be able to make their mutual recognition declarations publicly available online, provided that the mutual recognition declaration is easily accessible and is in a reliable format.

(23) The Commission should ensure that a template for the mutual recognition declaration and guidelines for completing it are made available on the Single Digital Gateway in all of the official languages of the Union.

(24) This Regulation should also apply to goods in respect of which only some aspects are covered by Union harmonisation legislation. Where, pursuant to Union harmonisation legislation, the economic operator is required to draw up an EU declaration of conformity to demonstrate compliance with that legislation, that economic operator should be permitted to attach the mutual recognition declaration provided for by this Regulation to the EU declaration of conformity.

(25) Where economic operators decide not to use the mutual recognition declaration, it should be for the competent authorities of the Member State of destination to make clearly defined requests for specific information that they consider to be necessary to assess the goods, with respect to the principle of proportionality.

(26) The economic operator should be given appropriate time within which to submit documents or any other information requested by the competent authority of the Member State of destination, or to submit any arguments or comments in relation to the assessment of the goods in question.

(27) Directive (EU) 2015/1535 of the European Parliament and of the Council[4] requires Member States to communicate to the Commission and to the other Member States any draft national technical regulation concerning any product, including any agricultural or fishery product, and a statement of the grounds on which the enactment of that regulation is necessary. It is necessary, however, to ensure that, following the adoption of such a national technical regulation,

---

[4] Directive (EU) 2015/1535 of the European Parliament and of the Council of 9 September 2015 laying down a procedure for the provision of information in the field of technical regulations and of rules on Information Society services (OJ L 241, 17.9.2015, p. 1).

the principle of mutual recognition is correctly applied to specific goods in individual cases. This Regulation should lay down procedures for the application of the principle of mutual recognition in individual cases, for example, by requiring Member States to indicate the national technical rules on which the administrative decision is based and the legitimate public interest grounds that justify the application of that national technical rule with respect to a good that has been lawfully marketed in another Member State. The proportionality of the national technical rule is the basis for demonstrating the proportionality of the administrative decision that is based on that rule. However, the means by which the proportionality of the administrative decision is to be demonstrated should be determined on a case-by-case basis.

(28) As administrative decisions restricting or denying market access for goods that are already lawfully marketed in another Member State should be exceptions to the fundamental principle of the free movement of goods, it is necessary to ensure that such decisions observe the existing obligations that derive from the principle of mutual recognition. It is therefore appropriate to establish a clear procedure for determining whether goods are lawfully marketed in that other Member State and, if so, whether the legitimate public interests covered by the applicable national technical rule of the Member State of destination are adequately protected, in accordance with Article 36 TFEU and the case-law of the Court of Justice of the European Union. Such procedure should ensure that any administrative decisions that are taken are proportionate and respect the principle of mutual recognition and are in accordance with this Regulation.

(29) Where a competent authority is assessing goods before deciding whether to restrict or deny market access, that authority should not be able to take decisions to suspend market access, except where rapid intervention is required to prevent harm to the safety or health of persons, to prevent harm to the environment, or to prevent the goods from being made available in cases where the making available of such goods is generally prohibited on grounds of public morality or public security, including, for example, the prevention of crime.

(30) Regulation (EC) No 765/2008 of the European Parliament and of the Council[5] establishes a system of accreditation which ensures the mutual acceptance of the level of competence of conformity assessment bodies. The competent authorities of Member States should therefore not refuse to accept test reports and certificates issued by an accredited conformity assessment body on grounds related to the competence of that body. Furthermore, in order to avoid as far as possible the duplication of tests and procedures which have been already carried out in another Member State, Member States should not refuse to accept test reports and certificates issued by other conformity assessment bodies in accordance with Union law. Competent authorities should take due account of the content of the test reports or certificates submitted.

(31) Directive 2001/95/EC of the European Parliament and of the Council[6] specifies that only safe products may be placed on the market and lays down the obligations of producers and distributors with respect to the safety of products. It entitles the competent authorities to ban any dangerous product with immediate effect or to ban products that could be dangerous temporarily for the period needed for the various safety evaluations, checks and controls. That Directive also describes the procedure for competent authorities to apply appropriate measures if products pose a risk, such as the measures referred to in points (b) to (f) of Article 8(1) of that Directive, and it also imposes an obligation on Member States to notify such measures to the Commission and the other Member States. Therefore, competent authorities should be able to continue applying that Directive and, in particular, points (b) to (f) of Article 8(1) and Article 8(3) of that Directive.

(32) Regulation (EC) No 178/2002 of the European Parliament and of the Council[7] establishes, inter alia, a rapid alert system for the notification of direct or indirect risks to human health deriving

---

[5] Regulation (EC) No 765/2008 of the European Parliament and of the Council of 9 July 2008 setting out the requirements for accreditation and market surveillance relating to the marketing of products and repealing Regulation (EEC) No 339/93 (OJ L 218, 13.8.2008, p. 30).

[6] Directive 2001/95/EC of the European Parliament and of the Council of 3 December 2001 on general product safety (OJ L 11, 15.1.2002, p. 4).

[7] Regulation (EC) No 178/2002 of the European Parliament and of the Council of 28 January 2002 laying down the general principles and requirements of food law, establishing the European Food Safety Authority and laying down procedures in matters of food safety (OJ L 31, 1.2.2002, p. 1).

from food or feed. It requires Member States to notify the Commission immediately, using the rapid alert system, of any measure they adopt which is aimed at restricting the placing on the market of food or feed, or withdrawing or recalling food or feed, for the purpose of protecting human health, and which requires rapid action. Competent authorities should be able to continue applying that Regulation and, in particular, Articles 50(3) and 54 of that Regulation.

(33) Regulation (EU) 2017/625 of European Parliament and of the Council[8] establishes a harmonised Union framework for the organisation of official controls, and for the organisation of official activities other than official controls, along the entire agri-food chain, taking into account the rules on official controls laid down in Regulation (EC) No 882/2004 of the European Parliament and of the Council[9] and in relevant Union sectoral legislation. Regulation (EU) 2017/625 lays down a specific procedure for ensuring that economic operators remedy situations of non-compliance with food and feed law, animal health rules or animal welfare rules. Competent authorities should be able to continue applying Regulation (EU) 2017/625 and, in particular, Article 138 thereof.

(34) Regulation (EU) No 1306/2013 of the European Parliament and of the Council[10] establishes a harmonised Union framework for carrying out checks in respect of the obligations laid down in Regulation (EU) No 1308/2013 of the European Parliament and of the Council[11] in accordance with the criteria laid down in Regulation (EC) No 882/2004 and specifies that Member States shall ensure that any operator complying with those obligations is entitled to be covered by a system of checks. Competent authorities should be able to continue applying Regulation (EU) No 1306/2013 and, in particular, Article 90 thereof.

(35) Any administrative decision taken by competent authorities of Member States pursuant to this Regulation should specify the remedies available to the economic operator, so that an economic operator is able, in accordance with national law, to appeal against the decision or bring proceedings before the competent national court or tribunal. The administrative decision should also refer to the possibility for economic operators to use the Internal Market Problem Solving Network (SOLVIT) and the problem-solving procedure provided for in this Regulation.

(36) Effective solutions for economic operators wishing for a business friendly alternative when challenging administrative decisions restricting or denying market access are essential to ensure the correct and consistent application of the principle of mutual recognition. In order to guarantee such solutions, and to avoid legal costs, especially for small and medium-sized enterprises (SMEs), a non-judicial problem-solving procedure should be available for economic operators.

(37) SOLVIT is a service provided by the national administration in each Member State that aims to find solutions for individuals and businesses when their rights have been breached by public authorities in another Member State. The principles governing the functioning of SOLVIT are set out in Commission Recommendation 2013/461/EU[12], according to which each Member State is to provide for a SOLVIT Centre that has adequate human and financial resources to ensure that the SOLVIT Centre takes part in SOLVIT. The Commission should increase awareness about the existence and benefits of SOLVIT, especially among businesses.

---

[8] Regulation (EU) 2017/625 of the European Parliament and of the Council of 15 March 2017 on official controls and other official activities performed to ensure the application of food and feed law, rules on animal health and welfare, plant health and plant protection products, amending Regulations (EC) No 999/2001, (EC) No 396/2005, (EC) No 1069/2009, (EC) No 1107/2009, (EU) No 1151/2012, (EU) No 652/2014, (EU) 2016/429 and (EU) 2016/2031 of the European Parliament and of the Council, Council Regulations (EC) No 1/2005 and (EC) No 1099/2009 and Council Directives 98/58/EC, 1999/74/EC, 2007/43/EC, 2008/119/EC and 2008/120/EC, and repealing Regulations (EC) No 854/2004 and (EC) No 882/2004 of the European Parliament and of the Council, Council Directives 89/608/EEC, 89/662/EEC, 90/425/EEC, 91/496/EEC, 96/23/EC, 96/93/EC and 97/78/EC and Council Decision 92/438/EEC (Official Controls Regulation) (OJ L 95, 7.4.2017, p. 1).

[9] Regulation (EC) No 882/2004 of the European Parliament and of the Council of 29 April 2004 on official controls performed to ensure the verification of compliance with feed and food law, animal health and animal welfare rules (OJ L 165, 30.4.2004, p. 1).

[10] Regulation (EU) No 1306/2013 of the European Parliament and of the Council of 17 December 2013 on the financing, management and monitoring of the common agricultural policy and repealing Council Regulations (EEC) No 352/78, (EC) No 165/94, (EC) No 2799/98, (EC) No 814/2000, (EC) No 1290/2005 and (EC) No 485/2008 (OJ L 347, 20.12.2013, p. 549).

[11] Regulation (EU) No 1308/2013 of the European Parliament and of the Council of 17 December 2013 establishing a common organisation of the markets in agricultural products and repealing Council Regulations (EEC) No 922/72, (EEC) No 234/79, (EC) No 1037/2001 and (EC) No 1234/2007 (OJ L 347, 20.12.2013, p. 671).

[12] Commission Recommendation 2013/461/EU of 17 September 2013 on the principles governing SOLVIT (OJ L 249, 19.9.2013, p. 10).

(38) SOLVIT is an effective non-judicial, problem-solving mechanism that is provided free of charge. It works under short deadlines and provides practical solutions to individuals and businesses when they are experiencing difficulties in the recognition of their Union rights by public authorities. Where the economic operator, the relevant SOLVIT Centre and the Member States involved all agree on the appropriate outcome, no further action should be required.

(39) However, where the SOLVIT's informal approach fails, and doubts remain regarding the compatibility of the administrative decision with the principle of mutual recognition, the Commission should be empowered to look into the matter at the request of any of the SOLVIT Centres involved. Following its assessment, the Commission should issue an opinion to be communicated through the relevant SOLVIT Centre to the economic operator concerned and to the competent authorities, which should be taken into account during the SOLVIT procedure. The Commission's intervention should be subject to a time-limit of 45 working days, which should not include the time necessary for the Commission to receive any additional information and documents that it considers necessary. If the case is solved during this period, the Commission should not be required to issue an opinion. Such SOLVIT cases should be subject to a separate workflow in the SOLVIT database and should not be included in the regular SOLVIT statistics.

(40) The opinion of the Commission as regards an administrative decision restricting or denying market access should only address whether the administrative decision is compatible with the principle of mutual recognition and with the requirements of this Regulation. This is without prejudice to the Commission's powers under Article 258 TFEU and the Member States' obligation to comply with Union law, when addressing systemic problems identified as regards the application of the principle of mutual recognition.

(41) It is important for the internal market for goods that businesses, in particular SMEs, can obtain reliable and specific information about the law in force in a given Member State. Product Contact Points should play an important role in facilitating communication between national authorities and economic operators by disseminating information about specific product rules and about how the principle of mutual recognition is applied in the territory of their Member State. Therefore, it is necessary to enhance the role of Product Contact Points as the principal providers of information on all product-related rules, including national technical rules covered by mutual recognition.

(42) In order to facilitate the free movement of goods, Product Contact Points should provide, free of charge, a reasonable level of information on their national technical rules and the application of the principle of mutual recognition. Product Contact Points should be adequately equipped and resourced. In accordance with Regulation (EU) 2018/1724 of the European Parliament and of the Council[13] they should provide such information through a website and should be subject to the quality criteria set out in that Regulation. The tasks of Product Contact Points related to the provision of any such information, including electronic copies of, or online access to, the national technical rules, should be performed without prejudice to the national rules governing the distribution of national technical rules. Furthermore, Product Contact Points should not be required to provide copies of, or online access to, standards which are subject to the intellectual property rights of standardisation bodies or organisations.

(43) Cooperation between competent authorities is essential for the smooth functioning of the principle of mutual recognition and for creating a mutual recognition culture. Product Contact Points and national competent authorities should therefore cooperate and exchange information and expertise in order to ensure the correct and consistent application of the principle of mutual recognition and this Regulation.

(44) For the purposes of notifying administrative decisions restricting or denying market access, allowing communication between Product Contact Points and ensuring administrative

---

[13] Regulation (EU) 2018/1724 of the European Parliament and of the Council of 2 October 2018 establishing a single digital gateway to provide access to information, to procedures and to assistance and problem-solving services and amending Regulation (EU) No 1024/2012 (OJ L 295, 21.11.2018, p. 1).

cooperation, it is necessary to provide Member States with access to an information and communication system.

(45) In order to ensure uniform conditions for the implementation of this Regulation, implementing powers should be conferred on the Commission. Those powers should be exercised in accordance with Regulation (EU) No 182/2011 of the European Parliament and of the Council[14].

(46) Where, for the purposes of this Regulation, it is necessary to process personal data, such processing should be carried out in accordance with Union law on the protection of personal data. Any processing of personal data under this Regulation is subject to Regulation (EU) 2016/679 of the European Parliament and of the Council[15] or Regulation (EU) 2018/1725 of the European Parliament and of the Council[16].

(47) Reliable and efficient monitoring mechanisms should be established to provide information on the application of this Regulation and on its impact on the free movement of goods. Such mechanisms should not go beyond what is necessary to achieve these objectives.

(48) For the purposes of raising awareness about the principle of mutual recognition and ensuring that this Regulation is applied correctly and consistently, provision should be made for Union financing of awareness-raising campaigns, trainings, exchange of officials and other related activities aiming at enhancing and supporting trust and cooperation between competent authorities, Product Contact Points and economic operators.

(49) In order to remedy the lack of accurate data related to the functioning of the principle of mutual recognition and its impact on the Single Market for goods, the Union should finance the collection of such data.

(50) The financial interests of the Union should be protected through proportionate measures throughout the expenditure cycle, including the prevention, detection and investigation of irregularities, the recovery of funds lost, wrongly paid or incorrectly used and, where appropriate, administrative and financial penalties.

(51) It is appropriate to defer the application of this Regulation in order to allow competent authorities and economic operators sufficient time to adapt to the requirements laid down herein.

(52) The Commission should carry out an evaluation of this Regulation in light of the objectives that it pursues. The Commission should use the data collected on the functioning of the principle of mutual recognition and its impact on the single market for goods and information available in the information and communication system to evaluate this Regulation. The Commission should be able to request Member States to provide additional information necessary for its evaluation. Pursuant to point 22 of the Interinstitutional Agreement of 13 April 2016 on Better Law Making[17], the evaluation of this Regulation, which should be based on efficiency, effectiveness, relevance, coherence and added value, should provide the basis for impact assessments of options for further action.

(53) Since the objective of this Regulation, namely to ensure the smooth, consistent and correct application of the principle of mutual recognition, cannot be sufficiently achieved by the Member States but can rather, by reason of its scale and effects, be better achieved at Union level, the Union may adopt measures, in accordance with the principle of subsidiarity as set out in Article 5 of the Treaty on European Union. In accordance with the principle of proportionality, as set out in that Article, this Regulation does not go beyond what is necessary in order to achieve that objective,

HAVE ADOPTED THIS REGULATION:

---

[14] Regulation (EU) No 182/2011 of the European Parliament and of the Council of 16 February 2011 laying down the rules and general principles concerning mechanisms for control by the Member States of the Commission's exercise of implementing powers (OJ L 55, 28.2.2011, p. 13).

[15] Regulation (EU) 2016/679 of the European Parliament and of the Council of 27 April 2016 on the protection of natural persons with regard to the processing of personal data and on the free movement of such data, and repealing Directive 95/46/EC (General Data Protection Regulation) (OJ L 119, 4.5.2016, p. 1).

[16] Regulation (EU) 2018/1725 of the European Parliament and of the Council of 23 October 2018 on the protection of natural persons with regard to the processing of personal data by the Union institutions, bodies, offices and agencies and on the free movement of such data, and repealing Regulation (EC) No 45/2001 and Decision No 1247/2002/EC (OJ L 295, 21.11.2018, p. 39).

[17] OJ L 123, 12.5.2016, p. 1.

Chapter I General provisions

Article 1 Subject matter

1. The aim of this Regulation is to strengthen the functioning of the internal market by improving the application of the principle of mutual recognition and by removing unjustified barriers to trade.

2. This Regulation lays down rules and procedures concerning the application by Member States of the principle of mutual recognition in individual cases in relation to goods which are subject to Article 34 TFEU and which are lawfully marketed in another Member State, having regard to Article 36 TFEU and the case-law of the Court of Justice of the European Union.

3. This Regulation also provides for the establishment and maintenance of Product Contact Points in Member States and for cooperation and exchange of information in the context of the principle of mutual recognition.

Article 2 Scope

1. This Regulation applies to goods of any type, including agricultural products within the meaning of the second subparagraph of Article 38(1) TFEU, and to administrative decisions that have been taken or are to be taken by a competent authority of a Member State of destination in relation to any such goods that are lawfully marketed in another Member State, where the administrative decision meets the following criteria:

    (a) the basis for the administrative decision is a national technical rule applicable in the Member State of destination; and

    (b) the direct or indirect effect of the administrative decision is to restrict or deny market access in the Member State of destination.

Administrative decision includes any administrative step that is based on a national technical rule and that has the same or substantially the same legal effect as the effect referred to in point (b).

2. For the purposes of this Regulation, a 'national technical rule' is any provision of a law, regulation or other administrative provision of a Member State which has the following characteristics:

    (a) it covers goods or aspects of goods that are not the subject of harmonisation at Union level;

    (b) it either prohibits the making available of goods, or goods of a given type, on the market in that Member State, or it makes compliance with the provision compulsory, de facto or de jure, whenever goods, or goods of a given type, are made available on that market; and

    (c) it does at least one of the following:

        (i) it lays down the characteristics required of goods or of goods of a given type, such as their levels of quality, performance or safety, or their dimensions, including the requirements applicable to those goods as regards the names under which they are sold, terminology, symbols, testing and test methods, packaging, marking or labelling and conformity assessment procedures;

        (ii) for the purpose of protecting consumers or the environment, it imposes other requirements on goods or goods of a given type that affect the life-cycle of the goods after they have been made available on the market in that Member State, such as conditions of use, recycling, reuse or disposal, where such conditions can significantly influence either the composition or nature of those goods, or the making available of them on the market in that Member State.

3. Point (c)(i) of paragraph 2 of this Article also covers production methods and processes used in respect of agricultural products as referred to in the second subparagraph of Article 38(1) TFEU, and in respect of products intended for human or animal consumption, as well as production methods and processes relating to other products, where these have an effect on their characteristics.

4. A prior authorisation procedure does not itself constitute a national technical rule for the purposes of this Regulation, but a decision to refuse prior authorisation based on a national technical

rule shall be considered to be an administrative decision to which this Regulation applies, if that decision fulfils the other requirements of the first subparagraph of paragraph 1.

5. This Regulation does not apply to:
 (a) decisions of a judicial nature taken by national courts or tribunals;
 (b) decisions of a judicial nature taken by law enforcement authorities in the course of the investigation or prosecution of a criminal offence as regards the terminology, symbols or any material reference to unconstitutional or criminal organisations or offences of a racist, discriminatory or xenophobic nature.

6. Articles 5 and 6 shall not affect the application of the following provisions:
 (a) points (b) to (f) of Article 8(1) and Article 8(3) of Directive 2001/95/EC;
 (b) point (a) of Article 50(3) and Article 54 of Regulation (EC) No 178/2002;
 (c) Article 90 of Regulation (EU) No 1306/2013; and
 (d) Article 138 of Regulation (EU) 2017/625.

7. This Regulation does not affect the obligation under Directive (EU) 2015/1535 to notify draft national technical regulations to the Commission and the Member States prior to their adoption.

Article 3 Definitions

For the purposes of this Regulation, the following definitions apply:

(1) 'lawfully marketed in another Member State' means that goods or goods of that type comply with the relevant rules applicable in that Member State or are not subject to any such rules in that Member State, and are made available to end users in that Member State;

(2) 'making available on the market' means any supply of goods for distribution, consumption or use on the market within the territory of a Member State in the course of a commercial activity, whether in return for payment or free of charge;

(3) 'restricting market access' means imposing conditions to be fulfilled before goods can be made available on the market in the Member State of destination, or conditions for keeping goods on that market, which in either case require the modification of one or more of the characteristics of those goods, as referred to in point (c)(i) of Article 2(2), or require the performance of additional testing;

(4) 'denying market access' means any of the following:
 (a) prohibiting goods from being made available on the market in the Member State of destination or from being kept on that market; or
 (b) requiring the withdrawal or recall of those goods from that market;

(5) 'withdrawal' means any measure aimed at preventing goods in the supply chain from being made available on the market;

(6) 'recall' means any measure aimed at achieving the return of goods that have already been made available to the end user;

(7) 'prior authorisation procedure' means an administrative procedure under the law of a Member State whereby the competent authority of that Member State is required, on the basis of an application by an economic operator, to give its formal approval before goods may be made available on the market in that Member State;

(8) 'producer' means:
 (a) any natural or legal person who manufactures goods or has goods designed or manufactured, or who produces goods which were not the result of a manufacturing process, including agricultural products, and markets them under that person's name or trademark,
 (b) any natural or legal person who modifies goods already lawfully marketed in a Member State in a way that might affect compliance with the relevant rules applicable in that Member State, or
 (c) any other natural or legal person who, by putting its name, trademark or other distinguishing feature on goods or on the documents that accompany those goods, presents itself as the producer of those goods;

(9) 'authorised representative' means any natural or legal person established within the Union who has received a written mandate from a producer to act on that producer's behalf with regard to the making available of goods on the market in question;

(10) 'importer' means any natural or legal person established within the Union who makes goods from a third country available on the Union market for the first time;

(11) 'distributor' means any natural or legal person in the supply chain, other than the producer or the importer, who makes goods available on the market in a Member State;

(12) 'economic operator' means any of the following in relation to goods: the producer, the authorised representative, the importer or the distributor;

(13) 'end user' means any natural or legal person residing or established in the Union, to whom the goods have been made available or are being made available, either as a consumer outside of any trade, business, craft or profession or as a professional end user in the course of its industrial or professional activities;

(14) 'legitimate public interest grounds' means any of the grounds set out in Article 36 TFEU or any other overriding reasons of public interest;

(15) 'conformity assessment body' means a conformity assessment body as defined in point 13 of Article 2 of Regulation (EC) No 765/2008.

Chapter II Procedures concerning application of the principle of mutual recognition in individual cases

Article 4   Mutual recognition declaration

1. The producer of goods, or of goods of a given type, that are being made or are to be made available on the market in the Member State of destination may draw up a voluntary declaration of lawful marketing of goods for the purposes of mutual recognition ('mutual recognition declaration') in order to demonstrate to the competent authorities of the Member State of destination that the goods, or the goods of that type, are lawfully marketed in another Member State.

The producer may mandate its authorised representative to draw up the mutual recognition declaration on its behalf.

The mutual recognition declaration shall follow the structure set out in Part I and Part II of the Annex and shall contain all the information specified therein.

The producer or its authorised representative, where mandated to do so, may fill in the mutual recognition declaration with only the information set out in Part I of the Annex. In such case the information set out in Part II of the Annex shall be filled in by the importer or by the distributor.

Alternatively, both parts of the mutual recognition declaration may be drawn up by the importer or by the distributor, provided that the signatory can supply the evidence referred to in point (a) of Article 5(4).

The mutual recognition declaration shall be drawn up in one of the official languages of the Union. Where that language is not the language required by the Member State of destination, the economic operator shall translate the mutual recognition declaration into a language required by the Member State of destination.

2. Economic operators who sign the mutual recognition declaration or a part of it shall be responsible for the content and accuracy of the information that they provide in the mutual recognition declaration, including the correctness of the information they translate. For the purposes of this paragraph, economic operators shall be liable in accordance with national laws.

3. Economic operators shall ensure that the mutual recognition declaration is kept up to date at all times, reflecting any changes in the information that they have provided in the mutual recognition declaration.

4. The mutual recognition declaration may be supplied to the competent authority of the Member State of destination for the purposes of an assessment to be carried out under Article 5. It may be supplied either in paper form or by electronic means or be made available online in accordance with the requirements of the Member State of destination.

5. Where economic operators make the mutual recognition declaration available online, the following conditions apply:

(a) the type of goods or the series to which the mutual recognition declaration applies shall be easily identifiable; and

(b) the technical means used shall ensure easy navigation and shall be monitored to ensure the availability of, and access to, the mutual recognition declaration.

6. Where the goods for which the mutual recognition declaration is being supplied are also subject to a Union act requiring an EU declaration of conformity, the mutual recognition declaration may be attached to the EU declaration of conformity.

Article 5   Assessment of goods

1. Where a competent authority of the Member State of destination intends to assess goods subject to this Regulation to establish whether the goods or goods of that type are lawfully marketed in another Member State, and, if so, whether the legitimate public interests covered by the applicable national technical rule of the Member State of destination are adequately protected, having regard to the characteristics of the goods in question, it shall contact the economic operator concerned without delay.

2. When entering into contact with the economic operator concerned, the competent authority of the Member State of destination shall inform the economic operator of the assessment, indicating the goods that are subject to that assessment and specifying the applicable national technical rule or prior authorisation procedure. The competent authority of the Member State of destination shall also inform the economic operator of the possibility of supplying a mutual recognition declaration in accordance with Article 4 for the purposes of that assessment.

3. The economic operator shall be allowed to make the goods available on the market in the Member State of destination while the competent authority carries out the assessment under paragraph 1 of this Article, and may continue to do so unless the economic operator receives an administrative decision restricting or denying market access for those goods. This paragraph shall not apply where the assessment is carried out in the framework of a prior authorisation procedure, or where the competent authority temporary suspends the making available on the market of the goods that are subject to that assessment in accordance with Article 6.

4. If a mutual recognition declaration is supplied to a competent authority of the Member State of destination in accordance with Article 4, then for the purposes of the assessment under paragraph 1 of this Article:

(a) the mutual recognition declaration, together with supporting evidence necessary to verify the information contained in it that was provided in response to a request by the competent authority, shall be accepted by the competent authority as sufficient to demonstrate that the goods are lawfully marketed in another Member State; and

(b) the competent authority shall not require any other information or documentation from any economic operator for the purpose of demonstrating that the goods are lawfully marketed in another Member State.

5. If a mutual recognition declaration is not supplied to a competent authority of the Member State of destination in accordance with Article 4, then for the purposes of the assessment under paragraph 1 of this Article, the competent authority may request the economic operators concerned to provide documentation and information that is necessary for that assessment concerning the following:

(a) the characteristics of the goods or type of goods in question; and

(b) lawful marketing of the goods in another Member State.

6. The economic operator concerned shall be allowed at least 15 working days following the request of the competent authority of the Member State of destination in which to submit the documents and information referred to in point (a) of paragraph 4 or in paragraph 5, or to submit any arguments or comments that the economic operator might have.

7. For the purposes of the assessment under paragraph 1 of this Article, the competent authority of the Member State of destination, in accordance with Article 10(3), may contact the competent

authorities or the Product Contact Points of the Member State in which an economic operator claims to be lawfully marketing its goods, if the competent authority needs to verify any information provided by the economic operator.

8. In carrying out the assessment under paragraph 1, the competent authorities of Member States of destination shall take due account of the content of test reports or certificates issued by a conformity assessment body that have been provided by any economic operator as part of the assessment. The competent authorities of Member States of destination shall not refuse test reports or certificates that were issued by a conformity assessment body accredited for the appropriate field of conformity assessment activity in accordance with Regulation (EC) No 765/2008 on grounds related to the competence of that body.

9. Where, on completion of an assessment under paragraph 1 of this Article, the competent authority of a Member State of destination takes an administrative decision with respect to the goods that it has assessed, it shall notify that administrative decision without delay to the economic operator referred to in paragraph 1 of this Article. The competent authority shall also notify that administrative decision to the Commission and to the other Member States no later than 20 working days after it took the decision. For that purpose, it shall use the system referred to in Article 11.

10. The administrative decision referred to in paragraph 9 shall set out the reasons for the decision in a manner that is sufficiently detailed and reasoned to facilitate an assessment of its compatibility with the principle of mutual recognition and with the requirements of this Regulation.

11. In particular, the following information shall be included in the administrative decision referred to in paragraph 9:

    (a) the national technical rule on which the administrative decision is based;

    (b) the legitimate public interest grounds justifying the application of the national technical rule on which the administrative decision is based;

    (c) the technical or scientific evidence that the competent authority of the Member State of destination considered, including, where applicable, any relevant changes in the state of the art that have occurred since the national technical rule came into force;

    (d) a summary of the arguments put forward by the economic operator concerned that are relevant for the assessment under paragraph 1, if any;

    (e) the evidence demonstrating that the administrative decision is appropriate for the purpose of achieving the objective pursued and that the administrative decision does not go beyond what is necessary in order to attain that objective.

12. The administrative decision referred to in paragraph 9 of this Article shall specify the remedies available under the national law of the Member State of destination and the time limits applicable to those remedies. It shall also include a reference to the possibility for economic operators to use SOLVIT and the procedure under Article 8.

13. The administrative decision referred to in paragraph 9 shall not take effect before it has been notified to the economic operator concerned under that paragraph.

Article 6   Temporary suspension of market access

1. When the competent authority of a Member State is carrying out an assessment of goods pursuant to Article 5, it may temporarily suspend the making available of those goods on the market in that Member State only if:

    (a) under normal or reasonably foreseeable conditions of use, the goods pose a serious risk to safety or health of persons or to the environment, including one where the effects are not immediate, which requires rapid intervention by the competent authority; or

    (b) the making available of the goods, or of goods of that type, on the market in that Member State is generally prohibited in that Member State on grounds of public morality or public security.

2. The competent authority of the Member State shall immediately notify the economic operator concerned, the Commission and the other Member States of any temporary suspension pursuant to paragraph 1 of this Article. The notification to the Commission and the other Member States shall be made by means of the system referred to in Article 11. In cases falling within point (a)

of paragraph 1 of this Article, the notification shall be accompanied by a detailed technical or scientific justification demonstrating why the case falls within the scope of that point.

Article 7   Notification through RAPEX or RASFF

If the administrative decision referred to in Article 5 or the temporary suspension referred to in Article 6 is also a measure which is to be notified through the Rapid Information Exchange System (RAPEX) in accordance with Directive 2001/95/EC or through the Rapid Alert System for Food and Feed (RASFF) in accordance with Regulation (EC) No 178/2002, a separate notification to the Commission and the other Member States under this Regulation shall not be required, provided that the following conditions are met:

(a) the RAPEX or RASFF notification indicates that the notification of the measure also serves as a notification under this Regulation; and

(b) the supporting evidence required for the administrative decision under Article 5 or for the temporary suspension under Article 6 is included with the RAPEX or RASFF notification.

Article 8   Problem-solving procedure

1. Where an economic operator affected by an administrative decision has submitted it to SOLVIT and where, during the SOLVIT procedure, the Home Centre or the Lead Centre requests the Commission to give an opinion in order to assist in solving the case, the Home Centre and the Lead Centre shall provide the Commission with all relevant documents relating to the administrative decision concerned.

2. After receiving the request referred to in paragraph 1, the Commission shall assess whether the administrative decision is compatible with the principle of mutual recognition and with the requirements of this Regulation.

3. For the purposes of the assessment referred to in paragraph 2 of this Article, the Commission shall consider the administrative decision notified in accordance with Article 5(9) and the documents and information provided within the SOLVIT procedure. Where additional information or documents are needed for the purposes of the assessment referred to in paragraph 2 of this Article, the Commission shall, without undue delay, request the relevant SOLVIT Centre to enter into communication with the economic operator concerned or with the competent authorities which took the administrative decision, for the purpose of obtaining such additional information or documents.

4. Within 45 working days of receipt of the request referred to in paragraph 1, the Commission shall complete its assessment and issue an opinion. Where appropriate, the Commission's opinion shall identify any concerns that should be addressed in the SOLVIT case or shall make recommendations to assist in solving the case. The 45 working day period does not include the time necessary for the Commission to receive the additional information and documents as provided for in paragraph 3.

5. Where the Commission has been informed that the case is solved during the assessment referred to in paragraph 2, the Commission shall not be required to issue an opinion.

6. The Commission's opinion shall be communicated through the relevant SOLVIT Centre to the economic operator concerned and to the relevant competent authorities. That opinion shall be notified by the Commission to all Member States by means of the system referred to in Article 11. The opinion shall be taken into account during the SOLVIT procedure referred to in paragraph 1 of this Article.

Chapter III Administrative cooperation, monitoring and communication

Article 9   Tasks of the Product Contact Points

1. Member States shall designate and maintain Product Contact Points on their territory and shall ensure that their Product Contact Points have sufficient powers and adequate resources for the proper performance of their tasks. They shall ensure that Product Contact Points deliver their services in accordance with Regulation (EU) 2018/1724.

2. Product Contact Points shall provide the following information online:

    (a) information on the principle of mutual recognition and the application of this Regulation in the territory of their Member State, including information on the procedure set out in Article 5;

    (b) the contact details, by means of which the competent authorities within that Member State may be contacted directly, including the particulars of the authorities responsible for supervising the implementation of the national technical rules applicable in the territory of their Member State;

    (c) the remedies and procedures available in the territory of their Member State in the event of a dispute between the competent authority and an economic operator, including the procedure set out in Article 8.

3. Where necessary to complement the information provided online under paragraph 2, Product Contact Points shall provide, at the request of an economic operator or a competent authority of another Member State, any useful information, such as electronic copies of, or online access to, the national technical rules and national administrative procedures applicable to specific goods or goods of a specific type in the territory in which the Product Contact Point is established or information on whether those goods or goods of that type are subject to prior authorisation under national law.

4. Product Contact Points shall respond within 15 working days of receiving any request under paragraph 3.

5. Product Contact Points shall not charge any fee for the provision of the information under paragraph 3.

Article 10   Administrative cooperation

1. The Commission shall provide for and ensure efficient cooperation among the competent authorities and the Product Contact Points of the various Member States through the following activities:

    (a) facilitating and coordinating the exchange and collection of information and best practices with regard to the application of the principle of mutual recognition;

    (b) supporting the functioning of the Product Contact Points and enhancing their cross-border cooperation;

    (c) facilitating and coordinating the exchange of officials among Member States and the organisation of common training and awareness raising programmes for authorities and businesses.

2. Member States shall ensure that their competent authorities and Product Contact Points participate in the activities referred to in paragraph 1.

3. Upon a request by a competent authority of the Member State of destination pursuant to Article 5(7), the competent authorities in the Member State in which an economic operator claims to be lawfully marketing its goods shall provide the competent authority of the Member State of destination within 15 working days with any information relevant for verifying data and documents supplied by the economic operator during the assessment under Article 5 relating to those goods. The Product Contact Points may be used to facilitate contacts between the relevant competent authorities in accordance with the time limit for providing the requested information set out in Article 9(4).

Article 11   Information and communication system

1. For the purposes of Articles 5, 6 and 10 of this Regulation, the information and communication system set out in Article 23 of Regulation (EC) No 765/2008 shall be used, except as provided in Article 7 of this Regulation.

2. The Commission shall adopt implementing acts specifying the details and functionalities of the system referred to in paragraph 1 of this Article for the purposes of this Regulation. Those implementing acts shall be adopted in accordance with the examination procedure referred to in Article 15(2).

Chapter IV Financing

Article 12   Financing of activities in support of this Regulation

1. The Union may finance the following activities in support of this Regulation:

   (a) awareness-raising campaigns;

   (b) education and training;

   (c) exchange of officials and of best practices;

   (d) cooperation among Product Contact Points and competent authorities, and the technical and logistic support for this cooperation;

   (e) the collection of data related to the functioning of the principle of mutual recognition and its impact on the Single Market for goods.

2. The Union's financial assistance with respect to activities in support of this Regulation shall be implemented in accordance with Regulation (EU, Euratom) 2018/1046 of the European Parliament and of the Council[18], either directly or by entrusting budget implementation tasks to the entities listed in point (c) of Article 62(1) of that Regulation.

3. The appropriations allocated to activities referred to in this Regulation shall be determined each year by the budgetary authority within the limits of the financial framework in force.

Article 13   Protection of the financial interests of the Union

1. The Commission shall take appropriate measures to ensure that, when activities financed under this Regulation are implemented, the financial interests of the Union are protected by the application of preventive measures against fraud, corruption and any other illegal activities, by effective checks and, if irregularities are detected, by the recovery of the amounts wrongly paid and, where appropriate, by effective, proportionate and dissuasive administrative and financial penalties.

2. The Commission or its representatives and the Court of Auditors shall have the power of audit, on the basis of documents and of on-the-spot inspections, over all grant beneficiaries, contractors and subcontractors who have received Union funds under this Regulation.

3. The European Anti-Fraud Office (OLAF) may carry out investigations, including on-the-spot checks and inspections, in accordance with the provisions and procedures laid down in Regulation (EU, Euratom) No 883/2013 of the European Parliament and of the Council[19] and Council Regulation (Euratom, EC) No 2185/96[20] with a view to establishing whether there has been fraud, corruption or any other illegal activity affecting the financial interests of the Union in connection with a grant agreement or grant decision or a contract funded under this Regulation.

4. Without prejudice to paragraphs 1, 2 and 3, cooperation agreements with third countries and with international organisations, contracts, grant agreements and grant decisions, resulting from the implementation of this Regulation shall contain provisions expressly empowering the Commission, the Court of Auditors and OLAF to conduct such audits and investigations, in accordance with their respective competences.

---

[18] Regulation (EU, Euratom) 2018/1046 of the European Parliament and of the Council of 18 July 2018 on the financial rules applicable to the general budget of the Union, amending Regulations (EU) No 1296/2013, (EU) No 1301/2013, (EU) No 1303/2013, (EU) No 1304/2013, (EU) No 1309/2013, (EU) No 1316/2013, (EU) No 223/2014, (EU) No 283/2014, and Decision No 541/2014/EU and repealing Regulation (EU, Euratom) No 966/2012 (OJ L 193, 30.7.2018, p. 1).

[19] Regulation (EU, Euratom) No 883/2013 of the European Parliament and of the Council of 11 September 2013 concerning investigations conducted by the European Anti-Fraud Office (OLAF) and repealing Regulation (EC) No 1073/1999 of the European Parliament and of the Council and Council Regulation (Euratom) No 1074/1999 (OJ L 248, 18.9.2013, p. 1).

[20] Council Regulation (Euratom, EC) No 2185/96 of 11 November 1996 concerning on-the-spot checks and inspections carried out by the Commission in order to protect the European Communities' financial interests against fraud and other irregularities (OJ L 292, 15.11.1996, p. 2.).

Chapter V   Evaluation and committee procedure

Article 14   Evaluation

1. By 20 April 2025, and every four years thereafter, the Commission shall carry out an evaluation of this Regulation in light of the objectives that it pursues and shall submit a report thereon to the European Parliament, to the Council and to the European Economic and Social Committee.

2. For the purposes of paragraph 1 of this Article, the Commission shall use the information available in the system referred to in Article 11 and any data collected in the course of activities referred to in point (e) of Article 12(1). The Commission may also ask Member States to submit any relevant information for evaluating the free movement of goods lawfully marketed in another Member State or for evaluating the effectiveness of this Regulation, as well as an assessment of the functioning of the Product Contact Points.

Article 15   Committee procedure

1. The Commission shall be assisted by a committee. That committee shall be a committee within the meaning of Regulation (EU) No 182/2011.

2. Where reference is made to this paragraph, Article 5 of Regulation (EU) No 182/2011 shall apply.

Chapter VI   Final provisions

Article 16   Repeal

Regulation (EC) No 764/2008 is repealed with effect from 19 April 2020.

References to the repealed Regulation shall be construed as references to this Regulation.

Article 17   Entry into force and application

This Regulation shall enter into force on the twentieth day following that of its publication in the *Official Journal of the European Union*.

It shall apply from 19 April 2020.

This Regulation shall be binding in its entirety and directly applicable in all Member States.

Done at Brussels, 19 March 2019.

Free movement of persons

Council Directive of 22 March 1977 to facilitate the effective exercise by lawyers of freedom to provide services (77/249/EEC)*

[OJ 1977 L78/17]

THE COUNCIL OF THE EUROPEAN COMMUNITIES,

Having regard to the Treaty establishing the European Economic Community, and in particular Articles 57 and 66 thereof,

Having regard to the proposal from the Commission,

Having regard to the opinion of the European Parliament,[1]

Having regard to the opinion of the Economic and Social Committee,[2]

---

* **Editor's Note:** As amended up to and including OJ 2013 L158/368.
[1] OJ No C 103, 5.10.1972, p. 19 and OJ No C 53, 8.3.1976, p. 33.
[2] OJ No C 36, 28.3.1970, p. 37 and OJ No C 50, 4.3.1976, p. 17.

Whereas, pursuant to the Treaty, any restriction on the provision of services which is based on nationality or on conditions of residence has been prohibited since the end of the transitional period;

Whereas this Directive deals only with measures to facilitate the effective pursuit of the activities of lawyers by way of provision of services;

Whereas more detailed measures will be necessary to facilitate the effective exercise of the right of establishment;

Whereas if lawyers are to exercise effectively the freedom to provide services host Member States must recognize as lawyers those persons practising the profession in the various Member States;

Whereas, since this Directive solely concerns provision of services and does not contain provisions on the mutual recognition of diplomas, a person to whom the Directive applies must adopt the professional title used in the Member State in which he is established, hereinafter referred to as 'the Member State from which he comes',

HAS ADOPTED THIS DIRECTIVE:

Article 1

1. This Directive shall apply, within the limits and under the conditions laid down herein, to the activities of lawyers pursued by way of provision of services.

Notwithstanding anything contained in this Directive, Member States may reserve to prescribed categories of lawyers the preparation of formal documents for obtaining title to administer estates of deceased persons, and the drafting of formal documents creating or transferring interests in land.

2. 'Lawyers' means any person entitled to pursue his professional activities under one of the following designations:*

Belgium:	Avocat/Advocaat
Bulgaria:	Адвокат
Croatia:	Odvjetnik/Odvjetnica
Czech Republic:	Advokát
Denmark:	Advokat
Germany:	Rechtsanwalt
Estonia:	Vandeadvokaat
Greece:	Δικηγόρος
France:	Avocat
Ireland:	Barrister
	Solicitor
Italy:	Avvocato
Cyprus:	Δικηγόρος
Latvia:	Zvērināts/advokāts
Lithuania:	Advokatas
Luxembourg:	Avocat-avoué
Hungary:	Ügyvéd
Malta:	Avukat/Prokuratur Legali
Netherlands:	Advocaat
Austria:	Rechtsanwalt

* **Editor's Note:** As amended by the Accession Acts.

Poland:	Adwokat/Radca prawny
Portugal:	Advogado
Romania:	Avocat
Slovenia:	Odvetnik/Odvetnica
Slovakia	Advokát/Komerčný právnik
Finland:	Asianajaja—Advokat
Spain:	Abogado
Sweden:	Advokat
United Kingdom:	Advocate
	Barrister
	Solicitor

Article 2
Each Member State shall recognise as a lawyer for the purpose of pursuing the activities specified in Article 1(1) any person listed in paragraph 2 of that Article.

Article 3
A person referred to in Article 1 shall adopt the professional title used in the Member State from which he comes, expressed in the language or one of the languages, of that State, with an indication of the professional organisation by which he is authorised to practise or the court of law before which he is entitled to practise pursuant to the laws of that State.

Article 4
1. Activities relating to the representation of a client in legal proceedings or before public authorities shall be pursued in each host Member State under the conditions laid down for lawyers established in that State, with the exception of any conditions requiring residence, or registration with a professional organisation, in that State.

2. A lawyer pursuing these activities shall observe the rules of professional conduct of the host Member State, without prejudice to his obligations in the Member State from which he comes.

3. When these activities are pursued in the United Kingdom, 'rules of professional conduct of the host Member State' means the rules of professional conduct applicable to solicitors, where such activities are not reserved for barristers and advocates. Otherwise the rules of professional conduct applicable to the latter shall apply. However, barristers from Ireland shall always be subject to the rules of professional conduct applicable in the United Kingdom to barristers and advocates.

When these activities are pursued in Ireland 'rules of professional conduct of the host Member State' means, in so far as they govern the oral presentation of a case in court, the rules of professional conduct applicable to barristers. In all other cases the rules of professional conduct applicable to solicitors shall apply. However, barristers and advocates from the United Kingdom shall always be subject to the rules of professional conduct applicable in Ireland to barristers.

4. A lawyer pursuing activities other than those referred to in paragraph 1 shall remain subject to the conditions and rules of professional conduct of the Member State from which he comes without prejudice to respect for the rules, whatever their source, which govern the profession in the host Member State, especially those concerning the incompatibility of the exercise of the activities of a lawyer with the exercise of other activities in that State, professional secrecy, relation with other lawyers, the prohibition on the same lawyer acting for parties with mutually conflicting interests, and publicity. The latter rules are applicable only if they are capable of being observed by a lawyer who is not established in the host Member State and to the extent to which their observance is objectively justified to ensure, in that State, the proper exercise of a lawyer's activities, the standing of the profession and respect for the rules concerning incompatibility.

Article 5

For the pursuit of activities relating to the representation of a client in legal proceedings, a Member State may require lawyers to whom Article 1 applies:
- to be introduced, in accordance with local rules or customs, to the presiding judge and, where appropriate, to the President of the relevant Bar in the host Member State;
- to work in conjunction with a lawyer who practises before the judicial authority in question and who would, where necessary, be answerable to that authority, or with an 'avoué' or 'procuratore' practising before it.

Article 6

Any Member State may exclude lawyers who are in the salaried employment of a public or private undertaking from pursuing activities relating to the representation of that undertaking in legal proceedings in so far as lawyers established in that State are not permitted to pursue those activities.

Article 7

1. The competent authority of the host Member State may request the person providing the services to establish his qualifications as a lawyer.

2. In the event of non-compliance with the obligations referred to in Article 4 and in force in the host Member State, the competent authority of the latter shall determine in accordance with its own rules and procedures the consequences of such non-compliance, and to this end may obtain an appropriate professional information concerning the person providing services. It shall notify the competent authority of the Member State from which the person comes of any decision taken. Such exchanges shall not affect the confidential nature of the information supplied.

(All remaining provisions omitted.)

Directive 96/71/EC of the European Parliament and of the Council of 16 December 1996 concerning the posting of workers in the framework of the provision of services

[OJ 1997 L18/1]

THE EUROPEAN PARLIAMENT AND THE COUNCIL OF THE EUROPEAN UNION,

Having regard to the Treaty establishing the European Community, and in particular Articles 57(2) and 66 thereof,

Having regard to the proposal from the Commission,[1]

Having regard to the opinion of the Economic and Social Committee,[2]

Acting in accordance with the procedure laid down in Article 189b of the Treaty,[3]

(1) Whereas, pursuant to Article 3 (c) of the Treaty, the abolition, as between Member States, of obstacles to the free movement of persons and services constitutes one of the objectives of the Community;

(2) Whereas, for the provision of services, any restrictions based on nationality or residence requirements are prohibited under the Treaty with effect from the end of the transitional period;

---

[1] OJ No C 225, 30.8.1991, p. 6 and OJ No C 187, 9.7.1993, p. 5.
[2] OJ No C 49, 24.2.1992, p. 41.
[3] Opinion of the European Parliament of 10 February 1993 (OJ No C 72, 15.3.1993, p. 78), Council common position of 3 June 1996 (OJ No C 220, 29.7.1996, p. 1) and Decision of the European Parliament of 18 September 1996 (not yet published in the Official Journal). Council Decision of 24 September 1996.

(3) Whereas the completion of the internal market offers a dynamic environment for the transnational provision of services, prompting a growing number of undertakings to post employees abroad temporarily to perform work in the territory of a Member State other than the State in which they are habitually employed;

(4) Whereas the provision of services may take the form either of performance of work by an undertaking on its account and under its direction, under a contract concluded between that undertaking and the party for whom the services are intended, or of the hiring-out of workers for use by an undertaking in the framework of a public or a private contract;

(5) Whereas any such promotion of the transnational provision of services requires a climate of fair competition and measures guaranteeing respect for the rights of workers;

(6) Whereas the transnationalization of the employment relationship raises problems with regard to the legislation applicable to the employment relationship; whereas it is in the interests of the parties to lay down the terms and conditions governing the employment relationship envisaged;

(7) Whereas the Rome Convention of 19 June 1980 on the law applicable to contractual obligations,[4] signed by 12 Member States, entered into force on 1 April 1991 in the majority of Member States;

(8) Whereas Article 3 of that Convention provides, as a general rule, for the free choice of law made by the parties; whereas, in the absence of choice, the contract is to be governed, according to Article 6 (2), by the law of the country, in which the employee habitually carries out his work in performance of the contract, even if he is temporarily employed in another country, or, if the employee does not habitually carry out his work in any one country, by the law of the country in which the place of business through which he was engaged is situated, unless it appears from the circumstances as a whole that the contract is more closely connected with another country, in which case the contract is to be governed by the law of that country;

(9) Whereas, according to Article 6 (1) of the said Convention, the choice of law made by the parties is not to have the result of depriving the employee of the protection afforded to him by the mandatory rules of the law which would be applicable under paragraph 2 of that Article in the absence of choice;

(10) Whereas Article 7 of the said Convention lays down, subject to certain conditions, that effect may be given, concurrently with the law declared applicable, to the mandatory rules of the law of another country, in particular the law of the Member State within whose territory the worker is temporarily posted;

(11) Whereas, according to the principle of precedence of Community law laid down in its Article 20, the said Convention does not affect the application of provisions which, in relation to a particular matter, lay down choice-of-law rules relating to contractual obligations and which are or will be contained in acts of the institutions of the European Communities or in national laws harmonized in implementation of such acts;

(12) Whereas Community law does not preclude Member States from applying their legislation, or collective agreements entered into by employers and labour, to any person who is employed, even temporarily, within their territory, although his employer is established in another Member State; whereas Community law does not forbid Member States to guarantee the observance of those rules by the appropriate means;

(13) Whereas the laws of the Member States must be coordinated in order to lay down a nucleus of mandatory rules for minimum protection to be observed in the host country by employers who post workers to perform temporary work in the territory of a Member State where the services are provided; whereas such coordination can be achieved only by means of Community law;

(14) Whereas a 'hard core' of clearly defined protective rules should be observed by the provider of the services notwithstanding the duration of the worker's posting;

---

[4] OJ No L 266, 9.10.1980, p. 1.

(15) Whereas it should be laid down that, in certain clearly defined cases of assembly and/or installation of goods, the provisions on minimum rates of pay and minimum paid annual holidays do not apply;

(16) Whereas there should also be some flexibility in application of the provisions concerning minimum rates of pay and the minimum length of paid annual holidays; whereas, when the length of the posting is not more than one month, Member States may, under certain conditions, derogate from the provisions concerning minimum rates of pay or provide for the possibility of derogation by means of collective agreements; whereas, where the amount of work to be done is not significant, Member States may derogate from the provisions concerning minimum rates of pay and the minimum length of paid annual holidays;

(17) Whereas the mandatory rules for minimum protection in force in the host country must not prevent the application of terms and conditions of employment which are more favourable to workers;

(18) Whereas the principle that undertakings established outside the Community must not receive more favourable treatment than undertakings established in the territory of a Member State should be upheld;

(19) Whereas, without prejudice to other provisions of Community law, this Directive does not entail the obligation to give legal recognition to the existence of temporary employment undertakings, nor does it prejudice the application by Member States of their laws concerning the hiring-out of workers and temporary employment undertakings to undertakings not established in their territory but operating therein in the framework of the provision of services;

(20) Whereas this Directive does not affect either the agreements concluded by the Community with third countries or the laws of Member States concerning the access to their territory of third-country providers of services; whereas this Directive is also without prejudice to national laws relating to the entry, residence and access to employment of third-country workers;

(21) Whereas Council Regulation (EEC) No 1408/71 of 14 June 1971 on the application of social security schemes to employed persons and their families moving within the Community[5] lays down the provisions applicable with regard to social security benefits and contributions;

(22) Whereas this Directive is without prejudice to the law of the Member States concerning collective action to defend the interests of trades and professions;

(23) Whereas competent bodies in different Member States must cooperate with each other in the application of this Directive;

whereas Member States must provide for appropriate remedies in the event of failure to comply with this Directive;

(24) Whereas it is necessary to guarantee proper application of this Directive and to that end to make provision for close collaboration between the Commission and the Member States;

(25) Whereas five years after adoption of this Directive at the latest the Commission must review the detailed rules for implementing this Directive with a view to proposing, where appropriate, the necessary amendments,

HAVE ADOPTED THIS DIRECTIVE:

Article 1 Scope

1. This Directive shall apply to undertakings established in a Member State which, in the framework of the transnational provision of services, post workers, in accordance with paragraph 3, to the territory of a Member State.

2. This Directive shall not apply to merchant navy undertakings as regards seagoing personnel.

3. This Directive shall apply to the extent that the undertakings referred to in paragraph 1 take one of the following transnational measures:

---

[5] OJ No L 149, 5.7.1971, p. 2; Special Edition 1971 (II), p. 416. Regulation as last amended by Regulation (EC) No 3096/95 (OJ No L 335, 30.12.1995, p. 10).

(a) post workers to the territory of a Member State on their account and under their direction, under a contract concluded between the undertaking making the posting and the party for whom the services are intended, operating in that Member State, provided there is an employment relationship between the undertaking making the posting and the worker during the period of posting; or

(b) post workers to an establishment or to an undertaking owned by the group in the territory of a Member State, provided there is an employment relationship between the undertaking making the posting and the worker during the period of posting; or

(c) being a temporary employment undertaking or placement agency, hire out a worker to a user undertaking established or operating in the territory of a Member State, provided there is an employment relationship between the temporary employment undertaking or placement agency and the worker during the period of posting.

4. Undertakings established in a non-member State must not be given more favourable treatment than undertakings established in a Member State.

Article 2   Definition

1. For the purposes of this Directive, 'posted worker' means a worker who, for a limited period, carries out his work in the territory of a Member State other than the State in which he normally works.

2. For the purposes of this Directive, the definition of a worker is that which applies in the law of the Member State to whose territory the worker is posted.

Article 3   Terms and conditions of employment

1. Member States shall ensure that, whatever the law applicable to the employment relationship, the undertakings referred to in Article 1(1) guarantee workers posted to their territory the terms and conditions of employment covering the following matters which, in the Member State where the work is carried out, are laid down:

– by law, regulation or administrative provision, and/or

– by collective agreements or arbitration awards which have been declared universally applicable within the meaning of paragraph 8, insofar as they concern the activities referred to in the Annex:

(a)   maximum work periods and minimum rest periods;

(b)   minimum paid annual holidays;

(c)   the minimum rates of pay, including overtime rates; this point does not apply to supplementary occupational retirement pension schemes;

(d)   the conditions of hiring-out of workers, in particular the supply of workers by temporary employment undertakings;

(e)   health, safety and hygiene at work;

(f)   protective measures with regard to the terms and conditions of employment of pregnant women or women who have recently given birth, of children and of young people;

(g)   equality of treatment between men and women and other provisions on non-discrimination.

For the purposes of this Directive, the concept of minimum rates of pay referred to in paragraph 1(c) is defined by the national law and/or practice of the Member State to whose territory the worker is posted.

2. In the case of initial assembly and/or first installation of goods where this is an integral part of a contract for the supply of goods and necessary for taking the goods supplied into use and carried out by the skilled and/or specialist workers of the supplying undertaking, the first subparagraph of paragraph 1(b) and (c) shall not apply, if the period of posting does not exceed eight days.

This provision shall not apply to activities in the field of building work listed in the Annex.

3. Member States may, after consulting employers and labour, in accordance with the traditions and practices of each Member State, decide not to apply the first subparagraph of paragraph 1(c) in the cases referred to in Article 1(3)(a) and (b) when the length of the posting does not exceed one month.

4. Member States may, in accordance with national laws and/or practices, provide that exemptions may be made from the first subparagraph of paragraph 1(c) in the cases referred to in Article 1(3)(a) and (b) and from a decision by a Member State within the meaning of paragraph 3 of this Article, by means of collective agreements within the meaning of paragraph 8 of this Article, concerning one or more sectors of activity, where the length of the posting does not exceed one month.

5. Member States may provide for exemptions to be granted from the first subparagraph of paragraph 1(b) and (c) in the cases referred to in Article 1(3)(a) and (b) on the grounds that the amount of work to be done is not significant.

Member States availing themselves of the option referred to in the first subparagraph shall lay down the criteria which the work to be performed must meet in order to be considered as 'non-significant'.

6. The length of the posting shall be calculated on the basis of a reference period of one year from the beginning of the posting.

For the purpose of such calculations, account shall be taken of any previous periods for which the post has been filled by a posted worker.

7. Paragraphs 1 to 6 shall not prevent application of terms and conditions of employment which are more favourable to workers.

Allowances specific to the posting shall be considered to be part of the minimum wage, unless they are paid in reimbursement of expenditure actually incurred on account of the posting, such as expenditure on travel, board and lodging.

8. 'Collective agreements or arbitration awards which have been declared universally applicable' means collective agreements or arbitration awards which must be observed by all undertakings in the geographical area and in the profession or industry concerned.

In the absence of a system for declaring collective agreements or arbitration awards to be of universal application within the meaning of the first subparagraph, Member States may, if they so decide, base themselves on:

- collective agreements or arbitration awards which are generally applicable to all similar undertakings in the geographical area and in the profession or industry concerned, and/ or
- collective agreements which have been concluded by the most representative employers and labour organizations at national level and which are applied throughout national territory,

provided that their application to the undertakings referred to in Article 1(1) ensures equality of treatment on matters listed in the first subparagraph of paragraph 1 of this Article between those undertakings and the other undertakings referred to in this subparagraph which are in a similar position.

Equality of treatment, within the meaning of this Article, shall be deemed to exist where national undertakings in a similar position:

- are subject, in the place in question or in the sector concerned, to the same obligations as posting undertakings as regards the matters listed in the first subparagraph of paragraph 1, and
- are required to fulfil such obligations with the same effects.

9. Member States may provide that the undertakings referred to in Article 1(1) must guarantee workers referred to in Article 1(3)(c) the terms and conditions which apply to temporary workers in the Member State where the work is carried out.

10. This Directive shall not preclude the application by Member States, in compliance with the Treaty, to national undertakings and to the undertakings of other States, on a basis of equality of treatment, of:

- terms and conditions of employment on matters other than those referred to in the first subparagraph of paragraph 1 in the case of public policy provisions,
- terms and conditions of employment laid down in the collective agreements or arbitration awards within the meaning of paragraph 8 and concerning activities other than those referred to in the Annex.

Article 4   Cooperation on information

1. For the purposes of implementing this Directive, Member States shall, in accordance with national legislation and/or practice, designate one or more liaison offices or one or more competent national bodies.

2. Member States shall make provision for cooperation between the public authorities which, in accordance with national legislation, are responsible for monitoring the terms and conditions of employment referred to in Article 3. Such cooperation shall in particular consist in replying to reasoned requests from those authorities for information on the transnational hiring-out of workers, including manifest abuses or possible cases of unlawful transnational activities. The Commission and the public authorities referred to in the first subparagraph shall cooperate closely in order to examine any difficulties which might arise in the application of Article 3(10).

Mutual administrative assistance shall be provided free of charge.

3. Each Member State shall take the appropriate measures to make the information on the terms and conditions of employment referred to in Article 3 generally available.

4. Each Member State shall notify the other Member States and the Commission of the liaison offices and/or competent bodies referred to in paragraph 1.

Article 5   Measures

Member States shall take appropriate measures in the event of failure to comply with this Directive.

They shall in particular ensure that adequate procedures are available to workers and/or their representatives for the enforcement of obligations under this Directive.

Article 6   Jurisdiction

In order to enforce the right to the terms and conditions of employment guaranteed in Article 3, judicial proceedings may be instituted in the Member State in whose territory the worker is or was posted, without prejudice, where applicable, to the right, under existing international conventions on jurisdiction, to institute proceedings in another State.

Article 7   Implementation

Member States shall adopt the laws, regulations and administrative provisions necessary to comply with this Directive by 16 December 1999 at the latest. They shall forthwith inform the Commission thereof.

When Member States adopt these provisions, they shall contain a reference to this Directive or shall be accompanied by such reference on the occasion of their official publication. The methods of making such reference shall be laid down by Member States.

Article 8   Commission review

By 16 December 2001 at the latest, the Commission shall review the operation of this Directive with a view to proposing the necessary amendments to the Council where appropriate.

Article 9

This Directive is addressed to the Member States.

Done at Brussels, 16 December 1996.

ANNEX

The activities mentioned in Article 3 (1), second indent, include all building work relating to the construction, repair, upkeep, alteration or demolition of buildings, and in particular the following work:
1. excavation
2. earthmoving

3. actual building work
4. assembly and dismantling of prefabricated elements
5. fitting out or installation
6. alterations
7. renovation
8. repairs
9. dismantling
10. demolition
11. maintenance
12. upkeep, painting and cleaning work
13. improvements.

Directive 98/5/EC of the European Parliament and of the Council of 16 February 1998 to facilitate practice of the profession of lawyer on a permanent basis in a Member State other than that in which the qualification was obtained*

[OJ 1998 L77/36]

THE EUROPEAN PARLIAMENT AND THE COUNCIL OF THE EUROPEAN UNION,

Having regard to the Treaty establishing the European Community, and in particular Article 49, Article 57(1) and the first and third sentences of Article 57(2) thereof,

Having regard to the proposal from the Commission,[1]

Having regard to the Opinion of the Economic and Social Committee,[2]

Acting in accordance with the procedure laid down in Article 189b of the Treaty,[3]

(1) Whereas, pursuant to Article 7a of the Treaty, the internal market is to comprise an area without internal frontiers; whereas, pursuant to Article 3(c) of the Treaty, the abolition, as between Member States, of obstacles to freedom of movement for persons and services constitutes one of the objectives of the Community; whereas, for nationals of the Member States, this means among other things the possibility of practising a profession, whether in a self-employed or a salaried capacity, in a Member State other than that in which they obtained their professional qualifications;

(2) Whereas, pursuant to Council Directive 89/48/EEC of 21 December 1988 on a general system for the recognition of higher-education diplomas awarded on completion of professional education and training of at least three years' duration,[4] a lawyer who is fully qualified in one Member State may already ask to have his diploma recognised with a view to establishing himself in another Member State in order to practise the profession of lawyer there under the professional title used in that State; whereas the objective of Directive 89/48/EEC is to ensure that a lawyer is integrated into the profession in the host Member State, and the Directive seeks neither to modify the rules regulating the profession in that State nor to remove such a lawyer from the ambit of those rules;

(3) Whereas while some lawyers may become quickly integrated into the profession in the host Member State, *inter alia* by passing an aptitude test as provided for in Directive 89/48/EEC, other

---

* **Editor's Note:** As amended up to and including Directive 2013/25 OJ 2013 L158/368.

[1] OJ No C128, 24.5.1995, p. 6 and OJ No C355, 25.11.1996, p. 19.

[2] OJ No C256, 2.10.1995, p. 14.

[3] Opinion of the European Parliament of 19 June 1996 (OJ No C198, 8.7.1996, p. 85), Council Common Position of 24 July 1997 (OJ No C297, 29.9.1997, p. 6), Decision of the European Parliament of 19 November 1997 (Council Decision of 15 December 1997).

[4] OJ No L19, 24.1.1989, p. 16.

fully qualified lawyers should be able to achieve such integration after a certain period of professional practice in the host Member State under their home-country professional titles or else continue to practise under their home-country professional titles;

(4) Whereas at the end of that period the lawyer should be able to integrate into the profession in the host Member States after verification that he possesses professional experience in that Member State;

(5) Whereas action along these lines is justified at Community level not only because, compared with the general system for the recognition of diplomas, it provides lawyers with an easier means whereby they can integrate into the profession in a host Member State, but also because, by enabling lawyers to practise under their home-country professional titles on a permanent basis in a host Member State, it meets the needs of consumers of legal services who, owing to the increasing trade flows resulting, in particular, from the internal market, seek advice when carrying out cross-border transactions in which international law, Community law and domestic laws often overlap;

(6) Whereas action is also justified at Community level because only a few Member States already permit in their territory the pursuit of activities of lawyers, otherwise than by way of provision of services, by lawyers from other Member States practising under their home-country professional titles; whereas, however, in the Member States where this possibility exists, the practical details concerning, for example, the area of activity and the obligation to register with the competent authorities differ considerably; whereas such a diversity of situations leads to inequalities and distortions in competition between lawyers from the Member States and constitutes an obstacle to freedom of movement; whereas only a directive laying down the conditions governing practice of the profession, otherwise than by way of provision of services, by lawyers practising under their home-country professional titles is capable of resolving these difficulties and of affording the same opportunities to lawyers and consumers of legal services in all Member States;

(7) Whereas, in keeping with its objective, this Directive does not lay down any rules concerning purely domestic situations, and where it does affect national rules regulating the legal profession it does so no more than is necessary to achieve its purpose effectively; whereas it is without prejudice in particular to national legislation governing access to and practice of the profession of lawyer under the professional title used in the host Member States;

(8) Whereas lawyers covered by the Directive should be required to register with the competent authority in the host Member State in order that that authority may ensure that they comply with the rules of professional conduct in force in that state; whereas the effect of such registration as regards the jurisdictions in which, and the levels and types of court before which lawyers may practise is determined by the law applicable to lawyers in the host Member States;

(9) Whereas lawyers who are not integrated into the profession in the host Member State should practise in that State under their home-country professional titles so as to ensure that consumers are properly informed and to distinguish between such lawyers and lawyers from the host Member State practising under the professional title used there;

(10) Whereas lawyers covered by this Directive should be permitted to give legal advice in particular on the law of their home Member States, on Community law, on international law and on the law of the host Member State; whereas this is already allowed as regards the provision of services under Council Directive 77/249/EEC of 22 March 1977 to facilitate the effective exercise by lawyers of freedom to provide services;[5] whereas, however, provision should be made, as in Directive 77/249/EEC, for the option of excluding from the activities

---

[5] OJ No L78, 26.3.1977, p. 17. Directive as last amended by the 1994 Act of Accession.

of lawyers practising under their home-country professional titles in the United Kingdom and Ireland the preparation of certain formal documents in the conveyancing and probate spheres; whereas this Directive in no way affects the provisions under which, in every Member State, certain activities are reserved for professions other than the legal profession; whereas the provision in Directive 77/249/EEC concerning the possibility of the host Member State to require a lawyer practising under his home-country professional title to work in conjunction with a local lawyer when representing or defending a client in legal proceedings should also be incorporated in this Directive; whereas the requirement must be interpreted in the light of the case law of the Court of Justice of the European Communities, in particular its judgment of 25 February 1988 in Case 427/85, Commission v. Germany;[6]

(11) Whereas to ensure the smooth operation of the justice system Member States should be allowed, by means of specific rules, to reserve access to their highest courts to specialist lawyers, without hindering the integration of Member States' lawyers fulfilling the necessary requirements;

(12) Whereas a lawyer registered under his home-country professional title in the host Member State must remain registered with the competent authority in his home Member State if he is to retain his status of lawyer and be covered by this Directive; whereas for that reason close collaboration between the competent authorities is indispensable, in particular in connection with any disciplinary proceedings;

(13) Whereas lawyers covered by this Directive, whether salaried or self-employed in their home Member States, may practise as salaried lawyers in the host Member State, where that Member State offers that possibility to its own lawyers;

(14) Whereas the purpose pursued by this Directive in enabling lawyers to practise in another Member State under their home-country professional titles is also to make it easier for them to obtain the professional title of that host Member State; whereas under Articles 48 and 52 of the Treaty as interpreted by the Court of Justice the host Member State must take into consideration any professional experience gained in its territory; whereas after effectively and regularly pursuing in the host Member State an activity in the law of that State including Community law for a period of three years, a lawyer may reasonably be assumed to have gained the aptitude necessary to become fully integrated into the legal profession there; whereas at the end of that period the lawyer who can, subject to verification, furnish evidence of his professional competence in the host Member State should be able to obtain the professional title of that Member State; whereas if the period of effective and regular professional activity of at least three years includes a shorter period of practice in the law of the host Member State, the authority shall also take into consideration any other knowledge of that State's law, which it may verify during an interview; whereas if evidence of fulfilment of these conditions is not provided, the decision taken by the competent authority of the host State not to grant the State's professional title under the facilitation arrangements linked to those conditions must be substantiated and subject to appeal under national law;

(15) Whereas, for economic and professional reasons, the growing tendency for lawyers in the Community to practise jointly, including in the form of associations, has become a reality; whereas the fact that lawyers belong to a grouping in their home Member State should not be used as a pretext to prevent or deter them from establishing themselves in the host Member States; whereas Member States should be allowed, however, to take appropriate measures with the legitimate aim of safeguarding the profession's independence; whereas certain guarantees should be provided in those Member States which permit joint practice,

HAVE ADOPTED THIS DIRECTIVE:

---

[6] [1988] ECR 1123.

Article 1 Object, scope and definitions

1. The purpose of this Directive is to facilitate practice of the profession of lawyer on a permanent basis in a self-employed or salaried capacity in a Member State other than that in which the professional qualification was obtained.

2. For the purposes of this Directive:

(a) 'lawyer' means any person who is a national of a Member State and who is authorised to pursue his professional activities under one of the following professional titles:

Belgium:	Avocat/Advocaat
Bulgaria:	АДВОКАТ
Czech Republic:	Advokát
Denmark:	Advokat
Germany:	Rechtsanwalt
Estonia:	Vandeadvokaat
Greece:	Dikigoros
France:	Avocat
Croatia:	Odvjetnik/Odvjetnica
Ireland:	Barrister Solicitor
Italy:	Avvocato
Cyprus:	Δικηγόρος
Latvia:	Zvērinats/Advokaāts
Lithuania:	Advokatas
Luxembourg:	Avocat-avoué
Hungary:	Ügyvéd
Malta:	Avukat/Prokuratur Legali
Netherlands:	Advocaat
Austria:	Rechtsanwalt
Poland:	Adwokat/Radca prawny
Portugal:	Advogado
Romania:	Avocat
Slovenia:	Odvetnik/Odvetnica
Slovakia:	Advokát/Komerčný právnik
Finland:	Asianajaja—Advokat
Spain:	Abogado
Sweden:	Advokat
United Kingdom:	Advocate
	Barrister
	Solicitor.

(b) 'home Member State' means the Member State in which a lawyer acquired the right to use one of the professional titles referred to in (a) before practising the profession of lawyer in another Member State;

(c) 'host Member State' means the Member State in which a lawyer practises pursuant to this Directive;

(d) 'home-country professional title' means the professional title used in the Member State in which a lawyer acquired the right to use that title before practising the profession of lawyer in the host Member State;

(e) 'grouping' means any entity, with or without legal personality, formed under the law of a Member State, within which lawyers pursue their professional activities jointly under a joint name;

(f) 'relevant professional title' or 'relevant profession' means the professional title or profession governed by the competent authority with whom a lawyer has registered under
Article 3, and 'competent authority' means that authority.

3. This Directive shall apply both to lawyers practising in a self-employed capacity and to lawyers practising in a salarial capacity in the home Member State and, subject to Article 8, in the host
Member State.

4. Practice of the profession of lawyer within the meaning of this Directive shall not include the
provision of services, which is covered by Directive 77/249/EEC.

Article 2   Right to practise under the home-country professional title

Any lawyer shall be entitled to pursue on a permanent basis, in any other Member State under his
home-country professional title, the activities specified in Article 5.

Integration into the profession of lawyer in the host Member State shall be subject to Article 10.

Article 3   Registration with the competent authority

1. A lawyer who wishes to practise in a Member State other than that in which he obtained his
professional qualification shall register with the competent authority in that State.

2. The competent authority in the host Member State shall register the lawyer upon presentation of a certificate attesting to his registration with the competent authority in the home Member
State. It may require that, when presented by the competent authority of the home Member State,
the certificate be not more than three months old. It shall inform the competent authority in the
home Member State of the registration.

3. For the purpose of applying paragraph 1:
   - in the United Kingdom and Ireland, lawyers practising under a professional title other
     than those used in the United Kingdom or Ireland shall register either with the authority
     responsible for the profession of barrister or advocate or with the authority responsible for
     the profession of solicitor,
   - in the United Kingdom, the authority responsible for a barrister from Ireland shall be that
     responsible for the profession of barrister or advocate, and the authority responsible for a
     solicitor from Ireland shall be that responsible for the profession of solicitor,
   - in Ireland, the authority responsible for a barrister or an advocate from the United Kingdom
     shall be that responsible for the profession of barrister, and the authority responsible for a
     solicitor from the United Kingdom shall be that responsible for the profession of solicitor.

4. Where the relevant competent authority in a host Member State publishes the names
of lawyers registered with it, it shall also publish the names of lawyers registered pursuant to
this Directive.

Article 4   Practice under the home-country professional title

1. A lawyer practising in a host Member State under his home-country professional title shall
do so under that title, which must be expressed in the official language or one of the official languages of his home Member State, in an intelligible manner and in such a way as to avoid confusion
with the professional title of the host Member State.

2. For the purpose of applying paragraph 1, a host Member State may require a lawyer practising under his home-country professional title to indicate the professional body of which he is a
member in his home Member State or the judicial authority before which he is entitled to practise
pursuant to the laws of his home Member State. A host Member State may also require a lawyer
practising under his home-country professional title to include a reference to his registration with
the competent authority in that State.

Article 5   Area of activity

1. Subject to paragraphs 2 and 3, a lawyer practising under his home-country professional title
carries on the same professional activities as a lawyer practising under the relevant processional
title used in the host Member State and may, *inter alia*, give advice on the law of his home Member
State, on Community law, on international law and on the law of the host Member State. He shall in
any event comply with the rules of procedure applicable in the national courts.

2. Member States which authorise in their territory a prescribed category of lawyers to prepare deeds for obtaining title to administer estates of deceased persons and for creating or transferring interests in land which, in other Member States, are reserved for professions other than that of lawyer may exclude from such activities lawyers practising under a home-country professional title conferred in one of the latter Member States.

3. For the pursuit of activities relating to the representation or defence of a client in legal proceedings and insofar as the law of the host Member State reserves such activities to lawyers practising under the professional title of that State, the latter may require lawyers practising under their home-country professional titles to work in conjunction with a lawyer who practises before the judicial authority in question and who would, where necessary, be answerable to that authority or with an 'avoué' practising before it.

Nevertheless, in order to ensure the smooth operation of the justice system, Member States may lay down specific rules for access to supreme courts, such as the use of specialist lawyers.

Article 6   Rules of professional conduct applicable

1. Irrespective of the rules of professional conduct to which he is subject in his home Member State, a lawyer practising under his home-country professional title shall be subject to the same rules of professional conduct as lawyers practising under the relevant professional title of the host Member State in respect of all the activities he pursues in its territory.

2. Lawyers practising under their home-country professional titles shall be granted appropriate representation in the professional associations of the host Member State. Such representation shall involve at least the right to vote in elections to those associations' governing bodies.

3. The host Member State may require a lawyer practising under his home country professional title either to take out professional indemnity insurance or to become a member of a professional guarantee fund in accordance with the rules which that State lays down for professional activities pursued in its territory. Nevertheless, a lawyer practising under his home-country professional title shall be exempted from that requirement if he can prove that he is covered by insurance taken out or a guarantee provided in accordance with the rules of his home Member State, insofar as such insurance or guarantee is equivalent in terms of the conditions and extent of cover. Where the equivalence is only partial, the competent authority in the host Member State may require that additional insurance or an additional guarantee be contacted to cover the elements which are not already covered by the insurance or guarantee contracted in accordance with the rules of the home Member States.

Article 7   Disciplinary proceedings

1. In the event of failure by a lawyer practising under his home-country professional title to fulfil the obligations in force in the host Member State, the rules of procedure, penalties and remedies provided for in the host Member State shall apply.

2. Before initiating disciplinary proceedings against a lawyer practising under his home-country professional title, the competent authority in the host Member State shall inform the competent authority in the home Member State as soon as possible, furnishing it with all the relevant details.

The first subparagraph shall apply *mutatis mutandis* where disciplinary proceedings are initiated by the competent authority of the home Member State, which shall inform the competent authority of the host Member State(s) accordingly.

3. Without prejudice to the decision-making power of the competent authority in the host Member State, that authority shall cooperate throughout the disciplinary proceedings with the competent authority in the home Member State. In particular, the host Member State shall take the measures necessary to ensure that the competent authority in the home Member State can make submissions to the bodies responsible for hearing any appeal.

4. The competent authority in the home Member State shall decide what action to take, under its own procedural and substantive rules, in the light of a decision of the competent authority in the host Member State concerning a lawyer practising under his home-country professional title.

5. Although it is not a prerequisite for the decision of the competent authority in the host Member State, the temporary or permanent withdrawal by the competent authority in the home

Member State of the authorisation to practise the profession shall automatically lead to the lawyer concerned being temporarily or permanently prohibited from practising under his home-country professional title in the host Member State.

Article 8   Salaried practice

A lawyer registered in a host Member State under his home-country professional title may practise as a salaried lawyer in the employ of another lawyer, an association or firm of lawyers, or a public or private enterprise to the extent that the host Member State so permits for lawyers registered under the professional title used in that State.

Article 9   Statement of reasons and remedies

Decisions not to effect the registration referred to in Article 3 or to cancel such registration and decisions imposing disciplinary measures shall state the reasons on which they are based.

A remedy shall be available against such decisions before a court or tribunal in accordance with the provisions of domestic law.

Article 10   Like treatment as a lawyer of the host Member State

1. A lawyer practising under his home-country professional title who has effectively and regularly pursued for a period of at least three years an activity in the host Member State in the law of that State including Community law shall, with a view to gaining admission to the profession of lawyer in the host Member State, be exempted from the conditions set out in Article 4(1)(b) of Directive 89/48/EEC, 'Effective and regular pursuit' means actual exercise of the activity without any interruption other than that resulting from the events of everyday life.

It shall be for the lawyer concerned to furnish the competent authority in the host Member State with proof of such effective regular pursuit for a period of at least three years of an activity in the law of the host Member State. To that end:

   (a) the lawyer shall provide the competent authority in the host Member State with any relevant information and documentation, notably on the number of matters he has dealt with and their nature;

   (b) the competent authority of the host Member State may verify the effective and regular nature of the activity pursued and may, if need be, request the lawyer to provide, orally or in writing, clarification of or further details on the information and documentation mentioned in point (a).

Reasons shall be given for a decision by the competent authority in the host Member State not to grant an exemption where proof is not provided that the requirements laid down in the first subparagraph have been fulfilled, and the decision shall be subject to appeal under domestic law.

2. A lawyer practising under his home-country professional title in a host Member State may, at any time, apply to have his diploma recognised in accordance with Directive 89/48/ EEC with a view to gaining admission to the profession of lawyer in the host Member State and practising it under the professional title corresponding to the profession in that Member State.

3. A lawyer practising under his home-country professional title who has effectively and regularly pursued a professional activity in the host Member State for a period of at least three years but for a lesser period in the law of that Member State may obtain from the competent authority of that State admission to the profession of lawyer in the host Member State and the right to practise it under the professional title corresponding to the profession in that Member State, without having to meet the conditions referred to in Article 4(1)(b) of Directive 89/48/ EEC, under the conditions and in accordance with the procedures set out below:

   (a) The competent authority of the host Member State shall take into account the effective and regular professional activity pursued during the abovementioned period and any knowledge and professional experience of the law of the host Member State, and any attendance at lectures or seminars on the law of the host Member State, including the rules regulating professional practice and conduct.

   (b) The lawyer shall provide the competent authority of the host Member State with any relevant information and documentation, in particular on the matters he has dealt with.

Assessment of the lawyer's effective and regular activity in the host Member State and assessment of his capacity to continue the activity he has pursued there shall be carried out by means of an interview with the competent authority of the host Member State in order to verify the regular and effective nature of the activity pursued.

Reasons shall be given for a decision by the competent authority in the host Member State not to grant authorisation where proof is not provided that the requirements laid down in the first subparagraph have been fulfilled, and the decision shall be subject to appeal under domestic law.

4. The competent authority of the host Member State may, by reasoned decision subject to appeal under domestic law, refuse to allow the lawyer the benefit of the provisions of this Article if it considers that this would be against public policy, in particular because of disciplinary proceedings, complaints or incidents of any kind.

5. The representatives of the competent authority entrusted with consideration of the application shall preserve the confidentiality of any information received.

6. A lawyer who gains admission to the profession of lawyer in the host Member State in accordance with paragraphs 1, 2 and 3 shall be entitled to use his home-country professional title, expressed in the official language or one of the official languages of his home Member State, alongside the professional title corresponding to the profession of lawyer in the host Member State.

Article 11   Joint practice

Where joint practice is authorised in respect of lawyers carrying on their activities under the relevant professional title in the host Member State, the following provisions shall apply in respect of lawyers wishing to carry on activities under that title or registering with the competent authority:

(1) One or more lawyers who belong to the same grouping in their home Member State and who practise under their home-country professional title in a host Member State may pursue their professional activities in a branch or agency of their grouping in the host Member State. However, where the fundamental rules governing that grouping in the home Member State are incompatible with the fundamental rules laid down by law, regulation or administrative action in the host Member State, the latter rules shall prevail insofar as compliance therewith is justified by the public interest in protecting clients and third parties.

(2) Each Member State shall afford two or more lawyers from the same grouping or the same home Member State who practise in its territory under their home-country professional titles access to a form of joint practice. If the host Member State gives its lawyers a choice between several forms of joint practice, those same forms shall also be made available to the aforementioned lawyers. The manner in which such lawyers practise jointly in the host Member State shall be governed by the laws, regulations and administrative provisions of that State.

(3) The host Member State shall take the measures necessary to permit joint practice also between:

(a) several lawyers from different Member States practising under their home-country professional titles;

(b) one or more lawyers covered by point (a) and one or more lawyers from the host Member State.

The manner in which such lawyers practise jointly in the host Member State shall be governed by the laws, regulations and administrative provisions of that State.

(4) A lawyer who wishes to practise under his home-country professional title shall inform the competent authority in the host Member State of the fact that he is a member of a grouping in his home Member State and furnish any relevant information on that grouping.

(5) Notwithstanding points 1 to 4, a host Member State, insofar as it prohibits lawyers practising under its own relevant professional title from practising the profession of lawyer within a grouping in which some persons are not members of the profession, may refuse to allow a lawyer registered under his home-country professional title to practise in its territory in his capacity as a member of his grouping. The grouping is deemed to include persons who are not members of the profession if

- the capital of the grouping is held entirely or partly, or
- the name under which it practises is used, or
- the decision-making power in that grouping is exercised, *de facto* or *de jure*,

by persons who do not have the status of lawyer within the meaning of Article 1(2).

Where the fundamental rules governing a grouping of lawyers in the home Member State are incompatible with the rules in force in the host Member State or with the provisions of the first sub-paragraph, the host Member State may oppose the opening of a branch or agency within its territory without the restrictions laid down in point (1).

Article 12   Name of the grouping

Whatever the manner in which lawyers practise under their home-country professional titles in the host Member State, they may employ the name of any grouping to which they belong in their home Member State.

The host Member State may require that, in addition to the name referred to in the first sub-paragraph, mention be made of the legal form of the grouping in the home Member State and/or of the names of any members of the grouping practising in the host Member State.

Article 13   Cooperation between the competent authorities in the home and host Member States and confidentiality

In order to facilitate the application of this Directive and to prevent its provisions from being misapplied for the sole purpose of circumventing the rules applicable in the host Member State, the competent authority in the host Member State and the competent authority in the home Member State shall collaborate closely and afford each other mutual assistance.

They shall preserve the confidentiality of the information they exchange.

Article 14   Designation of the competent authorities

Member States shall designate the competent authorities empowered to receive the applications and to take the decisions referred to in this Directive by 14 March 2000. They shall communicate this information to the other Member States and to the Commission.

Article 15   Report by the Commission

Ten years at the latest from the entry into force of this Directive, the Commission shall report to the European Parliament and to the Council on progress in the implementation of the Directive.

After having held all the necessary consultations, it shall on that occasion present its conclusions and any amendments which could be made to the existing system.

Article 16   Implementation

1. Member States shall bring into force the laws, regulations and administrative provisions necessary to comply with this Directive by 14 March 2000. They shall forthwith inform the Commission thereof.

When Member States adopt these measures, they shall contain a reference to this Directive or shall be accompanied by such reference on the occasion of their official publication. The methods of making such reference shall be adopted by Member States.

2. Member States shall communicate to the Commission the texts of the main provisions of domestic law which they adopt in the field covered by this Directive.

Article 17

This Directive shall enter into force on the date of its publication in the *Official Journal of the European Communities*.

Article 18   Addressees

This Directive is addressed to the Member States.

Done at Brussels, 16 February 1998.

Council Directive 2003/86/EC of 22 September 2003 on the right to family reunification

[OJ 2003 L251/12]

THE COUNCIL OF THE EUROPEAN UNION,

Having regard to the Treaty establishing the European Community, and in particular Article 63(3)(a) thereof,

Having regard to the proposal from the Commission,[1]

Having regard to the opinion of the European Parliament,[2]

Having regard to the opinion of the European Economic and Social Committee,[3]

Having regard to the opinion of the Committee of the Regions,[4]

Whereas:

(1) With a view to the progressive establishment of an area of freedom, security and justice, the Treaty establishing the European Community provides both for the adoption of measures aimed at ensuring the free movement of persons, in conjunction with flanking measures relating to external border controls, asylum and immigration, and for the adoption of measures relating to asylum, immigration and safeguarding the rights of third country nationals.

(2) Measures concerning family reunification should be adopted in conformity with the obligation to protect the family and respect family life enshrined in many instruments of international law. This Directive respects the fundamental rights and observes the principles recognised in particular in Article 8 of the European Convention for the Protection of Human Rights and Fundamental Freedoms and in the Charter of Fundamental Rights of the European Union.

(3) The European Council, at its special meeting in Tampere on 15 and 16 October 1999, acknowledged the need for harmonisation of national legislation on the conditions for admission and residence of third country nationals. In this context, it has in particular stated that the European Union should ensure fair treatment of third country nationals residing lawfully on the territory of the Member States and that a more vigorous integration policy should aim at granting them rights and obligations comparable to those of citizens of the European Union. The European Council accordingly asked the Council rapidly to adopt the legal instruments on the basis of Commission proposals. The need for achieving the objectives defined at Tampere have been reaffirmed by the Laeken European Council on 14 and 15 December 2001.

(4) Family reunification is a necessary way of making family life possible. It helps to create sociocultural stability facilitating the integration of third country nationals in the Member State, which also serves to promote economic and social cohesion, a fundamental Community objective stated in the Treaty.

(5) Member States should give effect to the provisions of this Directive without discrimination on the basis of sex, race, colour, ethnic or social origin, genetic characteristics, language, religion or beliefs, political or other opinions, membership of a national minority, fortune, birth, disabilities, age or sexual orientation.

(6) To protect the family and establish or preserve family life, the material conditions for exercising the right to family reunification should be determined on the basis of common criteria.

(7) Member States should be able to apply this Directive also when the family enters together.

(8) Special attention should be paid to the situation of refugees on account of the reasons which obliged them to flee their country and prevent them from leading a normal family life there.

---

[1] OJ C 116 E, 26.4.2000, p. 66, and OJ C 62 E, 27.2.2001, p. 99.
[2] OJ C 135, 7.5.2001, p. 174.
[3] OJ C 204, 18.7.2000, p. 40.
[4] OJ C 73, 26.3.2003, p. 16.

More favourable conditions should therefore be laid down for the exercise of their right to family reunification.

(9) Family reunification should apply in any case to members of the nuclear family, that is to say the spouse and the minor children.

(10) It is for the Member States to decide whether they wish to authorise family reunification for relatives in the direct ascending line, adult unmarried children, unmarried or registered partners as well as, in the event of a polygamous marriage, minor children of a further spouse and the sponsor. Where a Member State authorises family reunification of these persons, this is without prejudice of the possibility, for Member States which do not recognise the existence of family ties in the cases covered by this provision, of not granting to the said persons the treatment of family members with regard to the right to reside in another Member State, as defined by the relevant EC legislation.

(11) The right to family reunification should be exercised in proper compliance with the values and principles recognised by the Member States, in particular with respect to the rights of women and of children; such compliance justifies the possible taking of restrictive measures against applications for family reunification of polygamous households.

(12) The possibility of limiting the right to family reunification of children over the age of 12, whose primary residence is not with the sponsor, is intended to reflect the children's capacity for integration at early ages and shall ensure that they acquire the necessary education and language skills in school.

(13) A set of rules governing the procedure for examination of applications for family reunification and for entry and residence of family members should be laid down. Those procedures should be effective and manageable, taking account of the normal workload of the Member States' administrations, as well as transparent and fair, in order to offer appropriate legal certainty to those concerned.

(14) Family reunification may be refused on duly justified grounds. In particular, the person who wishes to be granted family reunification should not constitute a threat to public policy or public security. The notion of public policy may cover a conviction for committing a serious crime. In this context it has to be noted that the notion of public policy and public security covers also cases in which a third country national belongs to an association which supports terrorism, supports such an association or has extremist aspirations.

(15) The integration of family members should be promoted. For that purpose, they should be granted a status independent of that of the sponsor, in particular in cases of breakup of marriages and partnerships, and access to education, employment and vocational training on the same terms as the person with whom they are reunited, under the relevant conditions.

(16) Since the objectives of the proposed action, namely the establishment of a right to family reunification for third country nationals to be exercised in accordance with common rules, cannot be sufficiently achieved by the Member States and can therefore, by reason of the scale and effects of the action, be better achieved by the Community, the Community may adopt measures, in accordance with the principle of subsidiarity as set out in Article 5 of the Treaty. In accordance with the principle of proportionality as set out in that Article, this Directive does not go beyond what is necessary in order to achieve those objectives.

(17) In accordance with Articles 1 and 2 of the Protocol on the position of the United Kingdom and Ireland, annexed to the Treaty on European Union and to the Treaty establishing the European Community and without prejudice to Article 4 of the said Protocol these Member States are not participating in the adoption of this Directive and are not bound by or subject to its application.

(18) In accordance with Article 1 and 2 of the Protocol on the position of Denmark, annexed to the Treaty on European Union and the Treaty establishing the European Community, Denmark does not take part in the adoption of this Directive, and is not bound by it or subject to its application,

HAS ADOPTED THIS DIRECTIVE:

Chapter I General provisions

Article 1

The purpose of this Directive is to determine the conditions for the exercise of the right to family reunification by third country nationals residing lawfully in the territory of the Member States.

Article 2

For the purposes of this Directive:

(a) 'third country national' means any person who is not a citizen of the Union within the meaning of Article 17(1) of the Treaty;

(b) 'refugee' means any third country national or stateless person enjoying refugee status within the meaning of the Geneva Convention relating to the status of refugees of 28 July 1951, as amended by the Protocol signed in New York on 31 January 1967;

(c) 'sponsor' means a third country national residing lawfully in a Member State and applying or whose family members apply for family reunification to be joined with him/her;

(d) 'family reunification' means the entry into and residence in a Member State by family members of a third country national residing lawfully in that Member State in order to preserve the family unit, whether the family relationship arose before or after the resident's entry;

(e) 'residence permit' means any authorisation issued by the authorities of a Member State allowing a third country national to stay legally in its territory, in accordance with the provisions of Article 1(2)(a) of Council Regulation (EC) No 1030/2002 of 13 June 2002 laying down a uniform format for residence permits for third country nationals;[5]

(f) 'unaccompanied minor' means third country nationals or stateless persons below the age of eighteen, who arrive on the territory of the Member States unaccompanied by an adult responsible by law or custom, and for as long as they are not effectively taken into the care of such a person, or minors who are left unaccompanied after they entered the territory of the Member States.

Article 3

1. This Directive shall apply where the sponsor is holding a residence permit issued by a Member State for a period of validity of one year or more who has reasonable prospects of obtaining the right of permanent residence, if the members of his or her family are third country nationals of whatever status.

2. This Directive shall not apply where the sponsor is:

(a) applying for recognition of refugee status whose application has not yet given rise to a final decision;

(b) authorised to reside in a Member State on the basis of temporary protection or applying for authorisation to reside on that basis and awaiting a decision on his status;

(c) authorised to reside in a Member State on the basis of a subsidiary form of protection in accordance with international obligations, national legislation or the practice of the Member States or applying for authorisation to reside on that basis and awaiting a decision on his status.

3. This Directive shall not apply to members of the family of a Union citizen.

4. This Directive is without prejudice to more favourable provisions of:

(a) bilateral and multilateral agreements between the Community or the Community and its Member States, on the one hand, and third countries, on the other;

(b) the European Social Charter of 18 October 1961, the amended European Social Charter of 3 May 1987 and the European Convention on the legal status of migrant workers of 24 November 1977.

5. This Directive shall not affect the possibility for the Member States to adopt or maintain more favourable provisions.

---

[5] OJ L 157, 15.6.2002, p. 1.

Chapter II Family members

Article 4

1. The Member States shall authorise the entry and residence, pursuant to this Directive and subject to compliance with the conditions laid down in Chapter IV, as well as in Article 16, of the following family members:

(a) the sponsor's spouse;

(b) the minor children of the sponsor and of his/her spouse, including children adopted in accordance with a decision taken by the competent authority in the Member State concerned or a decision which is automatically enforceable due to international obligations of that Member State or must be recognised in accordance with international obligations;

(c) the minor children including adopted children of the sponsor where the sponsor has custody and the children are dependent on him or her. Member States may authorise the reunification of children of whom custody is shared, provided the other party sharing custody has given his or her agreement;

(d) the minor children including adopted children of the spouse where the spouse has custody and the children are dependent on him or her. Member States may authorise the reunification of children of whom custody is shared, provided the other party sharing custody has given his or her agreement.

The minor children referred to in this Article must be below the age of majority set by the law of the Member State concerned and must not be married.

By way of derogation, where a child is aged over 12 years and arrives independently from the rest of his/her family, the Member State may, before authorising entry and residence under this Directive, verify whether he or she meets a condition for integration provided for by its existing legislation on the date of implementation of this Directive.

2. The Member States may, by law or regulation, authorise the entry and residence, pursuant to this Directive and subject to compliance with the conditions laid down in Chapter IV, of the following family members:

(a) first-degree relatives in the direct ascending line of the sponsor or his or her spouse, where they are dependent on them and do not enjoy proper family support in the country of origin;

(b) the adult unmarried children of the sponsor or his or her spouse, where they are objectively unable to provide for their own needs on account of their state of health.

3. The Member States may, by law or regulation, authorise the entry and residence, pursuant to this Directive and subject to compliance with the conditions laid down in Chapter IV, of the unmarried partner, being a third country national, with whom the sponsor is in a duly attested stable long-term relationship, or of a third country national who is bound to the sponsor by a registered partnership in accordance with Article 5(2), and of the unmarried minor children, including adopted children, as well as the adult unmarried children who are objectively unable to provide for their own needs on account of their state of health, of such persons.

Member States may decide that registered partners are to be treated equally as spouses with respect to family reunification.

4. In the event of a polygamous marriage, where the sponsor already has a spouse living with him in the territory of a Member State, the Member State concerned shall not authorise the family reunification of a further spouse.

By way of derogation from paragraph 1(c), Member States may limit the family reunification of minor children of a further spouse and the sponsor.

5. In order to ensure better integration and to prevent forced marriages Member States may require the sponsor and his/her spouse to be of a minimum age, and at maximum 21 years, before the spouse is able to join him/her.

6. By way of derogation, Member States may request that the applications concerning family reunification of minor children have to be submitted before the age of 15, as provided for by its

existing legislation on the date of the implementation of this Directive. If the application is submitted after the age of 15, the Member States which decide to apply this derogation shall authorise the entry and residence of such children on grounds other than family reunification.

Chapter III Submission and examination
of the application

Article 5

1. Member States shall determine whether, in order to exercise the right to family reunification, an application for entry and residence shall be submitted to the competent authorities of the Member State concerned either by the sponsor or by the family member or members.

2. The application shall be accompanied by documentary evidence of the family relationship and of compliance with the conditions laid down in Articles 4 and 6 and, where applicable, Articles 7 and 8, as well as certified copies of family member(s)' travel documents.

If appropriate, in order to obtain evidence that a family relationship exists, Member States may carry out interviews with the sponsor and his/her family members and conduct other investigations that are found to be necessary.

When examining an application concerning the unmarried partner of the sponsor, Member States shall consider, as evidence of the family relationship, factors such as a common child, previous cohabitation, registration of the partnership and any other reliable means of proof.

3. The application shall be submitted and examined when the family members are residing outside the territory of the Member State in which the sponsor resides.

By way of derogation, a Member State may, in appropriate circumstances, accept an application submitted when the family members are already in its territory.

4. The competent authorities of the Member State shall give the person, who has submitted the application, written notification of the decision as soon as possible and in any event no later than nine months from the date on which the application was lodged.

In exceptional circumstances linked to the complexity of the examination of the application, the time limit referred to in the first subparagraph may be extended.

Reasons shall be given for the decision rejecting the application. Any consequences of no decision being taken by the end of the period provided for in the first subparagraph shall be determined by the national legislation of the relevant Member State.

5. When examining an application, the Member States shall have due regard to the best interests of minor children.

Chapter IV Requirements for the exercise of the
right to family reunification

Article 6

1. The Member States may reject an application for entry and residence of family members on grounds of public policy, public security or public health.

2. Member States may withdraw or refuse to renew a family member's residence permit on grounds of public policy or public security or public health.

When taking the relevant decision, the Member State shall consider, besides Article 17, the severity or type of offence against public policy or public security committed by the family member, or the dangers that are emanating from such person.

3. Renewal of the residence permit may not be withheld and removal from the territory may not be ordered by the competent authority of the Member State concerned on the sole ground of illness or disability suffered after the issue of the residence permit.

Article 7

1. When the application for family reunification is submitted, the Member State concerned may require the person who has submitted the application to provide evidence that the sponsor has:

   (a) accommodation regarded as normal for a comparable family in the same region and which meets the general health and safety standards in force in the Member State concerned;

   (b) sickness insurance in respect of all risks normally covered for its own nationals in the Member State concerned for himself/herself and the members of his/her family;

   (c) stable and regular resources which are sufficient to maintain himself/herself and the members of his/her family, without recourse to the social assistance system of the Member State concerned. Member States shall evaluate these resources by reference to their nature and regularity and may take into account the level of minimum national wages and pensions as well as the number of family members.

2. Member States may require third country nationals to comply with integration measures, in accordance with national law.

   With regard to the refugees and/or family members of refugees referred to in Article 12 the integration measures referred to in the first subparagraph may only be applied once the persons concerned have been granted family reunification.

Article 8

Member States may require the sponsor to have stayed lawfully in their territory for a period not exceeding two years, before having his/her family members join him/her.

By way of derogation, where the legislation of a Member State relating to family reunification in force on the date of adoption of this Directive takes into account its reception capacity, the Member State may provide for a waiting period of no more than three years between submission of the application for family reunification and the issue of a residence permit to the family members.

Chapter V Family reunification of refugees

Article 9

1. This Chapter shall apply to family reunification of refugees recognised by the Member States.

2. Member States may confine the application of this Chapter to refugees whose family relationships predate their entry.

3. This Chapter is without prejudice to any rules granting refugee status to family members.

Article 10

1. Article 4 shall apply to the definition of family members except that the third subparagraph of paragraph 1 thereof shall not apply to the children of refugees.

2. The Member States may authorise family reunification of other family members not referred to in Article 4, if they are dependent on the refugee.

3. If the refugee is an unaccompanied minor, the Member States:

   (a) shall authorise the entry and residence for the purposes of family reunification of his/her first-degree relatives in the direct ascending line without applying the conditions laid down in Article 4(2)(a);

   (b) may authorise the entry and residence for the purposes of family reunification of his/her legal guardian or any other member of the family, where the refugee has no relatives in the direct ascending line or such relatives cannot be traced.

Article 11

1. Article 5 shall apply to the submission and examination of the application, subject to paragraph 2 of this Article.

2. Where a refugee cannot provide official documentary evidence of the family relationship, the Member States shall take into account other evidence, to be assessed in accordance with national law, of the existence of such relationship. A decision rejecting an application may not be based solely on the fact that documentary evidence is lacking.

Article 12

1. By way of derogation from Article 7, the Member States shall not require the refugee and/or family member(s) to provide, in respect of applications concerning those family members referred to in Article 4(1), the evidence that the refugee fulfils the requirements set out in Article 7.

Without prejudice to international obligations, where family reunification is possible in a third country with which the sponsor and/or family member has special links, Member States may require provision of the evidence referred to in the first subparagraph.

Member States may require the refugee to meet the conditions referred to in Article 7(1) if the application for family reunification is not submitted within a period of three months after the granting of the refugee status.

2. By way of derogation from Article 8, the Member States shall not require the refugee to have resided in their territory for a certain period of time, before having his/her family members join him/her.

Chapter VI Entry and residence of family members

Article 13

1. As soon as the application for family reunification has been accepted, the Member State concerned shall authorise the entry of the family member or members. In that regard, the Member State concerned shall grant such persons every facility for obtaining the requisite visas.

2. The Member State concerned shall grant the family members a first residence permit of at least one year's duration. This residence permit shall be renewable.

3. The duration of the residence permits granted to the family member(s) shall in principle not go beyond the date of expiry of the residence permit held by the sponsor.

Article 14

1. The sponsor's family members shall be entitled, in the same way as the sponsor, to:
    (a) access to education;
    (b) access to employment and self-employed activity;
    (c) access to vocational guidance, initial and further training and retraining.

2. Member States may decide according to national law the conditions under which family members shall exercise an employed or self-employed activity. These conditions shall set a time limit which shall in no case exceed 12 months, during which Member States may examine the situation of their labour market before authorising family members to exercise an employed or self-employed activity.

3. Member States may restrict access to employment or self-employed activity by first-degree relatives in the direct ascending line or adult unmarried children to whom Article 4(2) applies.

Article 15

1. Not later than after five years of residence, and provided that the family member has not been granted a residence permit for reasons other than family reunification, the spouse or unmarried partner and a child who has reached majority shall be entitled, upon application, if required, to an autonomous residence permit, independent of that of the sponsor.

Member States may limit the granting of the residence permit referred to in the first subparagraph to the spouse or unmarried partner in cases of breakdown of the family relationship.

2. The Member States may issue an autonomous residence permit to adult children and to relatives in the direct ascending line to whom Article 4(2) applies.

3. In the event of widowhood, divorce, separation, or death of first-degree relatives in the direct ascending or descending line, an autonomous residence permit may be issued, upon application, if required, to persons who have entered by virtue of family reunification. Member States shall lay down provisions ensuring the granting of an autonomous residence permit in the event of particularly difficult circumstances.

4. The conditions relating to the granting and duration of the autonomous residence permit are established by national law.

Chapter VII Penalties and redress

Article 16

1. Member States may reject an application for entry and residence for the purpose of family reunification, or, if appropriate, withdraw or refuse to renew a family member's residence permit, in the following circumstances:

(a) where the conditions laid down by this Directive are not or are no longer satisfied. When renewing the residence permit, where the sponsor has not sufficient resources without recourse to the social assistance system of the Member State, as referred to in Article 7(1)(c), the Member State shall take into account the contributions of the family members to the household income;

(b) where the sponsor and his/her family member(s) do not or no longer live in a real marital or family relationship;

(c) where it is found that the sponsor or the unmarried partner is married or is in a stable long-term relationship with another person.

2. Member States may also reject an application for entry and residence for the purpose of family reunification, or withdraw or refuse to renew the family member's residence permits, where it is shown that:

(a) false or misleading information, false or falsified documents were used, fraud was otherwise committed or other unlawful means were used;

(b) the marriage, partnership or adoption was contracted for the sole purpose of enabling the person concerned to enter or reside in a Member State.

When making an assessment with respect to this point, Member States may have regard in particular to the fact that the marriage, partnership or adoption was contracted after the sponsor had been issued his/her residence permit.

3. The Member States may withdraw or refuse to renew the residence permit of a family member where the sponsor's residence comes to an end and the family member does not yet enjoy an autonomous right of residence under Article 15.

4. Member States may conduct specific checks and inspections where there is reason to suspect that there is fraud or a marriage, partnership or adoption of convenience as defined by paragraph 2. Specific checks may also be undertaken on the occasion of the renewal of family members' residence permit.

Article 17

Member States shall take due account of the nature and solidity of the person's family relationships and the duration of his residence in the Member State and of the existence of family, cultural and social ties with his/her country of origin where they reject an application, withdraw or refuse to renew a residence permit or decide to order the removal of the sponsor or members of his family.

Article 18

The Member States shall ensure that the sponsor and/or the members of his/her family have the right to mount a legal challenge where an application for family reunification is rejected or a residence permit is either not renewed or is withdrawn or removal is ordered.

The procedure and the competence according to which the right referred to in the first subparagraph is exercised shall be established by the Member States concerned.

Chapter VIII Final provisions

Article 19

Periodically, and for the first time not later than 3 October 2007, the Commission shall report to the European Parliament and the Council on the application of this Directive in the Member States and shall propose such amendments as may appear necessary. These proposals for amendments shall be made by way of priority in relation to Articles 3, 4, 7, 8 and 13.

Article 20

Member States shall bring into force the laws, regulations and administrative provisions necessary to comply with this Directive by not later than 3 October 2005. They shall forthwith inform the Commission thereof.

When Member States adopt these measures, they shall contain a reference to this Directive or be accompanied by such a reference on the occasion of their official publication. The methods of making such reference shall be laid down by the Member States.

Article 21

This Directive shall enter into force on the day of its publication in the *Official Journal of the European Union*.

Article 22

This Directive is addressed to the Member States in accordance with the Treaty establishing the European Community.

Done at Brussels, 22 September 2003.

Council Directive 2003/109/EC of 25 November 2003 concerning the status of third-country nationals who are long-term residents*

[OJ 2004 L16/44]

THE COUNCIL OF THE EUROPEAN UNION,

Having regard to the Treaty establishing the European Community, and in particular Article 63(3) and (4) thereof,

Having regard to the proposal from the Commission,[1]

Having regard to the opinion of the European Parliament,[2]

Having regard to the opinion of the European Economic and Social Committee,[3]

Having regard to the opinion of the Committee of the Regions,[4]

Whereas:

(1) With a view to the progressive establishment of an area of freedom, security and justice, the Treaty establishing the European Community provides both for the adoption of measures aimed at ensuring the free movement of persons, in conjunction with flanking measures relating to external

---

* **Editor's Note:** As amended up to Directive 2011/51 (OJ 2011 L132/1).
[1] OJ C 240 E, 28.8.2001, p. 79.
[2] OJ C 284 E, 21.11.2002, p. 102.
[3] OJ C 36, 8.2.2002, p. 59.
[4] OJ C 19, 22.1.2002, p. 18.

border controls, asylum and immigration, and for the adoption of measures relating to asylum, immigration and safeguarding the rights of third-country nationals.

(2) The European Council, at its special meeting in Tampere on 15 and 16 October 1999, stated that the legal status of third-country nationals should be approximated to that of Member States' nationals and that a person who has resided legally in a Member State for a period of time to be determined and who holds a long-term residence permit should be granted in that Member State a set of uniform rights which are as near as possible to those enjoyed by citizens of the European Union.

(3) This Directive respects the fundamental rights and observes the principles recognised in particular by the European Convention for the Protection of Human Rights and Fundamental Freedoms and by the Charter of Fundamental Rights of the European Union.

(4) The integration of third-country nationals who are long-term residents in the Member States is a key element in promoting economic and social cohesion, a fundamental objective of the Community stated in the Treaty.

(5) Member States should give effect to the provisions of this Directive without discrimination on the basis of sex, race, colour, ethnic or social origin, genetic characteristics, language, religion or beliefs, political or other opinions, membership of a national minority, fortune, birth, disabilities, age or sexual orientation.

(6) The main criterion for acquiring the status of long-term resident should be the duration of residence in the territory of a Member State. Residence should be both legal and continuous in order to show that the person has put down roots in the country. Provision should be made for a degree of flexibility so that account can be taken of circumstances in which a person might have to leave the territory on a temporary basis.

(7) To acquire long-term resident status, third-country nationals should prove that they have adequate resources and sickness insurance, to avoid becoming a burden for the Member State. Member States, when making an assessment of the possession of stable and regular resources may take into account factors such as contributions to the pension system and fulfilment of tax obligations.

(8) Moreover, third-country nationals who wish to acquire and maintain long-term resident status should not constitute a threat to public policy or public security. The notion of public policy may cover a conviction for committing a serious crime.

(9) Economic considerations should not be a ground for refusing to grant long-term resident status and shall not be considered as interfering with the relevant conditions.

(10) A set of rules governing the procedures for the examination of application for long-term resident status should be laid down. Those procedures should be effective and manageable, taking account of the normal workload of the Member States' administrations, as well as being transparent and fair, in order to offer appropriate legal certainty to those concerned. They should not constitute a means of hindering the exercise of the right of residence.

(11) The acquisition of long-term resident status should be certified by residence permits enabling those concerned to prove their legal status easily and immediately. Such residence permits should also satisfy high-level technical standards, notably as regards protection against falsification and counterfeiting, in order to avoid abuses in the Member State in which the status is acquired and in Member States in which the right of residence is exercised.

(12) In order to constitute a genuine instrument for the integration of long-term residents into society in which they live, long-term residents should enjoy equality of treatment with citizens of the Member State in a wide range of economic and social matters, under the relevant conditions defined by this Directive.

(13) With regard to social assistance, the possibility of limiting the benefits for long-term residents to core benefits is to be understood in the sense that this notion covers at least minimum income support, assistance in case of illness, pregnancy, parental assistance and long-term care. The modalities for granting such benefits should be determined by national law.

(14) The Member States should remain subject to the obligation to afford access for minors to the educational system under conditions similar to those laid down for their nationals.

(15) The notion of study grants in the field of vocational training does not cover measures which are financed under social assistance schemes. Moreover, access to study grants may be dependent on the fact that the person who applies for such grants fulfils on his/her own the conditions for acquiring long-term resident status. As regards the issuing of study grants, Member States may take into account the fact that Union citizens may benefit from this same advantage in the country of origin.

(16) Long-term residents should enjoy reinforced protection against expulsion. This protection is based on the criteria determined by the decisions of the European Court of Human Rights. In order to ensure protection against expulsion Member States should provide for effective legal redress.

(17) Harmonisation of the terms for acquisition of long-term resident status promotes mutual confidence between Member States. Certain Member States issue permits with a permanent or unlimited validity on conditions that are more favourable than those provided for by this Directive. The possibility of applying more favourable national provisions is not excluded by the Treaty. However, for the purposes of this Directive, it should be provided that permits issued on more favourable terms do not confer the right to reside in other Member States.

(18) Establishing the conditions subject to which the right to reside in another Member State may be acquired by third-country nationals who are long-term residents should contribute to the effective attainment of an internal market as an area in which the free movement of persons is ensured. It could also constitute a major factor of mobility, notably on the Union's employment market.

(19) Provision should be made that the right of residence in another Member State may be exercised in order to work in an employed or self-employed capacity, to study or even to settle without exercising any form of economic activity.

(20) Family members should also be able to settle in another Member State with a long-term resident in order to preserve family unity and to avoid hindering the exercise of the long-term resident's right of residence. With regard to the family members who may be authorised to accompany or to join the long-term residents, Member States should pay special attention to the situation of disabled adult children and of first-degree relatives in the direct ascending line who are dependent on them.

(21) The Member State in which a long-term resident intends to exercise his/her right of residence should be able to check that the person concerned meets the conditions for residing in its territory. It should also be able to check that the person concerned does not constitute a threat to public policy, public security or public health.

(22) To avoid rendering the right of residence nugatory, long-term residents should enjoy in the second Member State the same treatment, under the conditions defined by this Directive, they enjoy in the Member State in which they acquired the status. The granting of benefits under social assistance is without prejudice to the possibility for the Member States to withdraw the residence permit if the person concerned no longer fulfils the requirements set by this Directive.

(23) Third-country nationals should be granted the possibility of acquiring long-term resident status in the Member State where they have moved and have decided to settle under comparable conditions to those required for its acquisition in the first Member State.

(24) Since the objectives of the proposed action, namely the determination of terms for granting and withdrawing long-term resident status and the rights pertaining thereto and terms for the exercise of rights of residence by long-term residents in other Member States, cannot be sufficiently achieved by the Member States and can therefore, by reason of the scale and effects of the action, be better achieved by the Community, the Community may adopt measures, in accordance with the principle of subsidiarity as set out in Article 5 of the Treaty. In accordance with the principle of proportionality, as set out in that Article, this Directive does not go beyond what is necessary to achieve those objectives.

(25) In accordance with Articles 1 and 2 of the Protocol on the position of the United Kingdom and Ireland, annexed to the Treaty on European Union and to the Treaty establishing the European Community, and without prejudice to Article 4 of the said Protocol, these Member States are not participating in the adoption of this Directive and are not bound by or subject to its application.

(26) In accordance with Articles 1 and 2 of the Protocol on the position of Denmark, annexed to the Treaty on European Union and the Treaty establishing the European Community, Denmark does not take part in the adoption of this Directive, and is not bound by it or subject to its application,

HAS ADOPTED THIS DIRECTIVE:

Chapter I General provisions

Article 1 Subject matter
This Directive determines:
  (a) the terms for conferring and withdrawing long-term resident status granted by a Member State in relation to third-country nationals legally residing in its territory, and the rights pertaining thereto; and
  (b) the terms of residence in Member States other than the one which conferred long-term status on them for third-country nationals enjoying that status.

Article 2 Definitions
For the purposes of this Directive:
  (a) 'third-country national' means any person who is not a citizen of the Union within the meaning of Article 17(1) of the Treaty;
  (b) 'long-term resident' means any third-country national who has long-term resident status as provided for under Articles 4 to 7;
  (c) 'first Member State' means the Member State which for the first time granted long-term resident status to a third-country national;
  (d) 'second Member State' means any Member State other than the one which for the first time granted long-term resident status to a third-country national and in which that long-term resident exercises the right of residence;
  (e) 'family members' means the third-country nationals who reside in the Member State concerned in accordance with Council Directive 2003/86/EC of 22 September 2003 on the right to family reunification;[5]
  (f) 'international protection' means international protection as defined in Article 2(a) of Council Directive 2004/83/EC of 29 April 2004 on minimum standards for the qualification and status of third-country nationals or stateless persons as refugees or as persons who otherwise need international protection and the content of the protection granted;[6]
  (g) 'long-term resident's EC residence permit' means a residence permit issued by the Member State concerned upon the acquisition of long-term resident status.

Article 3 Scope
  1. This Directive applies to third-country nationals residing legally in the territory of a Member State.
  2. This Directive does not apply to third-country nationals who:
    (a) reside in order to pursue studies or vocational training;
    (b) are authorised to reside in a Member State on the basis of temporary protection or have applied for authorisation to reside on that basis and are awaiting a decision on their status;
    (c) are authorised to reside in a Member State on the basis of a form of protection other than international protection or have applied for authorisation to reside on that basis and are awaiting a decision on their status;
    (d) have applied for international protection and whose application has not yet given rise to a final decision;
    (e) reside solely on temporary grounds such as au pair or seasonal worker, or as workers posted by a service provider for the purposes of cross-border provision of services, or

---

[5] OJ L 251, 3.10.2003, p. 12.
[6] OJ L 304, 30.9.2004, p. 12.

as cross-border providers of services or in cases where their residence permit has been formally limited;

(f) enjoy a legal status governed by the Vienna Convention on Diplomatic Relations of 1961, the Vienna Convention on Consular Relations of 1963, the Convention of 1969 on Special Missions or the Vienna Convention on the Representation of States in their Relations with International Organisations of a Universal Character of 1975.

3. This Directive shall apply without prejudice to more favourable provisions of:

(a) bilateral and multilateral agreements between the Community or the Community and its Member States, on the one hand, and third countries, on the other;

(b) bilateral agreements already concluded between a Member State and a third country before the date of entry into force of this Directive;

(c) the European Convention on Establishment of 13 December 1955, the European Social Charter of 18 October 1961, the amended European Social Charter of 3 May 1987 and the European Convention on the Legal Status of Migrant Workers of 24 November 1977, paragraph 11 of the Schedule to the Convention Relating to the Status of Refugees of 28 July 1951, as amended by the Protocol signed in New York on 31 January 1967, and the European Agreement on Transfer of Responsibility for Refugees of 16 October 1980.

Chapter II Long-term resident status in a Member State

Article 4   Duration of residence

1. Member States shall grant long-term resident status to third-country nationals who have resided legally and continuously within its territory for five years immediately prior to the submission of the relevant application.

1a. Member States shall not grant long-term resident status on the basis of international protection in the event of the revocation of, ending of or refusal to renew international protection as laid down in Articles 14(3) and 19(3) of Directive 2004/83/EC.

2. Periods of residence for the reasons referred to in Article 3(2)(e) and (f) shall not be taken into account for the purposes of calculating the period referred to in paragraph 1.

Regarding the cases covered in Article 3(2)(a), where the third-country national concerned has acquired a title of residence which will enable him/her to be granted long-term resident status, only half of the periods of residence for study purposes or vocational training may be taken into account in the calculation of the period referred to in paragraph 1.

Regarding persons to whom international protection has been granted, at least half of the period between the date of the lodging of the application for international protection on the basis of which that international protection was granted and the date of the grant of the residence permit referred to in Article 24 of Directive 2004/83/EC, or the whole of that period if it exceeds 18 months, shall be taken into account in the calculation of the period referred to in paragraph 1.

3. Periods of absence from the territory of the Member State concerned shall not interrupt the period referred to in paragraph 1 and shall be taken into account for its calculation where they are shorter than six consecutive months and do not exceed in total 10 months within the period referred to in paragraph 1.

In cases of specific or exceptional reasons of a temporary nature and in accordance with their national law, Member States may accept that a longer period of absence than that which is referred to in the first subparagraph shall not interrupt the period referred to in paragraph 1. In such cases Member States shall not take into account the relevant period of absence in the calculation of the period referred to in paragraph 1.

By way of derogation from the second subparagraph, Member States may take into account in the calculation of the total period referred to in paragraph 1 periods of absence relating to secondment for employment purposes, including the provision of cross-border services.

Article 5   Conditions for acquiring long-term resident status

1. Member States shall require third-country nationals to provide evidence that they have, for themselves and for dependent family members:

- (a) stable and regular resources which are sufficient to maintain himself/herself and the members of his/her family, without recourse to the social assistance system of the Member State concerned. Member States shall evaluate these resources by reference to their nature and regularity and may take into account the level of minimum wages and pensions prior to the application for long-term resident status;
- (b) sickness insurance in respect of all risks normally covered for his/her own nationals in the Member State concerned.

2. Member States may require third-country nationals to comply with integration conditions, in accordance with national law.

Article 6   Public policy and public security

1. Member States may refuse to grant long-term resident status on grounds of public policy or public security.

When taking the relevant decision, the Member State shall consider the severity or type of offence against public policy or public security, or the danger that emanates from the person concerned, while also having proper regard to the duration of residence and to the existence of links with the country of residence.

2. The refusal referred to in paragraph 1 shall not be founded on economic considerations.

Article 7   Acquisition of long-term resident status

1. To acquire long-term resident status, the third-country national concerned shall lodge an application with the competent authorities of the Member State in which he/she resides. The application shall be accompanied by documentary evidence to be determined by national law that he/she meets the conditions set out in Articles 4 and 5 as well as, if required, by a valid travel document or its certified copy.

The evidence referred to in the first subparagraph may also include documentation with regard to appropriate accommodation.

2. The competent national authorities shall give the applicant written notification of the decision as soon as possible and in any event no later than six months from the date on which the application was lodged. Any such decision shall be notified to the third-country national concerned in accordance with the notification procedures under the relevant national legislation.

In exceptional circumstances linked to the complexity of the examination of the application, the time limit referred to in the first subparagraph may be extended.

In addition, the person concerned shall be informed about his/her rights and obligations under this Directive.

Any consequences of no decision being taken by the end of the period provided for in this provision shall be determined by national legislation of the relevant Member State.

3. If the conditions provided for by Articles 4 and 5 are met, and the person does not represent a threat within the meaning of Article 6, the Member State concerned shall grant the third-country national concerned long-term resident status.

Article 8   Long-term resident's EC residence permit

1. The status as long-term resident shall be permanent, subject to Article 9.

2. Member States shall issue a long-term resident's EC residence permit to long-term residents. The permit shall be valid at least for five years; it shall, upon application if required, be automatically renewable on expiry.

3. A long-term resident's EC residence permit may be issued in the form of a sticker or of a separate document. It shall be issued in accordance with the rules and standard model as set out in Council Regulation (EC) No 1030/2002 of 13 June 2002 laying down a uniform format for residence

permits for third-country nationals.[7] Under the heading 'type of permit', the Member States shall enter 'long-term resident—EC'.

4. Where a Member State issues a long-term resident's EU residence permit to a third-country national to whom it granted international protection, it shall enter the following remark in that long-term resident's EU residence permit, under the heading 'Remarks': 'International protection granted by [name of the Member State] on [date]'.

5. Where a long-term resident's EU residence permit is issued by a second Member State to a third-country national who already has a long-term resident's EU residence permit issued by another Member State which contains the remark referred to in paragraph 4, the second Member State shall enter the same remark in the long-term resident's EU residence permit.

Before the second Member State enters the remark referred to in paragraph 4, it shall request the Member State mentioned in that remark to provide information as to whether the long-term resident is still a beneficiary of international protection. The Member State mentioned in the remark shall reply no later than 1 month after receiving the request for information. Where international protection has been withdrawn by a final decision, the second Member State shall not enter that remark.

6. Where, in accordance with the relevant international instruments or national law, responsibility for the international protection of the long-term resident was transferred to the second Member State after the long-term resident's EU residence permit referred to in paragraph 5 was issued, the second Member State shall amend accordingly the remark referred to in paragraph 4 no later than 3 months after the transfer.

Article 9   Withdrawal or loss of status

1. Long-term residents shall no longer be entitled to maintain long-term resident status in the following cases:

    (a) detection of fraudulent acquisition of long-term resident status;

    (b) adoption of an expulsion measure under the conditions provided for in Article 12;

    (c) in the event of absence from the territory of the Community for a period of 12 consecutive months.

2. By way of derogation from paragraph 1(c), Member States may provide that absences exceeding 12 consecutive months or for specific or exceptional reasons shall not entail withdrawal or loss of status.

3. Member States may provide that the long-term resident shall no longer be entitled to maintain his/her long-term resident status in cases where he/she constitutes a threat to public policy, in consideration of the seriousness of the offences he/she committed, but such threat is not a reason for expulsion within the meaning of Article 12.

3a. Member States may withdraw the long-term resident status in the event of the revocation of, ending of or refusal to renew international protection as laid down in Articles 14(3) and 19(3) of Directive 2004/83/EC if the long-term resident status was obtained on the basis of international protection.

4. The long-term resident who has resided in another Member State in accordance with Chapter III shall no longer be entitled to maintain his/her long-term resident status acquired in the first Member State when such a status is granted in another Member State pursuant to Article 23.

In any case after six years of absence from the territory of the Member State that granted long-term resident status the person concerned shall no longer be entitled to maintain his/her long term resident status in the said Member State.

By way of derogation from the second subparagraph the Member State concerned may provide that for specific reasons the long-term resident shall maintain his/her status in the said Member State in case of absences for a period exceeding six years.

---

[7] OJ L 157, 15.6.2002, p. 1.

5. With regard to the cases referred to in paragraph 1(c) and in paragraph 4, Member States who have granted the status shall provide for a facilitated procedure for the re-acquisition of long-term resident status.

The said procedure shall apply in particular to the cases of persons that have resided in a second Member State on grounds of pursuit of studies.

The conditions and the procedure for the re-acquisition of long-term resident status shall be determined by national law.

6. The expiry of a long-term resident's EC residence permit shall in no case entail withdrawal or loss of long-term resident status.

7. Where the withdrawal or loss of long-term resident status does not lead to removal, the Member State shall authorise the person concerned to remain in its territory if he/she fulfils the conditions provided for in its national legislation and/or if he/she does not constitute a threat to public policy or public security.

Article 10   Procedural guarantees

1. Reasons shall be given for any decision rejecting an application for long-term resident status or withdrawing that status. Any such decision shall be notified to the third-country national concerned in accordance with the notification procedures under the relevant national legislation. The notification shall specify the redress procedures available and the time within which he/she may act.

2. Where an application for long-term resident status is rejected or that status is withdrawn or lost or the residence permit is not renewed, the person concerned shall have the right to mount a legal challenge in the Member State concerned.

Article 11   Equal treatment

1. Long-term residents shall enjoy equal treatment with nationals as regards:
   (a) access to employment and self-employed activity, provided such activities do not entail even occasional involvement in the exercise of public authority, and conditions of employment and working conditions, including conditions regarding dismissal and remuneration;
   (b) education and vocational training, including study grants in accordance with national law;
   (c) recognition of professional diplomas, certificates and other qualifications, in accordance with the relevant national procedures;
   (d) social security, social assistance and social protection as defined by national law;
   (e) tax benefits;
   (f) access to goods and services and the supply of goods and services made available to the public and to procedures for obtaining housing;
   (g) freedom of association and affiliation and membership of an organisation representing workers or employers or of any organisation whose members are engaged in a specific occupation, including the benefits conferred by such organisations, without prejudice to the national provisions on public policy and public security;
   (h) free access to the entire territory of the Member State concerned, within the limits provided for by the national legislation for reasons of security.

2. With respect to the provisions of paragraph 1, points (b), (d), (e), (f) and (g), the Member State concerned may restrict equal treatment to cases where the registered or usual place of residence of the long-term resident, or that of family members for whom he/she claims benefits, lies within the territory of the Member State concerned.

3. Member States may restrict equal treatment with nationals in the following cases:
   (a) Member States may retain restrictions to access to employment or self-employed activities in cases where, in accordance with existing national or Community legislation, these activities are reserved to nationals, EU or EEA citizens;

(b) Member States may require proof of appropriate language proficiency for access to education and training. Access to university may be subject to the fulfilment of specific educational prerequisites.

4. Member States may limit equal treatment in respect of social assistance and social protection to core benefits.

4a. As far as the Member State which granted international protection is concerned, paragraphs 3 and 4 shall be without prejudice to Directive 2004/83/EC.

5. Member States may decide to grant access to additional benefits in the areas referred to in paragraph 1.

Member States may also decide to grant equal treatment with regard to areas not covered in paragraph 1.

Article 12　Protection against expulsion

1. Member States may take a decision to expel a long-term resident solely where he/she constitutes an actual and sufficiently serious threat to public policy or public security.

2. The decision referred to in paragraph 1 shall not be founded on economic considerations.

3. Before taking a decision to expel a long-term resident, Member States shall have regard to the following factors:

(a) the duration of residence in their territory;

(b) the age of the person concerned;

(c) the consequences for the person concerned and family members;

(d) links with the country of residence or the absence of links with the country of origin.

3a. Where a Member State decides to expel a long-term resident whose long-term resident's EU residence permit contains the remark referred to in Article 8(4), it shall request the Member State mentioned in that remark to confirm whether the person concerned is still a beneficiary of international protection in that Member State. The Member State mentioned in the remark shall reply no later than 1 month after receiving the request for information.

3b. If the long-term resident is still a beneficiary of international protection in the Member State mentioned in the remark, that person shall be expelled to that Member State, which shall, without prejudice to the applicable Union or national law and to the principle of family unity, immediately readmit, without formalities, that beneficiary and his/her family members.

3c. By way of derogation from paragraph 3b, the Member State which adopted the expulsion decision shall retain the right to remove, in accordance with its international obligations, the long-term resident to a country other than the Member State which granted international protection where that person fulfils the conditions specified in Article 21(2) of Directive 2004/83/EC.

4. Where an expulsion decision has been adopted, a judicial redress procedure shall be available to the long-term resident in the Member State concerned.

5. Legal aid shall be given to long-term residents lacking adequate resources, on the same terms as apply to nationals of the State where they reside.

6. This Article shall be without prejudice to Article 21(1) of Directive 2004/83/EC.

Article 13　More favourable national provisions

Member States may issue residence permits of permanent or unlimited validity on terms that are more favourable than those laid down by this Directive. Such residence permits shall not confer the right of residence in the other Member States as provided by Chapter III of this Directive.

Chapter III　Residence in the other Member States

Article 14　Principle

1. A long-term resident shall acquire the right to reside in the territory of Member States other than the one which granted him/her the long-term residence status, for a period exceeding three months, provided that the conditions set out in this chapter are met.

2. A long-term resident may reside in a second Member State on the following grounds:
   (a) exercise of an economic activity in an employed or self-employed capacity;
   (b) pursuit of studies or vocational training;
   (c) other purposes.

3. In cases of an economic activity in an employed or self-employed capacity referred to in paragraph 2(a), Member States may examine the situation of their labour market and apply their national procedures regarding the requirements for, respectively, filling a vacancy, or for exercising such activities.

For reasons of labour market policy, Member States may give preference to Union citizens, to third-country nationals, when provided for by Community legislation, as well as to third-country nationals who reside legally and receive unemployment benefits in the Member State concerned.

4. By way of derogation from the provisions of paragraph 1, Member States may limit the total number of persons entitled to be granted right of residence, provided that such limitations are already set out for the admission of third-country nationals in the existing legislation at the time of the adoption of this Directive.

5. This chapter does not concern the residence of long-term residents in the territory of the Member States:
   (a) as employed workers posted by a service provider for the purposes of cross-border provision of services;
   (b) as providers of cross-border services.

Member States may decide, in accordance with national law, the conditions under which long-term residents who wish to move to a second Member State with a view to exercising an economic activity as seasonal workers may reside in that Member State. Cross-border workers may also be subject to specific provisions of national law.

6. This Chapter is without prejudice to the relevant Community legislation on social security with regard to third-country nationals.

Article 15   Conditions for residence in a second Member State

1. As soon as possible and no later than three months after entering the territory of the second Member State, the long-term resident shall apply to the competent authorities of that Member State for a residence permit.

Member States may accept that the long-term resident submits the application for a residence permit to the competent authorities of the second Member State while still residing in the territory of the first Member State.

2. Member States may require the persons concerned to provide evidence that they have:
   (a) stable and regular resources which are sufficient to maintain themselves and the members of their families, without recourse to the social assistance of the Member State concerned. For each of the categories referred to in Article 14(2), Member States shall evaluate these resources by reference to their nature and regularity and may take into account the level of minimum wages and pensions;
   (b) sickness insurance covering all risks in the second Member State normally covered for its own nationals in the Member State concerned.

3. Member States may require third-country nationals to comply with integration measures, in accordance with national law.

This condition shall not apply where the third-country nationals concerned have been required to comply with integration conditions in order to be granted long-term resident status, in accordance with the provisions of Article 5(2).

Without prejudice to the second subparagraph, the persons concerned may be required to attend language courses.

4. The application shall be accompanied by documentary evidence, to be determined by national law, that the persons concerned meets the relevant conditions, as well as by their long-term resident permit and a valid travel document or their certified copies.

The evidence referred to in the first subparagraph may also include documentation with regard to appropriate accommodation.

In particular:

    (a) in case of exercise of an economic activity the second Member State may require the persons concerned to provide evidence:

        (i) if they are in an employed capacity, that they have an employment contract, a statement by the employer that they are hired or a proposal for an employment contract, under the conditions provided for by national legislation. Member States shall determine which of the said forms of evidence is required;

        (ii) if they are in a self-employed capacity, that they have the appropriate funds which are needed, in accordance with national law, to exercise an economic activity in such capacity, presenting the necessary documents and permits;

    (b) in case of study or vocational training the second Member State may require the persons concerned to provide evidence of enrolment in an accredited establishment in order to pursue studies or vocational training.

Article 16   Family members

1. When the long-term resident exercises his/her right of residence in a second Member State and when the family was already constituted in the first Member State, the members of his/her family, who fulfil the conditions referred to in Article 4(1) of Directive 2003/86/EC shall be authorised to accompany or to join the long-term resident.

2. When the long-term resident exercises his/her right of residence in a second Member State and when the family was already constituted in the first Member State, the members of his/her family, other than those referred to in Article 4(1) of Directive 2003/86/EC may be authorised to accompany or to join the long-term resident.

3. With respect to the submission of the application for a residence permit, the provisions of Article 15(1) apply.

4. The second Member State may require the family members concerned to present with their application for a residence permit:

    (a) their long-term resident's EC residence permit or residence permit and a valid travel document or their certified copies;

    (b) evidence that they have resided as members of the family of the long-term resident in the first Member State;

    (c) evidence that they have stable and regular resources which are sufficient to maintain themselves without recourse to the social assistance of the Member State concerned or that the long-term resident has such resources and insurance for them, as well as sickness insurance covering all risks in the second Member State. Member States shall evaluate these resources by reference to their nature and regularity and may take into account the level of minimum wages and pensions.

5. Where the family was not already constituted in the first Member State, Directive 2003/86/EC shall apply.

Article 17   Public policy and public security

1. Member States may refuse applications for residence from long-term residents or their family members where the person concerned constitutes a threat to public policy or public security.

When taking the relevant decision, the Member State shall consider the severity or type of offence against public policy or public security committed by the long-term resident or his/her family member(s), or the danger that emanates from the person concerned.

2. The decision referred to in paragraph 1 shall not be based on economic considerations.

Article 18   Public health

1. Member States may refuse applications for residence from long-term residents or their family members where the person concerned constitutes a threat to public health.

2. The only diseases that may justify a refusal to allow entry or the right of residence in the territory of the second Member State shall be the diseases as defined by the relevant applicable instruments of the World Health Organisation's and such other infectious or contagious parasite-based diseases as are the subject of protective provisions in relation to nationals in the host country. Member States shall not introduce new more restrictive provisions or practices.

3. Diseases contracted after the first residence permit was issued in the second Member State shall not justify a refusal to renew the permit or expulsion from the territory.

4. A Member State may require a medical examination, for persons to whom this Directive applies, in order to certify that they do not suffer from any of the diseases referred to in paragraph 2. Such medical examinations, which may be free of charge, shall not be performed on a systematic basis.

Article 19   Examination of applications and issue of a residence permit

1. The competent national authorities shall process applications within four months from the date that these have been lodged.

If an application is not accompanied by the documentary evidence listed in Articles 15 and 16, or in exceptional circumstances linked with the complexity of the examination of the application, the time limit referred to in the first subparagraph may be extended for a period not exceeding three months. In such cases the competent national authorities shall inform the applicant thereof.

2. If the conditions provided for in Articles 14, 15 and 16 are met, then, subject to the provisions relating to public policy, public security and public health in Articles 17 and 18, the second Member State shall issue the long-term resident with a renewable residence permit. This residence permit shall, upon application, if required, be renewable on expiry. The second Member State shall inform the first Member State of its decision.

3. The second Member State shall issue members of the long-term resident's family with renewable residence permits valid for the same period as the permit issued to the long-term resident.

Article 19a   Amendments of long-term resident's EU residence permits

1. Where a long-term resident's EU residence permit contains the remark referred to in Article 8(4), and where, in accordance with the relevant international instruments or national law, responsibility for the international protection of the long-term resident is transferred to a second Member State before that Member State issues the long-term resident's EU residence permit referred to in Article 8(5), the second Member State shall ask the Member State which has issued the long-term resident's EU residence permit to amend that remark accordingly.

2. Where a long-term resident is granted international protection in the second Member State before that Member State issued the long-term resident's EU residence permit referred to in Article 8(5), that Member State shall ask the Member State which has issued the long-term resident's EU residence permit to amend it in order to enter the remark referred to in Article 8(4).

3. Following the request referred to in paragraphs 1 and 2, the Member State which has issued the long-term resident's EU residence permit shall issue the amended long-term resident's EU residence permit no later than 3 months after receiving the request from the second Member State.

Article 20   Procedural guarantees

1. Reasons shall be given for any decision rejecting an application for a residence permit. It shall be notified to the third-country national concerned in accordance with the notification procedures under the relevant national legislation. The notification shall specify the possible redress procedures available and the time limit for taking action.

Any consequences of no decision being taken by the end of the period referred to in Article 19(1) shall be determined by the national legislation of the relevant Member State.

2. Where an application for a residence permit is rejected, or the permit is not renewed or is withdrawn, the person concerned shall have the right to mount a legal challenge in the Member State concerned.

Article 21 Treatment granted in the second Member State

1. As soon as they have received the residence permit provided for by Article 19 in the second Member State, long-term residents shall in that Member State enjoy equal treatment in the areas and under the conditions referred to in Article 11.

2. Long-term residents shall have access to the labour market in accordance with the provisions of paragraph 1.

Member States may provide that the persons referred to in Article 14(2)(a) shall have restricted access to employed activities different than those for which they have been granted their residence permit under the conditions set by national legislation for a period not exceeding 12 months.

Member States may decide in accordance with national law the conditions under which the persons referred to in Article 14(2)(b) or (c) may have access to an employed or self-employed activity.

3. As soon as they have received the residence permit provided for by Article 19 in the second Member State, members of the family of the long-term resident shall in that Member State enjoy the rights listed in Article 14 of Directive 2003/86/EC.

Article 22 Withdrawal of residence permit and obligation to readmit

1. Until the third-country national has obtained long-term resident status, the second Member State may decide to refuse to renew or to withdraw the resident permit and to oblige the person concerned and his/her family members, in accordance with the procedures provided for by national law, including removal procedures, to leave its territory in the following cases:

(a) on grounds of public policy or public security as defined in Article 17;

(b) where the conditions provided for in Articles 14, 15 and 16 are no longer met;

(c) where the third-country national is not lawfully residing in the Member State concerned.

2. If the second Member State adopts one of the measures referred to in paragraph 1, the first Member State shall immediately readmit without formalities the long-term resident and his/her family members. The second Member State shall notify the first Member State of its decision.

3. Until the third-country national has obtained long-term resident status and without prejudice to the obligation to readmit referred to in paragraph 2, the second Member State may adopt a decision to remove the third-country national from the territory of the Union, in accordance with and under the guarantees of Article 12, on serious grounds of public policy or public security.

In such cases, when adopting the said decision the second Member State shall consult the first Member State.

When the second Member State adopts a decision to remove the third-country national concerned, it shall take all the appropriate measures to effectively implement it. In such cases the second Member State shall provide to the first Member State appropriate information with respect to the implementation of the removal decision.

3a. Unless, in the meantime, the international protection has been withdrawn or the person falls within one of the categories specified in Article 21(2) of Directive 2004/83/EC, paragraph 3 of this Article shall not apply to third-country nationals whose long-term resident's EU residence permit issued by the first Member State contains the remark referred to in Article 8(4) of this Directive.

This paragraph shall be without prejudice to Article 21(1) of Directive 2004/83/EC.

4. Removal decisions may not be accompanied by a permanent ban on residence in the cases referred to in paragraph 1(b) and (c).

5. The obligation to readmit referred to in paragraph 2 shall be without prejudice to the possibility of the long-term resident and his/her family members moving to a third Member State.

Article 23 Acquisition of long-term resident status in the second Member State

1. Upon application, the second Member State shall grant long-term residents the status provided for by Article 7, subject to the provisions of Articles 3, 4, 5 and 6. The second Member State shall notify its decision to the first Member State.

2. The procedure laid down in Article 7 shall apply to the presentation and examination of applications for long-term resident status in the second Member State. Article 8 shall apply for the issuance of the residence permit. Where the application is rejected, the procedural guarantees provided for by Article 10 shall apply.

Chapter IV Final provisions

Article 24 Report and rendez-vous clause

Periodically, and for the first time no later than 23 January 2011, the Commission shall report to the European Parliament and to the Council on the application of this Directive in the Member States and shall propose such amendments as may be necessary. These proposals for amendments shall be made by way of priority in relation to Articles 4, 5, 9, 11 and to Chapter III.

Article 25 Contact points

Member States shall appoint contact points who will be responsible for receiving and transmitting the information and documentation referred to in Articles 8, 12, 19, 19a, 22 and 23.

Member States shall provide appropriate cooperation in the exchange of the information and documentation referred to in the first paragraph.

Article 26 Transposition

Member States shall bring into force the laws, regulations and administrative provisions necessary to comply with this Directive by 23 January 2006 at the latest. They shall forthwith inform the Commission thereof.

When Member States adopt these measures, they shall contain a reference to this Directive or shall be accompanied by such reference on the occasion of their official publication. The methods of making such reference shall be laid down by Member States.

Article 27 Entry into force

This Directive shall enter into force on the day of its publication in the *Official Journal of the European Union*.

Article 28 Addressees

This Directive is addressed to the Member States in accordance with the Treaty establishing the European Community.

Done at Brussels, 25 November 2003.

Directive 2004/38/EC of the European Parliament and of the Council of 29 April 2004 on the right of citizens of the Union and their family members to move and reside freely within the territory of the Member States*

[OJ 2004 L158/77]

(Entry into force 30/4/2006 at which time Regulation (EEC) No 1612/68 is amended and Directives 64/221/EEC, 68/360/EEC, 72/194/EEC, 73/148/EEC, 75/34/EEC, 75/35/EEC, 90/364/EEC, 90/365/EEC and 93/96/EEC are repealed)

THE EUROPEAN PARLIAMENT AND THE COUNCIL OF THE EUROPEAN UNION,

Having regard to the Treaty establishing the European Community, and in particular Articles 12, 18, 40, 44 and 52 thereof,

Having regard to the proposal from the Commission,[1]

Having regard to the Opinion of the European Economic and Social Committee,[2]

Having regard to the Opinion of the Committee of the Regions,[3]

Acting in accordance with the procedure laid down in Article 251 of the Treaty,[4]

---

* **Editor's Note:** As corrected to OJ 2007 L 204/28 and amended by Regulation 492/2011 (OJ 2011 L141/1).

[1] OJ C 270 E, 25.9.2001, p. 150.

[2] OJ C 149, 21.6.2002, p. 46.

[3] OJ C 192, 12.8.2002, p. 17.

[4] Opinion of the European Parliament of 11 February (OJ C 43 E, 19.2.2004, p. 42), Council Common Position of 5 December (OJ C 54 E, 2.3.2004, p. 12) and Position of the European Parliament of 10 March 2004 (not yet published in the Official Journal).

Whereas:

(1) Citizenship of the Union confers on every citizen of the Union a primary and individual right to move and reside freely within the territory of the Member States, subject to the limitations and conditions laid down in the Treaty and to the measures adopted to give it effect.

(2) The free movement of persons constitutes one of the fundamental freedoms of the internal market, which comprises an area without internal frontiers, in which freedom is ensured in accordance with the provisions of the Treaty.

(3) Union citizenship should be the fundamental status of nationals of the Member States when they exercise their right of free movement and residence. It is therefore necessary to codify and review the existing Community instruments dealing separately with workers, self-employed persons, as well as students and other inactive persons in order to simplify and strengthen the right of free movement and residence of all Union citizens.

(4) With a view to remedying this sector-by-sector, piecemeal approach to the right of free movement and residence and facilitating the exercise of this right, there needs to be a single legislative act to amend Council Regulation (EEC) No 1612/68 of 15 October 1968 on freedom of movement for workers within the Community,[5] and to repeal the following acts: Council Directive 68/360/EEC of 15 October 1968 on the abolition of restrictions on movement and residence within the Community for workers of Member States and their families,[6] Council Directive 73/148/EEC of 21 May 1973 on the abolition of restrictions on movement and residence within the Community for nationals of Member States with regard to establishment and the provision of services,[7] Council Directive 90/364/EEC of 28 June 1990 on the right of residence,[8] Council Directive 90/365/EEC of 28 June 1990 on the right of residence for employees and self-employed persons who have ceased their occupational activity[9] and Council Directive 93/96/EEC of 29 October 1993 on the right of residence for students.[10]

(5) The right of all Union citizens to move and reside freely within the territory of the Member States should, if it is to be exercised under objective conditions of freedom and dignity, be also granted to their family members, irrespective of nationality. For the purposes of this Directive, the definition of 'family member' should also include the registered partner if the legislation of the host Member State treats registered partnership as equivalent to marriage.

(6) In order to maintain the unity of the family in a broader sense and without prejudice to the prohibition of discrimination on grounds of nationality, the situation of those persons who are not included in the definition of family members under this Directive, and who therefore do not enjoy an automatic right of entry and residence in the host Member State, should be examined by the host Member State on the basis of its own national legislation, in order to decide whether entry and residence could be granted to such persons, taking into consideration their relationship with the Union citizen or any other circumstances, such as their financial or physical dependence on the Union citizen.

(7) The formalities connected with the free movement of Union citizens within the territory of Member States should be clearly defined, without prejudice to the provisions applicable to national border controls.

(8) With a view to facilitating the free movement of family members who are not nationals of a Member State, those who have already obtained a residence card should be exempted from the requirement to obtain an entry visa within the meaning of Council Regulation (EC) No 539/2001 of 15 March 2001 listing the third countries whose nationals must be in possession of visas when crossing the external borders and those whose nationals are exempt from that requirement[11] or, where appropriate, of the applicable national legislation.

---

[5] OJ L 257, 19.10.1968, p. 2. Regulation as last amended by Regulation (EEC) No 2434/92 (OJ L 245, 26.8.1992, p. 1).
[6] OJ L 257, 19.10.1968, p. 13. Directive as last amended by the Act of Accession.
[7] OJ L 172, 28.6.1973, p. 14.
[8] OJ L 180, 13.7.1990, p. 26.
[9] OJ L 180, 13.7.1990, p. 28.
[10] OJ L 317, 18.12.1993, p. 59.
[11] OJ L 81, 21.3.2001, p. 1. Regulation as last amended by Regulation (EC) No 453/(OJ L 69, 13.3., p. 10).

(9) Union citizens should have the right of residence in the host Member State for a period not exceeding three months without being subject to any conditions or any formalities other than the requirement to hold a valid identity card or passport, without prejudice to a more favourable treatment applicable to job-seekers as recognised by the case-law of the Court of Justice.

(10) Persons exercising their right of residence should not, however, become an unreasonable burden on the social assistance system of the host Member State during an initial period of residence. Therefore, the right of residence for Union citizens and their family members for periods in excess of three months should be subject to conditions.

(11) The fundamental and personal right of residence in another Member State is conferred directly on Union citizens by the Treaty and is not dependent upon their having fulfilled administrative procedures.

(12) For periods of residence of longer than three months, Member States should have the possibility to require Union citizens to register with the competent authorities in the place of residence, attested by a registration certificate issued to that effect.

(13) The residence card requirement should be restricted to family members of Union citizens who are not nationals of a Member State for periods of residence of longer than three months.

(14) The supporting documents required by the competent authorities for the issuing of a registration certificate or of a residence card should be comprehensively specified in order to avoid divergent administrative practices or interpretations constituting an undue obstacle to the exercise of the right of residence by Union citizens and their family members.

(15) Family members should be legally safeguarded in the event of the death of the Union citizen, divorce, annulment of marriage or termination of a registered partnership. With due regard for family life and human dignity, and in certain conditions to guard against abuse, measures should therefore be taken to ensure that in such circumstances family members already residing within the territory of the host Member State retain their right of residence exclusively on a personal basis.

(16) As long as the beneficiaries of the right of residence do not become an unreasonable burden on the social assistance system of the host Member State they should not be expelled. Therefore, an expulsion measure should not be the automatic consequence of recourse to the social assistance system. The host Member State should examine whether it is a case of temporary difficulties and take into account the duration of residence, the personal circumstances and the amount of aid granted in order to consider whether the beneficiary has become an unreasonable burden on its social assistance system and to proceed to his expulsion. In no case should an expulsion measure be adopted against workers, self-employed persons or job-seekers as defined by the Court of Justice save on grounds of public policy or public security.

(17) Enjoyment of permanent residence by Union citizens who have chosen to settle long term in the host Member State would strengthen the feeling of Union citizenship and is a key element in promoting social cohesion, which is one of the fundamental objectives of the Union. A right of permanent residence should therefore be laid down for all Union citizens and their family members who have resided in the host Member State in compliance with the conditions laid down in this Directive during a continuous period of five years without becoming subject to an expulsion measure.

(18) In order to be a genuine vehicle for integration into the society of the host Member State in which the Union citizen resides, the right of permanent residence, once obtained, should not be subject to any conditions.

(19) Certain advantages specific to Union citizens who are workers or self-employed persons and to their family members, which may allow these persons to acquire a right of permanent residence before they have resided five years in the host Member State, should be maintained, as these constitute acquired rights, conferred by Commission Regulation (EEC) No 1251/70 of 29 June 1970 on the right of workers to remain in the territory of a Member State after having been employed in

that State[12] and Council Directive 75/34/EEC of 17 December 1974 concerning the right of nationals of a Member State to remain in the territory of another Member State after having pursued therein an activity in a self-employed capacity.[13]

(20) In accordance with the prohibition of discrimination on grounds of nationality, all Union citizens and their family members residing in a Member State on the basis of this Directive should enjoy, in that Member State, equal treatment with nationals in areas covered by the Treaty, subject to such specific provisions as are expressly provided for in the Treaty and secondary law.

(21) However, it should be left to the host Member State to decide whether it will grant social assistance during the first three months of residence, or for a longer period in the case of job-seekers, to Union citizens other than those who are workers or self-employed persons or who retain that status or their family members, or maintenance assistance for studies, including vocational training, prior to acquisition of the right of permanent residence, to these same persons.

(22) The Treaty allows restrictions to be placed on the right of free movement and residence on grounds of public policy, public security or public health. In order to ensure a tighter definition of the circumstances and procedural safeguards subject to which Union citizens and their family members may be denied leave to enter or may be expelled, this Directive should replace Council Directive 64/221/EEC of 25 February 1964 on the coordination of special measures concerning the movement and residence of foreign nationals, which are justified on grounds of public policy, public security or public health.[14]

(23) Expulsion of Union citizens and their family members on grounds of public policy or public security is a measure that can seriously harm persons who, having availed themselves of the rights and freedoms conferred on them by the Treaty, have become genuinely integrated into the host Member State. The scope for such measures should therefore be limited in accordance with the principle of proportionality to take account of the degree of integration of the persons concerned, the length of their residence in the host Member State, their age, state of health, family and economic situation and the links with their country of origin.

(24) Accordingly, the greater the degree of integration of Union citizens and their family members in the host Member State, the greater the degree of protection against expulsion should be. Only in exceptional circumstances, where there are imperative grounds of public security, should an expulsion measure be taken against Union citizens who have resided for many years in the territory of the host Member State, in particular when they were born and have resided there throughout their life. In addition, such exceptional circumstances should also apply to an expulsion measure taken against minors, in order to protect their links with their family, in accordance with the United Nations Convention on the Rights of the Child, of 20 November 1989.

(25) Procedural safeguards should also be specified in detail in order to ensure a high level of protection of the rights of Union citizens and their family members in the event of their being denied leave to enter or reside in another Member State, as well as to uphold the principle that any action taken by the authorities must be properly justified.

(26) In all events, judicial redress procedures should be available to Union citizens and their family members who have been refused leave to enter or reside in another Member State.

(27) In line with the case-law of the Court of Justice prohibiting Member States from issuing orders excluding for life persons covered by this Directive from their territory, the right of Union citizens and their family members who have been excluded from the territory of a Member State to submit a fresh application after a reasonable period, and in any event after a three year period from enforcement of the final exclusion order, should be confirmed.

(28) To guard against abuse of rights or fraud, notably marriages of convenience or any other form of relationships contracted for the sole purpose of enjoying the right of free movement and residence, Member States should have the possibility to adopt the necessary measures.

(29) This Directive should not affect more favourable national provisions.

---

[12] OJ L 142, 30.6.1970, p. 24.   [13] OJ L 14, 20.1.1975, p. 10.
[14] OJ 56, 4.4.1964, p. 850. Directive as last amended by Directive 75/35/EEC (OJ 14, 20.1.1975, p. 14).

(30) With a view to examining how further to facilitate the exercise of the right of free movement and residence, a report should be prepared by the Commission in order to evaluate the opportunity to present any necessary proposals to this effect, notably on the extension of the period of residence with no conditions.

(31) This Directive respects the fundamental rights and freedoms and observes the principles recognised in particular by the Charter of Fundamental Rights of the European Union. In accordance with the prohibition of discrimination contained in the Charter, Member States should implement this Directive without discrimination between the beneficiaries of this Directive on grounds such as sex, race, colour, ethnic or social origin, genetic characteristics, language, religion or beliefs, political or other opinion, membership of an ethnic minority, property, birth, disability, age or sexual orientation,

HAVE ADOPTED THIS DIRECTIVE:

Chapter I General provisions

Article 1 Subject
This Directive lays down:
- (a) the conditions governing the exercise of the right of free movement and residence within the territory of the Member States by Union citizens and their family members;
- (b) the right of permanent residence in the territory of the Member States for Union citizens and their family members;
- (c) the limits placed on the rights set out in (a) and (b) on grounds of public policy, public security or public health.

Article 2 Definitions
For the purposes of this Directive:
- (1) 'Union citizen' means any person having the nationality of a Member State;
- (2) 'Family member' means:
  - (a) the spouse;
  - (b) the partner with whom the Union citizen has contracted a registered partnership, on the basis of the legislation of a Member State, if the legislation of the host Member State treats registered partnerships as equivalent to marriage and in accordance with the conditions laid down in the relevant legislation of the host Member State;
  - (c) the direct descendants who are under the age of 21 or are dependants and those of the spouse or partner as defined in point (b);
  - (d) the dependent direct relatives in the ascending line and those of the spouse or partner as defined in point (b);
- (3) 'Host Member State' means the Member State to which a Union citizen moves in order to exercise his/her right of free movement and residence.

Article 3 Beneficiaries
1. This Directive shall apply to all Union citizens who move to or reside in a Member State other than that of which they are a national, and to their family members as defined in point 2 of Article 2 who accompany or join them.

2. Without prejudice to any right to free movement and residence the persons concerned may have in their own right, the host Member State shall, in accordance with its national legislation, facilitate entry and residence for the following persons:
- (a) any other family members, irrespective of their nationality, not falling under the definition in point 2 of Article 2 who, in the country from which they have come, are dependants or members of the household of the Union citizen having the primary right of residence, or where serious health grounds strictly require the personal care of the family member by the Union citizen;

(b) the partner with whom the Union citizen has a durable relationship, duly attested. The host Member State shall undertake an extensive examination of the personal circumstances and shall justify any denial of entry or residence to these people.

Chapter II Right of exit and entry

Article 4   Right of exit

1. Without prejudice to the provisions on travel documents applicable to national border controls, all Union citizens with a valid identity card or passport and their family members who are not nationals of a Member State and who hold a valid passport shall have the right to leave the territory of a Member State to travel to another Member State.

2. No exit visa or equivalent formality may be imposed on the persons to whom paragraph 1 applies.

3. Member States shall, acting in accordance with their laws, issue to their own nationals, and renew, an identity card or passport stating their nationality.

4. The passport shall be valid at least for all Member States and for countries through which the holder must pass when travelling between Member States. Where the law of a Member State does not provide for identity cards to be issued, the period of validity of any passport on being issued or renewed shall be not less than five years.

Article 5   Right of entry

1. Without prejudice to the provisions on travel documents applicable to national border controls, Member States shall grant Union citizens leave to enter their territory with a valid identity card or passport and shall grant family members who are not nationals of a Member State leave to enter their territory with a valid passport. No entry visa or equivalent formality may be imposed on Union citizens.

2. Family members who are not nationals of a Member State shall only be required to have an entry visa in accordance with Regulation (EC) No 539/2001 or, where appropriate, with national law. For the purposes of this Directive, possession of the valid residence card referred to in Article 10 shall exempt such family members from the visa requirement. Member States shall grant such persons every facility to obtain the necessary visas. Such visas shall be issued free of charge as soon as possible and on the basis of an accelerated procedure.

3. The host Member State shall not place an entry or exit stamp in the passport of family members who are not nationals of a Member State provided that they present the residence card provided for in Article 10.

4. Where a Union citizen, or a family member who is not a national of a Member State, does not have the necessary travel documents or, if required, the necessary visas, the Member State concerned shall, before turning them back, give such persons every reasonable opportunity to obtain the necessary documents or have them brought to them within a reasonable period of time or to corroborate or prove by other means that they are covered by the right of free movement and residence.

5. The Member State may require the person concerned to report his/her presence within its territory within a reasonable and non-discriminatory period of time. Failure to comply with this requirement may make the person concerned liable to proportionate and non-discriminatory sanctions.

Chapter III Right of residence

Article 6   Right of residence for up to three months

1. Union citizens shall have the right of residence on the territory of another Member State for a period of up to three months without any conditions or any formalities other than the requirement to hold a valid identity card or passport.

2. The provisions of paragraph 1 shall also apply to family members in possession of a valid passport who are not nationals of a Member State, accompanying or joining the Union citizen.

Article 7 Right of residence for more than three months

1. All Union citizens shall have the right of residence on the territory of another Member State for a period of longer than three months if they:
   - (a) are workers or self-employed persons in the host Member State; or
   - (b) have sufficient resources for themselves and their family members not to become a burden on the social assistance system of the host Member State during their period of residence and have comprehensive sickness insurance cover in the host Member State; or
   - (c) – are enrolled at a private or public establishment, accredited or financed by the host Member State on the basis of its legislation or administrative practice, for the principal purpose of following a course of study, including vocational training; and

     – have comprehensive sickness insurance cover in the host Member State and assure the relevant national authority, by means of a declaration or by such equivalent means as they may choose, that they have sufficient resources for themselves and their family members not to become a burden on the social assistance system of the host Member State during their period of residence; or
   - (d) are family members accompanying or joining a Union citizen who satisfies the conditions referred to in points (a), (b) or (c).

2. The right of residence provided for in paragraph 1 shall extend to family members who are not nationals of a Member State, accompanying or joining the Union citizen in the host Member State, provided that such Union citizen satisfies the conditions referred to in paragraph 1(a), (b) or (c).

3. For the purposes of paragraph 1(a), a Union citizen who is no longer a worker or self-employed person shall retain the status of worker or self-employed person in the following circumstances:
   - (a) he/she is temporarily unable to work as the result of an illness or accident;
   - (b) he/she is in duly recorded involuntary unemployment after having been employed for more than one year and has registered as a job-seeker with the relevant employment office;
   - (c) he/she is in duly recorded involuntary unemployment after completing a fixed-term employment contract of less than a year or after having become involuntarily unemployed during the first twelve months and has registered as a job-seeker with the relevant employment office. In this case, the status of worker shall be retained for no less than six months;
   - (d) he/she embarks on vocational training. Unless he/she is involuntarily unemployed, the retention of the status of worker shall require the training to be related to the previous employment.

4. By way of derogation from paragraphs 1(d) and 2 above, only the spouse, the registered partner provided for in Article 2(2)(b) and dependent children shall have the right of residence as family members of a Union citizen meeting the conditions under 1(c) above. Article 3(2) shall apply to his/her dependent direct relatives in the ascending lines and those of his/her spouse or registered partner.

Article 8 Administrative formalities for Union citizens

1. Without prejudice to Article 5(5), for periods of residence longer than three months, the host Member State may require Union citizens to register with the relevant authorities.

2. The deadline for registration may not be less than three months from the date of arrival. A registration certificate shall be issued immediately, stating the name and address of the person registering and the date of the registration. Failure to comply with the registration requirement may render the person concerned liable to proportionate and non-discriminatory sanctions.

3. For the registration certificate to be issued, Member States may only require that
   - – Union citizens to whom point (a) of Article 7(1) applies present a valid identity card or passport, a confirmation of engagement from the employer or a certificate of employment, or proof that they are self-employed persons;
   - – Union citizens to whom point (b) of Article 7(1) applies present a valid identity card or passport and provide proof that they satisfy the conditions laid down therein;

– Union citizens to whom point (c) of Article 7(1) applies present a valid identity card or passport, provide proof of enrolment at an accredited establishment and of comprehensive sickness insurance cover and the declaration or equivalent means referred to in point (c) of Article 7(1). Member States may not require this declaration to refer to any specific amount of resources.

4. Member States may not lay down a fixed amount which they regard as 'sufficient resources', but they must take into account the personal situation of the person concerned. In all cases this amount shall not be higher than the threshold below which nationals of the host Member State become eligible for social assistance, or, where this criterion is not applicable, higher than the minimum social security pension paid by the host Member State.

5. For the registration certificate to be issued to family members of Union citizens, who are themselves Union citizens, Member States may require the following documents to be presented:

   (a) a valid identity card or passport;

   (b) a document attesting to the existence of a family relationship or of a registered partnership;

   (c) where appropriate, the registration certificate of the Union citizen whom they are accompanying or joining;

   (d) in cases falling under points (c) and (d) of Article 2(2), documentary evidence that the conditions laid down therein are met;

   (e) in cases falling under Article 3(2)(a), a document issued by the relevant authority in the country of origin or country from which they are arriving certifying that they are dependants or members of the household of the Union citizen, or proof of the existence of serious health grounds which strictly require the personal care of the family member by the Union citizen;

   (f) in cases falling under Article 3(2)(b), proof of the existence of a durable relationship with the Union citizen.

Article 9   Administrative formalities for family members who are not nationals of a Member State

1. Member States shall issue a residence card to family members of a Union citizen who are not nationals of a Member State, where the planned period of residence is for more than three months.

2. The deadline for submitting the residence card application may not be less than three months from the date of arrival.

3. Failure to comply with the requirement to apply for a residence card may make the person concerned liable to proportionate and non-discriminatory sanctions.

Article 10   Issue of residence cards

1. The right of residence of family members of a Union citizen who are not nationals of a Member State shall be evidenced by the issuing of a document called 'Residence card of a family member of a Union citizen' no later than six months from the date on which they submit the application. A certificate of application for the residence card shall be issued immediately.

2. For the residence card to be issued, Member States shall require presentation of the following documents:

   (a) a valid passport;

   (b) a document attesting to the existence of a family relationship or of a registered partnership;

   (c) the registration certificate or, in the absence of a registration system, any other proof of residence in the host Member State of the Union citizen whom they are accompanying or joining;

   (d) in cases falling under points (c) and (d) of Article 2(2), documentary evidence that the conditions laid down therein are met;

   (e) in cases falling under Article 3(2)(a), a document issued by the relevant authority in the country of origin or country from which they are arriving certifying that they are dependants or members of the household of the Union citizen, or proof of the existence of serious health grounds which strictly require the personal care of the family member by the Union citizen;

(f) in cases falling under Article 3(2)(b), proof of the existence of a durable relationship with the Union citizen.

Article 11   Validity of the residence card

1. The residence card provided for by Article 10(1) shall be valid for five years from the date of issue or for the envisaged period of residence of the Union citizen, if this period is less than five years.

2. The validity of the residence card shall not be affected by temporary absences not exceeding six months a year, or by absences of a longer duration for compulsory military service or by one absence of a maximum of twelve consecutive months for important reasons such as pregnancy and childbirth, serious illness, study or vocational training, or a posting in another Member State or a third country.

Article 12   Retention of the right of residence by family members in the event of death or departure of the Union citizen

1. Without prejudice to the second subparagraph, the Union citizen's death or departure from the host Member State shall not affect the right of residence of his/her family members who are nationals of a Member State.

Before acquiring the right of permanent residence, the persons concerned must meet the conditions laid down in points (a), (b), (c) or (d) of Article 7(1).

2. Without prejudice to the second subparagraph, the Union citizen's death shall not entail loss of the right of residence of his/her family members who are not nationals of a Member State and who have been residing in the host Member State as family members for at least one year before the Union citizen's death.

Before acquiring the right of permanent residence, the right of residence of the persons concerned shall remain subject to the requirement that they are able to show that they are workers or self-employed persons or that they have sufficient resources for themselves and their family members not to become a burden on the social assistance system of the host Member State during their period of residence and have comprehensive sickness insurance cover in the host Member State, or that they are members of the family, already constituted in the host Member State, of a person satisfying these requirements. 'Sufficient resources' shall be as defined in Article 8(4).

Such family members shall retain their right of residence exclusively on a personal basis.

3. The Union citizen's departure from the host Member State or his/her death shall not entail loss of the right of residence of his/her children or of the parent who has actual custody of the children, irrespective of nationality, if the children reside in the host Member State and are enrolled at an educational establishment, for the purpose of studying there, until the completion of their studies.

Article 13   Retention of the right of residence by family members in the event of divorce, annulment of marriage or termination of registered partnership

1. Without prejudice to the second subparagraph, divorce, annulment of the Union citizen's marriage or termination of his/her registered partnership, as referred to in point 2(b) of Article 2 shall not affect the right of residence of his/her family members who are nationals of a Member State.

Before acquiring the right of permanent residence, the persons concerned must meet the conditions laid down in points (a), (b), (c) or (d) of Article 7(1).

2. Without prejudice to the second subparagraph, divorce, annulment of marriage or termination of the registered partnership referred to in point 2(b) of Article 2 shall not entail loss of the right of residence of a Union citizen's family members who are not nationals of a Member State where:

(a) prior to initiation of the divorce or annulment proceedings or termination of the registered partnership referred to in point 2(b) of Article 2, the marriage or registered partnership has lasted at least three years, including one year in the host Member State; or

(b) by agreement between the spouses or the partners referred to in point 2(b) of Article 2 or by court order, the spouse or partner who is not a national of a Member State has custody of the Union citizen's children; or

(c) this is warranted by particularly difficult circumstances, such as having been a victim of domestic violence while the marriage or registered partnership was subsisting; or

(d) by agreement between the spouses or partners referred to in point 2(b) of Article 2 or by court order, the spouse or partner who is not a national of a Member State has the right of access to a minor child, provided that the court has ruled that such access must be in the host Member State, and for as long as is required.

Before acquiring the right of permanent residence, the right of residence of the persons concerned shall remain subject to the requirement that they are able to show that they are workers or self-employed persons or that they have sufficient resources for themselves and their family members not to become a burden on the social assistance system of the host Member State during their period of residence and have comprehensive sickness insurance cover in the host Member State, or that they are members of the family, already constituted in the host Member State, of a person satisfying these requirements. 'Sufficient resources' shall be as defined in Article 8(4).

Such family members shall retain their right of residence exclusively on a personal basis.

Article 14   Retention of the right of residence

1. Union citizens and their family members shall have the right of residence provided for in Article 6, as long as they do not become an unreasonable burden on the social assistance system of the host Member State.

2. Union citizens and their family members shall have the right of residence provided for in Articles 7, 12 and 13 as long as they meet the conditions set out therein. In specific cases where there is a reasonable doubt as to whether a Union citizen or his/her family members satisfies the conditions set out in Articles 7, 12 and 13, Member States may verify if these conditions are fulfilled. This verification shall not be carried out systematically.

3. An expulsion measure shall not be the automatic consequence of a Union citizen's or his or her family member's recourse to the social assistance system of the host Member State.

4. By way of derogation from paragraphs 1 and 2 and without prejudice to the provisions of Chapter VI, an expulsion measure may in no case be adopted against Union citizens or their family members if:

(a) the Union citizens are workers or self-employed persons, or

(b) the Union citizens entered the territory of the host Member State in order to seek employment. In this case, the Union citizens and their family members may not be expelled for as long as the Union citizens can provide evidence that they are continuing to seek employment and that they have a genuine chance of being engaged.

Article 15   Procedural safeguards

1. The procedures provided for by Articles 30 and 31 shall apply by analogy to all decisions restricting free movement of Union citizens and their family members on grounds other than public policy, public security or public health.

2. Expiry of the identity card or passport on the basis of which the person concerned entered the host Member State and was issued with a registration certificate or residence card shall not constitute a ground for expulsion from the host Member State.

3. The host Member State may not impose a ban on entry in the context of an expulsion decision to which paragraph 1 applies.

Chapter IV   Right of permanent residence

Section I   Eligibility

Article 16   General rule for Union citizens and their family members

1. Union citizens who have resided legally for a continuous period of five years in the host Member State shall have the right of permanent residence there. This right shall not be subject to the conditions provided for in Chapter III.

2. Paragraph 1 shall apply also to family members who are not nationals of a Member State and have legally resided with the Union citizen in the host Member State for a continuous period of five years.

3. Continuity of residence shall not be affected by temporary absences not exceeding a total of six months a year, or by absences of a longer duration for compulsory military service, or by one absence of a maximum of twelve consecutive months for important reasons such as pregnancy and childbirth, serious illness, study or vocational training, or a posting in another Member State or a third country.

4. Once acquired, the right of permanent residence shall be lost only through absence from the host Member State for a period exceeding two consecutive years.

Article 17   Exemptions for persons no longer working in the host Member State and their family members

1. By way of derogation from Article 16, the right of permanent residence in the host Member State shall be enjoyed before completion of a continuous period of five years of residence by:

    (a) workers or self-employed persons who, at the time they stop working, have reached the age laid down by the law of that Member State for entitlement to an old age pension or workers who cease paid employment to take early retirement, provided that they have been working in that Member State for at least the preceding twelve months and have resided there continuously for more than three years.

    If the law of the host Member State does not grant the right to an old age pension to certain categories of self-employed persons, the age condition shall be deemed to have been met once the person concerned has reached the age of 60;

    (b) workers or self-employed persons who have resided continuously in the host Member State for more than two years and stop working there as a result of permanent incapacity to work.

    If such incapacity is the result of an accident at work or an occupational disease entitling the person concerned to a benefit payable in full or in part by an institution in the host Member State, no condition shall be imposed as to length of residence;

    (c) workers or self-employed persons who, after three years of continuous employment and residence in the host Member State, work in an employed or self-employed capacity in another Member State, while retaining their place of residence in the host Member State, to which they return, as a rule, each day or at least once a week.

    For the purposes of entitlement to the rights referred to in points (a) and (b), periods of employment spent in the Member State in which the person concerned is working shall be regarded as having been spent in the host Member State.

Periods of involuntary unemployment duly recorded by the relevant employment office, periods not worked for reasons not of the person's own making and absences from work or cessation of work due to illness or accident shall be regarded as periods of employment.

2. The conditions as to length of residence and employment laid down in point (a) of paragraph 1 and the condition as to length of residence laid down in point (b) of paragraph 1 shall not apply if the worker's or the self-employed person's spouse or partner as referred to in point 2(b) of Article 2 is a national of the host Member State or has lost the nationality of that Member State by marriage to that worker or self-employed person.

3. Irrespective of nationality, the family members of a worker or a self-employed person who are residing with him in the territory of the host Member State shall have the right of permanent residence in that Member State, if the worker or self-employed person has acquired himself the right of permanent residence in that Member State on the basis of paragraph 1.

4. If, however, the worker or self-employed person dies while still working but before acquiring permanent residence status in the host Member State on the basis of paragraph 1, his family members who are residing with him in the host Member State shall acquire the right of permanent residence there, on condition that:

    (a) the worker or self-employed person had, at the time of death, resided continuously on the territory of that Member State for two years; or

    (b) the death resulted from an accident at work or an occupational disease; or

(c) the surviving spouse lost the nationality of that Member State following marriage to the worker or self-employed person.

Article 18 Acquisition of the right of permanent residence by certain family members who are not nationals of a Member State

Without prejudice to Article 17, the family members of a Union citizen to whom Articles 12(2) and 13(2) apply, who satisfy the conditions laid down therein, shall acquire the right of permanent residence after residing legally for a period of five consecutive years in the host Member State.

Section II Administrative formalities

Article 19 Document certifying permanent residence for Union citizens

1. Upon application Member States shall issue Union citizens entitled to permanent residence, after having verified duration of residence, with a document certifying permanent residence.

2. The document certifying permanent residence shall be issued as soon as possible.

Article 20 Permanent residence card for family members who are not nationals of a Member State

1. Member States shall issue family members who are not nationals of a Member State entitled to permanent residence with a permanent residence card within six months of the submission of the application. The permanent residence card shall be renewable automatically every ten years.

2. The application for a permanent residence card shall be submitted before the residence card expires. Failure to comply with the requirement to apply for a permanent residence card may render the person concerned liable to proportionate and non-discriminatory sanctions.

3. Interruption in residence not exceeding two consecutive years shall not affect the validity of the permanent residence card.

Article 21 Continuity of residence

For the purposes of this Directive, continuity of residence may be attested by any means of proof in use in the host Member State. Continuity of residence is broken by any expulsion decision duly enforced against the person concerned.

Chapter V Provisions common to the right of residence and the right of permanent residence

Article 22 Territorial scope

The right of residence and the right of permanent residence shall cover the whole territory of the host Member State. Member States may impose territorial restrictions on the right of residence and the right of permanent residence only where the same restrictions apply to their own nationals.

Article 23 Related rights

Irrespective of nationality, the family members of a Union citizen who have the right of residence or the right of permanent residence in a Member State shall be entitled to take up employment or self-employment there.

Article 24 Equal treatment

1. Subject to such specific provisions as are expressly provided for in the Treaty and secondary law, all Union citizens residing on the basis of this Directive in the territory of the host Member State shall enjoy equal treatment with the nationals of that Member State within the scope of the Treaty. The benefit of this right shall be extended to family members who are not nationals of a Member State and who have the right of residence or permanent residence.

2. By way of derogation from paragraph 1, the host Member State shall not be obliged to confer entitlement to social assistance during the first three months of residence or, where appropriate, the longer period provided for in Article 14(4)(b), nor shall it be obliged, prior to acquisition of the right of permanent residence, to grant maintenance aid for studies, including vocational training,

consisting in student grants or student loans to persons other than workers, self-employed persons, persons who retain such status and members of their families.

Article 25   General provisions concerning residence documents

1. Possession of a registration certificate as referred to in Article 8, of a document certifying permanent residence, of a certificate attesting submission of an application for a family member residence card, of a residence card or of a permanent residence card, may under no circumstances be made a precondition for the exercise of a right or the completion of an administrative formality, as entitlement to rights may be attested by any other means of proof.

2. All documents mentioned in paragraph 1 shall be issued free of charge or for a charge not exceeding that imposed on nationals for the issuing of similar documents.

Article 26   Checks

Member States may carry out checks on compliance with any requirement deriving from their national legislation for non-nationals always to carry their registration certificate or residence card, provided that the same requirement applies to their own nationals as regards their identity card. In the event of failure to comply with this requirement, Member States may impose the same sanctions as those imposed on their own nationals for failure to carry their identity card.

Chapter VI Restrictions on the right of entry and the right of residence on grounds of public policy, public security or public health

Article 27   General principles

1. Subject to the provisions of this Chapter, Member States may restrict the freedom of movement and residence of Union citizens and their family members, irrespective of nationality, on grounds of public policy, public security or public health. These grounds shall not be invoked to serve economic ends.

2. Measures taken on grounds of public policy or public security shall comply with the principle of proportionality and shall be based exclusively on the personal conduct of the individual concerned.

Previous criminal convictions shall not in themselves constitute grounds for taking such measures.

The personal conduct of the individual concerned must represent a genuine, present and sufficiently serious threat affecting one of the fundamental interests of society. Justifications that are isolated from the particulars of the case or that rely on considerations of general prevention shall not be accepted.

3. In order to ascertain whether the person concerned represents a danger for public policy or public security, when issuing the registration certificate or, in the absence of a registration system, not later than three months from the date of arrival of the person concerned on its territory or from the date of reporting his/her presence within the territory, as provided for in Article 5(5), or when issuing the residence card, the host Member State may, should it consider this essential, request the Member State of origin and, if need be, other Member States to provide information concerning any previous police record the person concerned may have. Such enquiries shall not be made as a matter of routine. The Member State consulted shall give its reply within two months.

4. The Member State which issued the passport or identity card shall allow the holder of the document who has been expelled on grounds of public policy, public security, or public health from another Member State to re-enter its territory without any formality even if the document is no longer valid or the nationality of the holder is in dispute.

Article 28   Protection against expulsion

1. Before taking an expulsion decision on grounds of public policy or public security, the host Member State shall take account of considerations such as how long the individual concerned has resided on its territory, his/her age, state of health, family and economic situation, social and cultural integration into the host Member State and the extent of his/her links with the country of origin.

2. The host Member State may not take an expulsion decision against Union citizens or their family members, irrespective of nationality, who have the right of permanent residence on its territory, except on serious grounds of public policy or public security.

3. An expulsion decision may not be taken against Union citizens, except if the decision is based on imperative grounds of public security, as defined by Member States, if they:

(a) have resided in the host Member State for the previous ten years; or

(b) are a minor, except if the expulsion is necessary for the best interests of the child, as provided for in the United Nations Convention on the Rights of the Child of 20 November 1989.

Article 29   Public health

1. The only diseases justifying measures restricting freedom of movement shall be the diseases with epidemic potential as defined by the relevant instruments of the World Health Organisation and other infectious diseases or contagious parasitic diseases if they are the subject of protection provisions applying to nationals of the host Member State.

2. Diseases occurring after a three-month period from the date of arrival shall not constitute grounds for expulsion from the territory.

3. Where there are serious indications that it is necessary, Member States may, within three months of the date of arrival, require persons entitled to the right of residence to undergo, free of charge, a medical examination to certify that they are not suffering from any of the conditions referred to in paragraph 1. Such medical examinations may not be required as a matter of routine.

Article 30   Notification of decisions

1. The persons concerned shall be notified in writing of any decision taken under Article 27(1), in such a way that they are able to comprehend its content and the implications for them.

2. The persons concerned shall be informed, precisely and in full, of the public policy, public security or public health grounds on which the decision taken in their case is based, unless this is contrary to the interests of State security.

3. The notification shall specify the court or administrative authority with which the person concerned may lodge an appeal, the time limit for the appeal and, where applicable, the time allowed for the person to leave the territory of the Member State. Save in duly substantiated cases of urgency, the time allowed to leave the territory shall be not less than one month from the date of notification.

Article 31   Procedural safeguards

1. The persons concerned shall have access to judicial and, where appropriate, administrative redress procedures in the host Member State to appeal against or seek review of any decision taken against them on the grounds of public policy, public security or public health.

2. Where the application for appeal against or judicial review of the expulsion decision is accompanied by an application for an interim order to suspend enforcement of that decision, actual removal from the territory may not take place until such time as the decision on the interim order has been taken, except:

– where the expulsion decision is based on a previous judicial decision; or

– where the persons concerned have had previous access to judicial review; or

– where the expulsion decision is based on imperative grounds of public security under Article 28(3).

3. The redress procedures shall allow for an examination of the legality of the decision, as well as of the facts and circumstances on which the proposed measure is based. They shall ensure that the decision is not disproportionate, particularly in view of the requirements laid down in Article 28.

4. Member States may exclude the individual concerned from their territory pending the redress procedure, but they may not prevent the individual from submitting his/her defence in person, except when his/her appearance may cause serious troubles to public policy or public security or when the appeal or judicial review concerns a denial of entry to the territory.

Article 32   Duration of exclusion orders

1. Persons excluded on grounds of public policy or public security may submit an application for lifting of the exclusion order after a reasonable period, depending on the circumstances, and in any event after three years from enforcement of the final exclusion order which has been validly adopted in accordance with Community law, by putting forward arguments to establish that there has been a material change in the circumstances which justified the decision ordering their exclusion.

The Member State concerned shall reach a decision on this application within six months of its submission.

2. The persons referred to in paragraph 1 shall have no right of entry to the territory of the Member State concerned while their application is being considered.

Article 33   Expulsion as a penalty or legal consequence

1. Expulsion orders may not be issued by the host Member State as a penalty or legal consequence of a custodial penalty, unless they conform to the requirements of Articles 27, 28 and 29.

2. If an expulsion order, as provided for in paragraph 1, is enforced more than two years after it was issued, the Member State shall check that the individual concerned is currently and genuinely a threat to public policy or public security and shall assess whether there has been any material change in the circumstances since the expulsion order was issued.

Chapter VII   Final provisions

Article 34   Publicity

Member States shall disseminate information concerning the rights and obligations of Union citizens and their family members on the subjects covered by this Directive, particularly by means of awareness-raising campaigns conducted through national and local media and other means of communication.

Article 35   Abuse of rights

Member States may adopt the necessary measures to refuse, terminate or withdraw any right conferred by this Directive in the case of abuse of rights or fraud, such as marriages of convenience. Any such measure shall be proportionate and subject to the procedural safeguards provided for in Articles 30 and 31.

Article 36   Sanctions

Member States shall lay down provisions on the sanctions applicable to breaches of national rules adopted for the implementation of this Directive and shall take the measures required for their application. The sanctions laid down shall be effective and proportionate. Member States shall notify the Commission of these provisions not later than 30 April 2006 and as promptly as possible in the case of any subsequent changes.

Article 37   More favourable national provisions

The provisions of this Directive shall not affect any laws, regulations or administrative provisions laid down by a Member State which would be more favourable to the persons covered by this Directive.

Article 38   Repeals

(Paragraph 1 has been repealed.)

2. Directives 64/221/EEC, 68/360/EEC, 72/194/EEC, 73/148/EEC, 75/34/EEC, 75/35/EEC, 90/364/EEC, 90/365/EEC and 93/96/EEC shall be repealed with effect from 30 April 2006.

3. References made to the repealed provisions and Directives shall be construed as being made to this Directive.

Article 39   Report

No later than 30 April 2008 the Commission shall submit a report on the application of this Directive to the European Parliament and the Council, together with any necessary proposals, notably on the opportunity to extend the period of time during which Union citizens and their family members may reside in the territory of the host Member State without any conditions. The Member States shall provide the Commission with the information needed to produce the report.

Article 40   Transposition

1. Member States shall bring into force the laws, regulations and administrative provisions necessary to comply with this Directive by 30 April 2006.

When Member States adopt those measures, they shall contain a reference to this Directive or shall be accompanied by such a reference on the occasion of their official publication. The methods of making such reference shall be laid down by the Member States.

2. Member States shall communicate to the Commission the text of the provisions of national law which they adopt in the field covered by this Directive together with a table showing how the provisions of this Directive correspond to the national provisions adopted.

Article 41   Entry into force

This Directive shall enter into force on the day of its publication in the *Official Journal of the European Union*.

Article 42   Addressees

This Directive is addressed to the Member States.

Done at Brussels, 29 April 2004.

Directive 2005/36/EC of the European Parliament and of the Council of 7 September 2005 on the recognition of professional qualifications*

[OJ 2005 L255/22]

THE EUROPEAN PARLIAMENT AND THE COUNCIL OF THE EUROPEAN UNION,

Having regard to the Treaty establishing the European Community, and in particular Article 40, Article 47(1), the first and third sentences of Article 47(2), and Article 55 thereof,

Having regard to the proposal from the Commission,[1]

Having regard to the opinion of the European Economic and Social Committee,[2]

Acting in accordance with the procedure laid down in Article 251 of the Treaty,[3]

Whereas:

(1) Pursuant to Article 3(1)(c) of the Treaty, the abolition, as between Member States, of obstacles to the free movement of persons and services is one of the objectives of the Community. For nationals of the Member States, this includes, in particular, the right to pursue a profession, in a self-employed or employed capacity, in a Member State other than the one in which they have obtained their professional qualifications. In addition, Article 47(1) of the Treaty lays down that directives shall be issued for the mutual recognition of diplomas, certificates and other evidence of formal qualifications.

(2) Following the European Council of Lisbon on 23 and 24 March 2000, the Commission adopted a Communication on 'An Internal Market Strategy for Services', aimed in particular at making the free provision of services within the Community as simple as within an individual Member State. Further to the Communication from the Commission entitled 'New European Labour Markets, Open to All, with Access to All', the European Council of Stockholm on 23 and 24 March 2001 entrusted the Commission with presenting for the 2002 Spring European Council specific proposals for a more uniform, transparent and flexible regime of recognition of qualifications.

---

* **Editor's Note:** As amended following Bulgarian and Romanian entry to the EU (OJ 2006 L363/141) and corrected by OJ 2007 L271/18 and OJ 2008 L93/28. Further amended by OJ 2012 L180/9 (Regulation 632/2012), Directive 2013/25 (OJ 2013 L158/368), Directive 2013/55 (OJ 2013 L354/132), and Decision 2019/608 (OJ 2019 L104/1).

1 OJ C 181 E, 30.7.2002, p. 183.   2 OJ C 61, 14.3. 2003, p. 67.

3 Opinion of the European Parliament of 11 February 2004 (OJ C 97 E, 22.4.2004, p. 230), Council Common Position of 21 December 2004 (OJ C 58 E, 8.3.2005, p. 1) and Position of the European Parliament of 11 May 2005 (not yet published in the Official Journal). Council Decision of 6 June 2005.

(3) The guarantee conferred by this Directive on persons having acquired their professional qualifications in a Member State to have access to the same profession and pursue it in another Member State with the same rights as nationals is without prejudice to compliance by the migrant professional with any non-discriminatory conditions of pursuit which might be laid down by the latter Member State, provided that these are objectively justified and proportionate.

(4) In order to facilitate the free provision of services, there should be specific rules aimed at extending the possibility of pursuing professional activities under the original professional title. In the case of information society services provided at a distance, the provisions of Directive 2000/31/EC of the European Parliament and of the Council of 8 June 2000 on certain legal aspects of information society services, in particular electronic commerce, in the Internal Market[4], should also apply.

(5) In view of the different systems established for the cross-border provision of services on a temporary and occasional basis on the one hand, and for establishment on the other, the criteria for distinguishing between these two concepts in the event of the movement of the service provider to the territory of the host Member State should be clarified.

(6) The facilitation of service provision has to be ensured in the context of strict respect for public health and safety and consumer protection. Therefore, specific provisions should be envisaged for regulated professions having public health or safety implications, which provide cross-frontier services on a temporary or occasional basis.

(7) Host Member States may, where necessary and in accordance with Community law, provide for declaration requirements. These requirements should not lead to a disproportionate burden on service providers nor hinder or render less attractive the exercise of the freedom to provide services. The need for such requirements should be reviewed periodically in the light of the progress made in establishing a Community framework for administrative cooperation between Member States.

(8) The service provider should be subject to the application of disciplinary rules of the host Member State having a direct and specific link with the professional qualifications, such as the definition of the profession, the scope of activities covered by a profession or reserved to it, the use of titles and serious professional malpractice which is directly and specifically linked to consumer protection and safety.

(9) While maintaining, for the freedom of establishment, the principles and safeguards underlying the different systems for recognition in force, the rules of such systems should be improved in the light of experience. Moreover, the relevant directives have been amended on several occasions, and their provisions should be reorganised and rationalised by standardising the principles applicable. It is therefore necessary to replace Council Directives 89/48/EEC[5] and 92/51/ EEC,[6] as well as Directive 1999/42/EC of the European Parliament and of the Council[7] on the general system for the recognition of professional qualifications, and Council Directives 77/452/ EEC,[8] 77/453/EEC,[9] 78/686/EEC,[10] 78/687/EEC,[11] 78/1026/EEC,[12] 78/1027/EEC,[13] 80/154/EEC,[14] 80/155/EEC,[15] 85/384/EEC,[16] 85/432/EEC,[17] 85/433/EEC[18] and 93/16/EEC[19] concerning the professions of nurse

---

[4] OJ L 178, 17.7.2000, p. 1.

[5] OJ L 19, 24.1.1989, p. 16. Directive as amended by Directive 2001/19/EC of the European Parliament and of the Council (OJ L 206, 31.7.2001, p. 1).

[6] OJ L 209, 24.7.1992, p. 25. Directive as last amended by Commission Decision 2004/108/EC (OJ L 32, 5.2.2004, p. 15).

[7] OJ L 201, 31.7.1999, p. 77.

[8] OJ L 176, 15.7.1977, p. 1. Directive as last amended by the Act of Accession.

[9] OJ L 176, 15.7.1977, p. 8. Directive as last amended by Directive 2001/19/EC.

[10] OJ L 233, 24.8.1978, p. 1. Directive as last amended by the Act of Accession.

[11] OJ L 233, 24.8.1978, p. 10. Directive as last amended by the Act of Accession.

[12] OJ L 362, 23.12.1978, p. 1. Directive as last amended by Directive 2001/19/EC.

[13] OJ L 362, 23.12.1978, p. 7. Directive as last amended by Directive 2001/19/EC.

[14] OJ L 33, 11.2.1980, p. 1. Directive as last amended by the Act of Accession.

[15] OJ L 33, 11.2.1980, p. 8. Directive as last amended by Directive 2001/19/EC.

[16] OJ L 223, 21.8.1985, p. 15. Directive as last amended by the Act of Accession.

[17] OJ L 253, 24.9.1985, p. 34. Directive as amended by Directive 2001/19/EC.

[18] OJ L 253, 24.9.1985, p. 37. Directive as last amended by the Act of Accession.

[19] OJ L 165, 7.7.1993, p. 1. Directive as last amended by Regulation (EC) No 1882/2003 of the European Parliament and of the Council (OJ L 284, 31.10.2003, p. 1).

responsible for general care, dental practitioner, veterinary surgeon, midwife, architect, pharmacist and doctor, by combining them in a single text.

(10) This Directive does not create an obstacle to the possibility of Member States recognising, in accordance with their rules, the professional qualifications acquired outside the territory of the European Union by third country nationals. All recognition should respect in any case minimum training conditions for certain professions.

(11) In the case of the professions covered by the general system for the recognition of qualifications, hereinafter referred to as 'the general system', Member States should retain the right to lay down the minimum level of qualification required to ensure the quality of the services provided on their territory. However, pursuant to Articles 10, 39 and 43 of the Treaty, they should not require a national of a Member State to obtain qualifications, which they generally lay down only in terms of the diplomas awarded under their national educational system, where the person concerned has already obtained all or part of those qualifications in another Member State. As a result, it should be laid down that any host Member State in which a profession is regulated must take account of the qualifications obtained in another Member State and assess whether they correspond to those which it requires. The general system for recognition, however, does not prevent a Member State from making any person pursuing a profession on its territory subject to specific requirements due to the application of professional rules justified by the general public interest. Rules of this kind relate, for example, to organisation of the profession, professional standards, including those concerning ethics, and supervision and liability. Lastly, this Directive is not intended to interfere with Member States' legitimate interest in preventing any of their citizens from evading enforcement of the national law relating to professions.

(12) This Directive concerns the recognition by Member States of professional qualifications acquired in other Member States. It does not, however, concern the recognition by Member States of recognition decisions adopted by other Member States pursuant to this Directive. Consequently, individuals holding professional qualifications which have been recognised pursuant to this Directive may not use such recognition to obtain in their Member State of origin rights different from those conferred by the professional qualification obtained in that Member State, unless they provide evidence that they have obtained additional professional qualifications in the host Member State.

(13) In order to define the mechanism of recognition under the general system, it is necessary to group the various national education and training schemes into different levels. These levels, which are established only for the purpose of the operation of the general system, have no effect upon the national education and training structures nor upon the competence of Member States in this field.

(14) The mechanism of recognition established by Directives 89/48/EEC and 92/51/EEC remains unchanged. As a consequence, the holder of a diploma certifying successful completion of training at post-secondary level of a duration of at least one year should be permitted access to a regulated profession in a Member State where access is contingent upon possession of a diploma certifying successful completion of higher or university education of four years' duration, regardless of the level to which the diploma required in the host Member State belongs. Conversely, where access to a regulated profession is contingent upon successful completion of higher or university education of more than four years, such access should be permitted only to holders of a diploma certifying successful completion of higher or university education of at least three years' duration.

(15) In the absence of harmonisation of the minimum training conditions for access to the professions governed by the general system, it should be possible for the host Member State to impose a compensation measure. This measure should be proportionate and, in particular, take account of the applicant's professional experience. Experience shows that requiring the migrant to choose between an aptitude test or an adaptation period offers adequate safeguards as regards the latter's level of qualification, so that any derogation from that choice should in each case be justified by an imperative requirement in the general interest.

(16) In order to promote the free movement of professionals, while ensuring an adequate level of qualification, various professional associations and organisations or Member States should be

able to propose common platforms at European level. This Directive should take account, under certain conditions, in compliance with the competence of Member States to decide the qualifications required for the pursuit of professions in their territory as well as the contents and the organisation of their systems of education and professional training and in compliance with Community law, and in particular Community law on competition, of those initiatives, while promoting, in this context, a more automatic character of recognition under the general system. Professional associations which are in a position to submit common platforms should be representative at national and European level. A common platform is a set of criteria which make it possible to compensate for the widest range of substantial differences which have been identified between the training requirements in at least two-thirds of the Member States including all the Member States which regulate that profession. These criteria could, for example, include requirements such as additional training, an adaptation period under supervised practice, an aptitude test, or a prescribed minimum level of professional practice, or combinations thereof.

(17) In order to take into account all situations for which there is still no provision relating to the recognition of professional qualifications, the general system should be extended to those cases which are not covered by a specific system, either where the profession is not covered by one of those systems or where, although the profession is covered by such a specific system, the applicant does not for some particular and exceptional reason meet the conditions to benefit from it.

(18) There is a need to simplify the rules allowing access to a number of industrial, commercial and craft activities, in Member States where those professions are regulated, in so far as those activities have been pursued for a reasonable and sufficiently recent period of time in another Member State, while maintaining for those activities a system of automatic recognition based on professional experience.

(19) Freedom of movement and the mutual recognition of the evidence of formal qualifications of doctors, nurses responsible for general care, dental practitioners, veterinary surgeons, midwives, pharmacists and architects should be based on the fundamental principle of automatic recognition of the evidence of formal qualifications on the basis of coordinated minimum conditions for training. In addition, access in the Member States to the professions of doctor, nurse responsible for general care, dental practitioner, veterinary surgeon, midwife and pharmacist should be made conditional upon the possession of a given qualification ensuring that the person concerned has undergone training which meets the minimum conditions laid down. This system should be supplemented by a number of acquired rights from which qualified professionals benefit under certain conditions.

(20) To allow for the characteristics of the qualification system for doctors and dental practitioners and the related *acquis communautaire* in the area of mutual recognition, the principle of automatic recognition of medical and dental specialities common to at least two Member States should continue to apply to all specialities recognised on the date of adoption of this Directive. To simplify the system, however, automatic recognition should apply after the date of entry into force of this Directive only to those new medical specialities common to at least two-fifths of Member States. Moreover, this Directive does not prevent Member States from agreeing amongst themselves on automatic recognition for certain medical and dental specialities common to them but not automatically recognised within the meaning of this Directive, according to their own rules.

(21) Automatic recognition of formal qualifications of doctor with basic training should be without prejudice to the competence of Member States to associate this qualification with professional activities or not.

(22) All Member States should recognise the profession of dental practitioner as a specific profession distinct from that of medical practitioner, whether or not specialised in odontostomatology. Member States should ensure that the training given to dental practitioners equips them with the skills needed for prevention, diagnosis and treatment relating to anomalies and illnesses of the teeth, mouth, jaws and associated tissues. The professional activity of the dental practitioner should be carried out by holders of a qualification as dental practitioner set out in this Directive.

(23) It did not appear desirable to lay down standardised training for midwives for all the Member States. Rather, the latter should have the greatest possible freedom to organise their training.

(24) With a view to simplifying this Directive, reference should be made to the concept of 'pharmacist' in order to delimit the scope of the provisions relating to the automatic recognition of the qualifications, without prejudice to the special features of the national regulations governing those activities.

(25) Holders of qualifications as a pharmacist are specialists in the field of medicines and should, in principle, have access in all Member States to a minimum range of activities in this field. In defining this minimum range, this Directive should neither have the effect of limiting the activities accessible to pharmacists in the Member States, in particular as regards medical biology analyses, nor create a monopoly for those professionals, as this remains a matter solely for the Member States. The provisions of this Directive are without prejudice to the possibility for the Member States to impose supplementary training conditions for access to activities not included in the coordinated minimum range of activities. This means that the host Member State should be able to impose these conditions on the nationals who hold qualifications which are covered by automatic recognition within the meaning of this Directive.

(26) This Directive does not coordinate all the conditions for access to activities in the field of pharmacy and the pursuit of these activities. In particular, the geographical distribution of pharmacies and the monopoly for dispensing medicines should remain a matter for the Member States. This Directive leaves unchanged the legislative, regulatory and administrative provisions of the Member States forbidding companies from pursuing certain pharmacists' activities or subjecting the pursuit of such activities to certain conditions.

(27) Architectural design, the quality of buildings, their harmonious incorporation into their surroundings, respect for natural and urban landscapes and for the public and private heritage are a matter of public interest. Mutual recognition of qualifications should therefore be based on qualitative and quantitative criteria which ensure that the holders of recognised qualifications are in a position to understand and translate the needs of individuals, social groups and authorities as regards spatial planning, the design, organisation and realisation of structures, conservation and the exploitation of the architectural heritage, and protection of natural balances.

(28) National regulations in the field of architecture and on access to and the pursuit of the professional activities of an architect vary widely in scope. In most Member States, activities in the field of architecture are pursued, de jure or de facto, by persons bearing the title of architect alone or accompanied by another title, without those persons having a monopoly on the pursuit of such activities, unless there are legislative provisions to the contrary. These activities, or some of them, may also be pursued by other professionals, in particular by engineers who have undergone special training in the field of construction or the art of building. With a view to simplifying this Directive, reference should be made to the concept of 'architect' in order to delimit the scope of the provisions relating to the automatic recognition of the qualifications in the field of architecture, without prejudice to the special features of the national regulations governing those activities.

(29) Where a national and European-level professional organisation or association for a regulated profession makes a reasoned request for specific provisions for the recognition of qualifications on the basis of coordination of minimum training conditions, the Commission shall assess the appropriateness of adopting a proposal for the amendment of this Directive.

(30) In order to ensure the effectiveness of the system for the recognition of professional qualifications, uniform formalities and rules of procedure should be defined for its implementation, as well as certain details of the pursuit of the profession.

(31) Since collaboration among the Member States and between them and the Commission is likely to facilitate the implementation of this Directive and compliance with the obligations deriving from it, the means of collaboration should be organised.

(32) The introduction, at European level, of professional cards by professional associations or organisations could facilitate the mobility of professionals, in particular by speeding up the exchange of information between the host Member State and the Member State of origin. This professional

card should make it possible to monitor the career of professionals who establish themselves in various Member States. Such cards could contain information, in full respect of data protection provisions, on the professional's professional qualifications (university or institution attended, qualifications obtained, professional experience), his legal establishment, penalties received relating to his profession and the details of the relevant competent authority.

(33) The establishment of a network of contact points with the task of providing the citizens of the Member States with information and assistance will make it possible to ensure that the system of recognition is transparent. These contact points will provide any citizen who so requests and the Commission with all the information and addresses relevant to the recognition procedure. The designation of a single contact point by each Member State within this network does not affect the organisation of competencies at national level. In particular, it does not prevent the designation at national level of several offices, the contact point designated within the aforementioned network being in charge of coordinating with the other offices and informing the citizen, where necessary, of the details of the relevant competent office.

(34) Administering the various systems of recognition set up by the sectoral directives and the general system has proved cumbersome and complex. There is therefore a need to simplify the administration and updating of this Directive to take account of scientific and technical progress, in particular where the minimum conditions of training are coordinated with a view to automatic recognition of qualifications. A single committee for the recognition of professional qualifications should be set up for this purpose, and suitable involvement of representatives of the professional organisations, also at European level, should be ensured.

(35) The measures necessary for the implementation of this Directive should be adopted in accordance with Council Decision 1999/468/EC of 28 June 1999 laying down the procedures for the exercise of implementing powers conferred on the Commission.[20]

(36) The preparation by the Member States of a periodic report on the implementation of this Directive, containing statistical data, will make it possible to determine the impact of the system for the recognition of professional qualifications.

(37) There should be a suitable procedure for adopting temporary measures if the application of any provision of this Directive were to encounter major difficulties in a Member State.

(38) The provisions of this Directive do not affect the powers of the Member States as regards the organisation of their national social security system and determining the activities which must be pursued under that system.

(39) In view of the speed of technological change and scientific progress, life-long learning is of particular importance for a large number of professions. In this context, it is for the Member States to adopt the detailed arrangements under which, through suitable ongoing training, professionals will keep abreast of technical and scientific progress.

(40) Since the objectives of this Directive, namely the rationalisation, simplification and improvement of the rules for the recognition of professional qualifications, cannot be sufficiently achieved by the Member States and can therefore be better achieved at Community level, the Community may adopt measures, in accordance with the principle of subsidiarity as set out in Article 5 of the Treaty. In accordance with the principle of proportionality, as set out in that Article, this Directive does not go beyond what is necessary in order to achieve those objectives.

(41) This Directive is without prejudice to the application of Articles 39(4) and 45 of the Treaty concerning notably notaries.

(42) This Directive applies, concerning the right of establishment and the provision of services, without prejudice to other specific legal provisions regarding the recognition of professional qualifications, such as those existing in the field of transport, insurance intermediaries and statutory auditors. This Directive does not affect the operation of Council Directive 77/249/EEC of 22 March 1977 to facilitate the effective exercise by lawyers of freedom to provide services,[21] or of Directive 98/5/EC of the European Parliament and of the Council of 16 February 1998 to facilitate practice of the

---

[20] OJ L 184, 17.7.1999, p. 23.
[21] OJ L 78, 26.3.1977, p. 17. Directive as last amended by the Act of Accession.

profession of lawyer on a permanent basis in a Member State other than that in which the qualification was obtained.[22] The recognition of professional qualifications for lawyers for the purpose of immediate establishment under the professional title of the host Member State should be covered by this Directive.

(43) To the extent that they are regulated, this Directive includes also liberal professions, which are, according to this Directive, those practised on the basis of relevant professional qualifications in a personal, responsible and professionally independent capacity by those providing intellectual and conceptual services in the interest of the client and the public. The exercise of the profession might be subject in the Member States, in conformity with the Treaty, to specific legal constraints based on national legislation and on the statutory provisions laid down autonomously, within that framework, by the respective professional representative bodies, safeguarding and developing their professionalism and quality of service and the confidentiality of relations with the client.

(44) This Directive is without prejudice to measures necessary to ensure a high level of health and consumer protection,

HAVE ADOPTED THIS DIRECTIVE:

Title I General provisions

Article 1 Purpose
This Directive establishes rules according to which a Member State which makes access to or pursuit of a regulated profession in its territory contingent upon possession of specific professional qualifications (referred to hereinafter as the host Member State) shall recognise professional qualifications obtained in one or more other Member States (referred to hereinafter as the home Member State) and which allow the holder of the said qualifications to pursue the same profession there, for access to and pursuit of that profession. This Directive also establishes rules concerning partial access to a regulated profession and recognition of professional traineeships pursued in another Member State.

Article 2 Scope
1. This Directive shall apply to all nationals of a Member State wishing to pursue a regulated profession in a Member State, including those belonging to the liberal professions, other than that in which they obtained their professional qualifications, on either a self-employed or employed basis.

   This Directive shall also apply to all nationals of a Member State who have pursued a professional traineeship outside the home Member State.

2. Each Member State may permit Member State nationals in possession of evidence of professional qualifications not obtained in a Member State to pursue a regulated profession within the meaning of Article 3(1)(a) on its territory in accordance with its rules. In the case of professions covered by Title III, Chapter III, this initial recognition shall respect the minimum training conditions laid down in that Chapter.

3. Where, for a given regulated profession, other specific arrangements directly related to the recognition of professional qualifications are established in a separate instrument of Community law, the corresponding provisions of this Directive shall not apply.

4. This Directive shall not apply to notaries who are appointed by an official act of government.

Article 3 Definitions
1. For the purposes of this Directive, the following definitions apply:
   (a) 'regulated profession': a professional activity or group of professional activities, access to which, the pursuit of which, or one of the modes of pursuit of which is subject, directly or indirectly, by virtue of legislative, regulatory or administrative provisions to the possession of specific professional qualifications; in particular, the use of a professional

---

[22] OJ L 77, 14.3.1998, p. 36. Directive as amended by the Act of Accession.

title limited by legislative, regulatory or administrative provisions to holders of a given professional qualification shall constitute a mode of pursuit. Where the first sentence of this definition does not apply, a profession referred to in paragraph 2 shall be treated as a regulated profession;

(b) 'professional qualifications': qualifications attested by evidence of formal qualifications, an attestation of competence referred to in Article 11, point (a)(i) and/or professional experience;

(c) 'evidence of formal qualifications': diplomas, certificates and other evidence issued by an authority in a Member State designated pursuant to legislative, regulatory or administrative provisions of that Member State and certifying successful completion of professional training obtained mainly in the Community. Where the first sentence of this definition does not apply, evidence of formal qualifications referred to in paragraph 3 shall be treated as evidence of formal qualifications;

(d) 'competent authority': any authority or body empowered by a Member State specifically to issue or receive training diplomas and other documents or information and to receive the applications, and take the decisions, referred to in this Directive;

(e) 'regulated education and training': any training which is specifically geared to the pursuit of a given profession and which comprises a course or courses complemented, where appropriate, by professional training, or probationary or professional practice.

The structure and level of the professional training, probationary or professional practice shall be determined by the laws, regulations or administrative provisions of the Member State concerned or monitored or approved by the authority designated for that purpose;

(f) 'professional experience': the actual and lawful full-time or equivalent part-time pursuit of the profession concerned in a Member State;

(g) 'adaptation period': the pursuit of a regulated profession in the host Member State under the responsibility of a qualified member of that profession, such period of supervised practice possibly being accompanied by further training. This period of supervised practice shall be the subject of an assessment. The detailed rules governing the adaptation period and its assessment as well as the status of a migrant under supervision shall be laid down by the competent authority in the host Member State.

The status enjoyed in the host Member State by the person undergoing the period of supervised practice, in particular in the matter of right of residence as well as obligations, social rights and benefits, allowances and remuneration, shall be established by the competent authorities in that Member State in accordance with applicable Community law;

(h) 'aptitude test': a test of the professional knowledge, skills and competences of the applicant, carried out or recognised by the competent authorities of the host Member State with the aim of assessing the ability of the applicant to pursue a regulated profession in that Member State.

In order to permit this test to be carried out, the competent authorities shall draw up a list of subjects which, on the basis of a comparison of the education and training required in the host Member State and that received by the applicant, are not covered by the diploma or other evidence of formal qualifications possessed by the applicant.

The aptitude test must take account of the fact that the applicant is a qualified professional in the home Member State or the Member State from which the applicant comes. It shall cover subjects to be selected from those on the list, knowledge of which is essential in order to be able to pursue the profession in question in the host Member State. The test may also cover knowledge of the professional rules applicable to the activities in question in the host Member State.

The detailed application of the aptitude test and the status, in the host Member State, of the applicant who wishes to prepare himself for the aptitude test in that Member State shall be determined by the competent authorities in that Member State;

(i) 'manager of an undertaking': any person who in an undertaking in the occupational field in question has pursued an activity:

    (i)   as a manager of an undertaking or a manager of a branch of an undertaking; or

    (ii) as a deputy to the proprietor or the manager of an undertaking where that post involves responsibility equivalent to that of the proprietor or manager represented; or

    (iii) in a managerial post with duties of a commercial and/or technical nature and with responsibility for one or more departments of the undertaking.

(j) 'professional traineeship': without prejudice to Article 46(4), a period of professional practice carried out under supervision provided it constitutes a condition for access to a regulated profession, and which can take place either during or after completion of an education leading to a diploma;

(k) 'European Professional Card': an electronic certificate proving either that the professional has met all the necessary conditions to provide services in a host Member State on a temporary and occasional basis or the recognition of professional qualifications for establishment in a host Member State;

(l) 'lifelong learning': all general education, vocational education and training, non-formal education and informal learning undertaken throughout life, resulting in an improvement in knowledge, skills and competences, which may include professional ethics;

(m) 'overriding reasons of general interest': reasons recognised as such in the case-law of the Court of Justice of the European Union;

(n) 'European Credit Transfer and Accumulation System or ECTS credits': the credit system for higher education used in the European Higher Education Area.

2. A profession practised by the members of an association or organisation listed in Annex I shall be treated as a regulated profession.

The purpose of the associations or organisations referred to in the first subparagraph is, in particular, to promote and maintain a high standard in the professional field concerned. To that end they are recognised in a special form by a Member State and award evidence of formal qualifications to their members, ensure that their members respect the rules of professional conduct which they prescribe, and confer on them the right to use a title or designatory letters or to benefit from a status corresponding to those formal qualifications.

On each occasion that a Member State grants recognition to an association or organisation referred to in the first subparagraph, it shall inform the Commission. The Commission shall examine whether that association or organisation fulfils the conditions provided for in the second subparagraph. In order to take due account of regulatory developments in Member States, the Commission shall be empowered to adopt delegated acts in accordance with Article 57c in order to update Annex I where the conditions provided for in the second subparagraph are satisfied.

Where the conditions provided for in the second subparagraph are not satisfied, the Commission shall adopt an implementing act in order to reject the requested update of Annex I.

3. Evidence of formal qualifications issued by a third country shall be regarded as evidence of formal qualifications if the holder has three years' professional experience in the profession concerned on the territory of the Member State which recognised that evidence of formal qualifications in accordance with Article 2(2), certified by that Member State.

Article 4   Effects of recognition

1. The recognition of professional qualifications by the host Member State shall allow beneficiaries to gain access in that Member State to the same profession as that for which they are qualified in the home Member State and to pursue it in the host Member State under the same conditions as its nationals.

2. For the purposes of this Directive, the profession which the applicant wishes to pursue in the host Member State is the same as that for which he is qualified in his home Member State if the activities covered are comparable.

3. By way of derogation from paragraph 1, partial access to a profession in the host Member State shall be granted under the conditions laid down in Article 4f.

Article 4a   European Professional Card

1. Member States shall issue holders of a professional qualification with a European Professional Card upon their request and on condition that the Commission has adopted the relevant implementing acts provided for in paragraph 7.

2. When a European Professional Card has been introduced for a particular profession by means of relevant implementing acts adopted pursuant to paragraph 7, the holder of a professional qualification concerned may choose to apply for such a Card or to make use of the procedures provided for in Titles II and III.

3. Member States shall ensure that the holder of a European Professional Card benefits from all the rights conferred by Articles 4b to 4e.

4. Where the holder of a professional qualification intends to provide services under Title II other than those covered by Article 7(4), the competent authority of the home Member State shall issue the European Professional Card in accordance with Articles 4b and 4c. The European Professional Card shall, where applicable, constitute the declaration under Article 7.

5. Where the holder of a professional qualification intends to establish himself in another Member State under Chapters I to IIIa of Title III or to provide services under Article 7(4), the competent authority of the home Member State shall complete all preparatory steps with regard to the individual file of the applicant created within the Internal Market Information System (IMI) (IMI file) as provided for in Articles 4b and 4d. The competent authority of the host Member State shall issue the European Professional Card in accordance with Articles 4b and 4d.

For the purpose of establishment, the issuance of a European Professional Card shall not provide an automatic right to practise a particular profession if there are registration requirements or other control procedures already in place in the host Member State before a European Professional Card is introduced for that profession.

6. Member States shall designate competent authorities for dealing with IMI files and issuing European Professional Cards. Those authorities shall ensure an impartial, objective and timely processing of applications for European Professional Cards. The assistance centres referred to in Article 57b may also act in the capacity of a competent authority. Member States shall ensure that competent authorities and assistance centres inform citizens, including prospective applicants, about the functioning and the added value of a European Professional Card for the professions for which it is available.

7. The Commission shall, by means of implementing acts, adopt measures necessary to ensure the uniform application of the provisions on the European Professional Cards for those professions that meet the conditions laid down in the second subparagraph of this paragraph, including measures concerning the format of the European Professional Card, the processing of written applications, the translations to be provided by the applicant to support any application for a European Professional Card, details of the documents required pursuant to Article 7(2) or Annex VII to present a complete application and procedures for making and processing payments for a European Professional Card, taking into account the particularities of the profession concerned. The Commission shall also specify, by means of implementing acts, how, when and for which documents competent authorities may request certified copies in accordance with the second subparagraph of Article 4b(3), Articles 4d(2) and 4d(3) for the profession concerned.

The introduction of a European Professional Card for a particular profession by means of the adoption of relevant implementing acts referred to in the first subparagraph shall be subject to all of the following conditions:

    (a) there is significant mobility or potential for significant mobility in the profession concerned;

    (b) there is sufficient interest expressed by the relevant stakeholders;

    (c) the profession or the education and training geared to the pursuit of the profession is regulated in a significant number of Member States.

Those implementing acts shall be adopted in accordance with the examination procedure referred to in Article 58(2).

8. Any fees which applicants may incur in relation to administrative procedures to issue a European Professional Card shall be reasonable, proportionate and commensurate with the costs incurred by the home and the host Member States and shall not act as a disincentive to apply for a European Professional Card.

Article 4b   Application for a European Professional Card and creation of an IMI file

1. The home Member State shall enable a holder of a professional qualification to apply for a European Professional Card through an on-line tool, provided by the Commission, that automatically creates an IMI file for the particular applicant. Where a home Member State allows also for written applications, it shall put in place all necessary arrangements for the creation of the IMI file, any information to be sent to the applicant and the issuance of the European Professional Card.

2. Applications shall be supported by the documents required in the implementing acts to be adopted pursuant to Article 4a(7).

3. Within one week of receipt of the application, the competent authority of the home Member State shall acknowledge receipt of the application and inform the applicant of any missing document.

Where applicable, the competent authority of the home Member State shall issue any supporting certificate required under this Directive. The competent authority of the home Member State shall verify whether the applicant is legally established in the home Member State and whether all the necessary documents which have been issued in the home Member State are valid and authentic. In the event of duly justified doubts, the competent authority of the home Member State shall consult the relevant body and may request from the applicant certified copies of documents. In case of subsequent applications by the same applicant, the competent authorities of the home and the host Member States may not request the re-submission of documents which are already contained in the IMI file and which are still valid.

4. The Commission may, by means of implementing acts, adopt the technical specifications, the measures necessary to ensure integrity, confidentiality and accuracy of information contained in the European Professional Card and in the IMI file, and the conditions and the procedures for issuing a European Professional Card to its holder, including the possibility of downloading it or submitting updates for the IMI file. Those implementing acts shall be adopted in accordance with the examination procedure referred to in Article 58(2).

Article 4c   European Professional Card for the temporary and occasional provision of services other than those covered by Article 7(4)

1. The competent authority of the home Member State shall verify the application and the supporting documents in the IMI file and issue the European Professional Card for the temporary and occasional provision of services other than those covered by Article 7(4) within three weeks. That time period shall start upon receipt of the missing documents referred to in the first subparagraph of Article 4b(3) or, if no further documents were requested, upon the expiry of the one-week period referred to in that subparagraph. It shall then transmit the European Professional Card immediately to the competent authority of each host Member State concerned and shall inform the applicant accordingly. The host Member State may not require any further declaration under Article 7 for the following 18 months.

2. The decision of the competent authority of the home Member State, or the absence of a decision within the period of three weeks referred to in paragraph 1, shall be subject to appeal under national law.

3. If a holder of a European Professional Card wishes to provide services in Member States other than those initially mentioned in the application referred to in paragraph 1 that holder may apply for such extension. If the holder wishes to continue providing services beyond the period of 18 months referred to in paragraph 1, that holder shall inform the competent authority accordingly. In either case, that holder shall also provide any information on material changes in the situation substantiated in the IMI file that may be required by the competent authority in the home Member State in

accordance with the implementing acts to be adopted pursuant to Article 4a(7). The competent authority of the home Member State shall transmit the updated European Professional Card to the host Member States concerned.

4. The European Professional Card shall be valid in the entire territory of all the host Member States concerned for as long as its holder maintains the right to practice on the basis of the documents and information contained in the IMI file.

Article 4d   European Professional Card for establishment and for the temporary and occasional provision of services under Article 7(4)

1. The competent authority of the home Member State shall, within one month, verify the authenticity and validity of the supporting documents in the IMI file for the purpose of issuing a European Professional Card for establishment or for the temporary and occasional provision of services under Article 7(4). That time period shall start upon receipt of the missing documents referred to in the first subparagraph of Article 4b(3) or, if no further documents were requested, upon the expiry of the one-week period referred to in that subparagraph. It shall then transmit the application immediately to the competent authority of the host Member State. The home Member State shall inform the applicant of the status of the application at the same time as it transmits the application to the host Member State.

2. In the cases referred to in Articles 16, 21, 49a and 49b, a host Member State shall decide whether to issue a European Professional Card under paragraph 1 within one month of receipt of the application transmitted by the home Member State. In the event of duly justified doubts, the host Member State may request additional information from, or the inclusion of a certified copy of a document by, the home Member State, which the latter shall provide no later than two weeks after the submission of the request. Subject to the second subparagraph of paragraph 5, the period of one month shall apply, notwithstanding any such request.

3. In the cases referred to in Articles 7(4) and 14, a host Member State shall decide whether to issue a European Professional Card or to subject the holder of a professional qualification to compensation measures within two months of receipt of the application transmitted by the home Member State. In the event of duly justified doubts, the host Member State may request additional information from, or the inclusion of a certified copy of a document by, the home Member State which the latter shall provide no later than two weeks after the submission of the request. Subject to the second subparagraph of paragraph 5, the period of two months shall apply, notwithstanding any such request.

4. In the event that the host Member State does not receive the necessary information which it may require in accordance with this Directive for taking a decision on the issuance of the European Professional Card from either the home Member State or the applicant, it may refuse to issue the Card. Such refusal shall be duly justified.

5. Where the host Member State fails to take a decision within the time limits set out in paragraphs 2 and 3 of this Article or fails to organise an aptitude test in accordance with Article 7(4), the European Professional Card shall be deemed to be issued and shall be sent automatically, through IMI, to the holder of a professional qualification.

The host Member State shall have the possibility to extend by two weeks the deadlines set out in paragraphs 2 and 3 for the automatic issuance of the European Professional Card. It shall explain the reason for the extension and inform the applicant accordingly. Such an extension may be repeated once and only where it is strictly necessary, in particular for reasons relating to public health or the safety of the service recipients.

6. The actions taken by the home Member State in accordance with paragraph 1 shall replace any application for recognition of professional qualifications under the national law of the host Member State.

7. The decisions of the home and the host Member State adopted under paragraphs 1 to 5 or the absence of decision by the home Member State shall be subject to appeal under the national law of the Member State concerned.

Article 4e   Processing and access to data regarding the European Professional Card

1. Without prejudice to the presumption of innocence, the competent authorities of the home and the host Member States shall update, in a timely manner, the corresponding IMI file with information regarding disciplinary actions or criminal sanctions which relate to a prohibition or restriction and which have consequences for the pursuit of activities by the holder of a European Professional Card under this Directive. In so doing they shall respect personal data protection rules provided for in Directive 95/46/EC of the European Parliament and of the Council of 24 October 1995 on the protection of individuals with regard to the processing of personal data and on the free movement of such data[23] and Directive 2002/58/EC of the European Parliament and of the Council of 12 July 2002 concerning the processing of personal data and the protection of privacy in the electronic communications sector (Directive on privacy and electronic communications).[24] Such updates shall include the deletion of information which is no longer required. The holder of the European Professional Card as well as the competent authorities that have access to the corresponding IMI file shall be informed immediately of any updates. That obligation shall be without prejudice to the alert obligations for Member States under Article 56a.

2. The content of the information updates referred to in paragraph 1 shall be limited to the following:
   (a) the identity of the professional;
   (b) the profession concerned;
   (c) information about the national authority or court which has adopted the decision on restriction or prohibition;
   (d) the scope of the restriction or the prohibition; and
   (e) the period for which the restriction or the prohibition applies.

3. Access to the information in the IMI file shall be limited to the competent authorities of the home and the host Member States, in accordance with Directive 95/46/EC. The competent authorities shall inform the holder of the European Professional Card of the content of the IMI file upon that holder's request.

4. The information included in the European Professional Card shall be limited to the information that is necessary to ascertain its holder's right to exercise the profession for which it has been issued, namely the holder's name, surname, date and place of birth, profession, formal qualifications, and the applicable regime, competent authorities involved, Card number, security features and reference to a valid proof of identity. Information relating to professional experience acquired, or compensation measures passed, by the holder of the European Professional Card shall be included in the IMI file.

5. The personal data included in the IMI file may be processed for as long as it is needed for the purpose of the recognition procedure as such and as evidence of the recognition or of the transmission of the declaration required under Article 7. Member States shall ensure that the holder of a European Professional Card has the right at any time, and at no cost to that holder, to request the rectification of inaccurate or incomplete data, or the deletion or blocking of the IMI file concerned. The holder shall be informed of this right at the time the European Professional Card is issued, and reminded of it every two years thereafter. The reminder shall be sent automatically via IMI where the initial application for the European Professional Card was submitted online.

In the event of a request for deletion of an IMI file linked to a European Professional Card issued for the purpose of establishment or temporary and occasional provision of services under Article 7(4), the competent authorities of the host Member State concerned shall issue the holder of professional qualifications with evidence attesting to the recognition of his professional qualifications.

6. In relation to the processing of personal data in the European Professional Card and all IMI files, the relevant competent authorities of the Member States shall be regarded as controllers within the meaning of point (d) of Article 2 of Directive 95/46/EC. In relation to its responsibilities under paragraphs 1 to 4 of this Article and the processing of personal data involved therein, the Commission shall be regarded as a controller within the meaning of point (d) of Article 2 of

---

[23] OJ L 281, 23.11.1995, p. 31.
[24] OJ L 201, 31.7.2002, p. 37.

Regulation (EC) No 45/2001 of the European Parliament and of the Council of 18 December 2000 on the protection of individuals with regard to the processing of personal data by the Community institutions and bodies and on the free movement of such data.[25]

7. Without prejudice to paragraph 3, host Member States shall provide that employers, customers, patients, public authorities and other interested parties may verify the authenticity and validity of a European Professional Card presented to them by the Card holder.

The Commission shall, by means of implementing acts, lay down rules concerning access to the IMI file, and the technical means and the procedures for the verification referred to in the first subparagraph. Those implementing acts shall be adopted in accordance with the examination procedure referred to in Article 58(2).

Article 4f Partial access

1. The competent authority of the host Member State shall grant partial access, on a case-by-case basis, to a professional activity in its territory only when all the following conditions are fulfilled:

    (a) the professional is fully qualified to exercise in the home Member State the professional activity for which partial access is sought in the host Member State;

    (b) differences between the professional activity legally exercised in the home Member State and the regulated profession in the host Member State as such are so large that the application of compensation measures would amount to requiring the applicant to complete the full programme of education and training required in the host Member State to have access to the full regulated profession in the host Member State;

    (c) the professional activity can objectively be separated from other activities falling under the regulated profession in the host Member State.

For the purpose of point (c), the competent authority of the host Member State shall take into account whether the professional activity can be pursued autonomously in the home Member State.

2. Partial access may be rejected if such rejection is justified by overriding reasons of general interest, suitable for securing the attainment of the objective pursued, and does not go beyond what is necessary to attain that objective.

3. Applications for the purpose of establishment in a host Member State shall be examined in accordance with Chapters I and IV of Title III.

4. Applications for the purpose of providing temporary and occasional services in the host Member State concerning professional activities that have public health or safety implications shall be examined in accordance with Title II.

5. By derogation from the sixth subparagraph of Article 7(4) and Article 52(1), the professional activity shall be exercised under the professional title of the home Member State once partial access has been granted. The host Member State may require use of that professional title in the languages of the host Member State. Professionals benefiting from partial access shall clearly indicate to the service recipients the scope of their professional activities.

6. This Article shall not apply to professionals benefiting from automatic recognition of their professional qualifications under Chapters II, III and IIIa of Title III.

Title II Free provision of services

Article 5 Principle of the free provision of services

1. Without prejudice to specific provisions of Community law, as well as to Articles 6 and 7 of this Directive, Member States shall not restrict, for any reason relating to professional qualifications, the free provision of services in another Member State:

    (a) if the service provider is legally established in a Member State for the purpose of pursuing the same profession there (hereinafter referred to as the Member State of establishment), and

---

[25] OJ L 8, 12.1.2001, p. 1.

(b) where the service provider moves, if he has pursued that profession in one or several Member States for at least one year during the last 10 years preceding the provision of services when the profession is not regulated in the Member State of establishment. The condition of one year's pursuit shall not apply if the profession or the education and training leading to the profession is regulated.

2. The provisions of this title shall only apply where the service provider moves to the territory of the host Member State to pursue, on a temporary and occasional basis, the profession referred to in paragraph 1.

The temporary and occasional nature of the provision of services shall be assessed case by case, in particular in relation to its duration, its frequency, its regularity and its continuity.

3. Where a service provider moves, he shall be subject to professional rules of a professional, statutory or administrative nature which are directly linked to professional qualifications, such as the definition of the profession, the use of titles and serious professional malpractice which is directly and specifically linked to consumer protection and safety, as well as disciplinary provisions which are applicable in the host Member State to professionals who pursue the same profession in that Member State.

Article 6 Exemptions

Pursuant to Article 5(1), the host Member State shall exempt service providers established in another Member State from the requirements which it places on professionals established in its territory relating to:

(a) authorisation by, registration with or membership of a professional organisation or body. In order to facilitate the application of disciplinary provisions in force on their territory according to Article 5(3), Member States may provide either for automatic temporary registration with or for pro forma membership of such a professional organisation or body, provided that such registration or membership does not delay or complicate in any way the provision of services and does not entail any additional costs for the service provider. A copy of the declaration and, where applicable, of the renewal referred to in Article 7(1), accompanied, for professions which have implications for public health and safety referred to in Article 7(4) or which benefit from automatic recognition under Title III Chapter III, by a copy of the documents referred to in Article 7(2) shall be sent by the competent authority to the relevant professional organisation or body, and this shall constitute automatic temporary registration or pro forma membership for this purpose;

(b) registration with a public social security body for the purpose of settling accounts with an insurer relating to activities pursued for the benefit of insured persons.

The service provider shall, however, inform in advance or, in an urgent case, afterwards, the body referred to in point (b) of the services which he has provided.

Article 7 Declaration to be made in advance, if the service provider moves

1. Member States may require that, where the service provider first moves from one Member State to another in order to provide services, he shall inform the competent authority in the host Member State in a written declaration to be made in advance including the details of any insurance cover or other means of personal or collective protection with regard to professional liability. Such declaration shall be renewed once a year if the service provider intends to provide temporary or occasional services in that Member State during that year. The service provider may supply the declaration by any means.

2. Moreover, for the first provision of services or if there is a material change in the situation substantiated by the documents, Member States may require that the declaration be accompanied by the following documents:

(a) proof of the nationality of the service provider;

(b) an attestation certifying that the holder is legally established in a Member State for the purpose of pursuing the activities concerned and that he is not prohibited from practising, even temporarily, at the moment of delivering the attestation;

    (c) evidence of professional qualifications;

    (d) for cases referred to in point (b) of Article 5(1), any means of proof that the service provider has pursued the activity concerned for at least one year during the previous 10 years;

    (e) for professions in the security sector, in the health sector and professions related to the education of minors, including in childcare and early childhood education, where the Member State so requires for its own nationals, an attestation confirming the absence of temporary or final suspensions from exercising the profession or of criminal convictions;

    (f) for professions that have patient safety implications, a declaration about the applicant's knowledge of the language necessary for practising the profession in the host Member State;

    (g) for professions covering the activities referred to in Article 16 and which were notified by a Member State in accordance with Article 59(2), a certificate concerning the nature and duration of the activity issued by the competent authority or body of the Member State where the service provider is established.

    2a. Submission of a required declaration by the service provider in accordance with paragraph 1 shall entitle that service provider to have access to the service activity or to exercise that activity in the entire territory of the Member State concerned. A Member State may require additional information listed in paragraph 2 concerning the professional qualifications of the service provider if:

    (a) the profession is regulated in parts of that Member State's territory in a different manner;

    (b) such regulation is applicable also to all nationals of that Member State;

    (c) the differences in such regulation are justified by overriding reasons of general interest relating to public health or safety of service recipients; and

    (d) the Member State has no other means of obtaining such information.

    3. The service shall be provided under the professional title of the Member State of establishment, in so far as such a title exists in that Member State for the professional activity in question. That title shall be indicated in the official language or one of the official languages of the Member State of establishment in such a way as to avoid any confusion with the professional title of the host Member State. Where no such professional title exists in the Member State of establishment, the service provider shall indicate his formal qualification in the official language or one of the official languages of that Member State. By way of exception, the service shall be provided under the professional title of the host Member State for cases referred to in Title III Chapter III.

    4. For the first provision of services, in the case of regulated professions that have public health or safety implications which do not benefit from automatic recognition under Chapter II, III or IIIa of Title III, the competent authority of the host Member State may check the professional qualifications of the service provider prior to the first provision of services. Such a prior check shall be possible only where the purpose of the check is to avoid serious damage to the health or safety of the service recipient due to a lack of professional qualification of the service provider and where the check does not go beyond what is necessary for that purpose.

    No later than one month after receipt of the declaration and accompanying documents, referred to in paragraphs 1 and 2, the competent authority shall inform the service provider of its decision:

    (a) not to check his professional qualifications;

    (b) having checked his professional qualifications:

        (i) to require the service provider to take an aptitude test; or

        (ii) to allow the provision of services.

    Where there is a difficulty which would result in delay in taking a decision under the second subparagraph, the competent authority shall notify the service provider of the reason for the delay within the same deadline. The difficulty shall be solved within one month of that notification and the decision finalised within two months of resolution of the difficulty.

Where there is a substantial difference between the professional qualifications of the service provider and the training required in the host Member State, to the extent that that difference is such as to be harmful to public health or safety, and that it cannot be compensated by the service provider's professional experience or by knowledge, skills and competences acquired through lifelong learning formally validated to that end by a relevant body, the host Member State shall give that service provider the opportunity to show, by means of an aptitude test, as referred to in point (b) of the second subparagraph, that they have acquired the knowledge, skills or competence that were lacking. The host Member State shall take a decision on that basis on whether to allow the provision of services. In any case, it must be possible to provide the service within one month of the decision taken in accordance with the second subparagraph.

In the absence of a reaction of the competent authority within the deadlines set out in the second and third subparagraphs, the service may be provided.

In cases where professional qualifications have been verified under this paragraph, the service shall be provided under the professional title of the host Member State.

Article 8   Administrative cooperation

1. The competent authorities of the host Member State may ask the competent authorities of the Member State of establishment, in the event of justified doubts, to provide any information relevant to the legality of the service provider's establishment and good conduct, as well as the absence of any disciplinary or criminal sanctions of a professional nature. In the event that the competent authorities of the host Member State decide to check the service provider's professional qualifications, they may ask the competent authorities of the Member State of establishment for information about the service provider's training courses to the extent necessary to assess substantial differences likely to be harmful to public health or safety. The competent authorities of the Member State of establishment shall provide that information in accordance with Article 56. In the case of non-regulated professions in the home Member State, the assistance centres referred to in Article 57b may also provide such information.

2. The competent authorities shall ensure the exchange of all information necessary for complaints by a recipient of a service against a service provider to be correctly pursued. Recipients shall be informed of the outcome of the complaint.

Article 9   Information to be given to the recipients of the service

In cases where the service is provided under the professional title of the Member State of establishment or under the formal qualification of the service provider, in addition to the other requirements relating to information contained in Community law, the competent authorities of the host Member State may require the service provider to furnish the recipient of the service with any or all of the following information:

(a) if the service provider is registered in a commercial register or similar public register, the register in which he is registered, his registration number, or equivalent means of identification contained in that register;

(b) if the activity is subject to authorisation in the Member State of establishment, the name and address of the competent supervisory authority;

(c) any professional association or similar body with which the service provider is registered;

(d) the professional title or, where no such title exists, the formal qualification of the service provider and the Member State in which it was awarded;

(e) if the service provider performs an activity which is subject to VAT, the VAT identification number referred to in Article 22(1) of the sixth Council Directive 77/388/EEC of 17 May 1977 on the harmonisation of the laws of the Member States relating to turnover taxes—Common system of value added tax: uniform basis of assessment;[26]

(f) details of any insurance cover or other means of personal or collective protection with regard to professional liability.

[26] OJ L 145, 13.6.1977, p. 1. Directive as last amended by Directive 2004/66/EC (OJ L 168, 1.5.2004, p. 35).

Title III Freedom of establishment

Chapter I General system for the recognition of evidence of training

Article 10 Scope

This Chapter applies to all professions which are not covered by Chapters II and III of this Title and in the following cases in which the applicant, for specific and exceptional reasons, does not satisfy the conditions laid down in those Chapters:

(a) for activities listed in Annex IV, when the migrant does not meet the requirements set out in Articles 17, 18 and 19;

(b) for doctors with basic training, specialised doctors, nurses responsible for general care, dental practitioners, specialised dental practitioners, veterinary surgeons, midwives, pharmacists and architects, when the migrant does not meet the requirements of effective and lawful professional practice referred to in Articles 23, 27, 33, 37, 39, 43 and 49;

(c) for architects, when the migrant holds evidence of formal qualification not listed in Annex V, point 5.7;

(d) without prejudice to Articles 21(1), 23 and 27, for doctors, nurses, dental practitioners, veterinary surgeons, midwives, pharmacists and architects holding evidence of formal qualifications as a specialist, who must have taken part in the training leading to the possession of a title listed in Annex V, points 5.1.1, 5.2.2, 5.3.2, 5.4.2, 5.5.2, 5.6.2 and 5.7.1, and solely for the purpose of the recognition of the relevant specialty;

(e) for nurses responsible for general care and specialised nurses holding evidence of formal qualifications as a specialist who must have taken part in the training leading to the possession of a title listed in Annex V, point 5.2.2, when the migrant seeks recognition in another Member State where the relevant professional activities are pursued by specialised nurses without training as general care nurse;

(f) for specialised nurses without training as general care nurse, when the migrant seeks recognition in another Member State where the relevant professional activities are pursued by nurses responsible for general care, specialised nurses without training as general care nurse or specialised nurses holding evidence of formal qualifications as a specialist who must have taken part in the training leading to the possession of the titles listed in Annex V, point 5.2.2;

(g) for migrants meeting the requirements set out in Article 3(3).

Article 11 Levels of qualification

For the purposes of Article 13 and Article 14(6), professional qualifications shall be grouped under the following levels:

(a) an attestation of competence issued by a competent authority in the home Member State designated pursuant to legislative, regulatory or administrative provisions of that Member State, on the basis of:

(i) either a training course not forming part of a certificate or diploma within the meaning of points (b), (c), (d) or (e), or a specific examination without prior training, or full-time pursuit of the profession in a Member State for three consecutive years or for an equivalent duration on a part-time basis during the previous 10 years,

(ii) or general primary or secondary education, attesting that the holder has acquired general knowledge;

(b) a certificate attesting to a successful completion of a secondary course,

(i) either general in character, supplemented by a course of study or professional training other than those referred to in point (c) and/or by the probationary or professional practice required in addition to that course,

      (ii)   or technical or professional in character, supplemented where appropriate by a course of study or professional training as referred to in point (i), and/or by the probationary or professional practice required in addition to that course;

  (c)   a diploma certifying successful completion of

      (i)   either training at post-secondary level other than that referred to in points (d) and (e) of a duration of at least one year or of an equivalent duration on a part-time basis, one of the conditions of entry of which is, as a general rule, the successful completion of the secondary course required to obtain entry to university or higher education or the completion of equivalent school education of the second secondary level, as well as the professional training which may be required in addition to that post-secondary course; or

      (ii)   regulated education and training or, in the case of regulated professions, vocational training with a special structure, with competences going beyond what is provided for in level b, equivalent to the level of training provided for under point (i), if such training provides a comparable professional standard and prepares the trainee for a comparable level of responsibilities and functions provided that the diploma is accompanied by a certificate from the home Member State;

  (d)   a diploma certifying that the holder has successfully completed training at post-secondary level of at least three and not more than four years' duration, or of an equivalent duration on a part-time basis, which may in addition be expressed with an equivalent number of ECTS credits, at a university or establishment of higher education or another establishment of equivalent level and, where appropriate, that he has successfully completed the professional training required in addition to the post-secondary course;

  (e)   a diploma certifying that the holder has successfully completed a post-secondary course of at least four years' duration, or of an equivalent duration on a part-time basis, which may in addition be expressed with an equivalent number of ECTS credits, at a university or establishment of higher education or another establishment of equivalent level and, where appropriate, that he has successfully completed the professional training required in addition to the post-secondary course.

Article 12   Equal treatment of qualifications

Any evidence of formal qualifications or set of evidence of formal qualifications issued by a competent authority in a Member State, certifying successful completion of training in the Union, on a full or part-time basis, within or outside formal programmes, which is recognised by that Member State as being of an equivalent level and which confers on the holder the same rights of access to or pursuit of a profession or prepares for the pursuit of that profession, shall be treated as evidence of formal qualifications referred to in Article 11, including the level in question.

    Any professional qualification which, although not satisfying the requirements contained in the legislative, regulatory or administrative provisions in force in the home Member State for access to or the pursuit of a profession, confers on the holder acquired rights by virtue of these provisions, shall also be treated as such evidence of formal qualifications under the same conditions as set out in the first subparagraph. This applies in particular if the home Member State raises the level of training required for admission to a profession and for its exercise, and if an individual who has undergone former training, which does not meet the requirements of the new qualification, benefits from acquired rights by virtue of national legislative, regulatory or administrative provisions; in such case this former training is considered by the host Member State, for the purposes of the application of Article 13, as corresponding to the level of the new training.

Article 13   Conditions for recognition

    1.   If access to or pursuit of a regulated profession in a host Member State is contingent upon possession of specific professional qualifications, the competent authority of that Member State shall permit applicants to access and pursue that profession, under the same conditions as apply to its

nationals, if they possess an attestation of competence or evidence of formal qualifications referred to in Article 11, required by another Member State in order to gain access to and pursue that profession on its territory.

Attestations of competence or evidence of formal qualifications shall be issued by a competent authority in a Member State, designated in accordance with the laws, regulations or administrative provisions of that Member State.

2. Access to, and pursuit of, a profession as described in paragraph 1 shall also be granted to applicants who have pursued the profession in question on a full-time basis for one year or for an equivalent overall duration on a part-time basis during the previous 10 years in another Member State which does not regulate that profession, and who possess one or more attestations of competence or evidence of formal qualifications issued by another Member State which does not regulate the profession.

Attestations of competence and evidence of formal qualifications shall satisfy the following conditions:

   (a) they are issued by a competent authority in a Member State, designated in accordance with the laws, regulations or administrative provisions of that Member State;

   (b) they attest that the holder has been prepared for the pursuit of the profession in question.

The one year of professional experience referred to in the first subparagraph may not, however, be required if the evidence of formal qualifications which the applicant possesses certifies regulated education and training.

3. The host Member State shall accept the level attested under Article 11 by the home Member State, as well as the certificate by which the home Member State certifies that regulated education and training or vocational training with a special structure referred to in point (c)(ii) of Article 11 is equivalent to the level provided for in point (c)(i) of Article 11.

4. By way of derogation from paragraphs 1 and 2 of this Article and from Article 14, the competent authority of the host Member State may refuse access to, and pursuit of, the profession to holders of an attestation of competence classified under point (a) of Article 11 where the national professional qualification required to exercise the profession on its territory is classified under point (e) of Article 11.

Article 14 Compensation measures

1. Article 13 shall not preclude the host Member State from requiring the applicant to complete an adaptation period of up to three years or to take an aptitude test if:

   (a) the training the applicant has received covers substantially different matters than those covered by the evidence of formal qualifications required in the host Member State;

   (b) the regulated profession in the host Member State comprises one or more regulated professional activities which do not exist in the corresponding profession in the applicant's home Member State, and the training required in the host Member State covers substantially different matters from those covered by the applicant's attestation of competence or evidence of formal qualifications.

2. If the host Member State makes use of the option provided for in paragraph 1, it must offer the applicant the choice between an adaptation period and an aptitude test.

Where a Member State considers, with respect to a given profession, that it is necessary to derogate from the requirement, set out in the previous subparagraph, that it give the applicant a choice between an adaptation period and an aptitude test, it shall inform the other Member States and the Commission in advance and provide sufficient justification for the derogation.

Where the Commission considers that the derogation referred to in the second subparagraph is inappropriate or that it is not in accordance with Union law, it shall adopt an implementing act, within three months of receiving all necessary information, to ask the relevant Member State to refrain from taking the envisaged measure. In the absence of a response from the Commission within that deadline, the derogation may be applied.

3. By way of derogation from the principle of the right of the applicant to choose, as laid down in paragraph 2, for professions whose pursuit requires precise knowledge of national law and in respect of which the provision of advice and/or assistance concerning national law is an essential and constant aspect of the professional activity, the host Member State may stipulate either an adaptation period or an aptitude test.

This applies also to the cases provided for in Article 10 points (b) and (c), in Article 10 point (d) concerning doctors and dental practitioners, in Article 10 point (f) when the migrant seeks recognition in another Member State where the relevant professional activities are pursued by nurses responsible for general care or specialised nurses holding evidence of formal qualifications as a specialist who must have taken part in the training leading to the possession of the titles listed in Annex V, point 5.2.2 and in Article 10 point (g).

In the cases covered by Article 10 point (a), the host Member State may require an adaptation period or an aptitude test if the migrant envisages pursuing professional activities in a self-employed capacity or as a manager of an undertaking which require the knowledge and the application of the specific national rules in force, provided that knowledge and application of those rules are required by the competent authorities of the host Member State for access to such activities by its own nationals.

By way of derogation from the principle of the right of the applicant to choose, as laid down in paragraph 2, the host Member State may stipulate either an adaptation period or an aptitude test in the case of:

(a) a holder of a professional qualification referred to in point (a) of Article 11, who applies for recognition of his professional qualifications where the national professional qualification required is classified under point (c) of Article 11; or

(b) a holder of a professional qualification referred to in point (b) of Article 11, who applies for recognition of his professional qualifications where the national professional qualification required is classified under point (d) or (e) of Article 11.

In the case of a holder of a professional qualification referred to in point (a) of Article 11 who applies for recognition of his professional qualifications where the national professional qualification required is classified under point (d) of Article 11, the host Member State may impose both an adaptation period and an aptitude test.

4. For the purposes of paragraphs 1 and 5, 'substantially different matters' means matters in respect of which knowledge, skills and competences acquired are essential for pursuing the profession and with regard to which the training received by the migrant shows significant differences in terms of content from the training required by the host Member State.

5. Paragraph 1 shall be applied with due regard to the principle of proportionality. In particular, if the host Member State intends to require the applicant to complete an adaptation period or take an aptitude test, it must first ascertain whether the knowledge, skills and competences acquired by the applicant in the course of his professional experience or through lifelong learning, and formally validated to that end by a relevant body, in any Member State or in a third country, is of such nature as to cover, in full or in part, the substantially different matters defined in paragraph 4.

6. The decision imposing an adaptation period or an aptitude test shall be duly justified. In particular, the applicant shall be provided with the following information:

(a) the level of the professional qualification required in the host Member State and the level of the professional qualification held by the applicant in accordance with the classification set out in Article 11; and

(b) the substantial differences referred to in paragraph 4 and the reasons for which those differences cannot be compensated by knowledge, skills and competences acquired in the course of professional experience or through lifelong learning formally validated to that end by a relevant body.

7. Member States shall ensure that an applicant has the possibility of taking the aptitude test referred to in paragraph 1 not later than six months after the initial decision imposing an aptitude test on the applicant.

Chapter II Recognition of professional experience

Article 16   Requirements regarding professional experience

If, in a Member State, access to or pursuit of one of the activities listed in Annex IV is contingent upon possession of general, commercial or professional knowledge and aptitudes, that Member State shall recognise previous pursuit of the activity in another Member State as sufficient proof of such knowledge and aptitudes. The activity must have been pursued in accordance with Articles 17, 18 and 19.

Article 17   Activities referred to in list I of Annex IV

1. For the activities in list I of Annex IV, the activity in question must have been previously pursued:

(a) for six consecutive years on a self-employed basis or as a manager of an undertaking; or

(b) for three consecutive years on a self-employed basis or as a manager of an undertaking, where the beneficiary proves that he has received previous training of at least three years for the activity in question, evidenced by a certificate recognised by the Member State or judged by a competent professional body to be fully valid; or

(c) for four consecutive years on a self-employed basis or as a manager of an undertaking, where the beneficiary can prove that he has received, for the activity in question, previous training of at least two years' duration, attested by a certificate recognised by the Member State or judged by a competent professional body to be fully valid; or

(d) for three consecutive years on a self-employed basis, if the beneficiary can prove that he has pursued the activity in question on an employed basis for at least five years; or

(e) for five consecutive years in an executive position, of which at least three years involved technical duties and responsibility for at least one department of the company, if the beneficiary can prove that he has received, for the activity in question, previous training of at least three years' duration, as attested by a certificate recognised by the Member State or judged by a competent professional body to be fully valid.

2. In cases (a) and (d), the activity must not have finished more than 10 years before the date on which the complete application was submitted by the person concerned to the competent authority referred to in Article 56.

3. Paragraph 1(e) shall not apply to activities in Group ex 855, hairdressing establishments, of the ISIC Nomenclature.

Article 18   Activities referred to in list II of Annex IV

1. For the activities in list II of Annex IV, the activity in question must have been previously pursued:

(a) for five consecutive years on a self-employed basis or as a manager of an undertaking, or

(b) for three consecutive years on a self-employed basis or as a manager of an undertaking, where the beneficiary proves that he has received previous training of at least three years for the activity in question, evidenced by a certificate recognised by the Member State or judged by a competent professional body to be fully valid, or

(c) for four consecutive years on a self-employed basis or as a manager of an undertaking, where the beneficiary can prove that he has received, for the activity in question, previous training of at least two years' duration, attested by a certificate recognised by the Member State or judged by a competent professional body to be fully valid, or

(d) for three consecutive years on a self-employed basis or as a manager of an undertaking, if the beneficiary can prove that he has pursued the activity in question on an employed basis for at least five years, or

(e) for five consecutive years on an employed basis, if the beneficiary can prove that he has received, for the activity in question, previous training of at least three years' duration, as attested by a certificate recognised by the Member State or judged by a competent professional body to be fully valid, or

(f) for six consecutive years on an employed basis, if the beneficiary can prove that he has received previous training in the activity in question of at least two years' duration, as attested by a certificate recognised by the Member State or judged by a competent professional body to be fully valid.

2. In cases (a) and (d), the activity must not have finished more than 10 years before the date on which the complete application was submitted by the person concerned to the competent authority referred to in Article 56.

Article 19   Activities referred to in list III of Annex IV

1. For the activities in list III of Annex IV, the activity in question must have been previously pursued:

(a) for three consecutive years, either on a self-employed basis or as a manager of an undertaking, or

(b) for two consecutive years, either on a self-employed basis or as a manager of an undertaking, if the beneficiary can prove that he has received previous training for the activity in question, as attested by a certificate recognised by the Member State or judged by a competent professional body to be fully valid, or

(c) for two consecutive years, either on a self-employed basis or as a manager of an undertaking, if the beneficiary can prove that he has pursued the activity in question on an employed basis for at least three years, or

(d) for three consecutive years, on an employed basis, if the beneficiary can prove that he has received previous training for the activity in question, as attested by a certificate recognised by the Member State or judged by a competent professional body to be fully valid.

2. In cases (a) and (c), the activity must not have finished more than 10 years before the date on which the complete application was submitted by the person concerned to the competent authority referred to in Article 56.

Article 20   Adaptation of the lists of activities in Annex IV

The Commission shall be empowered to adopt delegated acts in accordance with Article 57c concerning the adaptation of the lists of activities set out in Annex IV which are the subject of recognition of professional experience pursuant to Article 16, with a view to updating or clarifying the activities listed in Annex IV in particular in order to further specify their scope and to take due account of the latest developments in the field of activity-based nomenclatures, provided that this does not involve any narrowing of the scope of the activities related to the individual categories and that there is no shift of activities between the existing lists I, II and III of Annex IV.

Chapter III   Recognition on the basis of coordination of minimum training conditions

Section 1   General provisions

Article 21   Principle of automatic recognition

1. Each Member State shall recognise evidence of formal qualifications as doctor giving access to the professional activities of doctor with basic training and specialised doctor, as nurse responsible for general care, as dental practitioner, as specialised dental practitioner, as veterinary surgeon, as pharmacist and as architect, listed in Annex V, points 5.1.1, 5.1.2, 5.2.2, 5.3.2, 5.3.3, 5.4.2, 5.6.2 and 5.7.1 respectively, which satisfy the minimum training conditions referred to in Articles 24, 25, 31, 34, 35, 38, 44 and 46 respectively, and shall, for the purposes of access to and pursuit of the professional activities, give such evidence the same effect on its territory as the evidence of formal qualifications which it itself issues.

Such evidence of formal qualifications must be issued by the competent bodies in the Member States and accompanied, where appropriate, by the certificates listed in Annex V, points 5.1.1, 5.1.2, 5.2.2, 5.3.2, 5.3.3, 5.4.2, 5.6.2 and 5.7.1 respectively.

The provisions of the first and second subparagraphs do not affect the acquired rights referred to in Articles 23, 27, 33, 37, 39 and 49.

2. Each Member State shall recognise, for the purpose of pursuing general medical practice in the framework of its national social security system, evidence of formal qualifications listed in Annex V, point 5.1.4 and issued to nationals of the Member States by the other Member States in accordance with the minimum training conditions laid down in Article 28.

The provisions of the previous subparagraph do not affect the acquired rights referred to in Article 30.

3. Each Member State shall recognise evidence of formal qualifications as a midwife, awarded to nationals of Member States by the other Member States, listed in Annex V, point 5.5.2, which complies with the minimum training conditions referred to in Article 40 and satisfies the criteria set out in Article 41, and shall, for the purposes of access to and pursuit of the professional activities, give such evidence the same effect on its territory as the evidence of formal qualifications which it itself issues. This provision does not affect the acquired rights referred to in Articles 23 and 43.

4. In respect of the operation of pharmacies that are not subject to territorial restrictions, a Member State may, by way of derogation, decide not to give effect to evidence of formal qualifications referred to in point 5.6.2 of Annex V, for the setting up of new pharmacies open to the public. For the purposes of this paragraph, pharmacies which have been open for less than three years shall also be considered as new pharmacies.

That derogation may not be applied in respect of pharmacists whose formal qualifications have already been recognised by the competent authorities of the host Member State for other purposes and who have been effectively and lawfully engaged in the professional activities of a pharmacist for at least three consecutive years in that Member State.

5. Evidence of formal qualifications as an architect referred to in Annex V, point 5.7.1, which is subject to automatic recognition pursuant to paragraph 1, proves completion of a course of training which began not earlier than during the academic reference year referred to in that Annex.

6. Each Member State shall make access to, and pursuit of, the professional activities of doctors, nurses responsible for general care, dental practitioners, veterinary surgeons, midwives and pharmacists subject to possession of evidence of formal qualifications referred to in points 5.1.1, 5.1.2, 5.1.4, 5.2.2, 5.3.2, 5.3.3, 5.4.2, 5.5.2 and 5.6.2 of Annex V respectively, attesting that the professional concerned, over the duration of his training, has acquired, as appropriate, the knowledge, skills and competences referred to in Articles 24(3), 31(6), 31(7), 34(3), 38(3), 40(3) and 44(3).

In order to take account of generally acknowledged scientific and technical progress, the Commission shall be empowered to adopt delegated acts in accordance with Article 57c to update the knowledge and skills referred to in Articles 24(3), 31(6), 34(3), 38(3), 40(3), 44(3) and 46(4) to reflect the evolution of Union law directly affecting the professionals concerned.

Such updates shall not entail an amendment of existing essential legislative principles in Member States regarding the structure of professions as regards training and conditions of access by natural persons. Such updates shall respect the responsibility of the Member States for the organisation of education systems, as set out in Article 165(1) of the Treaty on the Functioning of the European Union (TFEU).

Article 21a   Notification procedure

1. Each Member State shall notify the Commission of the laws, regulations and administrative provisions which it adopts with regard to the issuing of evidence of formal qualifications in the professions covered by this Chapter.

In the case of evidence of formal qualifications referred to in Section 8, notification in accordance with the first subparagraph shall also be addressed to the other Member States.

2. The notification referred to in paragraph 1 shall include information about the duration and content of the training programmes.

3. The notification referred to in paragraph 1 shall be transmitted via IMI.

4. In order to take due account of legislative and administrative developments in the Member States, and on condition that the laws, regulations and administrative provisions notified pursuant to paragraph 1 of this Article are in conformity with the conditions set out in this Chapter, the Commission shall be empowered to adopt delegated acts in accordance with Article 57c in order to amend points 5.1.1 to 5.1.4, 5.2.2, 5.3.2, 5.3.3, 5.4.2, 5.5.2, 5.6.2 and 5.7.1 of Annex V, concerning the updating of the titles adopted by the Member States for evidence of formal qualifications and, where appropriate, the body which issues the evidence of formal qualifications, the certificate which accompanies it and the corresponding professional title.

5. Where the legislative, regulatory and administrative provisions notified pursuant to paragraph 1 are not in conformity with the conditions set out in this Chapter, the Commission shall adopt an implementing act in order to reject the requested amendment of points 5.1.1 to 5.1.4, 5.2.2, 5.3.2, 5.3.3, 5.4.2, 5.5.2, 5.6.2 or 5.7.1 of Annex V.

Article 22 Common provisions on training

With regard to the training referred to in Articles 24, 25, 28, 31, 34, 35, 38, 40, 44 and 46:

(a) Member States may authorise part-time training under conditions laid down by the competent authorities; those authorities shall ensure that the overall duration, level and quality of such training is not lower than that of continuous full-time training;

(b) Member States shall, in accordance with the procedures specific to each Member State, ensure, by encouraging continuous professional development, that professionals whose professional qualification is covered by Chapter III of this Title are able to update their knowledge, skills and competences in order to maintain a safe and effective practice and keep abreast of professional developments.

Member States shall communicate to the Commission the measures taken pursuant to point (b) of the first paragraph by 18 January 2016.

Article 23 Acquired rights

1. Without prejudice to the acquired rights specific to the professions concerned, in cases where the evidence of formal qualifications as doctor giving access to the professional activities of doctor with basic training and specialised doctor, as nurse responsible for general care, as dental practitioner, as specialised dental practitioner, as veterinary surgeon, as midwife and as pharmacist held by Member States nationals does not satisfy all the training requirements referred to in Articles 24, 25, 31, 34, 35, 38, 40 and 44, each Member State shall recognise as sufficient proof evidence of formal qualifications issued by those Member States insofar as such evidence attests successful completion of training which began before the reference dates laid down in Annex V, points 5.1.1, 5.1.2, 5.2.2, 5.3.2, 5.3.3, 5.4.2, 5.5.2 and 5.6.2 and is accompanied by a certificate stating that the holders have been effectively and lawfully engaged in the activities in question for at least three consecutive years during the five years preceding the award of the certificate.

2. The same provisions shall apply to evidence of formal qualifications as doctor giving access to the professional activities of doctor with basic training and specialised doctor, as nurse responsible for general care, as dental practitioner, as specialised dental practitioner, as veterinary surgeon, as midwife and as pharmacist, obtained in the territory of the former German Democratic Republic, which does not satisfy all the minimum training requirements laid down in Articles 24, 25, 31, 34, 35, 38, 40 and 44 if such evidence certifies successful completion of training which began before:

(a) 3 October 1990 for doctors with basic training, nurses responsible for general care, dental practitioners with basic training, specialised dental practitioners, veterinary surgeons, midwives and pharmacists, and

(b) 3 April 1992 for specialised doctors.

The evidence of formal qualifications referred to in the first subparagraph confers on the holder the right to pursue professional activities throughout German territory under the same conditions as evidence of formal qualifications issued by the competent German authorities referred to in Annex V, points 5.1.1, 5.1.2, 5.2.2, 5.3.2, 5.3.3, 5.4.2, 5.5.2 and 5.6.2.

3. Without prejudice to the provisions of Article 37(1), each Member State shall recognise evidence of formal qualifications as doctor giving access to the professional activities of doctor with basic training and specialised doctor, as nurse responsible for general care, as veterinary surgeon, as midwife, as pharmacist and as architect held by Member States nationals and issued by the former Czechoslovakia, or whose training commenced, for the Czech Republic and Slovakia, before 1 January 1993, where the authorities of either of the two aforementioned Member States attest that such evidence of formal qualifications has the same legal validity within their territory as the evidence of formal qualifications which they issue and, with respect to architects, as the evidence of formal qualifications specified for those Member States in Annex VI, point 6, as regards access to the professional activities of doctor with basic training, specialised doctor, nurse responsible for general care, veterinary surgeon, midwife, pharmacist with respect to the activities referred to in Article 45 (2), and architect with respect to the activities referred to in Article 48, and the pursuit of such activities.

Such an attestation must be accompanied by a certificate issued by those same authorities stating that such persons have effectively and lawfully been engaged in the activities in question within their territory for at least three consecutive years during the five years prior to the date of issue of the certificate.

4. Each Member State shall recognise evidence of formal qualifications as doctor giving access to the professional activities of doctor with basic training and specialised doctor, as nurse responsible for general care, as dental practitioner, as specialised dental practitioner, as veterinary surgeon, as midwife, as pharmacist and as architect held by nationals of the Member States and issued by the former Soviet Union, or whose training commenced

    (a) for Estonia, before 20 August 1991,

    (b) for Latvia, before 21 August 1991,

    (c) for Lithuania, before 11 March 1990,

where the authorities of any of the three aforementioned Member States attest that such evidence has the same legal validity within their territory as the evidence which they issue and, with respect to architects, as the evidence of formal qualifications specified for those Member States in Annex VI, point 6, as regards access to the professional activities of doctor with basic training, specialised doctor, nurse responsible for general care, dental practitioner, specialised dental practitioner, veterinary surgeon, midwife, pharmacist with respect to the activities referred to in Article 45(2), and architect with respect to the activities referred to in Article 48, and the pursuit of such activities.

Such an attestation must be accompanied by a certificate issued by those same authorities stating that such persons have effectively and lawfully been engaged in the activities in question within their territory for at least three consecutive years during the five years prior to the date of issue of the certificate.

With regard to evidence of formal qualifications as veterinary surgeons issued by the former Soviet Union or in respect of which training commenced, for Estonia, before 20 August 1991, the attestation referred to in the preceding subparagraph must be accompanied by a certificate issued by the Estonian authorities stating that such persons have effectively and lawfully been engaged in the activities in question within their territory for at least five consecutive years during the seven years prior to the date of issue of the certificate.

5. Without prejudice to Article 43b, each Member State shall recognise evidence of formal qualifications as doctor giving access to the professional activities of doctor with basic training and specialised doctor, as nurse responsible for general care, as dental practitioner, as specialised dental practitioner, as veterinary surgeon, as midwife, as pharmacist and as architect held by nationals of the Member States and issued by the former Yugoslavia, or whose training commenced,

    (a) for Slovenia, before 25 June 1991; and

    (b) for Croatia, before 8 October 1991;

where the authorities of the aforementioned Member States attest that such evidence has the same legal validity within their territory as the evidence which they issue and, with respect to architects, as the evidence of formal qualifications specified for those Member States in Annex VI, point 6, as regards access to the professional activities of doctor with basic training, specialised doctor, nurse responsible for general care, dental practitioner, specialised dental practitioner, veterinary surgeon, midwife, pharmacist with respect to the activities referred to in Article 45(2), and architect with respect to the activities referred to in Article 48, and the pursuit of such activities.

Such an attestation must be accompanied by a certificate issued by those same authorities stating that such persons have effectively and lawfully been engaged in the activities in question within their territory for at least three consecutive years during the five years prior to the date of issue of the certificate.

6. Each Member State shall recognise as sufficient proof for Member State nationals whose evidence of formal qualifications as a doctor, nurse responsible for general care, dental practitioner, veterinary surgeon, midwife and pharmacist does not correspond to the titles given for that Member State in Annex V, points 5.1.1, 5.1.2, 5.1.3, 5.1.4, 5.2.2, 5.3.2, 5.3.3, 5.4.2, 5.5.2 and 5.6.2, evidence of formal qualifications issued by those Member States accompanied by a certificate issued by the competent authorities or bodies.

The certificate referred to in the first subparagraph shall state that the evidence of formal qualifications certifies successful completion of training in accordance with Articles 24, 25, 28, 31, 34, 35, 38, 40 and 44 respectively and is treated by the Member State which issued it in the same way as the qualifications whose titles are listed in Annex V, points 5.1.1, 5.1.2, 5.1.3, 5.1.4, 5.2.2, 5.3.2, 5.3.3, 5.4.2, 5.5.2 and 5.6.2.

Article 23a   Specific circumstances

1. By way of derogation from the present Directive, Bulgaria may authorise the holders of the qualification of 'ФеЛДШер' (feldsher) awarded in Bulgaria before 31 December 1999 and exercising this profession under the Bulgarian national social security scheme on 1 January 2000 to continue to exercise the said profession, even if parts of their activity fall under the provisions of the present Directive concerning doctors of medicine and nurses responsible for general care respectively.

2. The holders of the Bulgarian qualification of 'ФеЛДШер' (feldsher) referred to in paragraph 1 are not entitled to obtain professional recognition in other Member States as doctors of medicine nor as nurses responsible for general care under this Directive.

Section 2 Doctors of medicine

Article 24   Basic medical training

1. Admission to basic medical training shall be contingent upon possession of a diploma or certificate providing access, for the studies in question, to universities.

2. Basic medical training shall comprise a total of at least five years of study, which may in addition be expressed with the equivalent ECTS credits, and shall consist of at least 5 500 hours of theoretical and practical training provided by, or under the supervision of, a university.

For professionals who began their studies before 1 January 1972, the course of training referred to in the first subparagraph may comprise six months of full-time practical training at university level under the supervision of the competent authorities.

3. Basic medical training shall provide an assurance that the person in question has acquired the following knowledge and skills:

(a) adequate knowledge of the sciences on which medicine is based and a good understanding of the scientific methods including the principles of measuring biological functions, the evaluation of scientifically established facts and the analysis of data;

(b) sufficient understanding of the structure, functions and behaviour of healthy and sick persons, as well as relations between the state of health and physical and social surroundings of the human being;

(c) adequate knowledge of clinical disciplines and practices, providing him with a coherent picture of mental and physical diseases, of medicine from the points of view of prophylaxis, diagnosis and therapy and of human reproduction;

(d) suitable clinical experience in hospitals under appropriate supervision.

Article 25   Specialist medical training

1. Admission to specialist medical training shall be contingent upon completion and validation of a basic medical training programme as referred to in Article 24(2) in the course of which the trainee has acquired the relevant knowledge of basic medicine.

2. Specialist medical training shall comprise theoretical and practical training at a university or medical teaching hospital or, where appropriate, a medical care establishment approved for that purpose by the competent authorities or bodies.

The Member States shall ensure that the minimum duration of specialist medical training courses referred to in Annex V, point 5.1.3 is not less than the duration provided for in that point. Training shall be given under the supervision of the competent authorities or bodies. It shall include personal participation of the trainee specialised doctor in the activity and responsibilities entailed by the services in question.

3. Training shall be given on a full-time basis at specific establishments which are recognised by the competent authorities. It shall entail participation in the full range of medical activities of the department where the training is given, including duty on call, in such a way that the trainee specialist devotes all his professional activity to his practical and theoretical training throughout the entire working week and throughout the year, in accordance with the procedures laid down by the competent authorities. Accordingly, these posts shall be the subject of appropriate remuneration.

3a. Member States may provide, in national legislation, for partial exemptions from parts of the specialist medical training courses listed in point 5.1.3 of Annex V, to be applied on a case-by-case basis provided that that part of the training has been followed already during another specialist training course listed in point 5.1.3 of Annex V, for which the professional has already obtained the professional qualification in a Member State. Member States shall ensure that the granted exemption equates to not more than half of the minimum duration of the specialist medical training course in question.

Each Member State shall notify the Commission and the other Member States of the national legislation concerned for any such partial exemptions.

4. The Member States shall make the issuance of evidence of specialist medical training contingent upon possession of evidence of basic medical training referred to in Annex V, point 5.1.1.

5. The Commission shall be empowered to adopt delegated acts in accordance with Article 57c concerning the adaptation of the minimum periods of training referred to in point 5.1.3 of Annex V to scientific and technical progress.

Article 26   Types of specialist medical training

Evidence of formal qualifications as a specialised doctor referred to in Article 21 is such evidence awarded by the competent authorities or bodies referred to in Annex V, point 5.1.2 as corresponds, for the specialised training in question, to the titles in use in the various Member States and referred to in Annex V, point 5.1.3.

In order to take due account of changes in national legislation and with a view to updating this Directive, the Commission shall be empowered to adopt delegated acts in accordance with Article 57c concerning the inclusion in point 5.1.3 of Annex V of new medical specialties common to at least two-fifths of the Member States.

Article 27   Acquired rights specific to specialised doctors

1. A host Member State may require of specialised doctors whose part-time specialist medical training was governed by legislative, regulatory and administrative provisions in force as of 20 June 1975 and who began their specialist training no later than 31 December 1983 that their evidence of formal qualifications be accompanied by a certificate stating that they have been effectively and lawfully engaged in the relevant activities for at least three consecutive years during the five years preceding the award of that certificate.

2. Every Member State shall recognise the qualification of specialised doctors awarded in Spain to doctors who completed their specialist training before 1 January 1995, even if that training does not satisfy the minimum training requirements provided for in Article 25, in so far as that qualification is accompanied by a certificate issued by the competent Spanish authorities and attesting that

the person concerned has passed the examination in specific professional competence held in the context of exceptional measures concerning recognition laid down in Royal Decree 1497/99, with a view to ascertaining that the person concerned possesses a level of knowledge and skill comparable to that of doctors who possess a qualification as a specialised doctor defined for Spain in Annex V, points 5.1.2 and 5.1.3.

2a. Member States shall recognise the qualifications of specialised doctors awarded in Italy, and listed in points 5.1.2 and 5.1.3 of Annex V, to doctors who started their specialist training after 31 December 1983 and before 1 January 1991, despite the training concerned not satisfying all the training requirements set out in Article 25, if the qualification is accompanied by a certificate issued by the competent Italian authorities stating that the doctor concerned has effectively and lawfully been engaged, in Italy, in the activities of a medical specialist in the same specialist area concerned, for at least seven consecutive years during the 10 years preceding the award of the certificate.

3. Every Member State which has repealed its legislative, regulatory or administrative provisions relating to the award of evidence of formal qualifications as a specialised doctor referred to in Annex V, points 5.1.2 and 5.1.3 and which has adopted measures relating to acquired rights benefiting its nationals, shall grant nationals of other Member States the right to benefit from those measures, in so far as such evidence of formal qualifications was issued before the date on which the host Member State ceased to issue such evidence for the specialty in question.

The dates on which these provisions were repealed are set out in Annex V, point 5.1.3.

Article 28   Specific training in general medical practice

1. Admission to specific training in general medical practice shall be contingent upon completion and validation of a basic medical training programme as referred to in Article 24(2) in the course of which the trainee has acquired the relevant knowledge of basic medicine.

2. The specific training in general medical practice leading to the award of evidence of formal qualifications issued before 1 January 2006 shall be of a duration of at least two years on a full-time basis. In the case of evidence of formal qualifications issued after that date, the training shall be of a duration of at least three years on a full-time basis.

Where the training programme referred to in Article 24 comprises practical training given by an approved hospital possessing appropriate general medical equipment and services or as part of an approved general medical practice or an approved centre in which doctors provide primary medical care, the duration of that practical training may, up to a maximum of one year, be included in the duration provided for in the first subparagraph for certificates of training issued on or after 1 January 2006.

The option provided for in the second subparagraph shall be available only for Member States in which the specific training in general medical practice lasted two years as of 1 January 2001.

3. The specific training in general medical practice shall be carried out on a full-time basis, under the supervision of the competent authorities or bodies. It shall be more practical than theoretical.

The practical training shall be given, on the one hand, for at least six months in an approved hospital possessing appropriate equipment and services and, on the other hand, for at least six months as part of an approved general medical practice or an approved centre at which doctors provide primary health care.

The practical training shall take place in conjunction with other health establishments or structures concerned with general medicine. Without prejudice to the minimum periods laid down in the second subparagraph, however, the practical training may be given during a period of not more than six months in other approved establishments or health structures concerned with general medicine.

The training shall require the personal participation of the trainee in the professional activity and responsibilities of the persons with whom he is working.

4. Member States shall make the issuance of evidence of formal qualifications in general medical practice subject to possession of evidence of formal qualifications in basic medical training referred to in Annex V, point 5.1.1.

5. Member States may issue evidence of formal qualifications referred to in Annex V, point 5.1.4 to a doctor who has not completed the training provided for in this Article but who has completed a different, supplementary training, as attested by evidence of formal qualifications issued by the competent authorities in a Member State. They may not, however, award evidence of formal qualifications unless it attests knowledge of a level qualitatively equivalent to the knowledge acquired from the training provided for in this Article.

Member States shall determine, *inter alia*, the extent to which the complementary training and professional experience already acquired by the applicant may replace the training provided for in this Article.

The Member States may only issue the evidence of formal qualifications referred to in Annex V, point 5.1.4 if the applicant has acquired at least six months' experience of general medicine in a general medical practice or a centre in which doctors provide primary health care of the types referred to in paragraph 3.

Article 29   Pursuit of the professional activities of general practitioners

Each Member State shall, subject to the provisions relating to acquired rights, make the pursuit of the activities of a general practitioner in the framework of its national social security system contingent upon possession of evidence of formal qualifications referred to in Annex V, point 5.1.4.

Member States may exempt persons who are currently undergoing specific training in general medicine from this condition.

Article 30   Acquired rights specific to general practitioners

1. Each Member State shall determine the acquired rights. It shall, however, confer as an acquired right the right to pursue the activities of a general practitioner in the framework of its national social security system, without the evidence of formal qualifications referred to in Annex V, point 5.1.4, on all doctors who enjoy this right as of the reference date stated in that point by virtue of provisions applicable to the medical profession giving access to the professional activities of doctor with basic training and who are established as of that date on its territory, having benefited from the provisions of Articles 21 or 23.

The competent authorities of each Member State shall, on demand, issue a certificate stating the holder's right to pursue the activities of general practitioner in the framework of their national social security systems, without the evidence of formal qualifications referred to in Annex V, point 5.1.4, to doctors who enjoy acquired rights pursuant to the first subparagraph.

2. Every Member State shall recognise the certificates referred to in paragraph 1, second subparagraph, awarded to nationals of Member States by the other Member States, and shall give such certificates the same effect on its territory as evidence of formal qualifications which it awards and which permit the pursuit of the activities of a general practitioner in the framework of its national social security system.

Section 3 Nurses responsible for general care

Article 31   Training of nurses responsible for general care

1. Admission to training for nurses responsible for general care shall be contingent upon either:
   (a) completion of general education of 12 years, as attested by a diploma, certificate or other evidence issued by the competent authorities or bodies in a Member State or a certificate attesting success in an examination of an equivalent level and giving access to universities or to higher education institutions of a level recognised as equivalent; or
   (b) completion of general education of at least 10 years, as attested by a diploma, certificate or other evidence issued by the competent authorities or bodies in a Member State or a certificate attesting success in an examination of an equivalent level and giving access to a vocational school or vocational training programme for nursing.

2. Training of nurses responsible for general care shall be given on a full-time basis and shall include at least the programme described in Annex V, point 5.2.1.

The Commission shall be empowered to adopt delegated acts in accordance with Article 57c concerning amendments to the list set out in point 5.2.1 of Annex V with a view to adapting it to scientific and technical progress.

The amendments referred to in the second subparagraph shall not entail an amendment of existing essential legislative principles in Member States regarding the structure of professions as regards training and conditions of access by natural persons. Such amendments shall respect the responsibility of the Member States for the organisation of education systems, as set out in Article 165(1) TFEU.

3. The training of nurses responsible for general care shall comprise a total of at least three years of study, which may in addition be expressed with the equivalent ECTS credits, and shall consist of at least 4 600 hours of theoretical and clinical training, the duration of the theoretical training representing at least one third and the duration of the clinical training at least one half of the minimum duration of the training. Member States may grant partial exemptions to professionals who have received part of their training on courses which are of at least an equivalent level.

The Member States shall ensure that institutions providing nursing training are responsible for the coordination of theoretical and clinical training throughout the entire study programme.

4. Theoretical education is that part of nurse training from which trainee nurses acquire the professional knowledge, skills and competences required under paragraphs 6 and 7. The training shall be given by teachers of nursing care and by other competent persons, at universities, higher education institutions of a level recognised as equivalent or at vocational schools or through vocational training programmes for nursing.

5. Clinical training is that part of nurse training in which trainee nurses learn, as part of a team and in direct contact with a healthy or sick individual and/or community, to organise, dispense and evaluate the required comprehensive nursing care, on the basis of the knowledge, skills and competences which they have acquired. The trainee nurse shall learn not only how to work in a team, but also how to lead a team and organise overall nursing care, including health education for individuals and small groups, within health institutes or in the community.

This training shall take place in hospitals and other health institutions and in the community, under the responsibility of nursing teachers, in cooperation with and assisted by other qualified nurses. Other qualified personnel may also take part in the teaching process.

Trainee nurses shall participate in the activities of the department in question insofar as those activities are appropriate to their training, enabling them to learn to assume the responsibilities involved in nursing care.

6. Training for nurses responsible for general care shall provide an assurance that the professional in question has acquired the following knowledge and skills:

   (a) comprehensive knowledge of the sciences on which general nursing is based, including sufficient understanding of the structure, physiological functions and behaviour of healthy and sick persons, and of the relationship between the state of health and the physical and social environment of the human being;

   (b) knowledge of the nature and ethics of the profession and of the general principles of health and nursing;

   (c) adequate clinical experience; such experience, which should be selected for its training value, should be gained under the supervision of qualified nursing staff and in places where the number of qualified staff and equipment are appropriate for the nursing care of the patient;

   (d) the ability to participate in the practical training of health personnel and experience of working with such personnel;

   (e) experience of working together with members of other professions in the health sector.

7. Formal qualifications as a nurse responsible for general care shall provide evidence that the professional in question is able to apply at least the following competences regardless of whether the

training took place at universities, higher education institutions of a level recognised as equivalent or at vocational schools or through vocational training programmes for nursing:

(a) competence to independently diagnose the nursing care required using current theoretical and clinical knowledge and to plan, organise and implement nursing care when treating patients on the basis of the knowledge and skills acquired in accordance with points (a), (b) and (c) of paragraph 6 in order to improve professional practice;

(b) competence to work together effectively with other actors in the health sector, including participation in the practical training of health personnel on the basis of the knowledge and skills acquired in accordance with points (d) and (e) of paragraph 6;

(c) competence to empower individuals, families and groups towards healthy lifestyles and self-care on the basis of the knowledge and skills acquired in accordance with points (a) and (b) of paragraph 6;

(d) competence to independently initiate life-preserving immediate measures and to carry out measures in crises and disaster situations;

(e) competence to independently give advice to, instruct and support persons needing care and their attachment figures;

(f) competence to independently assure the quality of, and to evaluate, nursing care;

(g) competence to comprehensively communicate professionally and to cooperate with members of other professions in the health sector;

(h) competence to analyse the care quality to improve his own professional practice as a nurse responsible for general care.

Article 32   Pursuit of the professional activities of nurses responsible for general care

For the purposes of this Directive, the professional activities of nurses responsible for general care are the activities pursued on a professional basis and referred to in Annex V, point 5.2.2.

Article 33   Acquired rights specific to nurses responsible for general care

1. Where the general rules of acquired rights apply to nurses responsible for general care, the activities referred to in Article 23 must have included full responsibility for the planning, organisation and administration of nursing care delivered to the patient.

3. Member States shall recognise evidence of formal qualifications in nursing that:

(a) were awarded in Poland, to nurses who completed training before 1 May 2004, which did not comply with the minimum training requirements laid down in Article 31; and

(b) are attested by the diploma 'bachelor' which was obtained on the basis of a special upgrading programme contained in:

(i) Article 11 of the Act of 20 April 2004 on the amendment of the Act on professions of nurse and midwife and on some other legal acts (Official Journal of the Republic of Poland of 2004 No 92, pos. 885 and of 2007, No 176, pos. 1237) and the Regulation of the Minister of Health of 11 May 2004 on the detailed conditions of delivering studies for nurses and midwives, who hold a certificate of secondary school (final examination—matura) and are graduates of medical lyceum and medical vocational schools teaching in a profession of a nurse and a midwife (Official Journal of the Republic of Poland of 2004 No 110, pos. 1170 and of 2010 No 65, pos. 420); or

(ii) Article 52.3 point 2 of the Act of 15 July 2011 on professions of nurse and midwife (Official Journal of the Republic of Poland of 2011 No 174, pos. 1039) and the Regulation of the Minister of Health of 14 June 2012 on the detailed conditions of delivering higher education courses for nurses and midwives who hold a certificate of secondary school (final examination—matura) and are graduates of a medical secondary school or a post-secondary school teaching in a profession of a nurse and a midwife (Official Journal of the Republic of Poland of 2012, pos. 770),

for the purpose of verifying that the nurse concerned has a level of knowledge and competence comparable to that of nurses holding the qualifications listed for Poland in point 5.2.2 of Annex V.

Article 33(a)

As regards the Romanian qualification of nurse responsible for general care, only the following acquired rights provisions shall apply:

In the case of nationals of Member States who were trained as a nurse responsible for general care in Romania and whose training does not satisfy the minimum training requirements laid down in Article 31, Member States shall recognise the following evidence of formal qualifications as a nurse responsible for general care as being sufficient proof, provided that that evidence is accompanied by a certificate stating that those Member State nationals have effectively and lawfully been engaged in the activities of a nurse responsible for general care in Romania, including taking full responsibility for the planning, organisation and carrying out of the nursing care of patients, for a period of at least three consecutive years during the five years prior to the date of issue of the certificate:

    (a) Certificat de competențe profesionale de asistent medical generalist with post-secondary education obtained from a şcoală postliceală, attesting to training started before 1 January 2007;

    (b) Diplomă de absolvire de asistent medical generalist with short-time higher education studies, attesting to training started before 1 October 2003;

    (c) Diplomă de licență de asistent medical generalist with long-time higher education studies, attesting to training started before 1 October 2003.

Section 4 Dental practitioners

Article 34 Basic dental training

1. Admission to basic dental training presupposes possession of a diploma or certificate giving access, for the studies in question, to universities or higher institutes of a level recognised as equivalent, in a Member State.

2. Basic dental training shall comprise a total of at least five years of study, which may in addition be expressed with the equivalent ECTS credits, and shall consist of at least 5 000 hours of full-time theoretical and practical training that comprises at least the programme described in point 5.3.1 of Annex V and that is provided in a university, in a higher institute providing training recognised as being of an equivalent level or under the supervision of a university.

The Commission shall be empowered to adopt delegated acts in accordance with Article 57c concerning the amendment of the list set out in point 5.3.1 of Annex V with a view to adapting it to scientific and technical progress.

The amendments referred to in the second subparagraph shall not entail an amendment of existing essential legislative principles in Member States regarding the structure of professions as regards training and conditions of access by natural persons. Such amendments shall respect the responsibility of the Member States for the organisation of education systems, as set out in Article 165(1) TFEU.

3. Basic dental training shall provide an assurance that the person in question has acquired the following knowledge and skills:

    (a) adequate knowledge of the sciences on which dentistry is based and a good understanding of scientific methods, including the principles of measuring biological functions, the evaluation of scientifically established facts and the analysis of data;

    (b) adequate knowledge of the constitution, physiology and behaviour of healthy and sick persons as well as the influence of the natural and social environment on the state of health of the human being, in so far as these factors affect dentistry;

    (c) adequate knowledge of the structure and function of the teeth, mouth, jaws and associated tissues, both healthy and diseased, and their relationship to the general state of health and to the physical and social well-being of the patient;

    (d) adequate knowledge of clinical disciplines and methods, providing the dentist with a coherent picture of anomalies, lesions and diseases of the teeth, mouth, jaws and associated tissues and of preventive, diagnostic and therapeutic dentistry;

    (e) suitable clinical experience under appropriate supervision.

This training shall provide him with the skills necessary for carrying out all activities involving the prevention, diagnosis and treatment of anomalies and diseases of the teeth, mouth, jaws and associated tissues.

Article 35   Specialist dental training

1. Admission to specialist dental training shall be contingent upon completion and validation of basic dental training referred to in Article 34, or possession of the documents referred to in Articles 23 and 37.

2. Specialist dental training shall comprise theoretical and practical instruction in a university centre, in a treatment teaching and research centre or, where appropriate, in a health establishment approved for that purpose by the competent authorities or bodies.

Full-time specialist dental courses shall be of a minimum of three years' duration and shall be supervised by the competent authorities or bodies. They shall involve the personal participation of the dental practitioner training to be a specialist in the activity and in the responsibilities of the establishment concerned.

3. The Member States shall make the issuance of evidence of specialist dental training contingent upon possession of evidence of basic dental training referred to in Annex V, point 5.3.2.

4. The Commission shall be empowered to adopt delegated acts in accordance with Article 57c concerning the adaptation of the minimum period of training referred to in paragraph 2 to scientific and technical progress.

5. In order to take due account of changes in national legislation, and with a view to updating this Directive, the Commission shall be empowered to adopt delegated acts in accordance with Article 57c concerning the inclusion in point 5.3.3 of Annex V of new dental specialties common to at least two-fifths of the Member States.

Article 36   Pursuit of the professional activities of dental practitioners

1. For the purposes of this Directive, the professional activities of dental practitioners are the activities defined in paragraph 3 and pursued under the professional qualifications listed in Annex V, point 5.3.2.

2. The profession of dental practitioner shall be based on dental training referred to in Article 34 and shall constitute a specific profession which is distinct from other general or specialised medical professions. Pursuit of the activities of a dental practitioner requires the possession of evidence of formal qualifications referred to in Annex V, point 5.3.2. Holders of such evidence of formal qualifications shall be treated in the same way as those to whom Articles 23 or 37 apply.

3. The Member States shall ensure that dental practitioners are generally able to gain access to and pursue the activities of prevention, diagnosis and treatment of anomalies and diseases affecting the teeth, mouth, jaws and adjoining tissue, having due regard to the regulatory provisions and rules of professional ethics on the reference dates referred to in Annex V, point 5.3.2.

Article 37   Acquired rights specific to dental practitioners

1. Every Member State shall, for the purposes of the pursuit of the professional activities of dental practitioners under the qualifications listed in Annex V, point 5.3.2, recognise evidence of formal qualifications as a doctor issued in Italy, Spain, Austria, the Czech Republic, Slovakia and Romania to persons who began their medical training on or before the reference date stated in that Annex for the Member State concerned, accompanied by a certificate issued by the competent authorities of that Member State.

The certificate must show that the two following conditions are met:

    (a) that the persons in question have been effectively, lawfully and principally engaged in that Member State in the activities referred to in Article 36 for at least three consecutive years during the five years preceding the award of the certificate;

    (b) that those persons are authorised to pursue the said activities under the same conditions as holders of evidence of formal qualifications listed for that Member State in Annex V, point 5.3.2.

Persons who have successfully completed at least three years of study, certified by the competent authorities in the Member State concerned as being equivalent to the training referred to in Article 34, shall be exempt from the three-year practical work experience referred to in the second subparagraph, point (a).

With regard to the Czech Republic and Slovakia, evidence of formal qualifications obtained in the former Czechoslovakia shall be accorded the same level of recognition as Czech and Slovak evidence of formal qualifications and under the same conditions as set out in the preceding sub-paragraphs.

2. Each Member State shall recognise evidence of formal qualifications as a doctor issued in Italy to persons who began their university medical training after 28 January 1980 and no later than 31 December 1984, accompanied by a certificate issued by the competent Italian authorities.

The certificate must show that the three following conditions are met:

(a) that the persons in question passed the relevant aptitude test held by the competent Italian authorities with a view to establishing that those persons possess a level of knowledge and skills comparable to that of persons possessing evidence of formal qualifications listed for Italy in Annex V, point 5.3.2;

(b) that they have been effectively, lawfully and principally engaged in the activities referred to in Article 36 in Italy for at least three consecutive years during the five years preceding the award of the certificate;

(c) that they are authorised to engage in or are effectively, lawfully and principally engaged in the activities referred to in Article 36, under the same conditions as the holders of evidence of formal qualifications listed for Italy in Annex V, point 5.3.2.

Persons who have successfully completed at least three years of study certified by the competent authorities as being equivalent to the training referred to in Article 34 shall be exempt from the aptitude test referred to in the second subparagraph, point (a).

Persons who began their university medical training after 31 December 1984 shall be treated in the same way as those referred to above, provided that the abovementioned three years of study began before 31 December 1994.

3. As regards evidence of formal qualifications of dental practitioners, Member States shall recognise such evidence pursuant to Article 21 in cases where the applicants began their training on or before 18 January 2016.

4. Each Member State shall recognise evidence of formal qualifications as a doctor issued in Spain to professionals who began their university medical training between 1 January 1986 and 31 December 1997, accompanied by a certificate issued by the Spanish competent authorities.

The certificate shall confirm that the following conditions have been met:

(a) the professional in question has successfully completed at least three years of study, certified by the Spanish competent authorities as being equivalent to the training referred to in Article 34;

(b) the professional in question was effectively, lawfully and principally engaged in the activities referred to in Article 36 in Spain for at least three consecutive years during the five years preceding the award of the certificate;

(c) the professional in question is authorised to engage in or is effectively, lawfully and principally engaged in the activities referred to in Article 36, under the same conditions as the holders of evidence of formal qualifications listed for Spain in point 5.3.2 of Annex V.

Section 5 Veterinary surgeons

Article 38 The training of veterinary surgeons

1. The training of veterinary surgeons shall comprise a total of at least five years of full-time theoretical and practical study, which may in addition be expressed with the equivalent ECTS credits, at a university or at a higher institute providing training recognised as being of an equivalent level, or under the supervision of a university, covering at least the study programme referred to in point 5.4.1 of Annex V.

The Commission shall be empowered to adopt delegated acts in accordance with Article 57c concerning the amendment of the list set out in point 5.4.1 of Annex V with a view to adapting it to scientific and technical progress.

The amendments referred to in the second subparagraph shall not entail an amendment of existing essential legislative principles in Member States regarding the structure of professions as regards training and conditions of access by natural persons. Such amendments shall respect the responsibility of the Member States for the organisation of education systems, as set out in Article 165(1) TFEU.

2. Admission to veterinary training shall be contingent upon possession of a diploma or certificate entitling the holder to enter, for the studies in question, university establishments or institutes of higher education recognised by a Member State to be of an equivalent level for the purpose of the relevant study.

3. Training as a veterinary surgeon shall provide an assurance that the professional in question has acquired the following knowledge and skills:

(a) adequate knowledge of the sciences on which the activities of a veterinary surgeon are based and of the Union law relating to those activities;

(b) adequate knowledge of the structure, functions, behaviour and physiological needs of animals, as well as the skills and competences needed for their husbandry, feeding, welfare, reproduction and hygiene in general;

(c) the clinical, epidemiological and analytical skills and competences required for the prevention, diagnosis and treatment of the diseases of animals, including anaesthesia, aseptic surgery and painless death, whether considered individually or in groups, including specific knowledge of the diseases which may be transmitted to humans;

(d) adequate knowledge, skills and competences for preventive medicine, including competences relating to inquiries and certification;

(e) adequate knowledge of the hygiene and technology involved in the production, manufacture and putting into circulation of animal feedstuffs or foodstuffs of animal origin intended for human consumption, including the skills and competences required to understand and explain good practice in this regard;

(f) the knowledge, skills and competences required for the responsible and sensible use of veterinary medicinal products, in order to treat the animals and to ensure the safety of the food chain and the protection of the environment.

Article 39 Acquired rights specific to veterinary surgeons

Without prejudice to Article 23(4), with regard to nationals of Member States whose evidence of formal qualifications as a veterinary surgeon was issued by, or whose training commenced in, Estonia before 1 May 2004, Member States shall recognise such evidence of formal qualifications as a veterinary surgeon if it is accompanied by a certificate stating that such persons have effectively and lawfully been engaged in the activities in question in Estonia for at least five consecutive years during the seven years prior to the date of issue of the certificate.

Section 6 Midwives

Article 40 The training of midwives

1. The training of midwives shall comprise a total of at least:

(a) specific full-time training as a midwife comprising at least three years of theoretical and practical study (route I) comprising at least the programme described in Annex V, point 5.5.1, or

(b) specific full-time training as a midwife of 18 months' duration (route II), comprising at least the study programme described in Annex V, point 5.5.1, which was not the subject of equivalent training of nurses responsible for general care.

The Member States shall ensure that institutions providing midwife training are responsible for coordinating theory and practice throughout the programme of study.

The Commission shall be empowered to adopt delegated acts in accordance with Article 57c concerning the amendment of the list set out in point 5.5.1 of Annex V with a view to adapting it to scientific and technical progress.

The amendments referred to in the third subparagraph shall not entail an amendment of existing essential legislative principles in Member States regarding the structure of professions as regards training and conditions of access by natural persons. Such amendments shall respect the responsibility of the Member States for the organisation of education systems, as set out in Article 165(1) TFEU.

2. Admission to training as a midwife shall be contingent upon one of the following conditions:

(a) completion of at least 12 years of general school education or possession of a certificate attesting success in an examination, of an equivalent level, for admission to a midwifery school for route I;

(b) possession of evidence of formal qualifications as a nurse responsible for general care referred to in point 5.2.2 of Annex V for route II.

3. Training as a midwife shall provide an assurance that the professional in question has acquired the following knowledge and skills:

(a) detailed knowledge of the sciences on which the activities of midwives are based, particularly midwifery, obstetrics and gynaecology;

(b) adequate knowledge of the ethics of the profession and the legislation relevant for the practice of the profession;

(c) adequate knowledge of general medical knowledge (biological functions, anatomy and physiology) and of pharmacology in the field of obstetrics and of the newly born, and also knowledge of the relationship between the state of health and the physical and social environment of the human being, and of his behaviour;

(d) adequate clinical experience gained in approved institutions allowing the midwife to be able, independently and under his own responsibility, to the extent necessary and excluding pathological situations, to manage the antenatal care, to conduct the delivery and its consequences in approved institutions, and to supervise labour and birth, postnatal care and neonatal resuscitation while awaiting a medical practitioner;

(e) adequate understanding of the training of health personnel and experience of working with such personnel.

Article 41 Procedures for the recognition of evidence of formal qualifications as a midwife

1. The evidence of formal qualifications as a midwife referred to in point 5.5.2 of Annex V shall be subject to automatic recognition pursuant to Article 21 in so far as they satisfy one of the following criteria:

(a) full-time training of at least three years as a midwife, which may in addition be expressed with the equivalent ECTS credits, consisting of at least 4 600 hours of theoretical and practical training, with at least one third of the minimum duration representing clinical training;

(b) full-time training as a midwife of at least two years, which may in addition be expressed with the equivalent ECTS credits, consisting of at least 3 600 hours, contingent upon possession of evidence of formal qualifications as a nurse responsible for general care referred to in point 5.2.2 of Annex V;

(c) full-time training as a midwife of at least 18 months, which may in addition be expressed with the equivalent ECTS credits, consisting of at least 3 000 hours, contingent upon possession of evidence of formal qualifications as a nurse responsible for general care referred to in point 5.2.2 of Annex V, and followed by one year's professional practice for which a certificate has been issued in accordance with paragraph 2.

2. The certificate referred to in paragraph 1 shall be issued by the competent authorities in the home Member State. It shall certify that the holder, after obtaining evidence of formal qualifications

as a midwife, has satisfactorily pursued all the activities of a midwife for a corresponding period in a hospital or a health care establishment approved for that purpose.

Article 42   Pursuit of the professional activities of a midwife

1. The provisions of this section shall apply to the activities of midwives as defined by each Member State, without prejudice to paragraph 2, and pursued under the professional titles set out in Annex V, point 5.5.2.

2. The Member States shall ensure that midwives are able to gain access to and pursue at least the following activities:

(a) provision of sound family planning information and advice;

(b) diagnosis of pregnancies and monitoring normal pregnancies; carrying out the examinations necessary for the monitoring of the development of normal pregnancies;

(c) prescribing or advising on the examinations necessary for the earliest possible diagnosis of pregnancies at risk;

(d) provision of programmes of parenthood preparation and complete preparation for childbirth including advice on hygiene and nutrition;

(e) caring for and assisting the mother during labour and monitoring the condition of the foetus in utero by the appropriate clinical and technical means;

(f) conducting spontaneous deliveries including where required episiotomies and in urgent cases breech deliveries;

(g) recognising the warning signs of abnormality in the mother or infant which necessitate referral to a doctor and assisting the latter where appropriate; taking the necessary emergency measures in the doctor's absence, in particular the manual removal of the placenta, possibly followed by manual examination of the uterus;

(h) examining and caring for the new-born infant; taking all initiatives which are necessary in case of need and carrying out where necessary immediate resuscitation;

(i) caring for and monitoring the progress of the mother in the post-natal period and giving all necessary advice to the mother on infant care to enable her to ensure the optimum progress of the new-born infant;

(j) carrying out treatment prescribed by doctors;

(k) drawing up the necessary written reports.

Article 43   Acquired rights specific to midwives

1. Every Member State shall, in the case of Member State nationals whose evidence of formal qualifications as a midwife satisfies all the minimum training requirements laid down in Article 40 but, by virtue of Article 41, is not recognised unless it is accompanied by a certificate of professional practice referred to in Article 41(2), recognise as sufficient proof evidence of formal qualifications issued by those Member States before the reference date referred to in Annex V, point 5.5.2, accompanied by a certificate stating that those nationals have been effectively and lawfully engaged in the activities in question for at least two consecutive years during the five years preceding the award of the certificate.

1a. As regards evidence of formal qualifications of midwives, Member States shall recognise automatically those qualifications where the applicant started the training before 18 January 2016, and the admission requirement for such training was 10 years of general education or an equivalent level for route I, or completed training as a nurse responsible for general care as attested by evidence of formal qualification referred to in point 5.2.2 of Annex V before starting a midwifery training falling under route II.

2. The conditions laid down in paragraph 1 shall apply to the nationals of Member States whose evidence of formal qualifications as a midwife certifies completion of training received in the territory of the former German Democratic Republic and satisfying all the minimum training requirements laid down in Article 40 but where the evidence of formal qualifications, by virtue of Article 41, is not recognised unless it is accompanied by the certificate of professional experience referred to in Article 41(2), where it attests a course of training which began before 3 October 1990.

4. Member States shall recognise evidence of formal qualifications in midwifery that:

(a) were awarded in Poland, to midwives who completed training before 1 May 2004, which did not comply with the minimum training requirements laid down in Article 40; and

(b) are attested by the diploma 'bachelor' which was obtained on the basis of a special up-grading programme contained in:

(i) Article 11 of the Act of 20 April 2004 on the amendment of the Act on professions of nurse and midwife and on some other legal acts (Official Journal of the Republic of Poland of 2004 No 92, pos. 885 and of 2007 No 176, pos. 1237) and the Regulation of the Minister of Health of 11 May 2004 on the detailed conditions of delivering studies for nurses and midwives, who hold a certificate of secondary school (final examination—matura) and are graduates of medical lyceum and medical voca-tional schools teaching in a profession of a nurse and a midwife (Official Journal of the Republic of Poland of 2004 No 110, pos. 1170 and of 2010 No 65, pos. 420); or

(ii) Article 53.3 point 3 of the Act of 15 July 2011 on professions of nurse and mid-wife (Official Journal of the Republic of Poland of 2011 No 174, pos. 1039) and the Regulation of the Minister of Health of 14 June 2012 on the detailed conditions of delivering higher education courses for nurses and midwives who hold a certificate of secondary school (final examination—matura) and are graduates of a medical secondary school or a post-secondary school teaching in a profession of a nurse and a midwife (Official Journal of the Republic of Poland of 2012, pos. 770),

for the purpose of verifying that the midwife concerned has a level of knowledge and competence comparable to that of midwives holding the qualifications listed for Poland in point 5.5.2 of Annex V.

Article 43(a)

As regards the Romanian qualifications in midwifery, only the following acquired rights provisions will apply:

In the case of nationals of the Member States whose evidence of formal qualifications as a midwife (asistent medical obstetrică-ginecologie/obstetrics-gynaecology nurse) were awarded by Romania before the date of accession and which do not satisfy the minimum training requirements laid down in Article 40, Member States shall recognise the said evidence of formal qualifications as being suf-ficient proof for the purposes of carrying out the activities of midwife, if they are accompanied by a certificate stating that those Member State nationals have effectively and lawfully been engaged in the activities of midwife in Romania, for at least five consecutive years during the seven years prior to the issue of the certificate.

Article 43b

Acquired rights in midwifery shall not apply to the following qualifications which were obtained in Croatia before 1 July 2013: viša medicinska sestra ginekološko-opstetričkog smjera (High Gynaecology-Obstetrical Nurse), medicinska sestra ginekološko-opstetričkog smjera (Gynaecology-Obstetrical Nurse), viša medicinska sestra primaljskog smjera (High Nurse with Midwifery Degree), medicinska sestra primaljskog smjera (Nurse with Midwifery Degree), ginekološko-opstetrička primalja (Gynaecology-Obstetrical Midwife) and primalja (Midwife).

Section 7 Pharmacist

Article 44 Training as a pharmacist

1. Admission to a course of training as a pharmacist shall be contingent upon possession of a diploma or certificate giving access, in a Member State, to the studies in question, at universities or higher institutes of a level recognised as equivalent.

2. Evidence of formal qualifications as a pharmacist shall attest to training of at least five years' duration, which may in addition be expressed with the equivalent ECTS credits, comprising at least:

(a) four years of full-time theoretical and practical training at a university or at a higher institute of a level recognised as equivalent, or under the supervision of a university;

(b) during or at the end of the theoretical and practical training, six-month traineeship in a pharmacy which is open to the public or in a hospital under the supervision of that hospital's pharmaceutical department.

The training cycle referred to in this paragraph shall include at least the programme described in point 5.6.1 of Annex V. The Commission shall be empowered to adopt delegated acts in accordance with Article 57c concerning the amendment of the list set out in point 5.6.1 of Annex V with a view to adapting it to scientific and technical progress, including the evolution of pharmacological practice.

The amendments referred to in the second subparagraph shall not entail an amendment of existing essential legislative principles in Member States regarding the structure of professions as regards training and conditions of access by natural persons. Such amendments shall respect the responsibility of the Member States for the organisation of education systems, as set out in Article 165(1) TFEU.

3. Training for pharmacists shall provide an assurance that the person concerned has acquired the following knowledge and skills:

(a) adequate knowledge of medicines and the substances used in the manufacture of medicines;

(b) adequate knowledge of pharmaceutical technology and the physical, chemical, biological and microbiological testing of medicinal products;

(c) adequate knowledge of the metabolism and the effects of medicinal products and of the action of toxic substances, and of the use of medicinal products;

(d) adequate knowledge to evaluate scientific data concerning medicines in order to be able to supply appropriate information on the basis of this knowledge;

(e) adequate knowledge of the legal and other requirements associated with the pursuit of pharmacy.

Article 45   Pursuit of the professional activities of a pharmacist

1. For the purposes of this Directive, the activities of a pharmacist are those, access to which and pursuit of which are contingent, in one or more Member States, upon professional qualifications and which are open to holders of evidence of formal qualifications of the types listed in Annex V, point 5.6.2.

2. The Member States shall ensure that the holders of evidence of formal qualifications in pharmacy at university level or a level recognised as equivalent, which satisfies the requirements of Article 44, are able to gain access to and pursue at least the following activities, subject to the requirement, where appropriate, of supplementary professional experience:

(a) preparation of the pharmaceutical form of medicinal products;

(b) manufacture and testing of medicinal products;

(c) testing of medicinal products in a laboratory for the testing of medicinal products;

(d) storage, preservation and distribution of medicinal products at the wholesale stage;

(e) supply, preparation, testing, storage, distribution and dispensing of safe and efficacious medicinal products of the required quality in pharmacies open to the public;

(f) preparation, testing, storage and dispensing of safe and efficacious medicinal products of the required quality in hospitals;

(g) provision of information and advice on medicinal products as such, including on their appropriate use;

(h) reporting of adverse reactions of pharmaceutical products to the competent authorities;

(i) personalised support for patients who administer their medication;

(j) contribution to local or national public health campaigns.

3. If a Member State makes access to or pursuit of one of the activities of a pharmacist contingent upon supplementary professional experience, in addition to possession of evidence of formal qualifications referred to in Annex V, point 5.6.2, that Member State shall recognise as sufficient proof in

this regard a certificate issued by the competent authorities in the home Member State stating that the person concerned has been engaged in those activities in the home Member State for a similar period.

4. The recognition referred to in paragraph 3 shall not apply with regard to the two-year period of professional experience required by the Grand Duchy of Luxembourg for the grant of a State public pharmacy concession.

5. If, on 16 September 1985, a Member State had a competitive examination in place designed to select from among the holders referred to in paragraph 2, those who are to be authorised to become owners of new pharmacies whose creation has been decided on as part of a national system of geographical division, that Member State may, by way of derogation from paragraph 1, proceed with that examination and require nationals of Member States who possess evidence of formal qualifications as a pharmacist referred to in Annex V, point 5.6.2 or who benefit from the provisions of Article 23 to take part in it.

Section 8   Architect

Article 46   Training of architects

1. Training as an architect shall comprise:
    (a) a total of at least five years of full-time study at a university or a comparable teaching institution, leading to successful completion of a university-level examination; or
    (b) not less than four years of full-time study at a university or a comparable teaching institution leading to successful completion of a university-level examination, accompanied by a certificate attesting to the completion of two years of professional traineeship in accordance with paragraph 4.

2. Architecture must be the principal component of the study referred to in paragraph 1. The study shall maintain a balance between theoretical and practical aspects of architectural training and shall guarantee at least the acquisition of the following knowledge, skills and competences:
    (a) the ability to create architectural designs that satisfy both aesthetic and technical requirements;
    (b) adequate knowledge of the history and theories of architecture and the related arts, technologies and human sciences;
    (c) knowledge of the fine arts as an influence on the quality of architectural design;
    (d) adequate knowledge of urban design, planning and the skills involved in the planning process;
    (e) understanding of the relationship between people and buildings, and between buildings and their environment, and of the need to relate buildings and the spaces between them to human needs and scale;
    (f) understanding of the profession of architect and the role of the architect in society, in particular in preparing briefs that take account of social factors;
    (g) understanding of the methods of investigation and preparation of the brief for a design project;
    (h) understanding of the structural design, and constructional and engineering problems associated with building design;
    (i) adequate knowledge of physical problems and technologies and of the function of buildings so as to provide them with internal conditions of comfort and protection against the climate, in the framework of sustainable development;
    (j) the necessary design skills to meet building users' requirements within the constraints imposed by cost factors and building regulations;
    (k) adequate knowledge of the industries, organisations, regulations and procedures involved in translating design concepts into buildings and integrating plans into overall planning.

3. The number of years of academic study referred to in paragraphs 1 and 2 may in addition be expressed with the equivalent ECTS credits.

4. The professional traineeship referred to in point (b) of paragraph 1 shall take place only after completion of the first three years of the study. At least one year of the professional traineeship shall build upon knowledge, skills and competences acquired during the study referred to in paragraph 2. To that end, the professional traineeship shall be carried out under the supervision of a person or body that has been authorised by the competent authority in the home Member State. Such supervised traineeship may take place in any country. The professional traineeship shall be evaluated by the competent authority in the home Member State.

Article 47 Derogations from the conditions for the training of architects

By way of derogation from Article 46, the following shall also be recognised as complying with Article 21: training as part of social betterment schemes or part-time university studies which satisfies the requirements set out in Article 46(2), as attested by an examination in architecture passed by a professional who has been working for seven years or more in the field of architecture under the supervision of an architect or architectural bureau. The examination must be of university level and be equivalent to the final examination referred to in point (b) of Article 46(1).

Article 48 Pursuit of the professional activities of architects

1. For the purposes of this Directive, the professional activities of an architect are the activities regularly carried out under the professional title of 'architect'.

2. Nationals of a Member State who are authorised to use that title pursuant to a law which gives the competent authority of a Member State the power to award that title to Member States nationals who are especially distinguished by the quality of their work in the field of architecture shall be deemed to satisfy the conditions required for the pursuit of the activities of an architect, under the professional title of 'architect'. The architectural nature of the activities of the persons concerned shall be attested by a certificate awarded by their home Member State.

Article 49 Acquired rights specific to architects

1. Each Member State shall accept evidence of formal qualifications as an architect listed in Annex VI, point 6, awarded by the other Member States, and attesting a course of training which began no later than the reference academic year referred to in that Annex, even if they do not satisfy the minimum requirements laid down in Article 46, and shall, for the purposes of access to and pursuit of the professional activities of an architect, give such evidence the same effect on its territory as evidence of formal qualifications as an architect which it itself issues.

Under these circumstances, certificates issued by the competent authorities of the Federal Republic of Germany attesting that evidence of formal qualifications issued on or after 8 May 1945 by the competent authorities of the German Democratic Republic is equivalent to such evidence listed in that Annex, shall be recognised.

1a. Paragraph 1 shall also apply to evidence of formal qualifications as an architect listed in Annex V, where the training started before 18 January 2016.

2. Without prejudice to paragraph 1, every Member State shall recognise the following evidence of formal qualifications and shall, for the purposes of access to and pursuit of the professional activities of an architect performed, give them the same effect on its territory as evidence of formal qualifications which it itself issues: certificates issued to nationals of Member States by the Member States which have enacted rules governing the access to and pursuit of the activities of an architect as of the following dates:

(a) 1 January 1995 for Austria, Finland and Sweden;

(b) 1 May 2004 for the Czech Republic, Estonia, Cyprus, Latvia, Lithuania, Hungary, Malta, Poland, Slovenia and Slovakia;

(ba) 1 July 2013 for Croatia;

(c) 5 August 1987 for the other Member States.

The certificates referred to in paragraph 1 shall certify that the holder was authorised, no later than the respective date, to use the professional title of architect, and that he has been effectively engaged, in the context of those rules, in the activities in question for at least three consecutive years during the five years preceding the award of the certificate.

3. Each Member State shall give the following evidence the same effect on its territory as evidence of formal qualifications it itself issues for the purposes of access to and pursuit of the professional activities of an architect: evidence of completion of training existing as of 5 August 1985 and commenced no later than 17 January 2014, provided by 'Fachhochschulen' in the Federal Republic of Germany over a period of three years, satisfying the requirements set out in Article 46(2) and giving access to the activities referred to in Article 48 in that Member State under the professional title of 'architect', in so far as the training was followed by a four-year period of professional experience in the Federal Republic of Germany, as attested by a certificate issued by the competent authority in whose roll the name of the architect wishing to benefit from the provisions of this Directive appears.

Chapter IIIA Automatic recognition on the basis of common training principles

Article 49a Common training framework

1. For the purpose of this Article, 'common training framework' means a common set of minimum knowledge, skills and competences necessary for the pursuit of a specific profession. A common training framework shall not replace national training programmes unless a Member State decides otherwise under national law. For the purpose of access to and pursuit of a profession in Member States which regulate that profession, a Member State shall give evidence of professional qualifications acquired on the basis of such a framework the same effect in its territory as the evidence of formal qualifications which it itself issues, on condition that such framework fulfils the conditions laid down in paragraph 2.

2. A common training framework shall comply with the following conditions:

(a) the common training framework enables more professionals to move across Member States;

(b) the profession to which the common training framework applies is regulated, or the education and training leading to the profession is regulated in at least one third of the Member States;

(c) the common set of knowledge, skills and competences combines the knowledge, skills and competences required in the systems of education and training applicable in at least one third of the Member States; it shall be irrelevant whether the knowledge, skills and competences have been acquired as part of a general training course at a university or higher education institution or as part of a vocational training course;

(d) the common training framework shall be based on levels of the EQF, as defined in Annex II of the Recommendation of the European Parliament and of the Council of 23 April 2008 on the establishment of the European Qualifications Framework for lifelong learning[27];

(e) the profession concerned is neither covered by another common training framework nor subject to automatic recognition under Chapter III of Title III;

(f) the common training framework has been prepared following a transparent due process, including the relevant stakeholders from Member States where the profession is not regulated;

(g) the common training framework permits nationals from any Member State to be eligible for acquiring the professional qualification under such framework without first being required to be a member of any professional organisation or to be registered with such organisation.

3. Representative professional organisations at Union level, as well as national professional organisations or competent authorities from at least one third of the Member States, may submit to the Commission suggestions for common training frameworks which meet the conditions laid down in paragraph 2.

---

[27] OJ C 111, 6.5.2008, p. 1.

4. The Commission shall be empowered to adopt delegated acts in accordance with Article 57c to establish a common training framework for a given profession based on the conditions laid down in paragraph 2 of this Article.

5. A Member State shall be exempted from the obligation of introducing the common training framework referred to in paragraph 4 on its territory and from the obligation of granting automatic recognition to the professional qualifications acquired under that common training framework if one of the following conditions is fulfilled:

    (a) there are no education or training institutions available in its territory to offer such training for the profession concerned;

    (b) the introduction of the common training framework would adversely affect the organisation of its system of education and professional training;

    (c) there are substantial differences between the common training framework and the training required in its territory, which entail serious risks for public policy, public security, public health or for the safety of the service recipients or the protection of the environment.

6. Member States shall, within six months of the entry into force of the delegated act referred to in paragraph 4, notify to the Commission and to the other Member States:

    (a) the national qualifications, and where applicable the national professional titles, that comply with the common training framework; or

    (b) any use of the exemption referred to in paragraph 5, along with a justification of which conditions under that paragraph were fulfilled. The Commission may, within three months, request further clarification if it considers that a Member State has provided no or insufficient justification that one of these conditions has been fulfilled. The Member State shall reply within three months of any such request.

The Commission may adopt an implementing act to list the national professional qualifications and national professional titles benefiting from automatic recognition under the common training framework adopted in accordance with paragraph 4.

7. This Article also applies to specialties of a profession, provided such specialties concern professional activities the access to and the pursuit of which are regulated in Member States, where the profession is already subject to automatic recognition under Chapter III of Title III, but not the specialty concerned.

Article 49b   Common training tests

1. For the purpose of this Article, a 'common training test' means a standardised aptitude test available across participating Member States and reserved to holders of a particular professional qualification. Passing such a test in a Member State shall entitle the holder of a particular professional qualification to pursue the profession in any host Member State concerned under the same conditions as the holders of professional qualifications acquired in that Member State.

2. The common training test shall comply with the following conditions:

    (a) the common training test enables more professionals to move across Member States;

    (b) the profession to which the common training test applies is regulated, or the education and training leading to the profession concerned is regulated in at least one third of the Member States;

    (c) the common training test has been prepared following a transparent due process, including the relevant stakeholders from Member States where the profession is not regulated;

    (d) the common training test permits nationals from any Member State to participate in such a test and in the practical organisation of such tests in Member States without first being required to be a member of any professional organisation or to be registered with such organisation.

3. Representative professional organisations at Union level, as well as national professional organisations or competent authorities from at least one third of the Member States, may submit

to the Commission suggestions for common training tests which meet the conditions laid down in paragraph 2.

4. The Commission shall be empowered to adopt delegated acts in accordance with Article 57c to establish the contents of a common training test, and the conditions required for taking and passing the test.

5. A Member State shall be exempted from the obligation of organising the common training test referred to in paragraph 4 on its territory and from the obligation of granting automatic recognition to professionals who have passed the common training test if one of the following conditions is fulfilled:

    (a) the profession concerned is not regulated on its territory;

    (b) the contents of the common training test will not sufficiently mitigate serious risks for public health or the safety of the service recipients, which are relevant on its territory;

    (c) the contents of the common training test would render access to the profession significantly less attractive compared to national requirements.

6. Member States shall, within six months of the entry into force of the delegated act referred to in paragraph 4, notify to the Commission and to the other Member States:

    (a) the available capacity for organising such tests; or

    (b) any use of the exemption referred to in paragraph 5, along with the justification of which conditions under that paragraph were fulfilled. The Commission may, within three months, request further clarification, if it considers that a Member State has provided no or insufficient justification that one of these conditions has been fulfilled. The Member State shall reply within three months of any such request.

The Commission may adopt an implementing act to list the Member States in which the common training tests adopted in accordance with paragraph 4 are to be organised, the frequency during a calendar year and other arrangements necessary for organising common training tests across Member States.

Chapter IV Common provisions on establishment

Article 50 Documentation and formalities

1. Where the competent authorities of the host Member State decide on an application for authorisation to pursue the regulated profession in question by virtue of this Title, those authorities may demand the documents and certificates listed in Annex VII.

The documents referred to in Annex VII, point 1(d), (e) and (f), shall not be more than three months old by the date on which they are submitted.

The Member States, bodies and other legal persons shall guarantee the confidentiality of the information which they receive.

2. In the event of justified doubts, the host Member State may require from the competent authorities of a Member State confirmation of the authenticity of the attestations and evidence of formal qualifications awarded in that other Member State, as well as, where applicable, confirmation of the fact that the beneficiary fulfils, for the professions referred to in Chapter III of this Title, the minimum training conditions set out respectively in Articles 24, 25, 28, 31, 34, 35, 38, 40, 44 and 46.

3. In cases of justified doubt, where evidence of formal qualifications, as defined in Article 3(1)(c), has been issued by a competent authority in a Member State and includes training received in whole or in part in an establishment legally established in the territory of another Member State, the host Member State shall be entitled to verify with the competent body in the Member State of origin of the award:

    (a) whether the training course at the establishment which gave the training has been formally certified by the educational establishment based in the Member State of origin of the award;

(b) whether the evidence of formal qualifications issued is the same as that which would have been awarded if the course had been followed entirely in the Member State of origin of the award; and

(c) whether the evidence of formal qualifications confers the same professional rights in the territory of the Member State of origin of the award.

3a. In the event of justified doubts, the host Member State may require from the competent authorities of a Member State confirmation of the fact that the applicant is not suspended or prohibited from the pursuit of the profession as a result of serious professional misconduct or conviction of criminal offences relating to the pursuit of any of his professional activities.

3b. Exchange of information between competent authorities of different Member States under this Article shall take place via IMI

4. Where a host Member State requires its nationals to swear a solemn oath or make a sworn statement in order to gain access to a regulated profession, and where the wording of that oath or statement cannot be used by nationals of the other Member States, the host Member State shall ensure that the persons concerned can use an appropriate equivalent wording.

Article 51
Procedure for the mutual recognition of professional qualifications

1. The competent authority of the host Member State shall acknowledge receipt of the application within one month of receipt and inform the applicant of any missing document.

2. The procedure for examining an application for authorisation to practise a regulated profession must be completed as quickly as possible and lead to a duly substantiated decision by the competent authority in the host Member State in any case within three months after the date on which the applicant's complete file was submitted. However, this deadline may be extended by one month in cases falling under Chapters I and II of this Title.

3. The decision, or failure to reach a decision within the deadline, shall be subject to appeal under national law.

Article 52   Use of professional titles

1. If, in a host Member State, the use of a professional title relating to one of the activities of the profession in question is regulated, nationals of the other Member States who are authorised to practise a regulated profession on the basis of Title III shall use the professional title of the host Member State, which corresponds to that profession in that Member State, and make use of any associated initials.

2. Where a profession is regulated in the host Member State by an association or organisation within the meaning of Article 3(2), nationals of Member States shall not be authorised to use the professional title issued by that organisation or association, or its abbreviated form, unless they furnish proof that they are members of that association or organisation.

If the association or organisation makes membership contingent upon certain qualifications, it may do so, only under the conditions laid down in this Directive, in respect of nationals of other Member States who possess professional qualifications.

3. A Member State may not reserve the use of the professional title to the holders of professional qualifications if it has not notified the association or organisation to the Commission and to the other Member States in accordance with Article 3(2).

Title IV Detailed rules for pursuing the profession

Article 53   Knowledge of languages

1. Professionals benefiting from the recognition of professional qualifications shall have a knowledge of languages necessary for practising the profession in the host Member State.

2. A Member State shall ensure that any controls carried out by, or under the supervision of, the competent authority for controlling compliance with the obligation under paragraph 1 shall be

limited to the knowledge of one official language of the host Member State, or one administrative language of the host Member State provided that it is also an official language of the Union.

3. Controls carried out in accordance with paragraph 2 may be imposed if the profession to be practised has patient safety implications. Controls may be imposed in respect of other professions in cases where there is a serious and concrete doubt about the sufficiency of the professional's language knowledge in respect of the professional activities that that professional intends to pursue.

Controls may be carried out only after the issuance of a European Professional Card in accordance with Article 4d or after the recognition of a professional qualification, as the case may be.

4. Any language controls shall be proportionate to the activity to be pursued. The professional concerned shall be allowed to appeal such controls under national law.

Article 54   Use of academic titles

Without prejudice to Articles 7 and 52, the host Member State shall ensure that the right shall be conferred on the persons concerned to use academic titles conferred on them in the home Member State, and possibly an abbreviated form thereof, in the language of the home Member State. The host Member State may require that title to be followed by the name and address of the establishment or examining board which awarded it. Where an academic title of the home Member State is liable to be confused in the host Member State with a title which, in the latter Member State, requires supplementary training not acquired by the beneficiary, the host Member State may require the beneficiary to use the academic title of the home Member State in an appropriate form, to be laid down by the host Member State.

Article 55   Approval by health insurance funds

Without prejudice to Article 5(1) and Article 6, first subparagraph, point (b), Member States which require persons who acquired their professional qualifications in their territory to complete a preparatory period of in-service training and/or a period of professional experience in order to be approved by a health insurance fund, shall waive this obligation for the holders of evidence of professional qualifications of doctor and dental practitioner acquired in other Member States.

Article 55a   Recognition of professional traineeship

1. If access to a regulated profession in the home Member State is contingent upon completion of a professional traineeship, the competent authority of the home Member State shall, when considering a request for authorisation to exercise the regulated profession, recognise professional traineeships carried out in another Member State provided the traineeship is in accordance with the published guidelines referred to in paragraph 2, and shall take into account professional traineeships carried out in a third country. However, Member States may, in national legislation, set a reasonable limit on the duration of the part of the professional traineeship which can be carried out abroad.

2. Recognition of the professional traineeship shall not replace any requirements in place to pass an examination in order to gain access to the profession in question. The competent authorities shall publish guidelines on the organisation and recognition of professional traineeships carried out in another Member State or in a third country, in particular on the role of the supervisor of the professional traineeship.

Title V Administrative cooperation and responsibility for implementation

Article 56   Competent authorities

1. The competent authorities of the host Member State and of the home Member State shall work in close collaboration and shall provide mutual assistance in order to facilitate application of this Directive. They shall ensure the confidentiality of the information which they exchange.

2. The competent authorities of the home and the host Member States shall exchange information regarding disciplinary action or criminal sanctions taken or any other serious, specific

circumstances which are likely to have consequences for the pursuit of activities under this Directive. In so doing, they shall respect personal data protection rules provided for in Directives 95/46/EC and 2002/58/EC.

The home Member State shall examine the veracity of the circumstances and its authorities shall decide on the nature and scope of the investigations which need to be carried out and shall inform the host Member State of the conclusions which it draws from the information available to it.

2a. For the purposes of paragraphs 1 and 2, the competent authorities shall use IMI.

3. Each Member State shall, no later than 20 October 2007, designate the authorities and bodies competent to award or receive evidence of formal qualifications and other documents or information, and those competent to receive applications and take the decisions referred to in this Directive, and shall forthwith inform the other Member States and the Commission thereof.

4. Each Member State shall designate a coordinator for the activities of the competent authorities referred to in paragraph 1 and shall inform other Member States and the Commission thereof.

The coordinators' tasks shall be:

    (a) to promote uniform application of this Directive;

    (b) to collect all the information which is relevant for application of this Directive, such as on the conditions for access to regulated professions in the Member States;

    (c) to examine suggestions for common training frameworks and common training tests;

    (d) to exchange information and best practice for the purpose of optimising continuous professional development in Member States;

    (e) to exchange information and best practice on the application of compensation measures referred to in Article 14.

For the purpose of carrying out the task set out in point (b) of this paragraph, the coordinators may solicit the help of the assistance centres referred to in Article 57b.

Article 56a   Alert mechanism

1. The competent authorities of a Member State shall inform the competent authorities of all other Member States about a professional whose pursuit on the territory of that Member State of the following professional activities in their entirety or parts thereof has been restricted or prohibited, even temporarily, by national authorities or courts:

    (a) doctor of medicine and of general practice possessing evidence of a formal qualification referred to in points 5.1.1 and 5.1.4 of Annex V;

    (b) specialist doctor of medicine possessing a title referred to in point 5.1.3 of Annex V;

    (c) nurse responsible for general care possessing evidence of a formal qualification referred to in point 5.2.2 of Annex V;

    (d) dental practitioner possessing evidence of a formal qualification referred to in point 5.3.2 of Annex V;

    (e) specialist dentists possessing evidence of a formal qualification referred to in point 5.3.3 of Annex V;

    (f) veterinary surgeon possessing evidence of a formal qualification referred to in point 5.4.2 of Annex V;

    (g) midwife possessing evidence of a formal qualification referred to in point 5.5.2 of Annex V;

    (h) pharmacist possessing evidence of a formal qualification listed in point 5.6.2 of Annex V;

    (i) holders of certificates mentioned in point 2 of Annex VII attesting that the holder completed a training which satisfies the minimum requirements listed in Articles 24, 25, 31, 34, 35, 38, 40, or 44 respectively, but which started earlier than the reference dates of the qualifications listed in points 5.1.3, 5.1.4, 5.2.2, 5.3.2, 5.3.3, 5.4.2, 5.5.2, 5.6.2 of Annex V;

(j) holders of certificates of acquired rights as referred to in Articles 23, 27, 29, 33, 33a, 37, 43 and 43a;

(k) other professionals exercising activities that have patient safety implications, where the professional is pursuing a profession regulated in that Member State;

(l) professionals exercising activities relating to the education of minors, including in child-care and early childhood education, where the professional is pursuing a profession regulated in that Member State.

2. Competent authorities shall send the information referred to in paragraph 1 by way of alert via IMI at the latest within three days from the date of adoption of the decision restricting or prohibiting pursuit of the professional activity in its entirety or in part by the professional concerned. That information shall be limited to the following:

(a) the identity of the professional;

(b) the profession concerned;

(c) information about the national authority or court adopting the decision on restriction or prohibition;

(d) the scope of the restriction or the prohibition; and

(e) the period during which the restriction or the prohibition applies.

3. The competent authorities of a Member State concerned shall, at the latest within three days from the date of adoption of the court decision, inform the competent authorities of all other Member States, by way of alert via IMI, about the identity of professionals who have applied for the recognition of a qualification under this Directive and who have subsequently been found by courts to have used falsified evidence of professional qualifications in this context.

4. The processing of personal data for the purpose of the exchange of information referred to in paragraphs 1 and 3 shall be carried out in accordance with Directives 95/46/EC and 2002/58/EC. The processing of personal data by the Commission shall be carried out in accordance with Regulation (EC) No 45/2001.

5. The competent authorities of all Member States shall be informed without delay when a prohibition or a restriction referred to in paragraph 1 has expired. For that purpose, the competent authority of the Member State which provides the information in accordance with paragraph 1 shall also be required to provide the date of expiry as well as any subsequent change to that date.

6. Member States shall provide that professionals, in respect of whom alerts are sent to other Member States, are informed in writing of decisions on alerts at the same time as the alert itself, may appeal under national law against the decision or apply for rectification of such decisions and shall have access to remedies in respect of any damage caused by false alerts sent to other Member States, and in such cases the decision on the alert shall be qualified to indicate that it is subject to proceedings by the professional.

7. Data regarding alerts may be processed within IMI for as long as they are valid. Alerts shall be deleted within three days from the date of adoption of the revoking decision or from the expiry of the prohibition or the restriction referred to in paragraph 1.

8. The Commission shall adopt implementing acts for the application of the alert mechanism. Those implementing acts shall include provisions on the authorities entitled to send or receive alerts and on the withdrawal and closure of alerts, and measures to ensure the security of processing. Those implementing acts shall be adopted in accordance with the examination procedure referred to in Article 58(2).

Article 57   Contact points

1. Member States shall ensure that the following information is available online through the points of single contact, referred to in Article 6 of Directive 2006/123/EC of the European Parliament and of the Council of 12 December 2006 on services in the internal market[28] and regularly updated:

(a) a list of all regulated professions in the Member State including contact details of the competent authorities for each regulated profession and the assistance centres referred to in Article 57b;

---

[28] OJ L 376, 27.12.2006, p. 36.

(b) a list of the professions for which a European Professional Card is available, the functioning of that Card, including all related fees to be paid by professionals, and the competent authorities for issuing that Card;

(c) a list of all professions for which the Member State applies Article 7(4) under national laws, regulations and administrative provisions;

(d) a list of regulated education and training, and training with a special structure, referred to in point (c)(ii) of Article 11;

(e) the requirements and procedures referred to in Articles 7, 50, 51 and 53 for the professions regulated in the Member State, including all related fees to be paid by citizens and documents to be submitted by citizens to competent authorities;

(f) details on how to appeal, under national laws, regulations and administrative provisions, decisions of competent authorities adopted under this Directive.

2. Member States shall ensure that the information referred to in paragraph 1 is provided in a clear and comprehensive way for users, that it is easily accessible remotely and by electronic means and that it is kept up to date.

3. Member States shall ensure that any request for information addressed to the point of single contact is replied to as soon as possible.

4. Member States and the Commission shall take accompanying measures in order to encourage points of single contact to make the information provided for in paragraph 1 available in other official languages of the Union. This shall not affect the legislation of Member States on the use of languages in their territory.

5. Member States shall cooperate with each other and the Commission for the purpose of implementing paragraphs 1, 2 and 4.

Article 57a   Procedures by electronic means

1. Member States shall ensure that all requirements, procedures and formalities relating to matters covered by this Directive may be easily completed, remotely and by electronic means, through the relevant point of single contact or the relevant competent authorities. This shall not prevent competent authorities of Member States from requesting certified copies at a later stage in the event of justified doubts and where strictly necessary.

2. Paragraph 1 shall not apply to the carrying out of an adaptation period or aptitude test.

3. Where it is justified for Member States to ask for advanced electronic signatures, as defined in point 2 of Article 2 of Directive 1999/93/EC of the European Parliament and of the Council of 13 December 1999 on a Community framework for electronic signatures,[29] for the completion of procedures referred to in paragraph 1 of this Article, Member States shall accept electronic signatures in compliance with Commission Decision 2009/767/EC of 16 October 2009 setting out measures facilitating the use of procedures by electronic means through the points of single contact under Directive 2006/123/EC of the European Parliament and of the Council on services in the internal market[30] and provide for technical means to process documents with advanced electronic signature in formats defined by Commission Decision 2011/130/EU of 25 February 2011 establishing minimum requirements for the cross-border processing of documents signed electronically by competent authorities under Directive 2006/123/EC of the European Parliament and of the Council on services in the internal market.[31]

4. All procedures shall be carried out in accordance with Article 8 of Directive 2006/123/EC relating to the points of single contact. The procedural time limits set out in Article 7(4) and Article 51 of this Directive shall commence at the point when an application or any missing document has been submitted by a citizen to a point of single contact or directly to the relevant competent authority. Any request for certified copies referred to in paragraph 1 of this Article shall not be considered as a request for missing documents.

[29] OJ L 13, 19.1.2000, p. 12.
[30] OJ L 274, 20.10.2009, p. 36.
[31] OJ L 53, 26.2.2011, p. 66.

Article 57b   Assistance centres

1. Each Member State shall designate, no later than 18 January 2016, an assistance centre whose remit shall be to provide citizens, as well as assistance centres of the other Member States, with assistance concerning the recognition of professional qualifications provided for in this Directive, including information on the national legislation governing the professions and the pursuit of those professions, social legislation, and, where appropriate, the rules of ethics.

2. The assistance centres in host Member States shall assist citizens in exercising the rights conferred on them by this Directive, in cooperation, where appropriate, with the assistance centre in the home Member State and the competent authorities and the points of single contact in the host Member State.

3. Any competent authority in the home or host Member State shall be required to fully cooperate with the assistance centre in the host Member State and where appropriate the home Member State, and provide all relevant information about individual cases to such assistance centres upon their request and subject to data protection rules in accordance with Directives 95/46/EC and 2002/58/EC.

4. At the Commission's request, the assistance centres shall inform the Commission of the result of enquiries with which they are dealing within two months after receiving such a request.

Article 57c   Exercise of the delegation

1. The power to adopt delegated acts is conferred on the Commission subject to the conditions laid down in this Article.

2. The power to adopt delegated acts referred to in the third subparagraph of Article 3(2), Article 20, the second subparagraph of Article 21(6), Article 21a(4), Article 25(5), the second paragraph of Article 26, the second subparagraph of Article 31(2), the second subparagraph of Article 34(2), Article 35(4) and (5), the second subparagraph of Article 38(1), the third subparagraph of Article 40(1), the second subparagraph of Article 44(2), Article 49a(4) and Article 49b(4) shall be conferred on the Commission for a period of five years from 17 January 2014. The Commission shall draw up a report in respect of the delegation of power not later than nine months before the end of the five-year period. The delegation of power shall be tacitly extended for periods of an identical duration, unless the European Parliament or the Council opposes such extension not later than three months before the end of each period.

3. The power to adopt delegated acts referred to in the third subparagraph of Article 3(2), Article 20, the second subparagraph of Article 21(6), Article 21a(4), Article 25(5), the second paragraph of Article 26, the second subparagraph of Article 31(2), the second subparagraph of Article 34(2), Article 35(4) and (5), the second subparagraph of Article 38(1), the third subparagraph of Article 40(1), the second subparagraph of Article 44(2), Article 49a(4) and Article 49b(4) may be revoked at any time by the European Parliament or by the Council. A decision to revoke shall put an end to the delegation of the power specified in that decision. It shall take effect the day following the publication of the decision in the *Official Journal of the European Union* or at a later date specified therein. It shall not affect the validity of any delegated acts already in force.

4. As soon as it adopts a delegated act, the Commission shall notify it simultaneously to the European Parliament and to the Council.

5. A delegated act adopted pursuant to the third subparagraph of Article 3(2), Article 20, the second subparagraph of Article 21(6), Article 21a(4), Article 25(5), the second paragraph of Article 26, the second subparagraph of Article 31(2), the second subparagraph of Article 34(2), Article 35(4) and (5), the second subparagraph of Article 38(1), the third subparagraph of Article 40(1), the second subparagraph of Article 44(2), Article 49a(4) and Article 49b(4) shall enter into force only if no objection has been expressed either by the European Parliament or the Council within a period of two months of notification of that act to the European Parliament and the Council or if, before the expiry of that period, the European Parliament and the Council have both informed the Commission that they will not object. That period shall be extended by two months at the initiative of the European Parliament or of the Council.

Article 58   Committee procedure

1. The Commission shall be assisted by a Committee on the recognition of professional qualifications. That committee shall be a committee within the meaning of Regulation (EU) No 182/2011.

2. Where reference is made to this paragraph, Article 5 of Regulation (EU) No 182/2011 shall apply.

Article 59   Transparency

1. Member States shall notify to the Commission a list of existing regulated professions, specifying the activities covered by each profession, and a list of regulated education and training, and training with a special structure, referred to in point (c)(ii) of Article 11, in their territory by 18 January 2016. Any change to those lists shall also be notified to the Commission without undue delay. The Commission shall set up and maintain a publicly available database of regulated professions, including a general description of activities covered by each profession.

2. By 18 January 2016, Member States shall notify to the Commission the list of professions for which a prior check of qualifications is necessary under Article 7(4). Member States shall provide the Commission with a specific justification for the inclusion of each of those professions on that list.

3. Member States shall examine whether requirements under their legal system restricting the access to a profession or its pursuit to the holders of a specific professional qualification, including the use of professional titles and the professional activities allowed under such title, referred to in this Article as 'requirements' are compatible with the following principles:

   (a) requirements must be neither directly nor indirectly discriminatory on the basis of nationality or residence;
   (b) requirements must be justified by overriding reasons of general interest;
   (c) requirements must be suitable for securing the attainment of the objective pursued and must not go beyond what is necessary to attain that objective.

4. Paragraph 1 shall also apply to professions regulated in a Member State by an association or organisation within the meaning of Article 3(2) and any requirements for membership of those associations or organisations.

5. By 18 January 2016, Member States shall provide the Commission with information on the requirements they intend to maintain and the reasons for considering that those requirements comply with paragraph 3. Member States shall provide information on the requirements they subsequently introduced, and the reasons for considering that those requirements comply with paragraph 3, within six months of the adoption of the measure.

6. By 18 January 2016, and every two years thereafter, Member States shall also submit a report to the Commission about the requirements which have been removed or made less stringent.

7. The Commission shall forward the reports referred to in paragraph 6 to the other Member States which shall submit their observations within six months. Within the same period of six months, the Commission shall consult interested parties, including the professions concerned.

8. The Commission shall provide a summary report based on the information provided by Member States to the Group of Coordinators established under Commission Decision 2007/172/EC of 19 March 2007 setting up the group of coordinators for the recognition of professional qualifications[32] which may make observations.

9. In light of the observations provided for in paragraphs 7 and 8, the Commission shall, by 18 January 2017, submit its final findings to the European Parliament and the Council, accompanied where appropriate by proposals for further initiatives.

Title VI Other provisions

Article 60   Reports

1. As from 20 October 2007, Member States shall, every two years, send a report to the Commission on the application of the system. In addition to general observations, the report shall

---

[32] OJ L 79, 20.3.2007, p. 38.

contain a statistical summary of decisions taken and a description of the main problems arising from the application of this Directive.

As from 18 January 2016 the statistical summary of decisions taken referred to in the first subparagraph shall contain detailed information on the number and types of decisions taken in accordance with this Directive, including the types of decisions on partial access taken by competent authorities in accordance with Article 4f, and a description of the main problems arising from application of this Directive.

2. By 18 January 2019, and every five years thereafter, the Commission shall publish a report on the implementation of this Directive.

The first such report shall focus in particular on the new elements introduced in this Directive and consider in particular the following issues:

(a) the functioning of the European Professional Card;

(a) the modernisation of the knowledge, skills and competences for the professions covered by Chapter III of Title III, including the list of competences referred to in Article 31(7);

(c) the functioning of the common training frameworks and common training tests;

(d) the results of the special upgrading programme laid down under Romanian laws, regulations and administrative provisions for holders of the evidence of formal qualifications mentioned in Article 33a, as well as for holders of evidence of formal qualifications of post-secondary level, with a view to assessing the need to review the current provisions governing the acquired rights regime applicable to the Romanian evidence of formal qualifications as nurse responsible for general care.

Member States shall provide all necessary information for the preparation of that report.

Article 61 Derogation clause

If, for the application of one of the provisions of this Directive, a Member State encounters major difficulties in a particular area, the Commission shall examine those difficulties in collaboration with the Member State concerned.

Where appropriate, the Commission shall adopt an implementing act to permit the Member State in question to derogate from the relevant provision for a limited period of time.

Article 62 Repeal

Directives 77/452/EEC, 77/453/EEC, 78/686/EEC, 78/687/EEC, 78/1026/EEC, 78/1027/EEC, 80/154/EEC, 80/155/EEC, 85/384/EEC, 85/432/EEC, 85/433/EEC, 89/48/EEC, 92/51/EEC, 93/16/EEC and 1999/42/EC are repealed with effect from 20 October 2007. References to the repealed Directives shall be understood as references to this Directive and the acts adopted on the basis of those Directives shall not be affected by the repeal.

Article 63 Transposition

Member States shall bring into force the laws, regulations and administrative provisions necessary to comply with this Directive by 20 October 2007 at the latest. They shall forthwith inform the Commission thereof.

When Member States adopt these measures, they shall contain a reference to this Directive or be accompanied by such a reference on the occasion of their official publication. Member States shall determine how such reference is to be made.

Article 64 Entry into force

This Directive shall enter into force on the 20th day following its publication in the *Official Journal of the European Union*.

Article 65 Addressees

This Directive is addressed to the Member States.

Done at Strasbourg, 7 September 2005.

ANNEX I*

*List of professional associations or organisations fulfilling
the conditions of Article 3(2)*

Ireland[33]

1. The Institute of Chartered Accountants in Ireland
2. The Institute of Certified Public Accountants in Ireland
3. The Association of Certified Accountants
4. Institution of Engineers of Ireland
5. Irish Planning Institute

United Kingdom[34]

1. Institute of Chartered Accountants in England and Wales
2. Institute of Chartered Accountants of Scotland
3. Institute of Chartered Accountants in Ireland
4. Chartered Association of Certified Accountants
5. Chartered Institute of Loss Adjusters
6. Chartered Institute of Management Accountants
7. Institute of Chartered Secretaries and Administrators
8. Chartered Insurance Institute
9. Institute of Actuaries
10. Faculty of Actuaries
11. Chartered Institute of Bankers
12. Institute of Bankers in Scotland
13. Royal Institution of Chartered Surveyors
14. Royal Town Planning Institute
15. Chartered Society of Physiotherapy
16. Royal Society of Chemistry
17. British Psychological Society
18. Library Association
19. Institute of Chartered Foresters
20. Chartered Institute of Building
21. Engineering Council
22. Institute of Energy
23. Institution of Structural Engineers
24. Institution of Civil Engineers
25. Institution of Mining Engineers
26. Institution of Mining and Metallurgy

---

* **Editor's Note:** All other Annexes omitted.
[33] Only for the activity of auditing accounts.
[34] Irish nationals are also members of the following associations or organisations in the United Kingdom:
  – Institute of Chartered Accountants of Scotland
  – Institute of Actuaries
  – Faculty of Actuaries
  – The Chartered Institute of Management Accountants
  – Institute of Chartered Secretaries and Administrators
  – Royal Town Planning Institute
  – Royal Institution of Chartered Surveyors
  – Chartered Institute of Building.
  – Institute of Chartered Accountants in England and Wales

27. Institution of Electrical Engineers
28. Institution of Gas Engineers
29. Institution of Mechanical Engineers
30. Institution of Chemical Engineers
31. Institution of Production Engineers
32. Institution of Marine Engineers
33. Royal Institution of Naval Architects
34. Royal Aeronautical Society
35. Institute of Metals
36. Chartered Institution of Building Services Engineers
37. Institute of Measurement and Control
38. British Computer Society

Directive 2006/123/EC of the European Parliament and of the Council of 12 December 2006 on services in the internal market

[OJ 2006 L376/36]

THE EUROPEAN PARLIAMENT AND THE COUNCIL OF THE EUROPEAN UNION,

Having regard to the Treaty establishing the European Community, and in particular the first and third sentence of Article 47(2) and Article 55 thereof,

Having regard to the proposal from the Commission,

Having regard to the Opinion of the European Economic and Social Committee,[1]

Having regard to the opinion of the Committee of the Regions,[2]

Acting in accordance with the procedure laid down in Article 251 of the Treaty.[3]

Whereas:

(1) The European Community is seeking to forge ever closer links between the States and peoples of Europe and to ensure economic and social progress. In accordance with Article 14(2) of the Treaty, the internal market comprises an area without internal frontiers in which the free movement of services is ensured. In accordance with Article 43 of the Treaty the freedom of establishment is ensured. Article 49 of the Treaty establishes the right to provide services within the Community. The elimination of barriers to the development of service activities between Member States is essential in order to strengthen the integration of the peoples of Europe and to promote balanced and sustainable economic and social progress. In eliminating such barriers it is essential to ensure that the development of service activities contributes to the fulfilment of the task laid down in Article 2 of the Treaty of promoting throughout the Community a harmonious, balanced and sustainable development of economic activities, a high level of employment and of social protection, equality between men and women, sustainable and non-inflationary growth, a high degree of competitiveness and convergence of economic performance, a high level of protection and improvement of the quality of the environment, the raising of the standard of living and quality of life and economic and social cohesion and solidarity among Member States.

(2) A competitive market in services is essential in order to promote economic growth and create jobs in the European Union. At present numerous barriers within the internal market prevent providers, particularly small and medium-sized enterprises (SMEs), from extending their

---

[1] OJ C 221, 8.9.2005, p. 113.

[2] OJ C 43, 18.2.2005, p. 18.

[3] Opinion of the European Parliament of 16 February 2006 (not yet published in the Official Journal), Council Common Position of 24 July 2006 (OJ C 270 E, 7.11.2006, p. 1) and Position of the European Parliament of 15 November 2006. Council Decision of 11 December 2006.

operations beyond their national borders and from taking full advantage of the internal market. This weakens the worldwide competitiveness of European Union providers. A free market which compels the Member States to eliminate restrictions on cross-border provision of services while at the same time increasing transparency and information for consumers would give consumers wider choice and better services at lower prices.

(3) The report from the Commission on 'The State of the Internal Market for Services' drew up an inventory of a large number of barriers which are preventing or slowing down the development of services between Member States, in particular those provided by SMEs, which are predominant in the field of services. The report concludes that a decade after the envisaged completion of the internal market, there is still a huge gap between the vision of an integrated European Union economy and the reality as experienced by European citizens and providers. The barriers affect a wide variety of service activities across all stages of the provider's activity and have a number of common features, including the fact that they often arise from administrative burdens, the legal uncertainty associated with cross-border activity and the lack of mutual trust between Member States.

(4) Since services constitute the engine of economic growth and account for 70 % of GDP and employment in most Member States, this fragmentation of the internal market has a negative impact on the entire European economy, in particular on the competitiveness of SMEs and the movement of workers, and prevents consumers from gaining access to a greater variety of competitively priced services. It is important to point out that the services sector is a key employment sector for women in particular, and that they therefore stand to benefit greatly from new opportunities offered by the completion of the internal market for services. The European Parliament and the Council have emphasised that the removal of legal barriers to the establishment of a genuine internal market is a matter of priority for achieving the goal set by the European Council in Lisbon of 23 and 24 March 2000 of improving employment and social cohesion and achieving sustainable economic growth so as to make the European Union the most competitive and dynamic knowledge-based economy in the world by 2010, with more and better jobs. Removing those barriers, while ensuring an advanced European social model, is thus a basic condition for overcoming the difficulties encountered in implementing the Lisbon Strategy and for reviving the European economy, particularly in terms of employment and investment. It is therefore important to achieve an internal market for services, with the right balance between market opening and preserving public services and social and consumer rights.

(5) It is therefore necessary to remove barriers to the freedom of establishment for providers in Member States and barriers to the free movement of services as between Member States and to guarantee recipients and providers the legal certainty necessary for the exercise in practice of those two fundamental freedoms of the Treaty. Since the barriers in the internal market for services affect operators who wish to become established in other Member States as well as those who provide a service in another Member State without being established there, it is necessary to enable providers to develop their service activities within the internal market either by becoming established in a Member State or by making use of the free movement of services. Providers should be able to choose between those two freedoms, depending on their strategy for growth in each Member State.

(6) Those barriers cannot be removed solely by relying on direct application of Articles 43 and 49 of the Treaty, since, on the one hand, addressing them on a case-by-case basis through infringement procedures against the Member States concerned would, especially following enlargement, be extremely complicated for national and Community institutions, and, on the other hand, the lifting of many barriers requires prior coordination of national legal schemes, including the setting up of administrative cooperation. As the European Parliament and the Council have recognised, a Community legislative instrument makes it possible to achieve a genuine internal market for services.

(7) This Directive establishes a general legal framework which benefits a wide variety of services while taking into account the distinctive features of each type of activity or profession and its system of regulation. That framework is based on a dynamic and selective approach consisting in the removal, as a matter of priority, of barriers which may be dismantled quickly and, for the others,

the launching of a process of evaluation, consultation and complementary harmonisation of specific issues, which will make possible the progressive and coordinated modernisation of national regulatory systems for service activities which is vital in order to achieve a genuine internal market for services by 2010. Provision should be made for a balanced mix of measures involving targeted harmonisation, administrative cooperation, the provision on the freedom to provide services and encouragement of the development of codes of conduct on certain issues. That coordination of national legislative regimes should ensure a high degree of Community legal integration and a high level of protection of general interest objectives, especially protection of consumers, which is vital in order to establish trust between Member States. This Directive also takes into account other general interest objectives, including the protection of the environment, public security and public health as well as the need to comply with labour law.

(8) It is appropriate that the provisions of this Directive concerning the freedom of establishment and the free movement of services should apply only to the extent that the activities in question are open to competition, so that they do not oblige Member States either to liberalise services of general economic interest or to privatise public entities which provide such services or to abolish existing monopolies for other activities or certain distribution services.

(9) This Directive applies only to requirements which affect the access to, or the exercise of, a service activity. Therefore, it does not apply to requirements, such as road traffic rules, rules concerning the development or use of land, town and country planning, building standards as well as administrative penalties imposed for non-compliance with such rules which do not specifically regulate or specifically affect the service activity but have to be respected by providers in the course of carrying out their economic activity in the same way as by individuals acting in their private capacity.

(10) This Directive does not concern requirements governing access to public funds for certain providers. Such requirements include notably those laying down conditions under which providers are entitled to receive public funding, including specific contractual conditions, and in particular quality standards which need to be observed as a condition for receiving public funds, for example for social services.

(11) This Directive does not interfere with measures taken by Member States, in accordance with Community law, in relation to the protection or promotion of cultural and linguistic diversity and media pluralism, including the funding thereof. This Directive does not prevent Member States from applying their fundamental rules and principles relating to the freedom of press and freedom of expression. This Directive does not affect Member State laws prohibiting discrimination on grounds of nationality or on grounds such as those set out in Article 13 of the Treaty.

(12) This Directive aims at creating a legal framework to ensure the freedom of establishment and the free movement of services between the Member States and does not harmonise or prejudice criminal law. However, Member States should not be able to restrict the freedom to provide services by applying criminal law provisions which specifically affect the access to or the exercise of a service activity in circumvention of the rules laid down in this Directive.

(13) It is equally important that this Directive fully respect Community initiatives based on Article 137 of the Treaty with a view to achieving the objectives of Article 136 thereof concerning the promotion of employment and improved living and working conditions.

(14) This Directive does not affect terms and conditions of employment, including maximum work periods and minimum rest periods, minimum paid annual holidays, minimum rates of pay as well as health, safety and hygiene at work, which Member States apply in compliance with Community law, nor does it affect relations between social partners, including the right to negotiate and conclude collective agreements, the right to strike and to take industrial action in accordance with national law and practices which respect Community law, nor does it apply to services provided by temporary work agencies. This Directive does not affect Member States' social security legislation.

(15) This Directive respects the exercise of fundamental rights applicable in the Member States and as recognised in the Charter of fundamental Rights of the European Union and the accompanying explanations, reconciling them with the fundamental freedoms laid down in Articles 43 and

49 of the Treaty. Those fundamental rights include the right to take industrial action in accordance with national law and practices which respect Community law.

(16) This Directive concerns only providers established in a Member State and does not cover external aspects. It does not concern negotiations within international organisations on trade in services, in particular in the framework of the General Agreement on Trade in Services (GATS).

(17) This Directive covers only services which are performed for an economic consideration. Services of general interest are not covered by the definition in Article 50 of the Treaty and therefore do not fall within the scope of this Directive. Services of general economic interest are services that are performed for an economic consideration and therefore do fall within the scope of this Directive. However, certain services of general economic interest, such as those that may exist in the field of transport, are excluded from the scope of this Directive and certain other services of general economic interest, for example, those that may exist in the area of postal services, are the subject of a derogation from the provision on the freedom to provide services set out in this Directive. This Directive does not deal with the funding of services of general economic interest and does not apply to systems of aids granted by Member States, in particular in the social field, in accordance with Community rules on competition. This Directive does not deal with the follow-up to the Commission White Paper on Services of General Interest.

(18) Financial services should be excluded from the scope of this Directive since these activities are the subject of specific Community legislation aimed, as is this Directive, at achieving a genuine internal market for services. Consequently, this exclusion should cover all financial services such as banking, credit, insurance, including reinsurance, occupational or personal pensions, securities, investment funds, payments and investment advice, including the services listed in Annex I to Directive 2006/48/EC of the European Parliament and of the Council of 14 June 2006 relating to the taking up and pursuit of the business of credit institutions.[4]

(19) In view of the adoption in 2002 of a package of legislative instruments relating to electronic communications networks and services, as well as to associated resources and services, which has established a regulatory framework facilitating access to those activities within the internal market, notably through the elimination of most individual authorisation schemes, it is necessary to exclude issues dealt with by those instruments from the scope of this Directive.

(20) The exclusion from the scope of this Directive as regards matters of electronic communications services as covered by Directives 2002/19/EC of the European Parliament and of the Council of 7 March 2002 on access to, and interconnection of, electronic communications networks and associated facilities (Access Directive),[5] 2002/20/EC of the European Parliament and of the Council of 7 March 2002 on the authorisation of electronic communications networks and services (Authorisation Directive),[6] 2002/21/EC of the European Parliament and of the Council of 7 March 2002 on a common regulatory framework for electronic communications networks and services (Framework Directive),[7] 2002/22/EC of the European Parliament and of the Council of 7 March 2002 on universal service and users' rights relating to electronic communications networks and services (Universal Service Directive)[8] and 2002/58/EC of the European Parliament and of the Council of 12 July 2002 concerning the processing of personal data and the protection of privacy in the electronic communications sector (Directive on privacy and electronic communications)[9] should apply not only to questions specifically dealt with in these Directives but also to matters for which the Directives explicitly leave to Member States the possibility of adopting certain measures at national level.

(21) Transport services, including urban transport, taxis and ambulances as well as port services, should be excluded from the scope of this Directive.

---

[4] OJ L 177, 30.6.2006, p. 1.
[5] OJ L 108, 24.4.2002, p. 7.
[6] OJ L 108, 24.4.2002, p. 21.
[7] OJ L 108, 24.4.2002, p. 33.
[8] OJ L 108, 24.4.2002, p. 51.
[9] OJ L 201, 31.7.2002, p. 37. Directive as amended by Directive 2006/24/EC (OJ L 105, 13.4.2006, p. 54).

(22) The exclusion of healthcare from the scope of this Directive should cover healthcare and pharmaceutical services provided by health professionals to patients to assess, maintain or restore their state of health where those activities are reserved to a regulated health profession in the Member State in which the services are provided.

(23) This Directive does not affect the reimbursement of healthcare provided in a Member State other than that in which the recipient of the care is resident. This issue has been addressed by the Court of Justice on numerous occasions, and the Court has recognised patients' rights. It is important to address this issue in another Community legal instrument in order to achieve greater legal certainty and clarity to the extent that this issue is not already addressed in Council Regulation (EEC) No 1408/71 of 14 June 1971 on the application of social security schemes to employed persons, to self-employed persons and to members of their families moving within the Community.[10]

(24) Audiovisual services, whatever their mode of transmission, including within cinemas, should also be excluded from the scope of this Directive. Furthermore, this Directive should not apply to aids granted by Member States in the audiovisual sector which are covered by Community rules on competition.

(25) Gambling activities, including lottery and betting transactions, should be excluded from the scope of this Directive in view of the specific nature of these activities, which entail implementation by Member States of policies relating to public policy and consumer protection.

(26) This Directive is without prejudice to the application of Article 45 of the Treaty.

(27) This Directive should not cover those social services in the areas of housing, childcare and support to families and persons in need which are provided by the State at national, regional or local level by providers mandated by the State or by charities recognised as such by the State with the objective of ensuring support for those who are permanently or temporarily in a particular state of need because of their insufficient family income or total or partial lack of independence and for those who risk being marginalised. These services are essential in order to guarantee the fundamental right to human dignity and integrity and are a manifestation of the principles of social cohesion and solidarity and should not be affected by this Directive.

(28) This Directive does not deal with the funding of, or the system of aids linked to, social services. Nor does it affect the criteria or conditions set by Member States to ensure that social services effectively carry out a function to the benefit of the public interest and social cohesion. In addition, this Directive should not affect the principle of universal service in Member States' social services.

(29) Given that the Treaty provides specific legal bases for taxation matters and given the Community instruments already adopted in that field, it is necessary to exclude the field of taxation from the scope of this Directive.

(30) There is already a considerable body of Community law on service activities. This Directive builds on, and thus complements, the Community acquis. Conflicts between this Directive and other Community instruments have been identified and are addressed by this Directive, including by means of derogations. However, it is necessary to provide a rule for any residual and exceptional cases where there is a conflict between a provision of this Directive and a provision of another Community instrument. The existence of such a conflict should be determined in compliance with the rules of the Treaty on the right of establishment and the free movement of services.

(31) This Directive is consistent with and does not affect Directive 2005/36/EC of the European Parliament and of the Council of 7 September 2005 on the recognition of professional qualifications.[11] It deals with questions other than those relating to professional qualifications, for example professional liability insurance, commercial communications, multidisciplinary activities and administrative simplification. With regard to temporary cross-border service provision, a derogation from the provision on the freedom to provide services in this Directive ensures that Title II on the free provision of services of Directive 2005/36/EC is not affected. Therefore, none of

---

[10] OJ L 149, 5.7.1971, p. 2. Regulation as last amended by Regulation (EC) No 629/2006 of the European Parliament and of the Council (OJ L 114, 27.4.2006, p. 1).
[11] OJ L 255, 30.9.2005, p. 22.

the measures applicable under that Directive in the Member State where the service is provided is affected by the provision on the freedom to provide services.

(32) This Directive is consistent with Community legislation on consumer protection, such as Directive 2005/29/EC of the European Parliament and of the Council of 11 May 2005 concerning unfair business-to-consumer commercial practices in the internal market (the Unfair Commercial Practices Directive)[12] and Regulation (EC) No 2006/2004 of the European Parliament and of the Council of 27 October 2004 on cooperation between national authorities responsible for the enforcement of consumer protection laws (the Regulation on consumer protection cooperation).[13]

(33) The services covered by this Directive concern a wide variety of ever-changing activities, including business services such as management consultancy, certification and testing; facilities management, including office maintenance; advertising; recruitment services; and the services of commercial agents. The services covered are also services provided both to businesses and to consumers, such as legal or fiscal advice; real estate services such as estate agencies; construction, including the services of architects; distributive trades; the organisation of trade fairs; car rental; and travel agencies. Consumer services are also covered, such as those in the field of tourism, including tour guides; leisure services, sports centres and amusement parks; and, to the extent that they are not excluded from the scope of application of the Directive, household support services, such as help for the elderly. Those activities may involve services requiring the proximity of provider and recipient, services requiring travel by the recipient or the provider and services which may be provided at a distance, including via the Internet.

(34) According to the case-law of the Court of Justice, the assessment of whether certain activities, in particular activities which are publicly funded or provided by public entities, constitute a 'service' has to be carried out on a case by case basis in the light of all their characteristics, in particular the way they are provided, organised and financed in the Member State concerned. The Court of Justice has held that the essential characteristic of remuneration lies in the fact that it constitutes consideration for the services in question and has recognised that the characteristic of remuneration is absent in the case of activities performed, for no consideration, by the State or on behalf of the State in the context of its duties in the social, cultural, educational and judicial fields, such as courses provided under the national education system, or the management of social security schemes which do not engage in economic activity. The payment of a fee by recipients, for example, a tuition or enrolment fee paid by students in order to make a certain contribution to the operating expenses of a system, does not in itself constitute remuneration because the service is still essentially financed by public funds. These activities are, therefore, not covered by the definition of service in Article 50 of the Treaty and do not therefore fall within the scope of this Directive.

(35) Non-profit making amateur sporting activities are of considerable social importance. They often pursue wholly social or recreational objectives. Thus, they might not constitute economic activities within the meaning of Community law and should fall outside the scope of this Directive.

(36) The concept of 'provider' should cover any natural person who is a national of a Member State or any legal person engaged in a service activity in a Member State, in exercise either of the freedom of establishment or of the free movement of services. The concept of provider should thus not be limited solely to cross-border service provision within the framework of the free movement of services but should also cover cases in which an operator establishes itself in a Member State in order to develop its service activities there. On the other hand, the concept of a provider should not cover the case of branches in a Member State of companies from third countries because, under Article 48 of the Treaty, the freedom of establishment and free movement of services may benefit only companies constituted in accordance with the laws of a Member State and having their registered office, central administration or principal place of business within the Community. The concept of

[12] OJ L 149, 11.6.2005, p. 22.
[13] OJ L 364, 9.12.2004, p. 1. Regulation as amended by Directive 2005/29/EC.

'recipient' should also cover third country nationals who already benefit from rights conferred upon them by Community acts such as Regulation (EEC) No 1408/71, Council Directive/109/EC of 25 November concerning the status of third-country nationals who are long-term residents,[14] Council Regulation (EC) No 859/of 14 May extending the provisions of Regulation (EEC) No 1408/71 and Regulation (EEC) No 574/72 to nationals of third countries who are not already covered by those provisions solely on the ground of their nationality[15] and Directive 2004/38/EC of the European Parliament and of the Council of 29 April 2004 on the right of citizens of the Union and their family members to move and reside freely within the territory of the Member States.[16] Furthermore, Member States may extend the concept of recipient to other third country nationals that are present within their territory.

(37) The place at which a provider is established should be determined in accordance with the case-law of the Court of Justice according to which the concept of establishment involves the actual pursuit of an economic activity through a fixed establishment for an indefinite period. This requirement may also be fulfilled where a company is constituted for a given period or where it rents the building or installation through which it pursues its activity. It may also be fulfilled where a Member State grants authorisations for a limited duration only in relation to particular services. An establishment does not need to take the form of a subsidiary, branch or agency, but may consist of an office managed by a provider's own staff or by a person who is independent but authorised to act on a permanent basis for the undertaking, as would be the case with an agency. According to this definition, which requires the actual pursuit of an economic activity at the place of establishment of the provider, a mere letter box does not constitute an establishment. Where a provider has several places of establishment, it is important to determine the place of establishment from which the actual service concerned is provided. Where it is difficult to determine from which of several places of establishment a given service is provided, the location of the provider's centre of activities relating to this particular service should be that place of establishment.

(38) The concept of 'legal persons', according to the Treaty provisions on establishment, leaves operators free to choose the legal form which they deem suitable for carrying out their activity. Accordingly, 'legal persons', within the meaning of the Treaty, means all entities constituted under, or governed by, the law of a Member State, irrespective of their legal form.

(39) The concept of 'authorisation scheme' should cover, inter alia, the administrative procedures for granting authorisations, licences, approvals or concessions, and also the obligation, in order to be eligible to exercise the activity, to be registered as a member of a profession or entered in a register, roll or database, to be officially appointed to a body or to obtain a card attesting to membership of a particular profession. Authorisation may be granted not only by a formal decision but also by an implicit decision arising, for example, from the silence of the competent authority or from the fact that the interested party must await acknowledgement of receipt of a declaration in order to commence the activity in question or for the latter to become lawful.

(40) The concept of 'overriding reasons relating to the public interest' to which reference is made in certain provisions of this Directive has been developed by the Court of Justice in its case law in relation to Articles 43 and 49 of the Treaty and may continue to evolve. The notion as recognised in the case law of the Court of Justice covers at least the following grounds: public policy, public security and public health, within the meaning of Articles 46 and 55 of the Treaty; the maintenance of order in society; social policy objectives; the protection of the recipients of services; consumer protection; the protection of workers, including the social protection of workers; animal welfare; the preservation of the financial balance of the social security system; the prevention of fraud; the prevention of unfair competition; the protection of the environment and the urban environment, including town and country planning; the protection of creditors; safeguarding the sound

---

[14] OJ L 16, 23.1.2004, p. 44.
[15] OJ L 124, 20.5.2003, p. 1.
[16] OJ L 158, 30.4.2004, p. 77.

administration of justice; road safety; the protection of intellectual property; cultural policy objectives, including safeguarding the freedom of expression of various elements, in particular social, cultural, religious and philosophical values of society; the need to ensure a high level of education, the maintenance of press diversity and the promotion of the national language; the preservation of national historical and artistic heritage; and veterinary policy.

(41) The concept of 'public policy', as interpreted by the Court of Justice, covers the protection against a genuine and sufficiently serious threat affecting one of the fundamental interests of society and may include, in particular, issues relating to human dignity, the protection of minors and vulnerable adults and animal welfare. Similarly, the concept of public security includes issues of public safety.

(42) The rules relating to administrative procedures should not aim at harmonising administrative procedures but at removing overly burdensome authorisation schemes, procedures and formalities that hinder the freedom of establishment and the creation of new service undertakings therefrom.

(43) One of the fundamental difficulties faced, in particular by SMEs, in accessing service activities and exercising them is the complexity, length and legal uncertainty of administrative procedures. For this reason, following the example of certain modernising and good administrative practice initiatives undertaken at Community and national level, it is necessary to establish principles of administrative simplification, inter alia through the limitation of the obligation of prior authorisation to cases in which it is essential and the introduction of the principle of tacit authorisation by the competent authorities after a certain period of time elapsed. Such modernising action, while maintaining the requirements on transparency and the updating of information relating to operators, is intended to eliminate the delays, costs and dissuasive effects which arise, for example, from unnecessary or excessively complex and burdensome procedures, the duplication of procedures, the 'red tape' involved in submitting documents, the arbitrary use of powers by the competent authorities, indeterminate or excessively long periods before a response is given, the limited duration of validity of authorisations granted and disproportionate fees and penalties. Such practices have particularly significant dissuasive effects on providers wishing to develop their activities in other Member States and require coordinated modernisation within an enlarged internal market of twenty-five Member States.

(44) Member States should introduce, where appropriate, forms harmonised at Community level, as established by the Commission, which will serve as an equivalent to certificates, attestations or any other document in relation to establishment.

(45) In order to examine the need for simplifying procedures and formalities, Member States should be able, in particular, to take into account their necessity, number, possible duplication, cost, clarity and accessibility, as well as the delay and practical difficulties to which they could give rise for the provider concerned.

(46) In order to facilitate access to service activities and the exercise thereof in the internal market, it is necessary to establish an objective, common to all Member States, of administrative simplification and to lay down provisions concerning, inter alia, the right to information, procedures by electronic means and the establishment of a framework for authorisation schemes. Other measures adopted at national level to meet that objective could involve reduction of the number of procedures and formalities applicable to service activities and the restriction of such procedures and formalities to those which are essential in order to achieve a general interest objective and which do not duplicate each other in terms of content or purpose.

(47) With the aim of administrative simplification, general formal requirements, such as presentation of original documents, certified copies or a certified translation, should not be imposed, except where objectively justified by an overriding reason relating to the public interest, such as the protection of workers, public health, the protection of the environment or the protection of consumers. It is also necessary to ensure that an authorisation as a general rule permits access to, or exercise of, a service activity throughout the national territory, unless a new authorisation for each establishment, for example for each new hypermarket, or an authorisation that is restricted to a specific part of the national territory is objectively justified by an overriding reason relating to the public interest.

(48) In order to further simplify administrative procedures, it is appropriate to ensure that each provider has a single point through which he can complete all procedures and formalities (hereinafter referred to as 'points of single contact'). The number of points of single contact per Member State may vary according to regional or local competencies or according to the activities concerned. The creation of points of single contact should not interfere with the allocation of functions among competent authorities within each national system. Where several authorities at regional or local level are competent, one of them may assume the role of point of single contact and coordinator. Points of single contact may be set up not only by administrative authorities but also by chambers of commerce or crafts, or by the professional organisations or private bodies to which a Member State decides to entrust that function. Points of single contact have an important role to play in providing assistance to providers either as the authority directly competent to issue the documents necessary to access a service activity or as an intermediary between the provider and the authorities which are directly competent.

(49) The fee which may be charged by points of single contact should be proportionate to the cost of the procedures and formalities with which they deal. This should not prevent Member States from entrusting the points of single contact with the collection of other administrative fees, such as the fee of supervisory bodies.

(50) It is necessary for providers and recipients of services to have easy access to certain types of information. It should be for each Member State to determine, within the framework of this Directive, the way in which providers and recipients are provided with information. In particular, the obligation on Member States to ensure that relevant information is easily accessible to providers and recipients and that it can be accessed by the public without obstacle could be fulfilled by making this information accessible through a website. Any information given should be provided in a clear and unambiguous manner.

(51) The information provided to providers and recipients of services should include, in particular, information on procedures and formalities, contact details of the competent authorities, conditions for access to public registers and data bases and information concerning available remedies and the contact details of associations and organisations from which providers or recipients can obtain practical assistance. The obligation on competent authorities to assist providers and recipients should not include the provision of legal advice in individual cases. Nevertheless, general information on the way in which requirements are usually interpreted or applied should be given. Issues such as liability for providing incorrect or misleading information should be determined by Member States.

(52) The setting up, in the reasonably near future, of electronic means of completing procedures and formalities will be vital for administrative simplification in the field of service activities, for the benefit of providers, recipients and competent authorities. In order to meet that obligation as to results, national laws and other rules applicable to services may need to be adapted. This obligation should not prevent Member States from providing other means of completing such procedures and formalities, in addition to electronic means. The fact that it must be possible to complete those procedures and formalities at a distance means, in particular, that Member States must ensure that they may be completed across borders. The obligation as to results does not cover procedures or formalities which by their very nature are impossible to complete at a distance. Furthermore, this does not interfere with Member States' legislation on the use of languages.

(53) The granting of licences for certain service activities may require an interview with the applicant by the competent authority in order to assess the applicant's personal integrity and suitability for carrying out the service in question. In such cases, the completion of formalities by electronic means may not be appropriate.

(54) The possibility of gaining access to a service activity should be made subject to authorisation by the competent authorities only if that decision satisfies the criteria of non-discrimination, necessity and proportionality. That means, in particular, that authorisation schemes should be permissible only where an a posteriori inspection would not be effective because of the impossibility of ascertaining the defects of the services concerned a posteriori, due account being taken

of the risks and dangers which could arise in the absence of a prior inspection. However, the provision to that effect made by this Directive cannot be relied upon in order to justify authorisation schemes which are prohibited by other Community instruments such as Directive 1999/93/EC of the European Parliament and the Council of 13 December 1999 on a Community framework for electronic signatures,[17] or Directive 2000/31/EC of the European Parliament and of the Council of 8 June 2000 on certain legal aspects of information society services, in particular electronic commerce, in the internal market (Directive on electronic commerce).[18] The results of the process of mutual evaluation will make it possible to determine, at Community level, the types of activity for which authorisation schemes should be eliminated.

(55) This Directive should be without prejudice to the possibility for Member States to withdraw authorisations after they have been issued, if the conditions for the granting of the authorisation are no longer fulfilled.

(56) According to the case law of the Court of Justice, public health, consumer protection, animal health and the protection of the urban environment constitute overriding reasons relating to the public interest. Such overriding reasons may justify the application of authorisation schemes and other restrictions. However, no such authorisation scheme or restriction should discriminate on grounds of nationality. Further, the principles of necessity and proportionality should always be respected.

(57) The provisions of this Directive relating to authorisation schemes should concern cases where the access to or exercise of a service activity by operators requires a decision by a competent authority. This concerns neither decisions by competent authorities to set up a public or private entity for the provision of a particular service nor the conclusion of contracts by competent authorities for the provision of a particular service which is governed by rules on public procurement, since this Directive does not deal with rules on public procurement.

(58) In order to facilitate access to and exercise of service activities, it is important to evaluate and report on authorisation schemes and their justification. This reporting obligation concerns only the existence of authorisation schemes and not the criteria and conditions for the granting of an authorisation.

(59) The authorisation should as a general rule enable the provider to have access to the service activity, or to exercise that activity, throughout the national territory, unless a territorial limit is justified by an overriding reason relating to the public interest. For example, environmental protection may justify the requirement to obtain an individual authorisation for each installation on the national territory. This provision should not affect regional or local competences for the granting of authorisations within the Member States.

(60) This Directive, and in particular the provisions concerning authorisation schemes and the territorial scope of an authorisation, should not interfere with the division of regional or local competences within the Member States, including regional and local self-government and the use of official languages.

(61) The provision relating to the non-duplication of conditions for the granting of an authorisation should not prevent Member States from applying their own conditions as specified in the authorisation scheme. It should only require that competent authorities, when considering whether these conditions are met by the applicant, take into account the equivalent conditions which have already been satisfied by the applicant in another Member State. This provision should not require the application of the conditions for the granting of an authorisation provided for in the authorisation scheme of another Member State.

(62) Where the number of authorisations available for an activity is limited because of scarcity of natural resources or technical capacity, a procedure for selection from among several potential candidates should be adopted with the aim of developing through open competition the quality and conditions for supply of services available to users. Such a procedure should provide guarantees of

---

[17] OJ L 13, 19.1.2000, p. 12.
[18] OJ L 178, 17.7.2000, p. 1.

transparency and impartiality and the authorisation thus granted should not have an excessive duration, be subject to automatic renewal or confer any advantage on the provider whose authorisation has just expired. In particular, the duration of the authorisation granted should be fixed in such a way that it does not restrict or limit free competition beyond what is necessary in order to enable the provider to recoup the cost of investment and to make a fair return on the capital invested. This provision should not prevent Member States from limiting the number of authorisations for reasons other than scarcity of natural resources or technical capacity. These authorisations should remain in any case subject to the other provisions of this Directive relating to authorisation schemes.

(63) In the absence of different arrangements, failing a response within a time period, an authorisation should be deemed to have been granted. However, different arrangements may be put in place in respect of certain activities, where objectively justified by overriding reasons relating to the public interest, including a legitimate interest of third parties. Such different arrangements could include national rules according to which, in the absence of a response of the competent authority, the application is deemed to have been rejected, this rejection being open to challenge before the courts.

(64) In order to establish a genuine internal market for services, it is necessary to abolish any restrictions on the freedom of establishment and the free movement of services which are still enshrined in the laws of certain Member States and which are incompatible with Articles 43 and 49 of the Treaty respectively. The restrictions to be prohibited particularly affect the internal market for services and should be systematically dismantled as soon as possible.

(65) Freedom of establishment is predicated, in particular, upon the principle of equal treatment, which entails the prohibition not only of any discrimination on grounds of nationality but also of any indirect discrimination based on other grounds but capable of producing the same result. Thus, access to a service activity or the exercise thereof in a Member State, either as a principal or secondary activity, should not be made subject to criteria such as place of establishment, residence, domicile or principal provision of the service activity. However, these criteria should not include requirements according to which a provider or one of his employees or a representative must be present during the exercise of the activity when this is justified by an overriding reason relating to the public interest. Furthermore, a Member State should not restrict the legal capacity or the right of companies, incorporated in accordance with the law of another Member State on whose territory they have their primary establishment, to bring legal proceedings. Moreover, a Member State should not be able to confer any advantages on providers having a particular national or local socio-economic link; nor should it be able to restrict, on grounds of place of establishment, the provider's freedom to acquire, exploit or dispose of rights and goods or to access different forms of credit or accommodation in so far as those choices are useful for access to his activity or for the effective exercise thereof.

(66) Access to or the exercise of a service activity in the territory of a Member State should not be subject to an economic test. The prohibition of economic tests as a prerequisite for the grant of authorisation should cover economic tests as such, but not requirements which are objectively justified by overriding reasons relating to the public interest, such as the protection of the urban environment, social policy or public health. The prohibition should not affect the exercise of the powers of the authorities responsible for applying competition law.

(67) With respect to financial guarantees or insurance, the prohibition of requirements should concern only the obligation that the requested financial guarantees or insurance must be obtained from a financial institution established in the Member State concerned.

(68) With respect to pre-registration, the prohibition of requirements should concern only the obligation that the provider, prior to the establishment, be pre-registered for a given period in a register held in the Member State concerned.

(69) In order to coordinate the modernisation of national rules and regulations in a manner consistent with the requirements of the internal market, it is necessary to evaluate certain non-discriminatory national requirements which, by their very nature, could severely restrict or even prevent access to an activity or the exercise thereof under the freedom of establishment. This

evaluation process should be limited to the compatibility of these requirements with the criteria already established by the Court of Justice on the freedom of establishment. It should not concern the application of Community competition law. Where such requirements are discriminatory or not objectively justified by an overriding reason relating to the public interest, or where they are disproportionate, they must be abolished or amended. The outcome of this assessment will be different according to the nature of the activity and the public interest concerned. In particular, such requirements could be fully justified when they pursue social policy objectives.

(70) For the purposes of this Directive, and without prejudice to Article 16 of the Treaty, services may be considered to be services of general economic interest only if they are provided in application of a special task in the public interest entrusted to the provider by the Member State concerned. This assignment should be made by way of one or more acts, the form of which is determined by the Member State concerned, and should specify the precise nature of the special task.

(71) The mutual evaluation process provided for in this Directive should not affect the freedom of Member States to set in their legislation a high level of protection of the public interest, in particular in relation to social policy objectives. Furthermore, it is necessary that the mutual evaluation process take fully into account the specificity of services of general economic interest and of the particular tasks assigned to them. This may justify certain restrictions on the freedom of establishment, in particular where such restrictions pursue the protection of public health and social policy objectives and where they satisfy the conditions set out in Article 15(3)(a), (b) and (c). For example, with regard to the obligation to take a specific legal form in order to exercise certain services in the social field, the Court of Justice has already recognised that it may be justified to subject the provider to a requirement to be non-profit making.

(72) Services of a general economic interest are entrusted with important tasks relating to social and territorial cohesion. The performance of these tasks should not be obstructed as a result of the evaluation process provided for in this Directive. Requirements which are necessary for the fulfilment of such tasks should not be affected by this process while, at the same time, unjustified restrictions on the freedom of establishment should be addressed.

(73) The requirements to be examined include national rules which, on grounds other than those relating to professional qualifications, reserve access to certain activities to particular providers. These requirements also include obligations on a provider to take a specific legal form, in particular to be a legal person, to be a company with individual ownership, to be a non-profit making organisation or a company owned exclusively by natural persons, and requirements which relate to the shareholding of a company, in particular obligations to hold a minimum amount of capital for certain service activities or to have a specific qualification in order to hold share capital in or to manage certain companies. The evaluation of the compatibility of fixed minimum and/or maximum tariffs with the freedom of establishment concerns only tariffs imposed by competent authorities specifically for the provision of certain services and not, for example, general rules on price determination, such as for the renting of houses.

(74) The mutual evaluation process means that during the transposition period Member States will first have to conduct a screening of their legislation in order to ascertain whether any of the above mentioned requirements exists in their legal systems. At the latest by the end of the transposition period, Member States should draw up a report on the results of this screening. Each report will be submitted to all other Member States and interested parties. Member States will then have six months in which to submit their observations on these reports. At the latest by one year after the date of transposition of this Directive, the Commission should draw up a summary report, accompanied where appropriate by proposals for further initiatives. If necessary the Commission, in cooperation with the Member States, could assist them to design a common method.

(75) The fact that this Directive specifies a number of requirements to be abolished or evaluated by the Member States during the transposition period is without prejudice to any infringement proceedings against a Member State for failure to fulfil its obligations under Articles 43 or 49 of the Treaty.

(76) This Directive does not concern the application of Articles 28 to 30 of the Treaty relating to the free movement of goods. The restrictions prohibited pursuant to the provision on the freedom to provide services cover the requirements applicable to access to service activities or to the exercise thereof and not those applicable to goods as such.

(77) Where an operator travels to another Member State to exercise a service activity there, a distinction should be made between situations covered by the freedom of establishment and those covered, due to the temporary nature of the activities concerned, by the free movement of services. As regards the distinction between the freedom of establishment and the free movement of services, according to the case law of the Court of Justice the key element is whether or not the operator is established in the Member State where it provides the service concerned. If the operator is established in the Member State where it provides its services, it should come under the scope of application of the freedom of establishment. If, by contrast, the operator is not established in the Member State where the service is provided, its activities should be covered by the free movement of services. The Court of Justice has consistently held that the temporary nature of the activities in question should be determined in the light not only of the duration of the provision of the service, but also of its regularity, periodical nature or continuity. The fact that the activity is temporary should not mean that the provider may not equip itself with some forms of infrastructure in the Member State where the service is provided, such as an office, chambers or consulting rooms, in so far as such infrastructure is necessary for the purposes of providing the service in question.

(78) In order to secure effective implementation of the free movement of services and to ensure that recipients and providers can benefit from and supply services throughout the Community regardless of borders, it is necessary to clarify the extent to which requirements of the Member State where the service is provided can be imposed. It is indispensable to provide that the provision on the freedom to provide services does not prevent the Member State where the service is provided from imposing, in compliance with the principles set out in Article 16(1)(a) to (c), its specific requirements for reasons of public policy or public security or for the protection of public health or the environment.

(79) The Court of Justice has consistently held that Member States retain the right to take measures in order to prevent providers from abusively taking advantage of the internal market principles. Abuse by a provider should be established on a case by case basis.

(80) It is necessary to ensure that providers are able to take equipment which is integral to the provision of their service with them when they travel to provide services in another Member State. In particular, it is important to avoid cases in which the service could not be provided without the equipment or situations in which providers incur additional costs, for example, by hiring or purchasing different equipment to that which they habitually use or by needing to deviate significantly from the way they habitually carry out their activity.

(81) The concept of equipment does not refer to physical objects which are either supplied by the provider to the client or become part of a physical object as a result of the service activity, such as building materials or spare parts, or which are consumed or left in situ in the course of the service provision, such as combustible fuels, explosives, fireworks, pesticides, poisons or medicines.

(82) The provisions of this Directive should not preclude the application by a Member State of rules on employment conditions. Rules laid down by law, regulation or administrative provisions should, in accordance with the Treaty, be justified for reasons relating to the protection of workers and be non-discriminatory, necessary, and proportionate, as interpreted by the Court of Justice, and comply with other relevant Community law.

(83) It is necessary to ensure that the provision on the freedom to provide services may be departed from only in the areas covered by derogations. Those derogations are necessary in order to take into account the level of integration of the internal market or certain Community instruments relating to services pursuant to which a provider is subject to the application of a law other than that of the Member State of establishment. Moreover, by way of exception, measures against a given provider should also be adopted in certain individual cases and under certain strict procedural and substantive conditions. In addition, any restriction of the free movement

of services should be permitted, by way of exception, only if it is consistent with fundamental rights which form an integral part of the general principles of law enshrined in the Community legal order.

(84) The derogation from the provision on the freedom to provide services concerning postal services should cover both activities reserved to the universal service provider and other postal services.

(85) The derogation from the provision on the freedom to provide services relating to the judicial recovery of debts and the reference to a possible future harmonisation instrument should concern only the access to and the exercise of activities which consist, notably, in bringing actions before a court relating to the recovery of debts.

(86) This Directive should not affect terms and conditions of employment which, pursuant to Directive 96/71/EC of the European Parliament and of the Council of 16 December 1996 concerning the posting of workers in the framework of the provision of services,[19] apply to workers posted to provide a service in the territory of another Member State. In such cases, Directive 96/71/EC stipulates that providers have to comply with terms and conditions of employment in a listed number of areas applicable in the Member State where the service is provided. These are: maximum work periods and minimum rest periods, minimum paid annual holidays, minimum rates of pay, including overtime rates, the conditions of hiring out of workers, in particular the protection of workers hired out by temporary employment undertakings, health, safety and hygiene at work, protective measures with regard to the terms and conditions of employment of pregnant women or women who have recently given birth and of children and young people and equality of treatment between men and women and other provisions on non-discrimination. This not only concerns terms and conditions of employment which are laid down by law but also those laid down in collective agreements or arbitration awards that are officially declared or de facto universally applicable within the meaning of Directive 96/71/EC. Moreover, this Directive should not prevent Member States from applying terms and conditions of employment on matters other than those listed in Article 3(1) of Directive 96/71/EC on the grounds of public policy.

(87) Neither should this Directive affect terms and conditions of employment in cases where the worker employed for the provision of a cross-border service is recruited in the Member State where the service is provided. Furthermore, this Directive should not affect the right for the Member State where the service is provided to determine the existence of an employment relationship and the distinction between self-employed persons and employed persons, including 'false self-employed persons'. In that respect the essential characteristic of an employment relationship within the meaning of Article 39 of the Treaty should be the fact that for a certain period of time a person provides services for and under the direction of another person in return for which he receives remuneration. Any activity which a person performs outside a relationship of subordination must be classified as an activity pursued in a self-employed capacity for the purposes of Articles 43 and 49 of the Treaty.

(88) The provision on the freedom to provide services should not apply in cases where, in conformity with Community law, an activity is reserved in a Member State to a particular profession, for example requirements which reserve the provision of legal advice to lawyers.

(89) The derogation from the provision on the freedom to provide services concerning matters relating to the registration of vehicles leased in a Member State other than that in which they are used follows from the case law of the Court of Justice, which has recognised that a Member State may impose such an obligation, in accordance with proportionate conditions, in the case of vehicles used on its territory. That exclusion does not cover occasional or temporary rental.

(90) Contractual relations between the provider and the client as well as between an employer and employee should not be subject to this Directive. The applicable law regarding the contractual or non contractual obligations of the provider should be determined by the rules of private international law.

---

[19] OJ L 18, 21.1.1997, p. 1.

(91) It is necessary to afford Member States the possibility, exceptionally and on a case-by-case basis, of taking measures which derogate from the provision on the freedom to provide services in respect of a provider established in another Member State on grounds of the safety of services. However, it should be possible to take such measures only in the absence of harmonisation at Community level.

(92) Restrictions on the free movement of services, contrary to this Directive, may arise not only from measures applied to providers, but also from the many barriers to the use of services by recipients, especially consumers. This Directive mentions, by way of illustration, certain types of restriction applied to a recipient wishing to use a service performed by a provider established in another Member State. This also includes cases where recipients of a service are under an obligation to obtain authorisation from or to make a declaration to their competent authorities in order to receive a service from a provider established in another Member State. This does not concern general authorisation schemes which also apply to the use of a service supplied by a provider established in the same Member State.

(93) The concept of financial assistance provided for the use of a particular service should not apply to systems of aids granted by Member States, in particular in the social field or in the cultural sector, which are covered by Community rules on competition, nor to general financial assistance not linked to the use of a particular service, for example grants or loans to students.

(94) In accordance with the Treaty rules on the free movement of services, discrimination on grounds of the nationality of the recipient or national or local residence is prohibited. Such discrimination could take the form of an obligation, imposed only on nationals of another Member State, to supply original documents, certified copies, a certificate of nationality or official translations of documents in order to benefit from a service or from more advantageous terms or prices. However, the prohibition of discriminatory requirements should not preclude the reservation of advantages, especially as regards tariffs, to certain recipients, if such reservation is based on legitimate and objective criteria.

(95) The principle of non-discrimination within the internal market means that access by a recipient, and especially by a consumer, to a service on offer to the public may not be denied or restricted by application of a criterion, included in general conditions made available to the public, relating to the recipient's nationality or place of residence. It does not follow that it will be unlawful discrimination if provision were made in such general conditions for different tariffs and conditions to apply to the provision of a service, where those tariffs, prices and conditions are justified for objective reasons that can vary from country to country, such as additional costs incurred because of the distance involved or the technical characteristics of the provision of the service, or different market conditions, such as higher or lower demand influenced by seasonality, different vacation periods in the Member States and pricing by different competitors, or extra risks linked to rules differing from those of the Member State of establishment. Neither does it follow that the non-provision of a service to a consumer for lack of the required intellectual property rights in a particular territory would constitute unlawful discrimination.

(96) It is appropriate to provide that, as one of the means by which the provider may make the information which he is obliged to supply easily accessible to the recipient, he supply his electronic address, including that of his website. Furthermore, the obligation to make available certain information in the provider's information documents which present his services in detail should not cover commercial communications of a general nature, such as advertising, but rather documents giving a detailed description of the services proposed, including documents on a website.

(97) It is necessary to provide in this Directive for certain rules on high quality of services, ensuring in particular information and transparency requirements. These rules should apply both in cases of cross border provision of services between Member States and in cases of services provided in a Member State by a provider established there, without imposing unnecessary burdens on SMEs. They should not in any way prevent Member States from applying, in conformity with this Directive and other Community law, additional or different quality requirements.

(98) Any operator providing services involving a direct and particular health, safety or financial risk for the recipient or a third person should, in principle, be covered by appropriate professional liability insurance, or by another form of guarantee which is equivalent or comparable, which
means, in particular, that such an operator should as a general rule have adequate insurance cover
for services provided in one or more Member States other than the Member State of establishment.

(99) The insurance or guarantee should be appropriate to the nature and extent of the risk.
Therefore it should be necessary for the provider to have cross-border cover only if that provider actually provides services in other Member States. Member States should not lay down more detailed
rules concerning the insurance cover and fix for example minimum thresholds for the insured sum
or limits on exclusions from the insurance cover. Providers and insurance companies should maintain the necessary flexibility to negotiate insurance policies precisely targeted to the nature and extent of the risk. Furthermore, it is not necessary for an obligation of appropriate insurance to be laid
down by law. It should be sufficient if an insurance obligation is part of the ethical rules laid down
by professional bodies. Finally, there should be no obligation for insurance companies to provide
insurance cover.

(100) It is necessary to put an end to total prohibitions on commercial communications by the
regulated professions, not by removing bans on the content of a commercial communication but rather by removing those bans which, in a general way and for a given profession, forbid one or more
forms of commercial communication, such as a ban on all advertising in one or more given media.
As regards the content and methods of commercial communication, it is necessary to encourage
professionals to draw up, in accordance with Community law, codes of conduct at Community level.

(101) It is necessary and in the interest of recipients, in particular consumers, to ensure that
it is possible for providers to offer multidisciplinary services and that restrictions in this regard be
limited to what is necessary to ensure the impartiality, independence and integrity of the regulated
professions. This does not affect restrictions or prohibitions on carrying out particular activities
which aim at ensuring independence in cases in which a Member State entrusts a provider with
a particular task, notably in the area of urban development, nor should it affect the application of
competition rules.

(102) In order to increase transparency and promote assessments based on comparable criteria
with regard to the quality of the services offered and supplied to recipients, it is important that information on the meaning of quality labels and other distinctive marks relating to these services be
easily accessible. That obligation of transparency is particularly important in areas such as tourism,
especially the hotel business, in which the use of a system of classification is widespread. Moreover,
it is appropriate to examine the extent to which European standardisation could facilitate compatibility and quality of services. European standards are drawn up by the European standards-setting
bodies, the European Committee for Standardisation (CEN), the European Committee for
Electrotechnical Standardisation (CENELEC) and the European Telecommunications Standards
Institute (ETSI). Where appropriate, the Commission may, in accordance with the procedures laid
down in Directive 98/34/EC of the European Parliament and of the Council of 22 June 1998 laying
down a procedure for the provision of information in the field of technical standards and regulations[20] and of rules on Information Society services, issue a mandate for the drawing up of specific
European standards.

(103) In order to solve potential problems with compliance with judicial decisions, it is appropriate to provide that Member States recognise equivalent guarantees lodged with institutions
or bodies such as banks, insurance providers or other financial services providers established in
another Member State.

(104) The development of a network of Member States' consumer protection authorities, which
is the subject of Regulation (EC) No 2006/2004, complements the cooperation provided for in this
Directive. The application of consumer protection legislation in cross-border cases, in particular

---

[20] OJ L 204, 21.7.1998, p. 37. Directive as last amended by the Act of Accession.

with regard to new marketing and selling practices, as well as the need to remove certain specific obstacles to cooperation in this field, necessitates a greater degree of cooperation between Member States. In particular, it is necessary in this area to ensure that Member States require the cessation of illegal practices by operators in their territory who target consumers in another Member State.

(105) Administrative cooperation is essential to make the internal market in services function properly. Lack of cooperation between Member States results in proliferation of rules applicable to providers or duplication of controls for cross-border activities, and can also be used by rogue traders to avoid supervision or to circumvent applicable national rules on services. It is, therefore, essential to provide for clear, legally binding obligations for Member States to cooperate effectively.

(106) For the purposes of the Chapter on administrative cooperation, 'supervision' should cover activities such as monitoring and fact finding, problem solving, enforcement and imposition of sanctions and subsequent follow-up activities.

(107) In normal circumstances mutual assistance should take place directly between competent authorities. The liaison points designated by Member States should be required to facilitate this process only in the event of difficulties being encountered, for instance if assistance is required to identify the relevant competent authority.

(108) Certain obligations of mutual assistance should apply to all matters covered by this Directive, including those relating to cases where a provider establishes in another Member State. Other obligations of mutual assistance should apply only in cases of cross-border provision of services, where the provision on the freedom to provide services applies. A further set of obligations should apply in all cases of cross-border provision of services, including areas not covered by the provision on the freedom to provide services. Cross-border provision of services should include cases where services are provided at a distance and where the recipient travels to the Member State of establishment of the provider in order to receive services.

(109) In cases where a provider moves temporarily to a Member State other than the Member State of establishment, it is necessary to provide for mutual assistance between those two Member States so that the former can carry out checks, inspections and enquiries at the request of the Member State of establishment or carry out such checks on its own initiative if these are merely factual checks.

(110) It should not be possible for Member States to circumvent the rules laid down in this Directive, including the provision on the freedom to provide services, by conducting checks, inspections or investigations which are discriminatory or disproportionate.

(111) The provisions of this Directive concerning exchange of information regarding the good repute of providers should not pre-empt initiatives in the area of police and judicial cooperation in criminal matters, in particular on the exchange of information between law enforcement authorities of the Member States and on criminal records.

(112) Cooperation between Member States requires a well-functioning electronic information system in order to allow competent authorities easily to identify their relevant interlocutors in other Member States and to communicate in an efficient way.

(113) It is necessary to provide that the Member States, in cooperation with the Commission, are to encourage interested parties to draw up codes of conduct at Community level, aimed, in particular, at promoting the quality of services and taking into account the specific nature of each profession. Those codes of conduct should comply with Community law, especially competition law. They should be compatible with legally binding rules governing professional ethics and conduct in the Member States.

(114) Member States should encourage the setting up of codes of conduct, in particular, by professional bodies, organisations and associations at Community level. These codes of conduct should include, as appropriate to the specific nature of each profession, rules for commercial communications relating to the regulated professions and rules of professional ethics and conduct of the regulated professions which aim, in particular, at ensuring independence, impartiality and professional secrecy. In addition, the conditions to which the activities of estate agents are subject should be included in such codes of conduct. Member States should take accompanying measures

to encourage professional bodies, organisations and associations to implement at national level the codes of conduct adopted at Community level.

(115) Codes of conduct at Community level are intended to set minimum standards of conduct and are complementary to Member States' legal requirements. They do not preclude Member States, in accordance with Community law, from taking more stringent measures in law or national professional bodies from providing for greater protection in their national codes of conduct.

(116) Since the objectives of this Directive, namely the elimination of barriers to the freedom of establishment for providers in the Member States and to the free provision of services between Member States, cannot be sufficiently achieved by the Member States and can therefore, by reason of the scale of the action, be better achieved at Community level, the Community may adopt measures, in accordance with the principle of subsidiarity as set out in Article 5 of the Treaty. In accordance with the principle of proportionality, as set out in that Article, this Directive does not go beyond what is necessary in order to achieve those objectives.

(117) The measures necessary for the implementation of this Directive should be adopted in accordance with Council Decision 1999/468/EC of 28 June 1999 laying down the procedures for the exercise of implementing powers conferred on the Commission.[21]

(118) In accordance with paragraph 34 of the Interinstitutional Agreement on better law-making,[22] Member States are encouraged to draw up, for themselves and in the interest of the Community, their own tables, which will, as far as possible, illustrate the correlation between the Directive and the transposition measures, and to make them public,

HAVE ADOPTED THIS DIRECTIVE:

Chapter I General provisions

Article 1 Subject matter

1. This Directive establishes general provisions facilitating the exercise of the freedom of establishment for service providers and the free movement of services, while maintaining a high quality of services.

2. This Directive does not deal with the liberalisation of services of general economic interest, reserved to public or private entities, nor with the privatisation of public entities providing services.

3. This Directive does not deal with the abolition of monopolies providing services nor with aids granted by Member States which are covered by Community rules on competition.

This Directive does not affect the freedom of Member States to define, in conformity with Community law, what they consider to be services of general economic interest, how those services should be organised and financed, in compliance with the State aid rules, and what specific obligations they should be subject to.

4. This Directive does not affect measures taken at Community level or at national level, in conformity with Community law, to protect or promote cultural or linguistic diversity or media pluralism.

5. This Directive does not affect Member States' rules of criminal law. However, Member States may not restrict the freedom to provide services by applying criminal law provisions which specifically regulate or affect access to or exercise of a service activity in circumvention of the rules laid down in this Directive.

6. This Directive does not affect labour law, that is any legal or contractual provision concerning employment conditions, working conditions, including health and safety at work and the relationship between employers and workers, which Member States apply in accordance with national law which respects Community law. Equally, this Directive does not affect the social security legislation of the Member States.

---

[21] OJ L 184, 17.7.1999, p. 23. Decision as amended by Decision 2006/512/EC (OJ L 200, 22.7.2006, p. 11).
[22] OJ C 321, 31.12.2003, p. 1.

7. This Directive does not affect the exercise of fundamental rights as recognised in the Member States and by Community law. Nor does it affect the right to negotiate, conclude and enforce collective agreements and to take industrial action in accordance with national law and practices which respect Community law.

Article 2   Scope

1. This Directive shall apply to services supplied by providers established in a Member State.
2. This Directive shall not apply to the following activities:
    (a) non-economic services of general interest;
    (b) financial services, such as banking, credit, insurance and re-insurance, occupational or personal pensions, securities, investment funds, payment and investment advice, including the services listed in Annex I to Directive 2006/48/EC;
    (c) electronic communications services and networks, and associated facilities and services, with respect to matters covered by Directives 2002/19/EC, 2002/20/EC, 2002/21/EC, 2002/22/EC and 2002/58/EC;
    (d) services in the field of transport, including port services, falling within the scope of Title V of the Treaty;
    (e) services of temporary work agencies;
    (f) healthcare services whether or not they are provided via healthcare facilities, and regardless of the ways in which they are organised and financed at national level or whether they are public or private;
    (g) audiovisual services, including cinematographic services, whatever their mode of production, distribution and transmission, and radio broadcasting;
    (h) gambling activities which involve wagering a stake with pecuniary value in games of chance, including lotteries, gambling in casinos and betting transactions;
    (i) activities which are connected with the exercise of official authority as set out in Article 45 of the Treaty;
    (j) social services relating to social housing, childcare and support of families and persons permanently or temporarily in need which are provided by the State, by providers mandated by the State or by charities recognised as such by the State;
    (k) private security services;
    (l) services provided by notaries and bailiffs, who are appointed by an official act of government.
3. This Directive shall not apply to the field of taxation.

Article 3   Relationship with other provisions of Community law

1. If the provisions of this Directive conflict with a provision of another Community act governing specific aspects of access to or exercise of a service activity in specific sectors or for specific professions, the provision of the other Community act shall prevail and shall apply to those specific sectors or professions. These include:
    (a) Directive 96/71/EC;
    (b) Regulation (EEC) No 1408/71;
    (c) Council Directive 89/552/EEC of 3 October 1989 on the coordination of certain provisions laid down by law, regulation or administrative action in Member States concerning the pursuit of television broadcasting activities;[23]
    (d) Directive 2005/36/EC.
2. This Directive does not concern rules of private international law, in particular rules governing the law applicable to contractual and non contractual obligations, including those which guarantee that consumers benefit from the protection granted to them by the consumer protection rules laid down in the consumer legislation in force in their Member State.

---

[23] OJ L 298, 17.10.1989, p. 23. Directive as amended by Directive 97/36/EC of the European Parliament and of the Council (OJ L 202, 30.7.1997, p. 60).

3. Member States shall apply the provisions of this Directive in compliance with the rules of the Treaty on the right of establishment and the free movement of services.

Article 4   Definitions

For the purposes of this Directive, the following definitions shall apply:

1) 'service' means any self-employed economic activity, normally provided for remuneration, as referred to in Article 50 of the Treaty;

2) 'provider' means any natural person who is a national of a Member State, or any legal person as referred to in Article 48 of the Treaty and established in a Member State, who offers or provides a service;

3) 'recipient' means any natural person who is a national of a Member State or who benefits from rights conferred upon him by Community acts, or any legal person as referred to in Article 48 of the Treaty and established in a Member State, who, for professional or non-professional purposes, uses, or wishes to use, a service;

4) 'Member State of establishment' means the Member State in whose territory the provider of the service concerned is established;

5) 'establishment' means the actual pursuit of an economic activity, as referred to in Article 43 of the Treaty, by the provider for an indefinite period and through a stable infrastructure from where the business of providing services is actually carried out;

6) 'authorisation scheme' means any procedure under which a provider or recipient is in effect required to take steps in order to obtain from a competent authority a formal decision, or an implied decision, concerning access to a service activity or the exercise thereof;

7) 'requirement' means any obligation, prohibition, condition or limit provided for in the laws, regulations or administrative provisions of the Member States or in consequence of case-law, administrative practice, the rules of professional bodies, or the collective rules of professional associations or other professional organisations, adopted in the exercise of their legal autonomy; rules laid down in collective agreements negotiated by the social partners shall not as such be seen as requirements within the meaning of this Directive;

8) 'overriding reasons relating to the public interest' means reasons recognised as such in the case law of the Court of Justice, including the following grounds: public policy; public security; public safety; public health; preserving the financial equilibrium of the social security system; the protection of consumers, recipients of services and workers; fairness of trade transactions; combating fraud; the protection of the environment and the urban environment; the health of animals; intellectual property; the conservation of the national historic and artistic heritage; social policy objectives and cultural policy objectives;

9) 'competent authority' means any body or authority which has a supervisory or regulatory role in a Member State in relation to service activities, including, in particular, administrative authorities, including courts acting as such, professional bodies, and those professional associations or other professional organisations which, in the exercise of their legal autonomy, regulate in a collective manner access to service activities or the exercise thereof;

10) 'Member State where the service is provided' means the Member State where the service is supplied by a provider established in another Member State;

11) 'regulated profession' means a professional activity or a group of professional activities as referred to in Article 3(1)(a) of Directive 2005/36/EC;

12) 'commercial communication' means any form of communication designed to promote, directly or indirectly, the goods, services or image of an undertaking, organisation or person engaged in commercial, industrial or craft activity or practising a regulated profession. The following do not in themselves constitute commercial communications:

    (a) information enabling direct access to the activity of the undertaking, organisation or person, including in particular a domain name or an electronic-mailing address;

    (b) communications relating to the goods, services or image of the undertaking, organisation or person, compiled in an independent manner, particularly when provided for no financial consideration.

Chapter II Administrative simplification

Article 5 Simplification of procedures

1. Member States shall examine the procedures and formalities applicable to access to a service activity and to the exercise thereof. Where procedures and formalities examined under this paragraph are not sufficiently simple, Member States shall simplify them.

2. The Commission may introduce harmonised forms at Community level, in accordance with the procedure referred to in Article 40(2). These forms shall be equivalent to certificates, attestations and any other documents required of a provider.

3. Where Member States require a provider or recipient to supply a certificate, attestation or any other document proving that a requirement has been satisfied, they shall accept any document from another Member State which serves an equivalent purpose or from which it is clear that the requirement in question has been satisfied. They may not require a document from another Member State to be produced in its original form, or as a certified copy or as a certified translation, save in the cases provided for in other Community instruments or where such a requirement is justified by an overriding reason relating to the public interest, including public order and security.

The first subparagraph shall not affect the right of Member States to require non-certified translations of documents in one of their official languages.

4. Paragraph 3 shall not apply to the documents referred to in Article 7(2) and 50 of Directive 2005/36/EC, in Articles 45(3), 46, 49 and 50 of Directive 2004/18/EC of the European Parliament and of the Council of 31 March 2004 on the coordination of procedures for the award of public works contracts, public supply contracts and public service contracts,[24] in Article 3(2) of Directive 98/5/EC of the European Parliament and of the Council of 16 February 1998 to facilitate practice of the profession of lawyer on a permanent basis in a Member State other than that in which the qualification was obtained,[25] in the First Council Directive 68/151/EEC of 9 March 1968 on coordination of safeguards which, for the protection of the interests of members and others, are required by Member States of companies within the meaning of the second paragraph of Article 58 of the Treaty, with a view to making such safeguards equivalent throughout the Community[26] and in the Eleventh Council Directive 89/666/EEC of 21 December 1989 concerning disclosure requirements in respect of branches opened in a Member State by certain types of company governed by the law of another State.[27]

Article 6 Points of single contact

1. Member States shall ensure that it is possible for providers to complete the following procedures and formalities through points of single contact:

(a) all procedures and formalities needed for access to his service activities, in particular, all declarations, notifications or applications necessary for authorisation from the competent authorities, including applications for inclusion in a register, a roll or a database, or for registration with a professional body or association;

(b) any applications for authorisation needed to exercise his service activities.

2. The establishment of points of single contact shall be without prejudice to the allocation of functions and powers among the authorities within national systems.

Article 7 Right to information

1. Member States shall ensure that the following information is easily accessible to providers and recipients through the points of single contact:

(a) requirements applicable to providers established in their territory, in particular those requirements concerning the procedures and formalities to be completed in order to access and to exercise service activities;

---

[24] OJ L 134, 30.4.2004, p. 114. Directive as last amended by Commission Regulation (EC) No 2083/2005 (OJ L 333, 20.12.2005, p. 28).

[25] OJ L 77, 14.3.1998, p. 36. Directive as amended by the Act of Accession.

[26] OJ L 65, 14.3.1968, p. 8. Directive as last amended by Directive/58/EC of the European Parliament and of the Council (OJ L 221, 4.9.2003, p. 13).

[27] OJ L 395, 30.12.1989, p. 36.

    (b) the contact details of the competent authorities enabling the latter to be contacted directly, including the details of those authorities responsible for matters concerning the exercise of service activities;

    (c) the means of, and conditions for, accessing public registers and databases on providers and services;

    (d) the means of redress which are generally available in the event of dispute between the competent authorities and the provider or the recipient, or between a provider and a recipient or between providers;

    (e) the contact details of the associations or organisations, other than the competent authorities, from which providers or recipients may obtain practical assistance.

2. Member States shall ensure that it is possible for providers and recipients to receive, at their request, assistance from the competent authorities, consisting in information on the way in which the requirements referred to in point (a) of paragraph 1 are generally interpreted and applied. Where appropriate, such advice shall include a simple step-by-step guide. The information shall be provided in plain and intelligible language.

3. Member States shall ensure that the information and assistance referred to in paragraphs 1 and 2 are provided in a clear and unambiguous manner, that they are easily accessible at a distance and by electronic means and that they are kept up to date.

4. Member States shall ensure that the points of single contact and the competent authorities respond as quickly as possible to any request for information or assistance as referred to in paragraphs 1 and 2 and, in cases where the request is faulty or unfounded, inform the applicant accordingly without delay.

5. Member States and the Commission shall take accompanying measures in order to encourage points of single contact to make the information provided for in this Article available in other Community languages. This does not interfere with Member States' legislation on the use of languages.

6. The obligation for competent authorities to assist providers and recipients does not require those authorities to provide legal advice in individual cases but concerns only general information on the way in which requirements are usually interpreted or applied.

Article 8   Procedures by electronic means

1. Member States shall ensure that all procedures and formalities relating to access to a service activity and to the exercise thereof may be easily completed, at a distance and by electronic means, through the relevant point of single contact and with the relevant competent authorities.

2. Paragraph 1 shall not apply to the inspection of premises on which the service is provided or of equipment used by the provider or to physical examination of the capability or of the personal integrity of the provider or of his responsible staff.

3. The Commission shall, in accordance with the procedure referred to in Article 40(2), adopt detailed rules for the implementation of paragraph 1 of this Article with a view to facilitating the interoperability of information systems and use of procedures by electronic means between Member States, taking into account common standards developed at Community level.

Chapter III Freedom of establishment for providers

Section 1 Authorisations

Article 9   Authorisation schemes

1. Member States shall not make access to a service activity or the exercise thereof subject to an authorisation scheme unless the following conditions are satisfied:

    (a) the authorisation scheme does not discriminate against the provider in question;

    (b) the need for an authorisation scheme is justified by an overriding reason relating to the public interest;

(c) the objective pursued cannot be attained by means of a less restrictive measure, in particular because an a posteriori inspection would take place too late to be genuinely effective.

2. In the report referred to in Article 39(1), Member States shall identify their authorisation schemes and give reasons showing their compatibility with paragraph 1 of this Article.

3. This section shall not apply to those aspects of authorisation schemes which are governed directly or indirectly by other Community instruments.

Article 10   Conditions for the granting of authorisation

1. Authorisation schemes shall be based on criteria which preclude the competent authorities from exercising their power of assessment in an arbitrary manner.

2. The criteria referred to in paragraph 1 shall be:
   (a) non-discriminatory;
   (b) justified by an overriding reason relating to the public interest;
   (c) proportionate to that public interest objective;
   (d) clear and unambiguous;
   (e) objective;
   (f) made public in advance;
   (g) transparent and accessible.

3. The conditions for granting authorisation for a new establishment shall not duplicate requirements and controls which are equivalent or essentially comparable as regards their purpose to which the provider is already subject in another Member State or in the same Member State. The liaison points referred to in Article 28(2) and the provider shall assist the competent authority by providing any necessary information regarding those requirements.

4. The authorisation shall enable the provider to have access to the service activity, or to exercise that activity, throughout the national territory, including by means of setting up agencies, subsidiaries, branches or offices, except where an authorisation for each individual establishment or a limitation of the authorisation to a certain part of the territory is justified by an overriding reason relating to the public interest.

5. The authorisation shall be granted as soon as it is established, in the light of an appropriate examination, that the conditions for authorisation have been met.

6. Except in the case of the granting of an authorisation, any decision from the competent authorities, including refusal or withdrawal of an authorisation, shall be fully reasoned and shall be open to challenge before the courts or other instances of appeal.

7. This Article shall not call into question the allocation of the competences, at local or regional level, of the Member States' authorities granting authorisations.

Article 11   Duration of authorisation

1. An authorisation granted to a provider shall not be for a limited period, except where:
   (a) the authorisation is being automatically renewed or is subject only to the continued fulfilment of requirements;
   (b) the number of available authorisations is limited by an overriding reason relating to the public interest; or
   (c) a limited authorisation period can be justified by an overriding reason relating to the public interest.

2. Paragraph 1 shall not concern the maximum period before the end of which the provider must actually commence his activity after receiving authorisation.

3. Member States shall require a provider to inform the relevant point of single contact provided for in Article 6 of the following changes:
   (a) the creation of subsidiaries whose activities fall within the scope of the authorisation scheme;

(b) changes in his situation which result in the conditions for authorisation no longer being met.

4. This Article shall be without prejudice to the Member States' ability to revoke authorisations, when the conditions for authorisation are no longer met.

Article 12   Selection from among several candidates

1. Where the number of authorisations available for a given activity is limited because of the scarcity of available natural resources or technical capacity, Member States shall apply a selection procedure to potential candidates which provides full guarantees of impartiality and transparency, including, in particular, adequate publicity about the launch, conduct and completion of the procedure.

2. In the cases referred to in paragraph 1, authorisation shall be granted for an appropriate limited period and may not be open to automatic renewal nor confer any other advantage on the provider whose authorisation has just expired or on any person having any particular links with that provider.

3. Subject to paragraph 1 and to Articles 9 and 10, Member States may take into account, in establishing the rules for the selection procedure, considerations of public health, social policy objectives, the health and safety of employees or self-employed persons, the protection of the environment, the preservation of cultural heritage and other overriding reasons relating to the public interest, in conformity with Community law.

Article 13   Authorisation procedures

1. Authorisation procedures and formalities shall be clear, made public in advance and be such as to provide the applicants with a guarantee that their application will be dealt with objectively and impartially.

2. Authorisation procedures and formalities shall not be dissuasive and shall not unduly complicate or delay the provision of the service. They shall be easily accessible and any charges which the applicants may incur from their application shall be reasonable and proportionate to the cost of the authorisation procedures in question and shall not exceed the cost of the procedures.

3. Authorisation procedures and formalities shall provide applicants with a guarantee that their application will be processed as quickly as possible and, in any event, within a reasonable period which is fixed and made public in advance. The period shall run only from the time when all documentation has been submitted. When justified by the complexity of the issue, the time period may be extended once, by the competent authority, for a limited time. The extension and its duration shall be duly motivated and shall be notified to the applicant before the original period has expired.

4. Failing a response within the time period set or extended in accordance with paragraph 3, authorisation shall be deemed to have been granted. Different arrangements may nevertheless be put in place, where justified by overriding reasons relating to the public interest, including a legitimate interest of third parties.

5. All applications for authorisation shall be acknowledged as quickly as possible. The acknowledgement must specify the following:
(a) the period referred to in paragraph 3;
(b) the available means of redress;
(c) where applicable, a statement that in the absence of a response within the period specified, the authorisation shall be deemed to have been granted.

6. In the case of an incomplete application, the applicant shall be informed as quickly as possible of the need to supply any additional documentation, as well as of any possible effects on the period referred to in paragraph 3.

7. When a request is rejected because it fails to comply with the required procedures or formalities, the applicant shall be informed of the rejection as quickly as possible.

Section 2 Requirements prohibited or subject to evaluation

Article 14 Prohibited requirements

Member States shall not make access to, or the exercise of, a service activity in their territory subject to compliance with any of the following:

1) discriminatory requirements based directly or indirectly on nationality or, in the case of companies, the location of the registered office, including in particular:

(a) nationality requirements for the provider, his staff, persons holding the share capital or members of the provider's management or supervisory bodies;

(b) a requirement that the provider, his staff, persons holding the share capital or members of the provider's management or supervisory bodies be resident within the territory;

2) a prohibition on having an establishment in more than one Member State or on being entered in the registers or enrolled with professional bodies or associations of more than one Member State;

3) restrictions on the freedom of a provider to choose between a principal or a secondary establishment, in particular an obligation on the provider to have its principal establishment in their territory, or restrictions on the freedom to choose between establishment in the form of an agency, branch or subsidiary;

4) conditions of reciprocity with the Member State in which the provider already has an establishment, save in the case of conditions of reciprocity provided for in Community instruments concerning energy;

5) the case-by-case application of an economic test making the granting of authorisation subject to proof of the existence of an economic need or market demand, an assessment of the potential or current economic effects of the activity or an assessment of the appropriateness of the activity in relation to the economic planning objectives set by the competent authority; this prohibition shall not concern planning requirements which do not pursue economic aims but serve overriding reasons relating to the public interest;

6) the direct or indirect involvement of competing operators, including within consultative bodies, in the granting of authorisations or in the adoption of other decisions of the competent authorities, with the exception of professional bodies and associations or other organisations acting as the competent authority; this prohibition shall not concern the consultation of organisations, such as chambers of commerce or social partners, on matters other than individual applications for authorisation, or a consultation of the public at large;

7) an obligation to provide or participate in a financial guarantee or to take out insurance from a provider or body established in their territory. This shall not affect the possibility for Member States to require insurance or financial guarantees as such, nor shall it affect requirements relating to the participation in a collective compensation fund, for instance for members of professional bodies or organisations;

8) an obligation to have been pre-registered, for a given period, in the registers held in their territory or to have previously exercised the activity for a given period in their territory.

Article 15 Requirements to be evaluated

1. Member States shall examine whether, under their legal system, any of the requirements listed in paragraph 2 are imposed and shall ensure that any such requirements are compatible with the conditions laid down in paragraph 3. Member States shall adapt their laws, regulations or administrative provisions so as to make them compatible with those conditions.

2. Member States shall examine whether their legal system makes access to a service activity or the exercise of it subject to compliance with any of the following non-discriminatory requirements:

(a) quantitative or territorial restrictions, in particular in the form of limits fixed according to population or of a minimum geographical distance between providers;

(b) an obligation on a provider to take a specific legal form;

(c) requirements which relate to the shareholding of a company;

(d) requirements, other than those concerning matters covered by Directive 2005/36/EC or provided for in other Community instruments, which reserve access to the service activity in question to particular providers by virtue of the specific nature of the activity;

   (e) a ban on having more than one establishment in the territory of the same State;
   (f) requirements fixing a minimum number of employees;
   (g) fixed minimum and/or maximum tariffs with which the provider must comply;
   (h) an obligation on the provider to supply other specific services jointly with his service.
   3. Member States shall verify that the requirements referred to in paragraph 2 satisfy the following conditions:
   (a) non-discrimination: requirements must be neither directly nor indirectly discriminatory according to nationality nor, with regard to companies, according to the location of the registered office;
   (b) necessity: requirements must be justified by an overriding reason relating to the public interest;
   (c) proportionality: requirements must be suitable for securing the attainment of the objective pursued; they must not go beyond what is necessary to attain that objective and it must not be possible to replace those requirements with other, less restrictive measures which attain the same result.
   4. Paragraphs 1, 2 and 3 shall apply to legislation in the field of services of general economic interest only insofar as the application of these paragraphs does not obstruct the performance, in law or in fact, of the particular task assigned to them.
   5. In the mutual evaluation report provided for in Article 39(1), Member States shall specify the following:
   (a) the requirements that they intend to maintain and the reasons why they consider that those requirements comply with the conditions set out in paragraph 3;
   (b) the requirements which have been abolished or made less stringent.
   6. From 28 December 2006 Member States shall not introduce any new requirement of a kind listed in paragraph 2, unless that requirement satisfies the conditions laid down in paragraph 3.
   7. Member States shall notify the Commission of any new laws, regulations or administrative provisions which set requirements as referred to in paragraph 6, together with the reasons for those requirements. The Commission shall communicate the provisions concerned to the other Member States. Such notification shall not prevent Member States from adopting the provisions in question.
   Within a period of 3 months from the date of receipt of the notification, the Commission shall examine the compatibility of any new requirements with Community law and, where appropriate, shall adopt a decision requesting the Member State in question to refrain from adopting them or to abolish them.
   The notification of a draft national law in accordance with Directive 98/34/EC shall fulfil the obligation of notification provided for in this Directive.

Chapter IV Free movement of services

Section 1 Freedom to provide services and related derogations

Article 16 Freedom to provide services
   1. Member States shall respect the right of providers to provide services in a Member State other than that in which they are established.
   The Member State in which the service is provided shall ensure free access to and free exercise of a service activity within its territory.
   Member States shall not make access to or exercise of a service activity in their territory subject to compliance with any requirements which do not respect the following principles:
   (a) non-discrimination: the requirement may be neither directly nor indirectly discriminatory with regard to nationality or, in the case of legal persons, with regard to the Member State in which they are established;
   (b) necessity: the requirement must be justified for reasons of public policy, public security, public health or the protection of the environment;

(c) proportionality: the requirement must be suitable for attaining the objective pursued, and must not go beyond what is necessary to attain that objective.

2. Member States may not restrict the freedom to provide services in the case of a provider established in another Member State by imposing any of the following requirements:

    (a) an obligation on the provider to have an establishment in their territory;

    (b) an obligation on the provider to obtain an authorisation from their competent authorities including entry in a register or registration with a professional body or association in their territory, except where provided for in this Directive or other instruments of Community law;

    (c) a ban on the provider setting up a certain form or type of infrastructure in their territory, including an office or chambers, which the provider needs in order to supply the services in question;

    (d) the application of specific contractual arrangements between the provider and the recipient which prevent or restrict service provision by the self-employed;

    (e) an obligation on the provider to possess an identity document issued by its competent authorities specific to the exercise of a service activity;

    (f) requirements, except for those necessary for health and safety at work, which affect the use of equipment and material which are an integral part of the service provided;

    (g) restrictions on the freedom to provide the services referred to in Article 19.

3. The Member State to which the provider moves shall not be prevented from imposing requirements with regard to the provision of a service activity, where they are justified for reasons of public policy, public security, public health or the protection of the environment and in accordance with paragraph 1. Nor shall that Member State be prevented from applying, in accordance with Community law, its rules on employment conditions, including those laid down in collective agreements.

4. By 28 December 2011 the Commission shall, after consultation of the Member States and the social partners at Community level, submit to the European Parliament and the Council a report on the application of this Article, in which it shall consider the need to propose harmonisation measures regarding service activities covered by this Directive.

Article 17   Additional derogations from the freedom to provide services

Article 16 shall not apply to:

    1) services of general economic interest which are provided in another Member State, inter alia:

        (a) in the postal sector, services covered by Directive 97/67/EC of the European Parliament and of the Council of 15 December 1997 on common rules for the development of the internal market of Community postal services and the improvement of quality of service;[28]

        (b) in the electricity sector, services covered by Directive/54/EC[29] of the European Parliament and of the Council of 26 June concerning common rules for the internal market in electricity;

        (c) in the gas sector, services covered by Directive/55/EC of the European Parliament and of the Council of 26 June concerning common rules for the internal market in natural gas;[30]

        (d) water distribution and supply services and waste water services;

        (e) treatment of waste;

    2) matters covered by Directive 96/71/EC;

---

[28] OJ L 15, 21.1.1998, p. 14. Directive as last amended by Regulation (EC) No 1882/2003 (OJ L 284, 31.10.2003, p. 1).
[29] OJ L 176, 15.7.2003, p. 37. Directive as last amended by Commission Decision 2006/653/EC (OJ L 270, 29.9.2006, p. 72).
[30] OJ L 176, 15.7.2003, p. 57.

3) matters covered by Directive 95/46/EC of the European Parliament and of the Council of 24 October 1995 on the protection of individuals with regard to the processing of personal data and on the free movement of such data;[31]

4) matters covered by Council Directive 77/249/EEC of 22 March 1977 to facilitate the effective exercise by lawyers of freedom to provide services;[32]

5) the activity of judicial recovery of debts;

6) matters covered by Title II of Directive 2005/36/EC, as well as requirements in the Member State where the service is provided which reserve an activity to a particular profession;

7) matters covered by Regulation (EEC) No 1408/71;

8) as regards administrative formalities concerning the free movement of persons and their residence, matters covered by the provisions of Directive 2004/38/EC that lay down administrative formalities of the competent authorities of the Member State where the service is provided with which beneficiaries must comply;

9) as regards third country nationals who move to another Member State in the context of the provision of a service, the possibility for Member States to require visa or residence permits for third country nationals who are not covered by the mutual recognition regime provided for in Article 21 of the Convention implementing the Schengen Agreement of 14 June 1985 on the gradual abolition of checks at the common borders[33] or the possibility to oblige third country nationals to report to the competent authorities of the Member State in which the service is provided on or after their entry;

10) as regards the shipment of waste, matters covered by Council Regulation (EEC) No 259/93 of 1 February 1993 on the supervision and control of shipments of waste within, into and out of the European Community;[34]

11) copyright, neighbouring rights and rights covered by Council Directive 87/54/EEC of 16 December 1986 on the legal protection of topographies of semiconductor products[35] and by Directive 96/9/EC of the European Parliament and of the Council of 11 March 1996 on the legal protection of databases,[36] as well as industrial property rights;

12) acts requiring by law the involvement of a notary;

13) matters covered by Directive 2006/43/EC of the European Parliament and of the Council of 17 May 2006 on statutory audit of annual accounts and consolidated accounts;[37]

14) the registration of vehicles leased in another Member State;

15) provisions regarding contractual and non-contractual obligations, including the form of contracts, determined pursuant to the rules of private international law.

Article 18   Case-by-case derogations

1. By way of derogation from Article 16, and in exceptional circumstances only, a Member State may, in respect of a provider established in another Member State, take measures relating to the safety of services.

2. The measures provided for in paragraph 1 may be taken only if the mutual assistance procedure laid down in Article 35 is complied with and the following conditions are fulfilled:

(a) the national provisions in accordance with which the measure is taken have not been subject to Community harmonisation in the field of the safety of services;

(b) the measures provide for a higher level of protection of the recipient than would be the case in a measure taken by the Member State of establishment in accordance with its national provisions;

---

[31] OJ L 281, 23.11.1995, p. 31. Directive as amended by Regulation (EC) No 1882/2003.

[32] OJ L 78, 26.3.1977, p. 17. Directive as last amended by the Act of Accession.

[33] OJ L 239, 22.9.2000, p. 19. Convention as last amended by Regulation (EC) No 1160/2005 of the European Parliament and of the Council (OJ L 191, 22.7.2005, p. 18).

[34] OJ L 30, 6.2.1993, p. 1. Regulation as last amended by Commission Regulation (EC) No 2557/2001 (OJ L 349, 31.12.2001, p. 1).

[35] OJ L 24, 27.1.1987, p. 36.

[36] OJ L 77, 27.3.1996, p. 20.

[37] OJ L 157, 9.6.2006, p. 87.

(c) the Member State of establishment has not taken any measures or has taken measures which are insufficient as compared with those referred to in Article 35(2);

(d) the measures are proportionate.

3. Paragraphs 1 and 2 shall be without prejudice to provisions, laid down in Community instruments, which guarantee the freedom to provide services or which allow derogations therefrom.

Section 2 Rights of recipients of services

Article 19 Prohibited restrictions

Member States may not impose on a recipient requirements which restrict the use of a service supplied by a provider established in another Member State, in particular the following requirements:

(a) an obligation to obtain authorisation from or to make a declaration to their competent authorities;

(b) discriminatory limits on the grant of financial assistance by reason of the fact that the provider is established in another Member State or by reason of the location of the place at which the service is provided.

Article 20 Non-discrimination

1. Member States shall ensure that the recipient is not made subject to discriminatory requirements based on his nationality or place of residence.

2. Member States shall ensure that the general conditions of access to a service, which are made available to the public at large by the provider, do not contain discriminatory provisions relating to the nationality or place of residence of the recipient, but without precluding the possibility of providing for differences in the conditions of access where those differences are directly justified by objective criteria.

Article 21 Assistance for recipients

1. Member States shall ensure that recipients can obtain, in their Member State of residence, the following information:

(a) general information on the requirements applicable in other Member States relating to access to, and exercise of, service activities, in particular those relating to consumer protection;

(b) general information on the means of redress available in the case of a dispute between a provider and a recipient;

(c) the contact details of associations or organisations, including the centres of the European Consumer Centres Network, from which providers or recipients may obtain practical assistance.

Where appropriate, advice from the competent authorities shall include a simple step-by-step guide. Information and assistance shall be provided in a clear and unambiguous manner, shall be easily accessible at a distance, including by electronic means, and shall be kept up to date.

2. Member States may confer responsibility for the task referred to in paragraph 1 on points of single contact or on any other body, such as the centres of the European Consumer Centres Network, consumer associations or Euro Info Centres.

Member States shall communicate to the Commission the names and contact details of the designated bodies. The Commission shall transmit them to all Member States.

3. In fulfilment of the requirements set out in paragraphs 1 and 2, the body approached by the recipient shall, if necessary, contact the relevant body for the Member State concerned. The latter shall send the information requested as soon as possible to the requesting body which shall forward the information to the recipient. Member States shall ensure that those bodies give each other mutual assistance and shall put in place all possible measures for effective cooperation. Together with the Commission, Member States shall put in place practical arrangements necessary for the implementation of paragraph 1.

4. The Commission shall, in accordance with the procedure referred to in Article 40(2), adopt measures for the implementation of paragraphs 1, 2 and 3 of this Article, specifying the technical mechanisms for the exchange of information between the bodies of the various Member States and, in particular, the interoperability of information systems, taking into account common standards.

Chapter V Quality of services

Article 22   Information on providers and their services

1. Member States shall ensure that providers make the following information available to the recipient:

  (a) the name of the provider, his legal status and form, the geographic address at which he is established and details enabling him to be contacted rapidly and communicated with directly and, as the case may be, by electronic means;

  (b) where the provider is registered in a trade or other similar public register, the name of that register and the provider's registration number, or equivalent means of identification in that register;

  (c) where the activity is subject to an authorisation scheme, the particulars of the relevant competent authority or the single point of contact;

  (d) where the provider exercises an activity which is subject to VAT, the identification number referred to in Article 22(1) of Sixth Council Directive 77/388/EEC of 17 May 1977 on the harmonisation of the laws of the Member States relating to turnover taxes—Common system of value added tax: uniform basis of assessment;[38]

  (e) in the case of the regulated professions, any professional body or similar institution with which the provider is registered, the professional title and the Member State in which that title has been granted;

  (f) the general conditions and clauses, if any, used by the provider;

  (g) the existence of contractual clauses, if any, used by the provider concerning the law applicable to the contract and/or the competent courts;

  (h) the existence of an after-sales guarantee, if any, not imposed by law;

  (i) the price of the service, where a price is pre-determined by the provider for a given type of service;

  (j) the main features of the service, if not already apparent from the context;

  (k) the insurance or guarantees referred to in Article 23(1), and in particular the contact details of the insurer or guarantor and the territorial coverage.

2. Member States shall ensure that the information referred to in paragraph 1, according to the provider's preference:

  (a) is supplied by the provider on his own initiative;

  (b) is easily accessible to the recipient at the place where the service is provided or the contract concluded;

  (c) can be easily accessed by the recipient electronically by means of an address supplied by the provider;

  (d) appears in any information documents supplied to the recipient by the provider which set out a detailed description of the service he provides.

3. Member States shall ensure that, at the recipient's request, providers supply the following additional information:

  (a) where the price is not pre-determined by the provider for a given type of service, the price of the service or, if an exact price cannot be given, the method for calculating the price so that it can be checked by the recipient, or a sufficiently detailed estimate;

---

[38] OJ L 145, 13.6.1977, p. 1. Directive as last amended by Directive 2006/18/EC (OJ L 51, 22.2.2006, p. 12).

(b) as regards the regulated professions, a reference to the professional rules applicable in the Member State of establishment and how to access them;

(c) information on their multidisciplinary activities and partnerships which are directly linked to the service in question and on the measures taken to avoid conflicts of interest. That information shall be included in any information document in which providers give a detailed description of their services;

(d) any codes of conduct to which the provider is subject and the address at which these codes may be consulted by electronic means, specifying the language version available;

(e) where a provider is subject to a code of conduct, or member of a trade association or professional body which provides for recourse to a non-judicial means of dispute settlement, information in this respect. The provider shall specify how to access detailed information on the characteristics of, and conditions for, the use of non-judicial means of dispute settlement.

4. Member States shall ensure that the information which a provider must supply in accordance with this Chapter is made available or communicated in a clear and unambiguous manner, and in good time before conclusion of the contract or, where there is no written contract, before the service is provided.

5. The information requirements laid down in this Chapter are in addition to requirements already provided for in Community law and do not prevent Member States from imposing additional information requirements applicable to providers established in their territory.

6. The Commission may, in accordance with the procedure referred to in Article 40(2), specify the content of the information provided for in paragraphs 1 and 3 of this Article according to the specific nature of certain activities and may specify the practical means of implementing paragraph 2 of this Article.

Article 23   Professional liability insurance and guarantees

1. Member States may ensure that providers whose services present a direct and particular risk to the health or safety of the recipient or a third person, or to the financial security of the recipient, subscribe to professional liability insurance appropriate to the nature and extent of the risk, or provide a guarantee or similar arrangement which is equivalent or essentially comparable as regards its purpose.

2. When a provider establishes himself in their territory, Member States may not require professional liability insurance or a guarantee from the provider where he is already covered by a guarantee which is equivalent, or essentially comparable with regard to its purpose and the cover it provides in terms of the insured risk, the insured sum or a ceiling for the guarantee and possible exclusions from the cover, in another Member State in which the provider is already established. Where equivalence is only partial, Member States may require a supplementary guarantee to cover those aspects not already covered.

When a Member State requires a provider established in its territory to subscribe to professional liability insurance or to provide another guarantee, that Member State shall accept as sufficient evidence attestations of such insurance cover issued by credit institutions and insurers established in other Member States.

3. Paragraphs 1 and 2 shall not affect professional insurance or guarantee arrangements provided for in other Community instruments.

4. For the implementation of paragraph 1, the Commission may, in accordance with the regulatory procedure referred to in Article 40(2), establish a list of services which exhibit the characteristics referred to in paragraph 1 of this Article. The Commission may also, in accordance with the procedure referred to in Article 40(3), adopt measures designed to amend non-essential elements of this Directive by supplementing it by establishing common criteria for defining, for the purposes of the insurance or guarantees referred to in paragraph 1 of this Article, what is appropriate to the nature and extent of the risk.

5. For the purpose of this Article
   - 'direct and particular risk' means a risk arising directly from the provision of the service,
   - 'health and safety' means, in relation to a recipient or a third person, the prevention of death or serious personal injury,
   - 'financial security' means, in relation to a recipient, the prevention of substantial losses of money or of value of property,
   - 'professional liability insurance' means insurance taken out by a provider in respect of potential liabilities to recipients and, where applicable, third parties arising out of the provision of the service.

Article 24   Commercial communications by the regulated professions

1. Member States shall remove all total prohibitions on commercial communications by the regulated professions.

2. Member States shall ensure that commercial communications by the regulated professions comply with professional rules, in conformity with Community law, which relate, in particular, to the independence, dignity and integrity of the profession, as well as to professional secrecy, in a manner consistent with the specific nature of each profession. Professional rules on commercial communications shall be non-discriminatory, justified by an overriding reason relating to the public interest and proportionate.

Article 25   Multidisciplinary activities

1. Member States shall ensure that providers are not made subject to requirements which oblige them to exercise a given specific activity exclusively or which restrict the exercise jointly or in partnership of different activities.

However, the following providers may be made subject to such requirements:
   - (a) the regulated professions, in so far as is justified in order to guarantee compliance with the rules governing professional ethics and conduct, which vary according to the specific nature of each profession, and is necessary in order to ensure their independence and impartiality;
   - (b) providers of certification, accreditation, technical monitoring, test or trial services, in so far as is justified in order to ensure their independence and impartiality.

2. Where multidisciplinary activities between providers referred to in points (a) and (b) of paragraph 1 are authorised, Member States shall ensure the following:
   - (a) that conflicts of interest and incompatibilities between certain activities are prevented;
   - (b) that the independence and impartiality required for certain activities is secured;
   - (c) that the rules governing professional ethics and conduct for different activities are compatible with one another, especially as regards matters of professional secrecy.

3. In the report referred to in Article 39(1), Member States shall indicate which providers are subject to the requirements laid down in paragraph 1 of this Article, the content of those requirements and the reasons for which they consider them to be justified.

Article 26   Policy on quality of services

1. Member States shall, in cooperation with the Commission, take accompanying measures to encourage providers to take action on a voluntary basis in order to ensure the quality of service provision, in particular through use of one of the following methods:
   - (a) certification or assessment of their activities by independent or accredited bodies;
   - (b) drawing up their own quality charter or participation in quality charters or labels drawn up by professional bodies at Community level.

2. Member States shall ensure that information on the significance of certain labels and the criteria for applying labels and other quality marks relating to services can be easily accessed by providers and recipients.

3. Member States shall, in cooperation with the Commission, take accompanying measures to encourage professional bodies, as well as chambers of commerce and craft associations and

consumer associations, in their territory to cooperate at Community level in order to promote the quality of service provision, especially by making it easier to assess the competence of a provider.

4. Member States shall, in cooperation with the Commission, take accompanying measures to encourage the development of independent assessments, notably by consumer associations, in relation to the quality and defects of service provision, and, in particular, the development at Community level of comparative trials or testing and the communication of the results.

5. Member States, in cooperation with the Commission, shall encourage the development of voluntary European standards with the aim of facilitating compatibility between services supplied by providers in different Member States, information to the recipient and the quality of service provision.

Article 27 Settlement of disputes

1. Member States shall take the general measures necessary to ensure that providers supply contact details, in particular a postal address, fax number or e-mail address and telephone number to which all recipients, including those resident in another Member State, can send a complaint or a request for information about the service provided. Providers shall supply their legal address if this is not their usual address for correspondence.

Member States shall take the general measures necessary to ensure that providers respond to the complaints referred to in the first subparagraph in the shortest possible time and make their best efforts to find a satisfactory solution.

2. Member States shall take the general measures necessary to ensure that providers are obliged to demonstrate compliance with the obligations laid down in this Directive as to the provision of information and to demonstrate that the information is accurate.

3. Where a financial guarantee is required for compliance with a judicial decision, Member States shall recognise equivalent guarantees lodged with a credit institution or insurer established in another Member State. Such credit institutions must be authorised in a Member State in accordance with Directive 2006/48/EC and such insurers in accordance, as appropriate, with First Council Directive 73/239/EEC of 24 July 1973 on the coordination of laws, regulations and administrative provisions relating to the taking-up and pursuit of the business of direct insurance other than life assurance[39] and Directive 2002/83/EC of the European Parliament and of the Council of 5 November 2002 concerning life assurance.[40]

4. Member States shall take the general measures necessary to ensure that providers who are subject to a code of conduct, or are members of a trade association or professional body, which provides for recourse to a non-judicial means of dispute settlement inform the recipient thereof and mention that fact in any document which presents their services in detail, specifying how to access detailed information on the characteristics of, and conditions for, the use of such a mechanism.

Chapter VI Administrative cooperation

Article 28 Mutual assistance—general obligations

1. Member States shall give each other mutual assistance, and shall put in place measures for effective cooperation with one another, in order to ensure the supervision of providers and the services they provide.

2. For the purposes of this Chapter, Member States shall designate one or more liaison points, the contact details of which shall be communicated to the other Member States and the Commission. The Commission shall publish and regularly update the list of liaison points.

---

[39] OJ L 228, 16.8.1973, p. 3. Directive as last amended by Directive 2005/68/EC of the European Parliament and of the Council (OJ L 323, 9.12.2005, p. 1).

[40] OJ L 345, 19.12.2002, p. 1. Directive as last amended by Directive 2005/68/EC.

3. Information requests and requests to carry out any checks, inspections and investigations under this Chapter shall be duly motivated, in particular by specifying the reason for the request. Information exchanged shall be used only in respect of the matter for which it was requested.

4. In the event of receiving a request for assistance from competent authorities in another Member State, Member States shall ensure that providers established in their territory supply their competent authorities with all the information necessary for supervising their activities in compliance with their national laws.

5. In the event of difficulty in meeting a request for information or in carrying out checks, inspections or investigations, the Member State in question shall rapidly inform the requesting Member State with a view to finding a solution.

6. Member States shall supply the information requested by other Member States or the Commission by electronic means and within the shortest possible period of time.

7. Member States shall ensure that registers in which providers have been entered, and which may be consulted by the competent authorities in their territory, may also be consulted, in accordance with the same conditions, by the equivalent competent authorities of the other Member States.

8. Member States shall communicate to the Commission information on cases where other Member States do not fulfil their obligation of mutual assistance. Where necessary, the Commission shall take appropriate steps, including proceedings provided for in Article 226 of the Treaty, in order to ensure that the Member States concerned comply with their obligation of mutual assistance. The Commission shall periodically inform Member States about the functioning of the mutual assistance provisions.

Article 29   Mutual assistance—general obligations for the Member State of establishment

1. With respect to providers providing services in another Member State, the Member State of establishment shall supply information on providers established in its territory when requested to do so by another Member State and, in particular, confirmation that a provider is established in its territory and, to its knowledge, is not exercising his activities in an unlawful manner.

2. The Member State of establishment shall undertake the checks, inspections and investigations requested by another Member State and shall inform the latter of the results and, as the case may be, of the measures taken. In so doing, the competent authorities shall act to the extent permitted by the powers vested in them in their Member State. The competent authorities can decide on the most appropriate measures to be taken in each individual case in order to meet the request by another Member State.

3. Upon gaining actual knowledge of any conduct or specific acts by a provider established in its territory which provides services in other Member States, that, to its knowledge, could cause serious damage to the health or safety of persons or to the environment, the Member State of establishment shall inform all other Member States and the Commission within the shortest possible period of time.

Article 30   Supervision by the Member State of establishment in the event of the temporary movement of a provider to another Member State

1. With respect to cases not covered by Article 31(1), the Member State of establishment shall ensure that compliance with its requirements is supervised in conformity with the powers of supervision provided for in its national law, in particular through supervisory measures at the place of establishment of the provider.

2. The Member State of establishment shall not refrain from taking supervisory or enforcement measures in its territory on the grounds that the service has been provided or caused damage in another Member State.

3. The obligation laid down in paragraph 1 shall not entail a duty on the part of the Member State of establishment to carry out factual checks and controls in the territory of the Member State

where the service is provided. Such checks and controls shall be carried out by the authorities of the Member State where the provider is temporarily operating at the request of the authorities of the Member State of establishment, in accordance with Article 31.

Article 31   Supervision by the Member State where the service is provided in the event of the temporary movement of the provider

1. With respect to national requirements which may be imposed pursuant to Articles 16 or 17, the Member State where the service is provided is responsible for the supervision of the activity of the provider in its territory. In conformity with Community law, the Member State where the service is provided:

(a) shall take all measures necessary to ensure the provider complies with those require-ments as regards the access to and the exercise of the activity;

(b) shall carry out the checks, inspections and investigations necessary to supervise the ser-vice provided.

2. With respect to requirements other than those referred to in paragraph 1, where a provider moves temporarily to another Member State in order to provide a service without being established there, the competent authorities of that Member State shall participate in the supervision of the pro-vider in accordance with paragraphs 3 and 4.

3. At the request of the Member State of establishment, the competent authorities of the Member State where the service is provided shall carry out any checks, inspections and investi-gations necessary for ensuring the effective supervision by the Member State of establishment. In so doing, the competent authorities shall act to the extent permitted by the powers vested in them in their Member State. The competent authorities may decide on the most appropriate measures to be taken in each individual case in order to meet the request by the Member State of establishment.

4. On their own initiative, the competent authorities of the Member State where the service is provided may conduct checks, inspections and investigations on the spot, provided that those checks, inspections or investigations are not discriminatory, are not motivated by the fact that the provider is established in another Member State and are proportionate.

Article 32   Alert mechanism

1. Where a Member State becomes aware of serious specific acts or circumstances relating to a service activity that could cause serious damage to the health or safety of persons or to the environ-ment in its territory or in the territory of other Member States, that Member State shall inform the Member State of establishment, the other Member States concerned and the Commission within the shortest possible period of time.

2. The Commission shall promote and take part in the operation of a European network of Member States' authorities in order to implement paragraph 1.

3. The Commission shall adopt and regularly update, in accordance with the procedure re-ferred to in Article 40(2), detailed rules concerning the management of the network referred to in paragraph 2 of this Article.

Article 33   Information on the good repute of providers

1. Member States shall, at the request of a competent authority in another Member State, sup-ply information, in conformity with their national law, on disciplinary or administrative actions or criminal sanctions and decisions concerning insolvency or bankruptcy involving fraud taken by their competent authorities in respect of the provider which are directly relevant to the provider's competence or professional reliability. The Member State which supplies the information shall inform the provider thereof.

A request made pursuant to the first subparagraph must be duly substantiated, in particular as regards the reasons for the request for information.

2. Sanctions and actions referred to in paragraph 1 shall only be communicated if a final decision has been taken. With regard to other enforceable decisions referred to in paragraph 1, the Member State which supplies the information shall specify whether a particular decision is final or whether an appeal has been lodged in respect of it, in which case the Member State in question should provide an indication of the date when the decision on appeal is expected.

Moreover, that Member State shall specify the provisions of national law pursuant to which the provider was found guilty or penalised.

3. Implementation of paragraphs 1 and 2 must comply with rules on the provision of personal data and with rights guaranteed to persons found guilty or penalised in the Member States concerned, including by professional bodies. Any information in question which is public shall be accessible to consumers.

Article 34   Accompanying measures

1. The Commission, in cooperation with Member States, shall establish an electronic system for the exchange of information between Member States, taking into account existing information systems.

2. Member States shall, with the assistance of the Commission, take accompanying measures to facilitate the exchange of officials in charge of the implementation of mutual assistance and training of such officials, including language and computer training.

3. The Commission shall assess the need to establish a multi-annual programme in order to organise relevant exchanges of officials and training.

Article 35   Mutual assistance in the event of case-by-case derogations

1. Where a Member State intends to take a measure pursuant to Article 18, the procedure laid down in paragraphs 2 to 6 of this Article shall apply without prejudice to court proceedings, including preliminary proceedings and acts carried out in the framework of a criminal investigation.

2. The Member State referred to in paragraph 1 shall ask the Member State of establishment to take measures with regard to the provider, supplying all relevant information on the service in question and the circumstances of the case.

The Member State of establishment shall check, within the shortest possible period of time, whether the provider is operating lawfully and verify the facts underlying the request. It shall inform the requesting Member State within the shortest possible period of time of the measures taken or envisaged or, as the case may be, the reasons why it has not taken any measures.

3. Following communication by the Member State of establishment as provided for in the second subparagraph of paragraph 2, the requesting Member State shall notify the Commission and the Member State of establishment of its intention to take measures, stating the following:

(a) the reasons why it believes the measures taken or envisaged by the Member State of establishment are inadequate;

(b) the reasons why it believes the measures it intends to take fulfil the conditions laid down in Article 18.

4. The measures may not be taken until fifteen working days after the date of notification provided for in paragraph 3.

5. Without prejudice to the possibility for the requesting Member State to take the measures in question upon expiry of the period specified in paragraph 4, the Commission shall, within the shortest possible period of time, examine the compatibility with Community law of the measures notified.

Where the Commission concludes that the measure is incompatible with Community law, it shall adopt a decision asking the Member State concerned to refrain from taking the proposed measures or to put an end to the measures in question as a matter of urgency.

6. In the case of urgency, a Member State which intends to take a measure may derogate from paragraphs 2, 3 and 4. In such cases, the measures shall be notified within the shortest possible

period of time to the Commission and the Member State of establishment, stating the reasons for which the Member State considers that there is urgency.

Article 36 Implementing measures

In accordance with the procedure referred to in Article 40(3), the Commission shall adopt the implementing measures designed to amend non-essential elements of this Chapter by supplementing it by specifying the time-limits provided for in Articles 28 and 35. The Commission shall also adopt, in accordance with the procedure referred to in Article 40(2), the practical arrangements for the exchange of information by electronic means between Member States, and in particular the inter-operability provisions for information systems.

Chapter VII Convergence programme

Article 37 Codes of conduct at Community level

1. Member States shall, in cooperation with the Commission, take accompanying measures to encourage the drawing up at Community level, particularly by professional bodies, organisations and associations, of codes of conduct aimed at facilitating the provision of services or the establishment of a provider in another Member State, in conformity with Community law.

2. Member States shall ensure that the codes of conduct referred to in paragraph 1 are accessible at a distance, by electronic means.

Article 38 Additional harmonisation

The Commission shall assess, by 28 December 2010 the possibility of presenting proposals for harmonisation instruments on the following subjects:

(a) access to the activity of judicial recovery of debts;

(b) private security services and transport of cash and valuables.

Article 39 Mutual evaluation

1. By 28 December 2009 at the latest, Member States shall present a report to the Commission, containing the information specified in the following provisions:

(a) Article 9(2), on authorisation schemes;

(b) Article 15(5), on requirements to be evaluated;

(c) Article 25(3), on multidisciplinary activities.

2. The Commission shall forward the reports provided for in paragraph 1 to the Member States, which shall submit their observations on each of the reports within six months of receipt. Within the same period, the Commission shall consult interested parties on those reports.

3. The Commission shall present the reports and the Member States' observations to the Committee referred to in Article 40(1), which may make observations.

4. In the light of the observations provided for in paragraphs 2 and 3, the Commission shall, by 28 December 2010 at the latest, present a summary report to the European Parliament and to the Council, accompanied where appropriate by proposals for additional initiatives.

5. By 28 December 2009 at the latest, Member States shall present a report to the Commission on the national requirements whose application could fall under the third subparagraph of Article 16(1) and the first sentence of Article 16(3), providing reasons why they consider that the application of those requirements fulfil the criteria referred to in the third subparagraph of Article 16(1) and the first sentence of Article 16(3).

Thereafter, Member States shall transmit to the Commission any changes in their requirements, including new requirements, as referred to above, together with the reasons for them.

The Commission shall communicate the transmitted requirements to other Member States. Such transmission shall not prevent the adoption by Member States of the provisions in question. The

Commission shall on an annual basis thereafter provide analyses and orientations on the application of these provisions in the context of this Directive.

Article 40   Committee procedure

1. The Commission shall be assisted by a Committee.

2. Where reference is made to this paragraph, Articles 5 and 7 of Decision 1999/468/EC shall apply, having regard to the provisions of Article 8 thereof. The period laid down in Article 5(6) of Decision 1999/468/EC shall be set at three months.

3. Where reference is made to this paragraph, Article 5a(1) to (4), and Article 7 of Decision 1999/468/EC shall apply, having regard to the provisions of Article 8 thereof.

Article 41   Review clause

The Commission, by 28 December 2011 and every three years thereafter, shall present to the European Parliament and to the Council a comprehensive report on the application of this Directive. This report shall, in accordance with Article 16(4), address in particular the application of Article 16. It shall also consider the need for additional measures for matters excluded from the scope of application of this Directive. It shall be accompanied, where appropriate, by proposals for amendment of this Directive with a view to completing the Internal Market for services.

Article 42   Amendment of Directive 98/27/EC

In the Annex to Directive 98/27/EC of the European Parliament and of the Council of 19 May 1998 on injunctions for the protection of consumers' interests,[41] the following point shall be added:

'13. Directive 2006/123/EC of the European Parliament and of the Council of 12 December 2006 on services in the internal market (OJ L 376, 27.12.2006, p. 36)'.

Article 43   Protection of personal data

The implementation and application of this Directive and, in particular, the provisions on supervision shall respect the rules on the protection of personal data as provided for in Directives 95/46/EC and 2002/58/EC.

Chapter VIII   Final provisions

Article 44   Transposition

1. Member States shall bring into force the laws, regulations and administrative provisions necessary to comply with this Directive before 28 December 2009.

They shall forthwith communicate to the Commission the text of those measures.

When Member States adopt these measures, they shall contain a reference to this Directive or shall be accompanied by such a reference on the occasion of their official publication. The methods of making such reference shall be laid down by Member States.

2. Member States shall communicate to the Commission the text of the main provisions of national law which they adopt in the field covered by this Directive.

Article 45   Entry into force

This Directive shall enter into force on the day following that of its publication in the *Official Journal of the European Union*.

Article 46   Addressees

This Directive is addressed to the Member States.

Done at Strasbourg, 12 December 2006.

---

[41] OJ L 166, 11.6.1998, p. 51. Directive as last amended by Directive 2005/29/EC.

Regulation (EU) No 492/2011 of the European Parliament and of the Council of 5 April 2011 on freedom of movement for workers within the Union

[OJ 2011 L141/1]*

THE EUROPEAN PARLIAMENT AND THE COUNCIL OF THE EUROPEAN UNION,

Having regard to the Treaty on the Functioning of the European Union, and in particular Article 46 thereof,

Having regard to the proposal from the European Commission,

After transmission of the draft legislative act to the national parliaments,

Having regard to the opinion of the European Economic and Social Committee,[1]

Acting in accordance with the ordinary legislative procedure,[2]

Whereas:

(1) Regulation (EEC) No 1612/68 of the Council of 15 October 1968 on freedom of movement for workers within the Community[3] has been substantially amended several times.[4] In the interests of clarity and rationality the said Regulation should be codified.

(2) Freedom of movement for workers should be secured within the Union. The attainment of this objective entails the abolition of any discrimination based on nationality between workers of the Member States as regards employment, remuneration and other conditions of work and employment, as well as the right of such workers to move freely within the Union in order to pursue activities as employed persons subject to any limitations justified on grounds of public policy, public security or public health.

(3) Provisions should be laid down to enable the objectives laid down in Articles 45 and 46 of the Treaty on the Functioning of the European Union in the field of freedom of movement to be achieved.

(4) Freedom of movement constitutes a fundamental right of workers and their families. Mobility of labour within the Union must be one of the means by which workers are guaranteed the possibility of improving their living and working conditions and promoting their social advancement, while helping to satisfy the requirements of the economies of the Member States. The right of all workers in the Member States to pursue the activity of their choice within the Union should be affirmed.

(5) Such right should be enjoyed without discrimination by permanent, seasonal and frontier workers and by those who pursue their activities for the purpose of providing services.

(6) The right of freedom of movement, in order that it may be exercised, by objective standards, in freedom and dignity, requires that equality of treatment be ensured in fact and in law in respect of all matters relating to the actual pursuit of activities as employed persons and to eligibility for housing, and also that obstacles to the mobility of workers be eliminated, in particular as regards the conditions for the integration of the worker's family into the host country.

(7) The principle of non-discrimination between workers in the Union means that all nationals of Member States have the same priority as regards employment as is enjoyed by national workers.

(8) The machinery for vacancy clearance, in particular by means of direct cooperation between the central employment services and also between the regional services, as well as by coordination of the exchange of information, ensures in a general way a clearer picture of the labour market. Workers wishing to move should also be regularly informed of living and working conditions.

(9) Close links exist between freedom of movement for workers, employment and vocational training, particularly where the latter aims at putting workers in a position to take up concrete offers of employment from other regions of the Union. Such links make it necessary that the problems arising in this connection should no longer be studied in isolation but viewed as interdependent,

---

* **Editor's Note:** As amended by Directive 2016/589 (OJ 2016 L107/1) and Regulation 1149/2019 (OJ L186/21).

[1] OJ C 44, 11.2.2011, p. 170.

[2] Position of the European Parliament of 7 September 2010 (not yet published in the Official Journal) and decision of the Council of 21 March 2011.

[3] OJ L 257, 19.10.1968, p. 2.

[4] See Annex I.

account also being taken of the problems of employment at the regional level. It is therefore necessary to direct the efforts of Member States toward coordinating their employment policies,

HAVE ADOPTED THIS REGULATION:

Chapter I Employment, equal treatment and workers' families

Section 1 Eligibility for employment

Article 1

1. Any national of a Member State shall, irrespective of his place of residence, have the right to take up an activity as an employed person, and to pursue such activity, within the territory of another Member State in accordance with the provisions laid down by law, regulation or administrative action governing the employment of nationals of that State.

2. He shall, in particular, have the right to take up available employment in the territory of another Member State with the same priority as nationals of that State.

Article 2

Any national of a Member State and any employer pursuing an activity in the territory of a Member State may exchange their applications for and offers of employment, and may conclude and perform contracts of employment in accordance with the provisions in force laid down by law, regulation or administrative action, without any discrimination resulting therefrom.

Article 3

1. Under this Regulation, provisions laid down by law, regulation or administrative action or administrative practices of a Member State shall not apply:

    (a) where they limit application for and offers of employment, or the right of foreign nationals to take up and pursue employment or subject these to conditions not applicable in respect of their own nationals; or

    (b) where, though applicable irrespective of nationality, their exclusive or principal aim or effect is to keep nationals of other Member States away from the employment offered.

The first subparagraph shall not apply to conditions relating to linguistic knowledge required by reason of the nature of the post to be filled.

2. There shall be included in particular among the provisions or practices of a Member State referred to in the first subparagraph of paragraph 1 those which:

    (a) prescribe a special recruitment procedure for foreign nationals;

    (b) limit or restrict the advertising of vacancies in the press or through any other medium or subject it to conditions other than those applicable in respect of employers pursuing their activities in the territory of that Member State;

    (c) subject eligibility for employment to conditions of registration with employment offices or impede recruitment of individual workers, where persons who do not reside in the territory of that State are concerned.

Article 4

1. Provisions laid down by law, regulation or administrative action of the Member States which restrict by number or percentage the employment of foreign nationals in any undertaking, branch of activity or region, or at a national level, shall not apply to nationals of the other Member States.

2. When in a Member State the granting of any benefit to undertakings is subject to a minimum percentage of national workers being employed, nationals of the other Member States shall be counted as national workers, subject to Directive 2005/36/EC of the European Parliament and of the Council of 7 September 2005 on the recognition of professional qualifications.[5]

---

[5] OJ L 255, 30.9.2005, p. 22.

Article 5

A national of a Member State who seeks employment in the territory of another Member State shall receive the same assistance there as that afforded by the employment offices in that State to their own nationals seeking employment.

Article 6

1. The engagement and recruitment of a national of one Member State for a post in another Member State shall not depend on medical, vocational or other criteria which are discriminatory on grounds of nationality by comparison with those applied to nationals of the other Member State who wish to pursue the same activity.

2. A national who holds an offer in his name from an employer in a Member State other than that of which he is a national may have to undergo a vocational test, if the employer expressly requests this when making his offer of employment.

Section 2 Employment and equality of treatment

Article 7

1. A worker who is a national of a Member State may not, in the territory of another Member State, be treated differently from national workers by reason of his nationality in respect of any conditions of employment and work, in particular as regards remuneration, dismissal, and, should he become unemployed, reinstatement or re-employment.

2. He shall enjoy the same social and tax advantages as national workers.

3. He shall also, by virtue of the same right and under the same conditions as national workers, have access to training in vocational schools and retraining centres.

4. Any clause of a collective or individual agreement or of any other collective regulation concerning eligibility for employment, remuneration and other conditions of work or dismissal shall be null and void in so far as it lays down or authorises discriminatory conditions in respect of workers who are nationals of the other Member States.

Article 8

A worker who is a national of a Member State and who is employed in the territory of another Member State shall enjoy equality of treatment as regards membership of trade unions and the exercise of rights attaching thereto, including the right to vote and to be eligible for the administration or management posts of a trade union. He may be excluded from taking part in the management of bodies governed by public law and from holding an office governed by public law. Furthermore, he shall have the right of eligibility for workers' representative bodies in the undertaking.

The first paragraph of this Article shall not affect laws or regulations in certain Member States which grant more extensive rights to workers coming from the other Member States.

Article 9

1. A worker who is a national of a Member State and who is employed in the territory of another Member State shall enjoy all the rights and benefits accorded to national workers in matters of housing, including ownership of the housing he needs.

2. A worker referred to in paragraph 1 may, with the same right as nationals, put his name down on the housing lists in the region in which he is employed, where such lists exist, and shall enjoy the resultant benefits and priorities.

If his family has remained in the country whence he came, they shall be considered for this purpose as residing in the said region, where national workers benefit from a similar presumption.

Section 3 Workers' families

Article 10

The children of a national of a Member State who is or has been employed in the territory of another Member State shall be admitted to that State's general educational, apprenticeship and vocational training courses under the same conditions as the nationals of that State, if such children are residing in its territory.

Member States shall encourage all efforts to enable such children to attend these courses under the best possible conditions.

Chapter II Clearance of vacancies and applications for employment

Section 2 Machinery for vacancy clearance

Article 13*

1. The specialist service of each Member State shall regularly send to the specialist services of the other Member States and to the European Coordination Office referred to in Article 18:
    (a) details of vacancies which could be filled by nationals of other Member States;
    (b) details of vacancies addressed to third countries;
    (c) details of applications for employment by those who have formally expressed a wish to work in another Member State;
    (d) information, by region and by branch of activity, on applicants who have declared themselves actually willing to accept employment in another country.
The specialist service of each Member State shall forward this information to the appropriate employment services and agencies as soon as possible.

Chapter III Committees for ensuring close cooperation between the Member States in matters concerning the freedom of movement of workers and their employment

Section 1 The Advisory Committee

Article 21

The Advisory Committee shall be responsible for assisting the Commission in the examination of any questions arising from the application of the Treaty on the Functioning of the European Union and measures taken in pursuance thereof, in matters concerning the freedom of movement of workers and their employment.

Article 22

The Advisory Committee shall be responsible in particular for:
    (a) examining problems concerning freedom of movement and employment within the framework of national manpower policies, with a view to coordinating the employment policies of the Member States at Union level, thus contributing to the development of the economies and to an improved balance of the labour market;
    (b) making a general study of the effects of implementing this Regulation and any supplementary measures;

---

* **Editor's Note:** Deleted with effect from 13 May 2018.

(c) submitting to the Commission any reasoned proposals for revising this Regulation;

(d) delivering, either at the request of the Commission or on its own initiative, rea-soned opinions on general questions or on questions of principle, in particular on exchange of information concerning developments in the labour market, on the movement of workers between Member States, on programmes or measures to de-velop vocational guidance and vocational training which are likely to increase the possibilities of freedom of movement and employment, and on all forms of assis-tance to workers and their families, including social assistance and the housing of workers.

Article 23

1. The Advisory Committee shall be composed of six members for each Member State, two of whom shall represent the Government, two the trade unions and two the employers' associations.

2. For each of the categories referred to in paragraph 1, one alternate member shall be appointed by each Member State.

3. The term of office of the members and their alternates shall be 2 years. Their appointments shall be renewable.

On expiry of their term of office, the members and their alternates shall remain in office until replaced or until their appointments are renewed.

Article 24

The members of the Advisory Committee and their alternates shall be appointed by the Council, which shall endeavour, when selecting representatives of trade unions and employers' asso-ciations, to achieve adequate representation on the Committee of the various economic sectors concerned.

The list of members and their alternates shall be published by the Council for information in the *Official Journal of the European Union*.

Article 25

The Advisory Committee shall be chaired by a member of the Commission or his representa-tive. The Chairman shall not vote. The Committee shall meet at least twice a year. It shall be convened by its Chairman, either on his own initiative, or at the request of at least one third of the members.

Secretarial services shall be provided for the Committee by the Commission.

Article 26

The Chairman may invite individuals or representatives of bodies with wide experience in the field of employment or movement of workers to take part in meetings as observers or as experts. The Chairman may be assisted by expert advisers.

The European Labour Authority established by Regulation (EU) 2019/1149 of the European Parliament and of the Council shall participate in the meetings of the Advisory Committee as an observer, providing technical input and expertise as relevant.

Article 27

1. An opinion delivered by the Advisory Committee shall not be valid unless two thirds of the members are present.

2. Opinions shall state the reasons on which they are based; they shall be delivered by an abso-lute majority of the votes validly cast; they shall be accompanied by a written statement of the views expressed by the minority, when the latter so requests.

Article 28

The Advisory Committee shall establish its working methods by rules of procedure which shall enter into force after the Council, having received an opinion from the Commission, has given its approval. The entry into force of any amendment that the Committee decides to make thereto shall be subject to the same procedure.

Section 2 The Technical Committee*

Article 29
The Technical Committee shall be responsible for assisting the Commission in the preparation, promotion and follow-up of all technical work and measures for giving effect to this Regulation and any supplementary measures.

Article 30
The Technical Committee shall be responsible in particular for:
> (a) promoting and advancing cooperation between the public authorities concerned in the Member States on all technical questions relating to freedom of movement of workers and their employment;
> (b) formulating procedures for the organisation of the joint activities of the public authorities concerned;
> (c) facilitating the gathering of information likely to be of use to the Commission and the undertaking of the studies and research provided for in this Regulation, and encouraging exchange of information and experience between the administrative bodies concerned;
> (d) investigating at a technical level the harmonisation of the criteria by which Member States assess the state of their labour markets.

Article 31
1. The Technical Committee shall be composed of representatives of the Governments of the Member States. Each Government shall appoint as member of the Technical Committee one of the members who represent it on the Advisory Committee.

2. Each Government shall appoint an alternate from among its other representatives—members or alternates—on the Advisory Committee.

Article 32
The Technical Committee shall be chaired by a member of the Commission or his representative. The Chairman shall not vote. The Chairman and the members of the Committee may be assisted by expert advisers.

Secretarial services shall be provided for the Committee by the Commission.

Article 33
The proposals and opinions formulated by the Technical Committee shall be submitted to the Commission, and the Advisory Committee shall be informed thereof. Any such proposals and opinions shall be accompanied by a written statement of the views expressed by the various members of the Technical Committee, when the latter so request.

Article 34
The Technical Committee shall establish its working methods by rules of procedure which shall enter into force after the Council, having received an opinion from the Commission, has given its approval. The entry into force of any amendment which the Committee decides to make thereto shall be subject to the same procedure.

---

* **Editor's Note:** Articles 29–34 will be deleted on 1 August 2021.

Chapter IV Final provisions

Article 35

The rules of procedure of the Advisory Committee in force on 8 November 1968 shall continue to apply.

Article 36

1. This Regulation shall not affect the provisions of the Treaty establishing the European Atomic Energy Community which deal with eligibility for skilled employment in the field of nuclear energy, nor any measures taken in pursuance of that Treaty.

Nevertheless, this Regulation shall apply to the category of workers referred to in the first subparagraph and to members of their families in so far as their legal position is not governed by the above-mentioned Treaty or measures.

2. This Regulation shall not affect measures taken in accordance with Article 48 of the Treaty on the Functioning of the European Union.

3. This Regulation shall not affect the obligations of Member States arising out of special relations or future agreements with certain non-European countries or territories, based on institutional ties existing on 8 November 1968, or agreements in existence on 8 November 1968 with certain non-European countries or territories, based on institutional ties between them.

Workers from such countries or territories who, in accordance with this provision, are pursuing activities as employed persons in the territory of one of those Member States may not invoke the benefit of the provisions of this Regulation in the territory of the other Member States.

Article 37

Member States shall, for information purposes, communicate to the Commission the texts of agreements, conventions or arrangements concluded between them in the manpower field between the date of their being signed and that of their entry into force.

Article 38

The Commission shall adopt measures pursuant to this Regulation for its implementation. To this end it shall act in close cooperation with the central public authorities of the Member States.

Article 39

The administrative expenditure of the Advisory Committee shall be included in the general budget of the European Union in the section relating to the Commission.

Article 40

This Regulation shall apply to the Member States and to their nationals, without prejudice to Articles 2 and 3.

Article 41

Regulation (EEC) No 1612/68 is hereby repealed.

References to the repealed Regulation shall be construed as references to this Regulation and shall be read in accordance with the correlation table in Annex II.

Article 42

This Regulation shall enter into force on the 20th day following its publication in the *Official Journal of the European Union*.

This Regulation shall be binding in its entirety and directly applicable in all Member States.

Done at Strasbourg, 5 April 2011.

Social policy: equal pay and treatment

Council Directive of 19 December 1978 on the progressive implementation of the principle of equal treatment for men and women in matters of social security (79/7/EEC)

[OJ 1979 L6/24]

(Preamble omitted.)

Article 1

The purpose of this Directive is the progressive implementation, in the field of social security and other elements of social protection provided for in Article 3, of the principle of equal treatment for men and women in matters of social security, hereinafter referred to as 'the principle of equal treatment'.

Article 2

This Directive shall apply to the working population—including self-employed persons, workers and self-employed persons whose activity is interrupted by illness, accident or involuntary unemployment and persons seeking employment—and to retired or invalided workers and self-employed persons.

Article 3

1. This Directive shall apply to:
   (a) statutory schemes which provide protection against the following risks:
       – sickness,
       – invalidity,
       – old age,
       – accidents at work and occupational diseases,
       – unemployment;
   (b) social assistance, in so far as it is intended to supplement or replace the schemes referred to in (a).

2. This Directive shall not apply to the provisions concerning survivors' benefits nor to those concerning family benefits, except in the case of family benefits granted by way of increases of benefits due in respect of the risks referred to in paragraph 1(a).

3. With a view to ensuring implementation of the principle of equal treatment in occupational schemes, the Council, acting on a proposal from the Commission, will adopt provisions defining its substance, its scope and the arrangements for its application.

Article 4

1. The principle of equal treatment means that there shall be no discrimination whatsoever on ground of sex either directly, or indirectly by reference in particular to marital or family status, in particular as concerns:
    – the scope of the schemes and the conditions of access thereto,
    – the obligation to contribute and the calculation of contributions,
    – the calculation of benefits including increases due in respect of a spouse and for dependants and the conditions governing the duration and retention of entitlement to benefits.

2. The principle of equal treatment shall be without prejudice to the provisions relating to the protection of women on the grounds of maternity.

Article 5
Member States shall take the measures necessary to ensure that any laws, regulations and administrative provisions contrary to the principle of equal treatment are abolished.

Article 6
Member States shall introduce into their national legal systems such measures as are necessary to enable all persons who consider themselves wronged by failure to apply the principle of equal treatment to pursue their claims by judicial process, possibly after recourse to other competent authorities.

Article 7
1. This Directive shall be without prejudice to the right of Member States to exclude from its scope:
  (a) the determination of pensionable age for the purposes of granting old-age and retirement pensions and the possible consequences thereof for other benefits;
  (b) advantages in respect of old-age pension schemes granted to persons who have brought up children; the acquisition of benefit entitlements following periods of interruption of employment due to the bringing up of children;
  (c) the granting of old-age or invalidity benefit entitlements by virtue of the derived entitlements of a wife;
  (d) the granting of increases of long-term invalidity, old-age, accidents at work and occupational disease benefits for a dependent wife;
  (e) the consequences of the exercise, before the adoption of this Directive, of a right of option not to acquire rights or incur obligations under a statutory scheme.
2. Member States shall periodically examine matters excluded under paragraph 1 in order to ascertain, in the light of social developments in the matter concerned, whether there is justification for maintaining the exclusions concerned.

Article 8
1. Member States shall bring into force the laws, regulations and administrative provisions necessary to comply with this Directive within six years of its notification. They shall immediately inform the Commission thereof.
2. Member States shall communicate to the Commission the text of laws, regulations and administrative provisions which they adopt in the field covered by this Directive, including measures adopted pursuant to Article 7(2).

They shall inform the Commission of their reasons for maintaining any existing provisions on the matters referred to in Article 7(1) and of the possibilities for reviewing them at a later date.

Article 9
Within seven years of notification of this Directive, Member States shall forward all information necessary to the Commission to enable it to draw up a report on the application of this Directive for submission to the Council and to propose such further measures as may be required for the implementation of the principle of equal treatment.

Article 10
This Directive is addressed to the Member States.

Done at Brussels, 19 December 1978.

Council Directive 86/613 was repealed with effect from 5 August 2012 and replaced by Directive 2010/41 reproduced at the end of this section

Council Directive 2000/43/EC of 29 June 2000 implementing the principle of equal treatment between persons irrespective of racial or ethnic origin

[OJ 2000 L180/22]

THE COUNCIL OF THE EUROPEAN UNION,

Having regard to the Treaty establishing the European Community and in particular Article 13 thereof,

Having regard to the proposal from the Commission,[1]

Having regard to the opinion of the European Parliament,[2]

Having regard to the opinion of the Economic and Social Committee,[3]

Having regard to the opinion of the Committee of the Regions,[4]

Whereas:

(1) The Treaty on European Union marks a new stage in the process of creating an ever closer union among the peoples of Europe.

(2) In accordance with Article 6 of the Treaty on European Union, the European Union is founded on the principles of liberty, democracy, respect for human rights and fundamental freedoms, and the rule of law, principles which are common to the Member States, and should respect fundamental rights as guaranteed by the European Convention for the protection of Human Rights and Fundamental Freedoms and as they result from the constitutional traditions common to the Member States, as general principles of Community Law.

(3) The right to equality before the law and protection against discrimination for all persons constitutes a universal right recognised by the Universal Declaration of Human Rights, the United Nations Convention on the Elimination of all forms of Discrimination Against Women, the International Convention on the Elimination of all forms of Racial Discrimination and the United Nations Covenants on Civil and Political Rights and on Economic, Social and Cultural Rights and by the European Convention for the Protection of Human Rights and Fundamental Freedoms, to which all Member States are signatories.

(4) It is important to respect such fundamental rights and freedoms, including the right to freedom of association. It is also important, in the context of the access to and provision of goods and services, to respect the protection of private and family life and transactions carried out in this context.

(5) The European Parliament has adopted a number of Resolutions on the fight against racism in the European Union.

(6) The European Union rejects theories which attempt to determine the existence of separate human races. The use of the term 'racial origin' in this Directive does not imply an acceptance of such theories.

(7) The European Council in Tampere, on 15 and 16 October 1999, invited the Commission to come forward as soon as possible with proposals implementing Article 13 of the EC Treaty as regards the fight against racism and xenophobia.

(8) The Employment Guidelines 2000 agreed by the European Council in Helsinki, on 10 and 11 December 1999, stress the need to foster conditions for a socially inclusive labour market by

---

[1] Not yet published in the Official Journal.

[2] Opinion delivered on 18.5.2000 (not yet published in the Official Journal).

[3] Opinion delivered on 12.4.2000 (not yet published in the Official Journal).

[4] Opinion delivered on 31.5.2000 (not yet published in the Official Journal).

formulating a coherent set of policies aimed at combating discrimination against groups such as ethnic minorities.

(9) Discrimination based on racial or ethnic origin may undermine the achievement of the objectives of the EC Treaty, in particular the attainment of a high level of employment and of social protection, the raising of the standard of living and quality of life, economic and social cohesion and solidarity. It may also undermine the objective of developing the European Union as an area of freedom, security and justice.

(10) The Commission presented a communication on racism, xenophobia and anti-Semitism in December 1995.

(11) The Council adopted on 15 July 1996 Joint Action (96/443/JHA) concerning action to combat racism and xenophobia[5] under which the Member States undertake to ensure effective judicial cooperation in respect of offences based on racist or xenophobic behaviour.

(12) To ensure the development of democratic and tolerant societies which allow the participation of all persons irrespective of racial or ethnic origin, specific action in the field of discrimination based on racial or ethnic origin should go beyond access to employed and self-employed activities and cover areas such as education, social protection including social security and health-care, social advantages and access to and supply of goods and services.

(13) To this end, any direct or indirect discrimination based on racial or ethnic origin as regards the areas covered by this Directive should be prohibited throughout the Community. This prohibition of discrimination should also apply to nationals of third countries, but does not cover differences of treatment based on nationality and is without prejudice to provisions governing the entry and residence of third-country nationals and their access to employment and to occupation.

(14) In implementing the principle of equal treatment irrespective of racial or ethnic origin, the Community should, in accordance with Article 3(2) of the EC Treaty, aim to eliminate inequalities, and to promote equality between men and women, especially since women are often the victims of multiple discrimination.

(15) The appreciation of the facts from which it may be inferred that there has been direct or indirect discrimination is a matter for national judicial or other competent bodies, in accordance with rules of national law or practice. Such rules may provide in particular for indirect discrimination to be established by any means including on the basis of statistical evidence.

(16) It is important to protect all natural persons against discrimination on grounds of racial or ethnic origin. Member States should also provide, where appropriate and in accordance with their national traditions and practice, protection for legal persons where they suffer discrimination on grounds of the racial or ethnic origin of their members.

(17) The prohibition of discrimination should be without prejudice to the maintenance or adoption of measures intended to prevent or compensate for disadvantages suffered by a group of persons of a particular racial or ethnic origin, and such measures may permit organisations of persons of a particular racial or ethnic origin where their main object is the promotion of the special needs of those persons.

(18) In very limited circumstances, a difference of treatment may be justified where a characteristic related to racial or ethnic origin constitutes a genuine and determining occupational requirement, when the objective is legitimate and the requirement is proportionate. Such circumstances should be included in the information provided by the Member States to the Commission.

(19) Persons who have been subject to discrimination based on racial and ethnic origin should have adequate means of legal protection. To provide a more effective level of protection, associations or legal entities should also be empowered to engage, as the Member States so determine,

---

[5] OJ L 185, 24.7.1996, p. 5.

either on behalf or in support of any victim, in proceedings, without prejudice to national rules of procedure concerning representation and defence before the courts.

(20) The effective implementation of the principle of equality requires adequate judicial protection against victimisation.

(21) The rules on the burden of proof must be adapted when there is a prima facie case of discrimination and, for the principle of equal treatment to be applied effectively, the burden of proof must shift back to the respondent when evidence of such discrimination is brought.

(22) Member States need not apply the rules on the burden of proof to proceedings in which it is for the court or other competent body to investigate the facts of the case. The procedures thus referred to are those in which the plaintiff is not required to prove the facts, which it is for the court or competent body to investigate.

(23) Member States should promote dialogue between the social partners and with nongovernmental organisations to address different forms of discrimination and to combat them.

(24) Protection against discrimination based on racial or ethnic origin would itself be strengthened by the existence of a body or bodies in each Member State, with competence to analyse the problems involved, to study possible solutions and to provide concrete assistance for the victims.

(25) This Directive lays down minimum requirements, thus giving the Member States the option of introducing or maintaining more favourable provisions. The implementation of this Directive should not serve to justify any regression in relation to the situation which already prevails in each Member State.

(26) Member States should provide for effective, proportionate and dissuasive sanctions in case of breaches of the obligations under this Directive.

(27) The Member States may entrust management and labour, at their joint request, with the implementation of this Directive as regards provisions falling within the scope of collective agreements, provided that the Member States take all the necessary steps to ensure that they can at all times guarantee the results imposed by this Directive.

(28) In accordance with the principles of subsidiarity and proportionality as set out in Article 5 of the EC Treaty, the objective of this Directive, namely ensuring a common high level of protection against discrimination in all the Member States, cannot be sufficiently achieved by the Member States and can therefore, by reason of the scale and impact of the proposed action, be better achieved by the Community. This Directive does not go beyond what is necessary in order to achieve those objectives,

HAS ADOPTED THIS DIRECTIVE:

Chapter I General provisions

Article 1 Purpose
The purpose of this Directive is to lay down a framework for combating discrimination on the grounds of racial or ethnic origin, with a view to putting into effect in the Member States the principle of equal treatment.

Article 2 Concept of discrimination
1. For the purposes of this Directive, the principle of equal treatment shall mean that there shall be no direct or indirect discrimination based on racial or ethnic origin.

2. For the purposes of paragraph 1:
  (a) direct discrimination shall be taken to occur where one person is treated less favourably than another is, has been or would be treated in a comparable situation on grounds of racial or ethnic origin;
  (b) indirect discrimination shall be taken to occur where an apparently neutral provision, criterion or practice would put persons of a racial or ethnic origin at a particular disadvantage compared with other persons, unless that provision, criterion or practice is

objectively justified by a legitimate aim and the means of achieving that aim are appropriate and necessary.

3. Harassment shall be deemed to be discrimination within the meaning of paragraph 1, when an unwanted conduct related to racial or ethnic origin takes place with the purpose or effect of violating the dignity of a person and of creating an intimidating, hostile, degrading, humiliating or offensive environment. In this context, the concept of harassment may be defined in accordance with the national laws and practice of the Member States.

4. An instruction to discriminate against persons on grounds of racial or ethnic origin shall be deemed to be discrimination within the meaning of paragraph 1.

Article 3   Scope

1. Within the limits of the powers conferred upon the Community, this Directive shall apply to all persons, as regards both the public and private sectors, including public bodies, in relation to:

    (a) conditions for access to employment, to self-employment and to occupation, including selection criteria and recruitment conditions, whatever the branch of activity and at all levels of the professional hierarchy, including promotion;

    (b) access to all types and to all levels of vocational guidance, vocational training, advanced vocational training and retraining, including practical work experience;

    (c) employment and working conditions, including dismissals and pay;

    (d) membership of and involvement in an organisation of workers or employers, or any organisation whose members carry on a particular profession, including the benefits provided for by such organisations;

    (e) social protection, including social security and healthcare;

    (f) social advantages;

    (g) education;

    (h) access to and supply of goods and services which are available to the public, including housing.

2. This Directive does not cover difference of treatment based on nationality and is without prejudice to provisions and conditions relating to the entry into and residence of third-country nationals and stateless persons on the territory of Member States, and to any treatment which arises from the legal status of the third-country nationals and stateless persons concerned.

Article 4   Genuine and determining occupational requirements

Notwithstanding Article 2(1) and (2), Member States may provide that a difference of treatment which is based on a characteristic related to racial or ethnic origin shall not constitute discrimination where, by reason of the nature of the particular occupational activities concerned or of the context in which they are carried out, such a characteristic constitutes a genuine and determining occupational requirement, provided that the objective is legitimate and the requirement is proportionate.

Article 5   Positive action

With a view to ensuring full equality in practice, the principle of equal treatment shall not prevent any Member State from maintaining or adopting specific measures to prevent or compensate for disadvantages linked to racial or ethnic origin.

Article 6   Minimum requirements

1. Member States may introduce or maintain provisions which are more favourable to the protection of the principle of equal treatment than those laid down in this Directive.

2. The implementation of this Directive shall under no circumstances constitute grounds for a reduction in the level of protection against discrimination already afforded by Member States in the fields covered by this Directive.

Chapter II Remedies and enforcement

Article 7 Defence of rights

1. Member States shall ensure that judicial and/or administrative procedures, including where they deem it appropriate conciliation procedures, for the enforcement of obligations under this Directive are available to all persons who consider themselves wronged by failure to apply the principle of equal treatment to them, even after the relationship in which the discrimination is alleged to have occurred has ended.

2. Member States shall ensure that associations, organisations or other legal entities, which have, in accordance with the criteria laid down by their national law, a legitimate interest in ensuring that the provisions of this Directive are complied with, may engage, either on behalf or in support of the complainant, with his or her approval, in any judicial and/or administrative procedure provided for the enforcement of obligations under this Directive.

3. Paragraphs 1 and 2 are without prejudice to national rules relating to time limits for bringing actions as regards the principle of equality of treatment.

Article 8 Burden of proof

1. Member States shall take such measures as are necessary, in accordance with their national judicial systems, to ensure that, when persons who consider themselves wronged because the principle of equal treatment has not been applied to them establish, before a court or other competent authority, facts from which it may be presumed that there has been direct or indirect discrimination, it shall be for the respondent to prove that there has been no breach of the principle of equal treatment.

2. Paragraph 1 shall not prevent Member States from introducing rules of evidence which are more favourable to plaintiffs.

3. Paragraph 1 shall not apply to criminal procedures.

4. Paragraphs 1, 2 and 3 shall also apply to any proceedings brought in accordance with Article 7(2).

5. Member States need not apply paragraph 1 to proceedings in which it is for the court or competent body to investigate the facts of the case.

Article 9 Victimisation

Member States shall introduce into their national legal systems such measures as are necessary to protect individuals from any adverse treatment or adverse consequence as a reaction to a complaint or to proceedings aimed at enforcing compliance with the principle of equal treatment.

Article 10 Dissemination of information

Member States shall take care that the provisions adopted pursuant to this Directive, together with the relevant provisions already in force, are brought to the attention of the persons concerned by all appropriate means throughout their territory.

Article 11 Social dialogue

1. Member States shall, in accordance with national traditions and practice, take adequate measures to promote the social dialogue between the two sides of industry with a view to fostering equal treatment, including through the monitoring of workplace practices, collective agreements, codes of conduct, research or exchange of experiences and good practices.

2. Where consistent with national traditions and practice, Member States shall encourage the two sides of the industry without prejudice to their autonomy to conclude, at the appropriate level, agreements laying down anti-discrimination rules in the fields referred to in Article 3 which fall within the scope of collective bargaining. These agreements shall respect the minimum requirements laid down by this Directive and the relevant national implementing measures.

Article 12   Dialogue with non-governmental organisations

Member States shall encourage dialogue with appropriate non-governmental organisations which have, in accordance with their national law and practice, a legitimate interest in contributing to the fight against discrimination on grounds of racial and ethnic origin with a view to promoting the principle of equal treatment.

Chapter III   Bodies for the promotion of equal treatment

Article 13

1. Member States shall designate a body or bodies for the promotion of equal treatment of all persons without discrimination on the grounds of racial or ethnic origin. These bodies may form part of agencies charged at national level with the defence of human rights or the safeguard of individuals' rights.

2. Member States shall ensure that the competences of these bodies include:
   - without prejudice to the right of victims and of associations, organisations or other legal entities referred to in Article 7(2), providing independent assistance to victims of discrimination in pursuing their complaints about discrimination,
   - conducting independent surveys concerning discrimination,
   - publishing independent reports and making recommendations on any issue relating to such discrimination.

Chapter IV   Final provisions

Article 14   Compliance

Member States shall take the necessary measures to ensure that:
   (a) any laws, regulations and administrative provisions contrary to the principle of equal treatment are abolished;
   (b) any provisions contrary to the principle of equal treatment which are included in individual or collective contracts or agreements, internal rules of undertakings, rules governing profit-making or non-profit-making associations, and rules governing the independent professions and workers' and employers' organisations, are or may be declared, null and void or are amended.

Article 15   Sanctions

Member States shall lay down the rules on sanctions applicable to infringements of the national provisions adopted pursuant to this Directive and shall take all measures necessary to ensure that they are applied. The sanctions, which may comprise the payment of compensation to the victim, must be effective, proportionate and dissuasive. The Member States shall notify those provisions to the Commission by 19 July 2003 at the latest and shall notify it without delay of any subsequent amendment affecting them.

Article 16   Implementation

Member States shall adopt the laws, regulations and administrative provisions necessary to comply with this Directive by 19 July 2003 or may entrust management and labour, at their joint request, with the implementation of this Directive as regards provisions falling within the scope of collective agreements. In such cases, Member States shall ensure that by 19 July 2003, management and labour introduce the necessary measures by agreement, Member States being required to take any necessary measures to enable them at any time to be in a position to guarantee the results imposed by this Directive. They shall forthwith inform the Commission thereof.

When Member States adopt these measures, they shall contain a reference to this Directive or be accompanied by such a reference on the occasion of their official publication. The methods of making such a reference shall be laid down by the Member States.

Article 17   Report

1. Member States shall communicate to the Commission by 19 July 2005, and every five years thereafter, all the information necessary for the Commission to draw up a report to the European Parliament and the Council on the application of this Directive.

2. The Commission's report shall take into account, as appropriate, the views of the European Monitoring Centre on Racism and Xenophobia, as well as the viewpoints of the social partners and relevant non-governmental organisations. In accordance with the principle of gender mainstreaming, this report shall, inter alia, provide an assessment of the impact of the measures taken on women and men. In the light of the information received, this report shall include, if necessary, proposals to revise and update this Directive.

Article 18   Entry into force

This Directive shall enter into force on the day of its publication in the *Official Journal of the European Communities*.

Article 19   Addressees

This Directive is addressed to the Member States.

Done at Luxembourg, 29 June 2000.

Council Directive 2000/78/EC of 27 November 2000 establishing a general framework for equal treatment in employment and occupation

[OJ 2000 L303/16]

THE COUNCIL OF THE EUROPEAN UNION,

Having regard to the Treaty establishing the European Community, and in particular Article 13 thereof,

Having regard to the proposal from the Commission,[1]

Having regard to the Opinion of the European Parliament,[2]

Having regard to the Opinion of the Economic and Social Committee,[3]

Having regard to the Opinion of the Committee of the Regions,[4]

Whereas:

(1) In accordance with Article 6 of the Treaty on European Union, the European Union is founded on the principles of liberty, democracy, respect for human rights and fundamental freedoms, and the rule of law, principles which are common to all Member States and it respects fundamental rights, as guaranteed by the European Convention for the Protection of Human Rights and Fundamental Freedoms and as they result from the constitutional traditions common to the Member States, as general principles of Community law.

(2) The principle of equal treatment between women and men is well established by an important body of Community law, in particular in Council Directive 76/207/EEC of 9 February 1976 on the implementation of the principle of equal treatment for men and women as regards access to employment, vocational training and promotion, and working conditions.[5]

---

[1] OJ C 177 E, 27.6.2000, p. 42.
[2] Opinion delivered on 12 October 2000 (not yet published in the Official Journal).
[3] OJ C 204, 18.7.2000, p. 82.
[4] OJ C 226, 8.8.2000, p. 1.
[5] OJ L 39, 14.2.1976, p. 40.

(3) In implementing the principle of equal treatment, the Community should, in accordance with Article 3(2) of the EC Treaty, aim to eliminate inequalities, and to promote equality between men and women, especially since women are often the victims of multiple discrimination.

(4) The right of all persons to equality before the law and protection against discrimination constitutes a universal right recognised by the Universal Declaration of Human Rights, the United Nations Convention on the Elimination of All Forms of Discrimination against Women, United Nations Covenants on Civil and Political Rights and on Economic, Social and Cultural Rights and by the European Convention for the Protection of Human Rights and Fundamental Freedoms, to which all Member States are signatories. Convention No 111 of the International Labour Organisation (ILO) prohibits discrimination in the field of employment and occupation.

(5) It is important to respect such fundamental rights and freedoms. This Directive does not prejudice freedom of association, including the right to establish unions with others and to join unions to defend one's interests.

(6) The Community Charter of the Fundamental Social Rights of Workers recognises the importance of combating every form of discrimination, including the need to take appropriate action for the social and economic integration of elderly and disabled people.

(7) The EC Treaty includes among its objectives the promotion of coordination between employment policies of the Member States. To this end, a new employment chapter was incorporated in the EC Treaty as a means of developing a coordinated European strategy for employment to promote a skilled, trained and adaptable workforce.

(8) The Employment Guidelines for 2000 agreed by the European Council at Helsinki on 10 and 11 December 1999 stress the need to foster a labour market favourable to social integration by formulating a coherent set of policies aimed at combating discrimination against groups such as persons with disability. They also emphasise the need to pay particular attention to supporting older workers, in order to increase their participation in the labour force.

(9) Employment and occupation are key elements in guaranteeing equal opportunities for all and contribute strongly to the full participation of citizens in economic, cultural and social life and to realising their potential.

(10) On 29 June 2000 the Council adopted Directive 2000/43/EC[6] implementing the principle of equal treatment between persons irrespective of racial or ethnic origin. That Directive already provides protection against such discrimination in the field of employment and occupation.

(11) Discrimination based on religion or belief, disability, age or sexual orientation may undermine the achievement of the objectives of the EC Treaty, in particular the attainment of a high level of employment and social protection, raising the standard of living and the quality of life, economic and social cohesion and solidarity, and the free movement of persons.

(12) To this end, any direct or indirect discrimination based on religion or belief, disability, age or sexual orientation as regards the areas covered by this Directive should be prohibited throughout the Community. This prohibition of discrimination should also apply to nationals of third countries but does not cover differences of treatment based on nationality and is without prejudice to provisions governing the entry and residence of third-country nationals and their access to employment and occupation.

(13) This Directive does not apply to social security and social protection schemes whose benefits are not treated as income within the meaning given to that term for the purpose of applying Article 141 of the EC Treaty, nor to any kind of payment by the State aimed at providing access to employment or maintaining employment.

(14) This Directive shall be without prejudice to national provisions laying down retirement ages.

[6] OJ L 180, 19.7.2000, p. 22.

(15) The appreciation of the facts from which it may be inferred that there has been direct or indirect discrimination is a matter for national judicial or other competent bodies, in accordance with rules of national law or practice. Such rules may provide, in particular, for indirect discrimination to be established by any means including on the basis of statistical evidence.

(16) The provision of measures to accommodate the needs of disabled people at the workplace plays an important role in combating discrimination on grounds of disability.

(17) This Directive does not require the recruitment, promotion, maintenance in employment or training of an individual who is not competent, capable and available to perform the essential functions of the post concerned or to undergo the relevant training, without prejudice to the obligation to provide reasonable accommodation for people with disabilities.

(18) This Directive does not require, in particular, the armed forces and the police, prison or emergency services to recruit or maintain in employment persons who do not have the required capacity to carry out the range of functions that they may be called upon to perform with regard to the legitimate objective of preserving the operational capacity of those services.

(19) Moreover, in order that the Member States may continue to safeguard the combat effectiveness of their armed forces, they may choose not to apply the provisions of this Directive concerning disability and age to all or part of their armed forces. The Member States which make that choice must define the scope of that derogation.

(20) Appropriate measures should be provided, i.e. effective and practical measures to adapt the workplace to the disability, for example adapting premises and equipment, patterns of working time, the distribution of tasks or the provision of training or integration resources.

(21) To determine whether the measures in question give rise to a disproportionate burden, account should be taken in particular of the financial and other costs entailed, the scale and financial resources of the organisation or undertaking and the possibility of obtaining public funding or any other assistance.

(22) This Directive is without prejudice to national laws on marital status and the benefits dependent thereon.

(23) In very limited circumstances, a difference of treatment may be justified where a characteristic related to religion or belief, disability, age or sexual orientation constitutes a genuine and determining occupational requirement, when the objective is legitimate and the requirement is proportionate. Such circumstances should be included in the information provided by the Member States to the Commission.

(24) The European Union in its Declaration No 11 on the status of churches and nonconfessional organisations, annexed to the Final Act of the Amsterdam Treaty, has explicitly recognised that it respects and does not prejudice the status under national law of churches and religious associations or communities in the Member States and that it equally respects the status of philosophical and non-confessional organisations. With this in view, Member States may maintain or lay down specific provisions on genuine, legitimate and justified occupational requirements which might be required for carrying out an occupational activity.

(25) The prohibition of age discrimination is an essential part of meeting the aims set out in the Employment Guidelines and encouraging diversity in the workforce. However, differences in treatment in connection with age may be justified under certain circumstances and therefore require specific provisions which may vary in accordance with the situation in Member States. It is therefore essential to distinguish between differences in treatment which are justified, in particular by legitimate employment policy, labour market and vocational training objectives, and discrimination which must be prohibited.

(26) The prohibition of discrimination should be without prejudice to the maintenance or adoption of measures intended to prevent or compensate for disadvantages suffered by a group of persons of a particular religion or belief, disability, age or sexual orientation, and such measures may permit organisations of persons of a particular religion or belief, disability, age or sexual orientation where their main object is the promotion of the special needs of those persons.

(27) In its Recommendation 86/379/EEC of 24 July 1986 on the employment of disabled people in the Community,[7] the Council established a guideline framework setting out examples of positive action to promote the employment and training of disabled people, and in its Resolution of 17 June 1999 on equal employment opportunities for people with disabilities,[8] affirmed the importance of giving specific attention inter alia to recruitment, retention, training and lifelong learning with regard to disabled persons.

(28) This Directive lays down minimum requirements, thus giving the Member States the option of introducing or maintaining more favourable provisions. The implementation of this Directive should not serve to justify any regression in relation to the situation which already prevails in each Member State.

(29) Persons who have been subject to discrimination based on religion or belief, disability, age or sexual orientation should have adequate means of legal protection. To provide a more effective level of protection, associations or legal entities should also be empowered to engage in proceedings, as the Member States so determine, either on behalf or in support of any victim, without prejudice to national rules of procedure concerning representation and defence before the courts.

(30) The effective implementation of the principle of equality requires adequate judicial protection against victimisation.

(31) The rules on the burden of proof must be adapted when there is a prima facie case of discrimination and, for the principle of equal treatment to be applied effectively, the burden of proof must shift back to the respondent when evidence of such discrimination is brought. However, it is not for the respondent to prove that the plaintiff adheres to a particular religion or belief, has a particular disability, is of a particular age or has a particular sexual orientation.

(32) Member States need not apply the rules on the burden of proof to proceedings in which it is for the court or other competent body to investigate the facts of the case. The procedures thus referred to are those in which the plaintiff is not required to prove the facts, which it is for the court or competent body to investigate.

(33) Member States should promote dialogue between the social partners and, within the framework of national practice, with non-governmental organisations to address different forms of discrimination at the workplace and to combat them.

(34) The need to promote peace and reconciliation between the major communities in Northern Ireland necessitates the incorporation of particular provisions into this Directive.

(35) Member States should provide for effective, proportionate and dissuasive sanctions in case of breaches of the obligations under this Directive.

(36) Member States may entrust the social partners, at their joint request, with the implementation of this Directive, as regards the provisions concerning collective agreements, provided they take any necessary steps to ensure that they are at all times able to guarantee the results required by this Directive.

(37) In accordance with the principle of subsidiarity set out in Article 5 of the EC Treaty, the objective of this Directive, namely the creation within the Community of a level playing-field as regards equality in employment and occupation, cannot be sufficiently achieved by the Member States and can therefore, by reason of the scale and impact of the action, be better achieved at Community level. In accordance with the principle of proportionality, as set out in that Article, this Directive does not go beyond what is necessary in order to achieve that objective,

HAS ADOPTED THIS DIRECTIVE:

Chapter I General provisions

Article 1 Purpose

The purpose of this Directive is to lay down a general framework for combating discrimination on the grounds of religion or belief, disability, age or sexual orientation as regards employment and occupation, with a view to putting into effect in the Member States the principle of equal treatment.

---

[7] OJ L 180, 19.7.2000, p. 22.
[8] OJ L 225, 12.8.1986, p. 43.

Article 2   Concept of discrimination

1. For the purposes of this Directive, the 'principle of equal treatment' shall mean that there shall be no direct or indirect discrimination whatsoever on any of the grounds referred to in Article 1.

2. For the purposes of paragraph 1:

(a) direct discrimination shall be taken to occur where one person is treated less favourably than another is, has been or would be treated in a comparable situation, on any of the grounds referred to in Article 1;

(b) indirect discrimination shall be taken to occur where an apparently neutral provision, criterion or practice would put persons having a particular religion or belief, a particular disability, a particular age, or a particular sexual orientation at a particular disadvantage compared with other persons unless:

   (i) that provision, criterion or practice is objectively justified by a legitimate aim and the means of achieving that aim are appropriate and necessary, or

   (ii) as regards persons with a particular disability, the employer or any person or organisation to whom this Directive applies, is obliged, under national legislation, to take appropriate measures in line with the principles contained in Article 5 in order to eliminate disadvantages entailed by such provision, criterion or practice.

3. Harassment shall be deemed to be a form of discrimination within the meaning of paragraph 1, when unwanted conduct related to any of the grounds referred to in Article 1 takes place with the purpose or effect of violating the dignity of a person and of creating an intimidating, hostile, degrading, humiliating or offensive environment. In this context, the concept of harassment may be defined in accordance with the national laws and practice of the Member States.

4. An instruction to discriminate against persons on any of the grounds referred to in Article 1 shall be deemed to be discrimination within the meaning of paragraph 1.

5. This Directive shall be without prejudice to measures laid down by national law which, in a democratic society, are necessary for public security, for the maintenance of public order and the prevention of criminal offences, for the protection of health and for the protection of the rights and freedoms of others.

Article 3   Scope

1. Within the limits of the areas of competence conferred on the Community, this Directive shall apply to all persons, as regards both the public and private sectors, including public bodies, in relation to:

(a) conditions for access to employment, to self-employment or to occupation, including selection criteria and recruitment conditions, whatever the branch of activity and at all levels of the professional hierarchy, including promotion;

(b) access to all types and to all levels of vocational guidance, vocational training, advanced vocational training and retraining, including practical work experience;

(c) employment and working conditions, including dismissals and pay;

(d) membership of, and involvement in, an organisation of workers or employers, or any organisation whose members carry on a particular profession, including the benefits provided for by such organisations.

2. This Directive does not cover differences of treatment based on nationality and is without prejudice to provisions and conditions relating to the entry into and residence of third-country nationals and stateless persons in the territory of Member States, and to any treatment which arises from the legal status of the third-country nationals and stateless persons concerned.

3. This Directive does not apply to payments of any kind made by state schemes or similar, including state social security or social protection schemes.

4. Member States may provide that this Directive, in so far as it relates to discrimination on the grounds of disability and age, shall not apply to the armed forces.

Article 4   Occupational requirements

1. Notwithstanding Article 2(1) and (2), Member States may provide that a difference of treatment which is based on a characteristic related to any of the grounds referred to in Article 1 shall

not constitute discrimination where, by reason of the nature of the particular occupational activities concerned or of the context in which they are carried out, such a characteristic constitutes a genuine and determining occupational requirement, provided that the objective is legitimate and the requirement is proportionate.

2. Member States may maintain national legislation in force at the date of adoption of this Directive or provide for future legislation incorporating national practices existing at the date of adoption of this Directive pursuant to which, in the case of occupational activities within churches and other public or private organisations the ethos of which is based on religion or belief, a difference of treatment based on a person's religion or belief shall not constitute discrimination where, by reason of the nature of these activities or of the context in which they are carried out, a person's religion or belief constitute a genuine, legitimate and justified occupational requirement, having regard to the organisation's ethos. This difference of treatment shall be implemented taking account of Member States' constitutional provisions and principles, as well as the general principles of Community law, and should not justify discrimination on another ground.

Provided that its provisions are otherwise complied with, this Directive shall thus not prejudice the right of churches and other public or private organisations, the ethos of which is based on religion or belief, acting in conformity with national constitutions and laws, to require individuals working for them to act in good faith and with loyalty to the organisation's ethos.

Article 5   Reasonable accommodation for disabled persons

In order to guarantee compliance with the principle of equal treatment in relation to persons with disabilities, reasonable accommodation shall be provided. This means that employers shall take appropriate measures, where needed in a particular case, to enable a person with a disability to have access to, participate in, or advance in employment, or to undergo training, unless such measures would impose a disproportionate burden on the employer. This burden shall not be disproportionate when it is sufficiently remedied by measures existing within the framework of the disability policy of the Member State concerned.

Article 6   Justification of differences of treatment on grounds of age

1. Notwithstanding Article 2(2), Member States may provide that differences of treatment on grounds of age shall not constitute discrimination, if, within the context of national law, they are objectively and reasonably justified by a legitimate aim, including legitimate employment policy, labour market and vocational training objectives, and if the means of achieving that aim are appropriate and necessary.

Such differences of treatment may include, among others:

    (a) the setting of special conditions on access to employment and vocational training, employment and occupation, including dismissal and remuneration conditions, for young people, older workers and persons with caring responsibilities in order to promote their vocational integration or ensure their protection;

    (b) the fixing of minimum conditions of age, professional experience or seniority in service for access to employment or to certain advantages linked to employment;

    (c) the fixing of a maximum age for recruitment which is based on the training requirements of the post in question or the need for a reasonable period of employment before retirement.

2. Notwithstanding Article 2(2), Member States may provide that the fixing for occupational social security schemes of ages for admission or entitlement to retirement or invalidity benefits, including the fixing under those schemes of different ages for employees or groups or categories of employees, and the use, in the context of such schemes, of age criteria in actuarial calculations, does not constitute discrimination on the grounds of age, provided this does not result in discrimination on the grounds of sex.

Article 7   Positive action

1. With a view to ensuring full equality in practice, the principle of equal treatment shall not prevent any Member State from maintaining or adopting specific measures to prevent or compensate for disadvantages linked to any of the grounds referred to in Article 1.

2. With regard to disabled persons, the principle of equal treatment shall be without prejudice to the right of Member States to maintain or adopt provisions on the protection of health and safety at work or to measures aimed at creating or maintaining provisions or facilities for safeguarding or promoting their integration into the working environment.

Article 8   Minimum requirements

1. Member States may introduce or maintain provisions which are more favourable to the protection of the principle of equal treatment than those laid down in this Directive.

2. The implementation of this Directive shall under no circumstances constitute grounds for a reduction in the level of protection against discrimination already afforded by Member States in the fields covered by this Directive.

Chapter II Remedies and enforcement

Article 9   Defence of rights

1. Member States shall ensure that judicial and/or administrative procedures, including where they deem it appropriate conciliation procedures, for the enforcement of obligations under this Directive are available to all persons who consider themselves wronged by failure to apply the principle of equal treatment to them, even after the relationship in which the discrimination is alleged to have occurred has ended.

2. Member States shall ensure that associations, organisations or other legal entities which have, in accordance with the criteria laid down by their national law, a legitimate interest in ensuring that the provisions of this Directive are complied with, may engage, either on behalf or in support of the complainant, with his or her approval, in any judicial and/or administrative procedure provided for the enforcement of obligations under this Directive.

3. Paragraphs 1 and 2 are without prejudice to national rules relating to time limits for bringing actions as regards the principle of equality of treatment.

Article 10   Burden of proof

1. Member States shall take such measures as are necessary, in accordance with their national judicial systems, to ensure that, when persons who consider themselves wronged because the principle of equal treatment has not been applied to them establish, before a court or other competent authority, facts from which it may be presumed that there has been direct or indirect discrimination, it shall be for the respondent to prove that there has been no breach of the principle of equal treatment.

2. Paragraph 1 shall not prevent Member States from introducing rules of evidence which are more favourable to plaintiffs.

3. Paragraph 1 shall not apply to criminal procedures.

4. Paragraphs 1, 2 and 3 shall also apply to any legal proceedings commenced in accordance with Article 9(2).

5. Member States need not apply paragraph 1 to proceedings in which it is for the court or competent body to investigate the facts of the case.

Article 11   Victimisation

Member States shall introduce into their national legal systems such measures as are necessary to protect employees against dismissal or other adverse treatment by the employer as a reaction to a complaint within the undertaking or to any legal proceedings aimed at enforcing compliance with the principle of equal treatment.

Article 12   Dissemination of information

Member States shall take care that the provisions adopted pursuant to this Directive, together with the relevant provisions already in force in this field, are brought to the attention of the persons concerned by all appropriate means, for example, at the workplace, throughout their territory.

Article 13   Social dialogue

1. Member States shall, in accordance with their national traditions and practice, take adequate measures to promote dialogue between the social partners with a view to fostering equal treatment, including through the monitoring of workplace practices, collective agreements, codes of conduct and through research or exchange of experiences and good practices. ·

2. Where consistent with their national traditions and practice, Member States shall encourage the social partners, without prejudice to their autonomy, to conclude at the appropriate level agreements laying down anti-discrimination rules in the fields referred to in Article 3 which fall within the scope of collective bargaining. These agreements shall respect the minimum requirements laid down by this Directive and by the relevant national implementing measures.

Article 14   Dialogue with non-governmental organisations

Member States shall encourage dialogue with appropriate non-governmental organisations which have, in accordance with their national law and practice, a legitimate interest in contributing to the fight against discrimination on any of the grounds referred to in Article 1 with a view to promoting the principle of equal treatment.

Chapter III   Particular provisions

Article 15   Northern Ireland

1. In order to tackle the under-representation of one of the major religious communities in the police service of Northern Ireland, differences in treatment regarding recruitment into that service, including its support staff, shall not constitute discrimination insofar as those differences in treatment are expressly authorised by national legislation.

2. In order to maintain a balance of opportunity in employment for teachers in Northern Ireland while furthering the reconciliation of historical divisions between the major religious communities there, the provisions on religion or belief in this Directive shall not apply to the recruitment of teachers in schools in Northern Ireland in so far as this is expressly authorised by national legislation.

Chapter IV   Final provisions

Article 16   Compliance

Member States shall take the necessary measures to ensure that:
- (a) any laws, regulations and administrative provisions contrary to the principle of equal treatment are abolished;
- (b) any provisions contrary to the principle of equal treatment which are included in contracts or collective agreements, internal rules of undertakings or rules governing the independent occupations and professions and workers' and employers' organisations are, or may be, declared null and void or are amended.

Article 17   Sanctions

Member States shall lay down the rules on sanctions applicable to infringements of the national provisions adopted pursuant to this Directive and shall take all measures necessary to ensure that they are applied. The sanctions, which may comprise the payment of compensation to the victim, must be effective, proportionate and dissuasive. Member States shall notify those provisions to the Commission by 2 December 2003 at the latest and shall notify it without delay of any subsequent amendment affecting them.

Article 18   Implementation

Member States shall adopt the laws, regulations and administrative provisions necessary to comply with this Directive by 2 December 2003 at the latest or may entrust the social partners, at their joint request, with the implementation of this Directive as regards provisions concerning collective agreements. In such cases, Member States shall ensure that, no later than 2 December 2003, the social partners introduce the necessary measures by agreement, the Member States concerned being required to take any necessary measures to enable them at any time to be in a position to guarantee the results imposed by this Directive. They shall forthwith inform the Commission thereof.

In order to take account of particular conditions, Member States may, if necessary, have an additional period of 3 years from 2 December 2003, that is to say a total of 6 years, to implement the provisions of this Directive on age and disability discrimination. In that event they shall inform the Commission forthwith. Any Member State which chooses to use this additional period shall report annually to the Commission on the steps it is taking to tackle age and disability discrimination and on the progress it is making towards implementation. The Commission shall report annually to the Council.

When Member States adopt these measures, they shall contain a reference to this Directive or be accompanied by such reference on the occasion of their official publication. The methods of making such reference shall be laid down by Member States.

Article 19   Report

1. Member States shall communicate to the Commission, by 2 December 2005 at the latest and every five years thereafter, all the information necessary for the Commission to draw up a report to the European Parliament and the Council on the application of this Directive.

2. The Commission's report shall take into account, as appropriate, the viewpoints of the social partners and relevant non-governmental organisations. In accordance with the principle of gender mainstreaming, this report shall, inter alia, provide an assessment of the impact of the measures taken on women and men. In the light of the information received, this report shall include, if necessary, proposals to revise and update this Directive.

Article 20   Entry into force

This Directive shall enter into force on the day of its publication in the *Official Journal of the European Communities.*

Article 21   Addressees

This Directive is addressed to the Member States.

Done at Brussels, 27 November 2000.

Council Directive 2004/113/EC of 13 December 2004 implementing the principle of equal treatment between men and women in the access to and supply of goods and services

[OJ 2004 L373/37]

THE COUNCIL OF THE EUROPEAN UNION,

Having regard to the Treaty establishing the European Community and in particular Article 13(1) thereof,

Having regard to the proposal from the Commission,

Having regard to the Opinion of the European Parliament,[1]

Having regard to the Opinion of the European Economic and Social Committee,[2]

Having regard to the opinion of the Committee of the Regions,[3]

---

[1] Opinion delivered on 30 March 2004 (not yet published in the Official Journal).
[2] OJ C 241, 28.9.2004, p. 44.
[3] OJ C 121, 30.4.2004, p. 27.

Whereas:

(1) In accordance with Article 6 of the Treaty on European Union, the Union is founded on the principles of liberty, democracy, respect for human rights and fundamental freedoms and the rule of law, principles which are common to the Member States, and respects fundamental rights as guaranteed by the European Convention for the Protection of Human Rights and Fundamental Freedoms and as they result from the constitutional traditions common to the Member States as general principles of Community law.

(2) The right to equality before the law and protection against discrimination for all persons constitutes a universal right recognised by the Universal Declaration of Human Rights, the United Nations Convention on the Elimination of all forms of Discrimination Against Women, the International Convention on the Elimination of all forms of Racial Discrimination and the United Nations Covenants on Civil and Political Rights and on Economic, Social and Cultural Rights and by the Rights and Fundamental Freedoms, to which all Member States are signatories.

(3) While prohibiting discrimination, it is important to respect other fundamental rights and freedoms, including the protection of private and family life and transactions carried out in that context and the freedom of religion.

(4) Equality between men and women is a fundamental principle of the European Union. Articles 21 and 23 of the Charter of Fundamental Rights of the European Union prohibit any discrimination on grounds of sex and require equality between men and women to be ensured in all areas.

(5) Article 2 of the Treaty establishing the European Community provides that promoting such equality is one of the Community's essential tasks. Similarly, Article 3(2) of the Treaty requires the Community to aim to eliminate inequalities and to promote equality between men and women in all its activities.

(6) The Commission announced its intention of proposing a directive on sex discrimination outside of the labour market in its Communication on the Social Policy Agenda. Such a proposal is fully consistent with Council Decision 2001/51/EC of 20 December 2000 establishing a Programme relating to the Community framework strategy on gender equality (2001-2005),[4] covering all Community policies and aimed at promoting equality for men and women by adjusting these policies and implementing practical measures to improve the situation of men and women in society.

(7) At its meeting in Nice of 7 and 9 December 2000, the European Council called on the Commission to reinforce equality-related rights by adopting a proposal for a directive on promoting gender equality in areas other than employment and professional life.

(8) The Community has adopted a range of legal instruments to prevent and combat sex discrimination in the labour market. These instruments have demonstrated the value of legislation in the fight against discrimination.

(9) Discrimination based on sex, including harassment and sexual harassment, also takes place in areas outside of the labour market. Such discrimination can be equally damaging, acting as a barrier to the full and successful integration of men and women into economic and social life.

(10) Problems are particularly apparent in the area of the access to and supply of goods and services. Discrimination based on sex, should therefore be prevented and eliminated in this area. As in the case of Council Directive 2000/43/EC of 29 June 2000 implementing the principle of equal treatment between persons irrespective of racial and ethnic origin,[5] this objective can be better achieved by means of Community legislation.

(11) Such legislation should prohibit discrimination based on sex in the access to and supply of goods and services. Goods should be taken to be those within the meaning of the provisions of the Treaty establishing the European Community relating to the free movement of goods. Services should be taken to be those within the meaning of Article 50 of that Treaty.

(12) To prevent discrimination based on sex, this Directive should apply to both direct discrimination and indirect discrimination. Direct discrimination occurs only when one person is treated

---

[4] OJ L 17, 19.1.2001, p. 22.
[5] OJ L 180, 19.7.2000, p. 22.

less favourably, on grounds of sex, than another person in a comparable situation. Accordingly, for example, differences between men and women in the provision of healthcare services, which result from the physical differences between men and women, do not relate to comparable situations and therefore, do not constitute discrimination.

(13) The prohibition of discrimination should apply to persons providing goods and services, which are available to the public and which are offered outside the area of private and family life and the transactions carried out in this context. It should not apply to the content of media or advertising nor to public or private education.

(14) All individuals enjoy the freedom to contract, including the freedom to choose a contractual partner for a transaction. An individual who provides goods or services may have a number of subjective reasons for his or her choice of contractual partner. As long as the choice of partner is not based on that person's sex, this Directive should not prejudice the individual's freedom to choose a contractual partner.

(15) There are already a number of existing legal instruments for the implementation of the principle of equal treatment between men and women in matters of employment and occupation. Therefore, this Directive should not apply in this field. The same reasoning applies to matters of self-employment insofar as they are covered by existing legal instruments. The Directive should apply only to insurance and pensions which are private, voluntary and separate from the employment relationship.

(16) Differences in treatment may be accepted only if they are justified by a legitimate aim. A legitimate aim may, for example, be the protection of victims of sex-related violence (in cases such as the establishment of single-sex shelters), reasons of privacy and decency (in cases such as the provision of accommodation by a person in a part of that person's home), the promotion of gender equality or of the interests of men or women (for example single-sex voluntary bodies), the freedom of association (in cases of membership of single-sex private clubs), and the organisation of sporting activities (for example single-sex sports events). Any limitation should nevertheless be appropriate and necessary in accordance with the criteria derived from case law of the Court of Justice of the European Communities.

(17) The principle of equal treatment in the access to goods and services does not require that facilities should always be provided to men and women on a shared basis, as long as they are not provided more favourably to members of one sex.

(18) The use of actuarial factors related to sex is widespread in the provision of insurance and other related financial services. In order to ensure equal treatment between men and women, the use of sex as an actuarial factor should not result in differences in individuals' premiums and benefits. To avoid a sudden readjustment of the market, the implementation of this rule should apply only to new contracts concluded after the date of transposition of this Directive.

(19) Certain categories of risks may vary between the sexes. In some cases, sex is one but not necessarily the only determining factor in the assessment of risks insured. For contracts insuring those types of risks, Member States may decide to permit exemptions from the rule of unisex premiums and benefits, as long as they can ensure that underlying actuarial and statistical data on which the calculations are based, are reliable, regularly updated and available to the public. Exemptions are allowed only where national legislation has not already applied the unisex rule. Five years after transposition of this Directive, Member States should re-examine the justification for these exemptions, taking into account the most recent actuarial and statistical data and a report by the Commission three years after the date of transposition of this Directive.

(20) Less favourable treatment of women for reasons of pregnancy and maternity should be considered a form of direct discrimination based on sex and therefore prohibited in insurance and related financial services. Costs related to risks of pregnancy and maternity should therefore not be attributed to the members of one sex only.

(21) Persons who have been subject to discrimination based on sex should have adequate means of legal protection. To provide a more effective level of protection, associations, organisations and other legal entities should also be empowered to engage in proceedings, as the Member States so determine, either on behalf or in support of any victim, without prejudice to national rules of procedure concerning representation and defence before the courts.

(22) The rules on the burden of proof should be adapted when there is a prima facie case of discrimination and for the principle of equal treatment to be applied effectively, the burden of proof should shift back to the defendant when evidence of such discrimination is brought.

(23) The effective implementation of the principle of equal treatment requires adequate judicial protection against victimisation.

(24) With a view to promoting the principle of equal treatment, Member States should encourage dialogue with relevant stakeholders, which have, in accordance with national law and practice, a legitimate interest in contributing to the fight against discrimination on grounds of sex in the area of access to and supply of goods and services.

(25) Protection against discrimination based on sex should itself be strengthened by the existence of a body or bodies in each Member State, with competence to analyse the problems involved, to study possible solutions and to provide concrete assistance for the victims. The body or bodies may be the same as those with responsibility at national level for the defence of human rights or the safeguarding of individuals' rights, or the implementation of the principle of equal treatment.

(26) This Directive lays down minimum requirements, thus giving the Member States the option of introducing or maintaining more favourable provisions. The implementation of this Directive should not serve to justify any regression in relation to the situation, which already prevails in each Member State.

(27) Member States should provide for effective, proportionate and dissuasive penalties in cases of breaches of the obligations under this Directive.

(28) Since the objectives of this Directive, namely to ensure a common high level of protection against discrimination in all the Member States, cannot be sufficiently achieved by the Member States and can, therefore, by reason of the scale and effects of the action, be better achieved at Community level, the Community may adopt measures, in accordance with the principle of subsidiarity as set out in Article 5 of the Treaty. In accordance with the principle of proportionality, as set out in that Article, this Directive does not go beyond what is necessary in order to achieve those objectives.

(29) In accordance with paragraph 34 of the interinstitutional agreement on better law-making,[6] Member States are encouraged to draw up, for themselves and in the interest of the Community, their own tables, which will, as far as possible, illustrate the correlation between the Directive and the transposition measures and to make them public,

HAS ADOPTED THIS DIRECTIVE:

Chapter I General provisions

Article 1 Purpose

The purpose of this Directive is to lay down a framework for combating discrimination based on sex in access to and supply of goods and services, with a view to putting into effect in the Member States the principle of equal treatment between men and women.

Article 2 Definitions

For the purposes of this Directive, the following definitions shall apply:
  (a) direct discrimination: where one person is treated less favourably, on grounds of sex, than another is, has been or would be treated in a comparable situation;
  (b) indirect discrimination: where an apparently neutral provision, criterion or practice would put persons of one sex at a particular disadvantage compared with persons of the other sex, unless that provision, criterion or practice is objectively justified by a legitimate aim and the means of achieving that aim are appropriate and necessary;
  (c) harassment: where an unwanted conduct related to the sex of a person occurs with the purpose or effect of violating the dignity of a person and of creating an intimidating, hostile, degrading, humiliating or offensive environment;

---

[6] OJ C 321, 31.12.2003, p. 1.

(d) sexual harassment: where any form of unwanted physical, verbal, non-verbal or physical conduct of a sexual nature occurs, with the purpose or effect of violating the dignity of a person, in particular when creating an intimidating, hostile, degrading, humiliating or offensive environment.

Article 3 Scope

1. Within the limits of the powers conferred upon the Community, this Directive shall apply to all persons who provide goods and services, which are available to the public irrespective of the person concerned as regards both the public and private sectors, including public bodies, and which are offered outside the area of private and family life and the transactions carried out in this context.

2. This Directive does not prejudice the individual's freedom to choose a contractual partner as long as an individual's choice of contractual partner is not based on that person's sex.

3. This Directive shall not apply to the content of media and advertising nor to education.

4. This Directive shall not apply to matters of employment and occupation. This Directive shall not apply to matters of self-employment, insofar as these matters are covered by other Community legislative acts.

Article 4 Principle of equal treatment

1. For the purposes of this Directive, the principle of equal treatment between men and women shall mean that
   (a) there shall be no direct discrimination based on sex, including less favourable treatment of women for reasons of pregnancy and maternity;
   (b) there shall be no indirect discrimination based on sex.

2. This Directive shall be without prejudice to more favourable provisions concerning the protection of women as regards pregnancy and maternity.

3. Harassment and sexual harassment within the meaning of this Directive shall be deemed to be discrimination on the grounds of sex and therefore prohibited. A person's rejection of, or submission to, such conduct may not be used as a basis for a decision affecting that person.

4. Instruction to direct or indirect discrimination on the grounds of sex shall be deemed to be discrimination within the meaning of this Directive.

5. This Directive shall not preclude differences in treatment, if the provision of the goods and services exclusively or primarily to members of one sex is justified by a legitimate aim and the means of achieving that aim are appropriate and necessary.

Article 5 Actuarial factors

1. Member States shall ensure that in all new contracts concluded after 21 December 2007 at the latest, the use of sex as a factor in the calculation of premiums and benefits for the purposes of insurance and related financial services shall not result in differences in individuals' premiums and benefits.

2. Notwithstanding paragraph 1, Member States may decide before 21 December 2007 to permit proportionate differences in individuals' premiums and benefits where the use of sex is a determining factor in the assessment of risk based on relevant and accurate actuarial and statistical data. The Member States concerned shall inform the Commission and ensure that accurate data relevant to the use of sex as a determining actuarial factor are compiled, published and regularly updated. These Member States shall review their decision five years after 21 December 2007, taking into account the Commission report referred to in Article 16, and shall forward the results of this review to the Commission.

3. In any event, costs related to pregnancy and maternity shall not result in differences in individuals' premiums and benefits. Member States may defer implementation of the measures necessary to comply with this paragraph until two years after 21 December 2007 at the latest. In that case the Member States concerned shall immediately inform the Commission.

Article 6 Positive action

With a view to ensuring full equality in practice between men and women, the principle of equal treatment shall not prevent any Member State from maintaining or adopting specific measures to prevent or compensate for disadvantages linked to sex.

Article 7   Minimum requirements

1. Member States may introduce or maintain provisions which are more favourable to the protection of the principle of equal treatment between men and women than those laid down in this Directive.

2. The implementation of this Directive shall in no circumstances constitute grounds for a reduction in the level of protection against discrimination already afforded by Member States in the fields covered by this Directive.

Chapter II   Remedies and enforcement

Article 8   Defence of rights

1. Member States shall ensure that judicial and/or administrative procedures, including where they deem it appropriate conciliation procedures, for the enforcement of the obligations under this Directive are available to all persons who consider themselves wronged by failure to apply the principle of equal treatment to them, even after the relationship in which the discrimination is alleged to have occurred has ended.

2. Member States shall introduce into their national legal systems such measures as are necessary to ensure real and effective compensation or reparation, as the Member States so determine, for the loss and damage sustained by a person injured as a result of discrimination within the meaning of this Directive, in a way which is dissuasive and proportionate to the damage suffered. The fixing of a prior upper limit shall not restrict such compensation or reparation.

3. Member States shall ensure that associations, organisations or other legal entities, which have, in accordance with the criteria laid down by their national law, a legitimate interest in ensuring that the provisions of this Directive are complied with, may engage, on behalf or in support of the complainant, with his or her approval, in any judicial and/or administrative procedure provided for the enforcement of obligations under this Directive.

4. Paragraphs 1 and 3 shall be without prejudice to national rules on time limits for bringing actions relating to the principle of equal treatment.

Article 9   Burden of proof

1. Member States shall take such measures as are necessary, in accordance with their national judicial systems, to ensure that, when persons who consider themselves wronged because the principle of equal treatment has not been applied to them establish, before a court or other competent authority, facts from which it may be presumed that there has been direct or indirect discrimination, it shall be for the respondent to prove that there has been no breach of the principle of equal treatment.

2. Paragraph 1 shall not prevent Member States from introducing rules of evidence, which are more favourable to plaintiffs.

3. Paragraph 1 shall not apply to criminal procedures.

4. Paragraphs 1, 2 and 3 shall also apply to any proceedings brought in accordance with Article 8(3).

5. Member States need not apply paragraph 1 to proceedings in which it is for the court or other competent authority to investigate the facts of the case.

Article 10   Victimisation

Member States shall introduce into their national legal systems such measures as are necessary to protect persons from any adverse treatment or adverse consequence as a reaction to a complaint or to legal proceedings aimed at enforcing compliance with the principle of equal treatment.

Article 11   Dialogue with relevant stakeholders

With a view to promoting the principle of equal treatment, Member States shall encourage dialogue with relevant stakeholders which have, in accordance with national law and practice, a legitimate interest in contributing to the fight against discrimination on grounds of sex in the area of access to and supply of goods and services.

Chapter III Bodies for the promotion of equal treatment

Article 12

1. Member States shall designate and make the necessary arrangements for a body or bodies for the promotion, analysis, monitoring and support of equal treatment of all persons without discrimination on the grounds of sex. These bodies may form part of agencies charged at national level with the defence of human rights or the safeguard of individuals' rights, or the implementation of the principle of equal treatment.

2. Member States shall ensure that the competencies of the bodies referred to in paragraph 1 include:

(a) without prejudice to the rights of victims and of associations, organisations or other legal entities referred to in Article 8(3), providing independent assistance to victims of discrimination in pursuing their complaints about discrimination;

(b) conducting independent surveys concerning discrimination;

(c) publishing independent reports and making recommendations on any issue relating to such discrimination.

Chapter IV Final provisions

Article 13   Compliance

Member States shall take the necessary measures to ensure that the principle of equal treatment is respected in relation to the access to and supply of goods and services within the scope of this Directive, and in particular that:

(a) any laws, regulations and administrative provisions contrary to the principle of equal treatment are abolished;

(b) any contractual provisions, internal rules of undertakings, and rules governing profit-making or non-profit-making associations contrary to the principle of equal treatment are, or may be, declared null and void or are amended.

Article 14   Penalties

Member States shall lay down the rules on penalties applicable to infringements of the national provisions adopted pursuant to this Directive and shall take all measures necessary to ensure that they are applied. The penalties, which may comprise the payment of compensation to the victim, shall be effective, proportionate and dissuasive. Member States shall notify those provisions to the Commission by 21 December 2007 at the latest and shall notify it without delay of any subsequent amendment affecting them.

Article 15   Dissemination of information

Member States shall take care that the provisions adopted pursuant to this Directive, together with the relevant provisions already in force, are brought to the attention of the persons concerned by all appropriate means throughout their territory.

Article 16   Reports

1. Member States shall communicate all available information concerning the application of this Directive to the Commission, by 21 December 2009. and every five years thereafter. The Commission shall draw up a summary report, which shall include a review of the current practices of Member States in relation to Article 5 with regard to the use of sex as a factor in the calculation of premiums and benefits. It shall submit this report to the European Parliament and to the Council no later 21 December 2010. Where appropriate, the Commission shall accompany its report with proposals to modify the Directive.

2. The Commission's report shall take into account the viewpoints of relevant stakeholders.

Article 17   Transposition

1. Member States shall bring into force the laws, regulations and administrative provisions necessary to comply with this Directive by 21 December 2007 at the latest. They shall forthwith

communicate to the Commission the text of those provisions. When Member States adopt these measures, they shall contain a reference to this Directive or be accompanied by such a reference on the occasion of their official publication. The methods of making such publication of reference shall be laid down by the Member States.

2. Member States shall communicate to the Commission the text of the main provisions of national law which they adopt in the field covered by this Directive.

Article 18 Entry into force

This Directive shall enter into force on the day of its publication in the *Official Journal of the European Union*.

Article 19 Addressees

This Directive is addressed to the Member States.

Done at Brussels, 13 December 2004.

Directive 2006/54/EC of the European Parliament and of the Council of 5 July 2006 on the implementation of the principle of equal opportunities and equal treatment of men and women in matters of employment and occupation (recast)

[OJ 2006 L204/23]

THE EUROPEAN PARLIAMENT AND THE COUNCIL OF THE EUROPEAN UNION,

Having regard to the Treaty establishing the European Community, and in particular Article 141(3) thereof,

Having regard to the proposal from the Commission,

Having regard to the opinion of the European Economic and Social Committee,[1]

Acting in accordance with the procedure laid down in Article 251 of the Treaty,[2]

Whereas:

(1) Council Directive 76/207/EEC of 9 February 1976 on the implementation of the principle of equal treatment for men and women as regards access to employment, vocational training and promotion, and working conditions[3] and Council Directive 86/378/EEC of 24 July 1986 on the implementation of the principle of equal treatment for men and women in occupational social security schemes[4] have been significantly amended.[5] Council Directive 75/117/EEC of 10 February 1975 on the approximation of the laws of the Member States relating to the application of the principle of equal pay for men and women[6] and Council Directive 97/80/EC of 15 December 1997 on the burden of proof in cases of discrimination based on sex[7] also contain provisions which have as their purpose the implementation of the principle of equal treatment between men and women. Now that new amendments are being made to the said Directives, it is desirable, for reasons of clarity, that the provisions in question should be recast by bringing together in a single text the main provisions existing in this field as well as certain developments arising out of the case-law of the Court of Justice of the European Communities (hereinafter referred to as the Court of Justice).

---

[1] OJ C 157, 28.6.2005, p. 83.

[2] Opinion of the European Parliament of 6 July 2005 (not yet published in the Official Journal), Council Common Position of 10 March 2006 (OJ C 126 E, 30.5.2006, p. 33) and Position of the European Parliament of 1 June 2006 (not yet published in the Official Journal).

[3] OJ L 39, 14.2.1976, p. 40. Directive as amended by Directive 2002/73/EC of the European Parliament and of the Council (OJ L 269, 5.10.2002, p. 15).

[4] OJ L 225, 12.8.1986, p. 40. Directive as amended by Directive 96/97/EC (OJ L 46, 17.2.1997, p. 20).

[5] See Annex I Part A.

[6] OJ L 45, 19.2.1975, p. 19.

[7] OJ L 14, 20.1.1998, p. 6. Directive as amended by Directive 98/52/EC (OJ L 205, 22.7.1998, p. 66).

(2) Equality between men and women is a fundamental principle of Community law under Article 2 and Article 3(2) of the Treaty and the case-law of the Court of Justice. Those Treaty provisions proclaim equality between men and women as a 'task' and an 'aim' of the Community and impose a positive obligation to promote it in all its activities.

(3) The Court of Justice has held that the scope of the principle of equal treatment for men and women cannot be confined to the prohibition of discrimination based on the fact that a person is of one or other sex. In view of its purpose and the nature of the rights which it seeks to safeguard, it also applies to discrimination arising from the gender reassignment of a person.

(4) Article 141(3) of the Treaty now provides a specific legal basis for the adoption of Community measures to ensure the application of the principle of equal opportunities and equal treatment in matters of employment and occupation, including the principle of equal pay for equal work or work of equal value.

(5) Articles 21 and 23 of the Charter of Fundamental Rights of the European Union also prohibit any discrimination on grounds of sex and enshrine the right to equal treatment between men and women in all areas, including employment, work and pay.

(6) Harassment and sexual harassment are contrary to the principle of equal treatment between men and women and constitute discrimination on grounds of sex for the purposes of this Directive. These forms of discrimination occur not only in the workplace, but also in the context of access to employment, vocational training and promotion. They should therefore be prohibited and should be subject to effective, proportionate and dissuasive penalties.

(7) In this context, employers and those responsible for vocational training should be encouraged to take measures to combat all forms of discrimination on grounds of sex and, in particular, to take preventive measures against harassment and sexual harassment in the workplace and in access to employment, vocational training and promotion, in accordance with national law and practice.

(8) The principle of equal pay for equal work or work of equal value as laid down by Article 141 of the Treaty and consistently upheld in the case-law of the Court of Justice constitutes an important aspect of the principle of equal treatment between men and women and an essential and indispensable part of the acquis communautaire, including the case-law of the Court concerning sex discrimination. It is therefore appropriate to make further provision for its implementation.

(9) In accordance with settled case-law of the Court of Justice, in order to assess whether workers are performing the same work or work of equal value, it should be determined whether, having regard to a range of factors including the nature of the work and training and working conditions, those workers may be considered to be in a comparable situation.

(10) The Court of Justice has established that, in certain circumstances, the principle of equal pay is not limited to situations in which men and women work for the same employer.

(11) The Member States, in collaboration with the social partners, should continue to address the problem of the continuing gender-based wage differentials and marked gender segregation on the labour market by means such as flexible working time arrangements which enable both men and women to combine family and work commitments more successfully. This could also include appropriate parental leave arrangements which could be taken up by either parent as well as the provision of accessible and affordable child-care facilities and care for dependent persons.

(12) Specific measures should be adopted to ensure the implementation of the principle of equal treatment in occupational social security schemes and to define its scope more clearly.

(13) In its judgment of 17 May 1990 in Case C-262/88,[8] the Court of Justice determined that all forms of occupational pension constitute an element of pay within the meaning of Article 141 of the Treaty.

(14) Although the concept of pay within the meaning of Article 141 of the Treaty does not encompass social security benefits, it is now clearly established that a pension scheme for public servants falls within the scope of the principle of equal pay if the benefits payable under the scheme are paid to the worker by reason of his/her employment relationship with the public employer,

---

[8] C-262/88: *Barber v Guardian Royal Exchange Assurance Group* (1990 ECR I-1889).

notwithstanding the fact that such scheme forms part of a general statutory scheme. According to the judgments of the Court of Justice in Cases C-7/93[9] and C-351/00,[10] that condition will be satisfied if the pension scheme concerns a particular category of workers and its benefits are directly related to the period of service and calculated by reference to the public servant's final salary. For reasons of clarity, it is therefore appropriate to make specific provision to that effect.

(15) The Court of Justice has confirmed that whilst the contributions of male and female workers to a defined-benefit pension scheme are covered by Article 141 of the Treaty, any inequality in employers' contributions paid under funded defined-benefit schemes which is due to the use of actuarial factors differing according to sex is not to be assessed in the light of that same provision.

(16) By way of example, in the case of funded defined benefit schemes, certain elements, such as conversion into a capital sum of part of a periodic pension, transfer of pension rights, a reversionary pension payable to a dependant in return for the surrender of part of a pension or a reduced pension where the worker opts to take earlier retirement, may be unequal where the inequality of the amounts results from the effects of the use of actuarial factors differing according to sex at the time when the scheme's funding is implemented.

(17) It is well established that benefits payable under occupational social security schemes are not to be considered as remuneration insofar as they are attributable to periods of employment prior to 17 May 1990, except in the case of workers or those claiming under them who initiated legal proceedings or brought an equivalent claim under the applicable national law before that date. It is therefore necessary to limit the implementation of the principle of equal treatment accordingly.

(18) The Court of Justice has consistently held that the Barber Protocol[11] does not affect the right to join an occupational pension scheme and that the limitation of the effects in time of the judgment in Case C-262/88 does not apply to the right to join an occupational pension scheme. The Court of Justice also ruled that the national rules relating to time limits for bringing actions under national law may be relied on against workers who assert their right to join an occupational pension scheme, provided that they are not less favourable for that type of action than for similar actions of a domestic nature and that they do not render the exercise of rights conferred by Community law impossible in practice. The Court of Justice has also pointed out that the fact that a worker can claim retroactively to join an occupational pension scheme does not allow the worker to avoid paying the contributions relating to the period of membership concerned.

(19) Ensuring equal access to employment and the vocational training leading thereto is fundamental to the application of the principle of equal treatment of men and women in matters of employment and occupation. Any exception to this principle should therefore be limited to those occupational activities which necessitate the employment of a person of a particular sex by reason of their nature or the context in which they are carried out, provided that the objective sought is legitimate and complies with the principle of proportionality.

(20) This Directive does not prejudice freedom of association, including the right to establish unions with others and to join unions to defend one's interests. Measures within the meaning of Article 141(4) of the Treaty may include membership or the continuation of the activity of organisations or unions whose main objective is the promotion, in practice, of the principle of equal treatment between men and women.

(21) The prohibition of discrimination should be without prejudice to the maintenance or adoption of measures intended to prevent or compensate for disadvantages suffered by a group of persons of one sex. Such measures permit organisations of persons of one sex where their main object is the promotion of the special needs of those persons and the promotion of equality between men and women.

---

[9] C-7/93: *Bestuur van het Algemeen Burgerlijk Pensioenfonds v G. A. Beune* (1994 ECR I-4471).
[10] C-351/00: *Pirkko Niemi* (2002 ECR I-7007).
[11] Protocol 17 concerning Article 141 of the Treaty establishing the European Community (1992).

(22) In accordance with Article 141(4) of the Treaty, with a view to ensuring full equality in practice between men and women in working life, the principle of equal treatment does not prevent Member States from maintaining or adopting measures providing for specific advantages in order to make it easier for the under-represented sex to pursue a vocational activity or to prevent or compensate for disadvantages in professional careers. Given the current situation and bearing in mind Declaration No 28 to the Amsterdam Treaty, Member States should, in the first instance, aim at improving the situation of women in working life.

(23) It is clear from the case-law of the Court of Justice that unfavourable treatment of a woman related to pregnancy or maternity constitutes direct discrimination on grounds of sex. Such treatment should therefore be expressly covered by this Directive.

(24) The Court of Justice has consistently recognised the legitimacy, as regards the principle of equal treatment, of protecting a woman's biological condition during pregnancy and maternity and of introducing maternity protection measures as a means to achieve substantive equality. This Directive should therefore be without prejudice to Council Directive 92/85/EEC of 19 October 1992 on the introduction of measures to encourage improvements in the safety and health at work of pregnant workers and workers who have recently given birth or are breastfeeding.[12] This Directive should further be without prejudice to Council Directive 96/34/EC of 3 June 1996 on the framework agreement on parental leave concluded by UNICE, CEEP and the ETUC.[13]

(25) For reasons of clarity, it is also appropriate to make express provision for the protection of the employment rights of women on maternity leave and in particular their right to return to the same or an equivalent post, to suffer no detriment in their terms and conditions as a result of taking such leave and to benefit from any improvement in working conditions to which they would have been entitled during their absence.

(26) In the Resolution of the Council and of the Ministers for Employment and Social Policy, meeting within the Council, of 29 June 2000 on the balanced participation of women and men in family and working life,[14] Member States were encouraged to consider examining the scope for their respective legal systems to grant working men an individual and non-transferable right to paternity leave, while maintaining their rights relating to employment.

(27) Similar considerations apply to the granting by Member States to men and women of an individual and non-transferable right to leave subsequent to the adoption of a child. It is for the Member States to determine whether or not to grant such a right to paternity and/or adoption leave and also to determine any conditions, other than dismissal and return to work, which are outside the scope of this Directive.

(28) The effective implementation of the principle of equal treatment requires appropriate procedures to be put in place by the Member States.

(29) The provision of adequate judicial or administrative procedures for the enforcement of the obligations imposed by this Directive is essential to the effective implementation of the principle of equal treatment.

(30) The adoption of rules on the burden of proof plays a significant role in ensuring that the principle of equal treatment can be effectively enforced. As the Court of Justice has held, provision should therefore be made to ensure that the burden of proof shifts to the respondent when there is a *prima facie* case of discrimination, except in relation to proceedings in which it is for the court or other competent national body to investigate the facts. It is however necessary to clarify that the appreciation of the facts from which it may be presumed that there has been direct or indirect discrimination remains a matter for the relevant national body in accordance with national law or practice. Further, it is for the Member States to introduce, at any appropriate stage of the proceedings, rules of evidence which are more favourable to plaintiffs.

---

[12] OJ L 348, 28.11.1992, p. 1.
[13] OJ L 145, 19.6.1996, p. 4. Directive as amended by Directive 97/75/EC (OJ L 10, 16.1.1998, p. 24).
[14] OJ C 218, 31.7.2000, p. 5.

(31) With a view to further improving the level of protection offered by this Directive, associations, organisations and other legal entities should also be empowered to engage in proceedings, as the Member States so determine, either on behalf or in support of a complainant, without prejudice to national rules of procedure concerning representation and defence.

(32) Having regard to the fundamental nature of the right to effective legal protection, it is appropriate to ensure that workers continue to enjoy such protection even after the relationship giving rise to an alleged breach of the principle of equal treatment has ended. An employee defending or giving evidence on behalf of a person protected under this Directive should be entitled to the same protection.

(33) It has been clearly established by the Court of Justice that in order to be effective, the principle of equal treatment implies that the compensation awarded for any breach must be adequate in relation to the damage sustained. It is therefore appropriate to exclude the fixing of any prior upper limit for such compensation, except where the employer can prove that the only damage suffered by an applicant as a result of discrimination within the meaning of this Directive was the refusal to take his/her job application into consideration.

(34) In order to enhance the effective implementation of the principle of equal treatment, Member States should promote dialogue between the social partners and, within the framework of national practice, with non-governmental organisations.

(35) Member States should provide for effective, proportionate and dissuasive penalties for breaches of the obligations under this Directive.

(36) Since the objectives of this Directive cannot be sufficiently achieved by the Member States and can therefore be better achieved at Community level, the Community may adopt measures in accordance with the principle of subsidiarity as set out in Article 5 of the Treaty. In accordance with the principle of proportionality, as set out in that Article, this Directive does not go beyond what is necessary in order to achieve those objectives.

(37) For the sake of a better understanding of the different treatment of men and women in matters of employment and occupation, comparable statistics disaggregated by sex should continue to be developed, analysed and made available at the appropriate levels.

(38) Equal treatment of men and women in matters of employment and occupation cannot be restricted to legislative measures. Instead, the European Union and the Member States should continue to promote the raising of public awareness of wage discrimination and the changing of public attitudes, involving all parties concerned at public and private level to the greatest possible extent. The dialogue between the social partners could play an important role in this process.

(39) The obligation to transpose this Directive into national law should be confined to those provisions which represent a substantive change as compared with the earlier Directives. The obligation to transpose the provisions which are substantially unchanged arises under the earlier Directives.

(40) This Directive should be without prejudice to the obligations of the Member States relating to the time limits for transposition into national law and application of the Directives set out in Annex I, Part B.

(41) In accordance with paragraph 34 of the Interinstitutional agreement on better law-making,[15] Member States are encouraged to draw up, for themselves and in the interest of the Community, their own tables, which will, as far as possible, illustrate the correlation between this Directive and the transposition measures and to make them public,

HAVE ADOPTED THIS DIRECTIVE:

---

[15] OJ C 321, 31.12.2003, p. 1.

Title I General provisions

Article 1 Purpose

The purpose of this Directive is to ensure the implementation of the principle of equal opportunities and equal treatment of men and women in matters of employment and occupation.

To that end, it contains provisions to implement the principle of equal treatment in relation to:

(a) access to employment, including promotion, and to vocational training;

(b) working conditions, including pay;

(c) occupational social security schemes.

It also contains provisions to ensure that such implementation is made more effective by the establishment of appropriate procedures.

Article 2 Definitions

1. For the purposes of this Directive, the following definitions shall apply:

(a) 'direct discrimination': where one person is treated less favourably on grounds of sex than another is, has been or would be treated in a comparable situation;

(b) 'indirect discrimination': where an apparently neutral provision, criterion or practice would put persons of one sex at a particular disadvantage compared with persons of the other sex, unless that provision, criterion or practice is objectively justified by a legitimate aim, and the means of achieving that aim are appropriate and necessary;

(c) 'harassment': where unwanted conduct related to the sex of a person occurs with the purpose or effect of violating the dignity of a person, and of creating an intimidating, hostile, degrading, humiliating or offensive environment;

(d) 'sexual harassment': where any form of unwanted verbal, non-verbal or physical conduct of a sexual nature occurs, with the purpose or effect of violating the dignity of a person, in particular when creating an intimidating, hostile, degrading, humiliating or offensive environment;

(e) 'pay': the ordinary basic or minimum wage or salary and any other consideration, whether in cash or in kind, which the worker receives directly or indirectly, in respect of his/her employment from his/her employer;

(f) 'occupational social security schemes': schemes not governed by Council Directive 79/7/EEC of 19 December 1978 on the progressive implementation of the principle of equal treatment for men and women in matters of social security[16] whose purpose is to provide workers, whether employees or self-employed, in an undertaking or group of undertakings, area of economic activity, occupational sector or group of sectors with benefits intended to supplement the benefits provided by statutory social security schemes or to replace them, whether membership of such schemes is compulsory or optional.

2. For the purposes of this Directive, discrimination includes:

(a) harassment and sexual harassment, as well as any less favourable treatment based on a person's rejection of or submission to such conduct;

(b) instruction to discriminate against persons on grounds of sex;

(c) any less favourable treatment of a woman related to pregnancy or maternity leave within the meaning of Directive 92/85/EEC.

Article 3 Positive action

Member States may maintain or adopt measures within the meaning of Article 141(4) of the Treaty with a view to ensuring full equality in practice between men and women in working life.

---

[16] OJ L 6, 10.1.1979, p. 24.

Title II Specific provisions

Chapter 1 Equal pay

Article 4 Prohibition of discrimination

For the same work or for work to which equal value is attributed, direct and indirect discrimination on grounds of sex with regard to all aspects and conditions of remuneration shall be eliminated.

In particular, where a job classification system is used for determining pay, it shall be based on the same criteria for both men and women and so drawn up as to exclude any discrimination on grounds of sex.

Chapter 2 Equal treatment in occupational social security schemes

Article 5 Prohibition of discrimination

Without prejudice to Article 4, there shall be no direct or indirect discrimination on grounds of sex in occupational social security schemes, in particular as regards:

(a) the scope of such schemes and the conditions of access to them;

(b) the obligation to contribute and the calculation of contributions;

(c) the calculation of benefits, including supplementary benefits due in respect of a spouse or dependants, and the conditions governing the duration and retention of entitlement to benefits.

Article 6 Personal scope

This Chapter shall apply to members of the working population, including self-employed persons, persons whose activity is interrupted by illness, maternity, accident or involuntary unemployment and persons seeking employment and to retired and disabled workers, and to those claiming under them, in accordance with national law and/or practice.

Article 7 Material scope

1. This Chapter applies to:

(a) occupational social security schemes which provide protection against the following risks:

(i)   sickness,

(ii)   invalidity,

(iii) old age, including early retirement,

(iv) industrial accidents and occupational diseases,

(v)   unemployment;

(b) occupational social security schemes which provide for other social benefits, in cash or in kind, and in particular survivors' benefits and family allowances, if such benefits constitute a consideration paid by the employer to the worker by reason of the latter's employment.

2. This Chapter also applies to pension schemes for a particular category of worker such as that of public servants if the benefits payable under the scheme are paid by reason of the employment relationship with the public employer. The fact that such a scheme forms part of a general statutory scheme shall be without prejudice in that respect.

Article 8 Exclusions from the material scope

1. This Chapter does not apply to:

(a) individual contracts for self-employed persons;

(b) single-member schemes for self-employed persons;

(c) insurance contracts to which the employer is not a party, in the case of workers;

(d) optional provisions of occupational social security schemes offered to participants individually to guarantee them:

(i)   either additional benefits,

(ii) or a choice of date on which the normal benefits for self-employed persons will start, or a choice between several benefits;

(e) occupational social security schemes in so far as benefits are financed by contributions paid by workers on a voluntary basis.

2. This Chapter does not preclude an employer granting to persons who have already reached the retirement age for the purposes of granting a pension by virtue of an occupational social security scheme, but who have not yet reached the retirement age for the purposes of granting a statutory retirement pension, a pension supplement, the aim of which is to make equal or more nearly equal the overall amount of benefit paid to these persons in relation to the amount paid to persons of the other sex in the same situation who have already reached the statutory retirement age, until the persons benefiting from the supplement reach the statutory retirement age.

Article 9   Examples of discrimination

1. Provisions contrary to the principle of equal treatment shall include those based on sex, either directly or indirectly, for:

(a) determining the persons who may participate in an occupational social security scheme;

(b) fixing the compulsory or optional nature of participation in an occupational social security scheme;

(c) laying down different rules as regards the age of entry into the scheme or the minimum period of employment or membership of the scheme required to obtain the benefits thereof;

(d) laying down different rules, except as provided for in points (h) and (j), for the reimbursement of contributions when a worker leaves a scheme without having fulfilled the conditions guaranteeing a deferred right to long-term benefits;

(e) setting different conditions for the granting of benefits or restricting such benefits to workers of one or other of the sexes;

(f) fixing different retirement ages;

(g) suspending the retention or acquisition of rights during periods of maternity leave or leave for family reasons which are granted by law or agreement and are paid by the employer;

(h) setting different levels of benefit, except in so far as may be necessary to take account of actuarial calculation factors which differ according to sex in the case of defined-contribution schemes; in the case of funded defined-benefit schemes, certain elements may be unequal where the inequality of the amounts results from the effects of the use of actuarial factors differing according to sex at the time when the scheme's funding is implemented;

(i) setting different levels for workers' contributions;

(j) setting different levels for employers' contributions, except:

(i) in the case of defined-contribution schemes if the aim is to equalise the amount of the final benefits or to make them more nearly equal for both sexes,

(ii) in the case of funded defined-benefit schemes where the employer's contributions are intended to ensure the adequacy of the funds necessary to cover the cost of the benefits defined;

(k) laying down different standards or standards applicable only to workers of a specified sex, except as provided for in points (h) and (j), as regards the guarantee or retention of entitlement to deferred benefits when a worker leaves a scheme.

2. Where the granting of benefits within the scope of this Chapter is left to the discretion of the scheme's management bodies, the latter shall comply with the principle of equal treatment.

Article 10   Implementation as regards self-employed persons

1. Member States shall take the necessary steps to ensure that the provisions of occupational social security schemes for self-employed persons contrary to the principle of equal treatment are revised with effect from 1 January 1993 at the latest or for Member States whose accession took place after that date, at the date that Directive 86/378/EEC became applicable in their territory.

2. This Chapter shall not preclude rights and obligations relating to a period of membership of an occupational social security scheme for self-employed persons prior to revision of that scheme from remaining subject to the provisions of the scheme in force during that period.

Article 11   Possibility of deferral as regards self-employed persons

As regards occupational social security schemes for self-employed persons, Member States may defer compulsory application of the principle of equal treatment with regard to:

(a) determination of pensionable age for the granting of old-age or retirement pensions, and the possible implications for other benefits:
  (i) either until the date on which such equality is achieved in statutory schemes,
  (ii) or, at the latest, until such equality is prescribed by a directive;
(b) survivors' pensions until Community law establishes the principle of equal treatment in statutory social security schemes in that regard;
(c) the application of Article 9(1)(i) in relation to the use of actuarial calculation factors, until 1 January 1999 or for Member States whose accession took place after that date until the date that Directive 86/378/EEC became applicable in their territory.

Article 12   Retroactive effect

1. Any measure implementing this Chapter, as regards workers, shall cover all benefits under occupational social security schemes derived from periods of employment subsequent to 17 May 1990 and shall apply retroactively to that date, without prejudice to workers or those claiming under them who have, before that date, initiated legal proceedings or raised an equivalent claim under national law. In that event, the implementation measures shall apply retroactively to 8 April 1976 and shall cover all the benefits derived from periods of employment after that date. For Member States which acceded to the Community after 8 April 1976, and before 17 May 1990, that date shall be replaced by the date on which Article 141 of the Treaty became applicable in their territory.

2. The second sentence of paragraph 1 shall not prevent national rules relating to time limits for bringing actions under national law from being relied on against workers or those claiming under them who initiated legal proceedings or raised an equivalent claim under national law before 17 May 1990, provided that they are not less favourable for that type of action than for similar actions of a domestic nature and that they do not render the exercise of rights conferred by Community law impossible in practice.

3. For Member States whose accession took place after 17 May 1990 and which were on 1 January 1994 Contracting Parties to the Agreement on the European Economic Area, the date of 17 May 1990 in the first sentence of paragraph 1 shall be replaced by 1 January 1994.

4. For other Member States whose accession took place after 17 May 1990, the date of 17 May 1990 in paragraphs 1 and 2 shall be replaced by the date on which Article 141 of the Treaty became applicable in their territory.

Article 13   Flexible pensionable age

Where men and women may claim a flexible pensionable age under the same conditions, this shall not be deemed to be incompatible with this Chapter.

Chapter 3   Equal treatment as regards access to employment, vocational training and promotion and working conditions

Article 14   Prohibition of discrimination

1. There shall be no direct or indirect discrimination on grounds of sex in the public or private sectors, including public bodies, in relation to:

(a) conditions for access to employment, to self-employment or to occupation, including selection criteria and recruitment conditions, whatever the branch of activity and at all levels of the professional hierarchy, including promotion;
(b) access to all types and to all levels of vocational guidance, vocational training, advanced vocational training and retraining, including practical work experience;

(c) employment and working conditions, including dismissals, as well as pay as provided for in Article 141 of the Treaty;

(d) membership of, and involvement in, an organisation of workers or employers, or any organisation whose members carry on a particular profession, including the benefits provided for by such organisations.

2. Member States may provide, as regards access to employment including the training leading thereto, that a difference of treatment which is based on a characteristic related to sex shall not constitute discrimination where, by reason of the nature of the particular occupational activities concerned or of the context in which they are carried out, such a characteristic constitutes a genuine and determining occupational requirement, provided that its objective is legitimate and the requirement is proportionate.

Article 15   Return from maternity leave

A woman on maternity leave shall be entitled, after the end of her period of maternity leave, to return to her job or to an equivalent post on terms and conditions which are no less favourable to her and to benefit from any improvement in working conditions to which she would have been entitled during her absence.

Article 16   Paternity and adoption leave

This Directive is without prejudice to the right of Member States to recognise distinct rights to paternity and/or adoption leave. Those Member States which recognise such rights shall take the necessary measures to protect working men and women against dismissal due to exercising those rights and ensure that, at the end of such leave, they are entitled to return to their jobs or to equivalent posts on terms and conditions which are no less favourable to them, and to benefit from any improvement in working conditions to which they would have been entitled during their absence.

Title III Horizontal provisions

Chapter 1 Remedies and enforcement

Section 1 Remedies

Article 17   Defence of rights

1. Member States shall ensure that, after possible recourse to other competent authorities including where they deem it appropriate conciliation procedures, judicial procedures for the enforcement of obligations under this Directive are available to all persons who consider themselves wronged by failure to apply the principle of equal treatment to them, even after the relationship in which the discrimination is alleged to have occurred has ended.

2. Member States shall ensure that associations, organisations or other legal entities which have, in accordance with the criteria laid down by their national law, a legitimate interest in ensuring that the provisions of this Directive are complied with, may engage, either on behalf or in support of the complainant, with his/her approval, in any judicial and/or administrative procedure provided for the enforcement of obligations under this Directive.

3. Paragraphs 1 and 2 are without prejudice to national rules relating to time limits for bringing actions as regards the principle of equal treatment.

Article 18   Compensation or reparation

Member States shall introduce into their national legal systems such measures as are necessary to ensure real and effective compensation or reparation as the Member States so determine for the loss and damage sustained by a person injured as a result of discrimination on grounds of sex, in a way which is dissuasive and proportionate to the damage suffered. Such compensation or reparation may not be restricted by the fixing of a prior upper limit, except in cases where the employer can prove that the only damage suffered by an applicant as a result of discrimination within the meaning of this Directive is the refusal to take his/her job application into consideration.

Section 2 Burden of proof

Article 19 Burden of proof

1. Member States shall take such measures as are necessary, in accordance with their national judicial systems, to ensure that, when persons who consider themselves wronged because the principle of equal treatment has not been applied to them establish, before a court or other competent authority, facts from which it may be presumed that there has been direct or indirect discrimination, it shall be for the respondent to prove that there has been no breach of the principle of equal treatment.

2. Paragraph 1 shall not prevent Member States from introducing rules of evidence which are more favourable to plaintiffs.

3. Member States need not apply paragraph 1 to proceedings in which it is for the court or competent body to investigate the facts of the case.

4. Paragraphs 1, 2 and 3 shall also apply to:

    (a) the situations covered by Article 141 of the Treaty and, insofar as discrimination based on sex is concerned, by Directives 92/85/EEC and 96/34/EC;

    (b) any civil or administrative procedure concerning the public or private sector which provides for means of redress under national law pursuant to the measures referred to in (a) with the exception of out-of-court procedures of a voluntary nature or provided for in national law.

5. This Article shall not apply to criminal procedures, unless otherwise provided by the Member States.

Chapter 2 Promotion of equal treatment—Dialogue

Article 20 Equality bodies

1. Member States shall designate and make the necessary arrangements for a body or bodies for the promotion, analysis, monitoring and support of equal treatment of all persons without discrimination on grounds of sex. These bodies may form part of agencies with responsibility at national level for the defence of human rights or the safeguard of individuals' rights.

2. Member States shall ensure that the competences of these bodies include:

    (a) without prejudice to the right of victims and of associations, organisations or other legal entities referred to in Article 17(2), providing independent assistance to victims of discrimination in pursuing their complaints about discrimination;

    (b) conducting independent surveys concerning discrimination;

    (c) publishing independent reports and making recommendations on any issue relating to such discrimination;

    (d) at the appropriate level exchanging available information with corresponding European bodies such as any future European Institute for Gender Equality.

Article 21 Social dialogue

1. Member States shall, in accordance with national traditions and practice, take adequate measures to promote social dialogue between the social partners with a view to fostering equal treatment, including, for example, through the monitoring of practices in the workplace, in access to employment, vocational training and promotion, as well as through the monitoring of collective agreements, codes of conduct, research or exchange of experience and good practice.

2. Where consistent with national traditions and practice, Member States shall encourage the social partners, without prejudice to their autonomy, to promote equality between men and women, and flexible working arrangements, with the aim of facilitating the reconciliation of work and private life, and to conclude, at the appropriate level, agreements laying down anti-discrimination

rules in the fields referred to in Article 1 which fall within the scope of collective bargaining. These agreements shall respect the provisions of this Directive and the relevant national implementing measures.

3. Member States shall, in accordance with national law, collective agreements or practice, encourage employers to promote equal treatment for men and women in a planned and systematic way in the workplace, in access to employment, vocational training and promotion.

4. To this end, employers shall be encouraged to provide at appropriate regular intervals employees and/or their representatives with appropriate information on equal treatment for men and women in the undertaking.

Such information may include an overview of the proportions of men and women at different levels of the organisation; their pay and pay differentials; and possible measures to improve the situation in cooperation with employees' representatives.

Article 22　Dialogue with non-governmental organisations

Member States shall encourage dialogue with appropriate non-governmental organisations which have, in accordance with their national law and practice, a legitimate interest in contributing to the fight against discrimination on grounds of sex with a view to promoting the principle of equal treatment.

Chapter 3　General horizontal provisions

Article 23　Compliance

Member States shall take all necessary measures to ensure that:

(a) any laws, regulations and administrative provisions contrary to the principle of equal treatment are abolished;

(b) provisions contrary to the principle of equal treatment in individual or collective contracts or agreements, internal rules of undertakings or rules governing the independent occupations and professions and workers' and employers' organisations or any other arrangements shall be, or may be, declared null and void or are amended;

(c) occupational social security schemes containing such provisions may not be approved or extended by administrative measures.

Article 24　Victimisation

Member States shall introduce into their national legal systems such measures as are necessary to protect employees, including those who are employees' representatives provided for by national laws and/or practices, against dismissal or other adverse treatment by the employer as a reaction to a complaint within the undertaking or to any legal proceedings aimed at enforcing compliance with the principle of equal treatment.

Article 25　Penalties

Member States shall lay down the rules on penalties applicable to infringements of the national provisions adopted pursuant to this Directive, and shall take all measures necessary to ensure that they are applied. The penalties, which may comprise the payment of compensation to the victim, must be effective, proportionate and dissuasive. The Member States shall notify those provisions to the Commission by 5 October 2005 at the latest and shall notify it without delay of any subsequent amendment affecting them.

Article 26　Prevention of discrimination

Member States shall encourage, in accordance with national law, collective agreements or practice, employers and those responsible for access to vocational training to take effective measures to prevent all forms of discrimination on grounds of sex, in particular harassment and sexual harassment in the workplace, in access to employment, vocational training and promotion.

Article 27   Minimum requirements

1. Member States may introduce or maintain provisions which are more favourable to the protection of the principle of equal treatment than those laid down in this Directive.

2. Implementation of this Directive shall under no circumstances be sufficient grounds for a reduction in the level of protection of workers in the areas to which it applies, without prejudice to the Member States' right to respond to changes in the situation by introducing laws, regulations and administrative provisions which differ from those in force on the notification of this Directive, provided that the provisions of this Directive are complied with.

Article 28   Relationship to Community and national provisions

1. This Directive shall be without prejudice to provisions concerning the protection of women, particularly as regards pregnancy and maternity.

2. This Directive shall be without prejudice to the provisions of Directive 96/34/EC and Directive 92/85/EEC.

Article 29   Gender mainstreaming

Member States shall actively take into account the objective of equality between men and women when formulating and implementing laws, regulations, administrative provisions, policies and activities in the areas referred to in this Directive.

Article 30   Dissemination of information

Member States shall ensure that measures taken pursuant to this Directive, together with the provisions already in force, are brought to the attention of all the persons concerned by all suitable means and, where appropriate, at the workplace.

Title IV Final provisions

Article 31   Reports

1. By 15 February 2011, the Member States shall communicate to the Commission all the information necessary for the Commission to draw up a report to the European Parliament and the Council on the application of this Directive.

2. Without prejudice to paragraph 1, Member States shall communicate to the Commission, every four years, the texts of any measures adopted pursuant to Article 141(4) of the Treaty, as well as reports on these measures and their implementation. On the basis of that information, the Commission will adopt and publish every four years a report establishing a comparative assessment of any measures in the light of Declaration No 28 annexed to the Final Act of the Treaty of Amsterdam.

3. Member States shall assess the occupational activities referred to in Article 14(2), in order to decide, in the light of social developments, whether there is justification for maintaining the exclusions concerned. They shall notify the Commission of the results of this assessment periodically, but at least every 8 years.

Article 32   Review

By 15 February 2011 at the latest, the Commission shall review the operation of this Directive and if appropriate, propose any amendments it deems necessary.

Article 33   Implementation

Member States shall bring into force the laws, regulations and administrative provisions necessary to comply with this Directive by 15 August 2008 at the latest or shall ensure, by that date, that management and labour introduce the requisite provisions by way of agreement. Member States may, if necessary to take account of particular difficulties, have up to one additional year to comply with this Directive. Member States shall take all necessary steps to be able to guarantee the results imposed by this Directive. They shall forthwith communicate to the Commission the texts of those measures.

When Member States adopt these measures, they shall contain a reference to this Directive or be accompanied by such reference on the occasion of their official publication. They shall also include a statement that references in existing laws, regulations and administrative provisions to the Directives repealed by this Directive shall be construed as references to this Directive. Member States shall determine how such reference is to be made and how that statement is to be formulated.

The obligation to transpose this Directive into national law shall be confined to those provisions which represent a substantive change as compared with the earlier Directives. The obligation to transpose the provisions which are substantially unchanged arises under the earlier Directives.

Member States shall communicate to the Commission the text of the main provisions of national law which they adopt in the field covered by this Directive.

Article 34   Repeal

1. With effect from 15 August 2009 Directives 75/117/EEC, 76/207/EEC, 86/378/EEC and 97/80/EC shall be repealed without prejudice to the obligations of the Member States relating to the time-limits for transposition into national law and application of the Directives set out in Annex I, Part B.

2. References made to the repealed Directives shall be construed as being made to this Directive and should be read in accordance with the correlation table in Annex II.

Article 35   Entry into force

This Directive shall enter into force on the 20th day following its publication in the *Official Journal of the European Union.*

Article 36   Addressees

This Directive is addressed to the Member States.

Done at Strasbourg, 5 July 2006.

Annex II

Correlation table

Directive 75/117/EEC	Directive 76/207/EEC	Directive 86/378/EEC	Directive 97/80/EC	This Directive
—	Article 1(1)	Article 1	Article 1	Article 1
—	Article 1(2)	—	—	—
—	Article 2(2), first indent	—	—	Article 2(1), (a)
—	Article 2(2), second indent	—	Article 2(2)	Article 2(1), (b)
—	Article 2(2), third and fourth indents	—	—	Article 2(1), (c) and (d)
—	—	—	—	Article 2(1), (e)
—	—	Article 2(1)	—	Article 2(1), (f)
—	Article 2(3) and (4) and Article 2(7) third subparagraph	—	—	Article 2(2)
—	Article 2(8)	—	—	Article 3

Directive 75/117/EEC	Directive 76/207/EEC	Directive 86/378/EEC	Directive 97/80/EC	This Directive
Article 1	—	—	—	Article 4
—	—	Article 5(1)	—	Article 5
—	—	Article 3	—	Article 6
—	—	Article 4	—	Article 7(1)
—	—	—	—	Article 7(2)
		Article 2(2)		Article 8(1)
—	—	Article 2(3)	—	Article 8(2)
—	—	Article 6	—	Article 9
—	—	Article 8	—	Article 10
—	—	Article 9	—	Article 11
—	—	(Article 2 of Directive 96/97/EC)	—	Article 12
—	—	Article 9a	—	Article 13
—	Articles 2(1) and 3(1)	—	Article 2(1)	Article 14(1)
—	Article 2(6)	—	—	Article 14(2)
—	Article 2(7), second subparagraph	—	—	Article 15
—	Article 2(7), fourth subparagraph, second and third sentence	—	—	Article 16
Article 2	Article 6(1)	Article 10	—	Article 17(1)
—	Article 6(3)	—	—	Article 17(2)
—	Article 6(4)	—	—	Article 17(3)
—	Article 6(2)	—	—	Article 18
—	—	—	Articles 3 and 4	Article 19
—	Article 8a	—	—	Article 20
—	Article 8b	—	—	Article 21
—	Article 8c	—	—	Article 22
Articles 3 and 6	Article 3 (2)(a)	—	—	Article 23(a)
Article 4	Article 3(2)(b)	Article 7(a)	—	Article 23(b)
—	—	Article 7(b)	—	Article 23(c)
Article 5	Article 7	Article 11	—	Article 24
Article 6	—	—	—	—
—	Article 8d	—	—	Article 25
	Article 2(5)			Article 26
—	Article 8e(1)	—	Article 4(2)	Article 27(1)
—	Article 8e(2)	—	Article 6	Article 27(2)
—	Article 2(7) first subparagraph	Article 5(2)	—	Article 28(1)
—	Article 2(7) fourth subparagraph first sentence			Article 28(2)
—	Article 1(1a)			Article 29

Directive 75/117/EEC	Directive 76/207/EEC	Directive 86/378/EEC	Directive 97/80/EC	This Directive
Article 7	Article 8	—	Article 5	Article 30
Article 9	Article 10	Article 12(2)	Article 7, fourth subparagraph	Article 31(1) and (2)
—	Article 9(2)	—	—	Article 31(3)
—	—	—	—	Article 32
Article 8	Article 9(1), first subparagraph and 9 (2) and (3)	Article 12(1)	Article 7, first, second and third subparagraphs	Article 33
—	Article 9(1), second subparagraph	—	—	—
—	—	—	—	Article 34
—	—	—	—	Article 35
—	—	—	—	Article 36
—	—	Annex	—	—

Council Directive 2010/18/EU of 8 March 2010 implementing the revised Framework Agreement on parental leave concluded by BUSINESS EUROPE, UEAPME, CEEP and ETUC*

[OJ 2010 L68/13]

THE COUNCIL OF THE EUROPEAN UNION,

Having regard to the Treaty on the Functioning of the European Union, and in particular Article 155(2) thereof,

Having regard to the proposal from the European Commission,

Whereas:

(1) Article 153 of the Treaty on the Functioning of the European Union (the 'TFEU') enables the Union to support and complement the activities of the Member States, inter alia in the field of equality between men and women with regard to labour market opportunities and treatment at work.

(2) Social dialogue at Union level may, in accordance with Article 155(1) of the TFEU, lead to contractual relations, including agreements, should management and labour (the 'social partners') so desire. The social partners may, in accordance with Article 155(2) of the TFEU, request jointly that agreements concluded by them at Union level in matters covered by Article 153 of the TFEU be implemented by a Council decision on a proposal from the Commission.

(3) A Framework Agreement on parental leave was concluded by the European cross-industry social partner organisations (ETUC, UNICE and CEEP) on 14 December 1995 and was given legal effect by Council Directive 96/34/EC of 3 June 1996 on the framework agreement on parental leave concluded by UNICE, CEEP and the ETUC.[1] That Directive was amended and extended to the United Kingdom of Great Britain and Northern Ireland by Council Directive 97/75/EC.[2] Directive 96/34/EC

---

* **Editor's Note:** As amended by Directive 2013/62 (OJ 2013 L353/7).

[1] OJ L 145, 19.6.1996, p. 4.

[2] OJ L 10, 16.1.1998, p. 24.

contributed greatly to improving the opportunities available to working parents in the Member States to better reconcile their work and family responsibilities through leave arrangements.

(4) In accordance with Article 138(2) and (3) of the Treaty establishing the European Community (the 'EC Treaty'),* the Commission consulted the European social partners in 2006 and 2007 on ways of further improving the reconciliation of work, private and family life and, in particular, the existing Community legislation on maternity protection and parental leave, and on the possibility of introducing new types of family-related leave, such as paternity leave, adoption leave and leave to care for family members.

(5) The three European general cross-industry social partner organisations (ETUC, CEEP and BUSINESSEUROPE, formerly named UNICE) and the European cross-industry social partner organisation representing a certain category of undertakings (UEAPME) informed the Commission on 11 September 2008 of their wish to enter into negotiations, in accordance with Article 138(4) and Article 139 of the EC Treaty,** with a view to revising the Framework Agreement on parental leave concluded in 1995.

(6) On 18 June 2009, those organisations signed the revised Framework Agreement on parental leave (the 'revised Framework Agreement') and addressed a joint request to the Commission to submit a proposal for a Council decision implementing that revised Framework Agreement.

(7) In the course of their negotiations, the European social partners completely revised the 1995 Framework Agreement on parental leave. Therefore Directive 96/34/EC should be repealed and replaced by a new directive rather than being simply amended.

(8) Since the objectives of the Directive, namely to improve the reconciliation of work, private and family life for working parents and equality between men and women with regard to labour market opportunities and treatment at work across the Union, cannot be sufficiently achieved by the Member States and can therefore be better achieved at Union level, the Union may adopt measures, in accordance with the principle of subsidiarity as set out in Article 5 of the Treaty on European Union. In accordance with the principle of proportionality, as set out in that Article, this Directive does not go beyond what is necessary in order to achieve those objectives.

(9) When drafting its proposal for a Directive, the Commission took account of the representative status of the signatory parties to the revised Framework Agreement, their mandate and the legality of the clauses in that revised Framework Agreement and its compliance with the relevant provisions concerning small and medium-sized undertakings.

(10) The Commission informed the European Parliament and the European Economic and Social Committee of its proposal.

(11) Clause 1(1) of the revised Framework Agreement, in line with the general principles of Union law in the social policy area, states that the Agreement lays down minimum requirements.

(12) Clause 8(1) of the revised Framework Agreement states that the Member States may apply or introduce more favourable provisions than those set out in the Agreement.

(13) Clause 8(2) of the revised Framework Agreement states that the implementation of the provisions of the Agreement shall not constitute valid grounds for reducing the general level of protection afforded to workers in the field covered by the Agreement.

(14) Member States should provide for effective, proportionate and dissuasive penalties in the event of any breach of the obligations under this Directive.

(15) Member States may entrust the social partners, at their joint request, with the implementation of this Directive, as long as such Member States take all the steps necessary to ensure that they can at all times guarantee the results imposed by this Directive.

(16) In accordance with point 34 of the Interinstitutional agreement on better law-making,[3] Member States are encouraged to draw up, for themselves and in the interests of the Union, their own tables which will, as far as possible, illustrate the correlation between this Directive and the transposition measures, and to make them public,

HAS ADOPTED THIS DIRECTIVE:

---

* Renumbered: Article 154(2) and (3) of the TFEU.
** Renumbered: Articles 154(4) and 155 of the TFEU.
[3] OJ C 321, 31.12.2003, p. 1.

Article 1

This Directive puts into effect the revised Framework Agreement on parental leave concluded on 18 June 2009 by the European cross-industry social partner organisations (BUSINESSEUROPE, UEAPME, CEEP and ETUC), as set out in the Annex.

Article 2

Member States shall determine what penalties are applicable when national provisions enacted pursuant to this Directive are infringed. The penalties shall be effective, proportionate and dissuasive.

Article 3

1. Member States shall bring into force the laws, regulations and administrative provisions necessary to comply with this Directive or shall ensure that the social partners have introduced the necessary measures by agreement by 8 March 2012 at the latest. They shall forthwith inform the Commission thereof.

When those provisions are adopted by Member States, they shall contain a reference to this Directive or shall be accompanied by such reference on the occasion of their official publication. The methods of making such reference shall be laid down by Member States.

2. Member States may have a maximum additional period of one year to comply with this Directive, if this is necessary to take account of particular difficulties or implementation by collective agreement. They shall inform the Commission thereof by 8 March 2012 at the latest, stating the reasons for which an additional period is required. By way of derogation from the first subparagraph, the additional period referred to therein shall be extended to 31 December 2018 as regards Mayotte as an outermost region of the Union within the meaning of Article 349 TFEU.

3. Member States shall communicate to the Commission the text of the main provisions of national law which they adopt in the field covered by this Directive.

Article 4

Directive 96/34/EC shall be repealed with effect from 8 March 2012. References to Directive 96/34/EC shall be construed as references to this Directive.

Article 5

This Directive shall enter into force on the 20th day following its publication in the *Official Journal of the European Union*.

Article 6

This Directive is addressed to the Member States.

Done at Brussels, 8 March 2010.

Annex
Framework agreement on parental leave (revised)
18 June 2009

Preamble

This framework agreement between the European social partners, BUSINESSEUROPE, UEAPME, CEEP and ETUC (and the liaison committee Eurocadres/CEC) revises the framework agreement on parental leave, concluded on 14 December 1995, setting out the minimum requirements on parental leave, as an important means of reconciling professional and family responsibilities and promoting equal opportunities and treatment between men and women.

The European social partners request the Commission to submit this framework agreement to the Council for a Council decision making these requirements binding in the Member States of the European Union.

I. General considerations

1. Having regard to the EC Treaty and in particular Articles 138 and 139 thereof;*

2. Having regard to Articles 137(1)(c) and 141 of the EC Treaty** and the principle of equal treatment (Articles 2, 3 and 13 of the EC Treaty***) and the secondary legislation based on this, in particular Council Directive 75/117/EEC on the approximation of the laws of the Member States relating to the application of the principle of equal pay for men and women;[4] Council Directive 92/85/EEC on the introduction of measures to encourage improvements in the safety and health at work of pregnant workers and workers who have recently given birth or are breastfeeding;[5] Council Directive 96/97/EC amending Directive 86/378/EEC on the implementation of the principle of equal treatment for men and women in occupational social security schemes;[6] and Directive 2006/54/EC on the implementation of the principle of equal opportunities and equal treatment of men and women in matters of employment and occupation (recast);[7]

3. Having regard to the Charter of Fundamental Rights of the European Union of 7 December 2000 and Articles 23 and 33 thereof relating to equality between men and women and reconciliation of professional, private and family life;

4. Having regard to the 2003 Report from the Commission on the Implementation of Council Directive 96/34/EC of 3 June 1996 on the framework agreement on parental leave concluded by UNICE, CEEP and the ETUC;

5. Having regard to the objective of the Lisbon strategy on growth and jobs of increasing overall employment rates to 70 %, women's employment rates to 60 % and the employment rates of older workers to 50 %; to the Barcelona targets on the provision of childcare facilities; and to the contribution of policies to improve reconciliation of professional, private and family life in achieving these targets;

6. Having regard to the European social partners' Framework of Actions on Gender Equality of 22 March 2005 in which supporting work-life balance is addressed as a priority area for action, while recognising that, in order to continue to make progress on the issue of reconciliation, a balanced, integrated and coherent policy mix must be put in place, comprising of leave arrangements, working arrangements and care infrastructures;

7. Whereas measures to improve reconciliation are part of a broader policy agenda to address the needs of employers and workers and improve adaptability and employability, as part of a flexicurity approach;

8. Whereas family policies should contribute to the achievement of gender equality and be looked at in the context of demographic changes, the effects of an ageing population, closing the generation gap, promoting women's participation in the labour force and the sharing of care responsibilities between women and men;

9. Whereas the Commission has consulted the European social partners in 2006 and 2007 in a first and second stage consultation on reconciliation of professional, private and family life, and, among other things, has addressed the issue of updating the regulatory framework at Community level, and has encouraged the European social partners to assess the provisions of their framework agreement on parental leave with a view to its review;

10. Whereas the Framework agreement of the European social partners of 1995 on parental leave has been a catalyst for positive change, ensured common ground on work life balance in the Member States and played a significant role in helping working parents in Europe to achieve better

---

* Renumbered: Articles 154 and 155 of the TFEU.

** Renumbered: Articles 153(1)c and 157 of the TFEU.

*** Article 2 of the EC Treaty is repealed and replaced, in substance, by Article 3 of the Treaty on the European Union. Article 3(1) of the EC Treaty is repealed and replaced, in substance, by Articles 3 to 6 of the TFEU. Article 3(2) of the EC Treaty is renumbered as Article 8 of the TFEU. Article 13 of the EC Treaty is renumbered as Article 19 of the TFEU.

[4] OJ L 45, 19.2.1975, p. 19–20.

[5] OJ L 348, 28.11.1992, p. 1–8.

[6] OJ L 46, 17.2.1997, p. 20–24.

[7] OJ L 204, 26.7.2006, p. 23–36.

reconciliation; however, on the basis of a joint evaluation, the European social partners consider that certain elements of the agreement need to be adapted or revised in order to better achieve its aims;

11. Whereas certain aspects need to be adapted, taking into account the growing diversity of the labour force and societal developments including the increasing diversity of family structures, while respecting national law, collective agreements and/or practice;

12. Whereas in many Member States encouraging men to assume an equal share of family responsibilities has not led to sufficient results; therefore, more effective measures should be taken to encourage a more equal sharing of family responsibilities between men and women;

13. Whereas many Member States already have a wide variety of policy measures and practices relating to leave facilities, childcare and flexible working arrangements, tailored to the needs of workers and employers and aiming to support parents in reconciling their professional, private and family life; these should be taken into account when implementing this agreement;

14. Whereas this framework agreement provides one element of European social partners' actions in the field of reconciliation;

15. Whereas this agreement is a framework agreement setting out minimum requirements and provisions for parental leave, distinct from maternity leave, and for time off from work on grounds of force majeure, and refers back to Member States and social partners for the establishment of conditions for access and modalities of application in order to take account of the situation in each Member State;

16. Whereas the right of parental leave in this agreement is an individual right and in principle non-transferable, and Member States are allowed to make it transferable. Experience shows that making the leave non-transferable can act as a positive incentive for the take up by fathers, the European social partners therefore agree to make a part of the leave non-transferable;

17. Whereas it is important to take into account the special needs of parents with children with disabilities or long term illness;

18. Whereas Member States should provide for the maintenance of entitlements to benefits in kind under sickness insurance during the minimum period of parental leave;

19. Whereas Member States should also, where appropriate under national conditions and taking into account the budgetary situation, consider the maintenance of entitlements to relevant social security benefits as they stand during the minimum period of parental leave as well as the role of income among other factors in the take-up of parental leave when implementing this agreement;

20. Whereas experiences in Member States have shown that the level of income during parental leave is one factor that influences the take up by parents, especially fathers;

21. Whereas the access to flexible working arrangements makes it easier for parents to combine work and parental responsibilities and facilitates the reintegration into work, especially after returning from parental leave;

22. Whereas parental leave arrangements are meant to support working parents during a specific period of time, aimed at maintaining and promoting their continued labour market participation; therefore, greater attention should be paid to keeping in contact with the employer during the leave or by making arrangements for return to work;

23. Whereas this agreement takes into consideration the need to improve social policy requirements, to enhance the competitiveness of the European Union economy and to avoid imposing administrative, financial and legal constraints in a way which would hold back the creation and development of small and medium sized undertakings;

24. Whereas the social partners are best placed to find solutions that correspond to the needs of both employers and workers and shall therefore play a special role in the implementation, application, monitoring and evaluation of this agreement, in the broader context of other measures to improve the reconciliation of professional and family responsibilities and to promote equal opportunities and treatment between men and women.

THE SIGNATORY PARTIES HAVE AGREED THE FOLLOWING:

II. Content

Clause 1: Purpose and scope

1. This agreement lays down minimum requirements designed to facilitate the reconciliation of parental and professional responsibilities for working parents, taking into account the increasing diversity of family structures while respecting national law, collective agreements and/or practice.

2. This agreement applies to all workers, men and women, who have an employment contract or employment relationship as defined by the law, collective agreements and/or practice in force in each Member State.

3. Member States and/or social partners shall not exclude from the scope and application of this agreement workers, contracts of employment or employment relationships solely because they relate to part-time workers, fixed-term contract workers or persons with a contract of employment or employment relationship with a temporary agency.

Clause 2: Parental leave

1. This agreement entitles men and women workers to an individual right to parental leave on the grounds of the birth or adoption of a child to take care of that child until a given age up to eight years to be defined by Member States and/or social partners.

2. The leave shall be granted for at least a period of four months and, to promote equal opportunities and equal treatment between men and women, should, in principle, be provided on a non-transferable basis. To encourage a more equal take-up of leave by both parents, at least one of the four months shall be provided on a non-transferable basis. The modalities of application of the non-transferable period shall be set down at national level through legislation and/or collective agreements taking into account existing leave arrangements in the Member States.

Clause 3: Modalities of application

1. The conditions of access and detailed rules for applying parental leave shall be defined by law and/or collective agreements in the Member States, as long as the minimum requirements of this agreement are respected. Member States and/or social partners may, in particular:

   (a) decide whether parental leave is granted on a full-time or part-time basis, in a piecemeal way or in the form of a time-credit system, taking into account the needs of both employers and workers;

   (b) make entitlement to parental leave subject to a period of work qualification and/or a length of service qualification which shall not exceed one year; Member States and/or social partners shall ensure, when making use of this provision, that in case of successive fixed term contracts, as defined in Council Directive 1999/70/EC on fixed-term work, with the same employer the sum of these contracts shall be taken into account for the purpose of calculating the qualifying period;

   (c) define the circumstances in which an employer, following consultation in accordance with national law, collective agreements and/or practice, is allowed to postpone the granting of parental leave for justifiable reasons related to the operation of the organisation. Any problem arising from the application of this provision should be dealt with in accordance with national law, collective agreements and/or practice;

   (d) in addition to (c), authorise special arrangements to meet the operational and organisational requirements of small undertakings.

2. Member States and/or social partners shall establish notice periods to be given by the worker to the employer when exercising the right to parental leave, specifying the beginning and the end of the period of leave. Member States and/or social partners shall have regard to the interests of workers and of employers in specifying the length of such notice periods.

3. Member States and/or social partners should assess the need to adjust the conditions for access and modalities of application of parental leave to the needs of parents of children with a disability or a long-term illness.

Clause 4: Adoption

1. Member States and/or social partners shall assess the need for additional measures to address the specific needs of adoptive parents.

Clause 5: Employment rights and non-discrimination

1. At the end of parental leave, workers shall have the right to return to the same job or, if that is not possible, to an equivalent or similar job consistent with their employment contract or employment relationship.

2. Rights acquired or in the process of being acquired by the worker on the date on which parental leave starts shall be maintained as they stand until the end of parental leave. At the end of parental leave, these rights, including any changes arising from national law, collective agreements and/or practice, shall apply.

3. Member States and/or social partners shall define the status of the employment contract or employment relationship for the period of parental leave.

4. In order to ensure that workers can exercise their right to parental leave, Member States and/or social partners shall take the necessary measures to protect workers against less favourable treatment or dismissal on the grounds of an application for, or the taking of, parental leave in accordance with national law, collective agreements and/or practice.

5. All matters regarding social security in relation to this agreement are for consideration and determination by Member States and/or social partners according to national law and/or collective agreements, taking into account the importance of the continuity of the entitlements to social security cover under the different schemes, in particular health care.

All matters regarding income in relation to this agreement are for consideration and determination by Member States and/or social partners according to national law, collective agreements and/or practice, taking into account the role of income—among other factors—in the take-up of parental leave.

Clause 6: Return to work

1. In order to promote better reconciliation, Member States and/or social partners shall take the necessary measures to ensure that workers, when returning from parental leave, may request changes to their working hours and/or patterns for a set period of time. Employers shall consider and respond to such requests, taking into account both employers' and workers' needs.

The modalities of this paragraph shall be determined in accordance with national law, collective agreements and/or practice.

2. In order to facilitate the return to work following parental leave, workers and employers are encouraged to maintain contact during the period of leave and may make arrangements for any appropriate reintegration measures, to be decided between the parties concerned, taking into account national law, collective agreements and/or practice.

Clause 7: Time off from work on grounds of force majeure

1. Member States and/or social partners shall take the necessary measures to entitle workers to time off from work, in accordance with national legislation, collective agreements and/or practice, on grounds of force majeure for urgent family reasons in cases of sickness or accident making the immediate presence of the worker indispensable.

2. Member States and/or social partners may specify the conditions of access and detailed rules for applying clause 7.1 and limit this entitlement to a certain amount of time per year and/or per case.

Clause 8: Final provisions

1. Member States may apply or introduce more favourable provisions than those set out in this agreement.

2. Implementation of the provisions of this agreement shall not constitute valid grounds for reducing the general level of protection afforded to workers in the field covered by this agreement.

This shall not prejudice the right of Member States and/or social partners to develop different legislative, regulatory or contractual provisions, in the light of changing circumstances (including the introduction of non-transferability), as long as the minimum requirements provided for in the present agreement are complied with.

3. This agreement shall not prejudice the right of social partners to conclude, at the appropriate level including European level, agreements adapting and/or complementing the provisions of this agreement in order to take into account particular circumstances.

4. Member States shall adopt the laws, regulations and administrative provisions necessary to comply with the Council decision within a period of two years from its adoption or shall ensure that social partners introduce the necessary measures by way of agreement by the end of this period. Member States may, if necessary to take account of particular difficulties or implementation by collective agreements, have up to a maximum of one additional year to comply with this decision.

5. The prevention and settlement of disputes and grievances arising from the application of this agreement shall be dealt with in accordance with national law, collective agreements and/or practice.

6. Without prejudice to the respective role of the Commission, national courts and the European Court of Justice, any matter relating to the interpretation of this agreement at European level should, in the first instance, be referred by the Commission to the signatory parties who will give an opinion.

7. The signatory parties shall review the application of this agreement five years after the date of the Council decision if requested by one of the parties to this agreement.

Done at Brussels, 18 June 2009.

Directive 2010/41/EU of the European Parliament and of the Council of 7 July 2010 on the application of the principle of equal treatment between men and women engaged in an activity in a self-employed capacity

[OJ 2010 L180/1]

THE EUROPEAN PARLIAMENT AND THE COUNCIL OF THE EUROPEAN UNION,

Having regard to the Treaty on the Functioning of the European Union, and in particular Article 157(3) thereof,

Having regard to the proposal from the European Commission,

Having regard to the opinion of the European Economic and Social Committee,[1]

Acting in accordance with the ordinary legislative procedure,[2]

Whereas:

(1) Council Directive 86/613/EEC of 11 December 1986 on the application of the principle of equal treatment between men and women engaged in an activity, including agriculture, in a self-employed capacity, and on the protection of self-employed women during pregnancy and motherhood[3] ensures application in Member States of the principle of equal treatment as between men and women engaged in an activity in a self-employed capacity, or contributing to the pursuit of such activity. As far as self-employed workers and spouses of self-employed workers are concerned, Directive 86/613/EEC has not been very effective and its scope should be reconsidered, as discrimination based on sex and harassment also occur in areas outside salaried work. In the interest of clarity, Directive 86/613/EEC should be replaced by this Directive.

---

[1] OJ C 228, 22.9.2009, p. 107.
[2] Position of the European Parliament of 6 May 2009 (not yet published in the Official Journal), Position of the Council at first reading of 8 March 2010 (OJ C 123 E, 12.5.2010, p. 5), Position of the European Parliament of 18 May 2010.
[3] OJ L 359, 19.12.1986, p. 56.

(2) In its Communication of 1 March 2006 entitled 'Roadmap for equality between women and men', the Commission announced that in order to improve governance of gender equality, it would review the existing Union gender equality legislation not included in the 2005 recast exercise with a view to updating, modernising and recasting where necessary. Directive 86/613/EEC was not included in the recasting exercise.

(3) In its conclusions of 5 and 6 December 2007 on 'Balanced roles of women and men for jobs, growth and social cohesion', the Council called on the Commission to consider the need to revise, if necessary, Directive 86/613/EEC in order to safeguard the rights related to motherhood and fatherhood of self-employed workers and their helping spouses.

(4) The European Parliament has consistently called on the Commission to review Directive 86/613/EEC, in particular so as to boost maternity protection for self-employed women and to improve the situation of spouses of self-employed workers.

(5) The European Parliament has already stated its position on these matters in its resolution of 21 February 1997 on the situation of the assisting spouses of the self-employed.[4]

(6) In its Communication of 2 July 2008 entitled 'Renewed Social Agenda: Opportunities, access and solidarity in 21st century Europe', the Commission has affirmed the need to take action on the gender gap in entrepreneurship as well as to improve the reconciliation of private and professional life.

(7) There are already a number of existing legal instruments for the implementation of the principle of equal treatment which cover self-employment activities, in particular Council Directive 79/7/EEC of 19 December 1978 on the progressive implementation of the principle of equal treatment for men and women in matters of social security[5] and Directive 2006/54/EC of the European Parliament and of the Council of 5 July 2006 on the implementation of the principle of equal opportunities and equal treatment of men and women in matters of employment and occupation.[6] This Directive should therefore not apply to the areas already covered by other directives.

(8) This Directive is without prejudice to the powers of the Member States to organise their social protection systems. The exclusive competence of the Member States with regard to the organisation of their social protection systems includes, inter alia decisions on the setting up, financing and management of such systems and related institutions as well as on the substance and delivery of benefits, the level of contributions and the conditions for access.

(9) This Directive should apply to self-employed workers and to their spouses or, when and in so far as recognised by national law, their life partners, where they, under the conditions laid down by national law, habitually participate in the activities of the business. In order to improve the situation for these spouses and, when and in so far as recognised by national law, the life partners of self-employed workers, their work should be recognised.

(10) This Directive should not apply to matters covered by other Directives implementing the principle of equal treatment between men and women, notably Council Directive 2004/113/EC of 13 December 2004 implementing the principle of equal treatment between men and women in the access to and supply of goods and services,[7] inter alia, Article 5 of Directive 2004/113/EC on insurance and related financial services remains applicable.

(11) To prevent discrimination based on sex, this Directive should apply to both direct and indirect discrimination. Harassment and sexual harassment should be considered discrimination and therefore prohibited.

(12) This Directive should be without prejudice to the rights and obligations deriving from marital or family status as defined in national law.

(13) The principle of equal treatment should cover the relationships between the self-employed worker and third parties within the remit of this Directive, but not relationships between the self-employed worker and his or her spouse or life partner.

---

[4] OJ C 85, 17.3.1997, p. 186.
[5] OJ L 6, 10.1.1979, p. 24.
[6] OJ L 204, 26.7.2006, p. 23.
[7] OJ L 373, 21.12.2004, p. 37.

(14) In the area of self-employment, the application of the principle of equal treatment means that there must be no discrimination on grounds of sex, for instance in relation to the establishment, equipment or extension of a business or the launching or extension of any other form of self-employed activity.

(15) Member States may, under Article 157(4) of the Treaty on the Functioning of the European Union, maintain or adopt measures providing for specific advantages in order to make it easier for the under-represented sex to engage in self-employed activities or to prevent or compensate for disadvantages in their professional careers. In principle, measures such as positive action aimed at achieving gender equality in practice should not be seen as being in breach of the legal principle of equal treatment between men and women.

(16) It is necessary to ensure that the conditions for setting up a company between spouses or, when and in so far as recognised by national law, life partners, are not more restrictive than the conditions for setting up a company between other persons.

(17) In view of their participation in the activities of the family business, the spouses or, when and in so far as recognised by national law, the life partners of self-employed workers who have access to a system for social protection, should also be entitled to benefit from social protection. Member States should be required to take the necessary measures to organise this social protection in accordance with national law. In particular, it is up to Member States to decide whether this social protection should be implemented on a mandatory or voluntary basis. Member States may provide that this social protection may be proportional to the participation in the activities of the self-employed worker and/or the level of contribution.

(18) The economic and physical vulnerability of pregnant self-employed workers and pregnant spouses and, when and in so far as recognised by national law, pregnant life partners of self-employed workers, makes it necessary for them to be granted the right to maternity benefits. The Member States remain competent to organise such benefits, including establishing the level of contributions and all the arrangements concerning benefits and payments, provided the minimum requirements of this Directive are complied with. In particular, they may determine in which period before and/or after confinement the right to maternity benefits is granted.

(19) The length of the period during which female self-employed workers and female spouses or, when and in so far as recognised by national law, female life partners of self-employed workers, are granted maternity benefits is similar to the duration of maternity leave for employees currently in place at Union level. In case the duration of maternity leave provided for employees is modified at Union level, the Commission should report to the European Parliament and the Council assessing whether the duration of maternity benefits for female self-employed workers and female spouses and life partners referred to in Article 2 should also be modified.

(20) In order to take the specificities of self-employed activities into account, female self-employed workers and female spouses or, when and in so far as recognised by national law, female life partners of self-employed workers should be given access to any existing services supplying temporary replacement enabling interruptions in their occupational activity owing to pregnancy or motherhood, or to any existing national social services. Access to those services can be an alternative to or a part of the maternity allowance.

(21) Persons who have been subject to discrimination based on sex should have suitable means of legal protection. To provide more effective protection, associations, organisations and other legal entities should be empowered to engage in proceedings, as Member States so determine, either on behalf or in support of any victim, without prejudice to national rules of procedure concerning representation and defence before the courts.

(22) Protection of self-employed workers and spouses of self-employed workers and, when and in so far as recognised by national law, the life partners of self-employed workers, from discrimination based on sex should be strengthened by the existence of a body or bodies in each Member State with competence to analyse the problems involved, to study possible solutions and to provide practical assistance to the victims. The body or bodies may be the same as those with responsibility at national level for the implementation of the principle of equal treatment.

(23) This Directive lays down minimum requirements, thus giving the Member States the option of introducing or maintaining more favourable provisions.

(24) Since the objective of the action to be taken, namely to ensure a common high level of protection from discrimination in all the Member States, cannot be sufficiently achieved by the Member States and can be better achieved at Union level, the Union may adopt measures, in accordance with the principle of subsidiarity as set out in Article 5 of the Treaty on European Union. In accordance with the principle of proportionality, as set out in that Article, this Directive does not go beyond what is necessary in order to achieve that objective,

HAVE ADOPTED THIS DIRECTIVE:

Article 1   Subject matter

1. This Directive lays down a framework for putting into effect in the Member States the principle of equal treatment between men and women engaged in an activity in a self-employed capacity, or contributing to the pursuit of such an activity, as regards those aspects not covered by Directives 2006/54/EC and 79/7/EEC.

2. The implementation of the principle of equal treatment between men and women in the access to and supply of goods and services remains covered by Directive 2004/113/EC.

Article 2   Scope

This Directive covers:

(a) self-employed workers, namely all persons pursuing a gainful activity for their own account, under the conditions laid down by national law;

(b) the spouses of self-employed workers or, when and in so far as recognised by national law, the life partners of self-employed workers, not being employees or business partners, where they habitually, under the conditions laid down by national law, participate in the activities of the self-employed worker and perform the same tasks or ancillary tasks.

Article 3   Definitions

For the purposes of this Directive, the following definitions shall apply:

(a) 'direct discrimination': where one person is treated less favourably on grounds of sex than another is, has been or would be, treated in a comparable situation;

(b) 'indirect discrimination': where an apparently neutral provision, criterion or practice would put persons of one sex at a particular disadvantage compared with persons of the other sex, unless that provision, criterion or practice is objectively justified by a legitimate aim, and the means of achieving that aim are appropriate and necessary;

(c) 'harassment': where unwanted conduct related to the sex of a person occurs with the purpose, or effect, of violating the dignity of that person, and of creating an intimidating, hostile, degrading, humiliating or offensive environment;

(d) 'sexual harassment': where any form of unwanted verbal, non-verbal, or physical, conduct of a sexual nature occurs, with the purpose or effect of violating the dignity of a person, in particular when creating an intimidating, hostile, degrading, humiliating or offensive environment.

Article 4   Principle of equal treatment

1. The principle of equal treatment means that there shall be no discrimination whatsoever on grounds of sex in the public or private sectors, either directly or indirectly, for instance in relation to the establishment, equipment or extension of a business or the launching or extension of any other form of self-employed activity.

2. In the areas covered by paragraph 1, harassment and sexual harassment shall be deemed to be discrimination on grounds of sex and therefore prohibited. A person's rejection of, or submission to, such conduct may not be used as a basis for a decision affecting that person.

3. In the areas covered by paragraph 1, an instruction to discriminate against persons on grounds of sex shall be deemed to be discrimination.

Article 5   Positive action

Member States may maintain or adopt measures within the meaning of Article 157(4) of the Treaty on the Functioning of the European Union with a view to ensuring full equality in practice between men and women in working life, for instance aimed at promoting entrepreneurship initiatives among women.

Article 6   Establishment of a company

Without prejudice to the specific conditions for access to certain activities which apply equally to both sexes, the Member States shall take the measures necessary to ensure that the conditions for the establishment of a company between spouses, or between life partners when and in so far as recognised by national law, are not more restrictive than the conditions for the establishment of a company between other persons.

Article 7   Social protection

1. Where a system for social protection for self-employed workers exists in a Member State, that Member State shall take the necessary measures to ensure that spouses and life partners referred to in Article 2(b) can benefit from a social protection in accordance with national law.

2. The Member States may decide whether the social protection referred to in paragraph 1 is implemented on a mandatory or voluntary basis.

Article 8   Maternity benefits

1. The Member States shall take the necessary measures to ensure that female self-employed workers and female spouses and life partners referred to in Article 2 may, in accordance with national law, be granted a sufficient maternity allowance enabling interruptions in their occupational activity owing to pregnancy or motherhood for at least 14 weeks.

2. The Member States may decide whether the maternity allowance referred to in paragraph 1 is granted on a mandatory or voluntary basis.

3. The allowance referred to in paragraph 1 shall be deemed sufficient if it guarantees an income at least equivalent to:
   (a) the allowance which the person concerned would receive in the event of a break in her activities on grounds connected with her state of health and/or;
   (b) the average loss of income or profit in relation to a comparable preceding period subject to any ceiling laid down under national law and/or;
   (c) any other family related allowance established by national law, subject to any ceiling laid down under national law.

4. The Member States shall take the necessary measures to ensure that female self-employed workers and female spouses and life partners referred to in Article 2 have access to any existing services supplying temporary replacements or to any existing national social services. The Member States may provide that access to those services is an alternative to or a part of the allowance referred to in paragraph 1 of this Article.

Article 9   Defence of rights

1. The Member States shall ensure that judicial or administrative proceedings, including, where Member States consider it appropriate, conciliation procedures, for the enforcement of the obligations under this Directive are available to all persons who consider they have sustained loss or damage as a result of a failure to apply the principle of equal treatment to them, even after the relationship in which the discrimination is alleged to have occurred has ended.

2. The Member States shall ensure that associations, organisations and other legal entities which have, in accordance with the criteria laid down by their national law, a legitimate interest in ensuring that this Directive is complied with may engage, either on behalf or in support of the complainant, with his or her approval, in any judicial or administrative proceedings provided for the enforcement of obligations under this Directive.

3. Paragraphs 1 and 2 shall be without prejudice to national rules on time limits for bringing actions relating to the principle of equal treatment.

Article 10   Compensation or reparation

The Member States shall introduce such measures into their national legal systems as are necessary to ensure real and effective compensation or reparation, as Member States so determine, for the loss or damage sustained by a person as a result of discrimination on grounds of sex, such compensation or reparation being dissuasive and proportionate to the loss or damage suffered. Such compensation or reparation shall not be limited by the fixing of a prior upper limit.

Article 11   Equality bodies

1. The Member States shall take the necessary measures to ensure that the body or bodies designated in accordance with Article 20 of Directive 2006/54/EC are also competent for the promotion, analysis, monitoring and support of equal treatment of all persons covered by this Directive without discrimination on grounds of sex.

2. The Member States shall ensure that the tasks of the bodies referred to in paragraph 1 include:

   (a) providing independent assistance to victims of discrimination in pursuing their complaints of discrimination, without prejudice to the rights of victims and of associations, organisations and other legal entities referred to in Article 9(2);

   (b) conducting independent surveys on discrimination;

   (c) publishing independent reports and making recommendations on any issue relating to such discrimination;

   (d) exchanging, at the appropriate level, the information available with the corresponding European bodies, such as the European Institute for Gender Equality.

Article 12   Gender mainstreaming

The Member States shall actively take into account the objective of equality between men and women when formulating and implementing laws, regulations, administrative provisions, policies and activities in the areas referred to in this Directive.

Article 13   Dissemination of information

The Member States shall ensure that the provisions adopted pursuant to this Directive, together with the relevant provisions already in force, are brought by all appropriate means to the attention of the persons concerned throughout their territory.

Article 14   Level of protection

The Member States may introduce or maintain provisions which are more favourable to the protection of the principle of equal treatment between men and women than those laid down in this Directive.

The implementation of this Directive shall under no circumstances constitute grounds for a reduction in the level of protection against discrimination already afforded by Member States in the fields covered by this Directive.

Article 15   Reports

1. Member States shall communicate all available information concerning the application of this Directive to the Commission by 5 August 2015.

The Commission shall draw up a summary report for submission to the European Parliament and to the Council no later than 5 August 2016. That report should take into account any legal change concerning the duration of maternity leave for employees. Where appropriate, that report shall be accompanied by proposals for amending this Directive.

2. The Commission's report shall take the viewpoints of the stakeholders into account.

Article 16   Implementation

1. The Member States shall bring into force the laws, regulations and administrative provisions necessary to comply with this Directive by 5 August 2012 at the latest. They shall forthwith communicate to the Commission the text of those provisions.

When the Member States adopt those provisions, they shall contain a reference to this Directive or be accompanied by such a reference on the occasion of their official publication. Member States shall determine how such reference is to be made.

2. Where justified by particular difficulties, the Member States may, if necessary, have an additional period of two years until 5 August 2014 in order to comply with Article 7, and in order to comply with Article 8 as regards female spouses and life partners referred to in Article 2(b).

3. The Member States shall communicate to the Commission the text of the main provisions of national law which they adopt in the field covered by this Directive.

Article 17   Repeal

Directive 86/613/EEC shall be repealed, with effect from 5 August 2012.

References to the repealed Directive shall be construed as references to this Directive.

Article 18   Entry into force

This Directive shall enter into force on the 20th day following its publication in the *Official Journal of the European Union*.

Article 19   Addressees

This Directive is addressed to the Member States.

Done at Strasbourg, 7 July 2010

Social policy: worker protection

Council Directive 2001/23/EC of 12 March 2001 on the approximation of the laws of the Member States relating to the safeguarding of employees' rights in the event of transfers of undertakings, businesses or parts of undertakings or businesses*

[OJ 2001 L82/16]

THE COUNCIL OF THE EUROPEAN UNION,

Having regard to the Treaty establishing the European Community, and in particular Article 94 thereof,

Having regard to the proposal from the Commission,

Having regard to the opinion of the European Parliament,[1]

Having regard to the opinion of the Economic and Social Committee,[2]

Whereas:

(1) Council Directive 77/1877/EEC of 14 February 1977 on the approximation of the laws of the Member States relating to the safeguarding of employees' rights in the event of transfers of undertakings, businesses or parts of undertakings or businesses[3] has been substantially amended.[4] In the interests of clarity and rationality, it should therefore be codified.

(2) Economic trends are bringing in their wake, at both national and Community level, changes in the structure of undertakings, through transfers of undertakings, businesses or parts of undertakings or businesses to other employers as a result of legal transfers or mergers.

Editor's Note: This Directive repeals and replaces Council Directive 77/187/EEC (OJ L61, 5.3.1977, p. 26) and Council Directive 98/50/EC (OJ L201, 17.7.1998, p. 88). As amended by Directive 2015/1794 (OJ 2015 L263/1).

[1] Opinion delivered on 25 October 2000 (not yet published in the Official Journal).
[2] OJ C 367, 20.12.2000, p. 21.
[3] OJ L 61, 5.3.1977, p. 26.
[4] See Annex I, Part A.

(3) It is necessary to provide for the protection of employees in the event of a change of employer, in particular, to ensure that their rights are safeguarded.

(4) Differences still remain in the Member States as regards the extent of the protection of employees in this respect and these differences should be reduced.

(5) The Community Charter of the Fundamental Social Rights of Workers adopted on 9 December 1989 ('Social Charter') states, in points 7, 17 and 18 in particular that: 'The completion of the internal market must lead to an improvement in the living and working conditions of workers in the European Community. The improvement must cover, where necessary, the development of certain aspects of employment regulations such as procedures for collective redundancies and those regarding bankruptcies. Information, consultation and participation for workers must be developed along appropriate lines, taking account of the practice in force in the various Member States. Such information, consultation and participation must be implemented in due time, particularly in connection with restructuring operations in undertakings or in cases of mergers having an impact on the employment of workers'.

(6) In 1977 the Council adopted Directive 77/187/EEC to promote the harmonisation of the relevant national laws ensuring the safeguarding of the rights of employees and requiring transferors and transferees to inform and consult employees' representatives in good time.

(7) That Directive was subsequently amended in the light of the impact of the internal market, the legislative tendencies of the Member States with regard to the rescue of undertakings in economic difficulties, the case-law of the Court of Justice of the European Communities, Council Directive 75/129/EEC of 17 February 1975 on the approximation of the laws of the Member States relating to collective redundancies[5] and the legislation already in force in most Member States.

(8) Considerations of legal security and transparency required that the legal concept of transfer be clarified in the light of the case-law of the Court of Justice. Such clarification has not altered the scope of Directive 77/187/EEC as interpreted by the Court of Justice.

(9) The Social Charter recognises the importance of the fight against all forms of discrimination, especially based on sex, colour, race, opinion and creed.

(10) This Directive should be without prejudice to the time limits set out in Annex I Part B within which the Member States are to comply with Directive 77/187/EEC, and the act amending it,

HAS ADOPTED THIS DIRECTIVE:

Chapter I Scope and definitions

Article 1

1. (a) This Directive shall apply to any transfer of an undertaking, business, or part of an undertaking or business to another employer as a result of a legal transfer or merger.
   (b) Subject to subparagraph (a) and the following provisions of this Article, there is a transfer within the meaning of this Directive where there is a transfer of an economic entity which retains its identity, meaning an organised grouping of resources which has the objective of pursuing an economic activity, whether or not that activity is central or ancillary.
   (c) This Directive shall apply to public and private undertakings engaged in economic activities whether or not they are operating for gain. An administrative reorganisation of public administrative authorities, or the transfer of administrative functions between public administrative authorities, is not a transfer within the meaning of this Directive.

2. This Directive shall apply where and in so far as the undertaking, business or part of the undertaking or business to be transferred is situated within the territorial scope of the Treaty.

3. This Directive shall apply to a transfer of a seagoing vessel that is part of a transfer of an undertaking, business or part of an undertaking or business within the meaning of paragraphs 1

---

[5] OJ L 48, 22.2.1975, p. 29. Directive replaced by Directive 98/59/EC (OJ L 225, 12.8.1998, p. 6).

and 2, provided that the transferee is situated, or the transferred undertaking, business, or part of an undertaking or business remains, within the territorial scope of the Treaty.

This Directive shall not apply where the object of the transfer consists exclusively of one or more seagoing vessels.

Article 2

1. For the purposes of this Directive:
   (a) 'transferor' shall mean any natural or legal person who, by reason of a transfer within the meaning of Article 1(1), ceases to be the employer in respect of the undertaking, business or part of the undertaking or business;
   (b) 'transferee' shall mean any natural or legal person who, by reason of a transfer within the meaning of Article 1(1), becomes the employer in respect of the undertaking, business or part of the undertaking or business;
   (c) 'representatives of employees' and related expressions shall mean the representatives of the employees provided for by the laws or practices of the Member States;
   (d) 'employee' shall mean any person who, in the Member State concerned, is protected as an employee under national employment law.

2. This Directive shall be without prejudice to national law as regards the definition of contract of employment or employment relationship. However, Member States shall not exclude from the scope of this Directive contracts of employment or employment relationships solely because:
   (a) of the number of working hours performed or to be performed,
   (b) they are employment relationships governed by a fixed-duration contract of employment within the meaning of Article 1(1) of Council Directive 91/383/EEC of 25 June 1991 supplementing the measures to encourage improvements in the safety and health at work of workers with a fixed-duration employment relationship or a temporary employment relationship,[6] or
   (c) they are temporary employment relationships within the meaning of Article 1(2) of Directive 91/383/EEC, and the undertaking, business or part of the undertaking or business transferred is, or is part of, the temporary employment business which is the employer.

Chapter II Safeguarding of employees' rights

Article 3

1. The transferor's rights and obligations arising from a contract of employment or from an employment relationship existing on the date of a transfer shall, by reason of such transfer, be transferred to the transferee.

Member States may provide that, after the date of transfer, the transferor and the transferee shall be jointly and severally liable in respect of obligations which arose before the date of transfer from a contract of employment or an employment relationship existing on the date of the transfer.

2. Member States may adopt appropriate measures to ensure that the transferor notifies the transferee of all the rights and obligations which will be transferred to the transferee under this Article, so far as those rights and obligations are or ought to have been known to the transferor at the time of the transfer. A failure by the transferor to notify the transferee of any such right or obligation shall not affect the transfer of that right or obligation and the rights of any employees against the transferee and/or transferor in respect of that right or obligation.

3. Following the transfer, the transferee shall continue to observe the terms and conditions agreed in any collective agreement on the same terms applicable to the transferor under that agreement, until the date of termination or expiry of the collective agreement or the entry into force or

---

[6] OJ L 206, 29.7.1991, p. 19.

application of another collective agreement. Member States may limit the period for observing such terms and conditions with the proviso that it shall not be less than one year.

4. (a) Unless Member States provide otherwise, paragraphs 1 and 3 shall not apply in relation to employees' rights to old-age, invalidity or survivors' benefits under supplementary company or intercompany pension schemes outside the statutory social security schemes in Member States.

   (b) Even where they do not provide in accordance with sub-paragraph (a) that paragraphs 1 and 3 apply in relation to such rights, Member States shall adopt the measures necessary to protect the interests of employees and of persons no longer employed in the transferor's business at the time of the transfer in respect of rights conferring on them immediate or prospective entitlement to old age benefits, including survivors' benefits, under supplementary schemes referred to in subparagraph (a).

Article 4

1. The transfer of the undertaking, business or part of the undertaking or business shall not in itself constitute grounds for dismissal by the transferor or the transferee. This provision shall not stand in the way of dismissals that may take place for economic, technical or organisational reasons entailing changes in the workforce. Member States may provide that the first sub-paragraph shall not apply to certain specific categories of employees who are not covered by the laws or practice of the Member States in respect of protection against dismissal.

2. If the contract of employment or the employment relationship is terminated because the transfer involves a substantial change in working conditions to the detriment of the employee, the employer shall be regarded as having been responsible for termination of the contract of employment or of the employment relationship.

Article 5

1. Unless Member States provide otherwise, Articles 3 and 4 shall not apply to any transfer of an undertaking, business or part of an undertaking or business where the transferor is the subject of bankruptcy proceedings or any analogous insolvency proceedings which have been instituted with a view to the liquidation of the assets of the transferor and are under the supervision of a competent public authority (which may be an insolvency practitioner authorised by a competent public authority).

2. Where Articles 3 and 4 apply to a transfer during insolvency proceedings which have been opened in relation to a transferor (whether or not those proceedings have been instituted with a view to the liquidation of the assets of the transferor) and provided that such proceedings are under the supervision of a competent public authority (which may be an insolvency practitioner determined by national law) a Member State may provide that:

   (a) notwithstanding Article 3(1), the transferor's debts arising from any contracts of employment or employment relationships and payable before the transfer or before the opening of the insolvency proceedings shall not be transferred to the transferee, provided that such proceedings give rise, under the law of that Member State, to protection at least equivalent to that provided for in situations covered by Council Directive 80/987/EEC of 20 October 1980 on the approximation of the laws of the Member States relating to the protection of employees in the event of the insolvency of their employer,[7] and, or alternatively, that,

   (b) the transferee, transferor or person or persons exercising the transferor's functions, on the one hand, and the representatives of the employees on the other hand may agree alterations, in so far as current law or practice permits, to the employees' terms and conditions of employment designed to safeguard employment opportunities by ensuring the survival of the undertaking, business or part of the undertaking or business.

[7] OJ L 283, 20.10.1980, p. 23. Directive as last amended by the 1994 Act of Accession.

3. A Member State may apply paragraph 20(b) to any transfers where the transferor is in a situation of serious economic crisis, as defined by national law, provided that the situation is declared by a competent public authority and open to judicial supervision, on condition that such provisions already existed in national law on 17 July 1998.

The Commission shall present a report on the effects of this provision before 17 July 2003 and shall submit any appropriate proposals to the Council.

4. Member States shall take appropriate measures with a view to preventing misuse of insolvency proceedings in such a way as to deprive employees of the rights provided for in this Directive.

Article 6

1. If the undertaking, business or part of an undertaking or business preserves its autonomy, the status and function of the representatives or of the representation of the employees affected by the transfer shall be preserved on the same terms and subject to the same conditions as existed before the date of the transfer by virtue of law, regulation, administrative provision or agreement, provided that the conditions necessary for the constitution of the employee's representation are fulfilled.

The first subparagraph shall not apply if, under the laws, regulations, administrative provisions or practice in the Member States, or by agreement with the representatives of the employees, the conditions necessary for the reappointment of the representatives of the employees or for the reconstitution of the representation of the employees are fulfilled.

Where the transferor is the subject of bankruptcy proceedings or any analogous insolvency proceedings which have been instituted with a view to the liquidation of the assets of the transferor and are under the supervision of a competent public authority (which may be an insolvency practitioner authorised by a competent public authority), Member States may take the necessary measures to ensure that the transferred employees are properly represented until the new election or designation of representatives of the employees.

If the undertaking, business or part of an undertaking or business does not preserve its autonomy, the Member States shall take the necessary measures to ensure that the employees transferred who were represented before the transfer continue to be properly represented during the period necessary for the reconstitution or reappointment of the representation of employees in accordance with national law or practice.

2. If the term of office of the representatives of the employees affected by the transfer expires as a result of the transfer, the representatives shall continue to enjoy the protection provided by the laws, regulations, administrative provisions or practice of the Member States.

Chapter III Information and consultation

Article 7

1. The transferor and transferee shall be required to inform the representatives of their respective employees affected by the transfer of the following:
   – the date or proposed date of the transfer,
   – the reasons for the transfer,
   – the legal, economic and social implications of the transfer for the employees,
   – any measures envisaged in relation to the employees.

The transferor must give such information to the representatives of his employees in good time, before the transfer is carried out.

The transferee must give such information to the representatives of his employees in good time, and in any event before his employees are directly affected by the transfer as regards their conditions of works and employment.

2. Where the transferor or the transferee envisages measures in relation to his employees, he shall consult the representatives of his employees in good time on such measures with a view to reaching an agreement.

3. Member States whose laws, regulations or administrative provisions provide that representatives of the employees may have recourse to an arbitration board to obtain a decision on the

measures to be taken in relation to employees may limit the obligations laid down in paragraphs 1 and 2 to cases where the transfer carried out gives rise to a change in the business likely to entail serious disadvantages for a considerable number of the employees. The information and consultations shall cover at least the measures envisaged in relation to the employees.

The information must be provided and consultations take place in good time before the change in the business as referred to in the first subparagraph is effected.

4. The obligations laid down in this Article shall apply irrespective of whether the decision resulting in the transfer is taken by the employer or an undertaking controlling the employer.

In considering alleged breaches of the information and consultation requirements laid down by this Directive, the argument that such a breach occurred because the information was not provided by an undertaking controlling the employer shall not be accepted as an excuse.

5. Member States may limit the obligations laid down in paragraphs 1, 2 and 3 to undertakings or businesses which, in terms of the number of employees, meet the conditions for the election or nomination of a collegiate body representing the employees.

6. Member States shall provide that, where there are no representatives of the employees in an undertaking or business through no fault of their own, the employees concerned must be informed in advance of:
- the date or proposed date of the transfer,
- the reason for the transfer,
- the legal, economic and social implications of the transfer for the employees,
- any measures envisaged in relation to the employees.

Chapter IV Final provisions

Article 8

This Directive shall not affect the right of Member States to apply or introduce laws, regulations or administrative provisions which are more favourable to employees or to promote or permit collective agreements or agreements between social partners more favourable to employees.

Article 9

Member States shall introduce into their national legal systems such measures as are necessary to enable all employees and representatives of employees who consider themselves wronged by failure to comply with the obligations arising from this Directive to pursue their claims by judicial process after possible recourse to other competent authorities.

Article 10

The Commission shall submit to the Council an analysis of the effect of the provisions of this Directive before 17 July 2006. It shall propose any amendment which may seem necessary.

Article 11

Member States shall communicate to the Commission the texts of the laws, regulations and administrative provisions which they adopt in the field covered by this Directive.

Article 12

Directive 77/187/EEC, as amended by the Directive referred to in Annex I, Part A, is repealed, without prejudice to the obligations of the Member States concerning the time limits for implementation set out in Annex I, Part B.

References to the repealed Directive shall be construed as references to this Directive and shall be read in accordance with the correlation table in Annex II.

Article 13

This Directive shall enter into force on the 20th day following its publication in the *Official Journal of the European Communities*.

Article 14

This Directive is addressed to the Member States.

Done at Brussels, 12 March 2001.

Annex I

Part A

Repealed Directive and its amending Directive (referred to in Article 12)

Council Directive 77/ 187/EEC (OJ L 61, 5.3.1977, p. 26)
Council Directive 98/50/EC (OJ L 201, 17.7.1998, p. 88)

Part B

Deadlines for transposition into national law (referred to in Article 12)

Directive	Deadline for transposition
77/187/EEC	16 February 1979
98/50/EC	17 July 2001

Annex II Correlation table

Directive 77/187/EEC	This Directive
Article 1	Article 1
Article 2	Article 2
Article 3	Article 3
Article 4	Article 4
Article 4a	Article 5
Article 5	Article 6
Article 6	Article 7
Article 7	Article 8
Article 7a	Article 9
Article 7b	Article 10
Article 8	Article 11
–	Article 12
–	Article 13
–	Article 14
–	Annex I
–	Annex II

Council Directive of 12 June 1989 on the introduction of measures to encourage improvements in the safety and health of workers at work (89/391/EEC)*

[OJ 1989 L183/1]

THE COUNCIL OF THE EUROPEAN COMMUNITIES,

Having regard to the Treaty establishing the European Economic Community, and in particular Article 118a thereof,

(Recitals and Preamble omitted.)

HAS ADOPTED THIS DIRECTIVE:

Section I General provisions

Article 1 Object

1. The object of this Directive is to introduce measures to encourage improvements in the safety and health of workers at work.

2. To that end it contains general principles concerning the prevention of occupational risks, the protection of safety and health, the elimination of risk and accident factors, the informing, consultation, balanced participation in accordance with national laws and/or practices and training of workers and their representatives, as well as general guidelines for the implementation of the said principles.

3. This Directive shall be without prejudice to existing or future national and Community provisions which are more favourable to protection of the safety and health of workers at work.

Article 2 Scope

1. This Directive shall apply to all sectors of activity, both public and private (industrial, agricultural, commercial, administrative, service, educational, cultural, leisure, etc.).

2. This Directive shall not be applicable where characteristics peculiar to certain specific public service activities, such as the armed forces or the police, or to certain specific activities in the civil protection services inevitably conflict with it.

In that event, the safety and health of workers must be ensured as far as possible in the light of the objectives of this Directive.

Article 3 Definitions

For the purposes of this Directive, the following terms shall have the following meanings:

(a) worker: any person employed by an employer, including trainees and apprentices but excluding domestic servants;

(b) employer: any natural or legal person who has an employment relationship with the worker and has responsibility for the undertaking and/or establishment;

(c) workers' representative with specific responsibility for the safety and health of workers: any person elected, chosen or designated in accordance with national laws and/or practices to represent workers where problems arise relating to the safety and health protection of workers at work;

(d) prevention: all the steps or measures taken or planned at all stages of work in the undertaking to prevent or reduce occupational risks.

Article 4

1. Member States shall take the necessary steps to ensure that employers, workers and workers' representatives are subject to the legal provisions necessary for the implementation of this Directive.

2. In particular, Member States shall ensure adequate controls and supervision.

---

* **Editor's Note:** Amended by Regulation 2003/1882, OJ 2003 L284/1 and Directive 2007/30, OJ 2007 L165/21 and Regulation 1137/2008 OJ 2008 L311/1.

Section II Employers' obligations

Article 5 General provision

1. The employer shall have a duty to ensure the safety and health of workers in every aspect related to the work.

2. Where, pursuant to Article 7(3), an employer enlists competent external services or persons, this shall not discharge him from his responsibilities in this area.

3. The workers' obligations in the field of safety and health at work shall not affect the principle of the responsibility of the employer.

4. This Directive shall not restrict the option of Member States to provide for the exclusion or the limitation of employers' responsibility where occurrences are due to unusual and unforeseeable circumstances, beyond the employers' control, or to exceptional events, the consequences of which could not have been avoided despite the exercise of all due care.

Member States need not exercise the option referred to in the first subparagraph.

Article 6 General obligations on employers

1. Within the context of his responsibilities, the employer shall take the measures necessary for the safety and health protection of workers, including prevention of occupational risks and provision of information and training, as well as provision of the necessary organisation and means.

The employer shall be alert to the need to adjust these measures to take account of changing circumstances and aim to improve existing situations.

2. The employer shall implement the measures referred to in the first sub-paragraph of paragraph 1 on the basis of the following general principles of prevention:
   (a) avoiding risks;
   (b) evaluating the risks which cannot be avoided;
   (c) combating the risks at source;
   (d) adapting the work to the individual, especially as regards the design of work places, the choice of work equipment and the choice of working and production methods, with a view, in particular, to alleviating monotonous work and work at a predetermined work-rate and to reducing their effect on health;
   (e) adapting to technical progress;
   (f) replacing the dangerous by the non-dangerous or the less dangerous;
   (g) developing a coherent overall prevention policy which covers technology, organisation of work, working conditions, social relationships and the influence of factors related to the working environment;
   (h) giving collective protective measures priority over individual protective measures;
   (i) giving appropriate instructions to the workers.

3. Without prejudice to the other provisions of this Directive, the employer shall, taking into account the nature of the activities of the enterprise and/or establishment:
   (a) evaluate the risks to the safety and health of workers, *inter alia* in the choice of work equipment, the chemical substances or preparations used, and the fitting out of work places. Subsequent to this evaluation and as necessary, the preventive measures and the working and production methods implemented by the employer must:
   – assure an improvement in the level of protection afforded to workers with regard to safety and health,
   – be integrated into all the activities of the undertaking and/or establishment and at all hierarchical levels;
   (b) where he entrusts tasks to a worker, take into consideration the worker's capabilities as regards health and safety;
   (c) ensure that the planning and introduction of new technologies are the subject of consultation with the workers and/or their representatives, as regards the consequences of the choice of equipment, the working conditions and the working environment for the safety and health of workers;

(d) take appropriate steps to ensure that only workers who have received adequate instructions may have access to areas where there is serious and specific danger.

4. Without prejudice to the other provisions of this Directive, where several undertakings share a work place, the employers shall cooperate in implementing the safety, health and occupational hygiene provisions and, taking into account the nature of the activities, shall coordinate their actions in matters of the protection and prevention of occupational risks, and shall inform one another and their respective workers and/or workers' representatives of those risks.

5. Measures related to safety, hygiene and health at work may in no circumstances involve the workers in financial cost.

Article 7 Protective and preventive services

1. Without prejudice to the obligations referred to in Articles 5 and 6, the employer shall designate one or more workers to carry out activities related to the protection and prevention of occupational risks for the undertaking and/or establishment.

2. Designated workers may not be placed at any disadvantage because of their activities related to the protection and prevention of occupational risks.

Designated workers shall be allowed adequate time to enable them to fulfil their obligations arising from this Directive.

3. If such protective and preventive measures cannot be organised for lack of competent personnel in the undertaking and/or establishment, the employer shall enlist competent external services or persons.

4. Where the employer enlists such services or persons, he shall inform them of the factors known to affect, or suspected of affecting, the safety and health of the workers and they must have access to the information referred to in Article 10(2).

5. In all cases:
   - the workers designated must have the necessary capabilities and the necessary means,
   - the external services or persons consulted must have the necessary aptitudes and the necessary personal and professional means, and
   - the workers designated and the external services or persons consulted must be sufficient in number

to deal with the organisation of protective and preventive measures, taking into account the size of the undertaking and/or establishment and/or the hazards to which the workers are exposed and their distribution throughout the entire undertaking and/or establishment.

6. The protection from, and prevention of, the health and safety risks which form the subject of this Article shall be the responsibility of one or more workers, of one service or of separate services whether from inside or outside the undertaking and/or establishment.

The worker(s) and/or agency(ies) must work together whenever necessary.

7. Member States may define, in the light of the nature of the activities and size of the undertakings, the categories of undertakings in which the employer, provided he is competent, may himself take responsibility for the measures referred to in paragraph 1.

8. Member States shall define the necessary capabilities and aptitudes referred to in paragraph 5. They may determine the sufficient number referred to in paragraph 5.

Article 8 First aid, fire-fighting and evacuation of workers, serious and imminent danger

1. The employer shall:
   - take the necessary measures for first aid, fire-fighting and evacuation of workers, adapted to the nature of the activities and the size of the undertaking and/or establishment and taking into account other persons present,
   - arrange any necessary contacts with external services, particularly as regards first aid, emergency medical care, rescue work and fire-fighting.

2. Pursuant to paragraph 1, the employer shall, *inter alia*, for first aid, fire-fighting and the evacuation of workers, designate the workers required to implement such measures.

The number of such workers, their training and the equipment available to them shall be adequate, taking account of the size and/or specific hazards of the undertaking and/or establishment.

3. The employer shall:

(a) as soon as possible, inform all workers who are, or may be, exposed to serious and imminent danger of the risk involved and of the steps taken or to be taken as regards protection;

(b) take action and give instructions to enable workers in the event of serious, imminent and unavoidable danger to stop work and/or immediately to leave the work place and proceed to a place of safety;

(c) save in exceptional cases for reasons duly substantiated, refrain from asking workers to resume work in a working situation where there is still a serious and imminent danger.

4. Workers who, in the event of serious, imminent and unavoidable danger, leave their workstation and/or a dangerous area may not be placed at any disadvantage because of their action and must be protected against any harmful and unjustified consequences, in accordance with national laws and/or practices.

5. The employer shall ensure that all workers are able, in the event of serious and imminent danger to their own safety and/or that of other persons, and where the immediate superior responsible cannot be contacted, to take the appropriate steps in the light of their knowledge and the technical means at their disposal, to avoid the consequences of such danger.

Their actions shall not place them at any disadvantage, unless they acted carelessly or there was negligence on their part.

Article 9   Various obligations on employers

1. The employer shall:

(a) be in possession of an assessment of the risks to safety and health at work, including those facing groups of workers exposed to particular risks;

(b) decide on the protective measures to be taken and, if necessary, the protective equipment to be used;

(c) keep a list of occupational accidents resulting in a worker being unfit for work for more than three working days;

(d) draw up, for the responsible authorities and in accordance with national laws and/or practices, reports on occupational accidents suffered by his workers.

2. Member States shall define, in the light of the nature of the activities and size of the undertakings, the obligations to be met by the different categories of undertakings in respect of the drawing-up of the documents provided for in paragraph 1(a) and (b) and when preparing the documents provided for in paragraph 1(c) and (d).

Article 10   Worker information

1. The employer shall take appropriate measures so that workers and/or their representatives in the undertaking and/or establishment receive, in accordance with national laws and/or practices which may take account, *inter alia*, of the size of the undertaking and/or establishment, all the necessary information concerning:

(a) the safety and health risks and protective and preventive measures and activities in respect of both the undertaking and/or establishment in general and each type of workstation and/or job;

(b) the measures taken pursuant to Article 8(2).

2. The employer shall take appropriate measures so that employers of workers from any outside undertakings and/or establishments engaged in work in his undertaking and/or establishment receive, in accordance with national laws and/or practices, adequate information concerning the points referred to in paragraph 1(a) and (b) which is to be provided to the workers in question.

3. The employer shall take appropriate measures so that workers with specific functions in protecting the safety and health of workers, and workers' representatives with specific responsibility

for the safety and health of workers shall have access, to carry out their functions and in accordance with national laws and/or practices, to:

 (a) the risk assessment and protective measures referred to in Article 9(1)(a) and (b);

 (b) the list and reports referred to in Article 9(1)(c) and (d);

 (c) the information yielded by protective and preventive measures, inspection agencies and bodies responsible for safety and health.

Article 11   Consultation and participation of workers

1. Employers shall consult workers and/or their representatives and allow them to take part in discussions on all questions relating to safety and health at work.

 (a) This presupposes:

  – the consultation of workers,

  – the right of workers and/or their representatives to make proposals,

  – balanced participation in accordance with national laws and/or practices.

2. Workers or workers' representatives with specific responsibility for the safety and health of workers shall take part in a balanced way, in accordance with national laws and/or practices, or shall be consulted in advance and in good time by the employer with regard to:

 (a) any measure which may substantially affect safety and health;

 (b) the designation of workers referred to in Articles 7(1) and 8(2) and the activities referred to in Article 7(1);

 (c) the information referred to in Articles 9(1) and 10;

 (d) the enlistment, where appropriate, of the competent services or persons outside the undertaking and/or establishment, as referred to in Article 7(3);

 (e) the planning and organisation of the training referred to in Article 12.

3. Workers' representatives with specific responsibility for the safety and health of workers shall have the right to ask the employer to take appropriate measures and to submit proposals to him to that end to mitigate hazards for workers and/or to remove sources of danger.

4. The workers referred to in paragraph 2 and the workers' representatives referred to in paragraphs 2 and 3 may not be placed at a disadvantage because of their respective activities referred to in paragraphs 2 and 3.

5. Employers must allow workers' representatives with specific responsibility for the safety and health of workers adequate time off work, without loss of pay, and provide them with the necessary means to enable such representatives to exercise their rights and functions deriving from this Directive.

6. Workers and/or their representatives are entitled to appeal, in accordance with national law and/or practice, to the authority responsible for safety and health protection at work if they consider that the measures taken and the means employed by the employer are inadequate for the purposes of ensuring safety and health at work.

Workers' representatives must be given the opportunity to submit their observations during inspection visits by the competent authority.

Article 12   Training of workers

1. The employer shall ensure that each worker receives adequate safety and health training, in particular in the form of information and instructions specific to his workstation or job:

 – on recruitment,

 – in the event of a transfer or a change of job,

 – in the event of the introduction of new work equipment or a change in equipment,

 – in the event of the introduction of any new technology.

The training shall be:

 – adapted to take account of new or changed risks, and

 – repeated periodically if necessary.

2. The employer shall ensure that workers from outside undertakings and/or establishments engaged in work in his undertaking and/or establishment have in fact received appropriate instructions regarding health and safety risks during their activities in his undertaking and/or establishment.

3. Workers' representatives with a specific role in protecting the safety and health of workers shall be entitled to appropriate training.

4. The training referred to in paragraphs 1 and 3 may not be at the workers' expense or at that of the workers' representatives.

The training referred to in paragraph 1 must take place during working hours.

The training referred to in paragraph 3 must take place during working hours or in accordance with national practice either within or outside the undertaking and/or the establishment.

Section III Workers' obligations

Article 13

1. It shall be the responsibility of each worker to take care as far as possible of his own safety and health and that of other persons affected by his acts or omissions at work in accordance with his training and the instructions given by his employer.

2. To this end, workers must in particular, in accordance with their training and the instructions given by their employer:

    (a) make correct use of machinery, apparatus, tools, dangerous substances, transport equipment and other means of production;

    (b) make correct use of the personal protective equipment supplied to them and, after use, return it to its proper place;

    (c) refrain from disconnecting, changing or removing arbitrarily safety devices fitted, e.g., to machinery, apparatus, tools, plant and buildings, and use such safety devices correctly;

    (d) immediately inform the employer and/or the workers with specific responsibility for the safety and health of workers of any work situation they have reasonable grounds for considering represents a serious and immediate danger to safety and health and of any shortcomings in the protection arrangements;

    (e) cooperate, in accordance with national practice, with the employer and/or workers with specific responsibility for the safety and health of workers, for as long as may be necessary to enable any tasks or requirements imposed by the competent authority to protect the safety and health of workers at work to be carried out;

    (f) cooperate, in accordance with national practice, with the employer and/or workers with specific responsibility for the safety and health of workers, for as long as may be necessary to enable the employer to ensure that the working environment and working conditions are safe and pose no risk to safety and health within their field of activity.

Section IV Miscellaneous provisions

Article 14   Health surveillance

1. To ensure that workers receive health surveillance appropriate to the health and safety risks they incur at work, measures shall be introduced in accordance with national law and/or practices.

2. The measures referred to in paragraph 1 shall be such that each worker, if he so wishes, may receive health surveillance at regular intervals.

3. Health surveillance may be provided as part of a national health system.

Article 15   Risk groups

Particularly sensitive risk groups must be protected against the dangers which specifically affect them.

Article 16   Individual Directives—amendments—general scope of this Directive

1. The Council, acting on a proposal from the Commission based on Article 118a of the Treaty, shall adopt individual Directives, *inter alia*, in the areas listed in the Annex.

2. This Directive and, without prejudice to the procedure referred to in Article 17 concerning technical adjustments, the individual Directives may be amended in accordance with the procedure provided for in Article 118a of the Treaty.

3. The provisions of this Directive shall apply in full to all the areas covered by the individual Directives, without prejudice to more stringent and/or specific provisions contained in these individual Directives.

Article 17   Committee procedure

1. The Commission shall be assisted by a committee to make purely technical adjustments to the individual directives provided for in Article 16(1) in order to take account of:
  - (a) the adoption of directives in the field of technical harmonisation and standardisation;
  - (b) technical progress, changes in international regulations or specifications and new findings.

Those measures, designed to amend non-essential elements of the individual directives, shall be adopted in accordance with the regulatory procedure with scrutiny referred to in paragraph 2. On imperative grounds of urgency, the Commission may have recourse to the urgency procedure referred to in paragraph 3.

2. Where reference is made to this paragraph, Article 5a(1) to (4) and Article 7 of Decision 1999/468/EC shall apply, having regard to the provisions of Article 8 thereof.

3. Where reference is made to this paragraph, Article 5a(1), (2), (4) and (6) and Article 7 of Decision 1999/468 EC shall apply, having regard to the provisions of Article 8 thereof.

Article 17a   Implementation reports

1. Every five years, the Member States shall submit a single report to the Commission on the practical implementation of this Directive and individual Directives within the meaning of Article 16(1), indicating the points of view of the social partners. The report shall assess the various points related to the practical implementation of the different Directives and, where appropriate and available, provide data disaggregated by gender.

2. The structure of the report, together with a questionnaire specifying its content, shall be defined by the Commission, in cooperation with the Advisory Committee on Safety and Health at Work.

The report shall include a general part on the provisions of this Directive relating to the common principles and points applicable to all of the Directives referred to in paragraph 1.

To complement the general part, specific chapters shall deal with implementation of the particular aspects of each Directive, including specific indicators, where available.

3. The Commission shall submit the structure of the report, together with the above-mentioned questionnaire specifying its content, to the Member States at least six months before the end of the period covered by the report. The report shall be transmitted to the Commission within 12 months of the end of the five-year period that it covers.

4. Using these reports as a basis, the Commission shall evaluate the implementation of the Directives concerned in terms of their relevance, of research and of new scientific knowledge in the various fields in question. It shall, within 36 months of the end of the five-year period, inform the European Parliament, the Council, the European Economic and Social Committee and the Advisory Committee on Safety and Health at Work of the results of this evaluation and, if necessary, of any initiatives to improve the operation of the regulatory framework.

5. The first report shall cover the period 2007 to 2012.

Article 18   Final provisions

1. Member States shall bring into force the laws, regulations and administrative provisions necessary to comply with this Directive by 31 December 1992. They shall forthwith inform the Commission thereof.

2. Member States shall communicate to the Commission the texts of the provisions of national law which they have already adopted or adopt in the field covered by this Directive.

Article 19

This Directive is addressed to the Member States.

Done at Luxembourg, 12 June 1989.
(Signature omitted.)

Annex

List of areas referred to in Article 16(1) Work places[1]
- Work equipment
- Personal protective equipment
- Work with visual display units
- Handling of heavy loads involving risk of back injury
- Temporary or mobile work sites[2]
- Fisheries and agriculture

Council Directive 92/85/EEC of 19 October 1992 on the introduction of measures to encourage improvements in the safety and health at work of pregnant workers and workers who have recently given birth or are breastfeeding (tenth individual Directive within the meaning of Article 16(1) of Directive 89/391/EEC)*

[OJ 1992 L348/1]

The Council of the European Communities,

Having regard to the Treaty establishing the European Economic Community, and in particular Article 118a thereof,

Having regard to the proposal from the Commission, drawn up after consultation with the Advisory Committee on Safety, Hygiene and Health Protection at work,[1]

In cooperation with the European Parliament,[2]

Having regard to the opinion of the Economic and Social Committee,[3]

Whereas Article 118a of the Treaty provides that the Council shall adopt, by means of directives, minimum requirements for encouraging improvements, especially in the working environment, to protect the safety and health of workers;

Whereas this Directive does not justify any reduction in levels of protection already achieved in individual Member States, the Member States being committed, under the Treaty, to encouraging improvements in conditions in this area and to harmonising conditions while maintaining the improvements made;

Whereas, under the terms of Article 118a of the Treaty, the said directives are to avoid imposing administrative, financial and legal constraints in a way which would hold back the creation and development of small and medium-sized undertakings;

Whereas, pursuant to Decision 74/325/EEC,[4] as last amended by the 1985 Act of Accession, the Advisory Committee on Safety, Hygiene and Health protection at Work is consulted by the Commission on the drafting of proposals in this field;

Whereas the Community Charter of the fundamental social rights of workers, adopted at the Strasbourg European Council on 9 December 1989 by the Heads of State or Government of 11 Member States, lays down, in paragraph 19 in particular, that:

---

[1] Council Directive of 19 October 1992 (92/85/EEC) [No L 348/1] in the area of pregnant workers and workers who have recently given birth or are breastfeeding.

[2] Council Directive of 24 June 1992 (92/57/EEC) [No L 245/6] implementing minimum health and safety requirements in this area.

* **Editor's Note:** As amended by Directive 2007/30 (OJ 2007 L165/21) and Directive 2014/27 (OJ 2014 L65/7).

[1] OJ No C 281, 9 November 1990, p. 3 and OJ No C 25 1 February 1991, p. 9.

[2] OJ No C 19, 28 January 1992, p. 177 and OJ No C 150, 15 June 1992, p. 99.

[3] OJ No C 41, 18 February 1991, p. 29.

[4] OJ No L 185, 9 July 1974, p. 15.

'Every worker must enjoy satisfactory health and safety conditions in his working environment. Appropriate measures must be taken in order to achieve further harmonisation of conditions in this area while maintaining the improvements made';

Whereas the Commission, in its action programme for the implementation of the Community Charter of the fundamental social rights of workers, has included among its aims the adoption by the Council of a Directive on the protection of pregnant women at work;

Whereas Article 15 of Council Directive 89/391/EEC of 12 June 1989 on the introduction of measures to encourage improvements in the safety and health of workers at work[5] provides that particularly sensitive risk groups must be protected against the dangers which specifically affect them;

Whereas pregnant workers, workers who have recently given birth or who are breastfeeding must be considered a specific risk group in many respects, measures must be taken with regard to their safety and health;

Whereas the protection of the safety and health of pregnant workers, workers who have recently given birth or workers who are breastfeeding should not treat women on the labour market unfavourably nor work to the detriment of directives concerning equal treatment for men and women;

Whereas some types of activities may pose a specific risk, for pregnant workers, workers who have recently given birth or workers who are breastfeeding, of exposure to dangerous agents, processes or working conditions; whereas such risks must therefore be assessed and the result of such assessment communicated to female workers and/or their representatives;

Whereas, further, should the result of this assessment reveal the existence of a risk to the safety or health of the female worker, provision must be made for such worker to be protected;

Whereas pregnant workers and workers who are breastfeeding must not engage in activities which have been assessed as revealing a risk of exposure, jeopardizing safety and health, to certain particularly dangerous agents or working conditions;

Whereas provision should be made for pregnant workers, workers who have recently given birth or workers who are breastfeeding not to be required to work at night where such provision is necessary from the point of view of their safety and health;

Whereas the vulnerability of pregnant workers, workers who have recently given birth or who are breastfeeding makes it necessary for them to be granted the right to maternity leave of at least 14 continuous weeks, allocated before and/or after confinement, and renders necessary the compulsory nature of maternity leave of at least two weeks, allocated before and/or after confinement;

Whereas the risk of dismissal for reasons associated with their condition may have harmful effects on the physical and mental state of pregnant workers, workers who have recently given birth or who are breastfeeding; whereas provision should be made for such dismissal to be prohibited;

Whereas measures for the organisation of work concerning the protection of the health of pregnant workers, workers who have recently given birth or workers who are breastfeeding would serve no purpose unless accompanied by the maintenance of rights linked to the employment contract, including maintenance of payment and/or entitlement to an adequate allowance;

Whereas, moreover, provision concerning maternity leave would also serve no purpose unless accompanied by the maintenance of rights linked to the employment contract and/or entitlement to an adequate allowance;

Whereas the concept of an adequate allowance in the case of maternity leave must be regarded as a technical point of reference with a view to fixing the minimum level of protection and should in no circumstances be interpreted as suggesting an analogy between pregnancy and illness,

HAS ADOPTED THIS DIRECTIVE:

Section I Purpose and definitions

Article 1 Purpose

1. The purpose of this Directive, which is the tenth individual Directive within the meaning of Article 16(1) of Directive 89/391/EEC, is to implement measures to encourage improvements in the

[5] OJ No L183, 29 June 1989, p. 1.

safety and health at work of pregnant workers and workers who have recently given birth or who are breastfeeding.

2. The provisions of Directive 89/391/EEC, except for Article 2(2) thereof, shall apply in full to the whole area covered by paragraph 1, without prejudice to any more stringent and/or specific provisions contained in this Directive.

3. This Directive may not have the effect of reducing the level of protection afforded to pregnant workers, workers who have recently given birth or who are breastfeeding as compared with the situation which exists in each Member State on the date on which this Directive is adopted.

Article 2   Definitions

For the purposes of this Directive:

   (a) *pregnant worker* shall mean a pregnant worker who informs her employer of her condition, in accordance with national legislation and/or national practice;

   (b) *worker who has recently given birth* shall mean a worker who has recently given birth within the meaning of national legislation and/or national practice and who informs her employer of her condition, in accordance with that legislation and/or practice;

   (c) *worker who is breastfeeding* shall mean a worker who is breastfeeding within the meaning of national legislation and/or national practice and who informs her employer of her condition, in accordance with that legislation and/or practice.

Section II General provisions

Article 3   Guidelines

1. In consultation with the Member States and assisted by the Advisory Committee on Safety, Hygiene and Health Protection at Work, the Commission shall draw up guidelines on the assessment of the chemical, physical and biological agents and industrial processes considered hazardous for the safety or health of workers within the meaning of Article 2.

The guidelines referred to in the first sub-paragraph shall also cover movements and postures, mental and physical fatigue and other types of physical and mental stress connected with the work done by workers within the meaning of Article 2.

2. The purpose of the guidelines referred to in paragraph 1 is to serve as a basis for the assessment referred to in Article 4(1).

To this end, Member States shall bring these guidelines to the attention of all employers and all female workers and/or their representatives in the respective Member State.

Article 4   Assessment and information

1. For all activities liable to involve a specific risk of exposure to the agents, processes or working conditions of which a non-exhaustive list is given in Annex I, the employer shall assess the nature, degree and duration of exposure, in the undertaking and/or establishment concerned, of workers within the meaning of Article 2, either directly or by way of the protective and preventive services referred to in Article 7 of Directive 89/391/EEC, in order to:

   – assess any risks to the safety or health and any possible effect on the pregnancy or breastfeeding of workers within the meaning of Article 2,

   – decide what measures should be taken.

2. Without prejudice to Article 10 of Directive 89/391/EEC, workers within the meaning of Article 2 and workers likely to be in one of the situations referred to in Article 2 in the undertaking and/or establishment concerned and/or their representatives shall be informed of the results of the assessment referred to in paragraph 1 and of all measures to be taken concerning health and safety at work.

Article 5   Action further to the results of the assessment

1. Without prejudice to Article 6 of Directive 89/391/EEC, if the results of the assessment referred to in Article 4(1) reveal risk to the safety or health or an effect on the pregnancy or

breastfeeding of a worker within the meaning of Article 2, the employer shall take the necessary measures to ensure that, by temporarily adjusting the working conditions and/or the working hours of the worker concerned, the exposure of that worker to such risks is avoided.

2. If the adjustment of her working conditions and/or working hours is not technically and/or objectively feasible, or cannot reasonably be required on duly substantiated grounds, the employer shall take the necessary measures to move the worker concerned to another job.

3. If moving her to another job is not technically and/or objectively feasible or cannot reasonably be required on duly substantiated grounds, the worker concerned shall be granted leave in accordance with national legislation and/or national practice for the whole of the period necessary to protect her safety or health.

4. The provisions of this Article shall apply mutatis mutandis to the case where a worker pursuing an activity which is forbidden pursuant to Article 6 becomes pregnant or starts breastfeeding and informs her employer thereof.

Article 6   Cases in which exposure is prohibited

In addition to the general provisions concerning the protection of workers, in particular those relating to the limit values for occupational exposure:

1. pregnant workers within the meaning of Article 2(a) may under no circumstances be obliged to perform duties for which the assessment has revealed a risk of exposure, which would jeopardise safety or health, to the agents and working conditions listed in Annex II, Section A;

2. workers who are breastfeeding, within the meaning of Article 2(c), may under no circumstances be obliged to perform duties for which the assessment has revealed a risk of exposure, which would jeopardise safety or health, to the agents and working conditions listed in Annex II, Section B.

Article 7   Night work

1. Member States shall take the necessary measures to ensure that workers referred to in Article 2 are not obliged to perform night work during their pregnancy and for a period following childbirth which shall be determined by the national authority competent for safety and health, subject to submission, in accordance with the procedures laid down by the Member States, of a medical certificate stating that this is necessary for the safety or health of the worker concerned.

2. The measures referred to in paragraph 1 must entail the possibility, in accordance with national legislation and/or national practice, of:

    (a) transfer to daytime work; or

    (b) leave from work or extension of maternity leave where such a transfer is not technically and/or objectively feasible or cannot reasonably be required on duly substantiated grounds.

Article 8   Maternity leave

1. Member States shall take the necessary measures to ensure that workers within the meaning of Article 2 are entitled to a continuous period of maternity leave of at least 14 weeks allocated before and/or after confinement in accordance with national legislation and/or practice.

2. The maternity leave stipulated in paragraph 1 must include compulsory maternity leave of at least two weeks allocated before and/or after confinement in accordance with national legislation and/or practice.

Article 9   Time off for ante-natal examinations

Member States shall take the necessary measures to ensure that pregnant workers within the meaning of Article 2(a) are entitled to, in accordance with national legislation and/or practice, time off, without loss of pay, in order to attend ante-natal examinations, if such examinations have to take place during working hours.

Article 10   Prohibition of dismissal

In order to guarantee workers, within the meaning of Article 2, the exercise of their health and safety protection rights as recognised under this Article, it will be provided that:

1. Member States shall take the necessary measures to prohibit the dismissal of workers, within the meaning of Article 2, during the period from the beginning of their pregnancy to the end of the maternity leave referred to in Article 8(1), save in exceptional cases not connected with their condition which are permitted under national legislation and/or practice and, where applicable, provided that the competent authority has given its consent;

2. if a worker, within the meaning of Article 2, is dismissed during the period referred to in point 1, the employer must cite duly substantiated grounds for her dismissal in writing;

3. Member States shall take the necessary measures to protect workers, within the meaning of Article 2, from consequences of dismissal which is unlawful by virtue of point 1.

Article 11   Employment rights

In order to guarantee workers within the meaning of Article 2 the exercise of their health and safety protection rights as recognised in this Article, it shall be provided that:

1. in the cases referred to in Articles 5, 6 and 7, the employment rights relating to the employment contract, including the maintenance of a payment to, and/or entitlement to an adequate allowance for, workers within the meaning of Article 2, must be ensured in accordance with national legislation and/or national practice;

2. in the case referred to in Article 8, the following must be ensured:

   (a) the rights connected with the employment contract of workers within the meaning of Article 2, other than those referred to in point (b) below;

   (b) maintenance of a payment to, and/or entitlement to an adequate allowance for, workers within the meaning of Article 2;

3. the allowance referred to in point 2(b) shall be deemed adequate if it guarantees income at least equivalent to that which the worker concerned would receive in the event of a break in her activities on grounds connected with her state of health, subject to any ceiling laid down under national legislation;

4. Member States may make entitlement to pay or the allowance referred to in points 1 and 2(b) conditional upon the worker concerned fulfilling the conditions of eligibility for such benefits laid down under national legislation.

These conditions may under no circumstances provide for periods of previous employment in excess of 12 months immediately prior to the presumed date of confinement.

Article 12   Defence of rights

Member States shall introduce into their national legal systems such measures as are necessary to enable all workers who should themselves wronged by failure to comply with the obligations arising from the Directive to pursue their claims by judicial process (and/or, in accordance with national laws and/or practice) by recourse to other competent authorities.

Article 13   Amendments to Annex I

The Commission is empowered to adopt delegated acts in accordance with Article 13a to make strictly technical amendments to Annex I, in order to take account of technical progress, changes in international regulations or specifications and new findings.

Where, in duly justified and exceptional cases involving imminent, direct and serious risks to workers' and other persons' physical health and safety, imperative grounds of urgency require action in a very short timeframe, the procedure provided for in Article 13b shall apply to delegated acts adopted pursuant to this Article.

Article 13a   Exercise of the delegation

1. The power to adopt delegated acts is conferred on the Commission subject to the conditions laid down in this Article.

2. The power to adopt delegated acts referred to in Article 13 shall be conferred on the Commission for a period of five years from 26 July 2019. The Commission shall draw up a report in

respect of the delegation of power not later than nine months before the end of the five-year period. The delegation of power shall be tacitly extended for periods of an identical duration, unless the European Parliament or the Council opposes such extension not later than three months before the end of each period.

3. The delegation of power referred to in Article 13 may be revoked at any time by the European Parliament or by the Council. A decision to revoke shall put an end to the delegation of the power specified in that decision. It shall take effect the day following the publication of the decision in the *Official Journal of the European Union* or at a later date specified therein. It shall not affect the validity of any delegated acts already in force.

4. Before adopting a delegated act, the Commission shall consult experts designated by each Member State in accordance with the principles laid down in the Interinstitutional Agreement of 13 April 2016 on Better Law-Making[6].

5. As soon as it adopts a delegated act, the Commission shall notify it simultaneously to the European Parliament and to the Council.

6. A delegated act adopted pursuant to Article 13 shall enter into force only if no objection has been expressed either by the European Parliament or the Council within a period of two months of notification of that act to the European Parliament and the Council or if, before the expiry of that period, the European Parliament and the Council have both informed the Commission that they will not object. That period shall be extended by two months at the initiative of the European Parliament or of the Council.

Article 13b   Urgency procedure

1. Delegated acts adopted under this Article shall enter into force without delay and shall apply as long as no objection is expressed in accordance with paragraph 2. The notification of a delegated act to the European Parliament and to the Council shall state the reasons for the use of the urgency procedure.

2. Either the European Parliament or the Council may object to a delegated act in accordance with the procedure referred to in Article 13a(6). In such a case, the Commission shall repeal the act immediately following the notification of the decision to object by the European Parliament or by the Council.

Article 14   Final provisions

1. Member States shall bring into force the laws, regulations and administrative provisions necessary to comply with this Directive not later than two years after the adoption thereof or ensure, at the latest two years after adoption of this Directive, that the two sides of industry introduce the requisite provisions by means of collective agreements, with Member States being required to make all the necessary provisions to enable them at all times to guarantee the results laid down by this Directive. They shall forthwith inform the Commission thereof.

2. When Member States adopt the measures referred to in paragraph 1, they shall contain a reference of this Directive or shall be accompanied by such reference on the occasion of their official publication. The methods of making such a reference shall be laid down by the Member States.

3. Member States shall communicate to the Commission the texts of the essential provisions of national law which they have already adopted or adopt in the field governed by this Directive.

Article 15

This Directive is addressed to the Member States.

Done at Luxembourg, 19 October 1992.

---

[6] OJ L 123, 12.5.2016, p. 1.

Annex I

*Non-exhaustive list of agents, processes and working conditions
referred to in Article 4(1)*

A. Agents

1. *Physical agents* where these are regarded as agents causing foetal lesions and/or likely to disrupt placental attachment, and in particular:

    (a) shocks, vibration or movement;

    (b) handling of loads entailing risks, particularly of a dorsolumbar nature;

    (c) noise;

    (d) ionizing radiation;

    (e) non-ionizing radiation;

    (f) extremes of cold or heat;

    (g) movements and postures, travelling—either inside or outside the establishment—mental and physical fatigue and other physical burdens connected with the activity of the worker within the meaning of Article 2 of the Directive.

2. *Biological agents*

Biological agents of risk groups 2, 3 and 4 within the meaning of points 2, 3 and 4 of second paragraph of Article 2 of Directive 2000/54/EC of the European Parliament and of the Council,[7] in so far as it is known that such agents or the therapeutic measures necessitated by them endanger the health of pregnant women and the unborn child, and in so far as they do not yet appear in Annex II.

3. *Chemical agents*

The following chemical agents in so far as it is known that they endanger the health of pregnant women and the unborn child and in so far as they do not yet appear in Annex II:

    (a) substances and mixtures which meet the criteria for classification under Regulation (EC) No 1272/2008 of the European Parliament and of the Council[8] in one or more of the following hazard classes and hazard categories with one or more of the following hazard statements, in so far as they do not yet appear in Annex II;

      – germ cell mutagenicity, category 1A, 1B or 2 (H340, H341);

      – carcinogenicity, category 1A, 1B or 2 (H350, H350i, H351);

      – reproductive toxicity, category 1A, 1B or 2 or the additional category for effects on or via lactation (H360, H360D, H360FD, H360Fd, H360Df, H361, H361d, H361fd, H362);

      – specific target organ toxicity after single exposure, category 1 or 2 (H370, H371).

    (b) chemical agents in Annex I to Directive 2004/37/EC of the European Parliament and of the Council;

    (c) mercury and mercury derivatives;

    (d) antimitotic drugs;

    (e) carbon monoxide;

    (f) chemical agents of known and dangerous percutaneous absorption.

B. Processes

Industrial processes listed in Annex I to Directive 2004/37/EEC.

C. Working conditions

Underground mining work.

---

[7] Directive 2000/54/EC of the European Parliament and of the Council of 18 September 2000 on the protection of workers from risks related to exposure to biological agents at work (seventh individual directive within the meaning of Article 16(1) of Directive 89/391/EEC) (OJ L 262, 17.10.2000, p. 21).

[8] Regulation (EC) No 1272/2008 of the European Parliament and of the Council of 16 December 2008 on classification, labelling and packaging of substances and mixtures, amending and repealing Directives 67/548/EEC and 1999/45/EC, and amending Regulation (EC) No 1907/2006 (OJ L 353, 31.12.2008, p. 1).

Annex II

Non-exhaustive list of agents and working conditions referred to in Article 6

A. **Pregnant workers within the meaning of Article 2(a)**

1. *Agents*
   (a) Physical agents
       Work in hyperbaric atmosphere, e.g., pressurised enclosures and underwater diving.
   (b) Biological agents
       The following biological agents:
       – toxoplasma,
       – rubella virus,
       unless the pregnant workers are proved to be adequately protected against such agents by immunisation.
   (c) Chemical agents
       Lead and lead derivatives in so far as these agents are capable of being absorbed by the human organism.

2. *Working conditions*
   Underground mining work.

B. **Workers who are breastfeeding within the meaning of Article 2(c)**

1. *Agents*
   (a) Chemical agents
       Lead and lead derivatives in so far as these agents are capable of being absorbed by the human organism.

2. *Working conditions*
   Underground mining work.

Council Directive 94/33/EC of 22 June 1994 on the protection of young people at work*

[OJ 1994 L216/12]

THE COUNCIL OF THE EUROPEAN UNION,

Having regard to the Treaty establishing the European Community, and in particular Article 118a thereof,

Having regard to the proposal from the Commission,[1]

Having regard to the opinion of the Economic and Social Committee,[2]

Acting in accordance with the procedure referred to in Article 189c of the Treaty,[3]

Whereas Article 118a of the Treaty provides that the Council shall adopt, by means of directives, minimum requirements to encourage improvements, especially in the working environment, as regards the health and safety of workers;

---

* **Editor's Note:** As amended by Directive 2007/30 (OJ 2007 L165/21 (and Directive 2014/27 (OJ 2014 L65/7).

[1] OJ No C 84, 4.4.1992, p. 7.

[2] OJ No C 313, 30.11.1992, p. 70.

[3] Opinion of the European Parliament of 17 December 1992 (OJ No C 21, 25.1.1993, p. 167). Council Common Position of 23 November 1993 (not yet published in the Official Journal) and Decision of the European Parliament of 9 March 1994 (OJ No C 91, 28.3.1994, p. 89).

Whereas, under that Article, such directives must avoid imposing administrative, financial and legal constraints in a way which would hold back the creation and development of small and medium-sized undertakings;

Whereas points 20 and 22 of the Community Charter of the Fundamental Social Rights of Workers, adopted by the European Council in Strasbourg on 9 December 1989, state that:

'20. Without prejudice to such rules as may be more favourable to young people, in particular those ensuring their preparation for work through vocational training, and subject to derogations limited to certain light work, the minimum employment age must not be lower than the minimum school-leaving age and, in any case, not lower than 15 years;

22. Appropriate measures must be taken to adjust labour regulations applicable to young workers so that their specific development and vocational training and access to employment needs are met.

The duration of work must, in particular, be limited—without it being possible to circumvent this limitation through recourse to overtime—and night work prohibited in the case of workers of under eighteen years of age, save in the case of certain jobs laid down in national legislation or regulations.';

Whereas account should be taken of the principles of the International Labour Organisation regarding the protection of young people at work, including those relating to the minimum age for access to employment or work;

Whereas, in this Resolution on child labour,[4] the European Parliament summarised the various aspects of work by young people and stressed its effects on their health, safety and physical and intellectual development, and pointed to the need to adopt a Directive harmonising national legislation in the field;

Whereas Article 15 of Council Directive 89/391/EEC of 12 June 1989 on the introduction of measures to encourage improvements in the safety and health of workers at work[5] provides that particularly sensitive risk groups must be protected against the dangers which specifically affect them;

Whereas children and adolescents must be considered specific risk groups, and measures must be taken with regard to their safety and health;

Whereas the vulnerability of children calls for Member States to prohibit their employment and ensure that the minimum working or employment age is not lower than the minimum age at which compulsory schooling as imposed by national law ends or 15 years in any event; whereas derogations from the prohibition on child labour may be admitted only in special cases and under the conditions stipulated in this Directive;

Whereas, under no circumstances, may such derogations be detrimental to regular school attendance or prevent children benefiting fully from their education;

Whereas, in view of the nature of the transition from childhood to adult life, work by adolescents should be strictly regulated and protected;

Whereas every employer should guarantee young people working conditions appropriate to their age;

Whereas employers should implement the measures necessary to protect the safety and health of young people on the basis of an assessment of work-related hazards to the young;

Whereas Member States should protect young people against any specific risks arising from their lack of experience, absence of awareness of existing or potential risks, or from their immaturity;

Whereas Member States should therefore prohibit the employment of young people for the work specified by this Directive;

Whereas the adoption of specific minimal requirements in respect of the organisation of working time is likely to improve working conditions for young people;

Whereas the maximum working time of young people should be strictly limited and night work by young people should be prohibited, with the exception of certain jobs specified by national legislation or rules;

[4] OJ No C 190, 20.7.1987, p. 44.
[5] OJ No L 183, 29.6.1989, p. 1.

Whereas Member States should take the appropriate measures to ensure that the working time of adolescents receiving school education does not adversely affect their ability to benefit from that education;

Whereas time spent on training by young persons working under a theoretical and/or practical combined work/training scheme or an in-plant work-experience should be counted as working time;

Whereas, in order to ensure the safety and health of young people, the latter should be granted minimum daily, weekly and annual periods of rest and adequate breaks;

Whereas, with respect to the weekly rest period, due account should be taken of the diversity of cultural, ethnic, religious and other factors prevailing in the Member States;

Whereas in particular, it is ultimately for each Member State to decide whether Sunday should be included in the weekly rest period, and if so to what extent;

Whereas appropriate work experience may contribute to the aim of preparing young people for adult working and social life, provided it is ensured that any harm to their safety, health and development is avoided;

Whereas, although derogations from the bans and limitations imposed by this Directive would appear indispensable for certain activities or particular situations, applications thereof must not prejudice the principles underlying the established protection system;

Whereas this Directive constitutes a tangible step towards developing the social dimension of the internal market;

Whereas the application in practice of the system of protection laid down by this Directive will require that Member States implement a system of effective and proportionate measures;

Whereas the implementation of some provisions of this Directive poses particular problems for one Member State with regard to its system of protection for young people at work; whereas that Member State should therefore be allowed to refrain from implementing the relevant provisions for a suitable period,

HAS ADOPTED THIS DIRECTIVE:

Section I

Article 1 Purpose

1. Member States shall take the necessary measures to prohibit work by children. They shall ensure, under the conditions laid down by this Directive, that the minimum working or employment age is not lower than the minimum age at which compulsory full-time schooling as imposed by national law ends or 15 years in any event.

2. Member States ensure that work by adolescents is strictly regulated and protected under the conditions laid down in this Directive.

3. Member States shall ensure in general that employers guarantee that young people have working conditions which suit their age.

They shall ensure that young people are protected against economic exploitation and against any work likely to harm their safety, health or physical, mental, moral or social development or to jeopardise their education.

Article 2 Scope

1. This Directive shall apply to any person under 18 years of age having an employment contract or an employment relationship defined by the law in force in a Member State and/or governed by the law in force in a Member State.

2. Member States may make legislative or regulatory provision for this Directive not to apply, within the limits and under the conditions which they set by legislative or regulatory provision, to occasional work or short-term work involving:

    (a) domestic service in a private household, or

    (b) work regarded as not being harmful, damaging or dangerous to young people in a family undertaking.

Article 3   Definitions

For the purposes of this Directive:

(a) 'young person' shall mean any person under 18 years of age referred to in Article 2(1);

(b) 'child' shall mean any young person of less than 15 years of age or who is still subject to compulsory full-time schooling under national law;

(c) 'adolescent' shall mean any young person of at least 15 years of age but less than 18 years of age who is no longer subject to compulsory full-time schooling under national law;

(d) 'light work' shall mean all work which, on account of the inherent nature of the tasks which it involves and the particular conditions under which they are performed:

(i)   is not likely to be harmful to the safety, health or development of children, and

(ii) is not such as to be harmful to their attendance at school, their participation in vocational guidance or training programmes approved by the competent authority or their capacity to benefit from the instruction received;

(e) 'working time' shall mean any period during which the young person is at work, at the employer's disposal and carrying out his activity or duties in accordance with national legislation and/or practice;

(f) 'rest period' shall mean any period which is not working time.

Article 4   Prohibition of work by children

1. Member States shall adopt the measures necessary to prohibit work by children.

2. Taking into account the objectives set out in Article 1, Member States may make legislative or regulatory provision for the prohibition of work by children not to apply to:

(a) children pursuing the activities set out in Article 5;

(b) children of at least 14 years of age working under a combined work/training scheme or an in-plant work-experience scheme, provided that such work is done in accordance with the conditions laid down by the competent authority;

(c) children of at least 14 years of age performing light work other than that covered by Article 5; light work other than that covered by Article 5 may, however, be performed by children of 13 years of age for a limited number of hours per week in the case of categories of work determined by national legislation.

3. Member States that make use of the opinion referred to in paragraph 2(c) shall determine, subject to the provisions of this Directive, the working conditions relating to the light work in question.

Article 5   Cultural or similar activities

1. The employment of children for the purposes of performance in cultural, artistic, sports or advertising activities shall be subject to prior authorisation to be given by the competent authority in individual cases.

2. Member States shall by legislative or regulatory provision lay down the working conditions for children in the cases referred to in paragraph 1 and the details of the prior authorisation procedure, on condition that the activities:

(i)   are not likely to be harmful to the safety, health or development of children, and

(ii) are not such as to be harmful to their attendance at school, their participation in vocational guidance or training programmes approved by the competent authority or their capacity to benefit from the instruction received.

3. By way of derogation from the procedure laid down in paragraph 1, in the case of children of at least 13 years of age, Member States may authorise, by legislative or regulatory provision, in accordance with conditions which they shall determine, the employment of children for the purposes of performance in cultural, artistic, sports or advertising activities.

4. The Member States which have a specific authorisation system for modelling agencies with regard to the activities of children may retain that system.

Section II

Article 6   General obligations on employers

1. Without prejudice to Article 4(1), the employer shall adopt the measures necessary to protect the safety and health of young people, taking particular account of the specific risks referred to in Article 7(1).

2. The employer shall implement the measures provided for in paragraph 1 on the basis of an assessment of the hazards to young people in connection with their work. The assessment must be made before young people begin work and when there is any major change in working conditions and must pay particular attention to the following points:

    (a) the fitting-out and layout of the workplace and the workstation;

    (b) the nature, degree and duration of exposure to physical, biological and chemical agents;

    (c) the form, range and use of work equipment, in particular agents, machines, apparatus and devices, and the way in which they are handled;

    (d) the arrangement of work processes and operations and the way in which these are combined (organisation of work);

    (e) the level of training and instruction given to young people.

Where this assessment shows that there is a risk to the safety, the physical or mental health or development of young people, an appropriate free assessment and monitoring of their health shall be provided at regular intervals without prejudice to Directive 89/391/EEC. The free health assessment and monitoring may form part of a national health system.

3. The employer shall inform young people of possible risks and of all measures adopted concerning their safety and health.

Furthermore, he shall inform the legal representatives of children of possible risks and of all measures adopted concerning children's safety and health.

4. The employer shall involve the protective and preventive services referred to in Article 7 of Directive 89/391/EEC in the planning, implementation and monitoring of the safety and health conditions applicable to young people.

Article 7   Vulnerability of young people—prohibition of work

1. Member States shall ensure that young people are protected from any specific risks to their safety, health and development which are a consequence of their lack of experience, of absence of awareness of existing or potential risks or of the fact that young people have not yet fully matured.

2. Without prejudice to Article 4(1), Member States shall to this end prohibit the employment of young people for:

    (a) work which is objectively beyond their physical or psychological capacity;

    (b) work involving harmful exposure to agents which are toxic, carcinogenic, cause heritable genetic damage, or harm to the unborn child or which in any other way chronically affect human health;

    (c) work involving harmful exposure to radiation;

    (d) work involving the risk of accidents which it may be assumed cannot be recognised or avoided by young persons owing to their insufficient attention to safety or lack of experience or training; or

    (e) work in which there is a risk to health from extreme cold or heat, or from noise or vibration.

Work which is likely to entail specific risks for young people within the meaning of paragraph 1 includes:

    – work involving harmful exposure to the physical, biological and chemical agents referred to in point I of the Annex, and

    – processes and work referred to in point II of the Annex.

3. Member States may, by legislative or regulatory provision, authorise derogations from paragraph 2 in the case of adolescents where such derogations are indispensable for their vocational

training, provided that protection of their safety and health is ensured by the fact that the work is performed under the supervision of a competent person within the meaning of Article 7 of Directive 89/391/EEC and provided that the protection afforded by that Directive is guaranteed.

Section III

Article 8   Working time

1. Member States which make use of the option in Article 4(2)(b) or (c) shall adopt the measures necessary to limit the working time of children to:

   (a) eight hours a day and 40 hours a week for work performed under a combined work/training scheme or an in-plant work-experience scheme;

   (b) two hours on a school day and 12 hours a week for work performed in term-time outside the hours fixed for school attendance, provided that this is not prohibited by national legislation and/or practice; in no circumstances may the daily working time exceed seven hours; this limit may be raised to eight hours in the case of children who have reached the age of 15;

   (c) seven hours a day and 35 hours a week for work performed during a period of at least a week when school is not operating; these limits may be raised to eight hours a day and 40 hours a week in the case of children who have reached the age of 15;

   (d) seven hours a day and 35 hours a week for light work performed by children no longer subject to compulsory full-time schooling under national law.

2. Member States shall adopt the measures necessary to limit the working time of adolescents to eight hours a day and 40 hours a week.

3. The time spent on training by a young person working under a theoretical and/or practical combined work/training scheme or an in-plant work-experience scheme shall be counted as working time.

4. Where a young person is employed by more than one employer, working days and working time shall be cumulative.

5. Member States may, by legislative or regulatory provision, authorise derogations from paragraph 1(a) and paragraph 2 either by way of exception or where there are objective grounds for so doing. Member States shall, by legislative or regulatory provision, determine the conditions, limits and procedure for implementing such derogations.

Article 9   Night work

1. (a) Member States which make use of the option in Article 4(2)(b) or (c) shall adopt the measures necessary to prohibit work by children between 8 p.m. and 6 a.m.

   (b) Member States shall adopt the measures necessary to prohibit work by adolescents either between 10 p.m. and 6 a.m. or between 11 p.m. and 7 a.m.

2. (a) Member States may, by legislative or regulatory provision, authorise work by adolescents in specific areas of activity during the period in which night work is prohibited as referred to in paragraph 1(b). In that event, Member States shall take appropriate measures to ensure that the adolescent is supervised by an adult where such supervision is necessary for the adolescent's protection.

   (b) If point (a) is applied, work shall continue to be prohibited between midnight and 4 a.m.

However, Member States may, by legislative or regulatory provision, authorise work by adolescents during the period in which night work is prohibited in the following cases, where there are objective grounds for so doing and provided that adolescents are allowed suitable compensatory rest time and that the objectives set out in Article 1 are not called into question:

   – work performed in the shipping or fisheries sectors;

   – work performed in the context of the armed forces or the police;

   – work performed in hospitals or similar establishments;

   – cultural, artistic, sports or advertising activities.

3. Prior to any assignment to night work and at regular intervals thereafter, adolescents shall be entitled to a free assessment of their health and capacities, unless the work they do during the period during which work is prohibited is of an exceptional nature.

Article 10   Rest period

1. (a) Member States which make use of the option in Article 4(2)(b) or (c) shall adopt the measures necessary to ensure that, for each 24-hour period, children are entitled to a minimum rest period of 14 consecutive hours.

   (b) Member States shall adopt the measures necessary to ensure that, for each 24-hour period, adolescents are entitled to a minimum rest period of 12 consecutive hours.

2. Member States shall adopt the measures necessary to ensure that, for each seven-day period:
   - children in respect of whom they have made use of the option in Article 4(2)(b) or (c), and
   - adolescents

are entitled to a minimum rest period of two days, which shall be consecutive if possible. Where justified by technical or organisation reasons, the minimum rest period may be reduced, but may in no circumstances be less than 36 consecutive hours. The minimum rest period referred to in the first and second sub-paragraphs shall in principle include Sunday.

3. Member States may, by legislative or regulatory provision, provide for the minimum rest periods referred to in paragraphs 1 and 2 to be interrupted in the case of activities involving periods of work that are split up over the day or are of short duration.

4. Member States may make legislative or regulatory provision for derogations from paragraph 1(b) and paragraph 2 in respect of adolescents in the following cases, where there are objective grounds for so doing and provided that they are granted appropriate compensatory rest time and that the objectives set out in Article 1 are not called into question:

   (a) work performed in the shipping or fisheries sectors;
   (b) work performed in the context of the armed forces or the police;
   (c) work performed in hospitals or similar establishments;
   (d) work performed in agriculture;
   (e) work performed in the tourism industry or in the hotel, restaurant and café sector;
   (f) activities involving periods of work split up over the day.

Article 11   Annual rest

Member States which make use of the option referred to in Article 4(2)(b) or (c) shall see to it that a period free of any work is included, as far as possible, in the school holidays of children subject to compulsory full-time schooling under national law.

Article 12   Breaks

Member States shall adopt the measures necessary to ensure that, where daily working time is more than four and a half hours, young people are entitled to a break of at least 30 minutes, which shall be consecutive if possible.

Article 13   Work by adolescents in the event of force majeure

Member States may, by legislative or regulatory provision, authorise derogations from Article 8(2), Article 9(1)(b), Article 10(1)(b) and, in the case of adolescents, Article 12, for work in the circumstances referred to in Article 5(4) of Directive 89/391/EEC, provided that such work is of a temporary nature and must be performed immediately, that adult workers are not available and that the adolescents are allowed equivalent compensatory rest time within the following three weeks.

Section IV

Article 14   Measures

Each Member State shall lay down any necessary measures to be applied in the event of failure to comply with the provisions adopted in order to implement this Directive; such measures must be effective and proportionate.

Article 15   Adaptation of the Annex

Adaptations of a strictly technical nature to the Annex in the light of technical progress, changes in international rules or specifications and advances in knowledge in the field covered by this Directive shall be adopted in accordance with the procedure provided for in Article 17 of Directive 89/391/EEC.

Article 16   Non-reducing clause

Without prejudice to the right of Member States to develop, in the light of changing circumstances, different provisions on the protection of young people, as long as the minimum requirements provided for by this Directive are complied with, the implementation of this Directive shall not constitute valid grounds for reducing the general level of protection afforded to young people.

Article 17   Final provisions

1. (a) Member States shall bring into force the laws, regulations and administrative provisions necessary to comply with this Directive not later than 22 June 1996 or ensure, by that date at the latest, that the two sides of industry introduce the requisite provisions by means of collective agreements, with Member States being required to make all the necessary provisions to enable them at all times to guarantee the results laid down by this Directive.

   (b) The United Kingdom may refrain from implementing the first subparagraph of Article 8(1)(b) with regard to the provision relating to the maximum weekly working time, and also Article 8(2) and Article 9(1)(b) and (2) for a period of four years from the date specified in subparagraph (a).

      The Commission shall submit a report on the effects of this provision.

      The Council, acting in accordance with the conditions laid down by the Treaty, shall decide whether this period should be extended.

   (c) Member States shall forthwith inform the Commission thereof.

2. When Member States adopt the measures referred to in paragraph 1, such measures shall contain a reference to this Directive or shall be accompanied by such reference on the occasion of their official publication. The methods of making such reference shall be laid down by Member States.

3. Member States shall communicate to the Commission the texts of the main provisions of national law which they have already adopted or adopt in the field governed by this Directive.

Article 17a   Implementation report

Every five years, the Member States shall submit to the Commission a report on the practical implementation of this Directive in the form of a specific chapter of the single report referred to in Article 17a(1), (2) and (3) of Directive 89/391/EEC, which serves as a basis for the Commission's evaluation, in accordance with Article 17a(4) of that Directive.

Article 18

This Directive is addressed to the Member States.

Done at Luxembourg, 22 June 1994.

Council Directive 97/81/EC of 15 December 1997 concerning the framework agreement on part-time work concluded by UNICE, CEEP and the ETUC*

[OJ 1998 L14/9]

THE COUNCIL OF THE EUROPEAN UNION,

Having regard to the Agreement on social policy annexed to the Protocol (No 14) on social policy, annexed to the Treaty establishing the European Community, and in particular Article 4(2) thereof,

---

* **Editor's Note:** As extended to the UK by Council Directive 98/23/EC.

Having regard to the proposal from the Commission,

(1) Whereas on the basis of the Protocol on social policy annexed to the Treaty establishing the European Community, the Member States, with the exception of the United Kingdom of Great Britain and Northern Ireland (hereinafter referred to as 'the Member States'), wishing to continue along the path laid down in the 1989 Social Charter, have concluded an agreement on social policy;

(2) Whereas management and labour (the social partners) may, in accordance with Article 4(2) of the Agreement on social policy, request jointly that agreements at Community level be implemented by a Council decision on a proposal from the Commission;

(3) Whereas point 7 of the Community Charter of the Fundamental Social Rights of Workers provides, *inter alia*, that 'the completion of the internal market must lead to an improvement in the living and working conditions of workers in the European Community. This process must result from an approximation of these conditions while the improvement is being maintained, as regards in particular... forms of employment other than open-ended contracts, such as fixed-term contracts, part-time working, temporary work and seasonal work';

(4) Whereas the Council has not reached a decision on the proposal for a Directive on certain employment relationships with regard to distortions of competition,[1] as amended,[2] nor on the proposal for a Directive on certain employment relationships with regard to working conditions;[3]

(5) Whereas the conclusions of the Essen European Council stressed the need to take measures to promote employment and equal opportunities for women and men, and called for measures with a view to increasing the employment-intensiveness of growth, in particular by a more flexible organisation of work in a way which fulfils both the wishes of employees and the requirements of competition;

(6) Whereas the Commission, in accordance with Article 3(2) of the Agreement on social policy, has consulted management and labour on the possible direction of Community action with regard to flexible working time and job security;

(7) Whereas the Commission, considering after such consultation that Community action was desirable, once again consulted management and labour at Community level on the substance of the envisaged proposal in accordance with Article 3(3) of the said Agreement;

(8) Whereas the general cross-industry organisations, the Union of Industrial and Employer's Confederations of Europe (UNICE), the European Centre of Enterprises with Public Participation (CEEP) and the European Trade Union Confederation (ETUC) informed the Commission in their joint letter of 19 June 1996 of their desire to initiate the procedure provided for in Article 4 of the Agreement on social policy; whereas they asked the Commission, in a joint letter dated 12 March 1997, for a further three months; whereas the Commission complied with this request;

(9) Whereas the said cross-industry organisations concluded, on 6 June 1997, a Framework Agreement on part-time work; whereas they forwarded to the Commission their joint request to implement this Framework Agreement by a Council decision on a proposal from the Commission, in accordance with Article 4(2) of the said Agreement;

(10) Whereas the Council, in its Resolution of 6 December 1994 on prospects for a European Union social policy: contribution to economic and social convergence in the Union,[4] asked management and labour to make use of the opportunities for concluding agreements, since they are as a rule closer to social reality and to social problems;

(11) Whereas the signatory parties wished to conclude a framework agreement on part-time work setting out the general principles and minimum requirements for part-time working; whereas they have demonstrated their desire to establish a general framework for eliminating discrimination against part-time workers and to contribute to developing the potential for part-time work on a basis which is acceptable for employers and workers alike;

[1] OJ C 224, 8.9.1990, p. 6.
[2] OJ C 305, 5.12.1990, p. 8.
[3] OJ C 224, 8.9.1990, p. 4.
[4] OJ C 368, 23.12.1994, p. 6.

(12) Whereas the social partners wished to give particular attention to part-time work, while at the same time indicating that it was their intention to consider the need for similar agreements for other flexible forms of work;

(13) Whereas, in the conclusions of the Amsterdam European Council, the Heads of State and Government of the European Union strongly welcomed the agreement concluded by the social partners on part-time work;

(14) Whereas the proper instrument for implementing the Framework Agreement is a Directive within the meaning of Article 189 of the Treaty; whereas it therefore binds the Member States as to the result to be achieved, whilst leaving national authorities the choice of form and methods;

(15) Whereas, in accordance with the principles of subsidiarity and proportionality as set out in Article 3(b) of the Treaty, the objectives of this Directive cannot be sufficiently achieved by the Member States and can therefore be better achieved by the Community; whereas this Directive does not go beyond what is necessary for the attainment of those objectives;

(16) Whereas, with regard to terms used in the Framework Agreement which are not specifically defined therein, this Directive leaves Member States free to define those terms in accordance with national law and practice, as is the case for other social policy Directives using similar terms, providing that the said definitions respect the content of the Framework Agreement;

(17) Whereas the Commission has drafted its proposal for a Directive, in accordance with its Communication of 14 December 1993 concerning the application of the Protocol (No 14) on social policy and its Communication of 18 September 1996 concerning the development of the social dialogue at Community level, taking into account the representative status of the signatory parties and the legality of each clause of the Framework Agreement;

(18) Whereas the Commission has drafted its proposal for a Directive in compliance with Article 2 (2) of the Agreement on social policy which provides that Directives in the social policy domain 'shall avoid imposing administrative, financial and legal constraints in a way which would hold back the creation and development of small and medium-sized undertakings';

(19) Whereas the Commission, in accordance with its Communication of 14 December 1993 concerning the application of the Protocol (No 14) on social policy, informed the European Parliament by sending it the text of its proposal for a Directive containing the Framework Agreement;

(20) Whereas the Commission also informed the Economic and Social Committee;

(21) Whereas Clause 6.1 of the Framework Agreement provides that Member States and/or the social partners may maintain or introduce more favourable provisions;

(22) Whereas Clause 6.2 of the Framework Agreement provides that implementation of this Directive may not serve to justify any regression in relation to the situation which already exists in each Member State;

(23) Whereas the Community Charter of the Fundamental Social Rights of Workers recognises the importance of the fight against all forms of discrimination, especially based on sex, colour, race, opinion and creed;

(24) Whereas Article F(2) of the Treaty on European Union states that the Union shall respect fundamental rights, as guaranteed by the European Convention for the Protection of Human Rights and Fundamental Freedoms and as they result from the constitutional traditions common to the Member States, as general principles of Community law;

(25) Whereas the Member States may entrust the social partners, at their joint request, with the implementation of this Directive, provided that the Member States take all the necessary steps to ensure that they can at all times guarantee the results imposed by this Directive;

(26) Whereas the implementation of the Framework Agreement contributes to achieving the objectives under Article 1 of the Agreement on social policy,

HAS ADOPTED THIS DIRECTIVE:

Article 1

The purpose of this Directive is to implement the Framework Agreement on part-time work concluded on 6 June 1997 between the general cross-industry organisations (UNICE, CEEP and the ETUC) annexed hereto.

Article 2

1. Member States shall bring into force the laws, regulations and administrative provisions necessary to comply with this Directive not later than 20 January 2000, or shall ensure that, by that date at the latest, the social partners have introduced the necessary measures by agreement, the Member States being required to take any necessary measures to enable them at any time to be in a position to guarantee the results imposed by this Directive. They shall forthwith inform the Commission thereof.

Member States may have a maximum of one more year, if necessary, to take account of special difficulties or implementation by a collective agreement.

They shall inform the Commission forthwith in such circumstances. When Member States adopt the measures referred to in the first sub-paragraph, they shall contain a reference to this Directive or shall be accompanied by such reference on the occasion of their official publication. The methods of making such a reference shall be laid down by the Member States.

1a. As regards the United Kingdom of Great Britain and Northern Ireland, the date of 20 January 2000 in paragraph 1 shall be replaced by the date of 7 April 2000.

2. Member States shall communicate to the Commission the text of the main provisions of domestic law which they have adopted or which they adopt in the field governed by this Directive.

Article 3

This Directive shall enter into force on the day of its publication in the *Official Journal of the European Communities*.

Article 4

This Directive is addressed to the Member States.

Done at Brussels, 15 December 1997.

Annex

Union of Industrial and Employers' Confederations of Europe, European Trade Union Confederation, European Centre of Enterprises with Public Participation Framework Agreement on Part-time Work

Preamble

This Framework Agreement is a contribution to the overall European strategy on employment. Part-time work has had an important impact on employment in recent years. For this reason, the parties to this agreement have given priority attention to this form of work. It is the intention of the parties to consider the need for similar agreements relating to other forms of flexible work.

Recognising the diversity of situations in Member States and acknowledging that part-time work is a feature of employment in certain sectors and activities, this Agreement sets out the general principles and minimum requirements relating to part-time work. It illustrates the willingness of the social partners to establish a general framework for the elimination of discrimination against part-time workers and to assist the development of opportunities for part-time working on a basis acceptable to employers and workers.

This Agreement relates to employment conditions of part-time workers recognising that matters concerning statutory social security are for decision by the Member States. In the context of the principle of non-discrimination, the parties to this Agreement have noted the Employment Declaration of the Dublin European Council of December 1996, wherein the Council inter alia emphasised the need to make social security systems more employment-friendly by 'developing social protection systems capable of adapting to new patterns of work and of providing appropriate protection to people engaged in such work'. The parties to this Agreement consider that effect should be given to this Declaration.

ETUC, UNICE and CEEP request the Commission to submit this Framework Agreement to the Council for a decision making these requirements binding in the Member States which are party to the Agreement on social policy annexed to the Protocol (No 14) on social policy annexed to the Treaty establishing the European Community.

The parties to this Agreement ask the Commission, in its proposal to implement this Agreement, to request that Member States adopt the laws, regulations and administrative provisions necessary to comply with the Council decision within a period of two years from its adoption or ensure[5] that the social partners establish the necessary measures by way of agreement by the end of this period. Member States may, if necessary to take account of particular difficulties or implementation by collective agreement, have up to a maximum of one additional year to comply with this provision.

Without prejudice to the role of national courts and the Court of Justice, the parties to this agreement request that any matter relating to the interpretation of this agreement at European level should, in the first instance, be referred by the Commission to them for an opinion.

General considerations

1. Having regard to the Agreement on social policy annexed to the Protocol (No 14) on social policy annexed to the Treaty establishing the European Community, and in particular Articles 3(4) and 4(2) thereof;

2. Whereas Article 4(2) of the Agreement on social policy provides that agreements concluded at Community level may be implemented, at the joint request of the signatory parties, by a Council decision on a proposal from the Commission.

3. Whereas, in its second consultation document on flexibility of working time and security for workers, the Commission announced its intention to propose a legally binding Community measure;

4. Whereas the conclusions of the European Council meeting in Essen emphasised the need for measures to promote both employment and equal opportunities for women and men, and called for measures aimed at 'increasing the employment intensiveness of growth, in particular by more flexible organisation of work in a way which fulfils both the wishes of employees and the requirements of competition';

5. Whereas the parties to this agreement attach importance to measures which would facilitate access to part-time work for men and women in order to prepare for retirement, reconcile professional and family life, and take up education and training opportunities to improve their skills and career opportunities for the mutual benefit of employers and workers and in a manner which would assist the development of enterprises;

6. Whereas this Agreement refers back to Member States and social partners for the arrangements for the application of these general principles, minimum requirements and provisions, in order to take account of the situation in each Member State;

7. Whereas this Agreement takes into consideration the need to improve social policy requirements, to enhance the competitiveness of the Community economy and to avoid imposing administrative, financial and legal constraints in a way which would hold back the creation and development of small and medium-sized undertakings;

8. Whereas the social partners are best placed to find solutions that correspond to the needs of both employers and workers and must therefore be given a special role in the implementation and application of this Agreement.

THE SIGNATORY PARTIES HAVE AGREED THE FOLLOWING:

Clause 1:   Purpose

The purpose of this Framework Agreement is:

      (a) to provide for the removal of discrimination against part-time workers and to improve
         the quality of part-time work;

      (b) to facilitate the development of part-time work on a voluntary basis and to contribute to
         the flexible organisation of working time in a manner which takes into account the needs
         of employers and workers.

---

[5] Within the meaning of Article 2(4) of the Agreement on social policy of the Treaty establishing the European Community.

Clause 2:   Scope

1. This Agreement applies to part-time workers who have an employment contract or employment relationship as defined by the law, collective agreement or practice in force in each Member State.

2. Member States, after consultation with the social partners in accordance with national law, collective agreements or practice, and/or the social partners at the appropriate level in conformity with national industrial relations practice may, for objective reasons, exclude wholly or partly from the terms of this Agreement part-time workers who work on a casual basis. Such exclusions should be reviewed periodically to establish if the objective reasons for making them remain valid.

Clause 3:   Definitions

For the purpose of this agreement:

1. The term 'part-time worker' refers to an employee whose normal hours of work, calculated on a weekly basis or on average over a period of employment of up to one year, are less than the normal hours of work of a comparable full-time worker.

2. The term 'comparable full-time worker' means a full-time worker in the same establishment having the same type of employment contract or relationship, who is engaged in the same or a similar work/occupation, due regard being given to other considerations which may include seniority and qualification/skills.

Where there is no comparable full-time worker in the same establishment, the comparison shall be made by reference to the applicable collective agreement or, where there is no applicable collective agreement, in accordance with national law, collective agreements or practice.

Clause 4:   Principle of non-discrimination

1. In respect of employment conditions, part-time workers shall not be treated in a less favourable manner than comparable full-time workers solely because they work part time unless different treatment is justified on objective grounds.

2. Where appropriate, the principle of *pro rata temporis* shall apply.

3. The arrangements for the application of this clause shall be defined by the Member States and/or social partners, having regard to European legislation, national law, collective agreements and practice.

4. Where justified by objective reasons, Member States after consultation of the social partners in accordance with national law, collective agreements or practice and/or social partners may, where appropriate, make access to particular conditions of employment subject to a period of service, time worked or earnings qualification. Qualifications relating to access by part-time workers to particular conditions of employment should be reviewed periodically having regard to the principle of non-discrimination as expressed in Clause 4.1.

Clause 5:   Opportunities for part-time work

1. In the context of Clause 1 of this Agreement and of the principle of non-discrimination between part-time and full-time workers:
    (a) Member States, following consultations with the social partners in accordance with national law or practice, should identify and review obstacles of a legal or administrative nature which may limit the opportunities for part-time work and, where appropriate, eliminate them;
    (b) the social partners, acting within their sphere of competence and through the procedures set out in collective agreements, should identify and review obstacles which may limit opportunities for part-time work and, where appropriate, eliminate them.

2. A worker's refusal to transfer from full-time to part-time work or vice-versa should not in itself constitute a valid reason for termination of employment, without prejudice to termination in accordance with national law, collective agreements and practice, for other reasons such as may arise from the operational requirements of the establishment concerned.

3. As far as possible, employers should give consideration to:
    (a) requests by workers to transfer from full-time to part-time work that becomes available in the establishment;
    (b) requests by workers to transfer from part-time to full-time work or to increase their working time should the opportunity arise;

(c)   the provision of timely information on the availability of part-time and full-time positions in the establishment in order to facilitate transfers from full-time to part-time or vice versa;

(d)   measures to facilitate access to part-time work at all levels of the enterprise, including skilled and managerial positions, and where appropriate, to facilitate access by part-time workers to vocational training to enhance career opportunities and occupational mobility;

(e)   the provision of appropriate information to existing bodies representing workers about part-time working in the enterprise.

Clause 6:   Provisions on implementation

1. Member States and/or social partners may maintain or introduce more favourable provisions than set out in this agreement.

2. Implementation of the provisions of this Agreement shall not constitute valid grounds for reducing the general level of protection afforded to workers in the field of this agreement. This does not prejudice the right of Member States and/or social partners to develop different legislative, regulatory or contractual provisions, in the light of changing circumstances, and does not prejudice the application of Clause 5.1 as long as the principle of non-discrimination as expressed in Clause 4.1 is complied with.

3. This Agreement does not prejudice the right of the social partners to conclude, at the appropriate level, including European level, agreements adapting and/or complementing the provisions of this Agreement in a manner which will take account of the specific needs of the social partners concerned.

4. This Agreement shall be without prejudice to any more specific Community provisions, and in particular Community provisions concerning equal treatment or opportunities for men and women.

5. The prevention and settlement of disputes and grievances arising from the application of this Agreement shall be dealt with in accordance with national law, collective agreements and practice.

6. The signatory parties shall review this Agreement, five years after the date of the Council decision, if requested by one of the parties to this Agreement.

Council Directive 98/59/EC of 20 July 1998 on the approximation of the laws of the Member States relating to collective redundancies*

[OJ 1998 L225/16]

THE COUNCIL OF THE EUROPEAN UNION,

Having regard to the Treaty establishing the European Community, and in particular Article 100 thereof,

Having regard to the proposal from the Commission,

Having regard to the opinion of the European Parliament,[1]

Having regard to the opinion of the Economic and Social Committee,[2]

(1) Whereas for reasons of clarity and rationality Council Directive 75/129/EEC of 17 February 1975 on the approximation of the laws of the Member States relating to collective redundancies[3] should be consolidated;

(2) Whereas it is important that greater protection should be afforded to workers in the event of collective redundancies while taking into account the need for balanced economic and social development within the Community;

---

* **Editor's Note:** This repeals Directive 75/129 as amended by Directive 92/56. As corrected by OJ 2007 L59/84. As further amended by Directive 2015/1794 (OJ 2015 L263/1).
[1] OJ C 210, 6.7.1998.
[2] OJ C 158, 26.5.1997, p. 11.
[3] OJ L 48, 22.2.1975, p. 29. Directive as amended by Directive 92/56/EEC (OJ L 245, 26.8.1992, p. 3).

(3) Whereas, despite increasing convergence, differences still remain between the provisions in force in the Member States concerning the practical arrangements and procedures for such redundancies and the measures designed to alleviate the consequences of redundancy for workers;

(4) Whereas these differences can have a direct effect on the functioning of the internal market;

(5) Whereas the Council resolution of 21 January 1974 concerning a social action programme[4] made provision for a directive on the approximation of Member States' legislation on collective redundancies;

(6) Whereas the Community Charter of the fundamental social rights of workers, adopted at the European Council meeting held in Strasbourg on 9 December 1989 by the Heads of State or Government of 11 Member States, states, *inter alia*, in point 7, first paragraph, first sentence, and second paragraph; in point 17, first paragraph; and in point 18, third indent:

'7. The completion of the internal market must lead to an improvement in the living and working conditions of workers in the European Community.

The improvement must cover, where necessary, the development of certain aspects of employment regulations such as procedures for collective redundancies and those regarding bankruptcies.

17. Information, consultation and participation for workers must be developed along appropriate lines, taking account of the practices in force in the various Member States.

18. Such information, consultation and participation must be implemented in due time, particularly in the following cases:
   – in cases of collective redundancy procedures';

(7) Whereas this approximation must therefore be promoted while the improvement is being maintained within the meaning of Article 117 of the Treaty;

(8) Whereas, in order to calculate the number of redundancies provided for in the definition of collective redundancies within the meaning of this Directive, other forms of termination of employment contracts on the initiative of the employer should be equated to redundancies, provided that there are at least five redundancies;

(9) Whereas it should be stipulated that this Directive applies in principle also to collective redundancies resulting where the establishment's activities are terminated as a result of a judicial decision;

(10) Whereas the Member States should be given the option of stipulating that workers' representatives may call on experts on grounds of the technical complexity of the matters which are likely to be the subject of the informing and consulting;

(11) Whereas it is necessary to ensure that employers' obligations as regards information, consultation and notification apply independently of whether the decision on collective redundancies emanates from the employer or from an undertaking which controls that employer;

(12) Whereas Member States should ensure that workers' representatives and/or workers have at their disposal administrative and/or judicial procedures in order to ensure that the obligations laid down in this Directive are fulfilled;

(13) Whereas this Directive must not affect the obligations of the Member States concerning the deadlines for transposition of the Directives set out in Annex I, Part B.

HAS ADOPTED THIS DIRECTIVE:

Section I Definitions and scope

Article 1

1. For the purposes of this Directive:
   (a) 'collective redundancies' means dismissals effected by an employer for one or more reasons not related to the individual workers concerned where, according to the choice of the Member States, the number of redundancies is:
       (i) either, over a period of 30 days:

---

[4] OJ C 13, 12.2.1974, p. 1.

- at least 10 in establishments normally employing more than 20 and less than 100 workers,
- at least 10% of the number of workers in establishments normally employing at least 100 but less than 300 workers,
- at least 30 in establishments normally employing 300 workers or more,

(ii) or, over a period of 90 days, at least 20, whatever the number of workers normally employed in the establishments in question;

(b) 'workers' representatives means the workers' representatives provided for by the laws or practices of the Member States.

For the purpose of calculating the number of redundancies provided for in the first subparagraph of point (a), terminations of an employment contract which occur on the employer's initiative for one or more reasons not related to the individual workers concerned shall be assimilated to redundancies, provided that there are at least five redundancies.

2. This Directive shall not apply to:

(a) collective redundancies effected under contracts of employment concluded for limited periods of time or for specific tasks except where such redundancies take place prior to the date of expiry or the completion of such contracts;

(b) workers employed by public administrative bodies or by establishments governed by public law (or, in Member States where this concept is unknown, by equivalent bodies);

Section II Information and consultation

Article 2

1. Where an employer is contemplating collective redundancies, he shall begin consultations with the workers' representatives in good time with a view to reaching an agreement.

2. These consultations shall, at least, cover ways and means of avoiding collective redundancies or reducing the number of workers affected, and of mitigating the consequences by recourse to accompanying social measures aimed, *inter alia*, at aid for redeploying or retraining workers made redundant.

Member States may provide that the workers' representatives may call on the services of experts in accordance with national legislation and/or practice.

3. To enable workers' representatives to make constructive proposals, the employers shall in good time during the course of the consultations:

(a) supply them with all relevant information and

(b) in any event notify them in writing of:

(i)   the reasons for the projected redundancies;

(ii) the number of categories of workers to be made redundant;

(iii) the number and categories of workers normally employed;

(iv) the period over which the projected redundancies are to be effected;

(v)   the criteria proposed for the selection of the workers to be made redundant in so far as national legislation and/or practice confers the power therefore upon the employer;

(vi) the method for calculating any redundancy payments other than those arising out of national legislation and/or practice.

The employer shall forward to the competent public authority a copy of, at least, the elements of the written communication which are provided for in the first subparagraph, point (b), subpoints (i) to (v).

4. The obligations laid down in paragraphs 1, 2 and 3 shall apply irrespective of whether the decision regarding collective redundancies is being taken by the employer or by an undertaking controlling the employer.

In considering alleged breaches of the information, consultation and notification requirements laid down by this Directive, account shall not be taken of any defence on the part of the employer on the ground that the necessary information has not been provided to the employer by the undertaking which took the decision leading to collective redundancies.

Section III Procedure for collective redundancies

Article 3

1. Employers shall notify the competent public authority in writing of any projected collective redundancies.

However, Member States may provide that in the case of planned collective redundancies arising from termination of the establishment's activities as a result of a judicial decision, the employer shall be obliged to notify the competent public authority in writing only if the latter so requests.

This notification shall contain all relevant information concerning the projected collective redundancies and the consultations with workers' representatives provided for in Article 2, and particularly the reasons for the redundancies, the number of workers to be made redundant, the number of workers normally employed and the period over which the redundancies are to be effected.

Where the projected collective redundancy concerns members of the crew of a seagoing vessel, the employer shall notify the competent authority of the State of the flag which the vessel flies.

2. Employers shall forward to the workers' representatives a copy of the notification provided for in paragraph 1.

The workers' representatives may send any comments they may have to the competent public authority.

Article 4

1. Projected collective redundancies notified to the competent public authority shall take effect not earlier than 30 days after the notification referred to in Article 3(1) without prejudice to any provisions governing individual rights with regard to notice of dismissal.

Member States may grant the competent public authority the power to reduce the period provided for in the preceding subparagraph.

2. The period provided for in paragraph 1 shall be used by the competent public authority to seek solutions to the problems raised by the projected collective redundancies.

3. Where the initial period provided for in paragraph 1 is shorter than 60 days, Member States may grant the competent public authority the power to extend the initial period to 60 days following notification where the problems raised by the projected collective redundancies are not likely to be solved within the initial period.

Member States may grant the competent public authority wider powers of extension. The employer must be informed of the extension and the grounds for it before expiry of the initial period provided for in paragraph 1.

4. Member States need not apply this Article to collective redundancies arising from termination of the establishment's activities where this is the result of a judicial decision.

Section IV Final provisions

Article 5

This Directive shall not affect the right of Member States to apply or to introduce laws, regulations or administrative provisions which are more favourable to workers or to promote or to allow the application of collective agreements more favourable to workers.

Article 6

Member States shall ensure that judicial and/or administrative procedures for the enforcement of obligations under this Directive are available to the workers' representatives and/or workers.

Article 7

Member States shall forward to the Commission the text of any fundamental provisions of national law already adopted or being adopted in the area governed by this Directive.

Article 8

1. The Directives listed in Annex I, Part A, are hereby repealed without prejudice to the obligations of the Member States concerning the deadlines for transposition of the said Directive set out in Annex I, Part B.

2. References to the repealed Directives shall be construed as references to this Directive and shall be read in accordance with the correlation table in Annex II.

Article 9

This Directive shall enter into force on the 20th day following its publication in the *Official Journal of the European Communities*.

Article 10

This Directive is addressed to the Member States.

Done at Brussels, 20 July 1998.

Joint Declaration of the European Parliament, the Council and the Commission on Employee Representation

[OJ 2002 L80/34]

With regard to employee representation, the European Parliament, the Council and the Commission recall the judgements of the European Court of Justice of 8 June 1994 in Cases C-382/92 (Safeguarding of employees rights in the event of transfers of undertakings) and C-383/92 (Collective redundancies).

Directive 2003/88/EC of the European Parliament and of the Council of 4 November 2003 concerning certain aspects of the organisation of working time*

[OJ 2003 L299/9]

THE EUROPEAN PARLIAMENT AND THE COUNCIL OF THE EUROPEAN UNION,

Having regard to the Treaty establishing the European Community, and in particular Article 137(2) thereof,

Having regard to the proposal from the Commission,

Having regard to the opinion of the European Economic and Social Committee,[1]

Having consulted the Committee of the Regions,

Acting in accordance with the procedure referred to in Article 251 of the Treaty,[2]

Whereas:

(1) Council Directive 93/104/EC of 23 November 1993, concerning certain aspects of the organisation of working time,[3] which lays down minimum safety and health requirements for the organisation of working time, in respect of periods of daily rest, breaks, weekly rest, maximum weekly working time, annual leave and aspects of night work, shift work and patterns of work, has been significantly amended. In order to clarify matters, a codification of the provisions in question should be drawn up.

---

  * **Editor's Note:** This Directive repeals and replaces Directives 93/104 and 2000/34.

  [1] OJ C 61, 14.3.2003, p. 123.

  [2] Opinion of the European Parliament of 17 December 2002 (not yet published in the Official Journal) and Council Decision of 22 September 2003.

  [3] OJ L 307, 13.12.1993, p. 18. Directive as amended by Directive 2000/34/EC of the European Parliament and of the Council (OJ L 195, 1.8.2000, p. 41).

(2) Article 137 of the Treaty provides that the Community is to support and complement the activities of the Member States with a view to improving the working environment to protect workers' health and safety. Directives adopted on the basis of that Article are to avoid imposing administrative, financial and legal constraints in a way which would hold back the creation and development of small and medium-sized undertakings.

(3) The provisions of Council Directive 89/391/EEC of 12 June 1989 on the introduction of measures to encourage improvements in the safety and health of workers at work[4] remain fully applicable to the areas covered by this Directive without prejudice to more stringent and/or specific provisions contained herein.

(4) The improvement of workers' safety, hygiene and health at work is an objective which should not be subordinated to purely economic considerations.

(5) All workers should have adequate rest periods. The concept of 'rest' must be expressed in units of time, i.e. in days, hours and/or fractions thereof. Community workers must be granted minimum daily, weekly and annual periods of rest and adequate breaks. It is also necessary in this context to place a maximum limit on weekly working hours.

(6) Account should be taken of the principles of the International Labour Organisation with regard to the organisation of working time, including those relating to night work.

(7) Research has shown that the human body is more sensitive at night to environmental disturbances and also to certain burdensome forms of work organisation and that long periods of night work can be detrimental to the health of workers and can endanger safety at the workplace.

(8) There is a need to limit the duration of periods of night work, including overtime, and to provide for employers who regularly use night workers to bring this information to the attention of the competent authorities if they so request.

(9) It is important that night workers should be entitled to a free health assessment prior to their assignment and thereafter at regular intervals and that whenever possible they should be transferred to day work for which they are suited if they suffer from health problems.

(10) The situation of night and shift workers requires that the level of safety and health protection should be adapted to the nature of their work and that the organisation and functioning of protection and prevention services and resources should be efficient.

(11) Specific working conditions may have detrimental effects on the safety and health of workers. The organisation of work according to a certain pattern must take account of the general principle of adapting work to the worker.

(12) A European Agreement in respect of the working time of seafarers has been put into effect by means of Council Directive 1999/63/EC of 21 June 1999 concerning the Agreement on the organisation of working time of seafarers concluded by the European Community Ship-owners' Association (ECSA) and the Federation of Transport Workers' Unions in the European Union (FST)[5] based on Article 139(2) of the Treaty. Accordingly, the provisions of this Directive should not apply to seafarers.

(13) In the case of those 'share-fishermen' who are employees, it is for the Member States to determine, pursuant to this Directive, the conditions for entitlement to, and granting of, annual leave, including the arrangements for payments.

(14) Specific standards laid down in other Community instruments relating, for example, to rest periods, working time, annual leave and night work for certain categories of workers should take precedence over the provisions of this Directive.

(15) In view of the question likely to be raised by the organisation of working time within an undertaking, it appears desirable to provide for flexibility in the application of certain provisions of this Directive, whilst ensuring compliance with the principles of protecting the safety and health of workers.

(16) It is necessary to provide that certain provisions may be subject to derogations implemented, according to the case, by the Member States or the two sides of industry. As a general rule,

[4] OJ L 183, 29.6.1989, p. 1.
[5] OJ L 167, 2.7.1999, p. 33.

in the event of a derogation, the workers concerned must be given equivalent compensatory rest periods.

(17) This Directive should not affect the obligations of the Member States concerning the deadlines for transposition of the Directives set out in Annex I, part B,

HAVE ADOPTED THIS DIRECTIVE:

Chapter 1 Scope and definitions

Article 1   Purpose and scope

1. This Directive lays down minimum safety and health requirements for the organisation of working time.

2. This Directive applies to:

(a) minimum periods of daily rest, weekly rest and annual leave, to breaks and maximum weekly working time; and

(b) certain aspects of night work, shift work and patterns of work.

3. This Directive shall apply to all sectors of activity, both public and private, within the meaning of Article 2 of Directive 89/391/EEC, without prejudice to Articles 14, 17, 18 and 19 of this Directive.

This Directive shall not apply to seafarers, as defined in Directive 1999/63/EC without prejudice to Article 2(8) of this Directive.

4. The provisions of Directive 89/391/EEC are fully applicable to the matters referred to in paragraph 2, without prejudice to more stringent and/or specific provisions contained in this Directive.

Article 2   Definitions

For the purposes of this Directive, the following definitions shall apply:

1. 'working time' means any period during which the worker is working, at the employer's disposal and carrying out his activity or duties, in accordance with national laws and/or practice;

2. 'rest period' means any period which is not working time;

3. 'night time' means any period of not less than seven hours, as defined by national law, and which must include, in any case, the period between midnight and 5.00;

4. 'night worker' means:

(a) on the one hand, any worker, who, during night time, works at least three hours of his daily working time as a normal course; and

(b) on the other hand, any worker who is likely during night time to work a certain proportion of his annual working time, as defined at the choice of the Member State concerned:

(i)   by national legislation, following consultation with the two sides of industry; or

(ii) by collective agreements or agreements concluded between the two sides of industry at national or regional level;

5. 'shift work' means any method of organising work in shifts whereby workers succeed each other at the same work stations according to a certain pattern, including a rotating pattern, and which may be continuous or discontinuous, entailing the need for workers to work at different times over a given period of days or weeks;

6. 'shift worker' means any worker whose work schedule is part of shift work;

7. 'mobile worker' means any worker employed as a member of travelling or flying personnel by an undertaking which operates transport services for passengers or goods by road, air or inland waterway;

8. 'offshore work' means work performed mainly on or from offshore installations (including drilling rigs), directly or indirectly in connection with the exploration, extraction or exploitation of mineral resources, including hydrocarbons, and diving in connection with such activities, whether performed from an offshore installation or a vessel;

9. 'adequate rest' means that workers have regular rest periods, the duration of which is expressed in units of time and which are sufficiently long and continuous to ensure that, as a result of fatigue or other irregular working patterns, they do not cause injury to themselves, to fellow workers or to others and that they do not damage their health, either in the short term or in the longer term.

Chapter 2 Minimum rest periods—Other aspects of the organisation of working time

Article 3 Daily rest

Member States shall take the measures necessary to ensure that every worker is entitled to a minimum daily rest period of 11 consecutive hours per 24-hour period.

Article 4 Breaks

Member States shall take the measures necessary to ensure that, where the working day is longer than six hours, every worker is entitled to a rest break, the details of which, including duration and the terms on which it is granted, shall be laid down in collective agreements or agreements between the two sides of industry or, failing that, by national legislation.

Article 5 Weekly rest period

Member States shall take the measures necessary to ensure that, per each seven-day period, every worker is entitled to a minimum uninterrupted rest period of 24 hours plus the 11 hours' daily rest referred to in Article 3.

If objective, technical or work organisation conditions so justify, a minimum rest period of 24 hours may be applied.

Article 6 Maximum weekly working time

Member States shall take the measures necessary to ensure that, in keeping with the need to protect the safety and health of workers:

(a) the period of weekly working time is limited by means of laws, regulations or administrative provisions or by collective agreements or agreements between the two sides of industry;

(b) the average working time for each seven-day period, including overtime, does not exceed 48 hours.

Article 7 Annual leave

1. Member States shall take the measures necessary to ensure that every worker is entitled to paid annual leave of at least four weeks in accordance with the conditions for entitlement to, and granting of, such leave laid down by national legislation and/or practice.

2. The minimum period of paid annual leave may not be replaced by an allowance in lieu, except where the employment relationship is terminated.

Chapter 3 Night work—Shift work—Patterns of work

Article 8 Length of night work

Member States shall take the measures necessary to ensure that:

(a) normal hours of work for night workers do not exceed an average of eight hours in any 24-hour period;

(b) night workers whose work involves special hazards or heavy physical or mental strain do not work more than eight hours in any period of 24 hours during which they perform night work.

For the purposes of point (b), work involving special hazards or heavy physical or mental strain shall be defined by national legislation and/or practice or by collective agreements or agreements concluded between the two sides of industry, taking account of the specific effects and hazards of night work.

Article 9 Health assessment and transfer of night workers to day work

1. Member States shall take the measures necessary to ensure that:

(a) night workers are entitled to a free health assessment before their assignment and thereafter at regular intervals;

(b) night workers suffering from health problems recognised as being connected with the fact that they perform night work are transferred whenever possible to day work to which they are suited.

2. The free health assessment referred to in paragraph 1(a) must comply with medical confidentiality.

3. The free health assessment referred to in paragraph 1(a) may be conducted within the national health system.

Article 10   Guarantees for night-time working

Member States may make the work of certain categories of night workers subject to certain guarantees, under conditions laid down by national legislation and/or practice, in the case of workers who incur risks to their safety or health linked to night-time working.

Article 11   Notification of regular use of night workers

Member States shall take the measures necessary to ensure that an employer who regularly uses night workers brings this information to the attention of the competent authorities if they so request.

Article 12   Safety and health protection

Member States shall take the measures necessary to ensure that:

   (a) night workers and shift workers have safety and health protection appropriate to the nature of their work;
   (b) appropriate protection and prevention services or facilities with regard to the safety and health of night workers and shift workers are equivalent to those applicable to other workers and are available at all times.

Article 13   Pattern of work

Member States shall take the measures necessary to ensure that an employer who intends to organise work according to a certain pattern takes account of the general principle of adapting work to the worker, with a view, in particular, to alleviating monotonous work and work at a predetermined work-rate, depending on the type of activity, and of safety and health requirements, especially as regards breaks during working time.

Chapter 4 Miscellaneous provisions

Article 14   More specific Community provisions

This Directive shall not apply where other Community instruments contain more specific requirements relating to the organisation of working time for certain occupations or occupational activities.

Article 15   More favourable provisions

This Directive shall not affect Member States' right to apply or introduce laws, regulations or administrative provisions more favourable to the protection of the safety and health of workers or to facilitate or permit the application of collective agreements or agreements concluded between the two sides of industry which are more favourable to the protection of the safety and health of workers.

Article 16   Reference periods

Member States may lay down:

   (a) for the application of Article 5 (weekly rest period), a reference period not exceeding 14 days;
   (b) for the application of Article 6 (maximum weekly working time), a reference period not exceeding four months.
       The periods of paid annual leave, granted in accordance with Article 7, and the periods of sick leave shall not be included or shall be neutral in the calculation of the average;
   (c) for the application of Article 8 (length of night work), a reference period defined after consultation of the two sides of industry or by collective agreements or agreements concluded between the two sides of industry at national or regional level.

If the minimum weekly rest period of 24 hours required by Article 5 falls within that reference period, it shall not be included in the calculation of the average.

Chapter 5 Derogations and exceptions

Article 17 Derogations

1. With due regard for the general principles of the protection of the safety and health of workers, Member States may derogate from Articles 3 to 6, 8 and 16 when, on account of the specific characteristics of the activity concerned, the duration of the working time is not measured and/or predetermined or can be determined by the workers themselves, and particularly in the case of:

(a) managing executives or other persons with autonomous decision-taking powers;

(b) family workers; or

(c) workers officiating at religious ceremonies in churches and religious communities.

2. Derogations provided for in paragraphs 3, 4 and 5 may be adopted by means of laws, regulations or administrative provisions or by means of collective agreements or agreements between the two sides of industry provided that the workers concerned are afforded equivalent periods of compensatory rest or that, in exceptional cases in which it is not possible, for objective reasons, to grant such equivalent periods of compensatory rest, the workers concerned are afforded appropriate protection.

3. In accordance with paragraph 2 of this Article derogations may be made from Articles 3, 4, 5, 8 and 16:

(a) in the case of activities where the worker's place of work and his place of residence are distant from one another, including offshore work, or where the worker's different places of work are distant from one another;

(b) in the case of security and surveillance activities requiring a permanent presence in order to protect property and persons, particularly security guards and caretakers or security firms;

(c) in the case of activities involving the need for continuity of service or production, particularly:

    (i) services relating to the reception, treatment and/or care provided by hospitals or similar establishments, including the activities of doctors in training, residential institutions and prisons;

    (ii) dock or airport workers;

    (iii) press, radio, television, cinematographic production, postal and telecommunications services, ambulance, fire and civil protection services;

    (iv) gas, water and electricity production, transmission and distribution, household refuse collection and incineration plants;

    (v) industries in which work cannot be interrupted on technical grounds;

    (vi) research and development activities;

    (vii) agriculture;

    (viii) workers concerned with the carriage of passengers on regular urban transport services;

(d) where there is a foreseeable surge of activity, particularly in:

    (i) agriculture;

    (ii) tourism;

    (iii) postal services;

(e) in the case of persons working in railway transport:

    (i) whose activities are intermittent;

    (ii) who spend their working time on board trains; or

    (iii) whose activities are linked to transport timetables and to ensuring the continuity and regularity of traffic;

(f) in the circumstances described in Article 5(4) of Directive 89/391/EEC;

(g) in cases of accident or imminent risk of accident.

4. In accordance with paragraph 2 of this Article derogations may be made from Articles 3 and 5:

    (a) in the case of shift work activities, each time the worker changes shift and cannot take daily and/or weekly rest periods between the end of one shift and the start of the next one;

    (b) in the case of activities involving periods of work split up over the day, particularly those of cleaning staff.

5. In accordance with paragraph 2 of this Article, derogations may be made from Article 6 and Article 16(b), in the case of doctors in training, in accordance with the provisions set out in the second to the seventh subparagraphs of this paragraph.

With respect to Article 6 derogations referred to in the first subparagraph shall be permitted for a transitional period of five years from 1 August 2004.

Member States may have up to two more years, if necessary, to take account of difficulties in meeting the working time provisions with respect to their responsibilities for the organisation and delivery of health services and medical care. At least six months before the end of the transitional period, the Member State concerned shall inform the Commission giving its reasons, so that the Commission can give an opinion, after appropriate consultations, within the three months following receipt of such information. If the Member State does not follow the opinion of the Commission, it will justify its decision. The notification and justification of the Member State and the opinion of the Commission shall be published in the *Official Journal of the European Union* and forwarded to the European Parliament.

Member States may have an additional period of up to one year, if necessary, to take account of special difficulties in meeting the responsibilities referred to in the third subparagraph. They shall follow the procedure set out in that subparagraph.

Member States shall ensure that in no case will the number of weekly working hours exceed an average of 58 during the first three years of the transitional period, an average of 56 for the following two years and an average of 52 for any remaining period.

The employer shall consult the representatives of the employees in good time with a view to reaching an agreement, wherever possible, on the arrangements applying to the transitional period. Within the limits set out in the fifth subparagraph, such an agreement may cover:

    (a) the average number of weekly hours of work during the transitional period; and

    (b) the measures to be adopted to reduce weekly working hours to an average of 48 by the end of the transitional period.

With respect to Article 16(b) derogations referred to in the first subparagraph shall be permitted provided that the reference period does not exceed 12 months, during the first part of the transitional period specified in the fifth subparagraph, and six months thereafter.

Article 18   Derogations by collective agreements

Derogations may be made from Articles 3, 4, 5, 8 and 16 by means of collective agreements or agreements concluded between the two sides of industry at national or regional level or, in conformity with the rules laid down by them, by means of collective agreements or agreements concluded between the two sides of industry at a lower level.

Member States in which there is no statutory system ensuring the conclusion of collective agreements or agreements concluded between the two sides of industry at national or regional level, on the matters covered by this Directive, or those Member States in which there is a specific legislative framework for this purpose and within the limits thereof, may, in accordance with national legislation and/or practice, allow derogations from Articles 3, 4, 5, 8 and 16 by way of collective agreements or agreements concluded between the two sides of industry at the appropriate collective level.

The derogations provided for in the first and second subparagraphs shall be allowed on condition that equivalent compensating rest periods are granted to the workers concerned or, in exceptional cases where it is not possible for objective reasons to grant such periods, the workers concerned are afforded appropriate protection.

Member States may lay down rules:

(a) for the application of this Article by the two sides of industry; and

(b) for the extension of the provisions of collective agreements or agreements concluded in conformity with this Article to other workers in accordance with national legislation and/or practice.

Article 19   Limitations to derogations from reference periods

The option to derogate from Article 16(b), provided for in Article 17(3) and in Article 18, may not result in the establishment of a reference period exceeding six months.

However, Member States shall have the option, subject to compliance with the general principles relating to the protection of the safety and health of workers, of allowing, for objective or technical reasons or reasons concerning the organisation of work, collective agreements or agreements concluded between the two sides of industry to set reference periods in no event exceeding 12 months.

Before 23 November 2003, the Council shall, on the basis of a Commission proposal accompanied by an appraisal report, re-examine the provisions of this Article and decide what action to take.

Article 20   Mobile workers and offshore work

1. Articles 3, 4, 5 and 8 shall not apply to mobile workers.

Member States shall, however, take the necessary measures to ensure that such mobile workers are entitled to adequate rest, except in the circumstances laid down in Article 17(3)(f) and (g).

2. Subject to compliance with the general principles relating to the protection of the safety and health of workers, and provided that there is consultation of representatives of the employer and employees concerned and efforts to encourage all relevant forms of social dialogue, including negotiation if the parties so wish, Member States may, for objective or technical reasons or reasons concerning the organisation of work, extend the reference period referred to in Article 16(b) to 12 months in respect of workers who mainly perform offshore work.

3. Not later than 1 August 2005 the Commission shall, after consulting the Member States and management and labour at European level, review the operation of the provisions with regard to offshore workers from a health and safety perspective with a view to presenting, if need be, the appropriate modifications.

Article 21   Workers on board seagoing fishing vessels

1. Articles 3 to 6 and 8 shall not apply to any worker on board a seagoing fishing vessel flying the flag of a Member State.

Member States shall, however, take the necessary measures to ensure that any worker on board a seagoing fishing vessel flying the flag of a Member State is entitled to adequate rest and to limit the number of hours of work to 48 hours a week on average calculated over a reference period not exceeding 12 months.

2. Within the limits set out in paragraph 1, second subparagraph, and paragraphs 3 and 4 Member States shall take the necessary measures to ensure that, in keeping with the need to protect the safety and health of such workers:

(a) the working hours are limited to a maximum number of hours which shall not be exceeded in a given period of time; or

(b) a minimum number of hours of rest are provided within a given period of time.

The maximum number of hours of work or minimum number of hours of rest shall be specified by law, regulations, administrative provisions or by collective agreements or agreements between the two sides of the industry.

3. The limits on hours of work or rest shall be either:

(a) maximum hours of work which shall not exceed:

(i)   14 hours in any 24-hour period; and

(ii)   72 hours in any seven-day period;

or

(b) minimum hours of rest which shall not be less than:

    (i)   10 hours in any 24-hour period; and

    (ii) 77 hours in any seven-day period.

4. Hours of rest may be divided into no more than two periods, one of which shall be at least six hours in length, and the interval between consecutive periods of rest shall not exceed 14 hours.

5. In accordance with the general principles of the protection of the health and safety of workers, and for objective or technical reasons or reasons concerning the organisation of work, Member States may allow exceptions, including the establishment of reference periods, to the limits laid down in paragraph 1, second subparagraph, and paragraphs 3 and 4. Such exceptions shall, as far as possible, comply with the standards laid down but may take account of more frequent or longer leave periods or the granting of compensatory leave for the workers. These exceptions may be laid down by means of:

    (a) laws, regulations or administrative provisions provided there is consultation, where possible, of the representatives of the employers and workers concerned and efforts are made to encourage all relevant forms of social dialogue; or

    (b) collective agreements or agreements between the two sides of industry.

6. The master of a seagoing fishing vessel shall have the right to require workers on board to perform any hours of work necessary for the immediate safety of the vessel, persons on board or cargo, or for the purpose of giving assistance to other vessels or persons in distress at sea.

7. Member States may provide that workers on board seagoing fishing vessels for which national legislation or practice determines that these vessels are not allowed to operate in a specific period of the calendar year exceeding one month, shall take annual leave in accordance with Article 7 within that period.

Article 22   Miscellaneous provisions

1. A Member State shall have the option not to apply Article 6, while respecting the general principles of the protection of the safety and health of workers, and provided it takes the necessary measures to ensure that:

    (a) no employer requires a worker to work more than 48 hours over a seven-day period, calculated as an average for the reference period referred to in Article 16(b), unless he has first obtained the worker's agreement to perform such work;

    (b) no worker is subjected to any detriment by his employer because he is not willing to give his agreement to perform such work;

    (c) the employer keeps up-to-date records of all workers who carry out such work;

    (d) the records are placed at the disposal of the competent authorities, which may, for reasons connected with the safety and/or health of workers, prohibit or restrict the possibility of exceeding the maximum weekly working hours;

    (e) the employer provides the competent authorities at their request with information on cases in which agreement has been given by workers to perform work exceeding 48 hours over a period of seven days, calculated as an average for the reference period referred to in Article 16(b).

Before 23 November 2003, the Council shall, on the basis of a Commission proposal accompanied by an appraisal report, re-examine the provisions of this paragraph and decide on what action to take.

2. Member States shall have the option, as regards the application of Article 7, of making use of a transitional period of not more than three years from 23 November 1996, provided that during that transitional period:

    (a) every worker receives three weeks' paid annual leave in accordance with the conditions for the entitlement to, and granting of, such leave laid down by national legislation and/or practice; and

    (b) the three-week period of paid annual leave may not be replaced by an allowance in lieu, except where the employment relationship is terminated.

3. If Member States avail themselves of the options provided for in this Article, they shall forthwith inform the Commission thereof.

Chapter 6 Final provisions

Article 23   Level of protection
Without prejudice to the right of Member States to develop, in the light of changing circumstances, different legislative, regulatory or contractual provisions in the field of working time, as long as the minimum requirements provided for in this Directive are complied with, implementation of this Directive shall not constitute valid grounds for reducing the general level of protection afforded to workers.

Article 24   Reports
1. Member States shall communicate to the Commission the texts of the provisions of national law already adopted or being adopted in the field governed by this Directive.

2. Member States shall report to the Commission every five years on the practical implementation of the provisions of this Directive, indicating the viewpoints of the two sides of industry.

The Commission shall inform the European Parliament, the Council, the European Economic and Social Committee and the Advisory Committee on Safety, Hygiene and Health Protection at Work thereof.

3. Every five years from 23 November 1996 the Commission shall submit to the European Parliament, the Council and the European Economic and Social Committee a report on the application of this Directive taking into account Articles 22 and 23 and paragraphs 1 and 2 of this Article.

Article 25   Review of the operation of the provisions with regard to workers on board seagoing fishing vessels
Not later than 1 August 2009 the Commission shall, after consulting the Member States and management and labour at European level, review the operation of the provisions with regard to workers on board seagoing fishing vessels, and, in particular examine whether these provisions remain appropriate, in particular, as far as health and safety are concerned with a view to proposing suitable amendments, if necessary.

Article 26   Review of the operation of the provisions with regard to workers concerned with the carriage of passengers
Not later than 1 August 2005 the Commission shall, after consulting the Member States and management and labour at European level, review the operation of the provisions with regard to workers concerned with the carriage of passengers on regular urban transport services, with a view to presenting, if need be, the appropriate modifications to ensure a coherent and suitable approach in the sector.

Article 27   Repeal
1. Directive 93/104/EC, as amended by the Directive referred to in Annex I, part A, shall be repealed, without prejudice to the obligations of the Member States in respect of the deadlines for transposition laid down in Annex I, part B.

2. The references made to the said repealed Directive shall be construed as references to this Directive and shall be read in accordance with the correlation table set out in Annex II.

Article 28   Entry into force
This Directive shall enter into force on 2 August 2004.

Article 29   Addressees
This Directive is addressed to the Member States.

Done at Brussels, 4 November 2003.

Annex I

Part A Repealed Directive and its amendment (Article 27)

Council Directive 93/104/EC   (OJ L 307, 13.12.1993, p. 18)
Directive 2000/34/EC of the European Parliament and of the Council (OJ L 195, 1.8.2000, p. 41)

Part B Deadlines for transposition into national law (Article 27)

Directive	Deadline for transposition
93/104/EC	23 November 1996
2000/34/EC	1 August 2003[6]

Annex II

Correlation table

Directive 93/104/EC	This Directive
Articles 1 to 5	Articles 1 to 5
Article 6, introductory words	Article 6, introductory words
Article 6(1)	Article 6(a)
Article 6(2)	Article 6(b)
Article 7	Article 7
Article 8, introductory words	Article 8, introductory words
Article 8(1)	Article 8(a)
Article 8(2)	Article 8(b)
Articles 9, 10 and 11	Articles 9, 10 and 11
Article 12, introductory words	Article 12, introductory words
Article 12(1)	Article 12(a)
Article 12(2)	Article 12(b)
Articles 13, 14 and 15	Articles 13, 14 and 15
Article 16, introductory words	Article 16, introductory words
Article 16(1)	Article 16(a)
Article 16(2)	Article 16(b)
Article 16(3)	Article 16(c)
Article 17(1)	Article 17(1)
Article 17(2), introductory words	Article 17(2)
Article 17(2)(1)	Article 17(3)(a) to (e)
Article 17(2)(2)	Article 17(3)(f) to (g)
Article 17(2)(3)	Article 17(4)
Article 17(2)(4)	Article 17(5)
Article 17(3)	Article 18
Article 17(4)	Article 19

[6] August 2004 in the case of doctors in training. See Article 2 of Directive 2000/34/EC.

Directive 93/104/EC	This Directive
Article 17a(1)	Article 20(1), first subparagraph
Article 17a(2)	Article 20(1), second subparagraph
Article 17a(3)	Article 20(2)
Article 17a(4)	Article 20(3)
Article 17b(1)	Article 21(1), first subparagraph
Article 17b(2)	Article 21(1), second subparagraph
Article 17b(3)	Article 21(2)
Article 17b(4)	Article 21(3)
Article 17b(5)	Article 21(4)
Article 17b(6)	Article 21(5)
Article 17b(7)	Article 21(6)
Article 17b(8)	Article 21(7)
Article 18(1)(a)	—
Article 18(1)(b)(i)	Article 22(1)
Article 18(1)(b)(ii)	Article 22(2)
Article 18(1)(c)	Article 22(3)
Article 18(2)	—
Article 18(3)	Article 23
Article 18(4)	Article 24(1)
Article 18(5)	Article 24(2)
Article 18(6)	Article 24(3)
—	Article 25[7]
—	Article 26[8]
—	Article 27
Article 19	Article 28
—	Article 29
—	Annex 1

Competition

Regulation No 17—First Regulation implementing Articles 81 and 82 of the Treaty*

[OJ Sp. Ed. 1962, No 204/62, p. 87]

Article 8   Duration and revocation of decisions under Article 85(3)

3. The Commission may revoke or amend its decision or prohibit specified acts by the parties:
   (a) where there has been a change in any of the facts which were basic to the making of the decision;

---

[7] Directive 2000/34/EC, Article 3.

[8] Directive 2000/34/EC, Article 4.

* **Editor's Note:** Following the entry into force of Regulation No 1/2003, included below, Article 8(3) is the only Article which remains, temporarily, in force. To those who continue to question the inclusion of this foundational piece of legislation or believe Regulation 17 to be long dead, I can assure you the reports of its death are greatly exaggerated! This is still the case as of 31 March 2021 See http://data.europa.eu/eli/reg/1962/17/2004-05-01.

   (b) where the parties commit a breach of any obligation attached to the decision;

   (c) where the decision is based on incorrect information or was induced by deceit;

   (d) where the parties abuse the exemption from the provisions of Article 85(1) of the Treaty granted to them by the decision.

In cases to which subparagraphs (b), (c) or (d) apply, the decision may be revoked with retroactive effect.

Commission Notice on agreements of minor importance which do not appreciably restrict competition under Article 101(1) of the Treaty on the Functioning of the European Union (De Minimis Notice)

[OJ 2014 C291/01]*

I

1. Article 101(1) of the Treaty on the Functioning of the European Union prohibits agreements between undertakings which may affect trade between Member States and which have as their object or effect the prevention, restriction or distortion of competition within the internal market. The Court of Justice of the European Union has clarified that that provision is not applicable where the impact of the agreement on trade between Member States or on competition is not appreciable.[1]

2. The Court of Justice has also clarified that an agreement which may affect trade between Member States and which has as its object the prevention, restriction or distortion of competition within the internal market constitutes, by its nature and independently of any concrete effects that it may have, an appreciable restriction of competition.[2] This Notice therefore does not cover agreements which have as their object the prevention, restriction or distortion of competition within the internal market.

3. In this Notice the Commission indicates, with the help of market share thresholds, the circumstances in which it considers that agreements which may have as their effect the prevention, restriction or distortion of competition within the internal market do not constitute an appreciable restriction of competition under Article 101 of the Treaty. This negative definition of appreciability does not imply that agreements between undertakings which exceed the thresholds set out in this Notice constitute an appreciable restriction of competition. Such agreements may still have only a negligible effect on competition and may therefore not be prohibited by Article 101(1) of the Treaty.[3]

4. Agreements may also fall outside Article 101(1) of the Treaty because they are not capable of appreciably affecting trade between Member States. This Notice does not indicate what constitutes an appreciable effect on trade between Member States. Guidance to that effect is to be found in the Commission's Notice on effect on trade,[4] in which the Commission quantifies, with the help of the combination of a 5 % market share threshold and a EUR 40 million turnover threshold, which

---

* **Editor's Note:** Permission to reproduce this document is gratefully acknowledged but please note that 'Only the Official Journal published in electronic form shall be authentic and shall produce legal effects.' This notice replaces the 2001 *de minimis* notice. https://ec.europa.eu/competition/antitrust/legislation/deminimis.html.

[1] See Case C-226/11 *Expedia*, not yet reported, paragraphs 16 and 17.

[2] See Case C-226/11 *Expedia*, in particular paragraphs 35, 36 and 37.

[3] See, for instance, Joined Cases C-215/96 and C-216/96 *Bagnasco and Others* [1999] ECR I-135, paragraphs 34 and 35.

[4] Commission Notice—Guidelines on the effect on trade concept contained in Articles 81and 82 of the Treaty (OJ C 101, 27.4.2004, p. 81), in particular points 44 to 57.

agreements are in principle not capable of appreciably affecting trade between Member States.[5] Such agreements normally fall outside Article 101(1) of the Treaty even if they have as their object the prevention, restriction or distortion of competition.

5. In cases covered by this Notice, the Commission will not institute proceedings either upon a complaint or on its own initiative. In addition, where the Commission has instituted proceedings but undertakings can demonstrate that they have assumed in good faith that the market shares mentioned in points 8, 9, 10 and 11 were not exceeded, the Commission will not impose fines. Although not binding on them, this Notice is also intended to give guidance to the courts and competition authorities of the Member States in their application of Article 101 of the Treaty.[6]

6. The principles set out in this Notice also apply to decisions by associations of undertakings and to concerted practices.

7. This Notice is without prejudice to any interpretation of Article 101 of the Treaty which may be given by the Court of Justice of the European Union.

II

8. The Commission holds the view that agreements between undertakings which may affect trade between Member States and which may have as their effect the prevention, restriction or distortion of competition within the internal market, do not appreciably restrict competition within the meaning of Article 101(1) of the Treaty:

(a) if the aggregate market share held by the parties to the agreement does not exceed 10 % on any of the relevant markets affected by the agreement, where the agreement is made between undertakings which are actual or potential competitors on any of those markets (agreements between competitors);[7] or

(b) if the market share held by each of the parties to the agreement does not exceed 15 % on any of the relevant markets affected by the agreement, where the agreement is made between undertakings which are not actual or potential competitors on any of those markets (agreements between non-competitors).

9. In cases where it is difficult to classify the agreement as either an agreement between competitors or an agreement between non-competitors the 10 % threshold is applicable.

10. Where, in a relevant market, competition is restricted by the cumulative effect of agreements for the sale of goods or services entered into by different suppliers or distributors (cumulative foreclosure effect of parallel networks of agreements having similar effects on the market), the market share thresholds set out in point 8 and 9 are reduced to 5 %, both for agreements between competitors and for agreements between non-competitors. Individual suppliers or distributors with a market share not exceeding 5 %, are in general not considered to contribute significantly to a cumulative foreclosure effect.[8] A cumulative foreclosure effect is unlikely to exist if less than 30 % of the relevant market is covered by parallel (networks of) agreements having similar effects.

---

[5] It should be noted that agreements between small and medium sized undertakings (SMEs), as defined in the Commission Recommendation of 6 May 2003 concerning the definition of micro, small and medium-sized enterprises or any future recommendation replacing it (OJ L 124, 20.5.2003, p. 36), are also not normally capable of affecting trade between Member States. See in particular point 50 of the Notice on effect of trade.

[6] In particular, in order to determine whether or not a restriction of competition is appreciable, the competition authorities and the courts of Member States may take into account the thresholds established in this Notice but are not required to do so. See Case C-226/11 *Expedia*, paragraph 31.

[7] On the definition of actual or potential competitors, see the Communication from the Commission—Guidelines on the applicability of Article 101 of the Treaty on the Functioning of the European Union to horizontal cooperation agreements (OJ C 11, 14.1.2011, p. 1), point 10. Two undertakings are treated as actual competitors if they are active on the same relevant market. An undertaking is treated as a potential competitor of another undertaking if, in the absence of the agreement, in case of a small but permanent increase in relative prices it is likely that the former, within a short period of time, would undertake the necessary additional investments or other necessary switching costs to enter the relevant market on which the latter is active.

[8] See also the Guidelines on Vertical Restraints (OJ C 130, 19.5.2010, p. 1, in particular points 76, 134 and 179. While in the Guidelines on Vertical Restraints in relation to certain restrictions reference is made not only to the total but also to the tied market share of a particular supplier or buyer, in this Notice all market share thresholds refer to total market shares.

11. The Commission also holds the view that agreements do not appreciably restrict competition if the market shares of the parties to the agreement do not exceed the thresholds of respectively 10 %, 15 % and 5 % set out in points 8, 9 and 10 during two successive calendar years by more than 2 percentage points.

12. In order to calculate the market share, it is necessary to determine the relevant market. This consists of the relevant product market and the relevant geographic market. When defining the relevant market, reference should be had to the Notice on the definition of the relevant market.[9] The market shares are to be calculated on the basis of sales value data or, where appropriate, purchase value data. If value data are not available, estimates based on other reliable market information, including volume data, may be used.

13. In view of the clarification of the Court of Justice referred to in point 2, this Notice does not cover agreements which have as their object the prevention, restriction or distortion of competition within the internal market. The Commission will thus not apply the safe harbour created by the market share thresholds set out in points 8, 9, 10 and 11 to such agreements.[10] For instance, as regards agreements between competitors, the Commission will not apply the principles set out in this Notice to, in particular, agreements containing restrictions which, directly or indirectly, have as their object: a) the fixing of prices when selling products to third parties; b) the limitation of output or sales; or c) the allocation of markets or customers. Likewise, the Commission will not apply the safe harbour created by those market share thresholds to agreements containing any of the restrictions that are listed as hardcore restrictions in any current or future Commission block exemption regulation,[11] which are considered by the Commission to generally constitute restrictions by object.

14. The safe harbour created by the market share thresholds set out in points 8, 9, 10 and 11 is particularly relevant for categories of agreements not covered by any Commission block exemption regulation.[12] The safe harbour is also relevant for agreements covered by a Commission block exemption regulation to the extent that those agreements contain a so-called excluded restriction, that is a restriction not listed as a hardcore restriction but nonetheless not covered by the Commission block exemption regulation.[13]

15. For the purpose of this Notice, the terms 'undertaking', 'party to the agreement', 'distributor' and 'supplier' include their respective connected undertakings.

16. For the purpose of the Notice 'connected undertakings' are:
   (a) undertakings in which a party to the agreement, directly or indirectly:
      i.   has the power to exercise more than half the voting rights, or
      ii. has the power to appoint more than half the members of the supervisory board, board of management or bodies legally representing the undertaking, or
      iii. has the right to manage the undertaking's affairs;
   (b) undertakings which directly or indirectly have, over a party to the agreement, the rights or powers listed in (a);
   (c) undertakings in which an undertaking referred to in (b) has, directly or indirectly, the rights or powers listed in (a);

---

[9] Notice on the definition of the relevant market for the purposes of Community competition law (OJ C 372, 9.12.1997, p. 5).

[10] For these agreements, the Commission will exercise its discretion in deciding whether or not to institute proceedings.

[11] For supply and distribution agreements between non-competitors see in particular Article 4 of Commission Regulation (EU) No 330/2010 of 20 April 2010 on the application of Article 101(3) of the Treaty on the Functioning of the European Union to categories of vertical agreements and concerted practices (OJ L 102, 23.4.2010, p. 1) and for licensing agreements between non-competitors see in particular Article 4(2) of Commission Regulation (EU) No 316/2014 of 21 March 2014 on the application of Article 101(3) of the Treaty on the Functioning of the European Union to categories of technology transfer agreements (OJ L 93, 28.3.2014, p. 17). For agreements between competitors see in particular Article 5 of Commission Regulation (EU) No 1217/2010 of 14 December 2010 on the application of Article 101(3) of the Treaty on the Functioning of the European Union to certain categories of research and development agreements (OJ L 335, 18.12.2010, p. 36), and Article 4 of Commission Regulation (EU) No 1218/2010 of 14 December 2010 on the application of Article 101(3) of the Treaty on the Functioning of the European Union to certain categories of specialisation agreements (OJ L 335, 18.12.2010, p. 43) as well as Article 4(1) of Regulation (EU) No 316/2014.

[12] For instance, trade mark licence agreements and most types of agreements between competitors, with the exception of research and development agreements and specialisation agreements, are not covered by any block exemption regulation.

[13] For excluded restrictions see in particular Article 5 of Regulation (EU) No 330/2010, Article 5 of Regulation (EU) No 316/2014 and Article 6 of Regulation (EU) No 1217/2010.

(d) undertakings in which a party to the agreement together with one or more of the undertakings referred to in (a), (b) or (c), or in which two or more of the latter undertakings, jointly have the rights or powers listed in (a);

(e) undertakings in which the rights or the powers listed in (a) are jointly held by:

    i.   parties to the agreement or their respective connected undertakings referred to in (a) to (d), or

    ii.   one or more of the parties to the agreement or one or more of their connected undertakings referred to in (a) to (d) and one or more third parties.

17. For the purposes of point (e) in point 16, the market share held by these jointly held undertakings is apportioned equally to each undertaking having the rights or the powers listed in point (a) in point 16.

Commission Notice on the definition of relevant market for the purposes of Community competition law (97/C 372/03)*

[OJ 1997 C372/5]

I. INTRODUCTION

1. The purpose of this notice is to provide guidance as to how the Commission applies the concept of relevant product and geographic market in its ongoing enforcement of Community competition law, in particular the application of Council Regulation No 17 and (EEC) No 4064/89, their equivalents in other sectoral applications such as transport, coal and steel, and agriculture, and the relevant provisions of the EEA Agreement.[1] Throughout this notice, references to Articles 85 and 86 of the Treaty and to merger control are to be understood as referring to the equivalent provisions in the EEA Agreement and the ECSC Treaty.

2. Market definition is a tool to identify and define the boundaries of competition between firms. It serves to establish the framework within which competition policy is applied by the Commission. The main purpose of market definition is to identify in a systematic way the competitive constraints that the undertakings involved[2] face. The objective of defining a market in both its product and geographic dimension is to identify those actual competitors of the undertakings involved that are capable of constraining those undertakings' behaviour and of preventing them from behaving independently of effective competitive pressure. It is from this perspective that the market definition makes it possible *inter alia* to calculate market shares that would convey meaningful information regarding market power for the purposes of assessing dominance or for the purposes of applying Article 85.

3. It follows from point 2 that the concept of 'relevant market' is different from other definitions of market often used in other contexts. For instance, companies often use the term 'market' to refer to the area where it sells its products or to refer broadly to the industry or sector where it belongs.

4. The definition of the relevant market in both its product and its geographic dimensions often has a decisive influence on the assessment of a competition case. By rendering public the procedures

* **Editor's Note:** Permission to reproduce this document is gratefully acknowledged but please note that 'Only European Community legislation printed in the paper edition of the *Official Journal of the European Union* is deemed authentic' but from 1 July 2013 only the Official Journal published in electronic form shall be authentic and shall produce legal effects. https://ec.europa.eu/competition/antitrust/legislation/market.html.

[1] The focus of assessment in State aid cases is the aid recipient and the industry/sector concerned rather than identification of competitive constraints faced by the aid recipient. When consideration of market power and therefore of the relevant market are raised in any particular case, elements of the approach outlined here might serve as a basis for the assessment of State aid cases.

[2] For the purposes of this notice, the undertakings involved will be, in the case of a concentration, the parties to the concentration; in investigations within the meaning of Article 86 of the Treaty, the undertaking being investigated or the complainants; for investigations within the meaning of Article 85, the parties to the Agreement.

which the Commission follows when considering market definition and by indicating the criteria and evidence on which it relies to reach a decision, the Commission expects to increase the transparency of its policy and decision-making in the area of competition policy.

5. Increased transparency will also result in companies and their advisers being able to better anticipate the possibility that the Commission may raise competition concerns in an individual case. Companies could, therefore, take such a possibility into account in their own internal decision-making when contemplating, for instance, acquisitions, the creation of joint ventures, or the establishment of certain agreements. It is also intended that companies should be in a better position to understand what sort of information the Commission considers relevant for the purposes of market definition.

6. The Commission's interpretation of 'relevant market' is without prejudice to the interpretation which may be given by the Court of Justice or the Court of First Instance of the European Communities.

II. DEFINITION OF RELEVANT MARKET

Definition of relevant product market and relevant geographic market

7. The Regulations based on Article 85 and 86 of the Treaty, in particular in section 6 of Form A/B with respect to Regulation No 17, as well as in section 6 of Form CO with respect to Regulation (EEC) No 4064/89 on the control of concentrations having a Community dimension have laid down the following definitions, 'Relevant product markets' are defined as follows:

'A relevant product market comprises all those products and/or services which are regarded as interchangeable or substitutable by the consumer, by reason of the products' characteristics, their prices and their intended use'.

8. 'Relevant geographic markets' are defined as follows:

'The relevant geographic market comprises the area in which the undertakings concerned are involved in the supply and demand of products or services, in which the conditions of competition are sufficiently homogeneous and which can be distinguished from neighbouring areas because the conditions of competition are appreciably different in those area'.

9. The relevant market within which to assess a given competition issue is therefore established by the combination of the product and geographic markets. The Commission interprets the definitions in paragraphs 7 and 8 (which reflect the case-law of the Court of Justice and the Court of First Instance as well as its own decision-making practice) according to the orientations defined in this notice.

Concept of relevant market and objectives of Community competition policy

10. The concept of relevant market is closely related to the objectives pursued under Community competition policy. For example, under the Community's merger control, the objective in controlling structural changes in the supply of a product/service is to prevent the creation or reinforcement of a dominant position as a result of which effective competition would be significantly impeded in a substantial part of the common market. Under the Community's competition rules, a dominant position is such that a firm or group of firms would be in a position to behave to an appreciable extent independently of its competitors, customers and ultimately of its consumers.[3] Such a position would usually arise when a firm or group of firms accounted for a large share of the supply in any given market, provided that other factors analysed in the assessment (such as entry barriers, customers' capacity to react, etc.) point in the same direction.

11. The same approach is followed by the Commission in its application of Article 86 of the Treaty to firms that enjoy a single or collective dominant position. Within the meaning of Regulation No 17, the Commission has the power to investigate and bring to an end abuses of such a dominant

---

[3] Definition given by the Court of Justice in its judgment of 13 February 1979 in Case 85/76, Hoffmann-La Roche [1979] ECR 461, and confirmed in subsequent judgments.

position, which must also be defined by reference to the relevant market. Markets may also need to be defined in the application of Article 85 of the Treaty, in particular, in determining whether an appreciable restriction of competition exists or in establishing if the condition pursuant to Article 85(3)(b) for an exemption from the application of Article 85(1) is met.

12. The criteria for defining the relevant market are applied generally for the analysis of certain types of behaviour in the market and for the analysis of structural changes in the supply of products. This methodology, though, might lead to different results depending on the nature of the competition issue being examined. For instance, the scope of the geographic market might be different when analysing a concentration, where the analysis is essentially prospective, from an analysis of past behaviour. The different time horizon considered in each case might lead to the result that different geographic markets are defined for the same products depending on whether the Commission is examining a change in the structure of supply, such as a concentration or a cooperative joint venture, or examining issues relating to certain past behaviour.

Basic principles for market definition

Competitive constraints

13. Firms are subject to three main sources or competitive constraints: demand substitutability, supply substitutability and potential competition. From an economic point of view, for the definition of the relevant market, demand substitution constitutes the most immediate and effective disciplinary force on the suppliers of a given product, in particular in relation to their pricing decisions. A firm or a group of firms cannot have a significant impact on the prevailing conditions of sale, such as prices, if its customers are in a position to switch easily to available substitute products or to suppliers located elsewhere. Basically, the exercise of market definition consists in identifying the effective alternative sources of supply for the customers of the undertakings involved, in terms both of products/services and of geographic location of suppliers.

14. The competitive constraints arising from supply side substitutability other then those described in paragraphs 20 to 23 and from potential competition are in general less immediate and in any case require an analysis of additional factors. As a result such constraints are taken into account at the assessment stage of competition analysis.

Demand substitution

15. The assessment of demand substitution entails a determination of the range of products which are viewed as substitutes by the consumer. One way of making this determination can be viewed as a speculative experiment, postulating a hypothetical small, lasting change in relative prices and evaluating the likely reactions of customers to that increase. The exercise of market definition focuses on prices for operational and practical purposes, and more precisely on demand substitution arising from small, permanent changes in relative prices. This concept can provide clear indications as to the evidence that is relevant in defining markets.

16. Conceptually, this approach means that, starting from the type of products that the undertakings involved sell and the area in which they sell them, additional products and areas will be included in, or excluded from, the market definition depending on whether competition from these other products and areas affect or restrain sufficiently the pricing of the parties' products in the short term.

17. The question to be answered is whether the parties' customers would switch to readily available substitutes or to suppliers located elsewhere in response to a hypothetical small (in the range 5% to 10%) but permanent relative price increase in the products and areas being considered. If substitution were enough to make the price increase unprofitable because of the resulting loss of sales, additional substitutes and areas are included in the relevant market. This would be done until the set of products and geographical areas is such that small, permanent increases in relative prices would be profitable. The equivalent analysis is applicable in cases concerning the concentration of buying power, where the starting point would then be the supplier and the price test serves to identify the alternative distribution channels or outlets for the supplier's products. In the application of

these principles, careful account should be taken of certain particular situations as described within paragraphs 56 and 58.

18. A practical example of this test can be provided by its application to a merger of, for instance, soft-drink bottlers. An issue to examine in such a case would be to decide whether different flavours of soft drinks belong to the same market. In practice, the question to address would be whether consumers of flavour A would switch to other flavours when confronted with a permanent price increase of 5% to 10% for flavour A. If a sufficient number of consumers would switch to, say, flavour B, to such an extent that the price increase for flavour A would not be profitable owing to the resulting loss of sales, then the market would comprise at least flavours A and B. The process would have to be extended in addition to other available flavours until a set of products is identified for which a price rise would not induce a sufficient substitution in demand.

19. Generally, and in particular for the analysis of merger cases, the price to take into account will be the prevailing market price. This may not be the case where the prevailing price has been determined in the absence of sufficient competition. In particular for the investigation of abuses of dominant positions, the fact that the prevailing price might already have been substantially increased will be taken into account.

Supply substitution

20. Supply-side substitutability may also be taken into account when defining markets in those situations in which its effects are equivalent to those of demand substitution in terms of effectiveness and immediacy. This means that suppliers are able to switch production to the relevant products and market them in the short term[4] without incurring significant additional costs or risks in response to small and permanent changes in relative prices. When these conditions are met, the additional production that is put on the market will have a disciplinary effect on the competitive behaviour of the companies involved. Such an impact in terms of effectiveness and immediacy is equivalent to the demand substitution effect.

21. These situations typically arise when companies market a wide range of qualities or grades of one product; even if, for a given final customer or group of consumers, the different qualities are not substitutable, the different qualities will be grouped into one product market, provided that most of the suppliers are able to offer and sell the various qualities immediately and without the significant increases in costs described above. In such cases, the relevant product market will encompass all products that are substitutable in demand and supply, and the current sales of those products will be aggregated so as to give the total value or volume of the market. The same reasoning may lead to group different geographic areas.

22. A practical example of the approach to supply-side substitutability when defining product markets is to be found in the case of paper. Paper is usually supplied in a range of different qualities, from standard writing paper to high quality papers to be used, for instance, to publish art books. From a demand point of view, different qualities of paper cannot be used for any given use, i.e. an art book or a high quality publication cannot be based on lower quality papers. However, paper plants are prepared to manufacture the different qualities, and production can be adjusted with negligible costs and in a short time-frame. In the absence of particular difficulties in distribution, paper manufacturers are able therefore, to compete for orders of the various qualities, in particular if orders are placed with sufficient lead time to allow for modification of production plans. Under such circumstances, the Commission would not define a separate market for each quality of paper and its respective use. The various qualities of paper are included in the relevant market, and their sales added up to estimate total market value and volume.

23. When supply-side substitutability would entail the need to adjust significantly existing tangible and intangible assets, additional investments, strategic decisions or time delays, it will not be considered at the stage of market definition. Examples where supply-side substitution did not induce the Commission to enlarge the market are offered in the area of consumer products, in particular

---

[4] That is such a period that does not entail a significant adjustment of existing tangible and intangible assets (see paragraph 23).

for branded beverages. Although bottling plants may in principle bottle different beverages, there are costs and lead times involved (in terms of advertising, product testing and distribution) before the products can actually be sold. In these cases, the effects of supply-side substitutability and other forms of potential competition would then be examined at a later stage.

Potential competition

24. The third source of competitive constraint, potential competition, is not taken into account when defining markets, since the conditions under which potential competition will actually represent an effective competitive constraint depend on the analysis of specific factors and circumstances related to the conditions of entry. If required, this analysis is only carried out at a subsequent stage, in general once the position of the companies involved in the relevant market has already been ascertained, and when such position gives rise to concerns from a competition point of view.

III. EVIDENCE RELIED ON TO DEFINE RELEVANT MARKETS

The process of defining the relevant market in practice

Product dimension

25. There is a range of evidence permitting an assessment of the extent to which substitution would take place. In individual cases, certain types of evidence will be determinant, depending very much on the characteristics and specificity of the industry and products or services that are being examined. The same type of evidence may be of no importance in other cases. In most cases, a decision will have to be based on the consideration of a number of criteria and different items of evidence. The Commission follows an open approach to empirical evidence, aimed at making an effective use of all available information which may be relevant in individual cases. The Commission does not follow a rigid hierarchy of different sources of information or types of evidence.

26. The process of defining relevant markets may be summarized as follows: on the basis of the preliminary information available or information submitted by the undertakings involved, the Commission will usually be in a position to broadly establish the possible relevant markets within which, for instance, a concentration or a restriction of competition has to be assessed. In general, and for all practical purposes when handling individual cases, the question will usually be to decide on a few alternative possible relevant markets. For instance, with respect to the product market, the issue will often be to establish whether product A and product B belong or do not belong to the same product market. it is often the case that the inclusion of product B would be enough to remove any competition concerns.

27. In such situations it is not necessary to consider whether the market includes additional products, or to reach a definitive conclusion on the precise product market. If under the conceivable alternative market definitions the operation in question does not raise competition concerns, the question of market definition will be left open, reducing thereby the burden on companies to supply information.

Geographic dimension

28. The Commission's approach to geographic market definition might be summarized as follows: it will take a preliminary view of the scope of the geographic market on the basis of broad indications as to the distribution of market shares between the parties and their competitors, as well as a preliminary analysis of pricing and price differences at national and Community or EEA level. This initial view is used basically as a working hypothesis to focus the Commission's enquiries for the purposes of arriving at a precise geographic market definition.

29. The reasons behind any particular configuration of prices and market shares need to be explored. Companies might enjoy high market shares in their domestic markets just because of the weight of the past, and conversely, a homogeneous presence of companies throughout the EEA might

be consistent with national or regional geographic markets. The initial working hypothesis will therefore be checked against an analysis of demand characteristics (importance of national or local preferences, current patterns of purchases of customers, product differentiation/brands, other) in order to establish whether companies in different areas do indeed constitute a real alternative source of supply for consumers. The theoretical experiment is again based on substitution arising from changes in relative prices, and the question to answer is again whether the customers of the parties would switch their orders to companies located elsewhere in the short term and at a negligible cost.

30. If necessary, a further check on supply factors will be carried out to ensure that those companies located in differing areas do not face impediments in developing their sales on competitive terms throughout the whole geographic market. This analysis will include an examination of requirements for a local presence in order to sell in that area the conditions of access to distribution channels, costs associated with setting up a distribution network, and the presence or absence of regulatory barriers arising from public procurement, price regulations, quotas and tariffs limiting trade or production, technical standards, monopolies, freedom of establishment, requirements for administrative authorizations, packaging regulations, etc. In short, the Commission will identify possible obstacles and barriers isolating companies located in a given area from the competitive pressure of companies located outside that area, so as to determine the precise degree of market interpenetration at national, European or global level.

31. The actual pattern and evolution of trade flows offers useful supplementary indications as to the economic importance of each demand or supply factor mentioned above, and the extent to which they may or may not constitute actual barriers creating different geographic markets. The analysis of trade flows will generally address the question of transport costs and the extent to which these may hinder trade between different areas, having regard to plant location, costs of production and relative price levels.

Market integration in the Community

32. Finally, the Commission also takes into account the continuing process of market integration, in particular in the Community, when defining geographic markets, especially in the area of concentrations and structural joint ventures. The measures adopted and implemented in the internal market programme to remove barriers to trade and further integrate the Community markets cannot be ignored when assessing the effects on competition of a concentration or a structural joint venture. A situation where national markets have been artificially isolated from each other because of the existence of legislative barriers that have now been removed will generally lead to a cautious assessment of past evidence regarding prices, market shares or trade patterns. A process of market integration that would, in the short term, lead to wider geographic markets may therefore be taken into consideration when defining the geographic market for the purposes of assessing concentrations and joint ventures.

The process of gathering evidence

33. When a precise market definition is deemed necessary, the Commission will often contact the main customers and the main companies in the industry to enquire into their views about the boundaries of product and geographic markets and to obtain the necessary factual evidence to reach a conclusion. The Commission might also contact the relevant professional associations, and companies active in upstream markets, so as to be able to define, in so far as necessary, separate product and geographic markets, for different levels of production or distribution of the products/ services in question. It might also request additional information to the undertakings involved.

34. Where appropriate, the Commission will address written requests for information to the market players mentioned above. These requests will usually include questions relating to the perceptions of companies about reactions to hypothetical price increases and their views of the boundaries of the relevant market. They will also ask for provision of the factual information the Commission deems necessary to reach a conclusion on the extent of the relevant market. The Commission might also discuss with marketing directors or other officers of those companies to gain a better understanding on how negotiations between suppliers and customers take place and

better understand issues relating to the definition of the relevant market. Where appropriate, they might also carry out visits or inspections to the premises of the parties, their customers and/or their competitors, in order to better understand how products are manufactured and sold.

35. The type of evidence relevant to reach a conclusion as to the product market can be categorized as follows:

Evidence to define markets—product dimension

36. An analysis of the product characteristics and its intended use allows the Commission, as a first step, to limit the field of investigation of possible substitutes. However, product characteristics and intended use are insufficient to show whether two products are demand substitutes. Functional interchangeability or similarity in characteristics may not, in themselves, provide sufficient criteria, because the responsiveness of customers to relative price changes may be determined by other considerations as well. For example, there may be different competitive constraints in the original equipment market for car components and in spare parts, thereby leading to a separate delineation of two relevant markets. Conversely, differences in product characteristics are not in themselves sufficient to exclude demand substitutability, since this will depend to a large extent on how customers value different characteristics.

37. The type of evidence the Commission considers relevant to assess whether two products are demand substitutes can be categorized as follows:

38. *Evidence of substitution in the recent past.* In certain cases, it is possible to analyse evidence relating to recent past events or shocks in the market that offer actual examples of substitution between two products. When available, this sort of information will normally be fundamental for market definition. If there have been changes in relative prices in the past (all else being equal), the reactions in terms of quantities demanded will be determinant in establishing substitutability. Launches of new products in the past can also offer useful information, when it is possible to precisely analyse which products have lost sales to the new product.

39. There are a number of *quantitative* tests that have specifically been designed for the purpose of delineating markets. These tests consist of various econometric and statistical approaches estimates of elasticities and cross-price elasticities[5] for the demand of a product, tests based on similarity of price movements over time, the analysis of causality between price series and similarity of price levels and/or their convergence. The Commission takes into account the available quantitative evidence capable of withstanding rigorous scrutiny for the purposes of establishing patterns of substitution in the past.

40. *Views of customers and competitors.* The Commission often contacts the main customers and competitors of the companies involved in its enquiries, to gather their views on the boundaries of the product market as well as most of the factual information it requires to reach a conclusion on the scope of the market. Reasoned answers of customers and competitors as to what would happen if relative prices for the candidate products were to increase in the candidate geographic area by a small amount (for instance of 5% to 10%) are taken into account when they are sufficiently backed by factual evidence.

41. *Consumer preferences.* In the case of consumer goods, it may be difficult for the Commission to gather the direct views of end consumers about substitute products. *Marketing studies* that companies have commissioned in the past and that are used by companies in their own decision-making as to pricing of their products and/or marketing actions may provide useful information for the Commission's delineation of the relevant market. Consumer surveys on usage patterns and attitudes, data from consumer's purchasing patterns, the views expressed by retailers and more generally, market research studies submitted by the parties and their competitors are taken into account to establish whether an economically significant proportion of consumers consider two products as substitutable, also taking into account the importance of brands for the products in question.

---

[5] Own-price elasticity of demand for product X is a measure of the responsiveness of demand for X to percentage change in its own price. Cross-price elasticity between products X and Y is the responsiveness of demand for product X to percentage change in the price of product Y.

The methodology followed in consumer surveys carried out *ad hoc* by the undertakings involved or their competitors for the purposes of a merger procedure or a procedure pursuant to Regulation No 17 will usually be scrutinized with utmost care. Unlike pre-existing studies, they have not been prepared in the normal course of business for the adoption of business decisions.

42. *Barriers and costs associated with switching demand to potential substitutes.* There are a number of barriers and costs that might prevent the Commission from considering two *prima facie* demand substitutes as belonging to one single product market. It is not possible to provide an exhaustive list of all the possible barriers to substitution and of switching costs. These barriers or obstacles might have a wide range of origins, and in its decisions, the Commission has been confronted with regulatory barriers or other forms of State intervention, constraints arising in downstream markets, need to incur specific capital investment or loss in current output in order to switch to alternative inputs, the location of customers, specific investment in production process, learning and human capital investment, retooling costs or other investments, uncertainty about quality and reputation of unknown suppliers, and others.

43. *Different categories of customers and price discrimination.* The extent of the product market might be narrowed in the presence of distinct groups of customers. A distinct group of customers for the relevant product may constitute a narrower, distinct market when such a group could be subject to price discrimination. This will usually be the case when two conditions are met: (a) it is possible to identify clearly which group an individual customer belongs to at the moment of selling the relevant products to him, and (b) trade among customers or arbitrage by third parties should not be feasible.

Evidence for defining markets—geographic dimension

44. The type of evidence the Commission considers relevant to reach a conclusion as to the geographic market can be categorized as follows:

45. *Past evidence of diversion of orders to other areas.* In certain cases, evidence on changes in prices between different areas and consequent reactions by customers might be available. Generally, the same quantitative tests used for product market definition might as well be used in geographic market definition, bearing in mind that international comparisons of prices might be more complex due to a number of factors such as exchange rate movements, taxation and product differentiation.

46. *Basic demand characteristics.* The nature of demand for the relevant product may in itself determine the scope of the geographical market. Factors such as national preferences or preferences for national brands, language, culture and life style, and the need for a local presence have a strong potential to limit the geographic scope of competition.

47. *Views of customers and competitors.* Where appropriate, the Commission will contact the main customers and competitors of the parties in its enquiries, to gather their views on the boundaries of the geographic market as well as most of the factual information it requires to reach a conclusion on the scope of the market when they are sufficiently backed by factual evidence.

48. *Current geographic pattern of purchases.* An examination of the customers' current geographic pattern of purchases provides useful evidence as to the possible scope of the geographic market. When customers purchase from companies located anywhere in the Community or the EEA on similar terms, or they procure their supplies through effective tendering procedures in which companies from anywhere in the Community or the EEA submit bids, usually the geographic market will be considered to be Community-wide.

49. *Trade flows/pattern of shipments.* When the number of customers is so large that it is not possible to obtain through them a clear picture of geographic purchasing patterns, information on trade flows might be used alternatively, provided that the trade statistics are available with a sufficient degree of detail for the relevant products. Trade flows, and above all, the rationale behind trade flows provide useful insights and information for the purpose of establishing the scope of the geographic market but are not in themselves conclusive.

50. *Barriers and switching costs associated to divert orders to companies located in other areas.* The absence of trans-border purchases or trade flows, for instance, does not necessarily mean that

the market is at most national in scope. Still, barriers isolating the national market have to identified before it is concluded that the relevant geographic market in such a case is national. Perhaps the clearest obstacle for a customer to divert its orders to other areas is the impact of transport costs and transport restrictions arising from legislation or from the nature of the relevant products. The impact of transport costs will usually limit the scope of the geographic market for bulky, low-value products, bearing in mind that a transport disadvantage might also be compensated by a comparative advantage in other costs (labour costs or raw materials). Access to distribution in a given area, regulatory barriers still existing in certain sectors, quotas and custom tariffs might also constitute barriers isolating a geographic area from the competitive pressure of companies located outside that area. Significant switching costs in procuring supplies from companies located in other countries constitute additional sources of such barriers.

51. On the basis of the evidence gathered, the Commission will then define a geographic market that could range from a local dimension to a global one, and there are examples of both local and global markets in past decisions of the Commission.

52. The paragraphs above describe the different factors which might be relevant to define markets. This does not imply that in each individual case it will be necessary to obtain evidence and assess each of these factors. Often in practice the evidence provided by a subset of these factors will be sufficient to reach a conclusion, as shown in the past decisional practice of the Commission.

IV. CALCULATION OF MARKET SHARE

53. The definition of the relevant market in both its product and geographic dimensions allows the identification the suppliers and the customers/consumers active on that market. On that basis, a total market size and market shares for each supplier can be calculated on the basis of their sales of the relevant products in the relevant area. In practice, the total market size and market shares are often available from market sources, i.e. companies' estimates, studies commissioned from industry consultants and/or trade associations. When this is not the case, or when available estimates are not reliable, the Commission will usually ask each supplier in the relevant market to provide its own sales in order to calculate total market size and market shares.

54. If sales are usually the reference to calculate market shares, there are nevertheless other indications that, depending on the specific products or industry in question, can offer useful information such as, in particular, capacity, the number of players in bidding markets, units of fleet as in aerospace, or the reserves held in the case of sectors such as mining.

55. As a rule of thumb, both volume sales and value sales provide useful information. In cases of differentiated products, sales in value and their associated market share will usually be considered to better reflect the relative position and strength of each supplier.

V. ADDITIONAL CONSIDERATIONS

56. There are certain areas where the application of the principles above has to be undertaken with care. This is the case when considering primary and secondary markets, in particular, when the behaviour of undertakings at a point in time has to be analysed pursuant to Article 86. The method of defining markets in these cases is the same, i.e. assessing the responses of customers based on their purchasing decisions to relative price changes, but taking into account as well, constraints on substitution imposed by conditions in the connected markets. A narrow definition of market for secondary products, for instance, spare parts, may result when compatibility with the primary product is important. Problems of finding compatible secondary products together with the existence of high prices and a long lifetime of the primary products may render relative price increases of secondary products profitable. A different market definition may result if significant substitution between secondary products is possible or if the characteristics of the primary products make quick and direct consumer responses to relative price increases of the secondary products feasible.

57. In certain cases, the existence of chains of substitution might lead to the definition of a relevant market where products or areas at the extreme of the market are not directly substitutable. An example might be provided by the geographic dimension of a product with significant transport costs. In such cases, deliveries from a given plant are limited to a certain area around each plant by the impact of transport costs. In principle, such an area could constitute the relevant geographic market. However, if the distribution of plants is such that there are considerable overlaps between the areas around different plants, it is possible that the pricing of those products will be constrained by a chain substitution effect, and lead to the definition of a broader geographic market. The same reasoning may apply if product B is a demand substitute for products A and C. Even if products A and C are not direct demand substitutes, they might be found to be in the same relevant product market since their respective pricing might be constrained by substitution to B.

58. From a practical perspective, the concept of chains of substitution has to be corroborated by actual evidence, for instance related to price interdependence at the extremes of the chains of substitution, in order to lead to an extension of the relevant market in an individual case. Price levels at the extremes of the chains would have to be of the same magnitude as well.

Council Regulation (EC) No 1/2003 of 16 December 2002 on the implementation of the rules on competition laid down in Articles 81 and 82 of the Treaty*

[OJ 2003 L1/1]

THE COUNCIL OF THE EUROPEAN UNION,

Having regard to the Treaty establishing the European Community, and in particular Article 83 thereof,

Having regard to the proposal from the Commission,[1]

Having regard to the opinion of the European Parliament,[2]

Having regard to the opinion of the European Economic and Social Committee,[3]

Whereas:

(1) In order to establish a system which ensures that competition in the common market is not distorted, Articles 81 and 82 of the Treaty must be applied effectively and uniformly in the Community. Council Regulation No 17 of 6 February 1962, First Regulation implementing Articles 81 and 82[4] of the Treaty,[5] has allowed a Community competition policy to develop that has helped to disseminate a competition culture within the Community. In the light of experience, however, that Regulation should now be replaced by legislation designed to meet the challenges of an integrated market and a future enlargement of the Community.

(2) In particular, there is a need to rethink the arrangements for applying the exception from the prohibition on agreements, which restrict competition, laid down in Article 81(3) of the Treaty. Under Article 83(2)(b) of the Treaty, account must be taken in this regard of the need to ensure effective supervision, on the one hand, and to simplify administration to the greatest possible extent, on the other.

(3) The centralised scheme set up by Regulation No 17 no longer secures a balance between those two objectives. It hampers application of the Community competition rules by the courts and

---

* **Editor's Note:** This Regulation replaced Regulation 17 with effect from 1 May 2004, with the exception of Art 8 which remains in force. As amended by Regulation 411/2004 (OJ 2004 L68/1), Regulation 1419/2006 (OJ 2006 L269/1) and Regulations 169, 246 and 487/2009 (OJ 2009 L61/1, L79/1 and L148/1).

[1] OJ C 365 E, 19.12.2000, p. 284.

[2] OJ C 72 E, 21.3.2002, p. 305.

[3] OJ C 155, 29.5.2001, p. 73.

[4] The title of Regulation No 17 has been adjusted to take account of the renumbering of the Articles of the EC Treaty, in accordance with Article 12 of the Treaty of Amsterdam; the original reference was to Articles 85 and 86 of the Treaty.

[5] OJ 13, 21.2.1962, p. 204/62. Regulation as last amended by Regulation (EC) No 1216/1999 (OJ L 148, 15.6.1999, p. 5).

competition authorities of the Member States, and the system of notification it involves prevents the Commission from concentrating its resources on curbing the most serious infringements. It also imposes considerable costs on undertakings.

(4) The present system should therefore be replaced by a directly applicable exception system in which the competition authorities and courts of the Member States have the power to apply not only Article 81(1) and Article 82 of the Treaty, which have direct applicability by virtue of the case-law of the Court of Justice of the European Communities, but also Article 81(3) of the Treaty.

(5) In order to ensure an effective enforcement of the Community competition rules and at the same time the respect of fundamental rights of defence, this Regulation should regulate the burden of proof under Articles 81 and 82 of the Treaty. It should be for the party or the authority alleging an infringement of Article 81(1) and Article 82 of the Treaty to prove the existence thereof to the required legal standard. It should be for the undertaking or association of undertakings invoking the benefit of a defence against a finding of an infringement to demonstrate to the required legal standard that the conditions for applying such defence are satisfied. This Regulation affects neither national rules on the standard of proof nor obligations of competition authorities and courts of the Member States to ascertain the relevant facts of a case, provided that such rules and obligations are compatible with general principles of Community law.

(6) In order to ensure that the Community competition rules are applied effectively, the competition authorities of the Member States should be associated more closely with their application. To this end, they should be empowered to apply Community law.

(7) National courts have an essential part to play in applying the Community competition rules. When deciding disputes between private individuals, they protect the subjective rights under Community law, for example, by awarding damages to the victims of infringements. The role of the national courts here complements that of the competition authorities of the Member States. They should therefore be allowed to apply Articles 81 and 82 of the Treaty in full.

(8) In order to ensure the effective enforcement of the Community competition rules and the proper functioning of the cooperation mechanisms contained in this Regulation, it is necessary to oblige the competition authorities and courts of the Member States to also apply Articles 81 and 82 of the Treaty where they apply national competition law to agreements and practices which may affect trade between Member States. In order to create a level playing field for agreements, decisions by associations of undertakings and concerted practices within the internal market, it is also necessary to determine pursuant to Article 83(2)(e) of the Treaty the relationship between national laws and Community competition law. To that effect it is necessary to provide that the application of national competition laws to agreements, decisions or concerted practices within the meaning of Article 81(1) of the Treaty may not lead to the prohibition of such agreements, decisions and concerted practices if they are not also prohibited under Community competition law. The notions of agreements, decisions and concerted practices are autonomous concepts of Community competition law covering the coordination of behaviour of undertakings on the market as interpreted by the Community Courts. Member States should not under this Regulation be precluded from adopting and applying on their territory stricter national competition laws which prohibit or impose sanctions on unilateral conduct engaged in by undertakings. These stricter national laws may include provisions which prohibit or impose sanctions on abusive behaviour toward economically dependent undertakings. Furthermore, this Regulation does not apply to national laws which impose criminal sanctions on natural persons except to the extent that such sanctions are the means whereby competition rules applying to undertakings are enforced.

(9) Articles 81 and 82 of the Treaty have as their objective the protection of competition on the market. This Regulation, which is adopted for the implementation of these Treaty provisions, does not preclude Member States from implementing on their territory national legislation, which protects other legitimate interests provided that such legislation is compatible with general principles and other provisions of Community law. Insofar as such national legislation pursues predominantly an objective different from that of protecting competition on the market, the competition authorities and courts of the Member States may apply such legislation on their territory. Accordingly, Member States may under this

Regulation implement on their territory national legislation that prohibits or imposes sanctions on acts of unfair trading practice, be they unilateral or contractual. Such legislation pursues a specific objective, irrespective of the actual or presumed effects of such acts on competition on the market. This is particularly the case of legislation which prohibits undertakings from imposing on their trading partners, obtaining or attempting to obtain from them terms and conditions that are unjustified, disproportionate or without consideration.

(10) Regulations such as 19/65/EEC,[6] (EEC) No 2821/71,[7] (EEC) No 3976/87,[8] (EEC) No 1534/91,[9] or (EEC) No 479/92[10] empower the Commission to apply Article 81(3) of the Treaty by Regulation to certain categories of agreements, decisions by associations of undertakings and concerted practices. In the areas defined by such Regulations, the Commission has adopted and may continue to adopt so called 'block' exemption Regulations by which it declares Article 81(1) of the Treaty inapplicable to categories of agreements, decisions and concerted practices. Where agreements, decisions and concerted practices to which such Regulations apply nonetheless have effects that are incompatible with Article 81(3) of the Treaty, the Commission and the competition authorities of the Member States should have the power to withdraw in a particular case the benefit of the block exemption Regulation.

(11) For it to ensure that the provisions of the Treaty are applied, the Commission should be able to address decisions to undertakings or associations of undertakings for the purpose of bringing to an end infringements of Articles 81 and 82 of the Treaty. Provided there is a legitimate interest in doing so, the Commission should also be able to adopt decisions which find that an infringement has been committed in the past even if it does not impose a fine. This Regulation should also make explicit provision for the Commission's power to adopt decisions ordering interim measures, which has been acknowledged by the Court of Justice.

(12) This Regulation should make explicit provision for the Commission's power to impose any remedy, whether behavioural or structural, which is necessary to bring the infringement effectively to an end, having regard to the principle of proportionality. Structural remedies should only be imposed either where there is no equally effective behavioural remedy or where any equally effective behavioural remedy would be more burdensome for the undertaking concerned than the structural remedy. Changes to the structure of an undertaking as it existed before the infringement was committed would only be proportionate where there is a substantial risk of a lasting or repeated infringement that derives from the very structure of the undertaking.

(13) Where, in the course of proceedings which might lead to an agreement or practice being prohibited, undertakings offer the Commission commitments such as to meet its concerns, the Commission should be able to adopt decisions which make those commitments binding on the undertakings concerned. Commitment decisions should find that there are no longer grounds for

---

[6] Council Regulation No 19/65/EEC of 2 March 1965 on the application of Article 81(3) (the titles of the Regulations have been adjusted to take account of the renumbering of the Articles of the EC Treaty, in accordance with Article 12 of the Treaty of Amsterdam; the original reference was to Article 85(3) of the Treaty) of the Treaty to certain categories of agreements and concerted practices (OJ 36, 6.3.1965, p. 533). Regulation as last amended by Regulation (EC) No 1215/1999 (OJ L 148, 15.6.1999, p. 1).

[7] Council Regulation (EEC) No 2821/71 of 20 December 1971 on the application of Article 81(3) (the titles of the Regulations have been adjusted to take account of the renumbering of the Articles of the EC Treaty, in accordance with Article 12 of the Treaty of Amsterdam; the original reference was to Article 85(3) of the Treaty) of the Treaty to categories of agreements, decisions and concerted practices (OJ L 285, 29.12.1971, p. 46). Regulation as last amended by the Act of Accession of 1994.

[8] Council Regulation (EEC) No 3976/87 of 14 December 1987 on the application of Article 81(3) (the titles of the Regulations have been adjusted to take account of the renumbering of the Articles of the EC Treaty, in accordance with Article 12 of the Treaty of Amsterdam; the original reference was to Article 85(3) of the Treaty) of the Treaty to certain categories of agreements and concerted practices in the air transport sector (OJ L 374, 31.12.1987, p. 9). Regulation as last amended by the Act of Accession of 1994.

[9] Council Regulation (EEC) No 1534/91 of 31 May 1991 on the application of Article 81(3) (the titles of the Regulations have been adjusted to take account of the renumbering of the Articles of the EC Treaty, in accordance with Article 12 of the Treaty of Amsterdam; the original reference was to Article 85(3) of the Treaty) of the Treaty to certain categories of agreements, decisions and concerted practices in the insurance sector (OJ L 143, 7.6.1991, p. 1).

[10] Council Regulation (EEC) No 479/92 of 25 February 1992 on the application of Article 81(3) (the titles of the Regulations have been adjusted to take account of the renumbering of the Articles of the EC Treaty, in accordance with Article 12 of the Treaty of Amsterdam; the original reference was to Article 85(3) of the Treaty) of the Treaty to certain categories of agreements, decisions and concerted practices between liner shipping companies (Consortia) (OJ L 55, 29.2.1992, p. 3). Regulation amended by the Act of Accession of 1994.

action by the Commission without concluding whether or not there has been or still is an infringement. Commitment decisions are without prejudice to the powers of competition authorities and courts of the Member States to make such a finding and decide upon the case. Commitment decisions are not appropriate in cases where the Commission intends to impose a fine.

(14) In exceptional cases where the public interest of the Community so requires, it may also be expedient for the Commission to adopt a decision of a declaratory nature finding that the prohibition in Article 81 or Article 82 of the Treaty does not apply, with a view to clarifying the law and ensuring its consistent application throughout the Community, in particular with regard to new types of agreements or practices that have not been settled in the existing case-law and administrative practice.

(15) The Commission and the competition authorities of the Member States should form together a network of public authorities applying the Community competition rules in close cooperation. For that purpose it is necessary to set up arrangements for information and consultation. Further modalities for the cooperation within the network will be laid down and revised by the Commission, in close cooperation with the Member States.

(16) Notwithstanding any national provision to the contrary, the exchange of information and the use of such information in evidence should be allowed between the members of the network even where the information is confidential. This information may be used for the application of Articles 81 and 82 of the Treaty as well as for the parallel application of national competition law, provided that the latter application relates to the same case and does not lead to a different outcome. When the information exchanged is used by the receiving authority to impose sanctions on undertakings, there should be no other limit to the use of the information than the obligation to use it for the purpose for which it was collected given the fact that the sanctions imposed on undertakings are of the same type in all systems. The rights of defence enjoyed by undertakings in the various systems can be considered as sufficiently equivalent. However, as regards natural persons, they may be subject to substantially different types of sanctions across the various systems. Where that is the case, it is necessary to ensure that information can only be used if it has been collected in a way which respects the same level of protection of the rights of defence of natural persons as provided for under the national rules of the receiving authority.

(17) If the competition rules are to be applied consistently and, at the same time, the network is to be managed in the best possible way, it is essential to retain the rule that the competition authorities of the Member States are automatically relieved of their competence if the Commission initiates its own proceedings. Where a competition authority of a Member State is already acting on a case and the Commission intends to initiate proceedings, it should endeavour to do so as soon as possible. Before initiating proceedings, the Commission should consult the national authority concerned.

(18) To ensure that cases are dealt with by the most appropriate authorities within the network, a general provision should be laid down allowing a competition authority to suspend or close a case on the ground that another authority is dealing with it or has already dealt with it, the objective being that each case should be handled by a single authority. This provision should not prevent the Commission from rejecting a complaint for lack of Community interest, as the case-law of the Court of Justice has acknowledged it may do, even if no other competition authority has indicated its intention of dealing with the case.

(19) The Advisory Committee on Restrictive Practices and Dominant Positions set up by Regulation No 17 has functioned in a very satisfactory manner. It will fit well into the new system of decentralised application. It is necessary, therefore, to build upon the rules laid down by Regulation No 17, while improving the effectiveness of the organisational arrangements. To this end, it would be expedient to allow opinions to be delivered by written procedure. The Advisory Committee should also be able to act as a forum for discussing cases that are being handled by the competition authorities of the Member States, so as to help safeguard the consistent application of the Community competition rules.

(20) The Advisory Committee should be composed of representatives of the competition authorities of the Member States. For meetings in which general issues are being discussed, Member

States should be able to appoint an additional representative. This is without prejudice to members of the Committee being assisted by other experts from the Member States.

(21) Consistency in the application of the competition rules also requires that arrangements be established for cooperation between the courts of the Member States and the Commission. This is relevant for all courts of the Member States that apply Articles 81 and 82 of the Treaty, whether applying these rules in lawsuits between private parties, acting as public enforcers or as review courts. In particular, national courts should be able to ask the Commission for information or for its opinion on points concerning the application of Community competition law. The Commission and the competition authorities of the Member States should also be able to submit written or oral observations to courts called upon to apply Article 81 or Article 82 of the Treaty. These observations should be submitted within the framework of national procedural rules and practices including those safeguarding the rights of the parties. Steps should therefore be taken to ensure that the Commission and the competition authorities of the Member States are kept sufficiently well informed of proceedings before national courts.

(22) In order to ensure compliance with the principles of legal certainty and the uniform application of the Community competition rules in a system of parallel powers, conflicting decisions must be avoided. It is therefore necessary to clarify, in accordance with the case-law of the Court of Justice, the effects of Commission decisions and proceedings on courts and competition authorities of the Member States. Commitment decisions adopted by the Commission do not affect the power of the courts and the competition authorities of the Member States to apply Articles 81 and 82 of the Treaty.

(23) The Commission should be empowered throughout the Community to require such information to be supplied as is necessary to detect any agreement, decision or concerted practice prohibited by Article 81 of the Treaty or any abuse of a dominant position prohibited by Article 82 of the Treaty. When complying with a decision of the Commission, undertakings cannot be forced to admit that they have committed an infringement, but they are in any event obliged to answer factual questions and to provide documents, even if this information may be used to establish against them or against another undertaking the existence of an infringement.

(24) The Commission should also be empowered to undertake such inspections as are necessary to detect any agreement, decision or concerted practice prohibited by Article 81 of the Treaty or any abuse of a dominant position prohibited by Article 82 of the Treaty. The competition authorities of the Member States should cooperate actively in the exercise of these powers.

(25) The detection of infringements of the competition rules is growing ever more difficult, and, in order to protect competition effectively, the Commission's powers of investigation need to be supplemented. The Commission should in particular be empowered to interview any persons who may be in possession of useful information and to record the statements made. In the course of an inspection, officials authorised by the Commission should be empowered to affix seals for the period of time necessary for the inspection. Seals should normally not be affixed for more than 72 hours. Officials authorised by the Commission should also be empowered to ask for any information relevant to the subject matter and purpose of the inspection.

(26) Experience has shown that there are cases where business records are kept in the homes of directors or other people working for an undertaking. In order to safeguard the effectiveness of inspections, therefore, officials and other persons authorised by the Commission should be empowered to enter any premises where business records may be kept, including private homes. However, the exercise of this latter power should be subject to the authorisation of the judicial authority.

(27) Without prejudice to the case-law of the Court of Justice, it is useful to set out the scope of the control that the national judicial authority may carry out when it authorises, as foreseen by national law including as a precautionary measure, assistance from law enforcement authorities in order to overcome possible opposition on the part of the undertaking or the execution of the decision to carry out inspections in non-business premises. It results from the case-law that the

national judicial authority may in particular ask the Commission for further information which it needs to carry out its control and in the absence of which it could refuse the authorisation. The case-law also confirms the competence of the national courts to control the application of national rules governing the implementation of coercive measures.

(28) In order to help the competition authorities of the Member States to apply Articles 81 and 82 of the Treaty effectively, it is expedient to enable them to assist one another by carrying out inspections and other fact-finding measures.

(29) Compliance with Articles 81 and 82 of the Treaty and the fulfilment of the obligations imposed on undertakings and associations of undertakings under this Regulation should be enforceable by means of fines and periodic penalty payments. To that end, appropriate levels of fine should also be laid down for infringements of the procedural rules.

(30) In order to ensure effective recovery of fines imposed on associations of undertakings for infringements that they have committed, it is necessary to lay down the conditions on which the Commission may require payment of the fine from the members of the association where the association is not solvent. In doing so, the Commission should have regard to the relative size of the undertakings belonging to the association and in particular to the situation of small and medium sized enterprises. Payment of the fine by one or several members of an association is without prejudice to rules of national law that provide for recovery of the amount paid from other members of the association.

(31) The rules on periods of limitation for the imposition of fines and periodic penalty payments were laid down in Council Regulation (EEC) No 2988/74,[11] which also concerns penalties in the field of transport. In a system of parallel powers, the acts, which may interrupt a limitation period, should include procedural steps taken independently by the competition authority of a Member State. To clarify the legal framework, Regulation (EEC) No 2988/74 should therefore be amended to prevent it applying to matters covered by this Regulation, and this Regulation should include provisions on periods of limitation.

(32) The undertakings concerned should be accorded the right to be heard by the Commission, third parties whose interests may be affected by a decision should be given the opportunity of submitting their observations beforehand, and the decisions taken should be widely publicised. While ensuring the rights of defence of the undertakings concerned, in particular, the right of access to the file, it is essential that business secrets be protected. The confidentiality of information exchanged in the network should likewise be safeguarded.

(33) Since all decisions taken by the Commission under this Regulation are subject to review by the Court of Justice in accordance with the Treaty, the Court of Justice should, in accordance with Article 229 thereof be given unlimited jurisdiction in respect of decisions by which the Commission imposes fines or periodic penalty payments.

(34) The principles laid down in Articles 81 and 82 of the Treaty, as they have been applied by Regulation No 17, have given a central role to the Community bodies. This central role should be retained, whilst associating the Member States more closely with the application of the Community competition rules. In accordance with the principles of subsidiarity and proportionality as set out in Article 5 of the Treaty, this Regulation does not go beyond what is necessary in order to achieve its objective, which is to allow the Community competition rules to be applied effectively.

(35) In order to attain a proper enforcement of Community competition law, Member States should designate and empower authorities to apply Articles 81 and 82 of the Treaty as public enforcers. They should be able to designate administrative as well as judicial authorities to carry out the various functions conferred upon competition authorities in this Regulation. This Regulation recognises the wide variation which exists in the public enforcement systems of Member States. The effects of Article 11(6) of this Regulation should apply to all competition authorities. As an exception to this general rule, where a prosecuting authority brings a case before a separate judicial authority,

---

[11] Council Regulation (EEC) No 2988/74 of 26 November 1974 concerning limitation periods in proceedings and the enforcement of sanctions under the rules of the European Economic Community relating to transport and competition (OJ L 319, 29.11.1974, p. 1).

Article 11(6) should apply to the prosecuting authority subject to the conditions in Article 35(4) of this Regulation. Where these conditions are not fulfilled, the general rule should apply. In any case, Article 11(6) should not apply to courts insofar as they are acting as review courts.

(36) As the case-law has made it clear that the competition rules apply to transport, that sector should be made subject to the procedural provisions of this Regulation. Council Regulation No 141 of 26 November 1962 exempting transport from the application of Regulation No 17[12] should therefore be repealed and Regulations (EEC) No 1017/68,[13] (EEC) No 4056/86[14] and (EEC) No 3975/87[15] should be amended in order to delete the specific procedural provisions they contain.

(37) This Regulation respects the fundamental rights and observes the principles recognised in particular by the Charter of Fundamental Rights of the European Union. Accordingly, this Regulation should be interpreted and applied with respect to those rights and principles.

(38) Legal certainty for undertakings operating under the Community competition rules contributes to the promotion of innovation and investment. Where cases give rise to genuine uncertainty because they present novel or unresolved questions for the application of these rules, individual undertakings may wish to seek informal guidance from the Commission. This Regulation is without prejudice to the ability of the Commission to issue such informal guidance,

HAS ADOPTED THIS REGULATION:

Chapter I Principles

Article 1   Application of Articles 81 and 82 of the Treaty

1. Agreements, decisions and concerted practices caught by Article 81(1) of the Treaty which do not satisfy the conditions of Article 81(3) of the Treaty shall be prohibited, no prior decision to that effect being required.

2. Agreements, decisions and concerted practices caught by Article 81(1) of the Treaty which satisfy the conditions of Article 81(3) of the Treaty shall not be prohibited, no prior decision to that effect being required.

3. The abuse of a dominant position referred to in Article 82 of the Treaty shall be prohibited, no prior decision to that effect being required.

Article 2   Burden of proof

In any national or Community proceedings for the application of Articles 81 and 82 of the Treaty, the burden of proving an infringement of Article 81(1) or of Article 82 of the Treaty shall rest on the party or the authority alleging the infringement. The undertaking or association of undertakings claiming the benefit of Article 81(3) of the Treaty shall bear the burden of proving that the conditions of that paragraph are fulfilled.

Article 3   Relationship between Articles 81 and 82 of the Treaty and national competition laws

1. Where the competition authorities of the Member States or national courts apply national competition law to agreements, decisions by associations of undertakings or concerted practices within the meaning of Article 81(1) of the Treaty which may affect trade between Member States within the meaning of that provision, they shall also apply Article 81 of the Treaty to such agreements, decisions or concerted practices. Where the competition authorities of the Member States or

---

[12] OJ 124, 28.11.1962, p. 2751/62; Regulation as last amended by Regulation No 1002/67/EEC (OJ 306, 16.12.1967, p. 1).

[13] Council Regulation (EEC) No 1017/68 of 19 July 1968 applying rules of competition to transport by rail, road and inland waterway (OJ L 175, 23.7.1968, p. 1). Regulation as last amended by the Act of Accession of 1994.

[14] Council Regulation (EEC) No 4056/86 of 22 December 1986 laying down detailed rules for the application of Articles 81 and 82 (the title of the Regulation has been adjusted to take account of the renumbering of the Articles of the EC Treaty, in accordance with Article 12 of the Treaty of Amsterdam; the original reference was to Articles 85 and 86 of the Treaty) of the Treaty to maritime transport (OJ L 378, 31.12.1986, p. 4). Regulation as last amended by the Act of Accession of 1994.

[15] Council Regulation (EEC) No 3975/87 of 14 December 1987 laying down the procedure for the application of the rules on competition to undertakings in the air transport sector (OJ L 374, 31.12.1987, p. 1). Regulation as last amended by Regulation (EEC) No 2410/92 (OJ L 240, 24.8.1992, p. 18).

national courts apply national competition law to any abuse prohibited by Article 82 of the Treaty, they shall also apply Article 82 of the Treaty.

2. The application of national competition law may not lead to the prohibition of agreements, decisions by associations of undertakings or concerted practices which may affect trade between Member States but which do not restrict competition within the meaning of Article 81(1) of the Treaty, or which fulfil the conditions of Article 81(3) of the Treaty or which are covered by a Regulation for the application of Article 81(3) of the Treaty. Member States shall not under this Regulation be precluded from adopting and applying on their territory stricter national laws which prohibit or sanction unilateral conduct engaged in by undertakings.

3. Without prejudice to general principles and other provisions of Community law, paragraphs 1 and 2 do not apply when the competition authorities and the courts of the Member States apply national merger control laws nor do they preclude the application of provisions of national law that predominantly pursue an objective different from that pursued by Articles 81 and 82 of the Treaty.

Chapter II Powers

Article 4 Powers of the Commission

For the purpose of applying Articles 81 and 82 of the Treaty, the Commission shall have the powers provided for by this Regulation.

Article 5 Powers of the competition authorities of the Member States

The competition authorities of the Member States shall have the power to apply Articles 81 and 82 of the Treaty in individual cases. For this purpose, acting on their own initiative or on a complaint, they may take the following decisions:

- requiring that an infringement be brought to an end,
- ordering interim measures,
- accepting commitments,
- imposing fines, periodic penalty payments or any other penalty provided for in their national law.

Where on the basis of the information in their possession the conditions for prohibition are not met they may likewise decide that there are no grounds for action on their part.

Article 6 Powers of the national courts

National courts shall have the power to apply Articles 81 and 82 of the Treaty.

Chapter III Commission decisions

Article 7 Finding and termination of infringement

1. Where the Commission, acting on a complaint or on its own initiative, finds that there is an infringement of Article 81 or of Article 82 of the Treaty, it may by decision require the undertakings and associations of undertakings concerned to bring such infringement to an end. For this purpose, it may impose on them any behavioural or structural remedies which are proportionate to the infringement committed and necessary to bring the infringement effectively to an end. Structural remedies can only be imposed either where there is no equally effective behavioural remedy or where any equally effective behavioural remedy would be more burdensome for the undertaking concerned than the structural remedy. If the Commission has a legitimate interest in doing so, it may also find that an infringement has been committed in the past.

2. Those entitled to lodge a complaint for the purposes of paragraph 1 are natural or legal persons who can show a legitimate interest and Member States.

Article 8 Interim measures

1. In cases of urgency due to the risk of serious and irreparable damage to competition, the Commission, acting on its own initiative may by decision, on the basis of a prima facie finding of infringement, order interim measures.

2. A decision under paragraph 1 shall apply for a specified period of time and may be renewed in so far this is necessary and appropriate.

Article 9   Commitments

1. Where the Commission intends to adopt a decision requiring that an infringement be brought to an end and the undertakings concerned offer commitments to meet the concerns expressed to them by the Commission in its preliminary assessment, the Commission may by decision make those commitments binding on the undertakings. Such a decision may be adopted for a specified period and shall conclude that there are no longer grounds for action by the Commission.

2. The Commission may, upon request or on its own initiative, reopen the proceedings:

(a)   where there has been a material change in any of the facts on which the decision was based;

(b)   where the undertakings concerned act contrary to their commitments; or

(c)   where the decision was based on incomplete, incorrect or misleading information provided by the parties.

Article 10   Finding of inapplicability

Where the Community public interest relating to the application of Articles 81 and 82 of the Treaty so requires, the Commission, acting on its own initiative, may by decision find that Article 81 of the Treaty is not applicable to an agreement, a decision by an association of undertakings or a concerted practice, either because the conditions of Article 81(1) of the Treaty are not fulfilled, or because the conditions of Article 81(3) of the Treaty are satisfied.

The Commission may likewise make such a finding with reference to Article 82 of the Treaty.

Chapter IV   Cooperation

Article 11

Cooperation between the Commission and the competition authorities of the Member States

1. The Commission and the competition authorities of the Member States shall apply the Community competition rules in close cooperation.

2. The Commission shall transmit to the competition authorities of the Member States copies of the most important documents it has collected with a view to applying Articles 7, 8, 9, 10 and Article 29(1). At the request of the competition authority of a Member State, the Commission shall provide it with a copy of other existing documents necessary for the assessment of the case.

3. The competition authorities of the Member States shall, when acting under Article 81 or Article 82 of the Treaty, inform the Commission in writing before or without delay after commencing the first formal investigative measure. This information may also be made available to the competition authorities of the other Member States.

4. No later than 30 days before the adoption of a decision requiring that an infringement be brought to an end, accepting commitments or withdrawing the benefit of a block exemption Regulation, the competition authorities of the Member States shall inform the Commission. To that effect, they shall provide the Commission with a summary of the case, the envisaged decision or, in the absence thereof, any other document indicating the proposed course of action. This information may also be made available to the competition authorities of the other Member States. At the request of the Commission, the acting competition authority shall make available to the Commission other documents it holds which are necessary for the assessment of the case. The information supplied to the Commission may be made available to the competition authorities of the other Member States. National competition authorities may also exchange between themselves information necessary for the assessment of a case that they are dealing with under Article 81 or Article 82 of the Treaty.

5. The competition authorities of the Member States may consult the Commission on any case involving the application of Community law.

6. The initiation by the Commission of proceedings for the adoption of a decision under Chapter III shall relieve the competition authorities of the Member States of their competence to apply Articles 81 and 82 of the Treaty. If a competition authority of a Member State is already acting on a case, the Commission shall only initiate proceedings after consulting with that national competition authority.

Article 12   Exchange of information

1. For the purpose of applying Articles 81 and 82 of the Treaty the Commission and the competition authorities of the Member States shall have the power to provide one another with and use in evidence any matter of fact or of law, including confidential information.

2. Information exchanged shall only be used in evidence for the purpose of applying Article 81 or Article 82 of the Treaty and in respect of the subject-matter for which it was collected by the transmitting authority. However, where national competition law is applied in the same case and in parallel to Community competition law and does not lead to a different outcome, information exchanged under this Article may also be used for the application of national competition law.

3. Information exchanged pursuant to paragraph 1 can only be used in evidence to impose sanctions on natural persons where:
   – the law of the transmitting authority foresees sanctions of a similar kind in relation to an infringement of Article 81 or Article 82 of the Treaty or, in the absence thereof,
   – the information has been collected in a way which respects the same level of protection of the rights of defence of natural persons as provided for under the national rules of the receiving authority. However, in this case, the information exchanged cannot be used by the receiving authority to impose custodial sanctions.

Article 13   Suspension or termination of proceedings

1. Where competition authorities of two or more Member States have received a complaint or are acting on their own initiative under Article 81 or Article 82 of the Treaty against the same agreement, decision of an association or practice, the fact that one authority is dealing with the case shall be sufficient grounds for the others to suspend the proceedings before them or to reject the complaint. The Commission may likewise reject a complaint on the ground that a competition authority of a Member State is dealing with the case.

2. Where a competition authority of a Member State or the Commission has received a complaint against an agreement, decision of an association or practice which has already been dealt with by another competition authority, it may reject it.

Article 14   Advisory Committee

1. The Commission shall consult an Advisory Committee on Restrictive Practices and Dominant Positions prior to the taking of any decision under Articles 7, 8, 9, 10, 23, Article 24(2) and Article 29(1).

2. For the discussion of individual cases, the Advisory Committee shall be composed of representatives of the competition authorities of the Member States. For meetings in which issues other than individual cases are being discussed, an additional Member State representative competent in competition matters may be appointed. Representatives may, if unable to attend, be replaced by other representatives.

3. The consultation may take place at a meeting convened and chaired by the Commission, held not earlier than 14 days after dispatch of the notice convening it, together with a summary of the case, an indication of the most important documents and a preliminary draft decision. In respect of decisions pursuant to Article 8, the meeting may be held seven days after the dispatch of the operative part of a draft decision. Where the Commission dispatches a notice convening the meeting which gives a shorter period of notice than those specified above, the meeting may take place on the proposed date in the absence of an objection by any Member State. The Advisory Committee shall deliver a written opinion on the Commission's preliminary draft decision. It may deliver an opinion even if some members are absent and are not represented. At the request of one or several members, the positions stated in the opinion shall be reasoned.

4. Consultation may also take place by written procedure. However, if any Member State so requests, the Commission shall convene a meeting. In case of written procedure, the Commission shall determine a time-limit of not less than 14 days within which the Member States are to put forward their observations for circulation to all other Member States. In case of decisions to be taken pursuant to Article 8, the time-limit of 14 days is replaced by seven days. Where the Commission determines a time-limit for the written procedure which is shorter than those specified above, the proposed time-limit shall be applicable in the absence of an objection by any Member State.

5. The Commission shall take the utmost account of the opinion delivered by the Advisory Committee. It shall inform the Committee of the manner in which its opinion has been taken into account.

6. Where the Advisory Committee delivers a written opinion, this opinion shall be appended to the draft decision. If the Advisory Committee recommends publication of the opinion, the Commission shall carry out such publication taking into account the legitimate interest of undertakings in the protection of their business secrets.

7. At the request of a competition authority of a Member State, the Commission shall include on the agenda of the Advisory Committee cases that are being dealt with by a competition authority of a Member State under Article 81 or Article 82 of the Treaty. The Commission may also do so on its own initiative. In either case, the Commission shall inform the competition authority concerned.

A request may in particular be made by a competition authority of a Member State in respect of a case where the Commission intends to initiate proceedings with the effect of Article 11(6).

The Advisory Committee shall not issue opinions on cases dealt with by competition authorities of the Member States. The Advisory Committee may also discuss general issues of Community competition law.

Article 15   Cooperation with national courts

1. In proceedings for the application of Article 81 or Article 82 of the Treaty, courts of the Member States may ask the Commission to transmit to them information in its possession or its opinion on questions concerning the application of the Community competition rules.

2. Member States shall forward to the Commission a copy of any written judgment of national courts deciding on the application of Article 81 or Article 82 of the Treaty. Such copy shall be forwarded without delay after the full written judgment is notified to the parties.

3. Competition authorities of the Member States, acting on their own initiative, may submit written observations to the national courts of their Member State on issues relating to the application of Article 81 or Article 82 of the Treaty. With the permission of the court in question, they may also submit oral observations to the national courts of their Member State. Where the coherent application of Article 81 or Article 82 of the Treaty so requires, the Commission, acting on its own initiative, may submit written observations to courts of the Member States. With the permission of the court in question, it may also make oral observations.

For the purpose of the preparation of their observations only, the competition authorities of the Member States and the Commission may request the relevant court of the Member State to transmit or ensure the transmission to them of any documents necessary for the assessment of the case.

4. This Article is without prejudice to wider powers to make observations before courts conferred on competition authorities of the Member States under the law of their Member State.

Article 16   Uniform application of Community competition law

1. When national courts rule on agreements, decisions or practices under Article 81 or Article 82 of the Treaty which are already the subject of a Commission decision, they cannot take decisions running counter to the decision adopted by the Commission. They must also avoid giving decisions which would conflict with a decision contemplated by the Commission in proceedings it has initiated. To that effect, the national court may assess whether it is necessary to stay its proceedings. This obligation is without prejudice to the rights and obligations under Article 234 of the Treaty.

2. When competition authorities of the Member States rule on agreements, decisions or practices under Article 81 or Article 82 of the Treaty which are already the subject of a Commission decision, they cannot take decisions which would run counter to the decision adopted by the Commission.

Chapter V Powers of investigation

Article 17   Investigations into sectors of the economy and into types of agreements

1. Where the trend of trade between Member States, the rigidity of prices or other circumstances suggest that competition may be restricted or distorted within the common market, the Commission may conduct its inquiry into a particular sector of the economy or into a particular type

of agreements across various sectors. In the course of that inquiry, the Commission may request the undertakings or associations of undertakings concerned to supply the information necessary for giving effect to Articles 81 and 82 of the Treaty and may carry out any inspections necessary for that purpose.

The Commission may in particular request the undertakings or associations of undertakings concerned to communicate to it all agreements, decisions and concerted practices.

The Commission may publish a report on the results of its inquiry into particular sectors of the economy or particular types of agreements across various sectors and invite comments from interested parties.

2. Articles 14, 18, 19, 20, 22, 23 and 24 shall apply *mutatis mutandis*.

Article 18   Requests for information

1. In order to carry out the duties assigned to it by this Regulation, the Commission may, by simple request or by decision, require undertakings and associations of undertakings to provide all necessary information.

2. When sending a simple request for information to an undertaking or association of undertakings, the Commission shall state the legal basis and the purpose of the request, specify what information is required and fix the time-limit within which the information is to be provided, and the penalties provided for in Article 23 for supplying incorrect or misleading information.

3. Where the Commission requires undertakings and associations of undertakings to supply information by decision, it shall state the legal basis and the purpose of the request, specify what information is required and fix the time-limit within which it is to be provided. It shall also indicate the penalties provided for in Article 23 and indicate or impose the penalties provided for in Article 24. It shall further indicate the right to have the decision reviewed by the Court of Justice.

4. The owners of the undertakings or their representatives and, in the case of legal persons, companies or firms, or associations having no legal personality, the persons authorised to represent them by law or by their constitution shall supply the information requested on behalf of the undertaking or the association of undertakings concerned. Lawyers duly authorised to act may supply the information on behalf of their clients. The latter shall remain fully responsible if the information supplied is incomplete, incorrect or misleading.

5. The Commission shall without delay forward a copy of the simple request or of the decision to the competition authority of the Member State in whose territory the seat of the undertaking or association of undertakings is situated and the competition authority of the Member State whose territory is affected.

6. At the request of the Commission the governments and competition authorities of the Member States shall provide the Commission with all necessary information to carry out the duties assigned to it by this Regulation.

Article 19   Power to take statements

1. In order to carry out the duties assigned to it by this Regulation, the Commission may interview any natural or legal person who consents to be interviewed for the purpose of collecting information relating to the subject-matter of an investigation.

2. Where an interview pursuant to paragraph 1 is conducted in the premises of an undertaking, the Commission shall inform the competition authority of the Member State in whose territory the interview takes place. If so requested by the competition authority of that Member State, its officials may assist the officials and other accompanying persons authorised by the Commission to conduct the interview.

Article 20   The Commission's powers of inspection

1. In order to carry out the duties assigned to it by this Regulation, the Commission may conduct all necessary inspections of undertakings and associations of undertakings.

2. The officials and other accompanying persons authorised by the Commission to conduct an inspection are empowered:

    (a) to enter any premises, land and means of transport of undertakings and associations of undertakings;

(b) to examine the books and other records related to the business, irrespective of the medium on which they are stored;

(c) to take or obtain in any form copies of or extracts from such books or records;

(d) to seal any business premises and books or records for the period and to the extent necessary for the inspection;

(e) to ask any representative or member of staff of the undertaking or association of undertakings for explanations on facts or documents relating to the subject-matter and purpose of the inspection and to record the answers.

3. The officials and other accompanying persons authorised by the Commission to conduct an inspection shall exercise their powers upon production of a written authorisation specifying the subject matter and purpose of the inspection and the penalties provided for in Article 23 in case the production of the required books or other records related to the business is incomplete or where the answers to questions asked under paragraph 2 of the present Article are incorrect or misleading. In good time before the inspection, the Commission shall give notice of the inspection to the competition authority of the Member State in whose territory it is to be conducted.

4. Undertakings and associations of undertakings are required to submit to inspections ordered by decision of the Commission. The decision shall specify the subject matter and purpose of the inspection, appoint the date on which it is to begin and indicate the penalties provided for in Articles 23 and 24 and the right to have the decision reviewed by the Court of Justice. The Commission shall take such decisions after consulting the competition authority of the Member State in whose territory the inspection is to be conducted.

5. Officials of as well as those authorised or appointed by the competition authority of the Member State in whose territory the inspection is to be conducted shall, at the request of that authority or of the Commission, actively assist the officials and other accompanying persons authorised by the Commission. To this end, they shall enjoy the powers specified in paragraph 2.

6. Where the officials and other accompanying persons authorised by the Commission find that an undertaking opposes an inspection ordered pursuant to this Article, the Member State concerned shall afford them the necessary assistance, requesting where appropriate the assistance of the police or of an equivalent enforcement authority, so as to enable them to conduct their inspection.

7. If the assistance provided for in paragraph 6 requires authorisation from a judicial authority according to national rules, such authorisation shall be applied for. Such authorisation may also be applied for as a precautionary measure.

8. Where authorisation as referred to in paragraph 7 is applied for, the national judicial authority shall control that the Commission decision is authentic and that the coercive measures envisaged are neither arbitrary nor excessive having regard to the subject matter of the inspection. In its control of the proportionality of the coercive measures, the national judicial authority may ask the Commission, directly or through the Member State competition authority, for detailed explanations in particular on the grounds the Commission has for suspecting infringement of Articles 81 and 82 of the Treaty, as well as on the seriousness of the suspected infringement and on the nature of the involvement of the undertaking concerned. However, the national judicial authority may not call into question the necessity for the inspection nor demand that it be provided with the information in the Commission's file. The lawfulness of the Commission decision shall be subject to review only by the Court of Justice.

Article 21   Inspection of other premises

1. If a reasonable suspicion exists that books or other records related to the business and to the subject-matter of the inspection, which may be relevant to prove a serious violation of Article 81 or Article 82 of the Treaty, are being kept in any other premises, land and means of transport, including the homes of directors, managers and other members of staff of the undertakings and associations of undertakings concerned, the Commission can by decision order an inspection to be conducted in such other premises, land and means of transport.

2. The decision shall specify the subject matter and purpose of the inspection, appoint the date on which it is to begin and indicate the right to have the decision reviewed by the Court of Justice. It shall in particular state the reasons that have led the Commission to conclude that a suspicion in the

sense of paragraph 1 exists. The Commission shall take such decisions after consulting the competition authority of the Member State in whose territory the inspection is to be conducted.

3. A decision adopted pursuant to paragraph 1 cannot be executed without prior authorisation from the national judicial authority of the Member State concerned. The national judicial authority shall control that the Commission decision is authentic and that the coercive measures envisaged are neither arbitrary nor excessive having regard in particular to the seriousness of the suspected infringement, to the importance of the evidence sought, to the involvement of the undertaking concerned and to the reasonable likelihood that business books and records relating to the subject matter of the inspection are kept in the premises for which the authorisation is requested. The national judicial authority may ask the Commission, directly or through the Member State competition authority, for detailed explanations on those elements which are necessary to allow its control of the proportionality of the coercive measures envisaged.

However, the national judicial authority may not call into question the necessity for the inspection nor demand that it be provided with information in the Commission's file. The lawfulness of the Commission decision shall be subject to review only by the Court of Justice.

4. The officials and other accompanying persons authorised by the Commission to conduct an inspection ordered in accordance with paragraph 1 of this Article shall have the powers set out in Article 20(2)(a), (b) and (c). Article 20(5) and (6) shall apply *mutatis mutandis*.

Article 22   Investigations by competition authorities of Member States

1. The competition authority of a Member State may in its own territory carry out any inspection or other fact-finding measure under its national law on behalf and for the account of the competition authority of another Member State in order to establish whether there has been an infringement of Article 81 or Article 82 of the Treaty. Any exchange and use of the information collected shall be carried out in accordance with Article 12.

2. At the request of the Commission, the competition authorities of the Member States shall undertake the inspections which the Commission considers to be necessary under Article 20(1) or which it has ordered by decision pursuant to Article 20(4). The officials of the competition authorities of the Member States who are responsible for conducting these inspections as well as those authorised or appointed by them shall exercise their powers in accordance with their national law.

If so requested by the Commission or by the competition authority of the Member State in whose territory the inspection is to be conducted, officials and other accompanying persons authorised by the Commission may assist the officials of the authority concerned.

Chapter VI Penalties

Article 23   Fines

1. The Commission may by decision impose on undertakings and associations of undertakings fines not exceeding 1% of the total turnover in the preceding business year where, intentionally or negligently:

  (a) they supply incorrect or misleading information in response to a request made pursuant to Article 17 or Article 18(2);

  (b) in response to a request made by decision adopted pursuant to Article 17 or Article 18(3), they supply incorrect, incomplete or misleading information or do not supply information within the required time-limit;

  (c) they produce the required books or other records related to the business in incomplete form during inspections under Article 20 or refuse to submit to inspections ordered by a decision adopted pursuant to Article 20(4);

  (d) in response to a question asked in accordance with Article 20(2)(e),

   – they give an incorrect or misleading answer,

   – they fail to rectify within a time-limit set by the Commission an incorrect, incomplete or misleading answer given by a member of staff, or

    – they fail or refuse to provide a complete answer on facts relating to the subject-matter and purpose of an inspection ordered by a decision adopted pursuant to Article 20(4);

    (e) seals affixed in accordance with Article 20(2)(d) by officials or other accompanying persons authorised by the Commission have been broken.

2. The Commission may by decision impose fines on undertakings and associations of undertakings where, either intentionally or negligently:

    (a) they infringe Article 81 or Article 82 of the Treaty; or

    (b) they contravene a decision ordering interim measures under Article 8; or

    (c) they fail to comply with a commitment made binding by a decision pursuant to Article 9.

For each undertaking and association of undertakings participating in the infringement, the fine shall not exceed 10% of its total turnover in the preceding business year.

Where the infringement of an association relates to the activities of its members, the fine shall not exceed 10% of the sum of the total turnover of each member active on the market affected by the infringement of the association.

3. In fixing the amount of the fine, regard shall be had both to the gravity and to the duration of the infringement.

4. When a fine is imposed on an association of undertakings taking account of the turnover of its members and the association is not solvent, the association is obliged to call for contributions from its members to cover the amount of the fine.

Where such contributions have not been made to the association within a time-limit fixed by the Commission, the Commission may require payment of the fine directly by any of the undertakings whose representatives were members of the decision-making bodies concerned of the association.

After the Commission has required payment under the second subparagraph, where necessary to ensure full payment of the fine, the Commission may require payment of the balance by any of the members of the association which were active on the market on which the infringement occurred.

However, the Commission shall not require payment under the second or the third subparagraph from undertakings which show that they have not implemented the infringing decision of the association and either were not aware of its existence or have actively distanced themselves from it before the Commission started investigating the case.

The financial liability of each undertaking in respect of the payment of the fine shall not exceed 10% of its total turnover in the preceding business year.

5. Decisions taken pursuant to paragraphs 1 and 2 shall not be of a criminal law nature.

Article 24   Periodic penalty payments

1. The Commission may, by decision, impose on undertakings or associations of undertakings periodic penalty payments not exceeding 5% of the average daily turnover in the preceding business year per day and calculated from the date appointed by the decision, in order to compel them:

    (a) to put an end to an infringement of Article 81 or Article 82 of the Treaty, in accordance with a decision taken pursuant to Article 7;

    (b) to comply with a decision ordering interim measures taken pursuant to Article 8;

    (c) to comply with a commitment made binding by a decision pursuant to Article 9;

    (d) to supply complete and correct information which it has requested by decision taken pursuant to Article 17 or Article 18(3);

    (e) to submit to an inspection which it has ordered by decision taken pursuant to Article 20(4).

2. Where the undertakings or associations of undertakings have satisfied the obligation which the periodic penalty payment was intended to enforce, the Commission may fix the definitive

amount of the periodic penalty payment at a figure lower than that which would arise under the original decision. Article 23(4) shall apply correspondingly.

Chapter VII Limitation periods

Article 25 Limitation periods for the imposition of penalties

1. The powers conferred on the Commission by Articles 23 and 24 shall be subject to the following limitation periods:

    (a) three years in the case of infringements of provisions concerning requests for information or the conduct of inspections;

    (b) five years in the case of all other infringements.

2. Time shall begin to run on the day on which the infringement is committed. However, in the case of continuing or repeated infringements, time shall begin to run on the day on which the infringement ceases.

3. Any action taken by the Commission or by the competition authority of a Member State for the purpose of the investigation or proceedings in respect of an infringement shall interrupt the limitation period for the imposition of fines or periodic penalty payments. The limitation period shall be interrupted with effect from the date on which the action is notified to at least one undertaking or association of undertakings which has participated in the infringement. Actions which interrupt the running of the period shall include in particular the following:

    (a) written requests for information by the Commission or by the competition authority of a Member State;

    (b) written authorisations to conduct inspections issued to its officials by the Commission or by the competition authority of a Member State;

    (c) the initiation of proceedings by the Commission or by the competition authority of a Member State;

    (d) notification of the statement of objections of the Commission or of the competition authority of a Member State.

4. The interruption of the limitation period shall apply for all the undertakings or associations of undertakings which have participated in the infringement.

5. Each interruption shall start time running afresh. However, the limitation period shall expire at the latest on the day on which a period equal to twice the limitation period has elapsed without the Commission having imposed a fine or a periodic penalty payment. That period shall be extended by the time during which limitation is suspended pursuant to paragraph 6.

6. The limitation period for the imposition of fines or periodic penalty payments shall be suspended for as long as the decision of the Commission is the subject of proceedings pending before the Court of Justice.

Article 26 Limitation period for the enforcement of penalties

1. The power of the Commission to enforce decisions taken pursuant to Articles 23 and 24 shall be subject to a limitation period of five years.

2. Time shall begin to run on the day on which the decision becomes final.

3. The limitation period for the enforcement of penalties shall be interrupted:

    (a) by notification of a decision varying the original amount of the fine or periodic penalty payment or refusing an application for variation;

    (b) by any action of the Commission or of a Member State, acting at the request of the Commission, designed to enforce payment of the fine or periodic penalty payment.

4. Each interruption shall start time running afresh.

5. The limitation period for the enforcement of penalties shall be suspended for so long as:

    (a) time to pay is allowed;

    (b) enforcement of payment is suspended pursuant to a decision of the Court of Justice.

Chapter VIII Hearings and professional secrecy

Article 27   Hearing of the parties, complainants and others

1. Before taking decisions as provided for in Articles 7, 8, 23 and Article 24(2), the Commission shall give the undertakings or associations of undertakings which are the subject of the proceedings conducted by the Commission the opportunity of being heard on the matters to which the Commission has taken objection. The Commission shall base its decisions only on objections on which the parties concerned have been able to comment. Complainants shall be associated closely with the proceedings.

2. The rights of defence of the parties concerned shall be fully respected in the proceedings. They shall be entitled to have access to the Commission's file, subject to the legitimate interest of undertakings in the protection of their business secrets. The right of access to the file shall not extend to confidential information and internal documents of the Commission or the competition authorities of the Member States. In particular, the right of access shall not extend to correspondence between the Commission and the competition authorities of the Member States, or between the latter, including documents drawn up pursuant to Articles 11 and 14. Nothing in this paragraph shall prevent the Commission from disclosing and using information necessary to prove an infringement.

3. If the Commission considers it necessary, it may also hear other natural or legal persons. Applications to be heard on the part of such persons shall, where they show a sufficient interest, be granted. The competition authorities of the Member States may also ask the Commission to hear other natural or legal persons.

4. Where the Commission intends to adopt a decision pursuant to Article 9 or Article 10, it shall publish a concise summary of the case and the main content of the commitments or of the proposed course of action. Interested third parties may submit their observations within a time limit which is fixed by the Commission in its publication and which may not be less than one month. Publication shall have regard to the legitimate interest of undertakings in the protection of their business secrets.

Article 28   Professional secrecy

1. Without prejudice to Articles 12 and 15, information collected pursuant to Articles 17 to 22 shall be used only for the purpose for which it was acquired.

2. Without prejudice to the exchange and to the use of information foreseen in Articles 11, 12, 14, 15 and 27, the Commission and the competition authorities of the Member States, their officials, servants and other persons working under the supervision of these authorities as well as officials and civil servants of other authorities of the Member States shall not disclose information acquired or exchanged by them pursuant to this Regulation and of the kind covered by the obligation of professional secrecy. This obligation also applies to all representatives and experts of Member States attending meetings of the Advisory Committee pursuant to Article 14.

Chapter IX Exemption regulations

Article 29   Withdrawal in individual cases

1. Where the Commission, empowered by a Council Regulation, such as Regulations 19/65/ EEC, (EEC) No 2821/71, (EEC) No 3976/87, (EEC) No 1534/91 or (EEC) No 479/92, to apply Article 81(3) of the Treaty by regulation, has declared Article 81(1) of the Treaty inapplicable to certain categories of agreements, decisions by associations of undertakings or concerted practices, it may, acting on its own initiative or on a complaint, withdraw the benefit of such an exemption Regulation when it finds that in any particular case an agreement, decision or concerted practice to which the exemption Regulation applies has certain effects which are incompatible with Article 81(3) of the Treaty.

2. Where, in any particular case, agreements, decisions by associations of undertakings or concerted practices to which a Commission Regulation referred to in paragraph 1 applies have effects which are incompatible with Article 81(3) of the Treaty in the territory of a Member State, or in a

part thereof, which has all the characteristics of a distinct geographic market, the competition authority of that Member State may withdraw the benefit of the Regulation in question in respect of that territory.

Chapter X General provisions

Article 30   Publication of decisions

1. The Commission shall publish the decisions, which it takes pursuant to Articles 7 to 10, 23 and 24.

2. The publication shall state the names of the parties and the main content of the decision, including any penalties imposed. It shall have regard to the legitimate interest of undertakings in the protection of their business secrets.

Article 31   Review by the Court of Justice

The Court of Justice shall have unlimited jurisdiction to review decisions whereby the Commission has fixed a fine or periodic penalty payment. It may cancel, reduce or increase the fine or periodic penalty payment imposed.

Article 32   (Deleted by Regulation 1419/2006 OJ 2006 L269/1)

Article 33   Implementing provisions

1. The Commission shall be authorised to take such measures as may be appropriate in order to apply this Regulation. The measures may concern, *inter alia*:

    (a) the form, content and other details of complaints lodged pursuant to Article 7 and the procedure for rejecting complaints;

    (b) the practical arrangements for the exchange of information and consultations provided for in Article 11;

    (c) the practical arrangements for the hearings provided for in Article 27.

2. Before the adoption of any measures pursuant to paragraph 1, the Commission shall publish a draft thereof and invite all interested parties to submit their comments within the time-limit it lays down, which may not be less than one month. Before publishing a draft measure and before adopting it, the Commission shall consult the Advisory Committee on Restrictive Practices and Dominant Positions.

Chapter XI Transitional, amending and final provisions

Article 34   Transitional provisions

1. Applications made to the Commission under Article 2 of Regulation No 17, notifications made under Articles 4 and 5 of that Regulation and the corresponding applications and notifications made under Regulations (EEC) No 1017/68, (EEC) No 4056/86 and (EEC) No 3975/87 shall lapse as from the date of application of this Regulation.

2. Procedural steps taken under Regulation No 17 and Regulations (EEC) No 1017/68, (EEC) No 4056/86 and (EEC) No 3975/87 shall continue to have effect for the purposes of applying this Regulation.

Article 35   Designation of competition authorities of Member States

1. The Member States shall designate the competition authority or authorities responsible for the application of Articles 81 and 82 of the Treaty in such a way that the provisions of this regulation are effectively complied with. The measures necessary to empower those authorities to apply those Articles shall be taken before 1 May 2004. The authorities designated may include courts.

2. When enforcement of Community competition law is entrusted to national administrative and judicial authorities, the Member States may allocate different powers and functions to those different national authorities, whether administrative or judicial.

3. The effects of Article 11(6) apply to the authorities designated by the Member States including courts that exercise functions regarding the preparation and the adoption of the types of

decisions foreseen in Article 5. The effects of Article 11(6) do not extend to courts insofar as they act as review courts in respect of the types of decisions foreseen in Article 5.

4. Notwithstanding paragraph 3, in the Member States where, for the adoption of certain types of decisions foreseen in Article 5, an authority brings an action before a judicial authority that is separate and different from the prosecuting authority and provided that the terms of this paragraph are complied with, the effects of Article 11(6) shall be limited to the authority prosecuting the case which shall withdraw its claim before the judicial authority when the Commission opens proceedings and this withdrawal shall bring the national proceedings effectively to an end.

Article 36   (Repealed)

Article 37   Amendment of Regulation (EEC) No 2988/74

In Regulation (EEC) No 2988/74, the following Article is inserted:

'Article 7a   Exclusion

This Regulation shall not apply to measures taken under Council Regulation (EC) No 1/2003 of 16 December 2002 on the implementation of the rules on competition laid down in Articles 81 and 82 of the Treaty.'[16]

Article 38   Amendment of Regulation (EEC) No 4056/86

Regulation (EEC) No 4056/86 is amended as follows:

1. Article 7 is amended as follows:

    (a) Paragraph 1 is replaced by the following:

    '1. Breach of an obligation

    Where the persons concerned are in breach of an obligation which, pursuant to Article 5, attaches to the exemption provided for in Article 3, the Commission may, in order to put an end to such breach and under the conditions laid down in Council Regulation (EC) No 1/2003 of 16 December 2002 on the implementation of the rules on competition laid down in Articles 81 and 82 of the Treaty[17] adopt a decision that either prohibits them from carrying out or requires them to perform certain specific acts, or withdraws the benefit of the block exemption which they enjoyed.'

    (b) Paragraph 2 is amended as follows:

    (i)   In point (a), the words 'under the conditions laid down in Section II' are replaced by the words 'under the conditions laid down in Regulation (EC) No 1/ 2003';

    (ii) The second sentence of the second subparagraph of point (c)(i) is replaced by the following:

    'At the same time it shall decide, in accordance with Article 9 of Regulation (EC) No 1/2003, whether to accept commitments offered by the undertakings concerned with a view, inter alia, to obtaining access to the market for non-conference lines.'

2. Article 8 is amended as follows:

    (a) Paragraph 1 is deleted.

    (b) In paragraph 2 the words 'pursuant to Article 10' are replaced by the words 'pursuant to Regulation (EC) No 1/2003.'

    (c) Paragraph 3 is deleted;

3. Article 9 is amended as follows:

    (a) In paragraph 1, the words 'Advisory Committee referred to in Article 15' are replaced by the words 'Advisory Committee referred to in Article 14 of Regulation (EC) No 1/2003';

    (b) In paragraph 2, the words 'Advisory Committee as referred to in Article 15' are replaced by the words 'Advisory Committee referred to in Article 14 of Regulation (EC) No 1/2003';

---

[16] OJ L 1, 4.1.2003, p. 1.
[17] OJ L 1, 4.1.2003, p. 1.

4. Articles 10 to 25 are repealed with the exception of Article 13(3) which continues to apply to decisions adopted pursuant to Article 81(3) of the Treaty prior to the date of application of this Regulation until the date of expiration of those decisions;

5. in Article 26, the words 'the form, content and other details of complaints pursuant to Article 10, applications pursuant to Article 12 and the hearings provided for in Article 23(1) and (2)' are deleted.

Article 39   Amendment of Regulation (EEC) No 3975/87
Articles 3 to 19 of Regulation (EEC) No 3975/87 are repealed with the exception of Article 6(3) which continues to apply to decisions adopted pursuant to Article 81(3) of the Treaty prior to the date of application of this Regulation until the date of expiration of those decisions.

Article 40   Amendment of Regulations No 19/65/EEC, (EEC) No 2821/71 and (EEC) No 1534/91
Article 7 of Regulation No 19/65/EEC, Article 7 of Regulation (EEC) No 2821/71 and Article 7 of Regulation (EEC) No 1534/91 are repealed.

Article 41   (Repealed)

Article 42   (Repealed)

Article 43   Repeal of Regulations No 17 and No 141
1. Regulation No 17 is repealed with the exception of Article 8(3) which continues to apply to decisions adopted pursuant to Article 81(3) of the Treaty prior to the date of application of this Regulation until the date of expiration of those decisions.

2. Regulation No 141 is repealed.

3. References to the repealed Regulations shall be construed as references to this Regulation.

Article 44   Report on the application of the present Regulation
Five years from the date of application of this Regulation, the Commission shall report to the European Parliament and the Council on the functioning of this Regulation, in particular on the application of Article 11(6) and Article 17.

On the basis of this report, the Commission shall assess whether it is appropriate to propose to the Council a revision of this Regulation.

Article 45   Entry into force
This Regulation shall enter into force on the 20th day following that of its publication in the *Official Journal of the European Communities*.

It shall apply from 1 May 2004.

This Regulation shall be binding in its entirety and directly applicable in all Member States.

Done at Brussels, 16 December 2002.

Council Regulation (EC) No 139/2004 of 20 January 2004 on the control of concentrations between undertakings (the EC Merger Regulation)*

[OJ 2004 L24/22]

THE COUNCIL OF THE EUROPEAN UNION,

Having regard to the Treaty establishing the European Community, and in particular Articles 83 and 308 thereof,

---

* **Editor's Note:** This Regulation replaces and repeals Regulations 4064/89 and 1310/97.

Having regard to the proposal from the Commission,[1]

Having regard to the opinion of the European Parliament,[2]

Having regard to the opinion of the European Economic and Social Committee,[3]

Whereas:

(1) Council Regulation (EEC) No 4064/89 of 21 December 1989 on the control of concentrations between undertakings[4] has been substantially amended. Since further amendments are to be made, it should be recast in the interest of clarity.

(2) For the achievement of the aims of the Treaty, Article 3(1)(g) gives the Community the objective of instituting a system ensuring that competition in the internal market is not distorted. Article 4(1) of the Treaty provides that the activities of the Member States and the Community are to be conducted in accordance with the principle of an open market economy with free competition. These principles are essential for the further development of the internal market.

(3) The completion of the internal market and of economic and monetary union, the enlargement of the European Union and the lowering of international barriers to trade and investment will continue to result in major corporate reorganisations, particularly in the form of concentrations.

(4) Such reorganisations are to be welcomed to the extent that they are in line with the requirements of dynamic competition and capable of increasing the competitiveness of European industry, improving the conditions of growth and raising the standard of living in the Community.

(5) However, it should be ensured that the process of reorganisation does not result in lasting damage to competition; Community law must therefore include provisions governing those concentrations which may significantly impede effective competition in the common market or in a substantial part of it.

(6) A specific legal instrument is therefore necessary to permit effective control of all concentrations in terms of their effect on the structure of competition in the Community and to be the only instrument applicable to such concentrations. Regulation (EEC) No 4064/89 has allowed a Community policy to develop in this field. In the light of experience, however, that Regulation should now be recast into legislation designed to meet the challenges of a more integrated market and the future enlargement of the European Union. In accordance with the principles of subsidiarity and of proportionality as set out in Article 5 of the Treaty, this Regulation does not go beyond what is necessary in order to achieve the objective of ensuring that competition in the common market is not distorted, in accordance with the principle of an open market economy with free competition.

(7) Articles 81 and 82, while applicable, according to the case-law of the Court of Justice, to certain concentrations, are not sufficient to control all operations which may prove to be incompatible with the system of undistorted competition envisaged in the Treaty. This Regulation should therefore be based not only on Article 83 but, principally, on Article 308 of the Treaty, under which the Community may give itself the additional powers of action necessary for the attainment of its objectives, and also powers of action with regard to concentrations on the markets for agricultural products listed in Annex I to the Treaty.

(8) The provisions to be adopted in this Regulation should apply to significant structural changes, the impact of which on the market goes beyond the national borders of any one Member State. Such concentrations should, as a general rule, be reviewed exclusively at Community level, in application of a 'one-stop shop' system and in compliance with the principle of subsidiarity. Concentrations not covered by this Regulation come, in principle, within the jurisdiction of the Member States.

(9) The scope of application of this Regulation should be defined according to the geographical area of activity of the undertakings concerned and be limited by quantitative thresholds in order to cover those concentrations which have a Community dimension. The Commission should report to the Council on the implementation of the applicable thresholds and criteria so that the Council,

---

[1] OJ C 20, 28.1.2003, p. 4.

[2] Opinion delivered on 9.10.2003 (not yet published in the Official Journal).

[3] Opinion delivered on 24.10.2003 (not yet published in the Official Journal).

[4] OJ L 395, 30.12.1989, p. 1. Corrected version in OJ L 257, 21.9.1990, p. 13. Regulation as last amended by Regulation (EC) No 1310/97 (OJ L 180, 9.7.1997, p. 1). Corrigendum in OJ L 40, 13.2.1998, p. 17.

acting in accordance with Article 202 of the Treaty, is in a position to review them regularly, as well as the rules regarding pre-notification referral, in the light of the experience gained; this requires statistical data to be provided by the Member States to the Commission to enable it to prepare such reports and possible proposals for amendments. The Commission's reports and proposals should be based on relevant information regularly provided by the Member States.

(10) A concentration with a Community dimension should be deemed to exist where the aggregate turnover of the undertakings concerned exceeds given thresholds; that is the case irrespective of whether or not the undertakings effecting the concentration have their seat or their principal fields of activity in the Community, provided they have substantial operations there.

(11) The rules governing the referral of concentrations from the Commission to Member States and from Member States to the Commission should operate as an effective corrective mechanism in the light of the principle of subsidiarity; these rules protect the competition interests of the Member States in an adequate manner and take due account of legal certainty and the 'one-stop shop' principle.

(12) Concentrations may qualify for examination under a number of national merger control systems if they fall below the turnover thresholds referred to in this Regulation. Multiple notification of the same transaction increases legal uncertainty, effort and cost for undertakings and may lead to conflicting assessments. The system whereby concentrations may be referred to the Commission by the Member States concerned should therefore be further developed.

(13) The Commission should act in close and constant liaison with the competent authorities of the Member States from which it obtains comments and information.

(14) The Commission and the competent authorities of the Member States should together form a network of public authorities, applying their respective competences in close cooperation, using efficient arrangements for information-sharing and consultation, with a view to ensuring that a case is dealt with by the most appropriate authority, in the light of the principle of subsidiarity and with a view to ensuring that multiple notifications of a given concentration are avoided to the greatest extent possible. Referrals of concentrations from the Commission to Member States and from Member States to the Commission should be made in an efficient manner avoiding, to the greatest extent possible, situations where a concentration is subject to a referral both before and after its notification.

(15) The Commission should be able to refer to a Member State notified concentrations with a Community dimension which threaten significantly to affect competition in a market within that Member State presenting all the characteristics of a distinct market. Where the concentration affects competition on such a market, which does not constitute a substantial part of the common market, the Commission should be obliged, upon request, to refer the whole or part of the case to the Member State concerned. A Member State should be able to refer to the Commission a concentration which does not have a Community dimension but which affects trade between Member States and threatens to significantly affect competition within its territory. Other Member States which are also competent to review the concentration should be able to join the request. In such a situation, in order to ensure the efficiency and predictability of the system, national time limits should be suspended until a decision has been reached as to the referral of the case. The Commission should have the power to examine and deal with a concentration on behalf of a requesting Member State or requesting Member States.

(16) The undertakings concerned should be granted the possibility of requesting referrals to or from the Commission before a concentration is notified so as to further improve the efficiency of the system for the control of concentrations within the Community. In such situations, the Commission and national competition authorities should decide within short, clearly defined time limits whether a referral to or from the Commission ought to be made, thereby ensuring the efficiency of the system. Upon request by the undertakings concerned, the Commission should be able to refer to a Member State a concentration with a Community dimension which may significantly affect competition in a market within that Member State presenting all the characteristics of a distinct market; the undertakings concerned should not, however, be required to demonstrate that the effects of the concentration would be detrimental to competition. A concentration should not be referred from the Commission to a Member State which has expressed its disagreement to such a referral. Before notification to national authorities, the undertakings concerned should also be able to request that a concentration without

a Community dimension which is capable of being reviewed under the national competition laws of at least three Member States be referred to the Commission. Such requests for pre-notification referrals to the Commission would be particularly pertinent in situations where the concentration would affect competition beyond the territory of one Member State. Where a concentration capable of being reviewed under the competition laws of three or more Member States is referred to the Commission prior to any national notification, and no Member State competent to review the case expresses its disagreement, the Commission should acquire exclusive competence to review the concentration and such a concentration should be deemed to have a Community dimension. Such pre-notification referrals from Member States to the Commission should not, however, be made where at least one Member State competent to review the case has expressed its disagreement with such a referral.

(17) The Commission should be given exclusive competence to apply this Regulation, subject to review by the Court of Justice.

(18) The Member States should not be permitted to apply their national legislation on competition to concentrations with a Community dimension, unless this Regulation makes provision therefore. The relevant powers of national authorities should be limited to cases where, failing intervention by the Commission, effective competition is likely to be significantly impeded within the territory of a Member State and where the competition interests of that Member State cannot be sufficiently protected otherwise by this Regulation. The Member States concerned must act promptly in such cases; this Regulation cannot, because of the diversity of national law, fix a single time limit for the adoption of final decisions under national law.

(19) Furthermore, the exclusive application of this Regulation to concentrations with a Community dimension is without prejudice to Article 296 of the Treaty, and does not prevent the Member States from taking appropriate measures to protect legitimate interests other than those pursued by this Regulation, provided that such measures are compatible with the general principles and other provisions of Community law.

(20) It is expedient to define the concept of concentration in such a manner as to cover operations bringing about a lasting change in the control of the undertakings concerned and therefore in the structure of the market. It is therefore appropriate to include, within the scope of this Regulation, all joint ventures performing on a lasting basis all the functions of an autonomous economic entity. It is moreover appropriate to treat as a single concentration transactions that are closely connected in that they are linked by condition or take the form of a series of transactions in securities taking place within a reasonably short period of time.

(21) This Regulation should also apply where the undertakings concerned accept restrictions directly related to, and necessary for, the implementation of the concentration. Commission decisions declaring concentrations compatible with the common market in application of this Regulation should automatically cover such restrictions, without the Commission having to assess such restrictions in individual cases. At the request of the undertakings concerned, however, the Commission should, in cases presenting novel or unresolved questions giving rise to genuine uncertainty, expressly assess whether or not any restriction is directly related to, and necessary for, the implementation of the concentration. A case presents a novel or unresolved question giving rise to genuine uncertainty if the question is not covered by the relevant Commission notice in force or a published Commission decision.

(22) The arrangements to be introduced for the control of concentrations should, without prejudice to Article 86(2) of the Treaty, respect the principle of non-discrimination between the public and the private sectors. In the public sector, calculation of the turnover of an undertaking concerned in a concentration needs, therefore, to take account of undertakings making up an economic unit with an independent power of decision, irrespective of the way in which their capital is held or of the rules of administrative supervision applicable to them.

(23) It is necessary to establish whether or not concentrations with a Community dimension are compatible with the common market in terms of the need to maintain and develop effective competition in the common market. In so doing, the Commission must place its appraisal within the general framework of the achievement of the fundamental objectives referred to in Article 2 of the Treaty establishing the European Community and Article 2 of the Treaty on European Union.

(24) In order to ensure a system of undistorted competition in the common market, in further-ance of a policy conducted in accordance with the principle of an open market economy with free competition, this Regulation must permit effective control of all concentrations from the point of view of their effect on competition in the Community. Accordingly, Regulation (EEC) No 4064/89 established the principle that a concentration with a Community dimension which creates or strengthens a dominant position as a result of which effective competition in the common market or in a substantial part of it would be significantly impeded should be declared incompatible with the common market.

(25) In view of the consequences that concentrations in oligopolistic market structures may have, it is all the more necessary to maintain effective competition in such markets. Many oligopolistic mar- kets exhibit a healthy degree of competition. However, under certain circumstances, concentrations involving the elimination of important competitive constraints that the merging parties had exerted upon each other, as well as a reduction of competitive pressure on the remaining competitors, may, even in the absence of a likelihood of coordination between the members of the oligopoly, result in a significant impediment to effective competition. The Community courts have, however, not to date expressly interpreted Regulation (EEC) No 4064/89 as requiring concentrations giving rise to such non-coordinated effects to be declared incompatible with the common market. Therefore, in the inter-ests of legal certainty, it should be made clear that this Regulation permits effective control of all such concentrations by providing that any concentration which would significantly impede effective com-petition, in the common market or in a substantial part of it, should be declared incompatible with the common market. The notion of 'significant impediment to effective competition' in Article 2(2) and (3) should be interpreted as extending, beyond the concept of dominance, only to the anti-competitive effects of a concentration resulting from the non-coordinated behaviour of undertakings which would not have a dominant position on the market concerned.

(26) A significant impediment to effective competition generally results from the creation or strengthening of a dominant position. With a view to preserving the guidance that may be drawn from past judgments of the European courts and Commission decisions pursuant to Regulation (EEC) No 4064/89, while at the same time maintaining consistency with the standards of competitive harm which have been applied by the Commission and the Community courts regarding the compatibility of a concentration with the common market, this Regulation should accordingly establish the principle that a concentration with a Community dimension which would significantly impede effective com-petition, in the common market or in a substantial part thereof, in particular as a result of the creation or strengthening of a dominant position, is to be declared incompatible with the common market.

(27) In addition, the criteria of Article 81(1) and (3) of the Treaty should be applied to joint ventures performing, on a lasting basis, all the functions of autonomous economic entities, to the extent that their creation has as its consequence an appreciable restriction of competition between undertakings that remain independent.

(28) In order to clarify and explain the Commission's appraisal of concentrations under this Regulation, it is appropriate for the Commission to publish guidance which should provide a sound economic framework for the assessment of concentrations with a view to determining whether or not they may be declared compatible with the common market.

(29) In order to determine the impact of a concentration on competition in the common market, it is appropriate to take account of any substantiated and likely efficiencies put forward by the under-takings concerned. It is possible that the efficiencies brought about by the concentration counteract the effects on competition, and in particular the potential harm to consumers, that it might other-wise have and that, as a consequence, the concentration would not significantly impede effective competition, in the common market or in a substantial part of it, in particular as a result of the creation or strengthening of a dominant position. The Commission should publish guidance on the conditions under which it may take efficiencies into account in the assessment of a concentration.

(30) Where the undertakings concerned modify a notified concentration, in particular by offer-ing commitments with a view to rendering the concentration compatible with the common market, the Commission should be able to declare the concentration, as modified, compatible with the

common market. Such commitments should be proportionate to the competition problem and entirely eliminate it. It is also appropriate to accept commitments before the initiation of proceedings where the competition problem is readily identifiable and can easily be remedied. It should be expressly provided that the Commission may attach to its decision conditions and obligations in order to ensure that the undertakings concerned comply with their commitments in a timely and effective manner so as to render the concentration compatible with the common market. Transparency and effective consultation of Member States as well as of interested third parties should be ensured throughout the procedure.

(31) The Commission should have at its disposal appropriate instruments to ensure the enforcement of commitments and to deal with situations where they are not fulfilled. In cases of failure to fulfil a condition attached to the decision declaring a concentration compatible with the common market, the situation rendering the concentration compatible with the common market does not materialise and the concentration, as implemented, is therefore not authorised by the Commission. As a consequence, if the concentration is implemented, it should be treated in the same way as a non-notified concentration implemented without authorisation. Furthermore, where the Commission has already found that, in the absence of the condition, the concentration would be incompatible with the common market, it should have the power to directly order the dissolution of the concentration, so as to restore the situation prevailing prior to the implementation of the concentration. Where an obligation attached to a decision declaring the concentration compatible with the common market is not fulfilled, the Commission should be able to revoke its decision. Moreover, the Commission should be able to impose appropriate financial sanctions where conditions or obligations are not fulfilled.

(32) Concentrations which, by reason of the limited market share of the undertakings concerned, are not liable to impede effective competition may be presumed to be compatible with the common market. Without prejudice to Articles 81 and 82 of the Treaty, an indication to this effect exists, in particular, where the market share of the undertakings concerned does not exceed 25% either in the common market or in a substantial part of it.

(33) The Commission should have the task of taking all the decisions necessary to establish whether or not concentrations with a Community dimension are compatible with the common market, as well as decisions designed to restore the situation prevailing prior to the implementation of a concentration which has been declared incompatible with the common market.

(34) To ensure effective control, undertakings should be obliged to give prior notification of concentrations with a Community dimension following the conclusion of the agreement, the announcement of the public bid or the acquisition of a controlling interest. Notification should also be possible where the undertakings concerned satisfy the Commission of their intention to enter into an agreement for a proposed concentration and demonstrate to the Commission that their plan for that proposed concentration is sufficiently concrete, for example on the basis of an agreement in principle, a memorandum of understanding, or a letter of intent signed by all undertakings concerned, or, in the case of a public bid, where they have publicly announced an intention to make such a bid, provided that the intended agreement or bid would result in a concentration with a Community dimension. The implementation of concentrations should be suspended until a final decision of the Commission has been taken. However, it should be possible to derogate from this suspension at the request of the undertakings concerned, where appropriate. In deciding whether or not to grant a derogation, the Commission should take account of all pertinent factors, such as the nature and gravity of damage to the undertakings concerned or to third parties, and the threat to competition posed by the concentration. In the interest of legal certainty, the validity of transactions must nevertheless be protected as much as necessary.

(35) A period within which the Commission must initiate proceedings in respect of a notified concentration and a period within which it must take a final decision on the compatibility or incompatibility with the common market of that concentration should be laid down. These periods should be extended whenever the undertakings concerned offer commitments with a view to rendering the concentration compatible with the common market, in order to allow for sufficient time for the

analysis and market testing of such commitment offers and for the consultation of Member States as well as interested third parties. A limited extension of the period within which the Commission must take a final decision should also be possible in order to allow sufficient time for the investigation of the case and the verification of the facts and arguments submitted to the Commission.

(36) The Community respects the fundamental rights and observes the principles recognised in particular by the Charter of Fundamental Rights of the European Union.[5] Accordingly, this Regulation should be interpreted and applied with respect to those rights and principles.

(37) The undertakings concerned must be afforded the right to be heard by the Commission when proceedings have been initiated; the members of the management and supervisory bodies and the recognised representatives of the employees of the undertakings concerned, and interested third parties, must also be given the opportunity to be heard.

(38) In order properly to appraise concentrations, the Commission should have the right to request all necessary information and to conduct all necessary inspections throughout the Community. To that end, and with a view to protecting competition effectively, the Commission's powers of investigation need to be expanded. The Commission should, in particular, have the right to interview any persons who may be in possession of useful information and to record the statements made.

(39) In the course of an inspection, officials authorised by the Commission should have the right to ask for any information relevant to the subject matter and purpose of the inspection; they should also have the right to affix seals during inspections, particularly in circumstances where there are reasonable grounds to suspect that a concentration has been implemented without being notified; that incorrect, incomplete or misleading information has been supplied to the Commission; or that the undertakings or persons concerned have failed to comply with a condition or obligation imposed by decision of the Commission. In any event, seals should only be used in exceptional circumstances, for the period of time strictly necessary for the inspection, normally not for more than 48 hours.

(40) Without prejudice to the case-law of the Court of Justice, it is also useful to set out the scope of the control that the national judicial authority may exercise when it authorises, as provided by national law and as a precautionary measure, assistance from law enforcement authorities in order to overcome possible opposition on the part of the undertaking against an inspection, including the affixing of seals, ordered by Commission decision. It results from the case-law that the national judicial authority may in particular ask of the Commission further information which it needs to carry out its control and in the absence of which it could refuse the authorisation. The case-law also confirms the competence of the national courts to control the application of national rules governing the implementation of coercive measures. The competent authorities of the Member States should cooperate actively in the exercise of the Commission's investigative powers.

(41) When complying with decisions of the Commission, the undertakings and persons concerned cannot be forced to admit that they have committed infringements, but they are in any event obliged to answer factual questions and to provide documents, even if this information may be used to establish against themselves or against others the existence of such infringements.

(42) For the sake of transparency, all decisions of the Commission which are not of a merely procedural nature should be widely publicised. While ensuring preservation of the rights of defence of the undertakings concerned, in particular the right of access to the file, it is essential that business secrets be protected. The confidentiality of information exchanged in the network and with the competent authorities of third countries should likewise be safeguarded.

(43) Compliance with this Regulation should be enforceable, as appropriate, by means of fines and periodic penalty payments. The Court of Justice should be given unlimited jurisdiction in that regard pursuant to Article 229 of the Treaty.

(44) The conditions in which concentrations, involving undertakings having their seat or their principal fields of activity in the Community, are carried out in third countries should be observed, and provision should be made for the possibility of the Council giving the Commission an appropriate mandate for negotiation with a view to obtaining non-discriminatory treatment for such undertakings.

---

[5] OJ C 364, 18.12.2000, p. 1.

(45) This Regulation in no way detracts from the collective rights of employees, as recognised in the undertakings concerned, notably with regard to any obligation to inform or consult their recognised representatives under Community and national law.

(46) The Commission should be able to lay down detailed rules concerning the implementation of this Regulation in accordance with the procedures for the exercise of implementing powers conferred on the Commission. For the adoption of such implementing provisions, the Commission should be assisted by an Advisory Committee composed of the representatives of the Member States as specified in Article 23,

HAS ADOPTED THIS REGULATION:

Article 1   Scope

1. Without prejudice to Article 4(5) and Article 22, this Regulation shall apply to all concentrations with a Community dimension as defined in this Article.

2. A concentration has a Community dimension where:
   (a) the combined aggregate worldwide turnover of all the undertakings concerned is more than EUR 5000 million; and
   (b) the aggregate Community-wide turnover of each of at least two of the undertakings concerned is more than EUR 250 million,

unless each of the undertakings concerned achieves more than two-thirds of its aggregate Community-wide turnover within one and the same Member State.

3. A concentration that does not meet the thresholds laid down in paragraph 2 has a Community dimension where:
   (a) the combined aggregate worldwide turnover of all the undertakings concerned is more than EUR 2500 million;
   (b) in each of at least three Member States, the combined aggregate turnover of all the undertakings concerned is more than EUR 100 million;
   (c) in each of at least three Member States included for the purpose of point (b), the aggregate turnover of each of at least two of the undertakings concerned is more than EUR 25 million; and
   (d) the aggregate Community-wide turnover of each of at least two of the undertakings concerned is more than EUR 100 million,

unless each of the undertakings concerned achieves more than two-thirds of its aggregate Community-wide turnover within one and the same Member State.

4. On the basis of statistical data that may be regularly provided by the Member States, the Commission shall report to the Council on the operation of the thresholds and criteria set out in paragraphs 2 and 3 by 1 July 2009 and may present proposals pursuant to paragraph 5.

5. Following the report referred to in paragraph 4 and on a proposal from the Commission, the Council, acting by a qualified majority, may revise the thresholds and criteria mentioned in paragraph 3.

Article 2   Appraisal of concentrations

1. Concentrations within the scope of this Regulation shall be appraised in accordance with the objectives of this Regulation and the following provisions with a view to establishing whether or not they are compatible with the common market.

In making this appraisal, the Commission shall take into account:
   (a) the need to maintain and develop effective competition within the common market in view of, among other things, the structure of all the markets concerned and the actual or potential competition from undertakings located either within or outwith the Community;
   (b) the market position of the undertakings concerned and their economic and financial power, the alternatives available to suppliers and users, their access to supplies or markets, any legal or other barriers to entry, supply and demand trends for the relevant goods and services, the interests of the intermediate and ultimate consumers, and the development of technical and economic progress provided that it is to consumers' advantage and does not form an obstacle to competition.

2. A concentration which would not significantly impede effective competition in the common market or in a substantial part of it, in particular as a result of the creation or strengthening of a dominant position, shall be declared compatible with the common market.

3. A concentration which would significantly impede effective competition, in the common market or in a substantial part of it, in particular as a result of the creation or strengthening of a dominant position, shall be declared incompatible with the common market.

4. To the extent that the creation of a joint venture constituting a concentration pursuant to Article 3 has as its object or effect the coordination of the competitive behaviour of undertakings that remain independent, such coordination shall be appraised in accordance with the criteria of a Article 81(1) and (3) of the Treaty, with a view to establishing whether or not the operation is compatible with the common market.

5. In making this appraisal, the Commission shall take into account in particular:
   - whether two or more parent companies retain, to a significant extent, activities in the same market as the joint venture or in a market which is downstream or upstream from that of the joint venture or in a neighbouring market closely related to this market,
   - whether the coordination which is the direct consequence of the creation of the joint venture affords the undertakings concerned the possibility of eliminating competition in respect of a substantial part of the products or services in question.

Article 3   Definition of concentration

1. A concentration shall be deemed to arise where a change of control on a lasting basis results from:
   (a) the merger of two or more previously independent undertakings or parts of undertakings, or
   (b) the acquisition, by one or more persons already controlling at least one undertaking, or by one or more undertakings, whether by purchase of securities or assets, by contract or by any other means, of direct or indirect control of the whole or parts of one or more other undertakings.

2. Control shall be constituted by rights, contracts or any other means which, either separately or in combination and having regard to the considerations of fact or law involved, confer the possibility of exercising decisive influence on an undertaking, in particular by:
   (a) ownership or the right to use all or part of the assets of an undertaking;
   (b) rights or contracts which confer decisive influence on the composition, voting or decisions of the organs of an undertaking.

3. Control is acquired by persons or undertakings which:
   (a) are holders of the rights or entitled to rights under the contracts concerned; or
   (b) while not being holders of such rights or entitled to rights under such contracts, have the power to exercise the rights deriving therefrom.

4. The creation of a joint venture performing on a lasting basis all the functions of an autonomous economic entity shall constitute a concentration within the meaning of paragraph 1(b).

5. A concentration shall not be deemed to arise where:
   (a) credit institutions or other financial institutions or insurance companies, the normal activities of which include transactions and dealing in securities for their own account or for the account of others, hold on a temporary basis securities which they have acquired in an undertaking with a view to reselling them, provided that they do not exercise voting rights in respect of those securities with a view to determining the competitive behaviour of that undertaking or provided that they exercise such voting rights only with a view to preparing the disposal of all or part of that undertaking or of its assets or the disposal of those securities and that any such disposal takes place within one year of the date of acquisition; that period may be extended by the Commission on request where such institutions or companies can show that the disposal was not reasonably possible within the period set;

(b) control is acquired by an office-holder according to the law of a Member State relating to liquidation, winding up, insolvency, cessation of payments, compositions or analogous proceedings;

(c) the operations referred to in paragraph 1(b) are carried out by the financial holding companies referred to in Article 5(3) of Fourth Council Directive 78/660/EEC of 25 July 1978 based on Article 54(3)(g) of the Treaty on the annual accounts of certain types of companies[6] provided however that the voting rights in respect of the holding are exercised, in particular in relation to the appointment of members of the management and supervisory bodies of the undertakings in which they have holdings, only to maintain the full value of those investments and not to determine directly or indirectly the competitive conduct of those undertakings.

Article 4   Prior notification of concentrations and pre-notification referral at the request of the notifying parties

1. Concentrations with a Community dimension defined in this Regulation shall be notified to the Commission prior to their implementation and following the conclusion of the agreement, the announcement of the public bid, or the acquisition of a controlling interest.

Notification may also be made where the undertakings concerned demonstrate to the Commission a good faith intention to conclude an agreement or, in the case of a public bid, where they have publicly announced an intention to make such a bid, provided that the intended agreement or bid would result in a concentration with a Community dimension.

For the purposes of this Regulation, the term 'notified concentration' shall also cover intended concentrations notified pursuant to the second subparagraph. For the purposes of paragraphs 4 and 5 of this Article, the term 'concentration' includes intended concentrations within the meaning of the second subparagraph.

2. A concentration which consists of a merger within the meaning of Article 3(1)(a) or in the acquisition of joint control within the meaning of Article 3(1)(b) shall be notified jointly by the parties to the merger or by those acquiring joint control as the case may be. In all other cases, the notification shall be effected by the person or undertaking acquiring control of the whole or parts of one or more undertakings.

3. Where the Commission finds that a notified concentration falls within the scope of this Regulation, it shall publish the fact of the notification, at the same time indicating the names of the undertakings concerned, their country of origin, the nature of the concentration and the economic sectors involved. The Commission shall take account of the legitimate interest of undertakings in the protection of their business secrets.

4. Prior to the notification of a concentration within the meaning of paragraph 1, the persons or undertakings referred to in paragraph 2 may inform the Commission, by means of a reasoned submission, that the concentration may significantly affect competition in a market within a Member State which presents all the characteristics of a distinct market and should therefore be examined, in whole or in part, by that Member State.

The Commission shall transmit this submission to all Member States without delay. The Member State referred to in the reasoned submission shall, within 15 working days of receiving the submission, express its agreement or disagreement as regards the request to refer the case. Where that Member State takes no such decision within this period, it shall be deemed to have agreed.

Unless that Member State disagrees, the Commission, where it considers that such a distinct market exists, and that competition in that market may be significantly affected by the concentration, may decide to refer the whole or part of the case to the competent authorities of that Member State with a view to the application of that State's national competition law.

The decision whether or not to refer the case in accordance with the third subparagraph shall be taken within 25 working days starting from the receipt of the reasoned submission by the Commission. The Commission shall inform the other Member States and the persons or undertakings

---

[6] OJ L 222, 14.8.1978, p. 11. Directive as last amended by Directive 2003/51/EC of the European Parliament and of the Council (OJ L 178, 17.7.2003, p. 16).

concerned of its decision. If the Commission does not take a decision within this period, it shall be deemed to have adopted a decision to refer the case in accordance with the submission made by the persons or undertakings concerned.

If the Commission decides, or is deemed to have decided, pursuant to the third and fourth subparagraphs, to refer the whole of the case, no notification shall be made pursuant to paragraph 1 and national competition law shall apply. Article 9(6) to (9) shall apply *mutatis mutandis*.

5. With regard to a concentration as defined in Article 3 which does not have a Community dimension within the meaning of Article 1 and which is capable of being reviewed under the national competition laws of at least three Member States, the persons or undertakings referred to in paragraph 2 may, before any notification to the competent authorities, inform the Commission by means of a reasoned submission that the concentration should be examined by the Commission.

The Commission shall transmit this submission to all Member States without delay.

Any Member State competent to examine the concentration under its national competition law may, within 15 working days of receiving the reasoned submission, express its disagreement as regards the request to refer the case.

Where at least one such Member State has expressed its disagreement in accordance with the third subparagraph within the period of 15 working days, the case shall not be referred. The Commission shall, without delay, inform all Member States and the persons or undertakings concerned of any such expression of disagreement.

Where no Member State has expressed its disagreement in accordance with the third subparagraph within the period of 15 working days, the concentration shall be deemed to have a Community dimension and shall be notified to the Commission in accordance with paragraphs 1 and 2. In such situations, no Member State shall apply its national competition law to the concentration.

6. The Commission shall report to the Council on the operation of paragraphs 4 and 5 by 1 July 2009. Following this report and on a proposal from the Commission, the Council, acting by a qualified majority, may revise paragraphs 4 and 5.

Article 5   Calculation of turnover

1. Aggregate turnover within the meaning of this Regulation shall comprise the amounts derived by the undertakings concerned in the preceding financial year from the sale of products and the provision of services falling within the undertakings' ordinary activities after deduction of sales rebates and of value added tax and other taxes directly related to turnover. The aggregate turnover of an undertaking concerned shall not include the sale of products or the provision of services between any of the undertakings referred to in paragraph 4.

Turnover, in the Community or in a Member State, shall comprise products sold and services provided to undertakings or consumers, in the Community or in that Member State as the case may be.

2. By way of derogation from paragraph 1, where the concentration consists of the acquisition of parts, whether or not constituted as legal entities, of one or more undertakings, only the turnover relating to the parts which are the subject of the concentration shall be taken into account with regard to the seller or sellers.

However, two or more transactions within the meaning of the first subparagraph which take place within a two-year period between the same persons or undertakings shall be treated as one and the same concentration arising on the date of the last transaction.

3. In place of turnover the following shall be used:

   (a) for credit institutions and other financial institutions, the sum of the following income items as defined in Council Directive 86/635/EEC,[7] after deduction of value added tax and other taxes directly related to those items, where appropriate:

     (i)	interest income and similar income;

     (ii)	income from securities:

       – income from shares and other variable yield securities,

       – income from participating interests,

       – income from shares in affiliated undertakings;

---

[7] OJ L 372, 31.12.1986, p. 1. Directive as last amended by Directive 2003/51/EC of the European Parliament and of the Council.

(iii) commissions receivable;

(iv) net profit on financial operations;

(v) other operating income.

The turnover of a credit or financial institution in the Community or in a Member State shall comprise the income items, as defined above, which are received by the branch or division of that institution established in the Community or in the Member State in question, as the case may be;

(b) for insurance undertakings, the value of gross premiums written which shall comprise all amounts received and receivable in respect of insurance contracts issued by or on behalf of the insurance undertakings, including also outgoing reinsurance premiums, and after deduction of taxes and parafiscal contributions or levies charged by reference to the amounts of individual premiums or the total volume of premiums; as regards Article 1(2)(b) and (3)(b), (c) and (d) and the final part of Article 1(2) and (3), gross premiums received from Community residents and from residents of one Member State respectively shall be taken into account.

4. Without prejudice to paragraph 2, the aggregate turnover of an undertaking concerned within the meaning of this Regulation shall be calculated by adding together the respective turnovers of the following:

(a) the undertaking concerned;

(b) those undertakings in which the undertaking concerned, directly or indirectly:

(i) owns more than half the capital or business assets, or

(ii) has the power to exercise more than half the voting rights, or

(iii) has the power to appoint more than half the members of the supervisory board, the administrative board or bodies legally representing the undertakings, or

(iv) has the right to manage the undertakings' affairs;

(c) those undertakings which have in the undertaking concerned the rights or powers listed in (b);

(d) those undertakings in which an undertaking as referred to in (c) has the rights or powers listed in (b);

(e) those undertakings in which two or more undertakings as referred to in (a) to (d) jointly have the rights or powers listed in (b).

5. Where undertakings concerned by the concentration jointly have the rights or powers listed in paragraph 4(b), in calculating the aggregate turnover of the undertakings concerned for the purposes of this Regulation:

(a) no account shall be taken of the turnover resulting from the sale of products or the provision of services between the joint undertaking and each of the undertakings concerned or any other undertaking connected with any one of them, as set out in paragraph 4(b) to (e);

(b) account shall be taken of the turnover resulting from the sale of products and the provision of services between the joint undertaking and any third undertakings. This turnover shall be apportioned equally amongst the undertakings concerned.

Article 6 Examination of the notification and initiation of proceedings

1. The Commission shall examine the notification as soon as it is received.

(a) Where it concludes that the concentration notified does not fall within the scope of this Regulation, it shall record that finding by means of a decision.

(b) Where it finds that the concentration notified, although falling within the scope of this Regulation, does not raise serious doubts as to its compatibility with the common market, it shall decide not to oppose it and shall declare that it is compatible with the common market.

A decision declaring a concentration compatible shall be deemed to cover restrictions directly related and necessary to the implementation of the concentration.

(c) Without prejudice to paragraph 2, where the Commission finds that the concentration notified falls within the scope of this Regulation and raises serious doubts as to its compatibility with the common market, it shall decide to initiate proceedings. Without prejudice to Article 9, such proceedings shall be closed by means of a decision as provided for in Article 8(1) to (4), unless the undertakings concerned have demonstrated to the satisfaction of the Commission that they have abandoned the concentration.

2. Where the Commission finds that, following modification by the undertakings concerned, a notified concentration no longer raises serious doubts within the meaning of paragraph 1(c), it shall declare the concentration compatible with the common market pursuant to paragraph 1(b).

The Commission may attach to its decision under paragraph 1(b) conditions and obligations intended to ensure that the undertakings concerned comply with the commitments they have entered into vis-à-vis the Commission with a view to rendering the concentration compatible with the common market.

3. The Commission may revoke the decision it took pursuant to paragraph 1(a) or (b) where:

    (a) the decision is based on incorrect information for which one of the undertakings is responsible or where it has been obtained by deceit,

    or

    (b) the undertakings concerned commit a breach of an obligation attached to the decision.

4. In the cases referred to in paragraph 3, the Commission may take a decision under paragraph 1, without being bound by the time limits referred to in Article 10(1).

5. The Commission shall notify its decision to the undertakings concerned and the competent authorities of the Member States without delay.

Article 7   Suspension of concentrations

1. A concentration with a Community dimension as defined in Article 1, or which is to be examined by the Commission pursuant to Article 4(5), shall not be implemented either before its notification or until it has been declared compatible with the common market pursuant to a decision under Articles 6(1)(b), 8(1) or 8(2), or on the basis of a presumption according to Article 10(6).

2. Paragraph 1 shall not prevent the implementation of a public bid or of a series of transactions in securities including those convertible into other securities admitted to trading on a market such as a stock exchange, by which control within the meaning of Article 3 is acquired from various sellers, provided that:

    (a) the concentration is notified to the Commission pursuant to Article 4 without delay; and

    (b) the acquirer does not exercise the voting rights attached to the securities in question or does so only to maintain the full value of its investments based on a derogation granted by the Commission under paragraph 3.

3. The Commission may, on request, grant a derogation from the obligations imposed in paragraphs 1 or 2. The request to grant a derogation must be reasoned. In deciding on the request, the Commission shall take into account inter alia the effects of the suspension on one or more undertakings concerned by the concentration or on a third party and the threat to competition posed by the concentration. Such a derogation may be made subject to conditions and obligations in order to ensure conditions of effective competition. A derogation may be applied for and granted at any time, be it before notification or after the transaction.

4. The validity of any transaction carried out in contravention of paragraph 1 shall be dependent on a decision pursuant to Article 6(1)(b) or Article 8(1), (2) or (3) or on a presumption pursuant to Article 10(6).

This Article shall, however, have no effect on the validity of transactions in securities including those convertible into other securities admitted to trading on a market such as a stock exchange, unless the buyer and seller knew or ought to have known that the transaction was carried out in contravention of paragraph 1.

Article 8   Powers of decision of the Commission

1. Where the Commission finds that a notified concentration fulfils the criterion laid down in Article 2(2) and, in the cases referred to in Article 2(4), the criteria laid down in Article 81(3) of the Treaty, it shall issue a decision declaring the concentration compatible with the common market.

A decision declaring a concentration compatible shall be deemed to cover restrictions directly related and necessary to the implementation of the concentration.

2. Where the Commission finds that, following modification by the undertakings concerned, a notified concentration fulfils the criterion laid down in Article 2(2) and, in the cases referred to in Article 2(4), the criteria laid down in Article 81(3) of the Treaty, it shall issue a decision declaring the concentration compatible with the common market.

The Commission may attach to its decision conditions and obligations intended to ensure that the undertakings concerned comply with the commitments they have entered into vis-à-vis the Commission with a view to rendering the concentration compatible with the common market. A decision declaring a concentration compatible shall be deemed to cover restrictions directly related and necessary to the implementation of the concentration.

3. Where the Commission finds that a concentration fulfils the criterion defined in Article 2(3) or, in the cases referred to in Article 2(4), does not fulfil the criteria laid down in Article 81(3) of the Treaty, it shall issue a decision declaring that the concentration is incompatible with the common market.

4. Where the Commission finds that a concentration:

   (a) has already been implemented and that concentration has been declared incompatible with the common market, or

   (b) has been implemented in contravention of a condition attached to a decision taken under paragraph 2, which has found that, in the absence of the condition, the concentration would fulfil the criterion laid down in Article 2(3) or, in the cases referred to in Article 2(4), would not fulfil the criteria laid down in Article 81(3) of the Treaty, the Commission may:

   – require the undertakings concerned to dissolve the concentration, in particular through the dissolution of the merger or the disposal of all the shares or assets acquired, so as to restore the situation prevailing prior to the implementation of the concentration; in circumstances where restoration of the situation prevailing before the implementation of the concentration is not possible through dissolution of the concentration, the Commission may take any other measure appropriate to achieve such restoration as far as possible,

   – order any other appropriate measure to ensure that the undertakings concerned dissolve the concentration or take other restorative measures as required in its decision.

In cases falling within point (a) of the first subparagraph, the measures referred to in that subparagraph may be imposed either in a decision pursuant to paragraph 3 or by separate decision.

5. The Commission may take interim measures appropriate to restore or maintain conditions of effective competition where a concentration:

   (a) has been implemented in contravention of Article 7, and a decision as to the compatibility of the concentration with the common market has not yet been taken;

   (b) has been implemented in contravention of a condition attached to a decision under Article 6(1)(b) or paragraph 2 of this Article;

   (c) has already been implemented and is declared incompatible with the common market.

6. The Commission may revoke the decision it has taken pursuant to paragraphs 1 or 2 where:

   (a) the declaration of compatibility is based on incorrect information for which one of the undertakings is responsible or where it has been obtained by deceit; or

   (b) the undertakings concerned commit a breach of an obligation attached to the decision.

7. The Commission may take a decision pursuant to paragraphs 1 to 3 without being bound by the time limits referred to in Article 10(3), in cases where:

   (a) it finds that a concentration has been implemented

   (i) in contravention of a condition attached to a decision under Article 6(1)(b), or

   (ii) in contravention of a condition attached to a decision taken under paragraph 2 and in accordance with Article 10(2), which has found that, in the absence of the condition, the concentration would raise serious doubts as to its compatibility with the common market; or

    (b) a decision has been revoked pursuant to paragraph 6.

    8. The Commission shall notify its decision to the undertakings concerned and the competent authorities of the Member States without delay.

Article 9   Referral to the competent authorities of the Member States

    1. The Commission may, by means of a decision notified without delay to the undertakings concerned and the competent authorities of the other Member States, refer a notified concentration to the competent authorities of the Member State concerned in the following circumstances.

    2. Within 15 working days of the date of receipt of the copy of the notification, a Member State, on its own initiative or upon the invitation of the Commission, may inform the Commission, which shall inform the undertakings concerned, that:

    (a) a concentration threatens to affect significantly competition in a market within that Member State, which presents all the characteristics of a distinct market, or

    (b) a concentration affects competition in a market within that Member State, which presents all the characteristics of a distinct market and which does not constitute a substantial part of the common market.

    3. If the Commission considers that, having regard to the market for the products or services in question and the geographical reference market within the meaning of paragraph 7, there is such a distinct market and that such a threat exists, either:

    (a) it shall itself deal with the case in accordance with this Regulation; or

    (b) it shall refer the whole or part of the case to the competent authorities of the Member State concerned with a view to the application of that State's national competition law.

    If, however, the Commission considers that such a distinct market or threat does not exist, it shall adopt a decision to that effect which it shall address to the Member State concerned, and shall itself deal with the case in accordance with this Regulation.

    In cases where a Member State informs the Commission pursuant to paragraph 2(b) that a concentration affects competition in a distinct market within its territory that does not form a substantial part of the common market, the Commission shall refer the whole or part of the case relating to the distinct market concerned, if it considers that such a distinct market is affected.

    4. A decision to refer or not to refer pursuant to paragraph 3 shall be taken:

    (a) as a general rule within the period provided for in Article 10(1), second subparagraph, where the Commission, pursuant to Article 6(1)(b), has not initiated proceedings; or

    (b) within 65 working days at most of the notification of the concentration concerned where the Commission has initiated proceedings under Article 6(1)(c), without taking the preparatory steps in order to adopt the necessary measures under Article 8(2), (3) or (4) to maintain or restore effective competition on the market concerned.

    5. If within the 65 working days referred to in paragraph 4(b) the Commission, despite a reminder from the Member State concerned, has not taken a decision on referral in accordance with paragraph 3 nor has taken the preparatory steps referred to in paragraph 4(b), it shall be deemed to have taken a decision to refer the case to the Member State concerned in accordance with paragraph 3(b).

    6. The competent authority of the Member State concerned shall decide upon the case without undue delay.

    Within 45 working days after the Commission's referral, the competent authority of the Member State concerned shall inform the undertakings concerned of the result of the preliminary competition assessment and what further action, if any, it proposes to take. The Member State concerned may exceptionally suspend this time limit where necessary information has not been provided to it by the undertakings concerned as provided for by its national competition law.

    Where a notification is requested under national law, the period of 45 working days shall begin on the working day following that of the receipt of a complete notification by the competent authority of that Member State.

    7. The geographical reference market shall consist of the area in which the undertakings concerned are involved in the supply and demand of products or services, in which the conditions of

competition are sufficiently homogeneous and which can be distinguished from neighbouring areas because, in particular, conditions of competition are appreciably different in those areas. This assessment should take account in particular of the nature and characteristics of the products or services concerned, of the existence of entry barriers or of consumer preferences, of appreciable differences of the undertakings' market shares between the area concerned and neighbouring areas or of substantial price differences.

8. In applying the provisions of this Article, the Member State concerned may take only the measures strictly necessary to safeguard or restore effective competition on the market concerned.

9. In accordance with the relevant provisions of the Treaty, any Member State may appeal to the Court of Justice, and in particular request the application of Article 243 of the Treaty, for the purpose of applying its national competition law.

Article 10 Time limits for initiating proceedings and for decisions

1. Without prejudice to Article 6(4), the decisions referred to in Article 6(1) shall be taken within 25 working days at most. That period shall begin on the working day following that of the receipt of a notification or, if the information to be supplied with the notification is incomplete, on the working day following that of the receipt of the complete information. That period shall be increased to 35 working days where the Commission receives a request from a Member State in accordance with Article 9(2) or where, the undertakings concerned offer commitments pursuant to Article 6(2) with a view to rendering the concentration compatible with the common market.

2. Decisions pursuant to Article 8(1) or (2) concerning notified concentrations shall be taken as soon as it appears that the serious doubts referred to in Article 6(1)(c) have been removed, particularly as a result of modifications made by the undertakings concerned, and at the latest by the time limit laid down in paragraph 3.

3. Without prejudice to Article 8(7), decisions pursuant to Article 8(1) to (3) concerning notified concentrations shall be taken within not more than 90 working days of the date on which the proceedings are initiated. That period shall be increased to 105 working days where the undertakings concerned offer commitments pursuant to Article 8(2), second subparagraph, with a view to rendering the concentration compatible with the common market, unless these commitments have been offered less than 55 working days after the initiation of proceedings. The periods set by the first subparagraph shall likewise be extended if the notifying parties make a request to that effect not later than 15 working days after the initiation of proceedings pursuant to Article 6 (1)(c). The notifying parties may make only one such request. Likewise, at any time following the initiation of proceedings, the periods set by the first subparagraph may be extended by the Commission with the agreement of the notifying parties. The total duration of any extension or extensions effected pursuant to this subparagraph shall not exceed 20 working days.

4. The periods set by paragraphs 1 and 3 shall exceptionally be suspended where, owing to circumstances for which one of the undertakings involved in the concentration is responsible, the Commission has had to request information by decision pursuant to Article 11 or to order an inspection by decision pursuant to Article 13.

The first subparagraph shall also apply to the period referred to in Article 9(4)(b).

5. Where the Court of Justice gives a judgment which annuls the whole or part of a Commission decision which is subject to a time limit set by this Article, the concentration shall be re-examined by the Commission with a view to adopting a decision pursuant to Article 6(1).

The concentration shall be re-examined in the light of current market conditions.

The notifying parties shall submit a new notification or supplement the original notification, without delay, where the original notification becomes incomplete by reason of intervening changes in market conditions or in the information provided. Where there are no such changes, the parties shall certify this fact without delay.

The periods laid down in paragraph 1 shall start on the working day following that of the receipt of complete information in a new notification, a supplemented notification, or a certification within the meaning of the third subparagraph.

The second and third subparagraphs shall also apply in the cases referred to in Article 6(4) and Article 8(7).

6. Where the Commission has not taken a decision in accordance with Article 6(1)(b), (c), 8(1), (2) or (3) within the time limits set in paragraphs 1 and 3 respectively, the concentration shall be deemed to have been declared compatible with the common market, without prejudice to Article 9.

Article 11   Requests for information

1. In order to carry out the duties assigned to it by this Regulation, the Commission may, by simple request or by decision, require the persons referred to in Article 3(1)(b), as well as undertakings and associations of undertakings, to provide all necessary information.

2. When sending a simple request for information to a person, an undertaking or an association of undertakings, the Commission shall state the legal basis and the purpose of the request, specify what information is required and fix the time limit within which the information is to be provided, as well as the penalties provided for in Article 14 for supplying incorrect or misleading information.

3. Where the Commission requires a person, an undertaking or an association of undertakings to supply information by decision, it shall state the legal basis and the purpose of the request, specify what information is required and fix the time limit within which it is to be provided. It shall also indicate the penalties provided for in Article 14 and indicate or impose the penalties provided for in Article 15. It shall further indicate the right to have the decision reviewed by the Court of Justice.

4. The owners of the undertakings or their representatives and, in the case of legal persons, companies or firms, or associations having no legal personality, the persons authorised to represent them by law or by their constitution, shall supply the information requested on behalf of the undertaking concerned. Persons duly authorised to act may supply the information on behalf of their clients. The latter shall remain fully responsible if the information supplied is incomplete, incorrect or misleading.

5. The Commission shall without delay forward a copy of any decision taken pursuant to paragraph 3 to the competent authorities of the Member State in whose territory the residence of the person or the seat of the undertaking or association of undertakings is situated, and to the competent authority of the Member State whose territory is affected. At the specific request of the competent authority of a Member State, the Commission shall also forward to that authority copies of simple requests for information relating to a notified concentration.

6. At the request of the Commission, the governments and competent authorities of the Member States shall provide the Commission with all necessary information to carry out the duties assigned to it by this Regulation.

7. In order to carry out the duties assigned to it by this Regulation, the Commission may interview any natural or legal person who consents to be interviewed for the purpose of collecting information relating to the subject matter of an investigation. At the beginning of the interview, which may be conducted by telephone or other electronic means, the Commission shall state the legal basis and the purpose of the interview.

Where an interview is not conducted on the premises of the Commission or by telephone or other electronic means, the Commission shall inform in advance the competent authority of the Member State in whose territory the interview takes place. If the competent authority of that Member State so requests, officials of that authority may assist the officials and other persons authorised by the Commission to conduct the interview.

Article 12   Inspections by the authorities of the Member States

1. At the request of the Commission, the competent authorities of the Member States shall undertake the inspections which the Commission considers to be necessary under Article 13(1), or which it has ordered by decision pursuant to Article 13(4). The officials of the competent authorities of the Member States who are responsible for conducting these inspections as well as those authorised or appointed by them shall exercise their powers in accordance with their national law.

2. If so requested by the Commission or by the competent authority of the Member State within whose territory the inspection is to be conducted, officials and other accompanying persons authorised by the Commission may assist the officials of the authority concerned.

Article 13   The Commission's powers of inspection

1. In order to carry out the duties assigned to it by this Regulation, the Commission may conduct all necessary inspections of undertakings and associations of undertakings.

2. The officials and other accompanying persons authorised by the Commission to conduct an inspection shall have the power:

    (a) to enter any premises, land and means of transport of undertakings and associations of undertakings;

    (b) to examine the books and other records related to the business, irrespective of the medium on which they are stored;

    (c) to take or obtain in any form copies of or extracts from such books or records;

    (d) to seal any business premises and books or records for the period and to the extent necessary for the inspection;

    (e) to ask any representative or member of staff of the undertaking or association of undertakings for explanations on facts or documents relating to the subject matter and purpose of the inspection and to record the answers.

3. Officials and other accompanying persons authorised by the Commission to conduct an inspection shall exercise their powers upon production of a written authorisation specifying the subject matter and purpose of the inspection and the penalties provided for in Article 14, in the production of the required books or other records related to the business which is incomplete or where answers to questions asked under paragraph 2 of this Article are incorrect or misleading. In good time before the inspection, the Commission shall give notice of the inspection to the competent authority of the Member State in whose territory the inspection is to be conducted.

4. Undertakings and associations of undertakings are required to submit to inspections ordered by decision of the Commission. The decision shall specify the subject matter and purpose of the inspection, appoint the date on which it is to begin and indicate the penalties provided for in Articles 14 and 15 and the right to have the decision reviewed by the Court of Justice. The Commission shall take such decisions after consulting the competent authority of the Member State in whose territory the inspection is to be conducted.

5. Officials of, and those authorised or appointed by, the competent authority of the Member State in whose territory the inspection is to be conducted shall, at the request of that authority or of the Commission, actively assist the officials and other accompanying persons authorised by the Commission. To this end, they shall enjoy the powers specified in paragraph 2.

6. Where the officials and other accompanying persons authorised by the Commission find that an undertaking opposes an inspection, including the sealing of business premises, books or records, ordered pursuant to this Article, the Member State concerned shall afford them the necessary assistance, requesting where appropriate the assistance of the police or of an equivalent enforcement authority, so as to enable them to conduct their inspection.

7. If the assistance provided for in paragraph 6 requires authorisation from a judicial authority according to national rules, such authorisation shall be applied for. Such authorisation may also be applied for as a precautionary measure.

8. Where authorisation as referred to in paragraph 7 is applied for, the national judicial authority shall ensure that the Commission decision is authentic and that the coercive measures envisaged are neither arbitrary nor excessive having regard to the subject matter of the inspection. In its control of proportionality of the coercive measures, the national judicial authority may ask the Commission, directly or through the competent authority of that Member State, for detailed explanations relating to the subject matter of the inspection. However, the national judicial authority may not call into question the necessity for the inspection nor demand that it be provided with the information in the Commission's file. The lawfulness of the Commission's decision shall be subject to review only by the Court of Justice.

Article 14   Fines

1. The Commission may by decision impose on the persons referred to in Article 3(1)b, undertakings or associations of undertakings, fines not exceeding 1% of the aggregate turnover of the undertaking or association of undertakings concerned within the meaning of Article 5 where, intentionally or negligently:

    (a) they supply incorrect or misleading information in a submission, certification, notification or supplement thereto, pursuant to Article 4, Article 10(5) or Article 22(3);

    (b) they supply incorrect or misleading information in response to a request made pursuant to Article 11(2);

    (c) in response to a request made by decision adopted pursuant to Article 11(3), they supply incorrect, incomplete or misleading information or do not supply information within the required time limit;

    (d) they produce the required books or other records related to the business in incomplete form during inspections under Article 13, or refuse to submit to an inspection ordered by decision taken pursuant to Article 13(4);

    (e) in response to a question asked in accordance with Article 13(2)(e),

      – they give an incorrect or misleading answer,

      – they fail to rectify within a time limit set by the Commission an incorrect, incomplete or misleading answer given by a member of staff, or

      – they fail or refuse to provide a complete answer on facts relating to the subject matter and purpose of an inspection ordered by a decision adopted pursuant to Article 13(4);

    (f) seals affixed by officials or other accompanying persons authorised by the Commission in accordance with Article 13(2)(d) have been broken.

2. The Commission may by decision impose fines not exceeding 10% of the aggregate turnover of the undertaking concerned within the meaning of Article 5 on the persons referred to in Article 3(1)b or the undertakings concerned where, either intentionally or negligently, they:

    (a) fail to notify a concentration in accordance with Articles 4 or 22(3) prior to its implementation, unless they are expressly authorised to do so by Article 7(2) or by a decision taken pursuant to Article 7(3);

    (b) implement a concentration in breach of Article 7;

    (c) implement a concentration declared incompatible with the common market by decision pursuant to Article 8(3) or do not comply with any measure ordered by decision pursuant to Article 8(4) or (5);

    (d) fail to comply with a condition or an obligation imposed by decision pursuant to Articles 6(1)(b), Article 7(3) or Article 8(2), second subparagraph.

3. In fixing the amount of the fine, regard shall be had to the nature, gravity and duration of the infringement.

4. Decisions taken pursuant to paragraphs 1, 2 and 3 shall not be of a criminal law nature.

Article 15   Periodic penalty payments

1. The Commission may by decision impose on the persons referred to in Article 3(1)b, undertakings or associations of undertakings, periodic penalty payments not exceeding 5% of the average daily aggregate turnover of the undertaking or association of undertakings concerned within the meaning of Article 5 for each working day of delay, calculated from the date set in the decision, in order to compel them:

    (a) to supply complete and correct information which it has requested by decision taken pursuant to Article 11(3);

    (b) to submit to an inspection which it has ordered by decision taken pursuant to Article 13(4);

    (c) to comply with an obligation imposed by decision pursuant to Article 6(1)(b), Article 7(3) or Article 8(2), second subparagraph; or

    (d) to comply with any measures ordered by decision pursuant to Article 8(4) or (5).

2. Where the persons referred to in Article 3(1)(b), undertakings or associations of undertakings have satisfied the obligation which the periodic penalty payment was intended to enforce, the Commission may fix the definitive amount of the periodic penalty payments at a figure lower than that which would arise under the original decision.

Article 16   Review by the Court of Justice

The Court of Justice shall have unlimited jurisdiction within the meaning of Article 229 of the Treaty to review decisions whereby the Commission has fixed a fine or periodic penalty payments; it may cancel, reduce or increase the fine or periodic penalty payment imposed.

Article 17   Professional secrecy

1. Information acquired as a result of the application of this Regulation shall be used only for the purposes of the relevant request, investigation or hearing.

2. Without prejudice to Article 4(3), Articles 18 and 20, the Commission and the competent authorities of the Member States, their officials and other servants and other persons working under the supervision of these authorities as well as officials and civil servants of other authorities of the Member States shall not disclose information they have acquired through the application of this Regulation of the kind covered by the obligation of professional secrecy.

3. Paragraphs 1 and 2 shall not prevent publication of general information or of surveys which do not contain information relating to particular undertakings or associations of undertakings.

Article 18   Hearing of the parties and of third persons

1. Before taking any decision provided for in Article 6(3), Article 7(3), Article 8(2) to (6), and Articles 14 and 15, the Commission shall give the persons, undertakings and associations of undertakings concerned the opportunity, at every stage of the procedure up to the consultation of the Advisory Committee, of making known their views on the objections against them.

2. By way of derogation from paragraph 1, a decision pursuant to Articles 7(3) and 8(5) may be taken provisionally, without the persons, undertakings or associations of undertakings concerned being given the opportunity to make known their views beforehand, provided that the Commission gives them that opportunity as soon as possible after having taken its decision.

3. The Commission shall base its decision only on objections on which the parties have been able to submit their observations. The rights of the defence shall be fully respected in the proceedings. Access to the file shall be open at least to the parties directly involved, subject to the legitimate interest of undertakings in the protection of their business secrets.

4. In so far as the Commission or the competent authorities of the Member States deem it necessary, they may also hear other natural or legal persons. Natural or legal persons showing a sufficient interest and especially members of the administrative or management bodies of the undertakings concerned or the recognised representatives of their employees shall be entitled, upon application, to be heard.

Article 19   Liaison with the authorities of the Member States

1. The Commission shall transmit to the competent authorities of the Member States copies of notifications within three working days and, as soon as possible, copies of the most important documents lodged with or issued by the Commission pursuant to this Regulation. Such documents shall include commitments offered by the undertakings concerned vis-à-vis the Commission with a view to rendering the concentration compatible with the common market pursuant to Article 6(2) or Article 8(2), second subparagraph.

2. The Commission shall carry out the procedures set out in this Regulation in close and constant liaison with the competent authorities of the Member States, which may express their views upon those procedures. For the purposes of Article 9 it shall obtain information from the competent authority of the Member State as referred to in paragraph 2 of that Article and give it the opportunity to make known its views at every stage of the procedure up to the adoption of a decision pursuant to paragraph 3 of that Article; to that end it shall give it access to the file.

3. An Advisory Committee on concentrations shall be consulted before any decision is taken pursuant to Article 8(1) to (6), Articles 14 or 15 with the exception of provisional decisions taken in accordance with Article 18(2).

4. The Advisory Committee shall consist of representatives of the competent authorities of the Member States. Each Member State shall appoint one or two representatives; if unable to attend, they may be replaced by other representatives. At least one of the representatives of a Member State shall be competent in matters of restrictive practices and dominant positions.

5. Consultation shall take place at a joint meeting convened at the invitation of and chaired by the Commission. A summary of the case, together with an indication of the most important documents and a preliminary draft of the decision to be taken for each case considered, shall be sent with the invitation. The meeting shall take place not less than 10 working days after the invitation has been sent. The Commission may in exceptional cases shorten that period as appropriate in order to avoid serious harm to one or more of the undertakings concerned by a concentration.

6. The Advisory Committee shall deliver an opinion on the Commission's draft decision, if necessary by taking a vote. The Advisory Committee may deliver an opinion even if some members are absent and unrepresented. The opinion shall be delivered in writing and appended to the draft decision. The Commission shall take the utmost account of the opinion delivered by the Committee. It shall inform the Committee of the manner in which its opinion has been taken into account.

7. The Commission shall communicate the opinion of the Advisory Committee, together with the decision, to the addressees of the decision. It shall make the opinion public together with the decision, having regard to the legitimate interest of undertakings in the protection of their business secrets.

Article 20 Publication of decisions

1. The Commission shall publish the decisions which it takes pursuant to Article 8(1) to (6), Articles 14 and 15 with the exception of provisional decisions taken in accordance with Article 18(2) together with the opinion of the Advisory Committee in the *Official Journal of the European Union*.

2. The publication shall state the names of the parties and the main content of the decision; it shall have regard to the legitimate interest of undertakings in the protection of their business secrets.

Article 21 Application of the Regulation and jurisdiction

1. This Regulation alone shall apply to concentrations as defined in Article 3, and Council Regulations (EC) No 1/2003,[8] (EEC) No 1017/68,[9] (EEC) No 4056/86[10] and (EEC) No 3975/87[11] shall not apply, except in relation to joint ventures that do not have a Community dimension and which have as their object or effect the coordination of the competitive behaviour of undertakings that remain independent.

2. Subject to review by the Court of Justice, the Commission shall have sole jurisdiction to take the decisions provided for in this Regulation.

3. No Member State shall apply its national legislation on competition to any concentration that has a Community dimension.

The first subparagraph shall be without prejudice to any Member State's power to carry out any enquiries necessary for the application of Articles 4(4), 9(2) or after referral, pursuant to Article 9(3), first subparagraph, indent (b), or Article 9(5), to take the measures strictly necessary for the application of Article 9(8).

4. Notwithstanding paragraphs 2 and 3, Member States may take appropriate measures to protect legitimate interests other than those taken into consideration by this Regulation and compatible

---

[8] OJ L 1, 4.1.2003, p. 1.
[9] OJ L 175, 23.7.1968, p. 1. Regulation as last amended by Regulation (EC) No 1/2003 (OJ L 1, 4.1.2003, p. 1).
[10] OJ L 378, 31.12.1986, p. 4. Regulation as last amended by Regulation (EC) No 1/2003.
[11] OJ L 374. 31.12.1987, p. 1. Regulation as last amended by Regulation (EC) No 1/2003.

with the general principles and other provisions of Community law. Public security, plurality of the media and prudential rules shall be regarded as legitimate interests within the meaning of the first subparagraph.

Any other public interest must be communicated to the Commission by the Member State concerned and shall be recognised by the Commission after an assessment of its compatibility with the general principles and other provisions of Community law before the measures referred to above may be taken. The Commission shall inform the Member State concerned of its decision within 25 working days of that communication.

Article 22   Referral to the Commission

1. One or more Member States may request the Commission to examine any concentration as defined in Article 3 that does not have a Community dimension within the meaning of Article 1 but affects trade between Member States and threatens to significantly affect competition within the territory of the Member State or States making the request.

Such a request shall be made at most within 15 working days of the date on which the concentration was notified, or if no notification is required, otherwise made known to the Member State concerned.

2. The Commission shall inform the competent authorities of the Member States and the undertakings concerned of any request received pursuant to paragraph 1 without delay. Any other Member State shall have the right to join the initial request within a period of 15 working days of being informed by the Commission of the initial request.

All national time limits relating to the concentration shall be suspended until, in accordance with the procedure set out in this Article, it has been decided where the concentration shall be examined. As soon as a Member State has informed the Commission and the undertakings concerned that it does not wish to join the request, the suspension of its national time limits shall end.

3. The Commission may, at the latest 10 working days after the expiry of the period set in paragraph 2, decide to examine, the concentration where it considers that it affects trade between Member States and threatens to significantly affect competition within the territory of the Member State or States making the request. If the Commission does not take a decision within this period, it shall be deemed to have adopted a decision to examine the concentration in accordance with the request.

The Commission shall inform all Member States and the undertakings concerned of its decision. It may request the submission of a notification pursuant to Article 4.

The Member State or States having made the request shall no longer apply their national legislation on competition to the concentration.

4. Article 2, Article 4(2) to (3), Articles 5, 6, and 8 to 21 shall apply where the Commission examines a concentration pursuant to paragraph 3. Article 7 shall apply to the extent that the concentration has not been implemented on the date on which the Commission informs the undertakings concerned that a request has been made.

Regulation (EEC) No 4064/89	This Regulation
Article 1(1), (2) and (3)	Article 1(1), (2) and (3)
Article 1(4)	Article 1(4)
Article 1(5)	Article 1(5)
Article 2(1)	Article 2(1)
—	Article 2(2)
Article 2(2)	Article 2(3)
Article 2(3)	Article 2(4)
Article 2(4)	Article 2(5)
Article 3(1)	Article 3(1)
Article 3(1)	Article 3(4)
Article 3(4)	Article 3(3)

Regulation (EEC) No 4064/89	This Regulation
—	Article 3(4)
Article 3(5)	Article 3(5)
Article 4(1) first sentence	Article 4(1) first subparagraph
Article 4(1) second sentence	—
—	Article 4(1) second and third subparagraphs
Article 4(2) and (3)	Article 4(2) and (3)
—	Article 4(4) to (6)
Article 5(1) to (3)	Article 5(1) to (3)
Article 5(4), introductory words	Article 5(4), introductory words
Article 5(4) point (a)	Article 5(4) point (a)
Article 5(4) point (b), introductory words	Article 5(4) point (b), introductory words
Article 5(4) point (b), first indent	Article 5(4) point (b)(i)
Article 5(4) point (b), second indent	Article 5(4) point (b)(ii)
Article 5(4) point (b), third indent	Article 5(4) point (b)(iii)
Article 5(4) point (b), fourth indent	Article 5(4) point (b)(iv)
Article 5(4) points (c), (d) and (e)	Article 5(4) points (c), (d) and (e)
Article 5(5)	Article 5(5)
Article 6(1), introductory words	Article 6(1), introductory words
Article 6(1) points (a) and (b)	Article 6(1) points (a) and (b)
Article 6(1) point (c)	Article 6(1) point (c), first sentence
Article 6(2) to (5)	Article 6(2) to (5)
Article 7(1)	Article 7(1)
Article 7(3)	Article 7(2)
Article 7(4)	Article 7(3)
Article 7(5)	Article 7(4)
Article 8(1)	Article 6(1) point (c), second sentence
Article 8(2)	Article 8(1) and (2)
Article 8(3)	Article 8(3)
Article 8(4)	Article 8(4)
—	Article 8(5)
Article 8(5)	Article 8(6)
Article 8(6)	Article 8(7)
—	Article 8(8)
Article 9(1) to (9)	Article 9(1) to (9)
Article 9(10)	—
Article 10(1) and (2)	Article 10(1) and (2)
Article 10(3)	Article 10(3) first subparagraph, first sentence
—	Article 10(3) first subparagraph, second sentence
—	Article 10(3) second subparagraph
Article 10(4)	Article 10(4) first subparagraph
—	Article 10(4), second subparagraph
Article 10(5)	Article 10(5), first and fourth subparagraphs
—	Article 10(5), second, third and fifth subparagraphs
Article 10(6)	Article 10(6)
Article 11(1)	Article 11(1)
Article 11(2)	—
Article 11(3)	Article 11(2)
Article 11(4)	Article 11(4) first sentence
—	Article 11(4) first sentence
Article 11(5) first sentence	—

(cont.)

Regulation (EEC) No 4064/89	This Regulation
Article 11(5) second sentence	Article 11(3)
Article 11(6)	Article 11(5)
—	Article 11(6) and (7)
Article 12	Article 12
Article 13(1) first subparagraph	Article 13(1)
Article 13(1) second subparagraph, intro words	Article 13(2) introductory words
Article 13(1) second subparagraph, point (a)	Article 13(2) point (b)
Article 13(1) second subparagraph, point (b)	Article 13(2) point (c)
Article 13(1) second subparagraph, point (c)	Article 13(2) point (e)
Article 13(1) second subparagraph, point (d)	Article 13(2) point (a)
—	Article 13(2) point (d)
Article 13(2)	Article 13(3)
Article 13(3)	Article 13(4) first and second sentences
Article 13(4)	Article 13(4) third sentence
Article 13(5)	Article 13(5), first sentence
—	Article 13(5), second sentence
Article 13(6) first sentence	Article 13(6)
Article 13(6) second sentence	—
—	Article 13(7) and (8)
Article 14(1) introductory words	Article 14(1) introductory words
Article 14(1) point (a)	Article 14(2) point (a)
Article 14(1) point (b)	Article 14(1) point (a)
Article 14(1) point (c)	Article 14(1) points (b) and (c)
Article 14(1) point (d)	Article 14(1) point (d)
—	Article 14(1) points (e) and (f)
Article 14(2) introductory words	Article 14(2) introductory words
Article 14(2) point (a)	Article 14(2) point (d)
Article 14(2) points (b) and (c)	Article 14(2) points (b) and (c)
Article 14(3)	Article 14(3)
Article 14(4)	Article 14(4)
Article 15(1) introductory words	Article 15(1) introductory words
Article 15(1) points (a) and (b)	Article 15(1) points (a) and (b)
Article 15(2) introductory words	Article 15(1) introductory words
Article 15(2) point (a)	Article 15(1) point (c)
Article 15(2) point (b)	Article 15(1) point (d)
Article 15(3)	Article 15(2)
Articles 16 to 20	Articles 16 to 20
Article 21(1)	Article 21(2)
Article 21(2)	Article 21(3)
Article 21(3)	Article 21(4)
Article 22(1)	Article 21(1)
Article 22(3)	—
—	Article 22(1) to (3)
Article 22(4)	Article 22(4)
Article 22(5)	—
—	Article 22(5)
Article 23	Article 23(1)
—	Article 23(2)
Article 24	Article 24
—	Article 25
Article 25(1)	Article 26(1), first subparagraph

Where a notification pursuant to Article 4 is not required, the period set in Article 10(1) within which proceedings may be initiated shall begin on the working day following that on which the Commission informs the undertakings concerned that it has decided to examine the concentration pursuant to paragraph 3.

5. The Commission may inform one or several Member States that it considers a concentration fulfils the criteria in paragraph 1. In such cases, the Commission may invite that Member State or those Member States to make a request pursuant to paragraph 1.

Article 23   Implementing provisions

1. The Commission shall have the power to lay down in accordance with the procedure referred to in paragraph 2:

    (a) implementing provisions concerning the form, content and other details of notifications and submissions pursuant to Article 4;

    (b) implementing provisions concerning time limits pursuant to Article 4(4), (5) Articles 7, 9, 10 and 22;

    (c) the procedure and time limits for the submission and implementation of commitments pursuant to Article 6(2) and Article 8(2);

    (d) implementing provisions concerning hearings pursuant to Article 18.

2. The Commission shall be assisted by an Advisory Committee, composed of representatives of the Member States.

    (a) Before publishing draft implementing provisions and before adopting such provisions, the Commission shall consult the Advisory Committee.

    (b) Consultation shall take place at a meeting convened at the invitation of and chaired by the Commission. A draft of the implementing provisions to be taken shall be sent with the invitation. The meeting shall take place not less than 10 working days after the invitation has been sent.

    (c) The Advisory Committee shall deliver an opinion on the draft implementing provisions, if necessary by taking a vote. The Commission shall take the utmost account of the opinion delivered by the Committee.

Article 24   Relations with third countries

1. The Member States shall inform the Commission of any general difficulties encountered by their undertakings with concentrations as defined in Article 3 in a third country.

2. Initially not more than one year after the entry into force of this Regulation and, thereafter periodically, the Commission shall draw up a report examining the treatment accorded to undertakings having their seat or their principal fields of activity in the Community, in the terms referred to in paragraphs 3 and 4, as regards concentrations in third countries. The Commission shall submit those reports to the Council, together with any recommendations.

3. Whenever it appears to the Commission, either on the basis of the reports referred to in paragraph 2 or on the basis of other information, that a third country does not grant undertakings having their seat or their principal fields of activity in the Community, treatment comparable to that granted by the Community to undertakings from that country, the Commission may submit proposals to the Council for an appropriate mandate for negotiation with a view to obtaining comparable treatment for undertakings having their seat or their principal fields of activity in the Community.

4. Measures taken under this Article shall comply with the obligations of the Community or of the Member States, without prejudice to Article 307 of the Treaty, under international agreements, whether bilateral or multilateral.

Article 25   Repeal

1. Without prejudice to Article 26(2), Regulations (EEC) No 4064/89 and (EC) No 1310/97 shall be repealed with effect from 1 May 2004.

2. References to the repealed Regulations shall be construed as references to this Regulation and shall be read in accordance with the correlation table in the Annex.

Article 26 Entry into force and transitional provisions

1. This Regulation shall enter into force on the 20th day following that of its publication in the *Official Journal of the European Union*.

It shall apply from 1 May 2004.

2. Regulation (EEC) No 4064/89 shall continue to apply to any concentration which was the subject of an agreement or announcement or where control was acquired within the meaning of Article 4(1) of that Regulation before the date of application of this Regulation, subject, in particular, to the provisions governing applicability set out in Article 25(2) and (3) of Regulation (EEC) No 4064/89 and Article 2 of Regulation (EEC) No 1310/97.

3. As regards concentrations to which this Regulation applies by virtue of accession, the date of accession shall be substituted for the date of application of this Regulation.

This Regulation shall be binding in its entirety and directly applicable in all Member States.

Done at Brussels, 20 January 2004.

Commission Regulation (EC) No 773/2004 of 7 April 2004 relating to the conduct of proceedings by the Commission pursuant to Articles 81 and 82 of the EC Treaty*

[OJ 2004 L123/18]

THE COMMISSION OF THE EUROPEAN COMMUNITIES,

Having regard to the Treaty establishing the European Community,

Having regard to the Agreement on the European Economic Area,

Having regard to Council Regulation (EC) No 1/2003 of 16 December 2002 on the implementation of the rules on competition laid down in Articles 81 and 82 of the Treaty,[1] and in particular Article 33 thereof,

After consulting the Advisory Committee on Restrictive Practices and Dominant Positions,

Whereas:

(1) Regulation (EC) No 1/2003 empowers the Commission to regulate certain aspects of proceedings for the application of Articles 81 and 82 of the Treaty. It is necessary to lay down rules concerning the initiation of proceedings by the Commission as well as the handling of complaints and the hearing of the parties concerned.

(2) According to Regulation (EC) No 1/2003, national courts are under an obligation to avoid taking decisions which could run counter to decisions envisaged by the Commission in the same case. According to Article 11(6) of that Regulation, national competition authorities are relieved from their competence once the Commission has initiated proceedings for the adoption of a decision under Chapter III of Regulation (EC) No 1/2003. In this context, it is important that courts and competition authorities of the Member States are aware of the initiation of proceedings by the Commission. The Commission should therefore be able to make public its decisions to initiate proceedings.

(3) Before taking oral statements from natural or legal persons who consent to be interviewed, the Commission should inform those persons of the legal basis of the interview and its voluntary nature. The persons interviewed should also be informed of the purpose of the interview and of any record which may be made. In order to enhance the accuracy of the statements, the persons interviewed should also be given an opportunity to correct the statements recorded. Where information gathered from oral statements is exchanged pursuant to Article 12 of Regulation (EC) No 1/2003,

---

* **Editor's Note:** Read now Articles 101 and 102 TFEU. As amended by Regulations 1792/2006 (OJ 2006 L362/1) 622/2008 (OJ 2008 L171/3), 519/2013 (OJ 2013 L158/74), and 2015/1348 (OJ 2015 L208/3).

[1] OJ L 1, 4.1.2003, p. 1. Regulation as amended by Regulation (EC) No 411/2004 (OJ L 68, 6.3.2004, p. 1) and Regulation 1792/2006 OJ 2006 L 362/1.

that information should only be used in evidence to impose sanctions on natural persons where the conditions set out in that Article are fulfilled.

(4) Pursuant to Article 23(1)(d) of Regulation (EC) No 1/2003 fines may be imposed on undertakings and associations of undertakings where they fail to rectify within the time limit fixed by the Commission an incorrect, incomplete or misleading answer given by a member of their staff to questions in the course of inspections. It is therefore necessary to provide the undertaking concerned with a record of any explanations given and to establish a procedure enabling it to add any rectification, amendment or supplement to the explanations given by the member of staff who is not or was not authorised to provide explanations on behalf of the undertaking. The explanations given by a member of staff should remain in the Commission file as recorded during the inspection.

(5) Complaints are an essential source of information for detecting infringements of competition rules. It is important to define clear and efficient procedures for handling complaints lodged with the Commission.

(6) In order to be admissible for the purposes of Article 7 of Regulation (EC) No 1/2003, a complaint must contain certain specified information.

(7) In order to assist complainants in submitting the necessary facts to the Commission, a form should be drawn up. The submission of the information listed in that form should be a condition for a complaint to be treated as a complaint as referred to in Article 7 of Regulation (EC) No 1/2003.

(8) Natural or legal persons having chosen to lodge a complaint should be given the possibility to be associated closely with the proceedings initiated by the Commission with a view to finding an infringement. However, they should not have access to business secrets or other confidential information belonging to other parties involved in the proceedings.

(9) Complainants should be granted the opportunity of expressing their views if the Commission considers that there are insufficient grounds for acting on the complaint. Where the Commission rejects a complaint on the grounds that a competition authority of a Member State is dealing with it or has already done so, it should inform the complainant of the identity of that authority.

(10) In order to respect the rights of defence of undertakings, the Commission should give the parties concerned the right to be heard before it takes a decision.

(11) Provision should also be made for the hearing of persons who have not submitted a complaint as referred to in Article 7 of Regulation (EC) No 1/2003 and who are not parties to whom a statement of objections has been addressed but who can nevertheless show a sufficient interest. Consumer associations that apply to be heard should generally be regarded as having a sufficient interest, where the proceedings concern products or services used by the end-consumer or products or services that constitute a direct input into such products or services. Where it considers this to be useful for the proceedings, the Commission should also be able to invite other persons to express their views in writing and to attend the oral hearing of the parties to whom a statement of objections has been addressed. Where appropriate, it should also be able to invite such persons to express their views at that oral hearing.

(12) To improve the effectiveness of oral hearings, the Hearing Officer should have the power to allow the parties concerned, complainants, other persons invited to the hearing, the Commission services and the authorities of the Member States to ask questions during the hearing.

(13) When granting access to the file, the Commission should ensure the protection of business secrets and other confidential information. The category of 'other confidential information' includes information other than business secrets, which may be considered as confidential, insofar as its disclosure would significantly harm an undertaking or person. The Commission should be able to request undertakings or associations of undertakings that submit or have submitted documents or statements to identify confidential information.

(14) Where business secrets or other confidential information are necessary to prove an infringement, the Commission should assess for each individual document whether the need to disclose is greater than the harm which might result from disclosure.

(15) In the interest of legal certainty, a minimum time-limit for the various submissions provided for in this Regulation should be laid down.

(16) This Regulation replaces Commission Regulation (EC) No 2842/98 of 22 December 1998 on the hearing of parties in certain proceedings under Articles 85 and 86 of the EC Treaty,[2] which should therefore be repealed.

(17) This Regulation aligns the procedural rules in the transport sector with the general rules of procedure in all sectors. Commission Regulation (EC) No 2843/98 of 22 December 1998 on the form, content and other details of applications and notifications provided for in Council Regulations (EEC) No 1017/68, (EEC) No 4056/86 and (EEC) No 3975/87 applying the rules on competition to the transport sector[3] should therefore be repealed.

(18) Regulation (EC) No 1/2003 abolishes the notification and authorisation system. Commission Regulation (EC) No 3385/94 of 21 December 1994 on the form, content and other details of applications and notifications provided for in Council Regulation No 17[4] should therefore be repealed,

HAS ADOPTED THIS REGULATION:

Chapter I Scope

Article 1 Subject-matter and scope

This regulation applies to proceedings conducted by the Commission for the application of Articles 81 and 82 of the Treaty.

Chapter II Initiation of proceedings

Article 2 Initiation of proceedings

1. The Commission may decide to initiate proceedings with a view to adopting a decision pursuant to Chapter III of Regulation (EC) No 1/2003 at any point in time, but no later than the date on which it issues a preliminary assessment as referred to in Article 9(1) of that Regulation, a statement of objections or a request for the parties to express their interest in engaging in settlement discussions, or the date on which a notice pursuant to Article 27(4) of that Regulation is published, whichever is the earlier.

2. The Commission may make public the initiation of proceedings, in any appropriate way. Before doing so, it shall inform the parties concerned.

3. The Commission may exercise its powers of investigation pursuant to Chapter V of Regulation (EC) No 1/2003 before initiating proceedings.

4. The Commission may reject a complaint pursuant to Article 7 of Regulation (EC) No 1/2003 without initiating proceedings.

Chapter III Investigations by the Commission

Article 3 Power to take statements

1. Where the Commission interviews a person with his consent in accordance with Article 19 of Regulation (EC) No 1/2003, it shall, at the beginning of the interview, state the legal basis and the purpose of the interview, and recall its voluntary nature. It shall also inform the person interviewed of its intention to make a record of the interview.

2. The interview may be conducted by any means including by telephone or electronic means.

3. The Commission may record the statements made by the persons interviewed in any form.

A copy of any recording shall be made available to the person interviewed for approval. Where necessary, the Commission shall set a time-limit within which the person interviewed may communicate to it any correction to be made to the statement.

---

[2] OJ L 354, 30.12.1998, p. 18.
[3] OJ L 354, 30.12.1998, p. 22.
[4] OJ L 354, 31.12.1994, p. 28.

Article 4   Oral questions during inspections

1. When, pursuant to Article 20(2)(e) of Regulation (EC) No 1/2003, officials or other accompanying persons authorised by the Commission ask representatives or members of staff of an undertaking or of an association of undertakings for explanations, the explanations given may be recorded in any form.

2. A copy of any recording made pursuant to paragraph 1 shall be made available to the undertaking or association of undertakings concerned after the inspection.

3. In cases where a member of staff of an undertaking or of an association of undertakings who is not or was not authorised by the undertaking or by the association of undertakings to provide explanations on behalf of the undertaking or association of undertakings has been asked for explanations, the Commission shall set a time-limit within which the undertaking or the association of undertakings may communicate to the Commission any rectification, amendment or supplement to the explanations given by such member of staff. The rectification, amendment or supplement shall be added to the explanations as recorded pursuant to paragraph 1.

Article 4a   The Commission's Leniency Programme

1. The Commission may set the requirements and cooperation conditions under which it may reward undertakings that are or have been party to secret cartels, for their cooperation in disclosing the cartel and facilitating the establishment of an infringement, with immunity from fines or a reduction in fines which would otherwise be imposed under Article 23(2) of Regulation (EC) No 1/2003 (the Commission leniency programme).

Immunity from fines may be granted to the undertaking that is the first to submit evidence which in the Commission's view would enable it to carry out a targeted inspection or find an infringement of Article 101 of the Treaty in connection with the alleged cartel. A reduction in fines may be granted to undertakings which provide the Commission with evidence of the alleged infringement which represents significant added value with respect to the evidence already in the Commission's possession.

The Commission will only grant immunity from or a reduction of the fine under its leniency programme if, at the end of the administrative proceedings, the undertaking has met the requirements and cooperation conditions set out in the leniency programme. Those may cover, among others, the type of information and evidence the undertakings are required to submit and the further cooperation expected from the undertakings during the administrative proceedings.

2. In order to qualify for immunity from or reduction of the fine which would otherwise be imposed, undertakings shall provide the Commission with voluntary presentations of their knowledge of a secret cartel and their role therein, which may be also in the form of voluntary presentations of the knowledge of former or current employees or representatives of the undertaking (leniency corporate statements). Such leniency corporate statements shall be drawn up specifically for submission to the Commission with a view to obtaining immunity from or reduction of fines under the Commission's leniency programme.

3. The Commission will offer parties appropriate methods of providing leniency corporate statements other than by written submission, including orally. Oral corporate statements may be recorded and transcribed at the Commission's premises. The undertaking shall be granted an opportunity to check the technical accuracy of the recording of its oral statement at the Commission's premises, and, where necessary, to correct the substance of the statement without delay. The rules in this Regulation on leniency corporate statements shall apply to such statements irrespective of the medium on which they are stored. Pre-existing information, i.e. evidence that exists irrespective of the Commission proceedings and that is submitted to the Commission by an undertaking in the context of its application for immunity from or reduction of the fine, is not part of a leniency corporate statement.

Chapter IV   Handling of complaints

Article 5   Admissibility of complaints

1. Natural and legal persons shall show a legitimate interest in order to be entitled to lodge a complaint for the purposes of Article 7 of Regulation (EC) No 1/2003.

Such complaints shall contain the information required by Form C, as set out in the Annex. The Commission may dispense with this obligation as regards part of the information, including documents, required by Form C.

2. Three paper copies as well as, if possible, an electronic copy of the complaint shall be submitted to the Commission. The complainant shall also submit a non-confidential version of the complaint, if confidentiality is claimed for any part of the complaint.

3. Complaints shall be submitted in one of the official languages of the Community.

Article 6   Participation of complainants in proceedings

1. Where the Commission issues a statement of objections relating to a matter in respect of which it has received a complaint, it shall provide the complainant with a copy of the non-confidential version of the statement of objections, except in cases where the settlement procedure applies, where it shall inform the complainant in writing of the nature and subject matter of the procedure. The Commission shall also set a time limit within which the complainant may make known its views in writing.

2. The Commission may, where appropriate, afford complainants the opportunity of expressing their views at the oral hearing of the parties to which a statement of objections has been issued, if complainants so request in their written comments.

Article 7   Rejection of complaints

1. Where the Commission considers that on the basis of the information in its possession there are insufficient grounds for acting on a complaint, it shall inform the complainant of its reasons and set a time-limit within which the complainant may make known its views in writing. The Commission shall not be obliged to take into account any further written submission received after the expiry of that time-limit.

2. If the complainant makes known its views within the time-limit set by the Commission and the written submissions made by the complainant do not lead to a different assessment of the complaint, the Commission shall reject the complaint by decision.

3. If the complainant fails to make known its views within the time-limit set by the Commission, the complaint shall be deemed to have been withdrawn.

Article 8   Access to information

1. Where the Commission has informed the complainant of its intention to reject a complaint pursuant to Article 7(1) the complainant may request access to the documents on which the Commission bases its provisional assessment. For this purpose, the complainant may however not have access to business secrets and other confidential information belonging to other parties involved in the proceedings.

Article 9   Rejections of complaints pursuant to Article 13 of Regulation (EC) No 1/2003

Where the Commission rejects a complaint pursuant to Article 13 of Regulation (EC) No 1/2003, it shall inform the complainant without delay of the national competition authority which is dealing or has already dealt with the case.

Chapter V   Exercise of the right to be heard

Article 10   Statement of objections and reply

1. The Commission shall inform the parties concerned of the objections raised against them. The statement of objections shall be notified in writing to each of the parties against whom objections are raised.

2. The Commission shall, when notifying the statement of objections to the parties concerned, set a time-limit within which these parties may inform it in writing of their views. The Commission shall not be obliged to take into account written submissions received after the expiry of that time-limit.

3. The parties may, in their written submissions, set out all facts known to them which are relevant to their defence against the objections raised by the Commission. They shall attach any relevant documents as proof of the facts set out. They shall provide a paper original as well as an electronic copy or, where they do not provide an electronic copy, 31 paper copies of their submission and of the documents attached to it. They may propose that the Commission hear persons who may corroborate the facts set out in their submission.

Article 10a   Settlement procedure in cartel cases

1. After the initiation of proceedings pursuant to Article 11(6) of Regulation (EC) No 1/2003, the Commission may set a time limit within which the parties may indicate in writing that they are prepared to engage in settlement discussions with a view to possibly introducing settlement submissions. The Commission shall not be obliged to take into account replies received after the expiry of that time limit.

If two or more parties within the same undertaking indicate their willingness to engage in settlement discussions pursuant to the first subparagraph, they shall appoint a joint representation to engage in discussions with the Commission on their behalf. When setting the time limit referred to in the first subparagraph, the Commission shall indicate to the relevant parties that they are identified within the same undertaking, for the sole purpose of enabling them to comply with this provision.

2. Parties taking part in settlement discussions may be informed by the Commission of:
   (a) the objections it envisages to raise against them;
   (b) the evidence used to determine the envisaged objections;
   (c) non-confidential versions of any specified accessible document listed in the case file at that point in time, in so far as a request by the party is justified for the purpose of enabling the party to ascertain its position regarding a time period or any other particular aspect of the cartel; and
   (d) the range of potential fines.

This information shall be confidential vis-à-vis third parties, save where the Commission has given a prior explicit authorisation for disclosure.

Should settlement discussions progress, the Commission may set a time limit within which the parties may commit to follow the settlement procedure by introducing settlement submissions reflecting the results of the settlement discussions and acknowledging their participation in an infringement of Article 101 of the Treaty as well as their liability. These settlement submissions shall be specifically drawn up by the undertakings concerned as a formal request to the Commission to adopt any decision in their case following the settlement procedure. Before the Commission sets a time limit for the introduction of settlement submissions, the parties concerned shall be entitled to have the information specified in the first subparagraph, disclosed to them, upon request, in a timely manner. The Commission shall not be obliged to take into account settlement submissions received after the expiry of that time limit. The Commission will offer parties appropriate methods of providing settlement submissions other than by written submission, including orally. Oral settlement submissions may be recorded and transcribed at the Commission's premises. The undertaking shall be granted an opportunity to check the technical accuracy of the recording of its oral submission at the Commission's premises, and, where necessary, to correct the substance of their submission without delay. The rules in this Regulation on settlement submissions shall apply to settlement submissions irrespective of the medium on which they are stored.

3. When the statement of objections notified to the parties reflects the contents of their settlement submissions, the written reply to the statement of objections by the parties concerned shall, within a time limit set by the Commission, confirm that the statement of objections addressed to

them reflects the contents of their settlement submissions. The Commission may then proceed to the adoption of a Decision pursuant to Article 7 and Article 23 of Regulation (EC) No 1/2003 after consultation of the Advisory Committee on Restrictive Practices and Dominant Positions pursuant to Article 14 of Regulation (EC) No 1/2003.

4. The Commission may decide at any time during the procedure to discontinue settlement discussions altogether in a specific case or with respect to one or more of the parties involved, if it considers that procedural efficiencies are not likely to be achieved.

Article 11   Right to be heard

1. The Commission shall give the parties to whom it addresses a statement of objections the opportunity to be heard before consulting the Advisory Committee referred to in Article 14(1) of Regulation (EC) No 1/2003.

2. The Commission shall, in its decisions, deal only with objections in respect of which the parties referred to in paragraph 1 have been able to comment.

Article 12   Right to an oral hearing

1. The Commission shall give the parties to whom it addresses a statement of objections the opportunity to develop their arguments at an oral hearing, if they so request in their written submissions.

2. However, when introducing their settlement submissions the parties shall confirm to the Commission that they would only require having the opportunity to develop their arguments at an oral hearing, if the statement of objections does not reflect the contents of their settlement submissions.

Article 13   Hearing of other persons

1. If natural or legal persons other than those referred to in Articles 5 and 11 apply to be heard and show a sufficient interest, the Commission shall inform them in writing of the nature and subject matter of the procedure and shall set a time-limit within which they may make known their views in writing.

2. The Commission may, where appropriate, invite persons referred to in paragraph 1 to develop their arguments at the oral hearing of the parties to whom a statement of objections has been addressed, if the persons referred to in paragraph 1 so request in their written comments.

3. The Commission may invite any other person to express its views in writing and to attend the oral hearing of the parties to whom a statement of objections has been addressed. The Commission may also invite such persons to express their views at that oral hearing.

Article 14   Conduct of oral hearings

1. Hearings shall be conducted by a Hearing Officer in full independence.

2. The Commission shall invite the persons to be heard to attend the oral hearing on such date as it shall determine.

3. The Commission shall invite the competition authorities of the Member States to take part in the oral hearing. It may likewise invite officials and civil servants of other authorities of the Member States.

4. Persons invited to attend shall either appear in person or be represented by legal representatives or by representatives authorised by their constitution as appropriate. Undertakings and associations of undertakings may also be represented by a duly authorised agent appointed from among their permanent staff.

5. Persons heard by the Commission may be assisted by their lawyers or other qualified persons admitted by the Hearing Officer.

6. Oral hearings shall not be public. Each person may be heard separately or in the presence of other persons invited to attend, having regard to the legitimate interest of the undertakings in the protection of their business secrets and other confidential information.

7. The Hearing Officer may allow the parties to whom a statement of objections has been addressed, the complainants, other persons invited to the hearing, the Commission services and the authorities of the Member States to ask questions during the hearing.

8. The statements made by each person heard shall be recorded. Upon request, the recording of the hearing shall be made available to the persons who attended the hearing. Regard shall be had to the legitimate interest of the parties in the protection of their business secrets and other confidential information.

Chapter VI Access to the file and treatment of confidential information

Article 15 Access to the file

1. If so requested, the Commission shall grant access to the file to the parties to whom it has addressed a statement of objections. Access shall be granted after the notification of the statement of objections.

1a. After the initiation of proceedings pursuant to Article 11(6) of Regulation (EC) No 1/2003 and in order to enable the parties to introduce settlement submissions, the Commission shall disclose to them the evidence and documents described in Article 10a(2) upon request and subject to the conditions established in the relevant subparagraphs. In view thereof, when introducing their settlement submissions, the parties shall confirm to the Commission that they will only require access to the file pursuant to paragraph 1 after the receipt of the statement of objections, if the statement of objections does not reflect the contents of their settlement submissions. Where settlement discussions have been discontinued with one or more of the parties, such party shall be granted access to the file pursuant to paragraph 1 when a statement of objections has been addressed to it.

1b. Access pursuant to paragraph 1 or 1a to a leniency corporate statement within the meaning of Article 4a(2) or to a settlement submission within the meaning of Article 10a(2), shall only be granted at the premises of the Commission. The parties and their representatives shall not copy the leniency corporate statements or settlement submissions by any mechanical or electronic means.

2. The right of access to the file shall not extend to business secrets, other confidential information and internal documents of the Commission or of the competition authorities of the Member States. The right of access to the file shall also not extend to correspondence between the Commission and the competition authorities of the Member States or between the latter where such correspondence is contained in the file of the Commission.

3. Nothing in this Regulation prevents the Commission from disclosing and using information necessary to prove an infringement of Articles 81 or 82 of the Treaty.

Article 16 Identification and protection of confidential information

1. Information, including documents, shall not be communicated or made accessible by the Commission in so far as it contains business secrets or other confidential information of any person.

2. Any person which makes known its views pursuant to Article 6(1), Article 7(1), Article 10(2) and Article 13(1) and (3) or subsequently submits further information to the Commission in the course of the same procedure, shall clearly identify any material which it considers to be confidential, giving reasons, and provide a separate non-confidential version by the date set by the Commission for making its views known.

3. Without prejudice to paragraph 2 of this Article, the Commission may require undertakings and associations of undertakings which produce documents or statements pursuant to Regulation (EC) No 1/2003 to identify the documents or parts of documents which they consider to contain business secrets or other confidential information belonging to them and to identify the undertakings with regard to which such documents are to be considered confidential. The Commission may likewise require undertakings or associations of undertakings to identify any part of a statement of objections, a case summary drawn up pursuant to Article 27(4) of Regulation (EC) No 1/2003 or a decision adopted by the Commission which in their view contains business secrets.

The Commission may set a time-limit within which the undertakings and associations of undertakings are to:

(a) substantiate their claim for confidentiality with regard to each individual document or part of document, statement or part of statement;

(b) provide the Commission with a non-confidential version of the documents or statements, in which the confidential passages are deleted;

(c) provide a concise description of each piece of deleted information.

4. If undertakings or associations of undertakings fail to comply with paragraphs 2 and 3, the Commission may assume that the documents or statements concerned do not contain confidential information.

Chapter VIa   Limitations to the use of information obtained in the course of Commission proceedings

Article 16a

1. Information obtained pursuant to this Regulation shall only be used for the purposes of judicial or administrative proceedings for the application of Articles 101 and 102 of the Treaty.

2. Access to leniency corporate statements within the meaning of Article 4a(2) or to settlement submissions within the meaning of Article 10a(2) shall be granted only for the purposes of exercising the rights of defence in proceedings before the Commission. Information taken from such statements and submissions may be used by the party having obtained access to the file only where necessary for the exercise of its rights of defence in proceedings:

(a) before the European Union courts reviewing Commission decisions; or

(b) before the courts of the Member States in cases that are directly related to the case in which access has been granted, and which concern:

(i) the allocation between cartel participants of a fine imposed jointly and severally on them by the Commission; or

(ii) the review of a decision by which a competition authority of a Member State has found an infringement of Article 101 TFEU.

3. The following categories of information obtained pursuant to this Regulation shall not be used in proceedings before national courts until the Commission has closed its proceedings against all parties under investigation by adopting a decision pursuant to Article 7, 9 or 10 of Regulation (EC) No 1/2003 or has otherwise terminated its proceedings:

(a) information that was prepared by other natural or legal persons specifically for the proceedings of the Commission; and

(b) information that the Commission has drawn up and sent to the parties in the course of its proceedings.

Chapter VII   General and final provisions

Article 17   Time-limits

1. In setting the time limits provided for in Article 3(3), Article 4(3), Article 6(1), Article 7(1), Article 10(2), Article 10a(1), Article 10a(2), Article 10a(3) and Article 16(3), the Commission shall have regard both to the time required for preparation of the submission and to the urgency of the case.

2. The time-limits referred to in Article 6(1), Article 7(1) and Article 10(2) shall be at least four weeks. However, for proceedings initiated with a view to adopting interim measures pursuant to Article 8 of Regulation (EC) No 1/2003, the time-limit may be shortened to one week.

3. The time limits referred to in Article 4(3), Article 10a(1), Article 10a(2) and Article 16(3) shall be at least two weeks. The time limit referred to in Article 3(3) shall be at least two weeks, except for settlement submissions, for which corrections shall be made within one week. The time limit referred to in Article 10a(3) shall be at least two weeks.

4. Where appropriate and upon reasoned request made before the expiry of the original time-limit, time-limits may be extended.

Article 18 Repeals

Regulations (EC) No 2842/98, (EC) No 2843/98 and (EC) No 3385/94 are repealed.

References to the repealed regulations shall be construed as references to this regulation.

Article 19 Transitional provisions

Procedural steps taken under Regulations (EC) No 2842/98 and (EC) No 2843/98 shall continue to have effect for the purpose of applying this Regulation.

Article 20 Entry into force

This Regulation shall enter into force on 1 May 2004.

This Regulation shall be binding in its entirety and directly applicable in all Member States.

Done at Brussels, 7 April 2004.

Annex

Form C Complaint pursuant to Article 7 of Regulation (EC) No 1/2003

I. Information regarding the complainant and the undertaking(s) or association of undertakings giving rise to the complaint

1. Give full details on the identity of the legal or natural person submitting the complaint. Where the complainant is an undertaking, identify the corporate group to which it belongs and provide a concise overview of the nature and scope of its business activities. Provide a contact person (with telephone number, postal and e-mail-address) from which supplementary explanations can be obtained.

2. Identify the undertaking(s) or association of undertakings whose conduct the complaint relates to, including, where applicable, all available information on the corporate group to which the undertaking(s) complained of belong and the nature and scope of the business activities pursued by them. Indicate the position of the complainant vis-à-vis the undertaking(s) or association of undertakings complained of (e.g. customer, competitor).

II. Details of the alleged infringement and evidence

3. Set out in detail the facts from which, in your opinion, it appears that there exists an infringement of Article 81 or 82 of the Treaty and/or Article 53 or 54 of the EEA agreement. Indicate in particular the nature of the products (goods or services) affected by the alleged infringements and explain, where necessary, the commercial relationships concerning these products. Provide all available details on the agreements or practices of the undertakings or associations of undertakings to which this complaint relates. Indicate, to the extent possible, the relative market positions of the undertakings concerned by the complaint.

4. Submit all documentation in your possession relating to or directly connected with the facts set out in the complaint (for example, texts of agreements, minutes of negotiations or meetings, terms of transactions, business documents, circulars, correspondence, notes of telephone conversations...). State the names and address of the persons able to testify to the facts set out in the complaint, and in particular of persons affected by the alleged infringement. Submit statistics or other data in your possession which relate to the facts set out, in particular where they show developments in the marketplace (for example information relating to prices and price trends, barriers to entry to the market for new suppliers etc.).

5. Set out your view about the geographical scope of the alleged infringement and explain, where that is not obvious, to what extent trade between Member States or between the Community and one or more EFTA States that are contracting parties of the EEA Agreement may be affected by the conduct complained of.

III. Finding sought from the Commission and legitimate interest

6. Explain what finding or action you are seeking as a result of proceedings brought by the Commission.

7. Set out the grounds on which you claim a legitimate interest as complainant pursuant to Article 7 of Regulation (EC) No 1/2003. State in particular how the conduct complained of affects you and explain how, in your view, intervention by the Commission would be liable to remedy the alleged grievance.

IV. Proceedings before national competition authorities or national courts

8. Provide full information about whether you have approached, concerning the same or closely related subject-matters, any other competition authority and/or whether a lawsuit has been brought before a national court. If so, provide full details about the administrative or judicial authority contacted and your submissions to such authority.

Declaration that the information given in this form and in the Annexes thereto is given entirely in good faith.

Date and signature.

Commission Regulation (EU) No 330/2010 of 20 April 2010 on the application of Article 101(3) of the Treaty on the Functioning of the European Union to categories of vertical agreements and concerted practices

THE EUROPEAN COMMISSION,

Having regard to the Treaty on the Functioning of the European Union,

Having regard to Regulation No 19/65/EEC of the Council of 2 March 1965 on the application of Article 85(3) of the Treaty to certain categories of agreements and concerted practices,[1] and in particular Article 1 thereof,

Having published a draft of this Regulation,

After consulting the Advisory Committee on Restrictive Practices and Dominant Positions,

Whereas:

(1) Regulation No 19/65/EEC empowers the Commission to apply Article 101(3) of the Treaty on the Functioning of the European Union[*] by regulation to certain categories of vertical agreements and corresponding concerted practices falling within Article 101(1) of the Treaty.

(2) Commission Regulation (EC) No 2790/1999 of 22 December 1999 on the application of Article 81(3) of the Treaty to categories of vertical agreements and concerted practices[2] defines a category of vertical agreements which the Commission regarded as normally satisfying the conditions laid down in Article 101(3) of the Treaty. In view of the overall positive experience with the application of that Regulation, which expires on 31 May 2010, and taking into account further experience acquired since its adoption, it is appropriate to adopt a new block exemption regulation.

(3) The category of agreements which can be regarded as normally satisfying the conditions laid down in Article 101(3) of the Treaty includes vertical agreements for the purchase or sale of goods or services where those agreements are concluded between non-competing undertakings, between certain competitors or by certain associations of retailers of goods. It also includes vertical

---

[1] OJ 36, 6.3.1965, p. 533.

[*] With effect from 1 December 2009, Article 81 of the EC Treaty has become Article 101 of the Treaty on the Functioning of the European Union. The two Articles are, in substance, identical. For the purposes of this Regulation, references to Article 101 of the Treaty on the Functioning of the European Union should be understood as references to Article 81 of the EC Treaty where appropriate.

[2] OJ L 336, 29.12.1999, p. 21.

agreements containing ancillary provisions on the assignment or use of intellectual property rights. The term 'vertical agreements' should include the corresponding concerted practices.

(4) For the application of Article 101(3) of the Treaty by regulation, it is not necessary to define those vertical agreements which are capable of falling within Article 101(1) of the Treaty. In the individual assessment of agreements under Article 101(1) of the Treaty, account has to be taken of several factors, and in particular the market structure on the supply and purchase side.

(5) The benefit of the block exemption established by this Regulation should be limited to vertical agreements for which it can be assumed with sufficient certainty that they satisfy the conditions of Article 101(3) of the Treaty.

(6) Certain types of vertical agreements can improve economic efficiency within a chain of production or distribution by facilitating better coordination between the participating undertakings. In particular, they can lead to a reduction in the transaction and distribution costs of the parties and to an optimisation of their sales and investment levels.

(7) The likelihood that such efficiency-enhancing effects will outweigh any anti-competitive effects due to restrictions contained in vertical agreements depends on the degree of market power of the parties to the agreement and, therefore, on the extent to which those undertakings face competition from other suppliers of goods or services regarded by their customers as interchangeable or substitutable for one another, by reason of the products' characteristics, their prices and their intended use.

(8) It can be presumed that, where the market share held by each of the undertakings party to the agreement on the relevant market does not exceed 30%, vertical agreements which do not contain certain types of severe restrictions of competition generally lead to an improvement in production or distribution and allow consumers a fair share of the resulting benefits.

(9) Above the market share threshold of 30%, there can be no presumption that vertical agreements falling within the scope of Article 101(1) of the Treaty will usually give rise to objective advantages of such a character and size as to compensate for the disadvantages which they create for competition. At the same time, there is no presumption that those vertical agreements are either caught by Article 101(1) of the Treaty or that they fail to satisfy the conditions of Article 101(3) of the Treaty.

(10) This Regulation should not exempt vertical agreements containing restrictions which are likely to restrict competition and harm consumers or which are not indispensable to the attainment of the efficiency-enhancing effects. In particular, vertical agreements containing certain types of severe restrictions of competition such as minimum and fixed resale-prices, as well as certain types of territorial protection, should be excluded from the benefit of the block exemption established by this Regulation irrespective of the market share of the undertakings concerned.

(11) In order to ensure access to or to prevent collusion on the relevant market, certain conditions should be attached to the block exemption. To this end, the exemption of non-compete obligations should be limited to obligations which do not exceed a defined duration. For the same reasons, any direct or indirect obligation causing the members of a selective distribution system not to sell the brands of particular competing suppliers should be excluded from the benefit of this Regulation.

(12) The market-share limitation, the non-exemption of certain vertical agreements and the conditions provided for in this Regulation normally ensure that the agreements to which the block exemption applies do not enable the participating undertakings to eliminate competition in respect of a substantial part of the products in question.

(13) The Commission may withdraw the benefit of this Regulation, pursuant to Article 29(1) of Council Regulation (EC) No 1/2003 of 16 December 2002 on the implementation of the rules on competition laid down in Articles 81 and 82 of the Treaty[3], where it finds in a particular case that an agreement to which the exemption provided for in this Regulation applies nevertheless has effects which are incompatible with Article 101(3) of the Treaty.

(14) The competition authority of a Member State may withdraw the benefit of this Regulation pursuant to Article 29(2) of Regulation (EC) No 1/2003 in respect of the territory of that Member

---

[3] OJ L 1, 4.1.2003, p. 1.

State, or a part thereof where, in a particular case, an agreement to which the exemption provided for in this Regulation applies nevertheless has effects which are incompatible with Article 101(3) of the Treaty in the territory of that Member State, or in a part thereof, and where such territory has all the characteristics of a distinct geographic market.

(15) In determining whether the benefit of this Regulation should be withdrawn pursuant to Article 29 of Regulation (EC) No 1/2003, the anti-competitive effects that may derive from the existence of parallel networks of vertical agreements that have similar effects which significantly restrict access to a relevant market or competition therein are of particular importance. Such cumulative effects may for example arise in the case of selective distribution or non compete obligations.

(16) In order to strengthen supervision of parallel networks of vertical agreements which have similar anti-competitive effects and which cover more than 50% of a given market, the Commission may by regulation declare this Regulation inapplicable to vertical agreements containing specific restraints relating to the market concerned, thereby restoring the full application of Article 101 of the Treaty to such agreements,

HAS ADOPTED THIS REGULATION:

Article 1   Definitions

1. For the purposes of this Regulation, the following definitions shall apply:

  (a) 'vertical agreement' means an agreement or concerted practice entered into between two or more undertakings each of which operates, for the purposes of the agreement or the concerted practice, at a different level of the production or distribution chain, and relating to the conditions under which the parties may purchase, sell or resell certain goods or services;

  (b) 'vertical restraint' means a restriction of competition in a vertical agreement falling within the scope of Article 101(1) of the Treaty;

  (c) 'competing undertaking' means an actual or potential competitor; 'actual competitor' means an undertaking that is active on the same relevant market; 'potential competitor' means an undertaking that, in the absence of the vertical agreement, would, on realistic grounds and not just as a mere theoretical possibility, in case of a small but permanent increase in relative prices be likely to undertake, within a short period of time, the necessary additional investments or other necessary switching costs to enter the relevant market;

  (d) 'non-compete obligation' means any direct or indirect obligation causing the buyer not to manufacture, purchase, sell or resell goods or services which compete with the contract goods or services, or any direct or indirect obligation on the buyer to purchase from the supplier or from another undertaking designated by the supplier more than 80% of the buyer's total purchases of the contract goods or services and their substitutes on the relevant market, calculated on the basis of the value or, where such is standard industry practice, the volume of its purchases in the preceding calendar year;

  (e) 'selective distribution system' means a distribution system where the supplier undertakes to sell the contract goods or services, either directly or indirectly, only to distributors selected on the basis of specified criteria and where these distributors undertake not to sell such goods or services to unauthorised distributors within the territory reserved by the supplier to operate that system;

  (f) 'intellectual property rights' includes industrial property rights, know how, copyright and neighbouring rights;

  (g) 'know-how' means a package of non-patented practical information, resulting from experience and testing by the supplier, which is secret, substantial and identified: in this context, 'secret' means that the know-how is not generally known or easily accessible; 'substantial' means that the know-how is significant and useful to the buyer for the use, sale or resale of the contract goods or services; 'identified' means that the know-how is described in a sufficiently comprehensive manner so as to make it possible to verify that it fulfils the criteria of secrecy and substantiality;

(h) 'buyer' includes an undertaking which, under an agreement falling within Article 101(1) of the Treaty, sells goods or services on behalf of another undertaking;

(i) 'customer of the buyer' means an undertaking not party to the agreement which purchases the contract goods or services from a buyer which is party to the agreement.

2. For the purposes of this Regulation, the terms 'undertaking', 'supplier' and 'buyer' shall include their respective connected undertakings.

'Connected undertakings' means:

(a) undertakings in which a party to the agreement, directly or indirectly:
 (i) has the power to exercise more than half the voting rights, or
 (ii) has the power to appoint more than half the members of the supervisory board, board of management or bodies legally representing the undertaking, or
 (iii) has the right to manage the undertaking's affairs;

(b) undertakings which directly or indirectly have, over a party to the agreement, the rights or powers listed in point (a);

(c) undertakings in which an undertaking referred to in point (b) has, directly or indirectly, the rights or powers listed in point (a);

(d) undertakings in which a party to the agreement together with one or more of the undertakings referred to in points (a), (b) or (c), or in which two or more of the latter undertakings, jointly have the rights or powers listed in point (a);

(e) undertakings in which the rights or the powers listed in point (a) are jointly held by:
 (i) parties to the agreement or their respective connected undertakings referred to in points (a) to (d), or
 (ii) one or more of the parties to the agreement or one or more of their connected undertakings referred to in points (a) to (d) and one or more third parties.

Article 2   Exemption

1. Pursuant to Article 101(3) of the Treaty and subject to the provisions of this Regulation, it is hereby declared that Article 101(1) of the Treaty shall not apply to vertical agreements.

This exemption shall apply to the extent that such agreements contain vertical restraints.

2. The exemption provided for in paragraph 1 shall apply to vertical agreements entered into between an association of undertakings and its members, or between such an association and its suppliers, only if all its members are retailers of goods and if no individual member of the association, together with its connected undertakings, has a total annual turnover exceeding EUR 50 million. Vertical agreements entered into by such associations shall be covered by this Regulation without prejudice to the application of Article 101 of the Treaty to horizontal agreements concluded between the members of the association or decisions adopted by the association.

3. The exemption provided for in paragraph 1 shall apply to vertical agreements containing provisions which relate to the assignment to the buyer or use by the buyer of intellectual property rights, provided that those provisions do not constitute the primary object of such agreements and are directly related to the use, sale or resale of goods or services by the buyer or its customers. The exemption applies on condition that, in relation to the contract goods or services, those provisions do not contain restrictions of competition having the same object as vertical restraints which are not exempted under this Regulation.

4. The exemption provided for in paragraph 1 shall not apply to vertical agreements entered into between competing undertakings. However, it shall apply where competing undertakings enter into a non-reciprocal vertical agreement and:

(a) the supplier is a manufacturer and a distributor of goods, while the buyer is a distributor and not a competing undertaking at the manufacturing level; or

(b) the supplier is a provider of services at several levels of trade, while the buyer provides its goods or services at the retail level and is not a competing undertaking at the level of trade where it purchases the contract services.

5. This Regulation shall not apply to vertical agreements the subject matter of which falls within the scope of any other block exemption regulation, unless otherwise provided for in such a regulation.

Article 3   Market share threshold

1. The exemption provided for in Article 2 shall apply on condition that the market share held by the supplier does not exceed 30% of the relevant market on which it sells the contract goods or services and the market share held by the buyer does not exceed 30% of the relevant market on which it purchases the contract goods or services.

2. For the purposes of paragraph 1, where in a multi party agreement an undertaking buys the contract goods or services from one undertaking party to the agreement and sells the contract goods or services to another undertaking party to the agreement, the market share of the first undertaking must respect the market share threshold provided for in that paragraph both as a buyer and a supplier in order for the exemption provided for in Article 2 to apply.

Article 4   Restrictions that remove the benefit of the block exemption—hardcore restrictions

The exemption provided for in Article 2 shall not apply to vertical agreements which, directly or indirectly, in isolation or in combination with other factors under the control of the parties, have as their object:

(a) the restriction of the buyer's ability to determine its sale price, without prejudice to the possibility of the supplier to impose a maximum sale price or recommend a sale price, provided that they do not amount to a fixed or minimum sale price as a result of pressure from, or incentives offered by, any of the parties;

(b) the restriction of the territory into which, or of the customers to whom, a buyer party to the agreement, without prejudice to a restriction on its place of establishment, may sell the contract goods or services, except:

  (i)   the restriction of active sales into the exclusive territory or to an exclusive customer group reserved to the supplier or allocated by the supplier to another buyer, where such a restriction does not limit sales by the customers of the buyer,

  (ii)   the restriction of sales to end users by a buyer operating at the wholesale level of trade,

  (iii) the restriction of sales by the members of a selective distribution system to un-authorised distributors within the territory reserved by the supplier to operate that system, and

  (iv)   the restriction of the buyer's ability to sell components, supplied for the purposes of incorporation, to customers who would use them to manufacture the same type of goods as those produced by the supplier;

(c) the restriction of active or passive sales to end users by members of a selective distribution system operating at the retail level of trade, without prejudice to the possibility of prohibiting a member of the system from operating out of an unauthorised place of establishment;

(d) the restriction of cross-supplies between distributors within a selective distribution system, including between distributors operating at different level of trade;

(e) the restriction, agreed between a supplier of components and a buyer who incorporates those components, of the supplier's ability to sell the components as spare parts to end-users or to repairers or other service providers not entrusted by the buyer with the repair or servicing of its goods.

Article 5   Excluded restrictions

1. The exemption provided for in Article 2 shall not apply to the following obligations contained in vertical agreements:

(a) any direct or indirect non-compete obligation, the duration of which is indefinite or exceeds five years;

(b) any direct or indirect obligation causing the buyer, after termination of the agreement, not to manufacture, purchase, sell or resell goods or services;

(c) any direct or indirect obligation causing the members of a selective distribution system not to sell the brands of particular competing suppliers.

For the purposes of point (a) of the first subparagraph, a non-compete obligation which is tacitly renewable beyond a period of five years shall be deemed to have been concluded for an indefinite duration.

2. By way of derogation from paragraph 1(a), the time limitation of five years shall not apply where the contract goods or services are sold by the buyer from premises and land owned by the supplier or leased by the supplier from third parties not connected with the buyer, provided that the duration of the non-compete obligation does not exceed the period of occupancy of the premises and land by the buyer.

3. By way of derogation from paragraph 1(b), the exemption provided for in Article 2 shall apply to any direct or indirect obligation causing the buyer, after termination of the agreement, not to manufacture, purchase, sell or resell goods or services where the following conditions are fulfilled:

(a) the obligation relates to goods or services which compete with the contract goods or services;

(b) the obligation is limited to the premises and land from which the buyer has operated during the contract period;

(c) the obligation is indispensable to protect know-how transferred by the supplier to the buyer;

(d) the duration of the obligation is limited to a period of one year after termination of the agreement.

Paragraph 1(b) is without prejudice to the possibility of imposing a restriction which is unlimited in time on the use and disclosure of know-how which has not entered the public domain.

Article 6   Non-application of this Regulation

Pursuant to Article 1a of Regulation No 19/65/EEC, the Commission may by regulation declare that, where parallel networks of similar vertical restraints cover more than 50% of a relevant market, this Regulation shall not apply to vertical agreements containing specific restraints relating to that market.

Article 7   Application of the market share threshold

For the purposes of applying the market share thresholds provided for in Article 3 the following rules shall apply:

(a) the market share of the supplier shall be calculated on the basis of market sales value data and the market share of the buyer shall be calculated on the basis of market purchase value data. If market sales value or market purchase value data are not available, estimates based on other reliable market information, including market sales and purchase volumes, may be used to establish the market share of the undertaking concerned;

(b) the market shares shall be calculated on the basis of data relating to the preceding calendar year;

(c) the market share of the supplier shall include any goods or services supplied to vertically integrated distributors for the purposes of sale;

(d) if a market share is initially not more than 30% but subsequently rises above that level without exceeding 35%, the exemption provided for in Article 2 shall continue to apply for a period of two consecutive calendar years following the year in which the 30% market share threshold was first exceeded;

(e) if a market share is initially not more than 30% but subsequently rises above 35%, the exemption provided for in Article 2 shall continue to apply for one calendar year following the year in which the level of 35% was first exceeded;

(f) the benefit of points (d) and (e) may not be combined so as to exceed a period of two calendar years;

(g) the market share held by the undertakings referred to in point (e) of the second subparagraph of Article 1(2) shall be apportioned equally to each undertaking having the rights or the powers listed in point (a) of the second subparagraph of Article 1(2).

Article 8   Application of the turnover threshold

1. For the purpose of calculating total annual turnover within the meaning of Article 2(2), the turnover achieved during the previous financial year by the relevant party to the vertical agreement and the turnover achieved by its connected undertakings in respect of all goods and services, excluding all taxes and other duties, shall be added together. For this purpose, no account shall be taken of dealings between the party to the vertical agreement and its connected undertakings or between its connected undertakings.

2. The exemption provided for in Article 2 shall remain applicable where, for any period of two consecutive financial years, the total annual turnover threshold is exceeded by no more than 10%.

Article 9   Transitional period

The prohibition laid down in Article 101(1) of the Treaty shall not apply during the period from 1 June 2010 to 31 May 2011 in respect of agreements already in force on 31 May 2010 which do not satisfy the conditions for exemption provided for in this Regulation but which, on 31 May 2010, satisfied the conditions for exemption provided for in Regulation (EC) No 2790/1999.

Article 10   Period of validity

This Regulation shall enter into force on 1 June 2010.

It shall expire on 31 May 2022.

This Regulation shall be binding in its entirety and directly applicable in all Member States.

Done at Brussels, 20 April 2010.

Commission Regulation (EU) No 1217/2010 of 14 December 2010 on the application of Article 101(3) of the Treaty on the Functioning of the European Union to certain categories of research and development agreements

[OJ 2010 L335/36]

THE EUROPEAN COMMISSION,

Having regard to the Treaty on the Functioning of the European Union,

Having regard to Regulation (EEC) No 2821/71 of the Council of 20 December 1971 on application of Article 85(3) of the Treaty to categories of agreements, decisions and concerted practices[1],

Having published a draft of this Regulation,

After consulting the Advisory Committee on Restrictive Practices and Dominant Positions,

Whereas:

(1) Regulation (EEC) No 2821/71 empowers the Commission to apply Article 101(3) of the Treaty on the Functioning of the European Union* by regulation to certain categories of agreements, decisions and concerted practices falling within the scope of Article 101(1) of the Treaty which have as their object

---

[1] OJ L 285, 29.12.1971, p. 46.

* With effect from 1 December 2009, Article 81 of the EC Treaty has become Article 101 of the Treaty on the Functioning of the European Union (TFEU). The two Articles are, in substance, identical. For the purposes of this Regulation, references to Article 101 of the TFEU should be understood as references to Article 81 of the EC Treaty where appropriate. The TFEU also introduced certain changes in terminology, such as the replacement of 'Community' by 'Union' and 'common market' by 'internal market'. The terminology of the TFEU will be used throughout this Regulation.

the research and development of products, technologies or processes up to the stage of industrial application, and exploitation of the results, including provisions regarding intellectual property rights.

(2) Article 179(2) of the Treaty calls upon the Union to encourage undertakings, including small and medium-sized undertakings, in their research and technological development activities of high quality, and to support their efforts to cooperate with one another. This Regulation is intended to facilitate research and development while at the same time effectively protecting competition.

(3) Commission Regulation (EC) No 2659/2000 of 29 November 2000 on the application of Article 81(3) of the Treaty to categories of research and development agreements[2] defines categories of research and development agreements which the Commission regarded as normally satisfying the conditions laid down in Article 101(3) of the Treaty. In view of the overall positive experience with the application of that Regulation, which expires on 31 December 2010, and taking into account further experience acquired since its adoption, it is appropriate to adopt a new block exemption regulation.

(4) This Regulation should meet the two requirements of ensuring effective protection of competition and providing adequate legal security for undertakings. The pursuit of those objectives should take account of the need to simplify administrative supervision and the legislative framework to as great an extent as possible. Below a certain level of market power it can in general be presumed, for the application of Article 101(3) of the Treaty, that the positive effects of research and development agreements will outweigh any negative effects on competition.

(5) For the application of Article 101(3) of the Treaty by regulation, it is not necessary to define those agreements which are capable of falling within Article 101(1) of the Treaty. In the individual assessment of agreements under Article 101(1) of the Treaty, account has to be taken of several factors, and in particular the market structure on the relevant market.

(6) Agreements on the joint execution of research work or the joint development of the results of the research, up to but not including the stage of industrial application, generally do not fall within the scope of Article 101(1) of the Treaty. In certain circumstances, however, such as where the parties agree not to carry out other research and development in the same field, thereby forgoing the opportunity of gaining competitive advantages over the other parties, such agreements may fall within Article 101(1) of the Treaty and should therefore be included within the scope of this Regulation.

(7) The benefit of the exemption established by this Regulation should be limited to those agreements for which it can be assumed with sufficient certainty that they satisfy the conditions of Article 101(3) of the Treaty.

(8) Cooperation in research and development and in the exploitation of the results is most likely to promote technical and economic progress if the parties contribute complementary skills, assets or activities to the cooperation. This also includes scenarios where one party merely finances the research and development activities of another party.

(9) The joint exploitation of results can be considered as the natural consequence of joint research and development. It can take different forms such as manufacture, the exploitation of intellectual property rights that substantially contribute to technical or economic progress, or the marketing of new products.

(10) Consumers can generally be expected to benefit from the increased volume and effectiveness of research and development through the introduction of new or improved products or services, a quicker launch of those products or services, or the reduction of prices brought about by new or improved technologies or processes.

(11) In order to justify the exemption, the joint exploitation should relate to products, technologies or processes for which the use of the results of the research and development is decisive. Moreover, all the parties should agree in the research and development agreement that they will all have full access to the final results of the joint research and development, including any arising intellectual property rights and know-how, for the purposes of further research and development

---

[2] OJ L 304, 5.12.2000, p. 7.

and exploitation, as soon as the final results become available. Access to the results should generally not be limited as regards the use of the results for the purposes of further research and development. However, where the parties, in accordance with this Regulation, limit their rights of exploitation, in particular where they specialise in the context of exploitation, access to the results for the purposes of exploitation may be limited accordingly. Moreover, where academic bodies, research institutes or undertakings which supply research and development as a commercial service without normally being active in the exploitation of results participate in research and development, they may agree to use the results of research and development solely for the purpose of further research. Depending on their capabilities and commercial needs, the parties may make unequal contributions to their research and development cooperation. Therefore, in order to reflect, and to make up for, the differences in the value or the nature of the parties' contributions, a research and development agreement benefiting from this Regulation may provide that one party is to compensate another for obtaining access to the results for the purposes of further research or exploitation. However, the compensation should not be so high as to effectively impede such access.

(12) Similarly, where the research and development agreement does not provide for any joint exploitation of the results, the parties should agree in the research and development agreement to grant each other access to their respective pre-existing know-how, as long as this know-how is indispensable for the purposes of the exploitation of the results by the other parties. The rates of any licence fee charged should not be so high as to effectively impede access to the know-how by the other parties.

(13) The exemption established by this Regulation should be limited to research and development agreements which do not afford the undertakings the possibility of eliminating competition in respect of a substantial part of the products, services or technologies in question. It is necessary to exclude from the block exemption agreements between competitors whose combined share of the market for products, services or technologies capable of being improved or replaced by the results of the research and development exceeds a certain level at the time the agreement is entered into. However, there is no presumption that research and development agreements are either caught by Article 101(1) of the Treaty or that they fail to satisfy the conditions of Article 101(3) of the Treaty once the market share threshold set out in this Regulation is exceeded or other conditions of this Regulation are not met. In such cases, an individual assessment of the research and development agreement needs to be conducted under Article 101 of the Treaty.

(14) In order to ensure the maintenance of effective competition during joint exploitation of the results, provision should be made for the block exemption to cease to apply if the parties' combined share of the market for the products, services or technologies arising out of the joint research and development becomes too great. The exemption should continue to apply, irrespective of the parties' market shares, for a certain period after the commencement of joint exploitation, so as to await stabilisation of their market shares, particularly after the introduction of an entirely new product, and to guarantee a minimum period of return on the investments involved.

(15) This Regulation should not exempt agreements containing restrictions which are not indispensable to the attainment of the positive effects generated by a research and development agreement. In principle, agreements containing certain types of severe restrictions of competition such as limitations on the freedom of parties to carry out research and development in a field unconnected to the agreement, the fixing of prices charged to third parties, limitations on output or sales, and limitations on effecting passive sales for the contract products or contract technologies in territories or to customers reserved for other parties should be excluded from the benefit of the exemption established by this Regulation irrespective of the market share of the parties. In this context, field of use restrictions do not constitute limitations of output or sales, and also do not constitute territorial or customer restrictions.

(16) The market share limitation, the non-exemption of certain agreements and the conditions provided for in this Regulation normally ensure that the agreements to which the block exemption applies do not enable the parties to eliminate competition in respect of a substantial part of the products or services in question.

(17) The possibility cannot be ruled out that anti-competitive foreclosure effects may arise where one party finances several research and development projects carried out by competitors with regard to the same contract products or contract technologies, in particular where it obtains the exclusive right to exploit the results vis-à-vis third parties. Therefore the benefit of this Regulation should be conferred on such paid-for research and development agreements only if the combined market share of all the parties involved in the connected agreements, that is to say, the financing party and all the parties carrying out the research and development, does not exceed 25 %.

(18) Agreements between undertakings which are not competing manufacturers of products, technologies or processes capable of being improved, substituted or replaced by the results of the research and development will only eliminate effective competition in research and development in exceptional circumstances. It is therefore appropriate to enable such agreements to benefit from the exemption established by this Regulation irrespective of market share and to address any exceptional cases by way of withdrawal of its benefit.

(19) The Commission may withdraw the benefit of this Regulation, pursuant to Article 29(1) of Council Regulation (EC) No 1/2003 of 16 December 2002 on the implementation of the rules on competition laid down in Articles 81 and 82 of the Treaty[3], where it finds in a particular case that an agreement to which the exemption provided for in this Regulation applies nevertheless has effects which are incompatible with Article 101(3) of the Treaty.

(20) The competition authority of a Member State may withdraw the benefit of this Regulation pursuant to Article 29(2) of Regulation (EC) No 1/2003 in respect of the territory of that Member State, or a part thereof where, in a particular case, an agreement to which the exemption established by this Regulation applies nevertheless has effects which are incompatible with Article 101(3) of the Treaty in the territory of that Member State, or in a part thereof, and where such territory has all the characteristics of a distinct geographic market.

(21) The benefit of this Regulation could be withdrawn pursuant to Article 29 of Regulation (EC) No 1/2003, for example, where the existence of a research and development agreement substantially restricts the scope for third parties to carry out research and development in the relevant field because of the limited research capacity available elsewhere, where because of the particular structure of supply, the existence of the research and development agreement substantially restricts the access of third parties to the market for the contract products or contract technologies, where without any objectively valid reason, the parties do not exploit the results of the joint research and development vis-à-vis third parties, where the contract products or contract technologies are not subject in the whole or a substantial part of the internal market to effective competition from products, technologies or processes considered by users as equivalent in view of their characteristics, price and intended use, or where the existence of the research and development agreement would restrict competition in innovation or eliminate effective competition in research and development on a particular market.

(22) As research and development agreements are often of a long-term nature, especially where the cooperation extends to the exploitation of the results, the period of validity of this Regulation should be fixed at 12 years,

HAS ADOPTED THIS REGULATION:

Article 1   Definitions

1. For the purposes of this Regulation, the following definitions shall apply:
   (a) 'research and development agreement' means an agreement entered into between two or more parties which relate to the conditions under which those parties pursue:
      (i) joint research and development of contract products or contract technologies and joint exploitation of the results of that research and development;
      (ii) joint exploitation of the results of research and development of contract products or contract technologies jointly carried out pursuant to a prior agreement between the same parties;

---

[3] OJ L 1, 4.1.2003, p. 1.

  (iii) joint research and development of contract products or contract technologies excluding joint exploitation of the results;

  (iv) paid-for research and development of contract products or contract technologies and joint exploitation of the results of that research and development;

  (v) joint exploitation of the results of paid-for research and development of contract products or contract technologies pursuant to a prior agreement between the same parties; or

  (vi) paid-for research and development of contract products or contract technologies excluding joint exploitation of the results;

(b) 'agreement' means an agreement, a decision by an association of undertakings or a concerted practice;

(c) 'research and development' means the acquisition of know-how relating to products, technologies or processes and the carrying out of theoretical analysis, systematic study or experimentation, including experimental production, technical testing of products or processes, the establishment of the necessary facilities and the obtaining of intellectual property rights for the results;

(d) 'product' means a good or a service, including both intermediary goods or services and final goods or services;

(e) 'contract technology' means a technology or process arising out of the joint research and development;

(f) 'contract product' means a product arising out of the joint research and development or manufactured or provided applying the contract technologies;

(g) 'exploitation of the results' means the production or distribution of the contract products or the application of the contract technologies or the assignment or licensing of intellectual property rights or the communication of know-how required for such manufacture or application;

(h) 'intellectual property rights' means intellectual property rights, including industrial property rights, copyright and neighbouring rights;

(i) 'know-how' means a package of non-patented practical information, resulting from experience and testing, which is secret, substantial and identified;

(j) 'secret', in the context of know-how, means that the know-how is not generally known or easily accessible;

(k) 'substantial', in the context of know-how, means that the know-how is significant and useful for the manufacture of the contract products or the application of the contract technologies;

(l) 'identified', in the context of know-how, means that the know-how is described in a sufficiently comprehensive manner so as to make it possible to verify that it fulfils the criteria of secrecy and substantiality;

(m) 'joint', in the context of activities carried out under a research and development agreement, means activities where the work involved is:

  (i) carried out by a joint team, organisation or undertaking;

  (ii) jointly entrusted to a third party; or

  (iii) allocated between the parties by way of specialisation in the context of research and development or exploitation;

(n) 'specialisation in the context of research and development' means that each of the parties is involved in the research and development activities covered by the research and development agreement and they divide the research and development work between them in any way that they consider most appropriate; this does not include paid-for research and development;

(o) 'specialisation in the context of exploitation' means that the parties allocate between them individual tasks such as production or distribution, or impose restrictions upon each other regarding the exploitation of the results such as restrictions in relation to certain territories, customers or fields of use; this includes a scenario where only one party produces and distributes the contract products on the basis of an exclusive licence granted by the other parties;

(p) 'paid-for research and development' means research and development that is carried out by one party and financed by a financing party;

(q) 'financing party' means a party financing paid-for research and development while not carrying out any of the research and development activities itself;

(r) 'competing undertaking' means an actual or potential competitor;

(s) 'actual competitor' means an undertaking that is supplying a product, technology or process capable of being improved, substituted or replaced by the contract product or the contract technology on the relevant geographic market;

(t) 'potential competitor' means an undertaking that, in the absence of the research and development agreement, would, on realistic grounds and not just as a mere theoretical possibility, in case of a small but permanent increase in relative prices be likely to undertake, within not more than 3 years, the necessary additional investments or other necessary switching costs to supply a product, technology or process capable of being improved, substituted or replaced by the contract product or contract technology on the relevant geographic market;

(u) 'relevant product market' means the relevant market for the products capable of being improved, substituted or replaced by the contract products;

(v) 'relevant technology market' means the relevant market for the technologies or processes capable of being improved, substituted or replaced by the contract technologies.

2. For the purposes of this Regulation, the terms 'undertaking' and 'party' shall include their respective connected undertakings.

'Connected undertakings' means:

(a) undertakings in which a party to the research and development agreement, directly or indirectly:
  (i) has the power to exercise more than half the voting rights;
  (ii) has the power to appoint more than half the members of the supervisory board, board of management or bodies legally representing the undertaking; or
  (iii) has the right to manage the undertaking's affairs;

(b) undertakings which directly or indirectly have, over a party to the research and development agreement, the rights or powers listed in point (a);

(c) undertakings in which an undertaking referred to in point (b) has, directly or indirectly, the rights or powers listed in point (a);

(d) undertakings in which a party to the research and development agreement together with one or more of the undertakings referred to in points (a), (b) or (c), or in which two or more of the latter undertakings, jointly have the rights or powers listed in point (a);

(e) undertakings in which the rights or the powers listed in point (a) are jointly held by:
  (i) parties to the research and development agreement or their respective connected undertakings referred to in points (a) to (d); or
  (ii) one or more of the parties to the research and development agreement or one or more of their connected undertakings referred to in points (a) to (d) and one or more third parties.

Article 2   Exemption

1. Pursuant to Article 101(3) of the Treaty and subject to the provisions of this Regulation, it is hereby declared that Article 101(1) of the Treaty shall not apply to research and development agreements.

This exemption shall apply to the extent that such agreements contain restrictions of competition falling within the scope of Article 101(1) of the Treaty.

2. The exemption provided for in paragraph 1 shall apply to research and development agreements containing provisions which relate to the assignment or licensing of intellectual property rights to one or more of the parties or to an entity the parties establish to carry out the joint research

and development, paid-for research and development or joint exploitation, provided that those provisions do not constitute the primary object of such agreements, but are directly related to and necessary for their implementation.

Article 3 Conditions for exemption

1. The exemption provided for in Article 2 shall apply subject to the conditions set out in paragraphs 2 to 5.

2. The research and development agreement must stipulate that all the parties have full access to the final results of the joint research and development or paid-for research and development, including any resulting intellectual property rights and know-how, for the purposes of further research and development and exploitation, as soon as they become available. Where the parties limit their rights of exploitation in accordance with this Regulation, in particular where they specialise in the context of exploitation, access to the results for the purposes of exploitation may be limited accordingly. Moreover, research institutes, academic bodies, or undertakings which supply research and development as a commercial service without normally being active in the exploitation of results may agree to confine their use of the results for the purposes of further research. The research and development agreement may foresee that the parties compensate each other for giving access to the results for the purposes of further research or exploitation, but the compensation must not be so high as to effectively impede such access.

3. Without prejudice to paragraph 2, where the research and development agreement provides only for joint research and development or paid-for research and development, the research and development agreement must stipulate that each party must be granted access to any pre-existing know-how of the other parties, if this know-how is indispensable for the purposes of its exploitation of the results. The research and development agreement may foresee that the parties compensate each other for giving access to their pre-existing know-how, but the compensation must not be so high as to effectively impede such access.

4. Any joint exploitation may only pertain to results which are protected by intellectual property rights or constitute know-how and which are indispensable for the manufacture of the contract products or the application of the contract technologies.

5. Parties charged with the manufacture of the contract products by way of specialisation in the context of exploitation must be required to fulfil orders for supplies of the contract products from the other parties, except where the research and development agreement also provides for joint distribution within the meaning of point (m)(i) or (ii) of Article 1(1) or where the parties have agreed that only the party manufacturing the contract products may distribute them.

Article 4 Market share threshold and duration of exemption

1. Where the parties are not competing undertakings, the exemption provided for in Article 2 shall apply for the duration of the research and development. Where the results are jointly exploited, the exemption shall continue to apply for 7 years from the time the contract products or contract technologies are first put on the market within the internal market.

2. Where two or more of the parties are competing undertakings, the exemption provided for in Article 2 shall apply for the period referred to in paragraph 1 of this Article only if, at the time the research and development agreement is entered into:

    (a) in the case of research and development agreements referred to in point (a)(i), (ii) or (iii) of Article 1(1), the combined market share of the parties to a research and development agreement does not exceed 25 % on the relevant product and technology markets; or

    (b) in the case of research and agreements referred to in point (a)(iv), (v) or (vi) of Article 1(1), the combined market share of the financing party and all the parties with which the financing party has entered into research and development agreements with regard to the same contract products or contract technologies, does not exceed 25 % on the relevant product and technology markets.

3. After the end of the period referred to in paragraph 1, the exemption shall continue to apply as long as the combined market share of the parties does not exceed 25 % on the relevant product and technology markets.

Article 5   Hardcore restrictions

The exemption provided for in Article 2 shall not apply to research and development agreements which, directly or indirectly, in isolation or in combination with other factors under the control of the parties, have as their object any of the following:

(a) the restriction of the freedom of the parties to carry out research and development independently or in cooperation with third parties in a field unconnected with that to which the research and development agreement relates or, after the completion of the joint research and development or the paid-for research and development, in the field to which it relates or in a connected field;

(b) the limitation of output or sales, with the exception of:

    (i) the setting of production targets where the joint exploitation of the results includes the joint production of the contract products;

    (ii) the setting of sales targets where the joint exploitation of the results includes the joint distribution of the contract products or the joint licensing of the contract technologies within the meaning of point (m)(i) or (ii) of Article 1(1);

    (iii) practices constituting specialisation in the context of exploitation; and

    (iv) the restriction of the freedom of the parties to manufacture, sell, assign or license products, technologies or processes which compete with the contract products or contract technologies during the period for which the parties have agreed to jointly exploit the results;

(c) the fixing of prices when selling the contract product or licensing the contract technologies to third parties, with the exception of the fixing of prices charged to immediate customers or the fixing of licence fees charged to immediate licensees where the joint exploitation of the results includes the joint distribution of the contract products or the joint licensing of the contract technologies within the meaning of point (m)(i) or (ii) of Article 1(1);

(d) the restriction of the territory in which, or of the customers to whom, the parties may passively sell the contract products or license the contract technologies, with the exception of the requirement to exclusively license the results to another party;

(e) the requirement not to make any, or to limit, active sales of the contract products or contract technologies in territories or to customers which have not been exclusively allocated to one of the parties by way of specialisation in the context of exploitation;

(f) the requirement to refuse to meet demand from customers in the parties' respective territories, or from customers otherwise allocated between the parties by way of specialisation in the context of exploitation, who would market the contract products in other territories within the internal market;

(g) the requirement to make it difficult for users or resellers to obtain the contract products from other resellers within the internal market.

Article 6   Excluded restrictions

The exemption provided for in Article 2 shall not apply to the following obligations contained in research and development agreements:

(a) the obligation not to challenge after completion of the research and development the validity of intellectual property rights which the parties hold in the internal market and which are relevant to the research and development or, after the expiry of the research and development agreement, the validity of intellectual property rights which the parties hold in the internal market and which protect the results of the research and development, without prejudice to the possibility to provide for termination of the research and development agreement in the event of one of the parties challenging the validity of such intellectual property rights;

(b) the obligation not to grant licences to third parties to manufacture the contract products or to apply the contract technologies unless the agreement provides for the exploitation of the results of the joint research and development or paid-for research and development by at least one of the parties and such exploitation takes place in the internal market vis-à-vis third parties.

Article 7   Application of the market share threshold

For the purposes of applying the market share threshold provided for in Article 4 the following rules shall apply:

(a) the market share shall be calculated on the basis of the market sales value; if market sales value data are not available, estimates based on other reliable market information, including market sales volumes, may be used to establish the market share of the parties;

(b) the market share shall be calculated on the basis of data relating to the preceding calendar year;

(c) the market share held by the undertakings referred to in point (e) of the second subparagraph of Article 1(2) shall be apportioned equally to each undertaking having the rights or the powers listed in point (a) of that subparagraph;

(d) if the market share referred to in Article 4(3) is initially not more than 25 % but subsequently rises above that level without exceeding 30 %, the exemption provided for in Article 2 shall continue to apply for a period of two consecutive calendar years following the year in which the 25 % threshold was first exceeded;

(e) if the market share referred to in Article 4(3) is initially not more than 25 % but subsequently rises above 30 %, the exemption provided for in Article 2 shall continue to apply for a period of one calendar year following the year in which the level of 30 % was first exceeded;

(f) the benefit of points (d) and (e) may not be combined so as to exceed a period of two calendar years.

Article 8   Transitional period

The prohibition laid down in Article 101(1) of the Treaty shall not apply during the period from 1 January 2011 to 31 December 2012 in respect of agreements already in force on 31 December 2010 which do not satisfy the conditions for exemption provided for in this Regulation but which satisfy the conditions for exemption provided for in Regulation (EC) No 2659/2000.

Article 9   Period of validity

This Regulation shall enter into force on 1 January 2011.

It shall expire on 31 December 2022.

This Regulation shall be binding in its entirety and directly applicable in all Member States.

Done at Brussels, 14 December 2010.

Commission Regulation (EU) No 1218/2010 of 14 December 2010 on the application of Article 101(3) of the Treaty on the Functioning of the European Union to certain categories of specialisation agreements

[OJ 2010 L335/43]

THE EUROPEAN COMMISSION,

Having regard to the Treaty on the Functioning of the European Union,

Having regard to Regulation (EEC) No 2821/71 of the Council of 20 December 1971 on application of Article 85(3) of the Treaty to categories of agreements, decisions and concerted practices[1],

---

[1] OJ L 285, 29.12.1971, p. 46.

Having published a draft of this Regulation,

After consulting the Advisory Committee on Restrictive Practices and Dominant Positions,

Whereas:

(1) Regulation (EEC) No 2821/71 empowers the Commission to apply Article 101(3) of the Treaty on the Functioning of the European Union* by regulation to certain categories of agreements, decisions and concerted practices falling within the scope of Article 101(1) of the Treaty which have as their object specialisation, including agreements necessary for achieving it.

(2) Commission Regulation (EC) No 2658/2000 of 29 November 2000 on the application of Article 81(3) of the Treaty to categories of specialisation agreements[2] defines categories of specialisation agreements which the Commission regarded as normally satisfying the conditions laid down in Article 101(3) of the Treaty. In view of the overall positive experience with the application of that Regulation, which expires on 31 December 2010, and taking into account further experience acquired since its adoption, it is appropriate to adopt a new block exemption regulation.

(3) This Regulation should meet the two requirements of ensuring effective protection of competition and providing adequate legal security for undertakings. The pursuit of those objectives should take account of the need to simplify administrative supervision and the legislative framework to as great an extent as possible. Below a certain level of market power it can in general be presumed, for the application of Article 101(3) of the Treaty, that the positive effects of specialisation agreements will outweigh any negative effects on competition.

(4) For the application of Article 101(3) of the Treaty by regulation, it is not necessary to define those agreements which are capable of falling within Article 101(1) of the Treaty. In the individual assessment of agreements under Article 101(1) of the Treaty, account has to be taken of several factors, and in particular the market structure on the relevant market.

(5) The benefit of the exemption established by this Regulation should be limited to those agreements for which it can be assumed with sufficient certainty that they satisfy the conditions of Article 101(3) of the Treaty.

(6) Agreements on specialisation in production are most likely to contribute to improving the production or distribution of goods if the parties have complementary skills, assets or activities, because they can concentrate on the manufacture of certain products and thus operate more efficiently and supply the products more cheaply. The same can generally be said about agreements on specialisation in the preparation of services. Given effective competition, it is likely that consumers will receive a fair share of the resulting benefits.

(7) Such advantages can arise from agreements whereby one party fully or partly gives up the manufacture of certain products or preparation of certain services in favour of another party (unilateral specialisation), from agreements whereby each party fully or partly gives up the manufacture of certain products or preparation of certain services in favour of another party (reciprocal specialisation) and from agreements whereby the parties undertake to jointly manufacture certain products or prepare certain services (joint production). In the context of this Regulation, the concepts of unilateral and reciprocal specialisation do not require a party to reduce capacity, as it is sufficient if they reduce their production volumes. The concept of joint production, however, does not require the parties to reduce their individual production activities outside the scope of their envisaged joint production arrangement.

(8) The nature of unilateral and reciprocal specialisation agreements presupposes that the parties are active on the same product market. It is not necessary for the parties to be active on the same

---

* With effect from 1 December 2009, Article 81 of the EC Treaty has become Article 101 of the Treaty on the Functioning of the European Union (TFEU). The two Articles are, in substance, identical. For the purposes of this Regulation, references to Article 101 of the TFEU should be understood as references to Article 81 of the EC Treaty where appropriate. The TFEU also introduced certain changes in terminology, such as the replacement of 'Community' by 'Union' and 'common market' by 'internal market'. The terminology of the TFEU will be used throughout this Regulation.

[2] OJ L 304, 5.12.2000, p. 3.

geographic market. Consequently, the application of this Regulation to unilateral and reciprocal specialisation agreements should be limited to scenarios where the parties are active on the same product market. Joint production agreements can be entered into by parties who are already active on the same product market but also by parties who wish to enter a product market by way of the agreement. Therefore, joint production agreements should fall within the scope of this Regulation irrespective of whether the parties are already active in the same product market.

(9) To ensure that the benefits of specialisation will materialise without one party leaving the market downstream of production entirely, unilateral and reciprocal specialisation agreements should only be covered by this Regulation where they provide for supply and purchase obligations or joint distribution. Supply and purchase obligations may, but do not have to, be of an exclusive nature.

(10) It can be presumed that, where the parties' share of the relevant market for the products which are the subject matter of a specialisation agreement does not exceed a certain level, the agreements will, as a general rule, give rise to economic benefits in the form of economies of scale or scope or better production technologies, while allowing consumers a fair share of the resulting benefits. However, where the products manufactured under a specialisation agreement are intermediary products which one or more of the parties fully or partly use as an input for their own production of certain downstream products which they subsequently sell on the market, the exemption conferred by this Regulation should also be conditional on the parties' share on the relevant market for these downstream products not exceeding a certain level. In such a case, merely looking at the parties' market share at the level of the intermediary product would ignore the potential risk of foreclosing or increasing the price of inputs for competitors at the level of the downstream products. However, there is no presumption that specialisation agreements are either caught by Article 101(1) of the Treaty or that they fail to satisfy the conditions of Article 101(3) of the Treaty once the market share threshold set out in this Regulation is exceeded or other conditions of this Regulation are not met. In such cases, an individual assessment of the specialisation agreement needs to be conducted under Article 101 of the Treaty.

(11) This Regulation should not exempt agreements containing restrictions which are not indispensable to the attainment of the positive effects generated by a specialisation agreement. In principle, agreements containing certain types of severe restrictions of competition relating to the fixing of prices charged to third parties, limitation of output or sales, and allocation of markets or customers should be excluded from the benefit of the exemption established by this Regulation irrespective of the market share of the parties.

(12) The market share limitation, the non-exemption of certain agreements and the conditions provided for in this Regulation normally ensure that the agreements to which the block exemption applies do not enable the parties to eliminate competition in respect of a substantial part of the products or services in question.

(13) The Commission may withdraw the benefit of this Regulation, pursuant to Article 29(1) of Council Regulation (EC) No 1/2003 of 16 December 2002 on the implementation of the rules on competition laid down in Articles 81 and 82 of the Treaty[3], where it finds in a particular case that an agreement to which the exemption provided for in this Regulation applies nevertheless has effects which are incompatible with Article 101(3) of the Treaty.

(14) The competition authority of a Member State may withdraw the benefit of this Regulation pursuant to Article 29(2) of Regulation (EC) No 1/2003 in respect of the territory of that Member State, or a part thereof where, in a particular case, an agreement to which the exemption established by this Regulation applies nevertheless has effects which are incompatible with Article 101(3) of the Treaty in the territory of that Member State, or in a part thereof, and where such territory has all the characteristics of a distinct geographic market.

(15) The benefit of this Regulation could be withdrawn pursuant to Article 29 of Regulation (EC) No 1/2003 where, for example, the relevant market is very concentrated and competition is

---

[3] OJ L 1, 4.1.2003, p. 1.

already weak, in particular because of the individual market positions of other market participants or links between other market participants created by parallel specialisation agreements.

(16) In order to facilitate the conclusion of specialisation agreements, which can have a bearing on the structure of the parties, the period of validity of this Regulation should be fixed at 12 years,

HAS ADOPTED THIS REGULATION:

Article 1 Definitions

1. For the purposes of this Regulation, the following definitions shall apply:

(a) 'specialisation agreement' means a unilateral specialisation agreement, a reciprocal specialisation agreement or a joint production agreement;

(b) 'unilateral specialisation agreement' means an agreement between two parties which are active on the same product market by virtue of which one party agrees to fully or partly cease production of certain products or to refrain from producing those products and to purchase them from the other party, who agrees to produce and supply those products;

(c) 'reciprocal specialisation agreement' means an agreement between two or more parties which are active on the same product market, by virtue of which two or more parties on a reciprocal basis agree to fully or partly cease or refrain from producing certain but different products and to purchase these products from the other parties, who agree to produce and supply them;

(d) 'joint production agreement' means an agreement by virtue of which two or more parties agree to produce certain products jointly;

(e) 'agreement' means an agreement, a decision by an association of undertakings or a concerted practice;

(f) 'product' means a good or a service, including both intermediary goods or services and final goods or services, with the exception of distribution and rental services;

(g) 'production' means the manufacture of goods or the preparation of services and includes production by way of subcontracting;

(h) 'preparation of services' means activities upstream of the provision of services to customers;

(i) 'relevant market' means the relevant product and geographic market to which the specialisation products belong, and, in addition, where the specialisation products are intermediary products which one or more of the parties fully or partly use captively for the production of downstream products, the relevant product and geographic market to which the downstream products belong;

(j) 'specialisation product' means a product which is produced under a specialisation agreement;

(k) 'downstream product' means a product for which a specialisation product is used by one or more of the parties as an input and which is sold by those parties on the market;

(l) 'competing undertaking' means an actual or potential competitor;

(m) 'actual competitor' means an undertaking that is active on the same relevant market;

(n) 'potential competitor' means an undertaking that, in the absence of the specialisation agreement, would, on realistic grounds and not just as a mere theoretical possibility, in case of a small but permanent increase in relative prices be likely to undertake, within not more than 3 years, the necessary additional investments or other necessary switching costs to enter the relevant market;

(o) 'exclusive supply obligation' means an obligation not to supply a competing undertaking other than a party to the agreement with the specialisation product;

(p) 'exclusive purchase obligation' means an obligation to purchase the specialisation product only from a party to the agreement;

(q) 'joint', in the context of distribution, means that the parties:

(i) carry out the distribution of the products by way of a joint team, organisation or undertaking; or

(ii) appoint a third party distributor on an exclusive or non-exclusive basis, provided that the third party is not a competing undertaking;

(r) 'distribution' means distribution, including the sale of goods and the provision of services.

2. For the purposes of this Regulation, the terms 'undertaking' and 'party' shall include their respective connected undertakings.

'Connected undertakings' means:

(a) undertakings in which a party to the specialisation agreement, directly or indirectly:

(i) has the power to exercise more than half the voting rights;

(ii) has the power to appoint more than half the members of the supervisory board, board of management or bodies legally representing the undertaking; or

(iii) has the right to manage the undertaking's affairs;

(b) undertakings which directly or indirectly have, over a party to the specialisation agreement, the rights or powers listed in point (a);

(c) undertakings in which an undertaking referred to in point (b) has, directly or indirectly, the rights or powers listed in point (a);

(d) undertakings in which a party to the specialisation agreement together with one or more of the undertakings referred to in points (a), (b) or (c), or in which two or more of the latter undertakings, jointly have the rights or powers listed in point (a);

(e) undertakings in which the rights or the powers listed in point (a) are jointly held by:

(i) parties to the specialisation agreement or their respective connected undertakings referred to in points (a) to (d); or

(ii) one or more of the parties to the specialisation agreement or one or more of their connected undertakings referred to in points (a) to (d) and one or more third parties.

Article 2   Exemption

1. Pursuant to Article 101(3) of the Treaty and subject to the provisions of this Regulation, it is hereby declared that Article 101(1) of the Treaty shall not apply to specialisation agreements.

This exemption shall apply to the extent that such agreements contain restrictions of competition falling within the scope of Article 101(1) of the Treaty.

2. The exemption provided for in paragraph 1 shall apply to specialisation agreements containing provisions which relate to the assignment or licensing of intellectual property rights to one or more of the parties, provided that those provisions do not constitute the primary object of such agreements, but are directly related to and necessary for their implementation.

3. The exemption provided for in paragraph 1 shall apply to specialisation agreements whereby:

(a) the parties accept an exclusive purchase or exclusive supply obligation; or

(b) the parties do not independently sell the specialisation products but jointly distribute those products.

Article 3   Market share threshold

The exemption provided for in Article 2 shall apply on condition that the combined market share of the parties does not exceed 20 % on any relevant market.

Article 4   Hardcore restrictions

The exemption provided for in Article 2 shall not apply to specialisation agreements which, directly or indirectly, in isolation or in combination with other factors under the control of the parties, have as their object any of the following:

(a) the fixing of prices when selling the products to third parties with the exception of the fixing of prices charged to immediate customers in the context of joint distribution;

(b) the limitation of output or sales with the exception of:

(i) provisions on the agreed amount of products in the context of unilateral or reciprocal specialisation agreements or the setting of the capacity and production volume in the context of a joint production agreement; and

(ii) the setting of sales targets in the context of joint distribution;

(c) the allocation of markets or customers.

Article 5   Application of the market share threshold

For the purposes of applying the market share threshold provided for in Article 3 the following rules shall apply:

(a)   the market share shall be calculated on the basis of the market sales value; if market sales value data are not available, estimates based on other reliable market information, including market sales volumes, may be used to establish the market share of the parties;

(b)   the market share shall be calculated on the basis of data relating to the preceding calendar year;

(c)   the market share held by the undertakings referred to in point (e) of the second subparagraph of Article 1(2) shall be apportioned equally to each undertaking having the rights or the powers listed in point (a) of that subparagraph;

(d)   if the market share referred to in Article 3 is initially not more than 20 % but subsequently rises above that level without exceeding 25 %, the exemption provided for in Article 2 shall continue to apply for a period of 2 consecutive calendar years following the year in which the 20 % threshold was first exceeded;

(e)   if the market share referred to in Article 3 is initially not more than 20 % but subsequently rises above 25 %, the exemption provided for in Article 2 shall continue to apply for a period of 1 calendar year following the year in which the level of 25 % was first exceeded;

(f)   the benefit of points (d) and (e) may not be combined so as to exceed a period of 2 calendar years.

Article 6   Transitional period

The prohibition laid down in Article 101(1) of the Treaty shall not apply during the period from 1 January 2011 to 31 December 2012 in respect of agreements already in force on 31 December 2010 which do not satisfy the conditions for exemption provided for in this Regulation but which satisfy the conditions for exemption provided for in Regulation (EC) No 2658/2000.

Article 7   Period of validity

This Regulation shall enter into force on 1 January 2011.

It shall expire on 31 December 2022.

This Regulation shall be binding in its entirety and directly applicable in all Member States.

Done at Brussels, 14 December 2010.

Commission notice—Summary of the 'Guidelines on the effect on trade concept contained in Articles 81 and 82 of the Treaty' (Now Arts 101 and 102 TFEU)

[OJ 2004 C101]*

SUMMARY

Articles 101 and 102 of the Treaty on the Functioning of the European Union (TFEU) (ex-Articles 81 and 82 of the Treaty Establishing the European Community (TEC)) are applicable to horizontal and vertical agreements and practices on the part of undertakings which may affect trade between European Union (EU) countries.

* **Editor's Note:** This is a summary only of the c. 15-page full document. Summary: https://eur-lex.europa.eu/legal-content/EN/TXT/?uri=LEGISSUM:l26113; Full document: https://ec.europa.eu/competition/antitrust/legislation/trade.html.

The present guidelines spell out a rule indicating when agreements are in general unlikely to be capable of appreciably affecting trade between EU countries. They are not intended to be exhaustive. The aim is to set out the methodology for the application of the effect on trade concept and to provide guidance on its application in frequently occurring situations. Although not binding on them, these guidelines also intend to give guidance to the courts and authorities of the EU countries in their application of the effect on trade concept contained in Articles 101 and 102 TFEU.

The effect on trade criterion confines the scope of application of Articles 101 and 102 TFEU to agreements and practices that are capable of having a minimum level of cross-border effects within the EU.

In the case of Article 101 TFEU, it is the agreement that must be capable of affecting trade between EU countries. If the agreement as a whole is capable of affecting trade between EU countries, there is EU law jurisdiction in respect of the entire agreement, including any parts of the agreement that individually do not affect trade between EU countries. In cases where the contractual relations between the same parties cover several activities, these activities must, in order to form part of the same agreement, be directly linked and form an integral part of the same overall business arrangement. If not, each activity constitutes a separate agreement.

In the case of Article 102 TFEU, it is the abuse that must affect trade between EU countries. This does not imply, however, that each element of the behaviour must be assessed in isolation. Conduct that forms part of an overall strategy pursued by the dominant undertaking must be assessed in terms of its overall impact. Where a dominant undertaking adopts various practices in pursuit of the same aim, for instance practices that aim at eliminating or foreclosing competitors, in order for Article 102 TFEU to be applicable to all the practices forming part of this overall strategy, it is sufficient that at least one of these practices is capable of affecting trade between EU countries.

Analysis of the concept of affecting trade requires that three aspects in particular be addressed:

- **the concept of 'trade between EU countries'**: the concept of 'trade' is not limited to traditional exchanges of goods and services across borders. It is a wider concept, covering all cross-border economic activity including establishment. This interpretation is consistent with the fundamental objective of the Treaty to promote free movement of goods, services, persons and capital. The requirement that there must be an effect on trade 'between EU countries' implies that there must be an impact on cross-border economic activity involving at least two EU countries;
- **the notion 'may affect'**: the function of the notion 'may affect' is to define the nature of the required impact on trade between EU countries. According to the standard test developed by the Court of Justice, the notion 'may affect' implies that it must be possible to foresee with a sufficient degree of probability on the basis of a set of objective factors of law or fact that the agreement or practice may have an influence, direct or indirect, actual or potential, on the pattern of trade between EU countries. In cases where the agreement or practice is liable to affect the competitive structure inside the EU, EU law jurisdiction is established;
- **the concept of 'appreciability'**: the effect on trade criterion incorporates a quantitative element, limiting EU law jurisdiction to agreements and practices that are capable of having effects of a certain magnitude. Appreciability can be appraised in particular by reference to the position and the importance of the relevant undertakings on the market for the products concerned. The assessment of appreciability depends on the circumstances of each individual case, in particular the nature of the agreement and practice, the nature of the products covered and the market position of the undertakings concerned. In its notice on agreements of minor importance, the Commission states that agreements between small and medium-sized enterprises rarely affect trade between EU countries to a significant degree. The Commission holds the view that in principle agreements are not capable of appreciably affecting trade between EU countries when the following cumulative conditions are met:
  - the aggregate market share of the parties on any relevant market within the EU affected by the agreement does not exceed 5%;
  - in the case of horizontal agreements, the aggregate annual EU turnover of the undertakings concerned in the products covered by the agreement does not exceed EUR 40 million.

The threshold of EUR 40 million is calculated on the basis of total EU sales excluding tax during the previous financial year by the undertakings concerned, of the products covered by the agreement (the contract products). Sales between entities that form part of the same undertaking are excluded. In order to apply the market share threshold, it is necessary to determine the relevant market.

The Commission will apply the negative presumption to the application of the concept of affecting trade to all agreements, including agreements that by their very nature are capable of affecting trade between EU countries as well as agreements that involve trade with undertakings located in non-EU countries. Outside the scope of negative presumption, the Commission will take account of qualitative elements relating to the nature of the agreement or practice and the nature of the products that they concern.

The positive presumption relating to appreciability in the case of agreements also takes into account whether and how agreements and practices cover several EU countries, whether they are confined to a single EU country or to part of a single EU country. Agreements and practices involving non-EU countries are also dealt with. In the case of agreements and practices whose object is not to restrict competition inside the EU, it is normally necessary to proceed with a more detailed analysis of whether or not cross-border economic activity inside the EU, and thus patterns of trade between EU countries, are capable of being affected.

2006 Commission Notice on Immunity from fines and reduction of fines in cartel cases

[OJ 2006 C298/11]*

I. INTRODUCTION

(1) This notice sets out the framework for rewarding cooperation in the Commission investigation by undertakings which are or have been party to secret cartels affecting the Community. Cartels are agreements and/or concerted practices between two or more competitors aimed at co-ordinating their competitive behaviour on the market and/or influencing the relevant parameters of competition through practices such as the fixing of purchase or selling prices or other trading conditions, the allocation of production or sales quotas, the sharing of markets including bid-rigging, restrictions of imports or exports and/or anti-competitive actions against other competitors. Such practices are among the most serious violations of Article 81 EC.[1]

(2) By artificially limiting the competition that would normally prevail between them, undertakings avoid exactly those pressures that lead them to innovate, both in terms of product development and the introduction of more efficient production methods. Such practices also lead to more expensive raw materials and components for the Community companies that purchase from such producers. They ultimately result in artificial prices and reduced choice for the consumer. In the long term, they lead to a loss of competitiveness and reduced employment opportunities.

(3) By their very nature, secret cartels are often difficult to detect and investigate without the co-operation of undertakings or individuals implicated in them. Therefore, the Commission considers that it is in the Community interest to reward undertakings involved in this type of illegal practices which are willing to put an end to their participation and co-operate in the Commission's investigation, independently of the rest of the undertakings involved in the cartel. The interests of consumers and citizens in ensuring that secret cartels are detected and punished outweigh the interest in fining those undertakings that enable the Commission to detect and prohibit such practices.

---

* **Editor's Note:** Known as the Leniency Notice: As amended by Commission Communication (OJ 2015 C256/01) https://ec.europa.eu/competition/cartels/legislation/leniency_legislation.html.
[1] Reference in this text to Article 81 EC also covers Article 53 EEA when applied by the Commission according to the rules laid down in Article 56 of the EEA Agreement.

(4) The Commission considers that the collaboration of an undertaking in the detection of the existence of a cartel has an intrinsic value. A decisive contribution to the opening of an investigation or to the finding of an infringement may justify the granting of immunity from any fine to the undertaking in question, on condition that certain additional requirements are fulfilled.

(5) Moreover, co-operation by one or more undertakings may justify a reduction of a fine by the Commission. Any reduction of a fine must reflect an undertaking's actual contribution, in terms of quality and timing, to the Commission's establishment of the infringement. Reductions are to be limited to those undertakings that provide the Commission with evidence that adds significant value to that already in the Commission's possession.

(6) In addition to submitting pre-existing documents, undertakings may provide the Commission with voluntary presentations of their knowledge of a cartel and their role therein prepared specially to be submitted under this leniency programme. These initiatives have proved to be useful for the effective investigation and termination of cartel infringements and they should not be discouraged by discovery orders issued in civil litigation. Potential leniency applicants might be dissuaded from cooperating with the Commission under this Notice if this could impair their position in civil proceedings, as compared to companies who do not cooperate. Such undesirable effect would significantly harm the public interest in ensuring effective public enforcement of Article 81 EC in cartel cases and thus its subsequent or parallel effective private enforcement.

(7) The supervisory task conferred on the Commission by the Treaty in competition matters does not only include the duty to investigate and punish individual infringements, but also encompasses the duty to pursue a general policy. The protection of corporate statements in the public interest is not a bar to their disclosure to other addressees of the statement of objections in order to safeguard their rights of defence in the procedure before the Commission, to the extent that it is technically possible to combine both interests by rendering corporate statements accessible only at the Commission premises and normally on a single occasion following the formal notification of the objections. Moreover, the Commission will process personal data in the context of this notice in conformity with its obligations under Regulation (EC) No 45/2001.[2]

II. IMMUNITY FROM FINES

A. Requirements to qualify for immunity from fines

(8) The Commission will grant immunity from any fine which would otherwise have been imposed to an undertaking disclosing its participation in an alleged cartel affecting the Community if that undertaking is the first to submit information and evidence which in the Commission's view will enable it to:

(a) carry out a targeted inspection in connection with the alleged cartel;[3] or

(b) find an infringement of Article 81 EC in connection with the alleged cartel.

(9) For the Commission to be able to carry out a targeted inspection within the meaning of point (8)(a), the undertaking must provide the Commission with the information and evidence listed below, to the extent that this, in the Commission's view, would not jeopardize the inspections:

(a) A corporate statement[4] which includes, in so far as it is known to the applicant at the time of the submission:

– A detailed description of the alleged cartel arrangement, including for instance its aims, activities and functioning; the product or service concerned, the geographic scope, the duration of and the estimated market volumes affected by the alleged cartel; the specific dates, locations, content of and participants in alleged cartel contacts, and all relevant explanations in connection with the pieces of evidence provided in support of the application.

---

[2] OJ L 8, 12.1.2001, p. 1.

[3] The assessment of the threshold will have to be carried out ex ante, i.e. without taking into account whether a given inspection has or has not been successful or whether or not an inspection has or has not been carried out. The assessment will be made exclusively on the basis of the type and the quality of the information submitted by the applicant.

[4] Corporate statements may take the form of written documents signed by or on behalf of the undertaking or be made orally.

– The name and address of the legal entity submitting the immunity application as well as the names and addresses of all the other undertakings that participate(d) in the alleged cartel;

– The names, positions, office locations and, where necessary, home addresses of all individuals who, to the applicant's knowledge, are or have been involved in the alleged cartel, including those individuals which have been involved on the applicant's behalf;

– Information on which other competition authorities, inside or outside the EU, have been approached or are intended to be approached in relation to the alleged cartel; and

(b) Other evidence relating to the alleged cartel in possession of the applicant or available to it at the time of the submission, including in particular any evidence contemporaneous to the infringement.

(10) Immunity pursuant to point (8)(a) will not be granted if, at the time of the submission, the Commission had already sufficient evidence to adopt a decision to carry out an inspection in connection with the alleged cartel or had already carried out such an inspection.

(11) Immunity pursuant to point (8)(b) will only be granted on the cumulative conditions that the Commission did not have, at the time of the submission, sufficient evidence to find an infringement of Article 81 EC in connection with the alleged cartel and that no undertaking had been granted conditional immunity from fines under point (8)(a) in connection with the alleged cartel. In order to qualify, an undertaking must be the first to provide contemporaneous, incriminating evidence of the alleged cartel as well as a corporate statement containing the kind of information specified in point (9)(a), which would enable the Commission to find an infringement of Article 81 EC.

(12) In addition to the conditions set out in points (8)(a), (9) and (10) or in points (8)(b) and 11, all the following conditions must be met in any case to qualify for any immunity from a fine:

(a) The undertaking cooperates genuinely,[5] fully, on a continuous basis and expeditiously from the time it submits its application throughout the Commission's administrative procedure. This includes:

– providing the Commission promptly with all relevant information and evidence relating to the alleged cartel that comes into its possession or is available to it;

– remaining at the Commission's disposal to answer promptly to any request that may contribute to the establishment of the facts;

– making current (and, if possible, former) employees and directors available for interviews with the Commission;

– not destroying, falsifying or concealing relevant information or evidence relating to the alleged cartel; and

– not disclosing the fact or any of the content of its application before the Commission has issued a statement of objections in the case, unless otherwise agreed;

(b) The undertaking ended its involvement in the alleged cartel immediately following its application, except for what would, in the Commission's view, be reasonably necessary to preserve the integrity of the inspections;

(c) When contemplating making its application to the Commission, the undertaking must not have destroyed, falsified or concealed evidence of the alleged cartel nor disclosed the fact or any of the content of its contemplated application, except to other competition authorities.

(13) An undertaking which took steps to coerce other undertakings to join the cartel or to remain in it is not eligible for immunity from fines. It may still qualify for a reduction of fines if it fulfils the relevant requirements and meets all the conditions therefor.

B. Procedure

(14) An undertaking wishing to apply for immunity from fines should contact the Commission's Directorate General for Competition. The undertaking may either initially apply for a marker or

---

[5] This requires in particular that the applicant provides accurate, not misleading, and complete information. Cfr judgement of the European Court of Justice of 29 June 2006 in case C-301/04 P, Commission v SGL Carbon AG a.o., at paragraphs 68–70, and judgement of the European Court of Justice of 28 June 2005 in cases C-189/02 P, C-202/02 P, C-205/02 P, C-208/02 P and C-213/02 P, Dansk Rørindustri A/S a.o. v Commission, at paragraphs 395–399.

immediately proceed to make a formal application to the Commission for immunity from fines in order to meet the conditions in points (8)(a) or (8)(b), as appropriate. The Commission may disregard any application for immunity from fines on the ground that it has been submitted after the statement of objections has been issued.

(15) The Commission services may grant a marker protecting an immunity applicant's place in the queue for a period to be specified on a case-by-case basis in order to allow for the gathering of the necessary information and evidence. To be eligible to secure a marker, the applicant must provide the Commission with information concerning its name and address, the parties to the alleged cartel, the affected product(s) and territory(-ies), the estimated duration of the alleged cartel and the nature of the alleged cartel conduct. The applicant should also inform the Commission on other past or possible future leniency applications to other authorities in relation to the alleged cartel and justify its request for a marker. Where a marker is granted, the Commission services determine the period within which the applicant has to perfect the marker by submitting the information and evidence required to meet the relevant threshold for immunity. Undertakings which have been granted a marker cannot perfect it by making a formal application in hypothetical terms. If the applicant perfects the marker within the period set by the Commission services, the information and evidence provided will be deemed to have been submitted on the date when the marker was granted.

(16) An undertaking making a formal immunity application to the Commission must:

    (a) provide the Commission with all information and evidence relating to the alleged cartel available to it, as specified in points (8) and (9), including corporate statements; or

    (b) initially present this information and evidence in hypothetical terms, in which case the undertaking must present a detailed descriptive list of the evidence it proposes to disclose at a later agreed date. This list should accurately reflect the nature and content of the evidence, whilst safeguarding the hypothetical nature of its disclosure. Copies of documents, from which sensitive parts have been removed, may be used to illustrate the nature and content of the evidence. The name of the applying undertaking and of other undertakings involved in the alleged cartel need not be disclosed until the evidence described in its application is submitted. However, the product or service concerned by the alleged cartel, the geographic scope of the alleged cartel and the estimated duration must be clearly identified.

(17) If requested, the Directorate General for Competition will provide an acknowledgement of receipt of the undertaking's application for immunity from fines, confirming the date and, where appropriate, time of the application.

(18) Once the Commission has received the information and evidence submitted by the undertaking under point (16)(a) and has verified that it meets the conditions set out in points (8)(a) or (8)(b), as appropriate, it will grant the undertaking conditional immunity from fines in writing.

(19) If the undertaking has presented information and evidence in hypothetical terms, the Commission will verify that the nature and content of the evidence described in the detailed list referred to in point (16)(b) will meet the conditions set out in points (8)(a) or (8)(b), as appropriate, and inform the undertaking accordingly. Following the disclosure of the evidence no later than on the date agreed and having verified that it corresponds to the description made in the list, the Commission will grant the undertaking conditional immunity from fines in writing.

(20) If it becomes apparent that immunity is not available or that the undertaking failed to meet the conditions set out in points (8)(a) or (8)(b), as appropriate, the Commission will inform the undertaking in writing. In such case, the undertaking may withdraw the evidence disclosed for the purposes of its immunity application or request the Commission to consider it under section III of this notice. This does not prevent the Commission from using its normal powers of investigation in order to obtain the information.

(21) The Commission will not consider other applications for immunity from fines before it has taken a position on an existing application in relation to the same alleged infringement, irrespective of whether the immunity application is presented formally or by requesting a marker.

(22) If at the end of the administrative procedure, the undertaking has met the conditions set out in point (12), the Commission will grant it immunity from fines in the relevant decision. If

at the end of the administrative procedure, the undertaking has not met the conditions set out in point (12), the undertaking will not benefit from any favorable treatment under this Notice. If the Commission, after having granted conditional immunity ultimately finds that the immunity applicant has acted as a coercer, it will withhold immunity.

III. REDUCTION OF A FINE

A. Requirements to qualify for reduction of a fine

(23) Undertakings disclosing their participation in an alleged cartel affecting the Community that do not meet the conditions under section II above may be eligible to benefit from a reduction of any fine that would otherwise have been imposed.

(24) In order to qualify, an undertaking must provide the Commission with evidence of the alleged infringement which represents significant added value with respect to the evidence already in the Commission's possession and must meet the cumulative conditions set out in points (12)(a) to (12)(c) above.

(25) The concept of 'added value' refers to the extent to which the evidence provided strengthens, by its very nature and/or its level of detail, the Commission's ability to prove the alleged cartel. In this assessment, the Commission will generally consider written evidence originating from the period of time to which the facts pertain to have a greater value than evidence subsequently established. Incriminating evidence directly relevant to the facts in question will generally be considered to have a greater value than that with only indirect relevance. Similarly, the degree of corroboration from other sources required for the evidence submitted to be relied upon against other undertakings involved in the case will have an impact on the value of that evidence, so that compelling evidence will be attributed a greater value than evidence such as statements which require corroboration if contested.

(26) The Commission will determine in any final decision adopted at the end of the administrative procedure the level of reduction an undertaking will benefit from, relative to the fine which would otherwise be imposed. For the:

- first undertaking to provide significant added value: a reduction of 30–50%,
- second undertaking to provide significant added value: a reduction of 20–30%,
- subsequent undertakings that provide significant added value: a reduction of up to 20%.

In order to determine the level of reduction within each of these bands, the Commission will take into account the time at which the evidence fulfilling the condition in point (24) was submitted and the extent to which it represents added value.

If the applicant for a reduction of a fine is the first to submit compelling evidence in the sense of point (25) which the Commission uses to establish additional facts increasing the gravity or the duration of the infringement, the Commission will not take such additional facts into account when setting any fine to be imposed on the undertaking which provided this evidence.

B. Procedure

(27) An undertaking wishing to benefit from a reduction of a fine must make a formal application to the Commission and it must present it with sufficient evidence of the alleged cartel to qualify for a reduction of a fine in accordance with point (24) of this Notice. Any voluntary submission of evidence to the Commission which the undertaking that submits it wishes to be considered for the beneficial treatment of section III of this Notice must be clearly identified at the time of its submission as being part of a formal application for a reduction of a fine.

(28) If requested, the Directorate General for Competition will provide an acknowledgement of receipt of the undertaking's application for a reduction of a fine and of any subsequent submissions of evidence, confirming the date and, where appropriate, time of each submission. The Commission will not take any position on an application for a reduction of a fine before it has taken a position on any existing applications for conditional immunity from fines in relation to the same alleged cartel.

(29) If the Commission comes to the preliminary conclusion that the evidence submitted by the undertaking constitutes significant added value within the meaning of points (24) and (25), and that the undertaking has met the conditions of points (12) and (27), it will inform the undertaking in writing, no later than the date on which a statement of objections is notified, of its intention to apply a reduction of a fine within a specified band as provided in point (26). The Commission will also, within the same time frame, inform the undertaking in writing if it comes to the preliminary conclusion that the undertaking does not qualify for a reduction of a fine. The Commission may disregard any application for a reduction of fines on the grounds that it has been submitted after the statement of objections has been issued.

(30) The Commission will evaluate the final position of each undertaking which filed an application for a reduction of a fine at the end of the administrative procedure in any decision adopted. The Commission will determine in any such final decision:

    (a) whether the evidence provided by an undertaking represented significant added value with respect to the evidence in the Commission's possession at that same time;

    (b) whether the conditions set out in points (12)(a) to (12)(c) above have been met;

    (c) the exact level of reduction an undertaking will benefit from within the bands specified in point (26).

If the Commission finds that the undertaking has not met the conditions set out in point (12), the undertaking will not benefit from any favourable treatment under this Notice.

IV. CORPORATE STATEMENTS MADE TO QUALIFY UNDER THIS NOTICE

(31) A corporate statement is a voluntary presentation by or on behalf of an undertaking to the Commission of the undertaking's knowledge of a cartel and its role therein prepared specially to be submitted under this Notice. Any statement made vis-à-vis the Commission in relation to this notice, forms part of the Commission's file and can thus be used in evidence.

(32) Upon the applicant's request, the Commission may accept that corporate statements be provided orally unless the applicant has already disclosed the content of the corporate statement to third parties. Oral corporate statements will be recorded and transcribed at the Commission's premises. In accordance with Article 19 of Council Regulation (EC) No 1/2003[6] and Articles 3 and 17 of Commission Regulation (EC) No 773/2004,[7] undertakings making oral corporate statements will be granted the opportunity to check the technical accuracy of the recording, which will be available at the Commission's premises and to correct the substance of their oral statements within a given time limit. Undertakings may waive these rights within the said time-limit, in which case the recording will from that moment on be deemed to have been approved. Following the explicit or implicit approval of the oral statement or the submission of any corrections to it, the undertaking shall listen to the recordings at the Commission's premises and check the accuracy of the transcript within a given time limit. Non-compliance with the last requirement may lead to the loss of any beneficial treatment under this Notice.

(33) Access to corporate statements is only granted to the addressees of a statement of objections, provided that they commit,—together with the legal counsels getting access on their behalf—, not to make any copy by mechanical or electronic means of any information in the corporate statement to which access is being granted and to ensure that the information to be obtained from the corporate statement will solely be used for the purposes mentioned below. Other parties such as complainants will not be granted access to corporate statements. The Commission considers that this specific protection of a corporate statement is not justified as from the moment when the applicant discloses to third parties the content thereof.

(34) In accordance with the Commission Notice on rules for access to the Commission file,[8] access to the file is only granted to the addressees of a statement of objections on the condition that

---

[6] OJ L 1, 4.1.2003, p. 1.
[7] OJ L 123, 27.4.2004, p. 18.
[8] OJ C 325, 22.12.2005, p. 7.

the information thereby obtained may only be used for the purposes of judicial or administrative proceedings for the application of the Union competition rules. Any failure during the proceedings to comply with the provisions of Regulation (EC) No 773/2004[9] on the use of information obtained through access to the file may be regarded as lack of cooperation within the meaning of points (12) and (27) of this Notice. Under certain circumstances it is subject to penalties to be laid down under national law.[10] Moreover, if any such use is made after the Commission has already adopted a prohibition decision in the proceedings, the Commission may, in addition to applicable penalties under national law, in any legal proceedings before the Union Courts, ask the Court to increase the fine in respect of the responsible undertaking. Should any of the above limitations to the use of information be breached, at any point in time, with the involvement of an outside counsel, the Commission may report the incident to the bar of that counsel, with a view to disciplinary action.

(35) Corporate statements made under the present Notice will only be transmitted to the competition authorities of the Member States pursuant to Article 12 of Regulation No 1/2003, provided that the conditions set out in the Network Notice[11] are met and provided that the level of protection against disclosure awarded by the receiving competition authority is equivalent to the one conferred by the Commission.

(35a) In line with paragraph 26a of the Commission Notice on the co-operation between the Commission and the courts of the EU Member States in the application of Articles 101 and 102 of the Treaty, the Commission will not at any time transmit leniency corporate statements to national courts for use in actions for damages for breaches of those Treaty provisions.[12] This paragraph is without prejudice to the situation referred to in Article 6(7) of Directive 2014/104/EU.

V. GENERAL CONSIDERATIONS

(36) The Commission will not take a position on whether or not to grant conditional immunity, or otherwise on whether or not to reward any application, if it becomes apparent that the application concerns infringements covered by the five years limitation period for the imposition of penalties stipulated in Article 25(1)(b) of Regulation 1/2003, as such applications would be devoid of purpose.

(37) From the date of its publication in the Official Journal, this notice replaces the 2002 Commission notice on immunity from fines and reduction of fines in cartel cases for all cases in which no undertaking has contacted the Commission in order to take advantage of the favourable treatment set out in that notice. However, points (31) to (35) of the current notice will be applied from the moment of its publication to all pending and new applications for immunity from fines or reduction of fines.

(38) The Commission is aware that this notice will create legitimate expectations on which undertakings may rely when disclosing the existence of a cartel to the Commission.

(39) In line with the Commission's practice, the fact that an undertaking cooperated with the Commission during its administrative procedure will be indicated in any decision, so as to explain the reason for the immunity or reduction of the fine. The fact that immunity or reduction in respect of fines is granted cannot protect an undertaking from the civil law consequences of its participation in an infringement of Article 81 EC.

(40) The Commission considers that normally public disclosure of documents and written or recorded statements received in the context of this notice would undermine certain public or private interests, for example the protection of the purpose of inspections and investigations, within the meaning of Article 4 of Regulation (EC) No 1049/2001,[13] even after the decision has been taken.

---

[9] Article 16a of Regulation (EC) No 773/2004, as amended by Commission Regulation (EU) 2015/1348 (OJ L 208, 5.8.2015, p. 3).

[10] Articles 7 and 8 of Directive 2014/104/EU of the European Parliament and of the Council of 26 November 2014 on certain rules governing actions for damages under national law for infringements of the competition law provisions of the Member States and of the European Union (OJ L 349, 5.12.2014, p. 1).

[11] Commission Notice on cooperation within the Network of Competition Authorities, OJ C 101, 27.4.2004, p. 43.

[12] Commission Notice on the co-operation between the Commission and the courts of the EU Member States in the application of Articles 101 and 102 TFEU (OJ C 101, 27.4.2004, p. 54), as amended by the Communication from the Commission on Amendments to the Commission Notice on the cooperation between the Commission and courts of the EU Member States in the application of Articles 81 and 82 EC (OJ C 256, 5.8.2015, p. 5).

[13] OJ L 145, 31.5.2001, p. 43.

Commission Regulation (EU) No 316/2014 of 21 March 2014 on the application of Article 101(3) of the Treaty on the Functioning of the European Union to categories of technology transfer agreements

[OJ 2014 L93/17]*

THE EUROPEAN COMMISSION,

Having regard to the Treaty on the Functioning of the European Union,

Having regard to Regulation No 19/65/EEC of the Council of 2 March 1965 on application of Article 85(3) of the Treaty to certain categories of agreements and concerted practices,[1] and in particular Article 1 thereof,

Having published a draft of this Regulation,

After consulting the Advisory Committee on Restrictive Practices and Dominant Positions,

Whereas:

(1) Regulation No 19/65/EEC empowers the Commission to apply Article 101(3) of the Treaty by regulation to certain categories of technology transfer agreements and corresponding concerted practices to which only two undertakings are party which fall within Article 101(1) of the Treaty.

(2) Pursuant to Regulation No 19/65/EEC, the Commission has, in particular, adopted Commission Regulation (EC) No 772/2004.[2] Regulation (EC) No 772/2004 defines categories of technology transfer agreements which the Commission regarded as normally satisfying the conditions laid down in Article 101(3) of the Treaty. In view of the overall positive experience with the application of that Regulation, which expires on 30 April 2014, and taking into account further experience acquired since its adoption, it is appropriate to adopt a new block exemption regulation.

(3) This Regulation should meet the two requirements of ensuring effective protection of competition and providing adequate legal security for undertakings. The pursuit of those objectives should take account of the need to simplify administrative supervision and the legislative framework to as great an extent as possible.

(4) Technology transfer agreements concern the licensing of technology rights. Such agreements will usually improve economic efficiency and be pro-competitive as they can reduce duplication of research and development, strengthen the incentive for the initial research and development, spur incremental innovation, facilitate diffusion and generate product market competition.

(5) The likelihood that such efficiency-enhancing and pro-competitive effects will outweigh any anti-competitive effects due to restrictions contained in technology transfer agreements depends on the degree of market power of the undertakings concerned and, therefore, on the extent to which those undertakings face competition from undertakings owning substitute technologies or undertakings producing substitute products.

(6) This Regulation should cover only technology transfer agreements between a licensor and a licensee. It should cover such agreements even if the agreement contains conditions relating to more than one level of trade, for instance requiring the licensee to set up a particular distribution system and specifying the obligations the licensee must or may impose on resellers of the products produced under the licence. However, such conditions and obligations should comply with the competition rules applicable to supply and distribution agreements set out in Commission Regulation (EU) No 330/2010.[3] Supply and distribution agreements concluded between a licensee and buyers of its contract products should not be exempted by this Regulation.

---

* **Editor's Note:** This replaces Regulation 772 of 2004 on the same.

[1] OJ 36, 6.3.1965, p. 533/65.

[2] Commission Regulation (EC) No 772/2004 of 7 April 2004 on the application of Article 81(3) of the Treaty to categories of technology transfer agreements (OJ L 123, 27.4.2004, p. 11).

[3] Commission Regulation (EU) No 330/2010 of 20 April 2010 on the application of Article 101(3) of the Treaty on the Functioning of the European Union to categories of vertical agreements and concerted practices (OJ L 102, 23.4.2010, p. 1).

(7) This Regulation should only apply to agreements where the licensor permits the licensee and/or one or more of its sub-contractors to exploit the licensed technology rights, possibly after further research and development by the licensee and/or its sub-contractors, for the purpose of producing goods or services. It should not apply to licensing in the context of research and development agreements which are covered by Commission Regulation (EU) No 1217/2010[4] or to licensing in the context of specialisation agreements which are covered by Commission Regulation (EU) No 1218/2010.[5] It should also not apply to agreements, the purpose of which is the mere reproduction and distribution of software copyright protected products as such agreements do not concern the licensing of a technology to produce but are more akin to distribution agreements. Nor should it apply to agreements to set up technology pools, that is to say, agreements for the pooling of technologies with the purpose of licensing them to third parties, or to agreements whereby the pooled technology is licensed out to those third parties.

(8) For the application of Article 101(3) of the Treaty by regulation, it is not necessary to define those technology transfer agreements that are capable of falling within Article 101(1) of the Treaty. In the individual assessment of agreements pursuant to Article 101(1), account has to be taken of several factors, and in particular the structure and the dynamics of the relevant technology and product markets.

(9) The benefit of the block exemption established by this Regulation should be limited to those agreements which can be assumed with sufficient certainty to satisfy the conditions of Article 101(3) of the Treaty. In order to attain the benefits and objectives of technology transfer, this Regulation should not only cover the transfer of technology as such but also other provisions contained in technology transfer agreements if, and to the extent that, those provisions are directly related to the production or sale of the contract products.

(10) For technology transfer agreements between competitors it can be presumed that, where the combined share of the relevant markets accounted for by the parties does not exceed 20 % and the agreements do not contain certain severely anti-competitive restrictions, they generally lead to an improvement in production or distribution and allow consumers a fair share of the resulting benefits.

(11) For technology transfer agreements between non-competitors it can be presumed that, where the individual share of the relevant markets accounted for by each of the parties does not exceed 30 % and the agreements do not contain certain severely anti-competitive restrictions, they generally lead to an improvement in production or distribution and allow consumers a fair share of the resulting benefits.

(12) If the applicable market-share threshold is exceeded on one or more product or technology markets, the block exemption should not apply to the agreement for the relevant markets concerned.

(13) There can be no presumption that, above those market-share thresholds, technology transfer agreements fall within the scope of Article 101(1) of the Treaty. For instance, exclusive licensing agreements between non-competing undertakings often fall outside the scope of Article 101(1). There can also be no presumption that, above those market-share thresholds, technology transfer agreements falling within the scope of Article 101(1) will not satisfy the conditions for exemption. However, it can also not be presumed that they will usually give rise to objective advantages of such a character and size as to compensate for the disadvantages which they create for competition.

(14) This Regulation should not exempt technology transfer agreements containing restrictions which are not indispensable to the improvement of production or distribution. In particular, technology transfer agreements containing certain severely anti-competitive restrictions, such as the fixing of prices charged to third parties, should be excluded from the benefit of the block

---

[4] Commission Regulation (EU) No 1217/2010 of 14 December 2010 on the application of Article 101(3) of the Treaty on the Functioning of the European Union to certain categories of research and development agreements (OJ L 335, 18.12.2010, p. 36).

[5] Commission Regulation (EU) No 1218/2010 of 14 December 2010 on the application of Article 101(3) of the Treaty on the Functioning of the European Union to certain categories of specialisation agreements (OJ L 335, 18.12.2010, p. 43).

exemption established by this Regulation irrespective of the market shares of the undertakings concerned. In the case of such hardcore restrictions the whole agreement should be excluded from the benefit of the block exemption.

(15) In order to protect incentives to innovate and the appropriate application of intellectual property rights, certain restrictions should be excluded from the benefit of the block exemption. In particular certain grant back obligations and non-challenge clauses should be excluded. Where such a restriction is included in a licence agreement only the restriction in question should be excluded from the benefit of the block exemption.

(16) The market-share thresholds and the non-exemption of technology transfer agreements containing the severely anti-competitive restrictions and the excluded restrictions provided for in this Regulation will normally ensure that the agreements to which the block exemption applies do not enable the participating undertakings to eliminate competition in respect of a substantial part of the products in question.

(17) The Commission may withdraw the benefit of this Regulation, pursuant to Article 29(1) of Council Regulation (EC) No 1/2003,[6] where it finds in a particular case that an agreement to which the exemption provided for in this Regulation applies nevertheless has effects which are incompatible with Article 101(3) of the Treaty. This may occur in particular where the incentives to innovate are reduced or where access to markets is hindered.

(18) The competition authority of a Member State may withdraw the benefit of this Regulation pursuant to Article 29(2) of Regulation (EC) No 1/2003 in respect of the territory of that Member State, or a part thereof where, in a particular case, an agreement to which the exemption provided for in this Regulation applies nevertheless has effects which are incompatible with Article 101(3) of the Treaty in the territory of that Member State, or in a part thereof, and where such territory has all the characteristics of a distinct geographic market.

(19) In order to strengthen supervision of parallel networks of technology transfer agreements which have similar restrictive effects and which cover more than 50 % of a given market, the Commission may by regulation declare this Regulation inapplicable to technology transfer agreements containing specific restrictions relating to the market concerned, thereby restoring the full application of Article 101 of the Treaty to such agreements,

HAS ADOPTED THIS REGULATION:

Article 1   Definitions

1. For the purposes of this Regulation, the following definitions shall apply:
   (a) 'agreement' means an agreement, a decision of an association of undertakings or a concerted practice;
   (b) 'technology rights' means know-how and the following rights, or a combination thereof, including applications for or applications for registration of those rights:
      (i)   patents,
      (ii)   utility models,
      (iii) design rights,
      (iv)   topographies of semiconductor products,
      (v)   supplementary protection certificates for medicinal products or other products for which such supplementary protection certificates may be obtained,
      (vi)   plant breeder's certificates and
      (vii) software copyrights;
   (c) 'technology transfer agreement' means:
      (i)   a technology rights licensing agreement entered into between two undertakings for the purpose of the production of contract products by the licensee and/or its sub-contractor(s),

---

[6] Council Regulation (EC) No 1/2003 of 16 December 2002 on the implementation of the rules on competition laid down in Articles 81 and 82 of the Treaty (OJ L 1, 4.1.2003, p. 1).

(ii) an assignment of technology rights between two undertakings for the purpose of the production of contract products where part of the risk associated with the exploitation of the technology remains with the assignor;

(d) 'reciprocal agreement' means a technology transfer agreement where two undertakings grant each other, in the same or separate contracts, a technology rights licence, and where those licences concern competing technologies or can be used for the production of competing products;

(e) 'non-reciprocal agreement' means a technology transfer agreement where one undertaking grants another undertaking a technology rights licence, or where two undertakings grant each other such a licence but where those licences do not concern competing technologies and cannot be used for the production of competing products;

(f) 'product' means goods or a service, including both intermediary goods and services and final goods and services;

(g) 'contract product' means a product produced, directly or indirectly, on the basis of the licensed technology rights;

(h) 'intellectual property rights' includes industrial property rights, in particular patents and trademarks, copyright and neighbouring rights;

(i) 'know-how' means a package of practical information, resulting from experience and testing, which is:
  (i) secret, that is to say, not generally known or easily accessible,
  (ii) substantial, that is to say, significant and useful for the production of the contract products, and
  (iii) identified, that is to say, described in a sufficiently comprehensive manner so as to make it possible to verify that it fulfils the criteria of secrecy and substantiality;

(j) 'relevant product market' means the market for the contract products and their substitutes, that is to say all those products which are regarded as interchangeable or substitutable by the buyer, by reason of the products' characteristics, their prices and their intended use;

(k) 'relevant technology market' means the market for the licensed technology rights and their substitutes, that is to say all those technology rights which are regarded as interchangeable or substitutable by the licensee, by reason of the technology rights' characteristics, the royalties payable in respect of those rights and their intended use;

(l) 'relevant geographic market' means the area in which the undertakings concerned are involved in the supply of and demand for products or the licensing of technology rights, in which the conditions of competition are sufficiently homogeneous and which can be distinguished from neighbouring areas because the conditions of competition are appreciably different in those areas;

(m) 'relevant market' means the combination of the relevant product or technology market with the relevant geographic market;

(n) 'competing undertakings' means undertakings which compete on the relevant market, that is to say:
  (i) competing undertakings on the relevant market where the technology rights are licensed, that is to say, undertakings which license out competing technology rights (actual competitors on the relevant market),
  (ii) competing undertakings on the relevant market where the contract products are sold, that is to say, undertakings which, in the absence of the technology transfer agreement, would both be active on the relevant market(s) on which the contract products are sold (actual competitors on the relevant market) or which, in the absence of the technology transfer agreement, would, on realistic grounds and not just as a mere theroretical possibility, in response to a small and permanent

increase in relative prices, be likely to undertake, within a short period of time, the necessary additional investments or other necessary switching costs to enter the relevant market(s) (potential competitors on the relevant market);

(o) 'selective distribution system' means a distribution system where the licensor undertakes to license the production of the contract products, either directly or indirectly, only to licensees selected on the basis of specified criteria and where those licensees undertake not to sell the contract products to unauthorised distributors within the territory reserved by the licensor to operate that system;

(p) 'exclusive licence' means a licence under which the licensor itself is not permitted to produce on the basis of the licensed technology rights and is not permitted to license the licensed technology rights to third parties, in general or for a particular use or in a particular territory;

(q) 'exclusive territory' means a given territory within which only one undertaking is allowed to produce the contract products, but where it is nevertheless possible to allow another licensee to produce the contract products within that territory only for a particular customer where the second licence was granted in order to create an alternative source of supply for that customer;

(r) 'exclusive customer group' means a group of customers to which only one party to the technology transfer agreement is allowed to actively sell the contract products produced with the licensed technology.

2. For the purposes of this Regulation, the terms 'undertaking', 'licensor' and 'licensee' shall include their respective connected undertakings.

'Connected undertakings' means:

(a) undertakings in which a party to the technology transfer agreement, directly or indirectly:
   (i) has the power to exercise more than half the voting rights, or
   (ii) has the power to appoint more than half the members of the supervisory board, board of management or bodies legally representing the undertaking, or
   (iii) has the right to manage the undertaking's affairs;

(b) undertakings which directly or indirectly have, over a party to the technology transfer agreement, the rights or powers listed in point (a);

(c) undertakings in which an undertaking referred to in point (b) has, directly or indirectly, the rights or powers listed in point (a);

(d) undertakings in which a party to the technology transfer agreement together with one or more of the undertakings referred to in points (a), (b) or (c), or in which two or more of the latter undertakings, jointly have the rights or powers listed in point (a);

(e) undertakings in which the rights or the powers listed in point (a) are jointly held by:
   (i) parties to the technology transfer agreement or their respective connected undertakings referred to in points (a) to (d), or
   (ii) one or more of the parties to the technology transfer agreement or one or more of their connected undertakings referred to in points (a) to (d) and one or more third parties.

Article 2   Exemption

1. Pursuant to Article 101(3) of the Treaty and subject to the provisions of this Regulation, Article 101(1) of the Treaty shall not apply to technology transfer agreements.

2. The exemption provided for in paragraph 1 shall apply to the extent that technology transfer agreements contain restrictions of competition falling within the scope of Article 101(1) of the Treaty. The exemption shall apply for as long as the licensed technology rights have not expired, lapsed or been declared invalid or, in the case of know-how, for as long as the know-how remains secret. However, where know-how becomes publicly known as a result of action by the licensee, the exemption shall apply for the duration of the agreement.

3. The exemption provided for in paragraph 1 shall also apply to provisions, in technology transfer agreements, which relate to the purchase of products by the licensee or which relate to the licensing or assignment of other intellectual property rights or know-how to the licensee, if, and to the extent that, those provisions are directly related to the production or sale of the contract products.

Article 3   Market-share thresholds

1. Where the undertakings party to the agreement are competing undertakings, the exemption provided for in Article 2 shall apply on condition that the combined market share of the parties does not exceed 20 % on the relevant market(s).

2. Where the undertakings party to the agreement are not competing undertakings, the exemption provided for in Article 2 shall apply on condition that the market share of each of the parties does not exceed 30 % on the relevant market(s).

Article 4   Hardcore restrictions

1. Where the undertakings party to the agreement are competing undertakings, the exemption provided for in Article 2 shall not apply to agreements which, directly or indirectly, in isolation or in combination with other factors under the control of the parties, have as their object any of the following:

(a)   the restriction of a party's ability to determine its prices when selling products to third parties;

(b)   the limitation of output, except limitations on the output of contract products imposed on the licensee in a non-reciprocal agreement or imposed on only one of the licensees in a reciprocal agreement;

(c)   the allocation of markets or customers except:

(i)   the obligation on the licensor and/or the licensee, in a non-reciprocal agreement, not to produce with the licensed technology rights within the exclusive territory reserved for the other party and/or not to sell actively and/or passively into the exclusive territory or to the exclusive customer group reserved for the other party,

(ii)   the restriction, in a non-reciprocal agreement, of active sales by the licensee into the exclusive territory or to the exclusive customer group allocated by the licensor to another licensee provided the latter was not a competing undertaking of the licensor at the time of the conclusion of its own licence,

(iii)   the obligation on the licensee to produce the contract products only for its own use provided that the licensee is not restricted in selling the contract products actively and passively as spare parts for its own products,

(iv)   the obligation on the licensee, in a non-reciprocal agreement, to produce the contract products only for a particular customer, where the licence was granted in order to create an alternative source of supply for that customer;

(d)   the restriction of the licensee's ability to exploit its own technology rights or the restriction of the ability of any of the parties to the agreement to carry out research and development, unless such latter restriction is indispensable to prevent the disclosure of the licensed know-how to third parties.

2. Where the undertakings party to the agreement are not competing undertakings, the exemption provided for in Article 2 shall not apply to agreements which, directly or indirectly, in isolation or in combination with other factors under the control of the parties, have as their object any of the following:

(a)   the restriction of a party's ability to determine its prices when selling products to third parties, without prejudice to the possibility of imposing a maximum sale price or recommending a sale price, provided that it does not amount to a fixed or minimum sale price as a result of pressure from, or incentives offered by, any of the parties;

(b)   the restriction of the territory into which, or of the customers to whom, the licensee may passively sell the contract products, except:

    (i)   the restriction of passive sales into an exclusive territory or to an exclusive cus-
         tomer group reserved for the licensor,

    (ii) the obligation to produce the contract products only for its own use provided that
         the licensee is not restricted in selling the contract products actively and passively
         as spare parts for its own products,

    (iii) the obligation to produce the contract products only for a particular customer,
         where the licence was granted in order to create an alternative source of supply for
         that customer,

    (iv) the restriction of sales to end-users by a licensee operating at the wholesale level of
         trade,

    (v) the restriction of sales to unauthorised distributors by the members of a selective
         distribution system;

  (c) the restriction of active or passive sales to end-users by a licensee which is a member of a
       selective distribution system and which operates at the retail level, without prejudice to
       the possibility of prohibiting a member of the system from operating out of an unauthor-
       ised place of establishment.

3. Where the undertakings party to the agreement are not competing undertakings at the time of the conclusion of the agreement but become competing undertakings afterwards, paragraph 2 and not paragraph 1 shall apply for the full life of the agreement unless the agreement is subsequently amended in any material respect. Such an amendment includes the conclusion of a new technology transfer agreement between the parties concerning competing technology rights.

Article 5   Excluded restrictions

1. The exemption provided for in Article 2 shall not apply to any of the following obligations contained in technology transfer agreements:

  (a) any direct or indirect obligation on the licensee to grant an exclusive licence or to assign
       rights, in whole or in part, to the licensor or to a third party designated by the licensor
       in respect of its own improvements to, or its own new applications of, the licensed
       technology;

  (b) any direct or indirect obligation on a party not to challenge the validity of intellectual
       property rights which the other party holds in the Union, without prejudice to the possi-
       bility, in the case of an exclusive licence, of providing for termination of the technology
       transfer agreement in the event that the licensee challenges the validity of any of the
       licensed technology rights.

2. Where the undertakings party to the agreement are not competing undertakings, the exemption provided for in Article 2 shall not apply to any direct or indirect obligation limiting the licensee's ability to exploit its own technology rights or limiting the ability of any of the parties to the agreement to carry out research and development, unless such latter restriction is indispensable to prevent the disclosure of the licensed know-how to third parties.

Article 6   Withdrawal in individual cases

1. The Commission may withdraw the benefit of this Regulation, pursuant to Article 29(1) of Regulation (EC) No 1/2003, where it finds in any particular case that a technology transfer agreement to which the exemption provided for in Article 2 of this Regulation applies nevertheless has effects which are incompatible with Article 101(3) of the Treaty, and in particular where:

  (a) access of third parties' technologies to the market is restricted, for instance by the cumu-
       lative effect of parallel networks of similar restrictive agreements prohibiting licensees
       from using third parties' technologies;

  (b) access of potential licensees to the market is restricted, for instance by the cumulative
       effect of parallel networks of similar restrictive agreements prohibiting licensors from
       licensing to other licensees or because the only technology owner licensing out relevant
       technology rights concludes an exclusive license with a licensee who is already active on
       the product market on the basis of substitutable technology rights.

2. Where, in any particular case, a technology transfer agreement to which the exemption provided for in Article 2 of this Regulation applies has effects which are incompatible with Article 101(3) of the Treaty in the territory of a Member State, or in a part thereof, which has all the characteristics of a distinct geographic market, the competition authority of that Member State may withdraw the benefit of this Regulation, pursuant to Article 29(2) of Regulation (EC) No 1/2003, in respect of that territory, under the same circumstances as those set out in paragraph 1 of this Article.

Article 7   Non-application of this Regulation

1. Pursuant to Article 1a of Regulation (EC) No 19/65/EEC, the Commission may by regulation declare that, where parallel networks of similar technology transfer agreements cover more than 50 % of a relevant market, this Regulation is not to apply to technology transfer agreements containing specific restrictions relating to that market.

2. A regulation pursuant to paragraph 1 shall not become applicable earlier than six months following its adoption.

Article 8   Application of the market-share thresholds

For the purposes of applying the market-share thresholds laid down in Article 3 the following rules shall apply:

(a) the market share shall be calculated on the basis of market sales value data; if market sales value data are not available, estimates based on other reliable market information, including market sales volumes, may be used to establish the market share of the undertaking concerned;

(b) the market share shall be calculated on the basis of data relating to the preceding calendar year;

(c) the market share held by the undertakings referred to in point (e) of the second subparagraph of Article 1(2) shall be apportioned equally to each undertaking having the rights or the powers listed in point (a) of the second subparagraph of Article 1(2);

(d) the market share of a licensor on a relevant market for the licensed technology rights shall be calculated on the basis of the presence of the licensed technology rights on the relevant market(s) (that is the product market(s) and the geographic market(s)) where the contract products are sold, that is on the basis of the sales data relating to the contract products produced by the licensor and its licensees combined;

(e) if the market share referred to in Article 3(1) or (2) is initially not more than 20 % or 30 % respectively, but subsequently rises above those levels, the exemption provided for in Article 2 shall continue to apply for a period of two consecutive calendar years following the year in which the 20 % threshold or 30 % threshold was first exceeded.

Article 9   Relationship with other block exemption regulations

This Regulation shall not apply to licensing arrangements in research and development agreements which fall within the scope of Regulation (EU) No 1217/2010 or in specialisation agreements which fall within the scope of Regulation (EU) No 1218/2010.

Article 10   Transitional period

The prohibition laid down in Article 101(1) of the Treaty shall not apply from 1 May 2014 until 30 April 2015 to agreements already in force on 30 April 2014 which do not satisfy the conditions for exemption provided for in this Regulation but which, on 30 April 2014, satisfied the conditions for exemption provided for in Regulation (EC) No 772/2004.

Article 11   Period of validity

This Regulation shall enter into force on 1 May 2014.

It shall expire on 30 April 2026.

This Regulation shall be binding in its entirety and directly applicable in all Member States.

Done at Brussels, 21 March 2014.

Part III

UK Brexit-Related Legislation

European Communities Act 1972*

(1972 c. 68)

    1.—(1) This Act may be cited as the European Communities Act 1972.

    (2) In this Act

'the Communities' means the European Economic Community, the European Coal and Steel Community and the European Atomic Energy Community,

'the Treaties' or 'the EU Treaties' means, subject to subsection (3) below, the pre-accession treaties, that is to say, those described in Part I of Schedule I to this Act, taken with

>   *(a) the treaty relating to the accession of the United Kingdom to the European Economic Community and to the European Atomic Energy Community, signed at Brussels on the 22nd January 1972; and*

>   *(b) the decision, of the same date, of the Council of the European Communities relating to the accession of the United Kingdom to the European Coal and Steel Community; and*

and any other treaty entered into by the EU (except in so far as it relates to, or could be applied in relation to, the Common Foreign and Security Policy), with or without any of the member States, or entered into, as a treaty ancillary to any of the Treaties, by the United Kingdom;

    and any expression defined in Schedule I to this Act has the meaning there given to it.

    (3) If Her Majesty by Order in Council declares that a treaty specified in the Order is to be regarded as one of the EU Treaties as herein defined, the Order shall be conclusive that it is to be so regarded; but a treaty entered into by the United Kingdom after the 22nd January 1972, other than a pre-accession treaty to which the United Kingdom accedes on terms settled on or before that date, shall not be so regarded unless it is so specified, nor be so specified unless a draft of the Order in Council has been approved by resolution of each House of Parliament.

    (4) For purposes of subsections (2) and (3) above, 'treaty' includes any international agreement, and any protocol or annex to a treaty or international agreement.

2 General implementation of Treaties**

    2.—(1) All such rights, powers, liabilities, obligations and restrictions from time to time created or arising by or under the Treaties, and all such remedies and procedures from time to time provided for by or under the Treaties, as in accordance with the Treaties are without further enactment to be given legal effect or used in the United Kingdom shall be recognised and available in law, and be enforced, allowed and followed accordingly; and the expression 'enforceable EU right' and similar expressions shall be read as referring to one to which this subsection applies.

---

  * **Editor's Note:** Selected extracts are included, although the Act is now repealed, as they are of important historic interest in the relationship of the UK with the EU and some application survives according to s. 1 of the European Union (Withdrawal Agreement) Act 2020. The Schedules have not been retained.

  ** **Editor's Note:** Section 2(2)(a)(b) excluded (N.I.) by Northern Ireland Constitution Act 1973 (c. 36, SIF 29:3), s. 2(2), Sch. 2 para. 3. Reference in s. 2(5) to 'that subsection' means s. 2(2) of this Act. Reference to a Minister of the Government of Northern Ireland to be construed, as respects the discharge of functions, as a reference to the head of a Northern Ireland department: Northern Ireland Constitution Act 1973 (c. 36, SIF 29:3), Sch. 5 para. 7(2).

(2) Subject to Schedule 2 to this Act, at any time after its passing Her Majesty may by Order in Council, and any designated Minister or department may by order, rules, regulations or scheme, make provision—

    (a) for the purpose of implementing any EU obligation of the United Kingdom, or enabling any such obligation to be implemented, or of enabling any rights enjoyed or to be enjoyed by the United Kingdom under or by virtue of the Treaties to be exercised; or

    (b) for the purpose of dealing with matters arising out of or related to any such obligation or rights or the coming into force, or the operation from time to time, of subsection (1) above;

and in the exercise of any statutory power or duty, including any power to give directions or to legislate by means of orders, rules, regulations or other subordinate instrument, the person entrusted with the power or duty may have regard to the objects of the EU and to any such obligation or rights as aforesaid.

In this subsection 'designated Minister or department' means such Minister of the Crown or government department as may from time to time be designated by Order in Council in relation to any matter or for any purpose, but subject to such restrictions or conditions (if any) as may be specified by the Order in Council.

(3) There shall be charged on and issued out of the Consolidated Fund or, if so determined by the Treasury, the National Loans Fund the amounts required to meet any EU obligation to make payments to any of the EU or a member State, or any EU obligation in respect of contributions to the capital or reserves of the European Investment Bank or in respect of loans to the Bank, or to redeem any notes or obligations issued or created in respect of any such EU obligation; and, except as otherwise provided by or under any enactment,—

    (a) any other expenses incurred under or by virtue of the Treaties or this Act by any Minister of the Crown or government department may be paid out of moneys provided by Parliament and;

    (b) any sums received under or by virtue of the Treaties or this Act by any Minister of the Crown or government department save for such sums as may be required for disbursements permitted by any other enactment, shall be paid into the Consolidated Fund or, if so determined by the Treasury, the National Loans Fund.

(4) The provision that may be made under subsection (2) above includes, subject to Schedule 2 to this Act, any such provision (of any such extent) as might be made by Act of Parliament, and any enactment passed or to be passed, other than one contained in this part of this Act, shall be construed and have effect subject to the foregoing provisions of this section; but, except as may be provided by any Act passed after this Act, Schedule 2 shall have effect in connection with the powers conferred by this and the following sections of this Act to make Orders in Council or orders, rules, regulations or schemes.

(5) ...[1] and the references in that subsection to a Minister of the Crown or Government department and to a statutory power or duty shall include a Minister or department of the Government of Northern Ireland and a power or duty arising under or by virtue of an Act of the Parliament of Northern Ireland.

(6) A law passed by the legislature of any of the Channel Islands or of the Isle of Man, or a colonial Law (within the meaning of the Colonial Laws Validity Act 1865) passed or made for Gibraltar, if expressed to be passed or made in the implementation of the Treaties and of the obligations of the United Kingdom thereunder, shall not be void or inoperative by reason of any inconsistency with or repugnancy to an Act of Parliament, passed or to be passed, that extends to the Island or Gibraltar or any provision having the force and effect of an Act there (but not including this section), nor by reason of its having some operation outside the Island or Gibraltar; and any such Act or provision that extends to the Island or Gibraltar shall be construed and have effect subject to the provisions of any such law.

3 Decisions on, and proof of, Treaties and EU instruments etc.

3.—(1) For the purposes of all legal proceedings any question as to the meaning or effect of any of the Treaties, or as to the validity, meaning or effect of any EU instrument, shall be treated as a question

---

[1] Words repealed by the Northern Ireland Constitution Act 1973 (c. 36 SIF 29:3), Sch. 6 Pt. I.

of law (and, if not referred to the European Court, be for determination as such in accordance with the principles laid down by and any relevant decision of the European Court).

(2) Judicial notice shall be taken of the Treaties, of the Official Journal of the European Union and of any decision of, or expression of opinion by, the European Court on any such question as aforesaid; and the Official Journal shall be admissible as evidence of any instrument or other act thereby communicated of any of the EU or of any EU institution.

(3) Evidence of any instrument issued by a EU institution, including any judgment or order of the European Court, or of any document in the custody of a EU institution, or any entry in or extract from such a document, may be given in any legal proceedings by production of a copy certified as a true copy by an official of that institution; and any document purporting to be such a copy shall be received in evidence without proof of the official position or handwriting of the person signing the certificate.

(4) Evidence of any EU instrument may also be given in any legal proceedings—

    (a) by production of a copy purporting to be printed by the Queen's Printer;

    (b) where the instrument is in the custody of a government department (including a department of the Government of Northern Ireland), by production of a copy certified on behalf of the department to be a true copy by an officer of the department generally or specially authorised so to do;

and any document purporting to be such a copy as is mentioned in paragraph (b) above of an instrument in the custody of a department shall be received in evidence without proof of the official position or handwriting of the person signing the certificate, or of his authority to do so, or of the document being in the custody of the Department.

(5) In any legal proceedings in Scotland evidence of any matter given in a manner authorised by this section shall be sufficient evidence of it.

European Union (Withdrawal) Act 2018*

(2018 c. 16)

(Contents omitted.)

An Act to repeal the European Communities Act 1972 and make other provision in connection with the withdrawal of the United Kingdom from the EU.   [26th June 2018]

BE IT ENACTED by the Queen's most Excellent Majesty, by and with the advice and consent of the Lords Spiritual and Temporal, and Commons, in this present Parliament assembled, and by the authority of the same, as follows:—

Repeal of the ECA

1 Repeal of the European Communities Act 1972
The European Communities Act 1972 is repealed on exit day.

1A Saving for ECA for implementation period
(1) Subsections (2) to (4) have effect despite the repeal of the European Communities Act 1972 on exit day by section 1.

(2) The European Communities Act 1972, as it has effect in domestic law or the law of a relevant territory immediately before exit day, continues to have effect in domestic law or the law of the relevant territory on and after exit day so far as provided by subsections (3) to (5).

(3) The Act of 1972 has effect on and after exit day as if—

    (a) the definitions of 'the Treaties' and 'the EU Treaties' given by section 1(2) to (4) (interpretation)—

        (i) included Part 4 of the withdrawal agreement (implementation period), other than that Part so far as it relates to, or could be applied in relation to, the Common Foreign and Security Policy, but

        (ii) were otherwise limited to anything which falls within those definitions as at immediately before exit day so far as it is not excluded by regulations made on or after exit day by a Minister of the Crown under this sub-paragraph,

    (b) the reference in section 2(2) to the objects of the EU were a reference to those objects so far as they are applicable to and in the United Kingdom by virtue of Part 4 of the withdrawal agreement,

    (c) section 2(3) (payment of EU costs etc.) were omitted,

    (d) in section 3 (decisions on, and proof of, EU Treaties and EU instruments etc.)—

        (i) the references to the Treaties in subsections (1) and (2) included the withdrawal agreement, and

        (ii) the words in brackets in subsection (1) only applied so far as they are in accordance with Part 4 of the withdrawal agreement,

    (e) references in sections 5 and 6 (customs duties and common agricultural policy) to the common customs tariff of the EU, directly applicable EU provision, the exclusion of customs duties, EU arrangements and agricultural levies of the EU were to such things so far as they are applicable to and in the United Kingdom by virtue of Part 4 of the withdrawal agreement, and

    (f) in Part 2 of Schedule 1 (general definitions in relation to the EU)—

        (i) in the definition of 'EU customs duty', the reference to directly applicable EU provision were to such provision so far as it is applicable to and in the United Kingdom by virtue of Part 4 of the withdrawal agreement, and

        (ii) in the definition of 'Member' in the expression 'member State', after 'EU' there were inserted 'and for the purposes of this expression the United Kingdom is to be treated as if it were a member of the EU during the implementation period (within the meaning given by section 1A(6) of the European Union (Withdrawal) Act 2018)'.

(4) In this section 'relevant territory' means the Isle of Man, any of the Channel Islands or Gibraltar.

(5) Subsections (1) to (4) are repealed on IP completion day.

(6) In this Act—

'the implementation period' means the transition or implementation period provided for by Part 4 of the withdrawal agreement and beginning with exit day and ending on IP completion day;

'IP completion day' (and related expressions) have the same meaning as in the European Union (Withdrawal Agreement) Act 2020 (see section 39(1) to (5) of that Act);

'withdrawal agreement' has the same meaning as in that Act (see section 39(1) and (6) of that Act).

(7) In this Act—

    (a) references to the European Communities Act 1972 are to be read, so far as the context permits or requires, as being or (as the case may be) including references to that Act as it continues to have effect by virtue of subsections (2) to (4) above, and

    (b) references to any Part of the withdrawal agreement or the EEA EFTA separation agreement include references to any other provisions of that agreement so far as applying to that Part.

Retention of existing EU law

2 Saving for EU-derived domestic legislation

(1) EU-derived domestic legislation, as it has effect in domestic law immediately before IP completion day, continues to have effect in domestic law on and after IP completion day.

(2) This section is subject to section 5 and Schedule 1 (exceptions to savings and incorporation and section 5A (savings and incorporation: supplementary)).

3 Incorporation of direct EU legislation

(1) Direct EU legislation, so far as operative immediately before IP completion day, forms part of domestic law on and after IP completion day.

(2) In this Act 'direct EU legislation' means—

    (a) any EU regulation, EU decision or EU tertiary legislation, as it has effect in EU law immediately before IP completion day and so far as—

        (ai) it is applicable to and in the United Kingdom by virtue of Part 4 of the withdrawal agreement,

        (bi) it neither has effect nor is to have effect by virtue of section 7A or 7B,

        (i) it is not an exempt EU instrument (for which see section 20(1) and Schedule 6) and,

        (ii) its effect is not reproduced in an enactment to which section 2(1) applies,

    (b) any Annex to the EEA agreement, as it has effect in EU law immediately before IP completion day and so far as—

        (ai) it is applicable to and in the United Kingdom by virtue of Part 4 of the withdrawal agreement,

        (bi) it neither has effect nor is to have effect by virtue of section 7A or 7B,

        (i) it refers to, or contains adaptations of, anything falling within paragraph (a), and

        (ii) its effect is not reproduced in an enactment to which section 2(1) applies, or

    (c) Protocol 1 to the EEA agreement (which contains horizontal adaptations that apply in relation to EU instruments referred to in the Annexes to that agreement), as it has effect in EU law immediately before IP completion day and so far as—

        (i) it is applicable to and in the United Kingdom by virtue of Part 4 of the withdrawal agreement, and

        (ii) it neither has effect nor is to have effect by virtue of section 7A or 7B.

(3) For the purposes of this Act, any direct EU legislation is operative immediately before IP completion day if—

    (a) in the case of anything which comes into force at a particular time and is stated to apply from a later time, it is in force and applies immediately before IP completion day,

    (b) in the case of a decision which specifies to whom it is addressed, it has been notified to that person before IP completion day, and

    (c) in any other case, it is in force immediately before IP completion day.

(4) This section—

    (a) brings into domestic law any direct EU legislation only in the form of the English language version of that legislation, and

    (b) does not apply to any such legislation for which there is no such version, but paragraph (a) does not affect the use of the other language versions of that legislation for the purposes of interpreting it.

(5) This section is subject to section 5 and Schedule 1 (exceptions to savings and incorporation) and section 5A (savings and incorporation: supplementary).

4 Saving for rights etc. under section 2(1) of the ECA

(1) Any rights, powers, liabilities, obligations, restrictions, remedies and procedures which, immediately before IP completion day—

    (a) are recognised and available in domestic law by virtue of section 2(1) of the European Communities Act 1972, and

    (b) are enforced, allowed and followed accordingly,

continue on and after IP completion day to be recognised and available in domestic law (and to be enforced, allowed and followed accordingly).

(2) Subsection (1) does not apply to any rights, powers, liabilities, obligations, restrictions, remedies or procedures so far as they—

    (a) form part of domestic law by virtue of section 3,

      (aa) are, or are to be, recognised and available in domestic law (and enforced, allowed and followed accordingly) by virtue of section 7A or 7B, or

    (b) arise under an EU directive (including as applied by the EEA agreement) and are not of a kind recognised by the European Court or any court or tribunal in the United Kingdom in a case decided before IP completion day (whether or not as an essential part of the decision in the case).

(3) This section is subject to section 5 and Schedule 1 (exceptions to savings and incorporation) and section 5A (savings and incorporation: supplementary).

5 Exceptions to savings and incorporation

(1) The principle of the supremacy of EU law does not apply to any enactment or rule of law passed or made on or after IP completion day.

(2) Accordingly, the principle of the supremacy of EU law continues to apply on or after IP completion day so far as relevant to the interpretation, disapplication or quashing of any enactment or rule of law passed or made before IP completion day.

(3) Subsection (1) does not prevent the principle of the supremacy of EU law from applying to a modification made on or after IP completion day of any enactment or rule of law passed or made before IP completion day if the application of the principle is consistent with the intention of the modification.

(4) The Charter of Fundamental Rights is not part of domestic law on or after IP completion day.

(5) Subsection (4) does not affect the retention in domestic law on or after IP completion day in accordance with this Act of any fundamental rights or principles which exist irrespective of the Charter (and references to the Charter in any case law are, so far as necessary for this purpose, to be read as if they were references to any corresponding retained fundamental rights or principles).

(6) Schedule 1 (which makes further provision about exceptions to savings and incorporation) has effect.

(7) Subsections (1) to (6) and Schedule 1 are subject to relevant separation agreement law (for which see section 7C).

5A Savings and incorporation: supplementary

The fact that anything which continues to be, or forms part of, domestic law on or after IP completion day by virtue of section 2, 3 or 4 has an effect immediately before IP completion day which is time-limited by reference to the implementation period does not prevent it from having an indefinite effect on and after IP completion day by virtue of section 2, 3 or 4.

6 Interpretation of retained EU law

(1) A court or tribunal—

(a) is not bound by any principles laid down, or any decisions made, on or after IP completion day by the European Court, and

(b) cannot refer any matter to the European Court on or after IP completion day.

(2) Subject to this and subsections (3) to (6), a court or tribunal may have regard to anything done on or after IP completion day by the European Court, another EU entity or the EU so far as it is relevant to any matter before the court or tribunal.

(3) Any question as to the validity, meaning or effect of any retained EU law is to be decided, so far as that law is unmodified on or after IP completion day and so far as they are relevant to it—

(a) in accordance with any retained case law and any retained general principles of EU law, and

(b) having regard (among other things) to the limits, immediately before IP completion day, of EU competences.

(4) But—

(a) the Supreme Court is not bound by any retained EU case law,

(b) the High Court of Justiciary is not bound by any retained EU case law when—

(i) sitting as a court of appeal otherwise than in relation to a compatibility issue (within the meaning given by section 288ZA(2) of the Criminal Procedure (Scotland) Act 1995) or a devolution issue (within the meaning given by paragraph 1 of Schedule 6 to the Scotland Act 1998), or

(ii) sitting on a reference under section 123(1) of the Criminal Procedure (Scotland) Act 1995, (ba) a relevant court or relevant tribunal is not bound by any retained EU case law so far as is provided for by regulations under subsection (5A), and

(c) no court or tribunal is bound by any retained domestic case law that it would not otherwise be bound by.

(5) In deciding whether to depart from any retained EU case law by virtue of subsection (4)(a) or (b), the Supreme Court or the High Court of Justiciary must apply the same test as it would apply in deciding whether to depart from its own case law.

(5A) A Minister of the Crown may by regulations provide for—

(a) a court or tribunal to be a relevant court or (as the case may be) a relevant tribunal for the purposes of this section,

(b) the extent to which, or circumstances in which, a relevant court or relevant tribunal is not to be bound by retained EU case law,

(c) the test which a relevant court or relevant tribunal must apply in deciding whether to depart from any retained EU case law, or

(d) considerations which are to be relevant to—

(i) the Supreme Court or the High Court of Justiciary in applying the test mentioned in subsection (5), or

(ii) a relevant court or relevant tribunal in applying any test provided for by virtue of paragraph (c) above.

(5B) Regulations under subsection (5A) may (among other things) provide for—

(a) the High Court of Justiciary to be a relevant court when sitting otherwise than as mentioned in subsection (4)(b)(i) and (ii),

(b) the extent to which, or circumstances in which, a relevant court or relevant tribunal not being bound by retained EU case law includes (or does not include) that court or tribunal not being bound by retained domestic case law which relates to retained EU case law,

(c) other matters arising in relation to retained domestic case law which relates to retained EU case law (including by making provision of a kind which could be made in relation to retained EU case law), or

(d) the test mentioned in paragraph (c) of subsection (5A) or the considerations mentioned in paragraph (d) of that subsection to be determined (whether with or without the consent of a Minister of the Crown) by a person mentioned in subsection (5C)(a) to (e) or by more than one of those persons acting jointly.

(5C) Before making regulations under subsection (5A), a Minister of the Crown must consult—

(a) the President of the Supreme Court,

(b) the Lord Chief Justice of England and Wales,

(c) the Lord President of the Court of Session,

(d) the Lord Chief Justice of Northern Ireland,

(e) the Senior President of Tribunals, and

(f) such other persons as the Minister of the Crown considers appropriate.

(5D) No regulations may be made under subsection (5A) after IP completion day.

(6) Subsection (3) does not prevent the validity, meaning or effect of any retained EU law which has been modified on or after IP completion day from being decided as provided for in that subsection if doing so is consistent with the intention of the modifications.

(6A) Subsections (1) to (6) are subject to relevant separation agreement law (for which see section 7C).

(7) In this Act—

'retained case law' means—

(a) retained domestic case law, and

(b) retained EU case law;

'retained domestic case law' means any principles laid down by, and any decisions of, a court or tribunal in the United Kingdom, as they have effect immediately before IP completion day and so far as they—

(a) relate to anything to which section 2, 3 or 4 applies, and

(b) are not excluded by section 5 or Schedule 1,

(as those principles and decisions are modified by or under this Act or by other domestic law from time to time);

'retained EU case law' means any principles laid down by, and any decisions of, the European Court, as they have effect in EU law immediately before IP completion day and so far as they—

 (a) relate to anything to which section 2, 3 or 4 applies, and

 (b) are not excluded by section 5 or Schedule 1,

(as those principles and decisions are modified by or under this Act or by other domestic law from time to time);

'retained EU law' means anything which, on or after IP completion day, continues to be, or forms part of, domestic law by virtue of section 2, 3 or 4 or subsection (3) or (6) above (as that body of law is added to or otherwise modified by or under this Act or by other domestic law from time to time);

'retained general principles of EU law' means the general principles of EU law, as they have effect in EU law immediately before IP completion day and so far as they—

 (a) relate to anything to which section 2, 3 or 4 applies, and

 (b) are not excluded by section 5 or Schedule 1,

(as those principles are modified by or under this Act or by other domestic law from time to time).

7 Status of retained EU law

 (1) Anything which—

  (a) was, immediately before exit day, primary legislation of a particular kind, subordinate legislation of a particular kind or another enactment of a particular kind, and

  (b) continues to be domestic law on and after exit day by virtue of section 1A(2) or 1B(2),

continues to be domestic law as an enactment of the same kind.

 (1A) Anything which—

  (a) was, immediately before IP completion day, primary legislation of a particular kind, subordinate legislation of a particular kind or another enactment of a particular kind, and

  (b) continues to be domestic law on and after IP completion day by virtue of section 2,

continues to be domestic law as an enactment of the same kind.

 (2) Retained direct principal EU legislation cannot be modified by any primary or subordinate legislation other than—

  (a) an Act of Parliament,

  (b) any other primary legislation (so far as it has the power to make such a modification), or

  (c) any subordinate legislation so far as it is made under a power which permits such a modification by virtue of—

   (i) paragraph 3, 5(3)(a) or (4)(a), 8(3), 10(3)(a) or (4)(a), 11(2)(a) or 12(3) of Schedule 8,

   (ii) any other provision made by or under this Act,

   (iii) any provision made by or under an Act of Parliament passed before, and in the same Session as, this Act, or

   (iv) any provision made on or after the passing of this Act by or under primary legislation.

 (3) Retained direct minor EU legislation cannot be modified by any primary or subordinate legislation other than—

  (a) an Act of Parliament,

  (b) any other primary legislation (so far as it has the power to make such a modification), or

  (c) any subordinate legislation so far as it is made under a power which permits such a modification by virtue of—

   (i) paragraph 3, 5(2) or (4)(a), 8(3), 10(2) or (4)(a) or 12(3) of Schedule 8,

   (ii) any other provision made by or under this Act,

   (iii) any provision made by or under an Act of Parliament passed before, and in the same Session as, this Act, or

   (iv) any provision made on or after the passing of this Act by or under primary legislation.

 (4) Anything which is retained EU law by virtue of section 4 cannot be modified by any primary or subordinate legislation other than—

  (a) an Act of Parliament,

  (b) any other primary legislation (so far as it has the power to make such a modification), or

(c) any subordinate legislation so far as it is made under a power which permits such a modification by virtue of—

    (i) paragraph 3, 5(3)(b) or (4)(b), 8(3), 10(3)(b) or (4)(b), 11(2)(b) or 12(3) of Schedule 8,

    (ii) any other provision made by or under this Act,

    (iii) any provision made by or under an Act of Parliament passed before, and in the same Session as, this Act, or

    (iv) any provision made on or after the passing of this Act by or under primary legislation.

(5) For other provisions about the status of retained EU law, see—

    (a) section 5(1) to (3) and (7) (status of retained EU law in relation to other enactments or rules of law),

    (b) section 6 (status of retained case law and retained general principles of EU law),

    (ba) section 7C (status of case law of European Court etc in relation to retained EU law which is relevant separation agreement law),

    (c) section 15(2) and Part 2 of Schedule 5 (status of retained EU law for the purposes of the rules of evidence),

    (d) paragraphs 13 to 16 of Schedule 8 (affirmative and enhanced scrutiny procedure for, and information about, instruments which amend or revoke subordinate legislation under section 2(2) of the European Communities Act 1972 including subordinate legislation implementing EU directives),

    (e) paragraphs 19 and 20 of that Schedule (status of certain retained direct EU legislation for the purposes of the Interpretation Act 1978), and

    (f) paragraph 30 of that Schedule (status of retained direct EU legislation for the purposes of the Human Rights Act 1998).

(6) In this Act—

'retained direct minor EU legislation' means any retained direct EU legislation which is not retained direct principal EU legislation;

'retained direct principal EU legislation' means—

    (a) any EU regulation so far as it—

        (i) forms part of domestic law on and after IP completion day by virtue of section 3, and

        (ii) was not EU tertiary legislation immediately before IP completion day, or

    (b) any Annex to the EEA agreement so far as it—

        (i) forms part of domestic law on and after IP completion day by virtue of section 3, and

        (ii) refers to, or contains adaptations of, any EU regulation so far as it falls within paragraph (a),

(as modified by or under this Act or by other domestic law from time to time).

Further aspects of withdrawal

7A General implementation of remainder of withdrawal agreement

(1) Subsection (2) applies to—

    (a) all such rights, powers, liabilities, obligations and restrictions from time to time created or arising by or under the withdrawal agreement, and

    (b) all such remedies and procedures from time to time provided for by or under the withdrawal agreement, as in accordance with the withdrawal agreement are without further enactment to be given legal effect or used in the United Kingdom.

(2) The rights, powers, liabilities, obligations, restrictions, remedies and procedures concerned are to be—

    (a) recognised and available in domestic law, and

    (b) enforced, allowed and followed accordingly.

(3) Every enactment (including an enactment contained in this Act) is to be read and has effect subject to subsection (2).

(4) This section does not apply in relation to Part 4 of the withdrawal agreement so far as section 2(1) of the European Communities Act 1972 applies in relation to that Part.

(5) See also (among other things)—

(a) Part 3 of the European Union (Withdrawal Agreement) Act 2020 (further provision about citizens' rights),

(b) section 20 of that Act (financial provision),

(c) section 7C of this Act (interpretation of law relating to withdrawal agreement etc),

(d) section 8B of this Act (power in connection with certain other separation issues),

(e) section 8C of this Act (power in connection with the Protocol on Ireland/Northern Ireland in withdrawal agreement), and

(f) Parts 1B and 1C of Schedule 2 to this Act (powers involving devolved authorities in connection with certain other separation issues and the Ireland/Northern Ireland Protocol).

7B General implementation of EEA EFTA and Swiss agreements

(1) Subsection (2) applies to all such rights, powers, liabilities, obligations, restrictions, remedies and procedures as—

(a) would from time to time be created or arise, or (in the case of remedies or procedures) be provided for, by or under the EEA EFTA separation agreement or the Swiss citizens' rights agreement, and

(b) would, in accordance with Article 4(1) of the withdrawal agreement, be required to be given legal effect or used in the United Kingdom without further enactment,

if that Article were to apply in relation to the EEA EFTA separation agreement and the Swiss citizens' rights agreement, those agreements were part of EU law and the relevant EEA states and Switzerland were member States.

(2) The rights, powers, liabilities, obligations, restrictions, remedies and procedures concerned are to be—

(a) recognised and available in domestic law, and

(b) enforced, allowed and followed accordingly.

(3) Every enactment (other than section 7A but otherwise including an enactment contained in this Act) is to be read and has effect subject to subsection (2).

(4) See also (among other things)—

(a) Part 3 of the European Union (Withdrawal Agreement) Act 2020 (further provision about citizens' rights),

(b) section 7C of this Act (interpretation of law relating to the EEA EFTA separation agreement and the Swiss citizens' rights agreement etc),

(c) section 8B of this Act (power in connection with certain other separation issues), and

(d) Part 1B of Schedule 2 to this Act (powers involving devolved authorities in connection with certain other separation issues).

(5) In this section 'the relevant EEA states' means Norway, Iceland and Liechtenstein

(6) In this Act 'EEA EFTA separation agreement' and 'Swiss citizens' rights agreement' have the same meanings as in the European Union (Withdrawal Agreement) Act 2020 (see section 39(1) of that Act).

7C Interpretation of relevant separation agreement law

(1) Any question as to the validity, meaning or effect of any relevant separation agreement law is to be decided, so far as they are applicable—

(a) in accordance with the withdrawal agreement, the EEA EFTA separation agreement and the Swiss citizens' rights agreement, and

(b) having regard (among other things) to the desirability of ensuring that, where one of those agreements makes provision which corresponds to provision made by another of those agreements, the effect of relevant separation agreement law in relation to the matters dealt with by the corresponding provision in each agreement is consistent.

(2) See (among other things)—

(a) Article 4 of the withdrawal agreement (methods and principles relating to the effect, the implementation and the application of the agreement),

(b) Articles 158 and 160 of the withdrawal agreement (jurisdiction of the European Court in relation to Part 2 and certain provisions of Part 5 of the agreement),

(c) Articles 12 and 13 of the Protocol on Ireland/Northern Ireland in the withdrawal agreement (implementation, application, supervision and enforcement of the Protocol and common provisions),

(d) Article 4 of the EEA EFTA separation agreement (methods and principles relating to the effect, the implementation and the application of the agreement), and

(e) Article 4 of the Swiss citizens' rights agreement (methods and principles relating to the effect, the implementation and the application of the agreement).

(3) In this Act 'relevant separation agreement law' means—

  (a) any of the following provisions or anything which is domestic law by virtue of any of them—

    (i) section 7A, 7B, 8B or 8C or Part 1B or 1C of Schedule 2 or this section, or

    (ii) Part 3, or section 20, of the European Union (Withdrawal Agreement) Act 2020 (citizens' rights and financial provision), or

  (b) anything not falling within paragraph (a) so far as it is domestic law for the purposes of, or otherwise within the scope of—

    (i) the withdrawal agreement (other than Part 4 of that agreement),

    (ii) the EEA EFTA separation agreement, or

    (iii) the Swiss citizens' rights agreement,

as that body of law is added to or otherwise modified by or under this Act or by other domestic law from time to time.

Main powers in connection with withdrawal

8 Dealing with deficiencies arising from withdrawal

(1) A Minister of the Crown may by regulations make such provision as the Minister considers appropriate to prevent, remedy or mitigate—

  (a) any failure of retained EU law to operate effectively, or

  (b) any other deficiency in retained EU law,

arising from the withdrawal of the United Kingdom from the EU.

(2) Deficiencies in retained EU law are where the Minister considers that retained EU law—

  (a) contains anything which has no practical application in relation to the United Kingdom or any part of it or is otherwise redundant or substantially redundant,

  (b) confers functions on, or in relation to, EU entities which no longer have functions in that respect under EU law in relation to the United Kingdom or any part of it,

  (c) makes provision for, or in connection with, reciprocal arrangements between—

    (i) the United Kingdom or any part of it or a public authority in the United Kingdom, and

    (ii) the EU, an EU entity, a member State or a public authority in a member State, which no longer exist or are no longer appropriate,

  (d) makes provision for, or in connection with, other arrangements which—

    (i) involve the EU, an EU entity, a member State or a public authority in a member State, or

    (ii) are otherwise dependent upon the United Kingdom's membership of the EU or Part 4 of the withdrawal agreement, and which no longer exist or are no longer appropriate,

  (e) makes provision for, or in connection with, any reciprocal or other arrangements not falling within paragraph (c) or (d) which no longer exist, or are no longer appropriate, as a result of the United Kingdom ceasing to be a party to any of the EU Treaties or as a result of either the end of the implementation period or any other effect of the withdrawal agreement,

  (ea) is not clear in its effect as a result of the operation of any provision of sections 2 to 6 or Schedule 1,

  (f) does not contain any functions or restrictions which—

    (i) were in an EU directive and in force immediately before IP completion day (including any power to make EU tertiary legislation), and

(ii) it is appropriate to retain, or

(g) contains EU references which are no longer appropriate.

(3) There is also a deficiency in retained EU law where the Minister considers that there is—

(a) anything in retained EU law which is of a similar kind to any deficiency which falls within subsection (2), or

(b) a deficiency in retained EU law of a kind described, or provided for, in regulations made by a Minister of the Crown.

(4) But retained EU law is not deficient merely because it does not contain any modification of EU law which is adopted or notified, comes into force or only applies on or after IP completion day.

(5) Regulations under subsection (1) may make any provision that could be made by an Act of Parliament.

(6) Regulations under subsection (1) may (among other things) provide for functions of EU entities or public authorities in member States (including making an instrument of a legislative character or providing funding) to be—

(a) exercisable instead by a public authority (whether or not established for the purpose) in the United Kingdom, or

(b) replaced, abolished or otherwise modified.

(7) But regulations under subsection (1) may not—

(a) impose or increase taxation or fees,

(b) make retrospective provision,

(c) create a relevant criminal offence,

(d) establish a public authority,

(e)

(f) amend, repeal or revoke the Human Rights Act 1998 or any subordinate legislation made under it, or

(g) amend or repeal the Scotland Act 1998, the Government of Wales Act 2006 or the Northern Ireland Act 1998 (unless the regulations are made by virtue of paragraph 21(b) of Schedule 7 to this Act or are amending or repealing any provision of those Acts which modifies another enactment).

(8) No regulations may be made under this section after the end of the period of two years beginning with IP completion day.

(9) The reference in subsection (1) to a failure or other deficiency arising from the withdrawal of the United Kingdom from the EU includes a reference to any failure or other deficiency arising from—

(a) any aspect of that withdrawal, including (among other things)—

(i) the end of the implementation period, or

(ii) any other effect of the withdrawal agreement, or

(b) that withdrawal, or any such aspect of it, taken together with the operation of any provision, or the interaction between any provisions, made by or under this Act or the European Union (Withdrawal Agreement) Act 2020.

8A Supplementary power in connection with implementation period

(1) A Minister of the Crown may by regulations—

(a) provide for other modifications for the purposes of section 1B(3)(f)(i) (whether applying in all cases or particular cases or descriptions of case),

(b) provide for subsection (3) or (4) of section 1B not to apply to any extent in particular cases or descriptions of case,

(c) make different provision in particular cases or descriptions of case to that made by subsection (3) or (4) of that section,

(d) modify any enactment contained in this Act in consequence of any repeal made by section 1A(5) or 1B(6), or

(e) make such provision not falling within paragraph (a), (b), (c) or (d) as the Minister considers appropriate for any purpose of, or otherwise in connection with, Part 4 of the withdrawal agreement.

(2) The power to make regulations under subsection (1) may (among other things) be exercised by modifying any provision made by or under an enactment.

(3) In subsection (2) 'enactment' does not include primary legislation passed or made after IP completion day.

(4) No regulations may be made under subsection (1) after the end of the period of two years beginning with IP completion day.

8B Power in connection with certain other separation issues

(1) A Minister of the Crown may by regulations make such provision as the Minister considers appropriate—

    (a) to implement Part 3 of the withdrawal agreement (separation provisions),

    (b) to supplement the effect of section 7A in relation to that Part, or

    (c) otherwise for the purposes of dealing with matters arising out of, or related to, that Part (including matters arising by virtue of section 7A and that Part).

(2) A Minister of the Crown may by regulations make such provision as the Minister considers appropriate—

    (a) to implement Part 3 of the EEA EFTA separation agreement (separation provisions),

    (b) to supplement the effect of section 7B in relation to that Part, or

    (c) otherwise for the purposes of dealing with matters arising out of, or related to, that Part (including matters arising by virtue of section 7B and that Part).

(3) Regulations under this section may make any provision that could be made by an Act of Parliament.

(4) Regulations under this section may (among other things) restate, for the purposes of making the law clearer or more accessible, anything that forms part of domestic law by virtue of—

    (a) section 7A above and Part 3 of the withdrawal agreement, or

    (b) section 7B above and Part 3 of the EEA EFTA separation agreement.

(5) But regulations under this section may not—

    (a) impose or increase taxation or fees,

    (b) make retrospective provision,

    (c) create a relevant criminal offence,

    (d) establish a public authority,

    (e) amend, repeal or revoke the Human Rights Act 1998 or any subordinate legislation made under it, or

    (f) amend or repeal the Scotland Act 1998, the Government of Wales Act 2006 or the Northern Ireland Act 1998 (unless the regulations are made by virtue of paragraph 21(b) of Schedule 7 to this Act or are amending or repealing any provision of those Acts which modifies another enactment).

(6) In this section references to Part 3 of the withdrawal agreement or of the EEA EFTA separation agreement include references to any provision of EU law which is applied by, or referred to in, that Part (to the extent of the application or reference).

8C Power in connection with Ireland/Northern Ireland Protocol in withdrawal agreement

(1) A Minister of the Crown may by regulations make such provision as the Minister considers appropriate—

    (a) to implement the Protocol on Ireland/Northern Ireland in the withdrawal agreement,

    (b) to supplement the effect of section 7A in relation to the Protocol, or

    (c) otherwise for the purposes of dealing with matters arising out of, or related to, the Protocol (including matters arising by virtue of section 7A and the Protocol).

(2) Regulations under subsection (1) may make any provision that could be made by an Act of Parliament (including modifying this Act).

(3) Regulations under subsection (1) may (among other things) make provision facilitating the access to the market within Great Britain of qualifying Northern Ireland goods.

(4) Such provision may (among other things) include provision about the recognition within Great Britain of technical regulations, assessments, registrations, certificates, approvals and authorisations issued by—

    (a) the authorities of a member State, or

    (b) bodies established in a member State,

in respect of qualifying Northern Ireland goods.

(5) Regulations under subsection (1) may (among other things) restate, for the purposes of making the law clearer or more accessible, anything that forms part of domestic law by virtue of section 7A and the Protocol.

(6) A Minister of the Crown may by regulations define 'qualifying Northern Ireland goods' for the purposes of this Act.

(7) In this section any reference to the Protocol on Ireland/Northern Ireland includes a reference to—

    (a) any other provision of the withdrawal agreement so far as applying to the Protocol, and

    (b) any provision of EU law which is applied by, or referred to in, the Protocol (to the extent of the application or reference),

but does not include the second sentence of Article 11(1) of the Protocol (which provides that the United Kingdom and the Republic of Ireland may continue to make new arrangements that build on the provisions of the Belfast Agreement in other areas of North-South cooperation on the island of Ireland).

9 Implementing the withdrawal agreement [repealed by s. 36(a) EUWAA 2020]

Devolution

10 Protection for North-South co-operation and prevention of new border arrangements

(1) In exercising any of the powers under this Act, a Minister of the Crown or devolved authority must—

    (a) act in a way that is compatible with the terms of the Northern Ireland Act 1998, and

    (b) have due regard to the joint report from the negotiators of the EU and the United Kingdom Government on progress during phase 1 of negotiations under Article 50 of the Treaty on European Union.

(2) Nothing in section 8, or 23(1) or (6) of this Act authorises regulations which—

    (a) diminish any form of North-South cooperation provided for by the Belfast Agreement, or

    (b) create or facilitate border arrangements between Northern Ireland and the Republic of Ireland after exit day which feature physical infrastructure, including border posts, or checks and controls, that did not exist before exit day and are not in accordance with an agreement between the United Kingdom and the EU.

(3) A Minister of the Crown may not agree to the making of a recommendation by the Joint Committee under Article 11(2) of the Protocol on Ireland/Northern Ireland in the withdrawal agreement (recommendations as to North-South cooperation) to—

    (a) alter the arrangements for North-South co-operation as provided for by the Belfast Agreement,

    (b) establish a new implementation body, or

    (c) alter the functions of an existing implementation body.

(4) In this section—

'the Belfast Agreement' has the meaning given by section 98 of the Northern Ireland Act 1998;

'implementation body' has the meaning given by section 55(3) of that Act.

11 Powers involving devolved authorities corresponding to sections 8 to 8C

Schedule 2 (which confers powers to make regulations involving devolved authorities which correspond to the powers conferred by sections 8 to 8C) has effect.

12 Retaining EU restrictions in devolution legislation etc.

(1) In section 29(2)(d) of the Scotland Act 1998 (no competence for the Scottish Parliament to legislate incompatibly with EU law) for 'with EU law' substitute 'in breach of the restriction in section 30A(1)'.

(2) After section 30 of that Act (legislative competence: supplementary) insert—

'30A Legislative competence: restriction relating to retained EU law

(1) An Act of the Scottish Parliament cannot modify, or confer power by subordinate legislation to modify, retained EU law so far as the modification is of a description specified in regulations made by a Minister of the Crown.

(2) But subsection (1) does not apply to any modification so far as it would, immediately before exit day, have been within the legislative competence of the Parliament.

(3) A Minister of the Crown must not lay for approval before each House of the Parliament of the United Kingdom a draft of a statutory instrument containing regulations under this section unless—

(a) the Scottish Parliament has made a consent decision in relation to the laying of the draft, or

(b) the 40 day period has ended without the Parliament having made such a decision.

(4) For the purposes of subsection (3) a consent decision is—

(a) a decision to agree a motion consenting to the laying of the draft,

(b) a decision not to agree a motion consenting to the laying of the draft, or

(c) a decision to agree a motion refusing to consent to the laying of the draft;

and a consent decision is made when the Parliament first makes a decision falling within any of paragraphs (a) to (c) (whether or not it subsequently makes another such decision).

(5) A Minister of the Crown who is proposing to lay a draft as mentioned in subsection (3) must—

(a) provide a copy of the draft to the Scottish Ministers, and

(b) inform the Presiding Officer that a copy has been so provided.

(6) See also paragraph 6 of Schedule 7 (duty to make explanatory statement about regulations under this section including a duty to explain any decision to lay a draft without the consent of the Parliament).

(7) No regulations may be made under this section after the end of the period of two years beginning with exit day.

(8) Subsection (7) does not affect the continuation in force of regulations made under this section at or before the end of the period mentioned in that subsection.

(9) Any regulations under this section which are in force at the end of the period of five years beginning with the time at which they came into force are revoked in their application to any Act of the Scottish Parliament which receives Royal Assent after the end of that period.

(10) Subsections (3) to (8) do not apply in relation to regulations which only relate to a revocation of a specification.

(11) In this section—

'the 40 day period' means the period of 40 days beginning with the day on which a copy of the draft instrument is provided to the Scottish Ministers,

and, in calculating that period, no account is to be taken of any time during which the Parliament is dissolved or during which it is in recess for more than four days.'

(3) In section 108A(2)(e) of the Government of Wales Act 2006 (no competence for the National Assembly for Wales to legislate incompatibly with EU law) for 'with EU law' substitute 'in breach of the restriction in section 109A(1)'.

(4) After section 109 of that Act (legislative competence: supplementary) insert—

'109A Legislative competence: restriction relating to retained EU law

(1) An Act of the Assembly cannot modify, or confer power by subordinate legislation to modify, retained EU law so far as the modification is of a description specified in regulations made by a Minister of the Crown.

(2) But subsection (1) does not apply to any modification so far as it would, immediately before exit day, have been within the Assembly's legislative competence.

(3) No regulations are to be made under this section unless a draft of the statutory instrument containing them has been laid before, and approved by a resolution of, each House of Parliament.

(4) A Minister of the Crown must not lay a draft as mentioned in subsection (3) unless—

     (a) the Assembly has made a consent decision in relation to the laying of the draft, or

     (b) the 40 day period has ended without the Assembly having made such a decision.

(5) For the purposes of subsection (4) a consent decision is—

     (a) a decision to agree a motion consenting to the laying of the draft,

     (b) a decision not to agree a motion consenting to the laying of the draft, or

     (c) a decision to agree a motion refusing to consent to the laying of the draft;

and a consent decision is made when the Assembly first makes a decision falling within any of paragraphs (a) to (c) (whether or not it subsequently makes another such decision).

(6) A Minister of the Crown who is proposing to lay a draft as mentioned in subsection (3) must—

     (a) provide a copy of the draft to the Welsh Ministers, and

     (b) inform the Presiding Officer that a copy has been so provided.

(7) See also section 157ZA (duty to make explanatory statement about regulations under this section including a duty to explain any decision to lay a draft without the consent of the Assembly).

(8) No regulations may be made under this section after the end of the period of two years beginning with exit day.

(9) Subsection (8) does not affect the continuation in force of regulations made under this section at or before the end of the period mentioned in that subsection.

(10) Any regulations under this section which are in force at the end of the period of five years beginning with the time at which they came into force are revoked in their application to any Act of the Assembly which receives Royal Assent after the end of that period.

(11) Subsections (4) to (9) do not apply in relation to regulations which only relate to a revocation of a specification.

(12) In this section—

'the 40 day period' means the period of 40 days beginning with the day on which a copy of the draft instrument is provided to the Welsh Ministers,

and, in calculating that period, no account is to be taken of any time during which the Assembly is dissolved or during which it is in recess for more than four days.'

(5) In section 6(2)(d) of the Northern Ireland Act 1998 (no competence for the Northern Ireland Assembly to legislate incompatibly with EU law) for 'incompatible with EU law' substitute 'in breach of the restriction in section 6A(1)'.

(6) After section 6 of that Act (legislative competence) insert—

'6A Restriction relating to retained EU law

(1) An Act of the Assembly cannot modify, or confer power by subordinate legislation to modify, retained EU law so far as the modification is of a description specified in regulations made by a Minister of the Crown.

(2) But subsection (1) does not apply to any modification so far as it would, immediately before exit day, have been within the legislative competence of the Assembly.

(3) A Minister of the Crown must not lay for approval before each House of Parliament a draft of a statutory instrument containing regulations under this section unless—

     (a) the Assembly has made a consent decision in relation to the laying of the draft, or

     (b) the 40 day period has ended without the Assembly having made such a decision.

(4) For the purposes of subsection (3) a consent decision is—

     (a) a decision to agree a motion consenting to the laying of the draft,

     (b) a decision not to agree a motion consenting to the laying of the draft, or

     (c) a decision to agree a motion refusing to consent to the laying of the draft;

and a consent decision is made when the Assembly first makes a decision falling within any of paragraphs (a) to (c) (whether or not it subsequently makes another such decision).

(5) A Minister of the Crown who is proposing to lay a draft as mentioned in subsection (3) must—

(a) provide a copy of the draft to the relevant Northern Ireland department, and

(b) inform the Presiding Officer that a copy has been so provided.

(6) See also section 96A (duty to make explanatory statement about regulations under this section including a duty to explain any decision to lay a draft without the consent of the Assembly).

(7) No regulations may be made under this section after the end of the period of two years beginning with exit day.

(8) Subsection (7) does not affect the continuation in force of regulations made under this section at or before the end of the period mentioned in that subsection.

(9) Any regulations under this section which are in force at the end of the period of five years beginning with the time at which they came into force are revoked in their application to any Act of the Assembly which receives Royal Assent after the end of that period.

(10) Subsections (3) to (8) do not apply in relation to regulations which only relate to a revocation of a specification.

(11) Regulations under this section may include such supplementary, incidental, consequential, transitional, transitory or saving provision as the Minister of the Crown making them considers appropriate.

(12) In this section—

'the relevant Northern Ireland department' means such Northern Ireland department as the Minister of the Crown concerned considers appropriate;

'the 40 day period' means the period of 40 days beginning with the day on which a copy of the draft instrument is provided to the relevant Northern Ireland department,

and, in calculating that period, no account is to be taken of any time during which the Assembly is dissolved or during which it is in recess for more than four days.'

(7) Part 1 of Schedule 3 (which makes corresponding provision in relation to executive competence to that made by subsections (1) to (6) in relation to legislative competence) has effect.

(8) Part 2 of Schedule 3 (which imposes reporting obligations on a Minister of the Crown in recognition of the fact that the powers to make regulations conferred by subsections (1) to (6) and Part 1 of Schedule 3, and any restrictions arising by virtue of them, are intended to be temporary) has effect.

(9) A Minister of the Crown may by regulations—

(a) repeal any of the following provisions—

(i) section 30A or 57(4) to (15) of the Scotland Act 1998,

(ii) section 80(8) to (8L) or 109A of the Government of Wales Act 2006, or

(iii) section 6A or 24(3) to (15) of the Northern Ireland Act 1998, or

(b) modify any enactment in consequence of any such repeal.

(10) Until all of the provisions mentioned in subsection (9)(a) have been repealed, a Minister of the Crown must, after the end of each review period, consider whether it is appropriate—

(a) to repeal each of those provisions so far as it has not been repealed, or

(b) to revoke any regulations made under any of those provisions so far as they have not been revoked.

(11) In considering whether to exercise the power to make regulations under subsection (9), a Minister of the Crown must have regard (among other things) to—

(a) the fact that the powers to make regulations conferred by the provisions mentioned in subsection (9)(a), and any restrictions arising by virtue of them, are intended to be temporary and, where appropriate, replaced with other arrangements, and

(b) any progress which has been made in implementing those other arrangements.

(12) Part 3 of Schedule 3 (which contains amendments of devolution legislation not dealt with elsewhere) has effect.

(13) In this section—

'arrangement' means any enactment or other arrangement (whether or not legally enforceable);

'review period' means—
    (a) the period of three months beginning with the day on which subsection (10) comes into force, and
    (b) after that, each successive period of three months.

Parliamentary oversight of withdrawal

13 Parliamentary approval of the outcome of negotiations with the EU [repealed by s. 31 EUWAA 2020]

13A Review of EU legislation during implementation period

(1) Subsection (2) applies where the European Scrutiny Select Committee of the House of Commons ('the ESC') publishes a report in respect of any EU legislation made, or which may be made, during the implementation period and the report—
    (a) states that, in the opinion of the ESC, the EU legislation raises a matter of vital national interest to the United Kingdom,
    (b) confirms that the ESC has taken such evidence as it considers appropriate as to the effect of the EU legislation and has consulted any Departmental Select Committee of the House of Commons which the ESC considers also has an interest in the EU legislation, and
    (c) sets out the wording of a motion to be moved in the House of Commons in accordance with subsection (2).

(2) A Minister of the Crown must, within the period of 14 Commons sitting days beginning with the day on which the report is published, make arrangements for the motion mentioned in subsection (1)(c) to be debated and voted on by the House of Commons.

(3) Subsection (4) applies where the EU Select Committee of the House of Lords ('the EUC') publishes a report in respect of any EU legislation made, or which may be made, during the implementation period and the report—
    (a) states that, in the opinion of the EUC, the EU legislation raises a matter of vital national interest to the United Kingdom,
    (b) confirms that the EUC has taken such evidence as it considers appropriate as to the effect of the EU legislation, and
    (c) sets out the wording of a motion to be moved in the House of Lords in accordance with subsection (4).

(4) A Minister of the Crown must, within the period of 14 Lords sitting days beginning with the day on which the report is published, make arrangements for the motion mentioned in subsection (3)(c) to be debated and voted on by the House of Lords.

(5) In this section—
'EU legislation' means—
    (a) any amendment to the Treaty on European Union, the Treaty on the Functioning of the European Union, the Euratom Treaty or the EEA agreement,
    (b) any EU directive, or
    (c) any EU regulation or EU decision which is not EU tertiary legislation;
'the European Scrutiny Select Committee of the House of Commons' means the Select Committee of the House of Commons known as the European Scrutiny Select Committee or any successor of that committee;
'the EU Select Committee of the House of Lords' means the Select Committee of the House of Lords known as the EU Select Committee or any successor of that committee.

13B Certain dispute procedures under withdrawal agreement

(1) Subsection (2) applies if a request has been made under Article 170 of the withdrawal agreement to the other party in a dispute (request to establish an arbitration panel in relation to a dispute between the EU and the United Kingdom).

(2) A Minister of the Crown must, within the 14 day period beginning with the day on which the request is made, make a statement in writing to each House of Parliament that the request has been made and setting out the details of it.

(3) Subsection (4) applies if the European Court has given a ruling in response to a request by an arbitration panel under Article 174(1) of the withdrawal agreement (request for ruling by European Court on certain questions arising in a dispute submitted to arbitration).

(4) A Minister of the Crown must, within the 14 day period beginning with the publication in the Official Journal of the European Union of the ruling of the European Court, make a statement in writing to each House of Parliament that the ruling has been made and setting out the details of it contained in the Official Journal.

(5) After the end of each reporting period, a Minister of the Crown must lay before each House of Parliament a report setting out the number of times within the reporting period that the Joint Committee has been provided with notice under Article 169(1) of the withdrawal agreement (notice concerning the commencement of consultations in the Joint Committee to resolve a dispute between the EU and the United Kingdom about the interpretation and application of the withdrawal agreement).

(6) In this section—

'reporting period' means—

    (a) the period of one year beginning with the day on which IP completion day falls, and

    (b) each subsequent year;

'the 14 day period' means—

    (a) in relation to the House of Commons, the period of 14 Commons sitting days, and

    (b) in relation to the House of Lords, the period of 14 Lords sitting days.

*Financial and other matters**

15A Prohibition on extending implementation period

A Minister of the Crown may not agree in the Joint Committee to an extension of the implementation period.

15B Ministerial co-chairs of the Joint Committee

The functions of the United Kingdom's co-chair of the Joint Committee, under Annex VIII of the withdrawal agreement (rules of procedure of the Joint Committee and specialised committees), are to be exercised personally by a Minister of the Crown (and, accordingly, only a Minister of the Crown may be designated as a replacement under Rule 1(3)).

15C No use of written procedure in the Joint Committee

(1) The United Kingdom's co-chair of the Joint Committee may not consent to the Joint Committee using the written procedure provided for in Rule 9(1) of Annex VIII of the withdrawal agreement.

(2) In subsection (1) the reference to the United Kingdom's co-chair of the Joint Committee includes a reference to any designee of the co-chair designated under Rule 1(3) of Annex VIII of the withdrawal agreement.

16 Maintenance of environmental principles etc. [repealed by s. 36(b) EUWAA 2020]

17 Family unity for those seeking asylum or other protection in Europe

(1) A Minister of the Crown must, within the period of two months beginning with the day on which the European Union (Withdrawal Agreement) Act 2020 is passed, lay before Parliament a statement of policy in relation to any future arrangements between the United Kingdom and the EU about—

    (a) unaccompanied children, who make an application for international protection to a member State, coming to the United Kingdom where it is in their best interests to join a relative who—

        (i) is a lawful resident of the United Kingdom, or

        (ii) has made a protection claim which has not been decided, and

---

* **Editor's Note:** Sections 14 and 15 omitted.

(b) unaccompanied children in the United Kingdom, who make a protection claim, going to a member State to join a relative there in equivalent circumstances.

(2) For the purposes of subsection (1)(a)(i) a person is not a lawful resident of the United Kingdom if the person requires leave to enter or remain in the United Kingdom but does not have it.

(3) For the purposes of subsection (1)(a)(ii), a protection claim is decided—

(a) when the Secretary of State notifies the claimant of the Secretary of State's decision on the claim, unless the claimant appeals against the decision, or

(b) if the claimant appeals against the Secretary of State's decision on the claim, when the appeal is disposed of.

(4) In this section—

'application for international protection' has the meaning given by Article 2(h) of Directive 2011/95/EU of the European Parliament and of the Council on standards for the qualification of third-country nationals or stateless persons as beneficiaries of international protection, for a uniform status for refugees or for persons eligible for subsidiary protection, and for the content of the protection granted;

'protection claim' has the same meaning as in Part 5 of the Nationality, Immigration and Asylum Act 2002 (see section 82(2) of that Act);

'relative', in relation to an unaccompanied child, means—

(a) a spouse or civil partner of the child or any person with whom the child has a durable relationship that is similar to marriage or civil partnership, or

(b) a parent, grandparent, uncle, aunt, brother or sister of the child;

'unaccompanied child' means a person under the age of 18 ('the child') who is not in the care of a person who—

(a) is aged 18 or over, and

(b) by law or custom of the country or territory in which the child is present, has responsibility for caring for the child.

18 Customs arrangement as part of the framework for the future relationship [repealed by s. 36(b) EUWAA 2020]

19 Future interaction with the law and agencies of the EU [repealed by s. 36(c) EUWAA 2020]

General and final provision

20 Interpretation

(1) In this Act—

'Charter of Fundamental Rights' means the Charter of Fundamental Rights of the European Union of 7 December 2000, as adapted at Strasbourg on 12 December 2007;

'Commons sitting day' means a day on which the House of Commons is sitting (and a day is only a day on which the House of Commons is sitting if the House begins to sit on that day);

'devolved authority' means—

(a) the Scottish Ministers,

(b) the Welsh Ministers, or

(c) a Northern Ireland department;

'domestic law' means—

(a) in sections 3, 7A and 7B, the law of England and Wales, Scotland and Northern Ireland, and

(b) in any other case, the law of England and Wales, Scotland or Northern Ireland;

'the EEA' means the European Economic Area;

'enactment' means an enactment whenever passed or made and includes—

(a) an enactment contained in any Order in Council, order, rules, regulations, scheme, warrant, byelaw or other instrument made under an Act,

(b) an enactment contained in any Order in Council made in exercise of Her Majesty's Prerogative,

(c) an enactment contained in, or in an instrument made under, an Act of the Scottish Parliament,

(d) an enactment contained in, or in an instrument made under, a Measure or Act of the National Assembly for Wales,

(e) an enactment contained in, or in an instrument made under, Northern Ireland legislation,

(f) an enactment contained in any instrument made by a member of the Scottish Government, the Welsh Ministers, the First Minister for Wales, the Counsel General to the Welsh Government, a Northern Ireland Minister, the First Minister in Northern Ireland, the deputy First Minister in Northern Ireland or a Northern Ireland department in exercise of prerogative or other executive functions of Her Majesty which are exercisable by such a person on behalf of Her Majesty,

(g) an enactment contained in, or in an instrument made under, a Measure of the Church Assembly or of the General Synod of the Church of England, and

(h) except in sections 1B and 7 or where there is otherwise a contrary intention, any retained direct EU legislation;

'EU decision' means—

(a) a decision within the meaning of Article 288 of the Treaty on the Functioning of the European Union, or

(b) a decision under former Article 34(2)(c) of the Treaty on European Union;

'EU directive' means a directive within the meaning of Article 288 of the Treaty on the Functioning of the European Union;

'EU entity' means an EU institution or any office, body or agency of the EU;

'EU reference' means—

(a) any reference to the EU, an EU entity or a member State,

(b) any reference to an EU directive or any other EU law, or

(c) any other reference which relates to the EU;

'EU regulation' means a regulation within the meaning of Article 288 of the Treaty on the Functioning of the European Union;

'EU tertiary legislation' means—

(a) any provision made under—

(i) an EU regulation,

(ii) a decision within the meaning of Article 288 of the Treaty on the Functioning of the European Union, or

(iii) an EU directive,

by virtue of Article 290 or 291(2) of the Treaty on the Functioning of the European Union or former Article 202 of the Treaty establishing the European Community, or

(b) any measure adopted in accordance with former Article 34(2)(c) of the Treaty on European Union to implement decisions under former Article 34(2)(c),

but does not include any such provision or measure which is an EU directive;

'exempt EU instrument' means anything which is an exempt EU instrument by virtue of Schedule 6;

'exit day' means 29 March 2019 at 11.00 p.m. (and see subsections (2) to (5));

'Joint Committee' means the Joint Committee established by Article 164(1) of the withdrawal agreement;

'Lords sitting day' means a day on which the House of Lords is sitting (and a day is only a day on which the House of Lords is sitting if the House begins to sit on that day);

'member State' (except in the definitions of 'direct EU legislation' and 'EU reference') does not include the United Kingdom;

'Minister of the Crown' has the same meaning as in the Ministers of the Crown Act 1975 and also includes the Commissioners for Her Majesty's Revenue and Customs;

'modify' includes amend, repeal or revoke (and related expressions are to be read accordingly);

'Northern Ireland devolved authority' means the First Minister and deputy First Minister in Northern Ireland acting jointly, a Northern Ireland Minister or a Northern Ireland department;

'primary legislation' means—

(a) an Act of Parliament,

(b) an Act of the Scottish Parliament,

(c) a Measure or Act of the National Assembly for Wales, or

(d) Northern Ireland legislation;

'public authority' means a public authority within the meaning of section 6 of the Human Rights Act 1998;

'ratify', whether in relation to the withdrawal agreement or otherwise, has the same meaning as it does for the purposes of Part 2 of the Constitutional Reform and Governance Act 2010 in relation to a treaty (see section 25 of that Act);

'relevant criminal offence' means an offence for which an individual who has reached the age of 18 (or, in relation to Scotland or Northern Ireland, 21) is capable of being sentenced to imprisonment for a term of more than 2 years (ignoring any enactment prohibiting or restricting the imprisonment of individuals who have no previous convictions);

'retained direct EU legislation' means any direct EU legislation which forms part of domestic law by virtue of section 3 (as modified by or under this Act or by other domestic law from time to time, and including any instruments made under it on or after IP completion day);

'retrospective provision', in relation to provision made by regulations, means provision taking effect from a date earlier than the date on which the regulations are made;

'subordinate legislation' means—

(a) any Order in Council, order, rules, regulations, scheme, warrant, byelaw or other instrument made under any Act, or

(b) any instrument made under an Act of the Scottish Parliament, Northern Ireland legislation or a Measure or Act of the National Assembly for Wales,

and (except in section 7 or Schedule 2 or where there is a contrary intention) includes any Order in Council, order, rules, regulations, scheme, warrant, byelaw or other instrument made on or after IP completion day under any retained direct EU legislation;

'tribunal' means any tribunal in which legal proceedings may be brought;

'Wales' and 'Welsh zone' have the same meaning as in the Government of Wales Act 2006 (see section 158 of that Act);

(2) In this Act references to before, after or on exit day, or to beginning with exit day, are to be read as references to before, after or at 11.00 p.m. on 29 March 2019 or (as the case may be) to beginning with 11.00 p.m. on that day.

(3) Subsection (4) applies if the day or time on or at which the Treaties are to cease to apply to the United Kingdom in accordance with Article 50(3) of the Treaty on European Union is different from that specified in the definition of 'exit day' in subsection (1).

(4) A Minister of the Crown may by regulations—

(a) amend the definition of 'exit day' in subsection (1) to ensure that the day and time specified in the definition are the day and time that the Treaties are to cease to apply to the United Kingdom, and

(b) amend subsection (2) in consequence of any such amendment.

(5) In subsections (3) and (4) 'the Treaties' means the Treaty on European Union and the Treaty on the Functioning of the European Union.

(5A) In this Act references to anything which continues to be domestic law by virtue of section 1B(2) include—

(a) references to anything to which section 1B(2) applies which continues to be domestic law on or after exit day (whether or not it would have done so irrespective of that provision), and

(b) references to anything which continues to be domestic law on or after exit day by virtue of section 1B(2) (as that body of law is added to or otherwise modified by or under this Act or by other domestic law from time to time).

(6) In this Act references to anything which continues to be domestic law by virtue of section 2 include references to anything to which subsection (1) of that section applies which continues to be domestic law on or after IP completion day (whether or not it would have done so irrespective of that section).

(7) In this Act references to anything which is retained EU law by virtue of section 4 include references to any modifications, made by or under this Act or by other domestic law from time to time, of the rights, powers, liabilities, obligations, restrictions, remedies or procedures concerned.

(8) References in this Act (however expressed) to a public authority in the United Kingdom include references to a public authority in any part of the United Kingdom.

(9) References in this Act to former Article 34(2)(c) of the Treaty on European Union are references to that Article as it had effect at any time before the coming into force of the Treaty of Lisbon.

(10) Any other reference in this Act to—

    (a) an Article of the Treaty on European Union or the Treaty on the Functioning of the European Union, or

    (b) Article 10 of Title VII of Protocol 36 to those treaties,

includes a reference to that Article as applied by Article 106a of the Euratom Treaty.

21 Index of defined expressions [omitted]

22 Regulations

Schedule 7 (which makes provision about the scrutiny by Parliament and the devolved legislatures of regulations under this Act and contains other general provision about such regulations) has effect.

23 Consequential and transitional provision

(1) A Minister of the Crown may by regulations make such provision as the Minister considers appropriate in consequence of this Act.

(2) The power to make regulations under subsection (1) may (among other things) be exercised by modifying any provision made by or under an enactment.

(3) In subsection (2) 'enactment' does not include primary legislation passed or made after IP completion day.

(4) No regulations may be made under subsection (1) after the end of the period of 10 years beginning with IP completion day.

(5) Parts 1 and 2 of Schedule 8 (which contain consequential provision) have effect.

(6) A Minister of the Crown may by regulations make such transitional, transitory or saving provision as the Minister considers appropriate in connection with the coming into force of any provision of this Act (including its operation in connection with IP completion day).

(7) Parts 3 and 4 of Schedule 8 (which contain transitional, transitory and saving provision) have effect.

(8) The enactments mentioned in Schedule 9 (which contains repeals not made elsewhere in this Act) are repealed to the extent specified.

24 Extent

(1) Subject to subsections (2) and (3), this Act extends to England and Wales, Scotland and Northern Ireland.

(2) Any provision of this Act which amends or repeals an enactment has the same extent as the enactment amended or repealed.

(3) Regulations under section 8(1) or 23 may make provision which extends to Gibraltar—

    (a) modifying any enactment which—

        (i) extends to Gibraltar and relates to European Parliamentary elections, or

        (ii) extends to Gibraltar for any purpose which is connected with Gibraltar forming part of an electoral region, under the European Parliamentary Elections Act 2002, for the purposes of such elections, or

(b) which is supplementary, incidental, consequential, transitional, transitory or saving provision in connection with a modification within paragraph (a).

25 Commencement and short title*

(5) This Act may be cited as the European Union (Withdrawal) Act 2018.

Section 5(6)

SCHEDULE 1**

FURTHER PROVISION ABOUT EXCEPTIONS TO SAVINGS AND INCORPORATION

Challenges to validity of retained EU law

1.—(1) There is no right in domestic law on or after IP completion day to challenge any retained EU law on the basis that, immediately before IP completion day an EU instrument was invalid.

(2) Sub-paragraph (1) does not apply so far as—

(a) the European Court has decided before IP completion day that the instrument is invalid, or

(b) the challenge is of a kind described, or provided for, in regulations made by a Minister of the Crown.

(3) Regulations under sub-paragraph (2)(b) may (among other things) provide for a challenge which would otherwise have been against an EU institution to be against a public authority in the United Kingdom.

General principles of EU law

2. No general principle of EU law is part of domestic law on or after IP completion day if it was not recognised as a general principle of EU law by the European Court in a case decided before IP completion day (whether or not as an essential part of the decision in the case).

3.—(1) There is no right of action in domestic law on or after IP completion day based on a failure to comply with any of the general principles of EU law.

(2) No court or tribunal or other public authority may, on or after IP completion day—

(a) disapply or quash any enactment or other rule of law, or

(b) quash any conduct or otherwise decide that it is unlawful,

because it is incompatible with any of the general principles of EU law.

Rule in Francovich

4. There is no right in domestic law on or after IP completion day to damages in accordance with the rule in *Francovich*.

Interpretation

5.—(1) References in section 5 and this Schedule to the principle of the supremacy of EU law, the Charter of Fundamental Rights, any general principle of EU law or the rule in *Francovich* are to be read as references to that principle, Charter or rule so far as it would otherwise continue to be, or form part of, domestic law on or after IP completion day in accordance with this Act.

(2) Accordingly (among other things) the references to the principle of the supremacy of EU law in section 5(2) and (3) do not include anything which would bring into domestic law any modification of EU law which is adopted or notified, comes into force or only applies on or after IP completion day.

---

* **Editor's Note:** Omitted as the 2020 Act has amended this.
** **Editor's Note:** Other Schedules omitted.

Agreement on the Withdrawal of the United Kingdom of Great Britain and Northern Ireland from the European Union and the European Atomic Energy Community*

(Preambles and recitals omitted.)

THE EUROPEAN UNION AND THE EUROPEAN ATOMIC ENERGY COMMUNITY

AND

THE UNITED KINGDOM OF GREAT BRITAIN AND NORTHERN IRELAND, HAVE AGREED AS FOLLOWS:

PART ONE COMMON PROVISIONS

Article 1 Objective
This Agreement sets out the arrangements for the withdrawal of the United Kingdom of Great Britain and Northern Ireland ('United Kingdom') from the European Union ('Union') and from the European Atomic Energy Community ('Euratom').

Article 2 Definitions
For the purposes of this Agreement, the following definitions shall apply:
(a) 'Union law' means:
  (i) the Treaty on European Union ('TEU'), the Treaty on the Functioning of the European Union ('TFEU') and the Treaty establishing the European Atomic Energy Community ('Euratom Treaty'), as amended or supplemented, as well as the Treaties of Accession and the Charter of Fundamental Rights of the European Union, together referred to as 'the Treaties';
  (ii) the general principles of the Union's law;
  (iii) the acts adopted by the institutions, bodies, offices or agencies of the Union;
  (iv) the international agreements to which the Union is party and the international agreements concluded by the Member States acting on behalf of the Union;
  (v) the agreements between Member States entered into in their capacity as Member States of the Union;
  (vi) acts of the Representatives of the Governments of the Member States meeting within the European Council or the Council of the European Union ('Council');
  (vii) the declarations made in the context of intergovernmental conferences which adopted the Treaties;
(b) 'Member States' means the Kingdom of Belgium, the Republic of Bulgaria, the Czech Republic, the Kingdom of Denmark, the Federal Republic of Germany, the Republic of Estonia, Ireland, the Hellenic Republic, the Kingdom of Spain, the French Republic, the Republic of Croatia, the Italian Republic, the Republic of Cyprus, the Republic of Latvia, the Republic of Lithuania, the Grand Duchy of Luxembourg, Hungary, the Republic of Malta, the Kingdom of the Netherlands, the Republic of Austria, the Republic of Poland, the Portuguese Republic, Romania, the Republic of Slovenia, the Slovak Republic, the Republic of Finland and the Kingdom of Sweden;
(c) 'Union citizen' means any person holding the nationality of a Member State;
(d) 'United Kingdom national' means a national of the United Kingdom, as defined in the New Declaration by the Government of the United Kingdom of Great Britain and Northern Ireland of 31 December 1982 on the definition of the term 'nationals' together with Declaration No 63 annexed to the Final Act of the intergovernmental conference which adopted the Treaty of Lisbon;
(e) 'transition period' means the period provided in Article 126;

---

* **Editor's Note:** Selected Extracts (Arts 1–8; 9–29; 40–50; and 86–91). As taken from OJ 2020 L29/7. https://ec.europa.eu/info/relations-united-kingdom/eu-uk-withdrawal-agreement_en.

(f) 'day' means a calendar day, unless otherwise provided in this Agreement or in provisions of Union law made applicable by this Agreement.

Article 3   Territorial scope

1. Unless otherwise provided in this Agreement or in Union law made applicable by this Agreement, any reference in this Agreement to the United Kingdom or its territory shall be understood as referring to:

(a) the United Kingdom;

(b) Gibraltar, to the extent that Union law was applicable to it before the date of entry into force of this Agreement;

(c) the Channel Islands and the Isle of Man, to the extent that Union law was applicable to them before the date of entry into force of this Agreement;

(d) the Sovereign Base Areas of Akrotiri and Dhekelia in Cyprus, to the extent necessary to ensure the implementation of the arrangements set out in the Protocol on the Sovereign Base Areas of the United Kingdom of Great Britain and Northern Ireland in Cyprus annexed to the Act concerning the conditions of accession of the Czech Republic, the Republic of Estonia, the Republic of Cyprus, the Republic of Latvia, the Republic of Lithuania, the Republic of Hungary, the Republic of Malta, the Republic of Poland, the Republic of Slovenia and the Slovak Republic to the European Union;

(e) the overseas countries and territories listed in Annex II to the TFEU having special relations with the United Kingdom, where the provisions of this Agreement relate to the special arrangements for the association of the overseas countries and territories with the Union.

2. Unless otherwise provided in this Agreement or in Union law made applicable by this Agreement, any reference in this Agreement to Member States, or their territory, shall be understood as covering the territories of the Member States to which the Treaties apply as provided in Article 355 TFEU.

Article 4   Methods and principles relating to the effect, the implementation and the application of this Agreement

1. The provisions of this Agreement and the provisions of Union law made applicable by this Agreement shall produce in respect of and in the United Kingdom the same legal effects as those which they produce within the Union and its Member States.

Accordingly, legal or natural persons shall in particular be able to rely directly on the provisions contained or referred to in this Agreement which meet the conditions for direct effect under Union law.

2. The United Kingdom shall ensure compliance with paragraph 1, including as regards the required powers of its judicial and administrative authorities to disapply inconsistent or incompatible domestic provisions, through domestic primary legislation.

3. The provisions of this Agreement referring to Union law or to concepts or provisions thereof shall be interpreted and applied in accordance with the methods and general principles of Union law.

4. The provisions of this Agreement referring to Union law or to concepts or provisions thereof shall in their implementation and application be interpreted in conformity with the relevant case law of the Court of Justice of the European Union handed down before the end of the transition period.

5. In the interpretation and application of this Agreement, the United Kingdom's judicial and administrative authorities shall have due regard to relevant case law of the Court of Justice of the European Union handed down after the end of the transition period.

Article 5   Good faith

The Union and the United Kingdom shall, in full mutual respect and good faith, assist each other in carrying out tasks which flow from this Agreement.

They shall take all appropriate measures, whether general or particular, to ensure fulfilment of the obligations arising from this Agreement and shall refrain from any measures which could jeopardise the attainment of the objectives of this Agreement.

This Article is without prejudice to the application of Union law pursuant to this Agreement, in particular the principle of sincere cooperation.

Article 6   References to Union law

1. With the exception of Parts Four and Five, unless otherwise provided in this Agreement all references in this Agreement to Union law shall be understood as references to Union law, including as amended or replaced, as applicable on the last day of the transition period.

2. Where in this Agreement reference is made to Union acts or provisions thereof, such reference shall, where relevant, be understood to include a reference to Union law or provisions thereof that, although replaced or superseded by the act referred to, continue to apply in accordance with that act.

3. For the purposes of this Agreement, references to provisions of Union law made applicable by this Agreement shall be understood to include references to the relevant Union acts supplementing or implementing those provisions.

Article 7   References to the Union and to Member States

1. For the purposes of this Agreement, all references to Member States and competent authorities of Member States in provisions of Union law made applicable by this Agreement shall be understood as including the United Kingdom and its competent authorities, except as regards:

(a) the nomination, appointment or election of members of the institutions, bodies, offices and agencies of the Union, as well as the participation in the decision-making and the attendance in the meetings of the institutions;

(b) the participation in the decision-making and governance of the bodies, offices and agencies of the Union;

(c) the attendance in the meetings of the committees referred to in Article 3(2) of Regulation (EU) No 182/2011 of the European Parliament and of the Council, of Commission expert groups or of other similar entities, or in the meetings of expert groups or similar entities of bodies, offices and agencies of the Union, unless otherwise provided in this Agreement.

2. Unless otherwise provided in this Agreement, any reference to the Union shall be understood as including Euratom.

Article 8   Access to networks, information systems and databases

Unless otherwise provided in this Agreement, at the end of the transition period the United Kingdom shall cease to be entitled to access any network, any information system and any database established on the basis of Union law. The United Kingdom shall take appropriate measures to ensure that it does not access a network, information system or database which it is no longer entitled to access.

PART TWO   CITIZENS' RIGHTS

Title I   General provisions

Article 9   Definitions

For the purposes of this Part, and without prejudice to Title III, the following definitions shall apply:

(a) 'family members' means the following persons, irrespective of their nationality, who fall within the personal scope provided for in Article 10 of this Agreement:

(i) family members of Union citizens or family members of United Kingdom nationals as defined in point (2) of Article 2 of Directive 2004/38/EC of the European Parliament and of the Council;

(ii) persons other than those defined in Article 3(2) of Directive 2004/38/EC whose presence is required by Union citizens or United Kingdom nationals in order not to deprive those Union citizens or United Kingdom nationals of a right of residence granted by this Part;

(b) 'frontier workers' means Union citizens or United Kingdom nationals who pursue an economic activity in accordance with Article 45 or 49 TFEU in one or more States in which they do not reside;

(c) 'host State' means:

    (i) in respect of Union citizens and their family members, the United Kingdom, if they exercised their right of residence there in accordance with Union law before the end of the transition period and continue to reside there thereafter;

    (ii) in respect of United Kingdom nationals and their family members, the Member State in which they exercised their right of residence in accordance with Union law before the end of the transition period and in which they continue to reside thereafter;

(d) 'State of work' means:

    (i) in respect of Union citizens, the United Kingdom, if they pursued an economic activity as frontier workers there before the end of the transition period and continue to do so thereafter;

    (ii) in respect of United Kingdom nationals, a Member State in which they pursued an economic activity as frontier workers before the end of the transition period and in which they continue to do so thereafter;

(e) 'rights of custody' means rights of custody within the meaning of point (9) of Article 2 of Council Regulation (EC) No 2201/2003, including rights of custody acquired by judgment, by operation of law or by an agreement having legal effect.

Article 10   Personal scope

1. Without prejudice to Title III, this Part shall apply to the following persons:

(a) Union citizens who exercised their right to reside in the United Kingdom in accordance with Union law before the end of the transition period and continue to reside there thereafter;

(b) United Kingdom nationals who exercised their right to reside in a Member State in accordance with Union law before the end of the transition period and continue to reside there thereafter;

(c) Union citizens who exercised their right as frontier workers in the United Kingdom in accordance with Union law before the end of the transition period and continue to do so thereafter;

(d) United Kingdom nationals who exercised their right as frontier workers in one or more Member States in accordance with Union law before the end of the transition period and continue to do so thereafter;

(e) family members of the persons referred to in points (a) to (d), provided that they fulfil one of the following conditions:

    (i) they resided in the host State in accordance with Union law before the end of the transition period and continue to reside there thereafter;

    (ii) they were directly related to a person referred to in points (a) to (d) and resided outside the host State before the end of the transition period, provided that they fulfil the conditions set out in point (2) of Article 2 of Directive 2004/38/EC at the time they seek residence under this Part in order to join the person referred to in points (a) to (d) of this paragraph;

    (iii) they were born to, or legally adopted by, persons referred to in points (a) to (d) after the end of the transition period, whether inside or outside the host State, and fulfil the conditions set out in point (2)(c) of Article 2 of Directive 2004/38/EC at the time they seek residence under this Part in order to join the person referred to in points (a) to (d) of this paragraph and fulfil one of the following conditions:

      – both parents are persons referred to in points (a) to (d);

      – one parent is a person referred to in points (a) to (d) and the other is a national of the host State; or

– one parent is a person referred to in points (a) to (d) and has sole or joint rights of custody of the child, in accordance with the applicable rules of family law of a Member State or of the United Kingdom, including applicable rules of private international law under which rights of custody established under the law of a third State are recognised in the Member State or in the United Kingdom, in particular as regards the best interests of the child, and without prejudice to the normal operation of such applicable rules of private international law;

(f) family members who resided in the host State in accordance with Articles 12 and 13, Article 16(2) and Articles 17 and 18 of Directive 2004/38/EC before the end of the transition period and continue to reside there thereafter.

2. Persons falling under points (a) and (b) of Article 3(2) of Directive 2004/38/EC whose residence was facilitated by the host State in accordance with its national legislation before the end of the transition period in accordance with Article 3(2) of that Directive shall retain their right of residence in the host State in accordance with this Part, provided that they continue to reside in the host State thereafter.

3. Paragraph 2 shall also apply to persons falling under points (a) and (b) of Article 3(2) of Directive 2004/38/EC who have applied for facilitation of entry and residence before the end of the transition period, and whose residence is being facilitated by the host State in accordance with its national legislation thereafter.

4. Without prejudice to any right to residence which the persons concerned may have in their own right, the host State shall, in accordance with its national legislation and in accordance with point (b) of Article 3(2) of Directive 2004/38/EC, facilitate entry and residence for the partner with whom the person referred to in points (a) to (d) of paragraph 1 of this Article has a durable relationship, duly attested, where that partner resided outside the host State before the end of the transition period, provided that the relationship was durable before the end of the transition period and continues at the time the partner seeks residence under this Part.

5. In the cases referred to in paragraphs 3 and 4, the host State shall undertake an extensive examination of the personal circumstances of the persons concerned and shall justify any denial of entry or residence to such persons.

Article 11   Continuity of residence

Continuity of residence for the purposes of Articles 9 and 10 shall not be affected by absences as referred to in Article 15(2).

The right of permanent residence acquired under Directive 2004/38/EC before the end of the transition period shall not be treated as lost through absence from the host State for a period specified in Article 15(3).

Article 12   Non-discrimination

Within the scope of this Part, and without prejudice to any special provisions contained therein, any discrimination on grounds of nationality within the meaning of the first subparagraph of Article 18 TFEU shall be prohibited in the host State and the State of work in respect of the persons referred to in Article 10 of this Agreement.

Title II Rights and obligations

Chapter 1 Rights related to residence, residence documents

Article 13   Residence rights

1. Union citizens and United Kingdom nationals shall have the right to reside in the host State under the limitations and conditions as set out in Articles 21, 45 or 49 TFEU and in Article 6(1), points (a), (b) or (c) of Article 7(1), Article 7(3), Article 14, Article 16(1) or Article 17(1) of Directive 2004/38/EC.

2. Family members who are either Union citizens or United Kingdom nationals shall have the right to reside in the host State as set out in Article 21 TFEU and in Article 6(1), point (d) of Article 7(1), Article 12(1) or (3), Article 13(1), Article 14, Article 16(1) or 17(3) and (4) of Directive 2004/38/EC, subject to the limitations and conditions set out in those provisions.

3. Family members who are neither Union citizens nor United Kingdom nationals shall have the right to reside in the host State under Article 21 TFEU and as set out in Article 6(2), Article 7(2), Article 12(2) or (3), Article 13(2), Article 14, Article 16(2), Article 17(3) or (4) or Article 18 of Directive 2004/38/EC, subject to the limitations and conditions set out in those provisions.

4. The host State may not impose any limitations or conditions for obtaining, retaining or losing residence rights on the persons referred to in paragraphs 1, 2 and 3, other than those provided for in this Title. There shall be no discretion in applying the limitations and conditions provided for in this Title, other than in favour of the person concerned.

Article 14   Right of exit and of entry

1. Union citizens and United Kingdom nationals, their respective family members, and other persons, who reside in the territory of the host State in accordance with the conditions set out in this Title shall have the right to leave the host State and the right to enter it, as set out in Article 4(1) and the first subparagraph of Article 5(1) of Directive 2004/38/EC, with a valid passport or national identity card in the case of Union citizens and United Kingdom nationals, and with a valid passport in the case of their respective family members and other persons who are not Union citizens or United Kingdom nationals.

Five years after the end of the transition period, the host State may decide no longer to accept national identity cards for the purposes of entry to or exit from its territory if such cards do not include a chip that complies with the applicable International Civil Aviation Organisation standards related to biometric identification.

2. No exit visa, entry visa or equivalent formality shall be required of holders of a valid document issued in accordance with Article 18 or 26.

3. Where the host State requires family members who join the Union citizen or United Kingdom national after the end of the transition period to have an entry visa, the host State shall grant such persons every facility to obtain the necessary visas. Such visas shall be issued free of charge as soon as possible, and on the basis of an accelerated procedure.

Article 15   Right of permanent residence

1. Union citizens and United Kingdom nationals, and their respective family members, who have resided legally in the host State in accordance with Union law for a continuous period of 5 years or for the period specified in Article 17 of Directive 2004/38/EC, shall have the right to reside permanently in the host State under the conditions set out in Articles 16, 17 and 18 of Directive 2004/38/EC. Periods of legal residence or work in accordance with Union law before and after the end of the transition period shall be included in the calculation of the qualifying period necessary for acquisition of the right of permanent residence.

2. Continuity of residence for the purposes of acquisition of the right of permanent residence shall be determined in accordance with Article 16(3) and Article 21 of Directive 2004/38/EC.

3. Once acquired, the right of permanent residence shall be lost only through absence from the host State for a period exceeding 5 consecutive years.

Article 16   Accumulation of periods

Union citizens and United Kingdom nationals, and their respective family members, who before the end of the transition period resided legally in the host State in accordance with the conditions of Article 7 of Directive 2004/38/EC for a period of less than 5 years, shall have the right to acquire the right to reside permanently under the conditions set out in Article 15 of this Agreement once they have completed the necessary periods of residence. Periods of legal residence or work in accordance with Union law before and after the end of the transition period shall be included in the calculation of the qualifying period necessary for acquisition of the right of permanent residence.

Article 17   Status and changes

1. The right of Union citizens and United Kingdom nationals, and their respective family members, to rely directly on this Part shall not be affected when they change status, for example between student, worker, self-employed person and economically inactive person. Persons who, at the end of the transition period, enjoy a right of residence in their capacity as family members of Union citizens or United Kingdom nationals, cannot become persons referred to in points (a) to (d) of Article 10(1).

2. The rights provided for in this Title for the family members who are dependants of Union citizens or United Kingdom nationals before the end of the transition period, shall be maintained even after they cease to be dependants.

Article 18   Issuance of residence documents

1. The host State may require Union citizens or United Kingdom nationals, their respective family members and other persons, who reside in its territory in accordance with the conditions set out in this Title, to apply for a new residence status which confers the rights under this Title and a document evidencing such status which may be in a digital form.

Applying for such a residence status shall be subject to the following conditions:

(a) the purpose of the application procedure shall be to verify whether the applicant is entitled to the residence rights set out in this Title. Where that is the case, the applicant shall have a right to be granted the residence status and the document evidencing that status;

(b) the deadline for submitting the application shall not be less than 6 months from the end of the transition period, for persons residing in the host State before the end of the transition period.

For persons who have the right to commence residence after the end of the transition period in the host State in accordance with this Title, the deadline for submitting the application shall be 3 months after their arrival or the expiry of the deadline referred to in the first subparagraph, whichever is later.

A certificate of application for the residence status shall be issued immediately;

(c) the deadline for submitting the application referred to in point (b) shall be extended automatically by 1 year where the Union has notified the United Kingdom, or the United Kingdom has notified the Union, that technical problems prevent the host State either from registering the application or from issuing the certificate of application referred to in point (b). The host State shall publish that notification and shall provide appropriate public information for the persons concerned in good time;

(d) where the deadline for submitting the application referred to in point (b) is not respected by the persons concerned, the competent authorities shall assess all the circumstances and reasons for not respecting the deadline and shall allow those persons to submit an application within a reasonable further period of time if there are reasonable grounds for the failure to respect the deadline;

(e) the host State shall ensure that any administrative procedures for applications are smooth, transparent and simple, and that any unnecessary administrative burdens are avoided;

(f) application forms shall be short, simple, user friendly and adapted to the context of this Agreement; applications made by families at the same time shall be considered together;

(g) the document evidencing the status shall be issued free of charge or for a charge not exceeding that imposed on citizens or nationals of the host State for the issuing of similar documents;

(h) persons who, before the end of the transition period, hold a valid permanent residence document issued under Article 19 or 20 of Directive 2004/38/EC or hold a valid domestic immigration document conferring a permanent right to reside in the host State, shall have the right to exchange that document within the period referred to in point (b) of this paragraph for a new residence document upon application after a verification of their identity, a criminality and security check in accordance with point (p) of this paragraph and confirmation of their ongoing residence; such new residence documents shall be issued free of charge;

(i) the identity of the applicants shall be verified through the presentation of a valid passport or national identity card for Union citizens and United Kingdom nationals, and through the presentation of a valid passport for their respective family members and other persons who are not Union citizens or United Kingdom nationals; the acceptance of such identity documents shall not be made conditional upon any criteria other than that of the validity of the document. Where the identity document is retained by the competent authorities of the host State while the application is pending, the host State shall return that document upon application without delay, before the decision on the application has been taken;

(j) supporting documents other than identity documents, such as civil status documents, may be submitted in copy. Originals of supporting documents may be required only in specific cases where there is a reasonable doubt as to the authenticity of the supporting documents submitted;

(k) the host State may only require Union citizens and United Kingdom nationals to present, in addition to the identity documents referred to in point (i) of this paragraph, the following supporting documents as referred to in Article 8(3) of Directive 2004/38/EC:

(i) where they reside in the host State in accordance with point (a) of Article 7(1) of Directive 2004/38/EC as workers or self-employed, a confirmation of engagement from the employer or a certificate of employment, or proof that they are self-employed;

(ii) where they reside in the host State in accordance with point (b) of Article 7(1) of Directive 2004/38/EC as economically inactive persons, evidence that they have sufficient resources for themselves and their family members not to become a burden on the social assistance system of the host State during their period of residence and that they have comprehensive sickness insurance cover in the host State; or

(iii) where they reside in the host State in accordance with point (c) of Article 7(1) of Directive 2004/38/EC as students, proof of enrolment at an establishment accredited or financed by the host State on the basis of its legislation or administrative practice, proof of comprehensive sickness insurance cover, and a declaration or equivalent means of proof, that they have sufficient resources for themselves and their family members not to become a burden on the social assistance system of the host State during their period of residence. The host State may not require such declarations to refer to any specific amount of resources.

With regard to the condition of sufficient resources, Article 8(4) of Directive 2004/38/EC shall apply;

(l) the host State may only require family members who fall under point (e)(i) of Article 10(1) or Article 10(2) or (3) of this Agreement and who reside in the host State in accordance with point (d) of Article 7(1) or Article 7(2) of Directive 2004/38/EC to present, in addition to the identity documents referred to in point (i) of this paragraph, the following supporting documents as referred to in Article 8(5) or 10(2) of Directive 2004/38/EC:

(i) a document attesting to the existence of a family relationship or registered partnership;

(ii) the registration certificate or, in the absence of a registration system, any other proof that the Union citizen or the United Kingdom national with whom they reside actually resides in the host State;

(iii) for direct descendants who are under the age of 21 or who are dependants and dependent direct relatives in the ascending line, and for those of the spouse or registered partner, documentary evidence that the conditions set out in point (c) or (d) of Article 2(2) of Directive 2004/38/EC are fulfilled;

(iv) for the persons referred to in Article 10(2) or (3) of this Agreement, a document issued by the relevant authority in the host State in accordance with Article 3(2) of Directive 2004/38/EC.

With regard to the condition of sufficient resources as concerns family members who are themselves Union citizens or United Kingdom nationals, Article 8(4) of Directive 2004/38/EC shall apply;

(m) the host State may only require family members who fall under point (e)(ii) of Article 10(1) or Article 10(4) of this Agreement to present, in addition to the identity documents referred to in point (i) of this paragraph, the following supporting documents as referred to in Articles 8(5) and 10(2) of Directive 2004/38/EC:

  (i)   a document attesting to the existence of a family relationship or of a registered partnership;

  (ii) the registration certificate or, in the absence of a registration system, any other proof of residence in the host State of the Union citizen or of the United Kingdom nationals whom they are joining in the host State;

  (iii) for spouses or registered partners, a document attesting to the existence of a family relationship or a registered partnership before the end of the transition period;

  (iv) for direct descendants who are under the age of 21 or who are dependants and dependent direct relatives in the ascending line and those of the spouse or registered partner, documentary evidence that they were related to Union citizens or United Kingdom nationals before the end of the transition period and fulfil the conditions set out in point (c) or (d) of Article 2(2) of Directive 2004/38/EC relating to age or dependence;

  (v)   for the persons referred to in Article 10(4) of this Agreement, proof that a durable relationship with Union citizens or United Kingdom nationals existed before the end of the transition period and continues to exist thereafter;

(n) for cases other than those set out in points (k), (l) and (m), the host State shall not require applicants to present supporting documents that go beyond what is strictly necessary and proportionate to provide evidence that the conditions relating to the right of residence under this Title have been fulfilled;

(o) the competent authorities of the host State shall help the applicants to prove their eligibility and to avoid any errors or omissions in their applications; they shall give the applicants the opportunity to furnish supplementary evidence and to correct any deficiencies, errors or omissions;

(p) criminality and security checks may be carried out systematically on applicants, with the exclusive aim of verifying whether the restrictions set out in Article 20 of this Agreement may be applicable. For that purpose, applicants may be required to declare past criminal convictions which appear in their criminal record in accordance with the law of the State of conviction at the time of the application. The host State may, if it considers this essential, apply the procedure set out in Article 27(3) of Directive 2004/38/EC with respect to enquiries to other States regarding previous criminal records;

(q) the new residence document shall include a statement that it has been issued in accordance with this Agreement;

(r) the applicant shall have access to judicial and, where appropriate, administrative redress procedures in the host State against any decision refusing to grant the residence status. The redress procedures shall allow for an examination of the legality of the decision, as well as of the facts and circumstances on which the proposed decision is based. Such redress procedures shall ensure that the decision is not disproportionate.

2. During the period referred to in point (b) of paragraph 1 of this Article and its possible one-year extension under point (c) of that paragraph, all rights provided for in this Part shall be deemed to apply to Union citizens or United Kingdom nationals, their respective family members, and other persons residing in the host State, in accordance with the conditions and subject to the restrictions set out in Article 20.

3. Pending a final decision by the competent authorities on any application referred to in paragraph 1, and pending a final judgment handed down in case of judicial redress sought against any rejection of such application by the competent administrative authorities, all rights provided for in

this Part shall be deemed to apply to the applicant, including Article 21 on safeguards and right of appeal, subject to the conditions set out in Article 20(4).

4. Where a host State has chosen not to require Union citizens or United Kingdom nationals, their family members, and other persons, residing in its territory in accordance with the conditions set out in this Title, to apply for the new residence status referred to in paragraph 1 as a condition for legal residence, those eligible for residence rights under this Title shall have the right to receive, in accordance with the conditions set out in Directive 2004/38/EC, a residence document, which may be in a digital form, that includes a statement that it has been issued in accordance with this Agreement.

Article 19   Issuance of residence documents during the transition period

1. During the transition period, a host State may allow applications for a residence status or residence document as referred to in Article 18(1) and (4) to be made voluntarily from the date of entry into force of this Agreement.

2. Decisions to accept or refuse such applications shall be taken in accordance with Article 18(1) and (4). Decisions under Article 18(1) shall have no effect until after the end of the transition period.

3. If an application under Article 18(1) is accepted before the end of the transition period, the host State may not withdraw the decision granting the residence status before the end of the transition period on any grounds other than those set out in Chapter VI and Article 35 of Directive 2004/38/EC.

4. If an application is refused before the end of the transition period, the applicant may apply again at any time before the expiry of the period set out in point (b) of Article 18(1).

5. Without prejudice to paragraph 4, the redress procedures under point (r) of Article 18(1) shall be available from the date of any decision to refuse an application referred to in paragraph 2 of this Article.

Article 20   Restrictions of the rights of residence and entry

1. The conduct of Union citizens or United Kingdom nationals, their family members, and other persons, who exercise rights under this Title, where that conduct occurred before the end of the transition period, shall be considered in accordance with Chapter VI of Directive 2004/38/EC.

2. The conduct of Union citizens or United Kingdom nationals, their family members, and other persons, who exercise rights under this Title, where that conduct occurred after the end of the transition period, may constitute grounds for restricting the right of residence by the host State or the right of entry in the State of work in accordance with national legislation.

3. The host State or the State of work may adopt the necessary measures to refuse, terminate or withdraw any right conferred by this Title in the case of the abuse of those rights or fraud, as set out in Article 35 of Directive 2004/38/EC. Such measures shall be subject to the procedural safeguards provided for in Article 21 of this Agreement.

4. The host State or the State of work may remove applicants who submitted fraudulent or abusive applications from its territory under the conditions set out in Directive 2004/38/EC, in particular Articles 31 and 35 thereof, even before a final judgment has been handed down in the case of judicial redress sought against any rejection of such an application.

Article 21   Safeguards and right of appeal

The safeguards set out in Article 15 and Chapter VI of Directive 2004/38/EC shall apply in respect of any decision by the host State that restricts residence rights of the persons referred to in Article 10 of this Agreement.

Article 22   Related rights

In accordance with Article 23 of Directive 2004/38/EC, irrespective of nationality, the family members of a Union citizen or United Kingdom national who have the right of residence or the right of permanent residence in the host State or the State of work shall be entitled to take up employment or self-employment there.

Article 23 Equal treatment

1. In accordance with Article 24 of Directive 2004/38/EC, subject to the specific provisions provided for in this Title and Titles I and IV of this Part, all Union citizens or United Kingdom nationals residing on the basis of this Agreement in the territory of the host State shall enjoy equal treatment with the nationals of that State within the scope of this Part. The benefit of this right shall be extended to those family members of Union citizens or United Kingdom nationals who have the right of residence or permanent residence.

2. By way of derogation from paragraph 1, the host State shall not be obliged to confer entitlement to social assistance during periods of residence on the basis of Article 6 or point (b) of Article 14(4) of Directive 2004/38/EC, nor shall it be obliged, prior to a person's acquisition of the right of permanent residence in accordance with Article 15 of this Agreement, to grant maintenance aid for studies, including vocational training, consisting in student grants or student loans to persons other than workers, self-employed persons, persons who retain such status or to members of their families.

Chapter 2 Rights of workers and self-employed persons

Article 24 Rights of workers

1. Subject to the limitations set out in Article 45(3) and (4) TFEU, workers in the host State and frontier workers in the State or States of work shall enjoy the rights guaranteed by Article 45 TFEU and the rights granted by Regulation (EU) No 492/2011 of the European Parliament and of the Council. These rights include:

  (a) the right not to be discriminated against on grounds of nationality as regards employment, remuneration and other conditions of work and employment;
  (b) the right to take up and pursue an activity in accordance with the rules applicable to the nationals of the host State or the State of work;
  (c) the right to assistance afforded by the employment offices of the host State or the State of work as offered to own nationals;
  (d) the right to equal treatment in respect of conditions of employment and work, in particular as regards remuneration, dismissal and in case of unemployment, reinstatement or re-employment;
  (e) the right to social and tax advantages;
  (f) collective rights;
  (g) the rights and benefits accorded to national workers in matters of housing;
  (h) the right for their children to be admitted to the general educational, apprenticeship and vocational training courses under the same conditions as the nationals of the host State or the State of work, if such children are residing in the territory where the worker works.

2. Where a direct descendant of a worker who has ceased to reside in the host State is in education in that State, the primary carer for that descendant shall have the right to reside in that State until the descendant reaches the age of majority, and after the age of majority if that descendant continues to need the presence and care of the primary carer in order to pursue and complete his or her education.

3. Employed frontier workers shall enjoy the right to enter and exit the State of work in accordance with Article 14 of this Agreement and shall retain the rights they enjoyed as workers there, provided they are in one of the circumstances set out in points (a), (b), (c) and (d) of Article 7(3) of Directive 2004/38/EC, even where they do not move their residence to the State of work.

Article 25 Rights of self-employed persons

1. Subject to the limitations set out in Articles 51 and 52 TFEU, self-employed persons in the host State and self-employed frontier workers in the State or States of work shall enjoy the rights guaranteed by Articles 49 and 55 TFEU. These rights include:

(a) the right to take up and pursue activities as self-employed persons and to set up and man-age undertakings under the conditions laid down by the host State for its own nationals, as set out in Article 49 TFEU;

(b) the rights as set out in points (c) to (h) of Article 24(1) of this Agreement.

2. Article 24(2) shall apply to direct descendants of self-employed workers.

3. Article 24(3) shall apply to self-employed frontier workers.

Article 26   Issuance of a document identifying frontier workers' rights

The State of work may require Union citizens and United Kingdom nationals who have rights as frontier workers under this Title to apply for a document certifying that they have such rights under this Title. Such Union citizens and United Kingdom nationals shall have the right to be issued with such a document.

Chapter 3 Professional qualifications

Article 27   Recognised professional qualifications

1. The recognition, before the end of the transition period, of professional qualifications, as defined in point (b) of Article 3(1) of Directive 2005/36/EC of the European Parliament and of the Council, of Union citizens or United Kingdom nationals, and their family members, by their host State or their State of work shall maintain its effects in the respective State, including the right to pursue their profession under the same conditions as its nationals, where such recognition was made in accordance with any of the following provisions:

(a) Title III of Directive 2005/36/EC in respect of the recognition of professional qualifica-tions in the context of the exercise of the freedom of establishment, whether such rec-ognition fell under the general system for the recognition of evidence of training, the system for the recognition of professional experience or the system for the recognition on the basis of coordination of minimum training conditions;

(b) Article 10(1) and (3) of Directive 98/5/EC of the European Parliament and of the Council in respect of gaining admission to the profession of lawyer in the host State or State of work;

(c) Article 14 of Directive 2006/43/EC of the European Parliament and of the Council in respect of the approval of statutory auditors from another Member State;

(d) Council Directive 74/556/EEC in respect of the acceptance of evidence of the knowledge and ability necessary to take up or pursue the activities of self-employed persons and of intermediaries engaging in the trade and distribution of toxic products or activities in-volving the professional use of toxic products.

2. Recognitions of professional qualifications for the purposes of point (a) of paragraph 1 of this Article shall include:

(a) recognitions of professional qualifications which have benefited from Article 3(3) of Directive 2005/36/EC;

(b) decisions granting partial access to a professional activity in accordance with Article 4f of Directive 2005/36/EC;

(c) recognitions of professional qualifications for establishment purposes made under Article 4d of Directive 2005/36/EC.

Article 28   Ongoing procedures on the recognition of professional qualifications

Article 4, Article 4d in respect of recognitions of professional qualifications for establishment purposes, Article 4f and Title III of Directive 2005/36/EC, Article 10(1), (3) and (4) of Directive 98/5/EC, Article 14 of Directive 2006/43/EC and Directive 74/556/EEC shall apply in respect of the examination by a competent authority of the host State or State of work of any application for the recognition of professional qualifications introduced before the end of the transition period by Union citizens or United Kingdom nationals and in respect of the decision on any such application.

Articles 4a, 4b and 4e of Directive 2005/36/EC shall also apply to the extent relevant for the completion of the procedures for the recognitions of professional qualifications for establishment purposes under Article 4d of that Directive.

Article 29   Administrative cooperation on recognition of professional qualifications

1. With regard to the pending applications referred to in Article 28, the United Kingdom and the Member States shall cooperate in order to facilitate the application of Article 28. Cooperation may include the exchange of information, including information on disciplinary action or criminal sanctions taken or any other serious and specific circumstances which are likely to have consequences for the pursuit of the activities falling under the Directives referred to in Article 28.

2. By way of derogation from Article 8, for a period not exceeding 9 months from the end of the transition period, the United Kingdom shall be entitled to use the internal market information system in respect of applications referred to in Article 28 insofar as they concern procedures for the recognition of professional qualifications for establishment purposes under Article 4d of Directive 2005/36/EC.

PART THREE SEPARATION PROVISIONS

Title I Goods placed on the market

Article 40   Definitions

For the purposes of this Title, the following definitions shall apply:

    (a) 'making available on the market' means any supply of a good for distribution, consumption or use on the market in the course of a commercial activity, whether in return for payment or free of charge;

    (b) 'placing on the market' means the first making available of a good on the market in the Union or the United Kingdom;

    (c) 'supply of a good for distribution, consumption or use' means that an existing and individually identifiable good, after the stage of manufacturing has taken place, is the subject matter of a written or verbal agreement between two or more legal or natural persons for the transfer of ownership, any other property right, or possession concerning the good in question, or is the subject matter of an offer to a legal or natural person or persons to conclude such an agreement;

    (d) 'putting into service' means the first use of a good within the Union or the United Kingdom by the end user for the purposes for which it was intended or, in the case of marine equipment, placing on board;

    (e) 'market surveillance' means the activities carried out and measures taken by market surveillance authorities to ensure that goods comply with the applicable requirements and do not endanger health, safety or any other aspect of public interest protection;

    (f) 'market surveillance authority' means an authority of a Member State or of the United Kingdom responsible for carrying out market surveillance on its territory;

    (g) 'conditions for the marketing of goods' means requirements concerning the characteristics of goods such as levels of quality, performance, safety or dimensions, including on the composition of such goods or on the terminology, symbols, testing and testing methods, packaging, marking, labelling, and conformity assessment procedures used in relation to such goods; the term also covers requirements concerning production methods and processes, where these have an effect on product characteristics;

    (h) 'conformity assessment body' means a body that performs conformity assessment activities including calibration, testing, certification and inspection;

    (i) 'notified body' means a conformity assessment body authorised to carry out third-party conformity assessment tasks under Union law harmonising the conditions for the marketing of goods;

(j) 'animal products' means products of animal origin, animal by-products and derived products, as referred to in points (29), (30) and (31) of Article 4 of Regulation (EU) 2016/429 of the European Parliament and of the Council, respectively, feed of animal origin, and food and feed containing products of animal origin.

Article 41   Continued circulation of goods placed on the market

1. Any good that was lawfully placed on the market in the Union or the United Kingdom before the end of the transition period may:

   (a) be further made available on the market of the Union or of the United Kingdom and circulate between these two markets until it reaches its end-user;

   (b) where provided in the applicable provisions of Union law, be put into service in the Union or in the United Kingdom.

2. The requirements set out in Articles 34 and 35 TFEU and the relevant Union law governing the marketing of goods, including the conditions for the marketing of goods, applicable to the goods concerned shall apply in respect of the goods referred to in paragraph 1.

3. Paragraph 1 shall apply to all existing and individually identifiable goods within the meaning of Title II of Part Three of the TFEU, with the exception of the circulation between the Union market and the United Kingdom's market or vice-versa of:

   (a) live animals and germinal products;

   (b) animal products.

4. In respect of a movement of live animals or of germinal products between a Member State and the United Kingdom, or vice-versa, the provisions of Union law listed in Annex II shall apply, provided that the date of departure was before the end of the transition period.

5. This Article shall be without prejudice to the possibility for the United Kingdom, a Member State or the Union to take measures to prohibit or restrict the making available on its market of a good referred to in paragraph 1, or a category of such goods, where and to the extent permitted by Union law.

6. The provisions of this Title shall be without prejudice to any applicable rules on modalities of sale, intellectual property, customs procedures, tariffs and taxes.

Article 42   Proof of placing on the market

Where an economic operator relies on Article 41(1) with respect to a specific good, that operator shall bear the burden of proof of demonstrating, on the basis of any relevant document, that the good was placed on the market in the Union or the United Kingdom before the end of the transition period.

Article 43   Market surveillance

1. The market surveillance authorities of the Member States and the market surveillance authorities of the United Kingdom shall exchange without delay any relevant information collected with regard to the goods referred to in Article 41(1) in the context of their respective market surveillance activities. They shall, in particular, communicate to each other and to the European Commission any information relating to those goods presenting a serious risk, as well as any measures taken in relation to non-compliant goods, including relevant information drawn from networks, information systems and databases established under Union or United Kingdom law in relation to those goods.

2. The Member States and the United Kingdom shall transmit without delay any request from the market surveillance authorities of the United Kingdom or of a Member State, respectively, to a conformity assessment body established in their territory, where that request concerns a conformity assessment carried out by that body in its capacity as notified body before the end of the transition period. Member States and the United Kingdom shall ensure that any such request is promptly addressed by the conformity assessment body.

Article 44   Transfer of files and documents relating to ongoing procedures

The United Kingdom shall transfer without delay to the competent authority of a Member State designated in accordance with the procedures provided for in the applicable Union law all relevant files or documents in relation to assessments, approvals and authorisations ongoing on the day before the date of entry into force of this Agreement and led by a United Kingdom competent authority in accordance with Regulation (EU) No 528/2012, Regulation (EC) No 1107/2009, Directive 2001/83/EC and Directive 2001/82/EC of the European Parliament and of the Council.

Article 45   Making available of information in relation to past authorisation procedures for medicinal products

1. The United Kingdom shall, upon a reasoned request from a Member State or the European Medicines Agency, make available without delay the marketing authorisation dossier of a medicinal product authorised by a competent authority of the United Kingdom before the end of the transition period, where that dossier is necessary for the assessment of a marketing authorisation application in accordance with Articles 10 and 10a of Directive 2001/83/EC or Articles 13 and 13a of Directive 2001/82/EC.

2. A Member State shall, upon a reasoned request from the United Kingdom, make available without delay the marketing authorisation dossier of a medicinal product authorised by a competent authority of that Member State before the end of the transition period, where that dossier is necessary for the assessment of a marketing authorisation application in the United Kingdom in accordance with the United Kingdom's legislative requirements, to the extent that those legislative requirements replicate the circumstances of Articles 10 and 10a of Directive 2001/83/EC or Articles 13 and 13a of Directive 2001/82/EC.

Article 46   Making available of information held by notified bodies established in the United Kingdom or in a Member State

1. The United Kingdom shall ensure that information held by a conformity assessment body established in the United Kingdom in relation to its activities as a notified body under Union law before the end of the transition period is made available at the request of the certificate holder, without delay, to a notified body established in a Member State as indicated by the certificate holder.

2. Member States shall ensure that information held by a notified body established in the Member State concerned in relation to its activities before the end of the transition period is made available at the request of the certificate holder, without delay, to a conformity assessment body established in the United Kingdom as indicated by the certificate holder.

Title II Ongoing customs procedures

Article 47   Union status of goods

1. Regulation (EU) No 952/2013 of the European Parliament and of the Council shall apply in respect of Union goods referred to in point (23) of Article 5 of that Regulation, where such goods move from the customs territory of the United Kingdom to the customs territory of the Union, or vice versa, provided that the movement started before the end of the transition period and ended thereafter. A movement of goods which has started before the end of the transition period and ends thereafter shall be treated as an intra-Union movement regarding importation and exportation licencing requirements in Union law.

2. For the purposes of paragraph 1, the presumption of the customs status of Union goods as referred to in Article 153(1) of Regulation (EU) No 952/2013 shall not apply. The customs status of those goods as Union goods, as well as the fact that the movement referred to in paragraph 1 started before the end of the transition period, shall need to be proven for every movement by the person concerned by any of the means referred to in Article 199 of Commission Implementing Regulation (EU) 2015/2447. The proof of the start of the movement shall be provided by means of a transport document relating to the goods.

3. Paragraph 2 shall not apply in respect of Union goods that are carried by air and have been loaded or transhipped at an airport in the customs territory of the United Kingdom for consignment to the customs territory of the Union or have been loaded or transhipped at an airport in the customs territory of the Union for consignment to the customs territory of the United Kingdom, where such goods are carried under cover of a single transport document issued in either of the customs territories concerned, provided that the movement by air started before the end of the transition period and the movement ended thereafter.

4. Paragraph 2 shall not apply in respect of Union goods that are carried by sea and have been shipped between ports in the customs territory of the United Kingdom and ports in the customs territory of the Union by a regular shipping service, as referred to in Article 120 of Commission Delegated Regulation (EU) 2015/2446, provided that:

    (a) the voyage comprising the ports in the customs territory of the United Kingdom and ports in the customs territory of the Union started before the end of the transition period and ended thereafter; and

    (b) the regular shipping service vessel called at one or several ports in the customs territory of the United Kingdom or in the customs territory of the Union before the end of the transition period.

5. When during the voyage referred to in point (a) of paragraph 4 the regular shipping service vessel calls at one or several ports in the customs territory of the United Kingdom after the end of the transition period:

    (a) for goods loaded before the end of the transition period and unloaded in those ports, the customs status of Union goods shall not be altered;

    (b) for goods loaded in ports called after the end of the transition period, the customs status of Union goods shall not be altered provided that it is proven in accordance with paragraph 2.

Article 48   Entry summary declaration and pre-departure declaration

1. Regulation (EU) No 952/2013 shall apply in respect of entry summary declarations that were lodged at a customs office of first entry in accordance with Chapter I of Title IV of that Regulation before the end of the transition period, and those declarations shall produce the same legal effects in the customs territory of the Union and the customs territory of the United Kingdom after the end of the transition period.

2. Regulation (EU) No 952/2013 shall apply in respect of pre-departure declarations that were lodged in accordance with Chapter I of Title VIII of that Regulation before the end of the transition period and, where applicable, where the goods were released in accordance with Article 194 of that Regulation before the end of the transition period. Those declarations shall produce the same legal effects in the customs territory of the Union and the customs territory of the United Kingdom after the end of the transition period.

Article 49   Ending of temporary storage or customs procedures

1. Regulation (EU) No 952/2013 shall apply in respect of non-Union goods that were in temporary storage referred to in point (17) of Article 5 of that Regulation at the end of the transition period and in respect of goods that were under any of the customs procedures referred to in point (16) of Article 5 of that Regulation in the customs territory of the United Kingdom at the end of the transition period, until such temporary storage is ended, until one of the special customs procedures is discharged, until the goods are released for free circulation, or until the goods are taken out of the territory, provided that such event occurs after the end of the transition period but not later than within the corresponding time limit referred to in Annex III.

However, points (b) and (c) of Article 148(5) and Article 219 of Regulation (EU) No 952/2013 shall not apply in respect of movements of goods between the customs territory of the United Kingdom and the customs territory of the Union which end after the end of the transition period.

2. Regulation (EU) No 952/2013, Council Decision 2014/335/EU, Euratom, Council Regulation (EU, Euratom) No 608/2014 and Council Regulation (EU, Euratom) No 609/2014 shall apply in respect of any customs debt arising after the end of the transition period from the end of temporary storage or discharge referred to in paragraph 1.

3. Section 1 of Chapter 1 of Title II of Implementing Regulation (EU) 2015/2447 shall apply in respect of requests to benefit from tariff quotas which have been accepted by the customs authorities in the customs territory of the United Kingdom and where the required supporting documents have been provided in accordance with Article 50 of that Regulation by the customs authorities in the customs territory of the United Kingdom before the end of the transition period, and shall apply in respect of the cancellation of requests and returns of unused allocated quantities of such requests.

Article 50   Access to relevant networks, information systems and databases

By way of derogation from Article 8, the United Kingdom shall have access, to the extent strictly necessary to comply with its obligations under this Title, to the networks, information systems and databases listed in Annex IV. The United Kingdom shall reimburse the Union for the actual costs incurred by the Union as a consequence of facilitating that access. The Union shall communicate to the United Kingdom the amount of those costs by 31 March of each year until the end of the period referred to in Annex IV. In the event that the communicated amount of the actual costs incurred considerably diverges from the best estimates amount that was communicated by the Union to the United Kingdom before the signature of this Agreement, the United Kingdom shall pay without delay to the Union the best estimates amount and the Joint Committee shall determine the manner in which the difference between the actual costs incurred and the best estimates amount is to be addressed.

Title X Union judicial and administrative procedures

Chapter 1 Judicial procedures

Article 86   Pending cases before the Court of Justice of the European Union

1. The Court of Justice of the European Union shall continue to have jurisdiction in any proceedings brought by or against the United Kingdom before the end of the transition period. Such jurisdiction shall apply to all stages of proceedings, including appeal proceedings before the Court of Justice and proceedings before the General Court where the case is referred back to the General Court.

2. The Court of Justice of the European Union shall continue to have jurisdiction to give preliminary rulings on requests from courts and tribunals of the United Kingdom made before the end of the transition period.

3. For the purposes of this Chapter, proceedings shall be considered as having been brought before the Court of Justice of the European Union, and requests for preliminary rulings shall be considered as having been made, at the moment at which the document initiating the proceedings has been registered by the registry of the Court of Justice or the General Court, as the case may be.

Article 87   New cases before the Court of Justice

1. If the European Commission considers that the United Kingdom has failed to fulfil an obligation under the Treaties or under Part Four of this Agreement before the end of the transition period, the European Commission may, within 4 years after the end of the transition period, bring the matter before the Court of Justice of the European Union in accordance with the requirements laid down in Article 258 TFEU or the second subparagraph of Article 108(2) TFEU, as the case may be. The Court of Justice of the European Union shall have jurisdiction over such cases.

2. If the United Kingdom does not comply with a decision referred to in Article 95(1) of this Agreement, or fails to give legal effect in the United Kingdom's legal order to a decision, as referred to in that provision, that was addressed to a natural or legal person residing or established in the United Kingdom, the European Commission may, within 4 years from the date of the decision concerned, bring the matter to the Court of Justice of the European Union in accordance with the requirements laid down in Article 258 TFEU or the second subparagraph of Article 108(2) TFEU, as the case may be. The Court of Justice of the European Union shall have jurisdiction over such cases.

3. In deciding to bring matters under this Article, the European Commission shall apply the same principles in respect of the United Kingdom as in respect of any Member State.

Article 88   Procedural rules

The provisions of Union law governing the procedure before the Court of Justice of the European Union shall apply in respect of the proceedings and requests for preliminary rulings referred to in this Title.

Article 89   Binding force and enforceability of judgments and orders

1. Judgments and orders of the Court of Justice of the European Union handed down before the end of the transition period, as well as such judgments and orders handed down after the end of the transition period in proceedings referred to in Articles 86 and 87, shall have binding force in their entirety on and in the United Kingdom.

2. If, in a judgment referred to in paragraph 1, the Court of Justice of the European Union finds that the United Kingdom has failed to fulfil an obligation under the Treaties or this Agreement, the United Kingdom shall take the necessary measures to comply with that judgment.

3. Articles 280 and 299 TFEU shall apply in the United Kingdom in respect of the enforcement of the judgments and orders of the Court of Justice of the European Union referred to in paragraph 1 of this Article.

Article 90   Right to intervene and participate in the procedure

Until the judgments and orders of the Court of Justice of the European Union in all proceedings and requests for preliminary rulings referred to in Article 86 have become final, the United Kingdom may intervene in the same way as a Member State or, in the cases brought before the Court of Justice of the European Union in accordance with Article 267 TFEU, participate in the procedure before the Court of Justice of the European Union in the same way as a Member State. During that period, the Registrar of the Court of Justice of the European Union shall notify the United Kingdom, at the same time and in the same manner as the Member States, of any case referred to the Court of Justice of the European Union for a preliminary ruling by a court or tribunal of a Member State.

The United Kingdom may also intervene or participate in the procedure before the Court of Justice of the European Union in the same way as a Member State:

(a) in relation to cases which concern a failure to fulfil obligations under the Treaties, where the United Kingdom was subject to the same obligations before the end of the transition period, and where such cases are brought before the Court of Justice of the European Union in accordance with Articles 258 TFEU before the end of the period referred to in Article 87(1) or, as the case may be, until the moment, after the end of that period, at which the last judgment or order rendered by the Court of Justice of the European Union on the basis of Article 87(1) has become final;

(b) in relation to cases which concern acts or provisions of Union law which were applicable before the end of the transition period to and in the United Kingdom and which are brought before Court of Justice of the European Union in accordance with Article 267 TFEU before the end of the period referred to in Article 87(1) or, as the case may be, until the moment, after the end of that period, at which the last judgment or order rendered by the Court of Justice on the basis of Article 87(1) has become final; and

(c) in relation to the cases referred to in Article 95(3).

Article 91   Representation before the Court

1. Without prejudice to Article 88, where, before the end of the transition period, a lawyer authorised to practise before the courts or tribunals of the United Kingdom represented or assisted a party in proceedings before the Court of Justice of the European Union or in relation to requests for preliminary rulings made before the end of the transition period, that lawyer may continue to represent or assist that party in those proceedings or in relation to those requests. This right shall apply to all stages of proceedings, including appeal proceedings before the Court of Justice and proceedings before the General Court after a case has been referred back to it.

2. Without prejudice to Article 88, lawyers authorised to practise before the courts or tribunals of the United Kingdom may represent or assist a party before the Court of Justice of the European Union in the cases referred to in Article 87 and Article 95(3). Lawyers authorised to practise before the courts or tribunals of the United Kingdom may also represent or assist the United Kingdom in the proceedings covered by Article 90 in which the United Kingdom has decided to intervene or participate.

3. When representing or assisting a party before the Court of Justice of the European Union in the cases referred to in paragraphs 1 and 2, lawyers authorised to practise before the courts or

tribunals of the United Kingdom shall in every respect be treated as lawyers authorised to practise before courts or tribunals of Member States representing or assisting a party before the Court of Justice of the European Union.

(All other Articles omitted as these are covered in the Trade and Cooperation Agreement extracts of which are reproduced later.)

Protocol on Ireland/Northern Ireland*

The Union and the United Kingdom,

HAVING REGARD to the historic ties and enduring nature of the bilateral relationship between Ireland and the United Kingdom,

RECALLING that the United Kingdom's withdrawal from the Union presents a significant and unique challenge to the island of Ireland, and reaffirming that the achievements, benefits and commitments of the peace process will remain of paramount importance to peace, stability and reconciliation there,

RECOGNISING that it is necessary to address the unique circumstances on the island of Ireland through a unique solution in order to ensure the orderly withdrawal of the United Kingdom from the Union,

AFFIRMING that the Good Friday or Belfast Agreement of 10 April 1998 between the Government of the United Kingdom, the Government of Ireland and the other participants in the multi-party negotiations (the '1998 Agreement'), which is annexed to the British-Irish Agreement of the same date (the 'British-Irish Agreement'), including its subsequent implementation agreements and arrangements, should be protected in all its parts,

RECOGNISING that cooperation between Northern Ireland and Ireland is a central part of the 1998 Agreement and is essential for achieving reconciliation and the normalisation of relationships on the island of Ireland, and recalling the roles, functions and safeguards of the Northern Ireland Executive, the Northern Ireland Assembly and the North-South Ministerial Council (including cross-community provisions), as set out in the 1998 Agreement,

NOTING that Union law has provided a supporting framework for the provisions on Rights, Safeguards and Equality of Opportunity of the 1998 Agreement,

RECOGNISING that Irish citizens in Northern Ireland, by virtue of their Union citizenship, will continue to enjoy, exercise and have access to rights, opportunities and benefits, and that this Protocol should respect and be without prejudice to the rights, opportunities and identity that come with citizenship of the Union for the people of Northern Ireland who choose to assert their right to Irish citizenship, as defined in Annex 2 of the British-Irish Agreement 'Declaration on the Provisions of Paragraph (vi) of Article 1 in Relation to Citizenship',

EMPHASISING that in order to ensure democratic legitimacy, there should be a process to ensure democratic consent in Northern Ireland to the application of Union law under this Protocol,

RECALLING the commitment of the United Kingdom to protect North-South cooperation and its guarantee of avoiding a hard border, including any physical infrastructure or related checks and controls,

NOTING that nothing in this Protocol prevents the United Kingdom from ensuring unfettered market access for goods moving from Northern Ireland to the rest of the United Kingdom's internal market,

UNDERLINING the Union's and the United Kingdom's shared aim of avoiding controls at the ports and airports of Northern Ireland, to the extent possible in accordance with applicable legislation and taking into account their respective regulatory regimes as well as the implementation thereof,

RECALLING the commitments of the Union and the United Kingdom reflected in the Joint Report from the negotiators of the European Union and the United Kingdom Government on progress

---

* **Editor's Note:** Taken from OJ 2020 L29/102. Some provisions omitted as noted. Annexes omitted.

during phase 1 of negotiations under Article 50 TEU on the United Kingdom's orderly withdrawal from the European Union of 8 December 2017,

RECALLING that the Union and the United Kingdom have carried out a mapping exercise which shows that North-South cooperation relies to a significant extent on a common Union legal and policy framework,

NOTING that therefore the United Kingdom's withdrawal from the Union gives rise to substantial challenges to the maintenance and development of North-South cooperation,

RECALLING that the United Kingdom remains committed to protecting and supporting continued North-South and East-West cooperation across the full range of political, economic, security, societal and agricultural contexts and frameworks for cooperation, including the continued operation of the North-South implementation bodies,

ACKNOWLEDGING the need for this Protocol to be implemented so as to maintain the necessary conditions for continued North-South cooperation, including for possible new arrangements in accordance with the 1998 Agreement,

RECALLING the Union's and the United Kingdom's commitments to the North South PEACE and INTERREG funding programmes under the current multi-annual financial framework and to the maintaining of the current funding proportions for the future programme,

AFFIRMING the commitment of the United Kingdom to facilitate the efficient and timely transit through its territory of goods moving from Ireland to another Member State or to a third country, and vice versa,

DETERMINED that the application of this Protocol should impact as little as possible on the everyday life of communities in both Ireland and Northern Ireland,

UNDERLINING their firm commitment to no customs and regulatory checks or controls and related physical infrastructure at the border between Ireland and Northern Ireland,

RECALLING that Northern Ireland is part of the customs territory of the United Kingdom and will benefit from participation in the United Kingdom's independent trade policy,

HAVING REGARD to the importance of maintaining the integral place of Northern Ireland in the United Kingdom's internal market,

MINDFUL that the rights and obligations of Ireland under the rules of the Union's internal market and customs union must be fully respected,

HAVE AGREED UPON the following provisions, which shall be annexed to the Withdrawal Agreement:

Article 1   Objectives

1. This Protocol is without prejudice to the provisions of the 1998 Agreement in respect of the constitutional status of Northern Ireland and the principle of consent, which provides that any change in that status can only be made with the consent of a majority of its people.

2. This Protocol respects the essential State functions and territorial integrity of the United Kingdom.

3. This Protocol sets out arrangements necessary to address the unique circumstances on the island of Ireland, to maintain the necessary conditions for continued North-South cooperation, to avoid a hard border and to protect the 1998 Agreement in all its dimensions.

Article 2   Rights of individuals

1. The United Kingdom shall ensure that no diminution of rights, safeguards or equality of opportunity, as set out in that part of the 1998 Agreement entitled Rights, Safeguards and Equality of Opportunity results from its withdrawal from the Union, including in the area of protection against discrimination, as enshrined in the provisions of Union law listed in Annex 1 to this Protocol, and shall implement this paragraph through dedicated mechanisms.

2. The United Kingdom shall continue to facilitate the related work of the institutions and bodies set up pursuant to the 1998 Agreement, including the Northern Ireland Human Rights Commission, the Equality Commission for Northern Ireland and the Joint Committee of representatives of the Human Rights Commissions of Northern Ireland and Ireland, in upholding human rights and equality standards.

Article 3   Common Travel Area

1. The United Kingdom and Ireland may continue to make arrangements between themselves relating to the movement of persons between their territories (the 'Common Travel Area'), while fully respecting the rights of natural persons conferred by Union law.

2. The United Kingdom shall ensure that the Common Travel Area and the rights and privileges associated therewith can continue to apply without affecting the obligations of Ireland under Union law, in particular with respect to free movement to, from and within Ireland for Union citizens and their family members, irrespective of their nationality.

Article 4   Customs territory of the United Kingdom

Northern Ireland is part of the customs territory of the United Kingdom.

Accordingly, nothing in this Protocol shall prevent the United Kingdom from including Northern Ireland in the territorial scope of any agreements it may conclude with third countries, provided that those agreements do not prejudice the application of this Protocol.

In particular, nothing in this Protocol shall prevent the United Kingdom from concluding agreements with a third country that grant goods produced in Northern Ireland preferential access to that country's market on the same terms as goods produced in other parts of the United Kingdom.

Nothing in this Protocol shall prevent the United Kingdom from including Northern Ireland in the territorial scope of its Schedules of Concessions annexed to the General Agreement on Tariffs and Trade 1994.

Article 5   Customs, movement of goods

1. No customs duties shall be payable for a good brought into Northern Ireland from another part of the United Kingdom by direct transport, notwithstanding paragraph 3, unless that good is at risk of subsequently being moved into the Union, whether by itself or forming part of another good following processing.

The customs duties in respect of a good being moved by direct transport to Northern Ireland other than from the Union or from another part of the United Kingdom shall be the duties applicable in the United Kingdom, notwithstanding paragraph 3, unless that good is at risk of subsequently being moved into the Union, whether by itself or forming part of another good following processing.

No duties shall be payable by, as relief shall be granted to, residents of the United Kingdom for personal property, as defined in point (c) of Article 2(1) of Council Regulation (EC) No 1186/2009, brought into Northern Ireland from another part of the United Kingdom.

2. For the purposes of the first and second subparagraphs of paragraph 1, a good brought into Northern Ireland from outside the Union shall be considered to be at risk of subsequently being moved into the Union unless it is established that that good:

(a) will not be subject to commercial processing in Northern Ireland; and
(b) fulfils the criteria established by the Joint Committee in accordance with the fourth subparagraph of this paragraph.

For the purposes of this paragraph, 'processing' means any alteration of goods, any transformation of goods in any way, or any subjecting of goods to operations other than for the purpose of preserving them in good condition or for adding or affixing marks, labels, seals or any other documentation to ensure compliance with any specific requirements.

Before the end of the transition period, the Joint Committee shall by decision establish the conditions under which processing is to be considered not to fall within point (a) of the first subparagraph, taking into account in particular the nature, scale and result of the processing.

Before the end of the transition period, the Joint Committee shall by decision establish the criteria for considering that a good brought into Northern Ireland from outside the Union is not at risk of subsequently being moved into the Union. The Joint Committee shall take into consideration, *inter alia*:

(a) the final destination and use of the good;
(b) the nature and value of the good;
(c) the nature of the movement; and
(d) the incentive for undeclared onward-movement into the Union, in particular incentives resulting from the duties payable pursuant to paragraph 1.

The Joint Committee may amend at any time its decisions adopted pursuant to this paragraph.

In taking any decision pursuant to this paragraph, the Joint Committee shall have regard to the specific circumstances in Northern Ireland.

3. Legislation as defined in point (2) of Article 5 of Regulation (EU) No 952/2013 shall apply to and in the United Kingdom in respect of Northern Ireland (not including the territorial waters of the United Kingdom). However, the Joint Committee shall establish the conditions, including in quantitative terms, under which certain fishery and aquaculture products, as set out in Annex I to Regulation (EU) No 1379/2013 of the European Parliament and of the Council, brought into the customs territory of the Union defined in Article 4 of Regulation (EU) No 952/2013 by vessels flying the flag of the United Kingdom and having their port of registration in Northern Ireland are exempted from duties.

4. The provisions of Union law listed in Annex 2 to this Protocol shall also apply, under the conditions set out in that Annex, to and in the United Kingdom in respect of Northern Ireland.

5. Articles 30 and 110 TFEU shall apply to and in the United Kingdom in respect of Northern Ireland. Quantitative restrictions on exports and imports shall be prohibited between the Union and Northern Ireland.

6. Customs duties levied by the United Kingdom in accordance with paragraph 3 are not remitted to the Union.

Subject to Article 10, the United Kingdom may in particular:

(a) reimburse duties levied pursuant to the provisions of Union law made applicable by paragraph 3 in respect of goods brought into Northern Ireland;

(b) provide for circumstances in which a customs debt which has arisen is to be waived in respect of goods brought into Northern Ireland;

(c) provide for circumstances in which customs duties are to be reimbursed in respect of goods that can be shown not to have entered the Union; and

(d) compensate undertakings to offset the impact of the application of paragraph 3.

In taking decisions under Article 10, the European Commission shall take the circumstances in Northern Ireland into account as appropriate.

7. No duties shall be payable on consignments of negligible value, on consignments sent by one individual to another or on goods contained in travellers' personal baggage, under the conditions set out in the legislation referred to in paragraph 3.

Article 6 Protection of the UK internal market

1. Nothing in this Protocol shall prevent the United Kingdom from ensuring unfettered market access for goods moving from Northern Ireland to other parts of the United Kingdom's internal market. Provisions of Union law made applicable by this Protocol which prohibit or restrict the exportation of goods shall only be applied to trade between Northern Ireland and other parts of the United Kingdom to the extent strictly required by any international obligations of the Union. The United Kingdom shall ensure full protection under international requirements and commitments that are relevant to the prohibitions and restrictions on the exportation of goods from the Union to third countries as set out in Union law.

2. Having regard to Northern Ireland's integral place in the United Kingdom's internal market, the Union and the United Kingdom shall use their best endeavours to facilitate the trade between Northern Ireland and other parts of the United Kingdom, in accordance with applicable legislation and taking into account their respective regulatory regimes as well as the implementation thereof. The Joint Committee shall keep the application of this paragraph under constant review and shall adopt appropriate recommendations with a view to avoiding controls at the ports and airports of Northern Ireland to the extent possible.

3. Nothing in this Protocol shall prevent a product originating from Northern Ireland from being presented as originating from the United Kingdom when placed on the market in Great Britain.

4. Nothing in this Protocol shall affect the law of the United Kingdom regulating the placing on the market in other parts of the United Kingdom of goods from Northern Ireland that comply with or benefit from technical regulations, assessments, registrations, certificates, approvals or authorisations governed by provisions of Union law referred to in Annex 2 to this Protocol.

Article 7   Technical regulations, assessments, registrations, certificates, approvals and authorisations [7.1 and 7.2 omitted]

1. Without prejudice to the provisions of Union law referred to in Annex 2 to this Protocol, the lawfulness of placing goods on the market in Northern Ireland shall be governed by the law of the United Kingdom as well as, as regards goods imported from the Union, by Articles 34 and 36 TFEU.

The first subparagraph does not prevent the test and release by a qualified person in Northern Ireland of a batch of a medicinal product imported into or manufactured in Northern Ireland.

Articles 8 and 9   [Omitted]

Article 10   State aid

1. The provisions of Union law listed in Annex 5 to this Protocol shall apply to the United Kingdom, including with regard to measures supporting the production of and trade in agricultural products in Northern Ireland, in respect of measures which affect that trade between Northern Ireland and the Union which is subject to this Protocol.

2. Notwithstanding paragraph 1, the provisions of Union law referred to in that paragraph shall not apply with respect to measures taken by the United Kingdom authorities to support the production of and trade in agricultural products in Northern Ireland up to a determined maximum overall annual level of support, and provided that a determined minimum percentage of that exempted support complies with the provisions of Annex 2 to the WTO Agreement on Agriculture. The determination of the maximum exempted overall annual level of support and the minimum percentage shall be governed by the procedures set out in Annex 6.

3. Where the European Commission examines information regarding a measure by the United Kingdom authorities that may constitute unlawful aid that is subject to paragraph 1, it shall ensure that the United Kingdom is kept fully and regularly informed of the progress and outcome of the examination of that measure.

Article 11   Other areas of North-South cooperation

1. Consistent with the arrangements set out in Articles 5 to 10, and in full respect of Union law, this Protocol shall be implemented and applied so as to maintain the necessary conditions for continued North-South cooperation, including in the areas of environment, health, agriculture, transport, education and tourism, as well as in the areas of energy, telecommunications, broadcasting, inland fisheries, justice and security, higher education and sport.

In full respect of Union law, the United Kingdom and Ireland may continue to make new arrangements that build on the provisions of the 1998 Agreement in other areas of North-South cooperation on the island of Ireland.

2. The Joint Committee shall keep under constant review the extent to which the implementation and application of this Protocol maintains the necessary conditions for North-South cooperation. The Joint Committee may make appropriate recommendations to the Union and the United Kingdom in this respect, including on a recommendation from the Specialised Committee.

Article 12   Implementation, application, supervision and enforcement

1. Without prejudice to paragraph 4, the authorities of the United Kingdom shall be responsible for implementing and applying the provisions of Union law made applicable by this Protocol to and in the United Kingdom in respect of Northern Ireland.

2. Without prejudice to paragraph 4 of this Article, Union representatives shall have the right to be present during any activities of the authorities of the United Kingdom related to the implementation and application of provisions of Union law made applicable by this Protocol, as well as activities related to the implementation and application of Article 5, and the United Kingdom shall provide, upon request, all relevant information relating to such activities. The United Kingdom shall facilitate such presence of Union representatives and shall provide them with the information requested. Where the Union representative requests the authorities of the United Kingdom to carry out control measures in individual cases for duly stated reasons, the authorities of the United Kingdom shall carry out those control measures.

The Union and the United Kingdom shall exchange information on the application of Article 5 (1) and (2) on a monthly basis.

3. The practical working arrangements relating to the exercise of the rights of Union representatives referred to in paragraph 2 shall be determined by the Joint Committee, upon proposal from the Specialised Committee.

4. As regards the second subparagraph of paragraph 2 of this Article, Article 5 and Articles 7 to 10, the institutions, bodies, offices, and agencies of the Union shall in relation to the United Kingdom and natural and legal persons residing or established in the territory of the United Kingdom have the powers conferred upon them by Union law. In particular, the Court of Justice of the European Union shall have the jurisdiction provided for in the Treaties in this respect. The second and third paragraphs of Article 267 TFEU shall apply to and in the United Kingdom in this respect.

5. Acts of the institutions, bodies, offices, and agencies of the Union adopted in accordance with paragraph 4 shall produce in respect of and in the United Kingdom the same legal effects as those which they produce within the Union and its Member States.

6. When representing or assisting a party in relation to administrative procedures arising from the exercise of the powers of the institutions, bodies, offices, and agencies of the Union referred to in paragraph 4, lawyers authorised to practise before the courts or tribunals of the United Kingdom shall in every respect be treated as lawyers authorised to practise before courts or tribunals of Member States who represent or assist a party in relation to such administrative procedures.

7. In cases brought before the Court of Justice of the European Union pursuant to paragraph 4:

    (a) the United Kingdom may participate in the proceedings before the Court of Justice of the European Union in the same way as a Member State;

    (b) lawyers authorised to practise before the courts or tribunals of the United Kingdom may represent or assist a party before the Court of Justice of the European Union in such proceedings and shall in every respect be treated as lawyers authorised to practise before courts or tribunals of Member States representing or assisting a party before the Court of Justice of the European Union.

Article 13　Common provisions

1. For the purposes of this Protocol, any reference to the United Kingdom in the applicable provisions of the Withdrawal Agreement shall be read as referring to the United Kingdom or to the United Kingdom in respect of Northern Ireland, as the case may be.

Notwithstanding any other provisions of this Protocol, any reference to the territory defined in Article 4 of Regulation (EU) No 952/2013 in the applicable provisions of the Withdrawal Agreement and of this Protocol, as well as in the provisions of Union law made applicable to and in the United Kingdom in respect of Northern Ireland by this Protocol, shall be read as including the part of the territory of the United Kingdom to which Regulation (EU) No 952/2013 applies by virtue of Article 5(3) of this Protocol.

Titles I and III of Part Three and Part Six of the Withdrawal Agreement shall apply without prejudice to the provisions of this Protocol.

2. Notwithstanding Article 4(4) and (5) of the Withdrawal Agreement, the provisions of this Protocol referring to Union law or to concepts or provisions thereof shall in their implementation and application be interpreted in conformity with the relevant case law of the Court of Justice of the European Union.

3. Notwithstanding Article 6(1) of the Withdrawal Agreement, and unless otherwise provided, where this Protocol makes reference to a Union act, that reference shall be read as referring to that Union act as amended or replaced.

4. Where the Union adopts a new act that falls within the scope of this Protocol, but which neither amends nor replaces a Union act listed in the Annexes to this Protocol, the Union shall inform the United Kingdom of the adoption of that act in the Joint Committee. Upon the request of the Union or the United Kingdom, the Joint Committee shall hold an exchange of views on the implications of the newly adopted act for the proper functioning of this Protocol, within 6 weeks after the request.

As soon as reasonably practical after the Union has informed the United Kingdom in the Joint Committee, the Joint Committee shall either:

    (a) adopt a decision adding the newly adopted act to the relevant Annex to this Protocol; or

    (b) where an agreement on adding the newly adopted act to the relevant Annex to this Protocol cannot be reached, examine all further possibilities to maintain the good functioning of this Protocol and take any decision necessary to this effect.

If the Joint Committee has not taken a decision referred to in the second subparagraph within a reasonable time, the Union shall be entitled, after giving notice to the United Kingdom, to take appropriate remedial measures. Such measures shall take effect at the earliest 6 months after the Union informed the United Kingdom in accordance with the first subparagraph, but in no event shall such measures take effect before the date on which the newly adopted act is implemented in the Union.

5. By way of derogation from paragraph 1 of this Article and from Article 7 of the Withdrawal Agreement, unless the Union considers that full or partial access by the United Kingdom or the United Kingdom in respect of Northern Ireland, as the case may be, is strictly necessary to enable the United Kingdom to comply with its obligations under this Protocol, including where such access is necessary because access to the relevant information cannot be facilitated by the working group referred to in Article 15 of this Protocol or by any other practical means, in respect of access to any network, information system or database established on the basis of Union law, references to Member States and competent authorities of Member States in provisions of Union law made applicable by this Protocol shall not be read as including the United Kingdom or the United Kingdom in respect of Northern Ireland, as the case may be.

6. Authorities of the United Kingdom shall not act as leading authority for risk assessments, examinations, approvals and authorisation procedures provided for in Union law made applicable by this Protocol.

7. Articles 346 and 347 TFEU shall apply to this Protocol as regards measures taken by a Member State or by the United Kingdom in respect of Northern Ireland.

8. Any subsequent agreement between the Union and the United Kingdom shall indicate the parts of this Protocol which it supersedes. Once a subsequent agreement between the Union and the United Kingdom becomes applicable after the entry into force of the Withdrawal Agreement, this Protocol shall then, from the date of application of such subsequent agreement and in accordance with the provisions of that agreement setting out the effect of that agreement on this Protocol, not apply or shall cease to apply, as the case may be, in whole or in part.

Article 14   Specialised Committee

The Committee on issues related to the implementation of the Protocol on Ireland/Northern Ireland established by Article 165 of the Withdrawal Agreement ('Specialised Committee') shall:

    (a) facilitate the implementation and application of this Protocol;

    (b) examine proposals concerning the implementation and application of this Protocol from the North-South Ministerial Council and North-South Implementation bodies set up under the 1998 Agreement;

    (c) consider any matter of relevance to Article 2 of this Protocol brought to its attention by the Northern Ireland Human Rights Commission, the Equality Commission for Northern Ireland, and the Joint Committee of representatives of the Human Rights Commissions of Northern Ireland and Ireland;

    (d) discuss any point raised by the Union or the United Kingdom that is of relevance to this Protocol and gives rise to a difficulty; and

    (e) make recommendations to the Joint Committee as regards the functioning of this Protocol.

Article 15   Joint consultative working group

1. A joint consultative working group on the implementation of this Protocol ('working group') is hereby established. It shall serve as a forum for the exchange of information and mutual consultation.

2. The working group shall be composed of representatives of the Union and the United Kingdom and shall carry out its functions under the supervision of the Specialised Committee, to which it shall report. The working group shall have no power to take binding decisions other than the power to adopt its own rules of procedure referred to in paragraph 6.

3. Within the working group:

   (a) the Union and the United Kingdom shall, in a timely manner, exchange information about planned, ongoing and final relevant implementation measures in relation to the Union acts listed in the Annexes to this Protocol;

   (b) the Union shall inform the United Kingdom about planned Union acts within the scope of this Protocol, including Union acts that amend or replace the Union acts listed in the Annexes to this Protocol;

   (c) the Union shall provide to the United Kingdom all information the Union considers relevant to allow the United Kingdom to fully comply with its obligations under the Protocol; and

   (d) the United Kingdom shall provide to the Union all information that Member States are required to provide to one another or to the institutions, bodies, offices or agencies of the Union pursuant to the Union acts listed in the Annexes to this Protocol.

4. The working group shall be co-chaired by the Union and the United Kingdom.

5. The working group shall meet at least once a month, unless otherwise decided by the Union and the United Kingdom by mutual consent. Where necessary, the Union and the United Kingdom may exchange information referred to in points (c) and (d) of paragraph 3 between meetings.

6. The working group shall adopt its own rules of procedure by mutual consent.

7. The Union shall ensure that all views expressed by the United Kingdom in the working group and all information provided by the United Kingdom in the working group, including technical and scientific data, are communicated to the relevant institutions, bodies, offices and agencies of the Union without undue delay.

Article 16   Safeguards

1. If the application of this Protocol leads to serious economic, societal or environmental difficulties that are liable to persist, or to diversion of trade, the Union or the United Kingdom may unilaterally take appropriate safeguard measures. Such safeguard measures shall be restricted with regard to their scope and duration to what is strictly necessary in order to remedy the situation. Priority shall be given to such measures as will least disturb the functioning of this Protocol.

2. If a safeguard measure taken by the Union or the United Kingdom, as the case may be, in accordance with paragraph 1 creates an imbalance between the rights and obligations under this Protocol, the Union or the United Kingdom, as the case may be, may take such proportionate rebalancing measures as are strictly necessary to remedy the imbalance. Priority shall be given to such measures as will least disturb the functioning of this Protocol.

3. Safeguard and rebalancing measures taken in accordance with paragraphs 1 and 2 shall be governed by the procedures set out in Annex 7 to this Protocol.

Article 17   Protection of financial interests

The Union and the United Kingdom shall counter fraud and any other illegal activities affecting the financial interests of the Union or the financial interests of the United Kingdom.

Article 18   Democratic consent in Northern Ireland

1. Within 2 months before the end of both the initial period and any subsequent period, the United Kingdom shall provide the opportunity for democratic consent in Northern Ireland to the continued application of Articles 5 to 10.

2. For the purposes of paragraph 1, the United Kingdom shall seek democratic consent in Northern Ireland in a manner consistent with the 1998 Agreement. A decision expressing democratic consent shall be reached strictly in accordance with the unilateral declaration concerning the operation of the 'Democratic consent in Northern Ireland' provision of the Protocol on Ireland/Northern Ireland made by the United Kingdom on 17 October 2019, including with respect to the roles of the Northern Ireland Executive and Assembly.

3. The United Kingdom shall notify the Union before the end of the relevant period referred to in paragraph 5 of the outcome of the process referred to in paragraph 1.

4. Where the process referred to in paragraph 1 has been undertaken and a decision has been reached in accordance with paragraph 2, and the United Kingdom notifies the Union that the outcome of the process referred to in paragraph 1 is not a decision that the Articles of this Protocol referred to in that paragraph should continue to apply in Northern Ireland, then those Articles and other provisions of this Protocol, to the extent that those provisions depend on those Articles for their application, shall cease to apply 2 years after the end of the relevant period referred to in paragraph 5. In such a case the Joint Committee shall address recommendations to the Union and to the United Kingdom on the necessary measures, taking into account the obligations of the parties to the 1998 Agreement. Before doing so, the Joint Committee may seek an opinion from institutions created by the 1998 Agreement.

5. For the purposes of this Article, the initial period is the period ending 4 years after the end of the transition period. Where the decision reached in a given period was on the basis of a majority of Members of the Northern Ireland Assembly, present and voting, the subsequent period is the 4 year period following that period, for as long as Articles 5 to 10 continue to apply. Where the decision reached in a given period had cross-community support, the subsequent period is the 8-year period following that period, for as long as Articles 5 to 10 continue to apply.

6. For the purposes of paragraph 5, cross-community support means:
- (a) a majority of those Members of the Legislative Assembly present and voting, including a majority of the unionist and nationalist designations present and voting; or
- (b) a weighted majority (60 %) of Members of the Legislative Assembly present and voting, including at least 40 % of each of the nationalist and unionist designations present and voting.

Article 19   Annexes

Annexes 1 to 7 shall form an integral part of this Protocol.

(Annexes omitted.)

European Union (Withdrawal Agreement) Act 2020*

(2020 c. 1)

An Act to implement, and make other provision in connection with, the agreement between the United Kingdom and the EU under Article 50(2) of the Treaty on European Union which sets out the arrangements for the United Kingdom's withdrawal from the EU.   [23rd January 2020]

PART 3   CITIZENS' RIGHTS

Rights in relation to entry and residence

7   Rights related to residence: application deadline and temporary protection

(1) A Minister of the Crown may by regulations make such provision as the Minister considers appropriate for any of the following purposes—
- (a) specifying the deadline that applies for the purposes of—
  - (i) the first sub-paragraph of Article 18(1)(b) of the withdrawal agreement (deadline for the submission of applications for the new residence status described in Article 18(1));

---

* **Editor's Note:** The following sections which amended the EUWA 2018 (and can be found in situ within the 2018 Act) have been removed from here: ss. 1–6, 18–19, 21–24, 28–31, and 33–36. The Schedules have been omitted.

(ii) the first sub-paragraph of Article 17(1)(b) of the EEA EFTA separation agreement (deadline for the submission of applications for the new residence status described in Article 17(1));

(iii) the first sentence of Article 16(1)(b) of the Swiss citizens' rights agreement (deadline for the submission of applications for the new residence status described in Article 16(1));

(b) implementing Article 18(2) of the withdrawal agreement (protection for Union citizens etc. in the period prior to the deadline for the submission of applications for the new residence status described in Article 18(1));

(c) implementing Article 17(2) of the EEA EFTA separation agreement (protection for EEA EFTA nationals etc. in the period prior to the deadline for the submission of applications for the new residence status described in Article 17(1));

(d) implementing Article 16(2) of the Swiss citizens' rights agreement (protection for Swiss nationals etc. in the period prior to the deadline for the submission of applications for the new residence status described in Article 16(1));

(e) implementing Article 18(3) of the withdrawal agreement (protection for Union citizens etc. pending a final decision on an application for the new residence status described in Article 18(1));

(f) implementing Article 17(3) of the EEA EFTA separation agreement (protection for EEA EFTA nationals etc. pending a final decision on an application for the new residence status described in Article 17(1));

(g) implementing Article 16(3) of the Swiss citizens' rights agreement (protection for Swiss nationals etc. pending a final decision on an application for the new residence status described in Article 16(1)).

(2) If the Minister considers it appropriate, regulations under subsection (1) relating to the implementation of a provision mentioned in subsection (1)(b), (c) or (d) may be made so as to apply both to—

(a) persons to whom the provision in question applies, and

(b) persons to whom that provision does not apply but who may be granted leave to enter or remain in the United Kingdom by virtue of residence scheme immigration rules (see section 17) and who do not have such leave.

(3) If the Minister considers it appropriate, regulations under subsection (1) relating to the implementation of a provision mentioned in subsection (1)(e), (f) or (g) may be made so as to apply both to—

(a) persons to whom the provision in question applies, and

(b) persons to whom that provision does not apply but who make an application for leave to enter or remain in the United Kingdom by virtue of residence scheme immigration rules.

(4) The power to make regulations under subsection (1) may (among other things) be exercised by modifying any provision made by or under an enactment.

8 Frontier workers

(1) A Minister of the Crown may by regulations make such provision as the Minister considers appropriate for the purpose of implementing any of the following—

(a) Articles 24(3) and 25(3) of the withdrawal agreement (rights of employed and self-employed frontier workers) other than as regards rights enjoyed as workers (see section 14(1));

(b) Articles 23(3) and 24(3) of the EEA EFTA separation agreement (rights of employed and self-employed frontier workers) other than as regards rights enjoyed as workers (see section 14(2));

(c) Article 20(2) of the Swiss citizens' rights agreement (rights of frontier workers to enter and exit).

(2) A Minister of the Crown may by regulations make such provision as the Minister considers appropriate for the purpose of implementing any of the following—

  (a) Article 26 of the withdrawal agreement (issue of documents);

  (b) Article 25 of the EEA EFTA separation agreement (issue of documents);

  (c) Article 21(1)(a) and (2) of the Swiss citizens' rights agreement (issue of documents).

(3) The power to make regulations under subsection (1) or (2) may (among other things) be exercised by modifying any provision made by or under the Immigration Acts.

9 Restrictions of rights of entry and residence

(1) A Minister of the Crown may by regulations make such provision as the Minister considers appropriate for the purpose of implementing any of the following—

  (a) Article 20(1), (3) and (4) of the withdrawal agreement (restrictions of the rights of entry and residence);

  (b) Article 19(1), (3) and (4) of the EEA EFTA separation agreement (restrictions of the rights of entry and residence);

  (c) Articles 17(1) and (3) and 20(3) of the Swiss citizens' rights agreement (restrictions of the rights of entry and residence).

(2) If the Minister considers it appropriate, regulations under subsection (1) relating to the implementation of a provision mentioned in subsection (1)(a), (b) or (c) may be made so as to apply both to—

  (a) persons to whom the provision in question applies, and

  (b) persons to whom that provision does not apply but who—

    (i) have entry clearance granted by virtue of relevant entry clearance immigration rules (see section 17),

    (ii) have leave to enter or remain in the United Kingdom granted by virtue of residence scheme immigration rules (see section 17), or

    (iii) otherwise have leave to enter granted after arriving with entry clearance granted by virtue of relevant entry clearance immigration rules.

(3) In subsection (2)(b), references to a person who has entry clearance or leave to enter or remain include references to a person who would have had entry clearance or leave to enter or remain but for—

  (a) the making of a deportation order under section 5(1) of the Immigration Act 1971, or

  (b) the making of any other decision made in connection with restricting the right of the person to enter the United Kingdom.

(4) The power to make regulations under subsection (1) may (among other things) be exercised by modifying any provision made—

  (a) by or under the Immigration Acts, or

  (b) under other primary legislation.

10 Retention of existing grounds for deportation

(1) Section 3 of the Immigration Act 1971 (general provisions for regulation and control) is amended in accordance with subsections (2) to (4).

(2) After subsection (5) insert—

'(5A) The Secretary of State may not deem a relevant person's deportation to be conducive to the public good under subsection (5) if the person's deportation—

  (a) would be in breach of the obligations of the United Kingdom under Article 20 of the EU withdrawal agreement, Article 19 of the EEA EFTA separation agreement, or Article 17 or 20(3) of the Swiss citizens' rights agreement, or

  (b) would be in breach of those obligations if the provision in question mentioned in paragraph (a) applied in relation to the person.'

(3) After subsection (6) insert—

'(6A) A court may not recommend under subsection (6) that a relevant person be deported if the offence for which the person was convicted consisted of or included conduct that took place before IP completion day.'

(4) After subsection (9) insert—

'(10) For the purposes of this section, a person is a "relevant person"—

    (a) if the person is in the United Kingdom (whether or not they have entered within the meaning of section 11(1)) having arrived with entry clearance granted by virtue of relevant entry clearance immigration rules,

    (b) if the person has leave to enter or remain in the United Kingdom granted by virtue of residence scheme immigration rules,

    (c) if the person may be granted leave to enter or remain in the United Kingdom as a person who has a right to enter the United Kingdom by virtue of—

        (i) Article 32(1)(b) of the EU withdrawal agreement,

        (ii) Article 31(1)(b) of the EEA EFTA separation agreement, or

        (iii) Article 26a(1)(b) of the Swiss citizens' rights agreement,

        whether or not the person has been granted such leave, or

    (d) if the person may enter the United Kingdom by virtue of regulations made under section 8 of the European Union (Withdrawal Agreement) Act 2020 (frontier workers), whether or not the person has entered by virtue of those regulations.

(11) In this section—

"EEA EFTA separation agreement" and "Swiss citizens' rights agreement" have the same meanings as in the European Union (Withdrawal Agreement) Act 2020 (see section 39(1) of that Act);

"relevant entry clearance immigration rules" and "residence scheme immigration rules" have the meanings given by section 17 of the European Union (Withdrawal Agreement) Act 2020.'

(5) In section 33 of the UK Borders Act 2007 (exceptions to automatic deportation), after subsection (6A), insert—

'(6B) Exception 7 is where—

    (a) the foreign criminal is a relevant person, and

    (b) the offence for which the foreign criminal was convicted as mentioned in section 32(1)(b) consisted of or included conduct that took place before IP completion day.

(6C) For the purposes of subsection (6B), a foreign criminal is a "relevant person"—

    (a) if the foreign criminal is in the United Kingdom (whether or not they have entered within the meaning of section 11(1) of the Immigration Act 1971) having arrived with entry clearance granted by virtue of relevant entry clearance immigration rules,

    (b) if the foreign criminal has leave to enter or remain in the United Kingdom granted by virtue of residence scheme immigration rules,

    (c) if the foreign criminal may be granted leave to enter or remain in the United Kingdom as a person who has a right to enter the United Kingdom by virtue of—

        (i) Article 32(1)(b) of the EU withdrawal agreement,

        (ii) Article 31(1)(b) of the EEA EFTA separation agreement, or

        (iii) Article 26a(1)(b) of the Swiss citizens' rights agreement,

        whether or not the foreign criminal has been granted such leave, or

    (d) if the foreign criminal may enter the United Kingdom by virtue of regulations made under section 8 of the European Union (Withdrawal Agreement) Act 2020 (frontier workers), whether or not the foreign criminal has entered by virtue of those regulations.

(6D) In this section—

"EEA EFTA separation agreement" and "Swiss citizens' rights agreement" have the same meanings as in the European Union (Withdrawal Agreement) Act 2020 (see section 39(1) of that Act);

"relevant entry clearance immigration rules" and "residence scheme immigration rules" have the meanings given by section 17 of the European Union (Withdrawal Agreement) Act 2020.'

(6) In section 3(10) of the Immigration Act 1971 and section 33(6C) of the UK Borders Act 2007 (for which see subsections (4) and (5) above), references to having leave to enter or remain in the United Kingdom granted by virtue of residence scheme immigration rules include references to having such leave granted by virtue of those rules before section 17 comes into force.

11 Appeals etc. against citizens' rights immigration decisions

(1) A Minister of the Crown may by regulations make provision for, or in connection with, appeals against citizens' rights immigration decisions of a kind described in the regulations.

(2) For the purposes of this section, each of the following is a 'citizens' rights immigration decision'—

    (a) a decision made in connection with entry clearance by virtue of relevant entry clearance immigration rules (see section 17);

    (b) a decision made in connection with leave to enter or remain in the United Kingdom by virtue of residence scheme immigration rules (see section 17);

    (c) a decision made in connection with entry clearance for the purposes of acquiring leave to enter or remain in relation to a healthcare right of entry;

    (d) a decision made in connection with leave to enter or remain in the United Kingdom in relation to a healthcare right of entry;

    (e) a decision made in connection with a right to enter or remain in the United Kingdom by virtue of regulations made under section 8 (frontier workers);

    (f) a decision to make, or a refusal to revoke, a deportation order under section 5(1) of the Immigration Act 1971 in relation to a relevant person;

    (g) any other decision made in connection with restricting the right of a relevant person to enter the United Kingdom.

(3) A Minister of the Crown may also by regulations make provision for, or in connection with, reviews (including judicial reviews) of decisions within subsection (2)(g).

(4) The power to make regulations under subsection (1) or (3) may (among other things) be exercised by modifying any provision made by or under an enactment.

(5) Such regulations may, for example, apply with or without modifications any enactment which applies in relation to appeals under section 82 of the Nationality, Immigration and Asylum Act 2002 or section 2 of the Special Immigration Appeals Commission Act 1997.

(6) For the purposes of subsection (2), a 'healthcare right of entry' is a right to enter the United Kingdom that a person has by virtue of—

    (a) Article 32(1)(b) of the withdrawal agreement,

    (b) Article 31(1)(b) of the EEA EFTA separation agreement, or

    (c) Article 26a(1)(b) of the Swiss citizens' rights agreement.

(7) For the purposes of subsection (2)(f) and (g), a person is a 'relevant person' if—

    (a) Article 20 of the withdrawal agreement, Article 19 of the EEA EFTA separation agreement or (as the case may be) Articles 17 or 20(3) of the Swiss citizens' rights agreement (restrictions of the rights of entry and residence) applies to the person, or

    (b) the person is not within paragraph (a) but—

        (i) has entry clearance granted by virtue of relevant entry clearance immigration rules,

        (ii) has leave to enter or remain in the United Kingdom granted by virtue of residence scheme immigration rules, or

        (iii) otherwise has leave to enter granted after arriving with entry clearance granted by virtue of relevant entry clearance immigration rules.

(8) In subsection (7)(b), references to a person who has entry clearance or leave to enter or remain include references to a person who would have had entry clearance or leave to enter or remain but for—

    (a) the making of a deportation order under section 5(1) of the Immigration Act 1971, or

    (b) the making of any other decision made in connection with restricting the right of the person to enter the United Kingdom.

Professional qualifications

12 Recognition of professional qualifications

(1) An appropriate authority may by regulations make such provision as the authority considers appropriate—

    (a) to implement Chapter 3 of Title II of Part 2 of the withdrawal agreement (professional qualifications),

    (b) to supplement the effect of section 7A of the European Union (Withdrawal) Act 2018 in relation to that Chapter, or

    (c) otherwise for the purposes of dealing with matters arising out of, or related to, that Chapter (including matters arising by virtue of section 7A of that Act and that Chapter).

(2) An appropriate authority may by regulations make such provision as the authority considers appropriate—

    (a) to implement Chapter 3 of Title II of Part 2 of the EEA EFTA separation agreement (professional qualifications),

    (b) to supplement the effect of section 7B of the European Union (Withdrawal) Act 2018 in relation to that Chapter, or

    (c) otherwise for the purposes of dealing with matters arising out of, or related to, that Chapter (including matters arising by virtue of section 7B of that Act and that Chapter).

(3) An appropriate authority may by regulations make such provision as the authority considers appropriate—

    (a) to implement professional qualification provisions of the Swiss citizens' rights agreement,

    (b) to supplement the effect of section 7B of the European Union (Withdrawal) Act 2018 in relation to those provisions, or

    (c) otherwise for the purposes of dealing with matters arising out of, or related to, those provisions (including matters arising by virtue of section 7B of that Act and those provisions).

(4) For the purposes of subsection (3) the following are 'professional qualification provisions' of the Swiss citizens' rights agreement—

    (a) Part 4 of that agreement (mutual recognition of professional qualifications);

    (b) Article 23(4) of that agreement as regards the recognition of professional qualifications.

(5) If an appropriate authority considers it appropriate, regulations under subsection (1) or (2) relating to the implementation of a provision of Chapter 3 of Title II of Part 2 of the withdrawal agreement or of the EEA EFTA separation agreement may be made so as to apply both to—

    (a) persons to whom the provision in question applies, and

    (b) persons to whom that provision does not apply but who may be granted leave to enter or remain in the United Kingdom by virtue of residence scheme immigration rules, whether or not they have been granted such leave (see section 17).

(6) The power to make regulations under subsection (1), (2) or (3) may (among other things) be exercised by modifying any provision made by or under an enactment.

(7) In subsection (6) 'enactment' does not include primary legislation passed or made after IP completion day.

(8) In this section, 'appropriate authority' means—

    (a) a Minister of the Crown,

    (b) a devolved authority, or

    (c) a Minister of the Crown acting jointly with a devolved authority.

(9) Schedule 1 contains further provision about the power of devolved authorities to make regulations under this section.

Co-ordination of social security systems

13 Co-ordination of social security systems

(1) An appropriate authority may by regulations make such provision as the authority considers appropriate—

    (a) to implement Title III of Part 2 of the withdrawal agreement (co-ordination of social security systems),

    (b) to supplement the effect of section 7A of the European Union (Withdrawal) Act 2018 in relation to that Title, or

    (c) otherwise for the purposes of dealing with matters arising out of, or related to, that Title (including matters arising by virtue of section 7A of that Act and that Title).

(2) An appropriate authority may by regulations make such provision as the authority considers appropriate—

    (a) to implement Title III of Part 2 of the EEA EFTA separation agreement (co-ordination of social security systems),

    (b) to supplement the effect of section 7B of the European Union (Withdrawal) Act 2018 in relation to that Title, or

    (c) otherwise for the purposes of dealing with matters arising out of, or related to, that Title (including matters arising by virtue of section 7B of that Act and that Title).

(3) An appropriate authority may by regulations make such provision as the authority considers appropriate—

    (a) to implement social security co-ordination provisions of the Swiss citizens' rights agreement,

    (b) to supplement the effect of section 7B of the European Union (Withdrawal) Act 2018 in relation to those provisions, or

    (c) otherwise for the purposes of dealing with matters arising out of, or related to, those provisions (including matters arising by virtue of section 7B of that Act and those provisions).

(4) For the purposes of subsection (3) the following are 'social security co-ordination provisions' of the Swiss citizens' rights agreement—

    (a) Part 3 of that agreement (co-ordination of social security systems);

    (b) Article 23(4) of that agreement as regards social security co-ordination.

(5) The power to make regulations under subsection (1), (2) or (3) may (among other things) be exercised by modifying any provision made by or under an enactment.

(6) In this section, 'appropriate authority' means—

    (a) a Minister of the Crown,

    (b) a devolved authority, or

    (c) a Minister of the Crown acting jointly with a devolved authority.

(7) Schedule 1 contains further provision about the power of devolved authorities to make regulations under this section.

Equal treatment etc.

14 **Non-discrimination, equal treatment and rights of workers etc.**

(1) An appropriate authority may by regulations make such provision as the authority considers appropriate for the purpose of implementing any of the following provisions of the withdrawal agreement—

    (a) Article 12 (prohibition of discrimination on grounds of nationality);

    (b) Article 23 (right to equal treatment);

    (c) Articles 24(1) and 25(1) (rights of workers and the self-employed);

    (d) Articles 24(3) and 25(3) (rights of employed or self-employed frontier workers) as regards rights enjoyed as workers.

(2) An appropriate authority may by regulations make such provision as the authority considers appropriate for the purpose of implementing any of the following provisions of the EEA EFTA separation agreement—

    (a) Article 11 (prohibition of discrimination on grounds of nationality);

    (b) Article 22 (right to equal treatment);

    (c) Articles 23(1) and 24(1) (rights of workers and the self-employed);

    (d) Articles 23(3) and 24(3) (rights of employed or self-employed frontier workers) as regards rights enjoyed as workers.

(3) An appropriate authority may by regulations make such provision as the authority considers appropriate for the purpose of implementing any of the following provisions of the Swiss citizens' rights agreement—

    (a) Article 7 (prohibition of discrimination on grounds of nationality);

    (b) Article 18 (right to take up employment etc.);

(c) Article 19 (rights of employed or self-employed persons etc.);

(d) Article 20(1) (rights of frontier workers);

(e) Article 23(1) (rights of persons providing services).

(4) If the appropriate authority considers it appropriate, regulations under subsection (1), (2) or (3) relating to the implementation of a provision mentioned in that subsection, may be made so as to apply both to—

(a) persons to whom the provision in question applies, and

(b) persons to whom that provision does not apply but who may be granted leave to enter or remain in the United Kingdom by virtue of residence scheme immigration rules, whether or not they have been granted such leave (see section 17).

(5) The power to make regulations under subsection (1), (2) or (3) may (among other things) be exercised by modifying any provision made by or under an enactment.

(6) In this section, 'appropriate authority' means—

(a) a Minister of the Crown,

(b) a devolved authority, or

(c) a Minister of the Crown acting jointly with a devolved authority.

(7) Schedule 1 contains further provision about the power of devolved authorities to make regulations under this section.

Independent Monitoring Authority

15 Independent Monitoring Authority for the Citizens' Rights Agreements

(1) A body corporate called the Independent Monitoring Authority for the Citizens' Rights Agreements is established.

(2) In this Part that body is referred to as 'the IMA'.

(3) Schedule 2 contains provision relating to the IMA (including provisions about the IMA's constitution and functions).

General

16 Regulations: supplementary

(1) In sections 7, 8, 9 and 14—

(a) a power to make provision for the purpose of implementing a provision of the withdrawal agreement includes power to make provision to supplement the effect of section 7A of the European Union (Withdrawal) Act 2018 in relation to that provision of the agreement,

(b) a power to make provision for the purpose of implementing a provision of the EEA EFTA separation agreement includes power to make provision to supplement the effect of section 7B of that Act in relation to that provision of the agreement, and

(c) a power to make provision for the purpose of implementing a provision of the Swiss citizens' rights agreement includes power to make provision to supplement the effect of section 7B of that Act in relation to that provision of the agreement.

(2) The conferral of a power on a Minister of the Crown under section 7, 8, 9 or 11 does not affect the extent of any power of a devolved authority under section 12, 13 or 14 which overlaps with a power under section 7, 8, 9 or 11 by virtue of section 17(4).

(3) Regulations under this Part may not provide for the conferral of functions (including the conferral of a discretion) on, or the delegation of functions to, a person who is not a public authority (but may so provide if the person is a public authority).

(4) In subsection (3), 'public authority' means a person who exercises functions of a public nature.

17 Interpretation: Part 3

(1) In this Part, 'residence scheme immigration rules' means—

(a) Appendix EU to the immigration rules except those rules, or changes to that Appendix, which are identified in the immigration rules as not having effect in connection with the residence scheme that operates in connection with the withdrawal of the United Kingdom from the EU, and

(b) any other immigration rules which are identified in the immigration rules as having effect in connection with the withdrawal of the United Kingdom from the EU.

(2) In this Part, 'relevant entry clearance immigration rules' means any immigration rules which are identified in the immigration rules as having effect in connection with the granting of entry clearance for the purposes of acquiring leave to enter or remain in the United Kingdom by virtue of residence scheme immigration rules.

(3) In this Part, references to having leave to enter or remain in the United Kingdom granted by virtue of residence scheme immigration rules include references to having such leave granted by virtue of those rules before this section comes into force.

(4) In this Part, a reference to a Chapter, Title, Part or other provision of the withdrawal agreement, EEA EFTA separation agreement or Swiss citizens' rights agreement includes a reference to—

(a) any other provision of the agreement in question so far as relating to that Chapter, Title, Part or other provision, and

(b) any provision of EU law which is applied by, or referred to in, that Chapter, Title, Part or other provision (to the extent of the application or reference).

(5) In this Part—

'entry clearance' has the meaning given by section 33(1) of the Immigration Act 1971 (interpretation);

'immigration rules' has the same meaning as in the Immigration Act 1971.

PART 4 OTHER SUBJECT AREAS*

Main financial provision

20 Financial provision

(1) Any sum that is required to be paid to the EU or an EU entity to meet any obligation that the United Kingdom has by virtue of the withdrawal agreement is to be charged on and paid out of the Consolidated Fund or, if the Treasury so decides, the National Loans Fund.

(2) After 31 March 2021, subsection (1) does not apply in relation to any expenditure other than sums required to be paid in respect of the traditional own resources of the EU.

(3) Any money received by a Minister of the Crown or a government department by virtue of the withdrawal agreement is to be paid into the Consolidated Fund or, if the Treasury so decides, the National Loans Fund.

(4) A Minister of the Crown, government department or devolved authority may incur expenditure, for the purpose of, or in connection with, preparing for anything about which provision may be made under a power to make subordinate legislation conferred or modified by or under this Act, before any such provision is made.

(5) There is to be paid out of money provided by Parliament—

(a) any expenditure in relation to which subsection (1) does not apply which is incurred by a Minister of the Crown, government department or other public authority by virtue of this Act, and

(b) any increase attributable to this Act in the sums payable by virtue of any other Act out of money so provided.

(6) Subsections (1), (3) and (5) are subject to any other provision made by or under this Act or any other enactment.

(7) In this section—

'EU entity' means an EU institution or any office, body or agency of the EU;

'government department' means any department of the Government of the United Kingdom;

---

* **Editor's Note:** Sections 18 and 19 omitted.

'the traditional own resources of the EU' means the EU's traditional own resources referred to in Article 2(1)(a) of the Council Decision of 26 May 2014 on the system of own resources of the European Union (2014/335/EU, Euratom).

Relationship to EUWA 2018

25 Retention of saved EU law at end of implementation period [Amendments made]

26 Interpretation of retained EU law and relevant separation agreement law [Amendments made]

27 Dealing with deficiencies in retained EU law [Amendments made]

32 Requirements in Part 2 of CRAGA

Section 20 of the Constitutional Reform and Governance Act 2010 (treaties to be laid before Parliament before ratification) does not apply in relation to the withdrawal agreement (but this does not affect whether that section applies in relation to any modification of the agreement).

Other matters

37 Arrangements with EU about unaccompanied children seeking asylum [Amendments made]

PART 5 GENERAL AND FINAL PROVISION

Parliamentary sovereignty

38 Parliamentary sovereignty

    (1) It is recognised that the Parliament of the United Kingdom is sovereign.

    (2) In particular, its sovereignty subsists notwithstanding—

      (a) directly applicable or directly effective EU law continuing to be recognised and available in domestic law by virtue of section 1A or 1B of the European Union (Withdrawal) Act 2018 (savings of existing law for the implementation period),

      (b) section 7A of that Act (other directly applicable or directly effective aspects of the withdrawal agreement),

      (c) section 7B of that Act (deemed direct applicability or direct effect in relation to the EEA EFTA separation agreement and the Swiss citizens' rights agreement), and

      (d) section 7C of that Act (interpretation of law relating to the withdrawal agreement (other than the implementation period), the EEA EFTA separation agreement and the Swiss citizens' rights agreement).

    (3) Accordingly, nothing in this Act derogates from the sovereignty of the Parliament of the United Kingdom.

Interpretation

39 Interpretation

    (1) In this Act—

'devolved authority' means—

      (a) the Scottish Ministers,

      (b) the Welsh Ministers, or

      (c) a Northern Ireland department;

'EEA EFTA separation agreement' means (as modified from time to time in accordance with any provision of it) the Agreement on arrangements between Iceland, the Principality of Liechtenstein, the Kingdom of Norway and the United Kingdom of Great Britain and Northern Ireland following the withdrawal of the United Kingdom from the European Union, the EEA Agreement and other agreements applicable between the United Kingdom and the EEA EFTA States by virtue of the United Kingdom's membership of the European Union;

'enactment' means an enactment whenever passed or made and includes—

(a) an enactment contained in any Order in Council, order, rules, regulations, scheme, warrant, byelaw or other instrument made under an Act of Parliament,

(b) an enactment contained in any Order in Council made in exercise of Her Majesty's Prerogative,

(c) an enactment contained in, or in an instrument made under, an Act of the Scottish Parliament,

(d) an enactment contained in, or in an instrument made under, a Measure or Act of the National Assembly for Wales,

(e) an enactment contained in, or in an instrument made under, Northern Ireland legislation,

(f) an enactment contained in any instrument made by a member of the Scottish Government, the Welsh Ministers, the First Minister for Wales, the Counsel General to the Welsh Government, a Northern Ireland Minister, the First Minister in Northern Ireland, the deputy First Minister in Northern Ireland or a Northern Ireland department in exercise of prerogative or other executive functions of Her Majesty which are exercisable by such a person on behalf of Her Majesty,

(g) an enactment contained in, or in an instrument made under, a Measure of the Church Assembly or of the General Synod of the Church of England, and

(h) any retained direct EU legislation;

'IP completion day' means 31 December 2020 at 11.00 p.m (and see subsections (2) to (5));

'Minister of the Crown' has the same meaning as in the Ministers of the Crown Act 1975 and also includes the Commissioners for Her Majesty's Revenue and Customs;

'modify' includes amend, repeal or revoke (and related expressions are to be read accordingly);

'primary legislation' means—

(a) an Act of Parliament,

(b) an Act of the Scottish Parliament,

(c) a Measure or Act of the National Assembly for Wales, or

(d) Northern Ireland legislation;

'subordinate legislation' means any Order in Council, order, rules, regulations, scheme, warrant, byelaw or other instrument made under any primary legislation;

'Swiss citizens' rights agreement' means (as modified from time to time in accordance with any provision of it) the Agreement signed at Bern on 25 February 2019 between the United Kingdom of Great Britain and Northern Ireland and the Swiss Confederation on citizens' rights following the withdrawal of the United Kingdom from—

(a) the European Union, and

(b) the free movement of persons agreement,

so far as the Agreement operates for the purposes of the case where 'specified date' for the purposes of that Agreement has the meaning given in Article 2(b)(ii) of that Agreement;

'withdrawal agreement' means the agreement between the United Kingdom and the EU under Article 50(2) of the Treaty on European Union which sets out the arrangements for the United Kingdom's withdrawal from the EU (as that agreement is modified from time to time in accordance with any provision of it).

(2) In this Act references to before, after or on IP completion day, or to beginning with IP completion day, are to be read as references to before, after or at 11.00 p.m. on 31 December 2020 or (as the case may be) to beginning with 11.00 p.m. on that day.

(3) Subsection (4) applies if, by virtue of any change to EU summer-time arrangements, the transition or implementation period provided for by Part 4 of the withdrawal agreement is to end on a day or time which is different from that specified in the definition of 'IP completion day' in subsection (1).

(4) A Minister of the Crown may by regulations—

(a) amend the definition of 'IP completion day' in subsection (1) to ensure that the day and time specified in the definition are the day and time that the transition or implementation period provided for by Part 4 of the withdrawal agreement is to end, and

(b) amend subsection (2) in consequence of any such amendment.

(5) In subsection (3) 'EU summer-time arrangements' means the arrangements provided for by Directive 2000/84/EC of the European Parliament and of the Council of 19 January 2001 on summer-time arrangements.

(6) In this Act any reference to an Article of the Treaty on European Union includes a reference to that Article as applied by Article 106a of the Euratom Treaty.

Supplementary and final

40 Regulations

Schedule 4 contains provision about regulations under this Act (including provision about procedure).

41 Consequential and transitional provision etc.

(1) A Minister of the Crown may by regulations make such provision as the Minister considers appropriate in consequence of this Act.

(2) The power to make regulations under subsection (1) may (among other things) be exercised by modifying any provision made by or under an enactment.

(3) In subsection (2) 'enactment' does not include primary legislation passed or made after IP completion day.

(4) Parts 1 and 2 of Schedule 5 contain minor and consequential provision.

(5) A Minister of the Crown may by regulations make such transitional, transitory or saving provision as the Minister considers appropriate in connection with the coming into force of any provision of this Act (including its operation in connection with exit day or IP completion day).

(6) Part 3 of Schedule 5 contains transitional, transitory and saving provision.

42 Extent, commencement and short title

(1) Subject to subsections (2) to (5), this Act extends to England and Wales, Scotland and Northern Ireland.

(2) Any provision of this Act which amends or repeals an enactment has the same extent as the enactment amended or repealed.

(3) Accordingly, section 1 (but not section 2) also extends to the Isle of Man, the Channel Islands and Gibraltar.

(4) The power in section 36 of the Immigration Act 1971 or (as the case may be) section 60(4) of the UK Borders Act 2007 may be exercised so as to extend (with or without modifications) to the Isle of Man or any of the Channel Islands the modifications made to that Act by section 10 above.

(5) Paragraphs 1 and 2 of Schedule 5, so far as they relate to the modification of any provision in subordinate legislation which extends outside England and Wales, Scotland and Northern Ireland, also extend there.

(6) The following provisions—

(a) sections 3 and 4,

(b) sections 11, 16 and 17,

(c) sections 20, 29 and 31 to 40 (including Schedule 4),

(d) section 41(1) to (3) and (5),

(e) the following provisions of Schedule 5—

(i) paragraphs 1(3) to (6) and 2,

(ii) paragraph 3(2) to (8),

(iii) paragraph 4,

(iv) paragraphs 5 and 7(a) and (b),

(v) paragraphs 8 and 12(a) and (b),

(vi) paragraphs 17, 20, 22, 24, 27 and 31,

(vii) paragraphs 32, 36(a) and (b) and 37(b) and (c),

(viii) paragraphs 38, 41(1) and (3)(a), 42, 44(1), (2)(a), (d) and (e) and (3), 47(1), (2), (4) and (6) and 50,

(ix) paragraphs 51 and 56(1) and (7)(b) for the purposes of making regulations under section 8A of, or Part 1A of Schedule 2 to, the European Union (Withdrawal) Act 2018,

(x) paragraphs 52(1) and (3) to (7) and 53(1) to (4), (6), (7)(a), (8)(a) and (9) to (13),

(xi) paragraph 56(1) and (6)(b) to (d), and

(xii) paragraphs 65 to 68,

(and section 41(4) and (6) so far as relating to any provision so far as it falls within any of sub-paragraphs (i) to (xii)), and

(f) this section,

come into force on the day on which this Act is passed.

(7) The provisions of this Act, so far as they are not brought into force by subsection (6), come into force on such day as a Minister of the Crown may by regulations appoint; and different days may be appointed for different purposes.

(8) This Act may be cited as the European Union (Withdrawal Agreement) Act 2020.

The EU–UK Trade and Cooperation Agreement 2020* (Selected extracts)**

TRADE AND COOPERATION AGREEMENT

between the European Union and the European Atomic Energy Community, of the one part, and the United Kingdom of Great Britain and Northern Ireland, of the other part

Preamble

THE EUROPEAN UNION AND THE EUROPEAN ATOMIC ENERGY COMMUNITY

AND

THE UNITED KINGDOM OF GREAT BRITAIN AND NORTHERN IRELAND,

1. REAFFIRMING their commitment to democratic principles, to the rule of law, to human rights, to countering proliferation of weapons of mass destruction and to the fight against climate change, which constitute essential elements of this and supplementing agreements,

2. RECOGNISING the importance of global cooperation to address issues of shared interest,

3. RECOGNISING the importance of transparency in international trade and investment to the benefit of all stakeholders,

4. SEEKING to establish clear and mutually advantageous rules governing trade and investment between the Parties,

5. CONSIDERING that in order to guarantee the efficient management and correct interpretation and application of this Agreement and any supplementing agreement as well as compliance with the obligations under those agreements, it is essential to establish provisions ensuring overall governance, in particular dispute settlement and enforcement rules that fully respect the autonomy of the respective legal orders of the Union and of the United Kingdom, as well as the United Kingdom's status as a country outside the European Union,

6. BUILDING upon their respective rights and obligations under the Marrakesh Agreement Establishing the World Trade Organization, done on 15 April 1994, and other multilateral and bilateral instruments of cooperation,

7. RECOGNISING the Parties' respective autonomy and rights to regulate within their territories in order to achieve legitimate public policy objectives such as the protection and promotion of public health, social services, public education, safety, the environment including climate change, public morals, social or consumer protection, animal welfare, privacy and data protection and the

---

* **Editor's Note:** As published in OJ 2021 L149/10.
** **Editor's Note:** As indicated throughout the text.

promotion and protection of cultural diversity, while striving to improve their respective high levels of protection,

8. BELIEVING in the benefits of a predictable commercial environment that fosters trade and investment between the Parties and prevents the distortion of trade and unfair competitive advantages, in a manner conducive to sustainable development in its economic, social and environmental dimensions,

9. RECOGNISING the need for an ambitious, wide-ranging and balanced economic partnership to be underpinned by a level playing field for open and fair competition and sustainable development, through effective and robust frameworks for subsidies and competition and a commitment to uphold their respective high levels of protection in the areas of labour and social standards, environment, the fight against climate change, and taxation,

10. RECOGNISING the need to ensure an open and secure market for businesses, including small and medium-sized enterprises, and their goods and services through addressing unjustified barriers to trade and investment,

11. NOTING the importance of facilitating new opportunities for businesses and consumers through digital trade, and addressing unjustified barriers to data flows and trade enabled by electronic means, whilst respecting the Parties' personal data protection rules,

12. DESIRING that this Agreement contribute to consumer welfare through policies ensuring a high level of consumer protection and economic well-being, as well as encouraging cooperation between relevant authorities,

13. CONSIDERING the importance of cross-border connectivity by air, by road and by sea, for passengers and for goods, and the need to ensure high standards in the provision of transportation services between the Parties,

14. RECOGNISING the benefits of trade and investment in energy and raw materials and the importance of supporting the delivery of cost efficient, clean and secure energy supplies to the Union and the United Kingdom,

15. NOTING the interest of the Parties in establishing a framework to facilitate technical cooperation and to develop new trading arrangements for interconnectors which deliver robust and efficient outcomes for all timeframes,

16. NOTING that cooperation and trade between the Parties in these areas should be based on fair competition in energy markets and non-discriminatory access to networks,

17. RECOGNISING the benefits of sustainable energy, renewable energy, in particular offshore generation in the North Sea, and energy efficiency,

18. DESIRING to promote the peaceful use of the waters adjacent to their coasts and the optimum and equitable utilisation of the marine living resources in those waters including the continued sustainable management of shared stocks,

19. NOTING that the United Kingdom withdrew from the European Union and that with effect from 1 January 2021, the United Kingdom is an independent coastal State with corresponding rights and obligations under international law,

20. AFFIRMING that the sovereign rights of the coastal States exercised by the Parties for the purpose of exploring, exploiting, conserving and managing the living resources in their waters should be conducted pursuant to and in accordance with the principles of international law, including the United Nations Convention on the Law of the Sea, done at Montego Bay on 10 December 1982 (United Nations Convention on the Law of the Sea),

21. RECOGNISING the importance of the coordination of social security rights enjoyed by persons moving between the Parties to work, to stay or to reside, as well as the rights enjoyed by their family members and survivors,

22. CONSIDERING that cooperation in areas of shared interest, such as science, research and innovation, nuclear research and space, in the form of the participation of the United Kingdom in the corresponding Union programmes under fair and appropriate conditions will benefit both Parties,

23. CONSIDERING that cooperation between the United Kingdom and the Union relating to the prevention, investigation, detection or prosecution of criminal offences and to the execution of

criminal penalties, including the safeguarding against and prevention of threats to public security, will enable the security of the United Kingdom and the Union to be strengthened,

24. DESIRING that an agreement is concluded between the United Kingdom and the Union to provide a legal base for such cooperation,

25. ACKNOWLEDGING that the Parties may supplement this Agreement with other agreements forming an integral part of their overall bilateral relations as governed by this Agreement and that the Agreement on Security Procedures for Exchanging and Protecting Classified Information is concluded as such a supplementing agreement, and enables the exchange of classified information between the Parties under this Agreement or any other supplementing agreement,

HAVE AGREED AS FOLLOWS:

PART ONE COMMON AND INSTITUTIONAL PROVISIONS
Title I General provisions

Article 1 Purpose
This Agreement establishes the basis for a broad relationship between the Parties, within an area of prosperity and good neighbourliness characterised by close and peaceful relations based on cooperation, respectful of the Parties' autonomy and sovereignty.

Article 2 Supplementing agreements
1. Where the Union and the United Kingdom conclude other bilateral agreements between them, such agreements shall constitute supplementing agreements to this Agreement, unless otherwise provided for in those agreements. Such supplementing agreements shall be an integral part of the overall bilateral relations as governed by this Agreement and shall form part of the overall framework.

2. Paragraph 1 also applies to:
   (a) agreements between the Union and its Member States, of the one part, and the United Kingdom, of the other part; and
   (b) agreements between the European Atomic Energy Community, of the one part, and the United Kingdom, of the other part.

Article 3 Good faith
1. The Parties shall, in full mutual respect and good faith, assist each other in carrying out tasks that flow from this Agreement and any supplementing agreement.

2. They shall take all appropriate measures, whether general or particular, to ensure the fulfilment of the obligations arising from this Agreement and from any supplementing agreement, and shall refrain from any measures which could jeopardise the attainment of the objectives of this Agreement or any supplementing agreement.

Title II Principles of interpretation and definitions

Article 4 Public international law
1. The provisions of this Agreement and any supplementing agreement shall be interpreted in good faith in accordance with their ordinary meaning in their context and in light of the object and purpose of the agreement in accordance with customary rules of interpretation of public international law, including those codified in the Vienna Convention on the Law of Treaties, done at Vienna on 23 May 1969.

2. For greater certainty, neither this Agreement nor any supplementing agreement establishes an obligation to interpret their provisions in accordance with the domestic law of either Party.

3. For greater certainty, an interpretation of this Agreement or any supplementing agreement given by the courts of either Party shall not be binding on the courts of the other Party.

Article 5 Private rights

1. Without prejudice to Article SSC.67 of the Protocol on Social Security Coordination and with the exception, with regard to the Union, of Part Three of this Agreement, nothing in this Agreement or any supplementing agreement shall be construed as conferring rights or imposing obligations on persons other than those created between the Parties under public international law, nor as permitting this Agreement or any supplementing agreement to be directly invoked in the domestic legal systems of the Parties.

2. A Party shall not provide for a right of action under its law against the other Party on the ground that the other Party has acted in breach of this Agreement or any supplementing agreement.

Article 6 Definitions

1. For the purposes of this Agreement and any supplementing agreement, and unless otherwise specified, the following definitions apply:

(a) 'data subject' means an identified or identifiable natural person; an identifiable person being a person who can be identified, directly or indirectly, in particular by reference to an identifier such as a name, an identification number, location data or an online identifier, or to one or more factors specific to the physical, physiological, genetic, mental, economic, cultural or social identity of that natural person;

(b) 'day' means a calendar day;

(c) 'Member State' means a Member State of the European Union;

(d) 'personal data' means any information relating to a data subject;

(e) 'State' means a Member State or the United Kingdom, as the context requires;

(f) 'territory' of a Party means in respect of each Party the territories to which this Agreement applies in accordance with Article 774;

(g) 'the transition period' means the transition period provided for in Article 126 of the Withdrawal Agreement; and

(h) 'Withdrawal Agreement' means the Agreement on the withdrawal of the United Kingdom of Great Britain and Northern Ireland from the European Union and the European Atomic Energy Community, including its Protocols.

2. Any reference to the 'Union', 'Party' or 'Parties' in this Agreement or any supplementing agreement shall be understood as not including the European Atomic Energy Community, unless otherwise specified or where the context otherwise requires.

Title III Institutional framework

Article 7 Partnership Council

1. A Partnership Council is hereby established. It shall comprise representatives of the Union and of the United Kingdom. The Partnership Council may meet in different configurations depending on the matters under discussion.

2. The Partnership Council shall be co-chaired by a Member of the European Commission and a representative of the Government of the United Kingdom at ministerial level. It shall meet at the request of the Union or the United Kingdom, and, in any event, at least once a year, and shall set its meeting schedule and its agenda by mutual consent.

3. The Partnership Council shall oversee the attainment of the objectives of this Agreement and any supplementing agreement. It shall supervise and facilitate the implementation and application of this Agreement and of any supplementing agreement. Each Party may refer to the Partnership Council any issue relating to the implementation, application and interpretation of this Agreement or of any supplementing agreement.

4. The Partnership Council shall have the power to:

(a) adopt decisions in respect of all matters where this Agreement or any supplementing agreement so provides;

(b) make recommendations to the Parties regarding the implementation and application of this Agreement or of any supplementing agreement;

(c) adopt, by decision, amendments to this Agreement or to any supplementing agreement in the cases provided for in this Agreement or in any supplementing agreement;

(d) except in relation to Title III of Part One, until the end of the fourth year following the entry into force of this Agreement, adopt decisions amending this Agreement or any supplementing agreement, provided that such amendments are necessary to correct errors, or to address omissions or other deficiencies;

(e) discuss any matter related to the areas covered by this Agreement or by any supplementing agreement;

(f) delegate certain of its powers to the Trade Partnership Committee or to a Specialised Committee, except those powers and responsibilities referred to in point (g) of this paragraph;

(g) by decision, establish Trade Specialised Committees and Specialised Committees, other than those referred to in Article 8 (1), dissolve any Trade Specialised Committee or Specialised Committee, or change the tasks assigned to them; and

(h) make recommendations to the Parties regarding the transfer of personal data in specific areas covered by this Agreement or any supplementing agreement.

5. The work of the Partnership Council shall be governed by the rules of procedure set out in Annex 1. The Partnership Council may amend that Annex.

Article 8   Committees [8.3 and 8.4 omitted]

1. The following Committees are hereby established:

(a) the Trade Partnership Committee, which addresses matters covered by Titles I to VII, Chapter 4 of Title VIII, Titles IX to XII of Heading One of Part Two, Heading Six of Part Two, and Annex 27;

(b) the Trade Specialised Committee on Goods which addresses matters covered by Chapter 1 of Title I of Heading One of Part Two and Chapter 4 of Title VIII of Heading One of Part Two;

(c) the Trade Specialised Committee on Customs Cooperation and Rules of Origin, which addresses matters covered by Chapters 2 and 5 of Title I of Heading One of Part Two, the Protocol on mutual administrative assistance in customs matters and the provisions on customs enforcement of intellectual property rights, fees and charges, customs valuation and repaired goods;

(d) the Trade Specialised Committee on Sanitary and Phytosanitary Measures, which addresses matters covered by Chapter 3 of Title I of Heading One of Part Two;

(e) the Trade Specialised Committee on Technical Barriers to Trade, which addresses matters covered by Chapter 4 of Title I of Heading One of Part Two and Article 323;

(f) the Trade Specialised Committee on Services, Investment and Digital Trade, which addresses matters covered by Titles II to IV of Heading One of Part Two and Chapter 4 of Title VIII of Heading One of Part Two;

(g) the Trade Specialised Committee on Intellectual Property, which addresses matters covered by Title V of Heading One of Part Two;

(h) the Trade Specialised Committee on Public Procurement, which addresses matters covered by Title VI of Heading One of Part Two;

(i) the Trade Specialised Committee on Regulatory Cooperation, which addresses matters covered by Title X of Heading One of Part Two;

(j) the Trade Specialised Committee on Level Playing Field for Open and Fair Competition and Sustainable Development, which addresses matters covered by Title XI of Heading One of Part Two and Annex 27;

(k) the Trade Specialised Committee on Administrative Cooperation in VAT and Recovery of Taxes and Duties, which addresses matters covered by the Protocol on administrative cooperation and combating fraud in the field of Value Added Tax and on mutual assistance for the recovery of claims relating to taxes and duties;

(l) the Specialised Committee on Energy,

(i) which addresses matters covered by Title VIII of Heading One of Part Two, with the exception of Chapter 4, Article 323 and Annex 27, and

(ii) which can discuss and provide expertise to the relevant Trade Specialised Committee on matters pertaining to Chapter 4 and Article 323;

(m) the Specialised Committee on Air Transport, which addresses matters covered by Title I of Heading Two of Part Two;

(n) the Specialised Committee on Aviation Safety, which addresses matters covered by Title II of Heading Two of Part Two;

(o) the Specialised Committee on Road Transport, which addresses matters covered by Heading Three of Part Two;

(p) the Specialised Committee on Social Security Coordination, which addresses matters covered by Heading Four of Part Two and the Protocol on Social Security Coordination;

(q) the Specialised Committee on Fisheries, which addresses matters covered by Heading Five of Part Two;

(r) the Specialised Committee on Law Enforcement and Judicial Cooperation, which addresses matters covered by Part Three; and

(s) the Specialised Committee on Participation in Union Programmes, which addresses matters covered by Part Five.

2. With respect to issues related to Titles I to VII, Chapter 4 of Title VIII, Titles IX to XII of Heading One of Part Two, Heading Six of Part Two and Annex 27, the Trade Partnership Committee referred to in paragraph 1 of this Article shall have the power to:

(a) assist the Partnership Council in the performance of its tasks and, in particular, report to the Partnership Council and carry out any task assigned to it by the latter;

(b) supervise the implementation of this Agreement or any supplementing agreement;

(c) adopt decisions or make recommendations as provided for in this Agreement or any supplementing agreement or where such power has been delegated to it by the Partnership Council;

(d) supervise the work of the Trade Specialised Committees referred to in paragraph 1 of this Article;

(e) explore the most appropriate way to prevent or solve any difficulty that may arise in relation to the interpretation and application of this Agreement or any supplementing agreement, without prejudice to Title I of Part Six;

(f) exercise the powers delegated to it by the Partnership Council pursuant to point (f) of Article 7(4);

(g) establish, by decision, Trade Specialised Committees other than those referred to in paragraph 1 of this Article, dissolve any such Trade Specialised Committee, or change the tasks assigned to them; and

(h) establish, supervise, coordinate and dissolve Working Groups, or delegate their supervision to a Trade Specialised Committee.

5. Committees shall comprise representatives of each Party. Each Party shall ensure that its representatives on the Committees have the appropriate expertise with respect to the issues under discussion.

6. The Trade Partnership Committee shall be co-chaired by a senior representative of the Union and a representative of the United Kingdom with responsibility for trade-related matters, or their designees. It shall meet at the request of the Union or the United Kingdom, and, in any event, at least once a year, and shall set its meeting schedule and its agenda by mutual consent.

7. The Trade Specialised Committees and the Specialised Committees shall be co-chaired by a representative of the Union and a representative of the United Kingdom. Unless otherwise provided for in this Agreement, or unless the co-chairs decide otherwise, they shall meet at least once a year.

8. Committees shall set their meeting schedule and agenda by mutual consent.

9. The work of the Committees shall be governed by the rules of procedure set out in Annex 1.

10. By way of derogation from paragraph 9, a Committee may adopt and subsequently amend its own rules that shall govern its work.

Article 9   Working Groups

1. The following Working Groups are hereby established:

(a) the Working Group on Organic Products, under the supervision of the Trade Specialised Committee on Technical Barriers to Trade;

(b) the Working Group on Motor Vehicles and Parts, under the supervision of the Trade Specialised Committee on Technical Barriers to Trade;

(c) the Working Group on Medicinal Products, under the supervision of the Trade Specialised Committee on Technical Barriers to Trade;

(d) the Working Group on Social Security Coordination, under the supervision of the Specialised Committee on Social Security Coordination.

2. Working Groups shall, under the supervision of Committees, assist Committees in the performance of their tasks and, in particular, prepare the work of Committees and carry out any task assigned to them by the latter.

3. Working Groups shall comprise representatives of the Union and of the United Kingdom and shall be co-chaired by a representative of the Union and a representative of the United Kingdom.

4. Working Groups shall set their own rules of procedure, meeting schedule and agenda by mutual consent.

Article 10   Decisions and recommendations

1. The decisions adopted by the Partnership Council, or, as the case may be, by a Committee, shall be binding on the Parties and on all the bodies set up under this Agreement and under any supplementing agreement, including the arbitration tribunal referred to in Title I of Part Six. Recommendations shall have no binding force.

2. The Partnership Council or, as the case may be, a Committee, shall adopt decisions and make recommendations by mutual consent.

Article 11   Parliamentary cooperation

1. The European Parliament and the Parliament of the United Kingdom may establish a Parliamentary Partnership Assembly consisting of Members of the European Parliament and of Members of the Parliament of the United Kingdom, as a forum to exchange views on the partnership.

2. Upon its establishment, the Parliamentary Partnership Assembly:

(a) may request relevant information regarding the implementation of this Agreement and any supplementing agreement from the Partnership Council, which shall then supply that Assembly with the requested information;

(b) shall be informed of the decisions and recommendations of the Partnership Council; and

(c) may make recommendations to the Partnership Council.

Article 12   Participation of civil society

The Parties shall consult civil society on the implementation of this Agreement and any supplementing agreement, in particular through interaction with the domestic advisory groups and the Civil Society Forum referred to in Articles 13 and 14.

Article 13   Domestic advisory groups

1. Each Party shall consult on issues covered by this Agreement and any supplementing agreement its newly created or existing domestic advisory group or groups comprising a representation of independent civil society organisations including non-governmental organisations, business and employers' organisations, as well as trade unions, active in economic, sustainable development, social, human rights, environmental and other matters. Each Party may convene its domestic advisory group or groups in different configurations to discuss the implementation of different provisions of this Agreement or of any supplementing agreement.

2. Each Party shall consider views or recommendations submitted by its domestic advisory group or groups. Representatives of each Party shall aim to consult with their respective domestic advisory group or groups at least once a year. Meetings may be held by virtual means.

3. In order to promote public awareness of the domestic advisory groups, each Party shall endeavour to publish the list of organisations participating in its domestic advisory group or groups as well as the contact point for that or those groups.

4. The Parties shall promote interaction between their respective domestic advisory groups, including by exchanging where possible the contact details of members of their domestic advisory groups.

Article 14 Civil Society Forum

1. The Parties shall facilitate the organisation of a Civil Society Forum to conduct a dialogue on the implementation of Part Two. The Partnership Council shall adopt operational guidelines for the conduct of the Forum.

2. The Civil Society Forum shall meet at least once a year, unless otherwise agreed by the Parties. The Civil Society Forum may meet by virtual means.

3. The Civil Society Forum shall be open for the participation of independent civil society organisations established in the territories of the Parties, including members of the domestic advisory groups referred to in Article 13. Each Party shall promote a balanced representation, including non-governmental organisations, business and employers' organisations and trade unions, active in economic, sustainable development, social, human rights, environmental and other matters.

PART TWO TRADE, TRANSPORT, FISHERIES AND OTHER ARRANGEMENTS

HEADING ONE TRADE

Title I Trade in goods

Chapter 1 National treatment and market access for goods (including trade remedies)

Article 15 Objective

The objective of this Chapter is to facilitate trade in goods between the Parties and to maintain liberalised trade in goods in accordance with the provisions of this Agreement.

Article 16 Scope

Except as otherwise provided, this Chapter applies to trade in goods of a Party.

Article 17 Definitions

For the purposes of this Chapter, the following definitions apply:

- (a) 'consular transactions' means the procedure of obtaining from a consul of the importing Party in the territory of the exporting Party, or in the territory of a third party, a consular invoice or a consular visa for a commercial invoice, certificate of origin, manifest, shipper's export declaration or any other customs documentation in connection with the importation of the good;
- (b) 'Customs Valuation Agreement' means the Agreement on Implementation of Article VII of GATT 1994;
- (c) 'export licensing procedure' means an administrative procedure, whether or not referred to as licensing, used by a Party for the operation of export licensing regimes, requiring the submission of an application or other documentation, other than that generally required for customs clearance purposes, to the relevant administrative body as a prior condition for exportation from that Party;
- (d) 'import licensing procedure' means an administrative procedure, whether or not referred to as licensing, used by a Party for the operation of import licensing regimes, requiring the submission of an application or other documentation, other than that generally required for customs clearance purposes, to the relevant administrative body or bodies as a prior condition for importation into the territory of the importing Party;
- (e) 'originating goods' means, unless otherwise provided, a good qualifying under the rules of origin set out in Chapter 2 of this Title;
- (f) 'performance requirement' means a requirement that:
  - (i) a given quantity, value or percentage of goods be exported;
  - (ii) goods of the Party granting an import licence be substituted for imported goods;

(iii) a person benefiting from an import licence purchase other goods in the territory of the Party granting the import licence, or accord a preference to domestically produced goods;

(iv) a person benefiting from an import licence produce goods in the territory of the Party granting the import licence, with a given quantity, value or percentage of domestic content; or

(v) relates in whatever form to the volume or value of imports, to the volume or value of exports or to the amount of foreign exchange flows;

(g) 'remanufactured good' means a good classified under HS Chapters 32, 40, 84 to 90, 94 or 95 that:

(i) is entirely or partially composed of parts obtained from used goods;

(ii) has similar life expectancy and performance compared with such goods, when new; and

(iii) is given an equivalent warranty to as that applicable to such goods when new; and

(h) 'repair' means any processing operation undertaken on a good to remedy operating defects or material damage and entailing the re-establishment of the good to its original function or to ensure compliance with technical requirements for its use. Repair of a good includes restoration and maintenance, with a possible increase in the value of the good from restoring the original functionality of that good, but does not include an operation or process that:

(i) destroys the essential characteristics of a good, or creates a new or commercially different good;

(ii) transforms an unfinished good into a finished good; or

(iii) is used to improve or upgrade the technical performance of a good.

Article 18 Classification of goods

The classification of goods in trade between the Parties under this Agreement is set out in each Party's respective tariff nomenclature in conformity with the Harmonised System.

Article 19 National treatment on internal taxation and regulation

Each Party shall accord national treatment to the goods of the other Party in accordance with Article III of GATT 1994 including its Notes and Supplementary Provisions. To that end, Article III of GATT 1994 and its Notes and Supplementary Provisions are incorporated into and made part of this Agreement, *mutatis mutandis*.

Article 20 Freedom of transit

Each Party shall accord freedom of transit through its territory, via the routes most convenient for international transit, for traffic in transit to or from the territory of the other Party or of any other third country. To that end, Article V of GATT 1994 and its Notes and Supplementary Provisions are incorporated into and made part of this Agreement, *mutatis mutandis*. The Parties understand that Article V of GATT 1994 includes the movement of energy goods via *inter alia* pipelines or electricity grids.

Article 21 Prohibition of customs duties

Except as otherwise provided for in this Agreement, customs duties on all goods originating in the other Party shall be prohibited.

Article 22 Export duties, taxes or other charges

1. A Party may not adopt or maintain any duty, tax or other charge of any kind imposed on, or in connection with, the exportation of a good to the other Party; or any internal tax or other charge on a good exported to the other Party that is in excess of the tax or charge that would be imposed on like goods when destined for domestic consumption.

2. For the purpose of this Article, the term 'other charge of any kind' does not include fees or other charges that are permitted under Article 23.

Article 23   Fees and formalities

1. Fees and other charges imposed by a Party on or in connection with importation or exportation of a good of the other Party shall be limited in amount to the approximate cost of the services rendered, and shall not represent an indirect protection to domestic goods or taxation of imports or exports for fiscal purposes. A Party shall not levy fees or other charges on or in connection with importation or exportation on an *ad valorem* basis.

2. Each Party may impose charges or recover costs only where specific services are rendered, in particular, but not limited to, the following:

(a) attendance, where requested, by customs staff outside official office hours or at premises other than customs premises;

(b) analyses or expert reports on goods and postal fees for the return of goods to an applicant, particularly in respect of decisions relating to binding information or the provision of information concerning the application of the customs laws and regulations;

(c) the examination or sampling of goods for verification purposes, or the destruction of goods, where costs other than the cost of using customs staff are involved; and

(d) exceptional control measures, if these are necessary due to the nature of the goods or to a potential risk.

3. Each Party shall promptly publish all fees and charges it imposes in connection with importation or exportation via an official website in such a manner as to enable governments, traders and other interested parties, to become acquainted with them. That information shall include the reason for the fee or charge for the service provided, the responsible authority, the fees and charges that will be applied, and when and how payment is to be made. New or amended fees and charges shall not be imposed until information in accordance with this paragraph has been published and made readily available.

4. A Party shall not require consular transactions, including related fees and charges, in connection with the importation of any good of the other Party.

Article 24   Repaired goods

1. A Party shall not apply a customs duty to a good, regardless of its origin, that re-enters the Party's territory after that good has been temporarily exported from its territory to the territory of the other Party for repair.

2. Paragraph 1 does not apply to a good imported in bond, into free trade zones, or in similar status, that is then exported for repair and is not re-imported in bond, into free trade zones, or in similar status.

3. A Party shall not apply a customs duty to a good, regardless of its origin, imported temporarily from the territory of the other Party for repair.

Article 25   Remanufactured goods

1. A Party shall not accord to remanufactured goods of the other Party treatment that is less favourable than that which it accords to equivalent goods in new condition.

2. Article 26 applies to import and export prohibitions or restrictions on remanufactured goods. If a Party adopts or maintains import and export prohibitions or restrictions on used goods, it shall not apply those measures to remanufactured goods.

3. A Party may require that remanufactured goods be identified as such for distribution or sale in its territory and that they meet all applicable technical requirements that apply to equivalent goods in new condition.

Article 26   Import and export restrictions

1. A Party shall not adopt or maintain any prohibition or restriction on the importation of any good of the other Party or on the exportation or sale for export of any good destined for the territory of the other Party, except in accordance with Article XI of GATT 1994, including its Notes and Supplementary Provisions. To that end, Article XI of GATT 1994 and its Notes and Supplementary Provisions are incorporated into and made part of this Agreement, *mutatis mutandis*.

2. A Party shall not adopt or maintain:
  (a) export and import price requirements, except as permitted in enforcement of counter-vailing and anti-dumping duty orders and undertakings; or
  (b) import licensing conditioned on the fulfilment of a performance requirement.

Article 27   Import and export monopolies

A Party shall not designate or maintain an import or export monopoly. For the purposes of this Article, import or export monopoly means the exclusive right or grant of authority by a Party to an entity to import a good from, or export a good to, the other Party.

Article 28   Import licensing procedures

1. Each Party shall ensure that all import licensing procedures applicable to trade in goods be-tween the Parties are neutral in application, and are administered in a fair, equitable, non-discrim-inatory and transparent manner.

2. A Party shall only adopt or maintain licensing procedures as a condition for importation into its territory from the territory of the other Party, if other appropriate procedures to achieve an ad-ministrative purpose are not reasonably available.

3. A Party shall not adopt or maintain any non-automatic import licensing procedure, unless it is necessary to implement a measure that is consistent with this Agreement. A Party adopting such non-automatic import licensing procedure shall indicate clearly the measure being implemented through that procedure.

4. Each Party shall introduce and administer any import licensing procedure in accordance with Articles 1 to 3 of the WTO Agreement on Import Licensing Procedures ('the Import Licensing Agreement'). To that end, Articles 1 to 3 of the Import Licensing Agreement are incorporated into and made part of this Agreement *mutatis mutandis*.

5. Any Party introducing or modifying any import licensing procedure shall make all relevant information available online on an official website. That information shall be made available, when-ever practicable, at least 21 days prior to the date of the application of the new or modified licensing procedure and in any event no later than the date of application. That information shall contain the data required under Article 5 of the Import Licensing Agreement.

6. At the request of the other Party, a Party shall promptly provide any relevant information regarding any import licensing procedures that it intends to adopt or that it maintains, including the information referred to in Articles 1 to 3 of the Import Licensing Agreement.

7. For greater certainty, nothing in this Article requires a Party to grant an import licence, or prevents a Party from implementing its obligations or commitments under United Nations Security Council Resolutions or under multilateral non-proliferation regimes and import control arrangements.

Article 29   Export licensing procedures [29.2–29.4 omitted]

1. Each Party shall publish any new export licensing procedure, or any modification to an exist-ing export licensing procedure, in such a manner as to enable governments, traders and other interested parties to become acquainted with them. Such publication shall take place, whenever practicable, 45 days before the procedure or modification takes effect, and in any case no later than the date such procedure or modification takes effect and, where appropriate, publication shall take place on any relevant government websites.

Article 30   Customs valuation [omitted]

Article 31   Preference utilization [omitted]

Article 32   Trade remedies

1. The Parties affirm their rights and obligations under Article VI of GATT 1994, the Anti-Dumping Agreement, the SCM Agreement, Article XIX of GATT 1994, the Safeguards Agreement, and Article 5 of the Agreement on Agriculture.

2. Chapter 2 of this Title does not apply to anti-dumping, countervailing and safeguard investi-gations and measures.

3. Each Party shall apply anti-dumping and countervailing measures in accordance with the requirements of the Anti-Dumping Agreement and the SCM Agreement, and pursuant to a fair and transparent process.

4. Provided it does not unnecessarily delay the conduct of the investigation, each interested party in an anti-dumping or countervailing investigation[1] shall be granted a full opportunity to defend its interests.

5. Each Party's investigating authority may, in accordance with the Party's law, consider whether the amount of the anti-dumping duty to be imposed shall be the full margin of dumping or a lesser amount.

6. Each Party's investigating authority shall, in accordance with the Party's law, consider information provided as to whether imposing an anti-dumping or a countervailing duty would not be in the public interest.

7. A Party shall not apply or maintain, with respect to the same good, at the same time:

    (a) a measure pursuant to Article 5 of the Agreement on Agriculture; and

    (b) a measure pursuant to Article XIX of GATT 1994 and the Safeguards Agreement.

8. Title I of Part Six does not apply to paragraphs 1 to 6 of this Article.

Article 33   Use of existing WTO tariff rate quotas

1. Products originating in one Party shall not be eligible to be imported into the other Party under existing WTO Tariff Rate Quotas ('TRQs') as defined in paragraph 2. This shall include those TRQs as being apportioned between the Parties pursuant to Article XXVIII GATT negotiations initiated by the European Union in WTO document G/SECRET/42/Add.2 and by the United Kingdom in WTO document G/SECRET/44 and as set out in each Party's respective internal legislation. For the purposes of this Article, the originating status of the products shall be determined on the basis of non-preferential rules of origin applicable in the importing Party.

2. For the purposes of paragraph 1, 'existing WTO TRQs' means those tariff rate quotas which are WTO concessions of the European Union included in the draft EU28 schedule of concessions and commitments under GATT 1994 submitted to the WTO in document G/MA/TAR/RS/506 as amended by documents G/MA/TAR/RS/506/Add.1 and G/MA/TAR/RS/506/Add.2.

Article 34   Measures in case of breaches or circumventions of customs legislation

1. The Parties shall cooperate in preventing, detecting and combating breaches or circumventions of customs legislation, in accordance with their obligations under Chapter 2 of this Title and the Protocol on mutual administrative assistance in customs matters. Each Party shall take appropriate and comparable measures to protect its own and the other Party's financial interests regarding the levying of duties on goods entering the customs territories of the United Kingdom or the Union.

2. Subject to the possibility of exemption for compliant traders under paragraph 7, a Party may temporarily suspend the relevant preferential treatment of the product or products concerned in accordance with the procedure laid down in paragraphs 3 and 4 if:

    (a) that Party has made a finding, based on objective, compelling and verifiable information, that systematic and large-scale breaches or circumventions of customs legislation have been committed, and;

    (b) the other Party repeatedly and unjustifiably refuses or otherwise fails to comply with the obligations referred to in paragraph 1.

3. The Party which has made a finding as referred to in paragraph 2 shall notify the Trade Partnership Committee and shall enter into consultations with the other Party within the Trade Partnership Committee with a view to reaching a mutually acceptable solution.

4. If the Parties fail to agree on a mutually acceptable solution within three months after the date of notification, the Party which has made the finding may decide to suspend temporarily

---

[1] For the purpose of this Article, interested parties shall be defined as per Article 6.11 of the Anti-dumping Agreement and Article 12.9 of the SCM Agreement.

the relevant preferential treatment of the product or products concerned. In this case, the Party which made the finding shall notify the temporary suspension, including the period during which it intends the temporary suspension to apply, to the Trade Partnership Committee without delay.

5. The temporary suspension shall apply only for the period necessary to counteract the breaches or circumventions and to protect the financial interests of the Party concerned, and in any case not for longer than six months. The Party concerned shall keep the situation under review and, where it decides that the temporary suspension is no longer necessary, it shall bring it to an end before the end of the period notified to the Trade Partnership Committee. Where the conditions that gave rise to the suspension persist at the expiry of the period notified to the Trade Partnership Committee, the Party concerned may decide to renew the suspension. Any suspension shall be subject to periodic consultations within the Trade Partnership Committee.

6. Each Party shall publish, in accordance with its internal procedures, notices to importers about any decision concerning temporary suspensions referred to in paragraphs 4 and 5.

7. Notwithstanding paragraph 4, if an importer is able to satisfy the importing customs authority that such products are fully compliant with the importing Party's customs legislation, the requirements of this Agreement, and any other appropriate conditions related to the temporary suspension established by the importing Party in accordance with its laws and regulations, the importing Party shall allow the importer to apply for preferential treatment and recover any duties paid in excess of the applicable preferential tariff rates when the products were imported.

Article 35 Management of administrative errors [omitted]

Article 36 Cultural property

1. The Parties shall cooperate in facilitating the return of cultural property illicitly removed from the territory of a Party, having regard to the principles enshrined in the UNESCO Convention on the Means of Prohibiting and Preventing the Illicit Import, Export and Transfer of Ownership of Cultural Property signed in Paris on 17 November 1970.

2. For the purposes of this Article, the following definitions apply:
- (a) 'cultural property' means property classified or defined as being among the national treasures possessing artistic, historic or archaeological value under the respective rules and procedures of each Party; and
- (b) 'illicitly removed from the territory of a Party' means:
  - (i) removed from the territory of a Party on or after 1 January 1993 in breach of that Party's rules on the protection of national treasures or in breach of its rules on the export of cultural property; or
  - (ii) not returned at the end of a period of lawful temporary removal or any breach of another condition governing such temporary removal, on or after 1 January 1993.

3. The competent authorities of the Parties shall cooperate with each other in particular by:
- (a) notifying the other Party where cultural property is found in their territory and there are reasonable grounds for believing that the cultural property has been illicitly removed from the territory of the other Party;
- (b) addressing requests of the other Party for the return of cultural property which has been illicitly removed from the territory of that Party;
- (c) preventing any actions to evade the return of such cultural property, by means of any necessary interim measures; and
- (d) taking any necessary measures for the physical preservation of cultural property which has been illicitly removed from the territory of the other Party.

4. Each Party shall identify a contact point responsible for communicating with the contact point of the other Party with respect to any matters arising under this Article, including with respect to the notifications and requests referred to in points (a) and (b) of paragraph 3.

5. The envisaged cooperation between the Parties shall involve the customs authorities of the Parties responsible for managing export procedures for cultural property as appropriate and necessary.

6. Title I of Part Six does not apply to this Article.

Chapter 2   Rules of origin

Section 1 Rules of origin

Article 37   Objective

The objective of this Chapter is to lay down the provisions determining the origin of goods for the purpose of application of preferential tariff treatment under this Agreement, and setting out related origin procedures.

Article 38   Definitions

For the purposes of this Chapter, the following definitions apply:

(a) 'classification' means the classification of a product or material under a particular chapter, heading, or sub-heading of the Harmonised System;

(b) 'consignment' means products which are either sent simultaneously from one exporter to one consignee or covered by a single transport document covering their shipment from the exporter to the consignee or, in the absence of such a document, by a single invoice;

(c) 'exporter' means a person, located in a Party, who, in accordance with the requirements laid down in the laws and regulations of that Party, exports or produces the originating product and makes out a statement on origin;

(d) 'importer' means a person who imports the originating product and claims preferential tariff treatment for it;

(e) 'material' means any substance used in the production of a product, including any components, ingredients, raw materials, or parts;

(f) 'non-originating material' means a material which does not qualify as originating under this Chapter, including a material whose originating status cannot be determined;

(g) 'product' means the product resulting from the production, even if it is intended for use as a material in the production of another product;

(h) 'production' means any kind of working or processing including assembly.

Article 39   General requirements

1. For the purposes of applying the preferential tariff treatment by a Party to the originating good of the other Party in accordance with this Agreement, provided that the products satisfy all other applicable requirements of this Chapter, the following products shall be considered as originating in the other Party:

(a) products wholly obtained in that Party within the meaning of Article 41;

(b) products produced in that Party exclusively from originating materials in that Party; and

(c) products produced in that Party incorporating non-originating materials provided they satisfy the requirements set out in Annex 3.

2. If a product has acquired originating status, the non-originating materials used in the production of that product shall not be considered as non-originating when that product is incorporated as a material in another product.

3. The acquisition of originating status shall be fulfilled without interruption in the United Kingdom or the Union.

Article 40   Cumulation of origin

1. A product originating in a Party shall be considered as originating in the other Party if that product is used as a material in the production of another product in that other Party.

2. Production carried out in a Party on a non-originating material may be taken into account for the purpose of determining whether a product is originating in the other Party.

3. Paragraphs 1 and 2 do not apply if the production carried out in the other Party does not go beyond the operations referred to in Article 43.

4. In order for an exporter to complete the statement on origin referred to in point (a) of Article 54(2) for a product referred to in paragraph 2 of this Article, the exporter shall obtain from its

supplier a supplier's declaration as provided for in Annex 6 or an equivalent document that contains the same information describing the non-originating materials concerned in sufficient detail to enable them to be identified.

Article 41   Wholly obtained products

1. The following products shall be considered as wholly obtained in a Party:
  (a) mineral products extracted or taken from its soil or from its seabed;
  (b) plants and vegetable products grown or harvested there;
  (c) live animals born and raised there;
  (d) products obtained from live animals raised there;
  (e) products obtained from slaughtered animals born and raised there;
  (f) products obtained by hunting or fishing conducted there;
  (g) products obtained from aquaculture there if aquatic organisms, including fish, molluscs, crustaceans, other aquatic invertebrates and aquatic plants are born or raised from seed stock such as eggs, roes, fry, fingerlings, larvae, parr, smolts or other immature fish at a post-larval stage by intervention in the rearing or growth processes to enhance production such as regular stocking, feeding or protection from predators;
  (h) products of sea fishing and other products taken from the sea outside any territorial sea by a vessel of a Party;
  (i) products made aboard of a factory ship of a Party exclusively from products referred to in point (h);
  (j) products extracted from the seabed or subsoil outside any territorial sea provided that they have rights to exploit or work such seabed or subsoil;
  (k) waste and scrap resulting from production operations conducted there;
  (l) waste and scrap derived from used products collected there, provided that those products are fit only for the recovery of raw materials;
  (m) products produced there exclusively from the products specified in points (a) to (l).

2. The terms 'vessel of a Party' and 'factory ship of a Party' in points (h) and (i) of paragraph 1 mean a vessel and factory ship which:
  (a) is registered in a Member State or in the United Kingdom;
  (b) sails under the flag of a Member State or of the United Kingdom; and
  (c) meets one of the following conditions:
    (i) it is at least 50% owned by nationals of a Member State or of the United Kingdom; or
    (ii) it is owned by legal persons which each:
      (A) have their head office and main place of business in the Union or the United Kingdom; and
      (B) are at least 50% owned by public entities, nationals or legal persons of a Member State or the United Kingdom.

Articles 42–52   [Omitted]

Article 53   Review of drawback of, or exemption from, customs duties

Not earlier than two years from the entry into force of this Agreement, at the request of either Party, the Trade Specialised Committee on Customs Cooperation and Rules of Origin shall review the Parties' respective duty drawback and inward-processing schemes. For that purpose, at the request of a Party, no later than 60 days from that request, the other Party shall provide the requesting Party with available information and detailed statistics covering the period from the entry into force of this Agreement, or the previous five year period if that period is shorter, on the operation of its duty-drawback and inward-processing scheme. In the light of this review, the Trade Specialised Committee on Customs Cooperation and Rules of Origin may make recommendations to the Partnership Council for the amendment of the provisions of this Chapter and its Annexes, with a view to introducing limitations or restrictions with respect to drawback of or exemption from customs duties.

Section 2 Origin procedures

Articles 54–64   [Omitted]

Article 65   Administrative measures and sanctions

Each Party shall ensure the effective enforcement of this Chapter. Each Party shall ensure that the competent authorities are able to impose administrative measures, and, where appropriate, sanctions, in accordance with its laws and regulations, on any person who draws up a document, or causes a document to be drawn up, which contains incorrect information that was provided for the purpose of obtaining a preferential tariff treatment for a product, who does not comply with the requirements set out in Article 59, or who does not provide the evidence, or refuses to submit to a visit, as referred to in Article 62(3).

Section 3 Other Provisions

Articles 66–68   [Omitted]

Chapter 3 Sanitary and phytosanitary measures [omitted]

Chapter 4 Technical barriers to trade

Article 88   Objective

The objective of this Chapter is to facilitate trade in goods between the Parties by preventing, identifying and eliminating unnecessary technical barriers to trade.

Article 89   Scope

1. This Chapter applies to the preparation, adoption and application of all standards, technical regulations and conformity assessment procedures, which may affect trade in goods between the Parties.

2. This Chapter does not apply to:
   (a) purchasing specifications prepared by governmental bodies for production or consumption requirements of such bodies; or
   (b) SPS measures that fall within the scope of Chapter 3 of this Title.

3. The Annexes to this Chapter apply in addition to this Chapter in respect of products within the scope of those Annexes. Any provision in an Annex to this Chapter that an international standard or body or organisation is to be considered or recognised as relevant shall not prevent a standard developed by any other body or organisation from being considered to be a relevant international standard pursuant to Article 91(4) and (5).

Article 90   Relationship with the TBT Agreement

1. Articles 2 to 9 of and Annexes 1 and 3 to the TBT Agreement are incorporated into and made part of this Agreement *mutatis mutandis*.

2. Terms referred to in this Chapter and in the Annexes to this Chapter shall have the same meaning as they have in the TBT Agreement.

Article 91   Technical regulations

1. Each Party shall carry out impact assessments of planned technical regulations in accordance with its respective rules and procedures. The rules and procedures referred to in this paragraph and in paragraph 8 may provide for exceptions.

2. Each Party shall assess the available regulatory and non-regulatory alternatives to the proposed technical regulation that may fulfil the Party's legitimate objectives, in accordance with Article 2.2 of the TBT Agreement.

3. Each Party shall use relevant international standards as a basis for its technical regulations except when it can demonstrate that such international standards would be an ineffective or inappropriate means for the fulfilment of the legitimate objectives pursued.

4. International standards developed by the International Organization for Standardization (ISO), the International Electrotechnical Commission (IEC), the International Telecommunication

Union (ITU) and the Codex Alimentarius Commission (Codex) shall be the relevant international standards within the meaning of Article 2, Article 5 and Annex 3 of the TBT Agreement.

5. A standard developed by other international organisations may also be considered a relevant international standard within the meaning of Article 2, Article 5 and Annex 3 of the TBT Agreement, provided that:

    (a) it has been developed by a standardising body which seeks to establish consensus either:

        (i) among national delegations of the participating WTO Members representing all the national standardising bodies in their territory that have adopted, or expect to adopt, standards on the subject matter to which the international standardisation activity relates, or,

        (ii) among governmental bodies of participating WTO Members; and

    (b) it has been developed in accordance with the Decision of the WTO Committee on Technical Barriers to Trade on Principles for the Development of International Standards, Guides and Recommendations with relation to Articles 2, 5, and Annex 3 of the TBT Agreement.[2]

6. Where a Party does not use international standards as a basis for a technical regulation, on request of the other Party, it shall identify any substantial deviation from the relevant international standard, explain the reasons why such standards were judged inappropriate or ineffective for the objective pursued, and provide the scientific or technical evidence on which that assessment was based.

7. Each Party shall review its technical regulations to increase the convergence of those technical regulations with relevant international standards, taking into account, *inter alia*, any new developments in the relevant international standards or any changes in the circumstances that have given rise to divergence from any relevant international standards.

8. In accordance with its respective rules and procedures and without prejudice to Title X of this Heading, when developing a major technical regulation which may have a significant effect on trade, each Party shall ensure that procedures exist that allow persons to express their opinion in a public consultation, except where urgent problems of safety, health, environment or national security arise or threaten to arise. Each Party shall allow persons of the other Party to participate in such consultations on terms that are no less favourable than those accorded to its own nationals, and shall make the results of those consultations public.

Article 92   Standards

1. Each Party shall encourage the standardising bodies established within its territory, as well as the regional standardising bodies of which a Party or the standardising bodies established in its territory are members:

    (a) to participate, within the limits of their resources, in the preparation of international standards by relevant international standardising bodies;

    (b) to use relevant international standards as a basis for the standards they develop, except where such international standards would be ineffective or inappropriate, for example because of an insufficient level of protection, fundamental climatic or geographical factors or fundamental technological problems;

    (c) to avoid duplications of, or overlaps with, the work of international standardising bodies;

    (d) to review national and regional standards that are not based on relevant international standards at regular intervals, with a view to increasing the convergence of those standards with relevant international standards;

    (e) to cooperate with the relevant standardising bodies of the other Party in international standardisation activities, including through cooperation in the international standardising bodies or at regional level;

    (f) to foster bilateral cooperation with the standardising bodies of the other Party; and

    (g) to exchange information between standardising bodies.

2. The Parties shall exchange information on:

    (a) their respective use of standards in support of technical regulations; and

---

[2] G/TBT/9, 13 November 2000, Annex 4.

(b) their respective standardisation processes, and the extent to which they use international, regional or sub-regional standards as a basis for their national standards.

3. Where standards are rendered mandatory in a draft technical regulation or conformity assessment procedure, through incorporation or reference, the transparency obligations set out in Article 94 and in Article 2 or 5 of the TBT Agreement shall apply.

Articles 93–100   [Omitted]

Chapter 5 Customs and trade facilitation

Article 101   Objective

The objectives of this Chapter are:

(a) to reinforce cooperation between the Parties in the area of customs and trade facilitation and to support or maintain, where relevant, appropriate levels of compatibility of their customs legislation and practices with a view to ensuring that relevant legislation and procedures, as well as the administrative capacity of the relevant administrations, fulfil the objectives of promoting trade facilitation while ensuring effective customs controls and effective enforcement of customs legislation and trade related laws and regulations, the proper protection of security and safety of citizens and the respect of prohibitions and restrictions and financial interests of the Parties;

(b) to reinforce administrative cooperation between the Parties in the field of VAT and mutual assistance in claims related to taxes and duties;

(c) to ensure that the legislation of each Party is non-discriminatory and that customs procedures are based upon the use of modern methods and effective controls to combat fraud and to promote legitimate trade; and

(d) to ensure that legitimate public policy objectives, including in relation to security, safety and the fight against fraud are not compromised in any way.

Article 102   Definitions

For the purposes of this Chapter and Annex 18 and the Protocol on mutual administrative assistance in customs matters and the Protocol on administrative cooperation and combating fraud in the field of Value Added Tax and on mutual assistance for the recovery of claims relating to taxes and duties, the following definitions apply:

(a) 'Agreement on Pre-shipment Inspection' means the Agreement on Pre-shipment Inspection, contained in Annex 1A to the WTO Agreement;

(b) 'ATA and Istanbul Conventions' means the Customs Convention on the ATA Carnet for the Temporary Admission of Goods done in Brussels on 6 December 1961 and the Istanbul Convention on Temporary Admission done on 26 June 1990;

(c) 'Common Transit Convention' means the Convention of 20 May 1987 on a common transit procedure;

(d) 'Customs Data Model of the WCO' means the library of data components and electronic templates for the exchange of business data and compilation of international standards on data and information used in applying regulatory facilitation and controls in global trade, as published by the WCO Data Model Project Team from time to time;

(e) 'customs legislation' means any legal or regulatory provision applicable in the territory of either Party, governing the entry or import of goods, exit or export of goods, the transit of goods and the placing of goods under any other customs regime or procedure, including measures of prohibition, restriction and control;

(f) 'information' means any data, document, image, report, communication or authenticated copy, in any format, including in electronic format, whether or not processed or analysed;

(g) 'person' means any person as defined in point (l) of Article 512[3];

---

[3] For greater certainty, it is understood that, in particular for the purposes of this Chapter, the notion of 'person' includes any association of persons lacking the legal status of a legal person but recognized under applicable law as having the capacity to perform legal acts.

(h) 'SAFE Framework' means the SAFE Framework of Standards to Secure and Facilitate Global Trade adopted at the June 2005 World Customs Organisation Session in Brussels and as updated from time to time; and

(i) 'WTO Trade Facilitation Agreement' means the Agreement on Trade Facilitation annexed to the Protocol Amending the WTO Agreement (decision of 27 November 2014).

Article 103   Customs cooperation

1. The relevant authorities of the Parties shall cooperate on customs matters to support the objectives set out in Article 101, taking into account the resources of their respective authorities. For the purpose of this Title, the Convention of 20 May 1987 on the Simplification of Formalities in Trade in Goods applies.

2. The Parties shall develop cooperation, including in the following areas:

(a) exchanging information concerning customs legislation, the implementation of customs legislation and customs procedures; particularly in the following areas:

   (i)   the simplification and modernisation of customs procedures;

   (ii) the facilitation of transit movements and transhipment;

   (iii) relations with the business community; and

   (iv) supply chain security and risk management;

(b) working together on the customs-related aspects of securing and facilitating the international trade supply chain in accordance with the SAFE Framework;

(c) considering developing joint initiatives relating to import, export and other customs procedures including technical assistance, as well as towards ensuring an effective service to the business community;

(d) strengthening their cooperation in the field of customs in international organisations such as the WTO and the WCO, and exchanging information or holding discussions with a view to establishing where possible common positions in those international organisations and in UNCTAD, UNECE;

(e) endeavouring to harmonise their data requirements for import, export and other customs procedures by implementing common standards and data elements in accordance with the Customs Data Model of the WCO;

(f) strengthening their cooperation on risk management techniques, including sharing best practices, and, where appropriate, risk information and control results. Where relevant and appropriate, the Parties may also consider mutual recognition of risk management techniques, risk standards and controls and customs security measures; the Parties may also consider, where relevant and appropriate, the development of compatible risk criteria and standards, control measures and priority control areas;

(g) establishing mutual recognition of Authorised Economic Operator programmes to secure and facilitate trade;

(h) fostering cooperation between customs and other government authorities or agencies in relation to Authorised Economic Operator programmes, which may be achieved, *inter alia*, by agreeing on the highest standards, facilitating access to benefits and minimising unnecessary duplication;

(i) enforcing intellectual property rights by customs authorities, including exchanging information and best practices in customs operations focusing in particular on intellectual property rights enforcement;

(j) maintaining compatible customs procedures, where appropriate and practicable to do so, including the application of a single administrative document for customs declaration; and

(k) exchanging, where relevant and appropriate and under arrangements to be agreed, certain categories of customs-related information between the customs authorities of the Parties through structured and recurrent communication, for the purposes of improving risk management and the effectiveness of customs controls, targeting goods at risk in terms of revenue collection or safety and security, and facilitating legitimate trade; such exchanges may include export and import declaration data on trade between the Parties, with the possibility of exploring, through pilot initiatives, the development of interoperable mechanisms to avoid duplication in the submission of such information. Exchanges under this point shall be without prejudice to exchanges of information that may take place between the Parties pursuant to the Protocol on mutual administrative assistance in customs matters.

3. Without prejudice to other forms of cooperation envisaged in this Agreement, the customs authorities of the Parties shall provide each other with mutual administrative assistance in the matters covered by this Chapter in accordance with the Protocol on mutual administrative assistance in customs matters.

4. Any exchange of information between the Parties under this Chapter shall be subject to the confidentiality and protection of information set out in Article 12 of the Protocol on mutual administrative assistance in customs matters, *mutatis mutandis*, as well as to any confidentiality requirements set out in the legislation of the Parties.

Article 104   Customs and other trade related legislation and procedures

1. Each Party shall ensure that its customs provisions and procedures:

(a) are consistent with international instruments and standards applicable in the area of customs and trade, including the WTO Trade Facilitation Agreement, the substantive elements of the Revised Kyoto Convention on the Simplification and Harmonisation of Customs Procedures, the International Convention on the Harmonised Commodity Description and Coding System, as well as the SAFE Framework and the Customs Data Model of the WCO;

(b) provide the protection and facilitation of legitimate trade taking into account the evolution of trade practices through effective enforcement including in case of breaches of its laws and regulations, duty evasion and smuggling and through ensuring compliance with legislative requirements;

(c) are based on legislation that is proportionate and non-discriminatory, avoids unnecessary burdens on economic operators, provides for further facilitation for operators with high levels of compliance including favourable treatment with respect to customs controls prior to the release of goods, and ensures safeguards against fraud and illicit or damageable activities while ensuring a high level of protection of security and safety of citizens and the respect of prohibitions and restrictions and financial interests of the Parties; and

(d) contain rules that ensure that any penalty imposed for breaches of customs regulations or procedural requirements is proportionate and non-discriminatory and that the imposition of such penalties does not result in unjustified delays.

Each Party should periodically review its legislation and customs procedures. Customs procedures should also be applied in a manner that is predictable, consistent and transparent.

2. In order to improve working methods and to ensure non-discrimination, transparency, efficiency, integrity and the accountability of operations, each Party shall:

(a) simplify and review requirements and formalities wherever possible with a view to ensuring the rapid release and clearance of goods;

(b) work towards the further simplification and standardisation of the data and documentation required by customs and other agencies; and

(c) promote coordination between all border agencies, both internally and across borders, to facilitate border-crossing processes and enhance control, taking into account joint border controls where feasible and appropriate.

Article 105   Release of goods

1. Each Party shall adopt or maintain customs procedures that:

(a) provide for the prompt release of goods within a period that is no longer than necessary to ensure compliance with its laws and regulations;

(b) provide for advance electronic submission and processing of documentation and any other required information prior to the arrival of the goods, to enable the release of goods promptly upon arrival if no risk has been identified through risk analysis or if no random checks or other checks are to be performed;

(c) provide for the possibility, where appropriate and if the necessary conditions are satisfied, of releasing goods for free circulation at the first point of arrival; and

(d) allow for the release of goods prior to the final determination of customs duties, taxes, fees and charges, if such a determination is not done prior to, or upon arrival, or as rapidly as possible after arrival and provided that all other regulatory requirements have been met.

2. As a condition for such release, each Party may require a guarantee for any amount not yet determined in the form of a surety, a deposit or another appropriate instrument provided for in its laws and regulations. Such guarantee shall not be greater than the amount the Party requires to ensure payment of customs duties, taxes, fees and charges ultimately due for the goods covered by the guarantee. The guarantee shall be discharged when it is no longer required.

3. The Parties shall ensure that the customs and other authorities responsible for border controls and procedures dealing with importation, exportation and transit of goods cooperate with one another and coordinate their activities in order to facilitate trade and expedite the release of goods.

Article 106   Simplified customs procedures

1. Each Party shall work towards simplification of its requirements and formalities for customs procedures in order to reduce the time and costs thereof for traders or operators, including small and medium-sized enterprises.

2. Each Party shall adopt or maintain measures allowing traders or operators fulfilling criteria specified in its laws and regulations to benefit from further simplification of customs procedures. Such measures may include *inter alia*:

(a) customs declarations containing a reduced set of data or supporting documents;

(b) periodical customs declarations for the determination and payment of customs duties and taxes covering multiple imports within a given period after the release of those imported goods;

(c) self-assessment of and the deferred payment of customs duties and taxes until after the release of those imported goods; and

(d) the use of a guarantee with a reduced amount or a waiver from the obligation to provide a guarantee.

3. Where a Party chooses to adopt one of these measures, it will offer, where considered appropriate and practicable by that Party and in accordance with its laws and regulations, these simplifications to all traders who meet the relevant criteria.

Articles 107–109   [Omitted]

Article 110   Authorised Economic Operators

1. Each Party shall maintain a partnership programme for operators who meet the specified criteria in Annex 18.

2. The Parties shall recognise their respective programmes for Authorised Economic Operators in accordance with Annex 18.

Article 111–122   [Omitted]

Title II Services and investment

Chapter 1 General provisions

Article 123   Objective and scope

1. The Parties affirm their commitment to establish a favourable climate for the development of trade and investment between them.

2. The Parties reaffirm the right to regulate within their territories to achieve legitimate policy objectives, such as: the protection of public health; social services; public education; safety; the

environment, including climate change; public morals; social or consumer protection; privacy and data protection or the promotion and protection of cultural diversity.

3. This Title does not apply to measures affecting natural persons of a Party seeking access to the employment market of the other Party or to measures regarding nationality, citizenship, residence or employment on a permanent basis.

4. This Title shall not prevent a Party from applying measures to regulate the entry of natural persons into, or their temporary stay in, its territory, including those measures necessary to protect the integrity of its borders and to ensure the orderly movement of natural persons across them, provided that such measures are not applied in such a manner as to nullify or impair the benefits accruing to the other Party under the terms of this Title. The sole fact of requiring a visa for natural persons of certain countries and not for those of others shall not be regarded as nullifying or impairing benefits under this Title.

5. This Title does not apply to:

    (a) air services or related services in support of air services[4], other than:

        (i) aircraft repair and maintenance services;

        (ii) computer reservation system services;

        (iii) ground handling services;

        (iv) the following services provided using a manned aircraft, subject to compliance with the Parties' respective laws and regulations governing the admission of aircrafts to, departure from and operation within, their territory: aerial fire-fighting; flight training; spraying; surveying; mapping; photography; and other airborne agricultural, industrial and inspection services; and

        (v) the selling and marketing of air transport services;

    (b) audio-visual services;

    (c) national maritime cabotage[5]; and

    (d) inland waterways transport.

6. This Title does not apply to any measure of a Party with respect to public procurement of a good or service purchased for governmental purposes, and not with a view to commercial resale or with a view to use in the supply of a good or service for commercial sale, whether or not that procurement is 'covered procurement' within the meaning of Article 277.

7. Except for Article 132, this Title does not apply to subsidies or grants provided by the Parties, including government-supported loans, guarantees and insurance.

Article 124   Definitions

For the purposes of this Title, the following definitions apply:

    (a) 'activities performed in the exercise of governmental authority' means activities which are performed, including services which are supplied, neither on a commercial basis nor in competition with one or more economic operators;[6]

    (b) 'aircraft repair and maintenance services' means such activities when undertaken on an aircraft or a part thereof while it is withdrawn from service and does not include so-called line maintenance;

---

[4] Air services or related services in support of air services include, but are not limited to, the following services: air transportation; services provided by using an aircraft whose primary purpose is not the transportation of goods or passengers, such as aerial fire-fighting, flight training, sightseeing, spraying, surveying, mapping, photography, parachute jumping, glider towing, helicopter-lift for logging and construction, and other airborne agricultural, industrial and inspection services; the rental of aircraft with crew; and airport operation services.

[5] National maritime cabotage covers: for the Union, without prejudice to the scope of activities that may be considered cabotage under the relevant national legislation, transportation of passengers or goods between a port or point located in a Member State and another port or point located in that same Member State, including on its continental shelf, as provided for in the United Nations Convention on the Law of the Sea and traffic originating and terminating in the same port or point located in a Member State; for the United Kingdom, transportation of passengers or goods between a port or point located in the United Kingdom and another port or point located in the United Kingdom, including on its continental shelf, as provided for in the United Nations Convention on the Law of the Sea and traffic originating and terminating in the same port or point located in the United Kingdom.

[6] For greater certainty, the term 'activities performed in the exercise of governmental authority' when used in relation to measures of a Party affecting the supply of services, includes 'services supplied in the exercise of governmental authority' as defined in point (p) of Article 124.

(c) 'computer reservation system services' means services provided by computerised systems that contain information about air carriers' schedules, availability, fares and fare rules, through which reservations can be made or tickets may be issued;

(d) 'covered enterprise' means an enterprise in the territory of a Party established in accordance with point (h) by an investor of the other Party, in accordance with the applicable law, existing on the date of entry into force of this Agreement or established thereafter;

(e) 'cross-border trade in services' means the supply of a service:

    (i)   from the territory of a Party into the territory of the other Party; or

    (ii) in the territory of a Party to the service consumer of the other Party;

(f) 'economic activity' means any activity of an industrial, commercial or professional character or activities of craftsmen, including the supply of services, except for activities performed in the exercise of governmental authority;

(g) 'enterprise' means a legal person or a branch or a representative office of a legal person;

(h) 'establishment' means the setting up or the acquisition of a legal person, including through capital participation, or the creation of a branch or representative office in the territory of a Party, with a view to creating or maintaining lasting economic links;

(i) 'ground handling services' means the supply at an airport, on a fee or contract basis, of the following services: airline representation, administration and supervision; passenger handling; baggage handling; ramp services; catering; air cargo and mail handling; fuelling of an aircraft; aircraft servicing and cleaning; surface transport; and flight operations, crew administration and flight planning; ground handling services do not include: self-handling; security; aircraft repair and maintenance; or management or operation of essential centralised airport infrastructure, such as de-icing facilities, fuel distribution systems, baggage handling systems and fixed intra airport transport systems;

(j) 'investor of a Party' means a natural or legal person of a Party that seeks to establish, is establishing or has established an enterprise in accordance with point (h) in the territory of the other Party;

(k) 'legal person of a Party'[7] means:

    (i)   for the Union:

        (A) a legal person constituted or organised under the law of the Union or at least one of its Member States and engaged, in the territory of the Union, in substantive business operations, understood by the Union, in line with its notification of the Treaty establishing the European Community to the WTO (WT/REG39/1), as equivalent to the concept of 'effective and continuous link' with the economy of a Member State enshrined in Article 54 of the Treaty on the Functioning of the European Union (TFEU); and

        (B) shipping companies established outside the Union, and controlled by natural persons of a Member State, whose vessels are registered in, and fly the flag of, a Member State;

    (ii) for the United Kingdom:

        (A) a legal person constituted or organised under the law of the United Kingdom and engaged in substantive business operations in the territory of the United Kingdom; and

        (B) shipping companies established outside the United Kingdom and controlled by natural persons of the United Kingdom, whose vessels are registered in, and fly the flag of, the United Kingdom;

(l) 'operation' means the conduct, management, maintenance, use, enjoyment, or sale or other form of disposal of an enterprise;

(m) 'professional qualifications' means qualifications attested by evidence of formal qualification, professional experience, or other attestation of competence;

---

[7] For greater certainty, the shipping companies referred to in this point are only considered as legal persons of a Party with respect to their activities relating to the supply of maritime transport services.

(n) 'selling and marketing of air transport services' means opportunities for the air carrier concerned to sell and market freely its air transport services including all aspects of marketing such as market research, advertising and distribution, but not including the pricing of air transport services nor the applicable conditions;

(o) 'service' means any service in any sector except services supplied in the exercise of governmental authority;

(p) 'services supplied in the exercise of governmental authority' means any service which is supplied neither on a commercial basis, nor in competition with one or more service suppliers;

(q) 'service supplier' means any natural or legal person that seeks to supply or supplies a service;

(r) 'service supplier of a Party' means a natural or legal person of a Party that seeks to supply or supplies a service.

Article 125   Denial of benefits

1. A Party may deny the benefits of this Title and Title IV of this Heading to an investor or service supplier of the other Party, or to a covered enterprise, if the denying Party adopts or maintains measures related to the maintenance of international peace and security, including the protection of human rights, which:

(a) prohibit transactions with that investor, service supplier or covered enterprise; or

(b) would be violated or circumvented if the benefits of this Title and Title IV of this Heading were accorded to that investor, service supplier or covered enterprise, including where the measures prohibit transactions with a natural or legal person which owns or controls any of them.

2. For greater certainty, paragraph 1 is applicable to Title IV of this Heading to the extent that it relates to services or investment with respect to which a Party has denied the benefits of this Title.

Article 126   Review

1. With a view to introducing possible improvements to the provisions of this Title, and consistent with their commitments under international agreements, the Parties shall review their legal framework relating to trade in services and investment, including this Agreement, in accordance with Article 776.

2. The Parties shall endeavour, where appropriate, to review the non-conforming measures and reservations set out in Annexes 19, 20, 21 and 22 and the activities for short term business visitors set out in Annex 21, with a view to agreeing to possible improvements in their mutual interest.

3. This Article shall not apply with respect to financial services.

Chapter 2   Investment liberalisation

Article 127   Scope

This Chapter applies to measures of a Party affecting the establishment of an enterprise to perform economic activities and the operation of such an enterprise by:

(a) investors of the other Party;

(b) covered enterprises; and

(c) for the purposes of Article 132, any enterprise in the territory of the Party which adopts or maintains the measure.

Article 128   Market access

A Party shall not adopt or maintain, with regard to establishment of an enterprise by an investor of the other Party or by a covered enterprise, or operation of a covered enterprise, either on the basis of its entire territory or on the basis of a territorial sub-division, measures that:

(a) impose limitations on:

  (i) the number of enterprises that may carry out a specific economic activity, whether in the form of numerical quotas, monopolies, exclusive rights or the requirement of an economic needs test;

    (ii) the total value of transactions or assets in the form of numerical quotas or the requirement of an economic needs test;

    (iii) the total number of operations or on the total quantity of output expressed in terms of designated numerical units in the form of quotas or the requirement of an economic needs test;[8, 9]

    (iv) the participation of foreign capital in terms of maximum percentage limit on foreign shareholding or the total value of individual or aggregate foreign investment; or

    (v) the total number of natural persons that may be employed in a particular sector or that an enterprise may employ and who are necessary for, and directly related to, the performance of an economic activity, in the form of numerical quotas or the requirement of an economic needs test; or

(b) restrict or require specific types of legal entity or joint venture through which an investor of the other Party may perform an economic activity.

Article 129   National treatment

1. Each Party shall accord to investors of the other Party and to covered enterprises treatment no less favourable than that it accords, in like situations, to its own investors and to their enterprises, with respect to their establishment and operation in its territory.

2. The treatment accorded by a Party under paragraph 1 means:

(a) with respect to a regional or local level of government of the United Kingdom, treatment no less favourable than the most favourable treatment accorded, in like situations, by that level of government to investors of the United Kingdom and to their enterprises in its territory; and

(b) with respect to a government of, or in, a Member State, treatment no less favourable than the most favourable treatment accorded, in like situations, by that government to investors of that Member State and to their enterprises in its territory.

Article 130   Most-favoured-nation-treatment

1. Each Party shall accord to investors of the other Party and to covered enterprises treatment no less favourable than that it accords, in like situations, to investors of a third country and to their enterprises, with respect to establishment in its territory.

2. Each Party shall accord to investors of the other Party and to covered enterprises treatment no less favourable than that it accords, in like situations, to investors of a third country and to their enterprises, with respect to operation in its territory.

3. Paragraphs 1 and 2 shall not be construed as obliging a Party to extend to investors of the other Party or to covered enterprises the benefit of any treatment resulting from:

(a) an international agreement for the avoidance of double taxation or other international agreement or arrangement relating wholly or mainly to taxation; or

(b) measures providing for recognition, including the recognition of the standards or criteria for the authorisation, licencing, or certification of a natural person or enterprise to carry out an economic activity, or the recognition of prudential measures as referred to in paragraph 3 of the GATS Annex on Financial Services.

4. For greater certainty, the 'treatment' referred to in paragraphs 1 and 2 does not include investor-to-state dispute settlement procedures provided for in other international agreements.

5. For greater certainty, the existence of substantive provisions in other international agreements concluded by a Party with a third country, or the mere formal transposition of those provisions into domestic law to the extent that it is necessary in order to incorporate them into the domestic legal order, do not in themselves constitute the 'treatment' referred to in paragraphs 1 and 2. Measures of a Party pursuant to those provisions may constitute such treatment and thus give rise to a breach of this Article.

---

[8] Points (a)(i) to (iii) of Article 128 do not cover measures taken in order to limit the production of an agricultural or fishery product. Point (a)(iii) of Article 128 does not cover measures by a Party which limit inputs for the supply of services.

[9] Point (a)(iii) of Article 128 does not cover measures by a Party which limit inputs for the supply of services.

Article 131   Senior management and boards of directors

A Party shall not require a covered enterprise to appoint individuals of any particular nationality as executives, managers or members of boards of directors.

Article 132   Performance requirements

1. A Party shall not impose or enforce any requirement, or enforce any commitment or undertaking, in connection with the establishment or operation of any enterprise in its territory:

(a) to export a given level or percentage of goods or services;

(b) to achieve a given level or percentage of domestic content;

(c) to purchase, use or accord a preference to goods produced or services provided in its territory or to purchase goods or services from natural or legal persons or any other entities in its territory;

(d) to relate in any way the volume or value of imports to the volume or value of exports or to the amount of foreign exchange inflows associated with such enterprise;

(e) to restrict sales of goods or services in its territory that such enterprise produces or supplies, by relating those sales in any way to the volume or value of its exports or foreign exchange inflows;

(f) to transfer technology, a production process or other proprietary knowledge to a natural or legal person or any other entity in its territory;[10]

(g) to supply exclusively from the territory of that Party a good produced or a service supplied by the enterprise to a specific regional or world market;

(h) to locate the headquarters for a specific region of the world which is broader than the territory of the Party or the world market in its territory;

(i) to employ a given number or percentage of natural persons of that Party;

(j) to achieve a given level or value of research and development in its territory;

(k) to restrict the exportation or sale for export; or

(l) with regard to any licence contract in existence at the time the requirement is imposed or enforced, or any commitment or undertaking is enforced, or with regard to any future licence contract freely entered into between the enterprise and a natural or legal person or any other entity in its territory, if the requirement is imposed or enforced or the commitment or undertaking is enforced, in a manner that constitutes direct interference with that licence contract by an exercise of non-judicial governmental authority of a Party, to adopt:

   (i)   a rate or amount of royalty below a certain level; or

   (ii)   a given duration of the term of a licence contract.

This point does not apply where the licence contract is concluded between the enterprise and the Party. For the purposes of this point, a 'licence contract' means any contract concerning the licensing of technology, a production process, or other proprietary knowledge.

2. A Party shall not condition the receipt or continued receipt of an advantage, in connection with the establishment or operation of an enterprise in its territory, on compliance with any of the following requirements:

(a) achieving a given level or percentage of domestic content;

(b) purchasing, using or according a preference to goods produced or services supplied in its territory, or to purchase goods or services from natural or legal persons or any other entity in its territory;

(c) relating in any way the volume or value of imports to the volume or value of exports or to the amount of foreign exchange inflows associated with that enterprise;

(d) restricting the sales of goods or services in its territory that that enterprise produces or supplies by relating those sales in any way to the volume or value of its exports or foreign exchange inflows; or

---

[10] For greater certainty, point (f) of Article 132(1) is without prejudice to the provisions of Article 207.

(e) restricting the exportation or sale for export.

3. Paragraph 2 shall not be construed as preventing a Party from conditioning the receipt or continued receipt of an advantage, in connection with the establishment or operation of any enterprise in its territory, on compliance with a requirement to locate production, supply a service, train or employ workers, construct or expand particular facilities, or carry out research and development, in its territory.

4. Points (f) and (l) of paragraph 1 of this Article do not apply where:

(a) the requirement is imposed or enforced, or the commitment or undertaking is enforced, by a court or administrative tribunal, or by a competition authority pursuant to a Party's competition law to prevent or remedy a restriction or a distortion of competition; or

(b) a Party authorises the use of an intellectual property right in accordance with Article 31 or Article 31bis of the TRIPS Agreement, or adopts or maintains measures requiring the disclosure of data or proprietary information that fall within the scope of, and are consistent with, paragraph 3 of Article 39 of the TRIPS Agreement.

5. Points (a) to (c) of paragraph 1 and points (a) and (b) of paragraph 2 do not apply to qualification requirements for goods or services with respect to participation in export promotion and foreign aid programmes.

6. For greater certainty, this Article does not preclude the enforcement by the competent authorities of a Party of any commitment or undertaking given between persons other than a Party which was not directly or indirectly imposed or required by that Party.

7. For greater certainty, points (a) and (b) of paragraph 2 do not apply to requirements imposed by an importing Party in relation to the content of goods necessary to qualify for preferential tariffs or preferential quotas.

8. Point (l) of paragraph 1 does not apply if the requirement is imposed or enforced, or the commitment or undertaking is enforced, by a tribunal as equitable remuneration under the Party's copyright laws.

9. A Party shall neither impose nor enforce any measure inconsistent with its obligations under the Agreement on Trade-Related Investment Measures (TRIMs), even where such measure has been listed by that Party in Annex 19 or 20.

10. For greater certainty, this Article shall not be construed as requiring a Party to permit a particular service to be supplied on a cross-border basis where that Party adopts or maintains restrictions or prohibitions on such provision of services which are consistent with the reservations, conditions or qualifications specified with respect to a sector, subsector or activity listed in Annex 19 or 20.

11. A condition for the receipt or continued receipt of an advantage referred to in paragraph 2 does not constitute a requirement or a commitment or undertaking for the purposes of paragraph 1.

Article 133   Non-conforming measures and exceptions

1. Articles 128, 129, 130, 131 and 132 do not apply to:

(a) any existing non-conforming measure of a Party at the level of:

(i) for the Union:

(A) the Union, as set out in the Schedule of the Union in Annex 19;

(B) The central government of a Member State, as set out in the Schedule of the Union in Annex 19;

(C) a regional government of a Member State, as set out in the Schedule of the Union in Annex 19; or

(D) a local government, other than that referred to in point (C); and

(ii) for the United Kingdom:

(A) the central government, as set out in the Schedule of the United Kingdom in Annex 19;

(B) a regional government, as set out in the Schedule of the United Kingdom in Annex 19; or

(C) a local government;

(b) the continuation or prompt renewal of any non-conforming measure referred to in point (a) of this paragraph; or

(c) a modification to any non-conforming measure referred to in points (a) and (b) of this paragraph, to the extent that it does not decrease the conformity of the measure, as it existed immediately before the modification, with Article 128, 129, 130, 131 or 132.

2. Articles 128, 129, 130, 131 and 132 do not apply to a measure of a Party which is consistent with the reservations, conditions or qualifications specified with respect to a sector, subsector or activity listed in Annex 20.

3. Articles 129 and 130 of this Agreement do not apply to any measure that constitutes an exception to, or a derogation from, Article 3 or 4 of the TRIPS Agreement, as specifically provided for in Articles 3 to 5 of that Agreement.

4. For greater certainty, Articles 129 and 130 shall not be construed as preventing a Party from prescribing information requirements, including for statistical purposes, in connection with the establishment or operation of investors of the other Party or of covered enterprises, provided that it does not constitute a means to circumvent that Party's obligations under those Articles.

Chapter 3   Cross-border trade in services

Article 134   Scope
This Chapter applies to measures of a Party affecting the cross-border trade in services by service suppliers of the other Party.

Article 135   Market access
A Party shall not adopt or maintain, either on the basis of its entire territory or on the basis of a territorial sub-division, measures that:

(a) impose limitations on:
   (i) the number of service suppliers that may supply a specific service, whether in the form of numerical quotas, monopolies, exclusive service suppliers or the requirement of an economic needs test;
   (ii) the total value of service transactions or assets in the form of numerical quotas or the requirement of an economic needs test; or
   (iii) the total number of service operations or on the total quantity of service output expressed in the terms of designated numerical units in the form of quotas or the requirement of an economic needs test[11]; or

(b) restrict or require specific types of legal entity or joint venture through which a service supplier may supply a service.

Article 136   Local presence
A Party shall not require a service supplier of the other Party to establish or maintain an enterprise or to be resident in its territory as a condition for the cross-border supply of a service.

Article 137   National treatment
1. Each Party shall accord to services and service suppliers of the other Party treatment no less favourable than that it accords, in like situations, to its own services and service suppliers.

2. A Party may meet the requirement of paragraph 1 by according to services and service suppliers of the other Party either formally identical treatment or formally different treatment to that it accords to its own services and service suppliers.

3. Formally identical or formally different treatment shall be considered to be less favourable if it modifies the conditions of competition in favour of services or service suppliers of the Party compared to services or service suppliers of the other Party.

4. Nothing in this Article shall be construed as requiring either Party to compensate for inherent competitive disadvantages which result from the foreign character of the relevant services or service suppliers.

---

[11] Point (a)(iii) of Article 135 does not cover measures by a Party which limit inputs for the supply of services.

Article 138   Most-favoured-nation treatment

1. Each Party shall accord to services and service suppliers of the other Party treatment no less favourable than that it accords, in like situations, to services and service suppliers of a third country.

2. Paragraph 1 shall not be construed as obliging a Party to extend to services and service suppliers of the other Party the benefit of any treatment resulting from:

(a) an international agreement for the avoidance of double taxation or other international agreement or arrangement relating wholly or mainly to taxation; or

(b) measures providing for recognition, including of the standards or criteria for the authorisation, licencing, or certification of a natural person or enterprise to carry out an economic activity, or of prudential measures as referred to in paragraph 3 of the GATS Annex on Financial Services.

3. For greater certainty, the existence of substantive provisions in other international agreements concluded by a Party with a third country, or mere formal transposition of those provisions into domestic law to the extent that it is necessary in order to incorporate them into the domestic legal order, do not in themselves constitute the 'treatment' referred to in paragraph 1. Measures of a Party pursuant to those provisions may constitute such treatment and thus give rise to a breach of this Article.

Article 139   Non-conforming measures

1. Articles 135, 136, 137 and 138 do not apply to:

(a) any existing non-conforming measure of a Party at the level of:

    (i) for the Union:

        (A) the Union, as set out in the Schedule of the Union in Annex 19;

        (B) the central government of a Member State, as set out in the Schedule of the Union in Annex 19;

        (C) a regional government of a Member State, as set out in the Schedule of the Union in Annex 19; or

        (D) a local government, other than that referred to in point (C); and

    (ii) for the United Kingdom:

        (A) the central government, as set out in the Schedule of the United Kingdom in Annex 19;

        (B) a regional government, as set out in the Schedule of the United Kingdom in Annex 19; or

        (C) a local government;

(b) the continuation or prompt renewal of any non-conforming measure referred to in point (a) of this paragraph; or

(c) a modification to any non-conforming measure referred to in points (a) and (b) of this paragraph to the extent that it does not decrease the conformity of the measure, as it existed immediately before the modification, with Articles 135, 136, 137 and 138.

2. Articles 135, 136, 137 and 138 do not apply to any measure of a Party which is consistent with the reservations, conditions or qualifications specified with respect to a sector, subsector or activity listed in Annex 20.

Chapter 4   Entry and temporary stay of natural persons for business purposes

Article 140   Scope and definitions

1. This Chapter applies to measures of a Party affecting the performance of economic activities through the entry and temporary stay in its territory of natural persons of the other Party, who are business visitors for establishment purposes, contractual service suppliers, independent professionals, intra-corporate transferees and short-term business visitors.

2. To the extent that commitments are not undertaken in this Chapter, all requirements provided for in the law of a Party regarding the entry and temporary stay of natural persons shall continue to apply, including laws and regulations concerning the period of stay.

3. Notwithstanding the provisions of this Chapter, all requirements provided for in the law of a Party regarding work and social security measures shall continue to apply, including laws and regulations concerning minimum wages and collective wage agreements.

4. Commitments on the entry and temporary stay of natural persons for business purposes do not apply in cases where the intent or effect of the entry and temporary stay is to interfere with or otherwise affect the outcome of any labour or management dispute or negotiation, or the employment of any natural person who is involved in that dispute.

5. For the purposes of this Chapter:

    (a) 'business visitors for establishment purposes' means natural persons working in a senior position within a legal person of a Party, who:

        (i) are responsible for setting up an enterprise of such legal person in the territory of the other Party;

        (ii) do not offer or provide services or engage in any economic activity other than that which is required for the purposes of the establishment of that enterprise; and

        (iii) do not receive remuneration from a source located within the other Party;

    (b) 'contractual service suppliers' means natural persons employed by a legal person of a Party (other than through an agency for placement and supply services of personnel), which is not established in the territory of the other Party and has concluded a bona fide contract, not exceeding 12 months, to supply services to a final consumer in the other Party requiring the temporary presence of its employees who:

        (i) have offered the same type of services as employees of the legal person for a period of not less than one year immediately preceding the date of their application for entry and temporary stay;

        (ii) possess, on that date, at least three years professional experience, obtained after having reached the age of majority, in the sector of activity that is the object of the contract, a university degree or a qualification demonstrating knowledge of an equivalent level and the professional qualifications legally required to exercise that activity in the other Party[12]; and

        (iii) do not receive remuneration from a source located within the other Party;

    (c) 'independent professionals' means natural persons engaged in the supply of a service and established as self-employed in the territory of a Party who:

        (i) have not established in the territory of the other Party;

        (ii) have concluded a bona fide contract (other than through an agency for placement and supply services of personnel) for a period not exceeding 12 months to supply services to a final consumer in the other Party[13], requiring their presence on a temporary basis; and

        (iii) possess, on the date of their application for entry and temporary stay, at least six years professional experience in the relevant activity, a university degree or a qualification demonstrating knowledge of an equivalent level and the professional qualifications legally required to exercise that activity in the other Party[14];

    (d) 'intra-corporate transferees' means natural persons, who:

        (i) have been employed by a legal person of a Party, or have been partners in it, for a period, immediately preceding the date of the intra-corporate transfer, of not less than one year in the case of managers and specialists and of not less than six months in the case of trainee employees;

        (ii) at the time of application reside outside the territory of the other Party;

---

[12] Where the degree or qualification has not been obtained in the Party where the service is supplied, that Party may evaluate whether this is equivalent to a university degree required in its territory.

[13] Where the degree or qualification has not been obtained in the Party where the service is supplied, that Party may evaluate whether this is equivalent to a university degree required in its territory.

[14] Where the degree or qualification has not been obtained in the Party where the service is supplied, that Party may evaluate whether this is equivalent to a university degree required in its territory.

      (iii) are temporarily transferred to an enterprise of the legal person in the territory of the other Party which is a member of the same group as the originating legal person, including its representative office, subsidiary, branch or head company[15]; and

      (iv) belong to one of the following categories:

        (A) managers[16];

        (B) specialists; or

        (C) trainee employees;

  (e) 'manager' means a natural person working in a senior position, who primarily directs the management of the enterprise in the other Party, receiving general supervision or direction principally from the board of directors or from shareholders of the business or their equivalent and whose responsibilities include:

      (i) directing the enterprise or a department or subdivision thereof;

      (ii) supervising and controlling the work of other supervisory, professional or managerial employees; and

      (iii) having the authority to recommend hiring, dismissing or other personnel-related actions;

  (f) 'specialist' means a natural person possessing specialised knowledge, essential to the enterprise's areas of activity, techniques or management, which is to be assessed taking into account not only knowledge specific to the enterprise, but also whether the person has a high level of qualification, including adequate professional experience of a type of work or activity requiring specific technical knowledge, including possible membership of an accredited profession; and

  (g) 'trainee employee' means a natural person possessing a university degree who is temporarily transferred for career development purposes or to obtain training in business techniques or methods and is paid during the period of the transfer.[17]

  6. The service contract referred to in points (b) and (c) of paragraph 5 shall comply with the requirements of the law of the Party where the contract is executed.

Article 141 Intra-corporate transferees and business visitors for establishment purposes

  1. Subject to the relevant conditions and qualifications specified in Annex 21:

  (a) each Party shall allow:

      (i) the entry and temporary stay of intra-corporate transferees;

      (ii) the entry and temporary stay of business visitors for establishment purposes without requiring a work permit or other prior approval procedure of similar intent; and

      (iii) the employment in its territory of intra-corporate transferees of the other Party;

  (b) a Party shall not maintain or adopt limitations in the form of numerical quotas or economic needs tests regarding the total number of natural persons that, in a specific sector, are allowed entry as business visitors for establishment purposes or that an investor of the other Party may employ as intra-corporate transferees, either on the basis of a territorial subdivision or on the basis of its entire territory; and

  (c) each Party shall accord to intra-corporate transferees and business visitors for establishment purposes of the other Party, during their temporary stay in its territory, treatment no less favourable than that it accords, in like situations, to its own natural persons.

---

[15] Managers and specialists may be required to demonstrate they possess the professional qualifications and experience needed in the legal person to which they are transferred.

[16] While managers do not directly perform tasks concerning the actual supply of the services, this does not prevent them, in the course of executing their duties as described above, from performing such tasks as may be necessary for the provision of the services.

[17] The recipient enterprise may be required to submit a training programme covering the duration of the stay for prior approval, demonstrating that the purpose of the stay is for training. For AT, CZ, DE, FR, ES, HU and LT, training must be linked to the university degree which has been obtained.

2. The permissible length of stay shall be for a period of up to three years for managers and specialists, up to one year for trainee employees and up to 90 days within any six-month period for business visitors for establishment purposes.

Article 142 Short-term business visitors

1. Subject to the relevant conditions and qualifications specified in Annex 21, each Party shall allow the entry and temporary stay of short-term business visitors of the other Party for the purposes of carrying out the activities listed in Annex 21, subject to the following conditions:

(a) the short-term business visitors are not engaged in selling their goods or supplying services to the general public;

(b) the short-term business visitors do not, on their own behalf, receive remuneration from within the Party where they are staying temporarily; and

(c) the short-term business visitors are not engaged in the supply of a service in the framework of a contract concluded between a legal person that has not established in the territory of the Party where they are staying temporarily, and a consumer there, except as provided for in Annex 21.

2. Unless otherwise specified in Annex 21, a Party shall allow entry of short-term business visitors without the requirement of a work permit, economic needs test or other prior approval procedures of similar intent.

3. If short-term business visitors of a Party are engaged in the supply of a service to a consumer in the territory of the Party where they are staying temporarily in accordance with Annex 21, that Party shall accord to them, with regard to the supply of that service, treatment no less favourable than that it accords, in like situations, to its own service suppliers.

4. The permissible length of stay shall be for a period of up to 90 days in any six-month period.

Article 143 Contractual service suppliers and independent professionals

1. In the sectors, subsectors and activities specified in Annex 22 and subject to the relevant conditions and qualifications specified therein:

(a) a Party shall allow the entry and temporary stay of contractual service suppliers and independent professionals in its territory;

(b) a Party shall not adopt or maintain limitations on the total number of contractual service suppliers and independent professionals of the other Party allowed entry and temporary stay, in the form of numerical quotas or an economic needs test; and

(c) each Party shall accord to contractual service suppliers and independent professionals of the other Party, with regard to the supply of their services in its territory, treatment no less favourable than that it accords, in like situations, to its own service suppliers.

2. Access accorded under this Article relates only to the service which is the subject of the contract and does not confer entitlement to use the professional title of the Party where the service is provided.

3. The number of persons covered by the service contract shall not be greater than necessary to fulfil the contract, as it may be required by the law of the Party where the service is supplied.

4. The permissible length of stay shall be for a cumulative period of 12 months, or for the duration of the contract, whichever is less.

Article 144 Non-conforming measures

To the extent that the relevant measure affects the temporary stay of natural persons for business purposes, points (b) and (c) of Article 141(1), Article 142(3) and points (b) and (c) of Article 143(1) do not apply to:

(a) any existing non-conforming measure of a Party at the level of:

(i) for the Union:

(A) the Union, as set out in the Schedule of the Union in Annex 19;

(B) the central government of a Member State, as set out in the Schedule of the Union in Annex 19;

      (C) a regional government of a Member State, as set out in the Schedule of the Union in Annex 19; or

      (D) a local government, other than that referred to in point (C); and

    (ii) for the United Kingdom:

      (A) the central government, as set out in the Schedule of the United Kingdom in Annex 19;

      (B) a regional subdivision, as set out in the Schedule of the United Kingdom in Annex 19; or

      (C) a local government;

  (b) the continuation or prompt renewal of any non-conforming measure referred to in point (a) of this Article;

  (c) a modification to any non-conforming measure referred to in points (a) and (b) of this Article to the extent that it does not decrease the conformity of the measure, as it existed immediately before the modification, with points (b) and (c) of Article 141(1), Article 142(3) and points (b) and (c) of Article 143(1); or

  (d) any measure of a Party consistent with a condition or qualification specified in Annex 20.

Article 145   Transparency

1. Each Party shall make publicly available information on relevant measures that pertain to the entry and temporary stay of natural persons of the other Party, referred to in Article 140(1).

2. The information referred to in paragraph 1 shall, to the extent possible, include the following information relevant to the entry and temporary stay of natural persons:

  (a) categories of visa, permits or any similar type of authorisation regarding the entry and temporary stay;

  (b) documentation required and conditions to be met;

  (c) method of filing an application and options on where to file, such as consular offices or online;

  (d) application fees and an indicative timeframe of the processing of an application;

  (e) the maximum length of stay under each type of authorisation described in point (a);

  (f) conditions for any available extension or renewal;

  (g) rules regarding accompanying dependants;

  (h) available review or appeal procedures; and

  (i) relevant laws of general application pertaining to the entry and temporary stay of natural persons for business purposes.

3. With respect to the information referred to in paragraphs 1 and 2, each Party shall endeavour to promptly inform the other Party of the introduction of any new requirements and procedures or of the changes in any requirements and procedures that affect the effective application for the grant of entry into, temporary stay in and, where applicable, permission to work in the former Party.

Chapter 5   Regulatory framework

Section 1   Domestic regulation

Article 146   Scope and definitions

1. This Section applies to measures by the Parties relating to licensing requirements and procedures, qualification requirements and procedures, formalities and technical standards that affect:

  (a) cross-border trade in services;

  (b) establishment or operation; or

  (c) the supply of a service through the presence of a natural person of a Party in the territory of the other Party as set out in Article 140.

As far as measures relating to technical standards are concerned, this Section only applies to measures that affect trade in services. For the purposes of this Section, the term 'technical standards' does not include regulatory or implementing technical standards for financial services.

2. This Section does not apply to licensing requirements and procedures, qualification require-ments and procedures, formalities and technical standards pursuant to a measure:

> (a) that does not conform with Article 128 or 129 and is referred to in points (a) to (c) of Article 133(1) or with Article 135, 136 or 137 and is referred to in points (a) to (c) of Article 139(1) or with points (b) and (c) of Article 141(1), or Article 142(3) or with points (b) and (c) of Article 143(1) and is referred to in Article 144; or
>
> (b) referred to in Article 133(2) or Article 139(2).

3. For the purposes of this Section, the following definitions apply:

> (a) 'authorisation' means the permission to carry out any of the activities referred to in points (a) to (c) of paragraph 1 resulting from a procedure a natural or legal person must adhere to in order to demonstrate compliance with licensing requirements, qualification requirements, technical standards or formalities for the purposes of obtaining, main-taining or renewing that permission; and
>
> (b) 'competent authority' means a central, regional or local government or authority or non-governmental body in the exercise of powers delegated by central, regional or local governments or authorities, which is entitled to take a decision concerning the author-isation referred to in point (a).

Article 147   Submission of applications

Each Party shall, to the extent practicable, avoid requiring an applicant to approach more than one competent authority for each application for authorisation. If an activity for which authorisation is requested is within the jurisdiction of multiple competent authorities, multiple applications for au-thorisation may be required.

Article 148   Application timeframes

If a Party requires authorisation, it shall ensure that its competent authorities, to the extent prac-ticable, permit the submission of an application at any time throughout the year. If a specific time period for applying for authorisation exists, the Party shall ensure that the competent authorities allow a reasonable period of time for the submission of an application.

Article 149   Electronic applications and acceptance of copies

If a Party requires authorisation, it shall ensure that its competent authorities:

> (a) to the extent possible provide for applications to be completed by electronic means, in-cluding from within the territory of the other Party; and
>
> (b) accept copies of documents, that are authenticated in accordance with the Party's domestic law, in place of original documents, unless the competent authorities require original documents to protect the integrity of the authorisation process.

Article 150   Processing of applications

1. If a Party requires authorisation, it shall ensure that its competent authorities:

> (a) process applications throughout the year. Where that is not possible, this information should be made public in advance, to the extent practicable;
>
> (b) to the extent practicable, provide an indicative timeframe for the processing of an appli-cation. That timeframe shall be reasonable to the extent practicable;
>
> (c) at the request of the applicant, provide without undue delay information concerning the status of the application;
>
> (d) to the extent practicable, ascertain without undue delay the completeness of an applica-tion for processing under the Party's domestic laws and regulations;
>
> (e) if they consider an application complete for the purposes of processing under the Party's domestic laws and regulations,[18] within a reasonable period of time after the submission of the application ensure that:
>
> > (i)   the processing of the application is completed; and

---

[18] Balancing resource constraints against the potential burden on businesses, in cases where it is reasonable to do so, competent authorities may require that all information is submitted in a specified format to consider it 'complete for the purposes of processing'.

      (ii) the applicant is informed of the decision concerning the application, to the extent possible, in writing;[19]

  (f) if they consider an application incomplete for the purposes of processing under the Party's domestic laws and regulations, within a reasonable period of time, to the extent practicable:

      (i) inform the applicant that the application is incomplete;

      (ii) at the request of the applicant identify the additional information required to complete the application or otherwise provide guidance on why the application is considered incomplete; and

      (iii) provide the applicant with the opportunity to provide the additional information that is required to complete the application;[20]

    however, if none of the actions referred to in points (i), (ii) and (iii) is practicable, and the application is rejected due to incompleteness, the competent authorities shall ensure that they inform the applicant within a reasonable period of time; and

  (g) if an application is rejected, either upon their own initiative or upon request of the applicant, inform the applicant of the reasons for rejection and of the timeframe for an appeal against that decision and, if applicable, the procedures for resubmission of an application; an applicant shall not be prevented from submitting another application solely on the basis of a previously rejected application.

2. The Parties shall ensure that their competent authorities grant an authorisation as soon as it is established, on the basis of an appropriate examination, that the applicant meets the conditions for obtaining it.

3. The Parties shall ensure that, once granted, an authorisation enters into effect without undue delay, subject to the applicable terms and conditions.[21]

Article 151   Fees

1. For all economic activities other than financial services, each Party shall ensure that the authorisation fees charged by its competent authorities are reasonable and transparent and do not in themselves restrict the supply of the relevant service or the pursuit of any other economic activity. Having regard to the cost and administrative burden, each Party is encouraged to accept payment of authorisation fees by electronic means.

2. With regard to financial services, each Party shall ensure that its competent authorities, with respect to authorisation fees that they charge, provide applicants with a schedule of fees or information on how fee amounts are determined, and do not use the fees as a means of avoiding the Party's commitments or obligations.

3. Authorisation fees do not include fees for the use of natural resources, payments for auction, tendering or other non-discriminatory means of awarding concessions or mandated contributions to universal service provision.

Article 152   Assessment of qualifications

If a Party requires an examination to assess the qualifications of an applicant for authorisation, it shall ensure that its competent authorities schedule such an examination at reasonably frequent intervals and provide a reasonable period of time to enable applicants to request to take the examination. To the extent practicable, each Party shall accept requests in electronic format to take such examinations and shall consider the use of electronic means in other aspects of examination processes.

Article 153   Publication and information available

1. If a Party requires authorisation, the Party shall promptly publish the information necessary for persons carrying out or seeking to carry out the activities referred to in Article 146(1) for which

---

[19] Competent authorities may meet the requirement set out in point (ii) by informing an applicant in advance in writing, including through a published measure, that a lack of response after a specified period of time from the date of submission of the application indicates acceptance of the application. The reference to 'in writing' should be understood as including electronic format.

[20] Such 'opportunity' does not require a competent authority to provide extensions of deadlines.

[21] Competent authorities are not responsible for delays due to reasons outside their competence.

the authorisation is required to comply with the requirements, formalities, technical standards and procedures for obtaining, maintaining, amending and renewing such authorisation. Such information shall include, to the extent it exists:

    (a) the licensing and qualification requirements and procedures and formalities;

    (b) contact information of relevant competent authorities;

    (c) authorisation fees;

    (d) applicable technical standards;

    (e) procedures for appeal or review of decisions concerning applications;

    (f) procedures for monitoring or enforcing compliance with the terms and conditions of licences or qualifications;

    (g) opportunities for public involvement, such as through hearings or comments; and

    (h) indicative timeframes for the processing of an application.

For the purposes of this Section, 'publish' means to include in an official publication, such as an official journal, or on an official website. Parties shall consolidate electronic publications into a single online portal or otherwise ensure that competent authorities make them easily accessible through alternative electronic means.

    2. Each Party shall require each of its competent authorities to respond to any request for information or assistance, to the extent practicable.

Article 154 Technical standards

Each Party shall encourage its competent authorities, when adopting technical standards, to adopt technical standards developed through open and transparent processes, and shall encourage any body, including relevant international organisations, designated to develop technical standards to do so through open and transparent processes.

Article 155 Conditions for authorisation

    1. Each Party shall ensure that measures relating to authorisation are based on criteria which preclude the competent authorities from exercising their power of assessment in an arbitrary manner and may include, *inter alia*, competence and the ability to supply a service or any other economic activity, including to do so in compliance with a Party's regulatory requirements such as health and environmental requirements. For the avoidance of doubt, the Parties understand that in reaching decisions a competent authority may balance criteria.

    2. The criteria referred to in paragraph 1 shall be:

    (a) clear and unambiguous;

    (b) objective and transparent;

    (c) pre-established;

    (d) made public in advance;

    (e) impartial; and

    (f) easily accessible.

    3. If a Party adopts or maintains a measure relating to authorisation, it shall ensure that:

    (a) the competent authority concerned processes applications, and reaches and administers its decisions objectively and impartially and in a manner independent of the undue influence of any person carrying out the economic activity for which authorisation is required; and

    (b) the procedures themselves do not prevent fulfilment of the requirements.

Article 156 Limited numbers of licences

If the number of licences available for a given activity is limited because of the scarcity of available natural resources or technical capacity, a Party shall apply a selection procedure to potential candidates which provides full guarantees of impartiality, objectivity and transparency, including, in particular, adequate publicity about the launch, conduct and completion of the procedure. In establishing the rules for the selection procedure, a Party may take into account legitimate policy objectives, including considerations of health, safety, the protection of the environment and the preservation of cultural heritage.

Section 2   Provisions of general application

Article 157   Review procedures for administrative decisions

A Party shall maintain judicial, arbitral or administrative tribunals or procedures which provide, on request of an affected investor or service supplier of the other Party, for the prompt review of, and if justified appropriate remedies for, administrative decisions that affect establishment or operation, cross-border trade in services or the supply of a service through the presence of a natural person of a Party in the territory of the other Party. For the purposes of this Section, 'administrative decisions' means a decision or action with a legal effect that applies to a specific person, good or service in an individual case and covers the failure to take an administrative decision or take such action when that is so required by a Party's law. If such procedures are not independent of the competent authority entrusted with the administrative decision concerned, a Party shall ensure that the procedures in fact provide for an objective and impartial review.

Article 158   Professional qualifications

1. Nothing in this Article shall prevent a Party from requiring that natural persons possess the necessary professional qualifications specified in the territory where the activity is performed, for the sector of activity concerned[22].

2. The professional bodies or authorities, which are relevant for the sector of activity concerned in their respective territories, may develop and provide joint recommendations on the recognition of professional qualifications to the Partnership Council. Such joint recommendations shall be supported by an evidence-based assessment of:

  (a) the economic value of an envisaged arrangement on the recognition of professional qualifications; and
  (b) the compatibility of the respective regimes, that is, the extent to which the requirements applied by each Party for the authorisation, licensing, operation and certification are compatible.

3. On receipt of a joint recommendation, the Partnership Council shall review its consistency with this Title within a reasonable period of time. The Partnership Council may, following such review, develop and adopt an arrangement on the conditions for the recognition of professional qualifications by decision as an annex to this Agreement, which shall be considered to form an integral part of this Title.[23]

4. An arrangement referred to in paragraph 3 shall provide for the conditions for recognition of professional qualifications acquired in the Union and professional qualifications acquired in the United Kingdom relating to an activity covered by this Title and Title III of this Heading.

5. The Guidelines for arrangements on the recognition of professional qualifications set out in Annex 24 shall be taken into account in the development of the joint recommendations referred to in paragraph 2 of this Article and by the Partnership Council when assessing whether to adopt such an Arrangement, as referred to in paragraph 3 of this Article.

Section 3   Delivery services

Article 159   Scope and definitions

1. This Section applies to measures of a Party affecting the supply of delivery services in addition to Chapters 1, 2, 3 and 4 of this Title, and to Sections 1 and 2 of this Chapter.

2. For the purposes of this Section, the following definitions apply:

  (a) 'delivery services' means postal services, courier services, express delivery services or express mail services, which include the following activities: the collection, sorting, transport, and delivery of postal items;

---

[22] For greater certainty, this Article shall not be construed to prevent the negotiation and conclusion of one or more agreements between the Parties on the recognition of professional qualifications on conditions and requirements different from those provided for in this Article.
[23] For greater certainty, such arrangements shall not lead to the automatic recognition of qualifications but shall set, in the mutual interest of both Parties, the conditions for the competent authorities granting recognition.

(b) 'express delivery services' means the collection, sorting, transport and delivery of postal items at accelerated speed and reliability and may include value added elements such as collection from point of origin, personal delivery to the addressee, tracing, possibility of changing the destination and addressee in transit or confirmation of receipt;

(c) 'express mail services' means international express delivery services supplied through the EMS Cooperative, which is the voluntary association of designated postal operators under Universal Postal Union (UPU);

(d) 'licence' means an authorisation that a regulatory authority of a Party may require of an individual supplier in order for that supplier to offer postal or courier services;

(e) 'postal item' means an item up to 31.5 kg addressed in the final form in which it is to be carried by any type of supplier of delivery services, whether public or private and may include items such as a letter, parcel, newspaper or catalogue;

(f) 'postal monopoly' means the exclusive right to supply specified delivery services within a Party's territory or a subdivision thereof pursuant to the law of that Party; and

(g) 'universal service' means the permanent supply of a delivery service of specified quality at all points in the territory of a Party or a subdivision thereof at affordable prices for all users.

Article 160   Universal service

1. Each Party has the right to define the kind of universal service obligation it wishes to maintain and to decide on its scope and implementation. Any universal service obligation shall be administered in a transparent, non-discriminatory and neutral manner with regard to all suppliers subject to the obligation.

2. If a Party requires inbound express mail services to be supplied on a universal service basis, it shall not accord preferential treatment to those services over other international express delivery services.

Article 161   Universal service funding

A party shall not impose fees or other charges on the supply of a delivery service that is not a universal service for the purposes of funding the supply of a universal service. This Article does not apply to generally applicable taxation measures or administrative fees.

Article 162   Prevention of market distortive practices

Each party shall ensure that suppliers of delivery services subject to a universal service obligation or postal monopolies do not engage in market distortive practices such as:

(a) using revenues derived from the supply of the service subject to a universal service obligation or from a postal monopoly to cross-subsidise the supply of an express delivery service or any delivery service which is not subject to a universal service obligation; or

(b) unjustifiably differentiating between consumers with respect to tariffs or other terms and conditions for the supply of a service subject to a universal service or a postal monopoly.

Article 163   Licences

1. If a Party requires a licence for the provision of delivery services, it shall make publicly available:

(a) all the licensing requirements and the period of time normally required to reach a decision concerning an application for a licence; and

(b) the terms and conditions of licences.

2. The procedures, obligations and requirements of a licence shall be transparent, non-discriminatory and based on objective criteria.

3. If a licence application is rejected by the competent authority, it shall inform the applicant of the reasons for the rejection in writing. Each Party shall establish an appeal procedure through an independent body available to applicants whose licence has been rejected. That body may be a court.

Article 164   Independence of the regulatory body

1. Each Party shall establish or maintain a regulatory body which shall be legally distinct from and functionally independent from any supplier of delivery services. If a Party owns or controls a supplier of delivery services, it shall ensure the effective structural separation of the regulatory function from activities associated with ownership or control.

2. The regulatory bodies shall perform their tasks in a transparent and timely manner and have adequate financial and human resources to carry out the task assigned to them. Their decisions shall be impartial with respect to all market participants.

Section 4   Telecommunications services

Article 165   Scope

This Section applies to measures of a Party affecting the supply of telecommunications services in addition to Chapters 1, 2, 3 and 4 of this Title, and to Sections 1 and 2 of this Chapter.

Article 166   Definitions

For the purposes of this Section, the following definitions apply:

(a) 'associated facilities' means associated services, physical infrastructure and other facilities or elements associated with a telecommunications network or telecommunications service which enable or support the supply of services via that network or service or have the potential to do so;

(b) 'end user' means a final consumer of, or subscriber to, a public telecommunications service, including a service supplier other than a supplier of public telecommunications services;

(c) 'essential facilities' means facilities of a public telecommunications network or a public telecommunications service that:

(i)   are exclusively or predominantly provided by a single or limited number of suppliers; and

(ii) cannot feasibly be economically or technically substituted in order to provide a service;

(d) 'interconnection' means the linking of public telecommunications networks used by the same or different suppliers of telecommunications networks or telecommunications services in order to allow the users of one supplier to communicate with users of the same or another supplier or to access services provided by another supplier, irrespective of whether those services are provided by the suppliers involved or any other supplier who has access to the network;

(e) 'international mobile roaming service' means a commercial mobile service provided pursuant to a commercial agreement between suppliers of public telecommunications services that enables an end user to use its home mobile handset or other device for voice, data or messaging services while outside the territory in which the end user's home public telecommunications network is located;

(f) 'internet access service' means a public telecommunications service that provides access to the internet and thereby connectivity to virtually all end points of the internet, irrespective of the network technology and terminal equipment used;

(g) 'leased circuit' means telecommunications services or facilities, including those of a virtual nature, that set aside capacity for the dedicated use by, or availability to, a user between two or more designated points;

(h) 'major supplier' means a supplier of telecommunications networks or telecommunications services which has the ability to materially affect the terms of participation, having regard to price and supply, in a relevant market for telecommunications networks or telecommunications services as a result of control over essential facilities or the use of its position in that market;

(i) 'network element' means a facility or equipment used in supplying a telecommunications service, including features, functions and capabilities provided by means of that facility or equipment;

(j) 'number portability' means the ability of subscribers who so request to retain the same telephone numbers, at the same location in the case of a fixed line, without impairment of quality, reliability or convenience when switching between the same category of suppliers of public telecommunications services;

(k) 'public telecommunications network' means any telecommunications network used wholly or mainly for the provision of public telecommunications services which supports the transfer of information between network termination points;

(l) 'public telecommunications service' means any telecommunications service that is offered to the public generally;

(m) 'subscriber' means any natural or legal person which is party to a contract with a supplier of public telecommunications services for the supply of such services;

(n) 'telecommunications' means the transmission and reception of signals by any electromagnetic means;

(o) 'telecommunications network' means transmission systems and, where applicable, switching or routing equipment and other resources, including network elements which are not active, which permit the transmission and reception of signals by wire, radio, optical, or other electromagnetic means;

(p) 'telecommunications regulatory authority' means the body or bodies charged by a Party with the regulation of telecommunications networks and telecommunications services covered by this Section;

(q) 'telecommunications service' means a service which consists wholly or mainly in the transmission and reception of signals, including broadcasting signals, over telecommunications networks, including those used for broadcasting, but not a service providing, or exercising editorial control over, content transmitted using telecommunications networks and telecommunications services;

(r) 'universal service' means the minimum set of services of specified quality that must be made available to all users, or to a set of users, in the territory of a Party, or in a subdivision thereof, regardless of their geographical location and at an affordable price; and

(s) 'user' means any natural or legal person using a public telecommunications service.

Article 167   Telecommunications regulatory authority

1. Each Party shall establish or maintain a telecommunications regulatory authority that:

(a) is legally distinct and functionally independent from any supplier of telecommunications networks, telecommunications services or telecommunications equipment;

(b) uses procedures and issues decisions that are impartial with respect to all market participants;

(c) acts independently and does not seek or take instructions from any other body in relation to the exercise of the tasks assigned to it by law to enforce the obligations set out in Articles 169, 170, 171, 173 and 174;

(d) has the regulatory power, as well as adequate financial and human resources, to carry out the tasks mentioned in point (c) of this Article;

(e) has the power to ensure that suppliers of telecommunications networks or telecommunications services provide it, promptly upon request, with all the information[24], including financial information, which is necessary to enable it to carry out the tasks mentioned in point (c) of this Article; and

(f) exercises its powers transparently and in a timely manner.

2. Each Party shall ensure that the tasks assigned to the telecommunications regulatory authority are made public in an easily accessible and clear form, in particular where those tasks are assigned to more than one body.

---

[24] Information requested shall be treated in accordance with the requirements of confidentiality.

3. A Party that retains ownership or control of suppliers of telecommunications networks or telecommunications services shall ensure the effective structural separation of the regulatory function from activities associated with ownership or control.

4. Each Party shall ensure that a user or supplier of telecommunications networks or telecommunications services affected by a decision of the telecommunications regulatory authority has a right of appeal before an appeal body which is independent of the regulatory authority and other affected parties. Pending the outcome of the appeal, the decision shall stand, unless interim measures are granted in accordance with the Party's law.

Article 168   Authorisation to provide telecommunications networks or services

1. Each Party shall permit the provision of telecommunications networks or telecommunications services without a prior formal authorisation.

2. Each Party shall make publicly available all the criteria, applicable procedures and terms and conditions under which suppliers are permitted to provide telecommunications networks or telecommunications services.

3. Any authorisation criteria and applicable procedures shall be as simple as possible, objective, transparent, non-discriminatory and proportionate. Any obligations and conditions imposed on or associated with an authorisation shall be non-discriminatory, transparent and proportionate, and shall be related to the services or networks provided.

4. Each Party shall ensure that an applicant for an authorisation receives in writing the reasons for any denial or revocation of an authorisation or the imposition of supplier-specific conditions. In such cases, the applicant shall have a right of appeal before an appeal body.

5. Administrative fees imposed on suppliers shall be objective, transparent, non-discriminatory and commensurate with the administrative costs reasonably incurred in the management, control and enforcement of the obligations set out in this Section[25].

Article 169   Interconnection

Each Party shall ensure that a supplier of public telecommunications networks or public telecommunications services has the right and, when so requested by another supplier of public telecommunications networks or public telecommunications services, the obligation to negotiate interconnection for the purposes of providing public telecommunications networks or public telecommunications services.

Article 170   Access and use

1. Each Party shall ensure that any covered enterprise or service supplier of the other Party is accorded access to and use of public telecommunications networks or public telecommunications services on reasonable and non-discriminatory[26] terms and conditions. This obligation shall be applied, *inter alia*, to paragraphs 2 to 5.

2. Each Party shall ensure that covered enterprises or service suppliers of the other Party have access to and use of any public telecommunications network or public telecommunications service offered within or across its border, including private leased circuits, and to that end shall ensure, subject to paragraph 5, that such enterprises and suppliers are permitted:

(a) to purchase or lease and attach terminal or other equipment which interfaces with the network and which is necessary to conduct their operations;

(b) to interconnect private leased or owned circuits with public telecommunications networks or with circuits leased or owned by another covered enterprise or service supplier; and

(c) to use the operating protocols of their choice in their operations, other than as necessary to ensure the availability of telecommunications services to the public generally.

---

[25] Administrative fees do not include payments for rights to use scarce resources and mandated contributions to universal service provision.

[26] For the purposes of this Article, 'non-discriminatory' means most-favoured-nation and national treatment as defined in Articles 129, 130, 136 and 137, as well as under terms and conditions no less favourable than those accorded to any other user of like public telecommunications networks or services in like situations.

3. Each Party shall ensure that covered enterprises or service suppliers of the other Party may use public telecommunications networks and public telecommunications services for the movement of information within and across borders, including for their intra-corporate communications, and for access to information contained in databases or otherwise stored in machine-readable form in the territory of either Party.

4. Notwithstanding paragraph 3, a Party may take such measures as are necessary to ensure the security and confidentiality of communications, subject to the requirement that such measures are not applied in a manner which would constitute either a disguised restriction on trade in services or a means of arbitrary or unjustifiable discrimination or of nullification or impairment of benefits under this Title.

5. Each Party shall ensure that no condition is imposed on access to and use of public telecommunications networks or services other than as necessary:

  (a) to safeguard the public service responsibilities of suppliers of public telecommunications networks or public telecommunications services, in particular their ability to make their services available to the public generally; or

  (b) to protect the technical integrity of public telecommunications networks or services.

Article 171   Resolution of telecommunications disputes

1. Each Party shall ensure that, in the event of a dispute arising between suppliers of telecommunications networks or telecommunications services in connection with rights and obligations that arise from this Section, and upon request of either party involved in the dispute, the telecommunications regulatory authority issues a binding decision within a reasonable timeframe to resolve the dispute.

2. The decision by the telecommunications regulatory authority shall be made available to the public, having regard to the requirements of business confidentiality. The parties concerned shall be given a full statement of the reasons on which it is based and shall have the right of appeal referred to in Article 167(4).

3. The procedure referred to in paragraphs 1 and 2 shall not preclude either party concerned from bringing an action before a judicial authority.

Article 172   Competitive safeguards on major suppliers

Each Party shall introduce or maintain appropriate measures for the purpose of preventing suppliers of telecommunications networks or telecommunications services who, alone or together, are a major supplier from engaging in or continuing anti-competitive practices. These anti-competitive practices shall include in particular:

  (a) engaging in anti-competitive cross-subsidisation;

  (b) using information obtained from competitors with anti-competitive results; and

  (c) not making available to other service suppliers on a timely basis technical information about essential facilities and commercially relevant information which are necessary for them to provide services.

Article 173   Interconnection with major suppliers

1. Each Party shall ensure that major suppliers of public telecommunications networks or public telecommunications services provide interconnection at any technically feasible point in the network. Such interconnection shall be provided:

  (a) under non-discriminatory terms and conditions (including as regards rates, technical standards, specifications, quality and maintenance) and of a quality no less favourable than that provided for the own like services of such major supplier, or for like services of its subsidiaries or other affiliates;

  (b) in a timely fashion, on terms and conditions (including as regards rates, technical standards, specifications, quality and maintenance) that are transparent, reasonable, having regard to economic feasibility, and sufficiently unbundled so that the supplier need not pay for network elements or facilities that it does not require for the service to be provided; and

(c) upon request, at points in addition to the network termination points offered to the majority of users, subject to charges that reflect the cost of construction of necessary additional facilities.

2. The procedures applicable for interconnection to a major supplier shall be made publicly available.

3. Major suppliers shall make publicly available either their interconnection agreements or their reference interconnection offers as appropriate.

Article 174   Access to major suppliers' essential facilities

Each Party shall ensure that major suppliers in its territory make their essential facilities available to suppliers of telecommunications networks or telecommunications services on reasonable, transparent and non-discriminatory terms and conditions for the purpose of providing public telecommunications services, except where this is not necessary to achieve effective competition on the basis of the facts collected and the assessment of the market conducted by the telecommunications regulatory authority. The major supplier's essential facilities may include network elements, leased circuits services and associated facilities.

Article 175   Scarce resources

1. Each Party shall ensure that the allocation and granting of rights of use of scarce resources, including radio spectrum, numbers and rights of way, is carried out in an open, objective, timely, transparent, non-discriminatory and proportionate manner and by taking into account general interest objectives. Procedures, and conditions and obligations attached to rights of use, shall be based on objective, transparent, non-discriminatory and proportionate criteria.

2. The current use of allocated frequency bands shall be made publicly available, but detailed identification of radio spectrum allocated for specific government uses is not required.

3. Parties may rely on market-based approaches, such as bidding procedures, to assign spectrum for commercial use.

4. The Parties understand that measures of a Party allocating and assigning spectrum and managing frequency are not in and of themselves inconsistent with Articles 128 and 135. Each Party retains the right to establish and apply spectrum and frequency management measures that may have the effect of limiting the number of suppliers of telecommunications services, provided that it does so in a manner consistent with this Agreement. This includes the ability to allocate frequency bands taking into account current and future needs and spectrum availability.

Article 176   Universal service

1. Each Party has the right to define the kind of universal service obligations it wishes to maintain and to decide on their scope and implementation.

2. Each Party shall administer the universal service obligations in a proportionate, transparent, objective and non-discriminatory way, which is neutral with respect to competition and not more burdensome than necessary for the kind of universal service defined by the Party.

3. Each Party shall ensure that procedures for the designation of universal service suppliers are open to all suppliers of public telecommunications networks or public telecommunications services. Such designation shall be made through an efficient, transparent and non-discriminatory mechanism.

4. If a Party decides to compensate the universal service suppliers, it shall ensure that such compensation does not exceed the net cost caused by the universal service obligation.

Article 177   Number portability

Each Party shall ensure that suppliers of public telecommunications services provide number portability on reasonable terms and conditions.

Article 178   Open internet access

1. Each Party shall ensure that, subject to its laws and regulations, suppliers of internet access services enable users of those services to:

    (a) access and distribute information and content, use and provide applications and services of their choice, subject to non-discriminatory, reasonable, transparent and proportionate network management; and

    (b) use devices of their choice, provided that such devices do not harm the security of other devices, the network or services provided over the network.

2. For greater certainty, nothing in this Article shall prevent the Parties from adopting measures with the aim of protecting public safety with regards to users online.

Article 179   Confidentiality of information

1. Each Party shall ensure that suppliers that acquire information from another supplier in the process of negotiating arrangements pursuant to Articles 169, 170, 173 and 174 use that information solely for the purpose for which it was supplied and respect at all times the confidentiality of information transmitted or stored.

2. Each Party shall ensure the confidentiality of communications and related traffic data transmitted in the use of public telecommunications networks or public telecommunications services subject to the requirement that measures applied to that end do not constitute a means of arbitrary or unjustifiable discrimination or a disguised restriction on trade in services.

Article 180   Foreign shareholding

With regard to the provision of telecommunications networks or telecommunications services through establishment and notwithstanding Article 133, a Party shall not impose joint venture requirements or limit the participation of foreign capital in terms of maximum percentage limits on foreign shareholding or the total value of individual or aggregate foreign investment.

Article 181   International mobile roaming[27]

1. The Parties shall endeavour to cooperate on promoting transparent and reasonable rates for international mobile roaming services in ways that can help promote the growth of trade among the Parties and enhance consumer welfare.

2. Parties may choose to take steps to enhance transparency and competition with respect to international mobile roaming rates and technological alternatives to roaming services, such as:

    (a) ensuring that information regarding retail rates is easily accessible to end users; and

    (b) minimising impediments to the use of technological alternatives to roaming, whereby end users visiting the territory of a Party from the territory of the other Party can access telecommunications services using the device of their choice.

3. Each Party shall encourage suppliers of public telecommunications services in its territory to make publicly available information on retail rates for international mobile roaming services for voice, data and text messages offered to their end users when visiting the territory of the other Party.

4. Nothing in this Article shall require a Party to regulate rates or conditions for international mobile roaming services.

Section 5   Financial services

Article 182   Scope

1. This Section applies to measures of a Party affecting the supply of financial services in addition to Chapters 1, 2, 3 and 4 of this Title, and to Sections 1 and 2 of this Chapter.

2. For the purposes of this Section, the term 'activities performed in the exercise of governmental authority' referred to in point (f) of Article 124 means the following[28]:

    (a) activities conducted by a central bank or a monetary authority or by any other public entity in pursuit of monetary or exchange rate policies;

---

[27] This Article does not apply to intra-European Union roaming services, which are commercial mobile services provided pursuant to a commercial agreement between suppliers of public telecommunications services that enable an end user to use its home mobile handset or other device for voice, data or messaging services in a Member State other than that in which the end user's home public telecommunications network is located.

[28] For greater certainty, this modification applies to 'services supplied in the exercise of governmental authority' in point (o) of Article 124 as it applies to 'activities performed in the exercise of governmental authority' in point (f) of Article 124.

    (b) activities forming part of a statutory system of social security or public retirement plans; and

    (c) other activities conducted by a public entity for the account or with the guarantee or using the financial resources of the Party or its public entities.

3. For the purposes of the application of point (f) of Article 124 to this Section, if a Party allows any of the activities referred to in point (b) or (c) of paragraph 2 of this Article to be conducted by its financial service suppliers in competition with a public entity or a financial service supplier, 'activities performed in the exercise of governmental authority' does not include those activities.

4. Point (a) of Article 124 does not apply to services covered by this Section.

Article 183   Definitions

For the purposes of this Title, the following definitions apply:

    (a) 'financial service' means any service of a financial nature offered by a financial service supplier of a Party and includes the following activities:

        (i) insurance and insurance-related services:

            (A) direct insurance (including co-insurance):

                (aa) life;

                (bb) non-life;

            (B) reinsurance and retrocession;

            (C) insurance intermediation, such as brokerage and agency; and

            (D) services auxiliary to insurance, such as consultancy, actuarial, risk assessment and claim settlement services;

        (ii) banking and other financial services (excluding insurance):

            (A) acceptance of deposits and other repayable funds from the public;

            (B) lending of all types, including consumer credit, mortgage credit, factoring and financing of commercial transaction;

            (C) financial leasing;

            (D) all payment and money transmission services, including credit, charge and debit cards, travellers cheques and bankers drafts;

            (E) guarantees and commitments;

            (F) trading for own account or for account of customers, whether on an exchange, in an over-the-counter market or otherwise, the following:

                (aa) money market instruments (including cheques, bills, certificates of deposits);

                (bb) foreign exchange;

                (cc) derivative products including, but not limited to, futures and options;

                (dd) exchange rate and interest rate instruments, including products such as swaps, forward rate agreements;

                (ee) transferable securities; and

                (ff) other negotiable instruments and financial assets, including bullion;

            (G) participation in issues of all kinds of securities, including underwriting and placement as agent (whether publicly or privately) and provision of services related to such issues;

            (H) money broking;

            (I) asset management, such as cash or portfolio management, all forms of collective investment management, pension fund management, custodial, depository and trust services;

            (J) settlement and clearing services for financial assets, including securities, derivative products, and other negotiable instruments;

            (K) provision and transfer of financial information, and financial data processing and related software; and

            (L) advisory, intermediation and other auxiliary financial services on all the activities listed in points (A) to (K), including credit reference and analysis, investment and portfolio research and advice, advice on acquisitions and on corporate restructuring and strategy;

    (b) 'financial service supplier' means any natural or legal person of a Party that seeks to supply or supplies financial services and does not include a public entity;

    (c) 'new financial service' means a service of a financial nature including services related to existing and new products or the manner in which a product is delivered, that is not supplied by any financial service supplier in the territory of a Party but which is supplied in the territory of the other Party;

    (d) 'public entity' means:

        (i) a government, a central bank or a monetary authority, of a Party, or an entity owned or controlled by a Party, that is principally engaged in carrying out governmental functions or activities for governmental purposes, not including an entity principally engaged in supplying financial services on commercial terms; or

        (ii) a private entity, performing functions normally performed by a central bank or monetary authority, when exercising those functions;

    (e) 'self-regulatory organisation' means any non-governmental body, including a securities or futures exchange or market, clearing agency, other organisation or association, that exercises regulatory or supervisory authority over financial service suppliers by statute or delegation from central, regional or local governments or authorities, where applicable.

Article 184   Prudential carve-out

1. Nothing in this Agreement shall prevent a Party from adopting or maintaining measures for prudential reasons[29], such as:

    (a) the protection of investors, depositors, policy-holders or persons to whom a fiduciary duty is owed by a financial service supplier; or

    (b) ensuring the integrity and stability of a Party's financial system.

2. Where such measures do not conform with the provisions of this Agreement, they shall not be used as a means of avoiding the Party's commitments or obligations under this Agreement.

Article 185   Confidential information

Without prejudice to Part Three, nothing in this Agreement shall be construed to require a Party to disclose information relating to the affairs and accounts of individual consumers or any confidential or proprietary information in the possession of public entities.

Article 186   International standards

The Parties shall make their best endeavours to ensure that internationally agreed standards in the financial services sector for regulation and supervision, for the fight against money laundering and terrorist financing and for the fight against tax evasion and avoidance, are implemented and applied in their territory. Such internationally agreed standards are, *inter alia*, those adopted by: the G20; the Financial Stability Board; the Basel Committee on Banking Supervision, in particular its 'Core Principle for Effective Banking Supervision'; the International Association of Insurance Supervisors, in particular its 'Insurance Core Principles'; the International Organisation of Securities Commissions, in particular its 'Objectives and Principles of Securities Regulation'; the Financial Action Task Force; and the Global Forum on Transparency and Exchange of Information for Tax Purposes of the Organisation for Economic Cooperation and Development.

Article 187   Financial services new to the territory of a Party

1. Each Party shall permit a financial service supplier of the other Party established in its territory to supply any new financial service that it would permit its own financial service suppliers to supply in accordance with its law in like situations, provided that the introduction of the new financial service does not require the adoption of a new law or the amendment of an existing law. This does not apply to branches of the other Party established in the territory of a Party.

---

[29] For greater certainty, this shall not prevent a Party from adopting or maintaining measures for prudential reasons in relation to branches established in its territory by legal persons in the other Party.

2. A Party may determine the institutional and legal form through which the service may be supplied and require authorisation for the supply of the service. Where such authorisation is required, a decision shall be made within a reasonable time and the authorisation may only be refused for prudential reasons.

Article 188   Self-regulatory organisations

Where a Party requires membership of, participation in, or access to, any self-regulatory organisation in order for financial service suppliers of the other Party to supply financial services in its territory, the Party shall ensure observance by that self-regulatory organisation of the obligations under Articles 129, 130, 137 and 138.

Article 189   Clearing and payment systems

Under terms and conditions that accord national treatment, each Party shall grant to financial service suppliers of the other Party established in its territory access to payment and clearing systems operated by public entities, and to official funding and refinancing facilities available in the normal course of ordinary business. This Article does not confer access to the Party's lender of last resort facilities.

Section 6   International maritime transport services

Article 190   Scope and definitions

1. This Section applies to measures of a Party affecting the supply of international maritime transport services in addition to Chapters 1, 2, 3, 4 and Section 1 of this Chapter.

2. For the purposes of this Section and Chapters 1, 2, 3 and 4 of this Title, the following definitions apply:

    (a) 'international maritime transport services' means the transport of passengers or cargo by sea-going vessels between a port of one Party and a port of the other Party or of a third country, or between ports of different Member States, including the direct contracting with providers of other transport services, with a view to covering door-to-door or multimodal transport operations under a single transport document, but does not include the right to provide such other transport services;

    (b) 'door-to-door or multimodal transport operations' means the transport of international cargo using more than one mode of transport, that includes an international sea-leg, under a single transport document;

    (c) 'international cargo' means cargo transported between a port of one Party and a port of the other Party or of a third country, or between ports of different Member States;

    (d) 'maritime auxiliary services' means maritime cargo handling services, customs clearance services, container station and depot services, maritime agency services, maritime freight forwarding services and storage and warehousing services;

    (e) 'maritime cargo handling services' means activities exercised by stevedore companies, including terminal operators but not including the direct activities of dockers if the workforce is organised independently of the stevedoring or terminal operator companies; the activities covered include the organisation and supervision of:

        (i) loading or discharging of cargo to or from a ship;

        (ii) the lashing or unlashing of cargo; and

        (iii) the reception or delivery and safekeeping of cargoes before shipment or after discharge;

    (f) 'customs clearance services' means activities consisting in carrying out, on behalf of another party, customs formalities concerning import, export or through transport of cargoes, irrespective of whether these services are the main activity of the service supplier or a usual complement of its main activity;

    (g) 'container station and depot services' means activities that consist of storing, stuffing, stripping or repairing of containers and making containers available for shipment, whether in port areas or inland;

    (h) 'maritime agency services' means activities that consist of representing, within a given geographic area, as an agent the business interests of one or more shipping lines or shipping companies, for the following purposes:

        (i) marketing and sales of maritime transport and related services, from quotation to invoicing, issuance of bills of lading on behalf of the lines or companies, acquisition and resale of the necessary related services, preparation of documentation and provision of business information; and

        (ii) acting on behalf of the lines or companies organising the call of the ship or taking over cargoes when required;

    (i) 'feeder services' means, without prejudice to the scope of activities that may be considered as cabotage under the relevant national legislation, the pre- and onward transportation by sea of international cargo, including containerised, break bulk and dry or liquid bulk cargo, between ports located in the territory of a Party, provided such international cargo is 'en route', that is, directed to a destination, or coming from a port of shipment, outside the territory of that Party;

    (j) 'maritime freight forwarding services' means the activity consisting of organising and monitoring shipment operations on behalf of shippers, through the arrangement of transport and related services, preparation of documentation and provision of business information;

    (k) 'port services' means services provided inside a maritime port area or on the waterway access to such area by the managing body of a port, its subcontractors, or other service providers to support the transport of cargo or passengers; and

    (l) 'storage and warehousing services' means storage services of frozen or refrigerated goods, bulk storage services of liquids or gases, and other storage or warehousing services.

Article 191   Obligations

1. Without prejudice to non-conforming measures or other measures referred to in Articles 133 and 139, each Party shall implement the principle of unrestricted access to the international maritime markets and trades on a commercial and non-discriminatory basis by:

    (a) according to ships flying the flag of the other Party, or operated by service suppliers of the other Party, treatment no less favourable than that accorded to its own ships with regard to, *inter alia*:

        (i) access to ports;

        (ii) the use of port infrastructure;

        (iii) the use of maritime auxiliary services; and

        (iv) customs facilities and the assignment of berths and facilities for loading and unloading, including related fees and charges;

    (b) making available to international maritime transport service suppliers of the other Party, on terms and conditions which are both reasonable and no less favourable than those applicable to its own suppliers or vessels or to vessels or suppliers of a third country (including fees and charges, specifications and quality of the service to be provided), the following port services: pilotage, towing and tug assistance, provisioning, fuelling and watering, garbage collecting and ballast waste disposal, port captain's services, navigation aids, emergency repair facilities, anchorage, berth, berthing and unberthing services and shore-based operational services essential to ship operations, including communications, water and electrical supplies;

    (c) permitting international maritime transport service suppliers of the other Party, subject to the authorisation by the competent authority where applicable, to re-position owned or leased empty containers, which are not being carried as cargo against payment, between ports of the United Kingdom or between ports of a Member State; and

    (d) permitting international maritime transport service suppliers of the other Party to provide feeder services between ports of the United Kingdom or between ports of a Member State, subject to the authorisation by the competent authority where applicable.

2. In applying the principle referred to in paragraph 1, a Party shall:

   (a) not introduce cargo-sharing arrangements in future agreements with third countries concerning international maritime transport services, including dry and liquid bulk and liner trade, and terminate, within a reasonable period of time, such cargo-sharing arrangements in case they exist in previous agreements;

   (b) not adopt or maintain a measure that requires all or part of any international cargo to be transported exclusively by vessels registered in that Party or owned or controlled by natural persons of that Party;

   (c) abolish and abstain from introducing any unilateral measures or administrative, technical and other obstacles which could constitute a disguised restriction or have discriminatory effects on the free supply of international maritime transport services; and

   (d) not prevent international maritime transport service suppliers of the other Party from directly contracting with other transport service suppliers for door-to-door or multimodal transport operations.

Section 7   Legal services

Article 192   Scope

1. This Section applies to measures of a Party affecting the supply of designated legal services in addition to Chapters 1, 2, 3 and 4 of this Title and to Sections 1 and 2 of this Chapter.

2. Nothing in this Section shall affect the right of a Party to regulate and supervise the supply of designated legal services in its territory in a non-discriminatory manner.

Article 193   Definitions

For the purposes of this Section, the following definitions apply:

   (a) 'designated legal services' means legal services in relation to home jurisdiction law and public international law, excluding Union law;

   (b) 'home jurisdiction' means the jurisdiction (or a part of the jurisdiction) of the Member State or of the United Kingdom in which a lawyer acquired their home jurisdiction professional title or, in the case of a lawyer who has acquired a home jurisdiction professional title in more than one jurisdiction, any of those jurisdictions;

   (c) 'home jurisdiction law' means the law of the lawyer's home jurisdiction[30];

   (d) 'home jurisdiction professional title' means:

   (i) for a lawyer of the Union, a professional title acquired in a Member State authorising the supply of legal services in that Member State; or

   (ii) for a lawyer of the United Kingdom, the title of advocate, barrister or solicitor, authorising the supply of legal services in any part of the jurisdiction of the United Kingdom;

   (e) 'lawyer' means:

   (i) a natural person of the Union who is authorised in a Member State to supply legal services under a home jurisdiction professional title; or

   (ii) a natural person of the United Kingdom who is authorised in any part of the jurisdiction of the United Kingdom to supply legal services under a home jurisdiction professional title;

   (f) 'lawyer of the other Party' means:

   (i) where 'the other Party' is the Union, a lawyer referred to in point (e)(i); or

   (ii) where 'the other Party' is the United Kingdom, a lawyer referred to in point (e)(ii); and

   (g) 'legal services' means the following services:

   (i) legal advisory services; and

---

[30] For greater certainty, for the purposes of this Title, Union law is part of the home jurisdiction law of the lawyers referred to in point (e)(i) of this Article.

(ii) legal arbitration, conciliation and mediation services (but excluding such services when supplied by natural persons as set out in Article 140).[31]

'Legal services' do not include legal representation before administrative agencies, the courts, and other duly constituted official tribunals of a Party, legal advisory and legal authorisation, documentation and certification services supplied by legal professionals entrusted with public functions in the administration of justice such as notaries, 'huissiers de justice' or other 'officiers publics et ministériels', and services supplied by bailiffs who are appointed by an official act of government.

Article 194   Obligations

1. A Party shall allow a lawyer of the other Party to supply in its territory designated legal services under that lawyer's home jurisdiction professional title in accordance with Articles 128, 129, 135, 137 and 143.

2. Where a Party (the host jurisdiction) requires registration in its territory as a condition for a lawyer of the other Party to supply designated legal services pursuant to paragraph 1, the requirements and process for such registration shall not:

(a) be less favourable than those which apply to a natural person of a third country who is supplying legal services in relation to third country law or public international law under that person's third-country professional title in the territory of the host jurisdiction; and

(b) amount to or be equivalent to any requirement to requalify into or be admitted to the legal profession of the host jurisdiction.

3. Paragraph 4 applies to the supply of designated legal services pursuant to paragraph 1 through establishment.

4. A Party shall allow a legal person of the other Party to establish a branch in its territory through which designated legal services[32] are supplied pursuant to paragraph 1, in accordance with and subject to the conditions set out in Chapter 2 of this Title. This shall be without prejudice to requirements that a certain percentage of the shareholders, owners, partners, or directors of a legal person be qualified or practice a certain profession such as lawyers or accountants.

Article 195   Non-conforming measures

1. Article 194 does not apply to:

(a) any existing non-conforming measure of a Party at the level of:

(i) for the Union:

(A) the Union, as set out in the Schedule of the Union in Annex 19;

(B) the central government of a Member State, as set out in the Schedule of the Union in Annex 19;

(C) a regional government of a Member State, as set out in the Schedule of the Union in Annex 19; or

(D) a local government, other than that referred to in point (C); and

(ii) for the United Kingdom:

(A) the central government, as set out in the Schedule of the United Kingdom in Annex 19;

---

[31] 'Legal arbitration, conciliation and mediation services' means the preparation of documents to be submitted to, the preparation for and appearance before, an arbitrator, conciliator or mediator in any dispute involving the application and interpretation of law. It does not include arbitration, conciliation and mediation services in disputes not involving the application and interpretation of law, which fall under services incidental to management consulting. It also does not include acting as an arbitrator, conciliator or mediator. As a sub-category, international legal arbitration, conciliation or mediation services refers to the same services when the dispute involves parties from two or more countries.

[32] For greater certainty, for the purposes of this paragraph 'designated legal services' means, for services supplied in the Union, legal services in relation to the law of the United Kingdom or any part of it and public international law (excluding Union law), and for services supplied in the United Kingdom, legal services in relation to the law of the Member States (including Union law) and public international law (excluding Union law).

(B) a regional government, as set out in the Schedule of the United Kingdom in Annex 19; or

(C) a local government;

(b) the continuation or prompt renewal of any non-conforming measure referred to in point (a) of this paragraph; or

(c) a modification to any non-conforming measure referred to in points (a) and (b) of this paragraph to the extent that it does not decrease the conformity of the measure, as it existed immediately before the modification, with Article 194.

2. Article 194 does not apply to any measure of a Party which is consistent with the reservations, conditions or qualifications specified with respect to a sector, subsector or activity listed in Annex 20.

3. This Section applies without prejudice to Annex 22.

Title III Digital trade

Chapter 1 General provisions

Article 196 Objective

The objective of this Title is to facilitate digital trade, to address unjustified barriers to trade enabled by electronic means and to ensure an open, secure and trustworthy online environment for businesses and consumers.

Article 197 Scope

1. This Title applies to measures of a Party affecting trade enabled by electronic means.

2. This Title does not apply to audio-visual services.

Article 198 Right to regulate

The Parties reaffirm the right to regulate within their territories to achieve legitimate policy objectives, such as the protection of public health, social services, public education, safety, the environment including climate change, public morals, social or consumer protection, privacy and data protection, or the promotion and protection of cultural diversity.

Article 199 Exceptions

For greater certainty, nothing in this Title prevents the Parties from adopting or maintaining measures in accordance with Articles 184, 412 and 415 for the public interest reasons set out therein.

Article 200 Definitions

1. The definitions in Article 124 apply to this Title.

2. For the purposes of this Title, the following definitions apply:

(a) 'consumer' means any natural person using a public telecommunications service for other than professional purposes;

(b) 'direct marketing communication' means any form of commercial advertising by which a natural or legal person communicates marketing messages directly to a user via a public telecommunications service and covers at least electronic mail and text and multimedia messages (SMS and MMS);

(c) 'electronic authentication' means an electronic process that enables the confirmation of:

(i) the electronic identification of a natural or legal person, or

(ii) the origin and integrity of data in electronic form;

(d) 'electronic registered delivery service' means a service that makes it possible to transmit data between third parties by electronic means and provides evidence relating to the handling of the transmitted data, including proof of sending and receiving the data, and that protects transmitted data against the risk of loss, theft, damage or any unauthorised alterations;

(e) 'electronic seal' means data in electronic form used by a legal person which is attached to or logically associated with other data in electronic form to ensure the latter's origin and integrity;

(f) 'electronic signature' means data in electronic form which is attached to or logically associated with other data in electronic form that:

    (i)   is used by a natural person to agree on the data in electronic form to which it relates; and

    (ii) is linked to the data in electronic form to which it relates in such a way that any subsequent alteration in the data is detectable;

(g) 'electronic time stamp' means data in electronic form which binds other data in electronic form to a particular time establishing evidence that the latter data existed at that time;

(h) 'electronic trust service' means an electronic service consisting of:

    (i)   the creation, verification and validation of electronic signatures, electronic seals, electronic time stamps, electronic registered delivery services and certificates related to those services;

    (ii) the creation, verification and validation of certificates for website authentication; or

    (iii) the preservation of electronic signatures, seals or certificates related to those services;

(i) 'government data' means data owned or held by any level of government and by non-governmental bodies in the exercise of powers conferred on them by any level of government;

(j) 'public telecommunications service' means any telecommunications service that is offered to the public generally;

(k) 'user' means any natural or legal person using a public telecommunications service.

Chapter 2   Data flows and personal data protection

Article 201   Cross-border data flows

1. The Parties are committed to ensuring cross-border data flows to facilitate trade in the digital economy. To that end, cross-border data flows shall not be restricted between the Parties by a Party:

(a) requiring the use of computing facilities or network elements in the Party's territory for processing, including by imposing the use of computing facilities or network elements that are certified or approved in the territory of a Party;

(b) requiring the localisation of data in the Party's territory for storage or processing;

(c) prohibiting the storage or processing in the territory of the other Party; or

(d) making the cross-border transfer of data contingent upon use of computing facilities or network elements in the Parties' territory or upon localisation requirements in the Parties' territory.

2. The Parties shall keep the implementation of this provision under review and assess its functioning within three years of the date of entry into force of this Agreement. A Party may at any time propose to the other Party to review the list of restrictions listed in paragraph 1. Such a request shall be accorded sympathetic consideration.

Article 202   Protection of personal data and privacy

1. Each Party recognises that individuals have a right to the protection of personal data and privacy and that high standards in this regard contribute to trust in the digital economy and to the development of trade.

2. Nothing in this Agreement shall prevent a Party from adopting or maintaining measures on the protection of personal data and privacy, including with respect to cross-border data transfers, provided that the law of the Party provides for instruments enabling transfers under conditions of general application[33] for the protection of the data transferred.

3. Each Party shall inform the other Party about any measure referred to in paragraph 2 that it adopts or maintains.

---

[33] For greater certainty, 'conditions of general application' refer to conditions formulated in objective terms that apply horizontally to an unidentified number of economic operators and thus cover a range of situations and cases.

Chapter 3 Specific provisions

Article 203   Customs duties on electronic transmissions

1. Electronic transmissions shall be considered as the supply of a service within the meaning of Title II of this Heading.

2. The Parties shall not impose customs duties on electronic transmissions.

Article 204   No prior authorisation

1. A Party shall not require prior authorisation of the provision of a service by electronic means solely on the ground that the service is provided online, and shall not adopt or maintain any other requirement having an equivalent effect.

A service is provided online when it is provided by electronic means and without the parties being simultaneously present.

2. Paragraph 1 does not apply to telecommunications services, broadcasting services, gambling services, legal representation services or to the services of notaries or equivalent professions to the extent that they involve a direct and specific connection with the exercise of public authority.

Article 205   Conclusion of contracts by electronic means

1. Each Party shall ensure that contracts may be concluded by electronic means and that its law neither creates obstacles for the use of electronic contracts nor results in contracts being deprived of legal effect and validity solely on the ground that the contract has been made by electronic means.

2. Paragraph 1 does not apply to the following:
   (a) broadcasting services;
   (b) gambling services;
   (c) legal representation services;
   (d) the services of notaries or equivalent professions involving a direct and specific connection with the exercise of public authority;
   (e) contracts that require witnessing in person;
   (f) contracts that establish or transfer rights in real estate;
   (g) contracts requiring by law the involvement of courts, public authorities or professions exercising public authority;
   (h) contracts of suretyship granted, collateral securities furnished by persons acting for purposes outside their trade, business or profession; or
   (i) contracts governed by family law or by the law of succession.

Article 206   Electronic authentication and electronic trust services

1. A Party shall not deny the legal effect and admissibility as evidence in legal proceedings of an electronic document, an electronic signature, an electronic seal or an electronic time stamp, or of data sent and received using an electronic registered delivery service, solely on the ground that it is in electronic form.

2. A Party shall not adopt or maintain measures that would:
   (a) prohibit parties to an electronic transaction from mutually determining the appropriate electronic authentication methods for their transaction; or
   (b) prevent parties to an electronic transaction from being able to prove to judicial and administrative authorities that the use of electronic authentication or an electronic trust service in that transaction complies with the applicable legal requirements.

3. Notwithstanding paragraph 2, a Party may require that for a particular category of transactions, the method of electronic authentication or trust service is certified by an authority accredited in accordance with its law or meets certain performance standards which shall be objective, transparent and non-discriminatory and only relate to the specific characteristics of the category of transactions concerned.

Article 207   Transfer of or access to source code

1. A Party shall not require the transfer of, or access to, the source code of software owned by a natural or legal person of the other Party.

2. For greater certainty:

(a) the general exceptions, security exceptions and prudential carve-out referred to in Article 199 apply to measures of a Party adopted or maintained in the context of a certification procedure; and

(b) paragraph 1 of this Article does not apply to the voluntary transfer of, or granting of access to, source code on a commercial basis by a natural or legal person of the other Party, such as in the context of a public procurement transaction or a freely negotiated contract.

3. Nothing in this Article shall affect:

(a) a requirement by a court or administrative tribunal, or a requirement by a competition authority pursuant to a Party's competition law to prevent or remedy a restriction or a distortion of competition;

(b) a requirement by a regulatory body pursuant to a Party's laws or regulations related to the protection of public safety with regard to users online, subject to safeguards against unauthorised disclosure;

(c) the protection and enforcement of intellectual property rights; and

(d) the right of a Party to take measures in accordance with Article III of the GPA as incorporated by Article 277 of this Agreement.

Article 208   Online consumer trust

1. Recognising the importance of enhancing consumer trust in digital trade, each Party shall adopt or maintain measures to ensure the effective protection of consumers engaging in electronic commerce transactions, including but not limited to measures that:

(a) proscribe fraudulent and deceptive commercial practices;

(b) require suppliers of goods and services to act in good faith and abide by fair commercial practices, including through the prohibition of charging consumers for unsolicited goods and services;

(c) require suppliers of goods or services to provide consumers with clear and thorough information, including when they act through intermediary service suppliers, regarding their identity and contact details, the transaction concerned, including the main characteristics of the goods or services and the full price inclusive of all applicable charges, and the applicable consumer rights (in the case of intermediary service suppliers, this includes enabling the provision of such information by the supplier of goods or services); and

(d) grant consumers access to redress for breaches of their rights, including a right to remedies if goods or services are paid for and are not delivered or provided as agreed.

2. The Parties recognise the importance of entrusting their consumer protection agencies or other relevant bodies with adequate enforcement powers and the importance of cooperation between these agencies in order to protect consumers and enhance online consumer trust.

Article 209   Unsolicited direct marketing communications

1. Each Party shall ensure that users are effectively protected against unsolicited direct marketing communications.

2. Each Party shall ensure that direct marketing communications are not sent to users who are natural persons unless they have given their consent in accordance with each Party's laws to receiving such communications.

3. Notwithstanding paragraph 2, a Party shall allow natural or legal persons who have collected, in accordance with conditions laid down in the law of that Party, the contact details of a user in the context of the supply of goods or services, to send direct marketing communications to that user for their own similar goods or services.

4. Each Party shall ensure that direct marketing communications are clearly identifiable as such, clearly disclose on whose behalf they are made and contain the necessary information to enable users to request cessation free of charge and at any moment.

5. Each Party shall provide users with access to redress against suppliers of direct marketing communications that do not comply with the measures adopted or maintained pursuant to paragraphs 1 to 4.

Article 210 Open government data

1. The Parties recognise that facilitating public access to, and use of, government data contributes to stimulating economic and social development, competitiveness, productivity and innovation.

2. To the extent that a Party chooses to make government data accessible to the public, it shall endeavour to ensure, to the extent practicable, that the data:

(a) is in a format that allows it to be easily searched, retrieved, used, reused, and redistributed;

(b) is in a machine-readable and spatially-enabled format;

(c) contains descriptive metadata, which is as standard as possible;

(d) is made available via reliable, user-friendly and freely available Application Programming Interfaces;

(e) is regularly updated;

(f) is not subject to use conditions that are discriminatory or that unnecessarily restrict re-use; and

(g) is made available for re-use in full compliance with the Parties' respective personal data protection rules.

3. The Parties shall endeavour to cooperate to identify ways in which each Party can expand access to, and use of, government data that the Party has made public, with a view to enhancing and generating business opportunities, beyond its use by the public sector.

Article 211 Cooperation on regulatory issues with regard to digital trade

1. The Parties shall exchange information on regulatory matters in the context of digital trade, which shall address the following:

(a) the recognition and facilitation of interoperable authentication and electronic trust services;

(b) the treatment of direct marketing communications;

(c) the protection of consumers; and

(d) any other matter relevant for the development of digital trade, including emerging technologies.

2. Paragraph 1 shall not apply to a Party's rules and safeguards for the protection of personal data and privacy, including on cross-border transfers of personal data.

Article 212 Understanding on computer services

1. The Parties agree that, for the purpose of liberalising trade in services and investment in accordance with Title II of this Heading, the following services shall be considered as computer and related services, regardless of whether they are delivered via a network, including the internet:

(a) consulting, adaptation, strategy, analysis, planning, specification, design, development, installation, implementation, integration, testing, debugging, updating, support, technical assistance or management of or for computers or computer systems;

(b) computer programmes defined as the sets of instructions required to make computers work and communicate (in and of themselves), as well as consulting, strategy, analysis, planning, specification, design, development, installation, implementation, integration, testing, debugging, updating, adaptation, maintenance, support, technical assistance, management or use of or for computer programmes;

(c) data processing, data storage, data hosting or database services;

(d) maintenance and repair services for office machinery and equipment, including computers; and

(e) training services for staff of clients, related to computer programmes, computers or computer systems, and not elsewhere classified.

For greater certainty, services enabled by computer and related services, other than those listed in paragraph 1, shall not be regarded as computer and related services in themselves.

Title IV Capital movements, payments, transfers and temporary safeguard measures [omitted]

Title V Intellectual property

Chapter 1 General provisions

Article 219 Objectives

The objectives of this Title are to:

(a) facilitate the production, provision and commercialisation of innovative and creative products and services between the Parties by reducing distortions and impediments to such trade, thereby contributing to a more sustainable and inclusive economy; and

(b) ensure an adequate and effective level of protection and enforcement of intellectual property rights.

Article 220 Scope

1. This Title shall complement and further specify the rights and obligations of each Party under the TRIPS Agreement and other international treaties in the field of intellectual property to which they are parties.

2. This Title does not preclude either Party from introducing more extensive protection and enforcement of intellectual property rights than required under this Title, provided that such protection and enforcement does not contravene this Title.

Article 221 Definitions

For the purposes of this Title, the following definitions apply:

(a) 'Paris Convention' means the Paris Convention for the Protection of Industrial Property of 20 March 1883, as last revised at Stockholm on 14 July 1967;

(b) 'Berne Convention' means the Berne Convention for the Protection of Literary and Artistic Works of 9 September 1886 revised at Paris on 24 July 1971 and amended on 28 September 1979;

(c) 'Rome Convention' means the International Convention for the Protection of Performers, Producers of Phonograms and Broadcasting Organisations done at Rome on 26 October 1961;

(d) 'WIPO' means the World Intellectual Property Organisation;

(e) 'intellectual property rights' means all categories of intellectual property that are covered by Articles 225 to 255 of this Agreement or Sections 1 to 7 of Part II of the TRIPS Agreement. The protection of intellectual property includes protection against unfair competition as referred to in Article 10bis of the Paris Convention;

(f) 'national' means, in respect of the relevant intellectual property right, a person of a Party that would meet the criteria for eligibility for protection provided for in the TRIPS Agreement and multilateral agreements concluded and administered under the auspices of WIPO, to which a Party is a contracting party.

Article 222 International agreements

1. The Parties affirm their commitment to comply with the international agreements to which they are party:

(a) the TRIPS Agreement;

(b) the Rome Convention;

(c) the Berne Convention;

(d) the WIPO Copyright Treaty, adopted at Geneva on 20 December 1996;

(e) the WIPO Performances and Phonograms Treaty, adopted at Geneva on 20 December 1996;

(f) the Protocol Relating to the Madrid Agreement Concerning the International Registration of Marks, adopted at Madrid on 27 June 1989, as last amended on 12 November 2007;

(g) the Trademark Law Treaty, adopted at Geneva on 27 October 1994;

(h) the Marrakesh Treaty to Facilitate Access to Published Works for Persons Who Are Blind, Visually Impaired or Otherwise Print Disabled, adopted at Marrakesh on 27 June 2013;

(i) the Geneva Act of the Hague Agreement Concerning the International Registration of Industrial Designs, adopted at Geneva on 2 July 1999.

2. Each Party shall make all reasonable efforts to ratify or accede to the following international agreements:

(a) the Beijing Treaty on Audiovisual Performances, adopted at Beijing on 24 June 2012;

(b) the Singapore Treaty on the Law of Trademarks adopted at Singapore on 27 March 2006.

Article 223   Exhaustion

This Title does not affect the freedom of the parties to determine whether and under what conditions the exhaustion of intellectual property rights applies.

Article 224   National treatment

1. In respect of all categories of intellectual property covered by this Title, each Party shall accord to the nationals of the other Party treatment no less favourable than the treatment it accords to its own nationals with regard to the protection of intellectual property subject where applicable to the exceptions already provided for in, respectively, the Paris Convention, the Berne Convention, the Rome Convention and the Treaty on Intellectual Property in Respect of Integrated Circuits, done at Washington on 26 May 1989. In respect of performers, producers of phonograms and broadcasting organisations, this obligation only applies in respect of the rights provided for under this Agreement.

2. For the purposes of paragraph 1 of this Article, 'protection' shall include matters affecting the availability, acquisition, scope, maintenance, and enforcement of intellectual property rights as well as matters affecting the use of intellectual property rights specifically addressed in this Title, including measures to prevent the circumvention of effective technological measures as referred to in Article 234 and measures concerning rights management information as referred to in Article 235.

3. A Party may avail itself of the exceptions permitted pursuant to paragraph 1 in relation to its judicial and administrative procedures, including requiring a national of the other Party to designate an address for service in its territory, or to appoint an agent in its territory, if such exceptions are:

(a) necessary to secure compliance with the Party's laws or regulations which are not inconsistent with this Title; or

(b) not applied in a manner which would constitute a disguised restriction on trade.

4. Paragraph 1 does not apply to procedures provided in multilateral agreements concluded under the auspices of WIPO relating to the acquisition or maintenance of intellectual property rights.

Chapter 2   Standards concerning intellectual property rights

Section 1   Copyright and related rights

Article 225   Authors

Each Party shall provide authors with the exclusive right to authorise or prohibit:

(a) direct or indirect, temporary or permanent reproduction by any means and in any form, in whole or in part, of their works;

(b) any form of distribution to the public by sale or otherwise of the original of their works or of copies thereof;

(c) any communication to the public of their works by wire or wireless means, including the making available to the public of their works in such a way that members of the public may access them from a place and at a time individually chosen by them;

(d) the commercial rental to the public of originals or copies of their works; each Party may provide that this point does not apply to buildings or works of applied art.

Article 226   Performers

Each Party shall provide performers with the exclusive right to authorise or prohibit:

(a) the fixation of their performances;

(b) the direct or indirect, temporary or permanent reproduction by any means and in any form, in whole or in part, of fixations of their performances;

(c) the distribution to the public, by sale or otherwise, of the fixations of their performances;

(d) the making available to the public of fixations of their performances, by wire or wireless means, in such a way that members of the public may access them from a place and at a time individually chosen by them;

(e) the broadcasting by wireless means and the communication to the public of their performances, except where the performance is itself already a broadcast performance or is made from a fixation;

(f) the commercial rental to the public of the fixation of their performances.

Article 227   Producers of phonograms

Each Party shall provide phonogram producers with the exclusive right to authorise or prohibit:

(a) the direct or indirect, temporary or permanent, reproduction by any means and in any form, in whole or in part, of their phonograms;

(b) the distribution to the public, by sale or otherwise, of their phonograms, including copies thereof;

(c) the making available to the public of their phonograms, by wire or wireless means, in such a way that members of the public may access them from a place and at a time individually chosen by them;

(d) the commercial rental of their phonograms to the public.

Article 228   Broadcasting organisations

Each Party shall provide broadcasting organisations with the exclusive right to authorise or prohibit:

(a) the fixation of their broadcasts, whether these broadcasts are transmitted by wire or over the air, including by cable or satellite;

(b) the direct or indirect, temporary or permanent reproduction by any means and in any form, in whole or in part, of fixations of their broadcasts, whether those broadcasts are transmitted by wire or over the air, including by cable or satellite;

(c) the making available to the public, by wire or wireless means, of fixations of their broadcasts, whether those broadcasts are transmitted by wire or over the air, including by cable or satellite, in such a way that members of the public may access them from a place and at a time individually chosen by them;

(d) the distribution to the public, by sale or otherwise, of fixations, including copies thereof, of their broadcasts, whether these broadcasts are transmitted by wire or over the air, including by cable or satellite;

(e) the rebroadcasting of their broadcasts by wireless means, as well as the communication to the public of their broadcasts if such communication is made in places accessible to the public against payment of an entrance fee.

Article 229   Broadcasting and communication to the public of phonograms published for commercial purposes

1. Each Party shall provide a right in order to ensure that a single equitable remuneration is paid by the user to the performers and producers of phonograms, if a phonogram published for commercial purposes, or a reproduction of such phonogram, is used for broadcasting or any communication to the public.

2. Each Party shall ensure that the single equitable remuneration is shared between the relevant performers and phonogram producers. Each Party may enact legislation that, in the absence of an agreement between performers and producers of phonograms, sets the terms according to which performers and producers of phonograms shall share the single equitable remuneration.

3. Each Party may grant more extensive rights, as regards the broadcasting and communication to the public of phonograms published for commercial purposes, to performers and producers of phonograms.

Article 230   Term of protection

1. The rights of an author of a work shall run for the life of the author and for 70 years after the author's death, irrespective of the date when the work is lawfully made available to the public.

2. For the purpose of implementing paragraph 1, each Party may provide for specific rules on the calculation of the term of protection of musical composition with words, works of joint authorship as well as cinematographic or audiovisual works. Each Party may provide for specific rules on the calculation of the term of protection of anonymous or pseudonymous works.

3. The rights of broadcasting organisations shall expire 50 years after the first transmission of a broadcast, whether this broadcast is transmitted by wire or over the air, including by cable or satellite.

4. The rights of performers for their performances otherwise than in phonograms shall expire 50 years after the date of the fixation of the performance or, if lawfully published or lawfully communicated to the public during this time, 50 years from the first such publication or communication to the public, whichever is the earlier.

5. The rights of performers for their performances fixed in phonograms shall expire 50 years after the date of fixation of the performance or, if lawfully published or lawfully communicated to the public during this time, 70 years from such act, whichever is the earlier.

6. The rights of producers of phonograms shall expire 50 years after the fixation is made or, if lawfully published to the public during this time, 70 years from such publication. In the absence of a lawful publication, if the phonogram has been lawfully communicated to the public during this time, the term of protection shall be 70 years from such act of communication. Each Party may provide for effective measures in order to ensure that the profit generated during the 20 years of protection beyond 50 years is shared fairly between the performers and the producers of phonograms.

7. The terms laid down in this Article shall be counted from the first of January of the year following the year of the event which gives rise to them.

8. Each Party may provide for longer terms of protection than those provided for in this Article.

Article 231   Resale right

1. Each Party shall provide, for the benefit of the author of an original work of graphic or plastic art, a resale right, to be defined as an inalienable right, which cannot be waived, even in advance, to receive a royalty based on the sale price obtained for any resale of the work, subsequent to the first transfer of the work by the author.

2. The right referred to in paragraph 1 shall apply to all acts of resale involving as sellers, buyers or intermediaries art market professionals, such as salesrooms, art galleries and, in general, any dealers in works of art.

3. Each Party may provide that the right referred to in paragraph 1 shall not apply to acts of resale, where the seller has acquired the work directly from the author less than three years before that resale and where the resale price does not exceed a certain minimum amount.

4. The procedure for collection of the remuneration and their amounts shall be determined by the law of each Party.

Article 232   Collective management of rights

1. The Parties shall promote cooperation between their respective collective management organisations for the purpose of fostering the availability of works and other protected subject matter in their respective territories and the transfer of rights revenue between the respective collective management organisations for the use of such works or other protected subject matter.

2. The Parties shall promote the transparency of collective management organisations, in particular regarding the rights revenue they collect, the deductions they apply to the rights revenue they collect, the use of the rights revenue collected, the distribution policy and their repertoire.

3. The Parties shall endeavour to facilitate arrangements between their respective collective management organisations on non-discriminatory treatment of right holders whose rights these organisations manage under representation agreements.

4. The Parties shall cooperate to support the collective management organisations established in their territory and representing another collective management organisation established in the territory of the other Party by way of a representation agreement with a view to ensuring that they accurately, regularly and diligently pay amounts owed to the represented collective management organisations and provide the represented collective management organisation with the information on the amount of rights revenue collected on its behalf and any deductions made to that rights revenue.

Article 233 Exceptions and limitations

Each Party shall confine limitations or exceptions to the rights set out in Articles 225 to 229 to certain special cases which do not conflict with a normal exploitation of the work or other subject-matter and do not unreasonably prejudice the legitimate interests of the right holders.

Article 234 Protection of technological measures

1. Each Party shall provide adequate legal protection against the circumvention of any effective technological measures, which the person concerned carries out in the knowledge, or with reasonable grounds to know, that he or she is pursuing that objective. Each Party may provide for a specific regime for legal protection of technological measures used to protect computer programs.

2. Each Party shall provide adequate legal protection against the manufacture, import, distribution, sale, rental, advertisement for sale or rental, or possession for commercial purposes of devices, products or components or the provision of services which:

    (a) are promoted, advertised or marketed for the purpose of circumvention of;

    (b) have only a limited commercially significant purpose or use other than to circumvent; or

    (c) are primarily designed, produced, adapted or performed for the purpose of enabling or facilitating the circumvention of, any effective technological measures.

3. For the purposes of this Section, the expression 'technological measures' means any technology, device or component that, in the normal course of its operation, is designed to prevent or restrict acts, in respect of works or other subject-matter, which are not authorised by the right holder of any copyright or related right covered by this Section. Technological measures shall be deemed 'effective' where the use of a protected work or other subject matter is controlled by the right holders through application of an access control or protection process, such as encryption, scrambling or other transformation of the work or other subject-matter or a copy control mechanism, which achieves the protection objective.

4. Notwithstanding the legal protection provided for in paragraph 1 of this Article, each Party may take appropriate measures, as necessary, to ensure that the adequate legal protection against the circumvention of effective technological measures provided for in accordance with this Article does not prevent beneficiaries of exceptions or limitations provided for in accordance with Article 233 from enjoying such exceptions or limitations.

Article 235 Obligations concerning rights management information

1. Each Party shall provide adequate legal protection against any person knowingly performing without authority any of the following acts:

    (a) the removal or alteration of any electronic rights-management information;

    (b) the distribution, importation for distribution, broadcasting, communication or making available to the public of works or other subject-matter protected pursuant to this Section from which electronic rights-management information has been removed or altered without authority;

if such person knows, or has reasonable grounds to know, that by so doing he or she is inducing, enabling, facilitating or concealing an infringement of any copyright or any related rights as provided by the law of a Party.

2. For the purposes of this Article, 'rights-management information' means any information provided by right holders which identifies the work or other subject-matter referred to in this Article, the author or any other right holder, or information about the terms and conditions of use of the work or other subject-matter, and any numbers or codes that represent such information.

3. Paragraph 2 applies if any of these items of information is associated with a copy of, or appears in connection with the communication to the public of, a work or other subject-matter referred to in this Article.

Section 2   Trade marks

Article 236   Trade mark classification

Each Party shall maintain a trade mark classification system that is consistent with the Nice Agreement Concerning the International Classification of Goods and Services for the Purposes of the Registration of Marks of 15 June 1957, as amended and revised.

Article 237   Signs of which a trade mark may consist

A trade mark may consist of any signs, in particular words, including personal names, or designs, letters, numerals, colours, the shape of goods or of the packaging of goods, or sounds, provided that such signs are capable of:

(a) distinguishing the goods or services of one undertaking from those of other undertakings; and

(b) being represented on the respective trade mark register of each Party, in a manner which enables the competent authorities and the public to determine the clear and precise subject matter of the protection afforded to its proprietor.

Article 238   Rights conferred by a trade mark

1. Each Party shall provide that the registration of a trade mark confers on the proprietor exclusive rights therein. The proprietor shall be entitled to prevent all third parties not having the proprietor's consent from using in the course of trade:

(a) any sign which is identical with the registered trade mark in relation to goods or services which are identical with those for which the trade mark is registered;

(b) any sign where, because of its identity with, or similarity to, the registered trade mark and the identity or similarity of the goods or services covered by this trade mark and the sign, there exists a likelihood of confusion on the part of the public, including the likelihood of association between the sign and the registered trade mark.

2. The proprietor of a registered trade mark shall be entitled to prevent all third parties from bringing goods, in the course of trade, into the Party where the trade mark is registered without being released for free circulation there, where such goods, including packaging, come from other countries or the other Party and bear without authorisation a trade mark which is identical to the trade mark registered in respect of such goods, or which cannot be distinguished in its essential aspects from that trade mark.

3. The entitlement of the proprietor of a trade mark pursuant to paragraph 2 shall lapse if during the proceedings to determine whether the registered trade mark has been infringed, evidence is provided by the declarant or the holder of the goods that the proprietor of the registered trade mark is not entitled to prohibit the placing of the goods on the market in the country of final destination.

Article 239   Registration procedure

1. Each Party shall provide for a system for the registration of trade marks in which each final negative decision taken by the relevant trade mark administration, including partial refusals of registration, shall be communicated in writing to the relevant party, duly reasoned and subject to appeal.

2. Each Party shall provide for the possibility for third parties to oppose trade mark applications or, where appropriate, trade mark registrations. Such opposition proceedings shall be adversarial.

3. Each Party shall provide a publicly available electronic database of trade mark applications and trade mark registrations.

4. Each Party shall make best efforts to provide a system for the electronic application for and processing, registration and maintenance of trade marks.

Article 240   Well-known trade marks

For the purpose of giving effect to protection of well-known trade marks, as referred to in Article 6bis of the Paris Convention and Article 16(2) and (3) of the TRIPS Agreement, each Party shall apply the Joint Recommendation Concerning Provisions on the Protection of Well-Known Marks, adopted by the Assembly of the Paris Union for the Protection of Industrial Property and the General Assembly of the WIPO at the Thirty-Fourth Series of Meetings of the Assemblies of the Member States of WIPO on 20 to 29 September 1999.

Article 241   Exceptions to the rights conferred by a trade mark

1. Each Party shall provide for limited exceptions to the rights conferred by a trade mark such as the fair use of descriptive terms including geographical indications, and may provide other limited exceptions, provided such exceptions take account of the legitimate interests of the proprietor of the trade mark and of third parties.

2. The trade mark shall not entitle the proprietor to prohibit a third party from using, in the course of trade:

(a) the name or address of the third party, where the third party is a natural person;

(b) signs or indications concerning the kind, quality, quantity, intended purpose, value, geographical origin, the time of production of goods or of rendering of the service, or other characteristics of goods or services; or

(c) the trade mark for the purpose of identifying or referring to goods or services as those of the proprietor of that trade mark, in particular where the use of that trade mark is necessary to indicate the intended purpose of a product or service, in particular as accessories or spare parts, provided the third party uses them in accordance with honest practices in industrial or commercial matters.

3. The trade mark shall not entitle the proprietor to prohibit a third party from using, in the course of trade, an earlier right which only applies in a particular locality if that right is recognised by the laws of the Party in question and is used within the limits of the territory in which it is recognised.

Article 242   Grounds for revocation

1. Each Party shall provide that a trade mark shall be liable to revocation if, within a continuous period of five years it has not been put to genuine use in the relevant territory of a Party by the proprietor or with the proprietor's consent in relation to the goods or services for which it is registered, and there are no proper reasons for non-use.

2. Each Party shall also provide that a trade mark shall be liable to revocation if within the period of five years following the date of completion of the registration procedure it has not been put to genuine use in the relevant territory by the proprietor or with the proprietor's consent, in relation to the goods or services for which it is registered, and there are no proper reasons for non-use.

3. However, no person may claim that the proprietor's rights in a trade mark should be revoked where, during the interval between expiry of the five-year period and filing of the application for revocation, genuine use of the trade mark has been started or resumed. The commencement or resumption of use within a period of three months preceding the filing of the application for revocation which began at the earliest on expiry of the continuous period of five years of non-use, shall, however, be disregarded where preparations for the commencement or resumption occur only after the proprietor becomes aware that the application for revocation may be filed.

4. A trade mark shall also be liable to revocation if, after the date on which it was registered:

(a) as a consequence of acts or inactivity of the proprietor, it has become the common name in the trade for a good or service in respect of which it is registered;

(b) as a consequence of the use made of the trade mark by the proprietor of the trade mark or with the proprietor's consent in respect of the goods or services for which it is registered, it is liable to mislead the public, particularly as to the nature, quality or geographical origin of those goods or services.

Article 243 The right to prohibit preparatory acts in relation to the use of packaging or other means

Where the risk exists that the packaging, labels, tags, security or authenticity features or devices, or any other means to which the trade mark is affixed could be used in relation to goods or services and that use would constitute an infringement of the rights of the proprietor of the trade mark, the proprietor of that trade mark shall have the right to prohibit the following acts if carried out in the course of trade:

(a) affixing a sign identical with, or similar to, the trade mark on packaging, labels, tags, security or authenticity features or devices, or any other means to which the mark may be affixed; or

(b) offering or placing on the market, or stocking for those purposes, or importing or exporting, packaging, labels, tags, security or authenticity features or devices, or any other means to which the mark is affixed.

Article 244 Bad faith applications

A trade mark shall be liable to be declared invalid where the application for registration of the trade mark was made in bad faith by the applicant. Each Party may provide that such a trade mark shall not be registered.

Section 3 Design

Article 245 Protection of registered designs

1. Each Party shall provide for the protection of independently created designs that are new and original. This protection shall be provided by registration and shall confer exclusive rights upon their holders in accordance with this Section.

For the purposes of this Article, a Party may consider that a design having individual character is original.

2. The holder of a registered design shall have the right to prevent third parties not having the holder's consent at least from making, offering for sale, selling, importing, exporting, stocking the product bearing and embodying the protected design or using articles bearing or embodying the protected design where such acts are undertaken for commercial purposes.

3. A design applied to or incorporated in a product which constitutes a component part of a complex product shall only be considered to be new and original:

(a) if the component part, once it has been incorporated into the complex product, remains visible during normal use of the latter; and

(b) to the extent that those visible features of the component part fulfil in themselves the requirements as to novelty and originality.

4. For the purposes of point (a) of paragraph 3, 'normal use' means use by the end user, excluding maintenance, servicing or repair work.

Article 246 Duration of protection

The duration of protection available for registered designs, including renewals of registered designs, shall amount to a total term of 25 years from the date on which the application was filed[34].

Article 247 Protection of unregistered designs

1. Each Party shall confer on holders of an unregistered design the right to prevent the use of the unregistered design by any third party not having the holder's consent only if the contested use results from copying the unregistered design in their respective territory[35]. Such use shall at least cover the offering for sale, putting on the market, importing or exporting the product.

2. The duration of protection available for the unregistered design shall amount to at least three years as from the date on which the design was first made available to the public in the territory of the respective Party.

---

[34] Each Party may determine the relevant date of filing of the application in accordance with its own legislation.

[35] This section does not apply to the protection known in the United Kingdom as a design right.

Article 248   Exceptions and exclusions

1. Each Party may provide limited exceptions to the protection of designs, including unregis-tered designs, provided that such exceptions do not unreasonably conflict with the normal exploit-ation of designs, and do not unreasonably prejudice the legitimate interests of the holder of the design, taking account of the legitimate interests of third parties.

2. Protection shall not extend to designs solely dictated by technical or functional considera-tions. A design shall not subsist in features of appearance of a product which must necessarily be reproduced in their exact form and dimensions in order to permit the product in which the design is incorporated or to which it is applied to be mechanically connected to or placed in, around or against another product so that either product may perform its function.

3. By way of derogation from paragraph 2 of this Article, a design shall, in accordance with the conditions set out in Article 245(1), subsist in a design, which has the purpose of allowing the mul-tiple assembly or connection of mutually interchangeable products within a modular system.

Article 249   Relationship to copyright

Each Party shall ensure that designs, including unregistered designs, shall also be eligible for pro-tection under the copyright law of that Party as from the date on which the design was created or fixed in any form. The extent to which, and the conditions under which, such a protection is con-ferred, including the level of originality required, shall be determined by each Party.

Section 4   Patents

Article 250   Patents and public health

1. The Parties recognise the importance of the Declaration on the TRIPS Agreement and Public Health, adopted on 14 November 2001 by the Ministerial Conference of the WTO at Doha (the 'Doha Declaration'). In interpreting and implementing the rights and obligations under this Section, each Party shall ensure consistency with the Doha Declaration.

2. Each Party shall implement Article 31bis of the TRIPS Agreement, as well as the Annex to the TRIPS Agreement and the Appendix to the Annex to the TRIPS Agreement.

Article 251   Extension of the period of protection conferred by a patent on medicinal products and on plant protection products

1. The Parties recognise that medicinal products and plant protection products[36] protected by a patent in their respective territory may be subject to an administrative authorisation procedure before being put on their respective markets. The Parties recognise that the period that elapses be-tween the filing of the application for a patent and the first authorisation to place the product on the market, as defined for that purpose by the relevant legislation, may shorten the period of effective protection under the patent.

2. Each Party shall provide for further protection, in accordance with its laws and regulations, for a product which is protected by a patent and which has been subject to an administrative author-isation procedure referred to in paragraph 1 to compensate the holder of a patent for the reduction of effective patent protection. The terms and conditions for the provision of such further protection, including its length, shall be determined in accordance with the laws and regulations of the Parties.

3. For the purposes of this Title, 'medicinal product' means:

(a) any substance or combination of substances presented as having properties for treating or preventing disease in human beings or animals; or

(b) any substance or combination of substances which may be used in or administered to human beings or animals either with a view to restoring, correcting or modifying physiological functions by exerting a pharmacological, immunological or metabolic action, or to making a medical diagnosis.

---

[36] For the purposes of this Title, the term 'plant protection product' shall be defined for each Party by the respective legislations of the Parties.

Section 5 Protection of undisclosed information

Article 252 Protection of trade secrets

1. Each Party shall provide for appropriate civil judicial procedures and remedies for any trade secret holder to prevent, and obtain redress for, the acquisition, use or disclosure of a trade secret whenever carried out in a manner contrary to honest commercial practices.

2. For the purposes of this Section, the following definitions apply:

(a) 'trade secret' means information which meets all of the following requirements:

    (i)   it is secret in the sense that it is not, as a body or in the precise configuration and assembly of its components, generally known among or readily accessible to persons within the circles that normally deal with the kind of information in question;

    (ii) it has commercial value because it is secret; and

    (iii) it has been subject to reasonable steps under the circumstances, by the person lawfully in control of the information, to keep it secret;

(b) 'trade secret holder' means any natural or legal person lawfully controlling a trade secret.

3. For the purposes of this Section, at least the following conduct shall be considered contrary to honest commercial practices:

(a) the acquisition of a trade secret without the consent of the trade secret holder, whenever obtained by unauthorised access to, or by appropriation or copying of, any documents, objects, materials, substances or electronic files that are lawfully under the control of the trade secret holder, and that contain the trade secret or from which the trade secret can be deduced;

(b) the use or disclosure of a trade secret whenever it is carried out, without the consent of the trade secret holder, by a person who is found to meet any of the following conditions:

    (i)   having acquired the trade secret in a manner referred to in point (a);

    (ii) being in breach of a confidentiality agreement or any other duty not to disclose the trade secret; or

    (iii) being in breach of a contractual or any other duty to limit the use of the trade secret;

(c) the acquisition, use or disclosure of a trade secret whenever carried out by a person who, at the time of the acquisition, use or disclosure, knew, or ought to have known, under the circumstances that the trade secret had been obtained directly or indirectly from another person who was using or disclosing the trade secret unlawfully within the meaning of point (b).

4. Nothing in this Section shall be understood as requiring either Party to consider any of the following conducts as contrary to honest commercial practices:

(a) independent discovery or creation;

(b) the reverse engineering of a product that has been made available to the public or that is lawfully in the possession of the acquirer of the information, where the acquirer of the information is free from any legally valid duty to limit the acquisition of the trade secret;

(c) the acquisition, use or disclosure of a trade secret required or allowed by the law of each Party;

(d) the exercise of the right of workers or workers' representatives to information and consultation in accordance with the laws and regulations of that Party.

5. Nothing in this Section shall be understood as affecting the exercise of freedom of expression and information, including the freedom and pluralism of the media, as protected in each Party, restricting the mobility of employees, or as affecting the autonomy of social partners and their right to enter into collective agreements, in accordance with the laws and regulations of the Parties.

Article 253 Protection of data submitted to obtain an authorisation to put a medicinal product on the market

1. Each Party shall protect commercially confidential information submitted to obtain an authorisation to place medicinal products on the market ('marketing authorisation') against disclosure

to third parties, unless steps are taken to ensure that the data are protected against unfair commercial use or except where the disclosure is necessary for an overriding public interest.

2. Each Party shall ensure that for a limited period of time to be determined by its domestic law and in accordance with any conditions set out in its domestic law, the authority responsible for the granting of a marketing authorisation does not accept any subsequent application for a marketing authorisation that relies on the results of pre-clinical tests or clinical trials submitted in the application to that authority for the first marketing authorisation, without the explicit consent of the holder of the first marketing authorisation, unless international agreements to which the Parties are both party provide otherwise.

3. Each Party shall also ensure that, for a limited period of time to be determined by its domestic law and in accordance with any conditions set out in its domestic law, a medicinal product subsequently authorised by that authority on the basis of the results of the pre-clinical tests and clinical trials referred to in paragraph 2 is not placed on the market without the explicit consent of the holder of the first marketing authorisation, unless international agreements to which the Parties are both party provide otherwise.

4. This Article is without prejudice to additional periods of protection which each Party may provide in that Party's law.

Articles 254–255   [Omitted]

Chapter 3 Enforcement of intellectual property rights

Section 1   General provisions

Article 256   General obligations

1. Each Party shall provide under its respective law for the measures, procedures and remedies necessary to ensure the enforcement of intellectual property rights. For the purposes of Sections 1, 2 and 4 of this Chapter, the term 'intellectual property rights' does not include rights covered by Section 5 of Chapter 2.

2. The measures, procedures and remedies referred to in paragraph 1 shall:
    (a) be fair and equitable;
    (b) not be unnecessarily complicated or costly, or entail unreasonable time-limits or unwarranted delays;
    (c) be effective, proportionate and dissuasive;
    (d) be applied in such a manner as to avoid the creation of barriers to legitimate trade and to provide for safeguards against their abuse.

Article 257   Persons entitled to apply for the application of the measures, procedures and remedies

Each Party shall recognise as persons entitled to seek application of the measures, procedures and remedies referred to in Sections 2 and 4 of this Chapter:
    (a) the holders of intellectual property rights in accordance with the law of a Party;
    (b) all other persons authorised to use those rights, in particular licensees, in so far as permitted by and in accordance with the law of a Party; and
    (c) federations and associations[37], in so far as permitted by and in accordance with the law of a Party.

---

[37] For greater certainty, and in so far as permitted by the law of a Party, the term 'federations and associations' includes at least collective rights management bodies and professional defence bodies which are regularly recognised as having the right to represent holders of intellectual property rights.

Section 2   Civil and administrative enforcement [omitted]

Title VI Public procurement [omitted]
Title VII Small and medium-sized enterprises [omitted]
Title VIII Energy [omitted]

Title IX Transparency

Article 332   Objective

1. Recognising the impact that their respective regulatory environments may have on trade and investment between them, the Parties aim to provide a predictable regulatory environment and efficient procedures for economic operators, especially for small and medium-sized enterprises.

2. The Parties affirm their commitments in relation to transparency under the WTO Agreement, and build on those commitments in the provisions laid down in this Title.

Article 333   Definition

For the purposes of this Title, 'administrative decision' means a decision or action with legal effect that applies to a specific person, good or service in an individual case, and covers the failure to take a decision or take such action when that is so required by the law of a Party.

Article 334   Scope

This Title applies with respect to Titles I to VIII and Titles X to XII of this Heading and Heading Six.

Article 335   Publication

1. Each Party shall ensure that its laws, regulations, procedures and administrative rulings of general application are promptly published via an officially designated medium, and, where feasible, by electronic means, or are otherwise made available in such a manner as to enable any person to become acquainted with them.

2. To the extent appropriate, each Party shall provide an explanation of the objective of and rationale for measures referred to in paragraph 1.

3. Each Party shall provide a reasonable period of time between publication and entry into force of its laws and regulations, except when this is not possible for reasons of urgency.

Article 336   Enquiries

1. Each Party shall establish or maintain appropriate and proportionate mechanisms for responding to questions from any person regarding any laws or regulations.

2. Each Party shall promptly provide information and respond to questions by the other Party pertaining to any law or regulation whether in force or planned, unless a specific mechanism is established under another provision of this Agreement.

Article 337   Administration of measures of general application

1. Each Party shall administer its laws, regulations, procedures and administrative rulings of general application in an objective, impartial, and reasonable manner.

2. When administrative proceedings relating to persons, goods or services of the other Party are initiated in respect of the application of laws or regulations, each Party shall:

    (a) endeavour to provide persons who are directly affected by the administrative proceedings with reasonable notice in accordance with its laws and regulations, including a description of the nature of the proceedings, a statement of the legal authority under which the proceedings are initiated and a general description of any issues in controversy; and

    (b) afford such persons a reasonable opportunity to present facts and arguments in support of their positions prior to any final administrative decision insofar as time, the nature of the proceedings and the public interest permit.

Article 338 Review and appeal

1. Each Party shall establish or maintain judicial, arbitral or administrative tribunals and procedures for the purpose of the prompt review and, if warranted, correction of administrative decisions. Each Party shall ensure that its tribunals carry out procedures for appeal or review in a non-discriminatory and impartial manner. Those tribunals shall be impartial and independent of the authority entrusted with administrative enforcement.

2. Each Party shall ensure that the parties to the proceedings as referred to in paragraph 1 are provided with a reasonable opportunity to support or defend their respective positions.

3. In accordance with its law, each Party shall ensure that any decisions adopted in proceedings as referred to in paragraph 1 are based on the evidence and submissions of record or, where applicable, on the record compiled by the competent administrative authority.

4. Each Party shall ensure that decisions as referred to in paragraph 3 shall be implemented by the authority entrusted with administrative enforcement, subject to appeal or further review as provided for in its law.

Article 339 Relation to other Titles

The provisions set out in this Title supplement the specific transparency rules set out in those Titles of this Heading with respect to which this Title applies.

Title X Good regulatory practices and regulatory cooperation

Article 340 General principles

1. Each Party shall be free to determine its approach to good regulatory practices under this Agreement in a manner consistent with its own legal framework, practice, procedures and fundamental principles[38] underlying its regulatory system.

2. Nothing in this Title shall be construed as requiring a Party to:

    (a) deviate from its domestic procedures for preparing and adopting regulatory measures;

    (b) take actions that would undermine or impede the timely adoption of regulatory measures to achieve its public policy objectives; or

    (c) achieve any particular regulatory outcome.

3. Nothing in this Title shall affect the right of a Party to define or regulate its own levels of protection in pursuit or furtherance of its public policy objectives in areas such as:

    (a) public health;

    (b) human, animal or plant life and health, and animal welfare;

    (c) occupational health and safety;

    (d) labour conditions;

    (e) environment including climate change;

    (f) consumer protection;

    (g) social protection and social security;

    (h) data protection and cybersecurity;

    (i) cultural diversity;

    (j) integrity and stability of the financial system, and protection of investors;

    (k) energy security; and

    (l) anti-money laundering.

For greater certainty, for the purposes of in particular point (c) and (d) of the first subparagraph, the different models of industrial relations, including the role and autonomy of social partners, as provided for in the law or national practices of a Party, shall continue to apply, including laws and practices concerning collective bargaining and the enforcement of collective agreements.

4. Regulatory measures shall not constitute a disguised barrier to trade.

---

[38] For the Union, such principles include the precautionary principle.

Article 341   Definitions

For the purposes of this Title, the following definitions apply:

(a) 'regulatory authority' means:

    (i) for the Union, the European Commission; and

    (ii) for the United Kingdom, Her Majesty's Government of the United Kingdom of Great Britain and Northern Ireland, and the devolved administrations of the United Kingdom.

(b) 'regulatory measures' means:

    (i) for the Union:

        (A) regulations and directives, as provided for in Article 288 TFEU; and

        (B) implementing and delegated acts, as provided for in Articles 290 and 291 TFEU, respectively; and

    (ii) for the United Kingdom:

        (A) primary legislation; and

        (B) secondary legislation.

Article 342   Scope

1. This Title applies to regulatory measures proposed or issued, as relevant, by the regulatory authority of each Party in respect of any matter covered by Titles I to IX, Title XI and Title XII of this Heading and Heading Six.

2. Articles 351 and 352 also apply to other measures of general application issued or proposed by the regulatory authority of a Party in respect of any matter covered by the Titles referred to in paragraph 1 of this Article which are relevant to regulatory cooperation activities, such as guidelines, policy documents or recommendations.

3. This Title does not apply to regulatory authorities and regulatory measures, regulatory practices or approaches of the Member States.

4. Any specific provisions in the Titles referred to in paragraph 1 of this Article shall prevail over the provisions of this Title to the extent necessary for the application of the specific provisions.

Article 343   Internal coordination

Each Party shall have in place internal coordination or review processes or mechanisms with respect to regulatory measures that its regulatory authority is preparing. Such processes or mechanisms should seek, *inter alia*, to:

(a) foster good regulatory practices, including those set forth in this Title;

(b) identify and avoid unnecessary duplication and inconsistent requirements between the Party's own regulatory measures;

(c) ensure compliance with the Party's international trade and investment obligations; and

(d) promote the consideration of the impact of the regulatory measures under preparation, including the impact on small and medium-sized enterprises[39], in accordance with its respective rules and procedures.

Article 344   Description of processes and mechanisms

Each Party shall make publicly available descriptions of the processes or mechanisms used by its regulatory authority to prepare, evaluate or review regulatory measures. Those descriptions shall refer to relevant rules, guidelines or procedures, including those regarding opportunities for the public to provide comments.

Article 345   Early information on planned regulatory measures

1. Each Party shall make publicly available, in accordance with its respective rules and procedures on at least an annual basis, a list of planned major[40] regulatory measures that its regulatory authority reasonably expects to propose or adopt within a year. The regulatory authority of each

---

[39] For the United Kingdom, 'small and medium-sized enterprises' means small and micro-sized businesses.

[40] In the case of the United Kingdom, major regulatory measures shall be understood as significant regulatory measures in accordance with the definition of such measures in the United Kingdom's rules and procedures.

Party may determine what constitutes a major regulatory measure for the purposes of its obligations under this Title.

2. With respect to each major regulatory measure included in the list referred to in paragraph 1, each Party should also make publicly available, as early as possible:

(a) a brief description of its scope and objectives; and

(b) if available, the estimated time for its adoption, including any opportunities for public consultation.

Article 346   Public consultation

1. When preparing a major regulatory measure, each Party, in accordance with its respective rules and procedures, shall ensure that its regulatory authority:

(a) publishes either the draft regulatory measure or consultation documents providing sufficient details about the regulatory measure under preparation to allow any person to assess whether and how that person's interests might be significantly affected;

(b) offers, on a non-discriminatory basis, reasonable opportunities for any person to provide comments; and

(c) considers the comments received.

2. Each Party shall ensure that its regulatory authority makes use of electronic means of communication and shall seek to maintain online services that are available to the public free of charge for the purposes of publishing the relevant regulatory measures or documents of the kind referred to in point (a) of paragraph 1 and of receiving comments related to public consultations.

3. Each Party shall ensure that its regulatory authority makes publicly available, in accordance with its respective rules and procedures, a summary of the results of the public consultations referred to in this Article.

Article 347   Impact assessment

1. Each Party affirms its intention to ensure that its regulatory authority carries out, in accordance with its respective rules and procedures, impact assessments for any major regulatory measures it prepares. Such rules and procedures may provide for exceptions.

2. When carrying out an impact assessment, each Party shall ensure that its regulatory authority has processes and mechanisms in place that promote the consideration of the following factors:

(a) the need for the regulatory measure, including the nature and the significance of the problem that the regulatory measure intends to address;

(b) any feasible and appropriate regulatory or non-regulatory options that would achieve the Party's public policy objectives, including the option of not regulating;

(c) to the extent possible and relevant, the potential social, economic and environmental impact of those options, including the impact on international trade and investment and, in accordance with its respective rules and procedures, the impact on small and medium-sized enterprises; and

(d) where appropriate, how the options under consideration relate to relevant international standards, including the reasons for any divergence.

3. With respect to an impact assessment that a regulatory authority has conducted for a regulatory measure, each Party shall ensure that its regulatory authority prepares a final report detailing the factors it considered in its assessment and its relevant findings. To the extent possible, each Party shall make such reports publicly available no later than when the proposal for a regulatory measure as referred to in point (b)(i)(A) or (b)(ii(A) of Article 341 or a regulatory measure as referred to in point (b)(i)(B) or (b)(ii)(B) of that Article has been made publicly available.

Article 348   Retrospective evaluation

1. Each Party shall ensure that its regulatory authority has in place processes or mechanisms for the purpose of carrying out periodic retrospective evaluations of regulatory measures in force, where appropriate.

2. When conducting a periodic retrospective evaluation, each Party shall endeavour to consider whether there are opportunities to more effectively achieve its public policy objectives and to reduce unnecessary regulatory burdens, including on small and medium-sized enterprises.

3. Each Party shall ensure that its regulatory authority makes publicly available any existing plans for and the results of such retrospective evaluations.

Article 349   Regulatory register

Each Party shall ensure that regulatory measures that are in effect are published in a designated register that identifies regulatory measures and that is publicly available online free of charge. The register should allow searches for regulatory measures by citations or by word. Each Party shall periodically update its register.

Article 350   Exchange of information on good regulatory practices

The Parties shall endeavour to exchange information on their good regulatory practices as set out in this Title, including in the Trade Specialised Committee on Regulatory Cooperation.

Article 351   Regulatory cooperation activities

1. The Parties may engage in regulatory cooperation activities on a voluntary basis, without prejudice to the autonomy of their own decision-making and their respective legal orders. A Party may refuse to engage in or it may withdraw from regulatory cooperation activities. A Party that refuses to engage in or that withdraws from regulatory cooperation activities should explain the reasons for its decision to the other Party.

2. Each Party may propose a regulatory cooperation activity to the other Party. It shall present its proposal via the contact point designated in accordance with Article 353. The other Party shall review that proposal within a reasonable period and shall inform the proposing Party whether it considers the proposed activity to be suitable for regulatory cooperation.

3. In order to identify activities that are suitable for regulatory cooperation, each Party shall consider:

    (a) the list referred to in Article 345(1); and

    (b) proposals for regulatory cooperation activities submitted by persons of a Party that are substantiated and accompanied by relevant information.

4. If the Parties decide to engage in a regulatory cooperation activity, the regulatory authority of each Party shall endeavour, where appropriate:

    (a) to inform the regulatory authority of the other Party about the preparation of new or the revision of existing regulatory measures and other measures of general application referred to in Article 342(2) that are relevant to the regulatory cooperation activity;

    (b) on request, to provide information and discuss regulatory measures and other measures of general application referred to in Article 342(2) that are relevant to the regulatory cooperation activity; and

    (c) when preparing new or revising existing regulatory measures or other measures of general application referred to in Article 342(2), consider, to the extent feasible, any regulatory approach by the other Party on the same or a related matter.

Article 352   Trade Specialised Committee on Regulatory Cooperation

1. The Trade Specialised Committee on Regulatory Cooperation shall have the following functions:

    (a) enhancing and promoting good regulatory practices and regulatory cooperation between the Parties;

    (b) exchanging views with respect to the cooperation activities proposed or carried out under Article 351;

    (c) encouraging regulatory cooperation and coordination in international fora, including, when appropriate, periodic bilateral exchanges of information on relevant ongoing or planned activities.

2. The Trade Specialised Committee on Regulatory Cooperation may invite interested persons to participate in its meetings.

Article 353   Contact points

Within a month after the entry into force of this Agreement, each Party shall designate a contact point to facilitate the exchange of information between the Parties.

Article 354   Non-application of dispute settlement

Title I of Part Six does not apply in respect of disputes regarding the interpretation and application of this Title.

Title XI Level playing field for open and fair competition and sustainable development

Chapter 1 General provisions

Article 355   Principles and objectives

1. The Parties recognise that trade and investment between the Union and the United Kingdom under the terms set out in this Agreement require conditions that ensure a level playing field for open and fair competition between the Parties and that ensure that trade and investment take place in a manner conducive to sustainable development.

2. The Parties recognise that sustainable development encompasses economic development, social development and environmental protection, all three being interdependent and mutually reinforcing, and affirm their commitment to promoting the development of international trade and investment in a way that contributes to the objective of sustainable development.

3. Each Party reaffirms its ambition of achieving economy-wide climate neutrality by 2050.

4. The Parties affirm their common understanding that their economic relationship can only deliver benefits in a mutually satisfactory way if the commitments relating to a level playing field for open and fair competition stand the test of time, by preventing distortions of trade or investment, and by contributing to sustainable development. However the Parties recognise that the purpose of this Title is not to harmonise the standards of the Parties. The Parties are determined to maintain and improve their respective high standards in the areas covered by this Title.

Article 356   Right to regulate, precautionary approach[41] and scientific and technical information

1. The Parties affirm the right of each Party to set its policies and priorities in the areas covered by this Title, to determine the levels of protection it deems appropriate and to adopt or modify its law and policies in a manner consistent with each Party's international commitments, including its commitments under this Title.

2. The Parties acknowledge that, in accordance with the precautionary approach, where there are reasonable grounds for concern that there are potential threats of serious or irreversible damage to the environment or human health, the lack of full scientific certainty shall not be used as a reason for preventing a Party from adopting appropriate measures to prevent such damage.

3. When preparing or implementing measures aimed at protecting the environment or labour conditions that may affect trade or investment, each Party shall take into account relevant and available scientific and technical information, international standards, guidelines and recommendations.

Article 357   Dispute settlement

Title I of Part Six does not apply to this Chapter, except for Article 356(2). Articles 408 and 409 apply to Article 355(3).

Chapter 2   Competition policy

Article 358   Principles and definitions

1. The Parties recognise the importance of free and undistorted competition in their trade and investment relations. The Parties acknowledge that anticompetitive business practices may distort the proper functioning of markets and undermine the benefits of trade liberalisation.

2. For the purposes of this Chapter, an 'economic actor' means an entity or a group of entities constituting a single economic entity, regardless of its legal status, that is engaged in an economic activity by offering goods or services on a market.

---

[41] For greater certainty, in relation to the implementation of this Agreement in the territory of the Union, the precautionary approach refers to the precautionary principle.

Article 359 Competition law

1. In recognition of the principles set out in Article 358, each Party shall maintain a competition law which effectively addresses the following anticompetitive business practices:

(a) agreements between economic actors, decisions by associations of economic actors and concerted practices which have as their object or effect the prevention, restriction or distortion of competition;

(b) abuse by one or more economic actors of a dominant position; and

(c) for the United Kingdom, mergers or acquisitions and, for the Union, concentrations, between economic actors which may have significant anticompetitive effects.

2. The competition law referred to in paragraph 1 shall apply to all economic actors irrespective of their nationality or ownership status.

3. Each Party may provide for exemptions from its competition law in pursuit of legitimate public policy objectives, provided that those exemptions are transparent and are proportionate to those objectives.

Article 360 Enforcement

1. Each Party shall take appropriate measures to enforce its competition law in its territory.

2. Each Party shall maintain an operationally independent authority or authorities competent for the effective enforcement of its competition law.

3. Each Party shall apply its competition law in a transparent and non-discriminatory manner, respecting the principles of procedural fairness, including the rights of defence of the economic actors concerned, irrespective of their nationality or ownership status.

Article 361 Cooperation

1. To achieve the objectives of this Chapter and to enhance the effective enforcement of their respective competition law, the Parties recognise the importance of cooperation between their respective competition authorities with regard to developments in competition policy and enforcement activities.

2. For the purposes of paragraph 1, the European Commission or the competition authorities of the Member States, on the one side, and the United Kingdom's competition authority or authorities, on the other side, shall endeavour to cooperate and coordinate, with respect to their enforcement activities concerning the same or related conduct or transactions, where doing so is possible and appropriate.

3. To facilitate the cooperation and coordination referred to in paragraphs 1 and 2, the European Commission and the competition authorities of the Member States, on the one side, and the United Kingdom's competition authority or authorities, on the other side, may exchange information to the extent permitted by each Party's law.

4. To implement the objectives of this Article, the Parties may enter into a separate agreement on cooperation and coordination between the European Commission, the competition authorities of the Member States and the United Kingdom's competition authority or authorities, which may include conditions for the exchange and use of confidential information.

Article 362 Dispute settlement

This Chapter shall not be subject to dispute settlement under Title I of Part Six.

Chapters 3 to 5 [omitted]

Chapter 6 Labour and social standards

Article 386 Definition

1. For the purposes of this Chapter, 'labour and social levels of protection' means the levels of protection provided overall in a Party's law and standards[42], in each of the following areas:

(a) fundamental rights at work;

(b) occupational health and safety standards;

(c) fair working conditions and employment standards;

---

[42] For greater certainty, this Chapter and Article 411 do not apply to the Parties' law and standards relating to social security and pensions.

(d) information and consultation rights at company level; or

(e) restructuring of undertakings.

2. For the Union, 'labour and social levels of protection' means labour and social levels of protection that are applicable to and in, and are common to, all Member States.

Article 387   Non-regression from levels of protection

1. The Parties affirm the right of each Party to set its policies and priorities in the areas covered by this Chapter, to determine the labour and social levels of protection it deems appropriate and to adopt or modify its law and policies in a manner consistent with each Party's international commitments, including those under this Chapter.

2. A Party shall not weaken or reduce, in a manner affecting trade or investment between the Parties, its labour and social levels of protection below the levels in place at the end of the transition period, including by failing to effectively enforce its law and standards.

3. The Parties recognise that each Party retains the right to exercise reasonable discretion and to make bona fide decisions regarding the allocation of labour enforcement resources with respect to other labour law determined to have higher priority, provided that the exercise of that discretion, and those decisions, are not inconsistent with its obligations under this Chapter.

4. The Parties shall continue to strive to increase their respective labour and social levels of protection referred to in this Chapter.

Article 388   Enforcement

For the purposes of enforcement as referred to in Article 387 each Party shall have in place and maintain a system for effective domestic enforcement and, in particular, an effective system of labour inspections in accordance with its international commitments relating to working conditions and the protection of workers; ensure that administrative and judicial proceedings are available that allow public authorities and individuals with standing to bring timely actions against violations of the labour law and social standards; and provide for appropriate and effective remedies, including interim relief, as well as proportionate and dissuasive sanctions. In the domestic implementation and enforcement of Article 387, each Party shall respect the role and autonomy of the social partners at a national level, where relevant, in line with applicable law and practice.

Article 389   Dispute settlement

1. The Parties shall make all efforts through dialogue, consultation, exchange of information and cooperation to address any disagreement on the application of this Chapter.

2. By way of derogation from Title I of Part Six, in the event of a dispute between the Parties regarding the application of this Chapter, the Parties shall have recourse exclusively to the procedures established under Articles 408, 409 and 410.

Chapter 7   Environment and climate

Article 390   Definitions

1. For the purposes of this Chapter, 'environmental levels of protection' means the levels of protection provided overall in a Party's law which have the purpose of protecting the environment, including the prevention of a danger to human life or health from environmental impacts, including in each of the following areas:

(a) industrial emissions;

(b) air emissions and air quality;

(c) nature and biodiversity conservation;

(d) waste management;

(e) the protection and preservation of the aquatic environment;

(f) the protection and preservation of the marine environment;

(g) the prevention, reduction and elimination of risks to human health or the environment arising from the production, use, release or disposal of chemical substances; or

(h) the management of impacts on the environment from agricultural or food production, notably through the use of antibiotics and decontaminants.

2. For the Union, 'environmental levels of protection' means environmental levels of protection that are applicable to and in, and are common to, all Member States.

3. For the purposes of this Chapter, 'climate level of protection' means the level of protection with respect to emissions and removals of greenhouse gases and the phase-out of ozone depleting substances. With regard to greenhouse gases, this means:

    (a) for the Union, the 40% economy-wide 2030 target, including the Union's system of carbon pricing;

    (b) for the United Kingdom, the United Kingdom's economy-wide share of this 2030 target, including the United Kingdom's system of carbon pricing.

Article 391   Non-regression from levels of protection

1. The Parties affirm the right of each Party to set its policies and priorities in the areas covered by this Chapter, to determine the environmental levels of protection and climate level of protection it deems appropriate and to adopt or modify its law and policies in a manner consistent with each Party's international commitments, including those under this Chapter.

2. A Party shall not weaken or reduce, in a manner affecting trade or investment between the Parties, its environmental levels of protection or its climate level of protection below the levels that are in place at the end of the transition period, including by failing to effectively enforce its environmental law or climate level of protection.

3. The Parties recognise that each Party retains the right to exercise reasonable discretion and to make bona fide decisions regarding the allocation of environmental enforcement resources with respect to other environmental law and climate policies determined to have higher priorities, provided that the exercise of that discretion, and those decisions, are not inconsistent with its obligations under this Chapter.

4. For the purposes of this Chapter, insofar as targets are provided for in a Party's environmental law in the areas listed in Article 390, they are included in a Party's environmental levels of protection at the end of the transition period. These targets include those whose attainment is envisaged for a date that is subsequent to the end of the transition period. This paragraph shall also apply to ozone depleting substances.

5. The Parties shall continue to strive to increase their respective environmental levels of protection or their respective climate level of protection referred to in this Chapter.

Article 392   Carbon pricing

1. Each Party shall have in place an effective system of carbon pricing as of 1 January 2021.

2. Each system shall cover greenhouse gas emissions from electricity generation, heat generation, industry and aviation.

3. The effectiveness of the Parties' respective carbon pricing systems shall uphold the level of protection provided for by Article 391.

4. By way of derogation from paragraph 2, aviation shall be included within two years at the latest, if not included already. The scope of the Union system of carbon pricing shall cover departing flights from the European Economic Area to the United Kingdom.

5. Each Party shall maintain its system of carbon pricing insofar as it is an effective tool for each Party in the fight against climate change and shall in any event uphold the level of protection provided for by Article 391.

6. The Parties shall cooperate on carbon pricing. They shall give serious consideration to linking their respective carbon pricing systems in a way that preserves the integrity of these systems and provides for the possibility to increase their effectiveness.

Article 393   Environmental and climate principles

1. Taking into account the fact that the Union and the United Kingdom share a common biosphere in respect of cross-border pollution, each Party commits to respecting the internationally recognised environmental principles to which it has committed, such as in the Rio Declaration on Environment and Development, adopted at Rio de Janeiro on 14 June 1992 (the '1992 Rio Declaration on Environment and Development') and in multilateral environmental agreements, including in the United Nations Framework Convention on Climate Change, done at New York on

9 May 1992 (the 'UNFCCC') and the Convention on Biological Diversity, done at Rio de Janeiro on 5 June 1992 (the 'Convention on Biological Diversity'), in particular:

    (a) the principle that environmental protection should be integrated into the making of policies, including through impact assessments;

    (b) the principle of preventative action to avert environmental damage;

    (c) the precautionary approach referred to in Article 356(2);

    (d) the principle that environmental damage should as a priority be rectified at source; and

    (e) the polluter pays principle.

2. The Parties reaffirm their respective commitments to procedures for evaluating the likely impact of a proposed activity on the environment, and where specified projects, plans and programmes are likely to have significant environmental, including health, effects, this includes an environmental impact assessment or a strategic environmental assessment, as appropriate.

3. These procedures shall comprise, where appropriate and in accordance with a Party's laws, the determination of the scope of an environmental report and its preparation, the carrying out of public participation and consultations and the taking into account of the environmental report and the results of the public participation and consultations in the consented project, or adopted plan or programme.

Article 394   Enforcement

1. For the purposes of enforcement as referred to in Article 391, each Party shall, in accordance with its law, ensure that:

    (a) domestic authorities competent to enforce the relevant law with regard to environment and climate give due consideration to alleged violations of such law that come to their attention; those authorities shall have adequate and effective remedies available to them, including injunctive relief as well as proportionate and dissuasive sanctions, if appropriate; and

    (b) national administrative or judicial proceedings are available to natural and legal persons with a sufficient interest to bring actions against violations of such law and to seek effective remedies, including injunctive relief, and that the proceedings are not prohibitively costly and are conducted in a fair, equitable and transparent way.

Article 395   Cooperation on monitoring and enforcement

The Parties shall ensure that the European Commission and the supervisory bodies of the United Kingdom regularly meet with each other and co-operate on the effective monitoring and enforcement of the law with regard to environment and climate as referred to in Article 391.

Article 396   Dispute settlement

1. The Parties shall make all efforts through dialogue, consultation, exchange of information and cooperation to address any disagreement on the application of this Chapter.

2. By way of derogation from Title I of Part Six, in the event of a dispute between the Parties regarding the application of this Chapter, the Parties shall have recourse exclusively to the procedures established under Articles 408, 409 and 410.

Chapter 8   [Omitted]

Chapter 9   Horizontal and institutional provisions

Article 408   Consultations

1. A Party may request consultations with the other Party regarding any matter arising under Article 355(3), and Chapters 6, 7, and 8 by delivering a written request to the other Party. The complaining Party shall specify in its written request the reasons and basis for the request, including identification of the measures at issue, specifying the provisions that it considers applicable. Consultations must commence promptly after a Party delivers a request for consultations and in any event not later than 30 days after the date of delivery of the request, unless the Parties agree to a longer period.

2. The Parties shall enter into consultations with the aim of reaching a mutually satisfactory resolution of the matter. During consultations, each Party shall provide the other Party with sufficient information in its possession to allow a full examination of the matters raised. Each Party shall endeavour to ensure the participation of personnel of their competent authorities who have expertise in the matter subject to the consultations.

3. In matters relating to Article 355(3) or to the multilateral agreements or instruments referred to in Chapters 6, 7 or 8 the Parties shall take into account available information from the ILO or relevant bodies or organisations established under multilateral environmental agreements. Where relevant, the Parties shall jointly seek advice from such organisations or their bodies, or any other expert or body they deem appropriate.

4. Each Party may seek, when appropriate, the views of the domestic advisory groups referred to in Article 13 or other expert advice.

5. Any resolution reached by the Parties shall be made available to the public.

Article 409   Panel of experts

1. For any matter that is not satisfactorily addressed through consultations under Article 408, a Party may, after 90 days from the receipt of a request for consultations under that Article, request that a panel of experts be convened to examine that matter, by delivering a written request to the other Party. The request shall identify the measure at issue, specify and explain how that measure does not conform with the provisions of the relevant Chapter or Chapters in a manner sufficient to present the complaint clearly.

2. The panel of experts shall be composed of three panellists.

3. The Trade Specialised Committee on Level Playing Field for Open and Fair Competition and Sustainable Development shall, at its first meeting after the entry into force of this Agreement, establish a list of at least 15 individuals who are willing and able to serve as panellists. Each Party shall name at least five individuals to the list to serve as panellists. The Parties shall also name at least five individuals who are not nationals of either Party and who are willing and able to serve as chairperson of a panel of experts. The Trade Specialised Committee on Level Playing Field for Open and Fair Competition and Sustainable Development shall ensure that the list is kept up to date and that the number of experts is maintained at a minimum of 15 individuals.

4. The experts proposed as panellists must have specialised knowledge or expertise in labour or environmental law, other issues addressed in the relevant Chapter or Chapters, or in the resolution of disputes arising under international agreements. They must serve in their individual capacities and not take instructions from any organisation or government with regard to matters related to the dispute. They must not be affiliated with or take instructions from either Party. They shall not be persons who are members, officials or other servants of the Union institutions, of the Government of a Member State, or of the Government of the United Kingdom.

5. Unless the Parties agree otherwise within five days from the date of establishment of the panel of experts, the terms of reference shall be:

> 'to examine, in the light of the relevant provisions, the matter referred to in the request for the establishment of the panel of experts, and to deliver a report, in accordance with this Article that makes findings on the conformity of the measure with the relevant provisions.'

6. In respect of matters related to multilateral standards or agreements covered in this Title, the panel of experts should seek information from the ILO or relevant bodies established under those agreements, including any pertinent available interpretative guidance, findings or decisions adopted by the ILO and those bodies.

7. The panel of experts may request and receive written submissions or any other information from persons with relevant information or specialised knowledge.

8. The panel of experts shall make available such information to each Party allowing them to submit their comments within 20 days of its receipt.

9. The panel of experts shall issue to the Parties an interim report and a final report setting out the findings of fact, its determinations on the matter including as to whether the respondent Party

has conformed with its obligations under the relevant Chapter or Chapters and the rationale behind any findings and determinations that it makes. For greater certainty, the Parties share the understanding that if the Panel makes recommendations in its report, the respondent Party does not need to follow these recommendations in ensuring conformity with this Agreement.

10. The panel of experts shall deliver to the Parties the interim report within 100 days after the date of establishment of the panel of experts. When the panel of experts considers that this deadline cannot be met, the chairperson of the panel of experts shall notify the Parties in writing, stating the reasons for the delay and the date on which the panel of experts plans to deliver its interim report. The panel of experts shall, under no circumstances, deliver its interim report later than 125 days after the date of establishment of the panel of experts.

11. Each Party may deliver to the panel of experts a reasoned request to review particular aspects of the interim report within 25 days of its delivery. A Party may comment on the other's Party's request within 15 days of the delivery of the request.

12. After considering those comments, the panel of experts shall prepare the final report. If no request to review particular aspects of the interim report is delivered within the time period referred to in paragraph 11, the interim report shall become the final report of the panel of experts.

13. The panel of experts shall deliver its final report to the Parties within 175 days of the date of establishment of the panel of experts. When the panel of experts considers that this time limit cannot be met, its chairperson shall notify the Parties in writing, stating the reasons for the delay and the date on which the panel of experts plans to deliver its final report. The panel of experts shall, under no circumstances, deliver its final report later than 195 days after the date of establishment of the panel of experts.

14. The final report shall include a discussion of any written request by the Parties on the interim report and clearly address the comments of the Parties.

15. The Parties shall make the final report available to the public within 15 days of its delivery by the panel of experts.

16. If the final report of the panel of experts determines that a Party has not conformed with its obligations under the relevant Chapter or Chapters, the Parties shall, within 90 days of the delivery of the final report, discuss appropriate measures to be implemented taking into account the report of the panel of experts. No later than 105 days after the report has been delivered to the Parties, the respondent Party shall inform its domestic advisory groups established under Article 13 and the complaining Party of its decision on any measures to be implemented.

17. The Trade Specialised Committee on Level Playing Field for Open and Fair Competition and Sustainable Development shall monitor the follow-up to the report of the panel of experts. The domestic advisory groups of the Parties established under Article 13 may submit observations to the Trade Specialised Committee on Level Playing Field for Open and Fair Competition and Sustainable Development in that regard.

18. When the Parties disagree on the existence of, or the consistency with, the relevant provisions of any measure taken to address the non-conformity, the complaining Party may deliver a request, which shall be in writing, to the original panel of experts to decide on the matter. The request shall identify any measure at issue and explain how that measure is not in conformity with the relevant provisions in a manner sufficient to present the complaint clearly. The panel of experts shall deliver its findings to the Parties within 45 days of the date of the delivery of the request.

19. Except as otherwise provided for in this Article, Article 739(1), Article 740 and Articles 753 to 758, as well as Annexes 48 and 49, shall apply *mutatis mutandis*.

Article 410   Panel of experts for non-regression areas

1. Article 409 shall apply to disputes between the Parties concerning the interpretation and application of Chapters 6 and 7.

2. For the purposes of such disputes, in addition to the Articles listed in Article 409(19), Articles 749 and 750 shall apply *mutatis mutandis*.

3. The Parties recognise that, where the respondent Party chooses not [to] take any action to conform with the report of the panel of experts and with this Agreement, any remedies authorised under Article 749 continue to be available to the complaining Party.

Article 411   Rebalancing

1. The Parties recognise the right of each Party to determine its future policies and priorities with respect to labour and social, environmental or climate protection, or with respect to subsidy control, in a manner consistent with each Party's international commitments, including those under this Agreement. At the same time, the Parties acknowledge that significant divergences in these areas can be capable of impacting trade or investment between the Parties in a manner that changes the circumstances that have formed the basis for the conclusion of this Agreement.

2. If material impacts on trade or investment between the Parties are arising as a result of significant divergences between the Parties in the areas referred to in paragraph 1, either Party may take appropriate rebalancing measures to address the situation. Such measures shall be restricted with respect to their scope and duration to what is strictly necessary and proportionate in order to remedy the situation. Priority shall be given to such measures as will least disturb the functioning of this Agreement. A Party's assessment of those impacts shall be based on reliable evidence and not merely on conjecture or remote possibility.

3. The following procedures shall apply to rebalancing measures taken under paragraph 2:

(a) the concerned Party shall, without delay, notify the other Party through the Partnership Council of the rebalancing measures it intends to take, providing all relevant information. The Parties shall immediately enter into consultations. Consultations shall be deemed concluded within 14 days from the date of delivery of the notification, unless they are jointly concluded before that time limit;

(b) if no mutually acceptable solution is found, the concerned Party may adopt rebalancing measures no sooner than five days from the conclusion of the consultations, unless the notified Party requests within the same five day period, in accordance with Article 739(2)[43], the establishment of an arbitration tribunal by means of a written request delivered to the other Party in order for the arbitration tribunal to decide whether the notified rebalancing measures are consistent with paragraph 2 of this Article;

(c) the arbitration tribunal shall conduct its proceeding in accordance with Article 760 and deliver its final ruling within 30 days from its establishment. If the arbitration tribunal does not deliver its final ruling within that time period, the concerned Party may adopt the rebalancing measures no sooner than three days after the expiry of that 30 day time period. In that case, the other Party may take countermeasures proportionate to the adopted rebalancing measures until the arbitration tribunal delivers its ruling. Priority shall be given to such countermeasures as will least disturb the functioning of this Agreement. Point (a) shall apply *mutatis mutandis* to such countermeasures, which may be adopted no sooner than three days after the conclusion of consultations;

(d) if the arbitration tribunal has found the rebalancing measures to be consistent with paragraph 2, the concerned Party may adopt the rebalancing measures as notified to the other Party;

(e) if the arbitration tribunal has found the rebalancing measures to be inconsistent with paragraph 2 of this Article, the concerned Party shall, within three days from the delivery of the ruling, notify the complaining Party of the measures[44] it intends to adopt to comply with the ruling of the arbitration tribunal. Article 748(2) and Articles 749[45] and 750 shall apply *mutatis mutandis*, if the complaining Party considers that the notified measures are not in compliance with the ruling of the arbitration tribunal. The procedures under Article 748(2) and Articles 749 and 750 shall have no suspensive effect on the application of the notified measures pursuant to this paragraph;

(f) if rebalancing measures were adopted prior to the arbitration ruling in accordance with point (c), any countermeasures adopted pursuant to that point shall be withdrawn immediately, and in no case later than five days, after delivery of the ruling of the arbitration tribunal;

---

[43] For greater certainty, in this case the Party shall not have prior recourse to consultations in accordance with Article 738.
[44] Such measures may include withdrawal or adjustment of the rebalancing measures, as appropriate.
[45] Suspension of obligations under Article 749 shall be available only if rebalancing measures have in fact been applied.

(g) a Party shall not invoke the WTO Agreement or any other international agreement to preclude the other Party from taking measures pursuant to paragraphs 2 and 3, including when those measures consist of suspension of obligations under this Agreement;

(h) if the notified Party does not submit a request pursuant to point (b) of this paragraph within the time period laid down therein, that Party may without having prior recourse to consultations in accordance with Article 738 initiate the arbitration procedure referred to in Article 739. An arbitration tribunal shall treat the issue as a case of urgency for the purpose of Article 744.

4. In order to ensure an appropriate balance between the commitments made by the Parties in this Agreement on a more durable basis, either Party may request, no sooner than four years after the entry into force of this Agreement, a review of the operation of this Heading. The Parties may agree that other Headings of this Agreement may be added to the review.

5. Such a review shall commence at a Party's request, if that Party considers that measures under paragraph 2 or 3 have been taken frequently by either or both Parties, or if a measure that has a material impact on trade or investment between the Parties has been applied for a period of 12 months. For the purposes of this paragraph, the measures in question are those which were not challenged or not found by an arbitration tribunal to be strictly unnecessary pursuant to point (d) or (h) of paragraph 3. This review may commence earlier than four years after the entry into force of this Agreement.

6. The review requested pursuant to paragraph 4 or 5 shall begin within three months of the request and be completed within six months.

7. A review on the basis of paragraph 4 or 5 may be repeated at subsequent intervals of no less than four years after the conclusion of the previous review. If a Party has requested a review under paragraph 4 or 5, it may not request a further review under either paragraph 4 or 5 for at least four years from the conclusion of the previous review or, if applicable, from the entry into force of any amending agreement.

8. The review shall address whether this Agreement delivers an appropriate balance of rights and obligations between the Parties, in particular with regard to the operation of this Heading, and whether, as a result, there is a need for any modification of the terms of this Agreement.

9. The Partnership Council may decide that no action is required as a result of the review. If a Party considers that following the review there is a need for an amendment of this Agreement, the Parties shall use their best endeavours to negotiate and conclude an agreement making the necessary amendments. Such negotiations shall be limited to matters identified in the review.

10. If an amending agreement referred to in paragraph 9 is not concluded within one year from the date the Parties started negotiations, either Party may give notice to terminate this Heading or any other Heading of this Agreement that was added to the review, or the Parties may decide to continue negotiations. If a Party terminates this Heading, Heading Three shall be terminated on the same date. The termination shall take effect three months after the date of such notice.

11. If this Heading is terminated pursuant to paragraph 10 of this Article, Heading Two shall be terminated on the same date, unless the Parties agree to integrate the relevant parts of Title XI of this Heading in Heading Two.

12. Title I of Part Six does not apply to paragraphs 4 to 9 of this Article.

Title XII Exceptions [omitted]

HEADING TWO AVIATION

Title I Air transport

Article 417 Definitions
For the purposes of this Title, the following definitions apply:
(a) 'air carrier' means an air transport undertaking holding a valid operating licence or equivalent;

(b) 'air carrier of the Union' means an air carrier that fulfils the conditions laid down in point (b) of Article 422(1);

(c) 'air carrier of the United Kingdom' means an air carrier that fulfils the conditions laid down in point (a) of Article 422(1) or Article 422(2);

(d) 'air navigation services' means air traffic services, communication, navigation and sur-veillance services, meteorological services for air navigation, and aeronautical informa-tion services;

(e) 'air operator certificate' means a document issued to an air carrier which affirms that the air carrier in question has the professional ability and organisation to secure the safe operation of aircraft for the aviation activities specified in the certificate;

(f) 'air traffic management' means the aggregation of the airborne and ground-based func-tions (air traffic services, airspace management and air traffic flow management) required to ensure the safe and efficient movement of aircraft during all phases of operations;

(g) 'air transport' means the carriage by aircraft of passengers, baggage, cargo, and mail, separately or in combination, held out to the public for remuneration or hire;

(h) 'citizenship determination' means a finding that an air carrier proposing to operate air services under this Title satisfies the requirements of Article 422 regarding its owner-ship, effective control and principal place of business;

(i) 'competent authorities' means, for the United Kingdom, the authorities of the United Kingdom responsible for the regulatory and administrative functions incumbent on the United Kingdom under this Title; and for the Union, the authorities of the Union and of the Member States responsible for the regulatory and administrative functions incum-bent on the Union under this Title;

(j) 'the Convention' means the Convention on International Civil Aviation, done at Chicago on 7 December 1944, and includes:

(i) any amendment that has entered into force under Article 94(a) of the Convention and has been ratified by the United Kingdom and the Member State or Member States concerned, as is relevant to the issue in question; and

(ii) any Annex or any amendment thereto adopted under Article 90 of the Convention, insofar as such Annex or amendment is at any given time effective for the United Kingdom and the Member State or Member States concerned, as is relevant to the issue in question;

(k) 'discrimination' means differentiation of any kind without objective justification in re-spect of the supply of goods or services, including public services, employed for the op-eration of air transport services, or in respect of their treatment by public authorities relevant to such services;

(l) 'effective control' means a relationship constituted by rights, contracts or any other means which, either separately or jointly, and having regard to the considerations of fact or law involved, confer the possibility of directly or indirectly exercising a decisive influ-ence on an undertaking, in particular by:

(i) the right to use all or part of the assets of an undertaking;

(ii) rights or contracts which confer a decisive influence on the composition, voting or decisions of the bodies of an undertaking or otherwise confer a decisive influence on the running of the business of the undertaking;

(m) 'fitness determination' means a finding that an air carrier proposing to operate air ser-vices under this Title has satisfactory financial capability and adequate managerial ex-pertise to operate such services and is disposed to comply with the laws, regulations and requirements that govern the operation of such services;

(n) 'full cost' means the cost of the service provided, which may include appropriate amounts for cost of capital and depreciation of assets, as well as the costs of maintenance, oper-ation, management and administration;

(o) 'ICAO' means the United Nations International Civil Aviation Organization;

(p) 'principal place of business' means the head office or registered office of an air carrier within which the principal financial functions and operational control, including continued airworthiness management, of that air carrier are exercised;

(q) 'ramp inspection' means an examination by the competent authority of a Party or its designated representatives, on board and around an aircraft of the other Party, to check both the validity of the relevant aircraft documents and those of its crew members and the apparent condition of the aircraft and its equipment;

(r) 'self-handling' means the performance of ground handling operations by an air carrier directly for itself or for another air carrier where:
 (i) one holds the majority in the other; or
 (ii) a single body has a majority holding in each;

(s) 'scheduled air transport services' means air services which are scheduled and performed for remuneration according to a published timetable, or which are so regular or frequent as to constitute a recognisably systematic series, and which are open to direct booking by members of the public; and extra section flights occasioned by overflow traffic from scheduled flights;

(t) 'stop for non-traffic purposes' means a landing for any purpose other than taking on board or discharging passengers, baggage, cargo and/or mail in air transport;

(u) 'tariff' means any fare, rate or charge for the carriage of passengers, baggage or cargo (excluding mail) in air transport (including any other mode of transport in connection therewith) charged by air carriers, including their agents, and the conditions governing the availability of such fare, rate or charge;

(v) 'user charge' means a charge imposed on air carriers for the provision of airport, air navigation (including overflights), aviation security facilities or services including related services and facilities, or environment-related charges including noise-related charges and charges to address local air quality problems at or around airports.

Article 418 Route schedule

1. Subject to Article 419, the Union shall grant the United Kingdom the right for the air carriers of the United Kingdom to operate, while carrying out air transport, on the following routes:

Points in the territory of the United Kingdom—Intermediate Points—Points in the territory of the Union—Points Beyond.

2. Subject to Article 419, the United Kingdom shall grant the Union the right for the air carriers of the Union to operate, while carrying out air transport, on the following routes:

Points in the territory of the Union—Intermediate Points—Points in the territory of the United Kingdom—Points Beyond.

Article 419 Traffic rights

1. Each Party shall grant to the other Party the right for its respective air carriers, for the purpose of carrying out air transport on the routes laid down in Article 418, to:
 (a) fly across its territory without landing;
 (b) make stops in its territory for non-traffic purposes.

2. The United Kingdom shall enjoy the right for its air carriers to make stops in the territory of the Union to provide scheduled and non-scheduled air transport services between any points situated in the territory of the United Kingdom and any points situated in the territory of the Union (third and fourth freedom traffic rights).

3. The Union shall enjoy the right for its air carriers to make stops in the territory of the United Kingdom to provide scheduled and non-scheduled air transport services between any points situated in the territory of the Union and any points situated in the territory of the United Kingdom (third and fourth freedom traffic rights).

4. Notwithstanding paragraphs 1, 2 and 3 and without prejudice to paragraph 9, the Member States and the United Kingdom may, subject to the respective internal rules and procedures of the

Parties, enter into bilateral arrangements by which, as a matter of this Agreement, they grant each other the following rights:

(a) for the United Kingdom, the right for its air carriers to make stops in the territory of the Member State concerned to provide scheduled and non-scheduled all-cargo air transport services, between points situated in the territory of that Member State and points situated in a third country as part of a service with origin or destination in the territory of the United Kingdom (fifth freedom traffic rights);

(b) for the Member State concerned, the right for Union air carriers to make stops in the territory of the United Kingdom to provide scheduled and non-scheduled all-cargo air transport services between points situated in the territory of the United Kingdom and points situated in a third country, as part of a service with origin or destination in the territory of that Member State (fifth freedom traffic rights).

5. The rights mutually granted in accordance with paragraph 4 shall be governed by the provisions of this Title.

6. Neither Party shall unilaterally limit the volume of traffic, capacity, frequency, regularity, routing, origin or destination of the air transport services operated in accordance with paragraphs 2, 3 and 4, or the aircraft type or types operated for that purpose by the air carriers of the other Party, except as may be required for customs, technical, operational, air traffic management, safety, environmental or health protection reasons, in a non-discriminatory manner, or unless otherwise provided for in this Title.

7. Nothing in this Title shall be deemed to confer on the United Kingdom the right for its air carriers to take on board in the territory of a Member State passengers, baggage, cargo or mail carried for compensation and destined for another point in the territory of that Member State or any other Member State.

8. Nothing in this Title shall be deemed to confer on the Union the right for its air carriers to take on board in the territory of the United Kingdom passengers, baggage, cargo or mail carried for compensation and destined for another point in the territory of the United Kingdom.

9. Subject to the internal rules and procedures of the Parties, the competent authorities of the United Kingdom and of the Member States may authorise non-scheduled air transport services beyond the rights provided for in this Article provided that they do not constitute a disguised form of scheduled services, and may establish bilateral arrangements regarding the procedures to be followed for the handling of, and decisions on, air carriers' applications.

Article 420   Code-share and blocked space arrangements

1. Air transport services in accordance with Article 419 may be provided by means of blocked-space or code-share arrangements, as follows:

(a) an air carrier of the United Kingdom may act as the marketing carrier with any operating carrier that is an air carrier of the Union or an air carrier of the United Kingdom, or with any operating carrier of a third country which, under Union law or, as applicable, under the law of the Member State or Member States concerned, enjoys the necessary traffic rights as well as the right for its air carriers to exercise those rights by means of the arrangement in question;

(b) an air carrier of the Union may act as the marketing carrier with any operating carrier that is an air carrier of the Union or an air carrier of the United Kingdom, or with any operating carrier of a third country which, under United Kingdom law enjoys the necessary traffic rights as well as the right for its air carriers to exercise those rights by means of the arrangement in question;

(c) an air carrier of the United Kingdom may act as the operating carrier with any marketing carrier that is an air carrier of the Union or an air carrier of the United Kingdom, or with any marketing carrier of a third country which, under Union law or, as applicable, under the law of the Member State or Member States concerned, enjoys the necessary rights to enter into the arrangement in question;

(d) an air carrier of the Union may act as the operating carrier with any marketing carrier that is an air carrier of the Union or an air carrier of the United Kingdom, or with any marketing carrier of a third country which, under United Kingdom law, enjoys the necessary rights to enter into the arrangement in question;

(e) in the context of the arrangements provided under points (a) to (d), an air carrier of one Party may act as the marketing carrier in a blocked-space or code-share arrangement, in services between any pair of points of which both origin and destination are situated in the territory of the other Party provided that the following conditions are fulfilled:

   (i) the conditions laid down in point (a) or (b), as the case may be, as regards the operating carrier; and

   (ii) the transport service in question forms part of a carriage by the marketing carrier between a point in the territory of its Party and that destination point in the territory of the other Party.

2. An air carrier of one Party may act as the marketing carrier in a blocked-space or code-share arrangement, in services between any pair of points of which one is situated in the territory of the other Party and the other is situated in a third country, provided that the following conditions are fulfilled:

(a) the conditions laid down in point (a) or (b) of paragraph 1, as the case may be, as regards the operating carrier; and

(b) the transport service in question forms part of a carriage by the marketing carrier between a point in the territory of its Party and that point in a third country.

3. In respect of each ticket sold involving the arrangements referred to in this Article, the purchaser shall be informed upon reservation of which air carrier will operate each sector of the service. Where that is not possible, or in case of change after reservation, the identity of the operating carrier shall be communicated to the passenger as soon as it is established. In all cases, the identity of the operating carrier or carriers shall be communicated to the passenger at check-in, or before boarding where no check-in is required for a connecting flight.

4. The Parties may require the arrangements referred to in this Article to be approved by their competent authorities for the purpose of verifying compliance with the conditions set out therein and with other requirements provided for in this Agreement, in particular as regards competition, safety and security.

5. In no case shall recourse to code-share or blocked-space arrangements result in the air carriers of the Parties exercising traffic rights on the basis of this Agreement other than those provided for in Article 419.

Article 421   Operational flexibility

The rights mutually granted by the Parties in accordance with Article 419(2), (3) and (4) shall include, within the limits laid down therein, all of the following prerogatives:

(a) to operate flights in either or both directions;

(b) to combine different flight numbers within one aircraft operation;

(c) to serve points in the route schedule in any combination and in any order;

(d) to transfer traffic between aircraft of the same air carrier at any point (change of gauge);

(e) to carry stopover traffic through any points whether within or outside the territory of either Party;

(f) to carry transit traffic through the territory of the other Party;

(g) to combine traffic on the same aircraft regardless of where such traffic originates;

(h) to serve more than one point on the same service (co-terminalisation).

Article 422   Operating authorisations and technical permissions

1. On receipt of an application for an operating authorisation from an air carrier of a Party, in the form and manner prescribed, to operate air transport services under this Title, the other Party shall

grant the appropriate authorisations and technical permissions with minimum procedural delay, provided that all the following conditions are met:

    (a) in the case of an air carrier of the United Kingdom:

        (i)   the air carrier is owned, directly or through majority ownership, and is effectively controlled by the United Kingdom, its nationals, or both;

        (ii) the air carrier has its principal place of business in the territory of the United Kingdom, and is licenced in accordance with the law of the United Kingdom; and

        (iii) the air carrier holds an air operator certificate issued by the competent authority of the United Kingdom, which shall be clearly identified, and that authority exercises and maintains effective regulatory control of the air carrier;

    (b) in the case of an air carrier of the Union:

        (i)   the air carrier is owned, directly or through majority ownership, and is effectively controlled by one or more Member States, by other member states of the European Economic Area, by Switzerland, by nationals of such states, or by a combination thereof;

        (ii) the air carrier has its principal place of business in the territory of the Union and holds a valid operating licence in accordance with Union law; and

        (iii) the air carrier holds an air operator certificate issued by the competent authority of a Member State, or by a Union authority on its behalf, the certifying authority is clearly identified, and that Member State exercises and maintains effective regulatory control of the air carrier.

    (c) Articles 434 and 435 are being complied with, and

    (d) the air carrier meets the conditions prescribed under the laws and regulations normally applied to the operation of international air transport by the Party considering the application or applications.

2. Notwithstanding point (a)(i) of paragraph 1, the appropriate operating authorisations and permissions shall be granted to air carriers of the United Kingdom provided that all the following conditions are met:

    (a) the conditions laid down in points (a)(ii), (a)(iii), (c) and (d) of paragraph 1 are complied with;

    (b) the air carrier is owned, directly or through majority ownership, and is effectively controlled by one or more Member States, by other member states of the European Economic Area, by Switzerland, by nationals of such states, or by a combination thereof, whether alone or together with the United Kingdom and/or nationals of the United Kingdom;

    (c) on the day the transition period ended, the air carrier held a valid operating licence in accordance with Union Law.

3. For the purposes of paragraphs 1 and 2, evidence of effective regulatory control includes but is not limited to:

    (a) the air carrier concerned holding a valid operating licence or permit issued by the competent authority and meeting the criteria of the Party issuing the operating licence or permit for the operation of international air services; and

    (b) that Party having and maintaining safety and security oversight programmes for that air carrier in compliance with ICAO standards.

4. When granting operating authorisations and technical permissions, each Party shall treat all air carriers of the other Party in a non-discriminatory manner.

5. On receipt of an application for an operating authorisation from an air carrier of a Party, the other Party shall recognise any fitness determination or citizenship determination or both made by the first Party with respect to that air carrier as if such determination had been made by its own competent authorities, and shall not enquire further into such matters, except as provided for in Article 424(3).

Article 423   Operating plans, programmes and schedules

Notification of operating plans, programmes or schedules for air services operated under this Title may be required by a Party for information purposes only. Where a Party requires such notification, it shall minimise the administrative burden associated with its notification requirements and procedures that is borne by air transport intermediaries and the air carriers of the other Party.

Article 424   Refusal, revocation, suspension or limitation of operating authorisation

1. The Union may take action against an air carrier of the United Kingdom, in accordance with paragraphs 3, 4 and 5 of this Article, in any of the following cases:

   (a) in the case of authorisations and permissions granted in accordance with point (a) of Article 422(1), any of the conditions laid down therein is not met;

   (b) in the case of authorisations and permissions granted in accordance with Article 422(2), any of the conditions laid down therein is not met;

   (c) the air carrier has failed to comply with the laws and regulations referred to in Article 426; or

   (d) such action is necessary in order to prevent, protect against or control the spread of disease, or otherwise protect public health.

2. The United Kingdom may take action against an air carrier of the Union in accordance with paragraphs 3, 4 and 5 of this Article in any of the following cases:

   (a) any of the conditions laid down in point (b) of Article 422(1) is not met;

   (b) the air carrier has failed to comply with the laws and regulations referred to in Article 426; or

   (c) such action is necessary in order to prevent, protect against or control the spread of disease, or otherwise protect public health.

3. Where a Party has reasonable grounds to believe that an air carrier of the other Party is in any of the situations referred to in paragraph 1 or 2, as the case may be, and that action must be taken in that respect, that Party shall notify the other Party in writing as soon as possible of the reasons for the intended refusal, suspension or limitation of the operating authorisation or technical permission and request consultations.

4. Such consultations shall start as soon as possible and not later than 30 days from receipt of the request for consultations. Failure to reach a satisfactory agreement within 30 days or an agreed time period from the starting date of such consultations, or failure to take the agreed corrective action, shall constitute grounds for the Party that requested the consultations to take action to refuse, revoke, suspend, impose conditions on or limit the operating authorisation or technical permissions of the air carrier or air carriers concerned to ensure compliance with Articles 422 and 426. Where measures have been taken to refuse, revoke, suspend or limit the operating authorisation or technical permission of an air carrier, a Party may have recourse to arbitration in accordance with Article 739, without having prior recourse to consultations in accordance with Article 738. An arbitration tribunal shall treat the issue as a case of urgency for the purpose of Article 744. At the request of a Party, the tribunal may, pending its final ruling, order the adoption of interim relief measures, including the modification or suspension of measures taken by either Party under this Article.

5. Notwithstanding paragraphs 3 and 4, in the cases referred to in points (c) and (d) of paragraph 1, and in points (b) and (c) of paragraph 2, a Party may take immediate or urgent action where required by an emergency or to prevent further non-compliance. For the purposes of this paragraph, further non-compliance means that the question of non-compliance has already been raised between the competent authorities of the Parties.

6. This Article is without prejudice to the provisions of Title XI of Heading One, Article 427(4), Article 434(4), (6) and (8) and Article 435(12) and to the dispute settlement procedure laid down in Title I of Part Six or to the measures resulting therefrom.

Article 425   Ownership and control of air carriers

The Parties recognise the potential benefits of the continued liberalisation of ownership and control of their respective air carriers. The Parties agree to examine in the Specialised Committee on Air

Transport options for the reciprocal liberalisation of the ownership and control of their air carriers within 12 months from the entry into force of this Agreement, and thereafter within 12 months of receipt of a request to do so from one of the Parties. As a result of this examination, the Parties may decide to amend this Title.

Article 426   Compliance with laws and regulations

1. The laws and regulations of a Party relating to the admission to, operation within, and departure from its territory of aircraft engaged in international air transport shall be complied with by the air carriers of the other Party while entering, operating within, or leaving the territory of that Party, respectively.

2. The laws and regulations of a Party relating to the admission to, operation within, or departure from its territory of passengers, crew, baggage, cargo, or mail on aircraft (including regulations relating to entry, clearance, immigration, passports, customs and quarantine, or in the case of mail, postal regulations) shall be complied with by, or on behalf of, such passengers, crew, baggage, cargo, and mail carried by the air carriers of the other Party while entering, operating within, or leaving the territory of that Party, respectively.

3. The Parties shall permit, in their respective territory, the air carriers of the other Party to take appropriate measures to ensure that only persons with the travel documents required for entry into, or transit through, the territory of the other Party are carried.

Article 427   Non-Discrimination

1. Without prejudice to Title XI of Heading One, the Parties shall eliminate, within their respective jurisdictions, all forms of discrimination which would adversely affect the fair and equal opportunity of the air carriers of the other Party to compete in the exercise of the rights provided for in this Title.

2. A Party (the 'initiating Party') may proceed in accordance with paragraphs 3 to 6 where it considers that its air carriers' fair and equal opportunities to compete in the exercise of the rights provided for in this Title are adversely affected by discrimination prohibited by paragraph 1.

3. The initiating Party shall submit a written request for consultations to the other Party (the 'responding Party'). Consultations shall start within a period of 30 days from the receipt of the request, unless otherwise agreed by the Parties.

4. Where the initiating Party and the responding Party fail to reach agreement on the matter within 60 days from the receipt of the request for consultations referred to in paragraph 3, the initiating Party may take measures against all or part of the air carriers which have benefitted from discrimination prohibited by paragraph 1, including action to refuse, revoke, suspend, impose conditions on or limit the operating authorisations or technical permissions of the air carriers concerned.

5. The measures taken pursuant to paragraph 4 shall be appropriate, proportionate and restricted in their scope and duration to what is strictly necessary to mitigate the injury to the air carriers of the initiating Party and remove the undue advantage gained by the air carriers against which they are directed.

6. Where consultations have not resolved the matter or where measures have been taken pursuant to paragraph 4 of this Article, a Party may have recourse to arbitration in accordance with Article 739, without having prior recourse to consultations in accordance with Article 738. An arbitration tribunal shall treat the issue as a case of urgency for the purpose of Article 744. At the request of a Party, the tribunal may, pending its final ruling, order the adoption of interim relief measures, including the modification or suspension of measures taken by either Party under this Article.

7. Notwithstanding paragraph 2, the Parties shall not proceed under paragraphs 3 to 6 in relation to conduct falling under the scope of Title XI of Heading One.

Article 428   Doing business

1. The Parties agree that obstacles to doing business encountered by air carriers would hamper the benefits under this Title. The Parties agree to cooperate in removing obstacles to doing business for air carriers of both Parties where such obstacles may hamper commercial operations, create distortions to competition or affect equal opportunities to compete.

2. The Specialised Committee on Air Transport shall monitor progress in effectively addressing matters relating to obstacles to doing business for air carriers.

Article 429   Commercial operations

1. The Parties shall grant each other the rights laid down in paragraphs 2 to 7. For the purposes of the exercise of those rights, the air carriers of each Party shall not be required to retain a local sponsor.

2. As regards air carrier representatives:

(a) the establishment of offices and facilities by the air carriers of one Party in the territory of the other Party as necessary to provide services under this Title shall be allowed without restriction or discrimination;

(b) without prejudice to safety and security regulations, where such offices and facilities are located in an airport they may be subject to limitations on grounds of availability of space;

(c) each Party shall, in accordance with its laws and regulations relating to entry, residence and employment, authorise the air carriers of the other Party to bring in and maintain in the territory of the authorising Party those of their own managerial, sales, technical, operational and other specialist staff which the air carrier reasonably considers necessary for the provision of air transport services under this Title. Where employment authorisations are required for the personnel referred to in this paragraph, including those performing certain temporary duties, the Parties shall process applications for such authorisations expeditiously, subject to the relevant laws and regulations.

3. As regards ground handling:

(a) each Party shall permit the air carriers of the other Party to perform self-handling in its territory without restrictions other than those based on considerations of safety or security, or otherwise resulting from physical or operational constraints;

(b) each Party shall not impose on the air carriers of the other Party the choice of one or more providers of ground handling services among those which are present in the market in accordance with the laws and regulations of the Party where the services are provided;

(c) without prejudice to point (a), where the laws and regulations of a Party limit or restrict in any way free competition between providers of ground handling services, that Party shall ensure that all necessary ground handling services are available to the air carriers of the other Party and that they are provided under no less favourable terms than those under which they are provided to any other air carrier.

4. As regards the allocation of slots at airports, each Party shall ensure that its regulations, guidelines and procedures for allocation of slots at the airports in its territory are applied in a transparent, effective, non-discriminatory and timely manner.

5. As regards local expenses and transfer of funds and earnings:

(a) the provisions of Title IV of Heading One apply to the matters governed by this Title, without prejudice to Article 422;

(b) the Parties shall grant each other the benefits laid down in points (c) to (e);

(c) it shall be possible for the sale and purchase of transport and related services by the air carriers of the Parties, at the discretion of the air carrier, to be denominated in pounds sterling if the sale or purchase takes place in the territory of the United Kingdom, or, if the sale or purchase take place in the territory of a Member State, to be denominated in the currency of that Member State;

(d) the air carriers of each Party shall be permitted to pay for local expenses in local currency, at their discretion;

(e) the air carriers of each Party shall be permitted, on demand, to remit revenues obtained in the territory of the other Party from the sale of air transport services and associated activities directly linked to air transport in excess of sums locally disbursed, at any time, in any way, to the country of their choice. Prompt conversion and remittance shall be permitted without restrictions or taxation in respect thereof at the market rate of exchange applicable to current transactions and remittance on the date the carrier makes the initial application for remittance and shall not be subject to any charges except those normally made by banks for carrying out such conversion and remittance.

6. As regards intermodal transport:

    (a) in relation to the transport of passengers, the Parties shall not subject surface transport providers to laws and regulations governing air transport on the sole basis that such surface transport is held out by an air carrier under its own name;

    (b) subject to any conditions and qualifications set out in Title II of Heading One and its Annexes and in Title I of Heading Three and its Annex, air carriers of each Party shall be permitted, without restriction, to employ in connection with international air transport any surface transport for cargo to or from any points in the territories of the Parties, or in third countries, including transport to and from all airports with customs facilities, and including, where applicable, the right to transport cargo in bond under applicable laws and regulations. Such cargo, whether moving by surface or by air, shall have access to airport customs processing and facilities. Air carriers may elect to perform their own surface transport or to provide it through arrangements, including code share, with other surface transport providers, including surface transport operated by other air carriers and indirect providers of cargo air transport. Such inter-modal cargo services may be offered as a through service and at a single price for the air and surface transport combined, provided that shippers are informed as to the providers of the transport involved.

7. As regards leasing:

    (a) the Parties shall grant each other the right for their air carriers to provide air transport services in accordance with Article 419 in all the following ways:

        (i) using aircraft leased without crew from any lessor;

        (ii) in the case of air carriers of the United Kingdom, using aircraft leased with crew from other air carriers of the Parties;

        (iii) in the case of air carriers of the Union, using aircraft leased with crew from other air carriers of the Union;

        (iv) using aircraft leased with crew from air carriers other than those referred to in points (ii) and (iii), respectively, provided that the leasing is justified on the basis of exceptional needs, seasonal capacity needs or operational difficulties of the lessee, and the leasing does not exceed the duration which is strictly necessary to fulfil those needs or overcome those difficulties;

    (b) the Parties may require leasing arrangements to be approved by their competent authorities for the purpose of verifying compliance with the conditions set out in this paragraph and with the applicable safety and security requirements;

    (c) however, where a Party requires such approval, it shall endeavour to expedite the approval procedures and minimise the administrative burden on the air carriers concerned;

    (d) the provisions of this paragraph are without prejudice to the laws and regulations of a Party as regards the leasing of aircraft by air carriers of that Party.

Article 430   Fiscal provisions

1. On arriving in the territory of one Party, aircraft operated in international air transport by the air carriers of the other Party, their regular equipment, fuel, lubricants, consumable technical supplies, ground equipment, spare parts (including engines), aircraft stores (including but not limited to such items as food, beverages and liquor, tobacco and other products destined for sale to, or use by, passengers in limited quantities during flight) and other items intended for or used solely in connection with the operation or servicing of aircraft engaged in international air transport shall, on the basis of reciprocity, and provided that such equipment and supplies remain on board the aircraft, be exempt from all import restrictions, property taxes and capital levies, customs duties, excise taxes, inspection fees, value added tax or other similar indirect taxes, and similar fees and charges imposed by the national or local authorities or the Union.

2. The following goods shall also be exempt, on the basis of reciprocity, from the taxes, levies, duties, fees and charges referred to in paragraph 1:

    (a) aircraft stores introduced into or supplied in the territory of a Party and taken on board, within reasonable limits, for use on outbound aircraft of an air carrier of the other Party used in international air transport, even when these stores are to be used on a part of journey performed over the said territory;

(b) ground equipment and spare parts (including engines) introduced into the territory of a Party for the servicing, maintenance, or repair of aircraft of an air carrier of the other Party used in international air transport;

(c) lubricants and consumable technical supplies other than fuel introduced into or supplied in the territory of a Party for use in an aircraft of an air carrier of the other Party used in international air transport, even when those supplies are to be used on a part of the journey performed over the said territory; and

(d) printed matter, as provided for by the customs legislation of each Party, introduced into or supplied in the territory of one Party and taken on board for use on outbound aircraft of an air carrier of the other Party engaged in international air transport, even when those stores are to be used on a part of the journey performed over the said territory.

3. The regular airborne equipment, as well as the material, supplies and spare parts referred to in paragraph 1 normally retained on board aircraft operated by an air carrier of one Party may be unloaded in the territory of the other Party only with the approval of the customs authorities of that Party and may be required to be kept under the supervision or control of the said authorities up to such time as they are re-exported or otherwise disposed of in accordance with applicable regulations.

4. The relief from customs duties, national excise duties and similar national fees provided for in this Article shall also be available in situations where the air carrier or air carriers of one Party have entered into arrangements with another air carrier or air carriers for the loan or transfer in the territory of the other Party of the items specified in paragraphs 1 and 2, provided that such other air carrier or air carriers similarly enjoy such relief from that other Party.

5. Nothing in this Title shall prevent either Party from imposing taxes, levies, duties, fees or charges on goods sold other than for consumption on board to passengers during a sector of an air service between two points within its territory at which embarkation or disembarkation is permitted.

6. Baggage and cargo in direct transit across the territory of a Party shall be exempt from taxes, customs duties, fees and other similar charges.

7. Equipment and supplies referred to in paragraph 2 may be required to be kept under the supervision or control of the competent authorities.

8. The provisions of the respective conventions in force between the United Kingdom and Member States for the avoidance of double taxation on income and on capital remain unaffected by this Title.

9. The relief from customs duties, national excise duties and similar national fees shall not extend to charges based on the cost of services provided to an air carrier of a Party in the territory of the other Party.

Article 431 User charges

1. User charges that may be imposed by one Party on the air carriers of the other Party for the use of air navigation and air traffic control shall be cost-related and non-discriminatory. In any event, any such user charges shall be assessed on the air carriers of the other Party on terms not less favourable than the most favourable terms available to any other air carrier in like circumstances at the time the charges are applied.

2. Without prejudice to Article 429(5), each Party shall ensure that user charges other than those mentioned in paragraph 1 that may be imposed on the air carriers of the other Party are just, reasonable, not unjustly discriminatory, and equitably apportioned among categories of users. User charges imposed on the air carriers of the other Party may reflect, but not exceed, the full cost of providing appropriate airport, airport environmental and aviation security facilities and services at the airport or within the airport system. Such charges may include a reasonable return on assets after depreciation. Facilities and services for which user charges are imposed shall be provided on an efficient and economic basis. In any event, any such user charges shall be assessed on the air carrier of the other Party on terms no less favourable than the most favourable terms available to any other air carrier in like circumstances at the time the charges are applied.

3. In order to ensure the correct application of the principles set out in paragraphs 1 and 2, each Party shall ensure that consultations take place between the competent charging authorities

or bodies in its territory and the air carriers using the services and facilities concerned and that the competent charging authorities or bodies and the air carriers exchange such information as may be necessary. Each Party shall ensure that the competent charging authorities provide users with reasonable notice of any proposal for changes in user charges to enable users to express their views before any changes are made.

Article 432   Tariffs

1. The Parties shall allow tariffs to be freely established by the air carriers of the Parties on the basis of fair competition in accordance with this Title.

2. The Parties shall not subject the tariffs of each other's air carriers to approval.

Article 433   Statistics

1. The Parties shall cooperate within the framework of the Specialised Committee on Air Transport to facilitate the exchange of statistical information related to air transport under this Title.

2. Upon request, each Party shall provide the other Party with non-confidential and non-commercially sensitive available statistics related to air transport under this Title, as required by the respective laws and regulations of the Parties, on a non-discriminatory basis, and as may reasonably be required.

Article 434   Aviation safety

1. The Parties reaffirm the importance of close cooperation in the field of aviation safety.

2. Certificates of airworthiness, certificates of competency and licences issued or rendered valid by one Party and still in force shall be recognised as valid by the other Party and its competent authorities, for the purpose of operating air services under this Title, provided that such certificates or licences were issued or rendered valid pursuant to, and in conformity with, as a minimum, the relevant international standards established under the Convention.

3. Each Party may request consultations at any time concerning the safety standards maintained and administered by the other Party in areas relating to aeronautical facilities, flight crew, aircraft and the operation of aircraft. Such consultations shall take place within 30 days of the request.

4. If, following such consultations, one Party finds that the other Party does not effectively maintain and administer safety standards in the areas referred to in paragraph 2 that are at least equal to the minimum standards established at that time pursuant to the Convention, the first Party shall notify the other Party of those findings and the steps considered necessary to conform with those minimum standards, and the other Party shall take appropriate corrective action. Failure by the other Party to take appropriate action within 15 days or such other period as may be agreed shall be grounds for the requesting Party to refuse, revoke, suspend, impose conditions on or limit the operating authorisations or technical permissions, or to otherwise refuse, revoke, suspend, impose conditions on or limit the operations of the air carriers under the safety oversight of the other Party.

5. Any aircraft operated by, or under a lease arrangement on behalf of, an air carrier or air carriers of one Party may, while within the territory of the other Party, be made the subject of a ramp inspection, provided that this does not lead to unreasonable delay in the operation of the aircraft.

6. The ramp inspection or series of ramp inspections can give rise to:

   (a) serious concerns that an aircraft or the operation of an aircraft does not comply with the minimum standards established at that time pursuant to the Convention; or

   (b) serious concerns that there is a lack of effective maintenance and administration of safety standards established at that time pursuant to the Convention.

In the event that the Party that conducted the ramp inspection or inspections establishes serious concerns as referred to in point (a) or (b), it shall notify the competent authorities of the other Party that are responsible for the safety oversight of the air carrier operating the aircraft of such findings and inform them of the steps considered necessary to conform with those minimum standards. Failure to take appropriate corrective action within 15 days or such other period as may be agreed shall constitute grounds for the first Party to refuse, revoke, suspend, impose conditions on or limit the operating authorisations or technical permissions or to otherwise refuse, revoke, suspend, impose conditions on or limit the operations of the air carrier operating the aircraft.

7. In the event that access for the purpose of undertaking a ramp inspection of an aircraft operated by the air carrier or air carriers of one Party in accordance with paragraph 5 is denied, the other Party shall be free to infer that serious concerns as referred to in paragraph 6 arise and proceed in accordance with paragraph 6.

8. Each Party reserves the right to immediately revoke, suspend or limit the operating authorisations or technical permissions or to otherwise suspend or limit the operations of an air carrier or air carriers of the other Party, if the first Party concludes as a result of a ramp inspection, a series of ramp inspections, a denial of access for ramp inspection, consultation or otherwise, that immediate action is essential to the safety of an air carrier operation. The Party taking such measures shall promptly inform the other Party, providing reasons for its action.

9. Any action by one Party in accordance with paragraph 4, 6 or 8 shall be discontinued once the basis for the taking of that action ceases to exist.

10. Where measures have been taken by a Party pursuant to paragraph 4, 6 or 8, in the event of a dispute a Party may have recourse to arbitration in accordance with Article 739, without having prior recourse to consultations in accordance with Article 738. An arbitration tribunal shall treat the issue as a case of urgency for the purpose of Article 744. At the request of the complaining Party, the tribunal may, pending its final ruling, order the adoption of interim relief measures, including the modification or suspension of measures taken by either Party under this Article.

Article 435 Aviation security

1. The Parties shall provide upon request all necessary assistance to each other to address any threat to the security of civil aviation, including the prevention of acts of unlawful seizure of civil aircraft and other unlawful acts against the safety of such aircraft, of their passengers and crew, airports and air navigation facilities, and any other threat to the security of civil aviation.

2. The Parties shall, in their mutual relations, act in conformity with the aviation security standards established by ICAO. They shall require that operators of the aircraft in their registries and the operators of airports in their territory, act, at least, in conformity with such aviation security standards. Each Party shall, on request, provide the other Party notification of any difference between its laws, regulations and practices and the aviation security standards referred to in this paragraph. Each Party may at any time request consultations, to be held without delay, with the other Party to discuss those differences.

3. Each Party shall ensure that effective measures are taken within its territory to protect civil aviation against acts of unlawful interference, including, but not limited to, screening of passengers and their cabin baggage, screening of hold baggage, screening and security controls for persons other than passengers, including crew, and their items carried, screening and security controls for cargo, mail, in-flight and airport supplies, and access control to airside and security restricted areas. Each Party agrees that the security provisions of the other Party relating to the admission to, operating within, or departure from its territory of aircraft shall be observed.

4. The Parties shall endeavour to cooperate on aviation security matters to the highest extent, to exchange information on threat, vulnerability and risk, subject to the mutual agreement of appropriate arrangements for the secure transfer, use, storage and disposal of classified information, to discuss and share best practices, performance and detection standards of security equipment, compliance monitoring best practices and results, and in any other area that the Parties may identify. In particular, the Parties shall endeavour to develop and maintain cooperation arrangements between technical experts on the development and recognition of aviation security standards with the aim of facilitating such cooperation, reducing administrative duplication and fostering early notice and prior discussion of new security initiatives and requirements.

5. Each Party shall make available to the other Party on request the results of audits carried out by ICAO and the corrective actions taken by the audited state, subject to the mutual agreement of appropriate arrangements for the secure transfer, use, storage and disposal of such information.

6. The Parties agree to cooperate on security inspections undertaken by them in the territory of either Party through the establishment of mechanisms, including administrative arrangements, for the reciprocal exchange of information on results of such security inspections. The Parties agree to

consider positively requests to participate, as observers, in security inspections undertaken by the other Party.

7. Subject to paragraph 9, and with full regard and mutual respect for the other Party's sovereignty, a Party may adopt security measures for entry into its territory. Where possible, that Party shall take into account the security measures already applied by the other Party and any views that the other Party may offer. Each Party recognises that nothing in this Article limits the right of a Party to refuse entry into its territory of any flight or flights that it deems to present a threat to its security.

8. A Party may take emergency measures to meet a specific security threat. Such measures shall be notified immediately to the other Party. Without prejudice to the need to take immediate action in order to protect aviation security, when considering security measures, a Party shall evaluate possible adverse effects on international air transport and, unless constrained by law, shall take such effects into account when it determines what measures are necessary and appropriate to address the security concerns.

9. With regard to air services bound for its territory, a Party may not require security measures to be implemented in the territory of the other Party. Where a Party considers that a specific threat urgently requires the implementation of temporary measures in addition to the measures already in place in the territory of the other Party, it shall inform the other Party of the particulars of that threat to the extent consistent with the need to protect security information, and of the proposed measures. The other Party shall give positive consideration to such a proposal and may decide to implement additional measures as it deems necessary. Such measures shall be proportionate and limited in time.

10. When an incident or threat of an incident of unlawful seizure of civil aircraft or other unlawful acts against the safety of aircraft, passengers, crew, airports or air navigation facilities occurs, the Parties shall assist each other by facilitating communications and other appropriate measures intended to rapidly and safely terminate such incident or threat.

11. Each Party shall take all measures it finds practicable to ensure that an aircraft subjected to an act of unlawful seizure or other acts of unlawful interference which is on the ground in its territory is detained on the ground unless its departure is necessitated by the overriding duty to protect human life. Where practicable, such measures shall be taken on the basis of consultations between the Parties.

12. When a Party has reasonable grounds to believe that the other Party does not comply with this Article, that Party may request immediate consultations with the other Party. Such consultations shall start within 30 days of the receipt of such a request. Failure to reach a satisfactory agreement within 15 days or such other period as may be agreed from the date of such request shall constitute grounds for the Party that requested the consultations to take action to refuse, revoke, suspend, impose conditions on or limit the operating authorisation and technical permissions of an air carrier or air carriers of the other Party to ensure compliance with this Article. When required by an emergency, or to prevent further non-compliance with this Article, a Party may take interim action prior to the expiry of the 15 day-period referred to in this paragraph.

13. Any action taken in accordance with paragraph 8 shall be discontinued when the Party in question considers that the action is no longer required or has been superseded by other measures to mitigate the threat. Any action taken in accordance with paragraph 12 shall be discontinued upon compliance by the other Party with this Article. In the case of action taken in accordance with paragraph 8 or 12, this may be discontinued as mutually agreed by the Parties.

14. Where measures or actions have been taken in accordance with paragraph 7, 8, 9 or 12 of this Article, a Party may have recourse to the dispute settlement provisions of Title I of Part Six. An arbitration tribunal shall treat the issue as a case of urgency for the purpose of Article 744.

Article 436   Air traffic management

1. The Parties and their respective competent authorities and air navigation service providers shall cooperate with each other in such a way as to enhance the safe and efficient functioning of air traffic in the European region. The Parties shall seek interoperability between each other's service providers.

2. The Parties agree to cooperate on matters concerning the performance and charging of air navigation services and network functions, with a view to optimising overall flight efficiency, reducing costs, minimising environmental impact and enhancing the safety and capacity of air traffic flows between the existing air traffic management systems of the Parties.

3. The Parties agree to promote cooperation between their air navigation service providers in order to exchange flight data and coordinate traffic flows to optimise flight efficiency, with a view to achieving improved predictability, punctuality and service continuity for air traffic.

4. The Parties agree to cooperate on their air traffic management modernisation programmes, including research, development and deployment activities, and to encourage cross-participation in validation and demonstration activities with the goal of ensuring global interoperability.

Article 437   Air carrier liability

The Parties reaffirm their obligations under the Convention for the Unification of Certain Rules for International Carriage by Air, done at Montreal on 28 May 1999 (the 'Montreal Convention').

Article 438   Consumer protection

1. The Parties share the objective of achieving a high level of consumer protection and shall cooperate to that effect.

2. The Parties shall ensure that effective and non-discriminatory measures are taken to protect the interests of consumers in air transport. Such measures shall include the appropriate access to information, assistance including for persons with disabilities and reduced mobility, reimbursement and, if applicable, compensation in case of denied boarding, cancellation or delays, and efficient complaint handling procedures.

3. The Parties shall consult each other on any matter related to consumer protection, including their planned measures in that regard.

Article 439   Relationship to other agreements

1. Subject to paragraphs 4 and 5, earlier agreements and arrangements relating to the subject matter of this Title between the United Kingdom and the Member States, to the extent that they may not have been superseded by the law of the Union, shall be superseded by this Agreement.

2. The United Kingdom and a Member State may not grant each other any rights in connection with air transport to, from or within their respective territories other than those expressly laid down in this Title, save as provided for in Article 419(4) and (9).

3. If the Parties become party to a multilateral agreement, or endorse a decision adopted by ICAO or another international organisation that addresses matters covered by this Title, they shall consult in the Specialised Committee on Air Transport to determine whether this Title should be revised to take into account such developments.

4. Nothing in this Title shall affect the validity and application of existing and future air transport agreements between the Member States and the United Kingdom as regards territories under their respective sovereignty which are not covered by Article 774.

5. Nothing in this Title shall affect any rights available to the United Kingdom and Member States under the Multilateral Agreement on Commercial Rights of Non-Scheduled Air Services in Europe, signed at Paris on 30 April 1956, to the extent that such rights go beyond those laid down in this Title.

Article 440   Suspension and Termination

1. A suspension of this Title, in whole or in part, pursuant to Article 749, may be implemented no earlier than the first day of the International Air Transport Association (IATA) traffic season following the season during which the suspension has been notified.

2. Upon termination of this Agreement pursuant to Article 749 or upon termination of this Title pursuant to Article 441 or Article 521 or Article 509, the provisions governing the matters falling within the scope of this Title shall continue to apply beyond the date of cessation referred to in Article 779 or Article 441 or Article 521 or Article 509, until the end of the IATA traffic season in progress on that date.

3. The Party suspending this Title, in whole or in part, or terminating this Agreement or this Title shall inform ICAO thereof.

Article 441   Termination of this Title

Without prejudice to Article 779, Article 521, and Article 509 each Party may at any moment terminate this Title, by written notification through diplomatic channels. In that event, this Title shall cease to be in force on the first day of the ninth month following the date of notification.

Article 442   Registration of this Agreement

This Agreement and any amendments thereto shall, insofar as relevant, be registered with ICAO in accordance with Article 83 of the Convention.

Title II Aviation safety [omitted]

HEADING THREE ROAD TRANSPORT

Title I Transport of goods by road

Article 459   Objective

1. The objective of this Title is to ensure, as regards the transport of goods by road, continued connectivity between, through and within the territories of the Parties and to lay down the rules which are applicable to such transport.

2. The Parties agree not to take discriminatory measures when applying this Title.

3. Nothing in this Title shall affect the transport of goods by road within the territory of one of the Parties by a road haulage operator established in that territory.

Article 460   Scope

1. This Title applies to the transport of goods by road with a commercial purpose between, through and within the territories of the Parties and is without prejudice to the application of the rules established by the European Conference of Ministers of Transport.

2. Any transport of goods by road for which no direct or indirect remuneration is received and which does not directly or indirectly generate any income for the driver of the vehicle or for others, and which is not linked to professional activity shall be considered as the transport of goods for a non-commercial purpose.

Article 461   Definitions

For the purposes of this Title and in addition to the definitions set out in Article 124, the following definitions apply:

  (a) 'vehicle' means a motor vehicle registered in the territory of a Party, or a coupled combination of vehicles of which the motor vehicle is registered in the territory of a Party, and which is used exclusively for the transport of goods;

  (b) 'road haulage operator' means any natural or legal person engaged in the transport of goods with a commercial purpose, by means of a vehicle;

  (c) 'road haulage operator of a Party' means a road haulage operator which is a legal person established in the territory of a Party or a natural person of a Party;

  (d) 'party of establishment' means the Party in which a road haulage operator is established;

  (e) 'driver' means any person who drives a vehicle even for a short period, or who is carried in a vehicle as part of his duties to be available for driving if necessary;

  (f) 'transit' means the movement of vehicles across the territory of a Party without loading or unloading of goods;

  (g) 'regulatory measures' means:

    (i) for the Union:

      (A) regulations and directives, as provided for in Article 288 TFEU; and

      (B) delegated and implementing acts, as provided for in Articles 290 and 291 TFEU, respectively; and

    (ii) for the United Kingdom:

      (A) primary legislation; and

      (B) secondary legislation.

Article 462   Transport of goods between, through and within the territories of the Parties

1. Provided that the conditions in paragraph 2 are fulfilled, road haulage operators of a Party may undertake:

    (a) laden journeys with a vehicle, from the territory of the Party of establishment to the territory of the other Party, and vice versa, with or without transit through the territory of a third country;

    (b) laden journeys with a vehicle from the territory of the Party of establishment to the territory of the same Party with transit through the territory of the other Party;

    (c) laden journeys with a vehicle to or from the territory of the Party of establishment with transit through the territory of the other Party;

    (d) unladen journeys with a vehicle in conjunction with the journeys referred to in points (a), (b) and (c).

2. Road haulage operators of a Party may only undertake a journey referred to in paragraph 1 if:

    (a) they hold a valid licence issued in accordance with Article 463, except in the cases referred to in Article 464; and

    (b) the journey is carried out by drivers who hold a Certificate of Professional Competence in accordance with Article 465(1).

3. Subject to paragraph 6, and provided that the conditions in paragraph 2 are fulfilled, road haulage operators of the United Kingdom may undertake up to two laden journeys from one Member State to another Member State, without returning to the territory of the United Kingdom, provided that such journeys follow a journey from the territory of the United Kingdom permitted under point (a) of paragraph 1.

4. Without prejudice to paragraph 5, subject to paragraph 6 and provided that the conditions in paragraph 2 are fulfilled, road haulage operators of the United Kingdom may undertake one laden journey within the territory of a Member State provided that operation:

    (a) follows a journey from the territory of the United Kingdom permitted under point (a) of paragraph 1; and

    (b) is performed within seven days of the unloading in the territory of that Member State of goods carried on the journey referred to in point (a).

5. Subject to paragraph 6 and provided that the conditions in paragraph 2 are fulfilled, road haulage operators of the United Kingdom established in Northern Ireland may undertake up to two laden journeys within the territory of Ireland provided that such operations:

    (a) follow a journey from the territory of Northern Ireland permitted under point (a) of paragraph 1; and

    (b) are performed within seven days of the unloading in the territory of Ireland of goods carried on the journey referred to in point (a).

6. Road haulage operators of the United Kingdom shall be limited to a maximum of two journeys within the territory of the Union under paragraphs 3, 4 and 5 before returning to the territory of the United Kingdom.

7. Provided that the conditions in paragraph 2 are fulfilled, road haulage operators of the Union may undertake up to two laden journeys within the territory of the United Kingdom provided that such operations:

    (a) follow a journey from the territory of the Union permitted under point (a) of paragraph 1; and

    (b) are performed within seven days of the unloading in the territory of the United Kingdom of the goods carried on the journey referred to in point (a).

Articles 463–472   [Omitted]

Title II Transport of passengers by road

Article 473   Scope

1. The objective of this Title is to ensure, as regards the transport of passengers by road, continued connectivity between, through and within the territories of the Parties and to lay down the

rules which are applicable to such transport. It applies to the occasional, regular and special regular transport of passengers by coach and bus between, through and within the territories of the Parties.

2. The Parties agree not to take discriminatory measures when applying this Title.

3. Nothing in this Title shall affect the transport of passengers within the territory of one of the Parties by a road passenger transport operator established in that territory.

Article 474   Definitions

For the purposes of this Title and in addition to the definitions set out in Article 124, the following definitions apply:

   (a) 'coaches and buses' are vehicles which, by virtue of their construction and their equipment, are suitable for carrying more than nine persons, including the driver, and are intended for that purpose;

   (b) 'passenger transport services' means transport services by road for the public or for specific categories of users, supplied in return for payment by the person transported or by the transport organiser, by means of coaches and buses;

   (c) 'road passenger transport operator' means any natural person or any legal person, whether having its own legal personality or being dependent upon an authority having such a personality, which supplies passenger transport services;

   (d) 'road passenger transport operator of a Party' means a road passenger transport operator which is established in the territory of a Party;

   (e) 'regular services' means passenger transport services supplied at specified frequency along specified routes, whereby passengers may be picked up and set down at predetermined stopping points;

   (f) 'special regular services' means services by whomsoever organised, which provide for the transport of specified categories of passengers to the exclusion of other passengers, in so far as such services are operated under the conditions specified for regular services. Special regular services shall include:

     (i) the transport of workers between home and work, and

     (ii) the transport of school pupils and students to and from the educational institution. The fact that a special regular service may be varied according to the needs of users shall not affect its classification as a regular service;

   (g) 'group' means any of the following:

     (i) one or more associated natural or legal persons and their parent natural or legal person or persons,

     (ii) one or more associated natural person or legal persons which have the same parent natural or legal person or persons;

   (h) 'Interbus Agreement' means the Agreement on the international occasional carriage of passengers by coach and bus, as subsequently amended, which entered into force on 1 January 2003;

   (i) 'transit' means the movement of coaches and buses across the territory of a Party without picking up or setting down of passengers;

   (j) 'occasional services' means services which are not regular services or special regular services, and which are characterised above all by the fact that they carry groups of passengers assembled at the initiative of the customer or the road passenger transport operator.

Article 475   Passenger transport by coach and bus between, through and within the territories of the Parties

1. Road passenger transport operators of a Party may, when operating regular and special regular services, undertake laden journeys from the territory of a Party to the territory of the other Party, with or without transit through the territory of a third country, and unladen journeys related to such journeys.

2. Road passenger transport operators of a Party may, when operating regular and special regular services, undertake laden journeys from the territory of the Party, in which the road passenger transport operator is established, to the territory of the same Party with transit through the territory of the other Party, and unladen journeys related to such journeys.

3. A road passenger transport operator of a Party may not operate regular or special regular services with both origin and destination in the territory of the other Party.

4. Where the passenger transport service referred to in paragraph 1 is part of a service to or from the territory of the Party where the road passenger transport operator is established, passengers may be picked up or set down in the territory of the other Party en route, provided the stop is authorised in accordance with the rules applicable in that territory.

5. Where the passenger transport service referred to in this Article is part of an international regular or special regular service between Ireland and the United Kingdom in respect of Northern Ireland, passengers may be picked up and set down in one Party by a road passenger transport operator established in the other Party.

6. Road passenger transport operators established in the territory of one Party may, on a temporary basis, operate occasional services on the island of Ireland which pick up and set down passengers on the territory of the other Party.

7. Road passenger transport operators may, when operating occasional services, undertake a laden journey from the territory of a Party through the territory of the other Party to the territory of a non-Contracting Party to the Interbus Agreement, including a related unladen journey.

8. The passenger transport services referred to in this Article shall be performed using coaches and buses registered in the Party where the road passenger transport operator is established or resides. Those coaches and buses shall comply with the technical standards laid down in Annex 2 to the Interbus Agreement.

Articles 476–487 [Omitted]

HEADING FOUR SOCIAL SECURITY COORDINATION AND VISAS FOR SHORT-TERM VISITS

Title I Social security coordination

Article 488 Overview

Member States and the United Kingdom shall coordinate their social security systems in accordance with the Protocol on Social Security Coordination, in order to secure the social security entitlements of the persons covered therein.

Article 489 Legally residing

1. The Protocol on Social Security Coordination applies to persons legally residing in a Member State or the United Kingdom.

2. Paragraph 1 of this Article shall not affect entitlements to cash benefits which relate to previous periods of legal residence of persons covered by Article SSC.2 of the Protocol on Social Security Coordination.

Article 490 Cross-border situations

1. The Protocol on Social Security Coordination only applies to situations arising between one or more Member States and the United Kingdom.

2. The Protocol on Social Security Coordination shall not apply to persons whose situations are confined in all respects either to the United Kingdom, or to the Member States.

Article 491 Immigration applications

The Protocol on Social Security Coordination applies without prejudice to the right of a Member State or the United Kingdom to charge a health fee under national legislation in connection with an application for a permit to enter, to stay, to work, or to reside in that State.

Title II Visas for short-term visits

Article 492 Visas for short-term visits

1. The Parties note that on the date of entry into force of this Agreement both Parties provide for visa-free travel for short-term visits in respect of their nationals in accordance with their domestic

law. Each Party shall notify the other of any intention to impose a visa requirement for short-term visits by nationals of the other Party in good time and, if possible, at least three months before such a requirement takes effect.

2. Subject to paragraph 3 of this Article and to Article 781, in the event that the United Kingdom decides to impose a visa requirement for short-term visits on nationals of a Member State, that requirement shall apply to the nationals of all Member States.

3. This Article is without prejudice to any arrangements made between the United Kingdom and Ireland concerning the Common Travel Area.

HEADING FIVE FISHERIES
Chapter 1 Initial provisions

Article 493   Sovereign rights of coastal States exercised by the Parties
The Parties affirm that sovereign rights of coastal States exercised by the Parties for the purpose of exploring, exploiting, conserving and managing the living resources in their waters should be conducted pursuant to and in accordance with the principles of international law, including the United Nations Convention on the Law of the Sea.

Article 494   Objectives and principles
1. The Parties shall cooperate with a view to ensuring that fishing activities for shared stocks in their waters are environmentally sustainable in the long term and contribute to achieving economic and social benefits, while fully respecting the rights and obligations of independent coastal States as exercised by the Parties.

2. The Parties share the objective of exploiting shared stocks at rates intended to maintain and progressively restore populations of harvested species above biomass levels that can produce the maximum sustainable yield.

3. The Parties shall have regard to the following principles:
   (a) applying the precautionary approach to fisheries management;
   (b) promoting the long-term sustainability (environmental, social and economic) and optimum utilisation of shared stocks;
   (c) basing conservation and management decisions for fisheries on the best available scientific advice, principally that provided by the International Council for the Exploration of the Sea (ICES);
   (d) ensuring selectivity in fisheries to protect juvenile fish and spawning aggregations of fish, and to avoid and reduce unwanted bycatch;
   (e) taking due account of and minimising harmful impacts of fishing on the marine ecosystem and taking due account of the need to preserve marine biological diversity;
   (f) applying proportionate and non-discriminatory measures for the conservation of marine living resources and the management of fisheries resources, while preserving the regulatory autonomy of the Parties;
   (g) ensuring the collection and timely sharing of complete and accurate data relevant for the conservation of shared stocks and for the management of fisheries;
   (h) ensuring compliance with fisheries conservation and management measures, and combating illegal, unreported and unregulated fishing; and
   (i) ensuring the timely implementation of any agreed measures into the Parties' regulatory frameworks.

Article 495   Definitions
1. For the purposes of this Heading the following definitions apply:
   (a) 'EEZ' (of a Party) means, in accordance with the United Nations Convention on the Law of the Sea:
       (i) in the case of the Union, the exclusive economic zones established by its Member States adjacent to their European territories;
       (ii) the exclusive economic zone established by the United Kingdom;

(b) 'precautionary approach to fisheries management' means an approach according to which the absence of adequate scientific information does not justify postponing or failing to take management measures to conserve target species, associated or dependent species and non-target species and their environment;

(c) 'shared stocks' means fish, including shellfish of any kind that are found in the waters of the Parties, which includes molluscs and crustaceans;

(d) 'TAC' means the total allowable catch, which is the maximum quantity of a stock (or stocks) of a particular description that may be caught over a given period;

(e) 'non-quota stocks' means stocks which are not managed through TACs;

(f) 'territorial sea' (of a Party) means, in accordance with the United Nations Convention on the Law of the Sea:

    (i) in the case of the Union, by way of derogation from Article 774(1), the territorial sea established by its Member States adjacent to their European territories;

    (ii) the territorial sea established by the United Kingdom;

(g) 'waters' (of a Party) means:

    (i) in respect of the Union, by way of derogation from Article 774(1), the EEZs of the Member States and their territorial seas;

    (ii) in respect of the United Kingdom, its EEZ and its territorial sea, excluding for the purposes of Articles 500 and 501 and Annex 38 the territorial sea adjacent to the Bailiwick of Guernsey, the Bailiwick of Jersey and the Isle of Man;

(h) 'vessel' (of a Party) means:

    (i) in the case of the United Kingdom, a fishing vessel flying the flag of the United Kingdom, registered in the United Kingdom, the Bailiwick of Guernsey, the Bailiwick of Jersey or the Isle of Man, and licensed by a United Kingdom fisheries administration;

    (ii) in the case of the Union, a fishing vessel flying the flag of a Member State and registered in the Union.

Chapter 2   Conservation and sustainable exploitation

Article 496   Fisheries management

1. Each Party shall decide on any measures applicable to its waters in pursuit of the objectives set out in Article 494(1) and (2), and having regard to the principles referred to in Article 494(3).

2. A Party shall base the measures referred to in paragraph 1 on the best available scientific advice.

A Party shall not apply the measures referred to in paragraph 1 to the vessels of the other Party in its waters unless it also applies the same measures to its own vessels.

The second subparagraph is without prejudice to obligations of the Parties under the Port State Measures Agreement, the North East Atlantic Fisheries Commission Scheme of Control and Enforcement, the Northwest Atlantic Fisheries Organisation Conservation and Enforcement Measures, and Recommendation 18-09 by the International Commission for the Conservation of Atlantic Tunas on Port State Measures to Prevent, Deter and Eliminate Illegal, Unreported and Unregulated Fishing.

The Specialised Committee on Fisheries may amend the list of pre-existing international obligations referred to in the third subparagraph.

3. Each Party shall notify the other Party of new measures as referred to in paragraph 1 that are likely to affect the vessels of the other Party before those measures are applied, allowing sufficient time for the other Party to provide comments or seek clarification.

Article 497   Authorisations, compliance and enforcement

1. Where vessels have access to fish in the waters of the other Party pursuant to Article 500 and Article 502:

(a) each Party shall communicate in sufficient time to the other Party a list of vessels for which it seeks to obtain authorisations or licences to fish; and

(b) the other Party shall issue authorisations or licences to fish.

2. Each Party shall take all necessary measures to ensure compliance by its vessels with the rules applicable to those vessels in the other Party's waters, including authorisation or licence conditions.

Chapter 3   Arrangements on access to waters and resources

Article 498   Fishing opportunities

1. By 31 January of each year, the Parties shall cooperate to set the schedule for consultations with the aim of agreeing TACs for the stocks listed in Annex 35 for the following year or years.

That schedule shall take into account other annual consultations among coastal States that affect either or both of the Parties.

2. The Parties shall hold consultations annually to agree, by 10 December of each year, the TACs for the following year for the stocks listed in Annex 35. This shall include an early exchange of views on priorities as soon as advice on the level of the TACs is received. The Parties shall agree those TACs:

    (a) on the basis of the best available scientific advice, as well as other relevant factors, including socio-economic aspects; and

    (b) in compliance with any applicable multi-year strategies for conservation and management agreed by the Parties.

3. The Parties' shares of the TACs for the stocks listed in Annex 35 shall be allocated between the Parties in accordance with the quota shares set out in that Annex.

4. Annual consultations may also cover, *inter alia*:

    (a) transfers of parts of one Party's shares of TACs to the other Party;

    (b) a list of stocks for which fishing is prohibited;

    (c) the determination of the TAC for any stock which is not listed in Annex 35 or Annex 36 and the Parties' respective shares of those stocks;

    (d) measures for fisheries management, including, where appropriate, fishing effort limits;

    (e) stocks of mutual interest to the Parties other than those listed in the Annexes to this Heading.

5. The Parties may hold consultations with the aim of agreeing amended TACs if either Party so requests.

6. A written record documenting the arrangements made between the Parties as a result of consultations under this Article shall be produced and signed by the heads of delegation of the Parties.

7. Each Party shall give sufficient notice to the other Party before setting or amending TACs for the stocks listed in Annex 37.

8. The Parties shall set up a mechanism for voluntary in-year transfers of fishing opportunities between the Parties, to take place each year. The Specialised Committee on Fisheries shall decide on the details of this mechanism. The Parties shall consider making transfers of fishing opportunities for stocks which are, or are projected to be, underfished available at market value through that mechanism.

Article 499   Provisional TACs

1. If the Parties have not agreed a TAC for a stock listed in Annex 35 or tables A or B of Annex 36 by 10 December, they shall immediately resume consultations with the continued aim of agreeing the TAC. The Parties shall engage frequently with a view to exploring all possible options for reaching agreement in the shortest possible time.

2. If a stock listed in Annex 35 or in tables A and B of Annex 36 remains without an agreed TAC on 20 December, each Party shall set a provisional TAC corresponding to the level advised by ICES, applying from 1 January.

3. By way of derogation from paragraph 2, the TACs for special stocks shall be set in accordance with guidelines adopted under paragraph 5.

4. For the purposes of this Article, 'special stocks' means:

    (a) stocks where the ICES advice is for a zero TAC;

    (b) stocks caught in a mixed fishery, if that stock or another stock in the same fishery is vulnerable; or

    (c) other stocks which the Parties consider require special treatment.

5. The Specialised Committee on Fisheries shall adopt guidelines by 1 July 2021 for the setting of provisional TACs for special stocks.

6. Each year when advice is received from ICES on TACs, the Parties shall discuss, as a priority, the special stocks and the application of any guidelines set under paragraph 5 to the setting of provisional TACs by each Party.

7. Each Party shall set its share for each of the provisional TACs, which shall not exceed its share as set out in the corresponding Annex.

8. The provisional TACs and shares referred to in paragraphs 2, 3 and 7 shall apply until agreement is reached under paragraph 1.

9. Each Party shall, immediately, notify the other Party of its provisional TACs under paragraphs 2 and 3 and its provisional share of each of those TACs under paragraph 7.

Article 500   Access to waters

1. Provided that TACs have been agreed each Party shall grant vessels of the other Party access to fish in its waters in the relevant ICES sub-areas that year. Access shall be granted at a level and on conditions determined in those annual consultations.

2. The Parties may agree, in annual consultations, further specific access conditions in relation to:
   (a) the fishing opportunities agreed;
   (b) any multi-year strategies for non-quota stocks developed under point (c) of Article 508(1); and
   (c) any technical and conservation measures agreed by the Parties, without prejudice to Article 496.

3. The Parties shall conduct the annual consultations, including on the level and conditions of access referred to in paragraph 1, in good faith and with the objective of ensuring a mutually satisfactory balance between the interests of both Parties.

4. In particular, the outcome of the annual consultations should normally result in each Party granting:
   (a) access to fish the stocks listed in Annex 35 and tables A, B and F of Annex 36 in each other's EEZ (or if access is granted under point (c), in EEZs and in the divisions mentioned in that point) at a level that is reasonably commensurate with the Parties' respective shares of the TACs;
   (b) access to fish non-quota stocks in each other's EEZ (or if access is granted under point (c), in EEZs and in the divisions mentioned in that point), at a level that at least equates to the average tonnage fished by that Party in the waters of the other Party during the period 2012–2016; and
   (c) access to the waters of the Parties between six and twelve nautical miles from the baselines in ICES divisions 4c and 7d–g for qualifying vessels to the extent that Union fishing vessels and United Kingdom fishing vessels had access to those waters on 31 December 2020.
       For the purposes of point (c), 'qualifying vessel' means a vessel of a Party which fished in the zone mentioned in the previous sentence in four of the years between 2012 and 2016, or its direct replacement.
Annual consultations referred to in point (c) may include appropriate financial commitments and quota transfers between the Parties.

5. During the application of a provisional TAC, and pending an agreed TAC, the Parties shall grant provisional access to fish in the relevant ICES sub-areas as follows
   (a) for stocks listed in Annex 35 and non-quota stocks, from 1 January until 31 March at the levels provided for in points 4(a) and (b) of paragraph 4;
   (b) for stocks listed in Annex 36 from 1 January until 14 February at the levels provided for in point (a) of paragraph 4; and
   (c) in relation to access to fish in the six to twelve nautical miles zone, access in accordance with point (c) of paragraph 4 from 1 January to 31 January at a level equivalent to the average monthly tonnage fished in that zone in the previous three months.
Such access, for each of the relevant stocks in points (a) and (b), shall be in proportion to the average percentage of a Party's share of the annual TAC which that Party's vessels fished in the other Party's

waters in the relevant ICES sub-areas during the same period of the previous three calendar years. The same shall apply, *mutatis mutandis*, to access to fish non-quota stocks.

By 15 January in relation to the situation in point (c) of this paragraph, by 31 January in respect of the stocks listed in Annex 36, and by 15 March in respect of all other stocks, each Party shall notify the other Party of the change in the level and conditions of access to waters that will apply as of 1 February in relation to the situation in point (c) of this paragraph, as of 15 February in respect of the stocks listed in Annex 36, and as of 1 April in respect of all other stocks for the relevant ICES sub-areas.

6. Without prejudice to Article 499(1) and (8), after the period of one month in relation to the situation in point (c) of paragraph 5 of this Article, one and a half months in respect of the stocks listed in Annex 36 and three months in respect of all other stocks, the Parties shall seek to agree further provisional access arrangements at the appropriate geographical level with the aim of minimising disruption to fishing activities.

7. In granting access under paragraph 1 of this Article, a Party may take into account compliance of individual or groups of vessels with the applicable rules in its waters during the preceding year, and measures taken by the other Party pursuant to Article 497(2) during the preceding year.

8. This Article shall apply subject to Annex 38.

Articles 501–511   [Omitted]

HEADING SIX OTHER PROVISIONS [OMITTED]

PART THREE LAW ENFORCEMENT AND JUDICIAL COOPERATION IN CRIMINAL MATTERS [OMITTED]

PART FOUR THEMATIC COOPERATION [OMITTED]

PART FIVE PARTICIPATION IN UNION PROGRAMMES, SOUND FINANCIAL MANAGEMENT AND FINANCIAL PROVISIONS [OMITTED]

PART SIX DISPUTE SETTLEMENT AND HORIZONTAL PROVISIONS

Title I Dispute settlement

Chapter 1 General provisions

Article 734   Objective

The objective of this Title is to establish an effective and efficient mechanism for avoiding and settling disputes between the Parties concerning the interpretation and application of this Agreement and supplementing agreements, with a view to reaching, where possible, a mutually agreed solution.

Article 735   Scope

1. This Title applies, subject to paragraphs 2, 3, 4 and 5, to disputes between the Parties concerning the interpretation and application of the provisions of this Agreement or of any supplementing agreement ('covered provisions').

2. The covered provisions shall include all provisions of this Agreement and of any supplementing agreement with the exception of:

(a) Article 32 (1) to (6) and Article 36;

(b) Annex 12;

(c) Title VII of Heading one of Part Two;

(d) Title X of Heading One of Part Two;

(e) Article 355(1), (2) and (4), Article 356(1) and (3), Chapter 2 of Title XI of Heading One of Part Two, Articles 371 and 372, Chapter 5 of Title XI of Heading One of Part Two, and Article 411(4) to (9);

(f) Part Three, including when applying in relation to situations governed by other provisions of this Agreement;

(g) Part Four;

(h) Title II of Part Six;

(i) Article 782; and

(j) the Agreement on security procedures for exchanging and protecting classified information;

3. The Partnership Council may be seized by a Party with a view to resolving a dispute with respect to obligations arising from the provisions referred to in paragraph 2.

4. Article 736 applies to the provisions referred to in paragraph 2 of this Article.

5. Notwithstanding paragraphs 1 and 2, this Title shall not apply with respect to disputes concerning the interpretation and application of the provisions of the Protocol on Social Security Coordination or its annexes in individual cases.

Article 736   Exclusivity

The Parties undertake not to submit a dispute between them regarding the interpretation or application of provisions of this Agreement or of any supplementing agreement to a mechanism of settlement other than those provided for in this Agreement.

Article 737   Choice of forum in case of a substantially equivalent obligation under another international agreement

1. If a dispute arises regarding a measure allegedly in breach of an obligation under this Agreement or any supplementing agreement and of a substantially equivalent obligation under another international agreement to which both Parties are party, including the WTO Agreement, the Party seeking redress shall select the forum in which to settle the dispute.

2. Once a Party has selected the forum and initiated dispute settlement procedures either under this Title or under another international agreement, that Party shall not initiate such procedures under the other international agreement with respect to the particular measure referred to in paragraph 1, unless the forum selected first fails to make findings for procedural or jurisdictional reasons.

3. For the purposes of this Article:

(a) dispute settlement procedures under this Title are deemed to be initiated by a Party's request for the establishment of an arbitration tribunal under Article 739;

(b) dispute settlement procedures under the WTO Agreement are deemed to be initiated by a Party's request for the establishment of a panel under Article 6 of the Understanding on Rules and Procedure Governing the Settlement of Disputes of the WTO; and

(c) dispute settlement procedures under any other agreement are deemed to be initiated if they are initiated in accordance with the relevant provisions of that agreement.

4. Without prejudice to paragraph 2, nothing in this Agreement or any supplementing agreement shall preclude a Party from suspending obligations authorised by the Dispute Settlement Body of the WTO or authorised under the dispute settlement procedures of another international agreement to which the Parties are party. The WTO Agreement or any other international agreement between the Parties shall not be invoked to preclude a Party from suspending obligations under this Title.

Chapter 2   Procedure

Article 738   Consultations

1. If a Party ('the complaining Party') considers that the other Party ('the respondent Party') has breached an obligation under this Agreement or under any supplementing agreement, the Parties shall endeavour to resolve the matter by entering into consultations in good faith, with the aim of reaching a mutually agreed solution.

2. The complaining Party may seek consultations by means of a written request delivered to the respondent Party. The complaining Party shall specify in its written request the reasons for the request, including the identification of the measures at issue and the legal basis for the request, and the covered provisions it considers applicable.

3. The respondent Party shall reply to the request promptly, and in any case no later than 10 days after the date of its delivery. Consultations shall be held within 30 days of the date of delivery of the request in person or by any other means of communication agreed by the Parties. If held in person, consultations shall take place in the territory of the respondent Party, unless the Parties agree otherwise.

4. The consultations shall be deemed concluded within 30 days of the date of delivery of the request, unless the Parties agree to continue consultations.

5. Consultations on matters of urgency, including those regarding perishable goods or seasonal goods or services, shall be held within 20 days of the date of delivery of the request. The consultations shall be deemed concluded within those 20 days unless the Parties agree to continue consultations.

6. Each Party shall provide sufficient factual information to allow a complete examination of the measure at issue, including an examination of how that measure could affect the application of this Agreement or any supplementing agreement. Each Party shall endeavour to ensure the participation of personnel of their competent authorities who have expertise in the matter subject to the consultations.

7. For any dispute concerning an area other than Titles I to VII, Chapter 4 of Title VIII, Titles IX to XII of Heading One or Heading Six of Part Two, at the request of the complaining Party, the consultations referred to in paragraph 3 of this Article shall be held in the framework of a Specialised Committee or of the Partnership Council. The Specialised Committee may at any time decide to refer the matter to the Partnership Council. The Partnership Council may also seize itself of the matter. The Specialised Committee, or, as the case may be, the Partnership Council, may resolve the dispute by a decision. The time periods referred to in paragraph 3 of this Article shall apply. The venue of meetings shall be governed by the rules of procedure of the Specialised Committee or, as the case may be, the Partnership Council.

8. Consultations, and in particular all information designated as confidential and positions taken by the Parties during consultations, shall be confidential, and shall be without prejudice to the rights of either Party in any further proceedings.

Article 739   Arbitration procedure

1. The complaining Party may request the establishment of an arbitration tribunal if:
  (a) the respondent Party does not respond to the request for consultations within 10 days of the date of its delivery;
  (b) consultations are not held within the time periods referred to in Article 738(3), (4) or (5);
  (c) the Parties agree not to have consultations; or
  (d) consultations have been concluded without a mutually agreed solution having been reached.

2. The request for the establishment of the arbitration tribunal shall be made by means of a written request delivered to the respondent Party. In its request, the complaining Party shall explicitly identify the measure at issue and explain how that measure constitutes a breach of the covered provisions in a manner sufficient to present the legal basis for the complaint clearly.

Article 740   Establishment of an arbitration tribunal

1. An arbitration tribunal shall be composed of three arbitrators.

2. No later than 10 days after the date of delivery of the request for the establishment of an arbitration tribunal, the Parties shall consult with a view to agreeing on the composition of the arbitration tribunal.

3. If the Parties do not agree on the composition of the arbitration tribunal within the time period provided for in paragraph 2 of this Article, each Party shall appoint an arbitrator from the sub-list for that Party established pursuant to Article 752 no later than five days after the expiry of the time period provided for in paragraph 2 of this Article. If a Party fails to appoint an arbitrator

from its sub-list within that time period, the co-chair of the Partnership Council from the complaining Party shall select, no later than five days after the expiry of that time period, an arbitrator by lot from the sub-list of the Party that has failed to appoint an arbitrator. The co-chair of the Partnership Council from the complaining Party may delegate such selection by lot of the arbitrator.

4. If the Parties do not agree on the chairperson of the arbitration tribunal within the time period provided for in paragraph 2 of this Article, the co-chair of the Partnership Council from the complaining Party shall select, no later than five days after the expiry of that time period, the chairperson of the arbitration tribunal by lot from the sub-list of chairpersons established pursuant to Article 752. The co-chair of the Partnership Council from the complaining Party may delegate such selection by lot of the chairperson of the arbitration tribunal.

5. Should any of the lists provided for in Article 752 not be established or not contain sufficient names at the time a selection is made pursuant to paragraph 3 or 4 of this Article, the arbitrators shall be selected by lot from the individuals who have been formally proposed by one Party or both Parties in accordance with Annex 48.

6. The date of establishment of the arbitration tribunal shall be the date on which the last of the three arbitrators has notified to the Parties the acceptance of his or her appointment in accordance with Annex 48.

Article 741   Requirements for arbitrators

1. All arbitrators shall:
   (a) have demonstrated expertise in law and international trade, including on specific matters covered by Titles I to VII, Chapter 4 of Title VIII, Titles IX to XII of Heading One of Part Two or Heading Six of Part Two, or in law and any other matter covered by this Agreement or by any supplementing agreement and, in the case of a chairperson, also have experience in dispute settlement procedures;
   (b) not be affiliated with or take instructions from either Party;
   (c) serve in their individual capacities and not take instructions from any organisation or government with regard to matters related to the dispute; and
   (d) comply with Annex 49.

2. All arbitrators shall be persons whose independence is beyond doubt, who possess the qualifications required for appointment to high judicial office in their respective countries or who are jurisconsults of recognised competence.

3. In view of the subject-matter of a particular dispute, the Parties may agree to derogate from the requirements listed in point (a) of paragraph 1.

Article 742   Functions of the arbitration tribunal

The arbitration tribunal:
   (a) shall make an objective assessment of the matter before it, including an objective assessment of the facts of the case and the applicability of, and conformity of the measures at issue with, the covered provisions;
   (b) shall set out, in its decisions and rulings, the findings of facts and law and the rationale behind any findings that it makes; and
   (c) should consult regularly with the Parties and provide adequate opportunities for the development of a mutually agreed solution.

Article 743   Terms of reference

1. Unless the Parties agree otherwise no later than five days after the date of the establishment of the arbitration tribunal, the terms of reference of the arbitration tribunal shall be:

'to examine, in the light of the relevant covered provisions of this Agreement or of a supplementing agreement, the matter referred to in the request for the establishment of the arbitration tribunal, to decide on the conformity of the measure at issue with the provisions referred to in Article 735 and to issue a ruling in accordance with Article 745'.

2. If the Parties agree on terms of reference other than those referred to in paragraph 1, they shall notify the agreed terms of reference to the arbitration tribunal within the time period referred to in paragraph 1.

Article 744   Urgent proceedings

1. If a Party so requests, the arbitration tribunal shall decide, no later than 10 days after the date of its establishment, whether the case concerns matters of urgency.

2. In cases of urgency, the applicable time periods set out in Article 745 shall be half the time prescribed therein.

Article 745   Ruling of the arbitration tribunal

1. The arbitration tribunal shall deliver an interim report to the Parties within 100 days after the date of establishment of the arbitration tribunal. If the arbitration tribunal considers that this deadline cannot be met, the chairperson of the arbitration tribunal shall notify the Parties in writing, stating the reasons for the delay and the date on which the arbitration tribunal plans to deliver its interim report. The arbitration tribunal shall not deliver its interim report later than 130 days after the date of establishment of the arbitration tribunal under any circumstances.

2. Each Party may deliver to the arbitration tribunal a written request to review precise aspects of the interim report within 14 days of its delivery. A Party may comment on the other Party's request within six days of the delivery of the request.

3. If no written request to review precise aspects of the interim report is delivered within the time period referred to in paragraph 2, the interim report shall become the ruling of the arbitration tribunal.

4. The arbitration tribunal shall deliver its ruling to the Parties within 130 days of the date of establishment of the arbitration tribunal. When the arbitration tribunal considers that that deadline cannot be met, its chairperson shall notify the Parties in writing, stating the reasons for the delay and the date on which the arbitration tribunal plans to deliver its ruling. The arbitration tribunal shall not deliver its ruling later than 160 days after the date of establishment of the arbitration tribunal under any circumstances.

5. The ruling shall include a discussion of any written request by the Parties on the interim report and clearly address the comments of the Parties.

6. For greater certainty, a 'ruling' or 'rulings' as referred to in Articles 742, 743 and 753 and Article 754(1), (3), (4) and (6) shall be understood to refer also to the interim report of the arbitration tribunal.

Chapter 3   Compliance

Article 746   Compliance measures

1. If, in its ruling referred to in Article 745(4), the arbitration tribunal finds that the respondent Party has breached an obligation under this Agreement or under any supplementing agreement, that Party shall take the necessary measures to comply immediately with the ruling of the arbitration tribunal in order to bring itself in compliance with the covered provisions.

2. The respondent Party, no later than 30 days after delivery of the ruling, shall deliver a notification to the complaining Party of the measures which it has taken or which it envisages to take in order to comply.

Article 747   Reasonable Period of Time

1. If immediate compliance is not possible, the respondent Party, no later than 30 days after delivery of the ruling referred to in Article 745(4), shall deliver a notification to the complaining Party of the length of the reasonable period of time it will require for compliance with the ruling referred to in Article 745(4). The Parties shall endeavour to agree on the length of the reasonable period of time to comply.

2. If the Parties have not agreed on the length of the reasonable period of time, the complaining Party may, at the earliest 20 days after the delivery of the notification referred to in paragraph 1, request in writing that the original arbitration tribunal determines the length of the reasonable period of time. The arbitration tribunal shall deliver its decision to the Parties within 20 days of the date of delivery of the request.

3. The respondent Party shall deliver a written notification of its progress in complying with the ruling referred to in Article 745(4) to the complaining Party at least one month before the expiry of the reasonable period of time.

4. The Parties may agree to extend the reasonable period of time.

Article 748   Compliance Review

1. The respondent Party shall, no later than the date of expiry of the reasonable period of time, deliver a notification to the complaining Party of any measure that it has taken to comply with the ruling referred to in Article 745(4).

2. When the Parties disagree on the existence of, or the consistency with the covered provisions of, any measure taken to comply, the complaining Party may deliver a request, which shall be in writing, to the original arbitration tribunal to decide on the matter. The request shall identify any measure at issue and explain how that measure constitutes a breach of the covered provisions in a manner sufficient to present the legal basis for the complaint clearly. The arbitration tribunal shall deliver its decision to the Parties within 45 days of the date of delivery of the request.

Article 749   Temporary Remedies

1. The respondent Party shall, at the request of and after consultations with the complaining Party, present an offer for temporary compensation if:

    (a) the respondent Party delivers a notification to the complaining Party that it is not possible to comply with the ruling referred to in Article 745(4); or

    (b) the respondent Party fails to deliver a notification of any measure taken to comply within the deadline referred to in Article 746 or before the date of expiry of the reasonable period of time; or

    (c) the arbitration tribunal finds that no measure taken to comply exists or that the measure taken to comply is inconsistent with the covered provisions.

2. In any of the conditions referred to in points (a), (b) and (c) of paragraph 1, the complaining Party may deliver a written notification to the respondent Party that it intends to suspend the application of obligations under the covered provisions if:

    (a) the complaining Party decides not to make a request under paragraph 1; or

    (b) the Parties do not agree on the temporary compensation within 20 days after the expiry of the reasonable period of time or the delivery of the arbitration tribunal decision under Article 748 if a request under paragraph 1 of this Article is made.

The notification shall specify the level of intended suspension of obligations.

3. Suspension of obligations shall be subject to the following conditions:

    (a) Obligations under Heading Four of Part Two, the Protocol on Social Security Coordination or its annexes or Part Five may not be suspended under this Article;

    (b) By way of derogation from point (a), obligations under Part Five may be suspended only where the ruling referred to in Article 745(4) concerns the interpretation and implementation of Part Five;

    (c) Obligations outside Part Five may not be suspended where the ruling referred to in Article 745(4) concerns the interpretation and implementation of Part Five; and

    (d) Obligations under Title II of Heading One of Part Two in respect of financial services may not be suspended under this Article, unless the ruling referred to in Article 745(4) concerns the interpretation and application of obligations under Title II of Heading One of Part two in respect of financial services.

4. Where a Party persists in not complying with a ruling of an arbitration panel established under an earlier agreement concluded between the Parties, the other Party may suspend obligations under the covered provisions referred to in Article 735. With the exception of the rule in point (a) of paragraph 3 of this Article, all rules relating to temporary remedies in case of non-compliance and to review of any such measures shall be governed by the earlier agreement.

5. The suspension of obligations shall not exceed the level equivalent to the nullification or impairment caused by the violation.

6. If the arbitration tribunal has found the violation in Heading One or Heading Three of Part Two, the suspension may be applied in another Title of the same Heading as that in which the tribunal has found the violation, in particular if the complaining party is of the view that such suspension is effective in inducing compliance.

7. If the arbitration tribunal has found the violation in Heading Two of Part Two:

(a) the complaining party should first seek to suspend obligations in the same Title as that in which the arbitration tribunal has found the violation;

(b) if the complaining party considers that it is not practicable or effective to suspend obligations with respect to the same Title as that in which the tribunal has found the violation, it may seek to suspend obligations in the other Title under the same Heading.

8. If the arbitration tribunal has found the violation in Heading One, Heading Two, Heading Three or Heading Five of Part Two, and if the complaining party considers that it is not practicable or effective to suspend obligations within the same Heading as that in which the arbitration tribunal has found the violation, and that the circumstances are serious enough, it may seek to suspend obligations under other covered provisions.

9. In the case of point (b) of paragraph 7 and paragraph 8, the complaining Party shall state the reasons for its decision.

10. The complaining Party may suspend the obligations 10 days after the date of delivery of the notification referred to in paragraph 2 unless the respondent Party made a request under paragraph 11.

11. If the respondent Party considers that the notified level of suspension of obligations exceeds the level equivalent to the nullification or impairment caused by the violation or that the principles and procedures set forth in point (b) of paragraph 7, paragraph 8 or paragraph 9 have not been followed, it may deliver a written request to the original arbitration tribunal before the expiry of the 10 day period set out in paragraph 10 to decide on the matter. The arbitration tribunal shall deliver its decision on the level of the suspension of obligations to the Parties within 30 days of the date of the request. Obligations shall not be suspended until the arbitration tribunal has delivered its decision. The suspension of obligations shall be consistent with that decision.

12. The arbitration tribunal acting pursuant to paragraph 11 shall not examine the nature of the obligations to be suspended but shall determine whether the level of such suspension exceeds the level equivalent to the nullification or impairment caused by the violation. However, if the matter referred to arbitration includes a claim that the principles and procedures set forth in point (b) of paragraph 7, paragraph 8 or paragraph 9 have not been followed, the arbitration tribunal shall examine that claim. In the event the arbitration tribunal determines that those principles and procedures have not been followed, the complaining party shall apply them consistently with point (b) of paragraph 7, paragraph 8 and paragraph 9. The parties shall accept the arbitration tribunal's decision as final and shall not seek a second arbitration procedure. This paragraph shall under no circumstances delay the date as of which the complaining Party is entitled to suspend obligations under this Article.

13. The suspension of obligations or the compensation referred to in this Article shall be temporary and shall not be applied after:

(a) the Parties have reached a mutually agreed solution pursuant to Article 756;

(b) the Parties have agreed that the measure taken to comply brings the respondent Party into compliance with the covered provisions; or

(c) any measure taken to comply which the arbitration tribunal has found to be inconsistent with the covered provisions has been withdrawn or amended so as to bring the respondent Party into compliance with those covered provisions.

Article 750   Review of any measure taken to comply after the adoption of temporary remedies

1. The respondent Party shall deliver a notification to the complaining Party of any measure it has taken to comply following the suspension of obligations or following the application of temporary compensation, as the case may be. With the exception of cases under paragraph 2, the complaining Party shall terminate the suspension of obligations within 30 days from the delivery of the notification. In cases where compensation has been applied, with the exception of cases under paragraph 2, the respondent Party may terminate the application of such compensation within 30 days from the delivery of its notification that it has complied.

2. If the Parties do not reach an agreement on whether the notified measure brings the respondent Party into compliance with the covered provisions within 30 days of the date of delivery of the notification, the complaining Party shall deliver a written request to the original arbitration tribunal to decide on the matter. The arbitration tribunal shall deliver its decision to the Parties within 46 days of the date of the delivery of the request. If the arbitration tribunal finds that the measure taken to comply is in conformity with the covered provisions, the suspension of obligations or compensation, as the case may be, shall be terminated. When relevant, the level of suspension of obligations or of compensation shall be adjusted in light of the arbitration tribunal decision.

Chapter 4   Common procedural provisions

Articles 751–753   [Omitted]

Article 754   Arbitration tribunal decisions and rulings

1. The deliberations of the arbitration tribunal shall be kept confidential. The arbitration tribunal shall make every effort to draft rulings and take decisions by consensus. If this is not possible, the arbitration tribunal shall decide the matter by majority vote. In no case shall separate opinions of arbitrators be disclosed.

2. The decisions and rulings of the arbitration tribunal shall be binding on the Union and on the United Kingdom. They shall not create any rights or obligations with respect to natural or legal persons.

3. Decisions and rulings of the arbitration tribunal cannot add to or diminish the rights and obligations of the Parties under this Agreement or under any supplementing agreement.

4. For greater certainty, the arbitration tribunal shall have no jurisdiction to determine the legality of a measure alleged to constitute a breach of this Agreement or of any supplementing agreement, under the domestic law of a Party. No finding made by the arbitration tribunal when ruling on a dispute between the Parties shall bind the domestic courts or tribunals of either Party as to the meaning to be given to the domestic law of that Party.

5. For greater certainty, the courts of each Party shall have no jurisdiction in the resolution of disputes between the Parties under this Agreement.

6. Each Party shall make the rulings and decisions of the arbitration tribunal publicly available, subject to the protection of confidential information.

7. The information submitted by the Parties to the arbitration tribunal shall be treated in accordance with the confidentiality rules laid down in Annex 48.

Article 755   Suspension and termination of the arbitration proceedings

At the request of both Parties, the arbitration tribunal shall suspend its work at any time for a period agreed by the Parties and not exceeding 12 consecutive months. The arbitration tribunal shall resume its work before the end of the suspension period at the written request of both Parties, or at the end of the suspension period at the written request of either Party. The requesting Party shall deliver a notification to the other Party accordingly. If a Party does not request the resumption of the arbitration tribunal's work at the expiry of the suspension period, the authority of the arbitration tribunal shall lapse and the dispute settlement procedure shall be terminated. In the event of a suspension of the work of the arbitration tribunal, the relevant time periods shall be extended by the same time period for which the work of the arbitration tribunal was suspended.

Article 756   Mutually agreed solution

1. The Parties may at any time reach a mutually agreed solution with respect to any dispute referred to in Article 735.

2. If a mutually agreed solution is reached during panel proceedings, the Parties shall jointly notify the agreed solution to the chairperson of the arbitration tribunal. Upon such notification, the arbitration proceedings shall be terminated.

3. The solution may be adopted by means of a decision of the Partnership Council. Mutually agreed solutions shall be made publicly available. The version disclosed to the public shall not contain any information either Party has designated as confidential.

4. Each Party shall take the measures necessary to implement the mutually agreed solution within the agreed time period.

5. No later than the date of expiry of the agreed time period, the implementing Party shall inform the other Party in writing of any measures thus taken to implement the mutually agreed solution.

Article 757   Time Periods

1. All time periods laid down in this Title shall be counted in days from the day following the act to which they refer.

2. Any time period referred to in this Title may be modified by mutual agreement of the Parties.

3. The arbitration tribunal may at any time propose to the Parties to modify any time period referred to in this Title, stating the reasons for the proposal.

Articles 758–759   [Omitted]

Chapter 5   Specific arrangements for unilateral measures

Article 760   Special procedures for remedial measures and rebalancing

1. For the purposes of Article 374 and Article 411(2) and (3), this Title applies with the modifications set out in this Article.

2. By way of derogation from Article 740 and Annex 48, if the Parties do not agree on the composition of the arbitration tribunal within two days, the co-chair of the Partnership Council from the complaining Party shall select, no later than one day after the expiry of the two-day time period, an arbitrator by lot from the sub-list of each Party and the chairperson of the arbitration tribunal by lot from the sub-list of chairpersons established pursuant to Article 752. The co-chair of the Partnership Council from the complaining Party may delegate such selection by lot of the arbitrator or chairperson. Each individual shall confirm his or her availability to both Parties within two days from the date on which he or she was informed of his or her appointment. The organisational meeting referred to in Rule 10 of Annex 48 shall take place within two days from the establishment of the arbitration tribunal.

3. By way of derogation from Rule 11 of Annex 48 the complaining Party shall deliver its written submission no later than seven days after the date of establishment of the arbitration tribunal. The respondent Party shall deliver its written submission no later than seven days after the date of delivery of the written submission of the complaining Party. The arbitration tribunal shall adjust any other relevant time periods of the dispute settlement procedure as necessary to ensure the timely delivery of the report.

4. Article 745 does not apply and references to the ruling in this Title shall be read as references to the ruling referred to in Article 374(10) or point (c) of Article 411(3).

5. By way of derogation from Article 748(2), the arbitration tribunal shall deliver its decision to the Parties within 30 days from the date of delivery of the request.

Article 761   Suspension of obligations for the purposes of Article 374(12), Article 501(5) and Article 506(7)

1. The level of suspension of obligations shall not exceed the level equivalent to the nullification or impairment of benefits under this Agreement or under a supplementing agreement that is directly caused by the remedial or compensatory measures from the date the remedial or compensatory measures enter into effect until the date of the delivery of the arbitration ruling.

2. The level of suspension of obligations requested by the complaining Party and the determination of the level of suspension of obligations by the arbitration tribunal shall be based on facts demonstrating that the nullification or impairment arises directly from the application of the remedial or compensatory measure and affects specific goods, service suppliers, investors or other economic actors and not merely on allegation, conjecture or remote possibility.

3. The level of nullified or impaired benefits requested by the complaining Party or determined by the arbitration tribunal:

    (a) shall not include punitive damages, interest or hypothetical losses of profits or business opportunities;

(b) shall be reduced by any prior refunds of duties, indemnification of damages or other forms of compensation already received by the concerned operators or the concerned Party; and

(c) shall not include the contribution to the nullification or impairment by wilful or negligent action or omission of the concerned Party or any person or entity in relation to whom remedies are sought pursuant to the intended suspension of obligations.

Article 762   Conditions for rebalancing, remedial, compensatory and safeguard measures

Where a Party takes a measure under Article 374, Article 411, Article 469, Article 501, Article 506 or Article 773, that measure shall only be applied in respect of covered provisions within the meaning of Article 735 and shall comply, mutatis mutandis, with the conditions set out in Article 749(3).

Title II   Basis for cooperation

Article 763   Democracy, rule of law and human rights

1. The Parties shall continue to uphold the shared values and principles of democracy, the rule of law, and respect for human rights, which underpin their domestic and international policies. In that regard, the Parties reaffirm their respect for the Universal Declaration of Human Rights and the international human rights treaties to which they are parties.

2. The Parties shall promote such shared values and principles in international forums. The Parties shall cooperate in promoting those values and principles, including with or in third countries.

Article 764   Fight against climate change

1. The Parties consider that climate change represents an existential threat to humanity and reiterate their commitment to strengthening the global response to this threat. The fight against human-caused climate change as elaborated in the United Nations Framework Convention on Climate Change (UNFCCC) process, and in particular in the Paris Agreement adopted by the Conference of the Parties to the United Nations Framework Convention on Climate Change at its 21st session (the 'Paris Agreement'), inspires the domestic and external policies of the Union and the United Kingdom. Accordingly, each Party shall respect the Paris Agreement and the process set up by the UNFCCC and refrain from acts or omissions that would materially defeat the object and purpose of the Paris Agreement.

2. The Parties shall advocate the fight against climate change in international forums, including by engaging with other countries and regions to increase their level of ambition in the reduction of greenhouse emissions.

Articles 765–766   [Omitted]

Article 767   The most serious crimes of concern to the international community

1. The Parties reaffirm that the most serious crimes of concern to the international community as a whole must not go unpunished and that their effective prosecution must be ensured by taking measures at the national level and by enhancing international cooperation, including with the International Criminal Court. The Parties agree to fully support the universality and integrity of the Rome Statute of the International Criminal Court and related instruments.

2. The Parties agree to establish a regular dialogue on those matters.

Article 768   Counter-terrorism

1. The Parties shall cooperate at the bilateral, regional and international levels to prevent and combat acts of terrorism in all its forms and manifestations in accordance with international law, including, where applicable, international counterterrorism-related agreements, international humanitarian law and international human rights law, as well as in accordance with the principles of the Charter of the United Nations.

2. The Parties shall enhance cooperation on counter-terrorism, including preventing and countering violent extremism and the financing of terrorism, with the aim of advancing their common security interests, taking into account the United Nations Global Counter-Terrorism Strategy and relevant United Nations Security Council resolutions, without prejudice to law enforcement and judicial cooperation in criminal matters and intelligence exchanges.

3. The Parties agree to establish a regular dialogue on those matters. This dialogue will, *inter alia*, aim to promote and facilitate:

    (a) the sharing of assessments on the terrorist threat;

    (b) the exchange of best practices and expertise on counter terrorism;

    (c) operational cooperation and exchange of information; and

    (d) exchanges on cooperation in the framework of multilateral organisations.

Article 769   Personal data protection

1. The Parties affirm their commitment to ensuring a high level of personal data protection. They shall endeavour to work together to promote high international standards.

2. The Parties recognise that individuals have a right to the protection of personal data and privacy and that high standards in this regard contribute to trust in the digital economy and to the development of trade, and are a key enabler for effective law enforcement cooperation. To that end, the Parties shall undertake to respect, each in the framework of their respective laws and regulations, the commitments they have made in this Agreement in connection with that right.

3. The Parties shall cooperate at bilateral and multilateral levels, while respecting their respective laws and regulations. Such cooperation may include dialogue, exchanges of expertise, and cooperation on enforcement, as appropriate, with respect to personal data protection.

4. Where this Agreement or any supplementing agreement provide for the transfer of personal data, such transfer shall take place in accordance with the transferring Party's rules on international transfers of personal data. For greater certainty, this paragraph is without prejudice to the application of any specific provisions in this Agreement relating to the transfer of personal data, in particular Article 202 and Article 525, and to Title I of Part Six. Where needed, each Party will make best efforts, while respecting its rules on international transfers of personal data, to establish safeguards necessary for the transfer of personal data, taking into account any recommendations of the Partnership Council under point (h) of Article 7(4).

Article 770   Global cooperation on issues of shared economic, environmental and social interest

1. The Parties recognise the importance of global cooperation to address issues of shared economic, environmental and social interest. Where it is in their mutual interest, they shall promote multilateral solutions to common problems.

2. While preserving their decision-making autonomy, and without prejudice to other provisions of this Agreement or any supplementing agreement, the Parties shall endeavour to cooperate on current and emerging global issues of common interest such as peace and security, climate change, sustainable development, cross-border pollution, environmental protection, digitalisation, public health and consumer protection, taxation, financial stability, and free and fair trade and investment. To that end, they shall endeavour to maintain a constant and effective dialogue and to coordinate their positions in multilateral organisations and forums in which the Parties participate, such as the United Nations, the Group of Seven (G-7) and the Group of Twenty (G-20), the Organisation for Economic Co-operation and Development, the International Monetary Fund, the World Bank and the World Trade Organization.

Article 771   Essential elements

Article 763(1), Article 764(1) and Article 765(1) constitute essential elements of the partnership established by this Agreement and any supplementing agreement.

Title III Fulfillment of obligations and safeguard measures

Article 772   Fulfilment of obligations described as essential elements

1. If either Party considers that there has been a serious and substantial failure by the other Party to fulfil any of the obligations that are described as essential elements in Article 771, it may decide to terminate or suspend the operation of this Agreement or any supplementing agreement in whole or in part.

2. Before doing so, the Party invoking the application of this Article shall request that the Partnership Council meet immediately, with a view to seeking a timely and mutually agreeable solution. If no mutually agreeable solution is found within 30 days from the date of the request to the Partnership Council, the Party may take the measures referred to in paragraph 1.

3. The measures referred to in paragraph 1 shall be in full respect of international law and shall be proportionate. Priority shall be given to the measures which least disturb the functioning of this Agreement and of any supplementing agreements.

4. The Parties consider that, for a situation to constitute a serious and substantial failure to fulfil any of the obligations described as essential elements in Article 771, its gravity and nature would have to be of an exceptional sort that threatens peace and security or that has international repercussions. For greater certainty, an act or omission which materially defeats the object and purpose of the Paris Agreement shall always be considered as a serious and substantial failure for the purposes of this Article.

Article 773   Safeguard measures

1. If serious economic, societal or environmental difficulties of a sectoral or regional nature, including in relation to fishing activities and their dependent communities, that are liable to persist arise, the Party concerned may unilaterally take appropriate safeguard measures. Such safeguard measures shall be restricted with regard to their scope and duration to what is strictly necessary in order to remedy the situation. Priority shall be given to those measures which will least disturb the functioning of this Agreement.

2. The Party concerned shall, without delay, notify the other Party through the Partnership Council and shall provide all relevant information. The Parties shall immediately enter into consultations in the Partnership Council with a view to finding a mutually agreeable solution.

3. The Party concerned may not take safeguard measures until one month has elapsed after the date of notification referred to in paragraph 2, unless the consultation procedure pursuant to paragraph 2 has been jointly concluded before the expiration of the stated time limit. When exceptional circumstances requiring immediate action exclude prior examination, the Party concerned may apply forthwith the safeguard measures strictly necessary to remedy the situation.

The Party concerned shall, without delay, notify the measures taken to the Partnership Council and shall provide all relevant information.

4. If a safeguard measure taken by the Party concerned creates an imbalance between the rights and obligations under this Agreement or under any supplementing agreement, the other Party may take such proportionate rebalancing measures as are strictly necessary to remedy the imbalance. Priority shall be given to those measures which will least disturb the functioning of this Agreement. Paragraphs 2 to 4 shall apply *mutatis mutandis* to such rebalancing measures.

5. Either Party may, without having prior recourse to consultations pursuant to Article 738, initiate the arbitration procedure referred to in Article 739 to challenge a measure taken by the other Party in application of paragraphs 1 to 5 of this Article.

6. The safeguard measures referred to in paragraph 1 and the rebalancing measures referred to in paragraph 5 may also be taken in relation to a supplementing agreement, unless otherwise provided therein.

PART SEVEN FINAL PROVISIONS

Article 774   Territorial scope

1. This Agreement applies to:
   (a) the territories to which the TEU, the TFEU and the Treaty establishing the European Atomic Energy Community are applicable, and under the conditions laid down in those Treaties; and
   (b) the territory of the United Kingdom.

2. This Agreement also applies to the Bailiwick of Guernsey, the Bailiwick of Jersey and the Isle of Man to the extent set out in Heading Five of Part Two and Article 520.

3. This Agreement shall neither apply to Gibraltar nor have any effects in that territory.

4. This Agreement does not apply to the overseas territories having special relations with the United Kingdom: Anguilla; Bermuda; British Antarctic Territory; British Indian Ocean Territory; British Virgin Islands; Cayman Islands; Falkland Islands; Montserrat; Pitcairn, Henderson, Ducie and Oeno Islands; Saint Helena, Ascension and Tristan da Cunha; South Georgia and the South Sandwich Islands; and Turks and Caicos Islands.

Article 775   [Omitted]

Article 776   Review

The Parties shall jointly review the implementation of this Agreement and supplementing agreements and any matters related thereto five years after the entry into force of this Agreement and every five years thereafter.

Article 777   Classified information and sensitive non-classified information

Nothing in this Agreement or in any supplementing agreement shall be construed as requiring a Party to make available classified information.

Classified information or material provided by or exchanged between the Parties under this Agreement or any supplementing agreement shall be handled and protected in compliance with the Agreement on security procedures for exchanging and protecting classified information and any implementing arrangement concluded under it.

The Parties shall agree upon handling instructions to ensure the protection of sensitive non-classified information exchanged between them.

Article 778   Integral parts of this Agreement

1. The Protocols, Annexes, Appendices and footnotes to this Agreement shall form an integral part of this Agreement.

2. Each of the Annexes to this Agreement, including its appendices, shall form an integral part of the Section, Chapter, Title, Heading or Protocol that refers to that Annex or to which reference is made in that Annex.

   (*List of annexes omitted*)

Article 779   Termination

Either Party may terminate this Agreement by written notification through diplomatic channels. This Agreement and any supplementing agreement shall cease to be in force on the first day of the twelfth month following the date of notification.

Article 780   [Omitted]

Article 781   Future accessions to the Union

1. The Union shall notify the United Kingdom of any new request for accession of a third country to the Union.

2. During the negotiations between the Union and a third country regarding the accession of that country to the Union[46], the Union shall endeavour to:

    (a) on request of the United Kingdom and, to the extent possible, provide any information regarding any matter covered by this Agreement and any supplementing agreement; and

    (b) take into account any concerns expressed by the United Kingdom.

3. The Partnership Council shall examine any effects of accession of a third country to the Union on this Agreement and any supplementing agreement sufficiently in advance of the date of such accession.

4. To the extent necessary, the United Kingdom and the Union shall, before the entry into force of the agreement on the accession of a third country to the Union:

    (a) amend this Agreement or any supplementing agreement,

    (b) put in place by decision of the Partnership Council any other necessary adjustments or transitional arrangements regarding this Agreement or any supplementing agreement; or

    (c) decide within the Partnership Council whether:

        (i) to apply Article 492 to the nationals of that third country; or

        (ii) to establish transitional arrangements as regards Article 492 in relation to that third country and its nationals once it accedes to the Union.

5. In the absence of a decision under point (c)(i) or (ii) of paragraph 4 of this Article by the entry into force of the agreement on the accession of the relevant third country to the Union, Article 492 shall not apply to nationals of that third country.

6. In the event that the Partnership Council establishes transitional arrangements as referred to in point (c)(ii) of paragraph 4, it shall specify their duration. The Partnership Council may extend the duration of those transitional arrangements.

7. Before the expiry of the transitional arrangements referred to in point (c)(ii) of paragraph 4 of this Article, the Partnership Council shall decide whether to apply Article 492 to the nationals of that third country from the end of the transitional arrangements. In the absence of such a decision Article 492 shall not apply in relation to the nationals of that third country from the end of the transitional arrangements.

8. Point (c) of paragraph 4, and paragraphs 5 to 7 are without prejudice to the Union's prerogatives under its domestic legislation.

9. For greater certainty, without prejudice to point (c) of paragraph 4 and paragraphs 5 to 7, this Agreement shall apply in relation to a new Member State of the Union from the date of accession of that new Member State to the Union.

Article 782   [Omitted]

Article 783   Entry into force and provisional application

1. This Agreement shall enter into force on the first day of the month following that in which both Parties have notified each other that they have completed their respective internal requirements and procedures for establishing their consent to be bound.

2. The Parties agree to provisionally apply this Agreement from 1 January 2021 provided that prior to that date they have notified each other that their respective internal requirements and procedures necessary for provisional application have been completed. Provisional application shall cease on one of the following dates, whichever is the earliest:

    (a) 28 February 2021 or another date as decided by the Partnership Council; or

    (b) the day referred to in paragraph 1.

3. As from the date from which this Agreement is provisionally applied, the Parties shall understand references in this Agreement to 'the date of entry into force of this Agreement' or to 'the entry into force of this Agreement' as references to the date from which this Agreement is provisionally applied.

Done at Brussels and London on the thirtieth day of December in the year two thousand and twenty. *(Signatures and all annexes omitted.)*

---

[46] For greater certainty, paragraphs 2 to 9 apply in respect of negotiations between the Union and a third country for accession to the Union taking place after the entry into force of this Agreement, notwithstanding the fact a request for accession took place before the entry into force of this Agreement.

Index